2019 NHL DRAFT BLACK BOOK
PROSPECT SCOUTING REPORTS & DRAFT RANKINGS

BY HOCKEY PROSPECT

© 2019

ISBN: 978-1-9991552-1-6

INFORMATION	8	
2019 NHL DRAFT LIST	13	
2019 NHL DRAFT PROSPECTS	17	

AALTONEN, LEEVI	18		CARROLL, JOSEPH	60
ABRAMOV, MIKHAIL	18		CAUFIELD, COLE	60
ABRUZZESE, NICHOLAS	19		CAULFIELD, JUDD	64
AEBISCHER, DAVID	20		CEDERQVIST, FILIP	64
AFANASYEV, EGOR	20		CHISYAKOV, SEMYON	65
AHAC, LAYTON	21		CICCOLINI, ERIC	66
ALAMI, CADE	23		CLARKE, GRAEME	66
ALEXANDER, JACSON	23		CONNORS, LIAM	67
ALEXANDROV, NIKITA	24		CONSTANTINOU, WILLIAM	68
ALISHLALOV, MALIK	24		COSTMAR, ARVID	69
ALISTROV, VLADIMIR	25		COZENS, DYLAN	69
ALLENSEN, NATHAN	25		CROZIER, MAXWELL	71
ALNEFELT, HUGO	26		D'AMICO, DANIEL	72
ANDERSSON, ISAC	26		DACH, KIRBY	72
ANGLE, TYLER	27		DARIN, ALEXANDR	74
ANTROPOV, DANIL	27		DEL GAIZO, MARC	74
ASLANIDIS, ALEXANDROS	28		DOCTER, GRANT	75
ATTARD, RONALD	28		DONOVAN, RYDER	76
BAKER, JARRETT	29		DOROFEYEV, PAVEL	76
BARLAGE, LOGAN	29		DOYLE, BRADEN	78
BASSE, DOMINIC	30		DRKULEC, RYAN	78
BEATON, JOHN	30		EDMONDS, LUCAS	79
BEAUCAGE, ALEX	31		EGGENBERGER, NANDO	79
BECKMAN, ADAM	32		ELLIS, COLTEN	80
BEECHER, JOHN	33		FAGEMO, SAMUEL	80
BERGER, CARTER	34		FAIRBROTHER, GIANNI	81
BERGERON, JUSTIN	35		FARINACCI, JOHN	81
BERTUZZI, TAG	36		FENSORE, DOMENICK	82
BIBEAU, FELIX	36		FEUK, LUCAS	83
BIZIER, MATHIEU	37		FIRSTOV, VLADISLAV	84
BJERSELIUS, OSCAR	38		FOOTE, NOLAN	85
BJORNFOT, TOBIAS	38		FORD, PARKER	85
BLAISDELL, HARRISON	39		FRANCIS, WILLIAM	86
BLUMEL, MATEJ	40		FRISCH, ETHAN	87
BOHLSEN, KADEN	41		GAUCHER, JACOB	88
BOLDUC, SAMUEL	41		GAUTHIER, TAYLOR	88
BOLDY, MATTHEW	42		GILDON, MICHAEL	89
BRADY, COLE	44		GIRODAY, CHRISTOPHER	89
BREEN, LYDEN	45		GLOVER, TY	90
BREWER, MITCHELL	45		GNYP, SIMON	90
BRINK, BOBBY	46		GREWE, ALBIN	90
BRINKMAN, BENJAMIN	49		GRIFFIN, ROBERT	92
BROBERG, PHILIP	50		GRITSYUK, ARSENI	92
BRODZINSKI, BRYCE	52		GUENETTE, MAXENCE	93
BROWN, MATTHEW	53		GUSKOV, MATVEY	93
BROWN, MITCHELL	53		GUTIK, DANIIL	94
BUDY, BRENDAN	53		GUZDA, MACK	95
BUDGELL, BRETT	54		HAIDER, ETHAN	96
BUKES, COLBY	54		HAMALIUK, DILLON	96
BURZAN, LUKA	55		HANUS, CLAY	97
BYCHKOV, ROMAN	56		HARLEY, THOMAS	97
BYRAM, BOWEN	56		HARVEY-PINARD, RAFAËL	99
CAJKA, PETR	57		HAS, MARTIN	100
CAJKOVIC, MAXIM	58		HATAKKA, SANTERI	100
CAMPBELL, ALEXANDER	59		HEINOLA, VILLE	101

HELLESON, DREW	102	LOPONEN, KALLE	151	PIRONEN, KARI	187
HENRIKSSON, KARL	103	LUEDTKE, JOSH	152	PINARD, SIMON	187
HLAVAJ, SAMUEL	104	LUNDMARK, SIMON	152	PINONIEMI, GARRETT	188
HOGLANDER, NILS	105	LYCKÅSEN, ALBERT	153	PINTO, SHANE	188
HOLMSTROM, SIMON	106	MACCELLI, MATIAS	153	PITLICK, RHETT	189
HONKA, ANTTONI	107	MACK, SIMON	155	PLASEK, KAREL	190
HORNING, CONNOR	108	MACKAY, COLE	155	PODKOLZIN, VASILI	191
HUGHES, JACK	108	MAIER, NOLAN	156	PORCO, NICHOLAS	193
HUGLEN, AARON	111	MALONE, JACK	156	POULIN, SAMUEL	194
IINNALA, JERE	111	MARLEAU, VINCENT	157	PRIKRYL, FILIP	194
JANICKE, TREVOR	112	MASTROSIMONE, ROBERT	157	PRIMEAU, MASON	195
JACQUES, JÉRÉMY	113	MAZURA, TOMAS	158	PROCTOR, KIRBY	196
JENSEN, JACK	113	MCCARTHY, CASE	159	PROTAS, ALIAKSEI	196
JENTZSCH, TARO	114	MCCARTNEY, BEN	159	PUISTOLA, PATRIK	197
JOHANSSON, ALBERT	114	MCDONOUGH, AIDEN	160	RANNISTO, JASPER	198
JOHNSON, RYAN	115	MCMICHAEL, CONNOR	160	RASANEN, IIVARI	198
JONES, HUNTER	117	MEEHAN, BEN	162	RATY, AKU	199
JONES, ZACHARY	118	MEIER, SPENCER	162	REES, JAMIESON	199
JUNGELS, JETT	119	MERRITT, ARLO	163	RÉGIS, SAMUEL	202
JUTTING, JACKSON	120	MICHEL, JÉRÉMY	163	RIPPON, MERRICK	202
KAKKO, KAAPO	120	MILLAR, JACK	164	RIZZO, MASSIMO	203
KALIYEV, ARTHUR	123	MILLMAN, MASON	164	ROBERTSON, MATTHEW	203
KALLIONKIELI, MARCUS	125	MINER, TRENT	165	ROBERTSON, NICHOLAS	204
KALMIKOV, BROOKLYN	126	MIRONOV, ILYA	165	ROMANO, ANTHONY	205
KARLSTROM, DAVID	126	MISYUL, DANIL	166	ROSS, LIAM	206
KASTELIC, MARK	127	MOBERG, COLE	167	ROSS, RODDY	207
KEMP, BRETT	127	MOORE, COOPER	167	ROUSEK, LUKAS	207
KEPPEN, ETHAN	127	MOYNIHAN, PATRICK	168	ROWE, CAMERON	208
KINDER, NINO	128	MRAZIK, MICHAL	169	RYBINSKI, HENRIK	209
KNIAZEV, ARTEMI	129	MUIR, COLE	169	SAARELA, ANTTI	209
KNIGHT, SPENCER	129	MULLAHY, DEREK	170	SAMUELSSON, ADAM	210
KOCHETKOV, PYOTR	132	MURRAY, BLAKE	170	SAVILLE, ISAIAH	210
KOKKONEN, MIKKO	133	MUTALA, SASHA	171	SCHMIEMANN, QUINN	211
KOLYACHONOK, VLADISLAV	134	MUTTER, NAVRIN	172	SCHWINDT, COLE	212
KOPE, DAVID	136	MUZIK, RADEK	172	SEDOV, NIKITA	212
KORCZAK, KAEDAN	136	NAJAMAN, ADAM	173	SEIDER, MORITZ	213
KOSTER, MICHAEL	137	NESTERENKO, NIKITA	173	SERDYUK, EGOR	214
KRANNILA, JAMI	138	NEWHOOK, ALEX	174	SHESHIN, DMITRI	215
KREBS, PAYTON	138	NEWKIRK, REECE	176	SIEDEM, RYAN	215
KRYS, LUKE	140	NIKKANEN, HENRI	176	SILIANOFF, GRANT	216
LACOMBE, JACKSON	141	NIKOLAEV, ILYA	176	SILOVS, ARTURS	216
LADD, GRAYSON	142	NODLER, JOSHUA	177	SIMONEAU, XAVIER	217
LANG, MARTIN	142	NORLINDER, MATTIAS	178	SHASHKOV, NIKITA	218
LAROCHELLE, SEAN	143	NOUSIAINEN, KIM	178	SLEPETS, KIRILL	219
LAROSE, NATHAN	143	NUSSBAUMER, VALENTIN	179	SKINNER, HUNTER	220
LAVOIE, RAPHAEL	144	OKHOTYUK, NIKITA	180	SODERBLOM, ELMER	220
LEASON, BRETT	145	O'NEILL, RYAN	181	SODERSTROM, VICTOR	221
LEE, ANDRE	146	MERISIER-ORTIZ, CHRIS	181	SOGAARD, MADS	222
LEE, JAKE	147	PARENT, XAVIER	182	SPENCE, JORDAN	225
LEGARE, NATHAN	147	PARIK, LUKAS	182	SPIRIDONOV, YEGOR	225
LEGUERRIER, JACOB	148	PARSSINEN, JUSSO	183	SPOTT, TYLER	226
LEMIEUX, JONATHAN	149	PASIC, NIKOLA	183	STANGE, SAM	226
LIKHACHEV, YAROSLAV	149	PEACH, BAILEY	184	STANGE, SAM	227
LINDMARK, OWEN	150	PELLETIER, JAKOB	185	STARIKOV, LEV	228
LOPINA, JOSH	151	PHILLIPS, ETHAN	186	STEEVES, ALEXANDER	228

STEVENSON, KEEGAN	229	BLOMQVIST, JOEL	268	KUBICEK, SIMON	290
STIENBURG, MATTHEW	229	BOLTMANN, JAKE	268	KUNZ, JACKSON	290
STRONDALA, VOJTECH	230	BORDELEAU, THOMAS	269	KUZNETSOV, YAN	291
STRUBLE, JAYDEN	230	BOURQUE, MAVRIK	269	LAFRENIÈRE, ALEXIS	291
SUZUKI, RYAN	231	BOWEN, ETHAN	270	LAPIERRE, HENDRIX	292
SWANKLER, AUSTEN	233	BRISSON, BRENDAN	270	LAVALLÉE, CHARLES-ANTOINE	292
SWETLIKOFF, ALEX	234	BURNS, BRADY	270	LAWRENCE, JOSH	292
TANUS, KRISTIAN	234	BUTLER, CAMERON	271	LEVI, DEVON	293
TAPONEN, ROOPE	234	BYFIELD, QUINTON	271	LUNDELL, ANTON	293
TEPLY, MICHAL	235	CHABRIER, BRANDON	272	MALIK, NICK	294
TIEKSOLA, TUUKKA	235	CHOUPANI, MATT	272	MCCLENNON, CONNOR	294
THOMPSON, TYCE	236	CHROMIAK, MARTIN	272	MCDONALD, KYLE	295
THOMSON, LASSI	236	CIKHART, JAN	273	MEIERS, JOHNNY	295
THRUN, HENRY	238	CLANG, CALLE	273	MERCER, DAWSON	295
TOMASINO, PHILIP	238	COMMESSO, DREW	274	MERCURI, LUCAS	296
TOPOROWSKI, LUKE	239	CORMIER, LUKAS	274	MIETTINEN, VEETI	296
TRACEY, BRAYDEN	240	COULOMBE, ANTOINE	275	MILLER, JOE	297
TUOMISTO, ANTTI	241	CRNKOVIC, KYLE	275	MILLER, MITCHELL	297
TURAN, OLIVER	241	CUYLLE, WILL	275	MOORE, LLEYTON	297
TURCOTTE, ALEX	242	DAVID, ALEXANDRE	276	MORRISON, LOGAN	298
UBA, ERIC	243	DESNOYERS, ELLIOT	276	MUKHAMADULLIN, SHAKIR	298
VAN DE LEEST, JACKSON	244	DESROCHES, CHARLIE	276	MURRAY, JACOB	298
VLASIC, ALEX	244	DOUCET, ALEXANDRE	277	MYSAK, JAN	299
VORLICKY, MIKE	246	DRYSDALE, JAMIE	277	NEIGHBOURS, JAKE	299
VUKOJEVIC, MICHAEL	247	DUFOUR, WILLIAM	277	NIEMELA, TOPI	299
WANER, NATE	248	EVANGELISTA, LUKE	278	NOVAK, PAVEL	300
WARREN, MARSHALL	249	FABER, BROCK	278	NYBECK, ZION	300
WASHKURAK, KEEAN	250	FARRELL, SEAN	279	O'ROURKE, RYAN	301
WEBBER, CADE	250	FINLEY, JACK	279	OVCHINNIKOV, DMITRI	301
WEIGHT, DANNY	251	FOUDY, JEAN-LUC	280	PASHIN, ALEXANDER	301
WILDER, HENRY	251	FOWLER, HAYDEN	280	PERFETTI, COLE	302
WILLIAMS, JONATHAN	252	FRANCIS, RYAN	280	PERREAULT, JACOB	302
WILLIAMS, JOSH	252	GRANS, HELGE	281	PETERKA, JOHN-JASON	303
WOLF, DUSTIN	252	GREIG, RIDLEY	281	PETERSON, DYLAN	303
YAKOVENKO, ALEXANDER	253	GROSHEV, MAXIM	281	PIERCEY, RILEY	303
YANTSIS, JONATHAN	254	GUAY, PATRICK	282	PILLAR, JOSH	304
YORK, CAMERON	254	GUHLE, KAIDAN	282	POIRIER, JEREMIE	304
YORK, JACK	256	GUNLER, NOEL	283	PONOMARYOV, VASILI	304
YOUNG, TYLER	257	GUSHCHIN, DANIIL	283	PROKOP, LUKE	305
ZAYTSEV, OLEG	257	HALLIDAY, STEPHEN	284	PUUTIO, KASPER	305
ZAITSEV, DMITRI	258	HARDIE, JAMES	284	QUINN, JACK	305
ZEGRAS, TREVOR	258	HIRVONEN, RONI	284	RAFKIN, RUBEN	306
2020 NHL DRAFT TOP 31	**261**	HOLLOWAY, DYLAN	285	RATZLAFF, JAKE	306
2020 NHL DRAFT PROSPECTS 263		HOLTZ, ALEXANDER	285	RAYMOND, LUCAS	307
		HUNT, DAEMON	286	REID, LUKE	307
AMBROSIO, COLBY	264	IACOBO, FABIO	286	RENWICK, MICHAEL	308
AMIROV, RODION	264	JARVENTIE, ROBY	287	ROBINSON, DYLAN	308
ANDRAE, EMIL	264	JARVIS, SETH	287	ROCHETTE, THÉO	308
ASKAROV, YAROSLAV	265	JOHANNESSON, ANTON	287	ROEPKE, CASEY	309
BARRON, JUSTIN	265	KAISER, WYATT	288	ROLSTON, RYDER	309
BEAUDOIN, CHARLES	266	KEHRER, ANTHONY	288	ROODE, BENJAMIN	309
BEDNAR, JAN	266	KHUSNUTDINOV, MARAT	288	ROSSI, MARCO	310
BENNING, MICHAEL	267	KING, BEN	289	ROY, PIERRE-OLIVIER	310
BIAKABUTUKA, JEREMIE	267	KLEVEN, TYLER	289	SANDERSON, JAKE	311
BIONDI, BLAKE	268	KNAZKO, SAMUEL	289	SAVOIE, CARTER	311

SAVOIE, NICOLAS	311	GALLAGHER, TY	332	ROLOFS, STUART	351
SCHNEIDER, BRADEN	312	GAUCHER, NATHAN	332	ROUSSEAU, WILLIAM	352
SCHINGOETHE, WYATT	312	GAUDREAU, BEN	332	ROY, JOSHUA	352
SEBRANGO, DONOVAN	312	GILL, JUSTIN	333	ROY, TRISTAN	352
SEDOFF, CHRISTOFFER	313	GOURE, DENI	333	SAGANIUK, COLBY	353
SEED, NOLAN	313	GRATTON, DYLAN	333	SAMOSKEVICH, MATTHEW	353
SEELEY, RONAN	313	GRUSHNIKOV, ARTYOM	334	SAVAGE, REDMOND	354
SIMONTAIVEL, KASPER	314	GUENTHER, DYLAN	334	SAVOIE, CHARLES	354
SMILANIC, TY	314	GUÉVIN, JACOB	334	STANKOVEN, LOGAN	354
SMITH, JACK	314	HARRISON, BRETT	335	STILLMAN, CHASE	355
SOUCH, CARTER	315	HAYES, AVERY	335	STRINGER, ZACK	355
SOURDIF, JUSTIN	315	HÉBERT, JULIEN	335	TINLING, DOVAR	355
SPEARING, SHAWN	315	HOLMES, JACOB	336	WALLSTEDT, JESPER	356
STÜTZLE, TIM	316	HUCKINS, COLE	336	WHYNOT, CAMERON	356
STRANGES, ANTONIO	316	HUGHES, LUKE	336	WILMER, JEREMY	357
SVEJKOVSKY, LUKAS	317	JANICKE, JUSTIN	337	WINTERTON, RYAN	357
SZMAGAJ, ETHAN	317	JOHNSTON, WYATT	337	**GAME REPORTS 358**	
TERRY, ZACH	317	KIDNEY, RILEY	337	**CREDITS 581**	
THOMPSON, JACK	318	KUKKONEN, KYLE	338		
TOLNAI, CAMERON	318	LAMBOS, CARSON	338		
TUCH, LUKE	318	LANGLOIS, JÉRÉMY	338		
TULLIO, TYLER	319	LAVOIE, ELLIOT	339		
TUSSEY, NOAH	319	LEGAULT, CHARLES-ALEXIS	339		
VALADE, REID	319	L'HEUREUX, ZACHARY	339		
VEILLETTE, WILLIAM	320	LOCKHART, CONNOR	340		
VIERLING, EVAN	320	LUCIUS, CHAZ	340		
VILLENEUVE, WILLIAM	320	LYSELL, FABIAN	340		
WIESBLATT, OZZY	321	MACDONALD, CAMERON	341		
WILLIAMS, JACK	321	MAILLOUX, LOGAN	341		
WONG, NICHOLAS	322	MALATESTA, JAMES	342		
ZARY, CONNOR	322	MCCALLUM, LANDON	342		
2021 NHL DRAFT PROSPECTS 323		MCTAVISH, MASON	342		
		MELANSON, JACOB	343		
ALLEN, NOLAN	324	MIANSCUM, ISRAEL	343		
ARCURI, FRANCESCO	324	MITTELSTADT, LUKE	344		
AVON, JON-RANDALL	324	MOTORYGIN, MAKSIM	344		
BÉDARD, ANTHONY	325	MYKLUKHA, OLEKSII	344		
BEHRENS, SEAN	325	NADEAU, OLIVIER	345		
BELLIVEAU, ISAAC	325	NAUSE, EVAN	345		
BENIERS, MATTHEW	326	OLAUSSON, OSKAR	345		
BIGGAR, ZACH	326	ORR, ROBERT	346		
BOLDUC, ZACHARY	327	OTHMANN, BRENNAN	346		
BOUCHER, TYLER	327	PALODICHUK, JOE	346		
BOURGAULT, XAVIER	327	PAQUET, FÉLIX	347		
BOUTIN, CHARLES	328	PASTUJOV, SASHA	347		
BOUTIN, OLIVIER	328	PEART, JACK	348		
BROWN, CADEN	328	PELLERIN, MAXIME	348		
CHAYKA, DANIIL	329	PINELLI, FRANCESCO	348		
CLARKE, BRANDT	329	PLANDOWSKI, OSCAR	349		
DAIGLE, NICOLAS	330	POWER, OWEN	349		
DEAN, ZACHARY	330	PUNNETT, CONNOR	349		
DEL MASTRO, ETHAN	330	RATY, AATU	350		
DUKE, DYLAN	331	REYNOLDS, PETER	350		
EKLUND, WILLIAM	331	RICHARD, GUILLAUME	350		
ENRIGHT, ISAAC	331	ROBIDAS, JUSTIN	351		

INFORMATION

THE RANKINGS

This year we have made a change to our rankings we are including in the NHL Draft Black Book. Rather than rank 217 players, we wanted our list we put in this book to be the same as the rankings we give to NHL teams. The ranking will also more closely reflect the rankings of NHL teams. To give you an idea of what we're talking about we got some feedback from some teams. The feedback spans data from many years.

List Length

NHL teams draft lists length varied by the team and by year, but in general, the average team had anywhere from 85 players ranked (not including goalies)) to 120 players ranked. Teams also mentioned that in the average draft year, any player ranked in the 70+ range begins to have much less chance of actually being drafted.

Our draft list length will be at least 90 players and it will look much more like NHL teams lists. This year we will make a separate list for goalies. Of the teams we asked, all of them had goalies on a separate list. Previously we were going to combine goalies on our list, but for various reasons we have decided to do what the teams do.

Actual Draft Examples

To give you an idea of where a player is ranked and where that player might actually be drafted, we asked a few teams for some actual examples of where they had a player ranked on their list and where that player was selected by them on draft day. These examples are from multiple teams and go back as far as 10 years.

- **Example 1**
- Player Ranking was 29th on team list and was drafted 50th overall.
- **Example 2**
- Player Ranking was 40th on team list and was drafted 59th overall.
- **Example 3**
- Player Ranking was 30th on team list and was drafted 47th overall.
- **Example 4**
- Player Ranking was 33rd on team list and was drafted 56th overall.
- **Example 5**
- Player Ranking was 57th on team list and was drafted 93rd overall.
- **Example 6**
- Player Ranking was 43rd on team list and was drafted 65th overall.
- **Example 7**
- Player Ranking was 68th on team list and was drafted 144th overall.
- **Example 8**
- Player Ranking was 11th on team list and was drafted 25th overall.
- **Example 9**
- Player Ranking was 53rd on team list and was drafted 155th overall.
- **Example 10**
- Player Ranking was 61st on team list and was drafted 161st overall.

As you can see from these examples, a player who is #40 on our list does not equate to being the player we would select if we had the 40th pick in the draft.

Here is an example going back to the 1st round in 2018 using our own list:

Let's assume we were picking 9th overall in the New York Rangers spot. Although we had Kravtsov (NYR actual selection)ranked very high at 6th overall, we had Noah Dobson ranked one spot higher at 5th overall. Dobson would've been our selection in the Rangers 9th spot and also in the Edmonton Oilers 10th spot (Oilers selected Evan Bouchard and we had Dobson ranked 5th and Bouchard ranked 10th) We would have obviously been quite happy to get our 5th ranked prospect at 10th overall.

What is different with our rankings this year?

The simple answer is that the past we needed to include too many players in the 217 player list that we wouldn't actually draft ourselves. An example is a player like Reilly Damiani. We liked him as a possible 7th rounder. Last year he was ranked in the 200's on our list. On an actual NHL teams list that number needs to be closer to 75 at the latest to have a chance of selecting him. That's the range we would've ranked him in if we used this year's format in last year's Black Book. We've considered switching to this format for several years and regret not doing it sooner.

In our **2019 NHL Draft Black Book** our list will be the same as the average NHL team list*. If you see a player ranked by us, it tells you we would be willing to draft him. Team's will make adjustments during the draft based on live draft results.

*Sometimes teams have side lists. Some examples include small players lists or players with off ice concerns being listed separately As mentioned earlier, teams we've spoken to over the years use separate lists for goalies.

THE RATINGS (THE GRADES ARE BASED ON A 3-9 SCALE ALSO USED BY AN NHL TEAM.)

HOCKEY SENSE	COMPETE	SKILL	SKATING
Decision Making	Work Ethic	Shot Power	Quickness
Anticipation	Attack the net	Shot Release	Speed
Playmaking	Consistency	Shot Accuracy	Balance
	First on pucks	Puck Protection	Mobility
	Backcheck (BackPressure)	Passing	Mechanics
	Shot blocking	Stickhandling	Backwards
		Scoring ability	
Rated on 3-9 Scale	Rated on 3-9 Scale	Rated on 3-9 Scale	Rated on 3-9 Scale

We've included some areas we scout. There is no magical formula. We won't dock a defensman for not attacking the net.

3 -Poor, **4**- Below Average, **5** Average, **6** Good, **7** Very Good, **8** Excellent, **9** Elite

The "Average" grade is based on the player against his fellow draft eligibles in his current draft class. The grades simply give you an idea of where we see a player rate in several key aspects that we evaluate. There are obviously several tiers within a grade. Not all "6" skaters are created equal etc. We will take into account a players age and physical maturity when grading skating as an example. If we felt like a 99 birth was closer to his ceiling, he might get the same grade as a player who isn't quite at his level yet, but we project that it will get better. **NOTE:** We DO NOT add up the four grades for any type of score. There are other factors that carry weight into where a player ranks on our list, including off ice factors , size, level of competition etc.

The traits below are factored into our ratings for goalies and defensman.

DEFENSEMAN SPECIFIC	GOALIE SPECIFIC
Puck Retrieval	Angles & Positioning
Gap Control	Net Presence
Quarterbacking (Power Play)	Poise, confidence, big in net.
Defending	Lateral movement
	Recovery
	Rebound Control
	Glove
	Mental Toughness
	Playing the Puck
	Overall Quickness

DRAFT GRADES

We also include a draft grade in the player profiles this season. We use these draft grades as a sorting tool.

As a real life example, our Director of Scouting, Mark Edwards, could be making his first trip to the QMJHL in October. He would check the draft grades submitted by our local QMJHL area Scout, Jérôme Bérubé, for the draft eligible players he would see on the trip. This would give Mark an idea of which players and how many players he would be watching during the course of the trip. He might see three "A" players two "B" players and 5 "C" players. It obviously varies on each trip. As the season moves along, the number of players with draft grades drops. We use A.B.C,C+ Watch (Watch List) and ND (No Draft).

A - Round 1

B Rounds 2-3

C- Rounds 4-7

C+ Closer to round 4 than round 7

Not all the players we rate with a draftable grade will make our list. We will have several "C" rated players who don't crack our final list. Any players who we have rated with draftable grades who don't get drafted would start the next season as watch list. players. Note that actual NHL teams will be inviting some of their top rated players who went undrafted to their camps.

A common question:

Q: Why don't you have 31 "A" rated players when there are 31 players selected in the first round?

A: Because not all draft classes have 31 players that Scouts deem worthy of giving a 1st round grade.

In Speaking to several Scouts this season, the majority have told us they have between 18-23 "A" rated prospects.

2019 NHL DRAFT LIST

SKATERS

RANK	PLAYER	TEAM	LEAGUE	BIRTH	HEIGHT	WEIGHT	POS
1	HUGHES, JACK	USA U-18	NTDP	14-May-2001	5' 10.25"	168 lbs *	C
2	KAKKO, KAAPO	TPS	FINLAND	13-Feb-2001	6' 2.25"	194 lbs *	RW
3	BYRAM, BOWEN	VANCOUVER	WHL	13-Jun-2001	6' 0.5"	194 lbs *	D
4	TURCOTTE, ALEX	USA U-18	NTDP	26-Feb-2001	5' 11.0"	189 lbs *	C
5	ZEGRAS, TREVOR	USA U-18	NTDP	20-Mar-2001	6' 0.0"	166 lbs *	C
6	KREBS, PEYTON	KOOTENAY	WHL	26-Jan-2001	5' 11.25"	180 lbs *	C
7	PODKOLZIN, VASILI	SKA ST. PETERSBURG 2	RUSSIA-JR.	24-Jun-2001	6' 1.0"	190 lbs	RW
8	DACH, KIRBY	SASKATOON	WHL	21-Jan-2001	6' 3.5"	199 lbs *	C
9	BOLDY, MATTHEW	USA U-18	NTDP	05-Apr-2001	6' 1.5"	187 lbs *	LW
10	SEIDER, MORITZ	MANNHEIM	GERMANY	06-Apr-2001	6' 3.5"	183 lbs *	D
11	CAUFIELD, COLE	USA U-18	NTDP	02-Jan-2001	5' 7.25"	163 lbs *	RW
12	YORK, CAMERON	USA U-18	NTDP	05-Jan-2001	5' 11.25"	171 lbs *	D
13	SODERSTROM, VICTOR	BRYNAS	SWEDEN	26-Feb-2001	5' 11.0"	179 lbs *	D
14	COZENS, DYLAN	LETHBRIDGE	WHL	09-Feb-2001	6' 3.0"	181 lbs *	C
15	BRINK, BOBBY	SIOUX CITY	USHL	08-Jul-2001	5' 8.25"	159 lbs *	RW
16	HEINOLA, VILLE	LUKKO	FINLAND	03-Feb-2001	5' 11.25"	178 lbs *	D
17	NEWHOOK, ALEX	VICTORIA	BCHL	28-Jan-2001	5' 10.25"	195 lbs *	C
18	TOMASINO, PHILIP	NIAGARA	OHL	28-Jul-2001	5' 11.75"	178 lbs *	C
19	HARLEY, THOMAS	MISSISSAUGA	OHL	19-Aug-2001	6' 3.0"	188 lbs *	D
20	JOHNSON, RYAN	SIOUX FALLS	USHL	24-Jul-2001	6' 0.0"	173 lbs *	D
21	BROBERG, PHILIP	AIK	SWEDEN-2	25-Jun-2001	6' 2.75"	199 lbs *	D
22	KOLYACHONOK, VLADISLAV	FLINT	OHL	26-May-2001	6' 0.25"	176 lbs *	D
23	HOGLANDER, NILS	ROGLE	SWEDEN	20-Dec-2000	5' 9.0"	185 lbs	LW
24	POULIN, SAMUEL	SHERBROOKE	QMJHL	25-Feb-2001	6' 1.25"	206 lbs *	RW
25	LAVOIE, RAPHAEL	HALIFAX	QMJHL	25-Sep-2000	6' 3.5"	191 lbs *	C
26	SUZUKI, RYAN	BARRIE	OHL	28-May-2001	6' 0.25"	178 lbs *	C
27	DOROFEYEV, PAVEL	MAGNITOGORSK 2	RUSSIA-JR.	26-Oct-2000	6' 1.0"	167 lbs	LW
28	THOMSON, LASSI	KELOWNA	WHL	24-Sep-2000	6' 0.0"	188 lbs *	D
29	HELLESON, DREW	USA U-18	NTDP	26-Mar-2001	6' 2.25"	181 lbs *	D
30	BJORNFOT, TOBIAS	DJURGARDEN JR.	SWEDEN-JR.	06-Apr-2001	6' 0.0"	202 lbs *	D
31	REES, JAMIESON	SARNIA	OHL	26-Feb-2001	5' 10.0"	173 lbs *	C
32	MCMICHAEL, CONNOR	LONDON	OHL	15-Jan-2001	5' 10.75"	172 lbs *	C
33	HOLMSTROM, SIMON	HV 71 JR.	SWEDEN-JR.	24-May-2001	6' 1.0"	183 lbs	RW
34	KALIYEV, ARTHUR	HAMILTON	OHL	26-Jun-2001	6' 1.25"	190 lbs	RW
35	ROBERTSON, MATTHEW	EDMONTON	WHL	09-Mar-2001	6' 3.0"	201 lbs *	D
36	AHAC, LAYTON	PRINCE GEORGE	BCHL	22-Feb-2001	6' 1.75"	188 lbs *	D
37	VLASIC, ALEX	USA U-18	NTDP	05-Jun-2001	6' 5.75"	193 lbs *	D
38	JONES, ZACHARY	TRI-CITY	USHL	18-Oct-2000	5' 10.0"	172 lbs *	D
39	PELLETIER, JAKOB	MONCTON	QMJHL	07-Mar-2001	5' 9.0"	161 lbs *	LW
40	LACOMBE, JACKSON	SHATTUCK - ST.MARY'S	HIGH-MN	09-Jan-2001	6' 1.25"	171 lbs *	D
41	LEASON, BRETT	PRINCE ALBERT	WHL	30-Apr-1999	6' 3.75"	200 lbs *	C
42	MISYUL, DANIL	YAROSLAVL 2	RUSSIA-JR.	20-Oct-2000	6' 3.0"	176 lbs	D
43	PITLICK, RHETT	CHASKA	HIGH-MN	07-Feb-2001	5' 8.75"	160 lbs *	LW
44	PINTO, SHANE	LINCOLN	USHL	12-Nov-2000	6' 2.0"	192 lbs *	C
45	BEECHER, JOHN	USA U-18	NTDP	05-Apr-2001	6' 2.75"	204 lbs *	C
46	OKHOTYUK, NIKITA	OTTAWA	OHL	04-Dec-2000	6' 0.75"	191 lbs *	D
47	FARINACCI, JOHN	DEXTER SCHOOL	HIGH-MA	14-Feb-2001	5' 11.25"	185 lbs *	C
48	ROBERTSON, NICHOLAS	PETERBOROUGH	OHL	11-Sep-2001	5' 8.75"	162 lbs *	LW

49	JOHANSSON, ALBERT	FARJESTAD JR.	SWEDEN-JR.	04-Jan-2001	5' 10.75"	161 lbs *	D
50	PHILLIPS, ETHAN	SIOUX FALLS	USHL	07-May-2001	5' 9.25"	148 lbs *	C
51	NORLINDER, MATTIAS	MODO JR.	SWEDEN-JR.	12-Apr-2000	5' 11.0"	179 lbs	D
52	CAMPBELL, ALEXANDER	VICTORIA	BCHL	27-Feb-2001	5' 10.0"	151 lbs *	LW
53	ABRAMOV, MIKHAIL	VICTORIAVILLE	QMJHL	26-Mar-2001	5' 10.5"	154 lbs *	C
54	LEGARE, NATHAN	BAIE-COMEAU	QMJHL	11-Jan-2001	6' 0.0"	205 lbs *	RW
55	TRACEY, BRAYDEN	MOOSE JAW	WHL	28-May-2001	6' 0.0"	177 lbs *	LW
56	STRUBLE, JAYDEN	ST. SEBASTIANS SCHOOL	HIGH-MA	08-Sep-2001	6' 0.0"	194 lbs *	D
57	GRITSYUK, ARSENI	OMSK 2	RUSSIA-JR.	15-Mar-2001	5' 10.0"	169 lbs	RW
58	DARIN, ALEXANDR	YAROSLAVL 2	RUSSIA-JR.	16-Aug-2000	5' 11.0"	159 lbs	RW
59	AFANASYEV, EGOR	MUSKEGON	USHL	23-Jan-2001	6' 3.5"	201 lbs *	LW
60	RYBINSKI, HENRIK	SEATTLE	WHL	26-Jun-2001	6' 0.5"	176 lbs *	RW
61	BLAISDELL, HARRISON	CHILLIWACK	BCHL	18-Mar-2001	5' 11.0"	181 lbs *	C
62	HUGLEN, AARON	ROSEAU	HIGH-MN	06-Mar-2001	5' 11.25"	166 lbs *	RW
63	BECKMAN, ADAM	SPOKANE	WHL	10-May-2001	6' 0.5"	168 lbs *	LW
64	PROTAS, ALIAKSEI	PRINCE ALBERT	WHL	06-Jan-2001	6' 4.75"	205 lbs *	C
65	KORCZAK, KAEDAN	KELOWNA	WHL	29-Jan-2001	6' 2.75"	192 lbs *	D
66	SLEPETS, KIRILL	YAROSLAVL	RUSSIA	06-Apr-1999	5' 10.0"	165 lbs	LW
67	HENRIKSSON, KARL	FROLUNDA JR.	SWEDEN-JR.	05-Feb-2001	5' 8.75"	166 lbs *	C
68	KNIAZEV, ARTEMI	CHICOUTIMI	QMJHL	04-Jan-2001	5' 10.75"	176 lbs *	D
69	CHISTYAKOV, SEMYON	UFA 2	RUSSIA-JR.	07-Aug-2001	5' 10.0"	167 lbs	D
70	BERGER, CARTER	VICTORIA	BCHL	17-Sep-1999	6' 0.25"	200 lbs *	D
71	CAJKOVIC, MAXIM	SAINT JOHN	QMJHL	03-Jan-2001	5' 10.75"	185 lbs *	RW
72	RIZZO, MASSIMO	PENTICTON	BCHL	13-Jun-2001	5' 9.75"	175 lbs *	C
73	PUISTOLA, PATRIK	TAPPARA JR.	FINLAND-JR.	11-Jan-2001	6' 0.0"	174 lbs *	RW
74	NIKOLAEV, ILYA	YAROSLAVL 2	RUSSIA-JR.	26-Jun-2001	6' 0.0"	190 lbs	C
75	CLARKE, GRAEME	OTTAWA	OHL	24-Apr-2001	5' 11.5"	175 lbs *	RW
76	GUSKOV, MATVEY	LONDON	OHL	30-Jan-2001	6' 1.25"	177 lbs *	C
77	ALEXANDROV, NIKITA	CHARLOTTETOWN	QMJHL	16-Sep-2000	6' 0.0"	179 lbs *	C
78	HONKA, ANTTONI	JYP	FINLAND	05-Oct-2000	5' 10.25"	179 lbs *	D
79	CICCOLINI, ERIC	TORONTO JC	OJHL	14-Jan-2001	5' 10.5"	160 lbs *	RW
80	AALTONEN, LEEVI	KALPA JR.	FINLAND-JR.	24-Jan-2001	5' 8.75"	177 lbs *	RW
81	FOOTE, NOLAN	KELOWNA	WHL	29-Nov-2000	6' 3.5"	190 lbs *	LW
82	THRUN, HENRY	USA U-18	NTDP	12-Mar-2001	6' 2.0"	190 lbs *	D
83	FIRSTOV, VLADISLAV	WATERLOO	USHL	19-Jun-2001	6' 0.75"	181 lbs *	LW
84	HAMALIUK, DILLON	SEATTLE	WHL	30-Oct-2000	6' 2.75"	190 lbs *	LW
85	TEPLY, MICHAL	LIBEREC	CZREP	27-May-2001	6' 3.0"	187 lbs *	LW
86	NIKKANEN, HENRI	JUKURIT	FINLAND	28-Apr-2001	6' 3.5"	200 lbs *	C
87	BYCHKOV, ROMAN	YAROSLAVL 2	RUSSIA-JR.	10-Feb-2001	5' 11.0"	161 lbs	D
88	GREWE, ALBIN	DJURGARDEN JR.	SWEDEN-JR.	22-Mar-2001	5' 10.5"	187 lbs *	RW
89	FORD, PARKER	SIOUX CITY	USHL	20-Jul-2000	5' 8.5"	170 lbs *	C
90	KEPPEN, ETHAN	FLINT	OHL	20-Mar-2001	6' 1.75"	214 lbs *	LW
91	LINDMARK, OWEN	USA U-18	NTDP	17-May-2001	6' 0.0"	184 lbs *	C
92	KRANNILA, JAMI	SIOUX FALLS	USHL	03-Oct-2000	5' 10.0"	160 lbs *	C
93	MASTROSIMONE, ROBERT	CHICAGO	USHL	24-Jan-2001	5' 9.75"	158 lbs *	LW
94	GUTIK, DANIIL	YAROSLAVL 2	RUSSIA-JR.	31-Aug-2001	6' 3.0"	179 lbs	LW
95	MOYNIHAN, PATRICK	USA U-18	NTDP	23-Jan-2001	5' 10.75"	183 lbs *	RW
96	HANUS, CLAY	PORTLAND	WHL	25-Mar-2001	5' 10"	170 lbs	D
97	SPENCE, JORDAN	MONCTON	QMJHL	24-Feb-2001	5' 9.5"	164 lbs *	D
98	DEL GAIZO, MARC	UMASS	H-EAST	11-Oct-1999	5' 9.5"	188 lbs *	D
99	WARREN, MARSHALL	USA U-18	NTDP	20-Apr-2001	5' 10.5"	169 lbs *	D
100	TIEKSOLA, TUUKKA	KARPAT JR.	FINLAND-JR.	22-Jun-2001	5' 9.5"	146 lbs *	RW

101	BEAUCAGE, ALEX	ROUYN-NORANDA	QMJHL	25-Jul-2001	6' 1.0"	193 lbs *	RW
102	BOLDUC, SAMUEL	BLAINVILLE-BOISBRIAND	QMJHL	09-Dec-2000	6' 3.5"	210 lbs *	D
103	JANICKE, TREVOR	CENTRAL ILLINOIS	USHL	25-Dec-2000	5' 10.25"	193 lbs *	C
104	TUOMISTO, ANTTI	ASSAT JR.	FINLAND-JR.	20-Jan-2001	6' 4.0"	190 lbs	D
105	KOKKONEN, MIKKO	JUKURIT	FINLAND	18-Jan-2001	5' 11.0"	198 lbs *	D
106	LUNDMARK, SIMON	LINKOPING JR.	SWEDEN-JR.	08-Oct-2000	6' 2.0"	201 lbs	D
107	FAGEMO, SAMUEL	FROLUNDA	SWEDEN	14-Mar-2000	6' 0.0"	194 lbs	LW
108	GUENETTE, MAXENCE	VAL-D'OR	QMJHL	28-Apr-2001	6' 1.25"	181 lbs *	D

GOALIES

RANK	PLAYER	TEAM	LEAGUE	BIRTH	HEIGHT	WEIGHT	POS
1	KNIGHT, SPENCER	USA U-18	NTDP	19-Apr-2001	6' 3.0"	197 lbs *	G
2	SOGAARD, MADS	MEDICINE HAT	WHL	13-Dec-2000	6' 6.75"	192 lbs *	G
3	KOCHETKOV, PYOTR	RYAZAN	RUSSIA-2	25-Jun-1999	6' 3.0"	205 lbs	G
4	JONES, HUNTER	PETERBOROUGH	OHL	21-Sep-2000	6' 4.0"	196 lbs *	G
5	WOLF, DUSTIN	EVERETT	WHL	16-Apr-2001	5' 11.5"	156 lbs *	G
6	BASSE, DOMINIC	SELECTS U18 SOTH KENT	HIGH-CT	22-Apr-2001	6' 5.5"	179 lbs *	G

2019 NHL DRAFT PROSPECTS

	PLAYER	TEAM	LEAGUE	HEIGHT	WEIGHT	POS	GRADE
80	AALTONEN, LEEVI	KALPA JR.	FIN-JR.	5' 8.75"	177 *	RW	**C**
	HOCKEY SENSE	COMPETE		SKILL		SKATING	
	5	6		5		8	

Aaltonen spent the majority of the season playing for Kalpa's U20 team, where he was over a point-per-game player with 36 points in 29 games. During the season he also played 7 games in Liiga, registering one assist in those 7 games. He was a regular for Finland's U-18 team all year long in various tournaments, starting with the Hlinka-Gretzky Cup in August to the World Under-18 Hockey Championships in April.

The first thing you notice with Aaltonen is the pace at which he plays; he's got really quick feet, excellent acceleration and great top speed. If you combine his excellent skating abilities with his good compete level, you have a player who's very easy to notice on the ice. Despite his size, he competes hard, gets involved physically along the boards, and he's a very good forechecker. A significant portion of his offensive game came from his feet. By keeping his feet moving, he's tough to contain for opposing defensemen who can't keep up with him. He plays much bigger than his listed size, and his compete level mixed with his speed brings value to any penalty-killing unit. Offensively, he's a shoot-first type of forward who is not shy when it comes to putting pucks on net. He has a quick release and an above-average velocity on his wrist shot. However, he can be a bit too one-dimensional when he tries to create offense; he struggles with his decision-making, his passing game, and his vision is below-average. He can be ineffective during a game despite how hard he works, as his hockey IQ is poor and he can't always process the game quickly enough. If opponents are able to block his shooting lanes, he has trouble distributing pucks. Alternatively, if he does succeed in getting through, he's a bit too slow to find open teammates in the offensive zone. Aaltonen has good skills, quick hands, good shooting skills, and a solid compete level. The question marks surrounding him are related to his hockey IQ, playmaking abilities and his size.

	PLAYER	TEAM	LEAGUE	HEIGHT	WEIGHT	POS	GRADE
53	ABRAMOV, MIKHAIL	VICTORIAVILLE	QMJHL	5'10.5"	154 *	LC	**C+**
	HOCKEY SENSE	COMPETE		SKILL		SKATING	
	7	6		7		6	

Abramov came to Victoriaville from Russia this season after he was selected with the 97th overall pick in the CHL Import Draft last June. Before joining Victoriaville, he played for Russia at the Hlinka/Gretzky Cup in August, where he amassed 7 points in 5 games.

Abramov is a pass-first type of forward; he possesses excellent on-ice vision and he's always looking to find his teammates on the ice. He made a great duo with fellow Russian and draft-eligible Egor Serdyuk this season in Victoriaville. He's an above-average skater with average top speed, but has agility on his skates. Once he adds some mass to his frame, his speed will improve. His best attribute remains his hockey sense. He is a very smart hockey player at both ends of the ice and has a good compete level. On the forecheck, we've seen him steal the puck from a defenseman by using his quick stick on several occasions. Also, on the backcheck, there is always a strong effort, and he can cause turnovers with his quick stick and hustle. He has value as player that can be useful on the penalty kill for his team, as he possesses a great mix of hustle and anticipation, which makes him good shorthanded.

Offensively, as mentioned previously, he's a pass-first type of forward and didn't score a lot in the first half of the season. He only scored three goals before the Christmas break, but had more success when he used his shot, with 13 of his 16 goals coming in the 2nd half of the season. His wrist shot is pretty good, as it has good accuracy and can get off pretty quickly. He can pick corners if he has enough time to shoot it. On the power play, he likes to play from the half-wall on the right side of the ice. He has good poise with the puck, and as the season advanced, he became not only a threat to make great passes to his teammates, but also dangerous with his shot, firing pucks from the faceoff circle. Abramov will need to get stronger physically. This will make him even tougher to handle along the wall, and he would win more puck battles as well. There was a nice progression in his game this season, and we feel that he is only going to continue to improve and be better offensively next season (his second in the QMJHL) and possibly play for team Russia at the World Juniors.

"That Abramov kid was a letdown." - NHL Scout October 2018

"Not much talent surrounding him, big task for a rookie to try to carry this team." - NHL Scout, February 2019

"Late rounder for me." - NHL Scout, February 2019

"Not much in the Q (QMJHL) that I like but I have some time for this kid in the middle rounds." - NHL Scout, February 2019

"This player is better than some might think. He had a giant task to post big numbers on that team. I thought he started to shine later in the season. - HP Scout, Mark Edwards, May 2019

	PLAYER	TEAM	LEAGUE	HEIGHT	WEIGHT	POS	GRADE
NR	**ABRUZZESE, NICHOLAS**	**CHICAGO**	**USHL**	**5'9.25"**	**160 ***	**LC**	**C**
	HOCKEY SENSE	COMPETE		SKILL		SKATING	
	6	6		7		6	

Abruzzese is in his final year of draft eligibility as a 99' born. Nick started his sophomore campaign with the Steel on a torrid scoring pace and it didn't slow down as the year progressed. Abruzzese was an offensive catalyst for Chicago in their run to the Clark Cup Final, leading the USHL in scoring in the regular season with 29 goals and 51 Assists in 62 games, mostly playing alongside Robert Mastrosimone. Abruzzese is a bit of a late bloomer, as he played out all of his AAA eligibility, playing up through the North Jersey Avalanche program (T1EHL) through the U18 age group before heading to the Chicago Steel last season. Abruzzese has above average footwork and directional skating that allows him to play an up-tempo style and excels at making plays with the puck as he enters the offensive zone. Nick is a crafty playmaker that shows good patients and buy's time for his forwards to come into the zone and can adjust to what the defense does on the fly. Abruzzese is susceptible to committing turnovers in the neutral zone and near the offensive blueline as he can attempt some high-risk east-west plays instead of sometimes making the safe play and getting the puck in deep. Abruzzese is more of a passer and playmaking center than a goal scorer as his shot isn't going to beat a lot of NHL goalies one on one right now. Nick scores a lot of his goals in traffic, or in opportunistic odd man situations. Away from the puck, Abruzzese shows a good compete level but he still has a ways to go in the strength department, even as a 99 birthdate, he has a slight frame that keeps him from winning puck battles consistently and he can get pushed around along the walls and in front of the net. Abruzzese has the skill and skating to have a chance to play at the professional level, but much of it will depend on how he develops physically and if he is able to handle the rigors of pro hockey and potentially the NHL night in a night out. Abruzzese will be heading to Harvard this fall, where the longer developmental path and added Gym time that the NCAA route provides will be good for Nick's development path going forward.

"I think he'll go in the 4th or 5th round." - NHL Scout, May 2019

"He'll get drafted, no chance he doesn't. His game came around this year" - NHL Scout, May 2019

"I just don't see his game translating to the NHL as it sits right now." HP Scout, Dusten Braaksma

NR	PLAYER	TEAM	LEAGUE	HEIGHT	WEIGHT	POS	GRADE
	AEBISCHER, DAVID	GATINEAU	QMJHL	5'11"	183	RD	ND
	HOCKEY SENSE		COMPETE		SKILL		SKATING
	5		6		6		5

Aebischer came over from Switzerland to play for Gatineau in the QMJHL after the Olympiques drafted him with their 2nd pick in the CHL Import Draft (82nd overall). This season, he made some good progress during the season, ending the year with a good performance while facing a much better Drummondville team in the first round of the QMJHL playoffs. He also played for Switzerland at the World Junior Hockey Championships in Vancouver. When he returned, he was a much better player with Gatineau, as 19 of his 28 points in the 2019 calendar year were recorded (19 points in 30 games compared to 9 points in 29 games before the tournament).

As the season progressed, he started showing more confidence with the puck on his stick and was rewarded in terms of his offensive production. He's got some good feet, and can make some quick turns on the ice in order to avoid opposing players trying to take the puck away from him. With his boost in confidence, he would also skate more with the puck and make more plays with his feet, such as rushing the puck out of his zone and trying to create more offense using his feet. His point shot is average (either his slapshot or wrist shot) with good accuracy. He is a good puck-distributor on the power play, and is pretty smart with the puck. However, he is not an overly physical player, and it can be difficult for him versus bigger players down low in his own zone as a result. He needs to be more aggressive in those one-on-one battles. He's got some good tools offensively, but we are not sold on them converting to the NHL level as an offensive defenseman or power play guy. Because of this, it's important that he becomes a more dependable defensive defenseman who is capable of handling physical play. In January, Aebischer was rumoured to have a contract with a Swiss pro team for next season, which would mean he would not return to Gatineau. Those same reports were denied at the end of the season by local media.

"Much better in the second half of the season, didn't look like a prospect earlier in the year." - HP Scout Jerome Berube

59	PLAYER	TEAM	LEAGUE	HEIGHT	WEIGHT	POS	GRADE
	AFANASYEV, EGOR	MUSKEGON	USHL	6'3.5"	201 *	LW	C+
	HOCKEY SENSE		COMPETE		SKILL		SKATING
	5		6		7		5

Yegor just completed his 2nd full season with the Muskegon Lumberjacks after playing primarily a bottom six role last year. Afanasyev saw a significant jump in his point production this season. Finishing Top 10 in USHL scoring with 27 goals and 62 points in 58 games. Afanasyev came over to North America, from Russia at 14 years old and played at the Little Caesars program prior to joining Muskegon so he has had some time to adapt to the North American game and culture. Yegor has good size awareness and identifies when he has size and strength to his advantage. The issue up to this point has been his consistency in this area and can tend to blend into the game too often for a player his size. When Yegor is playing a fast, power forward style game, he has shown the ability to dominate games. Afanasyev has a good top gear and is hard for defenseman to handle once he gets a head of steam. Yegor's skating mechanics are ok, he lacks some explosiveness in his first few strides but is difficult to handle when he gets to top gear and has pretty good feet that can maneuver well in tight areas of the ice. Yegor can protect the puck well along the wall and below the dots and can create off the cycle by either finding teammates in the offensive zone or driving the puck to the net himself. Yegor has an NHL caliber shot but doesn't put it in play as much as he maybe should, instead deferring to driving himself and the puck to the net in a lot of situations as he entered the offensive zone. There are some red flags in his two-way game, but it doesn't come from lack of effort. Afansyev seems to understand his assignment both on the backcheck and in the defensive zone but lacks the foot speed to get there in some instances. He isn't quick to getting out to the points and his lack of footspeed keeps him from applying back pressure in the transition game. He is crafty with his stick when he gets there and has shown the ability to strip pucks from player in the neutral zone. Afanasyev is the definition of a raw prospect right now, he has a lot of physical tools and is blessed with NHL size and strength which will probably get him into the league at some point, but we believe it will come down to his ability to be more consistent that will determine what his pro upside will be down the road. Yegor was committed to Michigan State for this coming fall but there are signs he will be heading to Windsor (OHL) next season as they traded for his rights from Ottawa in December.

"He skates kinda like Kaliyev but he competes harder. Looked good this week." NHL Scout, September 2018

"He can score the way Kaliyev does but he's smarter, skates better and he competes much harder." - NHL Scout, September 2018

"I think there are some public lists that have this guy too high, much higher than I do. Average skater, doesn't make any plays or see the ice well. He does have good one on one skill and can shoot the puck." - NHL Scout, January 2019

"I worry about his pace and his brain." - NHL Scout, January 2019

"I didn't like him earlier but I've come around on him. He's a smarter player than I thought, the skating is ugly but he's powerful and competes hard. He's a top two rounder for sure." - NHL Scout, February 2019

"Seems like guys who rely on their shot to carry them seldom make it, especially if their skating is an issue." - NHL Scout, March 2019

"He's got a great shot but I don't like his skating." - NHL Scout, May 2019

"I wish I had seen more improvement over the course of the year. His stock dropped for me a lot since winter." - HP Scout, Michael Farkas

"I had time for him in Pittsburgh (USHL FallClassic) but I never liked him that much again the rest of the season. - HP Scout, Mark Edwards, May 2019

	PLAYER	TEAM	LEAGUE	HEIGHT	WEIGHT	POS	GRADE
36	AHAC, LAYTON	PRINCE GEORGE	BCHL	6'1.75"	188 *	LD	**B**
	HOCKEY SENSE		COMPETE		SKILL		SKATING
	7		6		6		6

Layton Ahac had a very good season for Prince George, as he became a contributor on both-special teams' units and produced 32 points in 53 games, including 4 goals. In the playoffs, he stepped up his production to a point-per-game, generating 17 points in 17 games, including 5 goals. His elevated play helped the Spruce Kings capture their first BCHL title. He is slated to play for the Ohio-State University in 2019-2020.

Ahac is an all-situations, minute-eating defenseman who has a strong two-way-game. In a draft that loses defensive-depth quickly due to a lack of offensive-talent on the backend; Ahac brings some significant potential. There's finesse to how he handles the puck; showing a set of soft-hands and a calculated approach that's matched by his poise. This gave him a high-rate of execution in all-three-zones when we viewed him. His feel for the game, affords him the opportunity to activate aggressively at the offensive line; displaying a good-degree of spatial-awareness and processing ability. This extends into his defensive-capabilities. Ahac is an initiator who looks to trap his opponents into pre-determined patterns based off his initial defensive-read, then overwhelm them with his leverage. His defensive-acumen expands to his stick-play. He's an aggressive poke-checker and one of the more impressive stick-pressers we've seen in this class. This makes him a handful to deal with around his blue-paint, where he can aggressively protect his net-area and box-out opponents effectively. His aggressiveness compliments his hockey-sense, rarely throwing himself out of the play as a result; it's another area where his attention to detail gives him the ability to defend in multiple ways. This includes maintaining a proper-gap, evaluating 2-on-1 plays properly, and assessing shooting lanes in advance so that he can position himself well. Although he's a rangy defenseman who hasn't filled out his frame, there's bite to his game; he's willing to stand up for himself and his teammates after play stops, and although he's not a heavy hitter, he knows how to use his weight effectively along the boards. He's not an easy defenseman to play against.

In a class that features a lot of shutdown defenseman, Ahac brings some raw offensive upside. As the year progressed, he started developing an offensive-attack built around his offensive-awareness. Ahac's hockey sense extends to his ability to hide his intentions with the puck. He's a difficult kid to read and uses his body mechanics to hide his release and his passing; there's a high-degree of coordination and this allows him to seamlessly transition to different offensive-play-types. Although his stat-line might suggest otherwise, Layton's shooting mechanics are a plus, getting his wrist-shots off quickly and more importantly, finding open-seams that allowed him to thread both shots and passes through traffic. If his offensive game doesn't develop as well as we think it could; he does have quality outlet-passing that extends over two-lines which can make him a useful transition option.

Although there's upside regarding Layton's game, there's still a significant flaw that he needs to work on in order to play regular minutes at the highest-level. His skating mechanics leave a lot to be desired. He's a taller kid whose posture is upright both from a take-off position and when skating at his top-gear. Additionally, his lower-body strength prevents him from driving through his stepping motion, which doesn't allow him to have an adequate knee-bend at this time. Despite his mechanics though, Layton still has a natural fluidity to his skating due to his coordination and impressive cross-overs. He's susceptible to getting beat wide when he miscalculates his gap due to his lack of two-step area quickness, yet he's surprisingly elusive under-pressure around his goal-line. When we view defenseman; we make it a priority to monitor how they handle puck-retrieval in their own end, and Layton's had a surprising amount of success by using his edges to form quick-stops and turns to escape the forecheck.

When looking at Ahac's trajectory, he became a more confident and consistent contributor in the offensive-zone towards the end of the season which bodes well for his continued development. As a result, there's potential for him to develop into a top-four defenseman but is unlikely to receive special-teams' responsibilities. His projection can't materialize unless he improves his skating though.

"Extremely smart defensive player. Skating is a little bit tricky to evaluate. Stronger in some areas than others." - NHL Scout, March 2019

"He's another player in this draft that is under the radar but I really like." - NHL Scout, May 2019

"This kid is a dark-horse prospect for me that I think has some real upside." - HP Scout, Brad Allen. March 2019

"Not much chatter on this player during the season. Most guys just told me they thought he was draftable, but some others had not even heard of him. That should change by the end of combine week." HP Scout, Mark Edwards, March 2019

"There were some really good prospects in the BCHL this season. This kid was right in the middle of it. He was a big reason for his team's success. Shares some traits with Seider as for as the way he shuts down forwards and projects to eat minutes." - HP Scout, Mark Edwards

	PLAYER	TEAM	LEAGUE	HEIGHT	WEIGHT	POS	GRADE
NR	ALAMI, CADE	BERKSHIRE	HIGH-MA	6'7.0"	190	RD	ND
	HOCKEY SENSE	COMPETE		SKILL		SKATING	
	5	5		4		5	

Cade Alami is a very tall and lanky right handed defenseman that can eat up a lot of time and space. Like most defenseman with his build there is a project that will need time to find out exactly the type of player he can be. Despite his size, Alami is far from clumsy on his skates. Alami possesses good knee bend and extends his stride nicely for such a big kid. There is no doubt his footwork and skating will need to develop for Cade to have a shot to extend his career after college but he has a good foundation to start from. One area of his game that will likely be the key for him going forward is his defensive acumen. Like many players his size in Prep School, Alami is dominate along the walls but it wasn't all due to his size advantage. Alami is very good in defending and winning battles in his own zone by being technically sound and smart as far as body positioning. His size is just an added advantage for him at this stage. His long reach and quick poke checking ability is a great asset and he utilizes it well in one on one situations. Alami doesn't project as a big puck rusher or a defenseman who will dominate the score sheet but he makes simple and reliable plays on the breakout and can handle the puck well in traffic. Predictably, Cade has a powerful shot from the point and if his agility and footwork develop he should be able to get into more situations to utilize it in the offensive end. Alami is as raw of a prospect as it gets and will need some time to grow into his tall frame but his game has some intriguing tools that have kept scouts interested throughout the year. Alami was a highly scouted prospect even in April at USA Nationals where he played for the Mid Fairfield Rangers. Alami will likely be returning to Berkshire School next season or the USHL before heading to Providence College in 2020.

	PLAYER	TEAM	LEAGUE	HEIGHT	WEIGHT	POS	GRADE
NR	ALEXANDER, JACSON	EDMONTON	WHL	5'9.25"	178 *	LD	ND
	HOCKEY SENSE	COMPETE		SKILL		SKATING	
	5	5		5		6	

Former 17th overall bantam draft pick moved from Swift Current to Edmonton this season. Alexander got off to a promising start with 5 points in 15 games before suffering a season ending injury. Standing only 5'9 Alexander makes up for his diminutive size with his strong skating ability. He really stood out defensively due to his good feet and ability to take away time and space from the opposition. With the puck Alexander was able to make plays using his skating. He had multiple end to end rushes and showcased the ability to beat opponents on the blueline with his agility. Over the course of the game Jacson is a player who makes a lot of good decisions with the puck and rarely makes big mistakes.

Not the most creative player, Jacson lacks somewhat in his puck skills for a smaller defenseman. There is a big possibility Jacson comes back even better next year on an Edmonton team that will be contending for the championship.

	PLAYER	TEAM	LEAGUE	HEIGHT	WEIGHT	POS	GRADE
77	ALEXANDROV, NIKITA	CHARLOTTETOWN	QMJHL	6'0.0"	179 *	LC	**C**
	HOCKEY SENSE		COMPETE		SKILL		SKATING
	6		5		6		6

Alexandrov was in his second season with Charlottetown in the QMJHL. After a good playoff run last year, he had a solid season, with 61 points in 64 games. He added 7 points in 6 playoff games. He was selected 50th overall in the 2017 CHL Import Draft. He's a dual-citizen; his father, a former pro hockey player who played a year in North America with Springfield in the mid-90s, played most of his career in Russia and Germany.

Alexandrov can play both down the middle and on the wing. He's better at center, but his defensive game and poor work in the faceoff circle might force him to play on the wing at the next level. He's a decent skater; his top speed and acceleration are good, but he needs to be stronger on his skates. This would help him protect the puck better along the boards. In our viewings, we saw fall down too often when challenged physically while in possession of the puck. He's got good puck skills, including good one-on-one abilities. He also likes to put pucks on net (217 shots on goal this year). He possesses an above-average shot with a quick release, but he needs to work on his consistency. This year with Charlottetown, he was a key player offensively, playing a top-6 role and getting top PP time. He missed last year's draft by one day, making him one of, if not the oldest from this draft class. In terms of upside, we're not sure there's enough offense there for him to be considered a top-6 forward. In order to be more effective at the next level in a more defensive role, he'll need to be better away from the puck. He's got one more season to go in the QMJHL before he can turn pro; look for him to continue to improve his two-way game.

	PLAYER	TEAM	LEAGUE	HEIGHT	WEIGHT	POS	GRADE
NR	ALISHLALOV, MALIK	WESTMINSTER	HIGH-CT	6'2.0"	195	LD	**ND**
	HOCKEY SENSE		COMPETE		SKILL		SKATING
	5		5		4		5

Malik is a 01' birthdate who has bounced around a little since coming to North America from Russia in 2016. Alishlalov started with the Colorado Revolution midget program in 16/17 before moving to the east coast and attending Westminster Prep School for the 17/18 season. Alishlalov has a smooth and effortless skating stride that gets to top gear rather quickly. Malik retrieves and moves pucks out of his own end well. He is quick to identify pressure and uses his skating mobility to elude pressure and turn plays north. Malik doesn't have much for dynamic puck moving ability and defaults to passing the puck out of his own end or going D to D rather than rushing the puck up the ice on his own.

Alishlalov defense against the rush well, his fluid mobility keeps him in good position on his man and keeps plays out of the middle of the ice with regularity. Where Alishlalov struggles defensively is when his team has been hemmed into his own end for a period of time, Malik can get caught puck watching and lose containment on his checks or be slow to pick up his assignments. Offensively, Alishlalov is effective moving the puck at the point, he can cover a lot of ground on the blue line and shows good poise with the puck under pressure. His shot is not a big threat from the point, mostly due to Malik not getting it off his tape quick enough. His size and physical maturity allows him to have a powerful slap shot but hasn't been in a lot of situations to utilize it yet. Malik's ceiling isn't incredibility high at his stage but has shown a slow but steady trajectory as far as his development. It's not unimaginable to see a team take a later round flyer on Alishlalov and see how he continues to develop at the NCAA level. We see him more as an NCAA Free Agent watch list prospect at this stage. Alishlalov was drafted by Youngstown in the 2017 USHL Phase 2 draft and is committed to the University of Connecticut.

	PLAYER	TEAM	LEAGUE	HEIGHT	WEIGHT	POS	GRADE
NR	ALISTROV, VLADIMIR	EDMONTON	WHL	6'1.75"	175 *	LW	ND
	HOCKEY SENSE		COMPETE		SKILL		SKATING
	6		4		6		5

After being taken 2nd overall in the import draft Vladimir Alistrov had a poor start to the year as he adapted to the WHL. As the year progressed Alistrov got more comfortable but still wound up finishing with only 38 points in 62 games.

Over the course of the year Alistrov's effort and compete level have been very inconsistent. In games where he was engaged he has looked like a draftable player but too often he was content to be a spectator. Vlad's hands are very good and allow him to possess the puck with a man on him. His vision and passing also stands out as strengths, he had multiple plays this year where he passed teammates in to empty nets by holding goalies and defensemen. Prefers to play the game from the outside and use his passing from there to set up teammates in dangerous areas. Not yet strong enough protecting the puck or quick enough to be consistently dangerous with this style. Play through the neutral zone was good as he was a threat to either skate it in or draw a defenseman and pass. Engagement without the puck was questionable as Alistrov did not show much will to make an impact defensively or in board battles.

	PLAYER	TEAM	LEAGUE	HEIGHT	WEIGHT	POS	GRADE
NR	ALLENSEN, NATHAN	BARRIE	OHL	5'11.5"	180 *	LD	ND
	HOCKEY SENSE		COMPETE		SKILL		SKATING
	5		6		5		7

Nathan Allensen had an average-season, developing more into a shutdown defensive-player as opposed to the two-way player that he showed flashes of becoming, after getting drafted 32nd overall in the OHL-draft. He managed some powerplay-time but finished with 20 points in 67 games, including 4 goals. Nathan is a mobile-shutdown defender who plays bigger than his size. His best attribute is his skating ability. He features a good set of mechanics and can stop and start on a dime. This led to him being able to maintain an adequate-gap when we watched him and he was good at racing down pucks off dump and chase sequences around his goal-line. Furthermore, his skating also allows him to pinch aggressively at the line and he can go end-to-end. Another impressive quality of Nathan's game is his willingness to physical-engage. He's not a tall defender but he's a powerful kid who can lay out bigger players than himself. His mean-streak works well in-front of the net, where he doesn't back down and makes life uncomfortable for forwards around the goal-line. There's a multi-faceted defensive approach to his game, where he also uses a good-stick and has anticipated lanes well when looking to intercept passes. The biggest drawbacks in Nathan's game are his anticipation with the puck on his stick and his passing execution-rate. We have seen him make quality decisions with limited time below the goal-line while getting heavily pressured, but they are not consistent. Additionally, when he interprets the forecheck correctly but can't skate the puck out, he has difficulty with his outlet passes. His passing can be too hard to handle and it led to several unforced turnovers since his accuracy is also average. His anticipation at the offensive-line is also a weakness. He has difficulty maintaining his poise under-pressure more at the offensive-line then when in his own-end, and as a result can make some poor plays with the puck. There isn't a whole lot of offensive-touch or offensive-awareness in Allensen's game, so he's going to have to rely on his high-compete level and skating ability in his own-zone to be a difference maker. The problem is that he hasn't shown a lot of consistency in being able to move the puck up the ice and he's not very big. In order for Nathan to take the next-step, he has to improve his playmaking ability and remain more composed when an opponent is bearing down on him, when he's in control of the puck.

NR	PLAYER	TEAM	LEAGUE	HEIGHT	WEIGHT	POS	GRADE
	ALNEFELT, HUGO	HV 71 JR.	SWE-JR.	6'2.0"	177*	G	C
	HOCKEY SENSE		COMPETE		SKILL		SKATING
	5		6		6		5

Hugo Alnefelt was the starter for HV71 in the SuperElit where he put up a 2.59 GAA and an .905 save percentage in 24 games. He also played 2 games in the J18 Elite where he put up a 2.01 GAA and an .943 save percentage.

In international play with team Sweden, he had a part in his teams successful season. Recording a 2.33 GAA and a save percentage of .922 in 3 games at the Ivan Hlinka tournament and then followed up that performance to win the gold at the U18's where he put up a 2.75 GAA and a .921 save percentage. Alnefelt's not the most technically gifted goaltender, but he gets the job done. He's got a big frame and often sits in his crease, in the butterfly position, just waiting for pucks to hit him. While in that position, he is strong along the ice and saves the first shot more often than not. However, his rebound-control and balance, often puts him in an awkward position where he is falling forwards and cant find the puck. That particular position also tends to open up big openings for the shooters to pick their shot just under the crossbar. An interesting aspect of his game is that he will come up big and make a big desperation save when his team needs it the most and at the same time he tends to concede cheap ones early in the games as well.

He possesses some pretty decent lateral quickness, but yet again, he doesn't recover well after that movement, but he doesn't give up on the play and competes hard to at least, try to make that impossible save. His skating and game around and behind the net, leaves much room for improvement, since he's not a very strong skater due to his balance being too much on his toes and his stickhandling needs to get worked on. He does read the dump-ins quickly and orders his defenders to come quickly to collect the puck.

NR	PLAYER	TEAM	LEAGUE	HEIGHT	WEIGHT	POS	GRADE
	ANDERSSON, ISAC	FRÖLUNDA J20	SWE JR	6'0.0"	190	LC	ND
	HOCKEY SENSE		COMPETE		SKILL		SKATING
	6		6		5		6

Andersson split this past season between two teams, Frölunda HC J18 and Frölunda HC J20 where he managed to put up 35 points in 51 games , both leagues combined. He also dressed for every single U18 tournament game for Sweden during the season where he put up a modest record of 1 goal and 2 assist for 3 points in 20 games despite his team winning the silver medal at the Hlinka tournament and the gold medal in he U18 world championships. He is a player that is 100% committed to team play and creating time and space for his team mates. There will be no flashy plays or glass breaking hits from him, but he will outwork most of his opponents every night. He is a decent skater, with good mobility and edge work, but he lacks top speed and power in his stride.

His size is average, but he is strong when making physical contact and is really effective at twisting and turning along the boards to come out with the puck on his stick to be able to deliver it to his line mates. He can maneuver his way into winning puck battles, but is not smart or fast enough to find the right areas to score himself. His offensive upsides are very limited, but he is a valuable team player.

	PLAYER	TEAM	LEAGUE	HEIGHT	WEIGHT	POS	GRADE
NR	ANGLE, TYLER	WINDSOR	OHL	5'9.5"	167 *	LC	ND
	HOCKEY SENSE		COMPETE		SKILL		SKATING
	6		7		5		5

Tyler Angle was one of the better players on the Spitfires this past season, finishing with 44 points in 58 games, including 20 goals. In the playoffs, he had 3 goals in 4 games and wasn't featured at international events. Angle was a player that impressed us due to his ability to elevate his game when his team needed him to. He's not the most skilled-kid, but he's more than the sum of his parts due to his drive and hockey-sense. Angle's good at evaluating his options quickly when holding the puck, and rarely forces play. This made him a good decision maker overall, and as a result, he had one of the better execution rates with the puck on the Spitfires squad in our viewings. On the powerplay, he was used along the half-wall where he drove play successfully and showed plus vision. He's a primary playmaker but also knows when he has a high-percentage shooting option in-front of him, which gave him the ability to score occasionally as well. His release point is average, but he can still take passes in one-motion and identifies angles on goalies at an above-average rate. Away from the play, Angle plays a 200-foot, detail-oriented game and was capable of helping support his defenseman at a decent-rate. Additionally, his impressive anticipation made him a threat on the penalty-kill; he was able to pressure correctly and generate takeaways.

Although Angle drove-play and was a plus contributor for his team in all-three-zones, he still has weaknesses that are unfortunately stoppers for us. Angle is a smaller-kid who has decent skating mechanics but lacks power. There isn't a lot of explosiveness to his game or much in the way of a separating gear. Though, when we describe his skating as average, it's a solid five as opposed to a fringe-five that some other prospects have, so there's a bit more room for his skating to improve compared to other average-skaters we have discussed. Regardless of how improved his skating becomes, he's not driving play at the NHL-level like he can in spurts for the Spitfires though. Furthermore, Angle doesn't a lotk of natural offensive-talent, relying primarily on his hockey-sense and determination which make him an unlikely candidate to translate.

"Angle was one of the more important players on the Spitfires roster."- HP Scout, Brad Allen

"I like him in the OHL. He's another one that can play for my Junior team anytime but I don't see NHL in him. He's 5'9" and not a great skater and not blessed with a ton of skill." - HP Scout, Mark Edwards

	PLAYER	TEAM	LEAGUE	HEIGHT	WEIGHT	POS	GRADE
NR	ANTROPOV, DANIL	OSHAWA	OHL	6'1.0"	185*	LW	ND
	HOCKEY SENSE		COMPETE		SKILL		SKATING
	5		5		5		5

The 6th player selected in the 2016 OHL Draft. The December 2000 birthdate makes him eligible for this years NHL Draft. Danil played a very vanilla game. While he did manage to post 15 goals and 52 points overall, there were too many of our viewings where he was difficult to find, especially for a player in his 3rd OHL season. Skating, Hockey IQ, competitiveness and skill were all just in that average range. In the end, there is just not enough about his game to warrant us giving him a draftable grade.

"I know one Gens staffer very well and the report was all positive about Danil off ice. 'Takes care of himself physically and got along well with the Vets in the room. Had a serious injury to his mouth where he lost some teeth and he didn't miss a game.'" - HP Scout, Mark Edwards

"Just too many games where I struggled to find him. Nothing about his game ever screamed draft me. He struggled to play with pace and create offence. I could've included several quotes from NHL Scouts but they primarily just echoed what I said or were even less flattering., so there was not much point. - HP Scout, Mark Edwards

	PLAYER	TEAM	LEAGUE	HEIGHT	WEIGHT	POS	GRADE
NR	ASLANIDIS, ALEXANDROS	AVON OLD FARMS	HIGH-CT	6'5.0"	220 *	G	**ND**
	HOCKEY SENSE	COMPETE		SKILL		SKATING	
	4	5		4		4	

Aslanidis spent most of 18/19 playing for Avon Old Farms School but did see one game of action with the USNTDP U18 team where he struggled. Aslanidis finished the season with the Mid Fairfield Rangers U18 squad at the USA National Tournament where he was a bit hot and cold in that tournament. Aslanidis is a big, thick goalie that when he plays at the top of his crease doesn't give a lot to shoot at but he isn't always positioned there and struggles playing too deep in the net a lot of the time. Aslanidis makes a lot of saves due to his size, but when forced to move laterally, he lacks some explosiveness and strength to get over and make the saves consistently. The 6'5" is intriguing but needs a lot of coaching and development going forward to get the most out of his impressive size. Alex is a Providence College commit but will need some seasoning and coaching in Junior hockey before he's ready for NCAA minutes.

"The kid is massive in the net but he needs a lot of time and coaching, very raw." - NHL Scout, April 2019

	PLAYER	TEAM	LEAGUE	HEIGHT	WEIGHT	POS	GRADE
NR	ATTARD, RONALD	TRI-CITY	USHL	6'3.0"	208 *	RD	**C**
	HOCKEY SENSE	COMPETE		SKILL		SKATING	
	5	6		6		5	

Aggressive, offensive defenseman. Attard's third USHL season was a revelation. After a combined 20 points in his first two seasons, the '99 birthday jumped to 30 goals, 65 points, and a USHL-best plus-47 while capturing Defenseman of the Year and Player of the Year honors in the league. It's a very shortlist of players (if any) that can lay claim to being on the ice as much as Attard and his defense partner Zac Jones this year. He plays a hyper-aggressive rover type game that carries him all over the ice. Very rarely does he back off the line defensively, and even when he does, he's just waiting for his next chance to step up and make a hit or try to make a steal. In the chase, it's not unheard of to find Attard in as F1 on the forecheck even. In the defensive zone, he is very impatient and, again, will chase the play all over the rink. He isn't hard to isolate, particularly when emerging from behind the net on a low-high setup. He often sets up outside the dot line against routine rush attempts and his body and stick positioning are as inconsistent and wonky as his gaps. His small-area footwork leaves a lot to be desired and it hinders his recovery ability. His skating stride isn't pretty and it looks like one foot is much more dominant than the other. He gets around the ice fine because he is moving a lot, but the inefficiencies in his stride prevent him from firing up an extra gear to shake defenders. His lateral skating and ability to walk the line don't generate enough power for him to really manipulate shooting lanes in terms of next-level prognostication (obviously, not as much of an issue at this level).

Attard offers a plus shot and the ability to one-time pucks. He was the triggerman on the power play and there was no secret about it. The green light that Ronnie had allowed him to travel down low, even at 5-on-5, to hunt for goals – that's part of how a defenseman ended up scoring on 20% of his 150 shots. Despite the gaudy production values, the stickhandling and overall technical skill level don't move the needle too much. His partner was a better puck carrier and playmaker – Attard was the finisher, or made the pinch to keep plays alive. All told, there isn't a lot of hockey sense to go around here and it will make undoing or fixing this very not-pro-style player a tough ask.

"For all of his offensive numbers he put up this year, I haven't heard many other scouts mention him at all." – HP Scout, Dusten Braaksma, May 2019

"Skating is interesting because he's ok going up and down the rink but he's kind of awkward and his overall agility is just ok at best." – HP Scout, Mark Edwards, May 2019

	PLAYER	TEAM	LEAGUE	HEIGHT	WEIGHT	POS	GRADE
NR	BAKER, JARRETT	DRUMMONDVILLE	QMJHL	5' 11.5"	181 *	LD	ND
	HOCKEY SENSE		COMPETE		SKILL		SKATING
	5		6		4		5

Baker is originally from Halifax and was selected by the Voltigeurs in the 5th round of the 2016 QMJHL Draft.

Baker is a defensive defenseman who can play a physical game in his own end, and who also doesn't mind dropping the gloves to defend a teammate if needed. He brings toughness to the Voltigeurs, and has value as penalty killer; he is a good shot blocker and can clear the front of the net. He has decent footwork, he's an above-average skater and can skate the puck out of his zone. He needs to do it more consistently, though; he needs to use his feet more to get the puck out of his zone. He lacks creativity with the puck in the neutral and offensive zones to be considered as being more than a defensive defenseman; his decision-making with the puck is only average and he struggles to move pucks quickly when he's under pressure. Offensively, he's limited; he lacks the necessary creativity and vision to play on the power play. However, he does have a good, hard shot, and can score from time to time from the point. In order to improve his game, he'll need to make smarter plays with the puck and think the game faster so that his transition and offensive game can both improve. We don't expect to see Baker get drafted, but with his toughness, he's a guy who could play in the lower levels of professional hockey at some point.

	PLAYER	TEAM	LEAGUE	HEIGHT	WEIGHT	POS	GRADE
NR	BARLAGE, LOGAN	LETHBRIDGE	WHL	6'3.75"	202 *	RC	ND
	HOCKEY SENSE		COMPETE		SKILL		SKATING
	5		5		6		4

Former 3rd overall bantam draft pick had a very hot start, before fading spastically after Lethbridge loaded up for a run. Ended the year with 15 goals and 39 points, mainly lining up on the third line and second powerplay.

Barlage is a supersized centre who stands over 6'4 and weighs over 200 pounds. His skating is clumsy and he is consistently one of the slower players on the ice. This especially stands out in situations that require quick directional changes or a burst of speed as he lacks the gear change to make an explosive play. This is largely due to a somewhat upright skating stance, with not enough knee bend. For such a big man Barlage has the puck skills to make some skill plays. Is very in control with the puck on his stick and does a great job of keeping it away from defenders. Can look dominant below the ringette line using his big body to hold off even the biggest defenders he came up against. On multiple occasions showed the ability to power himself to the net. Offensively Barlage makes an impact with his solid playmaking ability. While he is not a top level set up man, he was able to make plays through the defense and hit teammates in dangerous areas. Barlage still requires work on his shot release which comes a bit slow. Logan did not receive a ton of ice time this year, mainly playing a 3rd line role. With Lethbridge graduating a lot of forwards above him he should step in to a bigger role next year and have strong production.

#	PLAYER	TEAM	LEAGUE	HEIGHT	WEIGHT	POS	GRADE
6	BASSE, DOMINIC	SOUTH KENT	HIGH-CT	6'5.5"	179 *	G	C
	HOCKEY SENSE		COMPETE		SKILL		SKATING
	6		5		6		6

Massive goaltender who got into a lot of games for his level this season. Listed at 6'6", but Basse moves well in the net – he looks smooth and quite coordinated. He likes to remain upright in a very narrow stance. Even when he drops into the butterfly, he does a good job keeping his chest up and his shoulders back. This is especially helpful because of how concerned he appears with being anchored and not overlapping outside of his net, that he doesn't always show the ability to "complete" the push and get all the way to his post hard enough. As such, he doesn't cover the edges of the net very well. While he does a good job keeping his chest upright on the butterfly save selection, he doesn't do nearly as good of a job with that on his pushes or when shuffling. That's not uncommon for big young goalies who don't have the requisite core strength to support that capability. Dominic does a real good job tracking pucks at this slower, lower level where he got in the net more than 40 times this season. Coupled with his strong desire to track pucks, he really likes to be set on his mark to make saves and he makes his feet do that work for him. It's a good habit to have, but it does sometimes cost him some depth on shots. He doesn't show a lot of ability to challenge shooters from a depth perspective off of a pass. This potential flaw leaves him susceptible in the upper parts of the net, especially high glove, and even short side because of the aforementioned lack of finish on his pushes. He keeps a low glove hand, favoring a fingers-out posture. He gets the seal to the body with his elbow, but the glove placement and the wonky mechanics seem to hurt his ability to catch pucks routinely.

Basse is cool and confident with little sticks plays and setups behind the net for his defensemen and it augments the sense that he has a good feeling for the game. On the contrary, he does look a little quick to panic on pucks around his feet in rebound or shuffle situations. He makes it a point for pucks to hit him in the chest, but they don't stick to him enough. It's a product of his chest uprightness, but he needs to learn how to soften those shots so that he keeps more of them vacuum sealed. The Colorado College commit looks good using his blocker, especially just above his pad, to direct rebounds into the proper areas. As a huge goalie who just turned 18 but has the coordination of an older player, there is a big upside play here. He was selected in the 2018 USHL Entry Draft by Youngstown.

"I like him., he made my list. He's a later guy but solid." – NHL Scout, March 2019

#	PLAYER	TEAM	LEAGUE	HEIGHT	WEIGHT	POS	GRADE
NR	BEATON, JOHN	KEMPTVILLE	CCHL	6'0.5"	175 *	LC	ND
	HOCKEY SENSE		COMPETE		SKILL		SKATING
	5		6		5		5

Beaton is a hardworking, 200-foot player who played for Kemptville in the CCHL and recently committed to RPI for 2020-21. John competes every game, and was really effective for Kemptville when he got the puck down low and worked on the boards. He uses his size well to protect the puck; he also has a long reach which allows him to be more effective on the cycle. He ended the year with 47 points in 56 games. Overall, his skating is above average and he showed some good speed coming in off the rush. He showed the ability to beat defensemen wide and take pucks to the net. That said, he lacks acceleration, and he needs to improve his first couple steps. It takes him a little longer to join the rush from a stationary position than we'd like. He has exhibited a hard, accurate wrist shot that he can get off quickly. John is very reliable in his own end, as he understands his assignments and will make sure the puck is out safely before going on the attack. He has good size and plays the game well; by going the collegiate route he should be able to improve his speed and strength enough to be on the pro radar down the road.

	PLAYER	TEAM	LEAGUE	HEIGHT	WEIGHT	POS	GRADE
101	BEAUCAGE, ALEX	ROUYN-NORANDA	QMJHL	6'1.0"	193 *	RW	**C**
	HOCKEY SENSE	COMPETE		SKILL		SKATING	
	7	6		6		4	

Beaucage was the 22nd overall selection by Rouyn-Noranda in the 2017 QMJHL Draft. This season, he was one of the better players on his team, scoring 39 times and finishing the year with 79 points. He got a lot of ice time, playing on the top line with league-leading scorer Peter Abbandonato. He was a key player on the power play, playing on his off-wing for one-timer purposes. He scored many goals from the left wing/faceoff circle area.

Beaucage number one offensive weapon is his shot; he possesses one of the best shots among players available for this draft. He's got an excellent release, and his shot has NHL velocity. He's got to work a bit on his accuracy, or the consistency of his accuracy. He can pick corners very well, but his aim is not always on point. He can score from all sorts of angles; we saw him score goals from low-percentage angles a number of times this season. Beaucage's father (Marc Beaucage) was a long-time pro hockey player in the AHL, but mostly in Germany, where he played 7 seasons in the DEL. The younger Beaucage is not only a forward with a great shot, but one who thinks the game very well, using his above-average smarts. He's known for his shooting abilities, but he's an underrated passer and makes quick decisions with the puck in the neutral and offensive zones. Beaucage usually has a good compete level; even if he has a bad game, he works hard and doesn't quit on the ice. The biggest knock on Beaucage's game is by far in regards to his skating abilities. They are average at best, and on bad games, he might look below-average as a result of them. When he's playing in Rouyn-Noranda (smaller ice surface) his skating doesn't look too bad, but on the road, we see more problems in that department. In games against top teams with a lot of speed (Drummondville, for example) he really struggled to make an impact. The pace was too high for him, and he will definitely need to work really hard to improve his footwork and speed. Away from the puck, Beaucage is not a liability in his own zone (notably due to his smarts), but his lack of footspeed hurts his efficiency on the PK despite his good anticipation. For him, the name of the game will be his offense; in order to get to the NHL, he'll need to play on an offensive line. There's a lot of work ahead for him, but he's not afraid of it; his work ethic, NHL shot and smarts help his cause. His skating abilities will hurt his draft stock.

"Plays smart and that helps with the bad boots. He can flat out fire the puck." - NHL Scout, February 2019

"He's a first round talent." - NHL Scout, January 2019

"I'd take him in the 3rd, maybe the 2nd depending on who is still on the board when we pick." - NHL Scout, January 2019

"Mid Rounder." - NHL Scout, January 2019

"What's the difference between him and Kaliyev? Both having skating issues and this kid works harder and his shot is even better." - NHL Scout, February 2019

"He's maybe a late 6th or a 7th for us." - NHL Scout, May 2019

"Heard someone had Sam Reinhart as their comparable. A playmaking center vs scoring winger. If he's Sam Reinhardt then Toropchenko is Mario and I don't mean Tremblay." - NHL Scout, May 2019

"Tough to rank him because of the poor skating and I didn't see the same level of compete and hockey sense in my limited viewings as our area guy." - HP Scout, Mark Edwards, April 2019

"He had his share of scoring chances during the Memorial Cup, but didn't seem very confident shooting the puck during the tournament. His only goal, ironically, was from a backhand shot. Skating is a big issue with him, and it was again this week." HP Scout Jérôme Bérubé, June 2019

63	PLAYER	TEAM	LEAGUE	HEIGHT	WEIGHT	POS	GRADE
	BECKMAN, ADAM	SPOKANE	WHL	6'0.5"	168 *	LW	C+
	HOCKEY SENSE	COMPETE		SKILL		SKATING	
	7	5		6		6	

Beckman came into his first WHL season and worked his way up into a top 6 role for the Spokane Chiefs. Over the course of the season Beckman registered 32 goals and 62 points as one of the top rookies in the WHL.

Consistency was key for Beckman, as he made an impact in every single viewing we had. As a first year WHL player Beckman came in and over the course of the year constantly grew into a bigger role and showcased more skills. One of the better minds for the game amongst WHLers Beckman was often the driver on his line, constantly demanding the puck and getting in positions to make a play. Beckman has an excellent release and great sense for when to use it, beating goalies with consistency from the slot and from the circles. Beckman drove transition with his excellent ability to get pucks in to open spaces, took advantage of overcommitted defences to make cross ice passes to his teammates. In the offensive zone did not consistently display elite vision, but with more space on the powerplay made many clever passes. Skating is above average with good burst and a very slippery quality as he often manages to just wiggle through checks. Defensively Beckman has some work to do as he occasionally lapsed in his concentration and blew his assignment. Beckman was not overly physical but was impactful on the forecheck through excellent positioning and a great understanding of where he wanted to direct the play . Beckman is very cerebral making excellent decisions with the puck. Should become an even stronger player next year as he steps into an even larger role for Spokane.

"Liked him early but have questions with his work ethic...compete. I don't think we'll be drafting him where we have him." - NHL Scout, May 2019

"Pretty good skill. I like him in the late 2nd or later." - NHL Scout, May 2019

	PLAYER	TEAM	LEAGUE	HEIGHT	WEIGHT	POS	GRADE
45	BEECHER, JOHN	USA U-18	NTDP	6'2.75"	204 *	LC	B
	HOCKEY SENSE	COMPETE		SKILL		SKATING	
	5	6		5		8	

A big center who was used as a lower line player and penalty killer all year. The production was not there for Beecher in part because of his role, but also because of his own limitations as a player. He found just six goals and 20 points in 27 USHL games. At 6'3" and over 200 pounds, Beecher can get a good head of steam going after a couple strides. The first step is better than average too, for a player of his size. But it's the top speed after three or four power strides that impresses the most with his overall skating game. He has a really good understanding of how to use his body to shield pucks and win battles on the boards. Beecher's hits are powerful and useful for separating players from the puck.

He's a little less aggressive in the offensive zone than we'd like. He seems to fashion himself as more of a shooter and appears to try to make himself more available to get open than he does focusing on digging in and retrieving pucks and pressuring retrieving defensemen into mistakes. He would be better served in a cycling offense and working through a more "manufactured" style of attack than the freewheeling U18 Team's methods.

The skill level is about average for the big man. His passing game doesn't move the needle and his ability to accept passes is on the poorer side of average certainly. The latter will really need a lot of improvement if he wants to end up in the NHL. There are times when he looks really strong defensively and some games where he looks late to react to the play. As the year went on, he seemed to be less and less aware of his surroundings. This was really put on full display at the U18 World Junior Championships, where he had a disappointing outing in terms of his play away from the puck.

He has to be one of the best ready-made faceoff men in this draft class. While it could be argued that he wasn't given the opportunity to produce behind so many potential first round picks on the NTDP, he is going to jump to the University of Michigan in all likelihood in the fall where it's going to be really tough for him to be a featured scoring piece on the team. The collegiate game seems more tailored to his skill set, but this might be a tough ask for his offensive ceiling right now.

Ultimately, we feel this player doesn't offer enough upshot in the skill department to use a high pick on, but does bring other elements in his game that do translate well to the NHL, his size, skating ad faceoff prowess.

"Some of our guys like him more than I do. He's big and can skate but it ends right there for me." - NHL Scout, - September 2018

"Pretty much zero skill so he needs to be very good as far as other areas go. and I don't see it. Not physical at all." - NHL Scout, October 2018

"Tons of flash with the size/skating combo but he's not for me. He simply hasn't proven to me that he can score." - NHL Scout, October 2018

"He might be one of those players that plays better in the pro game." - NHL Scout, October 2018

"I like him. He can play on your PK and play down the middle on the 4th line for you. I'd take him in the 2nd" (round). - NHL Scout, January 2019

"I think he'll play. He can be a 3rd or 4th line type guy who kills penalties, will win faceoffs but there is a real lack of skill and hockey sense. Skating is great, he can fill a role." - NHL Scout, January 2019

" Reminds me of Freddie the Goat (Frédérik Gauthier) from Toronto except he's a much better skater than Gauthier. Projected 4th line Centre."- NHL Scout, January 2019

"I'd draft Hughes, Turcotte, Caufield, Boldy and Zegras. I wouldn't draft any other forwards on the team." - NHL Scout, March 2019

"I don't mind Beecher. I saw the program a ton and he didn't get much opportunity. He can play 3rd line and kill penalties. I like him in the late 3rd or 4th round." - NHL Scout, April 2019

" I like his faceoffs. He's a proven talent in that area." - NHL Scout, May 2019

" Needs to play with more physicality and use his body better to get the most out of his game." - HP Scout, Dusten Braaksma

" I like the size and he's a great skater. My issue is the lack of skill. If we were a real team we would be more focused on drafting skill guys ahead of big guys who we haven't seen score. I know he lacked opportunity, like many of the other USNTDP forwards, but I did see him with many good scoring opportunities and he could never seem to bury it. There is a spot where I would draft him because I think he'll play, but I'm guessing he'd be gone before I'd be willing to pull the trigger." - HP Scout, Mark Edwards, April 2019

" I got some really good feedback from Scouts regarding his interviews." - HP Scout, Mark Edwards, June 2019

	PLAYER	TEAM	LEAGUE	HEIGHT	WEIGHT	POS	GRADE
70	BERGER, CARTER	VICTORIA	BCHL	6'0.25"	200 *	LD	C
	HOCKEY SENSE	COMPETE		SKILL		SKATING	
	6	7		6		6	

Carter Berger had a very productive season for the Grizzlies. He was featured on the top-powerplay-unit with Newhook and Campbell but wasn't a by-product of their play; he complimented the top-unit well, which helped him produce 63 points in 54 games, including 27 goals. In the playoffs, he remained consistent, finishing with 18 points in 15 games, including 5 goals. He was also featured at the U19-World-Junior-A tournament, playing for Canada West, where he had 1 assist in 6 games.

Berger is a two-way defenseman who has excellent poise when walking the line. His best attribute is his anticipation in the offensive-zone; his ability to recognize in-coming pressure leaves him with the first-move. When he's getting pressured heavily, he's adept at getting his opponents to slow-down by using a variety of fakes; ranging from head-fakes, to shot-fakes and looks to use his lateral-skating to readjust his positioning. This gives him additional time and space to make plays. He's not a defenseman who looks to sit back and wait for his openings, instead he looks to activate aggressively which resulted in some impressive plays that led to points. He's got a good amount of skill and can make high-end dekes that he would look to use when rushing the puck. His lane recognition is good, and although he doesn't threaten with the amount of velocity he generates on most shot attempts, he does display a knack for getting them through traffic. There's a controlling-instinct when he's in possession of the puck and he has a versatile-attack at his disposal. Away from the puck, he shows an adequate compete-level and has no problem initiating along the boards, he was also responsible for one of the heaviest hits we saw this season in the neutral-zone. There is some sand-paper to his game and a decent amount of defensive-positioning as well.

Where we have trouble when identifying how Carter will translate, starts with his skating. This is his third-year of eligibility and although he has solid skating mechanics, his overall mobility ranks as a six. If this was his first year of draft-eligibility it would be a different-story, since he would have more time to develop this aspect of his game, but he doesn't. This point is confounded when taking into consideration his willingness to activate and become the puck-rushing, transport option for his team. He doesn't prefer looking for outlet-passes to the degree of some of the other defenseman we have ranked, yet his skating won't translate at the pro-level that allows him to use his current on-ice mentality. He will need to learn to be more adaptive when moving the puck up with his passing ability, as opposed to his rushing ability. That being said, he can pass the puck, which we have seen from him consistently throughout the season, he just needs to learn to use it as his initial instinct when holding into the puck more than he currently does. Another concerning element to Berger's game is his size. He's not the biggest defenseman who has to rely on his compete-level when battling in the corners or when attempting to clear out the front of the net, so he needs to find a way to further develop his active-stick when interpreting lanes, so that he doesn't rely on his frame as much as he did along the boards in our viewings.

Berger is an interesting defenseman who has some offensive-upside. In a draft where most defenseman after the top 20 players falls off dramatically in terms of their talent-level, we're left looking at Carter as someone who has already shown some offensive-talent, which is the reason he's made it on our list.

NR	PLAYER	TEAM	LEAGUE	HEIGHT	WEIGHT	POS	GRADE
	BERGERON, JUSTIN	ROUYN-NORANDA	QMJHL	6' 01"	180	LD	ND
	HOCKEY SENSE		COMPETE		SKILL		SKATING
	5		4		6		5

Bergeron went undrafted last year and came back even stronger this season as one of the top defensemen in the QMJHL, finishing the year with 16 goals and 57 points, good for 4th overall in scoring for defensemen in the league. This was particularly impressive when you take note of the acquisition of Noah Dobson. With the Huskies using four forwards and only one defenseman on the first power play unit, Bergeron lost a lot of the power play ice time that he had in the first half of the season, with Dobson taking his place.

Bergeron is an offensive defenseman who has excellent on-ice vision and flair in the offensive zone to create chances for his team. He did a really good job this season in terms of shot totals compared to last, as he finished the season with 223 shots on goal (2nd overall for defensemen in the league). He doesn't have a heavy shot from the point, but he has a good wrist shot with a quick release and does a good job finding shooting lanes by moving laterally on the blueline to get a better shooting angle. He had a lot of freedom to create offense this past season, often looking like a forward on the ice, as he was often deep in the offensive zone trying to create some opportunities. One area of his game that still needs lots of work: his skating abilities. He will need to get quicker and improve his footwork, as it's one of his biggest weaknesses at the moment. He did make some improvements this season in terms of his defensive play and compete level in his own end. He will never be known as a physical defenseman, but at least his compete level was much better this year. His play in his own end made some progress this year, but there are still developments that could be made there as well. He needs to assert himself more when battling for pucks along the boards and moving guys from the front of the net. When he was used on the PK, he didn't use his stick enough to block passing lanes in front of the net. Being more active with his stick in his own zone is also an element that will need improvement. Overall, his consistency and decision-making will need to be better as well. Bergeron might get a look late in the draft, and if not, he should get invitations for NHL rookie development camps over the summer.

"My question is how the f*** did Rouyn win the league? One stud D and five Tier 2 guys." – NHL Scout, May 2019

"Saw him in the offseason; he worked really hard to be better this season." – NHL Scout December 2018

"Don't get the feeling that there's a lot of support for him in the scouting community once again this year." – HP Scout Jérôme Bérubé

"Not a guy that has a chance to be on my list. Skating is average at best and he didn't show me anything my viewings to make me consider drafting him I'll say this about him though, he shoots the puck a lot. – HP Scout, Mark Edwards, April 2019

"Real tough showing for Bergeron at this event. He had so many tough shifts in his zone and never seemed to be able to get the puck out of his zone. Compared to his younger teammate Samuel Régis, he seemed intimidated by the big stage in Halifax" – HP Scout Jérôme Bérubé, June 2019

	PLAYER	TEAM	LEAGUE	HEIGHT	WEIGHT	POS	GRADE
NR	BERTUZZI, TAG	HAMILTON	OHL	5' 11.75"	203 *	LW	ND
	HOCKEY SENSE		COMPETE		SKILL		SKATING
	5		5		5		5

Bertuzzi was selected by the Guelph Storm second overall in the 2017 draft and is the son of former NHLer Todd Bertuzzi. We had limited viewings on Tag this season because he suffered a season ending injury. He was also injured last year, suffering from a concussion. When Tag was playing his numbers were not great he had 3 goals in 41 games last season and 4 goals in 30 games before his injury this season. The verdict after our viewings was a 'no draft' grade based on skating issues and an overall lack of higher end skill. We could not rank him on our list or give him a draftable grade based on what we saw this year. He was a high draft pick and only played one game in Hamilton before this seasons injury. Hopefully he is 100% healthy in September and can enjoy a productive fresh start in Hamilton.

"He can't skate well enough so he's not a draft for me." – NHL Scout, October 2018

"Don't see him as a draft, skating is not very good and not enough skill. – NHL Scout, November 2018

"I didn't see him much prior to the trade and his injury but his skating wasn't great. He was a no draft for me based on the lack of overly impressive aspects to his game in my limited viewings." – HP Scout, Mark Edwards, April 2019

	PLAYER	TEAM	LEAGUE	HEIGHT	WEIGHT	POS	GRADE
NR	BIBEAU, FELIX	ROUYN	QMJHL	6'0.0"	187	LC	ND
	HOCKEY SENSE		COMPETE		SKILL		SKATING
	7		7		5		5

Bibeau in his 3rd year of eligibility after being passed over in 2017 & 2018 NHL draft. He has made progress every year since entering the league with Rouyn-Noranda who drafted him with the 27th overall pick in the 2015 QMJHL Draft. He had a very good regular season this year amassing 69 points but had a monster playoff with the Huskies (29 points in 20 games) and was one of the top performers in the 2019 Memorial Cup scoring 5 goals in 5 games.

Bibeau is the kind of player who can play in all kind of situations on the ice, on the power play he can play all kind of roles either by being in front of the net to obstruct the goalie views and retrieve pucks or more in a shooting role where he can use his quick shot to beat goaltenders. Since coming in the QMJHL he has really work hard to improve his shot and his release. He's one of the best penalty killer in the league, has great anticipation and an avid shot blocker. He's the perfect type of player for every coach to have on their team because of his work ethic and smarts. He has a high compete level in all three zones and was a leader on Rouyn-Noranda this year as they end up winning the QMJHL president cup and Memorial Cup. For the pro level his offensive upside is limited but he plays such good all-around game that he could find a role in a good organization. He take pride in doing all the little details on the ice, good active stick in his zone and on the PK. He's also a pretty good faceoff guy as well. His skating ability and overall skill level are average but he's smart and has great work ethic. Bibeau is expected to play for Patrick Roy's Quebec Remparts next season and should be one of the top 20 years old in the league.

	PLAYER	TEAM	LEAGUE	HEIGHT	WEIGHT	POS	GRADE
NR	BIZIER, MATHIEU	GATINEAU	QMJHL	6' 1.0"	184 *	LC	**ND**
	HOCKEY SENSE	COMPETE			SKILL		SKATING
	6	6			5		5

Bizier was acquired by Gatineau at the QMJHL trade deadline from Rimouski. After a slow offensive start to the season, he did well with the Olympiques, racking up 27 points in 35 games after only getting 12 in 33 games Bizier was the 12th overall selection in the 2019 QMJHL Draft after playing one season with Lévis in the LHMAAAQ.

Bizier has good size and plays a strong overall game. He has a good hockey IQ at both ends of the ice. He always gives a strong effort away from the puck and on the backcheck. He will often act like a 3rd defenseman on the ice in his own zone, providing good support to retrieve pucks in his own zone. He's a good faceoff guy, even if his percentage is less than 50% this year; he was solid in that area in Midget AAA and should become one of the top faceoff guys next season. He's also not afraid to play a physical game, he has good size and he's a strong kid on his skates. He uses his size really well along the boards to protect the puck, demonstrating good technique when keeping the opponent as far as possible from it, using his back as a shield. He also won't hesitate to bring pucks to the net, even carrying defensemen on his back in order to do so. Bizier plays an honest two-way game that every coach loves and wants on their team. What he lacks is speed. His skating abilities are average at best, and he doesn't generate good enough speed. Plus, his feet are heavy. He needs to put in the work in order to improve his top speed and also be quicker in terms of his acceleration. This would help him reach his top speed faster and be more opportunistic when he has scoring chances in open ice. His skills are average, and he doesn't project as being higher than a 3rd- or 4th-liner at the next level. While his on-ice vision is fine and he has a good shot, he needs to improve his release. His hands are below-average; he's not a player who does well beating opponents one-on-one with just his hands. He will succeed more when using his body and strength. Bizier doesn't have the biggest upside, but does a lot of little things well at both ends of the ice. Obviously, his skill level and skating are areas in his game that he will need to work on. He could get a look from teams from the mid-to-late rounds who think he can improve on these elements in order to one day possibly become a grinder-type forward at the NHL level.

"He looked so much better with Gatineau than with Rimouski this year, he was brutal with Rimouski when I saw them in the first half of the season." - HP Scout Jérôme Bérubé

	PLAYER	TEAM	LEAGUE	HEIGHT	WEIGHT	POS	GRADE
NR	BJERSELIUS, OSCAR	DJURGARDEN JR.	SWE-JR.	5.11.0"	174	LC	ND
	HOCKEY SENSE		COMPETE		SKILL		SKATING
	6		6		5		5

Bjerselius had a really solid season where he did produce more points than expected on beforehand as he finished the season in the SuperElite league with 4 goals and 26 assists combining for 30 points in 45 regular season games. He stepped up when his team needed him the most in the playoffs and recorded 4 points in 3 J18 playoff games and 5 points in 8 J20 playoff games, where he eventually helped his club win the J20 bronze medal.

Even though he did produce a decent amount of points, his offensive upside is low. His shot is weak and he will often do whatever he can to avoid taking a shot, there were times where he passed the puck instead of shooting despite the net being open. His skating is very interesting, his foot speed is great and he is very mobile and maneuver quickly on tight areas, but even though his feet are moving quickly, his top speed on open ice is fairly unimpressive since his feet are moving up and down instead of in and out as stronger skaters strides.

He is extremely reliable and coaches seem to love his attention to detail, where he almost never is out of position defensively and got a nose for picking up loose pucks. His sloppy puck game along with his lack of offensive upside, will probably keep him out of the NHL, but he will likely turn in to a solid player in the SHL.

	PLAYER	TEAM	LEAGUE	HEIGHT	WEIGHT	POS	GRADE
30	BJORNFOT, TOBIAS	DJURGARDEN JR.	SWE-JR.	6.0.0"	202*	LD	B
	HOCKEY SENSE		COMPETE		SKILL		SKATING
	6		7		5		7

Björnfot had a strong development this season, where he was the leading player for his team in the SuperElite league as an underaged player. He put up 11 goals and 11 assists for 22 points from the blue line in 39 games. Thats the amount of points he can be expected to put up, since he can be labeled as a strong stay-at-home defenseman. His super solid play with the juniors got rewarded with 7 games in the SHL, where he didn't get much ice-time and did not record any points, but did not look out of place.

In international play he was the coaches go-to defender, even though higher ranked Broberg and Söderström were the biggest stars. He was the captain for team Sweden all season and he is a great leader and he leads by example. He only put up 8 points in 21 international games, despite being the quarterback on the first power play unit for the whole season, which is a role he wont be put in, in the NHL since his offensive upside aren't that big. Even internationally his puck retrieval is just fantastic, he never gets caught to forecheckers and has the ability to determine whether he should distribute the puck to his forwards or skate it himself. His outlet passes are accurate and crisp, but he rarely tries low-percentage passes.

His skating is powerful and he got some good leg strength at the same time as he can move effortlessly, in all directions. His strong skating is a big part of his defensive play, where he isn't the most physical player, but hes got a strong defensive stick with a long reach and if the opponents try to turn away from him, he easily locks him up by the boards. Hes also not afraid to block shots with his body or battle in front of the net which is attributes that makes him super strong on the box play. Björnfot will always compete hard, in every situation, for his team to get an opportunity to win games.

Offensively, he's not totally lost, but this is not where he excels. Yes, he's doing a solid job on the blue line and can really be a threat when he leaves the blue line as well, but he needs to keep it simple to be effective. He fires low, hard shots from the blue line for deflections and rebounds. Björnfot can stickhandle decently, but once again, its not one of his strengths, however, he has a tendency to knock down bouncing pucks anywhere on the ice. Björnfot is is superb physical shape and he is both strong and got good conditioning, this is a major asset that allows him to play such a solid and sturdy game as he does.

As far as a solid stay-at-home defenseman, he should be able to play in a second or third pairing in the NHL, but don't expect him to put up big offensive numbers.

He has signed a contract to play for Djurgården IF in the SHL next season.

" Zero offence but he's not without his value." - NHL Scout, February 2019

"Probably the top stay at home guy in this draft." - NHL Scout, April 2019

"You need guys like him. Not everyone needs to be a high octane points producer." - NHL Scout, April 2019

" I thought he really stepped it up after Christmas and everyone I have talked to says he's a great guy in the room." - HP Scout, Johan Karlsson, May 2019

" Our Swedish Scout Johan Karlsson talked about his fantastic puck retrieval skills in one of our conference calls and I think it's an extremely important component for Dmen." - HP Scout, Mark Edwards, May 2019

	PLAYER	TEAM	LEAGUE	HEIGHT	WEIGHT	POS	GRADE
61	BLAISDELL, HARRISON	CHILLIWACK	BCHL	5' 11.0"	181 *	LC	C+
	HOCKEY SENSE	COMPETE			SKILL		SKATING
	6	6			7		5

Harrison Blaisdell had a great season for the Chilliwack Chiefs by producing 56 points in 51 games, including 33 goals. In the playoffs his production slowed down, scoring 5 points in 11 games. He was featured at the world-junior-A challenge where he had 5 points in 6 games, including 4 goals. He's currently scheduled to play at the Univ. of North Dakota in the 2020-2021 season.

Blaisdell is a tenacious sniper who plays larger than his size. He has a compact frame, yet is a strong-kid who is capable of physically overwhelming larger players than himself. His willingness to physically engage extends to his willingness to enter heavy traffic areas. He's an aggressive player who looks to generate offense with his excellent wrist-shot. There's only a handful of players in this class that are as dangerous as Harrison when he's looking to shoot the puck. His release is the result of generating a ton of power though his shot motion. This is due to his dextrous wrists that allow him to flick through his shot, giving him a whip-like release. Through the release, he keeps his body static before driving through his fast-twitch to generate a lot of velocity. This makes it very difficult for netminders to react and get set before he finds his target. Furthermore, he can generate high-danger chances both when driving down the wing and when firing off one-timers from his wheel-house. Similar to his wrist-shot; his slapshot features a reduced wind-up and shows just how coordinated he is when moving through his release. There's specific shot-types that Blaisdell likes to take advantage of, such as going against the grain while moving laterally across the hash-marks and looking to pick the far-side corners on either wing when rushing down the ice. There's a level of creativity in his shot types as well; he looks to surprise with his spinning no-look shots and is good at placing his shots behind screens. Another important attribute for Blaisdell that synergizes well with his shot are his hands. His puck-skills are very-good; he can beat defenders with a variety of high-end dekes. Additionally, he doesn't force his move-set most of the time, instead using his hands to surprise and penetrate defenses. He also uses his hand-speed to generate turnovers away from the play; he's been good at stick-lifting unsuspecting players on the backcheck in our viewings. Although Blaisdell has a shoot-first mentality, he's also a capable passer who has good vision. The difference between himself and the other high-quality BCHL draft-eligible forwards is that he resorts to passing if he finds that he doesn't have a high-percentage shot, it's not his initial instinct when attacking. What encompasses Blaisdell's skill-set is how efficient he is when initiating an offensive-play. There's a high-level of dexterity, coordination and assertiveness when he has control of the puck; his talent-level allows him to generate before there's much of a reaction when he has a scoring chance. Like most gifted shooters, Blaisdell is good at finding soft-ice but wasn't as consistent at making himself a backdoor-option in some of our viewings.

Although Blaisdell has an offensive skill-set that can translate, other areas of his game might keep him from reaching his potential as a goal-scorer in the NHL. The biggest attribute holding him back is his skating ability. His skating mechanics are average; featuring a short-stride, an up-right posture, and a lack of fluidity in his start-up. However, he is a powerful kid who fights through his stride to generate an above-average amount of straight-line speed regardless of his mechanics. However, unless he cleans up his mechanics, it's going to be difficult for him to translate his game since he's most likely going to develop as a winger at the NHL-level. Another area of concern is in his consistency-levels. There are shifts where you notice him quickly out there, and then other shifts where you have to go looking for him. In the defensive-end, he can be too opportunistic when looking to direct the flow of play back up ice as well.

Although Blaisdell plays a plus 200-foot game and was used at center this past season, we view him as a winger. His most translatable skill is his shot but he needs to further refine his skating in order to put himself in positions where he can use it effectively. If he develops properly, we see Blaisdell as a potential top-9 scoring forward who can get some powerplay-time.

"He has one of the best releases in this class" - HP Scout, Brad Allen

NR	PLAYER	TEAM	LEAGUE	HEIGHT	WEIGHT	POS	GRADE
	BLUMEL, MATEJ	WATERLOO	USHL	5'11.5"	198 *	RW	ND
	HOCKEY SENSE	COMPETE		SKILL		SKATING	
	4	5		5		6	

Matej Blumel is a re-entry NHL draft prospect who just completed his sophomore campaign with Waterloo (USHL) after coming to North American in 2017 from the HC Dynamo program in the Czech Republic where he was a standout playing at the U18 level as an underage. Blumel represented the Czech Republic at both the Hlinka Gretzky and World Junior "A" challenge this year. Blumel is a quick skater and a fast paced player. His first couple strides are not blazing but he gets to a good top gear fairly quickly. He uses his speed well to attempt to gain the edge on defenseman and take the puck to the net. Blumel is a strong kid and is able to keep his balance while protecting the puck when he drives the crease. Matej has good quick skill where he moves the puck quickly in all three zones and is a very straight ahead player. Matej possesses a good arsenal of shots in the offensive zone and a shoot first mentality which allowed him to score 30 goals for Waterloo in 58 regular season games. Compete wise, blumel needs to still develop some consistency, in some viewings he was engaged in the game and effective on the fore-check and in front of the offensive net and others he played largely a perimeter game that didn't get involved much in the hard areas.

"Some games he couldn't be contained and some games you hardly noticed him, no clue what that's all about." HP Scout, Dusten Braaksma

	PLAYER	TEAM	LEAGUE	HEIGHT	WEIGHT	POS	GRADE
NR	**BOHLSEN, KADEN**	FARGO	USHL	6'3.0"	187	RW	**ND**
	HOCKEY SENSE	COMPETE		SKILL		SKATING	
	5	6		4		6	

Spent a few years in the Shattuck program before jumping into the USHL in 2017-18. His production had nowhere to go but up, but even then, it didn't get far off the mat. Bohlsen was dealt midseason from Des Moines to Fargo in a move that sparked nothing from the 6'3" center. He amassed just five goals, six points, and a minus-10 rating in his 30 games with the Force before being ousted from the playoffs by his former club. The looming question for Bohlsen is: What's his role? That's a question for the NHL level, but it's even a question at the USHL level. He's a husky center that can get around the rink pretty well. His top speed is better than his accelerator and he offers some physicality that fits his frame well. There are a number of games where he works to the best of his ability at both ends of the ice, but he leaves very little residue on the game at the end of the night. His skill level did not improve markedly over the course of the year. He's a little rigid in how he conducts himself. From the very predictable way he takes pucks off the boards to his inability to uncouple the top half of his body from the lower half to accept passes better; he makes no secret that there are a lot of subtleties to the game that he has yet to grasp. His hockey sense doesn't appear to be particularly noteworthy and it feels that the center ice position is a little too much ice for him to manage right now. Bohlsen is a better shooter than playmaker and a better body checker than backchecker, so perhaps a move to right wing would make more sense for him to get rolling. The lack of progress over the course of the season makes him a tough sell in this draft.

	PLAYER	TEAM	LEAGUE	HEIGHT	WEIGHT	POS	GRADE
102	**BOLDUC, SAMUEL**	BLAINVILLE	QMJHL	6'3.5"	210*	LD	**C**
	HOCKEY SENSE	COMPETE		SKILL		SKATING	
	5	5		7		7	

Bolduc was drafted in the 4th round (60th overall) by the Armada out of the LHPS (Quebec's prep school league) in 2016. After playing one Midget AAA season in 2016-2017 with Laval-Montréal, he has now played the past two seasons with the Armada.

Bolduc saw his role increase a lot this season due to several veteran defensemen from last year leaving. The Laval product has since established himself as the top defenseman on a struggling team. Bolduc's tools are very impressive; he's big, physically strong, and can really skate. He loves to rush the puck from his own zone. If he can reach his top speed without being touched, he can be very intimidating for opposing defensemen who have to defend against him one-on-one. His strides are very powerful; it can only take two or three steps for him to reach his top speed. Such a combination is very tough to defend against (for just about anyone in the league) when he's coming in at full speed. He has surprising hands when handling the puck; he can beat guys with some nice dekes as well. On the power play, he moves the puck well enough, but his bread and butter remain his shot (either his wrister or his slapshot). He tends to use his slapshot more often; it's very powerful and can beat any goalie. He does need to work a bit more on his accuracy and improve his shot selection (such as trying to find a better shooting angle rather than blindly shooting with the hope that it won't be blocked by the penalty killers in front of him). As mentioned, Bolduc's tools are very appealing, but he's very inconsistent and there are a lot of questions in regards to his decision-making and hockey sense. Decision-making is the area of his game that will need the most work. He can struggle while moving pucks under pressure and doesn't always use the best option available. Overall, he is very inconsistent as well; he can have a great game one night and struggle less than 24 hours later. He also doesn't impose himself physically like he should; we would like to see him take over games more and be more physically dominant, whereas sometimes he's the one getting mishandled along the boards in his own zone.

Bolduc remains intriguing as a prospect, but the question marks regarding his consistency and hockey sense will make teams worry about drafting him too high in this draft. He's definitely worth a pick in the mid-rounds, based purely on his tools.

"I always like to see top QMJHL prospects play well against top teams in the league. Bolduc had two horrible back-to-back games against Baie-Comeau and Rouyn-Noranda (two top teams in the league at the time) in front of a ton of scouts in one weekend." - HP Scout Jérôme Bérubé

"I like the tools and the size, but I'm not sure he'll be able to put them all together at the NHL level. There's a lot of if's and incertitude with him, definitely a risky pick. He'll need a great coach in the AHL to help him take the next steps in his development." - HP Scout Jérôme Bérubé, May 2019

"Very disappointed in his compete level playing against a top team, instead of setting the tempo physically for his team, he was the one getting dominated physically." - NHL Scout February 2019

"Saw him a ton this season, as I chased viewings of other prospects playing the Armada. I didn't like him in my first three viewings as he was very passive. Then he was great for two viewings, all the passive play was gone and he played aggressive and confident. He finished with at least four more viewings where he played very poorly in several aspects of the game. Nice size and skating and a wild but absolute cannon of a shot, but my confidence in him is pretty low right now. A Scout gave me some other info that scares me as well." - HP Scout, Mark Edwards, April 2019

	PLAYER	TEAM	LEAGUE	HEIGHT	WEIGHT	POS	GRADE
9	BOLDY, MATTHEW	USA U-18	NTDP	6'1.5"	187 *	LW	A
	HOCKEY SENSE		COMPETE		SKILL		SKATING
	7		6		8		5

Matthew Boldy has had a productive year for the USNTDP by generating 66 points in 53 games in the development program, and 40 points in 26 games in the USHL, including 15 goals. He's expected to commit to Boston College in the 2019-2020 season. On a team stacked with talent, Boldy wasn't over-shadowed and instead complimented his line-mates well, finding chemistry with Zegras throughout the season. He saved his best international performance at the end of the season, producing 12 points in 7 games, including 9 assists at the U18's.

Boldy is a multi-faceted forward who is one of the more talented players in this class. He has a unique-blend of size, skill, anticipation and vision. The combined attributes allow him to make some of the higher-end plays we've seen from any forward this season, as he's beaten multiple opponents one-on-one in the same sequence before making difficult spinning passes as an example. His length and quick reflexes allow him to make dekes that few other players can make, as well as shift the angle of his attack. This gives him an element of deception to his game when combined with his reactionary-style. It's very difficult to puck up his tells, due to the speed at which he can release the puck and the level of creativity he has shown. Matthew presents rare duel-threat offensive-attributes, showing the ability to be both a primary passer and shooter. He's capable of high-end technical passes while in motion and can make sharp passes through heavy traffic. As a shooter, he needs little time and space to elevate the puck off his stick, can score from severe-angles, and releases pucks in one-motion from stationary positions which gives him a plus slapshot. This allowed him to be dangerous both from a stationary position, when moving the puck with the man-advantage, as well as when he was going at top speeds. There are elements to his shot that he needs to continue to refine. His accuracy isn't always on point; sometimes he can miss the net by a large margin and he also tends to give up high-percentage shots in favour of finding his teammates. Boldy is at his best when he's taking direct approaches to the net and is able to cut aggressively while driving down the wings, yet it's an area that remains inconsistent. Lastly, he can use his frame effectively on the forecheck and has a good amount of leverage during board battling sequences, but his compete-level is hit and miss depending on the sequence and game.

Boldy looks to experiment on the ice, this was a double-edged sword though. On the one-hand, it kept his play from becoming telegraphed and it allowed him to flash a dynamic skill-set; on the other hand, it led to poor rates of execution at times. As an example, instead of making the simple yet more efficient shot, he would opt to attempt a low-percentage between the legs shot that would miss wide and would result in lost possession for his team. As the year progressed, this went from something we would mention briefly in our meetings, to an area of concern. There's been stretches this season, where his puck-management and consistency have become notable red-flags when evaluating the player. However, an area of improvement Matthew has shown is in his skating. He's a bigger kid and had a heavier stride at the beginning of the season, but as the season has progressed, he's managed to bring it to an average level. When projecting his skating going forward, it's become more fluid and there's still room for Boldy to continue to grow and gain power in his stride. The last area of concern with Boldy is that despite his size, he doesn't play as heavy a game as he theoretically should be able to. He's a finesse-oriented player that carries a great frame but hasn't developed the willingness to use it effectively when protecting the puck, on the forecheck, and when battling in-front of the net as consistently as we would like to see.

Boldy is a prospect with one of the higher-ceilings and presents a unique skill-set. When ranking him, we had to take into account that it's unlikely he can drive a line due to how his current skating projects and how he's capable of over-extending himself. His puck-management due to overextending his creativity has become a concern but he did show better puck-management down the stretch and at the U18's, where he showed an improved efficiency with the puck. Despite his drawbacks, we still project Matthew to become a versatile top-6-forward who can be used on the powerplay. In order for him to reach his potential, he will have to learn how to use his frame more effectively and dial down his creativity at times by self-containing when the situation calls for a simple yet more effective play.

"Boldy was really good last night with that stuff you've talked about. He had some 2 on 1's and he sold the shot, saw the D (defenseman) commit and moved it laterally but I've seen Boldy do some dumb sh** too." - NHL Scout, February 2019

"He's going to be interesting on draft day because he's been terrible in both international events so far. I wonder if that drops him." - NHL Scout, March 2019

"When is the last time a player sh** the bed in international events and was drafted in the top six?" - NHL Scout, March 2019

"He's 4th on my list." - NHL Scout, March 2019

"Terrible overseas and then he comes home and rips apart college teams. I've seen the best and the worst of him. I'm getting scared off of this kid as a top 10 pick." - NHL Scout, March 2019

"Two international tournaments and what does he have...two points or something? I'm probably not drafting that in the top 20 so top 10 is out of the question." - NHL Scout, March 2019

"I have him in the top 10 and actually have the same guys as you...I just don't like them. The draft ends at three.(laughs)." - NHL Scout, April 2019

"It took me a bit to completely come around on this player, but when I read through my game notes from September to now, he has improved in the areas that were concerns for me at the start of the year." - HP Scout, Dusten Braaksma, April, 2019

"Boldy is a dynamic player that has so many options when attacking that I think it's left him still trying to find his identity." - HP Scout, Brad Allen

"The U18 in April was the best I saw him all year. He had a knack for stinking out the joint whenever I would see him. Seriously, I'd see his numbers he was posting and I thought there was some other kid wearing his jersey in my viewings." - NHL Scout, May 2019

"Skilled player. He's great when he's playing inside because he has a knack for being able to score from in tight." - HP Scout, Mark Edwards

	PLAYER	TEAM	LEAGUE	HEIGHT	WEIGHT	POS	GRADE
NR	BRADY, COLE	JANESVILLE	NAHL	6'3.0"	165	G	C
	HOCKEY SENSE		COMPETE		SKILL		SKATING
	6		6		5		5

Brady is a tall, lanky goaltender out of the Ajax/Pickering midget program. Brady shared the crease last year for the Markham Royals (OJHL) and eventually found his way to Janesville (NAHL) this season where he was one of the more consistent goaltenders in the NAHL. Brady has NHL size at nearly 6'5" tall but has a ways to go to grow into his frame. Cole is still an extremely lanky kid that needs to add lower body strength in order to improve his explosiveness laterally, which is lacking at this stage. Brady has a calm presence in the crease and plays a solid technical game. You don't see Brady badly out of position and scrambling. Not the most aggressive goaltender as far as challenging shooters in one on one situations and is a very much a stay at home goaltender that relies on his size to make saves. Brady struggled with his glove at times throughout the season, seemed to battle with some routine saves. Brady isn't a dynamic playmaker with the puck but his skating is good enough that it allows him to get to hard rims and stop pucks for his defenseman behind his net. He can move it up the walls and off the glass efficiently but doesn't look to stretch the ice and find forward up the ice. Brady will likely spend one more season of Junior hockey before heading to Arizona State in 2020. Fargo owns his USHL rights, so a move to the USHL might be in the cards for Brady next year.

"He's on my list. He'll be a late pick by someone." - NHL Scout, April 2019

"Good goalie. Huge kid plays a blocking style, not overly athletic but he made my list." - NHL Scout, May 2019

"We won't be drafting him." - NHL Scout, May 2019

"I think he's one of the more talented North American based goaltenders for this draft." HP Scout, Dusten Braaksma

NR	PLAYER	TEAM	LEAGUE	HEIGHT	WEIGHT	POS	GRADE
	BREEN, LYDEN	CENTRAL ILLINOIS	USHL	5'9.25"	161 *	LC	ND
	HOCKEY SENSE	COMPETE		SKILL		SKATING	
	6	6		5		7	

Small, thin, energetic forward. Breen was born in New Brunswick, but played two years of prep school in New Hampshire. His first full year in the USHL saw him net 37 points for Central Illinois. Already a plus-plus skater, especially with his starts and stops, but he has the potential to be faster at the top-end with some added leg strength. The pull-away gear isn't quite there at the moment. Has a decent feel for the details of the game and looks to have the propensity to learn more, which is a big plus for the worker bees. It might be because there are some physical limitations, but he doesn't finish a lot of plays. He hustles to get to the right spots, and it looks like he means to be doing the right thing, but he doesn't fully complete enough objectives – offensively or defensively. Breen isn't hockey strong and can get knocked off his blades a good bit. Does a nice job not overhandling pucks and keeping plays alive; doesn't try to force plays and also doesn't handle the puck like a hot potato – he just knows his limitations. He might even be a little too aware of them even.

The skill level is just average overall, lessened by a weak shot. He could have had a bunch more goals this year based on how he was able to pop open in the slot or out-hustle to pucks, but his shot was too often weak and in the goalie chest. He does everything quickly though, right down to putting his stick down for faceoffs. To borrow a football analogy, he's a good running back – between the 20s. He'll need to specialize to make it as a role player; a move to left wing at the next level might make his life easier. Breen was claimed by Fargo in the USHL Dispersal Draft.

"Might only a good college player, but he could figure out a niche and claw his way up the ladder... that's a plausible out for him." - HP Scout, Michael Farkas

NR	PLAYER	TEAM	LEAGUE	HEIGHT	WEIGHT	POS	GRADE
	BREWER, MITCHELL	OSHAWA	OHL	6'0.25"	205 *	LD	ND
	HOCKEY SENSE	COMPETE		SKILL		SKATING	
	5	6		5		5	

A stay at home defenseman without any real projectable attributes for the NHL game. He is a solid contributor at the OHL level but never showed enough in his game to make us think he was a realistic NHL prospect. Skating is a weakness. as it is average at best. He lacks footspeed.

"Two viewings and he was pretty much off my list. He'll be a good Junior but I don't know what he is in the NHL." - NHL Scout, November 2018

"Skating isn't good enough for me and when I factor that with the other parts of his game he becomes a no draft grade on my list." - HP Scout, Mark Edwards, May 2019

	PLAYER	TEAM	LEAGUE	HEIGHT	WEIGHT	POS	GRADE
15	**BRINK, BOBBY**	**SIOUX CITY**	**USHL**	**5'8.25"**	**159 ***	**RW**	**A**
	HOCKEY SENSE		COMPETE		SKILL		SKATING
	8		8		8		5

Bobby Brink opted to join Sioux City full time this year and that proved to be the right decision. He Finished 2nd in USHL scoring with 35 goals in 43 games—including 9 game-winners—despite missing significant time with a foot-injury. After his injury, his line that featured both Marcus Kallionkieli and Martin Pospisil (CGY) had difficulty producing without him. This suggests that Bobby was the line-driver; he extended his driving of play to the World-Junior-A-Challenge where he produced 8 points in 6 games while capturing the MVP award. Brink has shown the ability to raise his game to another level time and time again. Going back to last season during Minnetonka's run to the Minnesota State Title, Brink saw his team down on a couple of different occasions throughout the playoffs and put the team on his back and took over hockey games. Our staff saw that same ability this season for Sioux City down the stretch, where his play helped push his team into the playoffs, scoring 11 goals and 10 Assists in the final 10 regular season games. He finished his 18/19 season by joining the NTDP team at the U18's in Sweden where he complimented a talented U.S squad, registering 3 goals and 3 assists in 5 games in helping USA win Bronze. Brink has little left to prove at the USHL level but is still a Junior in High School so it's possible we may see Brink back in the USHL next season before heading to Denver in 2020.

We have compared the differences between DeBrincat and Caufield, yet we find there's several similarities to discuss between DeBrincat and Brink which have made us believers in his ability to translate his game. However, there is one noticeable difference which Brink will have to overcome in order for him to convert his game at the highest-level. In DeBrincat's case, his average-skating was the result of his lack of strength and leg-extension, for Brink there's more concerning issues. There are few players in any class that have skating-mechanics as awkward as Brinks. He's extremely rigid, making him look like he's "trapped" within his frame when attempting to fully-extend. Despite this, his two-step area quickness is surprisingly above-average due to how he gains traction in his initial push-off. However, after the initial-steps, his skating breakdowns due to a lack of a deep-knee bend, inability to maintain proper posture, and his inability to kick-back in a straight-line. He can't stabilize when attempting to direct himself in a straight-line since he doesn't maintain a heel-to-toe motion when extending. When he kick's back during recovery extensions, he's off to the side as opposed to keeping a straight-line as well. Additionally, the inside-edge of his skate blade isn't always last to touch down on the ice with each subsequent stride. The above mechanics don't allow him to have a separating gear that can translate to the NHL-level. Though, when a player is looking to reconfigure a lane, they rely on their ability to pivot—reopening their hips—which gives them additional options; Brink is one of the better players in this class at doing just that. His size also lends well to having a lower-centre of gravity which does allow him to recover when attempting to re-balance himself after physical altercations. In conclusion; he can't maintain adequate straight-line speed but he does accelerate well, can pivot, and has decent cross-over mechanics, which help him get around the ice better than his core-skating-mechanics would suggest. Perhaps the biggest issue in projecting his skating is that it's not just a strength-concern, it's how comfortable he can become with cleaning up his skating fundamentals. The main takeaway though, is that if he can't clean up his mechanics, he still gets from point A-to-B at an adequate-level depending on the distance, and has a rare set of high-end attributes necessary to compensate for his glaring flaw.

The most important-skill that Brink has to compensate for the above concerns is a trait he shares with DeBrincat—they're both gifted at dynamically altering the tempo of a play by freezing their opponents. Much like a chess player manipulates his pieces to set-up traps for his opponent; Brink does the same with his deception. Defenseman at the highest-level will be able to close distance on him quickly, so it's vital to his success when translating that he has the ability to slow them down. The best way to stall an opponent is to remain difficult to read, which Brink is exceptional at. Much like DeBrincat, Bobby uses static body-posture, head fakes, shot-fakes, and pivoting mechanics to alter the perception of the intended play. If his fakes are read, his processing speed allows him to assess his time and space so that he can threaten by threading pucks past his opponents. We feel that Brink can make dynamic passes and that his playmaking is ahead of Alex's at the same age. This gives him the opportunity to generate high-percentage plays despite having his skating lanes cut-off from him. This leads to another very important trait that he shares with DeBrincat; they're as equally dangerous when in motion as they are from a stationary position. This extends to both their play with the man-advantage. Much like DeBrincat, Bobby is a duel-threat option. Over the past couple of seasons, Brinks shooting ability has improved; as he's now developed a varied arsenal of shots, including good one-timing ability from the circles, as well as the ability to rapidly shift-the-angle of his release point on his wrist-shot. His shooting mechanics allow him to generate a surprisingly powerful release for a smaller player. Though, DeBrincat's release point was slightly ahead at the same age and he opted to use a snap-shot more than Brink does. Where they did share similarities was how often they used screens to set-up their release. The last area to note with Brink's skill-set is in regards to his hands. Bobby is capable of beating his opponents one-on-one but more importantly uses his dekes at the right-times. This is another area that Bobby must excel in, since he needs to be able to guard the puck at a higher-rate than faster-forwards.

Away from the play, Brink and DeBrincat share another important aspect of hockey-sense, which is their ability to find-soft-ice. If Bobby can't drive play in the NHL to the extent he currently does in juniors, he has an excellent fall-back option, which is how quickly he can anticipate what his teammates are attempting to do with the puck. His skating will limit him more than some with his ability to lead the rush or attempt too many transitional-zone-entries, so he's going to have to rely on becoming the trailing option or finding backdoor lanes. Another plus attribute of Brinks, is his ability to anticipate off the forecheck. His frame isn't going to translate well at the NHL-level, yet his puck-tracking skills and motor allow him to reduce the amount of times he needs to physically initiate along the boards by beating opponents to the puck. Despite his skating concerns mentioned earlier and throughout this write-up, Brink keeps a very good-pace which is another element to his game that helps him compensate for his overall-average at best speed. There's a high-octane engine built into this kid, and it's made him one of the better overall competitors in this class. He plays a fearless brand-of-hockey, looking to attack in heavy traffic areas. Though, his competitive spirit doesn't completely translate as well in the defensive-zone as it does in the offensive-zone.

Brink left us with a defining feature to his game that can't be understated—he makes his teammates better. The hallmark of high-end hockey-sense is adaptability, and Brink has it in spades; adapting his current weaknesses should allow him to translate his game. As a result, we view Bobby as a cerebral duel-threat winger with the attributes needed to produce in a top-6 role at the NHL-level.

"So many of these guys in this league (USHL) are so overrated and over hyped. Look at Brink, he can't skate." - NHL Scout, September 2018

"He skates like he was at a Frat Party last night but I still like him." NHL Scout, September 2018

"Late rounder at best. Kid can't skate." - NHL Scout, October 2018

"He was my 2nd ranked player in the USHL but he probably just moved to #1 after that tournament (WJAC)." - NHL Scout, December 2018

"The small guys who can't skate that make it in the NHL are few and far between." - NHL Scout, December 2018

"He kinda reminds of a guy like Jake Guentzel because he doesn't fit that traditional look of a top prospect. All he does is get the puck more than anybody and make more plays than anybody. I've even come around a bit on his skating." - NHL Scout, December 2018

"Skating is important but it's not the end all be all. When you have what he has with the exception being skating, you can play in the NHL. Logan Couture comes to mind." - NHL Scout, December 2018

"He's so smart and plays such a mature game. He's a great playmaker and is such a determined player. he's an easy top 25 guy on my list." - NHL Scout, January 2019

"The brain and skill and compete level are so high that I am giving him a bit of a pass on his skating. - NHL Scout, February 2019

"Skating is obviously not a strength but lateral agility and in small areas he's not as bad as some people think." - NHL Scout, February 2019

"Barely a draft for me, maybe a late rounder. I don't see all this skill you see and his skating is a huge problem. - NHL Scout, March 2019

"Brink and Rees, two great players who are bad skaters." - NHL Scout, March 2019

"At the WJAC his skating scared me a bit but I've dug deeper to watch it a lot more. He does get separation for himself. It's not like he's got players catching him all the time. I saw some ridiculous forechecks too. He gets there." - NHL Scout, March 2019

"I'm sold and he looks bigger than 5'8". I think he's closer to 5'9.5" 5'10" 170." - NHL Scout, March, 2019

"How good was he (Brink) at the U18. Holy sh**, if only he could skate." - NHL Scout, May 2019

"He's Alexander DeBrincat." - NHL Scout, May 2019

"We'll see at the combine but I think he's closer to 5'10" 170." - NHL Scout, May 2019

"He's got that clutch gene that you look for, bigger the moment he seems to be able to elevate.- " HP Scout, Dusten Braaksma, March, 2019

"He's challenged himself and has excelled each and every time, whether it be playing Minnesota High School hockey in his bantam year, going to the USHL a year earlier than most MNHS kids do or jumping on a plane and going to the U18 tournament and performing well for USA team playing on very little rest, he's just been impressive since I started watching him 3 or so years ago." HP Scout, Dusten Braaksma May, 2019

"Saw him right from the get-go in Pittsburgh at the Fall Classic. Had a goal and an assist and showed plenty of his tools. At that point I was much more concerned about the skating than I am now." - HP Scout, Mark Edwards, March 2019

"He may not look like a speed demon off the rush but he has great lateral skating ability. He plays with great pace." - NHL Scout, March 2019

"I love Brink. I'd take him top 20 without even thinking about it and I think he'll go as high as 15 and won't slip past 25." - NHL Scout, April 2019

"The kid was puking before his flight overseas and still played on the day he arrived He's a gamer." - NHL Scout, May 2019

" I heard there is a team in the mid to late teens who loves him." - NHL Scout, May 2019

"I don't like Bobby Brink at all. He can't skate and he didn't do himself any good at the Under 18. It looked so bad on that big ice. He's smart and can make plays but that skating is non starter for me." - NHL Scout, June 2019

" I love that he can make plays under pressure. He thinks the game at such a high level and his playmaking and scoring abilities are high end. His hockey IQ helps offset some of his skating decencies. Most of the poor skating stars in the NHL think the game at a high level." - HP Scout, Mark Edwards April 2019

"There is another player I love in next year's draft who is also lacking in the skating department. Some ugly skaters can still be great when they are so high end in all the other facets of the game." HP Scout, Mark Edwards, April 2019

"Scouts I spoke to were all over the map on him. Some loved him and had had him ranked as a lock to be a first rounder. Others hated the skating and couldn't get past it. I know a few Scouts who saw him as a mid round prospect at best. I let them know my difference of opinion." - HP Scout, Mark Edwards, April 2019

" One of my personal faves in this draft class. He's so good that I'll accept his size/skating combo. He is high-end in the big three areas I look for: Smarts, Compete and Skilled. Skating is obviously not a strength but I think it's more visually ugly than bad. It isn't pretty to look at but I see him win a ton of puck races and I can't remember too many plays where his skating hurt him. An NHL Scout made a DeBrincat comparison to me yesterday and it was funny because we had mentioned several similarities in house earlier this season." - HP Scout, Mark Edwards, May 2019

"The first time I saw Kyle Connor play I loved his game and we ended up ranking him very high in his draft year. I felt the same way about Brink when I saw him for the first time. Compete and hockey sense stood out almost immediately with Brink." - HP Scout, Mark Edwards, May 2019

" Scouts liked him during combine interviews and gave me positive feedback but several noted that they wished he was a bit more aware of his need to have a plan this summer regarding his skating. I interviewed him and he is a very likeable kid, but when I asked him myself if he had any plans to work on anything this summer, I understood what the teams were talking about. He'll figure it out soon enough." - HP Scout, Mark Edwards, June 2019

	PLAYER	TEAM	LEAGUE	HEIGHT	WEIGHT	POS	GRADE
NR	BRINKMAN, BENNJAMIN	MINNESOTA	BIG 10	6'0.5"	215*	LD	C
	HOCKEY SENSE		COMPETE		SKILL		SKATING
	4		7		5		5

Ben Brinkman was the youngest player in college hockey this season after opting to pass on his senior season at Edina HS and Waterloo (USHL). Instead Ben escalate his schooling and enter the University of Minnesota this season. Brinkman was eased into the lineup early in the season, playing protected minutes for much of the first month but as the season progressed, Brinkman became one of the more relied upon defenseman for head coach Bob Motzko down the stretch. While Brinkman's offensive output isn't impressive, 1 goal 6 assists in 38 games, it's important to mention Brinkman hardly saw any Power Play time this season. Brinkman has good size and is a strong kid that showed the ability to handle the older opponents in college hockey. His board play and physicality down low and in front of his net allowed him to win important puck battles, stop cycles and transition the puck out of his own end. Brinkman quickly learned that he wasn't going to get away with some of the things he could in High School with the puck and adapted, made adjustments and simplified his game as the season progressed. Brinkman started to get more comfortable rushing the puck or joining the rush and showed better judgement in this regard later in the season. Brinkman possesses good footwork and agility in his skating but lacks some explosiveness and ability to separate from the fore-checker which can get him into trouble with speedy fore-checkers when he doesn't move the puck quick enough. Brinkman supports his defensive partner well and uses the boards well to move pucks D to D or find players up the ice. In the offensive end Brinkman has a heavy shot from the point but wasn't able to be in a lot of situations this season to utilize it and deferred to using a quick wrist shot that he can get through traffic consistently. He moves the puck quickly at the point and showed good poise under pressure. Brinkman has much more offensive ability than his numbers this season would suggest. The biggest question going forward is, with the blueliners Minnesota has coming in the next couple years, will Brinkman get the opportunity to develop his offensive game and see time on the power play or will he fit in better by being the stabilizing stay at home presence for some of the more offensively minded defenseman coming in to Minneapolis. He could be a prospect that takes some time to develop his offensive game.

"Personally I think some people dismissed him too early and didn't really look back in on him late in the year, he was Minnesota's best defenseman down the stretch and into the playoffs." - HP Scout, Dusten Braaksma, April, 2019

#	PLAYER	TEAM	LEAGUE	HEIGHT	WEIGHT	POS	GRADE
21	BROBERG, PHILIP	AIK	SWE-2	6'2.75"	199 *	LD	B
	HOCKEY SENSE		COMPETE		SKILL		SKATING
	5		6		5		8

Broberg has had his up and downs this season. He started out strong at the Hlinka Gretzky tournament where he recorded 3 goals and 1 assist. He's been playing in a somewhat sheltered role for AIK in the HockeyAllsvenskan, where he had 2 goals, and 7 assists in 41 games.

Broberg has got good size and excellent skating abilities, with a smooth, strong stride he likes to use to his advantage. He advances the puck up ice creating distance between him and his opponents, often going wide and around defenders. It's really his north-south skating that stands out as he often takes the shortest route towards his destination. He lacks some hockey sense but it should not be considered as bad. He will, however, try to make the same play over and over even though it hasn't been successful and the opposition has figured out what he's going to do. He needs to be able to adapt better. He does seem to be able to make up for that lack of hockey sense since he is very mobile and can adjust his skating accordingly.

However, against men and top international opponents, his defensive hockey sense gets easily exposed. He at times fails to read the situations properly which leads to dangerous scoring chances against his team. He can outmuscle opponents since he is big, strong and active in his own zone. with a good stick. There are times when he is cemented in front of his own net that he can be too passive.

Overall, his play in his own end is very inconsistent and he could benefit from better coaching/education in defensive play. He also tends to be a pusher, where he catches his guy and instead of tying him up along the boards or body checking him, he gives him a small push and nothing really happens.

Gap control could be better but he gets by as he can adjust his pace and angles with his flawless skating.

He should be considered as one of the stronger defenders in his age group but his offensive qualities in stickhandling and shot need to improve. He is a puck-transporting defenseman with decent defending abilities. He rarely plays the body but when he does his timing is perfect. Most of the time he outskates his opposing players and purely strips them of the puck with good reach and great speed. His puck retrieval is strong but he could really benefit from making the easy play after retrieving the puck. He creates offense with speed and power but not much with finesse and he seems to want to be the guy that's driving the play at all times. He just has this aura of confidence around him in everything he does. Broberg's passing play can at times be overlooked as he has a good hard first pass but since he prefers to skate the puck we don't get to see it as much as we probably should.

His passing play in the offensive zone is always a gamble as he is very likely to try a low percentage play. His shot is slightly above average. He's got some good power to his slapshot but it tends to be blocked and his wrist shot is accurate but lacks velocity.

Internationally, he was chosen best defenseman at the Under-18 World Championship; With 6 points in 7 games, he was a big contributor in Sweden's gold medal win. He also played for Sweden at the World Junior. He was the 7th defenseman who did not get a lot of ice time as Sweden lost in the quarterfinals to Switzerland. He had a point in 4 games.

Broberg is an intriguing prospect and may be considered as an unpolished long-term project as there still are a couple of aspects of his game that he needs to improve. Can his super-confident puck transporting skills be executed in the NHL with the same authority as he performs now? We are not as confident as some.Scouts.

"He skates the puck up ice, with blinders on, until he scores... or turns the puck over" -NHL Scout, April 2019

"Good player, but I'll tell you that I'm pretty confident Craig Button likes him a bit more than me." - NHL Scout, August 2018

"He can't move pucks, he tries to skate everything." - NHL Scout, August 2018

"People are getting caught up in his end to end rushes but ignore that he struggles at several important facets of the game." - NHL Scout, August 2018

"He really impressed me. Great tools ad he uses them. Thought he showed good hockey sense." - NHL Scout, August 2018

"He's too one-dimensional for me. He's in my second round." - NHL Scout, March 2019

"He turns over a lot of pucks. His Dzone exits are a big area of concern for me." - NHL Scout, March 2019

"He's more of a puck transporter than anything else. I like him because he competes but he's not without some issues. If someone takes him top 10 they will probably regret it. I think he's a great second round pick." - NHL Scout, April 2019

"He's kinda been living off the Hlinka but I thought he was good at the U18, not MVP good but good. nevertheless." - NHL Scout, May 2019

"I thought he stepped up in the U18 and Sweden doesn't win it without him." - NHL Scout, May 2019

"I love his skating because it's a long stride. The thing I dislike most (about his game) is that it's like he's playing with blinders like a horse wears." – HP Scout, Johan Karlsson, May 2019

"If you take the high end skating out of his game are we even talking about him in the top two rounds?" – HP Scout Jérôme Bérubé, May 2019

"If you look at our ratings they tell our version of his story. I think he lacks hockey sense and a great puck game. I didn't think he was nearly as fantastic at the Hlinka last summer as some scouts I spoke to did. To me he lacked hockey sense and it continued all season. Great size, skating combo but it goes downhill in a hurry after that in my opinion. I am far from alone on our staff with my assessment and I know numerous team scouts who also share our take. Hope I'm wrong. Seemed like a great kid. at the combine and I got good reviews on his interviews there." – HP Scout, Mark Edwards, June 2019

	PLAYER	TEAM	LEAGUE	HEIGHT	WEIGHT	POS	GRADE
NR	BRODZINSKI, BRYCE	BLAINE	HIGH-MN	5'11.75"	197 *	RW	**ND**
	HOCKEY SENSE	COMPETE		SKILL		SKATING	
	5	5		6		4	

Bryce Brodzinski – Hulking, goal-scorer who improved in his short time in the USHL at the end of the season. After winning the Mr. Hockey Award with Blaine High School, Brodzinski joined the Omaha Lancers and continued his impressive production. He can shoot the puck very well and he's willing to go to the net and battle for positioning. He has the ability to one-time pucks with some consistency. He doesn't show off his hands in open space too much – he's more deliberate and straightforward than many other modern skill players, but when he gets right up on defenders, he can flash a move that beats them from time to time and it sort of comes out of nowhere (typically it's a move that pulls the puck in towards his feet, rather than something outside of his shoulder plane and wide). The issue is that by not having hands in space, he fails to make a lot of room for himself and too often his feet stop churning when he's pulling off these elusive maneuvers.

Brodzinski's feet are his biggest red flag. While he looks better than even when he started late in the USHL, his wheels are still quite a ways below average. Mechanically, it's not smooth and he's a little stiff in his movements. Our early viewings pegged him as prohibitively slow; now, his skating has been upgraded to "a hindrance". He continues to play center at the USHL level, but this is almost certainly a winger at any level above this. The hockey sense is just average and he is prone to bad turnovers in his passing game. He's an August 2000 birthday that was passed over in 2018 - he's off to the University of Minnesota in the fall.

"Tore up Minnesota HS this year but it was a weak conference and he's a 00' born with size, he can shoot it but his skating hasn't progressed like I hoped it would, I don't think his feet will allow him to get into positions to utilize his shot at the next level." HP Scout, Dusten Braaksma, May 2019

NR	PLAYER	TEAM	LEAGUE	HEIGHT	WEIGHT	POS	GRADE
	BROWN, MATTHEW	DES MOINES	USHL	5'8.5"	184 *	LW	ND
	HOCKEY SENSE	COMPETE		SKILL		SKATING	
	6	6		4		4	

Though productive in lesser leagues, Matt Brown jumped seemingly out of nowhere to notch 30 goals and 57 points with Des Moines this season – a far cry from the six scoreless USHL games that got him dropped to the NAHL in 2017-18. He had a strong playoffs, but it seems as if he got onto the radar with his hot start (15 goals in his first 20 games; 34 points and a plus-20 in his first 26 games) and it became a little unsustainable in the second half on both counts. As a 5'9" player, with lower-end mobility, and having been passed over twice in the NHL Draft before, the deck is stacked against the New Jersey native. Though, he does continue to produce where ever he's at. Definitely more of a goal scorer than a playmaker, Brown doesn't wow anyone with his skills in open ice, but he burrows his way into the right areas of the rink and can get pucks off his blade quickly from in close. His technical skills to beat players or to make room for himself are low, especially when compared to his rate of production. His ability to finish on goalies is surprisingly high though. In fact, he had some oddly flashy finishes early in the year that seem uncharacteristic of this type of player. Brown competes hard and knows where to go, but the rest of his game is no better than average. Despite being a left winger, he has grown to take on faceoff duties regularly for the Buccaneers. His skating stride needs work and nothing about it pops or rises above the level of average. He participates defensively and isn't averse to throwing a hit. That said, he grinds without being a grinder in the traditional sense. He wants to play a skill game, but it seems like the law of diminishing returns will apply sooner than later and he's going to have to add a dimension. His ability to quickly adapt to the ever-rising level of play that he has participated in suggests that he may be able to train at and embrace a role that offers some security. To date, he certainly looks like a player who is greater than the sum of his parts.

"NCAA Free Agent watch list player for me" HP Scout, Dusten Braaksma, May 2019

NR	PLAYER	TEAM	LEAGUE	HEIGHT	WEIGHT	POS	GRADE
	BROWN, MITCHELL	TRI-CITY	WHL	6'3.0"	205 *	RD	ND
	HOCKEY SENSE	COMPETE		SKILL		SKATING	
	5	5		5		5	

Brown is a good size right handed defensemen who Tri-City drafted in the 2016 WHL Bantam draft with the 29th overall pick. Has the abilities to be a decent player at the WHL level, but Brown does not bring enough to project to be an NHLer in the future. Brown doesn't have any area of major strength and is instead an all-around average kind of player. He rarely stood out when we watched Tri-City this season and played in a bottom pairing role on the team with not much flashes or offensive skills that could translate for the next level.

NR	PLAYER	TEAM	LEAGUE	HEIGHT	WEIGHT	POS	GRADE
	BUDY, BRENDAN	TRI-CITY	USHL	5'10.0"	179	LW	ND
	HOCKEY SENSE	COMPETE		SKILL		SKATING	
	5	4		6		7	

Quick, offensive forward. Budy jumped right from the BCHL to the University of Denver – an eventual Frozen Four participant - as an 18 year old. He was used sparingly in the first half of the season and after six pointless games and a team-worst minus-5 rating, Budy left school for the Tri-City Storm. There, he was able to find some more ice time and get out of a bottom-six role and into more offensive situations. He was a point per game player with the Storm. Passed over in 2018, Brendan was invited to Carolina Hurricanes development camp last summer. He's a quick little forward with a short, compact stride. His first two steps are quite good and so is his closing speed. He carries a lower center of gravity, but he's not much for body contact in general. Budy has a skill level that's a bit above average but his game was a little mishmashed even once he got settled in. He looks like a better puck retriever as F1, but then he isn't the best board battler. He doesn't quite have the skill to carry the puck across lines, yet he's a better playmaker than finisher. Down the line, this player doesn't project to be a center necessarily, but being tasked with having to manage all of that ice would be a positive step for his overall development. He did come back defensively, but seemed just a quarter- to a half-beat late in terms of timing. The production was there, but he didn't seem to drive the bus as much as some others on the team. He needs more time at a lower level to maximize his development arc and the expectation is that he'll return to the USHL in 2019-20.

	PLAYER	TEAM	LEAGUE	HEIGHT	WEIGHT	POS	GRADE
NR	**BUDGELL, BRETT**	**CHARLOTTETOWN**	**QMJHL**	**5'10.75"**	**190 ***	**LW**	**ND**
	HOCKEY SENSE	COMPETE		SKILL		SKATING	
	5	6		5		5	

Budgell had his coming-out party in the 2018 QMJHL postseason, where he was one of the top performers for the Islanders in their great playoff run. We had hoped his great play would carry on into this season, but he had a slow start after being cut from Team Canada's U-18 squad for the Hlinka/Gretzky cup in August. Then, with the Islanders, he only had three goals in his first 17 games. For most of the season, his offensive performance was marked by inconsistency, and he finished the year with 18 goals and 33 points in 67 games. He started the year playing mostly on the wing, and was moved to center full time in the 2nd half. He didn't perform as we had thought he would offensively this year. However, he remains a pretty solid two-way player. He has decent size and decent skating abilities, as well as good work ethic at both ends of the ice, and also plays a physical game along the boards. What is surprising with Budgell's lack of offense this year is that he possesses an excellent shot, including a quick release, and his shot is heavy. He works hard on the forecheck and he's strong along the wall, but lacks a bit of creativity with the puck to create more offense for his line. He's also got an average hockey sense offensively. He's definitely a better shooter than he is a passer, a quality that would likely send him back to the wing if it translates to the professional level. He is a good player on the PK unit; he works hard away from the puck and pays attention to all the little details on the ice. His offensive game may not have progressed as expected this season, but he did become a very good two-way player this year and his move to center was a big reason why. As far as upside for the NHL, he's more in the mold of a grinder-type player. His lack of offense this year definitely hurt his stock for the draft. He could get picked late in the draft by a team that believes he'll have a big comeback season next year and replace himself as a decent NHL prospect.

"I was expecting so much more out of him after his great playoff run in the 2018 postseason, but he never was able to get it in gear 2 this year." - HP Scout Jérôme Bérubé, May 2019

	PLAYER	TEAM	LEAGUE	HEIGHT	WEIGHT	POS	GRADE
NR	**BUKES, COLBY**	**MUSKEGON**	**USHL**	**5'11.0"**	**192**	**RD**	**C**
	HOCKEY SENSE	COMPETE		SKILL		SKATING	
	6	6		6		7	

Mobile, offensive-minded defenseman with terrific transition ability. Bukes completed his third season with Muskegon with 36 points and a team-best plus-32 rating. He's a February 1999 birthday going to Minnesota State Mankato next year. Bukes' game is founded in mobility, puck retrievals, and quick, accurate outlet passes. He's a gifted skater: very agile, very good on his edges, good balance and escapability. His ability to change directions quickly with the puck to move against the flow of pressure is a major asset. He does sometimes try too hard to skirt away from hits after he releases the puck, which can put him in a worse spot than if he just had absorbed it in the first place. His timing and body positioning for puck retrievals is right on the money. He swoops in and scoops the puck up and deposits it where ever it needs to go next smoothly. His outlet passing is as quick as it is accurate. As an older, experienced player, he certainly has the advantage over many in the league, but from our vantage point, he's one of the most accurate outlet passers in the USHL. He does skate the puck sometimes, but that's a product of his wheels more than his hands and doesn't give off the vibe that it would transition to the pro game meaningfully. He smartly opens up for his partner readily, which is another feather in his transition-game cap.

Defensively, he does a fine job mitigating risk off the rush with his skating and pokecheck. He doesn't like to let poorly-conceived plays fester, so he'll play aggressive in the low neutral zone or highest layer of his defensive zone if something is just plodding along on his side of the rink. He has the luxury of good recovery ability because of his four-way mobility. He isn't a physical player by nature, but understands the value of applying body contact to disrupt plays along the boards. Oddly, he can get a little flat-footed against speed chances as he fails to match the speed of particularly fast forwards. He looks a little uncomfortable against layered attacks that cause him to have a looser gap. He has been beat a few times to the inside this season on over-ambitious, late crossovers. On the flip side, he does look comfortable jumping into the rush late but doesn't have the ability to bury pucks from distance, as his shot is not a positive attribute.

"No draft for me. More of a College free agent type player." – NHL Scout, May 2019

"A very good player but the 99' birthday is tough to overlook." – NHL Scout, June 2019

	PLAYER	TEAM	LEAGUE	HEIGHT	WEIGHT	POS	GRADE
NR	BURZAN, LUKA	BRANDON	WHL	6'0.0"	184 *	RW	**ND**
	HOCKEY SENSE	COMPETE		SKILL		SKATING	
	5	5		5		6	

Burzan put together a stronger season this year as a 2nd time eligible. the former 6th overall Bantam draft pick finished the year with 40 goals and 38 assists. There were major improvements in his game, but he still left some questions.

Burzan is an explosive skater who is extremely strong and well balanced on his edges. Can explode up ice and has pull away speed, never at risk from back pressure. On top of this open ice ability, Burzan is very quick and elusive in the corners. Burzan showcased the ability to make moves in tight on opponents this year while maintaining possession of the puck, allowing his explosiveness to be even more of a difference maker. Burzan also has a very heavy shot that he uses with frequency, as more of a shooter than playmaker. Burzan doesn't often display the ability to make complex plays through traffic, and sometimes can be too much of an individual on the ice. On top of this Burzan was often invisible for periods at a time before flashes of good play. Despite all the physical tools Burzan does not play with the fire and intensity to maximize his abilities.

87	PLAYER	TEAM	LEAGUE	HEIGHT	WEIGHT	POS	GRADE
	BYCHKOV, ROMAN	YAROSLAVL 2	RUS-JR.	5'11.0"	161	LD	C
	HOCKEY SENSE	COMPETE		SKILL		SKATING	
	6	6		6		6	

Roman Bychkov had a solid season while developing in Lokomotiv's program. He played the majority of the season with Loko Yaroslavl where he produced 15 points in 40 games, including 2 goals. He only factored into one playoff game during their run to the title, and had zero points. Internationally, he was featured at the Hlinka and World Junior A challenge, producing 2 combined points in 11 games. Bychkov is a two-way defenseman with some offensive-flare in his game. Unlike a lot of the Russian backend available in this class, Roman has legitimate offensive-tools that stood out. He can rush with the puck and use his hands in conjunction with his top-gear to beat opponents cleanly. He can execute between-the-legs drag dekes and rapidly shift the puck from his forehand to backhand and visa-versa. Additionally, despite his smaller stature, he also has a hard-shot from the point and is good at surveying the ice when looking for options. The biggest issue with Bychkov at this time is his size and skating combination. He's a good skater who has plus mechanics but he's also 5'10 and doesn't weigh a whole lot, so he's going to need to add another gear to his skating in order for his game to translate. Furthermore, he's less refined in his own-end, then in the offensive-zone, but does compete hard and isn't afraid to battle and finish checks against larger players. He also needs to continue how to identify his options below the goal-line under-pressure at a higher-rate then he currently does, but his anticipation when attacking in the offensive-zone, leads us to believe this area of his game can be developed if given enough time. There's some upside in this feisty defensive-player, but he will need extended-time for it to develop. .

3	PLAYER	TEAM	LEAGUE	HEIGHT	WEIGHT	POS	GRADE
	BYRAM, BOWEN	VANCOUVER	WHL	6'0.5"	194*	LD	A
	HOCKEY SENSE	COMPETE		SKILL		SKATING	
	8	6		8		7	

Bowen Byram turned into one of the most consistently impressive players we saw this year, developing an offensive-game that wasn't present in last years viewings. Byram finished with 71 points, and 26 goals which lead all defenseman in the CHL. He was voted as a Western Conference First Team All-Star, the only 2019 eligible player to make either WHL conferences first team. He also led The Giants to a final's appearance in the playoffs, where he accumulated

Byram is the most dynamic defenseman in this year's draft class. His stats were reflective of his talent which was largely generated through his combination of hockey sense, skill, and skating ability. Bowen thinks the game two-steps ahead of most of his opponents. This gives him the rare ability to force opponents to react to his play while not becoming reactive to there's. We've seen him chase down a puck below the goal-line in the defensive-end, then suddenly stop-up and fake a hit, this froze the forechecker who was skating down behind him which left him flat-footed, giving Byram the opportunity to peel off the pressure and carve his way through the neutral zone. Plays like that encompass his ability to dictate and control the tempo of a shift. The best aspect of his hockey-sense is his ability to rapidly process the play. This extends to all three-zones; in the defensive-end, it allows him to make excellent reads with little time and space behind his goal-line, rush the puck through heavy traffic in the neutral-zone, and breakdown opposing defenses in the offensive-zone. His hockey sense extends to his play away from the puck, managing to create time and space for his defensive partner, recognizing when play is transitioning, and when he needs to readjust his position to receive a pass. Furthermore, he was very good at defending off the rush with a strong gap and good stick-positioning which allowed him to neutralize the play. Although he's not the biggest defender, Bowen displayed the willingness to physically engage and even delivered some hard hits as players were attempting to transition over the defensive-line. When he has the puck on his stick in his own-end, he showcased excellent vision, especially in situations where he had the puck in the corners. This translated to quick, accurate and efficient outlet passes under heavy-pressure.

When he had the puck on his stick outside of the defensive-zone and in transition, he was one of the better defenders, if not the best defender we saw this year at generating high-end offensive-zone entries. As a result, plays rarely died on his stick which was one of the primary reasons he produced as many points as he did. After gaining the offensive-zone, Byram showed off a dynamic skill-set featured by excellent puck-skills that gave him the ability to beat players one-on-one. His hands compliment his skating ability. He has good skating mechanics, excellent two-step area quickness and solid straight-line speed which allows him to rush the puck. However, arguably the most impressive aspect of Byram's skating is his ability to pivot using his edges. There are very few players in this class who can be as elusive as Bowen is due to how suddenly he can shift his position. This gives him a rare level of escapability in-tight spaces and when walking-the-line. When you combine the aforementioned attributes with his hockey-sense, you get a defenseman who can drive-play in the offensive-end by using a multi-faceted attack. His wrist-shot was his preferred option in our viewings, featuring a plus release point, including the ability to suddenly shift the angle of his shot while in motion. Lastly, Bowen was very good at recognizing when he had closed and open lanes which allowed him to distribute the puck from the half-wall where he was primary used on the powerplay.

There were few players in this class who had a faster development-curve than Byram. He was a player who at the beginning of the season and much of last season looked like a potential two-way, top-four defenseman, but has now progressed into a dynamic top-pairing defenseman who can run a powerplay as his ceiling. In order for him to reach his ceiling, Bowen needs to continue to refine his play away from the puck in his own-end and continue to develop his intensity-level away from the puck, which at times can be inconsistent.

"You can't get players like this unless you draft them. Nobody trades them." - NHL Scout, March 2019

"Best Dman in the draft by a wide margin" - NHL Scout, March 2019

"Skating is a nine as far as his edgework." - HP Scout, Mark Edwards, January 2019

"He had 97 points this year which included 26 goals in regular season and 8 more in 26 playoff games. He was the biggest reason Vancouver went as far as they did. I think he has a chance to play in the NHL next season and Mark Hunter and Team Canada might be outta luck. I probably wouldn't rush him but it won't surprise me if he sticks." - HP Scout, Mark Edwards, May 2019

"Imagine if he goes 4th to Colorado. Makar and Byram. Game set, match." - HP Scout, Mark Edwards, May 2019 2019

"Several teams mentioned Byram to me as being one of their best interviews. Good on the ice and off ice." - HP Scout, Mark Edwards, June 2019

	PLAYER	TEAM	LEAGUE	HEIGHT	WEIGHT	POS	GRADE
NR	**CAJKA, PETR**	ERIE	OHL	5'11.75"	169 *	LC	**C**
	HOCKEY SENSE	COMPETE		SKILL		SKATING	
	5	5		6		6	

Cajka was selected 12th overall in the CHL-import-draft by the Erie Otters and had a respectable first-season. He finished with 38 points in 63 games, including 20 goals. He also played at both the U19 and U20 level for the Czech-

Republic, and had 1 assist in 7 combined games. Cajka is a skilled winger with some speed to his game. He was at his most dangerous off the rush and looked to take a direct-approach to the net. He wasn't a perimeter player but he also wasn't overly consistent either. There were viewings where he would threaten multiple times a game, showing an above-average release point and a set of soft-hands that he used to threaten one-on-one, but he also would go stretches without making much of an impact. One of the main reasons for this was due to his anticipation off the puck. There's still a raw element to his game in terms of identifying where he needs to be in order to receive a pass in a high-danger area, and this left opportunities on the board for him to put additional points up the board. This extends to his defensive-play, where he was average when we got to see him. There's some talent and skill, but he still needs more time to develop before he shows a translatable game towards the pro-levels.

"Skating was ok, at times he didn't move his feet, stood around too much." - NHL Scout February 2019

"There is some skill there. He made my list." - NHL Scout, May 2019

	PLAYER	TEAM	LEAGUE	HEIGHT	WEIGHT	POS	GRADE
71	CAJKOVIC, MAXIM	SAINT JOHN	QMJHL	5'10.75"	185 *	RW	C
	HOCKEY SENSE	COMPETE		SKILL		SKATING	
	5	5		7		6	

Cajkovic was the top pick in the CHL Import Draft last June after playing in Sweden last season. The Slovak forward joined Saint John in the QMJHL this season and didn't exactly have a stellar year. His low-ranked team encountered lots of difficulties in the first half, not winning many games. In the 2nd half, while things got a bit better, the Sea Dogs still finished 17th out of 18th teams in the league.

It was a tough first half of the season for Cajkovic. He would be a healthy scratch, unsuccessful offensively when he was in the lineup, and his overall body language was not good. Things got a bit better in the 2nd half of the season; he collected 26 points in 31 games and seemed to show more of his skill level on the ice. Cajkovic has average size, and his straight away skating is good. He does generate some speed on the ice; his top speed and acceleration are above average. He's agile on his feet, and he is able to beat guys one-on-one in the QMJHL, but he will still need to improve his speed for the next level. He's at his best on the power play with more room to manoeuvre. On the man-advantage, he often played on the point on the power play, as he has done for Slovakia on the international stage prior to joining the Sea Dogs. He's more of a shooter than he is a passer; he's got a very good shot from the point and is not shy to use it. He can either use his wrist shot or slapper, as he has a quick release and his puck poise is very good as well. He has the ability to beat guys one-on-one. His hands are above-average, and his patience with the puck can help him beat defensemen who are too aggressive while defending against him. His on-ice vision is not bad, but we've seen him miss some easy passes in our viewings. They can sometimes lack accuracy, and he also tends to hold onto the puck a bit too long. Talent-wise, Cajkovic has the talent needed to be a dominant player in the QMJHL for the next two seasons on a young (but talented) Saint John team. However, we want to see more maturity out of him. As far for the NHL goes, he'll need to play at a higher pace and his compete level will need to get better. The talent is there, but his lack of compete level and work ethic makes him a risky pick for the draft.

"Same as Nussbaumer as far as being a big disappointment this year in the QMJHL" - HP Scout Jérôme Bérubé

"A player we had ranked quite high prior to the season and has fallen on our list. He was even scratched for a couple games. That said, he has some talent and he was placed in a very poor *situation with the Sea Dogs. They are a mess right now and it made it that much difficult for him to succeed this year. He accounted for a huge chunk of his teams offensive output." - HP Scout, Mark Edwards, March 2019*

52	PLAYER	TEAM	LEAGUE	HEIGHT	WEIGHT	POS	GRADE
	CAMPBELL, ALEXANDER	VICTORIA	BCHL	5'10.0"	151 *	LW	C+
	HOCKEY SENSE	COMPETE		SKILL		SKATING	
	7	7		7		7	

Alex Campbell had a successful rookie season while playing for the Grizzles, producing 67 points in 53 games. In the playoffs, he continued being productive, generating 15 points in 14 games, including 8 goals. At the World-Junior-A-Challenge, he had 1 goal in 6 games. He's committed to play for Clarkson University at the beginning of the 2020-2021 season.

Campbell is a diminutive--yet elusive winger who comes equipped with an adaptable-attack. He features one of the slightest-frames out of any draft-eligible forward; yet has an excellent top-gear which is a testament to his skating mechanics. There are few players who are more technically refined coming out of the gate, and this allows him to compensate for his lack of power. His stride is very efficient; he leans further back, relying on his quads and he's adept at balancing himself when in full-flight as a result. The most significant aspect of his skating is in regards to his pivoting and edge-work. Due to his size, defenders look to physically initiate with him, but he's very good at angling himself away from physical contact while in motion as a result of his agility. His dexterity allows him to manipulate his frame generating misdirection when opponents are trying to identify his skating lane. This made him equally as effective when skating laterally, as it does when he skates north-south. His processing ability when determining what's available in open-ice is very good; few players recognize how to take advantage of soft-ice as much as Alex has in our viewings. When his lanes are closed-off; his puck-skills synergies well with his slippery-style of play. He can pull-the-puck rapidly while simultaneously contorting his frame to avoid players who are trying to initiate with him. Furthermore, like Newhook, he's not a kid who looks to use a pre-set list of moves given the context of a play-type; he's adaptive and feels off what his opponents are giving him. This translated to a lot of success in areas of the ice that his frame would theoretically put him at disadvantage in. Specifically, around the net-area and in high-traffic around the slot. He's more of a technically-sound passer who looks for high-percentage passing options than he is a multi-faceted one. This blends well with his willingness to enter high-traffic areas with the puck; looking to draw defenses towards himself before finding his open-teammates with crisp passes. Where Alex was less successful offensively was in regards to his shot-placement. Although his release is quick and he can take pucks in one-motion; in some of our viewings, he would miss the net frequently. There's still a lack of overall polish within how he follows through his shot.

One of the more impressive traits featured in Campbell's game is a mental-one but it could be to his long-term detriment. Given his stature, he should be less inclined to initiate contact than he is. He doesn't play afraid and does surprisingly well during board-battling sequences by out-working other players; this applies to his stick-lifting which is one of his best defensive-traits. Although his work-rate and compete-level are welcomed, he's going to have to gain a substantial amount of mass in order for his game to currently translate away from the puck. Additionally, when he attacks high-traffic areas -- it's critical for him to have a frame that can absorb some contact.

Although Campbell has a lot of raw-talent, he's part of the litmus test as to just how slight-a-frame can translate to the NHL-level. If he is able to overcome his physical limitations, then we see Alex as a top-9 energy-winger who can play the game at a high-speed.

"I'm not an overly big fan. Too light to play in a heavy style game and I don't see enough skill." - NHL Scout, December 2018

"He won't be joining an NHL lineup anytime soon at 150 lbs, but this Alex is smart skilled and competes. He plays bigger than his size with no fear." - HP Scout, Mark Edwards, February 2019

"Before I got to the NHL Combine and I had already been told by several Scouts how young and small Campbell looked. I saw for my own eyes on testing day." - HP Scout, Mark Edwards, June 2019

	PLAYER	TEAM	LEAGUE	HEIGHT	WEIGHT	POS	GRADE
NR	CARROLL, JOSEPH	SAULT STE. MARIE	OHL	6'2.0"	197 *	LC	ND
	HOCKEY SENSE	COMPETE		SKILL		SKATING	
	5	4		5		6	

Joe Carroll finished his season with 31 points in 65 games, including 9 goals. In the playoffs, he produced 3 points in 8 games.

Carroll is a large winger with an interesting tool-kit. Although he's slow out of the gate and doesn't produce much in the way of four-way mobility; the mechanics are above-average for his build. He's not the fastest player on the ice, but he still looks to use the skating to cut aggressively towards the goal-line and net area in some of the games we viewed him in. Furthermore, there's some raw-skill when he's carrying the puck. His height augments his length and he's capable of making extended dragging dekes as a result. His hands extend into his shot, which features the ability to shift-angles; his shot also comes off his stick quickly. Though he does lack a fluidity when using his hands at times, which resulted in him bobbling the puck and turning it over too. When driving down a wing, he's decent at anticipating the play and was capable of some impressive give-and-go sequences that resulted in points as well. Despite having a larger-frame with skating that theoretically should improve when he develops physically and has some skill, there's still an element to Carroll's game that holds him back. His pacing can be very-mixed depending on the shift and this is due to a lack of assertiveness on the ice. Considering the tools he brings to the table, we were left constantly wanting more from him. He lacks a take-over-mentality and plays with a passivity that trickles through the rest of his game; downgrading his tools as a result. Carroll will need to increase his intensity-levels and further refine his puck-skills by becoming more coordinated if he ever hopes to play. It wouldn't hurt if he extended his vision as well.

"Big and can skate but work ethic and compete are suspect. I'd like to see more passion in his game.- NHL Scout, May 2019

"I got texts from several Scouts who were surprised to see him invited to the Top Prospects Game." - HP Scout, Mark Edwards, December 2018

	PLAYER	TEAM	LEAGUE	HEIGHT	WEIGHT	POS	GRADE
11	CAUFIELD, COLE	USA U-18	NTDP	5'7.25"	163*	RW	A
	HOCKEY SENSE	COMPETE		SKILL		SKATING	
	7	6		9		6	

Cole Caufield had a historic season on the program by producing 72 goals in 65 games for a total of 100 points, beating Austin Matthews previous record. Of his 100 points, 41 were produced in the USHL and he had 29 goals in 28 games.

Internationally, he had his best performance at the end of the season by scoring 14 goals and 18 points in 7 games during the World U18's.

Caufield is a draft anomaly that forces a breakdown within our methodology for how we evaluate players. For starters, Cole is 5'7", historically that would make it incredibly unlikely that we would ever consider him for the first-round. Secondly, Cole's skating isn't high end, and if a player this size doesn't have excellent skating then he's likely to be moved down significantly in our rankings or given a no draft grade. Lastly, Cole's a smart player but lags behind some top-end players within regards to his vision, making him less of a duel-threat-option; he's more one-dimensional. Yet not only has he maintained his first-round status with us but he's actually significantly increased his status since we ranked him 16th overall way back in September. We don't usually do player comparable's for our write-ups, but for the nature of this assessment we feel it's obligatory to discuss him with another draft anomaly, Alex DeBrincat, due to their similar stature and goal-scoring ability.

DeBrincat and some other smaller players set a tone for scouting by not only proving doubters wrong, but by developing so rapidly that it's forced our hand when assessing elite offensive-talents who have less mobility relative to their size than we would like. When breaking down Alex DeBrincat and comparing him to Cole, we're going to look at the offensive-attributes that have made both successful. To start, Alex is a better playmaker and is more deceptive than Cole. What's meant by this is that DeBrincat's vision and ability to mask his intentions with the puck are at a higher-level than Caufield's at the same age. Alex had the ability to find players with backdoor options and thread passes through multiple players at a higher-rate than Cole did this season. More importantly, Alex was better at deceiving his opponents due to having more variation in his shot-types as well as a more hidden release point. Specifically, he threatened at a more consistent level with his backhand, snapshot and slapshot than Caufield does and used screens to mask his shot placement at a higher rate. From a stationary position, DeBrincat was more dangerous since it was more difficult to recognize his intentions with the puck due to the duel-threat options he presents. However, these above characteristics that we consider Alex more competent in, doesn't necessarily make him the better scoring threat. The initial counter-point that we argue when discussing Caufield's vision is that we don't want him passing the puck unless it's to put himself in a position to receive it back after the initial pass when a higher-percentage shot presents itself as a result. His shot counteracts the need for him to be a duel-threat option to the same degree that Alex was in his draft year.

When breaking down Caufield's inability to mask his intentions at the same-rate as DeBrincat's, it's due to how he releases the puck with his body mechanics behind the release point. Where DeBrincat opted primarily to use a snapshot that would beat goalies based on placement and how few tells there were in his shooting mechanics, Caufield looks to extend his drag in his release which gives a sudden-change in angle and a further change in angle than most of DeBrincat's shots. This results in goalies being able to pick up that Caufield is shooting before DeBrincat in some instances, yet the end result is the same. One of the most surprising aspects of Caufield is that you could make an argument that his footwork behind his shot isn't nearly as good as the rest of his mechanics. He can stand somewhat flat-footed at times before releasing the puck, yet the result is still a goal. The reason for this, is that Caufield is a master of manipulating his hips, core and shoulders in order to rotate and subsequently gain velocity on his shot. This is pronounced due to Caufield's height and weight. He theoretically shouldn't be able to generate nearly as much velocity as he does, yet has one of the hardest shots in this class which speaks volumes to his coordination behind his body rotation. This extends to his slapshot as well. Cole is excellent at lowering his posture by dropping to one-knee which further elevates the puck while gaining additional torque on his release-point. This has resulted in him being equally as dangerous from a stationary position as he is when in motion. The main takeaway is that DeBrincat and Caufield generate goals based off their release points in very different ways, yet the end results were very similar. With DeBrincat, there is hardly any delay in the start-up of his shot which gives him the initial advantage over Caufield by the slightest of margins, however the middle and end phase of the shot gives an advantage to Caufield due to how quickly he elevates the puck with his further rotation and extended drag. One fascinating area of development to note is that goalies in the

NHL have the ability to pick up extended release points a lot quicker than junior goalies, which theoretically indicates there's probably a slight advantage to DeBrincat in translating his goals, yet Caufield's so good at elevating the puck and changing his shooting angle that it might not matter.

Although DeBrincat was the superior playmaker and could mask his intentions better, the rest of Caufield's game is either equal to or ahead of where DeBrincat was at the same age with the exception of one other area. That area is in regards to DeBrincat's ability to change the tempo of a play, which was critical for his success due to his average foot-speed. He needed to be able to slow down his opponents more often than Caufield does. The reason for this is because Caufield is the superior skater at the same age. Cole's skating features solid mechanics, plus acceleration, a fluid-stride, and a good top-gear. Additionally, although he's not overly agile for his size, he does feature the ability to quickly side-step which gives him extended room to get off his release, an example being the high-end goal he scored against Russia at the U18's. As a result, Cole is usually in motion more than DeBrincat and can attack at a more aggressive pace at times. Perhaps Caufield's biggest area of strength next to his shot, is his ability to find soft-ice. When breaking down wingers who aren't expected to be line-drivers, we assess the importance of the player being able to put himself in a position to receive a pass, followed by the ability to assess how quickly he can put himself in a high-danger area after receiving the initial pass and lastly, how quickly he can generate a scoring chance. There's no other winger in this class who is ahead of Cole when breaking down the above criteria. Whether he's around the goal-line, trailing his center, driving down the wing, or finding a backdoor option, Cole is adept at anticipating where he can put himself in a position to score a goal and do it quickly. If he is challenged by a defender, Caufield has a soft set of hands that allow him to guard the puck, though due to his short stature, there's not a lot of length for him to make toe-drags and other dekes that can help separate him. It will be more difficult for him to challenge one-on-one aggressively against larger defenders with reach at the NHL-level. Lastly, there's an offensive efficiency to what Caufield does that goes beyond his attributes. He's one of the most naturally gifted junior scorers we've ever seen and apart of that is due to his bravado and willingness to challenge the goalie. Snipers generally go through droughts where you can see within their body language that their over-thinking the shot placement and have lost their confidence. That doesn't happen with Caufield, his confidence very rarely dips and if he does have off games, his ability to elevate his play back to his expected output is remarkably consistent.

Caufield is small, he's unlikely to drive a line, he's a competitor who will still get overwhelmed occasionally by larger defenseman, he's going to lose his share of board battles, but he has an offensive-gift that you can't teach which can still be a weapon for any team. The question will be if he can use that weapon as effectively in the playoffs.

"I just dropped him out of my first round. He scores but I'd like to see him create more and drive more play." - NHL Scout, December 2018

"I remember (Rocco) Grimaldi being more dynamic. He had the puck more and was way more competitive. Caufield doesn't skate great for his size and isn't as creative as Rocco was. Caufield wasn't my best interview either." - NHL Scout, January 2019

"He's going to be a great college player." - NHL Scout, April 2018

"Some of these list are hilarious, they have Caufield in the first round." - NHL Scout, November 2018

"Hard to take any list seriously that has Caufield in the first round." - NHL Scout, November 2018

(We informed both those Scout we are one of those lists.)

"He was probably the weakest interview of the top program guys. I didn't really care for the kid." - NHL Scout, January 2019

"Everyone is looking for the next DeBrincat now, but this kid isn't going to be him." - NHL Scout, February 2019

"Great player and he's way up on my list. The records are a bit tarnished for me though. When his coach puts PP one on the ice in blowouts all year, those guys are going to get more points. If having PP one on the ice for the 9th goal against Slovakia wasn't bad enough, they were on the ice for the 12th goal too. Embarrassing." - NHL Scout, April 2019

"He'll be a force on the powerplay right away." - NHL Scout, April 2019

"He is so smart. I love the way he finds the open areas." - NHL Scout, April 2019

"It's really tough to separate all these top guys." - NHL Scout, April 2019

"Big legs and thighs, he's a strong little ******. I was impressed when I interviewed him." - NHL Scout, April 2019

"There was a mini stretch where he wasn't scoring and in turn wasn't helping" - NHL Scout, April 2019

"He compared himself to DeBrincat (shocker) but I saw DeBrincat a lot and one difference for sure is I don't think he has the same jam at the same age. Alex would get pissed off and go after guys and take runs a them." - NHL Scout, May 2019

"Players that force your hand when evaluating them usually turn out to be impressive players at the NHL level, that was Caufield for me this season" - HP Scout, Brad Allen

"He scored a lot of goals but the one he scored at the U18's, short side over Yaroslav Askarov shoulder stands out. He made a quick move to his right that was a very high end play. That was a play that stood out for me on how talented he is." - HP Scout, Mark Edwards, April 2019

"I remember moving up Alex DeBrincat into the middle of the first round in the middle of his draft season and then moving him to the top of the 2nd round on our final list because of being wary of his size/skating combo. Caufield shares Alex DeBrincat's size but his skating is better at the same age - HP Scout, Mark Edwards, May 2019

"I asked a ton of Scouts over the past month where they had Caufield ranked. I was surprised how many of them still had him ranked in the 2nd round. The biggest reason I heard from numerous Scouts was - if he isn't scoring, what does he bring to the table.? Myself and others on our staff have that concern but in the end we think he'll score enough." HP Scout, Mark Edwards, June 2019

"Very likeable kid when I met him at the combine." - HP Scout, Mark Edwards, June 2019

	PLAYER	TEAM	LEAGUE	HEIGHT	WEIGHT	POS	GRADE
NR	CAULFIELD, JUDD	USA U-18	NTDP	6'3.0"	204 *	RW	ND
	HOCKEY SENSE	COMPETE		SKILL		SKATING	
	4	6		5		4	

Hulking, cycling winger. Judd Caufield was used on the lower lines for most of the USNTDP season and his stat line reflects that (6 goals, 25 points in 28 USHL games). He also failed to register a point at the U18 in seven games. The aura to Caulfield is that he's 6'3", 204 pounds but he's going to need a lot of polish to get where he needs to go. His skating leaves a lot to be desired: his agility, first-step quickness, and even balance are below average. With a head of steam, he gets around the ice okay and he's better at initiating contact than receiving it. Judd goes to the net readily and willingly, with or without the puck, he's taking it to the paint. It's tough to recall many goals this year from him that came from more than a stick length from the crease. He'll be better in that role when he can fine tune his skating, as it will allow him better angles to find loose pucks. He'll also be much tougher to move from the front if he can stay on his skates. The array of tricks in Caulfield's bag is also still pretty limited. He's a surprisingly adept passer and playmaker from down low, but in terms of taking on defenders with skill or even making a little room for himself – that's a bridge too far right now. Even his shooting and finishing ability near the net isn't very noteworthy, and if his bread and butter is going to be that of a workman like style of offense his scoring ability will need improvement. His cycle work and board play get pluses. We would like to see a little more engagement in the play more often, he doesn't have a great sense of urgency nor does he display much emotion on the ice. He has shown the capability to really unearth pucks by getting underneath opponents and prying them off the puck, but maybe not as often as he's capable. The hockey sense seems about average and the player, overall, seems raw with a lot of ground on his development arc to eat up. He's off to North Dakota in the fall, but Fargo also grabbed his rights in the 16th round just in case he craves some more time to collect himself at a lower level.

"The kid works his butt off but I don't see enough skill to be a highly effective offensive player in NHL and his feet scare me a bit." HP Scout, Dusten Braaksma, May 2019

	PLAYER	TEAM	LEAGUE	HEIGHT	WEIGHT	POS	GRADE
NR	CEDERQVIST, FILIP	VAXJO JR.	SWE-JR.	6'1.0"	187	LW	C
	HOCKEY SENSE	COMPETE		SKILL		SKATING	
	6	6		5		6	

Cederqvist has flown under the radar most of the season, a season that he split between two leagues. With his clubs U20 team in the SuperElite, he put up 14 goals and 18 assists for a total of 32 points in 26 games and he was a leader and a star on his team. He also played 33 games with his clubs men's team in the SHL where he managed to put up 4 goals and 4 assists for a total of 8 points. Cederqvist who was overlooked at last years draft has had a strong development this season and he really had a breakout year with his point producing. In the SuperElite he was a shining light on a blunt Växjö team and he led the first line both on the ice and off the ice. It was evident that he was a man against teens at times, where he was bigger and stronger than his opponents and could push through traffic with his heavy style of play.

Skillwise it's obvious when he's playing against juniors that he got a good offensive skill set with soft hands and a heavy shot and he has the ability to muscle through to get his shot off. His skating needs a bit of work but is totally viable and he's got a strong stride and is tough to stop. What's a bit worrying is his average hockey IQ, where he can be very inconsistent and doesn't seem to have a very good split vision. What's been interesting with his season is that he has been a point-producing star in the SuperElite and mixed it with a role as a fourth-line grinder in the SHL. He's been able to have success with both roles and has the ability to blend in everywhere on the roster. In a more defensive role with the SHL team, he's been good, but pretty far from great. Defensively he's struggled a bit against faster and smarter players and has shown a lack of defensive awareness, the defender he should have been marking has sneaked down to score a goal. His offensive game is decent at the SHL level, but he hasn't really gotten the chance to prove his worth offensively on a great offensive Växjö roster.

He is well built and is a strong player who can cope well with physical play, but he is a pusher and can often be seen with the stick in one hand to push the opposing player with the other hand, even in battles along the boards.

He got the opportunity to make his international debut this season with Swedens U19 team where he played 4 games and only managed to put up 1 assist and a total of 1 point, which was considered a disappointment considering his strong season up until that point.

#	PLAYER	TEAM	LEAGUE	HEIGHT	WEIGHT	POS	GRADE
69	CHISTYAKOV, SEMYON	UFA 2	RUS-JR.	5'10.0	167	LD	C
	HOCKEY SENSE		COMPETE		SKILL		SKATING
	6		7		5		7

Chistyakov is a two-way defenseman from the MHL, where he played 32 games with Tolpar Ufa and registered 11 points in the regular season. He was also a key player for the Russian U-18 national team all year, playing in various tournaments for them. He's an undersized defender who plays much bigger than his size; he likes to get involved physically and has great timing to deliver open-ice hits. At the World Under-18 event in April, he didn't get to play as physical as he did previously, though. It's possible that he was instructed to play safer, but he was less effective when deviating from his usual in-your-face formula to challenge puck-carriers. Internationally, he played his best hockey of the season at the Five Nations' tournament in February in Russia, where his physical play mixed with his skating and puck-moving abilities made him a threat on the ice. He can set the tempo or change the rhythm of a game with a bone-crunching open-ice hit, but he's limited in terms of what he can do down low in his zone due to his size. It's very difficult for him to contain big forwards along the boards and in front of the net, and he doesn't play with a long stick, making it even harder to take the puck away from opponents. He has a good compete level and he's a willing competitor, but needs to be very smart when defending due to his physical limitations. The best part of his game is his footwork; he's a good skater who is also very agile, making him quick to retrieve pucks in his own zone. He moves pucks well outside of his zone, making a quick pass or skating it out, away from the forecheck. He makes good decisions with the puck and helps his team's transition game with his puck-distribution from his own zone. There's some value to him on the power play, as he distributes pucks well enough at this level, but he's not super dynamic on the point and doesn't project as a power play quarterback at the NHL level.

Chistyakov is an energetic defenseman who could have value for an NHL team due to his physical game and ability to skate. His size is definitely a concern, and his lack of high-end skills might limit him to being used as a depth defenseman at the NHL level.

79	PLAYER	TEAM	LEAGUE	HEIGHT	WEIGHT	POS	GRADE
	CICCOLINI, ERIC	TORONTO JC	OJHL	5'10.5"	160 *	RW	C
	HOCKEY SENSE		COMPETE		SKILL		SKATING
	5		5		7		7

The Toronto Jr Canadiens forward has committed to the University of Michigan for 2020/2021. The skilled Right Winger had 62 points in 47 games which included 27 goals. He added a goal and 4 helpers in 5 OJHL Playoff games. Eric also participated in the WJAC in Bonnyville in December as a member of Team Canada East.

Eric Ciccolini is not lacking skill. Where we felt he did lack was in two other areas that carry a lot of weight for us. Those two areas were hockey sense and compete. There were times in some of our viewings where he seemingly didn't want the puck. He seemed to be in a rush to pass it to a teammate. His skating is definitely not a weakness and we often saw him streaking down the wing and letting his shot go on the fly. He lacked vision and creativity. He plays a very individual offensive game. He can make the odd play but it was not a regular occurrence in our viewings.

While we loved the skill and skating combination, the lack of competitiveness and drive from shift to shift is what makes him a later round option for us. He can become a very good hockey player, his ceiling is high but he'll need to improve in some important areas of his game.

"Sometimes I thought he was thinking too much and I'm not sure he processes the game quickly enough." - NHL Scout, March 2019

"Draft him late and hope fo the best in four years. Go Michigan. Secrets of the scouting world. (laughs)" -NHL Scout, May 2019

"One of the Assistant Coaches on the Jr Canadiens was a former player I coached. He told me back in December that they were working to improve Eric's decision making and that he was making progress." - HP Scout, Mark Edwards

75	PLAYER	TEAM	LEAGUE	HEIGHT	WEIGHT	POS	GRADE
	CLARKE, GRAEME	OTTAWA	OHL	5'11.5"	175 *	RW	C
	HOCKEY SENSE		COMPETE		SKILL		SKATING
	6		5		6		5

Coming off of a good rookie season for Ottawa, there were high expectations for Clarke coming into his second year. He started slow for the 67's this season - receiving limited ice time; he predominantly played on the 4th line because of the depth of older players on the team. He did play on the power play unit where he scored 8 of his 23 goals with the advantage. Clarke is at his best when he has the puck on his stick. While Clarke possesses a really good shot, his playmaking skills are underrated as he can create for his teammates despite his shoot-first mentality. Clarke shows above average puck skills with the ability to beat defensemen 1-on-1. Graeme's shot is his offensive weapon; he owns a lightning quick release with great velocity and strong accuracy. It doesn't take long for Clarke to shoot the puck when it is on his stick, he will shoot from anywhere in the offensive zone and needs very little time to get the puck off his stick. Clarke's skating is average, with decent top speed; but he needs to work on his quickness, his first couple of strides need to improve.

Defensively, Clarke needs to be more competitive in his own zone as he floats around and gets caught out of position or will try to leave the zone early to go on the attack. Clarke needs to be more committed to the defensive side of the game. Graeme's game could be more effective if he were to engage more in the offensive zone and go after pucks, he tends to shy away from the physicality. His game is played mostly on the perimeter and could, again, be more effective if he had a willingness to take pucks hard to the net. Graeme had a really strong playoff for Ottawa, as he was given more responsibility playing on the top line. He completed the playoffs with 14 points in 18 games. Clarke can be an offensive threat when he plays consistently, and going into next year Graeme should be one of the go-to guys for Ottawa and the points should come.

"Tough to see him. He barely plays." – NHL Scout, December 2018

"Skill is limited other than his shot." – NHL Scout, December 2018

"He competes at times but I've never seen him throw a body check." – NHL Scout, March 2019

"Skating has really improved since last year." – NHL Scout, March 2019

"Once he started to get more icetime, he got to show what he can do. I like him a lot, he's in my top 40." – NHL Scout, March 2019

"I like him, he's in my 2nd round." – NHL Scout, April 2019

"Third round guy for me. Love the shot and his skating has come a long way." – NHL Scout, May 2019

"I have him just behind Suzuki because he (Suzuki) works harder and has more skill." – NHL Scout, May 2019

"I think he's weak. He has a ton of work to do getting stronger before he'll ever have a chance. I think that's why he doesn't battle...he knows he can't win a one on one." – NHL Scout, May 2019

"I like the numbers, especially what he posted before he got increased ice time. My issue was he didn't work very hard in several of my viewings. He was hard to find out there at times. That said, I do have this small feeling in my gut that I might regret not ranking him a bit higher." – HP Scout, Mark Edwards

	PLAYER	TEAM	LEAGUE	HEIGHT	WEIGHT	POS	GRADE
NR	**CONNORS, LIAM**	**ST. SEBASTIANS**	**U.S PREP**	**5'8.0"**	**150**	**RW**	**ND**
	HOCKEY SENSE		COMPETE		SKILL		SKATING
	6		6		4		4

Connors was a 2nd round draft pick of Tri-City (USHL) in the 2017 Futures Draft but seen his rights traded to Muskegon. Connors has elected to stay in St. Sebastian's up to this point, putting up 14 goals and 29 assists in 29 games this year. Connors is a hard-working, two-way centerman but doesn't have the size or strength yet to be overly effective in this role. His offensive skill is just average at this time and can attempt plays that are above his skill set in certain situations. Liam's skating is ok but not overly agile for a player his size. Connors has pretty good awareness and hockey sense, he processes situations quickly at both ends of the ice. Liam is at is best when he simplifies his game and uses his work ethic to his advantage. Connors saw one game of USHL action last year for Muskegon. A move to the USHL against some older and stronger competition would be advantageous for Connors development at this stage. Connors is committed to Boston University for 2020.

NR	PLAYER	TEAM	LEAGUE	HEIGHT	WEIGHT	POS	GRADE
	CONSTANTINOU, WILLIAM	KINGSTON	OHL	5'11.75"	185 *	RD	ND
	HOCKEY SENSE		COMPETE		SKILL		SKATING
	4		6		7		7

Billy Constantinou had a sporadic season while playing both for the Niagara Ice-dogs and the Kingston Frontenacs. With Niagara, he generated 15 points in 22 games, including 4 goals. On Kingston, he was used in a prominent role including manning the top-powerplay, where he finished with 18 points in 44 games, including 6 goals. Constantinou is an offensively-gifted defenseman who uses impressive skating mechanics to rush the puck. When he has the puck on his stick, he can be an effective-player. Below the goal-line, he's very good at spinning off pressure and peeling off checking attempts which gives him an elusiveness to his game. His short-burst acceleration is also very-good, allowing him to escape in-tight areas of the ice when he's attempting to find his passing options. When he's taken off down the ice, he has good puck-skills that allow him guard the puck at an above-average-rate and beat opponents one-on-one. His skating when combined with his puck-skills make him a threat when he's walking the offensive-line, and he's shown the ability to deliver sharp passes, as well as creative-passes that require good vision. He's capable of extending his drag-dekes into his release point which can change his angle, and he's shown a good amount of coordination when attempting to fire off one-timers in his wheel-house. Although his shooting mechanics are above-average, he does have a tendency to over-commit on his shot after failing to identify that his lane has been taken away. This results in Billy hitting shin-pads more than we would like to see. What Billy does best, is activate using his speed followed by breaking down the defense with his skill, before generating a play towards the net-area. The problem is, when breaking down his hockey-sense, he doesn't play with a lot of poise and looks to take-over shifts which leaves his teammates trying to figure out how they can incorporate their play-style with his own. He doesn't have the offensive-IQ to drive play to the extent he currently wants to.

Although he's gifted offensively, and can keep a good pace at the offensive-line; his defensive-play leaves a lot to be desired. When he's not in possession of the puck, he's unengaged at times and doesn't show an attention to detail in his own-end. There's an assertiveness to his play-style when he's out of his own end but when he's forced to play defense – he has no structure to fall back on. He can play physically in-front of the net, and make a decent recovery play here and there, but it's not with any sort of sustained consistency. Furthermore, there's an erratic nature to his overall-performances in our viewings. He can look dialed in during one game while making plus plays; yet, fail to manage the puck properly and be a negative-player in others. There's some talent within this kid, but it's going to take a mental overhaul in order to un-tap it.

"Physical tools are good but he doesn't play consistent smart hockey." NHL Scout, October 2018

"He's all over the place on most shifts and plays too much solo hockey. I'd like to see him play with more structure and use his teammates more." - NHL Scout, December 2018

"If he would just settle his game down and realize that sometimes less is more he might be ok." - NHL Scout, January 2019

"Compete is all over the place. Some times it's great sometimes he is invisible" - NHL Scout, January 2019

"I can't help but ask myself why a guy with these tools gets traded from a team with bad defensemen." - NHL Scout, March 2019

"He won't be on our list." - NHL Scout, May 2019

"He forces plays, he's constantly trying to do too much. I don't think his hockey sense is actually as poor as he shows but it does show poorly. His compete level varies depending on if he has the puck or not. So that on ice plus plus everything else on his resume equals a no draft for me." - HP Scout, Mark Edwards

	PLAYER	TEAM	LEAGUE	HEIGHT	WEIGHT	POS	GRADE
NR	COSTMAR, ARVID	LINKOPING, JR.	SWE-JR.	5'10.75"	180 *	RC	**C**
	HOCKEY SENSE		COMPETE		SKILL		SKATING
	6		5		5		6

Costmar plays a fairly good two-way game where his offensive skills are slightly better than his defensive ones. He did have a productive season in the SuperElite league, as his teams second line centerman, where he put up 13 goals and 25 assist combining for 38 points and also got the opportunity to dress up for 4 SHL games this winter where he did not score any points, mostly due to lack of ice time.

He was a regular on team Sweden U18 all season and was a good point producer, especially on the power play. In 17 games he put up 13 points in international play and did miss the U18 world championships playoffs due to an unfortunate injury in the group stages.

His skating is not great, but it gets the job done, his first few strides needs to get a lot quicker and his top speed is not very good. However, he is mobile, has a low center of gravity and makes smart decisions and is smart enough to be at the right place at the right time. His defensive game is mostly cutting off passing lanes and picking up loose pucks, which he does effectively, but he lacks physicality, size and strength. His smartness makes him effective on the box play, where he can force the opposition to make hard plays, where his team mates can be aggressive and forcefully get the puck out.

Even though he has racked up some points this season, there is no real upside to his offense, other than his quick, low, hard one-timers from the slot. In those situations, hes often clinical and almost always hits the net, but he can not create any offense on his own, due to his average skating abilities and average stickhandling. His hockey sense is good enough, where as he can find a good pass if the lane is open and obvious, but he wont beat a defender 1 on 1 to be able to make a creative play. Costmar doesn't necessarily compete hard, but he competes smart.

	PLAYER	TEAM	LEAGUE	HEIGHT	WEIGHT	POS	GRADE
14	COZENS, DYLAN	LETHBRIDGE	WHL	6'3.0"	181 *	RC	**A**
	HOCKEY SENSE		COMPETE		SKILL		SKATING
	5		6		7		8

Dylan Cozens carried over from last season where he won the WHL-rookie-of-the-year award, by having another successful year, producing 84 points in 68 games with 34 goals. In the playoffs, he produced 8 points in 7 games. At international events he was mixed, having a solid-performance at the Hlinka, yet was underwhelming despite finishing with 9 points in 7 games at the U18's.

Cozens is an explosive duel-threat center who we think is more suited to the wing. The reason we suggest that he's more likely to translate as a winger is due to his hockey-sense. In order to become a dominant-center who can drive play like Cozens tools might suggest he could theoretically in the NHL; he needs an excellent-rate of anticipation and a high-degree of spatial awareness when carrying the puck. In Dylan's case, he falls short of either. His anticipation is above-average though, giving him the ability to recognize how to beat defenders one-on-one with his quick set of hands, as well as the ability to recognize the time and space he has when setting up his shot in the slot-area in most instances. Where his anticipation falls short, is when he's attempting to transition the puck. He's an explosive-skater with one of the best start-up gears in this class, which allows him to generate a ton of momentum as he barrels through the neutral-zone; however, he inadvertently skates himself into traffic, as he's unable to recognize soft-ice nearly at the rate needed to carry a line. He has trouble identifying movement dynamically when he's not looking for his passing option. He's a quality playmaker who has good-vision; this is where his anticipation comes through, yet if he's not attempting to identify his passing target—it falls short at too high a rate for us to feel comfortable. It's a situation where his speed is too much for his processing ability to handle. His lack of anticipation and spatial-awareness diminishes his sense for backwards pressure, which has made him vulnerable to turning the puck over as well in some of our viewings. His athleticism masks some of these deficiencies at the junior level. He's a well-built kid whose coordinated and features very impressive edge-work; when he skates himself into an area on the ice where he needs to re-calculate his options, these qualities give him a recovery-option. Though, at the NHL-level, he won't be able to have the same-rate of recovery that he currently has in the WHL. Furthermore, anticipation and spatial-awareness aren't attributes that are easy to enhance, which makes us believe that long-term, not enough development can take place in order for him to become a line-driving center.

Although there's concerns over his mental attributes, there are other qualities that make us a believer in him as a productive winger. We touched on his skating but haven't discussed his ability to execute with his shot or passing while going at top-speeds, which he can. He just executes at a much-higher rate when he has less-options presented to him. This fits well with why we believe that he can accomplish a lot more if given a straight-line to work with on the wing. His most successful plays for us this year have been when he only needs to identify a portion of the ice and has a linemate looking to feed off his playmaking ability. Furthermore, when put on the wing, he can use his excellent top-speed and frame to cut aggressively towards the front-of-the-net. Away from the play, he's a competitive kid who is willing to finish his checks and use his frame effectively, but there's still some pace concerns depending on the game. Part of this goes back to his anticipation; he looks to be defensively responsible and forecheck aggressively, but there's a slight-lag when determining what he wants to do depending on the play-type. Where there's far less lag in his responsiveness, is when he's identified a shooting-lane. He can really fire the puck, showing an advanced understanding of how to rotate through a shot, resulting in a good-amount of velocity both when stationary and when flying down the ice. His slapshot is a cannon as well; he had the most success with it on the powerplay which makes sense, since with less players to navigate around, he can find his soft-ice option quicker and get into a position to generate scoring chances. We feel that the less time he spends attempting to drive-play, and the more time he spends trying to put himself in a position to receive a pass and get off his shot will help him translate successfully. He's not just a primary shooter though, displaying rare-duel-threat-elements. His passing isn't as creative as some of the other high-end players in this class, but he can thread sharp passes at low-percentage angles. He can also play the half-wall on the powerplay, but at the NHL-level, we think he will be more suited to being a trigger-man with the man-advantage.

The problem with projecting him as a center is how many variables need to be accounted for. He would need to further enhance his anticipation, further increase his spatial-awareness, increase his overall-pace, and make decisions quicker overall. That's a lot of variables to take into account. What he does have going for him is his frame; he has arguably one of the best projectable-frames in this class, which will help when the game is going a bit too quick for him since he can over-power and run through smaller players at times. As a result, we still see Cozens as a 2nd-line, two-way winger who can get some powerplay-time, just not a line-driving, top-line center.

"I know he had a productive tournament (Hlinka) but I saw a lot of hope plays. I see questionable hockey sense. He's not up there with the big boys on my list." - NHL Scout, August, 2018

" I don't see him playing down the middle in the NHL so I'm not as high on him as some others seem to be." - NHL Scout, August 2018

"I'll give him this, he's got a great shot." - NHL Scout, November 2018

"He's not a player who is blessed with a ton of hockey sense. I think that effects his game more than anything else." - NHL Scout, January 2019

"I love his size and skating combo. Top 5 pick all day long. Too bad we have no shot at him." - NHL Scout, January 2019

"He plays too slow. I'm starting to think he's a winger." - NHL Scout, April 2019

"I think both he and Dach are good at hockey but I'm not sure they love hockey. Too many games where they don't show up." - NHL Scout, April 2019

"He had a chance to propel himself up into the top three with a good U18. He may have done the opposite and played his way out of the top 10. He was not good there. No clue why the coach didn't take away his ice and replace him on that line" - NHL Scout, April 2019

"There is a lot of media hype on this kid and I don't get it. They're not going to like your ranking (laughs)" - NHL Scout, May 2019

" Coles notes feedback from a few NHL Scouts regarding Cozen's interviews wasn't very positive. I have not been as high on his game as others going back to last season. To me he'll be a winger in the NHL and I never felt that he has the hockey sense that other players at the top of the draft have. Good player, but not enough to keep up with the top 10 guys. I'm not the only one of our Scouts who feels this way." - HP Scout, Mark Edwards, June 2019

	PLAYER	TEAM	LEAGUE	HEIGHT	WEIGHT	POS	GRADE
NR	CROZIER, MAXWELL	SIOUX FALLS	USHL	6'1.0"	195	D	ND
	HOCKEY SENSE	COMPETE		SKILL		SKATING	
	4	6		5		4	

Inconsistent offensive defenseman. Crozier jumped from Nanaimo of the BCHL to Sioux Falls (USHL) in 2018-19 where he became the team's main power play quarterback from the left point. His skill level doesn't match his production though. His hands are below average and he fails to elude or fool many defenders or forecheckers. Moreover, he's not a consistently accurate passer, nor do pucks really snap off his blade in this regard. His shot is above average and he's not shy about pulling the trigger either. That said, only two of his ten goals came at even strength this year. In fact, more than half of his points came on special teams. His stride is long and drawn out and not overly smooth. He gets around the ice fine, but it's just not natural looking. Fittingly, he is not very hockey strong either and is regularly knocked off his blades, even when he initiates contact. He really likes a good joust with opponents and gets into a considerable amount of penalty trouble as a result (7th in the USHL in PIMs), as he always wants to get the last word. Crozier is all over the place defensively. His body and stick positioning are inconsistent and rarely on point. His shoulder squareness and timing of pivots are a glaring weakness. His feet stop moving often when he tries to attack on-rushing forwards with whatever he's going to throw at them. He's quick to give up his leverage against speed, often leaving his feet or committing early to a play outside the dot line that allows the middle of the ice to open up. He does like to attack rushes up high, but it's a real risky style – these aren't 50/50 situations, they're closer to 20/80 situations in terms of them ever working out for him. Max makes bad pinches, but not so much when he's trying to keep plays alive offensively, but more so when the opponent is in possession of the puck and trying to execute a controlled breakout. It's not uncommon to see Crozier just buzzing through the neutral zone and end up jumping on some player's back just outside the top of their own circle. He's competitive and a needler, but his hockey sense is well below what we would like to see. The skating and skill combo doesn't do nearly enough to counterbalance it either.

"Our area guys are not fans and I'm not either." - HP Scout, Mark Edwards, May 2019

	PLAYER	TEAM	LEAGUE	HEIGHT	WEIGHT	POS	GRADE
NR	D'AMICO, DANIEL	WINDSOR	OHL	5'9.25"	184 *	LW	**ND**
	HOCKEY SENSE	COMPETE		SKILL		SKATING	
	6	6		5		4	

Daniel D'Amico had a productive season for the Spitfires, finishing with 46 points and 21 goals in 67 games. He produced 3 assists in 4 playoff games. Daniel displayed some solid chemistry with Angle this year, showing playmaking ability in the process. He's capable of generating one-touch passes under-pressure and was most effective around the goal-line where he could use his edges to his advantage when twisting and turning while exploring his passing lanes. Daniel also displayed the ability to find soft-ice, scoring several deflection goals along the ice by putting himself in a good position in-front of the net; though, there were games where he was largely kept to the perimeter as well. His shot isn't bad, It's an average release point that could threaten around the hash-mark area but not further out than that. The majority of points he scored in our viewings were around the goal-line. Which leads to his biggest issue, which is his size and skating package. He's a smaller kid who's willing to finish his checks and battle occasionally, but he was also easily over-powered when matched up against older and bigger defenseman. His skating leaves a lot to be desired. His two-step area quickness is just okay and his ability to pivot helped him stop-up to avoid physical contact but his straight-line speed for his size is poor. As a result, he was easily closed-off along the boards when attempting to transition the puck up the wing and isn't someone who can drive-play for extended periods. This was notable, since there were several viewings where Daniel wasn't involved in the play. D'Amico's skating needs to greatly improve, as does his consistency in order to be a quality-pro.

"Never really threatened to make my list this year." - HP Scout, Mark Edwards, May 2019

	PLAYER	TEAM	LEAGUE	HEIGHT	WEIGHT	POS	GRADE
8	DACH, KIRBY	SASKATOON	WHL	6'3.5"	199 *	RC	**A**
	HOCKEY SENSE	COMPETE		SKILL		SKATING	
	8	5		8		6	

Dach was selected 2nd overall by Saskatoon in the 2016 Bantam Draft. He posted 10 points in 19 games a 15 year old. In Kirby's first full year with the Blades he played in 52 games and posted 46 points. Kirby was named to the Canada roster for the Hlinka Gretzky Cup. During this tournament, Kirby played in 5 games and posted 2 goals and 5 assists for 7 points. This season he had 25 goals, including 3 on the power play and 48 assists and 40 PIM in 62 games. He also had 8 points in 10 playoff games this year.

Dach is a two-way, playmaking center with legitimate top-line upside. The most impressive element of his game is his hockey-sense. He has both tremendous anticipation with and without the puck. The most important aspect to Dach's anticipation is regarding his lane recognition. He's a pass-first player who instinctively looks for his teammates; so, it's vital for him to recognize open and closed seams while at top-speeds, and he can do this better than most in this class. If his lane isn't open, he's not a player who forces play; instead he shows a lot of poise and structure to his attack. His patience and awareness allow him to re-configure lanes when they are closed off, so that he can use the other very impressive aspect of his sense. That sense being, his playmaking ability; he's one of the top passers in this class and at times looks like a third-defenseman with his ability to thread sharp, yet accurate passes over extended distances. We've seen him fire passes to the same teammate, giving him multiple breakaways on the same shift, let alone the same game. This aspect gives Dach a special gift for being able to drive-a-line at this level, since he makes his teammates better as a result of them knowing, they just need to get into a high-danger area and he'll find them. One of the more impressive aspects of his pass, is that he rarely attempts a low-percentage pass unless it's the right play to make. This extends into his overall decision making; pucks rarely die on his stick. Another reason the play doesn't die with Dach is due to his hands. It's rare to see a player with his puck-skills given his size. He's a very coordinated kid with his wrists and can make unique dangles given his length and skill-level. This trait synergizes well with his frame, making it very difficult for Dach to be contained when he's guarding the puck. Although his shooting ability isn't as high-end as his passing ability, Kirby has shown growth regarding his shooting mechanics. He's learned how to use his length more effectively when in motion, giving him the ability to change angles and he gained more strength from the previous season, making his shot a lot harder than it was. His increased velocity on his shot, and his continued development, gives him room to potentially turn into a duel-threat player down the road, though at this time, he's a primary playmaker. Dach is not just an offensive-threat though, and has shown some versatility in his game as well. He's a capable stick-checker who can use his length in combination with his leverage to take-away pucks at a plus rate, and his anticipation allows him to identify offensive-threats quickly. He's mature in own-zone as well, showing an attention to-detail, he knows where he needs to be on the ice to help his defenseman and doesn't transition prematurely for the most part.

There's a tremendous tool-kit to work with in Dach's game, but our ranking of him reflects concerns that remained consistent throughout the season. Although he's one of the more talented players, his on-ice consistency in terms of his pacing, take-over-mentality, and production kept leaving us wanting more. His tools are built for hockey, but his mindset lacks an internal-drive. This can be seen when he's on the forecheck and loses a battle against a smaller player, or when he's disengaged during a secondary-scoring chance. There's been performances where he doesn't look like he wants to win the game for his team, and instead coasts. However, as the season progressed and towards the playoffs, he did seem to flip-a-switch by competing at a more consistent and aggressive-level. We just wish it didn't take playoff hockey for it to come out, we prefer players that have it innately. Another aspect of Dach's game that lags behind is in regards to his skating. He's a big kid with room to grow, but this has left him without much in the way of two-step area-quickness; he's slow out of the gate but once he gets going, he has an adequate top-gear. His mechanics aren't bad for a bigger player, so with extended time, this aspect of his game should be cleaned up.

Dach is a very intriguing center who could become a top-line contributor if his development goes really well. It's difficult for a kid to ignite a fire under himself to the degree we would be looking for though. In order to trust him enough with one of the top-picks, he needed to show that he wants to be the primary-driver more than he did past season; which is why our ranking of him reflects that we see him more as a 2nd-line-center who doesn't need to be as heavily relied upon as much as a star-player.

"Easily the most skill and highest upside amongst the WHL kids, Dach is the only thing that can hold Dach back from being a star." - NHL Scout, November 2019

"He has all the talent but I'd like to se more of a heartbeat." - NHL Scout, November 2018

"I think he's a lot like Ryan Johansen. He has all the skill but sometimes you can't find him." - WHL staffer, January 2019

"If he ever figures it all out he'll be a hell of a player." - NHL Scout, January 2019

"Other than Byram the west guys are all overrated." - NHL Scout, May 2019

"He was really good in the playoffs, especially versus Prince Albert. - NHL Scout, June 2019

"I think he has the skill and overall talent to be 4th on our list but he scares me a bit. I don't like how he has games where he becomes invisible. He was great on my trip out west and we ranked him 3rd overall after that but Byram passed him and he (Dach) slid for me because of a lack of drive at times. He's still way up our list which speaks to his talent. He's up with the best in this class when it comes to hockey sense and skill. If he ever flicks the switch to the 'on' position on a full time basis, look out he'll be fantastic." - HP Scout, Mark Edwards, June 2019

58	PLAYER	TEAM	LEAGUE	HEIGHT	WEIGHT	POS	GRADE
	DARIN, ALEXANDR	YAROSLAVL 2	RUS-JR.	5'11.0"	159	RW	C+
	HOCKEY SENSE	COMPETE		SKILL		SKATING	
	6	6		7		8	

Alexander Daryin (Alexandr Darin) had a season that put him on our radar after getting passed over in last years draft. He's a bit of a late-bloomer who brought his tools together this year that resulted in a productive season on the top MHL-team. He finished with 35 points in 47 games, including 20 goals, despite not always playing up high in the line-up. In the playoffs, he wasn't as successful, producing 4 points in 11 games, including just 1 goal. What makes Daryin stand out is his combination of skill and pace. He's an excellent skater who has an effortless-stride that features impressive skating-mechanics. More importantly, he's a deceptive skater who can change his skating trajectory rapidly, making him very elusive which is foundation to his game given his slight-frame. Despite his frame, he is willing to play hard around the goal-line and although he's not overly physical, he's good at recognizing and anticipating the forecheck so that he can use his skating ability to beat defenders to the puck. There's a lot of skill in his game, and he can use his speed with his hands to beat defenders cleanly one-on-one. His shot is more deceptive than it is strong. He uses his sharp-cuts to the net and masks his release well behind opponents, giving him a shot that's difficult to pick up. His playmaking is good overall as well, and he had some time playing on the powerplay along the half-wall, where he distributed the puck cleanly. Though we wouldn't label his passing as high-end. Daryin is still raw away from the play and had some moments that showed how green he can be in his own-zone. His speed makes him dangerous when threatening the point but to give an example, when his defenseman lost his stick on a sequence, Alexander didn't recognize the benefit of giving him his own and instead circled back to the outside. Despite his raw-defensive-game, there's a lot of skill and speed for Daryin to work with, he needs to bulk up a ton though.

98	PLAYER	TEAM	LEAGUE	HEIGHT	WEIGHT	POS	GRADE
	DEL GAIZO, MARC	UMASS	H-EAST	5'9.5"	188*	LD	C
	HOCKEY SENSE	COMPETE		SKILL		SKATING	
	6	6		6		7	

Del Gaizo is a late 99' that a couple of our scouts had on their draft lists last year when Marc was putting up impressive numbers for Muskegon (USHL). Del Gaizo stepped right into NCAA hockey this year and continued to show he can contribute at both ends of the ice. Del Gaizo registered an impressive 13 goals and 16 Assists in 41 games for UMASS. Which was 17th in the nation among all freshmen and 2nd in scoring among freshman defenseman? The most impressive thing about the offensive numbers Del Gaizo put up this year is they came from not getting a lot of #1 power play time, as Cale Makar absorbed much of the Power Play duties for the Minutemen. Del Gaizo doesn't have a lot of size but is incredibly strong and powerful on his skates. He protects the puck well with his body and can turn away and accelerate away from pressure nicely. Del Gaizo is a heads up player that makes good, quick reads out of his own end and committed very few turnovers for a freshman defenseman in a tough league. Del Gaizo plays with a good amount of sand paper in his own end and in one on one situations. He can be a bit careless with his stick and takes some unnecessary infractions at times. One area of Del Gaizo's game we wanted to see at the NCAA level was how he would be able to defend in an older bigger league and Del Gaizo showed that he is able to handle bigger players using his hockey smarts and footwork to his advantage. If Del Gaizo falls through the cracks in this year's NHL draft, we see him being a highly sought after NCAA Free Agent when his college career is complete, as he has the skating and puck moving ability to be effective in today's NHL.

"Bit of a late bloomer, in the last year he's come a long way physically and the way he stepped into a deep and talented defensive core at UMASS and made his presence known impressed me." HP Scout, Dusten Braaksma

"I think he goes (gets drafted) this year." - NHL Scout, April 2019

	PLAYER	TEAM	LEAGUE	HEIGHT	WEIGHT	POS	GRADE
NR	**DOCTER, GRANT**	**MINNETONKA**	**HIGH-MN**	**5'11.0"**	**190**	**LD**	**ND**
	HOCKEY SENSE	COMPETE		SKILL		SKATING	
	6	6		5		6	

Docter has been part of one of the best defensive pairing in Minnesota High School the last three seasons at Minnetonka HS, playing with fellow 2019 NHL Draft prospect Josh Luedtke. Docter doesn't have imposing size but he is a duel athlete, playing Lacrosse as well as hockey and possesses excellent upper and lower body strength and doesn't give a lot away physically against bigger players. Docter has plus all-around skating with the exception of his explosiveness which can come into question against quicker fore-checkers. Docter uses his upper body strength to have good power on his quick wrist shots from the point. In the last year, Docter has started to become more active on the offensive blueline as well as his willingness to be a part of the rush, contributing to his uptick in offensive production this season despite not have nearly as good of a team around him as last year. Docter can stretch the ice coming out of his own zone, he is a heads-up player that is able to go through his reads and get the puck up ice quickly. Defensively Docter excels at keeping a good gap against the rush, his skating allows him to be a bit more aggressive and still be able to recover if a player is able to gain the edge on him. Docter finished the season with 4 games with the Madison Capitols (USHL). Docter had an eye opening USHL experience playing against the USNTDP U18 team in his USHL debut but eventually settled into the league in his 3 remaining starts. Docter is a late 00' DOB so may be more of a NCAA Free Agent to keep an eye out down the road if he goes undrafted this spring. Grant is a Michigan Tech Commit for 2020.

"I have started to hear some draft chatter about him this year, I don't see it yet, but I haven't seen much of him yet this year." - NHL Scout, November 2018

NR	PLAYER	TEAM	LEAGUE	HEIGHT	WEIGHT	POS	GRADE
	DONOVAN, RYDER	DULUTH EAST	HIGH-MN	6'3.25"	184 *	RC	C
	HOCKEY SENSE		COMPETE		SKILL		SKATING
	4		4		6		7

Ryder Donovan elected to return to Duluth East (MNHS) for his senior season. Donovan saw a considerable dip in his point production from the previous season, mostly to do with the lack of players around him as most of the players from the year previous had moved on to junior hockey. Donovan registered 17 goals and 29 assists in 28 games this season. In many or our viewings Donovan was the best player on the ice and was forced to log a ton of minutes for his team as the season progressed. Donovan is a rangy centerman that has excellent skating speed and explosiveness. Donovan has a long stride that allows him to get to top gear quickly and is difficult to handle in the transition game when he gets speed through the neutral zone and is deceptively quick. Donovan has good hands and passing ability that allow him to create scoring chances and slide passes through tight lanes. Donovan has good shooting ability, he gets the puck off his tape quickly and has a heavy one-timer but Donovan could have benefitted from shooting the puck more, especially this season when in some viewings he would setup excellent scoring chances but didn't have the players around him to convert them into goals. One key area of Donovan's game that will need to improve before he's ready to play in professional hockey is his consistency, particularly when it comes to his compete factor. Donovan showed flashes of being engaged and using his size well to win pucks and when he played with a physical edge, he took over games but there were more than a few viewings this year where Donovan not only didn't compete but didn't engage in battles at all. There would be very little stops and starts in his game and too often would be waiting for the puck to find him. Donovan has a unique combination of size, skating and skill and if he ever puts it all together has a high ceiling at the professional level. Donovan recently changed his commitment from the University of North Dakota to the University of Wisconsin where he will be part of one of the more talented Freshman classes in college hockey this fall.

"He's out for a skate tonight, have you seen him in one puck battle." – NHL Scout, February, 2019

"If he could ever put it all together, the sky's the limit for this kid, with the physical tools he has! I just don't know if he will." – HP Scout, Dusten Braaksma

"If his mental game matched his physical game, he's a first round pick." – HP Scout, Michael Farkas

"I'm not a fan, our scout in the area, Dusten, has time for him but I can't get there." – HP Scout, Mark Edwards

27	PLAYER	TEAM	LEAGUE	HEIGHT	WEIGHT	POS	GRADE
	DOROFEYEV, PAVEL	MAGNITOGORSK 2	RUS-JR.	6'1.0"	167	LW	B
	HOCKEY SENSE		COMPETE		SKILL		SKATING
	7		5		7		6

Pavel Dorofeyev carried over his excellent play from last seasons U18-performance while playing on one of the top-lines in the MHL that consisted of Yegor Spiridonov and Dmitri Sheshin. His 31 points in 19 games, including 17 goals gave him a promotion to the KHL with Metallurg Magnitogorsk where he produced 2 points in 23 games. At the Spengler Cup, he produced zero points in 3 games and was unable to play at both the Hlinka and U18's due to his October birthday.

Dorofeyev is a cerebral sniper who out-thinks his opponents. His defining quality is his composure when in possession of the puck; and his composure arises from his high-panic-threshold. This threshold gives him the ability to rarely force or rush plays, which in turn allows him to make the right-decision on the ice at an excellent-rate. Opponents look to overwhelm him at times due to his physical limitations, yet rarely succeed. Pavel has an average-frame that he hasn't grown into yet, but he's learned how to compensate by altering the rhythm of play with his hockey-IQ and his skill-set. He uses static-body-posture and rarely exaggerates his movements, relying on a subtle approach that doesn't allow players to feel comfortable when engaging with him; as a result, his opponents slow-down giving Pavel time to bury the puck. For instance, when driving down the wing, he can slow down to make it look like he's passing the puck by using a head-fake, which forces the defender to attempt to cover for the passing lane, giving him additional space to make a play or look to use his shot. When we look at defining the upside of a sniper, we take into consideration how hard they can fire the puck before the goalie gets set. What makes Dorofeyev's release unique, is that it goes into the back of the net but he doesn't rely on the velocity of his shot as much as some other high-end shooters featured in this class. Instead, Pavel uses a rare-sense to pick up on the highest-percentage-angle when evaluating where to place the puck. This gives him a highly-accurate shot that finds its way in regardless if goalies are set. Additionally, where most shooters look to rush certain shot-types when they feel their window is closing; Dorofeyev looks to take advantage of that window and extend it. As an example, If he comes out from below the goal-line and is challenged aggressively before releasing his shot directly above the crease or slot, Pavel will look to out-wait the netminder before side-stepping to regain a better angle. This ability lends back to an attribute that was discussed earlier which is his panic-threshold, which blends will with his shot. His follow through features a sudden angle shift as he folds his hands over along his-stick depending on the shot-type as well. One of the more impressive aspects of his shot, is that he has identified his weakness and adapted. He tends to rely on his slapshot as opposed to his wrist-shot and snap-shot when above the hash-marks when we viewed him. This gave him an additional option which he generally lacks, which is the ability to over-power netminders. For this reason, he was used both along the point and along the half-wall on the powerplay for Stalnye. Together, these qualities form a shooter that can beat a goalie in multiple-ways and from an aesthetic point-of-view, made it look relatively easy at times. Although Dorofeyev is a primary shooter, he's also a capable distributor of the puck. He can thread saucer-passes across the ice, and has an element of creativity within his passing. Furthermore, his patience magnifies his ability to re-open lanes and find options. He's not a selfish player, and rarely shows tunnel-vision which is a credit to his offensive-awareness. Away from the puck, Dorofeyev is very good at recognizing soft-ice which is fundamental to his game transferring since he's unlikely to drive play in the NHL.

Dorofeyev is an offensively-gifted player with exceptional hockey-sense and a great shot, but there isn't a dynamic quality to his skill-set. He has a variety of dekes in his repertoire and is capable of pulling off high-end moves, but not as consistently as we would have liked to have seen. Furthermore, although he's good at receiving sharp passes and making quick moves with his hands while stationary; he has shown that he can bobble the puck at a decent-rate when in motion. The impression his hands leave you with, is that when dealing with higher-end defenseman, he's going to have some difficulty with his current puck-skills. We view pace as a very important trait, and this is something that Dorofeyev also lacks. His hockey-sense does account for some of this, since he has shown a tendency to engage at a more intense-level when the play calls for it at times, but overall, he can slow his own game down too much. Another concerning aspect which accounts for his inconsistent pace, is in regards to his skating. His mechanics are average, featuring an upright posture and a short-stride. Additionally, he lacks strength and this hampers his acceleration. Few players need to increase their two-steps area quickness more than Pavel in order for his game to manifest in the NHL; as he's not going to be able to rely on his frame or hands as much as some of the other more skilled-forwards in this class. Lastly, although he recognizes plays away from the puck in his own-end in advance, he's not going to be a reliable two-way player at this time; when he's not scoring, there's a lack of versatility to his game to compensate for it.

If Dorofeyev can increase his strength significantly, so that he can move more efficiently around the ice and improve his pace by increasing his intensity, while further refining his puck-skills; than he has a significant shot at developing into a top-6-scorer at the NHL-level. Our ranking of him reflects the fact that he's going to have to overcome several variables in order for that to happen. If he does fail to develop properly, there isn't going to be an opportunity for him to carve out a forechecking role.

"He has such a wide-range when it comes to his skill, he can look average on one play and then world-class on another" - HP Scout, Brad Allen, May 2019

"Reminded me of Suzuki at times because like Suzuki, he's very skilled but there were games where he really played a lot on perimeter." - HP Scout, Mark Edwards, May 2019

	PLAYER	TEAM	LEAGUE	HEIGHT	WEIGHT	POS	GRADE
NR	DOYLE, BRADEN	LAWRENCE ACAD	HIGH-MA	5'11.5"	167*	LD	ND
	HOCKEY SENSE	COMPETE		SKILL		SKATING	
	5	5		6		5	

Doyle is an average sized, puck moving defenseman out of the New England Prep Ranks, Braden got a look with Dubuque (USHL) at the end of the year but only saw spot duty, mainly dressing as a 7th defenseman as well as the Boston Jr. Bruins in the NCDC. Our scouts first saw Doyle a few years ago where he started playing for Shattuck St.Mary's in his bantam year before returning home and enrolling Lawrence Academy. Doyle has good hands that he uses to rush the puck effectively and elude fore-checkers under pressure. Doyle plays an aggressive transition game coming out of his own end, he looks for ways to stretch the ice and will gain zones with his feet if the need arises. He is an offensive minded defenseman and as a result can take some risky lanes coming up the ice and will rush the puck up ice with confidence. Defensively, Braden has a ways to go physically, which causes him to lose some situations in his own end but displays good compete and decent awareness in defensive situations. In the offensive end, Doyle shows creative playmaking abilities from the point, not only using his feet and good vision of the zone to open up lanes from the point but won't hesitate to look for opportunities to come down from the point looking to create scoring chances. His judgement can be questionable at times and Doyle takes unnecessary risks. Doyle has a way's to go to round out his complete game but his offensive skill set will give him a window to the NHL going forward. Doyle will be heading to Boston University in 2020 but will likely be playing in the USHL next season.

"I like this kid's confidence with the puck, I think with the right coaching he has a high ceiling." HP Scout, Dusten Braaksma

	PLAYER	TEAM	LEAGUE	HEIGHT	WEIGHT	POS	GRADE
NR	DRKULEC, RYAN	WATERLOO	USHL	6'5.0"	194	LW	ND
	HOCKEY SENSE	COMPETE		SKILL		SKATING	
	4	5		5		3	

Large-framed, tough winger with some untapped shooting upside. Druklec is a first-year USHL player who grew up in the Shattuck St. Mary's program. Things didn't break exactly the way we were hoping for the big Waterloo winger. Early in the season, there appeared be a really raw package that might smooth out and eat into a steep development arc, but by season's end it's clear that that never really materialized. Drkulec's skating did improve and he actually gets a little something out of his first three steps and his top speed and cruising speed were always on the plus side of average. He just never touches the puck in a game. In the extremely rare event that he caught a puck in the middle of the rink, his head would go down and he would stickhandle right into trouble at the closest advertisement he could find on the wall. Most of his game is spent ping-ponging from blue line to blue line. Between his hockey sense and his lacklustre acceleration, Ryan struggles to get involved. He has been offered no special teams time either. Watching him work off the wall, we see that the gears are spinning and he has a decent idea about what he should be doing in terms of puck protection and using his size and leverage, but he just doesn't have the coordination and timing of it down. This is seen in his hit attempts as well, many of them involve the feet not moving and are finished with a shove using the upper body – the proper weight transfer just isn't there consistently. He does have a pretty short fuse, which is kind of unexpected for the style of game he plays, as he does take some runs at guys and isn't afraid to paw someone's face after a whistle.

Bottom line: He has a plus shot and a huge frame, his hockey sense probably doesn't quite make it to average, and he still lacks the coordination to come off the wall or be a rebound machine despite being a September 2000 birthday. We would have more time for him if he had shown a greater level of improvement down the stretch.

"I think he works hard and is a good teammate and as much as I like his size and physicality, I just don't think there is enough there right now." HP Scout, Dusten Braaksma

	PLAYER	TEAM	LEAGUE	HEIGHT	WEIGHT	POS	GRADE
NR	EDMONDS, LUCAS	KARLSKRONA JR.	SWE-JR.	5'11.0	172	RW	ND
	HOCKEY SENSE	COMPETE		SKILL		SKATING	
	5	5		6		5	

Edmonds is a rather small, energetic forward. He was put in an offensive role in a mediocre team in the SuperElite league and put up 7 goals, 13 assists and 20 points in 37 games as a second line winger. He got the opportunity to play 10 games in HockeyAllsvenskan and managed to put up 3 points and did not look out of place. He likes to stickhandle the puck and there's where his strengths lie, but hes not more than a just above average stickhandler, since he often lose the puck and have to go retrieve it in the corners, or stickhandler until the opportunity to make a good pass goes away. He has a tendency to cheat defense to try to create offense and when he gets put under pressure in defense, he needs help and directions from his team mates. His skating is average, he needs way more explosiveness and speed to make up for his lack of size. His hockey sense can also be questioned since hes taking too long with the puck on his stick in all three zones and its not a good sign when a player is forced to cheat defense to get a head start on offense. Overall, there is not enough of anything to believe he will make it to the NHL. He has signed to play for Växjö Lakers U20 next season

	PLAYER	TEAM	LEAGUE	HEIGHT	WEIGHT	POS	GRADE
NR	EGGENBERGER, NANDO	OSHAWA	OHL	6'2.5"	205 *	LW	ND
	HOCKEY SENSE	COMPETE		SKILL		SKATING	
	5	5		5		5	

NHL Central has included Nando again this season but our opinion has not changed as far as making him a draft worthy prospect. He lacks the pace we like to see in players and tends to be average across the board as far as our main attributes we look for in a player. He's a good hockey player but just doesn't grade out as a projectable NHL player in our opinion.

"I didn't see it last year and I don't see it this season either. No draft again for me."- NHL Scout, March 2019

NR	PLAYER	TEAM	LEAGUE	HEIGHT	WEIGHT	POS	GRADE
	ELLIS, COLTEN	RIMOUSKI	QMJHL	6'0.75"	185 *	G	C
	HOCKEY SENSE		COMPETE		SKILL		SKATING
	6		6		6		6

Ellis had a second excellent season in the league; he was 3rd in the league for goals-against average and 5th for save percentage. The Nova Scotia product is a key player for the Océanic since coming over in a trade from Cape Breton during the 2017 QMJHL Draft.

Not the biggest goaltender (standing around 6'01"), Ellis sometimes has to fight hard to track the puck with heavy traffic in front of him, but usually does a good job seeing the puck coming towards him. As we well know, NHL teams are shying away with goaltenders under 6'02" early in the draft. He's very calm in his crease, doesn't get rattled by much on the ice, and he's quick to forget a bad goal he could give up or has good bounce back ability after a bad game. Good, above-average control of his rebounds, and he's smooth in his crease-movements. He's a good athlete, blessed with the ability to make look tough saves look easy. His glove-side is average, but he has an excellent blocker. Good work ethic; doesn't quit on any pucks and can make some good 2nd and 3rd saves. In addition to not having the ideal size for today's NHL goaltender, Ellis is not elite in any areas technically. He's a great junior goaltender, as he has showed in the past two seasons with Rimouski, but he's going to be challenged at the next level.

Quote: "He's has outplayed Olivier Rodrigue (Edmonton 2nd round pick in 2018) in the past 2 years in league play" - HP Scout Jérôme Bérubé, May 2019

107	PLAYER	TEAM	LEAGUE	HEIGHT	WEIGHT	POS	GRADE
	FAGEMO, SAMUEL	FROLUNDA	SWE	6'0.0"	194	LW	C
	HOCKEY SENSE		COMPETE		SKILL		SKATING
	5		5		7		6

Fagemo has an intriguing skillset where he got some big offensive flair to his game. He is not the best skater, but he can manage to gain some speed up the wing, despite a lack of explosiveness and does a good job on his zone entries where he can keep the puck under control, while being pressured to maintain the puck in his teams possession to create an attack.While in the offensive zone is where he really can excel and contribute to his team. His shot is great and he can score with his hard accurate slapshot or his quick-released wristshot. With his right-handed shot he can be absolutely lethal from the left face-off circle on the power play, where he can pick his shot with a little more time on his hands. He has a tendency of making love to the puck and not letting his teammates touch it, especially in the offensive zone he can be found circling around, looking for a shot and will not even consider making a pass. With that said, his vision and playmaking abilities are limited, since he really doesn't see anything but the net. He is a skilled, goal-scoring winger with good offensive upside, However, he does play on the perimeter and is highly unwilling to go to the dirty areas where there could be any kind of body contact, which is unfortunate since that would most likely increase his goal and point total.

Fagemo does his work from the offensive blue line and forwards, but in his defensive zone and the neutral zone he struggles to be a contributing factor to his teams play and his defensive play is very inconsistent.Fagemo was supposed to be a leading, point producing player at the U20 World championships for team Sweden, but he had a weak tournament overall and only managed to put up 1 point in 5 games in a tournament where a weak team Sweden lost in the quarterfinals.In domestic play he did exceed his expectations and scored 10 goals and 4 assist for a total of 14 points in 8 games in the SuperElite league and got rewarded with a promotion to his clubs SHL team. While in the SHL he also had a strong season with 14 goals and 11 assists for 25 points in 42 games in the regular season and 6 goals and 4 assists in 10 playoff games where his team were crowned as Swedish champions at the end of the season. In the Champions Hockey League he put up 10 points in 11 games, a tournament his team also won.

"I'm not a fan of him but I expect him to get drafted." – HP Scout, Johan Karlsson, May 2019

"He's improved for sure but still not a guy who is shooting up our list. He did have some support from one of our scouts though." – HP Scout, Mark Edwards

	PLAYER	TEAM	LEAGUE	HEIGHT	WEIGHT	POS	GRADE
NR	FAIRBROTHER, GIANNI	EVERETT	WHL	5'11.75"	194 *	LD	**ND**
	HOCKEY SENSE		COMPETE		SKILL		SKATING
	5		6		5		6

This year was big step forward for Fairbrother who played a prominent role on one of the league's top teams. The defenseman finished with 36 points, while playing a role on the penalty kill and 2nd Powerplay.

A very strong skater, Gianni gets low and has a strong stride, and the ability to easily move laterally. His speed often allowed him to jump up in the rush where he provided a great option for teammates, scoring multiple times on drives to the net or hanging back in the second wave for a one timer. Despite occasionally joining the rush he is not an offensive defenseman, as he was very effective in the defensive zone. Excelled defending off the rush where he used good feet, positioning, and instincts to contain opponents to the outside. These same strengths helped him defending out of the corners, in 1 on 1 situations he was rarely beat. Off the puck he showed good positional awareness, not getting caught up in no man's land. In transition Fairbrother was also effective, moving pucks up fast, and rarely getting his team pinned in their own end. Never made any creative reads, often making simple but effective plays to move the puck to a teammate. Fairbrother thinks the game alright, but rarely had moments where he showed a high end mind, mostly just making basic plays with consistency. Fairbrother is effective as a competent 2 way defender, but right now lacks the standout abilities and confidence of a true difference maker.

	PLAYER	TEAM	LEAGUE	HEIGHT	WEIGHT	POS	GRADE
47	FARINACCI, JOHN	DEXTER SCHOOL	HIGH-MA	5'11.25"	185 *	RC	**B**
	HOCKEY SENSE		COMPETE		SKILL		SKATING
	7		6		6		5

Farinacci kicked off his 18/19 campaign representing Team USA at the Hlinka Gretzky tournament where he played primarily a checking roll but still managed to register 2 goals and 3 assists in 5 games. Farinacci then returned to US Prep hockey for Dexter School where he was a dominating player. Throughout the course of the year, John saw two games with the NTDP U18 team as well as Muskegon (USHL) where he managed to put up 2 goals and an assist with the Lumberjacks. Farinacci is an average to slightly above average skater due to his good top gear. His hockey sense gets him to the right places on the ice quickly so his skating is not a big hindrance on his game at this time and he is fairly strong on his skates. Farinacci possesses a smart two-way game that finds a way to impact the game even if he is left off the score sheet. With his high hockey sense he is an effective penalty killer, as he picks the right spots to challenge the player with possession and can create shorthanded opportunities for his team. Farinacci's offensive skill doesn't jump out at you but he relies on his hockey sense and ability see a play develop in order to be in the right place at the right time to get his fair share of offensive chance. Farinacci is a fairly straight ahead player at this point, he won't try a lot of individual, one on one moves but see's the ice well uses his teammates to generate offense. His understanding of the game on the back check and in his own zone is an asset to his ability to be a strong two-way centermen at the next level. Not overly physical on the fore-check or in battles but comes away with the puck a lot. Farinacci reportedly battled some injuries at the end of the season that caused him to miss the USA Nationals Tournament where he was expected to play for the Boston Junior Eagles U18 team. Farinacci was also rumoured to join Muskegon for the Clark Cup playoffs in the spring but didn't see any ice time for the Lumberjacks. Farinacci will be heading to Harvard this fall.

"This player just never did enough for me this year, would have liked to have seen him in the USHL at the end of the year just to see how or if he progressed since the Hlinka, it's hard to gauge that at the Prep level." HP Scout, Dusten Braaksma

"He put some decent numbers in Prep League but he threw up some stinkers for games at times, I expected him to dominate that Prep Scene and he didn't." NHL Scout, April, 2019

"I spoke to the USA Coaches at the Hlinka and they loved the kid. Heart and soul kid with limited skill." - NHL Scout, August 2018

"Average skater, has some skill I guess but nothing special. His games is built on being a smart competitive kid." - NHL Scout, November 2018

"Who knows where he'll go. I see him like Drury's kid (Jack) and he went like 40 or something (42nd to Carolina)." - NHL Scout, January 2019

"I liked him at the Hlinka, was on the ice for all the big faceoffs. Played really well defensively at the Hlinka but chased the puck a bit on the controversial tying goal by Canada. Didn't like him as much in some games with Dexter. Felt he played down to the lower level of others at times and didn't compete as hard in that league." - HP scout, Mark Edwards

	PLAYER	TEAM	LEAGUE	HEIGHT	WEIGHT	POS	GRADE
NR	FENSORE, DOMENICK	USA U-18	NTDP	5'6.75"	153 *	LD	C
	HOCKEY SENSE		COMPETE		SKILL		SKATING
	5		6		5		7

Boston University commit who was better than a point-per-game and plus-per-game player against USHL opponents this season. His adaptability was on full display, he played LD and RD comfortably in all man-power situations. He even took a couple of spins at forward during the U18 in April. Fensore is a smooth skater. He has multi-directional mobility. His edgework is also solid. His first step quickness and agility often allowed him to skate out of problems. Despite his diminutive frame, his escapability allowed him to seldom get hit at this level. Fensore plays the entire game on his toes. Even at 5'7", he wants to take plays and players head on, as opposed to getting pushed back into areas where he does have the potential to lose a physical matchup. He's a clean player and not susceptible to PIMS, but he's not a shrinking violet either. He has no qualms taking or receiving hits. He uses a deep-knee bend, good leverage, and timing to knock rushers off of pucks when he needs to. His reliable body positioning is a staple to his defensive zone setup – he keeps himself between the puck and the net consistently. He has a good, aggressive stick and really likes to attack plays and not allow them to fester if he can help it. He is an intelligent player who makes reads in all three zones.

Offensively, Fensore brings a lot to the table from a puck rushing perspective. His ability to change gears and change directions quickly, even from a standing start, allows him to compensate a bit for his stature. When he's not rushing the puck, he can make a variety of passes accurately. He can confidently snap stretch passes across two lines if he needs to and he has the vision to pull it off. He can make a deceptive play at the attack line, where he can shake a checker and beat him to whatever the opposite of the defender's handedness is to work his way in close. The July '01 birthday very much prefers to pass instead of shoot – his shot is not strong, nor is it threatening from distance. It takes a little while to load up too. Carrying pucks in open ice and beating slower players at this level is one thing, but when his speed gets matched and he'll need to better protect pucks or make quicker plays before he gets stuck in traffic.

"No. Zero interest." - NHL Scout, December 2018

"Some guys talking about him in the 3rd round. C'mon now, let's get serious. Imagine him in these (NHL) playoffs right now. Healthy Scratch." - NHL Scout, April 2019

"Now people are talking about him at forward? Snap out of it. Until a few years ago, a 5'6" player had about as much chance at getting drafted as me dating a supermodel. Now guys are telling me I'm going to draft a 5'6" kid and change him to a position he's never played before. .It's laughable." - NHL Scout, April 2019

"Let's talk real life for a second. He's a 5'6" player who is weak and can barely defend now, but sure...let's match him up against Tom Wilson. Now we've gone and killed him" - NHL Scout, April 2019

"I'd love him on my Junior team but I question his hockey sense at times and he's 5'6" so it's all over for me right there, a non starter. One of our area guys loves him, so we made him a C grade but he's up against it as far as making our final list." - HP Scout, Mark Edwards, May 2019

	PLAYER	TEAM	LEAGUE	HEIGHT	WEIGHT	POS	GRADE
NR	FEUK, LUCAS	SODERTALE JR.	SWE-JR.	6' 0.0"	183	LW	ND
	HOCKEY SENSE	COMPETE		SKILL		SKATING	
	5	4		6		4	

Feuk had a strong season for Södertälje SK, where he played for three teams win three leagues. He was regularly found in the SuperElite league where he often was the first line right winger. He was his teams top scorer with 43 points in 43 games, 21 goals, and 22 assists. which is very impressive since he also was the youngest player on their roster. He was also registered for 84 penalty minutes. He disappeared during playoffs though and wasn't able to produce a single point in 5 games and had a -5 plus-minus rating in playoffs.

For his clubs U18 team he put up 8 points in 5 games, but he wasn't the dominating force you would expect your U20 points leader to be. The U18 league is less organized and this play to Feuk's favor. During playoffs, he did step up and produced another 8 points in 5 games, but did manage to control the play better. His team suffered a devastating loss to local rivals AIK in the quarterfinals. He also got the opportunity to play 5 games, where he put up 0 points for his club in the HockeyAllsvenskan, but did not get much ice time. He was awarded to play 8 games for Team Sweden during the season where his bad skating and inconsistent hockey sense got exposed against better competition, where the pace of the game was much faster than with his club, he put up a total of 2 points in these 8 games.

So Feuk's an offensive-minded forward with his strengths solely in the offensive zone, where he at times can dominate single shifts with great stickhandling and good body strength. He is a shot first type of player and his shot is both hard and comes with a quick release, he does miss the net a lot and his shots are often from too far away from the goal as he is rarely seen inside the perimeter. Even though he is a shot-first type of player, his playmaking skills cannot be neglected as he can find teammates in good scoring areas with crisp tape-to-tape passes. He tries flashy moves with the puck every time he got it on his stick and almost always tries the low-percentage play, but he is often able to pull them off since he is playing at a low pace due to his awful skating. He can stickhandle around both one and two opponents in tight areas and he is super strong at protecting the puck with his body and a strong core. His skating lacks both explosivity and top speed, his first few strides are okay, but then he is caught by the defenders and he has to begin the process of protecting the puck again. His skating might be the reason why he tends to be too eager to leave his own zone to try to create offense, he has too to create some separation and create time for him to attack, but it also leads to his own defenders getting exposed in their own zone. There are huge inconsistencies to his game, where his defensive game needs much work. This combined with bad body language when games don't go his way and he doesn't get the bounces makes him a gamble at this year's draft. He has signed a contract to play for Södertälje SK in the HockeyAllsvenskan next season.

83	PLAYER	TEAM	LEAGUE	HEIGHT	WEIGHT	POS	GRADE
	FIRSTOV, VLADISLAV	WATERLOO	USHL	6'0.75"	181 *	LW	C
	HOCKEY SENSE		COMPETE		SKILL		SKATING
	6		5		7		6

Firstov finished his first season in North America after being taken by Waterloo (USHL) in the Phase 2 USHL Draft last Spring. Firstov made an immediate impact for the Black Hawks. In his first season in North America, Firstov put up 26 goals and 58 points in 62 games for the Waterloo Black Hawks. His impressive offensive output as a USHL rookie speaks to his offensive skill and hockey sense, he is able to quickly identify areas of the ice he needs to get to and reads the play well in the offensive end. While not that having the fastest top gear, Firstov plays with good jump to his game, he is quick to loose pucks and moves the puck quickly in the transition game. Simply put, he plays a faster game than his skating would indicate. His biggest offensive threat is his shooting ability, while his shot is not overly powerful yet, it gets off his stick quickly and his shot placement is very good, especially in regard to his one-timer which can find the corners. With his wrist shot Firstov is able to use his quick hands to change the angle and manipulate the blade to fool goaltenders in one on one situations. Firstov uses his silky hands in traffic and shown the ability to make little feeds in the crease area to setup goals and can get his stick-on deflections well. Firstov isn't a straight line player and doesn't have a lot of stops and starts in his game at this stage, this makes him tough to keep track of offensively as he can get lost in the offensive zone and find holes in the defense, however this same style is a liability defensively. Vladislav stays on the outside of a lot of battles, hoping for the puck to pop out to him or will do a drive by attempt to poke the puck past everyone. In a few viewings Firstov showed the willingness to engage physically and get his nose over puck battles a bit more but this was not at all a consistent aspect of his game throughout the season. Firstov is an offensive minded winger with a smart approach to the game in the offensive end. If his compete level and willingness to be relentless over pucks becomes a big part of his game, he has a high pro ceiling. In too many viewings he relied upon others to get him the puck. Firstov will likely be off to the University of Connecticut this fall where the longer developmental path and defensively structured game should help him develop some of his deficiencies in his game.

"I think he has a better IQ than other USHL guys. I think his skill translates better than some other guys too." - NHL Scout, January 2019

"There were some spirited and physical games I saw that he wanted nothing to do with until he got on the Power Play, and then he would get engaged in the game again. Big red flag for me." - NHL Scout, March, 2019

"Some players you pay to score goals and anything else you get from them is a bonus, right now that's the type of player Firstov seems to be. Having said that, it was his first year in North

America, I'm willing to cut him some slack on some of the stuff away from the puck right now." - HP Scout, Dusten Braaksma

81	PLAYER	TEAM	LEAGUE	HEIGHT	WEIGHT	POS	GRADE
	FOOTE, NOLAN	KELOWNA	WHL	6'3.5"	190 *	LW	C
	HOCKEY SENSE	COMPETE		SKILL		SKATING	
	6	7		5		4	

As a third year WHLer and highly regarded prospect much was expected of Foote to start the year. Much like his team Foote's season was slightly underwhelming as he managed 63 points, below a point per game pace. As a late birthday Nolan didn't get a chance to showcase his abilities this year in any international events.

Foote has some areas that project him to play at a high level, but also possesses some major holes. Nolans skating is a pretty substantial weakness, he really struggles with acceleration and does not have very good lateral mobility. His top speed is average but he really takes a while to get going. This all limited a lot of his game to beneath the ringette line where a his strengths shone through. Foote is very physically strong and when protecting the puck was extremely difficult to take the puck from. This allowed him to showcase his offensive senses, threading passes through traffic and using his points when he drew extra attention. Foote also showed the ability to put his defender on his hip and assertively drive the puck to the net. Footes standout tool is his shot which was one of the strongest in the whole league. He gets a ton of velocity on his shots and excelled at picking corners, Foote could really snipe it off the rush when defensemen backed off and showed a lot of deception in his release. Another real positive is his compete level, Nolan battled night in and night out, back checking and banging for pucks on the board. Had a lot of intensity and showed natural leadership on the ice raising his game when his team needed it. If his skating develops Foote has a lot of intriguing pro tools.

89	PLAYER	TEAM	LEAGUE	HEIGHT	WEIGHT	POS	GRADE
	FORD, PARKER	SIOUX CITY	USHL	5'8.5"	170 *	RC	C
	HOCKEY SENSE	COMPETE		SKILL		SKATING	
	7	7		5		6	

Highly intelligent, hard working center. Ford is a complete package and likely played some of the most minutes in the USHL among forwards this season. His hockey sense is excellent. He makes great reads in all three zones and can really sense danger. The details in his game really present themselves from his sterling performance in the faceoff dot, to his stick positioning on the penalty kill, to his ability to go to the high traffic areas but avoid getting smashed with a hit. Ford is a puck magnet, which is a testament to his speed and smarts. He's a quick reaction player who works hard on every shift no matter the situation or his linemates. He's very adaptable, not only was he a top unit power play and top unit penalty killer, but he can work with guys like Bobby Brink and Marcus Kallionkieli, but also with the guys a tier below that while still creating positive shifts for his team. Ford is very fast, his stops and starts are really strong too, as is his change of direction skating. He can withstand contact from bigger players even when he's needling in for pucks heading towards the boards. His waterbug style of play doesn't inhibit him from initiating contact either. He doesn't pack a mean punch necessarily, but he is more than willing to mix it up if it contributes towards the shift being a successful one. He is surprisingly hockey strong for his average size.

The Sioux City captain has above average hands and his playmaking aptitude is good enough to keep plays alive and advance the puck. As the skill level goes up around him, it seems likely that he'll have to rely a little more on a chip and chase game than some of the carries that he's gotten away with this season, but he has the skill and guile to do something productive with it when he gets to loose pucks with his wheels. Doesn't have enough in his arsenal to regularly beat players one-on-one with his hands alone and his shot is pretty weak. He was used down low on the power play because he wasn't a big threat to shoot and because he was strong puck retriever. He is able to make some pretty slick cross-net-line passes though too, he certainly wasn't just a screener or a decoy. His defensive acumen is advanced for his age. The key to it is that he can really saddle up and get underneath a puck carrier and disrupt plays efficiently. One of the most telling characteristics of checkers being successful at the next level is their ability to mirror attackers, and Ford has that quality. He can match high skill players because he has such a good sense about what their next move is. He is always out protecting late leads for Sioux City. Even factoring in that he's a 2000 birthday, Ford is just about the most complete and balanced USHL draft eligible forward.

"Not a fan at all." - NHL Scout, March 2019

"No." - NHL Scout, March, 2019

"Some guys on our staff like him but I don't have him as a draft." - NHL Scout, April 2019

"I like him. I have him later on in the draft. Late pick though." - NHL Scout May 2019

"Who?" - NHL Scout, June 2019

"This kid just gets it. Been a fan of his game all year." - NHL Scout, Michael Farkas

"I don't think he will ever drive the offense on a line at the next level but his skating and hockey sense could give him the opportunity to be the worker bee on a skill line or an effective bottom six penalty killer, for me the question is, how do you value that in a draft." - HP Scout, Dusten Braaksma, May, 2019

"I liked him. He's one of those guys who makes you notice him. He's kind of a find a way to get it done player. Good compete, wish he was more skilled." - HP Scout, Mark Edwards

	PLAYER	TEAM	LEAGUE	HEIGHT	WEIGHT	POS	GRADE
NR	FRANCIS, WILLIAM	CEDAR RAPIDS	USHL	6'4.75"	207 *	RD	ND
	HOCKEY SENSE		COMPETE		SKILL		SKATING
	4		6		4		6

William Francis is a late 00' birthdate who elected to make the move to the USHL (Cedar Rapids) instead of returning to his Centennial HS team in Minnesota. Francis is a big, hulking defenseman with above average skating ability. Francis likes to play a physical stay at home defensive style. Francis doesn't join or lead the rush out of his own end. Francis lacks creativity on the backend, often defaulting off the glass to get puck out of his own end if his first outlet isn't available. Francis is a good one on one defender due to his size and long reach advantage. Shows decent awareness and defensive techniques in front of his own net and when defending in space. There isn't a lot of defensive lapses in his game and displays a strong understanding of coverages in his own end. In the offensive end, Francis is limited in his ability to create offense but possesses a booming right handed shot from the point that could be a weapon on the power play but doesn't get himself into too many situations where he can utilize it. Francis can move the puck effectively around the zone but lacks playmaking creativity to generate scoring chances. William will likely spend another season in the USHL before heading to Minnesota Duluth in 2020.

"I don't see enough skill or offensive upside to warrant a draft pick. I just ask myself would I really want to use a draft pick to develop a bottom pairing, stay at home defenseman?" - HP Scout Dusten Braaksma

NR	PLAYER	TEAM	LEAGUE	HEIGHT	WEIGHT	POS	GRADE
	FRISCH, ETHAN	GREEN BAY	USHL	5'11.25"	195 *	RD	ND
	HOCKEY SENSE	COMPETE		SKILL		SKATING	
	6	6		4		6	

Sturdy, defensive-minded defenseman. It was Frisch's first full season in the USHL after a long cup of coffee in 2017-18 with Green Bay. He was traded late in the season to Fargo, but his ice time was not reduced significantly as he quickly proved his worth to the Force. Ethan has improved his skating over the year and his foot churn is better and more productive. He plays a calm, cerebral game so his plus skating isn't always on full display – instead, he relies more on subtle angle adjustments. His skating could probably be graded half a point higher and be more accurate than the flat 6 represents. A little bit uncharacteristically of 5'11", smart, mobile defenseman is that Frisch can deliver some really crunching blows. He doesn't chase hits all over the map, but he has a tactical truculence to him that is hard not to notice. He is better at closing down rush chances that he directs into the gutter than he is battling in front of the net, but that seems more a product of inexperience than unwillingness or inability. He can be aggressive in the neutral zone as well: he has shown the propensity to identify single-man rush chances that are more designed to buy time for a change than they are to attack. He can also play a more passive style, with heavy stick usage and better puck retrieving. His pivots and close-off timing is usually right on the money.

Frisch is not very productive and it matches his skill level pretty well. He just doesn't exhibit a next-level skillset other than a plus slapshot. He doesn't panic with the puck and throw it away though; he does go through his reads on the breakout and is an efficient short passer. That's his best attribute from a skill perspective in all likelihood, just his ability to survey and make a smart play. The foundation of skating and hockey sense make him very palatable, but the skill level will need to improve if he is going to play at the NHL level one day.

"He's not a draft for me." - NHL Scout, March 2019

"He was pretty highly regarded coming into the year. I have him late." - NHL Scout, April 2019

"He didn't live up to what I was expecting from him this year. I just expect more and he didn't really get there this year, especially as a late 2000." - HP Scout, Dusten Braaksma

"He's not for me. Saw him versus Brink early in the season and late against the program (USNTDP) and he didn't show me enough to project him as an NHL prospect." - HP Scout, Mark Edwards, May 2019

NR	PLAYER	TEAM	LEAGUE	HEIGHT	WEIGHT	POS	GRADE
	GAUCHER, JACOB	VAL D'OR	QMJHL	6'3.0"	180	RC	ND
	HOCKEY SENSE		COMPETE		SKILL		SKATING
	6		6		4		4

Gaucher is defensive center from Val-d'Or who finished his rookie season in the QMJHL with 24 points in 68 games. Before this season, he played the past two years in Midget AAA with Saint-Hyacinthe, and was drafted in the 2nd round by the Foreurs during the 2017 QMJHL Draft.

A cerebral hockey player, Gaucher does a lot of little things well on the ice and away from the puck that make him such a useful asset for his team. He's always in good position; he doesn't cheat on the ice, uses a good and active stick in the defensive zone, and already has a solid understanding of his role and the kind of player he is. He has value on the PK and will soon be one of the more renowned players league-wide while shorthanded. He was over 50% in the faceoff circle this year. However, he's limited offensively; he is not a natural goal scorer and has average hands. He scored 12 goals this year after scoring only 4 in his first 28 games. He's smart with the puck, frequently demonstrating good puck-protection along the boards, and can be tough for opposing defensemen to handle in front of the net. A lot of his offensive chances are created when he does some good work down low. Skating is the biggest area of his game that needs work and improvement in order for him to have a better chance at the pro level. His feet are heavy, his top speed is currently below-average, and his acceleration is currently average. He struggled to play at a high pace versus quicker teams, but his good compete level can compensate for this, as he is rarely outworked on the ice. We don't expect Gaucher to be drafted, but he has size and plays well away from the puck. Should he be able to fix his skating issues and continue to improve his offensive skills, he could get a look at a lower level in professional hockey at some point.

"Reminds me of Andrew Coxhead (Québec) in last year's draft; big strong center with a ton of smarts and great work ethic, but just not enough skills and below-average skating, which translates to no draft for me." - HP Scout Jérôme Bérubé

NR	PLAYER	TEAM	LEAGUE	HEIGHT	WEIGHT	POS	GRADE
	GAUTHIER, TAYLOR	PRINCE GEORGE	WHL	6'1.0"	193 *	G	ND
	HOCKEY SENSE		COMPETE		SKILL		SKATING
	6		6		5		5

Gauthier has been highly touted for a long time, entering the WHL as the 10th overall bantam draft pick. Gauthier has two years under his belt playing close to starter minutes in the WHL already. This season Gauthier played 55 games for Prince George, with a 3.25 GAA and a .899 save percentage. Gauthier was also selected for Team Canada at the u-18s and Hlinka tournaments.

Gauthier has good size and looks how a top goalie prospect should. Gauthier plays with a ton of confidence, and always looks calm in between the pipes. Gauthier rarely appears flustered after a bad goal and does a good job at not letting his play snowball. He also has good explosiveness and the ability to recover from an aggressive position. Gauthier showed good determination this season battling through traffic to make a play on the puck. Gauthier does not always see the play developing and inconsistent tracking the puck, letting some weak goals that he would want back. While technically sound, decently sized, and athletic enough Gauthier lacks the standout level tools to be a top goalie prospect. He is also burdened with playing on a weak team without much support. Gauthier needs to further develop his hockey sense to maximize the rest of his abilities.

NR	PLAYER	TEAM	LEAGUE	HEIGHT	WEIGHT	POS	GRADE
	GILDON, MICHAEL	USA U-18	NTDP	6'1.0"	194 *	LW	ND
	HOCKEY SENSE	COMPETE		SKILL		SKATING	
	4	4		5		5	

Goal-scoring left winger. Bolstered a good bit by his time with Jack Hughes and at the net-front on the power play, Gildon notched 13 goals and 29 points in 26 USHL games. Half of his goals came on the power play. When used in a depth role, like he was at the U18 World Junior Championships, his single assist in seven games is probably a little better representation of the current toolkit. To his credit, Gildon did improve his feet over the course of the season. He was able to get to some pucks and areas later in the year that he could not have gotten to in October. He's a June 2001 birthday, so he's on the younger side of the draft class – though not significantly so. He does a fine job in front of the net and he can snap some pucks upstairs, but outside of that, Gildon doesn't bring much to the table. He still lumbers around a good bit and isn't a real strong worker to help compensate. His hockey sense is a little below average too, and that became a little more evident when paired with the freewheeling style of Jack Hughes and Cole Caufield. His technical skills are below the mark, as is his playmaking ability. He has a propensity to let plays die with him, as he just isn't a strong enough puck handler nor does he use his body to protect well enough. While he did play on the lower lines without much acclaim early in the season, he tried his best to embrace the puck-retriever/net-front-presence role on the top line later, but the overall success was middling. He is also not much of a physical presence, which is a little surprising given what he was tasked with in the second half and his rather meaty frame. His skating combined with mentally being a half-beat behind most plays is already a big strike, but when it's topped off with a seeming unwillingness to really push the pace of his own game, it creates a real tough situation for a potential suitor.

NR	PLAYER	TEAM	LEAGUE	HEIGHT	WEIGHT	POS	GRADE
	GIRODAY, CHRISTOPHER	GREEN BAY	USHL	6'1.0"	172 *	LD	ND
	HOCKEY SENSE	COMPETE		SKILL		SKATING	
	5	5		5		6	

Giroday battled some injuries this season in his 1st USHL season after joining Green Bay from Aurora (OJHL) in 18/19. Giroday is a Western Michigan University commit that was able to chip in with 8 goals and 6 assists in his 38 games with the Gamblers this year. At this stage Giroday is a good skating defenseman that can be relied upon for good defensive minutes but doesn't project to being a very offensive defenseman at the NHL level. His puck moving ability leaves a bit to be desired at times. Giroday can skate the puck out of trouble and use his defensive partner as an outlet but doesn't make a ton of plays that stretch the ice and can be slow in making reads out of his own end. Giroday has a plus shot from the blue line with good one-timing ability from the point. His footwork allows him to get into position for one-timers as well as create lanes at the top of the zone. Giroday shows good defensive acumen in his own end but lacks the puck skills at this stage to have a high ceiling at the NHL level.

"He was getting things going when he got hurt. He'll be an interesting one on draft day." - NHL Scout, June 2019

NR	PLAYER	TEAM	LEAGUE	HEIGHT	WEIGHT	POS	GRADE
	GLOVER, TY	BUFFALO	OJHL	6'1.5"	196 *	LC	ND
	HOCKEY SENSE	COMPETE		SKILL		SKATING	
	5	5		5		5	

Glover is a lanky winger with average skating abilities as his straight-line speed is decent although his lateral footwork and agility could use some improvement. He gets around the ice and uses his long reach to disrupt opposing defensemen on the forecheck. His stick skills are average as with 1-on-1 situations he sometimes struggles to generate any offense. Instead he plays a power forward game with skills that can be developed. He will power his way to the net rather than finesse and plays a strong game close to the net muscling goals and picking up rebounds using his larger frame. His shot is above average. Glover is a possible late round pick with developing body and skills. Overall Glover plays a solid 2-way style, with playmaking skills, and most likely fill as a bottom six forward role. He is verbally committed to WMU and was recently drafted high in USHL Phase II Draft by the Lincoln Stars, so will most likely spend another season in junior ranks as late '00 birthdate.

NR	PLAYER	TEAM	LEAGUE	HEIGHT	WEIGHT	POS	GRADE
	GNYP, SIMON	KÖLNER HAIE	GER	5'11.5"	179	LD	ND
	HOCKEY SENSE	COMPETE		SKILL		SKATING	
	5	5		5		6	

Along with top prospect Moritz Seider, Gnyp was another defenseman who got himself noticed at the DEL level, playing 14 games with Kölner Haie when injuries opened up a spot for him. He clearly needs more time at the junior level to mature, but that first look could have been a lot worse.

Gnyp is a strong skater with very good mobility, allowing him to defend the rush well and carry the puck. In juniors, he is the go-to breakout player and often manages to carry the puck from below his own goal line into the offensive zone. However, he often skates himself into traffic as well and doesn't have the puck skills to beat defenders consistently. He's more dangerous when he plays a breakout pass and jumps in on attacks without the puck, getting open again in the low slot for a shot. In the offensive zone, Gnyp gets a lot of responsibility as a puck distributor and offensive contributor. He can play accurate passes but his shot leaves a lot to be desired. He can get pucks at the net through traffic but his shot power is below average.

88	PLAYER	TEAM	LEAGUE	HEIGHT	WEIGHT	POS	GRADE
	GREWE, ALBIN	DJURGARDEN JR.	SWE-JR.	5'10.5"	187 *	RW	C
	HOCKEY SENSE	COMPETE		SKILL		SKATING	
	4	7		6		6	

Grewe has been one of Djurgårdens best players in the SuperElite league throughout this season. He has racked up the points, with 13 goals and 34 points in only 25 games at the same time as he is registered for 102 penalty minutes. His point producing combined with his grit and "take no prisoners" attitude got rewarded with 15 games in the SHL for Djurgården as well, where he failed to put up any points, but was a factor with his physical game during his few shifts and which also backfired when he was called for an illegal check to the head which resulted in him getting a three game suspension.

In international play, with team Sweden, he was a regular during the season, all the way from the Hlinka Gretzky tournament to start the season, to the U18 world championships to finish it. Here he put up 9 points in 17 games, including his 5 goals. Early during the season and up until the U18 world championships he was put on a big role for his country, a role where he didn't quite manage to excel and produce accordingly. At the Worlds where he played more on the second or even third line, he came up big with his high intensity, aggressive type game where he led the way against the Canadians with his physicality and then later against the Russians where he came up huge and scored the game winner with a hard, well-placed wrist shot. Sweden later went on to win the gold medal in this tournament.

There are times during his games where it looks like he is more interested in punishing the opponents with a bone-crushing hit than playing hockey and scoring goals and this usually leads to unnecessary penalties and sometimes, chaos. He has to be smarter in these situations and he must understand that he is more valuable to his team on the ice than in the penalty box. This is a testament that his hockey sense isn't all that high and overall his decisions are really inconsistent, where he can create a fantastic play with a great saucer pass in one shift and then take a stupid penalty in the offensive zone, away from the puck in the next shift. His vision is good and he sees the ice well, but when he has made his decision, he just won't change it and he will commit fully to his initial plan. An example of this is when he takes off on his right wing at full speed, he will more likely than not, go right into the middle of the ice just inside the blueline and it doesn't matter if there are 1 or 4 opponents there in his way. There are times when he will power his way straight through a single defender and there are times where he gets flat out killed when he goes there, but the decision has been made and nobody can make his change that.

His offensive skills are pretty decent. He's got a quick release and good velocity to his shot and his accuracy is also good. He can also be a threat with his passing play when he decides to even though he really could benefit from utilizing his linemates more since he tends to hold on to the puck and is trying to make it a one-man show at times. His skating is slightly above average, he can absolutely hit good top speed, but it isn't as smooth and effortless as you would like it to be, it looks a bit forced at times, with that said he is very powerful skating up his wing when he gets the speed up.

His defensive play is inconsistent where he switches between wanting to put guys through the wall deep in the corners and leaving the zone early to create offense. He does a decent job in reading the play defensively, but it would be good for him to be more dependable defensively.

Grewe is in very good physical shape and it's his conditioning and attitude that will make him excel at his role as a power forward, rather than his puck skills. However, if he wants to play in the NHL, that's the role he should embrace and develop.

"There is no hockey sense at all, it's awful. Seems like he's always going into the middle- skating into three guys. He plays with a lot of energy, but that doesn't mean he plays hard...he only plays hard when he think he can get the puck". HP Scout, Johan Karlsson, May 2019

"He has this ability to make his linemates worse." - HP Scout, Johan Karlsson, May 2019

"First time I saw him I liked him and I've liked him less with every viewing since. He lacks hockey sense and has selective hustle at times. He will chase hits at the expense of playing smart defensive hockey. He's not for me, not anywhere early (in the draft) at least." - HP Scout, Mark Edwards, January 2019

NR	PLAYER	TEAM	LEAGUE	HEIGHT	WEIGHT	POS	GRADE
	GRIFFIN, ROBERT	JR BRUINS	USPHL	6'0.0"	177*	RC	ND
	HOCKEY SENSE		COMPETE		SKILL		SKATING
	6		4		6		5

Griffin is average size forward that excels because of his high hockey IQ. He has had success through the years as he thinks the game well and usually a step or two ahead of most on the ice. With his intelligence he sees the ice well, so he can set up plays. Griffin is a pass first, playmaker rather than the pure goal scoring type. He does not play an overly aggressive game rather he reads the plays well using his positioning well and stick to gain possession. Griffin has good stick skills which makes him dangerous in the offensive zone with the pass or slipping around defenders for scoring opportunities. His skating ability is good with balance and agility although he lacks speed and explosiveness. He has played against older players at the junior level for the past two seasons in the USPHL and has produced although recently changed NCAA commit from Northeastern to UNH. Griffin was certainly above the rest two seasons ago might have hit his peak early and be a player to monitor in the college ranks to see his development path.

57	PLAYER	TEAM	LEAGUE	HEIGHT	WEIGHT	POS	GRADE
	GRITSYUK, ARSENI	OMSK 2	RUS-JR.	5'10.0"	169	RW	C+
	HOCKEY SENSE		COMPETE		SKILL		SKATING
	7		6		6		5

Arseni Gritsyuk had a productive season with Omskie Yastreby in the MHL. He produced 21 points in 30 games, including an additional 5 points in 8 playoff games. Internationally, he was successful both at the Hlinka tournament, where he produced 3 points in 5 games, including 2 goals, and at the U18-Five-Nations where he had some dominant performances. He capped off his season with a good U18's, finishing with 5 points in 7 games, with 3 goals. The hallmark of Gritsyuk's game is his hockey-sense. He's a player who can change the rhythm and flow of a shift with his ability to slow-down or speed up the game when he sees fit. There's a lot of poise when he controls the puck and he's demonstrated very-good spatial-awareness that allows him to put himself in position to generate high-danger scoring chances. Additionally, Arseni had shown duel-threat elements. He can adapt his role as a playmaker along the half-wall and when cycling, yet can also snipe the puck at a good-clip. His release is good but it's his recognition of what angle he has available that separates his shot from some of the other skilled euro-players. There's a versatile and highly-skilled game at Gritsyuk's disposal, but he's not a very big kid or very-strong at this time. He competes hard during puck-races and can out-pace opposing defenses but there's still a separating gear that he lacks at this time. This extends into his first-step which also doesn't have the power to remain as elusive as we would like, given his frame. However. his hockey-sense compensated for a lot of his weaknesses, which is why we have ranked him on the back-half of our list.

"Checks our boxes pretty well with the exception of his size and skating combination. He's not a bad skater, probably high in our five range but at 5'10" we'd always prefer to see better skating." - HP Scout, Mark Edwards, May 2019

	PLAYER	TEAM	LEAGUE	HEIGHT	WEIGHT	POS	GRADE
108	GUENETTE, MAXENCE	VAL-D'OR	QMJHL	6'1.25"	181 *	RD	**C**
	HOCKEY SENSE	COMPETE		SKILL		SKATING	
	6	6		6		6	

Guenette was the 5th overall pick in the 2017 QMJHL Draft and took part in the Hlinka/Gretzky tournament in August, representing Canada. He finished the 2018-2019 regular season with a respectable 32 points on a Val-d'Or team who once again finished in the bottom third of the league.

Guenette is a two-way defender with good skating abilities, good footwork and who has the ability to skate the puck out of his zone. His game still has inconsistencies to it; with his toolset, you would expect him to have more of an impact offensively. Instead, he opts to play a smart, safe, simple game and doesn't take many risks on the ice. Offensively, he flashes some of his skills with some good passes out of his zone and does a relatively good job moving pucks in transition, but in the offensive zone, he's usually not very noticeable. He needs to be more active and take charge of the play more often. Another thing would be for him to get more pucks on net, as he only had 106 shots this year. He doesn't have a powerful shot on net. While his accuracy is good, in order for him to be considered as more of a threat from the point, his shot's velocity should be improved. Offensively, he was never the number one option on the power play this season. It was mostly Félix Boivin (and, when healthy, David Noël). He remains a good defender with above-average footwork and a good active stick in his own zone. He's good at defending one-on-one, but can struggle down low against bigger players; Guenette is not overly physical and could stand to be stronger. We feel as though Guenette could be a late-round pick at the draft if a team believes that he has more to offer than what he has shown so far in his QMJHL career. He does have some decent skating abilities and is a smart two-way defender, but we do question if there are enough skills in him to make it as a regular NHLer.

"I remember a game in Drummondville the shots on goal after 40 minutes were 29-4, just a brutal game to scout a player. Many Val-d'Or games this year were like this, with them giving up 40+ shots in 36 games this year." - HP Scout Jérôme Bérubé

"He finished the year with 32 points, which is not terrible playing on a bad team, but I was expecting more out of him this year offensively-speaking. During a lot of viewings he just didn't get many puck touches to make any difference offensively for his team." - HP Scout Jérôme Bérubé

	PLAYER	TEAM	LEAGUE	HEIGHT	WEIGHT	POS	GRADE
76	GUSKOV, MATVEY	LONDON	OHL	6'1.25	177 *	LC	**C**
	HOCKEY SENSE	COMPETE		SKILL		SKATING	
	6	5		7		6	

Matvei (Matvey) Guskov may have had some difficulty adjusting in his first full-season with the London Knights. Despite his considerable talent, he only accumulated 30 points in 59 games, including 12 goals. In the playoffs, he produced 4 points in 11 games. Internationally, he was featured at the World-Junior-A challenge where he had a pretty solid showing despite only producing 1 assist in 4 games.

Guskov's an offensively-gifted player who thinks with a high-degree of creativity. Matvei can make difficult dekes look relatively easy and can execute them at a high-rate. His move-set is hard for his opponents to read and there's a good amount of fluidity within his movement. This blends into his skating mechanics which are a plus. He does have a tendency to slouch when going at top-speed since he lacks the strength to keep his core activated, but he does have good leg extension in his stride. The main focus for Matvei will be on improving his power so that he can shift into a secondary-gear at a higher-rate than he currently does but the base is there. His skating ability allows him to make difficult plays while in motion since he's balanced on his edges. Specifically, he was adept at finding his teammates who were trailing him, after making sharp-directional cuts; showing a good amount of awareness in regards to his lane recognition as well. Guskov is capable of slowing down the tempo of a play and can react quickly when under-pressure as well. His anticipation extends to all three-zones, where his ability to read the game helped him in own-end of the ice. He's a 200-foot-center who played responsibly in own-zone, helping support his defense, while showing the ability to engage physically most of the time.

Despite showing impressive playmaking ability and reading the game well overall, there's a significant flaw within Guskov's game that held him back when we evaluated our ranking of him. Although he can make dynamic plays, they are very fleeting; Guskov's had one of the more inconsistent seasons out of the OHL-talent available. He flashes a play that gets your attention but then goes invisible for long stretches of a game. The biggest area of development in order for Matvei to counteract his inconsistencies is within regards to his pace. His motor can look average and he hasn't shown a willingness to attempt to use his skill to take-over most games. There's enough talent for him to drive-play for extended-time at the CHL-level but he was a passenger far too often in our viewings. If Guskov can learn to play at a higher-tempo and increase his consistency, then he has enough talent to be a viable NHL-contributor but it's going to take a new, more assertive approach that we haven't seen from him yet.

"I've seen him a lot now and haven't seen any reason to draft him yet." - NHL Scout, January 2019

"No interest. This is a London Knight we won't be drafting." - NHL Scout, January 2019

"What does he do?" - NHL Scout, January 2019

"I thought he improved a lot by the time the season ended. He went from no draft to possibly a 5th or 6th rounder." - NHL Scout, April 2019

"Overall I got mostly poor reviews on him. Some scouts were a bit kinder late in the year but in general the feedback wasn't good." - HP Scout, Mark Edwards, April 2019

"I think there is something there. He began getting inside a bit more often later in the season and if that continues he'll have a lot more success." - HP Scout, Mark Edwards, April 2019

"I liked him a lot more in April than I did in October. I kept thinking the light switch was going to go on, it did a little bit, but not enough for me to push him up too high. I'd draft him though and it won't shock me if the light switch goes on next year and he posts some real numbers." - HP Scout, Mark Edwards, May 2019

	PLAYER	TEAM	LEAGUE	HEIGHT	WEIGHT	POS	GRADE
94	GUTIK, DANIIL	YAROSLAVL 2	RUS-JR.	6'3.0"	179	LW	C
	HOCKEY SENSE	COMPETE		SKILL		SKATING	
	7	4		8		4	

Daniil Gutik had an okay season but didn't live up his talent-level from our original viewings at the U17's last year. He played for both Loko-Yunior Yaroslavl of the NMHL where he produced 9 points in 9 games, and had 13 points in 36 games for Loko Yaroslavl of the MHL. He wasn't used in the playoffs with the exception of one game on their run to a championship, but he was used in the NMHL playoffs, producing 4 points in games. At the international-stage, he played on a line with Podkolzin, showing a natural chemistry between the two at the Hlinka and at the U19 World-Junior-

A-championships, producing a combined 8 points in 11 games, with 7 assists. Although his production didn't display it, Gutik is one of the most talented players featured in this class. Last season he was the player that stood out next to Podkolzin and showed higher-end hands and vision. His array of dekes and technical proficiency with his move-set is bordering on elite. He can beat two opponents simultaneously with his hands when attempting to guard the puck; his skill-set is extremely impressive given his size and length, it's very rare to find a player with his level of dexterity and coordination with handling the puck. Another impressive attribute of Daniil's is his vision, he sees the ice very well and can make some of the sharper and more accurate passes you will see out of the higher-skilled forwards. His shot isn't at the same level as his hands or playmaking ability but it still features plus mechanics, he just needs to learn how to create additional leverage with his length and frame through his release point. His decision making with the puck isn't bad either, he can assess his time and space quickly and shows a lot of poise when handling the puck.

Despite his impressive offensive-tool-kit, there's some notable red-flags that have kept Daniil back from developing into the offensive-force his skills suggest that he could become. For starters, he's knock-kneed and his inward knee-bend keeps him from pushing off correctly into his stride. He's also not a physically developed kid, so there's a lack of power when trying to gain traction on his skates when digging into the ice, which gives him a weak top-gear as well. His skating also effects his pace. He doesn't carry a high-intensity or a take-over mindset on the ice, he's the kind of player that can use his skills when a chance arrives but he's not going to will a chance out on the ice. Away from the puck, he doesn't like to battle very often along the boards and loses too many battles given his leverage. There's a low pace, a low compete-level and a severe problem with his skating mechanics. Together, these negative attributes greatly diminished his remarkable puck-skills, as he's failed to consistently assert himself into a game at the level he should theoretically be able to, given his skill-set. If he can develop a higher intensity-level and physically develop so that his legs don't diminish his stride, then he has a chance of becoming a special-player, but it's a long shot given the number of hurdles he needs to overcome.

"He was one of the most disappointing players for me this season but the talent level is still absurd." - HP Scout, Brad Allen, May 2019

NR	PLAYER	TEAM	LEAGUE	HEIGHT	WEIGHT	POS	GRADE
	GUZDA, MACK	OWEN SOUND	OHL	6'4.5"	217 *	G	ND
	HOCKEY SENSE	COMPETE		SKILL		SKATING	
	4	6		5		5	

Mack Guzda was taken 32nd overall in the 2017-OHL-Draft. He was put into the starting position during the mid-way point of his rookie season and faired-okay, yet had an underwhelming draft-season after starting as the number-one-option in net for the Attack. In 49 games, Guzda finished with a .878 and a 3.63 GAA, giving him 20 wins on the season. In 5 playoff games, he finished with a .873 save-percentage and a 4.25 GAA. Guzda is a large-netminder who moves at an above-average-rate for his size. His flexibility is impressive, and given his length, it allows him to take up the bottom part of the net away at a high-rate when dealing with plays down-low to the net. He looks to sprawl out and use his wing-span and overall length to block a lot of pucks but he relied on sprawling too often, putting himself in positions where he couldn't make recovery saves after the initial attempt. Although he showed some decent glove-saves earlier in the year, the mechanics weren't refined and he failed to develop his glove as the season progressed; this turned into one of his more liable traits and is something we consider important when evaluating a netminder. Additionally, Guzda does have decent movement and an impressive full-extension when kicking out his pads but he was very busy in net and as a result, threw himself out of position consistently. Lastly, his hockey-sense was average to below-average in most games we viewed him in; he would trail behind the play due to losing pucks in traffic. His hockey-sense also didn't allow him to evaluate high-end shooters to the extend he need's, this didn't allow him to absorb rebounds very effectively since he wasn't squared up to the initial shot as consistently as we need to see. There are some tools and and size in Mack's game, but there was too many variables when looking at his development, in order for us to consider him for the draft.

	PLAYER	TEAM	LEAGUE	HEIGHT	WEIGHT	POS	GRADE
NR	**HAIDER, ETHAN**	**MN MAGICIANS**	**NAHL**	**6'2.25"**	**207 ***	**G**	**ND**
	HOCKEY SENSE		COMPETE		SKILL		SKATING
	6		6		6		5

Haider left his highly talented Maple Grove High School team in Minnesota to make the move to Junior hockey to suit up for the Magicians. Haider got off to a rough start with Team USA at the Hlinka Gretzky Cup where he struggled but eventually settled into his game with the Magicians and was among the best goalies in the NAHL throughout the course of the season. Ethan put up a respectable 2.35 GAA and .926 Sv% in 37 Regular Season starts for the Magicians. Haider has high end technical skills when he is locked in and on his game but struggles with consistency in being able to string together starts at this stage. An aggressive goaltender, Haider plays bigger than his size in the net, especially in his lateral movements where his head height and posture stays level. Haider has good athleticism and competes hard in traffic to find and cover loose pucks. Haider controls the top of the crease; he competes for the ice he is entitled to well. Haider showed in multiple viewings of being able to lock things down after giving up a goal early. He is able to shake off bad goals and give his team an opportunity after a rough start which also speaks to his high compete. Haider brings a good attitude to the rink and a strong work ethic both on and off the ice. Haider is committed to Clarkson University in the ECAC but will likely spend one more season in Junior hockey before heading to Potsdam.

	PLAYER	TEAM	LEAGUE	HEIGHT	WEIGHT	POS	GRADE
84	**HAMALIUK, DILLON**	**SEATTLE**	**WHL**	**6'2.75"**	**190 ***	**LW**	**C**
	HOCKEY SENSE		COMPETE		SKILL		SKATING
	5		7		6		5

Unfortunately, Hamaliuk missed a lot of the year with injury. Hamaliuk started very strong before his pace slowed a bit as he battled through injuries to finish with 26 points in 31 games. He impressed enough at the start of the year to earn an invite to the Subway Super Series.

When playing he is one of the most physical players in the league, delivering huge hits each game. Hamaliuk imposes a physical presence on the game and capitalizes on every opportunity he has to deliver a hard check. He could chase the hit too much getting himself out of position in the process occasionally, but overall the positives of his physicality outweighed the negatives. Offensively he has very soft hands, and showed the ability to beat defenders one on one consistently. Hamaliuk was able to make plays through defenseman's sticks which allowed him to get in to high danger areas with the puck. His soft hands also made him a threat in tight which was very noticeable in his role as the net front player on the powerplay. Hamaliuk consistently had scoring chances, and his goal numbers were surprisingly low for the volume of chances he had. Hamaliuk also has the hockey sense to make plays for others, and showed the ability to make very good reads. Skating is the area in Hamaliuk's game that stands out as a weakness. He has above average top speed and he skates well enough that it doesn't hinder him at this level, but he doesn't have a great first couple steps. Hamaliuk's mobility and burst need work and he doesn't have an attractive stride, which combined with sometimes heavy feet makes his skating look awkward. Next season Hamaliuk will play with the Memorial Cup hosting Kelowna Rockets and will have the opportunity to be a star for the team.

96	PLAYER	TEAM	LEAGUE	HEIGHT	WEIGHT	POS	GRADE
	HANUS, CLAY	PORTLAND	WHL	5'10.0"	170	LD	C
	HOCKEY SENSE		COMPETE		SKILL		SKATING
	5		6		5		7

Second year WHLer out of Minnesota, steadily progressed into a top 4 role for Portland. Hanus progressed from 6 points last season to 27 this year with all but 3 points coming at even strength. Hanus is an offensively inclined puck moving defenseman who plays the game fast.

Watching Portland Hanus immediately stood out as one of the best pure skaters in the entire WHL. Hanus has NHL level speed and agility, with stellar edgework he left forecheckers in the dust on multiple occasions. When he decided to go for a skate he could easily gain the zone and was blowing by players in the neutral zone. With this skating ability Hanus has the ability to make plays deep into the offensive zone while maintaining the ability to recover into position. Defensively his skating helped him hold his own as he had the quickness to make up for the bad decisions and poor approach angles. Hanus battled very hard but was often simply overmatched by stronger players, with his small size giving him some difficulties. Defending without the puck he was error prone, getting caught watching the puck and losing his man on multiple occasions. While Hanus sometimes looks like an excellent puck mover he was inconsistent with his reads, making a lot of forced plays into coverage, was much more effective skating the puck than passing it. Offensively Hanus had games where he was awesome with his activation and games where he didn't do much. When he was involved he on occasion looked like a dominant player. Boosting his offensive abilities is a very hard and accurate shot, that he did an excellent job with getting on net and finding shooting lanes. Thanks to elite skating abilities Hanus has excellent long term potential, but there are still a lot of inconsistencies for him to iron out.

19	PLAYER	TEAM	LEAGUE	HEIGHT	WEIGHT	POS	GRADE
	HARLEY, THOMAS	MISSISSAUGA	OHL	6'3.0"	188 *	LD	A
	HOCKEY SENSE		COMPETE		SKILL		SKATING
	8		4		7		7

Thomas Harley had a productive season for Mississauga, quickly developing into their top offensive-option on the backend. He finished with the most points out of any 17-year-old defenseman in the OHL, generating 58 points in 66 games, including 11 goals. In the playoffs he had 4 assists in 4 games, while at the U18's he produced 4 points in 7 games.

Harley is a mobile puck-moving defenseman whose best skill-set is his ability to transition the puck out of his own-end and up the ice. The two primary attributes that allow him to be efficient in his transitional-play are his skating and his passing ability. Although Thomas is a tall kid who hasn't physically matured into his frame, he features a surprising amount of power which translates through his skating, giving him plus acceleration. Furthermore, although he can sometimes skate upright, he has an impressive knee-bend and a long-stride which gives him a good separating top-gear. Harley is also coordinated, fluid, and agile, this allows him to use his edges to escape pressure during forechecking sequences due to how elusive he can be despite his size. This also translated to when he's carrying the puck through the neutral-zone. His passing ability is some of the best in this class from the backend. He passes with a high-degree of execution by firing sharp and precise passes that can stretch from below the goal-line to the opposing teams-line. Thomas takes advantage of his gifted passing by thinking the game quickly under-pressure. His hockey sense when holding the puck is good and this allows him to make smart decisions which is one of the main reasons his rate of execution is high. Where his hockey-sense doesn't translate to the same degree is away from the play. He can occasionally get caught when attempting to activate at the offensive-line, he can respond late to transitional play in the neutral-zone, and he can miss defensive-assignments in his own-end as well. However, at the offensive-line, his mental-attributes come together to allow him to carry the puck and make high-end offensive-plays, making him one of the more talented offensive-minded defensemen in this class. He's poised, calm, and has shown a good-set of hands that allow him to fake his options. This allowed him to be a threat from the backend on the powerplay, since he has the ability to breakdown opponents who challenge him at the line. Lastly, although his shot doesn't generate a lot of power, he does have a plus release point which features a whip-like-release that he was able to get through heavy traffic consistently in most of the games we've seen him in.

Where Thomas had trouble in our viewings was in his consistency in his own-end. His biggest flaw as a player is in his pacing. Although there are games where he's increased his tempo, there's several other viewings where he leaves a lot left in the tank, playing at a one-gear pace. There were too many games for us where he looked both disinterested and lethargic in his own-zone. This caused him to have inconsistent gaps, inconsistent races for loose pucks on dump and chase sequences, and inconsistent box-outs. Additionally, he theoretically should be able to impose himself on most opponents due to having a significant size and reach advantage. Yet along the boards, he failed to use his leverage adequately at times, as well as failing to use his physical gifts to drain opposing forecheckers as often as we wanted to see. One of the more bazaar aspects to Thomas was his willingness to engage physically in some games, while avoiding physical play in others despite appearing healthy. Despite Harley's defensive concerns, he did show an active-stick that gave him well-timed takeaways and he was above average at keeping his opponents to the outside due to his skating ability being able to keep up with some of the fastest players in the league.

When Harley shows attention to detail in his own-end and plays with pace, he looks like a defenseman who can play in a top-four role. Though as of writing this, there's a significant amount of development needed in order for him to reach that ceiling.

"He doesn't compete. It's an issue for me. He's not the least bit physical either". – NHL Scout, October 2018

"Size and skating and passing is high high end. It gets uglier after that." – NHL Scout, October 2018

"Saw him in London last week and it was ugly. He turned over a ton of pucks. He was -4 for the night and earned it. He struggled with any pressure." NHL Scout, November 2018

"He has no desire to play defense and I didn't like my interview with him. He tended to make excuses." – NHL Scout, February 2019

"After Tomasino and Harley I have no idea who is next on my list (Eligibles from OHL) right now." – NHL Scout, March 2019

"He might be the best puck mover in the draft but he isn't without his warts." – NHL Scout, March 2019

"I thought he raised his level of compete in the second half and that got him into my top 20 because the other stuff in his game is very good." NHL Scout, March 2019

"He wasn't good at the U18 and I know from a few Scouts that the feedback on him wasn't great."– NHL Scout, April 2019

"On any given day, Thomas Harley can look like a completely different player depending on his engagement level. That's not the impression I want to be left with from one of our top ranked OHL player, but it also speaks volumes to the class of OHL-talent in this year's draft." - HP Scout, Brad Allen

" In December he was still frustrating me with laziness and no compete. Then I saw him in Barrie one night and he literally had a perfect game moving the puck, it was really impressive. He competed harder and actually took the body too. From that point I started a clean slate with him, watching more to see if he could repeat the Barrie game. He repeated the puck moving prowess of the Barrie game in my next four viewings. That was when his ranking went up and he cracked our top 31. He still showed lack of compete several times, which is frustrating, but his puck moving was so good, that he will probably hold his ranking. - HP Scout, Mark Edwards, May 2019

In short, he excels at skating, he is smart and has the skill to pass the puck very effectively. I don't project him as a high end power-play guy,but he is a high end puck mover. I don't rank questionable compete guys that high very often, so that speaks to how highly we think of other parts of his game - HP Scout, Mark Edwards, May 2019

" I spoke to numerous Scouts during combine week and the feedback was generally poor regarding their interviews with him. Several scouts from different teams referenced Harley, Kaliyev and McMichael amongst their weakest interviews of the week." -HP Scout, Mark Edwards, June 2019

NR	PLAYER	TEAM	LEAGUE	HEIGHT	WEIGHT	POS	GRADE
	HARVEY-PINARD, RAFAËL	ROUYN-NORANDA	QMJHL	5'9.0"	171	LW	ND
	HOCKEY SENSE		COMPETE		SKILL		SKATING
	7		7		5		5

Harvey-Pinard is in his 3rd year of NHL Entry Draft eligibility after being passed over in the last two. He's one of the most complete players in the QMJHL; he does just about everything well on the ice both with and without the puck. He's an on-ice leader as the captain of the Rouyn-Noranda Huskies, who put up an amazing regular season record and won the league playoff championship. Harvey-Pinard took his game to another level in the final, recording 14 points in 6 games after recording 13 in the previous three rounds combined. Harvey-Pinard is not the biggest or fastest guy, but he plays with a big heart and doesn't play on the perimeter at all. He's always in the tough areas of the ice, competing against all the top players in the league. He's more than willing to take some punishment in front of the net, in the slot or along the boards to make plays. He's extremely good along the boards for a player of his size; his compete level is elite and rarely gets outworked on the ice, making opponents pay when they take it too easy when facing him. He's a smart player who thinks the game quickly, and he's as good as a scorer as he is a playmaker. His offensive upside for the professional level is limited, though, as he doesn't have high-end skills. What makes him attractive for an NHL or AHL team is his two-way game, work ethic and solid PK play. He's one of the best players shorthanded in the QMJHL; his mix of hustle, anticipation and smarts makes him a threat. He's very courageous as well; he is not afraid to block shots and makes good use of his active stick to block passing or shooting lanes. The big knock on Harvey-Pinard is his speed in regards to his size; he has worked hard to improve it since joining the league, but it is still average. That lack of speed is probably why he hasn't been drafted so far in the NHL, because the rest of his game is solid. Even if he's not a speedster, there is not much doubt in our mind that Harvey-Pinard can be at least a good pro at the American Hockey League level, and a good player for an organization to have on their depth chart.

NR	PLAYER	TEAM	LEAGUE	HEIGHT	WEIGHT	POS	GRADE
	HAS, MARTIN	TAPPARA JR.	FIN-JR.	6'4.0"	192 *	RD	C
	HOCKEY SENSE	COMPETE		SKILL		SKATING	
	5	5		6		6	

Has is a big defenseman from the Czech Republic who has been playing in Finland for the last two seasons (in the Tappara system). This year, with the U-20 team he registered 9 goals, 16 points in 38 games and also played for his national U-18 and U-20 teams during the year. You can expect Has to challenge for a full roster spot in Liiga next season with Tappara. Has does possess above-average top speed for a 6'04" player, and this is arguably the most impressive thing about his skillset. He has decent footwork, but still has work to do in terms of his agility and backwards skating. Once he starts rushing the puck and reaches his top speed, it can be very impressive. He has good confidence with the puck on his stick; he likes to rush it of his zone with his good skating abilities. He needs to improve his puck-management and decision-making; his passes are not always accurate and he can be victim to turnovers when trying too much. He has value on the power play because of his above-average skills; he has a hard shot from the point, but needs to get it off faster, as opponents have more time to get in the shooting lane to block it (or goalies have enough time to get in position). In the defensive zone, he can be physical if needed along the boards and in front of the net, but there's inconsistency in that department. He does use his long reach well to block passing lanes. When combining this element with his skating abilities, he's able to cover a good amount of spaces in the defensive zone. The Czech defender has some good tools to work with, but needs to improve his decision-making and consistency in order to have a chance to reach the NHL in the future. Any NHL team would love to have a good 6'04" smooth-skating right-handed defenseman in their lineup. If he can fix those issues, he has a chance to play, but right now, he fits more in the "project" player prototype.

NR	PLAYER	TEAM	LEAGUE	HEIGHT	WEIGHT	POS	GRADE
	HATAKKA, SANTERI	JOKERIT JR.	FIN-JR.	6'0.0	174	LD	C
	HOCKEY SENSE	COMPETE		SKILL		SKATING	
	6	6		5		6	

Hatakka is a two-way defenseman from Finland who played this past season with Jokerit's U20 team. He's not a defenseman with a super-high upside, but he does just about everything well on the ice. He's solid at both ends of the rink; in his zone he can play a physical game and be tough to play against along the wall and in front of the net. He has good speed going forward when rushing the puck or jumping into the play. His best offensive weapon is his shot from the point, a good, hard slapper that can be useful on the power play. He's not very creative with the puck in the offensive zone, however, and that what is holding him back from the next level offensively. He usually keeps his play with the puck pretty simple. His transitional play is pretty good, as he has a good first pass and he's not shy to skate the puck out into the offensive zone. He also uses his good footwork to retrieve pucks quickly when dumped deep in his zone, and he is also strong on the puck and can absorb hits along the boards. Defensively, he uses his body well to win puck battles and covers a good amount of space thanks to his agility and good active stick. Hatakka is not a defenseman who will wow you with his superior offensive skills, but does a lot of good things that can be useful for his team. He has decent size, physicality, and skating abilities.

16	PLAYER	TEAM	LEAGUE	HEIGHT	WEIGHT	POS	GRADE
	HEINOLA, VILLIE	LUKKO	FIN	5'11.25"	178 *	LD	A
	HOCKEY SENSE	COMPETE		SKILL		SKATING	
	8	6		6		6	

Heinola spent all season playing in the top Finnish men's league with Luuko as one of their steadier defensemen. He also amassed 14 points, which is very good for a 17-year-old defenseman in this league. He missed some significant due to the World Juniors' in December, and also in January and February due to a knee injury suffered at this tournament.

Heinola is one of the smarter players from this draft class; he's very calm and rarely makes mistakes on the ice. He's confident with the puck on his stick, is calm under pressure and is also very good to activate the transition game for his team, using his passing or rushing abilities. He usually plays a safe game with the puck, making safe outlet passes. If there's no option available, he won't force the play to the point where it would result in a turnover. He's an average-sized defender; he'll need to work on getting stronger for the NHL. However, the way he defends in one of the top men's leagues in the world was pretty impressive this season. Offensively, he makes smart decisions with the puck, has excellent vision, and he's good at getting puck through on net. He doesn't have a hard shot from the point, but finds ways to hit the net. He has good accuracy and can create rebounds or make it easy for his teammates to tip pucks in front of the net. However, in order to be considered more threatening offensively at the NHL level, he'll need to add some power to his shot. He has good footwork and good lateral agility, which helps him defend well one-on-one. He lacks a bit of speed for a defenseman of his size, and we would like to see him add a bit of speed to his game: not only when he rushes the puck, but also when coming back to retrieve pucks in his zone. Once he adds some strength and he's stronger in his lower body, we think that we could see a bit more explosiveness with his skating. Heinola likes to have the puck on his stick. He offers a great balance between wanting to be a difference-maker with the puck on his stick and not being a defensive liability. He was a top performer all year long in our viewings, with his team during the season and at the World Juniors', but unfortunately he didn't have a good U-18 performance in April. It was a tough situation, with Finland not performing that well overall and missing some key guys in their lineup.

Heinola has a bright future ahead of him; he has the talent to be a top-4 defenseman at the NHL level if he continues to improve his skating and strength.

"He looked really poised at the Hlinka, really good getting pucks and with the puck. I didn't think he skated great for a smaller D but when the puck was on his stick his thought process was high-end." - NHL Scout, September 2018

"I'd want him to get stronger and quicker this year before I'd take him too high." - NHL Scout, September 2018

"He's a very good player. He wasn't as good in junior as he was vs men. That's not uncommon, he was anticipating things that the less talented players didn't. That will happen a lot less playing with NHL players" - NHL Scout, May 2019

#	PLAYER	TEAM	LEAGUE	HEIGHT	WEIGHT	POS	GRADE
29	HELLESON, DREW	USA U-18	NTDP	6'2.25"	181 *	RD	B
	HOCKEY SENSE	COMPETE		SKILL		SKATING	
	7	7		5		7	

Drew Helleson was a steady defender on the backend for the program, finishing with 23 points in 64 games. In the USHL, he produced 11 points in 28 games, including 4 goals. At international events, he wasn't a big point producer but did have 3 assists in 7 games at the U18's. He's slated to play for Boston College next season.

Helleson is a cerebral modern-day shutdown-defender who plays a competitive and efficient brand of hockey. What defines Drew's game is his hockey-sense and willingness to battle. When breaking down his hockey sense, his anticipation under-heavy pressure is well above-average. This allows him to make smart and effective plays around the boards during forechecking sequences and when he's getting pressured both through the neutral-zone and at the offensive-line. His hockey-sense extends to his decision making in all three-zones. In the defensive-end, he looks for the safest route either by skating the puck out of danger-areas or finding the open passing lane; in the neutral-zone he rarely forces plays and lets the play naturally flow; in the offensive-zone, he doesn't over-extend his skill-set which allows him to get pucks on net and turn it over at the blueline infrequently compared to some of the other defenders on both his team and overall in this class.

He's s a strong and tenacious player that enjoys the physical aspects of the game, which compliments his sturdy frame. This quality allowed him to come away a plus player during board-battling sequences; there's a fearlessness to his approach. His hockey-sense also extends to his spacing. Helleson kept an adequate-gap and was good at applying pressure and closing his gaps that forced further reactions to his play. His competitiveness and pace extend to his ability to recover. When he is caught out of position, he responds quickly and changes his gear to match the urgency of the play. Helleson wouldn't be able to defend as successfully as he did if it wasn't for his four-way mobility. He's an efficient and fluid skater who is capable of acceleration quickly and generates plus straight-line speed. This compliments his edges and pivoting mechanics which are a plus and this allowed him to keep up with some of the faster forwards who attempted sudden direction shifts on him.

Helleson's safer and more direct approach when dealing with the opposition in the defensive-end extends to the offensive-end, which doesn't leave him with a highly-creative or offensively proficient game. He does have the odd play where he shows flashes of some talent but it's not consistent. His hockey sense gives him the ability to make plus reads and activate at opportune times, but he's not a flashy or dynamic player. Furthermore, his vision isn't one of his better attributes in the offensive-zone. He can move the puck quickly and efficiently but it's rare to see him make a high-end pass that's threaded through multiple players. He hasn't developed the ability to freeze opponents who are attempting to cover him at the line. As a result, Drew looks to quickly get the puck either to his open-teammate or fire a simple wrist-shot through traffic. One major benefit of Helleson's clean and simple approach at the blueline is that he rarely makes mistakes that cause the play to go the wrong direction, which encompasses his style of play as a whole.

Helleson is the type of defender that consistently looks for the safe and effective play. It's not the most exciting summary of a player but it emphasizes the attributes that we think could allow him to become a useful bottom-pairing NHL defenseman who can shutdown some of the opposing teams more skilled players.

"There is always a group of program guys who don't get their chance to shine offensively. He's in that group this year. I'm not saying he's an offensive star but he has more to give." - NHL Scout, March 2019

"Really good interview. I think he's an underrated player too." - NHL Scout, May 2019

"Projects as good solid middle pairing guy and like you said, he has good structure to his game." - NHL Scout, May 2019

"I saw him a lot, he's ok but I'm not that high on him." - NHL Scout, June 2019

"Helleson was the structured force in chaotic situations when viewing the USNTD." HP scout, Brad Allen, May 2019

"Not much conversation about this player with other scouts this season but what I do know is there is a huge range of opinions on him. Scouts either had him high or seemed to have no time for him. Every year it seems like a player comes out of the USNTDP with little fanfare but ends up surprising. Helleson would probably be my pick to be that guy this year. Teams need the meat and potato guys too, not just the flashy offensive guys." - HP Scout, Mark Edwards, March 2019

"I spoke to a lot of scouts between the start of combine week and today, which is two days before our book release day. I can basically some up the comments in two ways: They either said something along the lines of -I like him, good player or they said something like - not a big fan." - HP Scout, Mark Edwards, June 2019

67	PLAYER	TEAM	LEAGUE	HEIGHT	WEIGHT	POS	GRADE
	HENRIKSSON, KARL	FROLUNDA JR.	SWE-JR.	5'8.75"	166 *	LC	C
	HOCKEY SENSE	COMPETE		SKILL		SKATING	
	7	7		6		5	

Henriksson has been sneaking in the weeds all season, where he has been a top producer for Frölunda in the SuperElit league and finished tied for first place in the leagues scoring race with 49 points divided in 13 goals and 36 assists in 45 games. He also had the best plus-minus rating of all the players, with a +35 in the SuperElit League. He was a big part of his club winning the U18 Swedish championships with his excellent playoff performance and leadership.

He was also rewarded with 2 games in the SHL for Frölunda in which he failed to score any point due to small amounts of ice time.

He has been playing on a strong line with 2020 top prospect Lucas Raymond all season with both his club team and for team Sweden and there is no doubt he can keep up with and play with superstar players. Henriksson's hockey IQ is very high and his reads are fantastic in all three zones. He can find passes that no one else can see and he will set up his linemates for one-timers in high scoring areas. He is most definitely a pass-first playmaker and really excels from the hash marks on the power play when he gets more time and space to thread his passes through the defending box. He rarely shoots the puck and his shot are very weak but somewhat accurate.

Henriksson's skills are somewhat underrated, mostly because he often makes the easy, smart play but also since he will get outshined by his super flashy linemate Lucas Raymond. However, his hands are soft and he can stickhandle well in tight situations and move the puck an inch to make a perfect tape-to-tape pass. He has this ability to always make it out of the corners with the puck on his stick, rolling away from his opponents his quick feet ability to evade getting hit.

He is a guy his teammates and coaches always can rely on since he always works hard and makes good reads all over the ice to help his team. He will never cheat defense to create offense and he is great at distributing the puck to his wingers from the defensive zone too.

Internationally he was one of the standouts for team Sweden at the U18 world championships where he centered the first line and led the way for his nation. His performance at the worlds showcased his brilliant hockey sense and loyalty towards his team, once again he didn't stand out in a flashy way, but rather with his ability to always make the right decision and he was the perfect link between his wingers and his defenders at all times. Team Sweden went on to win the gold medal in this tournament and Henriksson was his teams leading scorer with 3 goals and 9 points in 7 games. He put up a total of 19 points in 21 international games during the season

Henriksson is small, listed as 5'9" 174lbs and that's a big question mark to if he will be able to compete against big, strong adults going forward. He can be found having a hard time stripping the puck from bigger, stronger players, but somehow he manages to break up a pass or pickpocket the puck off another player.

His skating has to improve considering his lack of size, he is not necessarily a bad skater, his strides and technique are just fine, but there is not enough power or top speed for him to create the separation he will need. His footspeed is good and he moves very smoothly laterally.

Considering his high hockey IQ he could be a gamble worth making at the draft, but he will be a long-term project for whatever team picks him.

"He is one of my favourite players to watch in this draft. I enjoyed seeing him have success at the U18." - NHL Scout, May 2019

"Played really well at the U18 in April. Might've made himself a draft pick." - NHL Scout, May 2019

"He played with great players and some people think he's just a product of his linemates, but I've seen bad players ruin a line with two great players. Karl made his linemates even better." - HP Scout, Mark Edwards, April 2019

NR	PLAYER	TEAM	LEAGUE	HEIGHT	WEIGHT	POS	GRADE
	HLAVAJ, SAMUEL	SLOVAKIA U20	SVK	6'3.5"	187	G	ND
	HOCKEY SENSE	COMPETE		SKILL		SKATING	
	5	5		5		5	

Hlavaj joined Lincoln (USHL) after an impressive showing at the U20 World Juniors in Vancouver for Slovakia, despite his team being overmatched in many of the games. Joining the worst team in the USHL wasn't conducive to impressive numbers but was probably a good move in order to get more North American scout's eyes on him and was given a good amount of starts for Lincoln to do just that. Hlavaj plays an aggressive, athletic style where he challenges shooters at the top of the crease. He can be a bit too aggressive but has shown good recovery skills when he loses his crease. He carries his glove a bit awkwardly at times and is susceptible of getting picked apart over the glove, especially in one on one situations. Hlavaj needs to get better at staying big in the net, his head movement is inconsistent, especially when trying to around screens and his can get beat high as a result. Hlavaj has NHL size and athleticism but will need a long-term developmental path as he needs coaching to refine some of the technical aspects of his game. Hlavaj hasn't given an NCAA commitment yet to our knowledge so he will likely be spending next season in Junior hockey somewhere in North America. We wouldn't be shocked to see a CHL go after the talented netminder either.

	PLAYER	TEAM	LEAGUE	HEIGHT	WEIGHT	POS	GRADE
23	HOGLANDER, NILS	ROGLE	SWE	5'9.0"	185	LW	**B**
	HOCKEY SENSE	COMPETE			SKILL		SKATING
	6	7			8		5

Nils Höglander started the season with a new club, transferring from AIK in the HockeyAllsvenskan to Rögle BK in SHL. Since Höglander is not a physically big player, he struggled early on against bigger, stronger and faster opponents compared to the ones he faced the year prior. His debut season in the SHL ended with 7 goals and 14 points in 50 games; which is okay considering his age, size, and role on his team. He had a great U20 pre-season tournament for team Sweden in Örnsköldsvik, where he was his teams most dynamic offensive player and led his team in scoring. That's why it was a big surprise to see him get cut from the team just before the U20 world championships. In 8 international games, he managed to put up 4 goals and 7 assists but the odds are against him to make the team next season.

Hoglander is a dynamic winger who contains a high-octane motor. His pucks-skills are up there with the best in this class, as he has the best hands out of any draft eligible forward. His stickhandling can be mesmerizing and he uses this skill through most situations on the ice. There isn't a deke that he doesn't seem capable of doing; ranging from lacrosse-style moves behind the net, to side-stepping his opponents while simultaneously dragging the puck through their tri-pod. What makes his deking exceptional is how coordinated he is with his hands while in motion. This makes him look erratic at times, yet he's controlled and calculated within his movements, making him very difficult for opposing defenses to read. Another impressive aspect of his puck-skills are how he can use his skating in conjunction with his stick -- it gives him a rare-level of versatility within his move-set, since he can kick the puck back to his blade while trying a difficult move depending on the scenario. Another unique property of Nils hands, are in regards to where he likes to place the puck. A lot of players look to use inside-to-outside moves in order to guard the puck and gain separation, yet in Hoglander's case, it's the inverse with some of his moves; he looks to take-advantage of his rapid-hand speed by placing the puck directly into his opponent's skates. This allows him to maintain separation from active-sticks since defenders have to pivot and readjust with the puck underneath them. It speaks to his level of confidence and creativity with how truly diversified his move-set is. Hoglander isn't just a set of hands though. He possesses the intensity and competitiveness to be able to contribute in important games at a high level. He can take the role as a tough player to face when he is using his speed and aggressiveness to disrupt the opponent's puck-game. Despite his small size, he plays with great courage and attacks bravely. He will keep challenging the defenders no matter how much physical abuse he receives. No one can accuse him of playing on the perimeter. What we identified within his game, was that even though he's undersized, he was capable of forcing defenseman to play-heavy-weighted minutes against him. One of the primary reasons for this is due to his skating mechanics. Höglander's first few strides give him two-step area quickness; his edgework is superb and this gives him quite a bit of elusiveness. When combining his escapability with his hands and his pace, it starts painting a picture of why it's so difficult to handle him down-low. What brings his attributes together to form a dangerous forward is his anticipation. His move-set can't come together unless he's able to identify how his opponent is attempting to mirror-him in advance; he reads off his opponents and reacts dynamically to what's given to him. His playmaking lags behind his anticipation but it's still good and he's capable of making difficult passes in conjunction with his move-set; some of which are very creative. He can also identify soft-ice around the net area quickly due to his impressive level of spatial-awareness. His shot isn't as high-end as the rest of his offensive tool-kit, though due to his hand-speed, he is capable of shifting his shooting angle rapidly while in motion. The main area of growth for him with his shot will be in terms of increasing his velocity by learning how to bear down through the release point more than he currently does on most shot attempts. The last area to note regarding his skill-set is that he's a surprisingly heavy-hitter given his frame. We've seen him generate puck-separating hits on larger men than himself, though his aspect of his game will be harder for him to translate at the NHL-level.

There are areas where Hoglander has to develop in order to be an effective NHL contributor. His size makes it difficult for him to push his way towards the net, despite trying to enter heavy-traffic regularly. Sometimes, his play is too sporadic, resulting in his teammates having a difficult time reading what his intentions are. Although his edges and acceleration are plus attributes, he needs to produce more power in his stride so that he has a better top-gear. For a smaller player, there isn't as much separating speed as we would like to see. Reasons for his include a lack of leg-extension within his stride, making it appear short and he has an inability to dig his heel into the ice at times, making him look like he's skidding over the surface. Away from the puck, his defensive play lags behind his offensive-play but he has shown that he can strip the puck of unsuspecting players at times and doesn't shy away from some of his defensive-responsibilities. Lastly, for all of his offensive-gifts, he's yet to execute at the rate his skill-set suggests he should be able to, so it's important for him to increase his offensive-efficiency so that he doesn't rely on his hands as much as he can at times.

Höglander will most likely not be a big point producer in the NHL, but he is viable in most roles and positions in the forward-lineup and he will bring a good mindset and high compete to his team. For these reasons, we see Nils as a versatile 3rd-line energy winger who should be suited for playoff hockey.

"He plays the game with passion and it shows on the ice, this kid loves to play hockey." – HP Scout, Johan Karlsson

"The Swedish Bobby Brink." – NHL Scout, April 2019

33	PLAYER	TEAM	LEAGUE	HEIGHT	WEIGHT	POS	GRADE
	HOLMSTROM, SIMON	HV 71 JR.	SWE-JR.	6'1.0"	183	RW	B
	HOCKEY SENSE	COMPETE		SKILL		SKATING	
	6	7		6		6	

Holmströms season has been torn apart by injuries from the start. He came into the season from having hip surgery in the summer and by the time he was recovered from that he suffered another injury to his hand in the 5-nations tournament in Kravare, Check Republic in November and missed a big chunk of time due to that and when he finally recovered from that injury he got injured again.

He ended up playing only 21 games for HV71 in the SuperElit league and even though it was obvious he was a bit rusty, he still managed to put up 7 goals and 20 points and showed some flashes of brilliant offensive instincts at times. He excelled from behind the goal line where he successfully set up his teammates with excellent passing play and great creativity.

Holmströms skating is rather explosive, even though it has regressed a bit since his hip surgery, but he has great acceleration and his skating is smooth overall. He can keep his balance due to great edgework, a strong core and a lot of willpower, this combined with great hands and smooth puckhandling skills make him lethal in 1 on 1 situation. He often tries the low percentage play which leads to some turnovers, instead of making the easy play and keeping possession of the puck. His wrist shot is above average with a good quick release and a lot of power and it's also pretty accurate and he tends to fake the defenders and goaltenders well enough to make the shot look easy.

While his main strengths are in the offensive game, his two-way game cannot be denied. He competes superbly all over the ice and hates to not have the puck, this may lead to him overworking some defensive situations, but at least he is there contributing to team defense. His hockey sense is slightly above average, but he could really benefit from utilizing his skating even more than he already does. He is trusted to be on the ice in all situations and he is just as good on the box play as he is on the powerplay and will most likely be on the ice in important stages of the games.

Holmström is a beast along the boards and covers the puck very well with his body and he has the ability to deliver a well-timed offensive body check. His high level of competing along with his physicality and his explosive playmaking skill makes him very interesting for this year's draft. The biggest question mark is; can he stay healthy enough to be able to produce and contribute for a full season? This upcoming summer is undoubtedly a big one to be able to stay healthy and competitive.

Holmström got dressed in 9 games for Team Sweden during the season and put up 3 goals and 7 points in those games, including a big goal in the U18 world championship final against Russia where he helped his team clinch the gold medal on home soil. He held a somewhat low profile during this tournament though and it would have been great to see him take even more initiative and drive the play. Holmström also played in 1 game for HV71 in the SHL.He could be one of the surprises this summer, by going earlier than expected in the draft, if there's a team willing taking a risk.

"He's been hard to catch this season because of the injuries. When I have seen him he's been one of the best players on his team. Speaking to some of the guys on team, they had to drag him off the ice (during the time when he was injured) they rave about him." - HP Scout, Johan Karlsson, May 2019

"I really liked his skating last year and then he had the hip injury. Now I look at his skating and I don't think it's as good of an asset. I think it might have been affected by that injury." HP Scout, Jérôme Bérubé, May 2019

"Our Swede Johan is a big fan." - HP Scout, Mark Edwards, May 2019

78	PLAYER	TEAM	LEAGUE	HEIGHT	WEIGHT	POS	GRADE
	HONKA, ANTTONI	JYP	FIN	5'10.25"	179 *	RD	C
	HOCKEY SENSE		COMPETE		SKILL		SKATING
	5		5		7		7

Honka is the younger brother of Dallas Stars' defenseman Julius, a first-rounder from the 2014 NHL Entry Draft. The younger Honka had a difficult season, as he started in Liiga with JYP but was also loaned to Jukurit, Keupa HT from the Mestis league, and also saw action with JYP's U20 team in the junior league. For a prospect to bounce around like this in one calendar year, stability is hard to come by. Despite his struggles, he still made Team Finland for the World Juniors'. Unfortunately, his playing time was very limited there, and when he did see the ice, he really struggled in terms of his defensive play and was frequently outmatched physically in his own zone.

Honka's offensive skills are undeniable; he has really good puck skills and puck-distribution abilities from the point on the power play. He moves pucks quickly into transition from his own zone. In shooting situations in the offensive zone, he has a quick release and an accurate shot; the puck doesn't stay on his stick for too long. He has good skating skills, quick feet, and good, fluid footwork. His skillset screams power play potential for the NHL level. However, when Honka doesn't have the puck on his stick, things get complicated for him. He has issues defending in his own zone. His lack of size and strength makes it very hard for him to defend against bigger forwards. He has all kind of difficulties defending one-on-one, getting outmuscled too many times. Along the wall and in front of his net, he's not much help. It's mostly his compete level in his own zone that makes us doubt if he has really any future at the NHL level. It's one thing to struggle in your own zone and be outmuscled, but so far he has demonstrated a very low desire to play any defense in his own zone. His limited role at the World Juniors' was a big indication of how low his compete level is in that area. Right now, Honka is a one-dimensional defenseman with very good offensive skills. If he ever wants a chance to play at the NHL level, he will need to make big progress with his defensive game, get stronger and improve his willingness to play in his zone.

"Tough season, he struggled mightily. He can skate and he has skill but he makes too many mistakes, big mistakes. - NHL Scout, March 2019

"Never saw him play a good game this year and he was just ok when I saw him last year. He has talent but I'm not confident he's close enough to pulling it together to warrant drafting him." - NHL Scout, April 2019

"Poor decision making and low compete equals a big faller for me, despite having skill and the skating talent." - HP Scout, Mark Edwards

	PLAYER	TEAM	LEAGUE	HEIGHT	WEIGHT	POS	GRADE
NR	**HORNING, CONNOR**	**SWIFT CURRENT**	**WHL**	**6'2.75"**	**188 ***	**RD**	**ND**
	HOCKEY SENSE		COMPETE		SKILL		SKATING
	6		4		5		5

Horning was drafted in the 3rd round of the 2016 WHL Bantam Draft by Swift Current. This year in his second season he produced 31 points while playing a large role for a bottom feeding team.

Horning is a solid decision maker with the puck who can make effective passes. Did a solid job on the breakout and was steady on the offensive blueline. He also brings a strong shot to the table, that he showed good ability getting through traffic. Horning is a below average skater and was soft defensively and often beat to pucks in the corner. He'll need to improve his skating and his intensity level would make Horning a more attractive prospect or at least a better WHL player.

	PLAYER	TEAM	LEAGUE	HEIGHT	WEIGHT	POS	GRADE
1	**HUGHES, JACK**	**USA U-18**	**NTDP**	**5'10.25"**	**168 ***	**LC**	**A**
	HOCKEY SENSE		COMPETE		SKILL		SKATING
	8		7		8		9

Jack Hughes has had a record-breaking performance for the USNTDP U18 squad over the last 2 years, posting the most points out of any USNTDP player in history with 112 this season and 116 the previous season. He also played well at the U20 World Juniors where he had 4 assists in 4 games, getting better as the games progressed despite having an injury. He finished with his best international effort at the end of the season by producing 20 points in 7 games at the U18's, in Sweden breaking the previous scoring record held by Alex Ovechkin for combined points through this year's and last years performances. He also 3 assists in 7 games at the World Championships.

Hughes defining attribute is his ability to make dynamic plays while going at top-speeds. His edge work, agility, elusiveness, acceleration and top-gear are elite, managing to switch his stature from a disadvantage into an advantage and he generates deceptive levels of speed that throw defensive-units off due to his fluidity and the ability to change directions suddenly. This also applied to the boards, where Hughes uses his agility in tight-spaces that makes him surprisingly effective against larger opponents; he's not easy to pin. His skating alone isn't what make Hughes one of the top offensive-players in this class though, it's his processing ability on the ice which allows him to anticipate the play in advance that separates him from other draft-eligible players. He's constantly analyzing his options and adapting; he feels off what his opponent is giving him and needs very little time or space to make the smart and safe play or the skilled play. Hughes makes opposing teams uncomfortable due to being able to strike quickly and in a manner that isn't telegraphed. A fearless mentality defines his style, he's not a perimeter player in any sense of the word, opting instead to knife through heavy traffic at top-speed. Giving him very impressive clean-transitional zone-entries which will translate. This approach isn't possible if he doesn't recognize body positioning and lanes rapidly, which he does through his spatial awareness. It's an underrated trait that's essential for centerman to have if they are to efficiently drive play and Jack has it.

Hughes puck skills add another dynamic trait to his game, his hands are lightning quick, he can deke in-tight to his body and he can use them while going at top speeds. He also tends to use his move-set to not only beat players one-on-one but to also feel out the opposition and stall while looking for additional options. His vision is also bordering on elite. He's capable of making blind passes that his opponents fail to pick up on and routinely finds players behind defensive coverage. He's an accurate passer and he can make difficult passes look easy while on the ice. Furthermore, he's equally as dangerous passing on his backhand as he is on his forehand, which makes it very difficult to pick up on the direction he's passing from. Although his passing is impressive, his shot hasn't caught up to his playmaking ability yet, which reflected on the score-sheet. His release is quick and he has an accurate shot, but he still exaggerates his body mechanics to the point where goalies can read his release point at times. That being said, he still has plus footwork, uses advanced head fakes, and knows how to create leverage which gives him the ability to elevate the puck when attempting to shoot. His talent level should allow him the ability to develop a shot that comes within range of his passing ability at the pro-levels when given time.

The primary areas Jack needs to develop are mostly in his play away from the puck and his strength. It will be interesting to monitor how he continues to develop the ability to absorb physical contact when he carves through traffic the odd-time he is knocked off the puck and when competing along the boards. The biggest area of improvement that Jack needs to focus on is his play in the defensive-zone. He's capable of supporting his defense and has the awareness needed to translate into a solid defensive player but he had a tendency in some of our viewings to attempt to come out of his zone too early, showing impatience at times. Furthermore, he consistently looks to use his edges to turn and gain momentum when he's attempting to leave the zone. The problem is that this causes him to misread certain defensive-plays since he has his back to the play in some instances, when if he was more set in his positioning, it wouldn't occur as often as it does. Similar to his brother Quinn, he sometimes attempts high-skill plays in high-danger areas in his own-end, which has led to some turnovers, leading directly to goals-against. It's unlikely that Jack develops a defensive game that rivals his offensive-game but as long as he cleans up his decision making in terms of attempting high-skilled plays at inopportune times in his own-end and continues to develop a more detail-oriented approach away from the play, it won't be a concern.

Hughes is a special talent that dictates play and has tremendous potential as a franchise altering center at the NHL level. He has a take-over mentality every time he steps on the ice which is a testament to his mental game: he elevates his level of play during critical times which is the calling card for a star-player. As a result, the **worst-case** scenario we see, is that he might end up one of the better wingers in the league if he can't translate at the center position.

"I'm not the biggest Hughes fan compared to previous first overalls because I'm not sold he can play Center, but I haven't seen enough of the Finn to have an opinion on who is better." - NHL Scout, December, 2018

"Not sold on Hughes having good enough hockey sense to be talked about in the same breath with the big boys like Crosby." NHL Scout, December 2018

"Hughes will need at least a year on the wing. Kakko will make a bigger impact for the first two years if not more. The guys picking Hughes could be fired before Hughes catches up.- NHL Scout, December 2019

"All these experts pumping Kakko's tires need to zip it. Draft Hughes first overall and enjoy." - NHL Scout, January 2019

"I think sometimes he holds on to the puck way too long but when he went overseas (November) he was easily the best player there. I thought he made a statement there. That was really good for him." - NHL Scout, January 2019

"He'll need o learn to play with structure a bit more. He's left an opening to be overtaken at one. (overall). I haven't seen the guy that so many people are hyping him up to be." NHL Scout, January 2019

"He's a great player but I don't think he's the slam dunk at number one that media have put on him so far. Good news is he won't slip later than two (laughs)." - NHL Scout, January 2019

"He plays arrogant. I don't know if he thinks he's above some of this stuff but he plays some really dumb hockey on some shifts. The play dies on his stick a lot." - NHL Scout, January 2019

"He has his issues but I'm not going to overthink it. He's a really good Fu**ing player and he's going number one, I'd take him number one." - NHL Scout, January 2019

"Id rate him a slight notch behind (Nico) Hischier as far as recent top picks go. It's tight, but I like Hischier because he was way more complete at the same age." - NHL Scout, January 2019 (note the date of the quote and who now drafts first overall)

"Sometimes he doesn't play as smart as I think he, is because I think he's very smart...if that makes any sense. What I mean by that is that I think he can easily change making those occasional bad decisions where he needlessly turns over pucks."- HP Scout, Mark Edwards, January 2019

"He's a fantastic player that will not be going into as good of a situation as Kakko will get with the Rangers." - NHL Scout, May 2019

"He'll need to play on the wing for a bit, but he'll be great down the middle in time." - NHL Scout, May 2019

"Jersey is U.S based and will never take Kakko. The tough decision is going to be what to do with Hughes next season. He struggled against men." - NHL Scout, May 2019

"It' might be tough next year for him in Jersey. He'll be ok after that." - NHL Scout, May 2019

"I'm not convinced he can play down the middle. Look at the World Championships, he had a tough time there." - NHL Scout, May 2019

"Thought it was kinda funny when I heard that Hughes' parents were staying at the same hotel as the Devils brass at the U18 (in Sweden)" - NHL Scout, May 2019

"If they were both Centerman I'd take Kakko number one." - NHL Scout, May 2019

"They are two very different players but both are great." – HP Scout, Mark Edwards

"I've included a lot of comments that don't exactly praise Hughes but I want to state that Scouts are huge fans of his game and at least 80% of the Scouts I asked had Hughes over Kakko. That said, numerous Scouts stated (I'm included in this) that it was one of tightest gaps between the top two overall players in many years." – HP Scout, Mark Edwards, April 2019

"Very difficult picking the player to sit at the top of our rankings this year. I absolutely love the way Kakko plays the game but if Hughes can indeed play down the middle in the NHL he brings that positional value to his resume. Some people talk about Kakko at centre but he's a winger and he excels there." – HP Scout, Mark Edwards, April 2019.

	PLAYER	TEAM	LEAGUE	HEIGHT	WEIGHT	POS	GRADE
62	HUGLEN, AARON	ROSEAU	HIGH-MN	5'11.25"	166 *	RW	C+
	HOCKEY SENSE		COMPETE		SKILL		SKATING
	6		6		7		7

Aaron started and finished the season with Fargo (USHL) where he was a key two-way centerman in both his stints with the Force. Huglen also represented USA at the Hlinka Gretzky Cup where he played a similar role as well as scoring a notable Lacrosse style goal vs Canada. Huglen has an excellent top gear and explosiveness off the hop that is a cornerstone to his effectiveness at both ends of the ice. On top of his physical speed, he seems to think the game at a quicker level than most of his opponents which allows him to be in the right place at the right time and be an opportunistic player. Huglen offensive output was ok in his two stints in the USHL, totalling 4 goals and 10 assists in 28 games, however Huglen was mainly used as a 3rd line checking center and didn't get the bulk of the offensive opportunities that older players on the roster received, so his offensive skill has been a bit untapped at the upper levels to this point. Huglen is an excellent faceoff centerman who uses his body in the circle well to buy time for support when he doesn't win draws cleanly. Despite is slight frame at this stage, Huglen is strong on his skates and wins a good amount of his battles in the hard areas of the ice. He is smart in the way he positions his body to seal off his opponent. Huglen at least at this stage doesn't project as an elite offensive producer at the next level but he possesses enough skills and impressive hockey sense that gives him decent odds of making it to the NHL someday. Aaron is a player that can play in any situation and is a lead by example type of player. Huglen is committed to the University of Minnesota for the fall of 2020.

"He's one player I would really want to find a way to draft." – HP Scout, Dusten Braaksma

	PLAYER	TEAM	LEAGUE	HEIGHT	WEIGHT	POS	GRADE
NR	INNALA, JERE	HPK	FIN	5'09"	176	RW	ND
	HOCKEY SENSE		COMPETE		SKILL		SKATING
	6		5		6		6

Innala is in his 4th year of eligibility for the NHL Draft. He had a breakthrough season in Liiga, scoring 24 goals in 60 games for HPK. His 24 goals are the most by a U-21 player in Liiga since Saku Koivu had 27 in 1994-1995. Innala started the season slowly with 6 goals in his first 27 games, but finished really strong with 18 goals in his last 33 games. His offensive production exploded this season, seeing as he only put up 11 points in 48 games last year. He also saw his ice time increase from slightly above 12 minutes per game last season to almost 18 minutes per game this year.

Innala is not the biggest player physically, but he's a good skater with good top speed and good agility. He's as effective a scorer as he is a playmaker, making him unpredictable in the offensive zone. He's got above-average smarts and shooting abilities. He's got a quick release and good velocity on his wrist shot. He creates a lot of plays with his rapid feet, and his speed and quick decision-making make him a threat in the offensive zone. He lacks ideal size, however, and he's not a very physical player. He is also not a very good defensive player; his play away from the puck will need to improve before he can think about playing in the NHL. He's got nice puck poise, which makes him wait an extra second to find his teammates in scoring areas. His hands are above-average; he made some impressive plays in tight spaces this season. His confidence seemed to grow as the season progressed this season; he's really a late-bloomer. He was never on our radar the last three seasons for the NHL Draft, even though he played for Finland at the 2018 World Junior Hockey Championships.

	PLAYER	TEAM	LEAGUE	HEIGHT	WEIGHT	POS	GRADE
103	JANICKE, TREVOR	CENTRAL ILLINOIS	USHL	5'10.25"	193 *	RC	**C**
	HOCKEY SENSE		COMPETE		SKILL		SKATING
	6		7		5		5

Goal-scoring center who plays with an intriguing blend of skills and compete. His move out of the Program and into a captaincy with Central Illinois has allowed him to blossom. Owns a plus shot and is plenty capable of hitting a moving puck – a trait frequently utilized from the left side of the Flying Aces power play. Has enough moves to make some space for himself when he's got a head of steam, but isn't quite there skill-wise when he's working out of corners or tighter areas. He carries himself like a larger player. He's only 5'10" but looks pretty thick on the ice. He has a good gliding speed and then he constantly makes these swooping motions towards the areas that he wants to go with a strong one-foot push, which is a move normally reserved for larger players. His first step and his edges are better than his average top speed. Trevor is a better than average puck protector for his size and experience. He does a fine job on the forecheck, he takes the right angles, and there's a really good amount of competitiveness to it. He'll come back all the way in the defensive zone if you want to boot.

Despite all that, he looks like he'd probably be a winger at the next level given his style of play, plus with his shot, it stands to compliment his game more anyhow. We wonder how well he'll be able to manage and carry the puck in the middle of the ice and if that will be end up being a detrimental distraction. Though he carries himself like a bigger, hard-working player, he doesn't usually look for hits. He was a good faceoff taker in our viewings this year, but he also cheated a lot by never coming to a complete stop and not being called for it. The former USNTDP player demonstrates a willingness to learn and challenge himself to be better on and off the ice. Janicke doesn't have many pronounced weaknesses in his game, he's a sturdy competitor with good wheels, a plus shot, and a good skill level. He was claimed by Muskegon in the USHL Dispersal Draft.

"Might be a good college guy but that's about it. I like him, he has some game, but not for the NHL." – NHL Scout, June 2019

"He's a high compete kid. He made my list but late." – NHL Scout, June 2019

"He plays a bigger game than his physical stature and is strong on his skates, wouldn't shock me if he tests really well at the combine." HP Scout, Dusten Braaksma, May 2019

	PLAYER	TEAM	LEAGUE	HEIGHT	WEIGHT	POS	GRADE
NR	JACQUES, JÉRÉMY	SHERBROOKE	QMJHL	6'3.5"	182	RD	ND
	HOCKEY SENSE		COMPETE		SKILL		SKATING
	5		5		5		5

Jacques showed some promise during his QMJHL draft year with Magog, and then left for the USHL where he had some problems staying healthy and didn't get much ice time. He decided to join the QMJHL last October. Sherbrooke had previously acquired him from Moncton in the Anderson MacDonald trade last year.

Jacques has great size, standing at over 6'03", and still has plenty of room to add mass to his frame. He could become a more imposing defenseman when he's done maturing physically. His offensive game did not develop as well as we thought it would in his QMJHL draft year, and he did not show much in terms of offensive potential for the next level in 2018-2019. He mostly played a safe game, trying to minimize the amount of defensive mistakes and stay out of trouble. His decision-making is not bad, but it definitely needs to get quicker in order for him to process plays quicker and move pucks quicker into transition. He is not a big threat from the point to create offense, either. He can make some smart pinches offensively, but his shot is only average. He needs to get his shot off more rapidly, and find better shooting lanes, too. He didn't show good enough vision to project himself as a power play guy at the pro level. His game is still raw, as though his lack of playing time in the USHL really hurt his development and now he's trying to catch up to where he should be. Defensively, he does a good job defending one-on-one, has decent footwork for a big lanky defenseman, and a good active stick. He can play a physical game if need be; he's not very aggressive physically, but will take his man out when needed. We don't expect Jacques to get drafted this year, though he could possibly get some NHL rookie development camp invitations during the summer.

	PLAYER	TEAM	LEAGUE	HEIGHT	WEIGHT	POS	GRADE
NR	JENSEN, JACK	EDEN PRAIRIE	HIGH-MN	6'0.0"	194	LC	C
	HOCKEY SENSE		COMPETE		SKILL		SKATING
	4		7		5		6

Jack Jensen is another re-Entry NHL Draft prospect who elected to play out his senior year in the Minnesota High School ranks for Eden Prairie instead of heading for Junior hockey. Jensen was a key piece of Eden Prairie's success in getting all the way to the Minnesota Class AA State Championship game. Jensen scored 31 goals and 52 points in 24 Reg. Season games for Eden Prairie as well as being a dominate player in the State playoffs, registering 4 Goals and 5 Assists in 6 games in route to the State Title game. Jensen is a strong kid with a powerful skating base. He is an excellent all-around skater with a good top gear that he uses to affect the play at both ends of the ice. Jensen is often first in on the fore-check and does an excellent job pressuring the play and forcing turnovers. Jensen also brings a physical edge to his game, rarely missing an opportunity to finish his check. Jack plays with some reckless abandon at times and plays a game on the physical edge, sometime crossing the line but usually does a pretty good job of staying on the right side of the law. Jensen is a good 200-foot player, he comes back into the play hard and understand his coverages and role on the back-check. His speed is a threat at the top of the Penalty Kill where he can read the play to breakup passes and uses his speed to get to loose pucks behind the Power Play. Offensively Jensen doesn't display high end skill in the way of fancy stick handling moves or will beat guys one on one with Deke's but is effective in getting himself and the puck into scoring areas, can generate chances off the cycle and off the rush by driving the net and can finish on his opportunities. A lot of Jensen's goals are workmanlike, competing and battling in the slot area but can also be effective in finding the soft spots in coverage and getting shots off in tight areas. Jensen joined the Minnesota Magicians (NAHL) for their playoff run this Spring where he has been close to a Point Per Game player for the Magicians. Jensen is a fringe NHL Draft prospect as of now but his skating might give him a chance going forward and if he isn't taken in June draft will be a player to track and will likely have opportunities going forward. Jensen is committed to the University of Minnesota but will likely spend a full season in Junior hockey before heading to play for his hometown Gophers.

"I thought Jensen had a shot at getting drafted last year but he didn't have much help on his roster, this year was a different story and some of his skill was more identifiable with some players around him. He's on my list." - HP Scout, Dusten Braaksma

"I don't see the hockey IQ or skill and there isn't much else remaining in his game for me to pull the trigger on this 200 born player. Our Minnesota guy has time for him though." - HP Scout, Mark Edwards

	PLAYER	TEAM	LEAGUE	HEIGHT	WEIGHT	POS	GRADE
NR	JENTZSCH, TARO	SHERBROOKE	QMJHL	6'1.5"	154 *	RC	ND
	HOCKEY SENSE		COMPETE		SKILL		SKATING
	6		6		5		5

Jentzsch was a nice surprise with Sherbrooke this year, finishing with 42 points in 53 games and playing a top-6 role on the team. He came via the CHL Import Draft, where he was drafted with the 85th overall pick. The German center not only became a key player for Sherbrooke offensively, but brought a complete game to the table and some excellent play shorthanded.

He's got a good sense of anticipation mixed with a good compete level, a combination that makes him valuable shorthanded. He's got a good stick, which is valuable in his own zone to block passing lanes. At even-strength, he always does a good job to come back to help his defensemen deep in his own zone, often acting like a 3rd defenseman. Not an explosive skater, his top speed and acceleration are average at best. He was passed over in last year's draft while playing for the Red Bull Academy in the Czech U-18 league. His skill level is average; he doesn't stand out in any areas offensively, but he's smart and works hard. He will need to improve his faceoff percentage, as he only won 43% of his faceoffs this year. He doesn't have the upside to be an offensive player at the next level, but can fill in as more of role/defensive player. In order for him to be valuable as a defensive center, he'll need to improve on faceoffs to help him make it to the NHL. In addition, he'll need to keep getting stronger physically. He has a tall, lanky frame, but in order to be more effective along the boards and in front of the net he'll need to add some weight to it. Jentzsch is a good junior player and should be even better next season in his second QMJHL season, but his upside for the NHL is rather limited.

"Coming into this season I was thinking Oliver Okuliar would be the top euro on the Sherbrooke team but Jentzsch was the most consistent and better performer of the two rookie imports." - HP Scout Jérôme Bérubé, May 2019

	PLAYER	TEAM	LEAGUE	HEIGHT	WEIGHT	POS	GRADE
49	JOHANSSON, ALBERT	FARJESTAD JR.	SWE-JR.	5'10.75"	161 *	LD	B
	HOCKEY SENSE		COMPETE		SKILL		SKATING
	6		6		6		6

He is the son of former NHLer Roger Johansson. He had a good showing in the SuperElite this season, putting up 5 goals and 29 points in 40 games along with 63 penalty minutes in SuperElit. Given that he was up to two years younger than most of his teammates/opponents and the fact he was a defenseman, it was an impressive offensive season. He also scored 6 points in 5 games with his club's U18 team and one assist in 7 games at the U18 in April., where his team won gold. He dressed for 3 games in the SHL and looked like he belonged there.

Internationally, he played 21 games for Team Sweden where he put up 3 points, often on the third pairing. He was part of his country winning the gold medal at the U18 World Championship on home soil for the first time.

His skating was exposed at times playing internationally by getting burnt wide but he got acclimatized to the pace of international play at the end of the season and had a pretty decent U18 Worlds.

Thinking offense-first, he will leave his defensive responsibilities to join the rush even before he is certain that the zone exit is under control, leaving big gaps if the play gets overturned. While he does a good job of finding open space to receive a pass in the neutral zone, he prefers to transport it himself. There is absolutely nothing wrong with his self-confidence but his skills often don't match. His hockey sense offensively is very inconsistent, he can be a very strong puck transporting defenseman, or sloppy spreading it around. Johansson's has a hard shot from the blueline and he is not afraid to shoot the puck. He needs to improve his accuracy and his ability to avoid hitting the high forward, by moving the puck sideways before he releases the shot.

His stride has a good amount of power and sound technique but he lacks explosivity is his first couple; his feet aren't quick enough and he lacks a bit of lateral mobility. He plays with a lot of authority and he wants to lead his team. He demonstrates great potential but his whole game is unpolished. He's got a strong lower body, strong along the boards in bumping opponents off the puck, with a good stick that has a long reach.

He reads the play well defensively to break-up passes and pick-up loose pucks; his only problem defensively is that he leaves his responsibilities early

Johansson has a lot of unlocked potential. He can still can get much stronger. He has the ability to be a sleeper at this year's draft.

"He' not a flashy player but he is effective." - NHL Scout, May 2019

	PLAYER	TEAM	LEAGUE	HEIGHT	WEIGHT	POS	GRADE
20	JOHNSON, RYAN	SIOUX FALLS	USHL	6'0.0"	173 *	LD	**B**
	HOCKEY SENSE	COMPETE		SKILL		SKATING	
	7	7		6		8	

He's a modern, mobile two-way defenseman. The California product from the Anaheim Jr. Ducks, jumped right into a prominent USHL role on a top-flight team in his first season. Though he only notched 25 points in 54 games (21 of them at even strength), he did lead the team with a plus-24 rating. Johnson is one of the most fluid skaters in the draft class. He has effortless, multi-directional mobility with first-step quickness, terrific edgework and the ability to stop and turn against the flow of pressure easily and punctually. His escapability and poise with the puck makes him a calming presence in chaotic situations. The hockey sense is there in spades. He thinks and feels the game very well. Ryan has great spatial awareness, he understands where players have moved to even if he's not facing them, he understands the geometry of the rink perfectly. His skill level has improved over the course the season. Early in the year, he was able to beat players mostly on skating prowess, now he's able to make hands plays that really make an impact – both on the rush and when he's already in the offensive zone. The next challenge will be his ability to string consecutive technical skill plays together – whether it be beating F1 and threading a nice pass against the flow of pressure or making a move to work in down low in the attack zone and making a finishing pass or shot.

Johnson is a modern defender in the sense that he's a mobile, stick first rear guard who really doesn't like to get too engaged physically. He fronts a lot of plays as opposed to wallowing in the mire of a net-mouth battle. His stick positioning and timing are both excellent. To boot, he almost never gives up his leverage by leaving his feet – they're his best weapon and he knows it. While he has shown the ability to carry pucks, it didn't appear that that was in the Sioux Falls playbook very much. And if it was, Johnson didn't always look like he wanted to be tasked with that. While we have a lot of respect for his poise and calm demeanor, there is such a thing as too cool. We would have liked to have seen a little bit more of a take-charge attitude sometimes and not the let the game come to him quite so often. That lack of killer instinct may help to explain his somewhat disappointing point totals. Though, he wasn't used as the primary power play quarterback for much of the year (Max Crozier took that time for blueliners on a four-forward power play). Also, as the team's best defensive player, Johnson was used as a security blanket to insulate weaker players. His game is subtle and understated, even his skill plays are not that flashy – he has an exceptional grasp of "late touches" when accepting passes as a way to manipulate defenders and the space that he has in anticipation of the next step of the play. He really gets the game and that foundation in a fairly young player for this draft class is exciting. He still needs to improve his finishing passes (that is, passes in the mid- or lower-layer in the offensive zone that lead directly to high quality scoring chances) and his shot. All told though, there isn't a lot of lead-up time for Johnson before he'll ready to play in the NHL.

"Fantastic feet, he's raw but he's had a great showing this weekend." – NHL Scout, September 2018

"I've seen two periods and I can already see he's their best defensman. I wish they would play him more." – NHL Scout, September 2018

"I might move him above York if he keeps improving at this pace." – NHL Scout, December 2018

"He was really good in Bonnyville. When I say that about a player with zero points that tells you that I think he has a lot of upside." – NHL Scout, December 2018

"I like him. He's been lights out when I've seen him. I wish he had a bit more dynamic offensive ability for kid his size but his skating is elite and he's actually a really solid defensive player." – NHL Scout, December 2018

"He's probably one of the best players I've seen this year at retrieving pucks and making plays up ice. He was really good in my limited viewings so far." – NHL Scout, December 2018

"Right now I'd probably draft him ahead of York. More upside based on what I've seen so far.

"I have him as a 1st rounder now. Just moved him up. His feet are elite." – NHL Scout, January 2019

"He's been great in all of my viewings. One of the best skaters in the draft class and I'd rate him as an excellent defender." – NHL Scout, January 2019

"He needs some real coaching. They have him playing so basic it's embarrassing. It's like peewee AA out there at times the way they make him play. He was better last year when I saw him in Midget." – NHL Scout, April 2019

"I don't think he has that 'play for keeps' mentality. Maybe I value that more than others when evaluating defenseman. Having said that, I like him as a prospect, there's a place for his skill set on every NHL team right now." HP Scout, Dusten Braaksma

"I got a lot more feedback on him after the WJAC. and that feedback was very positive. We already had him ranked high before the tournament but I think his stock rose on some team's lists after that tournament." - HP Scout, Mark Edwards, December 2018

"I saw him last season in Midget AAA and really liked the way he played the game. His excellent skating is obvious, I liked how tight his gaps were. He's fantastic at stopping offence before it gets going, ruing breakouts and clogging the neutral zone. I like how he can both skate and pass the puck. I'm glad I saw him last year because he was able to flash some offensive potential that was not very evident this year. I don't see a future pp one player when I watch him but I still see a bright future. He is still raw with big upside." - HP Scout, Mark Edwards, February 2019

"Many of the NHL Scouts I spoke to who got to see Johnson a lot more often live than I did tended to blame his lack of numbers on his coaches mis use of his strengths as a player. We'll see how true that turns out to be in the years ahead. - HP Scout, Mark Edwards, May 2019

	PLAYER	TEAM	LEAGUE	HEIGHT	WEIGHT	POS	GRADE
4	JONES, HUNTER	PETERBOROUGH	OHL	6'4.0"	196 *	G	C+
	HOCKEY SENSE	COMPETE		SKILL		SKATING	
	6	6		7		6	

Hunter Jones came into the season more conditioned then last year after getting an opportunity to start for the Petes, but still had difficulty maintaining consistency and looked drained, which led to him having a poor second-half compared to his first-half. He finished with a .902 save-percentage and a 3.31 GAA in 57 starts before having a poor playoff, posting a .862 save-percentage and a 4.66GAA in 5 games.

Jones is built like a light-armoured vehicle when you see him in the crease, yet he has excellent reflexes for his size. His reflexes allow him to move rapidly from his butterfly to a standing position and visa-versa; complimenting his blocker and glove-side, where he's shown the ability to fully-extend and come away with some very impressive-saves. We've seen him look around a screen and quickly push-across into a wind-mill glove save on the other side of the net as an example. His recovery-rate for his size can be very-impressive when he's specifically in his butterfly and looking to re-extend, but if he has interpreted the initial angle correctly, it's rare that he doesn't absorb the shot. His rebound control expands to his glove-hand. When he's dialed in, he catches a lot of pucks and rarely fumbles them; it's one of his more impressive attributes. Another good quality of Jones is in regards to his skating; he keeps a tall and narrow stance that allows him to fluidly push off and cover a lot of net, though there are still times where he will over-commit and lose his crease. The other plus area regarding Jones technical skill-set is in terms of his post-integration. He's very fluid coming in and out of his reverse-VH and comes off his post well. Together, his reflexes and coordination compliment his huge-stature and make him an imposing netminder when he's on top of his game.

There's a lot of tools that translate with Jones; it's rare to see a goalie as reflexive as he is for his age and size, but there's also games where Hunter has being unable to use his tools effectively. There was basically two-versions of Jones this season. One of those versions could stand on his head and steal the Petes some games; while the other had difficulty just managing not to get pulled. He was doing a better job of maintaining his energy in the first half of the season but the Petes weren't able to keep a lot of pucks away from him, which we think drained him over-time. There's a confidence to his game when he's dialed in but when he's fatigued, it shows. Given his athletic talent and very impressive reflexes, he fails to extend as much as he needs to on certain shot-types. For instance, he prefers maintaining his butterfly position while keeping his limbs tight to him, even if the save requires him to extend his blocker into the top part of the net-instead. This is the most pronounced when he requires a full-extension with his pads. We've seen Jones in several games fail to stop secondary chances because he's unable to fully extend his legs; he doesn't have the flexibility at this time to take full advantage of his wing-span. Furthermore, he's good at anticipating play when he's dialed into the game, but when he's unable to remain focused, this attribute folds. The end result, is that Jones needed to rely on his reactionary ability which worked considerably better for him than some other goalies given his reaction-time but when you're facing 40 shots a night in some games, it's a difficult pace to keep and it got to Hunter. Another trait that needs improvement, is in regards to how compact he is in net. Similar to what we discussed with him not extending enough, he also doesn't come out of his net and cut down the angle as aggressively as he needs to. There are times where we've seen him cheat and not completely square up when he's expecting a pass that's moving laterally. Lastly, although he's a solid-skater who has fluidity, he hasn't learning how to error-correct using micro-adjustments during broken-plays in-front of him or when he doesn't read the initial play properly. It's a skill that would really help compliment his game given his reflexive tools and he hasn't learned how to use it enough.

Despite these concerns, Jones did have games where even if the score was 6-0 for the opposing team, he still battled and still made some impressive-saves. He's not a goalie who gave up during games, he got overwhelmed due to fatigue. The primary area of improvement to counteract his issues, lies in his ability to continue developing his off-ice conditioning so that he can increase his consistency as a starter. If he does become a well-conditioned goalie and puts in the work off the ice, then he has the chance of developing into an NHL-goalie.

"I love the tools and the kid's presence on the ice, but when he's off his game, he lacks the resources at this time to re-find it" - HP Scout, Brad Allen

38	PLAYER	TEAM	LEAGUE	HEIGHT	WEIGHT	POS	GRADE
	JONES, ZACHARY	TRI-CITY	USHL	5'10.0"	172 *	LD	B
	HOCKEY SENSE	COMPETE		SKILL		SKATING	
	6	7		7		6	

Jones is an offensive-minded defenseman. It's a very shortlist of players (if any) that can lay claim to being on the ice as much as Jones and his defense partner Ronnie Attard were this year. Jones, though, is a rookie out of Selects Academy (CT) paired with the veteran. The younger Jones was actually the clean-up man for the pair. As Attard pursued his roving, aggressive style, Jones tended to cover his tracks. Jones' communication on the rink became more evident, as he was often seen instructing a forward who was covering for Attard.

The fluidity and power of his skating did improve quite a bit over the course of the year - the problem was he started the season as an average slightly knock kneed skater. The speed of his leg churn became more impressive in the later months and he's improved in terms of four-way mobility. His edges and agility have been a staple all year. He was relied upon as a puck carrier and power play quarterback for his team as a first-year player. The skill level also improved over the course of the season to the point that he could challenge players 1-on-1 and net some rewarding territory. He started adding some moves to his repertoire, including a deceptive stick flinch move to try to get a checker to shift his weight quickly so that Jones can go against the grain on him. There are other weapons for defenses facing Tri-City to contend with that may have given Jones a little bit more room than he'd have in other situations, but the creative improvement was a great sign.

He wasn't counted on to shoot the puck much, he owns a decent wrist shot but nothing more than that. He really got thrown into the fire defensively and responded with really encouraging results. His stick positioning was strong. He learned how to close out plays that originate outside the dot line effectively later in the year and even found a few hip check attempts in the process. He competed in front and along the boards without getting bullied, but he obviously has a size disadvantage - his hockey strength is good though. We're upbeat on his hockey sense as he can sniff out plays and anticipate pretty well. His sense of urgency and danger are a positive. Though his partner normally beats him to the punch, Jones doesn't give up the offensive line quite so readily himself. He can fly in and knock a puck in deep while still having the recovery ability to field the rush defense if things go awry. He provides good partner support and outlet passes. His advancement over the year and his ability to babysit his partner for half a game was encouraging after an uneven start to the season from a skill perspective. Jones was recognized as the USHL Rookie of the Year and was a Second-Team All-Star.

"The Jones kid would be interesting if his skating was better." - NHL Scout, September 2018

"He's a good player, a bit wild with the puck at times but he's a rookie. Surprised there isn't more buzz on him." - NHL Scout, December 2018

"I like him but I think his skating will make him slide to the third. (Round)" - NHL Scout, May 2019

"Got paired with a '99 for support, but Jones ended up insulating him most of the time. Really improved as the year progressed." - HP Scout, Michael Farkas

"Zac Jones was a 2nd half riser for me, I didn't see him much early in the year. I think his awareness and hockey sense is very good." - HP Scout, Dusten Braaksma, May 2019

"Flashed a bit in the WJAC. He reminds me of (Cale) Makar a bit just the way he jumps around in the offensive zone. To be clear, no I'm not comparing him to Makar, he's a very good prospect but not close to the same tier of prospect as Cale." - HP Scout, Mark Edwards. December 2018

"I think his skating has improved a lot this year. Back in September in Pittsburgh, skating looked to be the only thing holding him back from being a legit NHL prospect. There is no denying he has offensive talent. He built off a solid offensive WJAC performance in December and kept getting better. He is still raw, but a very interesting prospect who became one of my favourite players to watch. All our staff that have seen thought he was trending upwards." - HP Scout, Mark Edwards, May 2019

	PLAYER	TEAM	LEAGUE	HEIGHT	WEIGHT	POS	GRADE
NR	JUNGELS, JETT	EDINA	HIGH-MN	5'10.0"	161	LW	ND
	HOCKEY SENSE	COMPETE		SKILL		SKATING	
	5	6		5		6	

Jungels was a key offensive player for Edina on their Run to the Minnesota Class AA State Championship in 2019. Jungels isn't a big player but plays an up tempo fearless style of game that made him difficult for opponents to contain all season long. Jungels registered 27 Goals and 27 Assists in 24 Reg. Season games for Edina HS and was dominate in the State playoffs with 5 goals and 3 assists in 6 games. Jungels has the ability to pop into the play at the right time, he gets lost in coverages and only needs a split second to capitalize on a mistake as he has an excellent release that is accurate and surprises goaltenders. Jungels isn't a fast skater, especially for his size and if anything limits his professional upside at this stage it's his skating when paired with his lack of size but Jungels plays the game quickly, especially in the neutral zone where he turns plays north by reading the play, making quick decisions and moving the puck quickly. Jett will need to get stronger as he can get outmuscled and separated from pucks rather easily in the corners, but he doesn't lack the willingness to go to these areas. As he gets stronger, he should become more effective along the walls and in front of the net. Jungels is a fringe NHL Draft prospect at this stage but has enough skill and the ability to be clutch in big moments to warrant a profile in this book.

"No chance for me and I doubt he gets drafted." - NHL Scout, April 2019

"I don't mind him. might be a late guy." - NHL Scout, April 2019

"He was awesome in the Fall Elite League and carried it over into his High School season. I like this kids swagger and the confidence he plays with, but he's a hit or miss type of prospect right now."- HP Scout, Dusten Braaksma

NR	PLAYER	TEAM	LEAGUE	HEIGHT	WEIGHT	POS	GRADE
	JUTTING, JACKSON	PRIOR LAKE	HIGH-MN	5'10.25"	185 *	LC	ND
	HOCKEY SENSE	COMPETE		SKILL		SKATING	
	4	6		4		5	

Jackson started the season at the Hlinka Gretzky Cup for Team USA where he played a key defensive role for Team USA but managed to chip in with some offense along the way. Jutting started and finished the season with the Minnesota Magicians (NAHL) where he has been a key offensive contributor in 26 regular season games (13 Goals and 10 Assists) as well as in the Robertson Cup Playoffs. Between stints with the Magicians, Jutting played for Prior Lake (MNHS) where he had a decent year for Lakers, putting up 14 goals and 28 assists in 24 games but didn't have a lot of help around him and was forced to do a lot of the heavy lifting when it came to the offense for much of the season. Jutting is a hard-working two-way forward that isn't going to make a lot of flashy plays. Instead relies upon his hockey sense and work ethic to create offense. Jutting possesses a low center of gravity and a strong skating base that makes him difficult to separate from the puck down low as he protects the puck well and can create off the cycle. Jutting has a heavy and accurate shot but doesn't get it off his tape very quick so there is certainly room for growth in this part of his game. Jutting has shown the willingness to drive the net off the rush, both with the puck and without and competes for ice when in the slot area. Jutting shows good awareness and competes at both ends of the ice and is an effective penalty killer. Jutting is able to read and anticipate plays at the top of the penalty kill and shows the willingness to sacrifice his body and block shots. Jutting is a player that doesn't off the page in any specific area of his game but does a lot of things right on a night in night out basis to help his team. Jutting is a Colorado College commit down the road, but it sounds like Jutting plans on playing out his senior season with Prior Lake next season as well as seeing some time in the USHL. Jutting was drafted by Cedar Rapids (USHL) in the 5th Round in the 2017 Futures Draft.

2	PLAYER	TEAM	LEAGUE	HEIGHT	WEIGHT	POS	GRADE
	KAKKO, KAAPO	TPS	FIN	6'2.25"	194 *	RW	A
	HOCKEY SENSE	COMPETE		SKILL		SKATING	
	8	9		8		7	

Kaapo kakko had a historic season while playing for TPS in Liiga, producing 38 points in 45 games, including 22 goals, which beat out the previous record set by Alexander Barkov in 2012-2013. He carried over his successful season by scoring 5 points in 5 playoff games before joining the World Championships where he produced 7 points in 10 games with 6 goals Kakko also secured the gold-medal for Finland at the U20's in Vancouver by scoring the golden goal while producing 5 points in 7 games.

Kakko is the most versatile forward featured in this class and as a result is the most dangerous forward when attacking from around the goal-line. The main attribute that contributes to his dominance along the boards and towards the net-area, is the same attribute that distinguishes him from everyone else. Simply put, Kaapo's puck protection skill-set is elite. There's several different criteria when breaking down a players ability to guard the puck, but it begins with his overall anticipation. Kakko is a cerebral player with some of the highest-end hockey-sense in this class; giving him the ability to identify and adapt to opposing defenses by anticipating lanes, body-positioning, active-sticks, pressure, plus the time and space he has to make a play. The end result, is that he's capable of reading opposing team defenses faster than they can read him in most instances. After identifying his options by thinking two-steps ahead, Kakko has the necessary physical-tools to take advantage. He's a naturally large and powerful kid, yet has a tremendous amount of escapeability given his stature. This is due to the most pronounced aspects of his skating, which is a combination of his agility and his balance. His elusiveness isn't just a by-product of his anticipation and his athleticism though. There's a sixth-sense to his game when identifying how he can use his leverage to his advantage after initiating physical-contact. When posturing back-on to his opponents, Kakko can dynamically react to their resistance. As an example, if he tosses his frame into a player whose either attempting to drive him into the boards or keep him to the outside, their reaction is to usually push back aggressively. This gives him an opportunity to redistribute his weight by using his edges which shifts them off-balance. This results in him maneuvering out of tight-areas, manipulating skating lanes while driving through heavy traffic, and coming away with the puck during physical sequences at a high-rate. It sounds like a secondary-trait, but for Kakko it defines him. It allows him the opportunity to force teams to play heavy minutes against him, which in a playoff series is critical. He can't just rely on his frame, so it doesn't hurt that he has an excellent set of hands. He uses a slightly shorter-stick which counter-intuitively works in his favour during moments where he's protecting the puck, since he's adept at deking in-tight to his body and is very strong on the puck. His hands extend his move-set in conjunction with his agility, allowing him to make side-step moves while handling the puck in transition. The skills highlighted above come together to form a player that's very hard to read. Kakko's hockey sense blends into his craftiness, leaving defenders without a lot of options when attempting to shutdown his game. What's even more frustrating for opposing players, is that when they do shutdown Kakko by reading his intentions correctly, he has the ability to recover through his compete, keeping the play alive in the process. There's an argument to be made that Kakko has the highest-rate of recovery out of any forward in this class. His recovery rate blends into his ability to magnetize to the puck; he's almost always around the puck in the offensive-zone, remaining consistently engaged.

Although Kakko is a great transitional player since he can identify the flow of the game at a very high-level, he's not as good in this area as Jack. Hughes is the superior-skater who has an unmatched efficiency to his stride. Kakko isn't as technically gifted a skater which causes him to come out of the gate slower and lacks the same separating gear that Hughes presents. That being said, he still has impressive overall skating with room to develop further. Another area where Hughes has an advantage is within his ability to find trailing teammates. Kakko is an exceptional playmaker like Hughes, but doesn't have the same-level of sense for trailing options. This could be attributed to how often Jack leads the rush and his pass-first mentality. Despite Hughes having the slight playmaking advantage, as well as the speed advantage, he lacks the shooting advantage. Kakko is a far more dangerous shooter from the hash-marks area and out. The significant difference between their shots is within regards to how they generate torque within their release. Kaapo's stick looks like it's going to break in-half on some shot attempts due to how much whip is generated as he bears down through the release point. This allows him to mask his shooting mechanics better than Hughes who has to rely on fully-extending himself through a shot-motion. The static body-posture of Kakko gives him a more deceptive release point, and the torque on his release allows him to generate a velocity that Jack's wrist-shot can't. This extends into their slapshots as well, giving Kaapo the advantage from a stationary position. As a result, Kakko is the more significant duel-threat option at this time. Hughes played his season on the program which didn't force him to develop his game away from the puck to the degree it did for Kakko. In Kakko's case, this was his first experience playing against men for a full season in Liiga. The end result, is that he learned how to be responsible while defending, where Jack could get away with a lot more due to the quality of competition being lower. So as of now, Kakko is the more developed 200-foot player. Despite their differences, there's mental aspects to both players that are very similar as well. Both have a take-over mentality that's necessary to drive-play and a confidence to their games that can't be taught. Though, the way they take games over is very different. Jack relies on his rapid gear-shifts to create a quick-strike offense, where Kakko imposes a heavy, yet varied-attack. Lastly, they're both intense competitors who keep a very good pace, but it's Kakko who will be the more effective player if neither one is producing during a game, since there's a physical element to his game that Hughes doesn't have.

Hughes had the top-spot in our rankings all season, but as the year progressed, Kakko not only closed the gap but made the first-overall spot a decision we were forced to spend much more time on than we would've predicted back in August. In January one of our Scouts moved Kakko to #1 on his list. In March another Scout joined him. Overall, we project Kakko to be a dynamic-first-line-winger who can help alter any franchise; it helps that he's also NHL-ready and doesn't' need further time before stepping into the show.

"You need to factor in the reality of the situation. New Jersey is an American team, they are not going to pass on the U.S kid who happens to be the media consensus #1 pick for a guy in Finland. Kakko is a stud but he's going second overall." - NHL scout, April 2019

"Pick Hughes (first overall) and be wrong and everyone on the planet was picking him so you're fine. Pick Kakko first and be wrong and you are fired. Easy decision." - NHL Scout, May 2019

"Hughes is a Center and Kakko showed at the Five Nations he can't play Center. Hughes goes first overall." NHL Scout, May 2019

"I haven't seen Kakko as much as you but I'd put Byram at #2 if I were you. You'll look smart in the end." OHL Scout, May 2019

"Two of our Scouts had Kakko ahead of Hughes but all the others had Hughes." - NHL Scout, May 2019

"Only two of our Scouts had Kakko number one overall. Wouldn't be enough if we had the first pick." - NHL Scout, May 2019

"Pretty sure only one of our guys had Kakko (over Hughes) - NHL Scout, May 2019

"He can play the game anyway he wants, it gives him an unmatched-level of adaptability" - HP Scout, Brad Allen, May 2019

"I feel like finding true power forwards is getting to be a more difficult task and when you find one it makes him more valuable. Kakko adds a ton to any teams roster. - HP Scout, Mark Edwards, April 2019

"Two of our Scouts have Kakko first overall. One since January and the other Scout since April. It's not making my decision on who to put first overall any easier, especially since Kakko plays the style of game I love." - HP Scout, Mark Edwards, April 2019

34	PLAYER	TEAM	LEAGUE	HEIGHT	WEIGHT	POS	GRADE
	KALIYEV, ARTHUR	HAMILTON	OHL	6'1.25"	190 *	RW	B
	HOCKEY SENSE		COMPETE		SKILL		SKATING
	7		4		8		5

Arthur Kaliyev had one of the best statistical draft eligible OHL seasons in recent memory. He became the 13th player in OHL history to record 50 goals as a 17-year-old. He is also the first Hamilton player to eclipse 100 points in a season and finished the year with the most shots on net in the OHL. He finished the regular season with 102 points in 67 regular season games, and 2 points in 4 playoff games.

Kaliyev has arguably the best shot in this draft class. He uses a longer-stick which allows him to gain additional torque on his release point, he's also highly coordinated and fluid when rotating his hips; this allows him to take poor passes in-tight to his skates, yet still find the angle necessary to bury the puck in one-motion. This ability made him dangerous on the powerplay, where he was capable of shooting the puck off passes that were difficult to handle. When he's shooting the puck after settling it on his blade, he has impressive-hands that allow him to suddenly shift the angle and allows him to extend his toe-drags into his shot. Furthermore, Arthur isn't a finesse shooter, it's primarily the amount of velocity he generates with his whip-like release, combined with his hockey-sense as a shooter that has led to his prolific scoring pace. Kaliyev identifies seams on opposing goalies very quickly and looks to over-power the puck past-them. Due to the amount of power he generates on his release, this made him one of the most threatening players from the hashmarks out. Though, near the front of the net, he was equally as dangerous, using his plus offensive-awareness to find soft-ice, while also showing the ability to fake his intentions with the puck on his stick before attempting wrap-arounds in-tight to the net, as well as cutting from the goal-line and elevating the puck quickly on the short-side. Arthur can score in multiple-ways and requires very little time and space to take advantage of his offensive-gifts. Lastly, he's a duel-threat player. It's rare to find a player who can shoot the puck like he can, yet isn't a prospect we would label as having tunnel-vision. He sees the ice pretty well, identifies his passing lanes quickly, and can make accurate and sharp passes. This was most pronounced on the powerplay, where he threaded soft-passes towards the goal-line consistently.

As good as Kaliyev is when he has the puck on his stick, he's equally as bad without the puck. We seek prospects who can blend their offensive-skill set with their compete-level. In Kaliyev's case, there are entire games where you can rank his compete as very-poor. Far too often, we have seen Kaliyev fail to forecheck effectively, or recognize when he needs to play with more urgency and pace. When we evaluate players we would want to draft, we ask ourselves, how will their game translate when the intensity-level increases during the playoffs? The answer as of today, is that Kaliyev would be a liability on the ice and someone who would require sheltered minutes. Another glaring flaw in Kaliyev's game is his skating mechanics. He skates upright and doesn't generate a lot of power due to a lack of a deep knee-bend which causes him to produce a heavy-stride. His edges can be hit or miss, sometimes inadvertently throwing himself off-balance. His cross-over mechanics are average due to a lack of fluidity, but once he gets up to his top-gear, it can look average to poor depending on the shift and the game. Which leads back to his compete-level and pace; Arthur's skating doesn't translate on paper to the ice. Which suggests there's more skating ability than he's shown, but it also suggests that there's a severe lack of effort as well.

Kaliyev is a great offensive-talent, capable of scoring highlight-reel goals, whose ceiling is a first-line forward who can slot in on a top powerplay. However, due to his compete-level and skating ability, we see Arthur as a player who's going to have to be given favourable match-ups and sheltered minutes. It's unlikely he will be able to drive a line and will need to be paired with the right teammates who can take advantage of his shot. He's going to have to reinvent himself away from the play in order to come close to maximizing his offensive potential.

"Skating is weak and he didn't show a whole lot of effort. Not a good showing out there" (Hlinka) - NHL Scout, August 2018

"He had three goals in five games and I still didn't like his game there (Hlinka). That tells me a lot." - NHL Scout, August 2018

"USA coaches didn't give me great reviews about him after that tourney. (Hlinka)" - NHL Scout, August 2018

"I've seen him three times so far and I don't really need to see him anymore because his game doesn't change." NHL Scout, November 2018

"He plays the same game as Pavel Brendl, weak skater, doesn't compete but scores a ton. Brendl had 60 plus goals in his draft year."(it was 73 goals) -NHL Scout, December 2018

"I check our spot in the standings and rank him him below that." - NHL Scout, January 2019

"His testing results at the Top Prospects game reminded me why I don't put any stock into the (on ice) testing at that crappy game." - NHL Scout, January 2019

"He can play on an NHL powerplay right now." - NHL Scout, January 2019

"How about the testing results in Red Deer....so basically they told us Kaliyev can skate and Suzuki can't. Got it. What a joke." - NHL Scout, February 2019

"I put zero stock into that testing (Top Prospects Game) Look at Kaliyev. They might want to think about doing a test that makes them skate for more than 10 seconds. There is a reason few scouts even bother attending the testing anymore." - NHL Scout, February 2019

"He's Pavel Brendl. The _____(named another team) can have him." - NHL Scout, February 2019

"Kaliyev does what others don't do and that F***ing score." NHL Scout, March 2019

"He actually looked like he gave a crap in my last viewing but it's too little and too late for me. He won't be a _____(his team)" - NHL Scout, March 2019

"At least his skating is better than (Matt) Strome's." - NHL Scout, March 2019

"I have him behind Tomasino, Rees, Harley, Suzuki, McMichael, Robertson, Kolyachonok, Okhotyuk and the goalie." - NHL Scout, March 2019

"No motor, no pace of play, only plays in spurts when he thinks he might be able to score. He doesn't engage physically...guys like him drive me nuts. So much talent but too much risk for me." NHL Scout, April 2019

"50 goals and 50 assists on sh** team. You can't forget about that, it needs to have some weight on your ranking. I even saw him work hard on a few shifts in one of my last viewings. I saw him drive the net." - NHL Scout, May 2019

"I don't think I've been more uninterested in a player who can score the way he can. You can tell me that he can improve his compete-level, but I'm still waiting for Alex Semin to translate his talent-level and give a crap on a shift." - HP Scout, Brad Allen

"Nobody denies his ability to score goals, it's elite ability. I just don't like the lack of compete in his game and it also translates to his skating. I've coached at the Junior level and one thing that always frustrated me was players who played a lazy game with selective compete. I had my share of them over the years and they always hurt our team." - HP Scout, Mark Edwards, March 2019

"I got some poor feedback from a few scouts during combine week regarding his interviews." - HP Scout, Mark Edwards, June 2019

NR	PLAYER	TEAM	LEAGUE	HEIGHT	WEIGHT	POS	GRADE
	KALLIONKIELI, MARCUS	SIOUX CITY	USHL	6'2.25"	193 *	LW	C
	HOCKEY SENSE	COMPETE		SKILL		SKATING	
	5	4		6		6	

Rangy winger who holds some degree of intrigue because he seems pretty far from a finished product. The Finnish import went from a complete unknown to scoring ten goals in his first nine USHL games as a rookie, which started the roller coaster ride in terms of his perception. One thing that Kallionkieli has had is linemates – he regularly saw time with Martin Pospisil, Bobby Brink, and Parker Ford, some of the premier names in the USHL. He did put that time to good use by potting 29 goals in 58 games. He was used on the left side of the power play (despite being a left-handed shot) at times and down near the post at other times. However, he did not factor much into the zone entry strategy at even strength or with the man advantage. He can place his shots pretty well, but it's not a bullet or at all overpowering. He gets around the ice well with his long, almost exaggerated stride. He can withstand contact despite his still somewhat lanky, but athletic frame.

There isn't too much about Marcus's game that is consistent though, from his skating, to his defensive play, to his offensive prowess, to his work rate…nothing seems the same from the night before. There are games where he is only slightly effective on the forecheck and then doesn't really participate defensively. Then there are games where he's coming back hard pickpocketing players in the neutral zone. Offensively, especially earlier in the season, he would try to take on some guys on the rush – as the season wore on, he settled in to being the late, third-layer winger who is just trying to get a shot through. Some viewings saw him always be the first player off the ice from his line and never really get engaged, while others saw him really working. He is not effective along the boards no matter what game he's playing though. His hockey sense is no better than average and he displays a fair bit of tunnel vision with the puck on his stick. He cannot reliably slow up and make plays against the grain or across multiple lanes. He wants to play the game as fast as he can regardless of the situation. He ends up being in a hurry, but sometimes with no place to go. It's an interesting mix of athleticism and potential, but ultimately, it's hard to see what he could do for an NHL team, that game seems like it will be too fast for him.

"He made my list but I think he really rode the coattails of Brink and Pospisil." - NHL Scout, March 2019

"The production is there, but I think you have to ask yourself what will he really be able to do in an NHL game?" - HP Scout, Michael Farkas

"I started high on this kid, he came over here with a lot of hype in the scouting community and he performed early but the more I watched the more I started to like him less and less, too many plays die on his tape but he can shoot it, I'll give him that." HP Scout, Dusten Braaksma, April 2019

"I got some poor interview reports from scouts at the combine." HP Scout, Mark Edwards, June 2019

NR	PLAYER	TEAM	LEAGUE	HEIGHT	WEIGHT	POS	GRADE
	KALMIKOV, BROOKLYN	CAPE BRETON	QMJHL	5'11.75"	165 *	LC	ND
	HOCKEY SENSE	COMPETE		SKILL		SKATING	
	5	5		6		6	

After a solid first season in the QMJHL where he amassed 36 points in 58 games, it was a more disappointing season this year for the young winger, as his production regressed. He scored 19 times and collected 29 points total. Kalmikov was a surprise performer as a 16-year-old rookie last year, but didn't live up to the hype this year.

Kalmikov is a good skater who generates some decent speed, and he's also strong on his skates. He's continuing to get stronger each year; he was less than 150 pounds in his QMJHL draft year and has put on at least 15-20 pounds since he got drafted by the Screaming Eagles. He's a good athlete with a good skill level, quick hands and an above-average shot. He can score with his great wrist shot, but he doesn't use it enough. This year, he had 104 shots in 61 games compared to 105 shots in 58 games last year. Offensively, he could be more dangerous and successful if he would take more shots on net. He's agile on his feet, can be dangerous one-on-one with his quick hands and a quick burst of speed to beat defensemen wide. His on-ice vision is average, as he doesn't always see the best option in front of him. His decision-making is also average at best, which can explain his low assist numbers this year. Defensively, he'll never be known as a defensive forward or specialist, but he did make some nice strides this year in that department. He's versatile, can play all three forward positions, and took over 450 faceoffs this year (49% success rate). He needs to improve his compete level and consistency. These two areas of his game will be key if he wants to produce more in the QMJHL, and next season will be huge for him. Kalmikov is talented and should get drafted based on his skill level, but his poor season is going to hurt him.

"The kid has skills but his lack of production in the QMJHL is an issue, with his talent level you need to produce in this league" - HP Scout Jérôme Bérubé

NR	PLAYER	TEAM	LEAGUE	HEIGHT	WEIGHT	POS	GRADE
	KARLSTROM, DAVID	AIK JR.	SWE-JR.	6'1.0"	187	LC	ND
	HOCKEY SENSE	COMPETE		SKILL		SKATING	
	6	5		4		5	

Karlström is a defensive, third line center for AIK U20 in the SuperElite league. In 41 games he put up 9 goals and 11 assists on a team that was a big, positive surprise during the regular season. He also played 3 games with his club's U18 team and had 2 points in 3 games.

Karlström plays with great maturity and thinks the game quite well. Every move seems to be calculated and thought out beforehand. He does a good job at standing in the right defensive lane and is quite responsible in the defensive zone. When he gets control of the puck, he easily distributes it to the wings with speed. He can struggle at times with transporting the puck up ice but given time he does a good job with that as well. His skating needs much improvement. His stride is long and he gets decent power but his technique isn't good and his foot speed needs significant improvement. The biggest downside to his game is that he totally lacks offense. Even though his stickhandling is average and he can control the puck well while skating under pressure, he won't be a big threat to the opposing goaltender. His shot is very weak, the velocity below average and most of his shots end up in the stomach of the goaltender. He has the ability to make some good offensive passes but mostly arrives as the third forward over the blueline. He will more than likely end up in front of the net battling defenders to create space for his linemates with a more explosive offensive skill set than him.

	PLAYER	TEAM	LEAGUE	HEIGHT	WEIGHT	POS	GRADE
NR	KASTELIC, MARK	CALGARY	WHL	6'3.5"	213 *	RC	**ND**
	HOCKEY SENSE		COMPETE		SKILL		SKATING
	5		6		5		5

A 1999 Born, Kastelic made a major breakthrough this season. Kastelic lead the Hitmen in goals with 47 and points with 77 while serving as the teams captain. Kastelic was a WHL Eastern Conference second team all-star.

Kastelic is a big power winger who plays a physical style. Offensively Kastelic's game revolves around a heavy wristlet that he was adept at using after muscling his way in to a dangerous area, beating multiple goals with his shot. Kastelic was an excellent goalscorer this season as well in part due to his willingness to get to the dirty areas around the net. Kastelic has enough speed for the WHL level but his lack of agility will make it harder to make an impact as he moves up a level. Kastelic also lacks high end senses and hockey IQ, getting tunnel vision while barrelling in to the zone on occasion. Kastelic brings a major physical element to his game, playing a tough in your face style of game and using his big body to deliver punishing checks. Next season Kastelic will be dominant as an overager if he is back in the WHL.

	PLAYER	TEAM	LEAGUE	HEIGHT	WEIGHT	POS	GRADE
NR	KEMP, BRETT	MEDICINE HAT	WHL	6'0.5"	162*	RC	**ND**
	HOCKEY SENSE		COMPETE		SKILL		SKATING
	5		6		5		6

Kemp had an eventful season this year while having a breakout in the midst of playing for two teams. Kemp recorded 60 points in 64 games spread between the Edmonton Oil Kings and Medicine Hat Tigers. In both locations he played high in the lineup and on the powerplay.

Kemps best asset right now is his skating, with the ability to quickly jet up ice and good use of lateral crossovers. Kemp is deceptive skating through the neutral zone and combines that ability with quick hands allowing him to gain the zone easily. Kemp also possesses an above average shot with a quick release that allowed him to score 33 goals this season. Kemp showed growth defensively after moving to Medicine Hat where he played with strong positioning and effort. Kemp's IQ is average and he still has room to improve on his offensive awareness in order to become an even better goalscorer. Kemp has the potential for a very big junior season next year.

	PLAYER	TEAM	LEAGUE	HEIGHT	WEIGHT	POS	GRADE
90	KEPPEN, ETHAN	FLINT	OHL	6'1.75"	214 *	LW	**C**
	HOCKEY SENSE		COMPETE		SKILL		SKATING
	6		6		5		5

Ethan Keppen was drafted 10th overall in the priority selection and lived up to his draft-position this past season. He was one of the leading players both on and off the ice for Flint, producing 30 goals and 59 points in 68 games. Despite his impressive output, he wasn't featured at any International events for Canada. Ethan is a two-way, power-forward who plays with a fearless approach. His best attribute is a mental-one, which is his compete-level; he thrives in the tough-areas on the ice and is at his best when attacking around the net area. His straight-ahead style of play forced defenseman to gravitate towards him which helped open up the ice for his linemates. He's not a high-end playmaker but has above-average anticipation away from the play which allows him to find soft-ice in heavy traffic, where he scored the majority of his goals in our viewings. He's not just a net-crasher though, he has above-average hands and can beat opponents one-on-one, however there will be a limit to how often he can challenge against pro-defenseman. Ethan's a powerful kid who has a good amount of velocity on his shots as a result, with a release point that hovers between average and above-average depending on the game. Where he will make his money is on the forecheck and during the penalty-kill though. He's shown a good defensive-presence and as a result, has generated takeaways at the defensive-line. His frame and willingness to physically engage made him an impressive forechecker as well. Where Ethan needs to clean up his game the most in order to translate, is within regards to his skating ability. His fluidity is a plus due to his balance and cross-over mechanics but his stride is short. It's going to be difficult for him to be an impactful forechecker and a penalty-kill specialist, if he can't create pressure with a further increase in his overall speed. If Keppen can improve his skating mechanics, then he can potentially develop into a checking line winger, who generates down-low and off the forecheck.

"Bad boots." - NHL Scout, December 2018

"Big fish in a small pond. I've made that mistake before. He won't make my list." January 2019

"Has size and he skates and he works but he's not without his warts." - NHL Scout, February 2019

"Poor hockey sense but when it comes to guys in the OHL this year, at least he looks the part of an NHL player." - NHL Scout, March 2019

"Decent player but he didn't make my list." - NHL Scout, May 2019

"Saw him more early before he got hot. When I saw him late his feet were a bit better than I remembered. Had him has a no draft for half the year but moved him to a 'C' rating in the second half." - HP scout, Mark Edwards

	PLAYER	TEAM	LEAGUE	HEIGHT	WEIGHT	POS	GRADE
NR	**KINDER, NINO**	**EISBAREN BER JR.**	**GER-JR.**	**6'0.0"**	**165 ***	**LC**	**ND**
	HOCKEY SENSE	COMPETE		SKILL		SKATING	
	5	5		5		5	

Kinder broke into the U19 DNL at 15 and has now played three seasons in the league. In 2018-19, he also made his pro debut, appearing in five DEL games for Eisbären Berlin. Coming into the DNL at a young age, hopes were always high for Kinder, but he hasn't been able to live up to the hype. He's developed into an excellent offensive player for German standards, leading the U18 national team with nine points in five games at the U18 Div. 1 A worlds, but nothing more.

Kinder is a shifty and agile skater with good hands, allowing him to carry the puck through the neutral zone and into the offensive zone. However, his stride lacks power, costing him speed. He has a nose for the net and strong awareness, frequently finding openings to move into for scoring chances, but his shot, while accurate, lacks power as well. Kinder plays a smart two-way game, as he's quick on the forecheck and backcheck and angles puck-carriers very well, but his offensive ability isn't where it needs to be if he wants to be considered an NHL prospect.

68	PLAYER	TEAM	LEAGUE	HEIGHT	WEIGHT	POS	GRADE
	KNIAZEV, ARTEMI	CHICOUTIMI	QMJHL	5'10.75"	176 *	LD	C
	HOCKEY SENSE	COMPETE		SKILL		SKATING	
	6	6		5		7	

This i   Kniazev was a key player in Chicoutimi's rebuilding year. The Saguenéens had a strong core of 16-year-old and 17-year-old players on their team. Kniazev came over from Russia after the Saguenéens drafted him this past June in the CHL Import Draft with the 9th overall pick.

An above-average skater, the young Russian defenseman likes to carry the puck from his own zone. Chicoutimi was a great place to play for him, as they play on a wider ice surface there. He likes to take advantage of the additional space on the ice that's available to him by rushing the puck as often as he can. He scored 10 of his 13 goals on home ice this season. He's quick to get the puck out of his zone, either by using his feet or making a quick passes in transition. His decision-making is quick; he has a good first pass out of his zone and he's very helpful for his team's transition game. Offensively, he creates a lot of plays with his skating abilities. He's quite active in the offensive zone, trying to create scoring chances for himself or a teammate. He scored 7 of his 13 goals on the power play this season. What he lacks in order to be considered a premiere offensive defenseman is that great on-ice vision, as his is only average. We would like to see him create more plays with his passing plays and vision. He's capable of making some high-end passing plays, but there's some inconsistency with him there. He's got a good wrist shot with good velocity and accuracy. He prefers using his wrist shot over his slapper, as there is a lot more accuracy and velocity with his wrist shot. He can contribute offensively, as shown with his 13 goals, but for an offensive defenseman in the QMJHL, his assist and point totals are a bit low (21 assists and 34 points). Defensively, he made some good strides this year. He looked a bit like a liability at the beginning of the season, but the more the season progressed, the more he was confident as a defender. He uses his good footwork well to retrieve pucks in his zone and he's quick to apply pressure on the puck-carrier entering his zone. Even if he's not big, he competes well along the boards and is unafraid. He won't ever be known as a physical defenseman, but at least he competes well along the boards and can dish out some hits here and there. His one-on-one defensive coverage has gotten better over the course of the season. He just needs to get stronger physically so that he can compete better versus bigger and stronger players along the boards and in front of the net. Kniazev has a lot of good things going for him, including good offensive potential and the fact that he is pretty mobile on the ice. Starting next season, he should be one of the top offensive defensemen in the QMJHL, playing on a good, young and talented team in Chicoutimi.

"No doubt he's the best D prospects out of the QMJHL this year. Playing on the big ice in Chicoutimi was a match made in heaven for him this year." - HP Scout Jérôme Bérubé

1	PLAYER	TEAM	LEAGUE	HEIGHT	WEIGHT	POS	GRADE
	KNIGHT, SPENCER	USA U-18	NTDP	6'3.0"	197 *	G	A
	HOCKEY SENSE	COMPETE		SKILL		SKATING	
	8	7		7		7	

Spencer Knight had a solid overall season for the USNTDP despite having some inconsistencies towards the second-half, finishing with a 2.36GAA and a .913 save percentage in 33 games within the program and a 2.21GAA and a .903 save percentage in 16 starts in the USHL. Although his play was average at the Five-Nations tournament in February, he stepped up and played well at the U18's, finishing with a 1.51GAA and a .936 save-percentage in 6 starts. He's slated to play for Boston College next season.

Knight is one of the more technically proficient goalies for his age group in recent years and is one of the most talented goalie prospects of the last couple of drafts. His biggest strength is a mental-one, specifically his ability to interpret dynamic offensive-plays in advance; it's rare for Knight to fall behind the play and he's excellent at recognizing backdoor passing-options. When he's evaluating what a player is going to do with the puck, he's adept at reading backhand options. For instance, we've seen Knight consistently evaluate different passing lanes correctly as a result of recognizing when a player slides his stick from a forehand to a backhand passing option while driving down the wing or attempting to cut out behind the net area while looking for an open-man. His tall stature allows him to read the point well by looking over screens, and he's very good at angling himself around-screens while remaining square to the shooter. Furthermore, he rarely over-commits when interpreting passing-angles by reading the space of the puck before it hits a shooter. Another plus mental attribute of Knight is his ability to interpret shooting angles, specifically from high-danger areas that require him to take the bottom part of the net away. The above mental attributes give Spencer a significant presence whose calm and composed demeanor could be felt when evaluating him.

If there was one area of concern with his mental approach, it was the following; as the season progressed, one of his better strengths which was his ability to remain engaged in games for extended periods of inaction dissipated. There were several games in the first couple of months of the season where Knight was inactive but then was forced to make a high-danger save, yet he did so successfully. However, as the season progressed, Knight lost focus at times and as a result let in some very poor goals. We consider Knight a goalie who can brush off a bad goal and recover quickly from a bad showing but his confidence did regress in the second-half. This resulted in one of his better attributes, which is his ability to contain himself in the net by rarely over-committing becoming a double-edged sword. When Knight is on his game, his lack of aggression plays to his advantage for the most part, yet when he's lost his confidence, he has a tendency to misplay his shooting angles by not cutting off the angle as rapidly as he should. This was most noticeable when wingers were driving down the right-wing and shooting on Knights blocker-side. That being said, Knight was in a unique spot as a goalie since he was on the best team in junior hockey. This resulted in him not getting large shot volumes and having to remain focused when games were out of reach for their opponents by the midway point at times, which is not an easy task for a young netminder.

His level of inactivity leads to our next impressive attribute for Knight which most likely developed as a by-product of needing to come up with creative ways to stay active in the net when his team was dominating games. That skill-set is his stick-handling. Knight is arguably one of the most impressive stick-handlers we've ever seen at his age for his position. In today's game, it can't be understated how much of an impact a good puck-handling goalie can have when mitigating the forecheck and generating transitional play through stretch-passes. His stick-work and hockey-sense aside, Knight also features some very impressive technical and athletic ability. When we evaluate goalies, we give them a height to reflexes ratio and Knights is excellent. He's a big kid who has the ability to dynamically react to high-danger shots directly in-front of him as a result of his reaction-time. This trait matches well with his high-compete level which allows him to make high-end recovery and secondary saves. Though secondary saves aren't very common for Knight due to his impressive technical butterfly. He rarely presents any seam for a shooter when falling into his butterfly and is good at absorbing pucks in it. Furthermore, when he is on his knees, he keeps his posture and rarely shrinks when challenging a shooter which allows him to use his shoulders to deflect high-shots. That being said, Knight is better at taking the lower part of the net away then he is at taking the top-part. This is largely due to his ability to fully extend his legs which makes it very difficult to wrap the puck around him. His blocker hand has good technical rebound control, where he has shown the ability to angle his elbow 90-degrees parallel to the ice which lets him deflect pucks away from the net or absorb them enough so that they drop directly in-front of him. His glove-hand is solid but it's not as high-end as some of his other attributes. Part of this has to do with his stance, where he keeps his glove somewhat low but that can be corrected over time through development. His overall stance is a modern-day stance used for improved mobility; meaning it's somewhat narrow and he stands more upright. This allows him to gain traction when moving laterally during cross-ice saves so he can push off with more power. Knight is a good skater who can make rapid adjustments that allow him to error-correct when he does misinterpret the initial release point on a shot as well. The last area regarding his skating is his ability to use edges properly when integrating into his post from a reverse-VH. The allows him to seamlessly come out of his reverse-VH and into his butterfly which was important when dealing with passes that came from behind the net and were directed towards the crease area. Lastly, Knight rarely let in soft-short-side goals in our viewings due to his ability to seal off the post consistently.

Overall, the above technical attributes, athletic traits, and mature mental approach allowed Knight to develop into a fluid goaltender who was consistently composed, yet had the ability to react dynamically to difficult shots. Spencer Knight is one of the most developed goalies for his age in a long time, and although he didn't have as good a season as his abilities suggest he could have had, we still believe that he has the making of an above-average number one goalie in the NHL if he can maintain a more consistent level of play. We'd be willing to select him somewhere in the 2nd round.

"Suzuki is sliding, Lavoie has not been good at all. This kid is going to go higher than a lot of people think because too many other players are sucking." - NHL Scout, January 2019

"The more you watch him the more you realize it's not an accident that he's this good. He's tenth on my list." - NHL Scout, January 2019

"Goalies on good teams have always scared me." - OHL Staffer, January 2019

"Everywhere I dig he comes up smelling like a rose. Character and work ethic to match his ability on the ice. Love the way he plays the puck too. he can stop it and pass it." - NHL Scout, January 2019

"Fantastic interview. ten outta ten." - NHL Scout, January 2019

"I've already interviewed him and it was one of the better interviews I've done." - NHL Scout, January 2019

"I think he's unbelievable. Once the slam dunk skaters are gone and different teams will have different opinions of where that happens on their lists, I think this kid goes (gets picked)." - NHL Scout, January 2019

"I think he's easily a first rounder and I'd project him to be a future starter in the NHL." NHL Scout, April 2019

"He'll be gone by pick 20." - NHL Scout, April 2019

"I thought he had a good season. He thinks the game so well and that is what allows him to be so good." - NHL Scout, April 2019

"Having to assess a goalie on the program which was essentially an all-star team was challenging, and it led to far more projection by the end of the process than we were hoping." - HP Scout, Brad Allen

"I got plenty of good reviews but I also got a couple of poor reviews from Scouts on their interviews with him. I didn't speak to him." - HP Scout, Mark Edwards, June 2019

	PLAYER	TEAM	LEAGUE	HEIGHT	WEIGHT	POS	GRADE
3	KOCHETKOV, PYOTR	RYAZAN	RUS-2	6'3.0"	205	G	**B**
	HOCKEY SENSE		COMPETE		SKILL		SKATING
	7		8		6		6

Pyotr Kochetkov had some time in the spotlight by taking the starting role at the World-Junior U20's after getting passed over in the previous two-drafts. He played on an average-team in the MHL which put him under-the-radar but this season was different for him. In 5 games, he finished with a .953 save-percentage and a 1.45GAA which earned him the award for best goalie of the tournament, and put him on the map internationally. In league games, he played for HK Ryazan of the VHL, finishing with a .930 save-percentage and a 2.13 GAA in 18 games, and in the playoffs continued his success, finishing with a .955 save-percentage and 1.61GAA in 3 starts. He also ended up getting experience at the highest Russian-level in the KHL, playing two games with HK Sochi. He was traded to SKA St. Petersburg where he will be fighting for a backup job in the KHL starting next season.

Kochetkov is a cerebral – blocking style – netminder, who relies on his consistent-focus to interpret plays dynamically around the goal-line, that sets himself apart from most of the other goalies available. He's a massive-goalie, whose broadness compliments his height, and he takes up a tremendous amount of the net when he cuts down an angle properly. Pyotr rarely shrinks in his net which allows him to take full-advantage of his frame. He relies on his size since his reflexes are good but not excellent. We prefer more reflexive netminder's, since we identify them having a higher probability of making it to the show, but Pyotr is gifted at reading high-percentage shots in advance that's put him in the conversation with some of the other top-goalies available. When he reads the play properly, there's very little to shoot at and he relies on keeping tight-seams in all his technical positions, ranging from his reverse-VH when he integrates with his post, to pushing across in his butterfly; this allows him to absorb pucks in his frame at a very-high-rate, showing solid rebound control. There were few goals that were the result of his technique breaking in terms of keeping himself sealed-up. This was most pronounced on his blocker-side; he's excellent at moving into a shots trajectory while angling his elbow and blocker so that he can absorb the puck and have it fall in-front of him or have it deflected into the corner. It's rare to see him have to extend his blocker-outwards, this speaks volumes to how efficient he can be at interpreting angles when the shooter is aiming far-side on his blocker when coming down the right-wing. Kochetkov is the best goalie in this class at breaking his own-technique when he misidentifies an initial play-type and requires a secondary-save; we've seen him toss his stick out of the play and enter a "swimming-mode" where he uses his frame and limbs to try and come away with a high-end recovery-save off his back. His poise and panic-threshold are second-to-none on recovery save attempts; this isn't to be mistaken for what looks like chaotic movements around his crease area. Although he looks like he's lost in the crease during second and third shot attempts at times, there's a calculated approach and he's unyielding in the net, showing a very high-compete level. His compete-level blends into his net-presence; there's a calming effect when he's in net regardless of how he makes certain desperation-saves. One of the primary reasons for this, is due to the fact that he makes the initial read properly most of the time. The most important aspect of his reads and what really stood out for us, was his ability to make reads dynamically on high-skilled players around his goal-line. The main attribute that allows him to follow quick-stick motions and interpret his shooting-angle in-tight rapidly is his processor; which allows him to track-pucks at an excellent-rate.

Kochetkov has some very interesting attributes that have already helped him translate against men, but to play in the NHL, there's certain aspects of his game that need further developing. Although he's very-good at interpreting angles on opponents shooting from the right-wing and slot-area, he specifically has trouble identifying his shooting angle when shots are labelled towards his glove-side, when a player is shooting on his left-wing. He tends to over-commit on the short-side, which gives a shooter a lot of room to work with on the far-side with his glove-hand. Pyotr has flashed an above-average glove when we've seen him, but his tendency to misidentify this specific angle needs to be corrected if he doesn't want it to be exploited by top-shooters. Although, his stance is very good for creating a tight-seal in his butterfly quickly and his glove is kept-low; this does allow him to create a secondary seal when he's extending his left-pad since he has his glove attached to it, taking away the bottom part of the net when shooters do aim for the far-side when coming down the left-wing. This does help compensate for his misreads. Kochetkov, like other top-Russian goalies has good skating mechanics and his narrow stance allows him to push off-correctly, but this is where his lack of high-end athleticism troubles us. Specifically, when he does over-commit on an initial shot, his push-off isn't very explosive. That's not to say he isn't fluid, he is; Kochetkov is a coordinated netminder. but there's a lack of fast-twitch that accompanies the initial push-off, that leaves him without the extension needed when he does mis-assess shots that require a lot of movement laterally across the crease. However, he's able to reach post-to-post with his legs when sitting in the net and this does allow him to still make high-end saves after a lateral-pass in-tight to him, just not at the level required for him to make difficult lateral saves in the NHL consistently enough as of writing this.

Although there's some concerns with Kochetkov misinterpreting a select-angle and lacking the explosive mobility needed; he still has a very-good physical and mental-package to work with. For these reasons, he's a goalie we would consider drafting and has the potential to backup a team at the NHL-level.

"I think someone steps up in the 2nd round to make sure they get him." - NHL Scout, February 2019

"Even though Jones has the superior athletic trait I look for, Kochetkov has a rare set of mental-tools that put him ahead of Jones athletic traits." - HP Scout, Brad Allen. May 2019

105	PLAYER	TEAM	LEAGUE	HEIGHT	WEIGHT	POS	GRADE
	KOKKONEN, MIKKO	JUKURIT	FIN	5'11.0"	198 *	LD	C
	HOCKEY SENSE		COMPETE		SKILL		SKATING
	6		6		5		5

Kokkonen had a solid season in the top men's league in Finland this year, with 19 points in 56 games for Jukurit. This was the 3rd-highest point total amassed by a U-18 defenseman in league history. He was a regular for Finland internationally at the U-18 level, playing good minutes for them at the Hlinka-Gretzky Cup and the more recent World Under-18 Hockey Championships. He also played at the U20 level for them in November, at the Four Nations' tournament in Russia.

Kokkonen has always been more physically advanced compared to his peers. When he was 15 years old, he played with the National U-17 team. When he was 16, he played with the National U-18 team. He has not grown much since he was 15 years old, as he was already 5'10" or close to 5'11" at that age. He always had that thick body frame that helps him in inferior levels when it comes to winning puck battles. However, the physical advantage he used to have over his peers is now gone, and he was surpassed by others such as Ville Heinola from his home country this year. He had a decent tournament in August (the Hlinka-Gretzky Cup in Edmonton); he did a good job advancing the puck and making quick decisions with it. We were critical of him last season in this regard. At the tournament he also showed a good ability to get his shot through to the net. In November, he played at the U-20 Four Nations' tournament in Russia instead of playing with the U-18 team at the Five Nations' tournament in the Czech Republic. It was an average tournament for him there; he was able to make good passes into transition, but really struggled with the pace of the game. He was beaten wide because of his poor footwork and caught flat-footed in the neutral zone. He also struggled when attempting to retrieve pucks quickly deep in his zone, once again due to his slow footwork. He did not make Team Finland for the World Junior Hockey Championships in December. At the last event of the year in Sweden for the World Under-18 Hockey Championships, Finland did not have a good tournament overall (with no Kaapo Kakko there to help them) but Kokkonen was a disappointment. He struggled with the pace of the game, and his decision-making was poor all tournament long. In league play, judging by his stats, he did well in terms of putting points on the board, but he's never going to be a big point-producer at the next level. What he did well in Liiga was playing a smart and effective game with the puck. He made a good safe pass out of his zone and made good decisions in the offensive zone. He's got a good shot from the point, and has that good ability to find shooting lanes to get it on net. He can score with his shot when keeping it low most of the time; it can either create rebound opportunities for his teammates or be tipped in front of the net. He's not an overly creative or flashy player with the puck, though. He has battled consistency issues all year from his Liiga play and international play (decision-making and quickness when moving pucks). He's not overly physical, even if he's a strong kid physically, but can lean on guys when he has to along the boards.

Kokkonen is a player whose numbers in Liiga are a bit odd for us, as they don't really represent the type of player we see. We see him as someone with limited potential; for example, at the U-18s in April, he didn't do much, and in some games he barely touched the puck or made any kind of impact. When you look at this development curve, it makes you wonder how much better he will become in the years ahead. He has peaked physically, and usually that's not necessarily good news for the development path of a player. The biggest drawback for us with Kokkonen: his skating abilities. They have not made a lot of progress in the last two seasons since we first saw him at the U-17s in 2016-2017. His footwork is average to decent, and he makes good use of his active stick to break up some plays in the defensive zone, but his lack of speed hurts him when rushing the puck or when he jumps into the play. He has trouble creating separation between himself and his coverage. In the years ahead, Kokkonen should continue to really work hard on improving his footspeed; it's going to be vital for him to do so in order to become a NHL player down the road. He's going to continue to be a solid player in the Liiga in the years ahead, and should be a strong candidate for Finland at the World Juniors' in the next two seasons.

	PLAYER	TEAM	LEAGUE	HEIGHT	WEIGHT	POS	GRADE
22	KOLYACHONOK, VLAD	FLINT	OHL	6'0.25"	176 *	LD	B
	HOCKEY SENSE	COMPETE		SKILL		SKATING	
	5	7		6		9	

Vladislav Kolyachonok was waived from London at the beginning of the season due to the arrival of Adam Boqvist and Matvei Guskov; giving Flint an opportunity to acquire him, where he became their most impactful player on the backend while playing in all situations. He finished the season with 29 points in 53 games, including 4 goals. At the World U18's, he produced 5 points in 5 games while captaining Belarus.

Kolyachonok is a mobile, two-way defender who plays with an edge. When breaking down the top skaters in this class; we view Kolyachonok as the best from the backend. His skating ability is elite and it starts with his mechanics. He has excellent posture that features proper leg extension, giving him a fluid heel-to-toe motion when stepping. When he takes off from a stand-still position, he looks weightless. When discussing short-bursts of acceleration, we describe it as two-step area quickness, but Vladislav has that rare one-step area quickness where he gains a lot of momentum in short order, making him look effortless when gear-shifting. His stride is so efficient that it doesn't break down regardless of the distance required; this gives him arguably the best recovery rate out of any defender in the draft. This aspect is critical to Kolyachonok specifically, since he does have mixed decision making depending on how dialed into the game he is. He can measure his options at a decent-level and has shown a good-rate of anticipation on most play-types but at times can make a decision that isn't warranted. For instance, on the powerplay, we've seen him rush his shooting-options by shooting a low-percentage shot off-angle when he could have just as easily held the puck and used his sublime skating to re-position himself; extending his options. This applies to the defensive-zone as well, where he can make errant pass attempts that require him to hustle back into position. Despite having average-decision-making at times, his compete-level synced well with his skating to counter-act the damage. In a draft that features several defensemen who rely primarily on their stick-work to defend; Kolyachonok has a good mix of physicality and an active-stick. He likes to initiate contact, and is willing to expend his gas-tank while competing along the boards. He might have an average-build, but he plays with a mean-streak and is a volatile defender at times in one-on-one battles. When he isn't engaging physically, he uses his impressive puck-tracking ability to close off lanes and gaps abruptly, using aggressive-stick-play to generate takeaways. One of the more impressive aspects to his compete-level, is his willingness to sacrifice his body away from the play. In our viewings, we've seen him come away with multiple shot-blocks in the same sequence and he is good at angling-himself correctly to deflect them. With the puck, Kolyachonok is an excellent transporting option due to his speed but doesn't prefer driving-play for extended periods. Instead, he looks for his highest-percentage passing option but his vision isn't always consistent. At the NHL-level it's more important to make a quality two-line pass from your own-end than skating it out but in Vladislav's case, he might have to rely on his skating ability which could leave him at a disadvantage depending on the play. Another factor when evaluating his transporting ability is his poise, which is above-average in most games. However, even when calm, he can still be prone to making errors around the goal-line under-pressure. That being said, his escapability is second-to-none which does give him a bit more time to further evaluate his options.

At the offensive-line, Kolyachonok has a good offensive-skill set but not one we would label as high-end. He looks to stutter-step while simultaneously pulling the puck from his backhand to his forehand to re-configure his options; but, he doesn't activate as often as he could, given his skating. There was a hesitancy to his game at times, not always looking confident enough to drive-play to the extend his tools should theoretically allow him to. That said, when he was playing for his international team, there was a more assertive approach to his game. When that assertiveness is present, he becomes more of a threat; using a plus wrist-shot that features above-average mechanics and a quick-release point. Although he can miss his passing options at times, we've seen him deliver some impressive passes as well in the offensive-zone, threading sharp passes through tight-seams. He's not going to make too many dynamic offensive-plays but he can contribute due to how efficiently he can re-open lanes and get his shot through traffic. Another area to note, is that he's a defender you can pair with a high-end offensive-defenseman, since his recovery is so impressive. This is important if his partner looks to activate a lot, since Kolyachonok has shown that he can defend against odd-man rushes properly. The question is how much untapped offensive potential is in Vladislav's game given his tools, and we think there could be more that hasn't surfaced yet due to the circumstances he plays under in the OHL. Flint is one of the weakest teams in the CHL let alone the OHL, and as a result, Kolyachonok doesn't get a lot of extended time with the puck on his stick offensively since his team is always on their heels.

There's an intriguing tool-kit to work with in Kolyachonok's game, but he's going to need the right development in order for it to blossom. If he can develop properly, then Kolyachonok can be a puck-moving, minute-eating defenseman that you can put on your top penalty-kill but he's probably unlikely to see much NHL powerplay-time.

"He struggles to stay between the dots and to be honest, I question his hockey sense. Too many instances this year that left me scratching my head." – NHL Scout, November 2018

"A lot of big hitters at some of his games recently. I think he may get drafted way earlier than I would be willing to take him." – NHL Scout, December 2018

"I saw him twice this week. He was good in one (game) and not good at all in the other. I'll need to see him more. This much I know, the kid can skate." – NHL Scout, December 2018

"I love the tools but I'm not sure about the brain. He makes some really bad plays with the puck and chases too often." – NHL Scout, January 2019

"He's a work in progress. He can skate but he hasn't got much better this season. Not sure I want to draft him if he's headed back to Flint next season." – NHL Scout, February 2019

"Do you really want to draft a player from Flint? All you need to do is watch Dellandrea this year and that should make the decision easier." – NHL Scout, February 2019

"He made some head scratching plays at times ...even when he had time, but one thing i love about him is his compete. He's got compete coming out his ears." – NHL Scout, May 2019

"I have faith in his game but his hockey sense is just ok. Upside is limited." NHL Scout, May 2019

"Looked great overseas on the big ice where he had a bit more time and space." – HP Scout, Mark Edwards, April 2019

"I spoke to him at the NHL Combine and was impressed." – HP Scout, Mark Edwards June 2019

	PLAYER	TEAM	LEAGUE	HEIGHT	WEIGHT	POS	GRADE
NR	KOPE, DAVID	EDMONTON	WHL	6'3.75"	170 *	RW	**ND**
	HOCKEY SENSE	COMPETE		SKILL		SKATING	
	4	5		5		5	

Kope is late 2000 born forward who has 2 WHL seasons under his belt. He didn't make much improvement statistically speaking this year, scored 14 goals for a second straight year and had 3 more points overall. He's a raw and rangy winger with decent skating ability and skills. The Edmonton native has some projectable abilities and occasionally looked like a force on the ice. Kope can sometimes look a bit sped up on the ice and looks like he cannot always process the play at high pace. He's more of a long term project because of his size and raw abilities. He's got to work on improving his decision making, his consistency and compete level. The size and skating combo is the most intriguing part about Kope potential as a pro.

	PLAYER	TEAM	LEAGUE	HEIGHT	WEIGHT	POS	GRADE
65	KORCZAK, KAEDAN	KELOWNA	WHL	6'2.75"	192 *	RD	**C**
	HOCKEY SENSE	COMPETE		SKILL		SKATING	
	6	7		5		6	

Korczak was the 11th overall selection in the 2016 WHL Draft. He came into the year as one of the leagues better prospects; he was solid but unspectacular with the Rockets finishing with 33 points in 68 games on a fairly low scoring team. He also played on Canada U-18 team this season in August at the Hlinka/Gretzky cup and this past April in Sweden at the World Under-18 hockey championship.

Korczak has the outline of a very good all-round defenseman. He skates very well for his size, occasionally demonstrating the ability to take the puck end to end with impressive speed through the neutral zone. Passing was his biggest weakness as he often missed open options, and wrong sided forwards and his partners on passes. Has an okay shot that he does a good job finding holes with, though he didn't always get himself in the best spots to use it. His hands and overall skill level do not really stand out. Korczak is very strong and a high compete player who displayed a lot of will to win. He's very good defensively with great range and mobility to stifle the opposition on the rush and contain offence's to the outside. He plays with a bit of a physical edge and was especially tough in front of the net.

"I'm not a big fan. He was very inconsistent and he lacks skill." – NHL Scout, January 2019

"I have a lot of time for him. He is a steady player and can eat minutes going forward." - NHL Scout, February 2019

"Just a steady reliable guy on the back end. I'll take guys like him every year." - NHL Scout, March 2019

"No real weakness and I think he's just scratching the surface. I see a lot of room to grow." - NHL Scout, March 2019

"I'm not nearly as high on him as most of the scouts I have spoken to about him. In fact a few gave me grief when I told them I'd draft Helleson before him. I don't dislike Korczak but there are plenty of defensemen I'd draft before him." - HP Scout, Mark Edwards, April 2019

	PLAYER	TEAM	LEAGUE	HEIGHT	WEIGHT	POS	GRADE
NR	KOSTER, MICHAEL	CHASKA	HIGH-MN	5'9.25"	171 *	LD	C
	HOCKEY SENSE		COMPETE		SKILL		SKATING
	6		6		7		5

Koster got off to a slow start to the season with Team USA at the Hlinka Gretzky Cup where he struggled in a couple of outings. His game never really got in a groove in that tournament and he struggled to find a roll with that squad. Koster's game started to take off about the midpoint of his season with Chaska HS where he finished 2nd on his team in points with 59 and 1st in assists with 40. Koster has always had excellent offensive ability but up until this year his interest and willingness to improve his defensive game hasn't been there. Koster started to turn a corner in regard to his all-around game and started to pay more attention to his play in his own end. Koster is not a physically imposing defenseman, either in regards to his size or style of play, much of his defense comes from him having the puck much of the time but Koster showed growth in his gap control as well as his willingness to compete below his own goal line and along the walls. While Koster has excellent east-west mobility and footwork his skating lacks some explosiveness off the hop, and he can be susceptible to being caught by speedy fore-checkers and forced into turnovers as a result. When Koster is rushing the puck, he can make things happen, he has quick hands and can make plays with pace through the neutral zone. He is very effective as he enters the offensive zone and knows how to create off the rush and can look like a forward with the puck in the offensive zone at times. Koster showed good versatility in running the power play both from the point and on the half-wall position. Does a good job getting into position to utilize his one-timer. Simply put, Koster is a creative playmaker in the offensive zone, uses head fakes and quick hands to open up lanes and uses the walls and the geometry of the rink well to get pucks where he needs to.

Koster finished the season with Tri-City this spring where he was forced to take on more of a stay at home shutdown role with the Storm due to their two defenseman Ronnie Attard and Zac Jones who really like to lead and join the rush up ice. Koster showed the ability to adapt and excel in this role and often was Tri-City's best defensive defenseman. If Koster can get stronger over the next few seasons at the University of Minnesota and his skating gains some explosiveness, Koster has the skill to be an effective puck moving defenseman at the next level.

"Thought he started to come on later in the year from a defensive perspective, but his overall pace needs to quicken." - HP Scout, Michael Farkas

"I think his game has matured in the last year or so, he is more than just a Power Play specialist now, needs to get a lot stronger but there is enough talent there for me." HP Scout, Dusten Braaksma

"I have time for him but his skating is subpar for me at his size. He's a later round pick for me at best" – HP Scout, Mark Edwards, January 2019

92	PLAYER	TEAM	LEAGUE	HEIGHT	WEIGHT	POS	GRADE
	KRANNILA, JAMI	SIOUX FALLS	USHL	5'10.0"	160 *	LC	C
	HOCKEY SENSE	COMPETE		SKILL		SKATING	
	6	5		6		6	

Quick and industrious, two-way center. Krannila brings a complete, 200-foot game to the table on a nightly basis. He developed in the Tappara junior system, but only played in five career games at the highest junior level before embarking on his North American hockey career. His hockey IQ and his quickness combine to make him a highly effective forechecker and backchecker. His first couple steps see him flying off the blocks and his top speed is really strong to boot. Despite playing at the pace that he does, we seldom ever see him overplay the game or over-skate situations. His angles and body position are definite pluses. He has shown the propensity to up his defensive game, even against elite talent. In particular, his ability to routinely sniff out fanciful USNTDP attacks in a February matchup really showed his worth as a two-way talent at this level. We would surmise that very few USHL players can claim they have skated end line to end line with purpose as much as Krannila did this season. His work rate is infectious and he doesn't back down from a battle. Despite his rather slight frame and low center of gravity that makes him look even smaller on the ice, the Finn fights his own battles out there. He regularly finishes hits and doesn't mind mixing it up after whistles if the situation calls for it. He's a feisty bugger.

Definitely more of a playmaker than a shooter, Krannila was relied upon to be a puck carrier from the center ice position as his linemates were not able to advance the puck over a line consistently. His skill level is above average, but it's unlikely that he'll be able to beat players one-on-one at the pro level without having built up a significant amount of speed first. The shot is not threatening and he doesn't seem to own any go-to finishing moves. His stick is maybe a little too long for his own good, which may be disruptive to his offensive game, but it seems to augment his defensive game. He can look off defenders and make subtle passes that setup high-quality scoring chances consistently. Jami can execute one-touch passes with regularity as well. He played at the point on the power play for a lot of the year. A fairly natural spot for him given how readily he would cover for pinching d-men when the situation arose. We had Krannila in really good standing for most of the year, but something happened down the stretch and the bottom just sort of fell out for him from a production standpoint. He has spent some time at left wing in the playoffs. The details in his game combined with all the compete, skating, and skills boxes that he checks off make him a very worthy player. His hockey IQ could easily be half a point higher in our grading and represent him well, and maybe his work ethic too.9

6	PLAYER	TEAM	LEAGUE	HEIGHT	WEIGHT	POS	GRADE
	KREBS, PEYTON	KOOTENAY	WHL	5'11.25"	180 *	LC	A
	HOCKEY SENSE	COMPETE		SKILL		SKATING	
	8	9		7		7	

Looking purely at stats some could be underwhelmed by Krebs 68 points, and -50 rating. In the context of playing on one of the worst teams in the CHL with little support these numbers look a lot better. His season started strong with a good showing at the Ivan Hlinka, and at the u-18 Worlds, Krebs captained team Canada and played a leading role on the team's top line.

Krebs is one of the high-end playmakers in this draft, and a constant difference maker, who brings almost everything you could want in a player to the table. He excels as a playmaker, where he demonstrated very good vision to find teammates open in coverage and the touch to find the hole to pass through. There's a variety of passes at his disposal, showing an excellent combination of no look passes, saucer passes, and slip passes to make unexpected plays for his teammates. He excelled at making these kinds of plays in traffic where he quickly recognizes his options while assessing which layer of the ice he wanted to penetrate. Krebs isn't only a playmaker though, showing a multi-threat attack. There's variety to his shot selection, often opting to rip it low blocker and high-glove as his preferred options. His mechanics are good, showing a quick release point and static body posture which reduces the goalie's ability to recognize when the shot is coming. This is vital for him since he doesn't generate a lot of torque since he uses a pushing movement into his wrist instead of pulling the puck back. He wasn't only dangerous on his forehand though, showing off an exceptional ability to make plays on his backhand with a high level of finesse.

There's an energy to Peyton that forces defenses to magnetize to him which opens up options to his teammates, this quality made him an effective line-driver on Kootenay. He couldn't drive a line without solid skating; Krebs is a very good skater in the open ice with a quick burst to his top speed and great use of lateral crossovers to make himself unpredictable. His agility allowed him to be shifty on the ice which extends to transitional play. This made him a dangerous zone-entry threat as his vision and elusiveness allowed him to see the gaps and holes in the other team's structure and hit them like an NFL running back. He also has excellent utilization of the 10-2 stance with the ability to shake defenders out of the corner from it with his multidirectional ability. There's a deceptive element to his game, which caught the opposition off guard on many occasions. One of the primary reasons he can mask his intentions with the puck is due to his high-end creativity. This allows him to make unique plays, as he often recognizes patterns, and has the confidence to execute plays others can rarely see. Payton has the ability to force reactions, putting opposing teams behind the play and on their heels. His head works in conjunction with his hands; his puck handling is high end with the ability to embarrass players with the puck, often going through the tripod and between players legs. On top of this Krebs is very strong on his stick, rarely being stripped of the puck despite his average size.

Despite being a complete 200-foot player with a good skill-set, there's still some concerns with how Krebs will translate at the NHL-level. His frame might keep him from being able to dictate play at the same rate he currently does. He's an excellent board-battler who plays much larger than his size, but there's not a lot of extra room for Krebs to grow and that could diminish his effectiveness theoretically. Although he's a quality-skater, there's still an extra-gear that he lacks for his size which could reduce the amount of pressure he generates on the forecheck and how well he can carry the puck going forward. There's also a lack of an exceptional skill-level to Peyton's game. He's a well-rounded and versatile forward but he's not going to blow you away with his skill-level, it's very good but not as high-end as some of the other top-end talents in this class.

With the above slight drawbacks to his game pointed out above, Krebs is good everywhere but not exceptionally dynamic anywhere, yet he seems to be the definition of a player who exceeds his talent-level. The Kootenay ice were one of the worst teams in the CHL, it was Peyton who single-handily willed them into respectability during games due to his relentless-drive. There isn't a more competitive player who brings it on a shift-to-shift basis, and this defines his game. His team had little to no chance but his presence was always felt, leading the charge, and willing results into existence that he or his team has no business having on some nights. His effort-level extends to every-facet of the game both with the puck and away from the play in all three-zones; he's one of the most naturally gifted leaders in this class. Krebs ability to elevate his play based off his drive leads us to believe that he might become one of the most natural playoff performers we've seen from this year's crop of talent.

Moving forward, Peyton projects very comfortably as a top-6-level forward in the NHL. We are confident he will make an impact at a high level as a 200-foot playmaking center and displays the hockey sense to contribute in all areas of the game. We are optimistic in his ability to stick as a center as he shows all the traits you want in the middle of the ice.

"Krebs had the best game out of all the guys at the Top Prospects game." - NHL Scout, January 2019

"He was basically playing for the WHL equivalent of Kingston and look what he did this year. I give the kid all the credit in the world." - NHL Scout, January 2019

"He's the heart and soul guy of this draft class. I think he's going to go high and some people will think it's a bad pick and then he's going to prove that he was worthy of going as high as he did." - He has nothing with him on that team." - NHL Scout, January 2019

"I like Krebs, he works his ass off. He's my next guy after Byram from out west." - NHL Scout, March 2019

"I really like the kid but he had crappy shift at the end of that Sweden game. (April U18) - NHL Scout, April 2019

"Had one of the most impressive performances I have seen in a game all year. It was against Dach in Saskatoon where he almost singlehandedly won Kootenay the game."- HP Scout Liam Loeb

"To me he's a lot like Turcotte. Just a very slightly lesser version. He's not quite as skilled or as good of a skater, but he's smart and probably competes even a bit harder than Turcotte. Both are players that their future coaches will love and will rely on in all facets of the game. Both may also be future Captains of their NHL teams." - HP Scout, Mark Edwards, May 2019

NR	PLAYER	TEAM	LEAGUE	HEIGHT	WEIGHT	POS	GRADE
	KRYS, LUKE	SALISBURY	HIGH-CT	6'1.5"	185 *	RD	ND
	HOCKEY SENSE	COMPETE		SKILL		SKATING	
	5	5		4		5	

Luke played for Salisbury in the New England prep ranks this season. Despite putting up decent offensive numbers with 9 goals and 23 assists in 30 Games, Luke doesn't have the same playmaking and skill game as older brother Chad (CHI, 2nd Rd.) but doesn't play the same type of game either. What Krys does well is understand his game and limitations and plays to his strengths, which is in large a sound defensive game. Krys can handle the puck and break out of his own zone adequately but lacks the playmaking skill to be an offensive catalyst at the next level. Krys also has more size and defensive acumen than his older brother. He is able to handle things from a physical standpoint in his own end and understand coverages and assignments in his own end well. Luke's skating is adequate for the player he projects to be, he doesn't project as a puck rusher but can escape pressure and moves the puck out of his own end quickly and accurately. Krys's NHL projection is a few years away and he has some skills to take with him into Junior hockey and the NCAA that will give him an opportunity to develop. Krys is drafted by Madison (USHL) and was also drafted by Quebec in the 2nd Round of the 2018 QMJHL American Draft. Krys is committed to Brown University.

"He might be a late rounder for someone, his game has made some great strides the last couple of years."- USHL Scout

	PLAYER	TEAM	LEAGUE	HEIGHT	WEIGHT	POS	GRADE
40	LACOMBE, JACKSON	SHATTUCK	HIGH-MN	6'1.25"	171 *	LD	**B**
	HOCKEY SENSE	COMPETE		SKILL		SKATING	
	5	6		7		8	

LaCombe is a very intriguing prospect for the 2019 Draft. Just a couple years ago LaCombe missed making the Shattuck St. Mary's U16 Team as a forward and was playing on the AAA squad. A switch to defense has him in line to be an early round selection in this year's NHL Draft. LaCombe is a very gifted skater, particularly in regards to his edgework and four way mobility. Jackson has effortless edges and turns that allow him to change directions on a dime and close on opponents quickly. His stride is long and fluid; he excels nicely from his crossovers and leaves fore checkers in the dust as he comes out from behind his own net. LaCombe is a very offensive minded defenseman. He won't hesitate to rush the puck up the ice and carry it deep into the offensive zone. What comes next is what separates him from a lot of the other top defenseman in this draft. Jackson's playmaking ability off the rush and as he enters the offensive zone. Being only a couple year removed from playing forward, a lot of those instincts with the puck are easily noticeable in his game. It's not uncommon for LaCombe to drive wide on a defender and take the puck to the net; much like a winger would and has great ability to find guys coming into the zone off the rush. LaCombe has shown good growth in his judgement, he has learned to pick his spots better and supports his defensive partner much more than he used to. LaCombe fits into the category of today's defenseman who can be part of the attack. In the offensive zone, Jackson is able to set the table from the point position. His mobility and hands open up opportunities all over the zone and Shattuck had a very dangerous power play as a result.

For all his offensive ability from the back end, his defensive game has come a long way in such a short time. Jackson has shown excellent coach-ability and willingness to learn the defensive aspects of the position. LaCombe has good size and reach advantage which he is still learning to use in his own end. His stick positioning can be sloppy at times, especially on the penalty kill as lanes open up down low as a result but being so new to the position, this is something that should improve through over time through coaching. One small area of concern right now is on the breakout. Lacombe defaults to skating the puck out of his own end if his first read isn't available, he will need to learn to show more poise with the puck and use his defensive partner as a way to relieve pressure going forward. Some of this might come from LaCombe reverting back to his comfort zone and simply not being used to looking at the ice from a defenseman's viewpoint. His skating and skills are all there for him to excel in this area, it may just be a case of needing the repetitions and coaching. Lacombe saw a couple of games for Chicago (USHL) in the Clark Cup playoffs and didn't look at all out of place. He was confident with the puck and the faster paced games compared to Prep School didn't seem to be an issue from an adjustment standpoint. LaCombe will likely spend next season in the USHL before heading to the University of Minnesota in the fall of 2020.

"Skating is really high end." - NHL Scout, May 2019

"He leads the rush a lot but my argument is because he can playing at that level." - NHL Scout, May 2019

"Saw him a few times. Played like an extra forward in three of my four viewings. He defended ok in the game where he was clearly holding back from jumping in as 4th forward." - NHL Scout, May 2019

"I'm a big fan of this kid, I think his understanding of the position has taken major strides as this season progressed." HP Scout, Dusten Braaksma

"I'm not sure about his hockey sense. My viewings were limited but that was my concern." -HP Scout, Mark Edwards

NR	PLAYER	TEAM	LEAGUE	HEIGHT	WEIGHT	POS	GRADE
	LADD, GRAYSON	WINDSOR	OHL	6'1.0"	172	RD	ND
	HOCKEY SENSE	COMPETE		SKILL		SKATING	
	5	5		5		6	

Injuries ended Ladd's season early which was probably even more disappointing for the Grayson considering it's his draft year. We managed to see Ladd a few times before he was lost for the season with the broken thumb and dislocation. He's a good player but tends to be one of those players who is just solid in a lot of areas but doesn't overly excel in any one part of his game. In other words, we felt like he lacks in talent that we would see translating to the NHL game. Skating is good but not a conversation starter and he never flashed a whole lot of offensive potential that would make you think he could fill an offensive role in the NHL.

Grayson is the type of player that makes scouts ask, what is he going to be at the next level? When scouts ask that question it's usually not a good sign for their draft hopes. We feel that the former 1st round pick of the Kitchener Rangers will continue to be valuable OHL player but he is not a player that feel projects to the NHL at this time.

"There isn't really a part of his game that he excels at...maybe his skating." - NHL Scout, October 2018

"Just a solid OHL defenseman. i like him in the OHL but he's often very vanilla and nothing stands out about his game to make him project well to the next level." - HP Scout, Mark Edwards

NR	PLAYER	TEAM	LEAGUE	HEIGHT	WEIGHT	POS	GRADE
	LANG, MARTIN	KAMLOOPS	WHL	5'10.75"	163 *	RW	ND
	HOCKEY SENSE	COMPETE		SKILL		SKATING	
	6	5		5		4	

Coming over from the Czech Republic as the 14th pick in the CHL import draft, much was expected of Lang who had been one of the best skaters in his country for his age group. Lang had a somewhat underwhelming year finishing with only 33 points on the year. Lang is however a very late birthday, born on September 15, the last day eligible for this years draft.

Lang seemed to have some difficulty with the speed of the WHL game at first, lacking the skating ability to consistently make a difference. Lang doesn't get much power out of a short stride, and was pretty easily knocked off balance. Does however have a decent amount of wiggle and deceptiveness along the board. Lang in large part lacks strength, and really had to rely on his hockey sense to make a difference without these standout physical tools. Over the course of the season did an excellent job giving his teammates options and getting in to open ice. With the puck on his stick Martin is calm and liked to slow it down and play on the outside looking for penetrating passes, showing great vision on multiple occasions. Lang posted low goal totals, but actually has a pretty decent shot with good accuracy and a ton of deception as he hides whether he is shooting or passing well. Needs further physical development to become more of an impact player in the WHL.

NR	PLAYER	TEAM	LEAGUE	HEIGHT	WEIGHT	POS	GRADE
	LAROCHELLE, SEAN	VICTORIAVILLE	QMJHL	5'9.5"	164 *	RD	ND
	HOCKEY SENSE	COMPETE		SKILL		SKATING	
	6	5		6		5	

Larochelle is from Varennes, located on the South Shore of Montreal. After playing his QMJHL draft year with St-Hyacinthe in Quebec Midget AAA, he made move to Stanstead, a Canadian prep school, and then joined Victoriaville this season. The Tigres had drafted Larochelle with the 20th overall pick in the 2017 QMJHL Draft.

This season had some ups and downs for Larochelle offensively. After starting the season on fire with 15 points in his first 19 games, he cooled off for a while and then had a strong finish with 10 points in his last 16 games. If you break down his stats for the rest of the season, he only had 4 points in 33 games. Larochelle finished with 29 points in 68 games, which was good for 33rd overall among defensemen, but 4th among rookie defensemen. There was a lot of inconsistency in his game in his first QMJHL season, due to learning a new league and also because physically, he has a ways to go before even thinking about the pro game. He's undersized and struggles in his own zone while battling in front of his net and along the boards to retrieve pucks there, due to his lack of strength. His best tools are his vision with the puck and ability to make things happen for his team in the transition game and in the offensive zone. He's got some quick feet which help him make quick zone exits and rush the puck into the offensive zone. He's agile and fluid on his skates, but his top speed is only average. He can run a power play in the QMJHL, making quick decisions with the puck and using his above-average vision. His shot is average, as it lacks velocity to it, but it does have a quick release and it's accurate. When he was at his best this season, Larochelle looked like a potential pick for the NHL Entry Draft. Other times, he looked like a guy who could just be a good junior defenseman. He could get a look late in the draft due to his puck moving ability, footwork and offensive game.

NR	PLAYER	TEAM	LEAGUE	HEIGHT	WEIGHT	POS	GRADE
	LAROSE, NATHAN	CAPE BRETON	QMJHL	6'1.0"	194 *	RD	ND
	HOCKEY SENSE	COMPETE		SKILL		SKATING	
	5	5		5		5	

Larose was acquired by Cape Breton in a trade with Saint John for 16-year-old Alex Drover in late December during the QMJHL trade deadline. This was Larose's third team in three seasons in the QMJHL, and he finished the year with 19 points in 53 games. He was originally drafted by Chicoutimi in the 2016 QMJHL Draft in the 2nd round (30th overall). Larose has got good size. Physically, he's pretty strong. He's a decent skater for his size, and likes to rush the puck out of his zone and bring it to the offensive zone. In the offensive zone, he can be a threat on the point because of his heavy shot. However, he's got to improve his decision-making with the puck in the offensive and defensive zones. He can be victim to turnovers when he makes bad passing plays and tries to force the play. He's got to make better reads in both offensive and defensive zone as well. Larose has some offensive potential, but has been unable to fully materialize this in his QMJHL career thus far. The rest of his game needs still lot of work, such as defending, but mostly his decision-making.

25	PLAYER	TEAM	LEAGUE	HEIGHT	WEIGHT	POS	GRADE
	LAVOIE, RAPHAEL	HALIFAX	QMJHL	6'3.5"	191 *	RC	B
	HOCKEY SENSE		COMPETE		SKILL		SKATING
	6		4		8		6

Lavoie was in his third seasons in the QMJHL this year and didn't have the type of season a lot of peoples expected out of him. He improved on last year numbers but he was not nearly as dominant in the regular season as we expected but did had a good playoff run with the Mooseheads. Lavoie was drafted 29th overall in the 2016 QMJHL draft by Halifax even though he was ranked as a first round prospect.

Lavoie's toolbox is very impressive; he's a big kid who has made some nice progress with his skating ability over the past 3 seasons. He's not a high end skater but for a 6'04" kid his skating won't hinder him at the next level. He played mostly at center in midget but in the major junior he has moved mostly on the wing and projects more as a winger at the NHL level. His play away from the puck lacks consistency to be an effective center at the NHL level, on the wing he has fewer responsibilities in his own end and more freedom to try to create offense. Lavoie is at his best when he competes hard and is involved in the play. Our biggest issue with him as he's not a consistently hard worker and you don't know what you're going to get out of him each game. With his skill level, size and being one of the older players from this draft class we expected him to be a dominant player in the league, but he was just barely over a point per game player over the course of the year. This is a bit concerning when you consider he played in the QMJHL which was weak this year and played often against Saint-John and Acadie-Bathurst, two teams he should have dominated but didn't. He only had 16 points in 15 games against those two teams.

When he's on, Lavoie is a threat. He has a big time shot and can score from almost anywhere in the offensive zone. It's an NHL caliber shot which is accurate, has great velocity and he's quick to get it off. He's got above average vision, can make plays for his teammate with some high caliber passes. He does good work using his big frame to protect pucks along the boards and with his long reach, it's tough to take the puck away from him. He's also good with his stick. Often will retrieve pucks along the boards with his long reach and quick stick. That said, even with his big frame he's not a physical player, he lacks a good compete level and won't throw many hits on the ice. To be at his best, he needs to be more involved in the play and his compete level needs to be upgraded. Lavoie is a bit of wild card in this draft, he has all the talent in the world but his lack of commitment is a concern.

"He was only good for one period. I'll say this though, he was really good in that period." - NHL Scout, October 2018

"He has talent but the compete level is not good." - NHL Scout, December, 2018

"He is playing bad teams a lot and he isn't exactly lighting up the league. The Sea Dogs and Acadie are like tier II teams and he's invisible." - NHL Scout, December 2018

"I'd take Pelletier ahead of him." - NHL Scout, December 2018

"Between his lack of eye popping numbers given his tools and birthdate and everything else I'm hearing I'd have hard time taking him very early." - NHL Scout, January 2019

"I have a story to tell you about my interview with him." - NHL Scout, February 2019

"A lot of his skill is individual skill. He doesn't see the ice well and didn't make guys around him better. He isn't good at all defensively but the hope is you could fix that." - NHL Scout, April 2019

"His defensive game stinks. He's good with the puck on his tape but even that stuff is all one on one stuff. He doesn't make many plays off the rush or show creativity." - NHL Scout, April 2019

"I'm not really a big fan." - NHL Scout, May 2019

"I'd have no problem taking him later in the 1st round." - NHL Scout, May 2019

"I'm not going to erase what I saw for six months for one month of good play." HP Scout, Jérôme Bérubé, April 2019

"He's been an interesting player all season long for me both on ice and getting feedback from a ton of Scouts. They gave me their thoughts of his game and several of them told me about their interviews with him. We included a quote from one Scout above who told me all about his meeting with the player and he actually spoke to the coach as well. I wanted the player a bit less after getting feedback from him and other Scouts." - HP Scout, Mark Edwards, April 2019

"He has tools but I don't like the lack of compete so I'm guessing he'd be gone before I'd be willing to select him. I will give him props for a much stronger second half. All my live viewings were prior to February. I only saw him on video after that." - HP Scout, Mark Edwards, May 2019

"His Memorial Cup performance was representative of his regular season, a couple of nice flashes here and there but some disappearing acts as well. One of the most frustrating players I have scouted in years. The talent is there but too many question marks come with it. - HP Scout, Jérôme Bérubé, June 2019

"Had two scouts mention him to me as one of their weaker interviews." - HP Scout, Mark Edwards, June 2019

	PLAYER	TEAM	LEAGUE	HEIGHT	WEIGHT	POS	GRADE
41	LEASON, BRETT	PRINCE ALBERT	WHL	6'3.75"	200 *	RC	**B**
	HOCKEY SENSE		COMPETE		SKILL		SKATING
	6		5		7		5

Leason had one of the more unique paths to the draft in recent history this season. After 50 points combined in his previous two WHL seasons, Leason exploded this season with 89 points in 55 games. One of the driving forces between the powerhouse Prince Albert Raiders team, Leason played heavy minutes in all situations. Leason had such an impressive opening to the season that he managed to make Team Canada for the World Junior Championship. At the tournament he scored 5 points in 5 games.

Leason is a big and powerful winger who was physically dominant against WHLers this season. He is heavy on his stick and very difficult to budge off the puck, using his strength to get to any spot he wants on the ice. Leason has great instincts for getting in to scoring positions and moves well to gain speed before receiving pucks. Because of this ability Leason can play a bit faster than he is. As a skater he lacks standout top speed and infrequently shows high end edge work. At the world juniors this lack of speed was more evident and is an issue that will affect him more as the levels move up. For his age group his skating is below average for a top prospect. Leason can also be too dependant on physical domination and doesn't really have special senses with the puck, rarely did he display the ability to make advanced passes. For a player his size Leason has soft hands and can keep the puck away from defenders with his touch, reach, and physicality. Leason possesses an above average shot that is heavy and accurate. He does a good job of getting his momentum in to his shot and shooting off the rush. Defensively he is reliable and does a great job getting in defensemen's shooting lanes, blocking multiple shots that lead to breakaways. He also uses his strength and good stick to frequently steal pucks from opponents .With Leason it's important to remember he is 2 years ahead of most other players that will be drafted. In these 2 crucial developmental years a lot can change and we believe certain others like Adam Beckman in Spokane or Henry Rybinski in Seattle have the potential to be better than what Leason is now in 2 years' time.

"He's going to go in the first round." - NHL Scout, November 2018

"Our guys like him a lot. Guessing late first (round)." - NHL Scout, December 2018

"Big power forward who can skate and plays hard. I'll take an older player like him when he brings those tools." - NHL Scout, January 2019

"(Number)21 is better than (number) 20 and he's a lot younger." - NHL Scout, February 2019

"I hope someone takes him in the first round. He's a mid round pick for me. He's an average skater and he plays soft." - NHL Scout, March 2019

"He's big and he can score a bit but 1999's are supposed to score in the WHL. Skating isn't good." - NHL Scout, March 2019

"Get someone to check his heartbeat monitor." - NHL Scout, May 2019

"Leason wasn't very good. Not many of them (Raiders) were though....well actually I thought Gregor was good." - NHL Scout, May 2019

"Most of my viewings were in the 2nd half of the season and I'm not as big a fan of his game as some scouts I've spoken to. He is a 1999 birth and his skating might be an issue. The heavy feet translated to a very sluggish look in too many shifts during my viewings. His speed is fine once he gets rolling but his first few steps are weak." - HP Scout, Mark Edwards, April 2019

"Didn't think his skating was too bad in Halifax...I saw him win some puck races, but his skating won't get much better than this as an older prospect. No finish around the net in the three games he played." - HP Scout, Jérôme Bérubé, June 2019

	PLAYER	TEAM	LEAGUE	HEIGHT	WEIGHT	POS	GRADE
NR	LEE, ANDRE	SIOUX FALLS	USHL	6'4.5"	206 *	LW	**ND**
	HOCKEY SENSE		COMPETE		SKILL		SKATING
	5		5		6		4

Massive, goal scoring winger from the Swedish junior system. Lee is every bit of 6'4", 201 pounds and he packs a big shot that has the potential to bore a hole in some goalies. Common to a lot of the rest of his game, his shot takes a little while to load up. While he isn't terribly coordinated yet, he generates some straight line speed when he is able to get a head of steam going. His stride is really sloppy, and will likely prohibit a lot of growth from an acceleration perspective. His starts and stops are elongated and his turning radius is cause for concern. In terms of forechecking, he has some good ideas, but the speed and dexterity sometimes eludes him even when his mental game comes through. He gets caught in between plays a lot. By the time he changes directions and figures out where he ought to be, the play is often tracking back in the other direction. As a result, Lee finds himself blending into the ice on a lot of nights. He isn't a very physical player, particularly for his size meaning that we're left with just a goal scoring winger of limited dimension. Unfortunately, Andre has yet to fully embrace his role as a shooter and a net-front guy. In fact, he spends too much time in the margins of the rink. Given his seemingly late bloom in the Swedish junior ranks, his jump from there to the USHL to the NCAA next season will be telling about how adaptable and palatable he might be in years to come. The shot and size are of interest, but ultimately the skill level, hockey sense, and skating outweigh the former by enough. A full dedication to his one true area of strength would benefit him immensely.

	PLAYER	TEAM	LEAGUE	HEIGHT	WEIGHT	POS	GRADE
NR	LEE, JAKE	SEATTLE	WHL	6'1.75"	216 *	LD	C
	HOCKEY SENSE	COMPETE		SKILL		SKATING	
	5	6		5		5	

Former first round WHL draft pick took a major step forward for the Seattle Thunderbirds this season. Lee stepped up playing a first pairing role and registering 24 points. Lee played all situations for his teams.

Had a very promising start to the season but really faded over the course of the year. Lee has prototypical shut down defenseman size and the strength of a man already. Consistently looked physically dominant in the corners and in his ability to hold forecheckers off. He excelled defensively in large part due to this as he could stonewall opposing players trying to beat him on the rush. The only times he was beat were on quick change of direction plays where his lateral agility was challenged. With the puck made a lot of good breakout decisions, rarely forcing the play early in the year. In later viewings his decision making was not nearly as good, throwing too many pucks in to traffic and losing a lot of the calm he'd had earlier in the year. Too frequently he telegraphed his passes making in easy for the other team to read where the play was going. Can struggle to assert himself offensively as Lee generally didn't do much to standout in this area. Lee does have a bomb of a point shot when given the time and space to get it off. Lee also showed very good instincts for when to make a pinch offensively, and was very effective at this skill. Lee's skating is below average for the next level, especially in his acceleration as he was often exposed by speedier forwards on dump ins. Lee does however have strong edgework for a player his size, making some great tight turns to beat forechecks through out the year. It looked as if his confidence faded throughout the year. When Lee was at his best he looked like an NHL level prospect.

	PLAYER	TEAM	LEAGUE	HEIGHT	WEIGHT	POS	GRADE
54	LEGARE, NATHAN	BAIE-COMEAU	QMJHL	6'0.0"	205 *	RW	C+
	HOCKEY SENSE	COMPETE		SKILL		SKATING	
	5	6		6		5	

Legaré was the 6th overall pick by Baie-Comeau in the 2017 QMJHL Draft after playing his QMJHL draft year with the St-Eustache Vikings on a line with Alexis Lafrenière. Legaré had a decent first season in the league but really exploded offensively this season finishing up with 45 goals (tie for 2nd in the league) and 87 points (tie for 8th in the league). Legaré draft year didn't start well when he was cut in August from team Canada U-18 for the Hlinka/Gretzky cup.

He started the year with Baie-Comeau and made a big impact right from the get go with 17 points in his first 8 games and his strong play continued the rest of the year. Most of the year he played on the top line for the Drakkar and got first power play unit, often paired with Ivan Chekhovich (San Jose prospect) and Gabriel Fortier (Tampa Bay prospect) and was consistently one of the top lines in the QMJHL this season. Obviously he got a lot of help on his line with those two players. Chekhovich is a high IQ player with great offensive creativity and Fortier brings a tremendous work ethic and speed to the line.

Legaré was the shooter on the line and really understood his role well and took a ton of shots on goal. He took 271 shots on net in 68 games this year (3.98 per game) compared to his rookie season where he had 95 shots in 62 games (1.53 per game). He's got a good wrist shot, good accuracy and velocity. One thing he improved from his rookie season was his release, this year he was able to get his shot off more quickly which was important as he was closely watch by other teams as the season progressed. In the offensive zone he likes to shoot from anywhere, he's not shy to put pucks on net but he's dangerous if I can find dead spaces in the slot and get the puck there, he's got an excellent one-timer. He also scored many times this year from the point on the power play with one-timer from there.

Legaré's skating is an area of his game that he'll need to improve; his stride is not terrible but he has tough time generating speed on a long stretch with it. His skating didn't looked terrible versus QMJHL teams but when he played vs Russia in November his skating looked below average versus that quick team. Just by playing at a lesser weight, we think you would see his skating improve a bit. Important thing for Legaré is to keep his feet moving in the offensive zone, that makes him tougher to defend and less predictable. He has a good work ethic, a good compete level but at some points during the season where he was scoring a lot, he didn't work as hard and became a one-dimensional offensive player. Meaning that he was waiting after his chances but didn't work to retrieve pucks along the wall like he did earlier.

Hockey sense it's a strong part of his game but it's not huge flaw either, it's kind of in the middle for him as he's not dumb but also doesn't have a high hockey IQ either. He can set up some plays for his teammate as well, not an outstanding playmaker but can make some nice passes in the offensive zone even though he's a shoot first type of player. Overall his playmaking abilities are a bit underrated as we always focusing on his shot and scoring ability but we've seen make some great passes this year. He's got a big frame, he doesn't use it well along the board to win puck possession and retrieve pucks. He doesn't mind the physical game, can throw some good hits but to improve his efficiency on the forecheck and be more of a threat for opposing defensemen he'll need to get quicker because he can't always catch up with speedy defensemen.

He's a capable scorer with decent size. He's got parts of his games to improve though to have success at the pro level like skating & conditioning.

	PLAYER	TEAM	LEAGUE	HEIGHT	WEIGHT	POS	GRADE
NR	LEGEURRIER, JACOB	SAULT STE. MARIE	OHL	6'1.0"	200 *	LD	C
	HOCKEY SENSE	COMPETE		SKILL		SKATING	
	5	6		5		6	

Jacob LeGuerrier had a solid year for the Greyhounds. He had 16 points in 68 games, including 6 goals and an additional 2 assists in 11 playoff games. Although his points totals aren't overly impressive, he wasn't given extended power-play time and doesn't project as an offensive-defenseman. What Jacob does do pretty well is move the puck. He's plays a decisive game. If he feels there's an opportunity to impose himself physically by closing his gap on a player, he'll do it. If he thinks he can weave through the neutral-zone and generate a transitional-entry, he'll do that too. He's a kid who thinks the game at a plus-rate in most of our viewings and when combined with his poise, it allows him to use his tools to take advantage of his skill-set. He's not going to wow anyone with his puck-skills and rarely will flash a high-level of play; however, he will make clean and intelligent plays that extend through all three-zones. His skating is above-average for his size. He's a powerful kid who has some fluidity in his stride and this allows him to skate the puck up the ice and feel comfortable when walking the line. His lateral mobility isn't as good as his top-end speed, but he does have above-average lane recognition which allows him to get shots through traffic regardless if he can't re-orchestrate his lanes. His slapshot carries a reduced-wind-up and his wrist-shot features a lot of velocity which made it harder for goalies to absorb.

He doesn't have high-end vision, opting for efficient and high-percentage passing attempts; he's not going to make a highlight-reel with a dynamic pass. That's okay though given his skill-set. His hockey-IQ is high-enough, that he understands his limitations and seems to play within the confines of what he's capable of doing to help his team. There's a decent-base to work with in LeGuerrier's game -- he doesn't have the highest-offensive ceiling, and can mismanage his defensive-reads at times, but if he can continue to evolve his skating to where it gets closer to a 7 on our rating scale, then he has a chance of becoming a bottom-pairing defenseman.

"Like his skating and compete level but not sure if there is enough ceiling there." – NHL Scout, May 2019

"A few Ontario based scouts I spoke to had him as a possible option in the 7th round and that was pretty much my take. Good Junior player for sure and probably worthy of a late round grade but might be in tight to make our list." – HP Scout, Mark Edwards, April 2019

	PLAYER	TEAM	LEAGUE	HEIGHT	WEIGHT	POS	GRADE
NR	LEMIEUX, JONATHAN	VAL-D'OR	QMJHL	5'11.75"	187 *	G	C
	HOCKEY SENSE	COMPETE		SKILL		SKATING	
	6	7		6		6	

Lemieux had a real tough first season in the QMJHL last year, playing on a very bad team. This season, he bounced back with some great performances, winning 19 games in 40 starts and posting a save percentage of over 90% on a struggling team. He saw an average of 36 shots per 60 minutes played this season, which kept him busy.

He was the 42nd overall pick in the 2017 QMJHL Draft (3rd goalie picked) out of the St-Hyacinthe Gaulois midget program. Lemieux has decent athletic abilities and possesses a quick glove. He's a great competitor in net; he doesn't quit on any pucks and will make some great 2nd and 3rd saves. However, he does have a hard time with his rebound-control at times. He'll need to work on this and control them better to stop giving extra opportunities to opposing teams. He's got quick reflexes and quick pads, so he covers the lower part of the net well. For today's NHL, he would be considered a small goaltender, standing at 6 feet tall. He struggles when tracking pucks coming from the point with traffic in front of him, due to his average height. He's aggressive in his net; he doesn't stay too deep and tends to challenge shooters at the top of his crease. Many NHL teams have shied away from drafting goaltenders less than 6'02" so that could hurt Lemieux at the draft. He had some really good performances in the opening round of the playoff vs. Victoriaville doing his best to help his stock for the draft.

	PLAYER	TEAM	LEAGUE	HEIGHT	WEIGHT	POS	GRADE
NR	LIKHACHEV, YAROSLAV	GATINEAU	QMJHL	5'10.0"	168 *	LW	ND
	HOCKEY SENSE	COMPETE		SKILL		SKATING	
	4	5		8		5	

Likhachev came to Gatineau after he was drafted with the 22nd overall pick in the CHL Import Draft, and had a good amount of hype surrounding him after his good 2017-2018 season and a good showing in August's Hlinka/Gretzky tournament (7 points in 5 games).

When you watch Likhachev, it's easy to notice that he has really quick and soft hands. He likes to handle the puck a lot, and has a great arsenal of dekes that he likes to show off in one-on-one confrontations when facing opposing defensemen. He's an average skater, but he's slippery on the ice and can get around defenders. He can play on both wings, but as a right-shooting winger, he likes come down on his off-wing often. Unfortunately, to say that his season was a disappointment would be an understatement. The young Russian forward finished the regular season with only 24 points in 57 games. He showed some flashes of his talent during the season in certain games, but overall, he was not able to transfer his game to the QMJHL and his lack of production in this league was a red flag. With his skillset and the fact that the QMJHL is usually a great place for small, skilled forwards, it's a bit shocking how his season went. He tends to rely on his stickhandling too often; he will make a highlight-reel play here and there, but needs to learn to use his teammates more and share the puck. He would frequently try to beat opposing players on his own with his quick stickhandling work. This would be successful on some occasions, but on others he would lose possession of the puck and cause turnovers. He's got a quick release and his wrist shot has above-average velocity. For his size, he lacks that good, top speed and acceleration that creates separation. Players of his stature usually need this attribute in order to reach the NHL. He's not strong enough physically, either, and it shows when it comes to keeping possession of the puck along the boards. His compete level is also average at best. The best thing about Likhachev's game is his hands, and they are excellent. Players need more than this to succeed at the NHL level, though. There's a ton of work in other areas of Likhachev's game that need to be worked on before he can get there.

"A lot of individual plays out of him, he tries too much to beat everyone on the ice instead of using his teammates. Lack of scoring in a weaker league is worrisome for a player like Likhachev, no draft for me." - HP Scout Jerome Berube

	PLAYER	TEAM	LEAGUE	HEIGHT	WEIGHT	POS	GRADE
91	**LINDMARK, OWEN**	USA U-18	NTDP	6'0.0"	184 *	RC	**C**
	HOCKEY SENSE	COMPETE		SKILL		SKATING	
	6	7		5		6	

Savvy, two-way center. Lindmark's 14 points in 24 USHL contests is just about the bottom of the barrel for the U18 team, but it's hardly indicative of his contribution. The Chicago Mission product played lower line center all year and really embraced it and owned it every night. Lindmark has a terrific feel for the game and is very detailed oriented for such a young player. He shows a great sense of where the danger is defensively and then uses a real quick stick to shut down would-be scoring chances. He plays a 200 foot game and does a lot of work on the penalty kill. He's a plus faceoff taker in our viewings as well. Owen has good mobility underneath a worthwhile frame, he gives off the impression that he's pretty hockey strong even without being filled out yet. His top- and closing-speeds are pretty impressive. The big plus for Lindmark's stock is that he displays a lot of untapped upside outside of being a work-a-day checking forward. He didn't always play with the most confidence, especially early in the season – but he flashed some legitimately useful hands and finishing ability in the limited even strength ice time that he was given. He has a nice little forehand-backhand move that seems highly effective. Many checking line players have to grind their way to goals, but Lindmark looks pretty comfortable in rush situations too – which is another clue that there's more here than meets the eye. His hockey sense and adaptability are really something. He has the ability to mirror talented offensive players too, which gives him a huge advantage in defensive situations. While well-rounded, Owen still needs to improve his playmaking ability, his overall technical skills, and his first-step quickness if he wants to realize the top-end of his potential. This is a player who may have generated more draft buzz had he been a featured piece on an average USHL team as opposed to being an afterthought on a juggernaut squad.

NR	PLAYER	TEAM	LEAGUE	HEIGHT	WEIGHT	POS	GRADE
	LOPINA, JOSH	LINCOLN	USHL	6'2.0"	165	RC	ND
	HOCKEY SENSE	COMPETE		SKILL		SKATING	
	4	5		5		6	

Average, meandering center. Was dealt a pretty poor hand by playing on a Lincoln team that struggled all year and their main catalyst for offense (Shane Pinto) was traded midway through the season, leaving the team on just fumes. Lopina was given the opportunity to step up and take on a larger role, but even though he played more than twice as many games as Pinto in Lincoln, he still couldn't pass him in scoring. The right-handed center is about as average of a prospect as we're going to see in the USHL – a slight plus for skating, a slight minus for hockey sense. The rest of his game doesn't move the needle one way or the other. While he does try to come back defensively, he doesn't have a great feel on what to do or the timing of it. He doesn't have the skill to take on players at this level and struggled to manage all the ice that he had as a center. On a team that was starved for any semblance of skill to step up, Lopina left us wanting more. It's also important to note that he's first year player coming out of the Chicago Mission AAA program – a league he wasn't exactly lighting up either. He'll go to UMass-Amherst in the fall of 2020.

NR	PLAYER	TEAM	LEAGUE	HEIGHT	WEIGHT	POS	GRADE
	LOPONEN, KALLE	KARPAT JR.	FIN-JR.	5'9.5"	186 *	RD	ND
	HOCKEY SENSE	COMPETE		SKILL		SKATING	
	5	6		6		5	

Loponen split the past season between the Mestis league (Finland's 2nd-tier men's league) and the Jr. A SM-Liiga for Karpat's U20 team. Loponen has some good offensive skills. He's good on the power play, as he can move pucks efficiently, and has good shooting skills as well. He's not afraid to put pucks on net from the point, as he does a good job finding shooting lanes and getting pucks through. On the point, he can either use his wrist shot or a good one-timer on the point. He's got a pretty quick release, which helps him get pucks on net quickly without being blocked by opponents. He's an average-sized defender but he's very competitive, and not afraid to engage physically along the boards in addition to having good timing with his hits. For his size, his skating and footwork are average. His footwork is not very fluid and he doesn't generate a lot of speed from his strides. When he's rushing the puck from his own zone, he doesn't create enough separation between himself and the forechecker. That size and lack of speed combination is a bit problematic for Loponen, and he'll need to work hard in the years to come in order to improve his chances of playing in the NHL. He's a good puck-mover, has a good first pass out of his zone, and quick transition out of his zone. His defensive positioning is a work-in-progress, as he can be caught out of place and running around a bit too often in his own zone. At his size, he can have problems against bigger players in front of the net or along the boards. Over the course of the season, he saw regular ice time internationally for Finland in all tournaments. In April, however, he saw his ice time cut down by a lot, and was basically Finland's 7th defenseman to start the tournament. Loponen has some offensive upside, but in order for him to have a chance to play at the NHL level, he will need to get quicker and be more efficient in his zone.

NR	PLAYER	TEAM	LEAGUE	HEIGHT	WEIGHT	POS	GRADE
	LUEDTKE, JOSH	MINNETONKA	HIGH-MN	5'8.25"	165	RD	ND
	HOCKEY SENSE	COMPETE		SKILL		SKATING	
	4	5		6		6	

Luedtke is a September 2000 born prospect out of Minnetonka HS. Luedtke doesn't have a lot of size or strength at this stage. But what he lacks physically he makes up for with skating and skill. Luedtke has been the other half of one of the top defensive pairs in Minnesota HS hockey the last couple years, paired with Grand Docter. Josh has been the more offensive defenseman of the pair. Luedtke likes to get involved in the rush or leading it coming out of own zone. His combination of skating and skill with the puck allow him to be effective creating off the rush. One major concern in Luedtke's game up to this point is his judgement. He has started to turn the corner in regards to picking his spots better and not jumping into the play each and every time his team brings the puck out their own end. His defensive awareness in his own end still has a ways to go, as he can get puck watching at times and misses his coverage in front of his own net but he doesn't back down against bigger players and competes in the hard areas, despite the likely size disadvantage he faces in a lot of situations. For as undersized Luedtke is, he plays with a good amount of physicality. He has displayed on a number of occasions the ability to time his hits and connect on some big open ice hits in the neutral zone and can finish guys along the wall when they try to go wide on him. The power play for the skippers has run through Luedtke for a couple of season's now. He is very much a shoot first point man on the power play. He looks for ways to open up lanes and get pucks on net. He can peel off to the half wall position and fire one-timers as well as well as make moves around the defenseman that are challenging the points and come down in the zone as well. His shot still needs some work, while it's fairly accurate, the release and velocity are in the average category right now. Luedtke recently switched his commitment from Northern Michigan to Denver University where he is heading this fall.

106	PLAYER	TEAM	LEAGUE	HEIGHT	WEIGHT	POS	GRADE
	LUNDMARK, SIMON	LINKOPING JR.	SWE-JR.	6'2.0"	201	RD	C
	HOCKEY SENSE	COMPETE		SKILL		SKATING	
	6	5		5		5	

Lundmark is a late-born 2000. He split the season between two leagues, starting with Linköping HC's U20s where he played 25 games. He put up 2 goals and 15 assists before getting promoted to that club's SHL team, where he dressed in 28 games in which he had 3 assists and a plus-minus rating of -9 . He also played 4 games for Team Sweden U19 and had 1 goal and 1 assist and was one of the leading players on that team.

He has recently signed a 2-year contract to play for Linköping in the SHL. Lundmark is always very calm and composed, as if it's impossible for him to become stressed. He has very good defensive reads and is always very well positioned. He wins himself time by being perfectly positioned when he gets the puck. He plays safe with the puck, always trying the high percentage play instead of going for the decisive pass or transporting the puck by himself. However, it would benefit him if he could be more active in transition and take a little more initiative with the puck as he has good vision and smooth hands. Lundmark's stride is long and smooth but he lacks explosiveness. He is mobile and can maneuver very well on the offensive blueline but he can be beaten on the outside against small quick forwards. Because he has just one gear he can also be vulnerable in the open ice. Though not physical, he is smart enough to get away with it as he stays close enough to limit the opposition's time and space and he has the ability to read plays and intercept passes.

His offensive skills are somewhat underrated, at least in part because he's not as active offensively as he should be. His wrist shot is really good with good velocity and accuracy especially when he joins the attack and is fed the puck in the slot. His short passing game in the offensive zone is also very solid as he tends to keep it simple and goes for the high percentage play. He also has a knack for getting his teammates the puck in open spaces Big and strong, he will need to become more active all over the ice and he needs to be able to step up physically and be more aggressive in his own zone.

Lundmark has the attributes of a modern two-way, smart defenseman; he is a puck-mover and if he can be aggressive and physical defensively and less passive in the transition game, he give himself a much better chance at becoming a viable player in the NHL going forward.

	PLAYER	TEAM	LEAGUE	HEIGHT	WEIGHT	POS	GRADE
NR	LYCKÅSEN, ALBERT	LINKÖPING HC J20	SWE-JR	5'11.0"	187	RD	C
	HOCKEY SENSE		COMPETE		SKILL		SKATING
	6		5		6		6

Lyckåsen was a regular for Linköping HC in the SuperElite where he put up 7 goals 9 helpers for 16 points in 44 games. He was mostly on the second pairing and was an important piece when they won a silver medal in the Swedish championship. He also appeared in 5 games with his club's U18 team in which he registered 5 assists. He also appeared in 17 games for Team Sweden during the season, recording 3 assists and he was a part of the team that won the gold medal at the U18 World Championship. There's a good possibility that we will see Lyckåsen make the jump to play for Linköping in the SHL next season.

He is a smallish, right-handed defenseman with a good two-way game. Although he can get pushed around a bit by bigger opponents, he reads the game well and reacts quickly when an opportunity to steal a puck, or pick up a loose one appears. His biggest asset is his skating, which is super smooth. He skates with a low center of gravity, is nicely balanced and he can move around with great mobility, both laterally and when turning around from skating forward to backward.

While he takes his defensive duties seriously, he loves to join the attack on the rush. He creates offense and supports his forwards but he does not project to be a consistent point-producing defenseman. His passing game can be a bit sloppy at times, but he will deliver great outlet passes, even under pressure and his short passing game in the offensive zone is underrated. On offense, Lyckåsen has a tendency of getting frustrated if things aren't working and he will then start to try to skate the puck up ice by himself with a mixed success rate. His shot is not very hard but he keeps his the puck low and rarely gets blocked, He does a very good job at moving the puck sideways before releasing his shots from the blueline.

Lyckåsen needs to get much stronger to be able to handle his defensive responsibilities better, such as in battles in front of the net and in the corners.

	PLAYER	TEAM	LEAGUE	HEIGHT	WEIGHT	POS	GRADE
NR	MACCELLI, MATIAS	DUBUQUE	USHL	5'11.0"	165 *	LW	C
	HOCKEY SENSE		COMPETE		SKILL		SKATING
	4		4		8		5

Maccelli had an impressive offensive season in his sophomore year for Dubuque after coming over in the middle of the season last year from the TPS U20 Jr. A program. Maccelli finished 3rd in USHL scoring in the regular season, registering 31 goals and 41 assists in 62 games for the Fighting Saints. Maccelli is a very offensively minded winger that struggles with consistency in regard to his compete and two-way game. Maccelli isn't an overly quick or agile player but he shows good vision and passing ability from the perimeter in the offensive zone as well as off the rush, but he can be caught flat footed and when his time and space is taken away, he can be neutralized fairly easily and had some games where he wasn't really a factor. Matias has shown the ability to expose gaps in defenses and has good finishing ability where he capitalizes on his scoring chances. Maccelli likes to pull up and distribute the puck from the half wall position or will circle the offensive zone with the puck, looking for passing lanes and holes in coverages. There is very little North-South or power in his offensive game. Maccelli darts in and out of holes in the offensive zone, looking for scoring opportunities but doesn't like staying in the slot area or paying a price in front to score goals. Matias started to show more of a desire to compete and get involved on the back check later in the year, but this remains the big concern in his game. In too many viewings Maccelli was unengaged away from the puck, he was slow coming back into his own end, seemed to be hoping to stay behind the defense hoping the puck would come to him for a breakaway opportunity or he would exit his own zone often, looking for outlet passes before his team had possession in the defensive zone. Matias's straight-line skating is not at the level it needs to be a factor in the transition game; however, he moved the puck quickly in the neutral zone and can find guys with speed. Maccelli uses the geometry of the rink well in regard to indirect passing and shows good creativity in this regard. Maccelli still very much plays a European style and needs time and space to be effective but doesn't show great ability to create it for himself or his line mates. Maccelli has signed a contract to play in Europe next season, which may not help his development in the short term, as he needs to learn to be effective with less space, not more, so whichever team that drafts him will need to figure out a developmental path for him that can get him to transition to the North American game at some point. There is no denying Maccelli's playmaking and his ability to cash in on his scoring chances and that skill will give him a shot at NHL at some point, but there is a ways to go for him before his game is ready and before he is ready physically, as he is still very slight of frame and can get separated from pucks in battles rather easily.

"Late round pick at best." - NHL Scout, March 2019

"He'll get drafted for sure. Good player." - NHL Scout, March 2019

"I know one of our guys really liked him but I wouldn't draft him." - NHL Scout, March 2019

"I'm not a big fan. I think He'll play overseas when all is said and done." - USHL Staffer, March 2019

"There is skill there but he's a ways off in the compete and hockey sense category, and how often do those things develop late? Maybe a late round flyer for me but that's about it." HP Scout, Dusten Braaksma

"I don't think any player in the USHL turns the puck over more than Maccelli." - HP Scout, Michael Farkas

"To be ranked anywhere high by us when players have low compete they need to be pretty special in several other areas." - HP Scout, Mark Edwards, May 2019

NR	PLAYER	TEAM	LEAGUE	HEIGHT	WEIGHT	POS	GRADE
	MACK, SIMON	BROCKVILLE	CCHL	5'9.25"	180 *	RD	ND
	HOCKEY SENSE		COMPETE		SKILL		SKATING
	6		6		6		6

Simon is a smaller, puck-moving defenseman who was one of the top blueliners in the CCHL this year. He is a Penn State commit for the 2020-21 season. Simon is a good skater. His skating ability and smart angles on puck retrievals, allow him to win a lot of races cleanly enough to turn the puck north quickly. Simon handles the puck well and makes good, crisp, accurate passes, and shows the ability to rush the puck up the ice to create offensive chances for his team. Although he is undersized for a defenseman, he makes up for it with his hockey IQ. He has shown great awareness with or without the puck. He is an offensive-minded defenseman but did look good in 1-on-1 situations and maintained proper gap control with a good, active stick. In the offensive end, Simon does a really good job of distributing the puck from the point to his forwards, he doesn't have a heavy shot from back there, but it's a very accurate and seems to be imminently tip-able. Simon will need plenty of time to develop his game. Going to Penn State for four years may allow him to be a good player at the pro level down the road.

NR	PLAYER	TEAM	LEAGUE	HEIGHT	WEIGHT	POS	GRADE
	MACKAY, COLE	SAULT STE. MARIE	OHL	5'10.0"	188 *	RW	ND
	HOCKEY SENSE		COMPETE		SKILL		SKATING
	6		6		5		5

Mackay had a productive year for the Greyhounds and showed some chemistry when he had an opportunity to play with the more skilled players featured on the team, such as Frost and Hayton. He finished the season with 61 points in 65 games, including 27 goals. He was less successful in the playoffs and finished with 4 points in 11 games. He didn't play internationally.

Mackay is a playmaking winger who can attack all three-layers of the ice in the offensive-end. His vision was impressive both at even-strength and the powerplay; where he was used predominantly around the goal-line. He's capable of quick-one-touch passes and can make technical no-look passes that land on the tape. If there was one complaint with his passing, it was that he was more dangerous when passing from a stationary position than when he was carrying the puck. Part of this could be attributed to his skating which is average. His stride is choppy and he doesn't have a lot of separating speed given his average-build. His lack of gear-shifting reduces his ability to reorganize his passing lanes. Although Cole is a good playmaker, he can shoot the puck too. His shot extends past the hash-marks, where he has the ability to mix up his options with a powerful slapshot, as well as his wrist-shot. His release point is generated primarily through his wrists, demonstrating a quick-flicking motion that allows the start-up phase of his shot to stay hidden. Although his wrist-shot still lacks some velocity and he didn't elevate the puck in-tight to the net as much as we wanted to see. His hockey-sense allows him to take advantage of the above-attributes. He has good lane-recognition even if he can't take advantage of it at times due to his skating; there was also a consistency to his game when identifying soft-ice around the crease-area. Furthermore, he's shown poise when handling the puck and this allows him the opportunity to slow the play down, which helps compensate for his speed.

Mackay hasn't always been consistent and didn't have the best playoff performance. There is some talent but he needs to further increase his speed and become a more consistent player on a shift-to-shift basis in order to have a shot at making it.

"Worry about his skating and I see a player who is good at some things but not elite at anything." - NHL Scout, May 2019

NR	PLAYER	TEAM	LEAGUE	HEIGHT	WEIGHT	POS	GRADE
	MAIER, NOLAN	SASKATOON	WHL	6'0.0"	170	G	ND
	HOCKEY SENSE	COMPETE		SKILL		SKATING	
	5	7		5		7	

Maier just completed his second year starting in the WHL with the Saskatoon Blazers. This season he backstopped one of the leagues strongest teams with a 2.64 GAA and .910 save percentage. Maier was also given the opportunity to represent Canada at the Hlinka and u-18 tournaments.

Maier is an undersized goalie who makes up for this deficiency with excellent athleticism and compete. He is the type of goalie who never gives up on a play and has the athleticism to steal a goal back from the other team. Maier plays a very aggressive style and is a gambler who will occasionally put himself in positions where he has to rely on those desperation saves. While he is constantly engaged he can sometimes misread the play and leave himself very exposed. Maier also runs hot and cold, with games where he is unbeatable, and games where he lets in multiple soft goals and allows his play to snowball. Sometimes he can also try to do too much with the puck and he had frequent puck handling miscues this season. While Maier has exceptional athletic ability he could stand to refine his game to put himself in less situations where he has to scramble. As a smaller goalie his margin for error is not very big and he has to give himself every advantage he can.

NR	PLAYER	TEAM	LEAGUE	HEIGHT	WEIGHT	POS	GRADE
	MALONE, JACK	YOUNGSTOWN	USHL	6'0.75"	191 *	RW	C
	HOCKEY SENSE	COMPETE		SKILL		SKATING	
	6	6		5		5	

A well-rounded forward who can do a lot of things well. The former Delbarton (NJ-HS) standout quadrupled his production in his second USHL season. His 40 helpers were good for sixth in the entire USHL. Malone wouldn't take all the credit for that, as he spent a lot of time with Brett Murray (2016 4th Rd – BUF) perhaps the most lethal offensive weapon in the USHL this year. Murray was in on 37 of Malone's 59 points, including 18 of Murray's goals. Malone's skill level did seem to perk up as the year went on and he looked a little more comfortable handling the disc. He exhibits good, strong puck protection ability and is really tough to knock off his skates. His playmaking ability is improving, but it's not next-level yet. He did a better job finding passing lanes that were hidden from him earlier in the year, but the creation of those lanes is still a bit lacking. The puck poise is on the rise; he uses his body and skating to buy some extra time for himself that he can't necessarily make with pure skill. His hands don't really move the needle still, but he also doesn't press the issue to the point that he creates negative outcomes for himself. The player type that Malone purports to be is typically a much better finisher, especially in tight spaces – but that's not the case for the California-born Malone, quite the opposite actually. Jack's finishing ability in tight, or off one-timers left us wanting more all season long. He just doesn't connect consistently enough with good wood to make him a noteworthy lamplighter.

Malone's skating posture is a little awkward with how far he hunches forward instead of sitting back on his quads. That said, he gets around the rink with aplomb. He's quick and pretty industrious. The small-area footwork and his stops have gotten sharper. His balance is excellent, no matter who initiates contact, he can absorb it and not give much ground. While not an overtly physical player, he does throw some hits as necessary and they land well. As the year went on, he seemed to trade some defensive acumen for offensive forays but he still killed penalties and could cover for a center caught up ice as needed. He can play center and right wing and he continued to take faceoffs on his strong side or in special teams situations. He takes good, smart angles on the forecheck and supports plays well. His IQ and compete could probably both be given an extra half a point than the flat sixes we have. He doesn't quite have the viscosity that the best defensive players have, but then again, nothing about Malone is close to a finished product yet –as it's unclear what his development path is going to direct him toward. Given his smarts, skating, sturdy frame and good size, Jack represents an intriguing chunk of clay to mold; the technical skills will need to get up another tier in order for him to be a real play-driver at the next levels.

"I think he's an average skater and has average skill too. Not a guy I'd push for." - NHL Scout, February 2019

"He plays pretty hard and he's got decent hockey sense. He's a draft." - NHL Scout, February 2019

"I think he'll get drafted. I liked him but later on in the draft." - NHL Scout, April 2019

	PLAYER	TEAM	LEAGUE	HEIGHT	WEIGHT	POS	GRADE
NR	MARLEAU, VINCENT	ROUYN-NORANDA	QMJHL	6'2"	188	RC	**ND**
	HOCKEY SENSE		COMPETE		SKILL		SKATING
	-		-		-		-

Marleau went undrafted in the QMJHL Draft. He was signed as a free agent by the Huskies after a strong start to the season in the collegial league, back in 2016-2017. He's a classic late-bloomer type of prospect. After playing last year mostly on the 4th line, he saw his role increase this year. He had an excellent first half, with 34 of his 39 points coming before the Christmas break. After the trade period, the Huskies acquired two key forwards (Joël Teasdale and Louis-Filip Coté). Marleau then saw his ice time drop and only recorded 5 points (including two goals) in his last 26 games. Marleau can play both at center and on the wing, has great size and he's also an above-average skater. He has great work ethic, and doesn't mind getting involved in the physical game. There's value with him as a defensive forward. He can be an asset for a team on the PK unit. His lack of production in the second half is a bit concerning, and because of it, we don't expect him to get drafted. He'll be back next season as an overage player in the league. He's starting to use his size a bit more; he had a late growth spurt after Midget AAA and is still working on getting comfortable in his big frame. Next season, we expect him to get more ice time and a boost in confidence to start producing like he did in the first half of the season. There's a lot to like with him, as he's smart, has good size, skates well and plays a solid two-way game. Offensive upside is still the main question mark with him going forward.

	PLAYER	TEAM	LEAGUE	HEIGHT	WEIGHT	POS	GRADE
93	MASTROSIMONE, ROBERT	CHICAGO	USHL	5'9.75"	158 *	LW	**C**
	HOCKEY SENSE		COMPETE		SKILL		SKATING
	5		6		7		5

Quick, goal-scoring winger. Mastrosimone followed up on his All-Rookie Team campaign in 2017-18 by adding a Third-Team All-Star nod this season. He finished fourth in the league in goals (31) and led the USHL in playoff points (15) en route to a Clark Cup Final appearance. A speedy forward, Mastrosimone can get a lot of mileage out of streaking down the wing and ripping a shot high on a goalie. He has a quick release and can whiz one by a goalie's ear without a lot of wind-up. His north-south game is when he's at his most effective. While he does flash some moves from time to time, he's just as likely to have a puck roll off of his stick as he is to finish the move successfully. He is prone to turnovers from trying to do a little too much sometimes, particularly when circling the attack zone with the puck. To make matters worse, there's some tunnel vision from him when he's on one of these east-west missions and he seldom ever calls on support – he wants to get into an area and shoot, even if he's lost ground from his starting point. He can, however, skate himself out of some trouble. His straight-line skating offers a lot of pluses and he darts around the ice quickly. Where he lacks a little bit is the small-area footwork and using his feet to properly position himself for a puck battle or for good body positioning. He sometimes will over-skate those situations and end up giving away his advantage or leverage. Mastrosimone has the tendency to chase the play a lot, which works fine for now because of his skating gifts, but it will get tougher to overcome as he moves up. The bulk of his defensive game comes from chasing down players from behind and picking their pocket. This event occurs much more often before the opponents gain the zone, or even center ice. In the defensive zone proper, Mastrosimone doesn't offer too much. Robert's hockey sense is best described as a bit below average and he's oddly not physical for being as energized as he normally is. He acts as more of an outlet for the players playing defense than an actual, in-zone tactical threat. He just doesn't quite have the angles and puck support methods figured out. That said, he does have a pretty infectious work rate (mostly when the puck seems reachable) and he competes like a player that wants to be a winner. His board play needs to improve, not only for winning battles but how he gets off the wall. He has one head-fake shimmy that seems reasonably effective, but he's going to need to grow that out as a winger. Mastrosimone also needs to be better at pass catching, too many pucks get away from him even when they hit his tape – pucks in his feet are a misadventure. He was used on his off-wing at times this season to get his shot into the interior of the surface. Rather than trying to fully round out this type of player, it might end up being better for all parties to just lean in to the curve and focus the development on the dimensions that he offers: speed and shooting.

"I think his all-around game made some strides this year, he will probably be off the board by the time I'd be interested in drafting him." H/P Scout, Dusten Braaksma

	PLAYER	TEAM	LEAGUE	HEIGHT	WEIGHT	POS	GRADE
NR	MAZURA, TOMAS	KIMBALL	HIGH-NH	6'2.5	170 *	LC	**ND**
	HOCKEY SENSE	COMPETE		SKILL		SKATING	
	5	4		6		6	

Tomas came a bit out of nowhere this year to get on the 2019 NHL Draft Radar. Mazura wasn't even on the varsity roster last year at Kimball Academy but a late growth spirt and some skating development saw his game really excel in the last year, earning him an offer and commitment to Providence College for the fall of 2020. Tomas is a native of the Czech Republic and came over to North America in 16/17 to play at Kimball Academy. Tomas has a good blend of size and skill and the added pop in his skating made him difficult to defend at the prep level this year. Mazura has a good set of hands that allows him to buy time and make slick feeds in traffic to open areas of the ice. His style almost seems like he tries to draw defenders in close in order to expose the ice they free up and slips passes through their sticks and feet. Tomas can power down the wing and use his size to drive the net on defenders and has shown the ability to make slick passes while driving or circling behind the net. There are still some areas of concern when it comes to this play. He doesn't offer real high compete away from the puck and doesn't bring a lot physically so he squanders some of his size advantage without the puck. For a player his size in prep school, he wasn't winning a large amount of his puck battles. Mazura has some intriguing offensive tools but is still very much a project that will need some time at the junior, NCAA and probably the AHL level before he could be ready for NHL minutes. Oddly, Mazura was overlooked in the USHL

Phase 2 draft this past spring, but it's hard to imagine him not getting a Camp invite, especially if he gets drafted in Vancouver or he could always return to Kimball Academy for his senior year.

"He probably goes in the 3rd or 4th round." - NHL Scout, April 2019

NR	PLAYER	TEAM	LEAGUE	HEIGHT	WEIGHT	POS	GRADE
	MCCARTHY, CASE	USA U-18	NTDP	6'0.5	194 *	RD	C
	HOCKEY SENSE	COMPETE		SKILL		SKATING	
	5	6		4		5	

Traditional, defensive defenseman. The Boston University commit is the shutdown righty for the USNTDP and his game won't be measured by the boxscore most nights. Skating is in the average category, it's not prohibitive to his style, but his feet don't necessarily make his job any easier either. He actually looks to get a bit antsy if there's a lot of lead-up time to a rush chance against and he'll take a deeper C-cut than necessary and get himself a little off his mark. His recovery ability is on the weaker side, so he's swimming upstream until he can get his stick or physicality involved. McCarthy is a battler, he'll scrap and claw and block shots as necessary. He's a no-frills player who offers little offensive upside. He may have a little bit of a plus shot, but he's cautious to really step into plays offensively – the sequence has to demonstrate firm, controlled offensive possession before he'll stray more than five feet in off the attack line. He needs to do a better job of keeping his shot down, he's not going to score from 60 feet at any level. His ability to break the puck out when coupled with his puck poise are just not up to snuff. We think that the pressure of playing on a Globetrotter-like team when he's a Washington General at heart actually created more undue consternation for Case. In a more structured environment, the 6'1" rearguard might be able to more reliably make D-to-D or short breakout passes, but that's yet to be proven, of course. His anticipation is a useful attribute when facing in-zone attacks, but it's his vision with the puck that fails him. McCarthy is a willing competitor, but the technical tools need to fall into a reliable range.

NR	PLAYER	TEAM	LEAGUE	HEIGHT	WEIGHT	POS	GRADE
	MCCARTNEY, BEN	BRANDON	WHL	6'0.0"	182*	LW	C
	HOCKEY SENSE	COMPETE		SKILL		SKATING	
	5	6		5		6	

McCartney had a major breakout for Brandon this year going from 12 points last season to 41 this year, while improving his goals from 2 to 21. This was made all the more impressive considering he was not on the top powerplay and his most common line mate was a 16 year old rookie. Something of a skilled grinder at this point McCartney could play up and down the line up.

McCartney is an exciting player to watch with a combination of physicality and skill. Consistently willing to throw the body on the forecheck, and created a lot of turnovers using his body. Was always in the corners quick, making it difficult for defensemen to move the puck up clean. McCartneys skating also stood out as he has very good acceleration and a strong low base that makes him very powerful when engaging in contact. He easily took contact while maintaining his balance, allowing him to make plays in to high traffic areas. On top of this he has the hands to occasionally beat defensemen one on one. His handling ability sometimes suffered from a lack of creativity as he mostly used the same basic toe drag moves. McCartneys shot is good with a very quick release and solid accuracy. Scored multiple goals in our viewings where he shot around defensemen who he used as screens. Effort was consistently strong and in our viewings didn't take shifts off. McCartney hasn't shown great senses with the puck and was not a consistently noticeable offensive player, more relying on individual ability and hustle to generate most of his chances. He plays the game fast constantly putting pressure on the opposition defensemen with and without the puck, but there is room for growth as he learns to sometimes slow the game down with the puck. The tools are there for further progress in the coming years as McCartney shows a lot of natural ability and work ethic.

	PLAYER	TEAM	LEAGUE	HEIGHT	WEIGHT	POS	GRADE
NR	MCDONOUGH, AIDEN	CEDAR RAPIDS	USHL	6'2.0"	201	LW	**C**
	HOCKEY SENSE	COMPETE		SKILL		SKATING	
	6	7		6		5	

McDonough is a player we liked for the draft in last year's Black Book so it was surprising to us that the late 99' DOB forward went undrafted. As a result he was a player that was on our watch list at the start of the year as a re-entry prospect. We were eager to see what the powerful winger could accomplish in his transition to junior hockey from the New England prep school scene. McDonough didn't disappoint us in many viewings this year. He has added tremendous strength in the last year and has a good combination of size, speed and power in his game. McDonough very much plays a north-south, straight line power forward game. While his skill isn't eye popping, and he lacks the high end playmaking ability of some of the players at the top of draft lists, he possesses decent hands off the rush and the ability to quickly get his shot off, whether it is in traffic or in shooting in stride off the rush. McDonough likes to try to gain the middle of the ice with the puck and use the defenseman as a screen off the rush but doesn't hesitate to lower his shoulder and drive the net when the need arises. McDonough scored 21 goals and 21 assists in 50 games for Cedar Rapids this season, and many of them were of the power forward variety. McDonough was Cedar Rapids best player in the playoffs, registering 4 goals and 3 assists in 6 games. His ability to elevate his game in the playoffs impressed our staff as well. Aidan doesn't shy away from physical contact and in many instances initiates it. His first couple strides are average and has a good top gear that is difficult for a lot of opponents to handle. While nothing about his game oozes high end, there isn't a lot of glaring flaws in McDonough's all-around game at this stage as he works hard at both ends of the ice, both near and away from the puck and gives an honest effort night in and night out. His offensive ceiling is maybe limited at the NHL level but he checks enough boxes right now to be in this year's Black Book McDonough is physically ready for college hockey and is heading to Northeastern this fall.

"Can't say for sure but one of the reasons McDonough might have been passed over last year was many possibly thought he benefitted too much by playing with Jay O'Brien. I'm not sure that was the case, looking back at it now. I would have drafted him last year and he's on my list for this year as well.- HP Scout, Dusten Braaksma"

	PLAYER	TEAM	LEAGUE	HEIGHT	WEIGHT	POS	GRADE
32	MCMICHAEL, CONNOR	LONDON	OHL	5'10.75"	172 *	LC	**B**
	HOCKEY SENSE	COMPETE		SKILL		SKATING	
	7	5		7		6	

Connor McMichael had a breakout season for London. He finished 2nd in scoring in the OHL among all 17-year-old players, collecting 72 points in 67 games, including 36 goals. In the playoffs, he produced # in # of games. At the U18's heMcMichael is a cerebral two-way center who can put the puck in the back of the net. His best attribute is his hockey sense. When breaking down his hockey-sense, it's his combination of anticipating plays in advance and decision making that really stand-out. His anticipation gives him the ability to put himself in scoring positions by finding soft-ice and getting behind defensive-coverage consistently. This extends to the defensive-zone, where he's good at recognizing play-types unfold and reacts accordingly by getting in the way of both passing and shooting lanes. His decision-making when combined with how rapidly he can process the play allows him to make high-end one-touch passes to his teammates both in motion and from stationary positions. This also made him effective at keeping plays alive and not running out of room when protecting the puck. Connor's capable of thinking two-steps ahead of the play, which emphasized his efficiency on the powerplay and when attempting to generate in-tight spaces at even-strength. He's also a capable defender in his own-end of the ice due to his intelligence. We have seen him make some great defensive-reads, and intercept pucks that most other players wouldn't recognize in-time. Regarding his scoring ability, he's not a heavy framed player, but manages to generate a good amount of velocity on his release. Additionally, he's capable of handling difficult passes while going at top-speeds which made him effective off the rush when attempting to use his shot. Another impressive aspect of McMichael's goal scoring ability is that he can score in multiple-ways. He generates enough power to score from the hash-marks and out, yet has the hockey-sense necessary to find rebounds in-tight to the net before his opponents. Lastly, Connor has a good set-of-hands that allow him to drag the puck quickly, giving him the ability to beat opponents one-on-one as well as shift the angle of his shot.

What keeps McMichael from being higher in our rankings, is that he can go invisible for long-durations of a game. There's been far too many viewings where you're looking for him out on the ice and waiting for him to generate a play. In games where he's assertive, he looks like a completely different player than he is when he's not engaged. There's a lack of hustle when he's not as engaged and overall has shown us a very inconsistent motor as a result. Furthermore, he's not always willing to forecheck or play physical, displaying a lack of sandpaper to his game. Another area of concern is that when things aren't going his way, he has shown poor body-language which extends to his lack of competitiveness on a shift-to-shift basis. We've seen him argue with a referee while in the middle of a forecheck which made his attempt ineffective, as an example. Lastly, he has good fundamental skating mechanics. He's not an all-out burner, but he has solid straight-line speed, and his skating should translate when given time to add strength to his frame. So, if he's willing to compete more consistently over the course of his development, he has shown the translatable skating necessary to make it as a center at the next level.

Although we see McMichael as a center instead of a winger due to having better engagement-levels in our viewings down the middle, it's unlikely he will develop the mental attributes necessary to drive a line. As a result, we see McMichael as a potential 3rd-line center who can match-up well against other skilled-players if he continues to develop a better overall pace but is unlikely to become a primary offensive player.

"I want to draft players that are engaged and work hard. He waited for everyone else to do the work." - NHL Scout, December 2018

"He doesn't do any of the heavy lifting out there." NHL Scout, December 2018

"Loved him down the middle and didn't like him at all on the wing. It was like watching two different players. He's a top 25 pick at Centre and might not be top 60 for me as winger." NHL Scout, December 2018

"He has high end hockey sense and high end skill. Not much of that in the OHL (eligibles) this year. Compete could use some work." NHL Scout, January 2019

"Skating is hard to judge. I've seen him blow past guys and other nights I think his skating is average at best." - NHL Scout, January 2019

"Too much talent to drop too far down but he does frustrate you." - NHL Scout, January 2019

"McMichael had games where he looks like a top-6 scoring talent, and had other games where you needed to look at the line-up sheet to see if he was actually playing" - HP Scout, Brad Allen

"I think I managed to see him 10 times before I saw a game that looked like it matched his stats." - HP Scout, Mark Edwards, May 2019

"He won't be wearing a _____ jersey anytime soon." - NHL Scout, May 2019

"His skating grade would've been a seven if he put more effort into it on a consistent basis. He skated like a five grade at times. Compete was a four rating in several of my viewings. We kept it at five though. I found him difficult to rank because he played so poorly in my personal viewings but the goal totals are real. - HP scout, Mark Edwards, May 2019

"I'm not as high as some team scouts that I've talked to about Connor, but compared to the rest of our own scouts it's like I'm practically the president of his fan club. Not much support for one of my OHL guys from our crew." - HP Scout, Mark Edwards, May 2019

	PLAYER	TEAM	LEAGUE	HEIGHT	WEIGHT	POS	GRADE
NR	**MEEHAN, BEN**	**DEXTER**	**HIGH-MA**	**6'0.0"**	**163**	**LD**	**ND**
	HOCKEY SENSE	COMPETE			SKILL		SKATING
	6	6			5		4

Meehan is a player that has quietly gained more traction and eyes this season even though he has been verbally committed to UMass-Lowell since September 2017. He tripled his production from the previous two season at Dexter School this past season. His footwork has steadily improved over the years and plays steady game making smooth outlets and chipping in on the offense as well. He will maneuver at the blue line to find shooting lanes, makes good puck decisions in both ends, and defensively positions himself well and has an active stick to break play up. He is decent size though could develop additional muscle mass to be more effective in physical battles as he progresses into juniors and college levels. Meehan is intriguing as he is just starting to scratch the surface in potential and has many tools and mind to become a blue liner at the next levels.

	PLAYER	TEAM	LEAGUE	HEIGHT	WEIGHT	POS	GRADE
NR	**MEIER, SPENCER**	**ST CLOUD ST**	**NCAA**	**6'3.25"**	**193**	**RD**	**ND**
	HOCKEY SENSE	COMPETE			SKILL		SKATING
	6	6			4		5

Meier was a key piece to Fargo's run to the Clark Cup title last spring and is coming off a pretty successful freshman season for the St. Cloud State Huskies. Despite mostly being used as a bottom pair defenseman for the Huskies, Meier managed to chip in offensively with 1 goal and 9 assists in 38 games. Meier is a 99' born that looks the part of a shutdown defenseman with his impressive size and range with his stick. Meier uses his body and size effectively, both to shield the puck as well as in order to box guys out and defend in front of his own net. Where Meier struggles defensively is when he is on an island, defending one on one. His footwork and four-way change of direction struggles vs more agile opponents. His long and active stickwork can be a negating factor for him at this level but his footwork will need to improve if Meier is going to be an effective shut down defenseman at the NHL level. At this stage Meier doesn't project as a big offensive contributing at the next level but he shoes good poise with the puck and decent hands in traffic which allows him to move the puck away from pressure effectively. Meier isn't on our draft board but should be a player to trade as a potential NCAA Free Agent down the road.

"Very much a meat and potatos kind of defenseman. Not much there in the way of offense that I see translating to the NHL. He might get drafted though." - HP Scout, Dusten Braaksma

NR	PLAYER	TEAM	LEAGUE	HEIGHT	WEIGHT	POS	GRADE
	MERRITT, ARLO	KIMBALL UNION	HIGH-NH	6'3.0"	190	LC	ND
	HOCKEY SENSE	COMPETE		SKILL		SKATING	
	4	6		4		7	

The rangy, speedy Merritt completed his third year with Kimball Union Academy by narrowly eclipsing his previous season totals. He finished the year by getting a handful of shifts with the Lincoln Stars, scoring once in four games. The Halifax native was selected in the 7th round by both the Mooseheads (QMJHL) and the Stars (USHL). To preserve his collegiate commitment to Ohio State, he elected to go the USHL route. Merritt is a fairly lanky looking player who gives the impression he is every bit of 6'3". His best asset is his speed; his top-end speed is probably just about an 8, but the rest of his footwork drags the grade down a bit. His edgework and body control do not match his top gear. He needs speed to compensate for below average hockey sense. Arlo, quite simply, just looks a little lost in all three zones. He chases the game around quite a bit. He looks pretty comfortable going to the front of the net and watching his pointman defensively, but those attributes are hardly award winning. In the event that he can make a play on a puck, his skill level is below expectation. He fumbles quite a few pucks away and over-skates quite a few more. He gives off the feeling that he's not too comfortable with the puck on his blade and feels rushed to get rid of it. It looks like he has a plus shot and he can hack some pucks out of danger with his really long reach, but those are the only redeeming qualities at the present. He looks pretty game and athletic, he'll throw body checks if that's what the cue card says. Even for a project pick, there really doesn't seem like there would be upside beyond that of a low-end depth player.

NR	PLAYER	TEAM	LEAGUE	HEIGHT	WEIGHT	POS	GRADE
	MICHEL, JÉRÉMY	VAL D'OR	QMJHL	6'1.0"	150	LW	ND
	HOCKEY SENSE	COMPETE		SKILL		SKATING	
	5	5		6		6	

Michel was in his second season with the Foreurs. He had a decent year, with 16 goals and 42 points on a team that struggled to win games and score goals. He was the 17th overall selection in the 2017 QMJHL Draft after playing one midget season with Lévis in the LHMAAAQ. Michel is a good skater with above-average hands who is going to be a good point producer in the QMJHL in the next two or three seasons. Physically, he still has ways to go; he needs to get stronger in order to compete better along the boards to win more puck battles and in front of the net. Due to his current lack of strength, he tends to stay on the perimeter too often and doesn't engage himself in one-on-one battles with enough frequency. He's a good skater who generates some good speed and can surprise opposing defensemen with a quick burst of speed. He's got to improve his play away from the puck, showing better involvement in his own zone. Right now, he's a one-dimensional forward with a good offensive touch, but needs to improve his play away from the puck and physical involvement.

NR	PLAYER	TEAM	LEAGUE	HEIGHT	WEIGHT	POS	GRADE
	MILLAR, JACK	CEDAR RAPIDS	USHL	6'2.0"	179	RD	ND
	HOCKEY SENSE	COMPETE		SKILL		SKATING	
	5	5		4		5	

Docile, defensive defenseman with a big frame. Millar's move out of midget hockey didn't even require him to change his stationery, as he graduated to the Cedar Rapids RoughRiders from the Rocky Mountain RoughRiders program. The modest stat line matches his game pretty well. He had just 14 points in 61 games, with a minus-5 rating. The right-handed defenseman has just average mobility. He doesn't generate a lot of power when moving laterally and there is no mechanism in his game to really wheel. He can over-exert a little bit with his upper body when trying to battle leaving him vulnerable to end up on the ice. He's a loose gap, conservative player who really lets the game come to him – almost to a fault sometimes. His general lack of aggression allows some plays to fester that would have been shut down by rearguards who play more aggressive Despite his frame, he's not a commit-to-hit player, nor does he have a penchant to exert his strength in almost any situation. His skill level is below the mark. The one plus is that he seems to have a good sense of when and where to move the puck on the breakout and off of retrievals. He really doesn't get into a lot of trouble there, despite his fairly limited skill/skating package. The rest of his game, however, doesn't give us a lot of confidence about his hockey intelligence. He's no dummy, but he also gives himself a lot of time to diagnose plays because of the gap that he keeps – based on how he manages his spacing with the puck and potential threats, he looks to have only an average feel for the game and even less confidence in himself. His shot takes a while to load up, and while he has decent leverage because of his frame, it's not much of a threat. To his credit, he was used a lot in the postseason against one of the better duos in the league (Nick Abruzzese and Robert Mastrosimone) and he acquitted himself well. Even with that, this late 2000 birthday looks no better than a watchlist player for us right now.

NR	PLAYER	TEAM	LEAGUE	HEIGHT	WEIGHT	POS	GRADE
	MILLMAN, MASON	SAGINAW	OHL	6'0.75"	175 *	LD	C
	HOCKEY SENSE	COMPETE		SKILL		SKATING	
	6	6		5		6	

Mason Millman had a solid, yet maybe slightly under-the-radar rookie season for Saginaw. He produced 25 points in 66 games, and had an additional 5 points in 13 playoff games. Millman's best quality is his willingness to initiate physically. He's a competitive kid who keeps a good pace and makes life uncomfortable for opposing teams who attempt to cut around him. His defensive-reads were a plus overall, recognizing most offensive-plays in advance which gave him the ability to keep opposing players largely to the outside. When he was beaten-wide or made a defensive-error, his recovery-rate was impressive thanks to his ability to switch his intensity when the play called for it. Behind the goal-line, he was calm under-pressure and was capable of moving the puck quickly in most of our viewings. In-front of the net, he knows how to use his frame effectively, and was able to get under his opponent's skin, this included more offensively-gifted players as well. His outlet passes were hit or miss but he is capable of making a quality two-line pass and also has the ability to skate the puck up the ice. His skating is a six in our rating system. He features a powerful-stride but it can be a bit short at times when he's attempting to enter another gear. Additionally, he's not the most agile player and carries a thicker-frame which reduces his escapability both when in his own-end and when attempting to weave through the neutral-zone. In the offensive-zone, he flashes some skill on occasion; including the ability to thread passes after activating at the line and uses shot-fakes to re-adjust his lane. He's never going to be misinterpreted for an offensive-defenseman, but Millman brings a lot of poise to his game and has shown good overall decision making. There might be an untapped two-way defender in MIllman, but he's going to need extended development time in order to for him to take-advantage of his hockey-sense in the offensive-zone more than he currently does.

"There might be some untapped potential in Mason, he kept forcing me to recognize him out on the ice" - HP Scout, Brad Allen

"He's on my list but I doubt we'd take him." - NHL Scout, March, 2019

"He's a good skater and he's competitive. He gets involved. i'm taking him over a lot of the other later round OHL guys."- NHL Scout, March 2019

"I like him in the OHL but I don't know what he'll be at the next level so he didn't make my list." - NHL Scout, May 2019

"I couldn't warm up to him. I mean I know he skates well but I don't know what in his game translates to the next level...what's he gonna be? I watched him three times in the playoffs trying to figure him out." - NHL Scout, June 2019

"Didn't make my list but there's not much doubt he will be a late selection. Skating will get him drafted."- NHL Scout, June 2019

"Skating is solid and he shows some poise with the puck. I gave him a draftable grade but it's probably tight for him to make our list late right now." - HP Scout, Mark Edwards, May 2019

	PLAYER	TEAM	LEAGUE	HEIGHT	WEIGHT	POS	GRADE
NR	**MINER, TRENT**	**VANCOUVER**	**WHL**	**6'0.5"**	**182 ***	**G**	**ND**
	HOCKEY SENSE	COMPETE		SKILL		SKATING	
	6	5		5		5	

A former 1st round WHL draft pick, Miner had a phenomenal rookie season this year. Coming in to the year as a backup, Miner pushed Arizona draft pick David Tendeck all year and finished with a 1.98 GAA and a .924 save percentage.

Miner is undersized but excels with excellent positioning. He does an excellent job of reading the play as it develops and is great at putting himself in a position to make the save. Miner is rarely caught scrambling and has a calming effect on his team when he's in net. Miner is fluid post to post but isn't explosive, and is not the type to make the highlight reel desperation save. He frequently has the saves he should make but lacks the ability to steal a goal from the opposition. He is a plus puck handler who does a good job coming out to stop the puck behind his net and puts his defensemen in good positions. Miner has an excellent understanding of the game and is an excellent junior goalie, however his lack of size or elite athleticism could be a hindrance at higher levels of play.

	PLAYER	TEAM	LEAGUE	HEIGHT	WEIGHT	POS	GRADE
NR	**MIRONOV, ILYA**	**YAROSLAVL 2**	**RUS-JR.**	**6'3.0"**	**201**	**LD**	**ND**
	HOCKEY SENSE	COMPETE		SKILL		SKATING	
	5	5		5		5	

Ilya Mironov had a decent year while playing for the best team in the MHL. He was featured more in a depth-role at times, while generating 6 points in 36 games, including 1 goal. In the playoffs, he produced 2 points in 10 games on there way to a championship. At international events. Ilya stood out at the beginning of the season by producing 4 points in 5 games at the Hlinka, and had an additional assist at the U19-World-Junior-A-Challenge. Mironov is a large-defender with a good point-shot. He has some length and has aggressive defensive-instincts, though this can get him in trouble at times since he can mis-assess or fail to anticipate the play as it's developing, which can put him at a disadvantage. He's an okay skater given his size, but he relies on his pivots and edges more than pure straight-line, transitioning speed. He does use frame effectively in the corners, and is willing to battle to get the puck back. At the offensive-line, he can activate into the play, has decent playmaking ability and a powerful point shot that he rarely got through traffic when we got to watch him play.

	PLAYER	TEAM	LEAGUE	HEIGHT	WEIGHT	POS	GRADE
42	MISYUL, DANIL	YAROSLAVL 2	RUS-JR.	6'3.0"	176	LD	B
	HOCKEY SENSE	COMPETE		SKILL		SKATING	
	6	7		5		8	

Daniil Misyul had a very good season while developing in Lokomotiv's program. He played the majority of his hockey with Loko Yaroslavl of the MHL, finishing with 10 points in 46 games, including 4 goals. In the playoffs he produced no points in 10 games but was trusted in critical situations when protecting the lead late during their run to the championship. His play earned him a small call-up to Lokomotiv Yaroslavl of the KHL, where he finished with 2 points including 1 goal in 9 combined games between the regular season and post season.

Misyul is a mobile, two-way defenseman who can play a nasty-game in-front of the net. His long and lanky-frame, combined with his upward stance doesn't leave you with an impression that he can move very-well but when he takes off, he shows very impressive mechanics. There's few skaters in this class who have a more translatable skating package considering the amount of room that Daniil still has to grow into his frame. He's a powerful and fluid skater who has very little wasted efficiency in his stride; so when he matures, he should develop into one of the better overall skaters in this class. His four-way mobility blends well with his aggressive and fast-paced game when hes' defending. He looks to magnetize to his opponents in coverage and uses his leverage and tenacity to make life difficult for them. He's not afraid to use his size and can already deliver solid hits. He's a multi-dimensional player in his own-end and has an excellent stick that's extended through his length and good defensive-awareness, which allows him to interpret lanes and deflect passes. He can lose his man in coverage and get too aggressive at times but his skating ability and compete allow him to recover very well. There's few defenders in this class who can close a gap like Daniil and impose themselves on an opponent using his wing-span. Misyul is also good in breakout situations. He has the option of either transporting the puck up the ice or finding his outlet-pass, and he's capable of both. There's a good amount of poise and confidence when he's rushing the puck and he's not a player who gets rattled under-pressure below the goal-line. He's also a player who's willing to get engaged after the play and doesn't mind dropping the gloves; he doesn't back down and has the mentality needed to play a mean-game in-front of the net.

Misyul does make good decisions overall, and he's an excellent skater, but there's still a lot of room for growth in the offensive-zone. He doesn't feature a very-hard wrist-shot or much in the way of a quality fast-release, and still needs to continue to learn how to recognize when he has an opening to get his release through traffic. That said, he does have good coordination and uses it within his slapshot so create more momentum in his release. What's already translatable in the offensive-zone is his understanding of when to activate at the line at the right times, and his poise when holding the puck for extended time when identifying options; he's more raw in the offensive-end in terms of finishing then some of the other high-ranked defenders in this class. Furthermore, he doesn't use fakes at the line, as often as we would like, but again, these are developmental traits that we think he can add to his offensive-game over time.

Misyul already carries a sound defensive-presence on the ice and we think the majority of his tools are translatable and they're packed into a projectable NHL-frame. Though, we also see some limits to what he's most likely going to be capable of. We think he is going to be a smart-two-way-defender who can keep a high-pace, but is unlikely to receive powerplay-time, but he can definitely kill penalties. Since the offense isn't up there with the top defensive-players, even though the tools are, we have him in this middle-range.

> *"I'll never forget watching him last season and remembering he was one of the few kids who could slow down Jack Hughes offensive-game when basically no other defenders at the U18's could." - HP Scout, Brad Allen*

NR	PLAYER	TEAM	LEAGUE	HEIGHT	WEIGHT	POS	GRADE
	MOBERG, COLE	PRINCE GEORGE	WHL	6'2.5"	187*	RD	ND
	HOCKEY SENSE		COMPETE		SKILL		SKATING
	5		4		5		5

Moberg is a late 2000 born player from North Vancouver who was in his 2nd full season in the WHL. He went undrafted in the WHL bantam Draft and signed with Prince George after a strong training camp in 2016.

He took a major leap this year going from a marginal defenseman with 11 points, to a 40 point scorer who played an integral power play role with the Cougars this season. Moberg has a strong shot and good instincts with the puck. He got lot of his goals this year thanks to his strong shot from the point. We saw him get shots through the goaltender thanks to the high velocity of his shot. He's not shy to rush the puck and be active from the blueline with the puck trying to create offense. He's a decent skater for his size; he generate some decent speed in straight lines but has average fluidity and agility. His compete level in the defensive zone need to improve for Moberg to become more of a quality NHL level prospect in the years ahead.

NR	PLAYER	TEAM	LEAGUE	HEIGHT	WEIGHT	POS	GRADE
	MOORE, COOPER	BRUNSWICK PREP	HIGH-CT	6'1.25"	175 *	LD	ND
	HOCKEY SENSE		COMPETE		SKILL		SKATING
	4		4		5		7

Cooper Moore played for Brunswick Prep School this year where he was over a PPG defenseman with 13 goals and 18 assists in 28 games. Moore has good size with strong skating abilities. Moore provides a strong and mobile base that protects the puck well which makes him hard to pressure into mistakes on the breakout. Moore lacks some ability to defend consistently in his own end; he can lose battles and coverages around the net but shows that he cares and puts forth the effort so the defensive deficiencies might work themselves out over time. Offensively Cooper shows flashes of some dynamic puck moving ability and can defeat guys one on one but makes a fair amount of high risk decisions and can commit turnovers in key areas of the ice. Moore has plus puck shooting ability with a versatile arsenal of shots from the point position. His quick snap shot is impressive and has good velocity, get through to the net and can find the corners. Moore will be off the Chilliwack (BCHL) this year before heading to The University of North Dakota in 2020.

95	PLAYER	TEAM	LEAGUE	HEIGHT	WEIGHT	POS	GRADE
	MOYNIHAN, PATRICK	USA U-18	NTDP	5'10.75"	183 *	RW	C
	HOCKEY SENSE		COMPETE		SKILL		SKATING
	6		6		5		6

Energetic, but savvy forward. While his point totals weren't as gaudy in the USHL circuit as some of his world-class teammates, Moynihan made a really positive impression most nights. Not a lot of bad things happened when he was out there either, his plus-32 rating in 28 USHL games was tops among all forwards on the team (Cam York at plus-40, the only player better).

Moynihan has an infectious work rate and enthusiasm on the ice no matter what role or line he was offered. He works hard, but more importantly, he works smart – even when he's up playing with elite talent, he doesn't miss a beat. His skating is a major plus; his first-step quickness is especially impressive. His closing speed isn't bad either, as he has a good feel for the game and neutralizing threats against his club. His feet are always moving and he's poised and ready to go as soon as he jumps on the ice, which suggests he's really invested in the game – even from the bench. He plays the game at a really good pace – a pro pace. His baseline for detail work is already high-end, as readily covers for pinching defensemen or he provides overlap support or center-lane drive to prevent rush chances from stagnating with parallelism. Moynihan fetches pucks from anywhere on the ice and he moves them quickly. One of Patrick's finest traits is that plays seldom die with him – maybe he can't deke a quality defender every single time he has possession, but he'll find someone or he'll whip a good shot on net. He has a plus shot and he can get it off quickly from anywhere, almost regardless of his body position. It's not uncommon to see Moynihan take one off his back skate and zip it on net, or get a "late touch" on one that crosses the plane of his body before he lets it go.

Moynihan is no slouch in open space either. He has above average hands, looks good making "finishing" passes down near the net, and does a fine job looking off defenders to offer some misdirection. The talent level certainly isn't elite; he projects to be better as a complementary piece than someone who drives the play of a line. That said, this feels like a "utility-plus" player, in that he projects to be able to fill a lot of slots in the lineup when called upon. While he looks to be able to play up and down a lineup across multiple positions, his lack of specialization, lack of elite talent, and just average size and strength prevent him from being a more highly-regarded prospect. Given some of his linemates over the course of the season, he doesn't get to handle the puck or carry it across lines as much as we'd like. He also doesn't get the full attention of opposing defenses to challenge from a skill perspective – that will be the next big hurdle for the Providence College commit.

"There aren't 186 top-six talents in the NHL, those spots that don't have top-six talent are filled in by Patrick Moynihans." – HP Scout, Michael Farkas

"I think he's a really smart player, he knows where he needs to be on the ice, reads the play extremely well, he really moved up my rankings the 2nd half of the season." – HP Scout, Dusten Braaksma

NR	PLAYER	TEAM	LEAGUE	HEIGHT	WEIGHT	POS	GRADE
	MRAZIK, MICHAL	RÖGLE JR.	SWE-JR.	6'4.0"	183 *	RW	ND
	HOCKEY SENSE	COMPETE		SKILL		SKATING	
	5	4		6		4	

The big Slovakia born winger moved to Sweden this season to play for Rögle BK and their U20 team in the SuperElit league where he put up 11 goals and 13 assists in 40 games in his debut season. Mrazik also played 8 games for his new club's U18 team and put up 7 goals and 12 assists.

Mrazik is very unpolished and lacks tactical understanding. It's obvious that he's got some offensive skills and has never really had to defend before arriving in Sweden. Even though he can actually defend pretty decent on 1-on-1 situations, the few times he is on the right side of the puck in the defensive zone, he leaves early almost every time to try to create odd-man rushes the other way. Though it's rare he puts himself in the proper position to do so, he utilizes his big frame to stand in the lane to block shots and gets in the way for opposing defenders trying to join the attack. While in the defensive zone, he gives the impression of being somewhat passive and unwilling to participate, but he reads the play very well

His game really starts from the red line going forward, where he does a good job at entering the offensive zone with control of the puck. He plays with a rather short stick and his stickhandling really benefits from it, where he can dangle his way around opponents and keep the puck close to his body. He can also manage the puck at full speed but that top speed is pretty slow as his skating is choppy and is his Achilles heel. His first few strides lack explosivity and his foot speed leaves much room for improvement. He is easy to catch on the backcheck but he is very strong and he can sustain his balance as well as the control of the puck despite being caught. . He has a clear knack of finding the open areas to get a pass for a one-timer and often finds loose pucks around the net and in the corners. His shots are often from the slot and often result in a high danger scoring chance. But he needs to be more consistent in getting shots off. Right now, he often either fans on one-timers, misses the net, or goes bar-down and in.

In international play, he appeared in 13 games for Slovakia where he put up 9 goals and 15 points. He had a very rough tournament at the U18 Worlds, managing just a goal in 7 games; He was a -10 in the plus-minus category in a tournament where his team got relegated from the A group.

NR	PLAYER	TEAM	LEAGUE	HEIGHT	WEIGHT	POS	GRADE
	MUIR, COLE	KOOTENAY	WHL	6'2.5"	205 *	LC	ND
	HOCKEY SENSE	COMPETE		SKILL		SKATING	
	5	6		5		4	

Big powerful centre who's play was stronger than his 27 points on a weak Kootenay team would suggest. Muir is strong in board battles and made assertive net drives from down low and off the half wall. Muir possesses a heavy shot that he liked to utilize off the rush and in the slot, could stand to speed up his release and become a bit less predictable. Does not have pro level skating yet, as Muir lacks strong edgework to make elusive moves. Takes a bit too much time to really get up to top speed which was a bit limiting for his game as well. Offensively did not show many high end instincts, generating most of his chances off defensive miscues and basic reads rather than creating something out of nothing. Was trusted defensively spending a lot of time matched up against stronger opponents and on the penalty kill where he played a strong positional game. Muir also brings a strong physical element crashing hard on the forecheck and finishing his checks whenever the opportunity is there. Will be interesting to see how much he can develop his offensive game and skating over the offseason, could be one to watch for next year.

NR	PLAYER	TEAM	LEAGUE	HEIGHT	WEIGHT	POS	GRADE
	MULLAHY, DEREK	DEXTER SCHOOL	HIGH-MA	6'0.0"	178 *	G	ND
	HOCKEY SENSE	COMPETE		SKILL		SKATING	
	5	6		6		6	

Mullahy was rivalling Spencer Knight as one of the other top goalies in this class in his U15 year but never hit a second growth spirt. What Mullahy lacks in size, he makes up for in athleticism as well as being an aggressive goalie that comes out and challenges shooters. Mullahy's athleticism and quick lateral movements allow him to recover and adjust in the crease after challenging shooters. Mullahy is barely over 6 feet tall but plays much larger in the net in regards to his posture and style of play. He doesn't leave much for shooters to shoot for when he is in one on one situations. With any small goalie, holes open up when you get him moving laterally which is just a downfall of being an undersized goalie but Mullahy has the skill set to overcome his size and has a better than average shot at playing professional hockey down the road. Derek is committed to Harvard University for 2020 so will likely be playing junior hockey this fall. Mullahy was drafted in the 3rd Round by Cedar Rapids as well as a 1st Round, 15th overall pick by Rimouski (QMJHL) in 2017.

NR	PLAYER	TEAM	LEAGUE	HEIGHT	WEIGHT	POS	GRADE
	MURRAY, BLAKE	SUDBURY	OHL	6'1.75"	187 *	LC	ND
	HOCKEY SENSE	COMPETE		SKILL		SKATING	
	5	4		7		5	

Blake Murray had a disappointing season despite having pretty solid production. He finished the year with 30 goals, which was the most of any player on the Wolves, and had 50 points overall. In the playoffs, he continued scoring, producing 4 goals and 5 points in 8 games. We thought highly of Murray entering the season due to his talent-level. The kid has a pro-release. He has static posturing, good-footwork, understands how to generate torque through his initial shot-phase, and can mask where he's intending to place the puck. These attributes formed a dangerous sniper who needed little time and space to beat goalies. Furthermore, he's capable of generating power, resulting in his shot threatening from beyond the hash-mark area. His hands are good as well, which contributed to his release since he could seamlessly transition from guarding the puck into following through on his shot. Despite having a high-skill level and a pro-element to his game that created production, the rest of Blake's game never evolved over the course of the season. For such a naturally gifted shooter, he's as unnatural as they come away from the puck. He doesn't like physical contact and doesn't like to compete in-front of the net; as a result, he largely stays to the perimeter. What's more concerning, is that he was validated when he would enter into more dangerous shooting areas, yet this never increased his consistency. Blake is willing to do the right thing on the ice when he feels like it, not when it's required. This extends to his pacing. He keeps a very inconsistent-pace; one shift, he can make a solid defensive play, or strip the puck off an opponent on the forecheck; on another, he can be a detriment to his team by routinely turning over the puck or losing his man in-coverage. He's a bigger kid, but you wouldn't know it by his play-style, so he has to rely on the finesse elements of his game. Yet, in order to find high-percentage shooting areas to take advantage of his soft-touch with the puck, he needs to skate to them. Blakes skating mechanics are average and it takes him some time to get up to his okay top-gear. This wouldn't be so concerning if his motor was above-average, but it isn't. Furthermore, he lacks agility and has trouble dealing with aggressive defenders in-tight spaces.

"He had 20 goals last year. How does he not make the Hlinka team?" - NHL Scout, August 2018

"I didn't see much of him last season because of the lack of draft worthy players in Sudbury but liked him in his OHL Draft year, especially his shot. I saw him vs Guelph in his first game of the season. He played so soft and didn't compete at all. Our former Scout Ryan Yessie (now with

Sudbury) was at the game and after two periods I told him what I thought. What I didn't know was that the Wolves Director of Scouting was standing beside Ryan. Nicely inserted foot in mouth. It was all good though. We moved on to other players." - HP scout, Mark Edwards, September 2018

"I just saw him last week. Not a fan of his game at all. Already a no draft for me if that's possible." - NHL Scout, September 2018

"Skating isn't fantastic and he is a one trick pony. He can shoot a puck though." - NHL Scout, November 2018

"He can score. If he would just work harder he would really have something." NHL Scout, November 2018

"30 goals is 30 goals. You can't take that away from him and goal scorers don't grow on trees. I'd draft him late with no hesitation at all." - NHL Scout, April 2019

"Skating is just ok and he struggles to compete. I thought he had a few flashes in the playoffs but a bit too little too late. - NHL Scout, May 2019

"He can shoot the puck and he scores. Keep it simple when scouting him. Forget the all the other noise" - NHL Scout, May 2019

"If you only saw Murray play against Ottawa in the playoffs it would've given you a good snapshot of what scouts saw and talked about all year. I saw the two games in Ottawa and his soft play led to two goals for Ottawa. It put a bow on what I had seen all year long. Despite the 30 goals he's a no draft for me. Poor decisions and what I almost interpreted as fear on the ice." - HP Scout, Mark Edwards, April 2019

	PLAYER	TEAM	LEAGUE	HEIGHT	WEIGHT	POS	GRADE
NR	MUTALA, SASHA	TRI-CITY	WHL	6'0.5"	195 *	RW	C
	HOCKEY SENSE		COMPETE		SKILL		SKATING
	5		5		6		5

As a former 5th overall WHL draft pick, and member of Canada's Ivan Hlinka team, Mutala began the year highly touted. His season likely didn't go as well as many saw it going finishing with 41 points for the Tri-City Americans. However Mutala still managed to wear a letter as an assistant captain as one of the youngest players on his team.

Mutala is a physically strong two way winger with above average skating ability. He skates with an excellent knee bend making him difficult to knock off the puck. He shows good speed darting up the ice and on the back check. Mutala always competes defensively and pressures the point, taking away shooting lanes very well. Offensively Mutala makes some good reads, getting in to smart positions without the puck, and committing defenders before making a play. However, doesn't consistently display high end offensive instincts and seems to be missing some sense of timing to make plays. Mutala has above average puck handling ability, making plays through the tripod and beating defenseman off the rush. Mutala also has a dangerous shot with a quick release. With all of his tools Mutala should have more of an offensive impact but can defer and fade in to background too often.

NR	PLAYER	TEAM	LEAGUE	HEIGHT	WEIGHT	POS	GRADE
	MUTTER, NAVRIN	HAMILTON	OHL	6'3.0"	190 *	LW	ND
	HOCKEY SENSE	COMPETE		SKILL		SKATING	
	4	6		3		6	

A big kid from Lucan Ontario. He was selected by Hamilton in Round 5, 83rd overall, in the 2017 OHL Draft.

Mutter is a huge kid who plays a very physical game . Ontario Hockey League coaches voted him the second best body checker in the Eastern Conference Mutter lacks quickness but is a decent skater. We gave him a six rating because his skating will probably continue to improve He has value on the forecheck, opposing defensemen want to move the puck quickly. His work ethic is good, and his physical game is his strength. He lacks skill and hockey sense. He plays a simple game using his body to create space. He's a throwback player but more often these days third and 4th line NHL'ers are often players who piled up points in junior but can't crack top 6 roles. Those players alter their game to stay in the league. Even back in the early 90's this would happen. Jody Hull scored 50 goals and had a 94 point season in the OHL. He was selected 18th overall in the 1987 NHL Draft He told us a few years ago that he realized quickly that he better be willing to change his game if he wanted to stay in the NHL because he wasn't good enough to play up the lineup. He adapted and filled a bottom forward role. We're not saying players like Mutter can't make it, there are always exceptions but it's increasingly less likely these days.

"He's big and he can skate and he' tough. Someone might draft him." - NHL Scout, May 2019

"Not for me but I wouldn't be surprised if someone drafted him." NHL Scout, May 2019

"30 years ago he might've been a top three round pick." - NHL Scout, May 2019

"He's a gamer but he lacks skill and hockey sense so he won't be on our list." - HP Scout, Mark Edwards, May 2019

NR	PLAYER	TEAM	LEAGUE	HEIGHT	WEIGHT	POS	GRADE
	MUZIK, RADEK	LULEA JR.	SWE-JR.	6'2.75"	179 *	LW	ND
	HOCKEY SENSE	COMPETE		SKILL		SKATING	
	5	6		5		4	

Muzik came to Sweden and Luleå HF prior to this season and has been a breath of fresh air to his organization. He was a regular and an important piece in Luleå's U20 team in the SuperElit league where he played 38 games and managed to put up 8 goals and 14 assists in 38 games for a total of 22 points. He also starred in 8 games with the U18 team where he recorded 8 goals and 6 assists for a total of 14 points in just 8 games and he looked really good.

Muzik skating technique leaves much room for improvement, but he gets the job done and he can assemble really good top speed when he gets the opportunity to gain speed up the wing. He accelerates very well considering his big frame and he plays a very energetic and intense game, where he takes the puck to the net and doesn't shy away from the physical play in the high danger areas in the offensive zone. He could benefit from using his physical gifts even more on the forecheck, where he is able to catch up easily, but just skates by and don't finish the hit. There is no complaining over his work ethic since he will give his 100% every shift he is on the ice.

Offensively he is more annoying for the defenders than a threat for the goaltender, he reacts quickly to loose pucks and wins battles for the puck by playing physical against his opponents to bump them off the puck. His wrist shot is actually very hard and precise, but he tends not to shoot often enough as he tries to power his way to the net instead of trying to find space and time to get a shot off. He will try to find openings high on the short side and will eventually catch the goaltender off guard. His hands and stickhandling are average and need some improvement, but he will get by since he can control the puck at high speed and won't try to play a flashy game.

Muzik has figured as the captain of his nation as the Czech Republic has played against the international competition during the season and he has taken his responsibilities very seriously and has certainly been a leader to his team with his work rate and intensity. During the season he played 33 games for the Team Czech Republic in which he put up 11 goals and 12 assists for 23 points in international play.

He has signed to play for HC Plzen in the domestic Czech league the Extraliga next season.

	PLAYER	TEAM	LEAGUE	HEIGHT	WEIGHT	POS	GRADE
NR	NAJAMAN, ADAM	BENATKY N. J.	CZE-2	5'10.75	176 *	LC	ND
	HOCKEY SENSE		COMPETE		SKILL		SKATING
	6		5		6		4

Najman played this past season in the 2nd-tier men's league in the Czech Republic, and had 10 points in 40 games. He was a regular internationally for the Czech U-18 team. He's not the biggest player, but he's strong on his skates and is good to protect the puck along the boards. In terms of skating, he's not very dynamic or explosive, and can be a bit invisible on the ice due to his lack of speed. In the offensive zone, he can be dangerous because he has an above-average shot and can surprise goaltenders with it. He has good hands and can be dangerous one-on-one. He also handles the puck well in tight spaces. There's a lot of inconsistency with him from game to game; he can be invisible on the ice. Even in his better performances, he doesn't jump out at you with his skill level (and obviously his skating). He's not a player we would draft based on his skating ability, skill level or compete level.

	PLAYER	TEAM	LEAGUE	HEIGHT	WEIGHT	POS	GRADE
NR	NESTERENKO, NIKITA	LAWRENCEVILLE	HIGH-NJ	5'10.25"	140 *	LC	ND
	HOCKEY SENSE		COMPETE		SKILL		SKATING
	5		5		6		5

Nesterenko is not the biggest body in mass as on the thinner, lanky side yet it does not stop the forward from trying to make plays. He is a gifted offense player as he possesses above-average stick skills whereby he can make plays in traffic and tight areas. Sometimes it can be his downfall as well, as at times he should opt for a more simple and unselfish play, rather than the slick skilled move that sometimes leads to turnovers. He is an offensive minded player with very good instincts in the offensive zone that likes to make plays with speed and attack with the puck. At times he can play a bit on the perimeter and will go unnoticed unless the puck is on his stick. Nesterenko will also need to develop his defensive awareness along with gaining strength. He is set to play in the BCHL next season with Chilliwack before enrolling at Brown University for 2020-21 season.

	PLAYER	TEAM	LEAGUE	HEIGHT	WEIGHT	POS	GRADE
17	NEWHOOK, ALEX	VICTORIA	BCHL	5'10.25"	195 *	LC	**A**
	HOCKEY SENSE	COMPETE		SKILL		SKATING	
	6	7		6		7	

Alex Newhook captained the Grizzlies while leading by example on the ice with 102 points in 53 regular season games. In the playoffs he scored 24 points in 15 games before getting knocked out by the Prince George Spruce Kings. He had a slow start internationally after getting cut at the Hlinka and under-performing at the World-Junior-A-Challenge but did rebound at the U18's with a solid effort. He scored 10 points in 5 games, including 5 goals in an important performance considering his quality of competition in league play. Alex is scheduled to play for Boston College next season.

Newhook is an explosive two-way center who keeps an overwhelming-pace. What makes Alex unique is his high-octane motor. He's magnetized to the puck in the offensive-end and is constantly in motion which generates pressure on opposing defenses. The tools that gives him his pace are his skating ability and willingness to be a difference maker. Newhook is a well-built kid who features a powerful-stride. He pushes off correctly and is one of the better players in this class at shifting his-weight when taking off, giving him a ton of forward momentum. His ability to gear-shift rapidly is his defining feature when breaking down opposing defenses. This led him to being the main transport option during transitional-zone-entry attempts on the powerplay and allowed him to drive one of the better lines in the BCHL. When shifting over the offensive-line, his cross-over mechanics and edge-work allow him to drive-wide and aggressively cut-towards soft-ice. After creating space, Newhook has a multi-faceted attack at his disposal. His primary offensive-attribute is his playmaking ability, which resulted in impressive give-and-go sequences off the rush. He's a very-good passer who can occasionally make a dynamic and unexpected pass, but not with the same consistency as some of the other high-end playmakers featured in this class. Most of his passes have purpose and are accurate though. This extends below the goal-line where Newhook has shown the ability to deceive with his passing-options by using body-fakes to mask his passing lane. His shot isn't far behind his playmaking but is still a notch-lower overall. Earlier in the season and last season, Alex didn't always move inside his shot motion as a result having inconsistent footwork when setting up his release. Though, as the season progressed, he became more consistent with his footwork. This is an important aspect of his shot since he doesn't always extend through his motion when releasing the puck. His lack of extension can be seen within the angle of his release points; rarely rocking-his-blade and pulling it back and extending his shot motion. This does allow him to release the puck quicker though while maintaining a high-level of accuracy. Although his shot lacks power as a result of some of the above mechanics, it does present few tells which is why he was still a capable goal-scorer. He was most dangerous with his shot when given time in the right-circle to pick the far-side. Away from the play, Newhook is a 200-foot player who looks to support his defenseman and can play a physical-brand of hockey when required. He has no problem initiating contact and has shown a good amount of compete when battling in the corners. There's a well-rounded approach to his game that extends to his own end of the ice.

Although Alex is a versatile and quick-striking player, he does have some issues when projecting his ceiling. The majority of Newhook's production is a by-product of his vision, skating, and motor, it's not primarily because of his puck-skills. When comparing him to the rest of the high-end forwards, Alex's puck skills are good but not in anyway dynamic. Few high-end players in this class ended up losing the puck off their stick when attempting to challenge one-on-one as much as Alex did in our viewings. He did have success putting the puck between his opponents tri-pod when shifting his own posture; but when attempting higher-end dekes, he lost the puck frequently. For Newhook's shot to translate well, he's going to need to be able to identify when to release it behind-screens, yet this puts him in a position where he will need to guard the puck under heavy pressure by using his hands in most instances. At the BCHL-level it wasn't as much of a concern, but it will be at the pro level if he doesn't continue refining his puck-skills. Although beating opponents one-on-one cleanly is considered a secondary-trait; due to Newhook's line-driving instincts, it becomes more important. Regarding his hockey-sense, Alex sees the ice-well and this allows him to identify his passing and skating lanes, however there is a slight lag in his overall anticipation of the play. He's a reactive player who doesn't use predetermined moves which is a great quality in a player with good anticipation but he's not as unpredictable as he should be given this quality. What holds back his unpredictability is his lack of altering his tempo as consistently as he needs to. Alex stays at a very high-pace which can be a great asset but also a detriment at times; players at the NHL-level will adapt to his one-paced style of play. His pace and line-driving mentality have allowed him to generate a lot of scoring chances but he does have a tendency to overhandle the puck, extending as the carry option for his line too frequently as a result. Though, this aspect of his game should be less refined in theory since he's playing in a league that plays a bit slower overall than the CHL, which allows him to get away with some of the concerns discussed.

An area of significance that helps alleviate some of the above concerns, is that Newhook has shown some adaptability in the BCHL which is critical for him to translate his game. In our final viewings, he started using his skating more than his hands, relying on his two-step area quickness to shift the tempo and alter the flow of the game more than he previously was. Furthermore, he's learned how to use the boards to extend his hands by banking the puck back to himself. Generating foot-races as opposed to challenging with his hands will be important for him to translate. The last area to note for Newhook's development is in regards to his body-posture. He's going to have to continue to refine his body-mechanics when attempting to alter his skating-lanes, which will make him a harder player to read on the ice. If he can become more difficult to read when skating aggressively, he can translate his game.

We don't see Alex as a 1st-line scoring forward at the NHL-level. There isn't a dynamic element to his game and we feel that will hold him back when projecting him. If he does refine his puck-skills and continues to learn how to identify options a bit quicker, than he could translate as a potential middle-6 center or winger who can help at both ends of the ice.

"He wasn't healthy at the WJAC. He's much better than what he showed there." - NHL Scout, December 2018

"He's a great player. You need to go back and keep watching. I've got him ahead of a bunch of guys in your top 15. - January 2019

"I've never seen him play well. I can't warm up to him. Other guys on our staff really like him though." - NHL Scout, January 2019

"Every time I see him he play he doesn't dominate. He's playing tier II." -NHL Scout, January 2019

"He's a second rounder for me. Not enough skill." - NHL Scout, January 2019

"I think he's faster than quick." - NHL Scout, May 2019

"He's a powerful skater but his mechanics aren't as refined, if he can clean them up, then he has a better chance of making it" - HP Scout, Brad Allen

"I like Newhook but prior to the season I thought he was better than I saw this season. He's not quite as skilled or dynamic as I thought he was in my limited viewings in his OHL Draft year and last season. He's a good player, but it also concerns me a bit that I didn't see him dominate BCHL games as much as Tyson Jost did in the same league and Jost has had some struggles so far." - HP Scout, Mark Edwards

NR	PLAYER	TEAM	LEAGUE	HEIGHT	WEIGHT	POS	GRADE
	NEWKIRK, REECE	PORTLAND	WHL	5'10.75"	172 *	LC	C
	HOCKEY SENSE	COMPETE		SKILL		SKATING	
	6	7		5		5	

This year Newkirk put himself on the map as he upped his point production from 11 to 59 points. Newkirk filled multiple roles over the course of the year from playing on Cody Glass' wing to centering his own line with rookie wingers.

Extremely versatile and low maintenance, Newkirk fit wherever he was placed. He spent parts of the year on glass' wing and parts anchoring the 2nd line as a center. Stands out for an extremely high hockey IQ, over the course of a game constantly makes all the right little plays. Utilized his teammates very well and also does a great job at giving them options when he's without the puck. On top of this Newkirk is feisty and intense, playing unafraid and chippy style. Newkirk is not afraid to come in hard on the forecheck, and is giving the goalie an extra poke every chance he gets. Newkirk lacks signature physical skills to hang his hat on. Skates well enough but does not have standout speed or agility. Offensively does not make the flashy highlight plays, did not burn the goalies with an elite release or dangle through multiple players. Newkirk instead makes his impact through his fearless style and consistent good decisions. Only question would be how he translates up a level with his physical tools and skill.

86	PLAYER	TEAM	LEAGUE	HEIGHT	WEIGHT	POS	GRADE
	NIKKANEN, HENRI	JUKURIT	FIN	6'3.5"	200 *	LC	C
	HOCKEY SENSE	COMPETE		SKILL		SKATING	
	5	5		5		5	

Nikkanen is a good-sized center from Finland who missed some significant time this season with injuries, as he only played 14 games in the junior league and 9 games in Liiga. In international play, he performed well this season at the Hlinka-Gretzky Cup in August and the November Five Nations' tournament, but missed the February Five Nations' and the World Under-18 Hockey Championships in April because of his injuries. However, whether he was in junior or in the men's league, he didn't live up to expectations in league play. He's a big center with average skating abilities. He has above-average smarts at both ends of the ice. His best asset offensively is his vision; he's not known for his scoring abilities and is rather inconsistent in that area. He's able to take advantage of his size when battling for pucks along the boards or trying to gain position in the slot. He has a pretty good puck-protection game along the boards that helps him win a lot of puck battles due to his size advantage at this level. He's solid in his zone, has a good hockey IQ and pays attention to all the little details. He's limited offensively, however, and doesn't have a high upside for the next level. If he has a good bounce-back year next season and stays healthy, it's possible that he could one day challenge for a depth role at the NHL level.

74	PLAYER	TEAM	LEAGUE	HEIGHT	WEIGHT	POS	GRADE
	NIKOLAEV, ILYA	YAROSLAVL 2	RUS-JR.	6'0.0"	190	LC	C
	HOCKEY SENSE	COMPETE		SKILL		SKATING	
	6	5		6		6	

Nikolaev played this past season in the MHL with Loko Yaroslavl where he had 25 points in 41 games and on the international stage he played in every U-18 tournaments for Russia and also the World Junior A Challenge in December.

Nikolaev is a good size two-way center who often in tournaments would end up centering Russia top line and playing with Vasili Podkolzin. He's physically mature and it shows when he battles for loose pucks along the board and also has very good puck protection skills. He's not a high end offensive player but does a lot of good things away from the puck. He's very good in his own zone and on the penalty killing unit. He's got a good compete level away from the puck and a good active stick in his zone to blocker passes or passing lanes. Nikolaev plays a heavy game, he's strong on his skate and his shot is deceptive and heavy. Offensively he can score with his shot but we wish he would use it more often, as above average vision offensively but his offensive effort have been inconsistent this year from tournament to tournament. His offensive output in the MHL has been average as well. He lacks ideal skating, he's very powerful on his skate but lacks an extra gear and his acceleration is only average. We see Nikolaev has more as a 3rd line forward due to his size, smart and attention to details but we're not sold on him if he has enough upside to be a top 6 forwards.

"Skating is good but he seems to need to work really hard to get to his top speed. Not a very efficient skater." - NHL Scout, January 2019

"It was interesting that myself and others on our staff all really backed off on Nikolaev. We seldom had long conversations about him because it seemed like every conference call he was falling on all our lists. The more I watched the more I thought he played too much on the outside and failed to really compete. - HP Scout, Mark Edwards, May 2019

	PLAYER	TEAM	LEAGUE	HEIGHT	WEIGHT	POS	GRADE
NR	NODLER, JOSHUA	FARGO	USHL	5'11.25"	194 *	RC	C
	HOCKEY SENSE		COMPETE		SKILL		SKATING
	6		7		5		5

Worker bee forward, with some niche potential. Nodler jumped out of the Honeybaked program to be a full-time USHL player for the first time. He saw a couple games with the USNTDP and Fargo in 2018. The Michigan State commit jumped on to the scene with a 42-point campaign, netting All-Rookie Second Team honors in the process. Nodler is very active on the ice, which includes a lot of jump and eagerness but also a lot of overplaying. He means well, but he halves his own cause for various reasons. He's a shade short of six-foot and 200 pounds, but he is very light on his feet. His mobility is a plus and it's aided by his work ethic. His stride is a little straight-legged, but he gets around the ice fine and can transition in and out of backwards skating without a hiccup. His wheels in space are a plus, but he seems to a lack a little bit of body control – which may be a product of him seemingly gliding atop the ice when he skates. For his size, he's a little easier to move off his spot than we'd like. His biggest drawback is that he overplays or over-skates the game often. Defensively, he can't quite stop in the right spot. Physically, he can't quite get the right leverage in a battle. Offensively, he tends to fumble pucks away as a result of his jumpiness.

Nodler has just "C" level hands still. He still tends to chop the puck up a little bit and his hands are not smooth. His posture and style causes his heel to leave the ice an awful lot, which may be a root cause. Certainly a pass-first player, Josh seems a little shy to shoot – particularly as a center. The shot and finishing ability do not move the needle in a noteworthy way, but they aren't detriment. He struggles to work pucks into the middle if he's coming from outside the dot line. The technical skills, puck protection ability, and guile are just not good enough for him to reliably get to the useful areas of the sheet. His hockey sense and decision making doesn't stray too far from average. Josh is a gentlemanly, honest player who never takes liberties or has any interest in post-whistle activities. He gives off the vibe of a player that might fill a niche role of some sort down the line, provided he's willing to embrace it, because there might not be enough meat on the bone for him to be a more well-rounded NHL player.

"He's a good below the dots, net front guy. He's very strong on his skates but his foot speed is a concern and the game is only going to get faster from here." HP Scout, Dusten Braaksma

"He gives off the vibe of a player that might fill a niche role of some sort down the line, provided he's willing to embrace it." – HP Scout, Mike Farkas

	PLAYER	TEAM	LEAGUE	HEIGHT	WEIGHT	POS	GRADE
51	NORLINDER, MATTIAS	MODO JR.	SWE-JR.	5'11.0"	179	LD	**C+**
	HOCKEY SENSE		COMPETE		SKILL		SKATING
	6		7		6		7

Norlinder made clear progress this season. He started the season with his club's U20 team Modo?) in the SuperElit league and recorded 5 goals and 16 assists in 30 games. He then got promoted to play for his club's men's team in the HockeyAllsvenskan. His development exploded after the promotion. He recorded 2 goals and 4 assists playing up with men but his skating and poise were his biggest attributes that showed he was ready to make the jump.

He's an excellent skater and he has a beautiful stride which allows him to gain a lot of speed. His great edgework allows him to maintain the speed in most situations. He is especially good at taking advantage of his skating to gain time and space and to pressure the puck.

Offensively he can create havoc in the offensive zone when he decides to jump into the play. He creates space for himself on the blueline by flawless lateral movement to find an open lane to shoot or find a pass. His sticking-handling is decent, passing is underrated; his first pass is usually accurate and stretches out the opposition and he can make sneaky, shorts passes in the offensive zone as well. He can be difficult to play against defensively, even though he doesn't play a physical game. He is generally well positioned but even when he is not, he will get back quickly. He also has a great stick and compete level in his own zone. By not getting stuck in battles along the boards, he can really take off and his zone exits are superb, when both passing and transporting the puck.

Norlinder came back down to the juniors after his team missed qualifying for the SHL. He was a dominant force. In his 5 games, he scored 2 goals and 4 assists and was a leader on his team. The club ended up winning the championship title and Norlinder was the well-deserved SuperElit playoffs MVP.

The second-year draft-eligible Norlinder will be attractive and if his development during the season is an indication of where he is going, he might end up to be a steal. His upside is to become a good, solid two-way defenseman with great skating abilities.

	PLAYER	TEAM	LEAGUE	HEIGHT	WEIGHT	POS	GRADE
NR	NOUSIAINEN, KIM	KALPA JR.	FIN-JR.	5'9.0"	169	LD	**ND**
	HOCKEY SENSE		COMPETE		SKILL		SKATING
	6		5		6		5

Nousiainen spent the majority of the season in the U20 league with Kalpa, where he had 28 points in 32 games. He had the 3rd-best point-per-game ratio among all defensemen league-wide. He also saw ice time in Liiga, playing 6 games with Kalpa's top team and in the Mestis league playing 8 games with IPK. He also participated in the Spengler Cup with Kalpa, scoring 1 goal in 3 games. He was named to the tournament's All-Star team.

He's an undersized offensive defenseman who likes being active on the ice, rushing the puck into the offensive zone and jumping into the rush, often acting as a 4th forward on the ice. He's an agile skater with above-average footwork who currently lacks the great acceleration and top speed that you want to see from a defenseman of his stature. With that extra gear, he could create more space for himself and could distance himself away from forechecking pressure more rapidly. He's good puck-distributor on the ice; he makes quick, accurate passes to his teammates in the offensive zone. He's quick to move pucks out of his zone, either by making a quick first pass or just by skating it out. His best asset in the offensive zone is his vision; he sees the ice very well and his decision-making is also good. He doesn't possess a powerful shot from the point, but finds way to get his shot through with good accuracy. In the junior league, he was really good at creating offense at even-strength. Of his 28 points, only 7 came on the power play. It's a good sign when a player like him produces at a high level at even-strength. There's a lot of work to do with his defensive game, however. With his size and lack of strength, it's tough for him to defend in front of his net or along the boards, as he can get outmuscled by bigger opponents. He's not afraid of the physical play, but he has limitations in terms of what he can do out there. One thing he needs to improve on is his compete level in his own end. We need to see him care a bit more about playing well in his own zone. Overall, Nousiainen is a creative offensive defenseman but needs to bring up his defensive game. His size and speed limitations are big question marks for him when projecting him in the NHL.

	PLAYER	TEAM	LEAGUE	HEIGHT	WEIGHT	POS	GRADE
NR	**NUSSBAUMER, VALENTIN**	SHAWINIGAN	QMJHL	5'10.5"	167 *	LC	**ND**
	HOCKEY SENSE		COMPETE		SKILL		SKATING
	6		5		6		5

Nussbaumer was the 4th overall pick in the CHL Import Draft in June 2018, and came over to Shawinigan with some good hype surrounding him after playing at the World Juniors at age 17. He was also named captain of the Swiss U-18 team. He came into a rough situation in Shawinigan, as they are in the early process of their rebuild. He collected a modest 38 points in 58 games with the Cataractes this season, which was considered to be a disappointment. He was viewed as one of the top rookies in the league at the beginning of the year (and also one of the older ones) as he missed last year's draft by only 10 days (born on September 25th, 2000).

The Swiss forward played both on the wing and at center, but his lack of success in the faceoff circle (42%) and his lack of a strong two-way game has us projecting him as a winger at the pro level. His lack of success offensively is mostly due to playing on a bad team in the league (they clinched the last playoff spot in the last game of the season). Aside from 16-year-old Mavrik Bourque, there were not a lot of talented offensive players on the Shawinigan roster. With the puck, Nussbaumer is very creative and sees the ice well, but it was tough for him to create offense with teammates possessing limited offensive talent. He's got quick hands and a quick shot. The velocity on his shot needs to improve, but he has a quick release. He's agile on his skates, and with his quick hands, he can be a threat one-on-one. He had some success at the World Juniors in Vancouver, flashing some of his talent (3 points in 7 games for the surprising Swiss team). What Nussbaumer needs to improve on is his intensity on the ice; he tends to stay away from the physical game. He needs to get stronger physically, which will help him be stronger on pucks and have more of an impact in the more physical aspects of the game. Bottom line: he needs to be tougher to play against. His skating abilities will need to get better as well. Currently they are average at best, and at his size, it's not good enough. He's agile on his skates, but his top speed is not good enough, and the same goes for his acceleration. His play away from the puck will need to get upgraded as well; one reason he ends up playing more on the wing than at center is due to his attention to detail in his zone. This needs to be better if he wants to play center at the next level. There are some good and bad things about Nussbaumer's game, but his skill and creativity with the puck might be enough for him to hear his name late in the draft. There is, however, no doubt that his combination of size, skating and lack of production as an 18-year-old rookie in the QMJHL are all concerns in his case.

"He played better at the World Juniors than he did in the QMJHL" - HP Scout Jérôme Bérubé

"I saw him early in the year vs Blainville and thought maybe he could be a late round pick. Took another look in Gatineau on a trip later in the season and made him a no draft. Not high enough skill or compete combined with what I thought was very average skating equaled a no draft grade for me." - HP Scout, Mark Edwards, February 2019

"I made two sperate trips to see him this year, one early on and then another a few months later. Neither viewings showed me much in the way of making me confident he had a lot of translatable NHL talent.". - HP Scout, Mark Edwards, April 2019

	PLAYER	TEAM	LEAGUE	HEIGHT	WEIGHT	POS	GRADE
46	OKHOTYUK, NIKITA	OTTAWA	OHL	6'0.75"	191 *	LD	B
	HOCKEY SENSE		COMPETE		SKILL		SKATING
	6		7		5		6

A late 2000-born defenseman, Okhotyuk was arguably Ottawa's most consistent defenseman all year. You knew what you were going to get every game. He is a very solid, physical defender in his own zone; he showed some offensive ability throughout the year with 17 points from the backend. He was an excellent penalty killer for Ottawa as well. He shows good mobility on the defensive side of the rush and exhibits an active stick which was good for knocking pucks off of opponents' sticks. In transition, Nikita shows very strong gap control and has the ability to angle his opponents into low percentage areas of the ice allowing him to separate players from the puck with contact. His reaction time in the defensive zone is what stands out for him; he is always hard on puck carriers entering the zone and really physical with forwards in the corners when they want to cycle the puck. His awareness in the defensive zone is really good. He's tough in front of the net and allows the goalie to see shots from the point. Opposing forwards need to keep their head up skating through the neutral zone as the tough Russian was good for at least one nice open-ice hit per game. He makes a high percentage of accurate passes and he's really good at not forcing pucks up the wall in to the winger's feet, or forcing pucks into the middle of the ice. He can slow the play down in front of him and if there aren't any options, he'll safely put the puck off the glass and out. While Okhotyuk would benefit from improving his puck skills, he plays within himself and doesn't need to be a flashy offensive defenseman to be effective. Offensively, he has shown a good, hard, low, and accurate shot from the point; he needs to quicken his release and improve his ability to open more shooting lanes for himself. I would classify Nikita as a hard-nosed North American type defenseman with a Russian name. With more strength on his frame, and continued work on his skating, Nikita projects to be a bottom three defenseman in the NHL.

"When he was pressured he struggled to make plays." - NHL Scout October 2018

"You don't notice him very often because he's smart and doesn't make many mistakes." - NHL Scout, October 2018

"Strays outside the dots and struggles with passing accuracy. He is a bit of a mess as far as his Dzone coverage goes." - NHL Scout, March 2019

"When he kept things simple he was outstanding. He's very physical and has a cannon for a shot. Accuracy could be better though. Puck game is inconsistent." - HP Scout, Mark Edwards, May 2019

NR	PLAYER	TEAM	LEAGUE	HEIGHT	WEIGHT	POS	GRADE
	O'NEILL, RYAN	ST. THOMAS	HIGH-MN	5'10.5"	154	RC	ND
	HOCKEY SENSE	COMPETE		SKILL		SKATING	
	6	4		7		5	

Creative, playmaking center. A three-year player at St. Thomas Academy in the Minnesota high school circuit, O'Neill had a little bit of a coming out party in the 2018 playoffs and state tournament for the Cadets. In 2018-19 he ended up leading his team in points with 43 while taking zero penalties (down from two the previous season). The Roseville native is rather resourceful with his playmaking abilities. He can really make some interesting passing lanes appear and thread some slick passes through them. No question he's guilty of being a little too adventurous in this regard and costing his team with turnovers, he'll overhandle the puck in traffic a little too much for our liking too. One noteworthy thing about O'Neill's puck play is that he's a significantly better attack zone passer than he is a puck carrier or distributor in the neutral zone. He can make the "finishing pass", if you will, but his puck carrying skills are less than we would expect from this style of player. He's also a noted beaver tapper, despite not being a shooter – he wants the puck all the time, just to give it to someone else immediately thereafter. He does seem like an intelligent player because of his vision, but he does not apply this to the defensive zone whatsoever. He cheats and flies the zone constantly, even on the penalty kill he'll start giving the one-leg push towards his own blueline if he gets the sense his defensemen can throw a bomb to him. When he does come back defensively, he does so very indiscriminately. He'll usually just take a lap and chase the puck around and because he never stops on a puck or plays physically, Ryan will just take himself right back out to the top of the zone again. He's a little better than average skater who could probably provide more production from his stride if he's constantly working to get himself open, that's when gears start to really churn: when he can get the puck. He does have very good technical skills in tight spots and his passing is in the upper tier of the Minnesota high school level. His shot is only average and there doesn't appear to be a lot of real, transferrable finishing ability for now, he'd rather pass the puck into the net. O'Neill is a very incomplete player at the moment – willfully so – but skill level makes him worth a discussion. Sioux Falls (USHL) drafted him in the 10th round of the USHL Entry Draft.

NR	PLAYER	TEAM	LEAGUE	HEIGHT	WEIGHT	POS	GRADE
	MERISIER-ORTIZ, CHRIS	BAIE-COMEAU	QMJHL	5'11"	165	LD	ND
	HOCKEY SENSE	COMPETE		SKILL		SKATING	
	5	5		6		6	

Ortiz was the 7th overall selection in the 2017 QMJHL Draft, one spot behind teammate Nathan Legaré. The St-Eustache native is a skilled offensive defenseman who finished this season with 33 points and also had 4 points in 7 games in the playoffs.

Ortiz has some good value on the power play; he sees the ice well and can make some good passes to open teammates in scoring areas. He's an above-average skater with some good feet; he can rush the puck in the offensive zone and get it away from the pressure of the opposing team. He doesn't have a big shot from the point. He needs to be more patient with the puck and find better shooting lanes, as he'll often get his shot blocked in front of the net. When his shot does hit the net, it is usually accurate, but lacks some velocity behind it. His release is above-average. Ortiz's biggest problem when creating offense: we would like to see a bit more poise out of him in order to manage the puck better. His hockey IQ is poor; he needs to make better decisions with the puck and play a smarter game. The same goes for his defensive game, which needs to be simplified in order for him to be less of a liability there. His compete level in his zone could also be better. He is not a physical player by any means, and needs to compete more in order to retrieve those loose pucks and play with more jam in his own zone. There's no doubt that Ortiz has some skills, but his poor hockey IQ is hurting his game and potential for the NHL. There's a possibility that he could hear his name late in the draft if a team thinks that there are enough skills there, but his hockey sense would scare me, and that's why we think he could also go undrafted.

	PLAYER	TEAM	LEAGUE	HEIGHT	WEIGHT	POS	GRADE
NR	**PARENT, XAVIER**	HALIFAX	QMJHL	5'7.75"	171 *	LW	**ND**
	HOCKEY SENSE	COMPETE		SKILL		SKATING	
	4	6		6		5	

Parent came into the QMJHL with a lot of hype; he was talked about since he was in pee-wee as the "next dominant player from Quebec." After two solid seasons in Midget AAA with Collège Esther-Blondin, he was drafted 4th overall by Halifax in the 2017 QMJHL Draft.

So far in the QMJHL, he has not been the dominant player some had hoped he'd be. In his first season, he did fine with limited playing time. This year, things did start pretty well for him, as he did a fine job with Team Canada at the Hlinka/Gretzky Cup in August. However, with Halifax, it was not a very positive year. He barely beat last year's point totals with 34 points compared to 29. His best asset coming through minor hockey was always his speed, but in our viewings this year, we thought it only looked average. We're not sure where that great speed went; maybe he bulked up too much in the offseason (we thought it looked like he was playing a bit heavy). Nevertheless, his top asset was definitely missing this year. At his size, it's crucial for him to get it back in order to have any chance at the NHL in the future. He's got a quick release on his wrist shot, and if he can keep his feet moving in the offensive zone, this is how he'll get those scoring chances. He's got a good compete level; despite his size, he doesn't play a timid game on the ice and will battle. He puts in the work, but sometimes he doesn't work smartly out there. He's talented, but sometimes he has a bit of tunnel vision. He doesn't make players around him better, and his hockey IQ is not a strong trait in his game. But we still feel as though Parent will bounce back next season and put up some big numbers statistically for the Mooseheads, with a strong offseason and a bigger role on the team. Because of that as well as his talent, we think there's a chance that an NHL team could take a chance on him late in the draft. At the same time, his size and with his skating abilities have not been very strong, and his lack of success this year offensively could also mean he goes undrafted as well.

"Will probably post some good numbers in the QMJHL in the next 2 or 3 seasons, but as far as the NHL draft goes (and his NHL potential), he's not someone I would draft." - HP Scout Jérôme Bérubé

	PLAYER	TEAM	LEAGUE	HEIGHT	WEIGHT	POS	GRADE
NR	**PARIK, LUKAS**	LIBEREC JR.	CZE-JR.	6'4.0"	185	G	**C**
	HOCKEY SENSE	COMPETE		SKILL		SKATING	
	6	6		5		5	

Parik is a big goaltender from the Czech Republic. He was not featured in August during the Hlinka-Gretzky tournament, but had his coming-out party at the November Five Nations' tournament. From there on out, he was clearly the Czechs' top goaltender for the rest of the year during U-18 events. We love his quickness and agility in net. He's quick to move from post to post and his compete level is really good, in addition to the fact that he doesn't quit on any puck. He covers a lot of net with his big frame; he is square to shooters and does not provide much net to shoot at. His athleticism could be better, however, which would allow him to be quick enough to get back in his position. The biggest area he needs to work on in the next couple of years is improving his rebound-control. As the year went on, we saw some flaws from Parik; he would have trouble with his rebounds and give up some juicy ones in the slot. We also noticed some trouble in terms of him catching pucks with his glove, often resulting in more rebounds in the slot. Parik has some good tools to work on with his size and agility, as he's still a bit raw and will need time to develop. Still, we like the potential here.

NR	PLAYER	TEAM	LEAGUE	HEIGHT	WEIGHT	POS	GRADE
	PARSSINEN, JUUSO	TPS JR.	FIN-JR.	6'2.0"	203 *	LC	ND
	HOCKEY SENSE	COMPETE		SKILL		SKATING	
	6	6		5		5	

Parssinen spent the majority of the season in the junior league with TPS' U20 team, where he scored 13 goals and 22 points in 36 games. He also scored one goal in 7 games in Liiga and played in various international tournaments for Finland at the U-18 level, notably scoring 9 goals and 15 points in 24 games.

The big center is not a player with big upside offensively. Nevertheless, he has above-average smarts and he's also good away from the puck. He lacks some footspeed as well, but has great anticipation on the ice and a good active stick. These attributes make him an asset on the PK unit. His quick stick also helps him create some turnovers on the ice, stealing pucks away from opponents. He's got a good compete level in the defensive zone and has a strong positional game. He has a good work ethic as well, and is not best quickest skater, but he's good on the forecheck and takes good pursuit angles. In his zone, he often acted like a 3rd defenseman on the ice. He provided strong support down low, helping his defensemen retrieve pucks. However, he'll need to add some speed to his game. His top speed and acceleration leave something to be desired at the moment. Despite this, he's quick to change directions, which can make it tough for defenders to face him along the boards when he's controlling the puck from there. He's also offensively limited. His skill level is decent, but lacks some consistency and he has not showed enough skills to warrant a top-6 projection. His hands and shot are also decent, but he has never showed anything that could lead us to believe that he can be an offensive player at the next level. He can be useful on the power play when using his size in front of the net. Parssinen has value as a possible late pick because of his work ethic, defensive game and smarts, but lacks the necessary offensive upside to be taken higher in the draft.

NR	PLAYER	TEAM	LEAGUE	HEIGHT	WEIGHT	POS	GRADE
	PASIC, NIKOLA	LINKOPING JR.	SWE-JR.	5'10.0"	187	RW	C
	HOCKEY SENSE	COMPETE		SKILL		SKATING	
	5	5		7		7	

Pasic is a small-sized winger with an interesting set of skills. He has mainly been playing in the SuperElite league for Linköping HC where he was a point-a-game player with 18 goals and 18 assists in 36 games. His offensive skills led to 15 games in the SHL, where he managed to score 1 goal and 1 assist on a Linköping team that struggled to produce any offense. He was also loaned to BIK Karlskoga in the HockeyAllsvenskan for a short conditioning stint where he put up 1 point in 2 games. He is set to play for BIK Karlskoga in the HockeyAllsvenskan next season.

When Pasic plays against players his own age, he is a dynamic offensive dynamo at times. But he tends to be very inconsistent and doesn't seem to come to play every night, or even every shift. He's amazing in close because he can utilize his excellent skating abilities and strong stickhandling. He skates with a low center of gravity and has excellent edgework. He can slip away from defenders easily by using his good foot speed. Even though he is small and has an average stride length, he can gain a lot of speed in open ice Pasic is a dangler, where he uses his stickhandling to dazzle opponents and gets around them using fast hands and great balance. He has been used at center but his game translates better to the wing.

He is inconsistent in his work ethic and defensive reads. He can create havoc in the offensive zone since he has a great wrist shot with good velocity and quick release. The problem is that he shoots all the time, even when it's obvious that the shot is going to get blocked or the angle is non-existent. He can give the impression at times that he plays like he only cares about his own point total. He can thread through a good pass here and there, but he is a shot-first type of player. This is concerning since it shows a lack of hockey sense even though he has a nose for sniffing up good areas to get his one-timer off.

There is a lot of skill to this player, but his compete level is low and he has little interest in going to the corners or any other physical battles. He is great on the power play when he doesn't get pressured as much and gets more time to process his next move. He often operates from a low position at the right side of the net. Pasic played 4 games for Team Sweden U19s during the season and put up 1 goal and 3 assists.

He has a lot of offensive upsides but the biggest question mark here is if he can find a way to translate his offensive game to the professional ranks without shying away due to his small sized frame.

	PLAYER	TEAM	LEAGUE	HEIGHT	WEIGHT	POS	GRADE
NR	**PEACH, BAILEY**	**SHERBROOKE**	**QMJHL**	**5'9.5"**	**175 ***	**LW**	**ND**
	HOCKEY SENSE		COMPETE		SKILL		SKATING
	5		5		6		6

Peach was Sherbrooke's 2nd first-round pick in the 2017 QMJHL Draft (11th overall) out of the Cole Harbour midget program in Nova Scotia. He missed a month and a half at the beginning of the season after dislocating his shoulder in the 2nd game of the year. He came back in November, and his season was plagued by inconsistent play. As a result, he didn't bring the offense the team had expected out of him. He finished the season with 11 goals, 35 points in 54 games. Peach has the talent to be a point-per-game producer in the QMJHL, and should be one starting next season.

Peach's skillset is intriguing. First of all, he's one of the best skaters in the QMJHL. His top speed is very good and is acceleration is impressive. He can easily beat guys wide with his speed, and can be dangerous when he uses it and decides to cut to the net. He's a left-handed shot, but mostly will play on the right wing. Not many players in this league can make those plays, but we also don't see him make them often enough. He's got good hands and a quick shot. His lack of production this year is a bit of a concern, since we know that the talent is there. His hockey IQ is also slightly lacking, as he doesn't always process information quickly enough on the ice. His work ethic also is inconsistent. Some nights he'll work hard, and in other games he is barely noticeable on the ice. He's still got a lot to learn with his play away from the puck, as he can be a bit of liability in his own zone. He is not a very physical player, either; after his injury, he shied away from the physical game. Right now, he's a one-dimensional player because of his offensive skills and great skating abilities. He has one main quality that is good enough for him to reach the NHL: his skating. He now needs to work on improving other parts of his game. Because of that one quality, there is a chance that one team could take a flyer on him in the late rounds of the NHL Draft. He's got one big season ahead of him to help him establish himself as a premier offensive player on his team (and in the league) to the level anticipated in his QMJHL draft year.

"Great skater, but still waiting for rest of his game to catch up." - HP Scout Jérôme Bérubé

	PLAYER	TEAM	LEAGUE	HEIGHT	WEIGHT	POS	GRADE
39	**PELLETIER, JAKOB**	**MONCTON**	**QMJHL**	**5'9.0"**	**161 ***	**LW**	**B**
	HOCKEY SENSE		COMPETE		SKILL		SKATING
	7		7		5		5

Moncton drafted Jakob Pelletier with the 3rd overall pick in the 2017 QMJHL Draft behind Alexis Lafrenière and Samuel Poulin. Last season, Pelletier didn't take long to adjust to the QMJHL in his first season. He was a point-per-game player and also played a big role in Moncton upsetting Rimouski in the opening round of the QMJHL playoffs. He started 2018-2019 by making Team Canada (Hlinka-Gretzky Cup in August) but unfortunately broke his wrist after hitting the boards hard, missing the rest of the tournament and all of the Wildcats' training camp thereafter. Nevertheless, Pelletier had a great season, finishing with 89 points in his second year in the league, good for 7th overall in the scoring race. Not to take anything away from his points total this year, but he did get 36 of his 89 points against Acadie-Bathurst and Saint John, the two worst teams in the league. We don't feel that these totals reflect well on how we project him as a player at the NHL level.

Pelletier is a smart, hard-working forward who can play on any line on a team's lineup. Since coming into the league, he has mostly played on the wing, but has some experience playing center prior to the QMJHL. We wouldn't be surprised to see Moncton try him at center at some point next year. He's got the smarts and vision to be a good center at the junior level, but he projects more as a winger at the NHL level. Pelletier is a very good forward away from the puck; one of the best defensive forwards in the league already. He has a high compete level in all three zones, is quick on the forecheck and has a good ability to pressure the puck-carrier. On the penalty-kill, he keeps his feet active and his motor doesn't stop. What makes him very good shorthanded is his good sense of anticipation. He's not the biggest guy, but his compete level is very good and he's got great work ethic. Even at his size, he wins the majority of his one-on-one battles. He uses his good puck-protection skills down low and scores the majority of his goals close to the net. There's a bit of Brendan Gallagher in him, although the Habs' forward has a better shot. Pelletier battles hard close to the net so that he can jump on rebounds or tip in some pucks. We very much like the enthusiasm that he plays with on the ice. He is a very positive energy guy, and it's always good for a team to have a leader like him. One thing that he'll surely need to improve: his skating abilities. He's agile on his feet and elusive, but for his size, he needs to be faster. His top speed is average at best, and in order to take better advantage of opposing teams' mistakes and create more space on the ice, his top speed needs to improve. His best asset offensively remains his on-ice vision; he sees the ice well and makes players around him better. Meanwhile, his shooting skills and hands are average. He has a quick shot, but needs to improve its velocity. He didn't score a lot from far; most of his goals came from 5 to 10 feet away from the net.

In conclusion, Pelletier is a player that we like due to his good hockey IQ and great work ethic. However, we don't see that high-end offensive skillset that is necessary to be a top offensive player in the NHL. When you look at the goals he scored this year, not many were based on pure skill, but rather great work ethic (rebounds and hard work around the net). We do see a lot of value in him as a two-way forward who brings good energy to his team but more in a 3rd line role on a good NHL team.

"I like the work ethic but not sure about his offensive upside right now." – NHL Scout, September 2018

"Plays like Phillip Danault at the same age." – NHL Scout, December 2018

"Scores more because of hard work than skill. That doesn't always translate to the NHL. I'd take him ahead of Lavoie though." – NHL Scout, December 2018

"Skating concerns me." NHL Scout, March 2019

"Skill needs to be more high end to compensate for his size and skating deficiencies." - NHL Scout, May 2019

"Love this kid, he can play on my team." - HP Scout Jérôme Bérubé, April 2019

"Interesting to look at his stats breakdown this season versus the top 9 & bottom 9 teams of the league. 54 points in 30 games against the bottom 9 and 35 points in 35 games against the top 9." - HP Scout, Jérôme Bérubé, April 2019

"Skating is probably a 5.5 but we went with the lower rating because it really hurt him in some viewings. He works hard but skill isn't high end and neither is the skating. When I combine that with being a smaller guy he slips on my list. - HP Scout, Mark Edwards. April 2019

	PLAYER	TEAM	LEAGUE	HEIGHT	WEIGHT	POS	GRADE
50	PHILLIPS, ETHAN	SIOUX FALLS	USHL	5'9.25"	148 *	RC	C+
	HOCKEY SENSE	COMPETE		SKILL		SKATING	
	6	6		6		7	

Ethan joined the USHL early in the season from his midget program (Selects Hockey Academy – South Kent School) and wasted no time acclimating himself – as he scored in each of his first 11 USHL games. He's an industrious, speedy forward who unearths a lot of pucks for himself. Phillips does a really good job with his angles of attack and as a result, he ends up with a lot of pucks in tough areas despite his rather slight frame. His hockey sense carries him just as expeditiously as his feet do. He thinks the game very well and when matched with his higher-end compete level, there's a strong foundation for a player to grow into a really strong prospect. He has the skill level and the playmaking ability to play right wing with lesser linemates and still make things work offensively. He also was entrusted with the left point of the power play because of his passing ability and vision. Though he can be a little too antsy with moving the puck with lower percentage, cross-lane plays, he is an adept one-touch passer. He doesn't overhandle the puck, if he's going to give it away, it's going to be because he is over-passed it or rushed a pass. Somewhat conversely, his best skill is probably his ability to catch passes. He was thrown a number of bad passes this year and found a way to corral them in with his stick, skate or hand and not miss a beat. Ethan's skating certainly boosts his profile. His change of direction skating is slippery and makes him difficult to contain in open space. He's a plus player in all other aspects from his edges and first step to his top speed, he motors around the rink very well.

Defensively he works smart and covers readily for defensemen. Just like in the offensive zone, Phillips is willing and able in the tougher areas to take a hit to make a play. On the forecheck, too, Ethan is a nuisance to many defensemen attempting to break out. The angles that he takes and his stick positioning help neutralize some otherwise potent first-passers. There are some contests where he's pushing it a little too hard for his own good and he can overplay the game a little bit, trying to do too much. While he did carry pucks often this year, his skill level is only above average overall and he needs some space to show off his hands. He appears to lose some confidence in his abilities with the disc in tighter checking games. He has shown some ability to one-time pucks, but his goal scoring prowess is not noteworthy. Phillips wasn't as strong of an even strength producer as we'd like to see

	PLAYER	TEAM	LEAGUE	HEIGHT	WEIGHT	POS	GRADE
NR	PIRONEN, KARI	WINDSOR	OHL	6'1.0"	171 *	G	ND
	HOCKEY SENSE		COMPETE		SKILL		SKATING
	5		6		5		6

Kari Piiroinen had an average-season for the Spitfires after getting selected 30th-overall in the CHL Import Draft. He finished with a .423 GAA and a .875 save-percentage in 27 games. In the playoffs and at international events, he didn't fair much better, but did okay at the Hlinka, registering a .906 save-percentage and a 2.98 GAA in 2 starts. Piiroinen is a technically proficient goalie who relies on his butterfly and skating ability to keep the puck out. He's good on his edges while maintaining a semi-narrow stance which allows him to push-off laterally fluidly; we've seen him push off from post-to-post and make some highlight-reel saves, while also containing himself in his crease. His skating mechanics allow him to make micro-adjustments in the crease area at times as well. He stands tall in his butterfly and doesn't shrink down in his net most of the time, which is critical for Kari, since he's not a very large netminder. Although Piiroinen shows good fundamental mechanics in a couple of notable places, his hockey-sense was average to below-average. He had difficulty determining shooting-angles, would mis-read passes, and had difficulty tracking pucks through screens. Although his reflexes are decent, they also are not at the level we look for when determining if a smaller-netminder can make it. There's a decent base, but there was multiple stoppers for us as well.

	PLAYER	TEAM	LEAGUE	HEIGHT	WEIGHT	POS	GRADE
NR	PINARD, SIMON	BLAINVILLE	QMJHL	5'10"	160	LW	ND
	HOCKEY SENSE		COMPETE		SKILL		SKATING
	-		-		-		-

Pinard went undrafted in his first year of eligibility for the QMJHL Draft, but was picked this past June in the 2nd round (22nd overall) after a remarkable 2nd season with Magog in Midget AAA, where he notably won postseason MVP honours.

Similar to his Midget AAA career, Pinard had a slow start to his QMJHL career. He only had 5 points before the Christmas break (in 30 games). He came back very strong in the second half of the season, with 23 points in 35 games. He's not a super-skilled player, but he's pretty smart at both ends of the ice, and has a great work ethic as well. He's an average skater, but has showed a quick burst of speed with the puck on his stick, and this helps him beat guys wide when rushing the puck. He plays a pretty mature two-way game; he played in every situation for the Armada and, offensively speaking, his second half leaves us hoping for a big year from him next year. He might just be a good junior player, but there's hope that if everything goes well, with his smarts, he could challenge to become a depth player down the line. A defined example of what he could accomplish is Danick Martel of the Tampa Bay Lightning. Martel went undrafted after playing three seasons in the QMJHL, also with the Armada, and also grew up in Drummondville (on the same street as Pinard). We don't feel as though Pinard will be drafted this year, but if he can explode offensively like he did in the second half of the season (also like in his second Midget season in Magog) he could really help his chances for next year's draft.

	PLAYER	TEAM	LEAGUE	HEIGHT	WEIGHT	POS	GRADE
NR	PINONIEMI, GARRETT	HOLY FAMILY	HIGH-MN	5'11.5"	147 *	LC	**ND**
	HOCKEY SENSE		COMPETE		SKILL		SKATING
	6		4		6		5

Pinoniemi had the option to play junior hockey this season, being a 1st Rd Draft pick of Lincoln (USHL) in 2017 but elected to return to the Minnesota High School ranks as he had a pretty good team returning for Holy Family that had an opportunity to make the Minnesota State Tournament. Pinoniemi started the season in the Midwest HS Elite League for Team Northeast where he far and away lead his team in points. Pinoniemi continued his impressive points pace for Holy Family HS where he dominated his conference with 26 goals and 66 points in 24 games. Pinoniemi plays largely a perimeter game with the puck in the offensive zone and struggles penetrating the slot area and hardly ever drives the net, instead electing to pull up at the half wall and catch teammates entering the zone with speed, driving the net. He is highly effective in this approach at the high school level but will need to develop more of a desire to go to the hard areas to be as effective. His straight-line skating is good enough but struggles in tight areas due to lack of agility, as he gets stronger, especially in the lower body his skating should improve. A lot of times his hands move faster than his feet which gets him in trouble against good defenders. Pinoniemi thinks the game very offensively, sometimes cheating in the defensive zone and will get caught on the wrong side of the puck or attempting to get behind the defense too early. His offensive skill is good, and he is an opportunistic player that will finish on his opportunities. Pinoniemi is still a very lanky kid that has a ways to go physically and it shows in areas of the ice where he can easily be separated from pucks in the corners. Pinoniemi has the skill but lacks the compete and willingness to go to the areas necessary to be effective at the professional level. If Garrett is able to grow into his frame in the next couple of years, and show he is willing to go to the hard areas and compete more, he will have an opportunity to play beyond the NCAA level. Pinoniemi was another St. Cloud commit that changed his commitment to University of Minnesota when head coach Bob Motzko took the job at UM. Pinoniemi is at least one maybe two years away from being ready for college hockey.

"Gifted in the skill department but doesn't check enough boxes beyond that for me." HP Scout, Dusten Braaksma

	PLAYER	TEAM	LEAGUE	HEIGHT	WEIGHT	POS	GRADE
44	PINTO, SHANE	LINCOLN	USHL	6'2.0"	192 *	RC	**B**
	HOCKEY SENSE		COMPETE		SKILL		SKATING
	6		6		6		7

Strong, adaptable offensive forward. Pinto is one of the top players in the USHL not playing for the USNTDP. With his slick hands, wrist shot and heady playmaking ability, he shows good offensive potential. He consistently turned in a strong effort whether on first place Tri-City or last place Lincoln. He posted points in 75% of the games he played this season and despite leaving Lincoln 30 games into the 62-game docket, even at season's end, he's still the team leader in points – no one passed him. He acclimated into the robust Tri-City lineup very well midway through the season. His role on the power play was altered though. With Ronnie Attard as the triggerman, Pinto was forced into a net-front and puck retriever role which he seemed to embrace despite it limiting his puck touches in open space. One thing it did show off is Pinto's phenomenal hand-eye coordination. Between deflections and pass acceptances, he seems to never fail to get a stick on the puck.

Shane's a thick player who can be tough to move from the front of the net or the slot. He wins a lot of puck battles with his timing and body positioning. Despite only being an average skater with a long stride, Pinto does have good closing speed which might be enough to bump him up a half point. He is carried primarily by his ability to anticipate plays. He finds some sneaky passing lanes to unleash crisp passes through. He can finish with authority from in-close or mid-range with his powerful wrist shot and snappy release. Despite his size, he doesn't seem like a naturally physical player but he will make a hit to help out defensively. His defensive play is inconsistent overall, some nights he seems more attentive to it than others. On the plus side, he is an expert in the dot and does a good job communicating to teammates what he wants to have happen off the draw. He was mostly used at center this year, but has shown the ability to play the wing.

Pinto didn't look out of place no matter what team or situation he was put in or on. Going from being a one-man show on a desolate Lincoln team, to having to fit into the best team in the league thereafter: he really looked the part all season. He was in on half of all of Tri-City's playoff goals. Between his balanced attacking tools, size and hockey IQ, this player has all the makings of being very useful to a pro organization.

"Beecher, Pinto and maybe a guy like Ryder Donovan will probably all be mid to late second rounders and none of them have top two line upside. Just big." - NHL Scout, October 2018

"I think he's miscast as a Centre. He doesn't see the ice or distribute very well. He just uses his size and he competes." - NHL Scout, December 2018

"I didn't like him out west (Bonnyville WJAC). Didn't show me enough skill and played in a tunnel. He's not in the same league as the other top USHL guys like (Ryan) Johnson or (Bobby) Brink." - NHL Scout, December 2018

"He has the tools to be a goal scorer at the next level, has a ways to go if he's going to drive a line though." HP Scout, Dusten Braaksma

"I had a scout single him out as one of his teams better interviews. I missed him at the combine." - HP Scout, Mark Edwards, June 2019

	PLAYER	TEAM	LEAGUE	HEIGHT	WEIGHT	POS	GRADE
43	PITLICK, RHETT	CHASKA	HIGH-MN	5'8.75"	160 *	LW	B
	HOCKEY SENSE	COMPETE		SKILL		SKATING	
	6	7		7		7	

Rhett Pitlick is the son of former NHLer Lance Pitlick, the younger brother of current Nashville Predators prospect Rem Pitlick and cousin to current Dallas Stars forward Tyler, so he has the hockey lineage on his side. Pitlick is his own player when it comes to the family however, and probably has the most offensive tools of any of the three. Rhett Pitlick was an offensive catalyst for the Chaska Hawks this past season. When his team needed a goal, chances are Rhett Pitlick was in on it. Pitlick has high end skill and playmaking ability that allows him to create time and space on the wing. His hands and feet are both equally quick which made him very difficult to contain at the High School level this season for Chaska High School (21 Goals, 33 Assists in 25 Reg. Season Games). He proved to be elusive with the puck and difficult for defenseman to lock down along the wall and rarely absorbed direct hits with the puck. Pitlick sees the ice well and is a playmaker with quick strike ability that will identify and take advantage of defensive lapses by the opposition. His top skating gear is good and is an equally fast skater with the puck on his stick. There is still a ways to go in terms of his 200-foot game but Pitlick displays a consistent work ethic to win puck battles and uses his crafty stick work to strip pucks off players. Pitlick is a pest and a puck hound, he shows good second efforts for pucks and shows very little tentativeness to go up against bigger, stronger players, this is an area of his game that has improved immensely in the last couple of seasons. Pitlick is not the biggest player but plays above his weight class a lot of the time. Rhett is far from a physical player in the way of initiating body contact or delivering big hits when entering puck races, but he very much plays a physical game in the sense that he is over top of pucks and constantly competing against his opponent. Pitlick struggles with playing a straight-line game with the puck on his tape, he likes to have the puck on his stick and his level of competition in a lot of cases was conducive to him hanging onto the puck for long stretches and circling the ice in order to reset the play. Pitlick learned in the Spring with his short stint with Omaha (USHL) that this approach will not be effective a lot of the time at the higher levels. Having said that, in his stretch of 7 regular season games with the Lancers, Pitlick registered 1 goal and 4 assists in limited minutes and adapted well to the older, tougher league and by the end of the year, his north-south game had shown improvement. While Pitlick can place his shot accurately, it is not the strongest part of his game and will need to continue to improve his release and velocity if his goal scoring ability is going to translate to the NHL. Pitlick scored a lot of his goals in close, by the net, using his hockey sense in order to be opportunistic and his quick stick and hands to put home rebounds and dirty goals in the crease area. Off the rush Pitlick likes to be the setup guy, rather than the finisher and can be tentative in pulling the trigger and gives up scoring opportunities for that extra pass in some cases. Rhett doesn't project as an NHL prospect that can carve out a roll in a bottom six at this stage, he has the look of a prospect that will best serve in offensive opportunities and situations. If he hits a late growth spirt and adds some much-needed strength over the next few years, he may become a more versatile prospect. Pitlick's plans for 19/20 are a bit unknown at this stage but he will likely return to Chaska High School for his Senior year, while also spending some time with Omaha (USHL) at some point as well. Pitlick is a University of Minnesota commit for the fall of 2020.

"I'm a fan, has good sense and is competitive, He'll grow, he's a player." NHL Scout, November 2018

"He can fly and he has a really good brain and skill. He'll be in Omaha to finish the year. We'll see if he can be like some of the other high school guys that finished their draft season with a strong USHL debut." - NHL Scout, January 2019

"He'll be a late pick." - NHL Scout, January 2019

"He can make plays at high speed." - NHL Scout, January 2019

"He seems to be the best high school player this year." - NHL Scout, January 2019

"Not on our radar." NHL Scout, January 2019

"Do you mean Rem? He's drafted already." - NHL Scout, January 2019

"No draft for me." - NHL Scout, March 2019

"I think he needs to simplify his game at times, but he's got the skill." HP Scout, Dusten Braaksma

	PLAYER	TEAM	LEAGUE	HEIGHT	WEIGHT	POS	GRADE
NR	PLASEK, KAREL	BRNO	CZE	5'11.0"	154	RW	ND
	HOCKEY SENSE		COMPETE		SKILL		SKATING
	6		4		5		6

Plasek was undrafted last year, and he's looking to get drafted this time around as a second time eligible player. He split this past season in the top men's league and the Czech U-19 league. He had 6 points in 29 games in the top league, and was a goal-per-game player in the U-19 league. He also played for the Czech Republic at the World Junior Hockey

Championships in Vancouver, where he had only 1 assist in 5 games. Last year, Plasek captained the Czech at the U-18 World Hockey Championships, scoring 4 goals in 7 games.

He's an above-average skater who is able to create most of his offense from the rush. He's not very strong physically, and has a harder time creating with less room to operate, such as along the boards where he can be physically overmatched. He's got above-average puck skills and good one-on-one abilities with his quick and agile hands. He can beat goalies from various ways in the offensive zone; he has a good one-timer that he uses on the power play or with his quick hands in close one-on-one with the goalie. One of the biggest issues we have with him has been his inconsistency from shift to shift; he can be too invisible on the ice and doesn't make an impact in the game if he's not creating offense. More often than not, he will flash some skills in games, but at the end of the day he left viewers wanting more out of him. With his speed and anticipation, he creates some value for himself when his team is a man short. Overall, Plasek is a decent winger, but there are holes in his game and we don't expect to see him get drafted this year.

	PLAYER	TEAM	LEAGUE	HEIGHT	WEIGHT	POS	GRADE
7	PODKOLZIN, VASILI	SKA ST. PETRSBRG	RUS-JR	6'1.0"	190	RW	A
	HOCKEY SENSE	COMPETE		SKILL		SKATING	
	7	9		7		6	

Vasili Podkolzin played for three different teams while getting developed in SKA's system. In the MHL, he produced 8 points in 12 games, highlighted by 6 goals, and had 3 points in 3 playoff games. In the VHL, Vasili produced 5 points in 14 games and an additional 3 points in 8 playoff games. He had a cup of coffee in the KHL, recording zero points in 3 games. On the international stage, Podkolzin dominated the Hlinka and World Junior A challenge, producing a combined 19 points in 11 games, including 11 goals. At the U20's, despite being one of the youngest players featured, he managed to solidify his spot under Valeri Bragin while generating 3 assists in 8 games. After his U20 performance, his play at international events dipped, performing poorly at the U18-Five-Nations and World U18's, where he produced 4 points in 7 games.

Podkolzin has a rare level of tenacious—in your face hockey—mixed with a lot of talent. When discussing compete-levels, only a handful of players come close to matching Vasili's. Although he has a high-octane motor that's emphasized through his aggressiveness; it's his willingness to play with an edge that really separate's him. His hockey-sense and energy give him the ability to manipulate the momentum of a shift in different-facets, complimenting his 200-foot-game. As examples, he can bulldoze through a defenseman on his way to the net, get into heated altercations, or finish a devastating check which forces opposing teams to take notice. His compete blends into his leadership qualities, which gave him the opportunity to be the Captain of Russia at international events. He doesn't back down an inch, showing a rare primal-instinct when physically engaging both before and after the whistle. This makes him an uncomfortable player to play against and a natural agitator. He's the type of player that's willing to challenge defenseman, yet has the anticipation and spatial-awareness to identify open-lanes and take advantage. This gives him a varied attack when he has the puck. He can barrel down the wing and cut directly towards the net-area, or stop-up and contort his frame while simultaneously using his impressive-hands to change directions while knifing through an alternate-route. His ability to cut through lanes is magnified by his skating mechanics which improved over the course of the season. At the beginning of the year, Podkolzin skated very low to the ice which made it more difficult for him to be knocked off balance but didn't allow him to maintain separating straight-line speed; there was a heaviness to his stride and he would stay hunched over at times. As the season progressed, his strength increased and he started skating with better posture, which resulted in a marked increase in his fluidity.

After breaking down defenses, Vasili has demonstrated in our viewings that he's a primary shooter. He's highly coordinated and this compliments his release which generates a good amount of velocity; activating his hips, core and legs to drive through his initial phase of the shot. Much like some other high-end shooters in this class, he understands how to fully rotate through the release point. He drives through the point of contact with the puck during his slapshot as well, giving him different options both when in motion and from stationary positions. When his shooting lanes are taken-away, Podkolzin has shown an excellent array of dekes to bypass defenses. He can put pucks quickly through an opponents tripod, pull pucks around frames while going at top speeds, and can rapidly change from his forehand to backhand and visa-versa. His puck-skills give him a dynamic element to his game from an aesthetic perspective; he's not the type of player who you have to go searching for, which summarizes his skill. Despite his impact in most games and having one of the higher floor-to-ceiling ratios featured in this class, there's elements to Podkolzin's game that might set him back from developing into the theoretical line-driver we envision.

In contrast to his shot, Podkolzin doesn't look to pass the puck as often. One of the main reasons for this is due to his take-over mentality which gives him tunnel-vision at times. This makes him less effective when looking for backdoor passing options or when evaluating tight-seams parallel to him. Though, he consistently makes clean-transitional zone-entries when attempting to drive-play, and as a result has to find his teammates trailing him. Due to this trait, he has displayed impressive vision when identifying players lagging behind him off the rush. Another aspect of his playmaking, is his ability to generate dynamic passes on occasion. They're not frequent but he is capable of making highly-technical no-look passes and can thread sharp-passes through traffic, just not as consistently as we would like. The biggest problem with his playmaking is in regards to his body-mechanics. There's a lack of deception in-terms of Podkolzin's posturing when faking a pass at times; this can extend to his release as well. As an example, he doesn't use head-fakes as often as we would like when attempting to mask where he's intending to place the puck after identifying his passing option. When he does release the puck, there at times where he exaggerates his posture which gives netminders a tell. This looks like a smaller issue, but's its magnified for players who attempt to drive-a-line to the degree Vasili does. He needs to further develop his unpredictability. Another aspect of Vasili's game that could have trouble translating is in regards to his frame. He's a powerful-kid who has a tremendous forechecking and backchecking skill-set due to how strong he can be on the puck, but his frame isn't very large given his projection as a power-winger. Lastly, depending on his line-mates, Podkolzin has difficulty at times making the players around him better. His willingness to dictate play is one aspect of his game that makes him a gifted player, but he needs to further refine his take-over mentality so that he can better involve his teammates if he wants his game to translate.

Podkolzin is a unique and highly sought-after player-type and we believe he has the determination and drive needed to dictate play at the highest levels regardless of some of his concerns. In conclusion, we see Vasili developing into a complete power-winger who can be used on both special-teams units which should make him an effective playoff contributor.

"Fantastic player. He plays a lot harder than most Russians." - NHL Scout, August, 2018

"Top three in June: Hughes, Kakko and Podkolzin 3rd. Nobody is touching them so book it. - NHL Scout, January 2019

"He's a great player. He competes so hard, he's skilled. - NHL Scout, May 2019

"Skilled and hard to play against. He's a big pest. Good on the walls and along the half-boards." - NHL Scout, May 2019 - NHL Scout, May 2019

"He doesn't need to put up as many points as some of these other highly ranked kids in order to be a difference maker" - HP Scout, Brad Allen

NR	PLAYER	TEAM	LEAGUE	HEIGHT	WEIGHT	POS	GRADE
	PORCO, NICHOLAS	SAGINAW	OHL	5'11.75"	177 *	LW	ND
	HOCKEY SENSE	COMPETE		SKILL		SKATING	
	4	5		5		6	

Nicholas Porco, a 4th overall selection in the OHL Draft, had an okay season for Saginaw. He started out of the gate with 18 points, including 10 goals in his first 20 games but then cooled off significantly for the majority of the season. He finished the year with 36 points in 67 games, including 20 goals. In the playoffs, he generated 7 points in 16 games, with 3 goals and wasn't featured at international events.

Porco's game is based around his speed. He's a surprisingly awkward skater who has an upright-posture and can look off-balance at times when attempting to start up. Despite his unorthodox stride, he generates a lot of power which gives him separating speed. He took advantage of this speed both at even-strength and when short-handed, making him a threat at the defensive-blueline. He doesn't need a lot of time to get up to his top-gear and this allowed him to cut aggressively when switching his speeds after transitioning over the offensive-blueline, putting defense on their heels. He's got some length and likes to use it to try and wrap pucks in-tight but has an average-skill-set so quite a few of his high-percentage chances didn't result in goals. Furthermore, Nicholas can have tunnel-vision at times and lacks the anticipation and poise to slow the game down to better take-advantage of his skating. This made it difficult for him to involve his linemates at times; instead he would opt to attempt to drive-play with mixed results.

He skates aggressively, but rarely switches the tempo of the play, consistently staying in one-gear which makes him easier to read. He prefers his shot, which can get off his stick at an okay-rate but it's not a refined release and like his skating, can look uncoordinated depending on the shot. Although he has flashed the occasional high-end pass, it's never consistent. Which leads to the biggest problem with Porco's game, which is his inability to show up on a game-to-game basis. In some games, he would display good-compete level and make some impressive plays both on the forecheck and in-front of the net. In other games, he would be invisible and stay largely disengaged, floating around the perimeter. There's some talent in Porco and he has the potential to be an even better skater down the road if he can continue to refine his mechanics going forward, but we don't see his overall-hockey-sense or puck-skills translating at this time.

"He's a decent skater, it's not great mechanically but he get's there." - NHL Scout, March 2019

"I didn't have him very high anyway but he played really poorly down the stretch." - NHL Scout, May 2019

"I saw one game where he didn't touch the F***ing puck. Oh wait, sorry...he had a shot from way outside." - NHL Scout, April 2019

"He plays with some energy in spurts but no real compete or toughness. I think his hockey sense is an issue. Offensively he plays a pretty simple drive up the wing and shoot type of game. We had him ranked much later than he was drafted in the OHL Draft and he's not on my list in this draft. He's a decent OHL player but not for me as far as the NHL goes." - HP Scout, Mark Edwards

24	PLAYER	TEAM	LEAGUE	HEIGHT	WEIGHT	POS	GRADE
	POULIN, SAMUEL	SHERBROOKE	QMJHL	6'1.25"	206 *	RW	B
	HOCKEY SENSE		COMPETE		SKILL		SKATING
	7		7		6		6

Poulin was the 2nd overall pick in the 2017 QMJHL Draft, after Alexis Lafrenière. In the month of February 2019, he was named the captain of the Sherbrooke Phoenix, making him the youngest captain in the QMJHL this season. The son of former NHLer Patrick Poulin is a power forward who plays a heavy and smart game at both ends of the ice. Before this season started, he played mostly a bottom 6 role for Canada at the Hlinka/Gretzky Cup.

This season with the Phoenix, he averaged over a point per game in the regular season and was really good in the opening round of the playoffs against Blainville-Boisbriand, averaging close to two points per game in that series. Poulin is not a high-end scorer, though; we project him more as a 3rd-line type of winger for the NHL. He plays a smart game, is strong on the puck along the wall and doesn't mind going to the net with it. He plays a physical game when need be, but he's not overly aggressive physically. He will use his body and strength to win his puck battles and create space for his teammates. His skating abilities are fine for a kid of his age who is over 200 pounds, but depending on the game, they go from average to above-average. It's not a strong part of his game, but it's also not going to hold him back for the next level. He's got a decent shot that is heavy but lacks some accuracy. He is not a natural goal scorer, but has enough skills that will enable him to be a good point-producer at the junior level. It's once he turns pro that he'll be more renowned for his two-way game, his physical attributes and his attention to all the little details on the ice. There's not a lot to dislike about him, other than the fact that we wish he had a higher upside at the NHL level. Overall, we like the player and we're pretty confident that he'll be a good pro down the road.

"I really like him a lot. No huge weakness and he's got a ton of character." - NHL Scout, March 2019

"Top guy for me out of the Q this year." - NHL Scout, March 2019

"A good, safe bet that he can be an NHL'er playing in a supporting role. I think he understands his game very well." - HP Scout Jérôme Bérubé

"I saw him when his team was getting spanked and the game was over early. You never would've know it with this kid. He played like it was overtime in game 7. Upside might not through the roof but he's smart, goes to the dirty areas and finds a way to get his points." - HP Scout, Mark Edwards

NR	PLAYER	TEAM	LEAGUE	HEIGHT	WEIGHT	POS	GRADE
	PRIKRYL, FILIP	SAINT JOHN	QMJHL	6'0.75"	165 *	LC	ND
	HOCKEY SENSE		COMPETE		SKILL		SKATING
	6		6		5		4

Prikryl was the 2nd European pick by the Sea Dogs this past June (after Maxim Cajkovic). The Czech forward was selected with the 61st overall pick.

Prikryl's adjustment to the QMJHL was a bit rough in the first half, and it didn't help that he was playing on one of the worst teams in the league. Offensively, the Czech center did much better in the 2nd half, amassing 23 of his 31 points after the Christmas break. Prikryl is a good-sized two-way forward who can contribute at both ends of the ice. He can play both at center and on the wing. We liked him as a center more than a winger, but his faceoff work will need to get better. Away from the puck, he provides a good effort while backchecking and in his zone. When playing center, he does a good job supporting his defensemen down low to retrieve pucks. Good active stick in the defensive zone; he's got good smarts while playing in a defensive role. Offensively, he's not a high-end skills guy, but will work hard down low and in front of the net to get his goals and points. He doesn't have the skill level or skating abilities needed to play a high-tempo game, and won't be a flashy player out there. His skating needs a lot of work. Notably, he should improve the quickness of his feet, as they looked heavy and his starts are slow. His fluidity also needs improvement, as well as his explosiveness. Overall, skating is his biggest flaw in his game right now. Due to not having a high ceiling and his skating being below-average, we don't see Prikryl being a high draft pick. We could see a team take a chance on him late in the draft following his decent second half of the season, or he could also go undrafted.

	PLAYER	TEAM	LEAGUE	HEIGHT	WEIGHT	POS	GRADE
NR	PRIMEAU, MASON	NORTH BAY	OHL	6'5.0"	205 *	LC	C
	HOCKEY SENSE	COMPETE		SKILL		SKATING	
	5	6		4		6	

Primeau had a tale-of-two-seasons type of year. He started off with Guelph and had some difficulties getting minutes, he generated 7 points in 20 games, including 3 goals. However, after getting traded to North-Bay, he asserted himself into games at a much higher-rate, leading to an increase in production. He generated 26 points in his final 49 games, including 10 goals; and in the playoffs, he had 3 points in 5 games. Primeau is a tall, two-way center who has some versatility in his game. He's a decently coordinated kid given his size and this extends to his skating mechanics that are above-average. Though, there's still a lot of frame left to fill out and as a result he's not a powerful skater and has difficulty gaining traction on the ice. There is some fluidity in him that helps compensate, and this did allow him to recover and support his defenseman away from the play; his impressive length led to several stick-on-puck plays.

One of the better qualities that Mason developed this year was his ability to assess high-percentage plays. He learned how to generate more offensively at a better clip in the second-half, due to being more assertive on the ice, and took advantage of soft-ice at a better-rate. His shot is decent; it doesn't feature much in the way of a follow through, and he has difficulty with his footwork but there's some flexibility in his wrists that give him an okay release point, in terms of the speed it comes off his stick. His passing is ahead of where his shot is; he can thread difficult passes while in motion but his vision has limitations. He still has trouble identifying seams depending on the play-type. At the beginning of the season, his pace was very-average at times – yet, he became a more competitive player after his trade, showing an improved motor. His improved energy helped Primeau develop into a multi-faceted player that became an important cog for the Battalion. He's not a kid who is going to beat pro-defenseman one-on-one or end up on a highlight-reel, but if he can fill out his frame and use it more often, continue to develop his pace, and increase his speed, then he has an outside shot at the bottom of a line-up.

"I don't know many Scouts who have him as draft." - NHL Scout, February 2019

"If you can't produce in this league what are you going to do in the NHL? I'm not drafting him to be my 3rd line checker." - NHL Scout, March 2019

"There is just not enough there as far as offence goes. I actually didn't see this player in his OHL Draft year but I remember our OHL Draft Scouts telling me his team was better when he missed some games. Most were not high on him." - HP Scout, Mark Edwards, April 2019

I found myself wanting to like him. I went to extra playoff games just to see him but in the end I don't see much there." – HP Scout, Mark Edwards, May 2019

NR	PLAYER	TEAM	LEAGUE	HEIGHT	WEIGHT	POS	GRADE
	PROCTOR, KIRBY	DES MOINES	USHL	6'3.25"	190 *	LD	ND
	HOCKEY SENSE		COMPETE		SKILL		SKATING
	4		6		3		5

Jumping from Bonnyville (AJHL) to the Buccaneers to preserve NCAA eligibility, Proctor did fine with the transition. His 17 assists and 18 points were second on his club in defense scoring and he kept a surprisingly tidy PIM number of 35 (15 of which came in one game) despite his prodding style. The Alberta native checks in at 6'3", 190 pounds but throws his weight around like he's much heavier than that. As the season wore on, his time seemed to dwindle a bit on average. Proctor is just an average skater and his technical skills leave a lot to be desired even for a player of his style. He has shown some ability to make short outlet passes or move a puck against the grain, but his puck poise under even moderate pressure is discouraging. He likes to be an aggressive style defender and make hits up at the point of attack. Not atypical of this type of blueliner, Proctor tends to chase hits all over the map. He doesn't maintain enough positional integrity because he leans outside the dot line anticipating a hit attempt, and it leaves him vulnerable against skilled players who can pilot their way back to the middle of the ice. He doesn't have the agility or smarts to recover well enough either. He took his physical game to another level in the playoff and very annoying for opposing players after most whistles. The size and physicality are obvious, and while he isn't a total relic to a bygone era, Kirby will really need to improve his technical abilities to garner attention.

64	PLAYER	TEAM	LEAGUE	HEIGHT	WEIGHT	POS	GRADE
	PROTAS, ALIAKSEI	PRINCE ALBERT	WHL	6'4.75"	205 *	LC	C
	HOCKEY SENSE		COMPETE		SKILL		SKATING
	7		5		6		5

Protas moved to the WHL from Belarus for the year after being taken with the 26th pick in the CHL import draft. Protas had an okay regular season finishing with 40 points. In the playoffs Protas really turned it on and consistently displayed his abilities as one of the top performers, tallying 22 points in 23 games.

Protas is a player of massive strengths and massive weaknesses. His standout flaw is in his skating ability. Protas has an extremely awkward looking stride and fails to reach a good top speed. Just getting to his top speed also takes far too long often leaving him a bit behind the play. Does have some short area natural elusiveness that enables his weak skating to not handicap him offensively. In this zone Protas displays high end vision, making an impact as a passer for others. He has a knack for making the unexpected pass and showed a great ability to catch defenders sleeping off the puck to feather dangerous passes to his teammates. When this ability is tied in with his great ability to protect the puck using his deceptive hands and massive frame, he was able to make a massive offensive impact that was stronger than his stats would show. Protas was also surprisingly a major threat through the neutral zone, making great leading passes to teammates and often being far enough behind the play to get a drop pass and attack a flat defense. In the defensive zone he effectively played his role, relying on smart positioning and his reach to make an impact. Beyond this did an excellent job getting pucks out with possession. He does not make much of a physical impact, more preferring to swallow up puck carriers with his reach than to engage for a check. While the skating is difficult to get past, Protas is one of the more intriguing prospects as he progressed at a high level through out the year and has some hard to learn natural abilities.

"For a big guy he plays a very soft game. He's not a guy I'd push for." - NHL Scout, February 2019

"He's the better player for me (over Leason) but he plays a soft game like Leason. His skating is ugly but considering Leason is a 99 (birth) I'd rate it better than Leason." - NHL Scout, March 2019

"I know he had the big playoffs but he's still a later round pick. Someone will take him to early with a recency bias though. - NHL Scout, May 2019

"I like him more than Leason. He'll be better than Leason in two years." - NHL Scout, May 2019

"Lots of work to do with his skating, but he's still pretty young compared to his linemate Leason. Really loved his vision in the offensive zone and how good he was along the wall during the Memorial Cup." - HP Scout, Jérôme Bérubé, June 2019

	PLAYER	TEAM	LEAGUE	HEIGHT	WEIGHT	POS	GRADE
73	PUISTOLA, PATRIK	TAPPARA JR.	FIN-JR.	6'0.0"	174 *	RW	C
	HOCKEY SENSE		COMPETE		SKILL		SKATING
	6		4		7		5

Puistola is one of the most skilled players from Finland in this draft class. This season, he split his playing time between three levels. In Finland's 2nd-tier men's league with LeKi in the Mestis league, he was over a point-per-game player, finishing first in scoring among U-18 players. With Tappara's U20 team in the junior league, he was just under a point per game, with 22 points in 25 games. He also played 16 games in Liiga with Tappara, where he only had 1 assist in limited playing time. On the international stage, he was a threat offensively, scoring 14 goals in 21 games with the U-18 team. Despite Finland having a tough U-18 tournament in April, he still managed to score 5 goals in 5 games.

What makes Puistola a prospect is: his hands. They are excellent in tight areas and have the ability to make defenders miss, and he's a threat one-on-one. He lacks some speed to be even more dangerous one-on-one, as he doesn't play at a high pace and when faced with a higher level of competition, that lack of speed will hurt him. One thing with Puistola was that he liked to challenge players one-on-one, but to the point where he would be victim to turnovers when trying to beat those defensemen. If there are too many such turnovers in the neutral zone or just inside the offensive zone, he might not end up being one of the coach's favourites. He possesses an excellent wrist shot that has allowed him to score many goals this season. His shot has great velocity, and he can also release it in no time. He's a good passer and has above-average vision, but he's definitely a shoot-first type of winger. He needs to get stronger, but he does some good work along the boards anyway. He can hold onto the puck and use his size and good technique to keep possession of the puck, using his back to shield opponents away and making quick turns to get away from defenders. There was a great sequence at the recent U-18s against the Czech team where he did exactly that, maintaining possession of the puck against three Czech players trying to take it away from him. There's still some inconsistency in terms of his effort from game to game, and he is still too one-dimensional at times.

With Puistola, you're going to hope that the rest of his game and effort level will catch up to his skill level in the years ahead. He has the talent and scoring potential to be a very good top-6 winger at the NHL level, but his skating and overall game will need to get better.

NR	PLAYER	TEAM	LEAGUE	HEIGHT	WEIGHT	POS	GRADE
	RANNISTO, JASPER	BLAINVILLE-BOIS	QMJHL	6'1.0"	179 *	LD	ND
	HOCKEY SENSE	COMPETE		SKILL		SKATING	
	5	5		4		4	

Rannisto came over from Finland this season, selected 52nd overall in the 2018 CHL Import Draft. He struggled to make an impact on the Armada this past season; he's a defensive defenseman with limited upside. Rarely will he rush the puck out of his zone. When he did, he didn't show a lot of creativity creating offensive plays. He has a decent shot from the point, but takes too much time to get his shots off, often resulting in them being blocked in front of the net. He has to play a very safe game in order to be effective on the ice. He lacks good footwork, meaning that he needs to back up every time a player comes down his wing. His gap control is also not good enough. He can play a physical game along the boards, has good size and plays a good North American game in terms of physicality. He can be useful on the PK, mainly because he's strong to battle in front of the net or along the boards, in addition to having a good active stick in front of the net. He struggles against speedy wingers, as he doesn't have the footwork to compete against them. He gets caught flat-footed too many times. Rannisto is not a player we would draft, and there's a good chance he won't be back with the Armada next season.

"Our four ratings say it all. I saw this team a lot and it was pretty much over for him as far as b making my list after a couple of viewings." - HP Scout, Mark Edwards, May 2019

NR	PLAYER	TEAM	LEAGUE	HEIGHT	WEIGHT	POS	GRADE
	RASANEN, IIVARI	TAPPARA U20	FIN-JR.	5'11.5"	204	LD	ND
	HOCKEY SENSE	COMPETE		SKILL		SKATING	
	5	6		5		6	

Rasanen was Finland's captain at the U-18 tournament in April. During the season, he played all year in the junior league, posting 31 points in 49 games with Tappara's U20 team.

Even if he posted some decent numbers this year in the junior league, Rasanen is not a highly offensive defenseman, more like a stay-at-home type with not much flash to his game. He's a good penalty-killer with a good active stick that is willing to block shots in front of his goaltender. He's got a good compete level in his own zone and is a good competitor that was used in a shutdown role by Finland in international competition this season. He's quick to apply pressure to the puck-carrier in the defensive zone. He's not a creative offensive player with the puck; he makes a good pass to get the puck out of his zone, but once in the offensive zone, he's limited in what he can do. He has good mobility, good footwork and with his agility he can cover a good amount of ice in his own zone. He can use his good skating abilities to rush the puck out of his zone. His speed is adequate; it lacks a bit of explosiveness, but it's not a weakness. Rasanen is a low-upside stay-at-home defenseman who we're hoping to see improve his offensive skills in order to assert himself as an impact prospect at the next level.

NR	PLAYER	TEAM	LEAGUE	HEIGHT	WEIGHT	POS	GRADE
	RATY, AKU	KARPAT JR.	FIN-JR.	5'11.5"	170 *	RW	ND
	HOCKEY SENSE		COMPETE		SKILL		SKATING
	5		7		5		6

Raty is a high-energy player in the Kalpat system. This year in his rookie season in the U20 league, he amassed 45 points in 52 games, good for 4th among all U-18 players in this league. Even if he had very nice offensive numbers this season, Raty won't be known as an offensive player if he wants to reach the NHL. He's an up-and-down player that has great work ethic. He plays hard, and loves to get engaged physically with a good forecheck. There are skills there, no doubt. However, he doesn't have enough to be a top-6 guy at the NHL level. If he makes it, he's going to be a depth-role player that can skate on a 4th, possibly 3rd line. He's an effective forechecker; he has quick feet, good acceleration, and good top speed to apply quick pressure on the puck-carrier. He can be a bit of a pest on the ice at times with his aggressive style of play. He keeps his feet moving in the offensive zone and gets open for scoring chances this way. He has a quick and accurate shot, but he's not a high-end skills guy, nor is he very creative. His hockey IQ is only average, limiting his potential offensively. He's aggressive on the ice and will get his nose dirty in front of the net. With his speed and hustle, he has good value to become an effective penalty-killer at the next level. Raty plays the game the right way; he's your classic prospect from Finland with limited skills but great work ethic and compete level.

31	PLAYER	TEAM	LEAGUE	HEIGHT	WEIGHT	POS	GRADE
	REES, JAMIESON	SARNIA	OHL	5'10.0"	173 *	LC	B
	HOCKEY SENSE		COMPETE		SKILL		SKATING
	6		8		7		6

Jamieson Rees had a difficult start to the season after suffering a lacerated kidney that put him out of the line-up for an extended period of time. When he returned, he started producing at a good-clip, finishing the season with 32 points in 37 games. Although he didn't manage to produce in the playoffs, he was one of the best players for Canada at the U18's, where he produced 8 points in 7 games.

Rees is a multi-threat forward who treats every shift like it's his last. There's few players who blend his tenacity and skill. His best quality is his pace, which he keeps on a shift-to-shift basis that's generated through a high-voltage engine. We always take into account a kid's physical tools, yet Rees reminds us that there's a select few players who have the ability to elevate their physical presence regardless of their size. He's a tenacious and relentless player who is capable of out-competing much larger and bigger players than himself. This made Rees a difficult player to deal with on the forecheck since his high-tempo style of play resulted in relentless pressure. Despite his frame, he also delivered some massive-open ice-hits and he's willing to throw his entire body into his opponents; his fearless mentality allows him to penetrate through heavy-traffic as well. When he does have the puck on his stick, he shows a highly-creative and versatile attack. There's limitations to how physical he can be so he's adapted a less-stream-lined approach when he has the puck, then when he doesn't. This has made him difficult to read since he uses his edges and body-posturing to remain elusive and unpredictable when weaving through opposing defenses. His plus agility is essential in order for him to avoid contact, and he's very good at contorting his frame while simultaneously using his stick to generate dekes that help him guard the puck while in full-flight. His creativity melds into his hands which are very-good. He can drag the puck rapidly in-tight to his body and can beat defenders one-on-one. His hands also compliment his release. He can take the puck in one-motion both from a stationary position and when aggressively skating, making him a threat with the man-advantage. Despite his size, he can generate a surprising amount of leverage on most of his shot attempts; his release also features the ability to suddenly shift-angles. Although he can shoot the puck, it's not his initial instinct, as Rees is a primary playmaker. Much like the rest of his game, his vision is enhanced through his creativity. He looks to make highly technical no-look passes around the goal-line and can find his teammates through tight-seams in heavy-traffic. His execution-rate with his passes has been good in our viewings overall. The most significant aspect of his offensive-skill set is his anticipation. He's a player that feels off what the opposition is giving him and doesn't use many pre-set moves; he out thinks his opponents when setting up his attack and sets a pace that overwhelms them without overwhelming himself.

There's a ton to like about Rees's game but there's also reservations when projecting him at the highest-level. For a player his size, it's essential that he can skate well, yet we find his skating to be average in some aspects. His motor compensates for some of his skating concerns but not enough for us to feel comfortable ranking him as one of the A-rated players in this class. He features a slouched back when he's attempting to generate an increased speed, and due to the length of his legs, his stride is short. It didn't prevent him from generating at this level, but it might at the NHL-level if he doesn't refine his mechanics and continue to increase his overall speed. Another important area to consider is just how much of Rees's overall game can translate. He's not a player who's going to back down from other physical players, but he's at a disadvantage given his build which could reduce his efficiency when attempting to be impactful away from the puck.

Lastly, Rees attempts a lot of interesting and imaginative plays when he's on the ice due to how often he was capable of driving play in the OHL, but at the next-level, he's not going to be able to carry play for extended periods like he did this past season. There's going to be an adjustment period for him when determining how long he can hang onto the puck. Despite the concerns addressed, there's a saying we use that encompasses why we think Rees can make it, simply put, he's a "hockey player". If Rees can increase his separating speed and fill-out, then we think he can develop into an effective two-way energy forward, whose drive could make him an important piece, especially come playoff time.

"When I attempted to cap his skill-level, he would make a play that would force me to extend the cap" – HP Scout, Brad Allen

"You could argue he was the best player on the ice during Hlinka camp." – NHL Scout, August 2018

"This kid competes his butt off. I've watched him a lot. Skating is the weakness but he finds a way to get it done." – NHL Scout, August 2018

"Could he be a Brad Marchant? What about Brendan Gallagher?" – NHL Scout, August 2018

"He's a poor man's Travis Konecny." – NHL Scout, December 2018

"He's good with the puck, he can make plays in small areas." – NHL Scout, December 2018

"A lot of his game reminds me of Travis Konecny including the injuries."– OHL Staffer, January 2019

"I like him a lot. Not sure my ranking will match our team ranking and even if it does it might not match with where we are picking." – NHL Scout, January 2019

"He's an enigma. All I know is I can't drop a guy who works that hard too far down my list." –NHL Scout, January 2019

"Not an option for me in the 2nd round because I think there will be too many better players but if you're talking 3rd or 4th round I'd take him in a heartbeat." – NHL Scout, January 2019

"Sometimes his skating looked putrid, like he was pulling a house. Then I'd see him a month later and it looked good enough to make it work in the NHL."– NHL Scout, January 2019

"This kid is tough to rank. I think he'll go mid second but I feel better about early third." – NHL Scout, February 2019

"I don't know what to do with him on my list." NHL Scout, February 2019

"After Harley it's just a big f***ing mess in the OHL this year. I do like Rees in the 3rd or 4th round but I have a strong feeling he won't get there." – NHL Scout, March 2019

"I have Robertson (Nick) just ahead of him right now. He's 8th or 9th on my OHL list." – NHL Scout, March 2019

"I'd take him in the 3rd but after his U18 I think he'll go in the 2nd round." NHL Scout, May 2019

"He wasn't great with Sarnia but he's done it twice (played great) with Canada now (Hlinka & U18) and remember that the Hlinka wasn't on big ice." – NHL Scout, May 2019

"He was great in the Summer, shi### in Sarnia and good again in Sweden. Welcome to NHL Draft Scouting." – NHL Scout, May 2019

"I like the player but he's 5'9" and can't skate. He'll be long gone before I'd be willing to move on him." – NHL Scout, May 2019

"Injuries, suspension, playing out of position...there were a lot of things that hurt him. If Sarnia plays him on the wing all year he's getting drafted earlier." – NHL Scout, May 2019

"I've moved him into my 2nd round now but not sure where he'll be on our overall list." – NHL Scout, May 2019

"My only concern is injuries, he plays hard and has struggled to stay healthy." – NHL Scout, May 2019

"Issues with wing versus Center, No clue what happened in Sarnia...he wasn't great there when you compare his play to international games." – NHL Scout, May 2019

"His short area quickness looked ok in Sweden but he still got caught from behind just like he did in Sarnia. If I could get him in the 3rd I'd risk the skating." – NHL scout, May 2019

"Didn't like all the stupid penalties at the U18. He was good there but the tournament was weak this year. I didn't really like his self evaluation in my interview with him." – NHL Scout, May 2019

"I've been a fan for a while. I love the compete and he has skill. It's the skating that keeps him from being even higher on my list. There are times when it really held him back and then other times where it didn't look as bad. I think he might be one of those guys who can will his way into the league despite his average size/skating combo." – HP Scout, Mark Edwards, February 2019

"Hockey sense was between a six and a seven (rating) for me and his skating looked like a six at times, and even looking better so far at the Under 18, but was probably closer to a five more often in the OHL. That said, I saw him twice right after he returned from the lacerated kidney It's been tricky to figure his skating out Short area quickness is pretty good. though." – HP Scout, Mark Edwards, April 2019

"One thing to note is that I have always liked his game better on the wing and for our rankings we are projecting him as a winger. in the NHL." – HP Scout, Mark Edwards, May 2019

	PLAYER	TEAM	LEAGUE	HEIGHT	WEIGHT	POS	GRADE
NR	**RÉGIS, SAMUEL**	ROUYN-NORANDA	QMJHL	5'11"	194	LD	**ND**
	HOCKEY SENSE	COMPETE		SKILL		SKATING	
	6	6		5		5	

Régis is a smart stay-at-home defenseman who had a great first year in the league, playing top-4 minutes with the Rouyn-Noranda Huskies, often paired with Noah Dobson in the second half. Régis is very comfortable playing that shutdown role, as we have seen since his midget days with Châteauguay. In his QMJHL draft year, he was a big reason his team was able to shut down Alexis Lafrenière and his St-Eustache team in the opening round of the playoffs and pull off a big upset. Rouyn-Noranda picked Régis in the 4th round of the 2017 QMJHL Draft, and he is yet another name that they can add to their growing list of solid mid-round selections.

He's not the biggest defenseman, but doesn't mind playing a physical game in his own zone. He's not very tall, but he's strong on his skates. He's solid along the wall when it comes to retrieving pucks, he's also good at using a good, quick stick to block passing lanes. This season, he became a key player for Rouyn-Noranda while shorthanded. With the puck on his stick, he plays a simple game. He knows his limits well and understands his game well. He makes the simple play with the puck; if easy pass out of his zone is unavailable, he won't try to make a high-risk play that could become a turnover in the neutral zone. He had some power play time during the year, which is not his specialty, but he's smart with the puck and moves it adequately. The biggest area of his game that needs work: his footspeed and overall skating abilities. These are all average, and he will need to improve them for the next level. His shot from the point could see some improvement as well. It's fairly accurate, but its velocity could stand to be better. Overall, we like this player because of his competitive nature and solid hockey IQ, but there are some doubts with him in regards to his NHL upside and footwork.

"Smart, smart, smart." – HP Scout Jérôme Bérubé, May 2019

"He played a lot of big minutes with Jacob Neveu out of the lineup during the Memorial Cup. After Dobson, he was their most efficient defenseman in the defensive zone during this tournament. He was not intimated by the big stage." HP Scout Jérôme Bérubé, June 2019

	PLAYER	TEAM	LEAGUE	HEIGHT	WEIGHT	POS	GRADE
NR	**RIPPON, MERRICK**	OTTAWA	OHL	6'0.0"	191	LD	**ND**
	HOCKEY SENSE	COMPETE		SKILL		SKATING	
	5	6		5		5	

Rippon was coming into his third season in the OHL and was looking to build off of his strong finish in 2017-18. With all of Ottawa's top D returning, he was put in a depth role for the 67's and played well for them. Rippon did put up a lot of points this year, but he was used in more of a shutdown role. Rippon is a physical defenseman who uses his body and strength well in battle, and plays a very simple but effective game. Merrick was good this year at using his leverage to separate forwards from the puck. His skating is above average and his timing and awareness away from the puck are good. This allows him to keep players to the outside and finish checks along the boards. Merrick has shown some offensive upside in his game, but he tends to force pucks into tight windows on the rush. He isn't overly creative with the puck and his puck-related decisions were average at best. He has shown a good, low, accurate shot from the point. He'll have to be quicker with his decisions with the puck. He needs to improve his play with the puck and make simpler plays instead of trying to insert himself into the rush on offense. His game is more of a stay at home defensemen that plays with an edge.

	PLAYER	TEAM	LEAGUE	HEIGHT	WEIGHT	POS	GRADE
72	RIZZO, MASSIMO	PENTICTON	BCHL	5'9.75"	175 *	LC	C
	HOCKEY SENSE	COMPETE		SKILL		SKATING	
	6	5		7		6	

Rizzo was the captain of Penticton Vees this season and even though he missed some significant time with a shoulder injury at the beginning of the season he amassed over a point per game. This was Rizzo second season in the BCHL and he's committed to play college hockey at the University of North Dakota. The Burnaby native also played for team Canada West at the World junior A championship this past December but didn't had a particular good showing at this event.

He's a talented offensive player with good skating skills and plays the game at a good pace. He's very good on the power play, has great vision and makes players around him better with his ability to pass the puck. This year he had 21 of his 40 points on the power play and of those 21 points, 20 were assists which was the highest on the team even though he missed 20 plus games due to injury. He's good two-way forward, good puck support all over the ice and he's good in the faceoff circle. He has soft hands and can score his share of goals as well, good one on one ability. He plays in all situations, power play and penalty killing. To become a better player we would like to see improve his compete level and showed more grit to win more puck battles and being tougher to play against. Rizzo is a bit on the small side listed at 5'10" and will need to continue to add mass to his frame to compete better against tougher competition which he will have time to do at the NCAA level on a great program and also by getting stronger physically hopefully he can stay away from the injury list.

" Plays to the outside too much for me to take him very early." NHL Scout, March 2019

" Hockey sense for offensive zone is good, hockey sense away from the puck is not great." NHL Scout, March 2019

" I think he is better defensively than some people give him credit. He likes playing up and down the walls."- NHL Scout, April 2019

" He's a 6th or 7th rounder." - NHL Scout, May 2019

	PLAYER	TEAM	LEAGUE	HEIGHT	WEIGHT	POS	GRADE
35	ROBERTSON, MATTHEW	EDMONTON	WHL	6'3.0"	210 *	LD	B
	HOCKEY SENSE	COMPETE		SKILL		SKATING	
	6	6		6		7	

Matthew stood out as a key player for a strong Edmonton team this year, wearing a letter as an 18 year old. Their worst stretch of the year came when he was out of the lineup due to an injury. He finished the year with 33 points in only 52 games. He was the 7th overall pick in the 2016 WHL draft. He played internationally for Canada at the 2018 World Under-18 hockey championship as an underager and in this past August at the Hlinka/Gretzky cup in Edmonton.

Watching Robertson, he immediately stands out for his excellent skating ability at his size with speed and agility that allow him to play a very confident game. Robertson clearly trusts his tools, often times attempted moves at the blueline and sometimes even in the d zone. In our viewings lacked touch on both his passes and stickhandling, often bobbling the puck and whiffing on passes. Offensively he had games where he was engaged, making cuts into the slot, demanding the puck at the point, and finding lanes; as well as games where he sat back content to not make a huge impact in this area. Defensively he was a rock, with an excellent stick and gap on the rush, and strong in the corners with great board work. Decision making with the puck was not always good, with a lot of turnovers on bad reads and forced plays. The skating and length combination is enticing but Robertson needs to fine tune his decision making and refine his skills.

"I had time for him but didn't get much support fo where I wanted to rank him." - NHL Scout, May 2019

"I spoke to a few western based scouts who seem to like him less than the eastern based Scouts. We were a bit split on him as far as being a high end prospect. If he turns out to be really good, I'm in the group that gets the blame for dropping him out of our top thirty one." - HP Scout, Mark Edwards

48	PLAYER	TEAM	LEAGUE	HEIGHT	WEIGHT	POS	GRADE
	ROBERTSON, NICHOLAS	PETERBOROUGH	OHL	5'8.75"	162 *	LW	B
	HOCKEY SENSE	COMPETE		SKILL		SKATING	
	6	7		8		5	

Nick Robertson had a great start to the year by putting up point-per-game numbers at the Hlinka before suffering a wrist-injury that gave him some difficulties for the first 2 months of the season with Peterborough. That didn't stop him from generating 55 points in 54 games, including 27 goals. In the playoffs, he had 2 points in 5 games.

Robertson is a diminutive-winger with an excellent offensive-skill set, combining tenacity with dynamic puck-skills. There are few players in this class who blend his combination of compete and talent-level. The end result is a forward capable of making highlight-reel plays. We've seen him beat defenders one-on-one regularly using advanced outside-to-inside moves, between-the-leg dekes, and extended drag-moves. He's also capable of generating dangerous-shots off of his move-set. Specifically, his drag-dekes give him leverage when he pulls in-tight to his body which gives him a release point that can shift-angles rapidly and is surprisingly powerful. Additionally, his release is dangerous from the hashmarks and out, and he can shoot both from a stationary position and when going at top-speeds. His mental-game is strong; he's a competitor who looks to drive-play and as a result, when he's on his game, he makes his teammates around him better and plays fearless when attempting to cut through heavy-traffic. Nick also features duel-threat elements to his game, showing the ability to be both a primary shooter and passer. His vision can be hit or miss depending on the game though. In some viewings, he looks to extend and carry the play for too long, resulting in turnovers. That being said, he can thread both sharp and soft-passes through multiple-players and when he's playing well, mixes up his options effectively. His plus-motor extends away from the puck, where we've watched him stick-lift larger unsuspecting opponents during forechecking and backchecking sequences. His hockey-sense doesn't just allow him to process the play in-tight spaces with the puck on his stick either; he has good awareness in the defensive-zone and has intercepted passes at an impressive level in some of our viewings. Though in other viewings, he can have defensive-games where he's ineffective as well.

Despite Nick's offensive-gifts, his physical-limitations leave him with a severe development curve when attempting to project him at the next-level. Robertson is one of the weakest kids in this draft class who routinely gets knocked down to the ice and against larger more experienced defenseman, has a difficult time penetrating through lanes, which forces him to the outside. Furthermore, it's difficult to see how Robertson can be effective along the boards when taking into account his current frame. There's room for him to grow and he's one of the youngest kids in this class, but he's going to have to put on significant-mass and strength. Which leads to the next glaring flaw in Robertson's game which is his skating. He has difficulty pushing off correctly, generates little power, and has balance-issues that don't allow him to produce much in the way of straight-line speed. The end result is a player whose both very small and can't skate overly well. He compensates for his flaws by showing significant puck-protection skills by using his hands to counteract players who pressure him, and has a low-centre of gravity which allows him to mitigate defense who attempt to push him off the puck to a degree, but in every viewing, his size and skating package has continued to concern us.

When we evaluate Robertson based on his talent, he projects as a middle-6 scoring winger at the next level. However, there's few players in any class that overcome the size and skating disadvantages that he currently has. In order for him to translate as a pro, he's going to need extended-time to get a lot stronger and fix his skating mechanics, in order to have any shot at the show.

"He's a 3rd rounder for me. I'm not taking him earlier than that." - NHL Scout, December 2018

"I love him. He's going to make it because he wants it bad. Great interview." - NHL Scout, January 2019

"Numerous Scouts made a point to tell me how strong he interviewed." HP scouts, Mark Edwards, March 2019

"I've seen him a lot and he's not for me. He barely made my list." - NHL Scout, April 2019

"I can't really put my finger on one thing about him but I could never get on board with him all season. I kept going back to watch him but at the end of the day he's probably at a spot on my list where I'd never draft him." - NHL Scout, April 2019

"He'll be first or second on my list of OHL (eligible) players." NHL Scout, April 2019

"In this industry, if you're small and just an average skater, then you're usually going to be battling to make it, but Nick brings a rare drive that might allow him to beat the odds" - HP Scout, Brad Allen

"He has no issues with his compete and is clearly skilled. The reason he drops a bit on my list is his size strength and skating package. I watched him a lot late in the season and he never made me want to push him up my list. Won't be shocked if he makes it because of his skill and compete, but there are several OHL'ers I'd select before him." - HP Scout, Mark Edwards, May 2019

	PLAYER	TEAM	LEAGUE	HEIGHT	WEIGHT	POS	GRADE
NR	ROMANO, ANTHONY	SIOUX FALLS	USHL	5'10.75"	182 *	LC	**C**
	HOCKEY SENSE		COMPETE		SKILL		SKATING
	6		6		5		5

Net driving, high motor forward. Moved from the Toronto Jr. Canadiens to the Aurora Tigers in Ontario Jr. A, but to preserve NCAA eligibility did not pursue an opportunity with the Sarnia Sting. He tied for the team-lead in goals with 26 on a strong Sioux Falls club. A competitive player armed with a lot of drive to his game. Let's cut right to the chase: Romano's ticket to the show is being a net-front man in the mold of Patric Hornqvist. Though miscast as a center at times this year in Sioux Falls, Romano is more effective as a right winger where he can simplify his game by driving the net and make a mess at the top of the crease. At center, he gets away from his strengths and tries a lot of passes that simply aren't in his repertoire. He needs to be a player who can get it, shoot, and then tuck home the rebound. When he tripods in front of the net, it's like moving a fire hydrant – he can really cement himself in front of a goalie. He hasn't fully developed and embraced all that there is to that role, but the early signs are there. He has the work ethic, build, and determination to develop it.

His skating and shot can be described as slightly above average, his hands are on the wrong side of that average axis. The small area footwork and edges will need to improve. He's not slick, so he absorbs a lot of hits at maximum impact, as he hasn't developed the ability to roll-off of brute force contact. His ability to fight through contact without being knocked off stride in the cycle game and along the boards in general will be a major factor in his success – right now, that isn't there either, but again, this is a player that probably hasn't fully embraced his suggested future role, which is completely understandable (if not a positive) given the level he's playing at and where he's at on his development arc. Defensively he means well, because he does come back pretty hard but there's no nuance or purpose to his backchecks. He doesn't sense where the puck is going to be next in the defensive zone nearly enough – another good indicator that he shouldn't be asked to manage the middle of the ice. His on-ice demeanor looks professional and well-tempered while still keeping up his workman-like game.

	PLAYER	TEAM	LEAGUE	HEIGHT	WEIGHT	POS	GRADE
NR	ROSS, LIAM	SUDBURY	OHL	6'1.75"	197 *	LD	ND
	HOCKEY SENSE	COMPETE		SKILL		SKATING	
	4	6		5		5	

Liam Ross had a decent season for Sudbury, generating 29 points in 68 games, including 7 goals. In the playoffs, he finished with 1 assist in 8 games. What Ross did well was use his thick-frame to impose a physical presence on the ice. He's good at weighing heavy on opponents along the boards and battles aggressively. His aggressive style in his own-end blended together with his recovery-rate; he's willing to expend his tank in order to make a defensive recovery-play. He needed to make more recovery plays than he did though. His ability to recognize transitional play was mixed, resulting in Liam losing a step against some of the faster-players. When he was positioned well, he was able to drive most players to the outside and was a defender who could use his stick in conjunction with his frame. The biggest area of improvement for Ross in his own-end will be reacting to pressure at a more consistent-level. There were games where his outlet passing was good when given limited time and space, but also games where it was poor. His anticipation at the offensive-line was better than behind his own-goal line. He activated and made plus decisions in some viewings, and was very good at keeping pucks in; recognizing when he needed to move the puck quickly.

Where he had difficulty was when attempting to breakdown defenses. He rarely showed a skill-level that was capable of making high-end offensive-plays, and relied more on getting his quick wrist-shot through traffic in order to generate offense. It's his combination of grit, determination, and size that translates at this time, not so much his puck-game or ability to transition. He's going to need to continue to develop offensively and develop more poise under pressure in order to translate.

"The bulk of the scouts I have spoken to don't see him as a draftable prospect." – HP Scout, Mark Edwards, January 2019

"I don't mind the offensive numbers but he made so many mistakes in my viewings that I never got a feeling of confidence that he can make the jump to the next level. Multiple bad puck decisions in every one of my viewings. - HP Scout, Mark Edwards, May 2019

NR	PLAYER	TEAM	LEAGUE	HEIGHT	WEIGHT	POS	GRADE
	ROSS, RODDY	SEATTLE	WHL	6'4.0"	174	G	C

HOCKEY SENSE	COMPETE	SKILL	SKATING
5	6	6	6

Ross had a whirlwind of a season, beginning the year with Camrose in the AJHL before signing with Seattle midway through the year. Ross' arrival was a game changer for the Thunderbirds as he came in and seized the starting job, leading them to an excellent second half and playoff berth. Ross posted a 2.76 GAA and .919 save percentage over 25 games in the WHL this year.

Ross is a big goaltender with great athleticism. He is explosive getting across the crease and has the ability to make saves that wow you. Ross thrives under pressure and is at his best when he is getting peppered with shots. When he is locked in Ross is tough to beat and can win his team a game. Ross is extremely raw and not the most technically refined goaltender, relying on his athleticism and natural shot stopping ability. Ross can play a bit out of control at times and is sometimes chasing the play too much. Some of this can be attributed to his lack of high end playing experience and limited training. Ross came out of nowhere this season and has a limited track record of play at a high level. With this being said there is a question of how sustainable his high end performance is. On the flip side, there is also the potential for a ton of growth as he gets top training for the first time. Ross has a lot of unteachable ability and the size and athleticism to develop into a high level prospect.

NR	PLAYER	TEAM	LEAGUE	HEIGHT	WEIGHT	POS	GRADE
	ROUSEK, LUKAS	SPARTA	CZE	5'11.0"	161	RW	ND

HOCKEY SENSE	COMPETE	SKILL	SKATING
5	6	5	6

Rousek is a 1999-born Czech forward who played mostly in the Czech top men's league this year, amassing 9 points in 34 games and 5 points in 4 playoff games. He's versatile, as he can play either at center or on the wing. He's an above-average skater with good acceleration. He can make things happen by keeping his feet moving constantly. He's quick to retrieve pucks in the offensive zone due to his compete level and skating abilities. He has good vision and nice smarts at both ends of ice. He's valuable shorthanded with his anticipation and work ethic. He's inconsistent in his offensive performances, as he had ups and downs throughout international tournaments during the year. However, he did have a good second half of the season with his team. His hands remain average, and he doesn't possess a lot of offensive potential for the NHL. He creates a lot of scoring chances for himself with his speed and by going hard to the net, but he's not a finisher. He does well along the boards to protect the puck with his size, using his back to shield opponents away. His potential is more as a 3rd- or 4th-line winger with value on the penalty killing unit.

NR	PLAYER	TEAM	LEAGUE	HEIGHT	WEIGHT	POS	GRADE
	ROWE, CAMERON	USA U-18	NTDP	6'1.75"	201 *	G	C
	HOCKEY SENSE		COMPETE		SKILL		SKATING
	4		6		7		5

Cameron Rowe – Inconsistent, frenetic goaltender who gets by chiefly on athleticism. Rowe served as the backup for Spencer Knight on Team USA, but in USHL play they ended up in the same number of games. Rowe gave up nearly a goal per game more (3.05 vs. 2.21) and lost the save percentage battle handily by a score of .903 to .884. Naturally, Knight is a tough comparison for any goalie in this draft class, but Rowe lagged far behind on the scoresheet and on the ice. Rowe is quick on his skates in the crease and gets good pushes. He can make one big push to the far post quickly. Cameron can also swing back to the post from the top of his crease at terrific pace. He plays a very athletic game and he's a battler in the crease.

He's a battler to a fault, in fact. As way too many shots are an adventure for him. His movement in the crease and the subtle little feet adjustments that he makes and how often he checks his marks on the rink to calibrate his depth properly look pretty good, almost rehearsed, and everything is fine right up until the shot is taken. Once a shot is released, all technique seems to just drain out of the equation. He has not shown the ability to read shots off of sticks, so he guesses and just has to react. He has a natural built-in mechanism to deal with that as no matter what depth he initially establishes, he's very easy to push back deeper into his net in virtually any situation. This gives him an eighth of a beat more time to react, but it's a vulnerability. His constant movement also manifests itself as really poor anchoring. He almost never makes a save from his "mark", he's also sliding in a direction and hoping that it's with the direction of the play. Because Rowe has fairly poor balance, it's difficult for him to remain upright with his shoulders up on bigger pushes. He can sit back on his heels in a compact butterfly and absorb a shot to the belly pad, but that's not enough to give us confidence in his skills transferring to the pro level. He has high glove placement and his fingers look upright in there, which is pretty common for American goaltenders. However, because of Rowe's unpolished ability to read shots, he leaves himself really susceptible to pucks going through his body – another thing that happens far too often for a goalie of his height. At 6'7", it's a little more understandable and we'd track how those holes get sealed over time – but at 6'2", it's a little less excusable to the degree that it happens. Because he fights the puck so often, rebound control is unpredictable. His stick play is also a weakness. Rowe's panic threshold is very low, so he begins swimming immediately after a rebound or a deflection – that really bucks an overwhelming trend in the world of goaltending these days. At the end of the day, there isn't anything to latch on to for the North Dakota commit. Everything about him is so inconsistent, right down to how wide his stance is in his setups – there just isn't enough of a foundation to reasonably work with here. The one potential out for Rowe is that he might look better and feel more comfortable as a goalie on a team that is constantly under siege defensively. If he's put in a situation to make crazy acrobatic save after crazy acrobatic save, there might be some appeal there. The idea of him playing on a tight, competitive team that gives up 23 shots a game and he has just be reliable seems remote right now. Unrelated, he was drafted 8th overall by Des Moines in the USHL Entry Draft.

"Future London Knight." – NHL Scout, September 2018

"He's blessed with tools but he's all over the place." – NHL Scout, October 2018

"Incredibly athletic but not very structured. No draft." – NHL Scout December 2018

"If you could combine the two goalies (Knight and him) you would have a great prospect." – NHL Scout, December 2018

*"He went to sh** in the 2nd half, good goalie but may have played his way out of being drafted. Picked by Des Moines so it wouldn't shock me if he went to London next year. He probably should, he needs to play." - NHL Scout, May 2019*

60	PLAYER	TEAM	LEAGUE	HEIGHT	WEIGHT	POS	GRADE
	RYBINSKI, HENRIK	SEATTLE	WHL	6'0.5"	176 *	RW	C+
	HOCKEY SENSE	COMPETE		SKILL		SKATING	
	6	7		6		5	

Rybinski had quite the journey this season, beginning in a bottom 6 role with Medicine Hat, before requesting a trade, spending half the year in the BCHL, then becoming a top line player for the Seattle Thunderbirds. Overall Rybinski had 38 points in 47 games overall, however 35 of those came in the 33 games he played with Seattle where he emerged as an excellent play maker and offensive leader.

Rybinski creates a ton of space with good edges but lacks in breakaway speed. He plays with a deceptive pace and in combination with above average puckhandling is very elusive. Great at finding the hole to get passes through. Rarely gives away where he's going with his passing, making a lot of creative feeds some of which his teammates aren't ready for due to the sheer difficulty of the attempt. Is very reluctant as a shooter and clearly needs to add more power on his shot, it is obvious he wants to pass in any odd man or even situation. Not a passive player and is proactive in acquiring the puck, doing a great job using his hands and anticipation to receive dump ins and make up for his lack of size. Rybinski is mostly a perimeter player offensively right now but is not a guy who plays afraid, and is willing to engage physically. Defensively positioning is okay and he is not a liability whatsoever as he clearly buys in to his teams concepts. Can gain the zone in transition mainly in situations where he sets up a d to the inside then beats them to the wide lane but does not have the speed or assertiveness to turn and drive the net. Went from a bottom 6 player in Medicine Hat to top line driver on Seattle, gaining confidence and showing added wrinkles to his game with each viewing.

"Henry is a versatile player with high compete and he plays a complete 200 foot game. He possesses deceptive speed with quickness and has shown the ability to beat defenders 1 on 1." - Jason Fortier, Head Coach, Coquitlam Express

"One of the best examples of how big of a role opportunity plays in performance. After a midseason move to Seattle and promotion to the first line he looked like a different player. With better linemates and more opportunity his playmaking ability thrived." - HP Scout Liam Loeb

NR	PLAYER	TEAM	LEAGUE	HEIGHT	WEIGHT	POS	GRADE
	SAARELA, ANTTI	LUKKO JR.	FIN-JR.	5'10.75"	183 *	LC	C
	HOCKEY SENSE	COMPETE		SKILL		SKATING	
	5	6		5		6	

Saarela split this past season between the junior league and Liiga, where he had respectable offensive success. His 10 points in 24 games was the 3rd-highest point-per-game ratio for U-18 players in the league. His older brother Aleksi is playing in the AHL with the Charlotte Checkers; he was a 3rd-round pick of the New York Rangers in the 2015 NHL Draft.

Saarela can play all three forward positions. He was mostly featured on the right wing this season and projects more as a winger than a center at the next level. He has a slight frame and will need to continue to get stronger physically in order to compete better along the boards when facing bigger and stronger opponents. He plays with a good pace; he has a good compete level and good skating abilities. He keeps his feet moving and his acceleration is above-average when it comes time to taking advantage of slower defensemen, beating them wide frequently. He is also good at creating turnovers with a quick forecheck. He's a good two-way forward who plays well in all three zones. However, he plays a bit too much on the perimeter in the offensive zone and doesn't have good velocity on his shot. He's not a good goal scorer, and his offensive output at the next level will be limited because of the lack of velocity on his shot. He's also limited physically, and his body frame doesn't suggest he'll get much bigger in the future. He's not strong enough on the puck, either. He needs to protect it better along the wall and be tougher to play against. He takes care of his play in his zone, showing good support in his zone and good puck-retrieval abilities. He can play in all situations; he can do some good things on the PK due to his speed and anticipation. Offensively, he's not someone who will drive his line; he's more of a complementary player. His best tools are his compete level and skating abilities. He projects more as a 3rd- or 4th-line player if he can get stronger and bigger physically.

	PLAYER	TEAM	LEAGUE	HEIGHT	WEIGHT	POS	GRADE
NR	SAMUELSSON, ADAM	SIOUX CITY	USHL	6'5.75"	240	LD	ND
	HOCKEY SENSE		COMPETE		SKILL		SKATING
	4		6		3		5

Huge defender who has improved his mobility in the last 12 months. At 6'6" and 240 pounds, there are no secrets about what keeps Samuelsson on the radar. He's a conservative, defensive defenseman who has some toughness in his game. Though, most of that toughness comes after the fact and isn't used quite as much as a weapon to shut down plays. He tries to bully some guys in corners or get a little sticky after whistles to mix it up, but when facing a rush chance, he plays with a loose gap and is hoping to just push the play wide with his reach. He will troll around the neutral zone waiting for a lesser skill player who is trying to hit the red line to dump it in and clobber him, but against legitimate skill and speed, he can't get the timing of that right to make a physical play. He gets around the ice better than he did last year, but his pivots and small-area footwork against quicker players leaves a good bit to be desired. Some of it is physical, some of it is poor timing from a mental perspective. Often, when Samuelsson commits and opens up his hips to a wide rush, he allows a lane back underneath him to the net that an attacker with good edges and puck protection ability could exploit. He just isn't agile or nimble enough to compensate for his clunky processor.

Samuelsson is low on puck skills and because he plays so much of the game on his heels, he fails to get good wood on a lot of shots and passes that should be routine for a 2000 birthday with this degree of playing experience. He doesn't offer reliable technical skills in any zone and his overly conservative nature makes him a nightmare in terms of partner support. In fact, his puck support in any zone is off-putting and poorly executed. While the skating and his cruising speed have improved, his hockey sense doesn't seem any better from last year and he remains a beat behind the action. He left Boston College to re-join the USHL in the winter, which we think was a wise move from a technical development perspective – but the bloodlines and the size aren't enough to offset the on-ice product for us.

	PLAYER	TEAM	LEAGUE	HEIGHT	WEIGHT	POS	GRADE
NR	SAVILLE, ISAIAH	TRI-CITY	USHL	6'1.0"	193 *	G	C
	HOCKEY SENSE		COMPETE		SKILL		SKATING
	6		6		6		6

Compact, butterfly goaltender who is very consistent in his blocking style technique. Saville is on a hot streak from an accolades standpoint. He won a championship with the Colorado Thunderbirds, he was a second-team all-star in his first and only NAHL season, and then jumped to Tri-City and helped them to the best record in the league, while capturing

USHL Goaltender of the Year honors. At 25-4-3, Saville's record speaks for itself. He was also the lone goalie in the league to have a sub-2.00 GAA (1.90, the next best netminder gave up a quarter of a goal more per game) while posting the league's second best save pct. at .925.

The Alaska native is married to his technique. He plays the entire game from his knees with focus on getting square to shots. His positioning is sharp and consistent. He slides well in his crease and improved on his ability to remain more upright on his pushes to cover as much net as possible without allowing holes through his body. The right-glove goalie was able to challenge shooters better on rush chances and his proper back-side shoulder rotation showed some depth and maturity to his technical skills that we weren't too sure about earlier in the year. His post integrations are always RVH and given how tight he looks in the net – purposeful as it may be – he may be susceptible to the new en vogue shot of short-side high to combat the RVH setup. At 6'1", Saville doesn't have as much room for error in this regard. His glove mechanics and positioning are less than stellar. There's a lot of hip overlap and his fingers seem to point towards the interior of the ice, which is odd. It's not in his toolbox to telescope out for a lot for shots, and he shows some signs as having lazy hands in conjunction with that methodology. While he doesn't have a lot of save selections to choose from, he does a really good job making his rebound control predictable and manageable. One of his more impressive traits is his ability to remain square, calm, and poised on second- and third-chance opportunities. He sticks with the plan to the very end. It's a very distinct rarity to see Saville panic swimming in the crease. To this end, he rarely even comes out of the crease to play the puck. His focus is just on being efficient, tracking well, and having pucks hit him the chest as often as possible. He'll test himself once again in the fall, as he moves to the University of Nebraska-Omaha.

"Steady goalie." – NHL Scout, April 2019

"Don't see it myself but others say maybe a late guy." – NHL Scout, April 2019

	PLAYER	TEAM	LEAGUE	HEIGHT	WEIGHT	POS	GRADE
NR	**SCHMIEMANN, QUINN**	**KAMLOOPS**	**WHL**	**6'1.75"**	**185 ***	**LD**	**ND**
	HOCKEY SENSE		COMPETE		SKILL		SKATING
	6		5		5		5

Schmiemann was quietly effective all season long, making consistent decisions and rarely putting himself in bad positions. Does not immediately jump off the page for any standout tools but the combination of hockey IQ, mobility, and skill allows him to play greater than the sum of his parts. Schmiemann skates well enough, with a solid side that allows him to get up the ice and retrieve pucks in the corner before pressure is right on him. Schmiemann could stand to work on his edgework as he did not show much escape-ability with the puck. Schmiemann rarely found himself in positions where he had to cleanly beat a forechecker as he kept very good positioning to retrieve pucks and often executed passes quickly to open outlets. Very reliable and consistent in his passing, rarely throwing his teammates grenades and mostly hitting tape to tape passes. Offensively lacked dynamism but made some impact thanks to a heavy shot that he often got through traffic, and the basic instincts to make himself available for passes. Schmiemann even was able to play a role on his teams powerplay thanks to his calm and efficient puck distribution. Schmiemann plays a solid positional game defensively, keeping himself in between his man and the net, and rarely losing track off the puck. Was rarely proactive in taking the puck off the opposition, and could use his frame and play with physicality more often.

NR	PLAYER	TEAM	LEAGUE	HEIGHT	WEIGHT	POS	GRADE
	SCHWINDT, COLE	MISSISSAUGA	OHL	6'2.25"	182 *	RW	C
	HOCKEY SENSE	COMPETE		SKILL		SKATING	
	6	7		5		6	

Cole Schwindt had a solid season for Mississauga, showing good chemistry with Keean Washkurak when they were together; he contributed 49 points in 68 games, including 19 goals. In the playoffs, he had 1 goal in 4 games.

Schwindt can be a bit off-balance at times, since he doesn't have the strongest base, but he keeps his back relatively straight given his height and has a deep-knee-bend; he sits back into his stride and allows his quads to do the rest. There's an efficiency to his mechanics as well within his upper-frame and together with his lower-frame, they come together to form a skater who doesn't get easily fatigued during a shift which is critical to his game. Due to his height, Cole is capable of using his leverage when initiating contact and as a result was a very-effective board battler in our viewings. He's not just a capable forechecker off the puck though. Schwindt features a good sense for finding soft-ice away from the play and has shown plus playmaking ability. This allowed him to be at his most effective when either entering heavy traffic while looking to find soft-ice in the slot—and around the goal-line when he was identifying his passing options. His compete melds into his defensive-acumen, where he's shown a good attention to detail away from the puck and is willing to battle in order to support his defense down-low.

Although Cole is an aggressive and competitive player who can make good decisions with the puck, he's not overly skilled. He's at his best when he's hitting a straight-line and using a stream-lined approach, such as chip and chase sequences where he can use his most effective attributes. There's a lack of overall creativity and he lacks a shot that can threaten from the hash-marks out on a consistent basis. We love his competitive-spirit, but it's difficult to see him developing as an NHL-contributor, given his current level of skill.

"I saw him last week and I don't think he touched the puck." - NHL Scout, October 2018

"No skill. He looks like he could be a pro in warmup but he is hard to find once the game starts. Late pick at best for me right now." - NHL Scout, October 2018

"Three goals every 20 games in the OHL equals no draft." - NHL Scout, November 2018

"I was high on him coming into the season and he didn't do much of anything in my first five viewings. At that point I figured I would have him as a no draft. When I circled back to get more viewings of Harley after Christmas Cole started to show up. He finished the season closer to what I had expected to see in October. Earned a draftable grade in my second half viewings." - HP Scout, Mark Edwards

NR	PLAYER	TEAM	LEAGUE	HEIGHT	WEIGHT	POS	GRADE
	SEDOV, NIKITA	REGINA.	WHL	6'1.0"	192	LD	C
	HOCKEY SENSE	COMPETE		SKILL		SKATING	
	6	5		5		6	

Sedov came to the WHL through the import draft after previously playing for the Colorado Evolution. Playing for a low scoring team Sedov registered 19 points despite not registering a single goal.

He is a much better player than his stats would indicate. On a very weak team he often stood apart for his abilities. Sedov looked natural leading a breakout, rarely panicking and displaying the ability to beat a forechecker before finding a tape to tape pass. Sedov skates easily with strong edges and a smooth, long, stride. Sedov has shown the ability to contain well off the rush and displayed a strong stick in the corners. Offensively Sedov showed good abilities on the point, distributing pucks well and doing a fine job at getting pucks through and not hitting shin pads. There are some issues with his game as he still needs to add strength, being easily outmuscled in the corners by stronger players. He also did not consistently play engaged and would not consistently compete for pucks especially in games where his team was being blown out. There is a really smooth and calm nature to Sedov's game, and with above average skating and decision making he is an interesting long term prospect.

10	PLAYER	TEAM	LEAGUE	HEIGHT	WEIGHT	POS	GRADE
	SEIDER, MORITZ	MANNHEIM	GER	6'3.5"	183 *	RD	A
	HOCKEY SENSE	COMPETE		SKILL		SKATING	
	8	7		6		7	

Seider broke into Germany's U19 junior league (DNL) at 15, made his pro debut at 16, and played his first full DEL season with Adler Mannheim at 17. In his draft year, he won the DEL championship and the league's rookie of the year award as well as gold with Team Germany at the U20 Div 1 A world championship. To top it all off, Seider played for Germany at the men's world championship.

When he first played in the DNL, Seider was an extremely dynamic puck-carrier who could go end to end and ridicule opponents. Since then, he's had a growth spurt and lost a lot of that dynamic ability, but he's still a very good skater and has become a much more reliable two-way player. What stands out the most about Seider is his excellent ability to defend the rush. His backward speed and mobility allow him to play a tight gap in the neutral zone before quickly jumping at oncoming attackers with an active stick once they hit the blue line. From there, he's able to transition quickly and join in on the attack. In the defensive zone, Seider impresses with a high compete level and excellent physical play. He is always quick to the puck in corner and board battles, where he uses his stick and body to free pucks and cause turnovers, rarely taking himself out of position. Measuring 6-foot-4 and 200 pounds, Seider has a pro frame and he knows very well how to use it to his advantage. When gets the puck in the defensive zone, Seider displays great poise, always trying to make a high-percentage play. He always makes sure to be aware of his surroundings before moving the puck. He has strong puck protection and can execute quick turns to shake off opponents before playing accurate breakout passes, but he doesn't take unnecessary risks and rather chips the puck out than allowing dangerous defensive-zone turnovers. However, his puck skills are only slightly above average and he doesn't have the ability to beat defenders one-on-one, often resulting in dump-ins after carrying the puck through the neutral zone.

Playing his first pro season, Seider started out as a safety-first stay-at-home player but gained confidence as well as the coaches' trust as the season progressed. Especially after recording a goal and seven points in five games at the U20 worlds, Seider started to contribute more and more offensively. He has excellent defensive anticipation, allowing him to see turnovers before they happen and jump in on attacks either as a puck-carrier and set-up man or getting open for a shot himself. When he's trying to accelerate quickly, Seider often abandons his usually strong skating technique and falls into sloppy forward jumps, but once he's at full stride, his speed is good and he can gain separation from opponents. His first steps and mechanics should be easy to fix with a skating coach as well.

In the offensive zone, Seider displays strong vision and can distribute pucks with accurate passes. He occasionally tries to execute fakes and beat defenders when he gets the puck on the blue line, but he struggles to actually fool opponents. He can get shots through to the net, but his shot power has room for improvement for a player his size. Seider has excellent offensive awareness and sees open spaces extremely well, often moving in to create scoring chances for himself and his teammates. He also does an excellent job pinching up the boards when the opportunity arises, keeping his team in possession while preventing counter attacks.

Seider is not the player he was in junior, but the player he is now promises to have a smooth transition to the NHL level. He's a strong skater with a large frame and excellent hockey IQ. Like with any German-developed prospect, parts of his skill set are still raw, but he has all the tools to become a minute-munching NHL defenseman.

"Seider won't be a dynamic offensive threat but his responsible defensive play and smarts make him a sure-fire top-4 defenseman who can play 25 minutes a night." HP Scout Janik Beichler, May 2019

"Not much in the way of quotes I can share on this player. The general consensus was very positive and the majority of the Scouts had him rated as 1st rounder which probably doesn't surprise anyone at this point." - HP Scout, Mark Edwards, April 2019

"Much like Kravtsov last season, I've been forced to watch Seider on video only this year. I am a big fan of this player. He's smart, has size and can really skate. He's a competitor and is a very effective shutdown guy. I think he'll get some points 5 on 5 in the NHL because he's a very good puck mover. He can pass it and skate it. He might slide into a second powerplay role at some point but my projection is based on him logging big minutes against the oppositions top forwards. I also think his value will also get an uptick in the playoffs." - HP Scout, Mark Edwards, May 2019

"It's so hard to get high end defensman. That's why guys like Byram, Seider and York have so much value. After they are drafted they won't be available again for a long time. Best way to get high end D is to draft them." - HP Scout, Mark Edwards, May 2019

"Met him at the combine and it was extremely easy to see why almost every team I spoke to said he was one of, if not their top interview. Kid is mature beyond his years. Fantastic." - HP Scout, Mark Edwards, June 2019

	PLAYER	TEAM	LEAGUE	HEIGHT	WEIGHT	POS	GRADE
NR	**SERDYUK, EGOR**	**VICTORIAVILLE**	**QMJHL**	**5'10.0**	**158 ***	**RW**	**C**
	HOCKEY SENSE	COMPETE		SKILL		SKATING	
	6	6		6		5	

Serdyuk was the 37th overall selection last June in the CHL Import Draft. He was the top rookie scorer in the QMJHL this season with 25 goals, 65 points in 63 games. The young Russian played the majority of the year on a line with fellow Russian and draft-eligible Mikhail Abramov. They showed great chemistry all year long.

Serdyuk's top quality is his ability to score goals and manufacture offense; he has a great touch around the net and does a good job finding holes in the defensive zone. He's got a good wrist shot and a decent release, but his shot is also deceptive and tough to track for goaltenders. He's a smart hockey player, regularly demonstrating good IQ in the offensive zone to know where to be on the ice to get open, added to the fact that he's an above-average playmaker. He's not huge, but he's strong in his lower body. That helps him protect the puck along the boards and be strong on his skates. However, his skating abilities are not good enough for a player of his size. They are average at best, and he doesn't play with a lot of pace; he always seems to skate at the same speed. We wish he was more active on the ice; battling more frequently for loose pucks and showing a better compete level. His play away from the puck will need some improvement as well. He needs to provide a better effort on the backcheck and a better compete level in his zone. To us, Serdyuk looks like a pretty good junior player right now; we know that he can score, but the rest of his game is lacking. He could hear his name called late in the draft if a team really likes his scoring potential and think they can work on the other parts of his game.

"A good junior player for me." – HP Scout Jérôme Bérubé, May 2019

NR	PLAYER	TEAM	LEAGUE	HEIGHT	WEIGHT	POS	GRADE
	SHESHIN, DMITRI	MAGNITOGORSK	MHL	5'8.0"	143 *	RW	ND
	HOCKEY SENSE	COMPETE		SKILL		SKATING	
	6	6		5		6	

Sheshin is a tiny Russian forward who had ton of success this season in the MHL with 43 points in 45 games. The 3rd most point by a U18 players in this league (1st in point per game). However when he played internationally he was more of depth player for Russia playing mostly on the 3rd or 4th line and getting limited time on the power play but became a top penalty killer.

He'll need to get a whole lot stronger before thinking about making the jump to the NHL, he's not tall and also very light on his skates. However we do appreciate his compete level and he's not afraid to play in high traffic. Although at his weight he gets pushed over easily by opposing defensemen and very tough for him to win a lot of puck battles along the board. He's got good speed, above average top speed and acceleration .He also does a good job keeping his feet moving all the time, when he does this this is where he's the most effective. Even if he put great numbers at the MHL level he never showed internationally the skills and the upside to be that kind of player at the next level. He did show however some good work on the PK, energetic and some good smart. With his size he's definitely a long term project that NHL teams will need to be patient with to let him get bigger and stronger. With the CBA rule and the fact they will need to sign him 2 years after drafting him doesn't really help his cause as in two years he's likely to still be undersize and not ready for the pro North American game. A risky pick for a team based on his lack of size and lack of big success on the international stage this season.

NR	PLAYER	TEAM	LEAGUE	HEIGHT	WEIGHT	POS	GRADE
	SIEDEM, RYAN	CENTRAL ILLINOIS	USHL	6'2.25"	191 *	RD	ND
	HOCKEY SENSE	COMPETE		SKILL		SKATING	
	4	4		5		5	

Ryan Siedem – Siedem has been a bit all over the place in his lead-up to his draft year. He played prep school at Delbarton and then Avon Old Farms. Then he left the USNTDP for Central Illinois. He de-committed from Boston College and he's headed for Harvard next season. A rather lackadaisical offensive defenseman who doesn't offer enough dynamic skill to offset his flaws. Quarterbacks the power play from the top, which is where he is most effective by far. Just an average skater, which is probably dragged down a touch by just how stiff he looks out there. He doesn't carry the puck, nor does he seem to own the confidence or desire to carry. His defensive positioning and posture is generally poor, if not lazy. He fails to square his shoulders up against a rush, he'll turn away from the puck/attack often and he doesn't exhibit a lot of urgency near his net. Against sustained attacks, he'll switch sides at his leisure and not call it out, which often causes some degree of chaos. He does try to bait forecheckers in and make passes against the grain to make for an easier breakout for his forwards, and when it works, it's effective – however, there were more than a few times in our viewings where he tied himself in a knot and gave the puck away in a place where the puck just can't be given away. He still fumbles too many pucks and doesn't catch as many passes as you'd like for a player that needs to be a power play specialist. Siedem isn't very high on hockey sense and doesn't offer enough technical or physical traits to compensate for it. He was claimed by Fargo in the USHL Dispersal Draft.

NR	PLAYER	TEAM	LEAGUE	HEIGHT	WEIGHT	POS	GRADE
	SILIANOFF, GRANT	CEDAR RAPIDS	USHL	5'11.0"	169 *	RW	ND
	HOCKEY SENSE		COMPETE		SKILL		SKATING
	6		6		4		5

Silianoff joined Cedar Rapids this season after being drafted 1st overall by the Rough Riders out of Shattuck St. Mary's in the 2017 USHL Phase 1 draft. Silianoff represented to United States this year at the Hlinka Gretzky Cup as well as the World Junior A Challenge. Silianoff plays a hard-working two-way game on the wing. His skating speed and explosiveness are not eye popping at this stage, however Silianoff possesses decent agility and is very strong on his skates which allows him to be effective in puck battles as well as protecting the puck down low and along the walls. As he develops physically his skating could develop some pop as his mechanics are not terrible. Silianoff lacks high end playmaking ability but is able to move the puck quickly and accurately in all three zones and plays a reliable, risk free game with the puck on his tape. You won't see Grant often attempting fancy stick handling moves around the bluelines and is very much a pucks out and pucks in type of winger. He will chip pucks into the offensive zone that gives his team a good opportunity to pressure the defenseman on the fore-check and create turnovers. Silianoff has plus shooting ability and release but doesn't get a lot of opportunities to use it as he was primarily stationed as the net front guy on the power play and is usually the person working down low to get his team the puck in the offensive zone. Silianoff scored a lot of his goals down around the crease area where he works to get position on his defenseman and showcases a quick stick and puck hounding ability in traffic to put home rebounds. Silianoff excels on the penalty kill, is willing to blocks shots and has good awareness to not waste time and simply clear pucks out of his zone on the penalty kill. Silianoff doesn't project as a big offensive producer at the next level but he does a lot of things night in night out that help his team win games. Silianoff will likely be spending one more season in the USHL before he heads to the University of Notre Dame.

NR	PLAYER	TEAM	LEAGUE	HEIGHT	WEIGHT	POS	GRADE
	SILOVS, ARTURS	HS RIGA	LATVIA	6'4.0"	203	G	C
	HOCKEY SENSE		COMPETE		SKILL		SKATING
	6		7		6		5

Arturs Silovs had an interesting year; moving from junior hockey to men's hockey in preparation for the U18's. He was also mentored under the Dinamo Riga goalie coach and practised with them before moving to HS Riga in the Latvian league. He posted a .920 save-percentage and a 2.45GAA in 7 games for HK Riga in the MHL, followed by a .914 save-percentage and a 3.26GAA in 20 games for HS Riga in the Latvian league. At the U18's, he started 5 games, posting a 3.32 GAA and a .918 save-percentage, and was named best player against Russia before shutting out Slovakia.

Silovs is an athletic netminder who has a good-frame. He's coordinated and capable of fully-extending through his lower-body, which allows him to make impressive kick-saves that are labelled for the far-sides of the net. Furthermore, his length and extension allows him to make some unique-lateral saves that require a lot of flexibility. At the beginning portions of the season while playing in the MHL, Arturs showed a couple of deficiencies within his game. His stance was wide, which resulted in him not been able to take full advantage of his lateral mobility. Furthermore, he's capable of making micro-adjustments but could only make them at a reduced-rate, since they require a narrower stance unless they are occurring from a half-butterfly. Another concern, was regarding his post-integration; he would come off his post too late when crouched down in his reverse-VH and didn't always seal his posts off, which resulted in some bad goals against. After making the transition to HS Riga in the Latvian league, we started seeing improvements. He's began the process of narrowing his stance, which has helped his skating and he stands-taller in net as opposed to more crouched-down, which took away his size advantage. He also learned how to integrate along the post better than he previously was. One tool that he's consistently maintained and flashed throughout the year is his glove-hand. He's got an above-average-glove and can make difficult saves when relying upon it. Another impressive attribute of Arturs, is his willingness to use his stick when players are cutting directly into his net-area. We've seen him use his poke-checks instinctively, resulting in several broken up plays that would have been high-danger-shots otherwise. Additionally, Arturs has displayed a good compete-level and is willing to battle through secondary-scoring chances. His rebound control has been above-average as well, absorbing pucks in his large-frame at a good-rate; this includes off-angle shots that were harder to absorb. His mechanics and frame come together to form a goaltender who can take away a large portion of the bottom part of the net away in short order.

The biggest concern for us when evaluating Silovs game, is in regards to his reflexes given his height. His athleticism is more a by-product of his ability to fully-extend, plus his coordination. It's not primarily his reflexes which are good for the quality of competition he's currently facing, but not at the level-needed to be identified as an NHL-goalie as of writing this. Furthermore, he still has tendencies that need to be cleaned-up. He loses balance too often, and falls in positions that leave him susceptible to elevated shots off of rebounds as a result. Additionally, he still commits too often to his butterfly and remains in the position too long, though this isn't nearly as hard to fix as his reflexes will be. In order to improve his fast-twitch, he's going to need extensive strength-and-conditioning coaching that could help him further take advantage of his frame and athletic gifts.

His mechanics and frame come together to form a goaltender who can take away a large portion of the bottom part of the net away in short order. There's a solid-base to work with when evaluating Silovs but improving his reflexes, which will subsequently improve his reaction-time, is a tall-task. Due to these concerns, we have him as a watch for next-year as opposed to a goalie we would draft this season. Arturs is currently scheduled to come over and play in the CHL which will help his exposure if he does get passed over at the NHL draft.

"I think he's going to have a lot of success in the CHL and get more attention" - HP Scout, Brad Allen

	PLAYER	TEAM	LEAGUE	HEIGHT	WEIGHT	POS	GRADE
NR	**SIMONEAU, XAVIER**	**DRUMMONDVILLE**	**QMJHL**	**5'6.25"**	**169 ***	**LC**	**ND**
	HOCKEY SENSE		COMPETE		SKILL		SKATING
	7		8		6		5

Simoneau was the 9th overall selection in the 2017 QMJHL Draft out of the Gatineau Midget program. This year, on a stacked team in Drummondville, he was able to average over a point per game, playing mostly on the 2nd line and getting regular power play time.

He's very good shorthanded, where his work ethic and anticipation make him a dangerous player (he notably scored twice shorthanded this season). On the power play, with more space available on the ice, he also did well. He was able to control the puck more freely from the half-wall area on the right side of the ice. He possesses excellent on-ice vision and excellent passing abilities. He can make some high-caliber passes to his teammates for quality scoring chances. His shot is accurate, but he could stand to add more velocity to it; he doesn't possess the type of shot that can lead to goals from long distances. He needs to be closer to the net to get his shot past the opposing goaltender. Despite being just 5'07", Simoneau always plays like he's 6'04", 220 pounds. He's one of the most annoying players to play against in the

QMJHL. He's very tenacious on the forecheck, and his compete level is often unmatched by the opposition. Not only can he play a skilled game out there, but he's also such a pest on the ice. He doesn't back down from anyone and loves to talk. For his size, his skating is average, his speed is fine for the junior level but he will need to work on getting faster if he wants to reach the NHL. He lacks a good top speed; his acceleration could be quicker, but at least he keeps his feet moving all the time. This makes him tough to contain along the boards. There's some concern due to the combination of his style of play and his size; injuries could be a factor down the road for him (he'll need to pick his spots better, as he plays against bigger and stronger players). If Simoneau is drafted, we see him as a late pick. He could go undrafted as well. The team that drafts him will need to place a lot of faith in their Quebec scout, as the rationale usually points to him being a player teams would pass on due to size and speed. But with his skill level, excellent work ethic and compete level, he could be part of the next wave of Quebec players to beat the odds and make it to the NHL (as Desharnais, Gourde, Marchessault and others have done before him).

"Great compete level and he's super smart, but his lack of speed and being 5'07" really hurts him for the NHL." - HP Scout Jérôme Bérubé

"He's a pain in the ass to play against and a productive player for his team but in no way shape or form is he an NHL Draft pick." - NHL Scout, January 2019

"One of our guys likes him but he's a clear no draft for me." - NHL Scout, January 2019

"He annoys the opposition but the tiny size and skating issues makes him a no draft for me." - HP Scout Mark Edwards, March 2019

	PLAYER	TEAM	LEAGUE	HEIGHT	WEIGHT	POS	GRADE
NR	SHASHKOV NIKITA	SIBIR NOVOSIBIRS	RUSSIA	5'11.0"	179	LW	**C**
	HOCKEY SENSE	COMPETE		SKILL		SKATING	
	7	6		6		6	

Nikita Shashkov had an excellent season in his third-year of eligibility, and did enough to show up on our scouting radar. He played the majority of his season with Sibir Novosibirsk of the KHL, producing 4 points in 25 games, including 3 goals. Although he didn't produce very often, his game did translate successfully in our viewings. In the MHL, he played for Sibirskie and produced 9 points in 7 games, including 5 goals. He also had an excellent performance at the U20's for Russia in a depth-role, producing 5 points in 5 games, including 2 goals. Shashkov is a two-way, cerebral forward who has an excellent sense for the game away from the puck. His spatial-awareness and timing around the goal-line is very impressive, and this made him a threat during plays where he could get behind defensive-coverage and become a backdoor passing option. It also made him difficult to deal with on the forecheck, since he can anticipate defenseman and read off of them quickly. Additionally, he makes a lot of good decisions with the puck on his stick. He rarely forces play, and is good at evaluating when he has a high-danger scoring chance. His shot can threaten from above the hash-marks and he can use it while going at top-speeds as well. There's a good maturity to his game and he's developed a detail-oriented approach as a result. Shashkov blends his hockey-sense with some skill as well. He's not a dynamic offensive-player who is going to beat opponents clean very often with his hands, but he does feature an impressive release point and is good at masking his shot behind screens and in heavy-traffic. He's also a duel-threat player who can pass as well as he shoots, giving him a versatile-attack. In the defensive-end, he's engaged and he keeps a good-pace which generates pressure on his opponents. His skating mechanics are also technically-refined, featuring proper posture, a deep-knee bend and little wasted movement. The biggest area of concern with Shashkov, is how translatable can his game be in the NHL? He doesn't have any stand-out quality with the exception of his hockey-sense, so he's likely able to play only in a depth-role; but he could be a useful and versatile forward for a team.

"I think Shashkov's game could translate, he's such a well-rounded player and plays a North-American brand of hockey" - HP Scout, Brad Allen, May 2019

66	PLAYER	TEAM	LEAGUE	HEIGHT	WEIGHT	POS	GRADE
	SLEPETS KIRILL	YAROSLAVL	RUSSIA	5'10.0"	165	LW	C
	HOCKEY SENSE		COMPETE		SKILL		SKATING
	6		7		6		8

After getting passed over in two previous drafts, due to his size and initial lack of production, Kirill had a season that put himself back on our radar. He had a successful season, starting with his play for Loko Yaroslavl in the MHL, where he produced 18 points in 17 games, including 12 goals. In the playoffs he produced 10 points in 17 games, with 4 goals. He also played for Lada Togliatta of the VHL, producing 3 assists and had some playing time with Lokomotiv Yaroslavl of the KHL, producing 1 goal in 10 games. His best performance was at the World-Junior U20's, after he had a good super-series set that afforded him a spot on the roster. Valeri Bragin sensed he could use Slepets talents and he was right, as he produced 7 points in 7 games, including 5 goals, and was one of the best performers at the event on the world-stage.

Slepets is one of the oldest draft-eligible players featured, yet has translatable-tools; Kirill is an excellent skater and has one of the most impressive motors as a result of his speed. The pace he keeps and the subsequent pressure he can maintain on opposing defenders is what separates Slepets from some of the other players who have been passed over. His skating features fantastic cross-over mechanics and an explosive-first-step which allows him to gear-shift rapidly. He's a winger that can't be identified late in transition or he's already blown by the defender. He uses his speed to threaten both with and without the puck. He can make high-skilled plays while going at top-speed, yet shows patience and the offensive-awareness needed to slow-down the play and mix-up his options. He's always had the tools but didn't know how to meld them together to form a cohesive-player, yet this past season, he's begun to develop into what we consider a specialist-type of player. He can use his speed and anticipation to pressure the blueline on the penalty-kill but has enough talent and pace to be featured on an energy-line responsible for aggressively forechecking. That's not to say he can't score though, he can. His shot is his most impressive offensive-skill and his speed allows him to change the trajectory of his release without having to pull the puck; this allows him to shoot with a quick snapping motion, where he relies on his accuracy and ability to release the puck before the goalie is completely-set. Although he's very thin, he's also very elusive because of his edge-work and his hands. He can contort and manipulate his-frame while simultaneously making highly-technical dekes and this gives him a more multi-dimensional attack as opposed to a player who just skates aggressively north-south.

The biggest issue when projecting Slepets is regarding his frame. He can pressure on the forecheck and use his stick and has had success at the junior-level using his body, but at the NHL-level, there's a risk in terms of how much of his physical-tool-kit can really translate. Furthermore, he's not a line-driver, and he's not a player that makes his teammates better when he's controlling the puck; he's a quick-striking forward who uses his tools at a more individual-rate. That said, he's not someone who hurts a team, it's been the opposite this past season. He's identified his game, and has learned how to take-advantage of his speed. Although our attribute scores of him might suggest a higher ranking in terms of draft-position, keep in mind that he's almost 20, so there isn't as much room to continue to develop. When we view a player like Rhett Pitlick, there's some similarities in terms of their skill and speed, but we would take Pitlick ahead due to the potential boon in development over a player like Slepets.

We value pace and Slepets has it. There's a lot of translatable tools that make him an interesting late-round selection and we think he has the potential to become a specialist-player who can be used on the top-penalty-kill as a result.

NR	PLAYER	TEAM	LEAGUE	HEIGHT	WEIGHT	POS	GRADE
	SKINNER, HUNTER	LINCOLN	USHL	6'2.5"	176 *	RD	ND
	HOCKEY SENSE	COMPETE		SKILL		SKATING	
	5	6		5		6	

Hunter Skinner is a rangy, smooth skating defenseman who was traded from one of the top teams in the USHL (Muskegon) to the bottom team in the league in Lincoln and still managed to put up similar numbers, despite having much less talent around him with the Stars. Hunter put up 3 goals and 8 assists in 24 games with Muskegon and 2 goals and 9 assists with the Lincoln Stars. Skinner has some developing to go in regard to his straight-line skating and explosiveness, but he has excellent four-way mobility for a kid his size and as he adds on strength to his lanky frame, his skating should add some pop with the right instruction. Hunter makes up for his lack of footspeed with a high-end hockey sense. He makes quick decisions and moves the puck out of his own zone well. He identifies pressure well and uses his defensive partner and the boards well to escape the forecheck. Hunter is an accurate passer and hits his outlets on the tape and in stride consistently in our viewings. He protects the puck well with his body to fend off fore-checkers and is strong on his skates. Skinner has showcased a heavy shot from the point, he uses his lanky frame to generate leverage and power on his wrist shot. Hunter needs to commit to his shots quicker and develop a bit of a quicker release, as he can give defenses and goaltenders too much time to adjust, especially when on the Power Play. Defensively, Skinner excels in one on one situations, he has an active stick and uses his reach and size to his advantage when defending in open space. Skinner possesses a lot of intriguing tools; his pro ceiling will likely depend on how his skating smoothens out going forward. While his offensive skills are not eye popping at this stage, he is efficient and reliable with the puck at both ends of the ice. Skinner will likely spend one more season in the USHL before heading to Western Michigan in 2020.

"Nothing about his game jumps out at you as high end." - HP Scout, Dusten Braaksma

NR	PLAYER	TEAM	LEAGUE	HEIGHT	WEIGHT	POS	GRADE
	SODERBLOM, ELMER	FROLUNDA JR.	SWE-JR.	6'6.25	219 *	RW	C
	HOCKEY SENSE	COMPETE		SKILL		SKATING	
	5	5		6		4	

Söderblom is a mountain of a man, listed as 6'7" 220 pounds. He split his season between Frölunda HC's U18s and U20s. He was a regular on the U20s in the SuperElite, where he put up 9 goals and 8 assists in 44 games. He had 11 appearances on his U18 team, where he put up 3 goals and 3 assists.

Söderblom has surprisingly decent hands and coordination for a kid his size and the length of his stick. He can handle the puck well and make some incredible dekes when he decides to and he can combine his fluid stickhandling with his superb reach to beat defenders 1-on-1. If he could use his reach with his enormous frame to power his way towards the net and/or through opponents, he could be an offensive powerhouse. But he completely lacks that killer mentality, or even the awareness that he could do it. His hockey sense and vision are somewhat underrated too since he makes good reads, but his terrible skating doesn't allow him to get there on time.

It's no surprise a guy his size lacks the ability to skate. He did make improvements during the season but his skating technique is poor and so is his power which combine to make his acceleration top speed both below average. Another problem is his weak stabilizing muscles: ankles, core and his glutes. These weaknesses directly effects his balance and he tends to lose puck battles against much smaller players when getting hit especially when reaching for pucks.

Söderblom must figure out how he can be most effective. With his extraordinary size we would like to see him play more physically and he should possess dominate games with his size and strength.

He has been an amazing playoff performer. While his regular season was average, at best. He really stepped up in time for playoffs and was a dominating force for Frölunda HC U18 on their way to win gold at the Swedish championship. He recorded 4 goals and 2 assists in 7 games during that run.

He appeared in 17 games for Team Sweden during the season where he put up a total of 5 points, but he was mostly used on a third or fourth line. He has problems keeping us with the pace of the stronger nations in international play. During the U18 Worlds, he was a key piece to a gritty third line and he managed to hit another gear in the elimination games, playing with more authority than earlier in the tournament. His team won the tournament on home soil and he was a strong contributor on the ice but not on the scoresheet.

	PLAYER	TEAM	LEAGUE	HEIGHT	WEIGHT	POS	GRADE
13	SODERSTROM, VICTOR	BRYNAS	SWE	5'11.0	179 *	RD	A
	HOCKEY SENSE		COMPETE		SKILL		SKATING
	8		7		7		7

Söderström is one of the highest touted Swedish prospects coming into this summers draft. He started the season with Brynäs U20 team in the SuperElite league where he put up 1 goal and 7 assist for a total of 8 points in 14 games, in which he was completely dominant in most of them. He then got called up to the men's team in the SHL where he played 44 games and recorded 4 goals and 3 assists in a season where his team was fighting for survival to stay away from relegation play.

When he played against men in the SHL he really had to show how smart he is. Since he's both young and rather small, he had to outsmart his opponents and did so successfully. There were times when he looked like he had played in the league for 10 years even though he had his cage on. He makes great decisions and has the ability to know what to do with the puck, way before he has it, this makes him able to avoid getting forechecked and he wins extra time for his teammates. Söderström plays with great maturity and he's always very calm and composed even in the most stressful of situations.In the rare occasions when he gets pressured and makes a mistake, he learns from it as he rarely makes the same mistake twice.

Söderström survives with his defending, even against bigger, stronger opponents due to his intelligence, as he anticipates the play very well and adapts to the situation. His defensive awareness is excellent but he will get overpowered and lose battles in front of the net since he is small and not strong enough yet. He does what he can by lifting sticks and trying not to stand in his goaltenders line of sight.

His passing game is fantastic as his first pass is hard and accurate and he always seems to make the safest play and his vision is more than good enough to thread through long breakaway passes too. He is a two-way defenseman with great puck skills overall, his stickhandling is underrated and he tends to always keep control of the puck even if he is under pressure and has to make dekes or has to make other lateral movements with the puck.

His shot is by no means the hardest, but he is very good at moving the puck laterally to create lanes to avoid getting his shots blocked. He always hits the net with his shots and his slapshot is not really that bad either. In the SHL he's had to tone his offense down a bit since they were playing to avoid relegation and he had to play it very safe to avoid turnovers, but this has led to him being able to help him teammates getting to scoring chances by setting them up with superb short passes.

We would like to see him utilize his puck skills and offensive instincts even more since he was a dominating offensive force in the SuperElite league, but given the circumstances, it's understandable that he didn't showcase it as much as he used too prior getting called up. He was awarded as the U18 player with the best point total in the SHL this season.

Söderström is an excellent skater, while he might lack a bit of top speed, he skates fluidly and flawlessly and can move around easily in all directions all over the ice. His stride is not very long or powerful, but it's so smooth and it really looks like he skates effortlessly. He's got a low center of gravity which helps him keep his balance and he can skate while keeping the puck close to his body.

One problem is that Söderström's stride is very wide which strains his groins and kills some power in his stride and may be the reason why he has missed a couple of international tournaments due to an injury to the groin.

Söderstrom was expected to be a star for Team Sweden this season and he was when he was healthy enough to dress up for the games. He only played 7 games for his country recording 3 points in the form of 1 goal and 2 assists. He was a star player and the alternate captain for Team Sweden at the U18 world championships which unfortunately ended earlier than expected for him due to a concussion he suffered in the game against team Russia in the group stage. His team did go on to win the gold anyway, and even though he missed the playoffs, he was a part of that winning team.

Victor is a very solid two-way defenseman. He competes very hard, as this kid hates losing. He will adapt in any system and do what is necessary for his team to win. Even if he is not very big and doesn't usually play super physical, don't get yourself fooled, he is tough and has a strong enough core to throw a big hit.

"He's smart. He plays better with the pro players because he is used to them being smarter. It's always easier to play with smarter players." - NHL Scout, April 2019

"Our Swede likes him. Thinks he is a top 20 pick." - NHL Scout, May 2019

	PLAYER	TEAM	LEAGUE	HEIGHT	WEIGHT	POS	GRADE
2	**SOGAARD, MADS**	**MEDICINE HAT**	**WHL**	**6'6.75"**	**192 ***	**G**	**A**
	HOCKEY SENSE	COMPETE		SKILL		SKATING	
	7	8		7		7	

Mads Sogaard had an excellent season for the Medicine Hat Tigers and was the primary reason they made the playoffs. He finished the regular season with a 2.64 GAA and a .921 save percentage in 37 games. In the playoffs, he finished with a 3.16 GAA and a .919 save percentage. Internationally Sogaard struggled at the U20's but was featured on a team that was largely over-matched. He finished that event with a 6.16 GAA and a .802 save percentage in 5 games.

Sogaard is an intriguing netminder with an excellent tool-set given his enormous stature. It's rare to find a goalie that's been gifted with the reflexes and subsequent reaction-time he possesses at his size. This has allowed him the ability to make saves that very few other goalies of any class can make. Mads reflexes augment his coordination, giving him a fluidity that bleeds into most facets of his game. When dropping into his butterfly, he's adept at reversing out of the movement, giving him the necessary ingredients to make back-to-back saves while transitioning into and out of the technique. Though his butterfly isn't as technically sound as Spencer Knight's. For starters, Mads does have the tendency on some sequences to shrink into himself, specifically by not keeping his core activated which doesn't allow him to maintain his posture. However, when Mads does shrink into himself, he's at a size where he still takes up extended-space; so if he can develop the ability to remain more consistent when "looking tall" in his butterfly, it will allow him to take up a tremendous amount of the net when on his knees. Additionally, his butterfly doesn't contain many seams for shots to leak through; it's tightly-sealed off in most games which allowed him to absorb rebounds at a plus rate when we viewed him. Usually when Sogaard let's in a goal from his butterfly, it's a by-product of over-committing on a shot which gives him less opportunity to react when transitioning into it. Another important aspect when discussing Mads butterfly is in relation to his hockey-sense. Bigger Goaltenders are more susceptible to injuries when they move into their butterfly more frequently and when they push off laterally from the position. However, Sogaard has demonstrated a good sense for when a shot is getting blocked in a lane. This allows him to stay more upright, which prevents him from overusing the technique. It seems subtle, but it's vital when projecting his long-term durability. You can't afford to draft a goalie that you project as a starter if he's not able to play the games required to fill his role.

When breaking down Sogaard's hockey-sense overall, it's not as high-end as Knight's but it's still well above-average. He's good at recognizing the intent of shooters in-tight to the net which allowed him to make several point-blank saves and stop breakaway scoring chances in our viewings. Furthermore, his height gives him a distinct advantage when analyzing the trajectory of point-shots, and he rarely loses track of the puck as a result of being able to look around screens in a half-crouch when he can't afford to stand-tall. Where he tends to lose-track the most, is in the same position Knight loses the puck, and that's behind the goal-line. There's games where Mads is late to anticipate plays coming out from below the goal-line and this has resulted in some poor goals-against. However, when Mads is on his game, his inability to anticipate around the goal-line diminishes. Arguably the most important aspect of Mads development in terms of recognizing play-types will be learning how to assess skilled fakes, such as a fake-shot into a pass. Despite this, he can come away with impressive lateral saves when he's out of position but needs to continue to refine how he identifies dynamic passes so that he doesn't need to make high-end saves as frequently as he currently does. Regardless if he sometimes misidentifies plays, his other technical areas are a plus and help compensate, with the exception of how often he's willing to use his V-H when dealing with wingers who are driving down on the right-side of the ice. That being said, his reverse V-H is used optimally in most games we've watched. His fluidity and coordination allow him to integrate into his post seamlessly and he takes up a tremendous amount of the net when in it. His length compliments his reverse V-H since he can use an aggressive stick to counter-act players attempting to drive in-tight on him as well. His glove-hand is above-average and doesn't require a lot of rotation when approaching high-shots due to his size, but his rebound control can be inconsistent in terms of catching the puck depending on the sequence. His blocker-side has more refined mechanics than his glove-side, sealing it in tight to his body within his stance, while showing much of the same attributes that Knight presents by being able to extend his elbow 90-degrees parallel to the ice which gives him the ability to deflect and absorb pucks properly. The most important technical element of new modern-day-netminders is in regards to their skating and that's where Sogaard has shown growth this past season. His stance is still not as narrow at it needs to be in order for him to take advantage of his edges to the degree he theoretically should be able to later in his development; but for such a large kid, he shows impressive rapid-adjustments when misinterpreting initial play-types or when broken plays occur. This synergies well with Mads compete-level and ability to recover.

An area of significant difference between Sogaard and Knight is in regards to their willingness to break their own form in order to make recovery saves. Spencer Knight is the more technically proficient of the two netminders; this makes him less comfortable contorting his frame and extending himself as often as Mads. That's not to say that Knight can't break his own technique, we've seen him do it several times throughout the season to make a save, just not as often as we would have liked. One argument that could be made, is that Knight doesn't need to break his own technique in order to extend himself since he reads the play better overall. This is true to a degree, but it still leaves Knight letting in goals that he could have stopped if he was willing to make a more unorthodox save; compared to Sogaard who shows a higher-comfort level when extending himself as a result of not anticipating certain play-types as well. When looking at it from an aesthetic point of view, Mads has the higher-rate of making saves that look like sure goals. Where Knight and Sogaard have similarities, is in regards to how they handle-pressure. There were games where Sogaard was under a heavy sustained attack, yet thrived in that environment, much like Knight was better in games where he was given more volume to work with as well. They both carry a significant net-presence as a result of their poise and confidence.

Our main takeaway, is that Sogaard isn't as technically refined as Spencer Knight and doesn't stay ahead of the play as consistently as Knight, but he does have fascinating physical and mental tools with a remarkably large and projectable frame. This leads us to believe that he's the 2nd best goalie in this class and has the potential to start in the NHL with the proper development. We expect his development to take longer than Knight's but the finished product could be an exciting one if he learns how to refine how aggressively he cuts down his angles at times, narrow's his stance further to optimize his skating, and becomes more consistent in his evaluations of certain play-types. We'd be willing to select him somewhere in the late first to early 2nd round range.

"Six foot six guys have a lot more room for error than the six foot one guys. The smaller goalies like DiPietro need to be so perfect and that's why I'm not convinced a guy like him will make it in the NHL." - NHL Scout, January 2019

"I won't say the goalies name, but he was drafted reasonably high and is in the six foot range. The day I dropped him on my list was after he let in a goal where he did everything perfect but couldn't get there to stop the shot. Sogaard will make some saves easily that smaller guys need to be almost perfect on. It's not apples to apples at that point. It's unfair. - NHL Scout, March 2019

"He got better as the year went on. In November I thought we could steal the kid in the mid rounds, now I think he'll go late in the first round." - NHL Scout, April 2019

"At worst he's a 2nd rounder." - NHL Scout, April 2019

"I have him just outside my first round." - NHL Scout, April 2019

"He made my top 31 and not at the bottom (of the list)" - NHL Scout, April 2019

"I haven't seen him but I know our guys like him, he's been a big riser." - NHL Scout, April 2019

"I think he has more upside than (Spencer) Knight I'd be willing to take him late first." - NHL Scout, May 2019

"His movement when he's closer to his developmental peak might make him one of the most unique, yet exciting netminders to watch down the road." - HP Scout, Brad Allen

"I walked out of the Scout's room in Medicine Hat just as he walked out of the dressing room and we almost collided. I'm 6'5" and I had to look way up because he is 6'6" and was on skates. He wasn't starting that night but right then I hoped he would play the next night because I was in town for back to back games. He started the next night and was fantastic." -HP Scout, Mark Edwards, November 2018

"After just one viewing on a trip west in November I thought he was impressive enough to consider him as an "A" prospect. The thing that really stood out in that game was his ability to move the way he did for a kid that size. From that first viewing until now in April, he only cemented himself more as a high level prospect in this draft." - HP Scout, Mark Edwards, April 2019

"I spoke to approximately fifteen Scouts about Sogaard and none of them had anything bad to say about him." - HP Scout, Mark Edwards, May 2019

"I spoke to a few

"Multiple rave reviews about his interviews at the NHL Combine. He was listed in the top three by several teams" - HP Scout, Mark Edwards, June 2019

97	PLAYER	TEAM	LEAGUE	HEIGHT	WEIGHT	POS	GRADE
	SPENCE, JORDAN	MONCTON	QMJHL	5'9.5"	164 *	RD	C
	HOCKEY SENSE	COMPETE		SKILL		SKATING	
	6	5		6		5	

Spence was passed over in his first year of eligibility for the QMJHL Draft. After a great year playing Junior A with the Summerside Western Capitals, he was selected 20th overall by Moncton this past June. He didn't take much time to adjust to the QMJHL this season and established himself from the get-go as one of the top rookies in the league, and a key piece of the Moncton Wildcats. Spence was named the rookie in the QMJHL this season. The P.E.I. native finished the season with 49 points, good for 4th overall in rookie scoring. He was also 9th among defensemen league-wide.

Spence is an undersized defenseman with good offensive potential. He's an excellent passer with really good on-ice vision. He's at his best on the power play, where he often shows good puck poise and solid abilities as a puck-distributor. He's has a decent shot with good accuracy, but his shot could have more velocity to it. He is clearly more of a passer than he is a shooter. By improving his shot, he could improve on his goal total. He only scored 6 goals this season compared to his 43 assists. He's also got to work on his consistency a bit; there were some ups and downs in our viewings this past season in this regard. His play at 5-on-5 was the most inconsistent part of his game in our viewings, as he didn't always stand out the way he did on the man-advantage. For a smaller defender, Spencer doesn't have the best skating abilities that you would want to see. He's has decent mobility and footwork, but his top speed is average and he can struggle to create space for himself when rushing the puck. Defensively, due to his size, he's going to be challenged against bigger forwards down low in his zone and in front of his net. He'll need to get stronger physically in order to compete better in the physical part of the game, but he's a pretty smart player with a smart stick and good positioning in his own zone (he is not a liability). Overall, we like Spence's hockey sense and puck-moving abilities, although there are some question marks in terms of his size and skating abilities when combined.

" Love a lot of things about Spence's game, but his size and skating combination scares me a bit. That, and the fact that he was never great when I saw him this year." - HP Scout Jérôme Bérubé

" Played poorly in my viewings of him. Made poor decisions with the puck. With his size/skating combo I would want him to be much better in several aspects of his game." - HP Scout, Mark Edwards, March 2019

NR	PLAYER	TEAM	LEAGUE	HEIGHT	WEIGHT	POS	GRADE
	SPIRIDONOV, YEGOR	MAGNITOGORSK 2	RUS-JR.	6'3.0"	192 *	RC	ND
	HOCKEY SENSE	COMPETE		SKILL		SKATING	
	6	6		5		5	

Spiridonov was the 4th-leading scorer in the MHL for U-18 players this season, even though he's not known for his superior offensive skills. He's more known for his excellent two-way game and attention to the little details on the ice. He plays a very unselfish game. He does a lot of dirty work along the boards, using his big frame well to win puck battles and also protect the puck when he has possession of it. He has excellent defensive awareness in his own zone, including good anticipation and a good active stick in his own zone to block passes. He is also not afraid to block shots. He has value as penalty-killer, and he's a good faceoff man. He makes good use of his long reach. He demonstrates good puck-protection, using his big frame and long reach to make it tough for opposing players to take the puck away from him. Offensively, most of his chances come from his hard work in front of the net or when he is working the puck down low and going to the net. As previously mentioned, he doesn't have any elite offensive skills and doesn't project as top-6 forward at the NHL. The biggest knock on him: his skating abilities. His top speed is only average and he doesn't have quick feet. He needs to work to improve his explosiveness and agility on the ice. His skating (or his lack thereof) will play a big role in determining whether or not NHL teams will draft him. He projects more as a bottom-6 forward at the NHL level, but will need to show that he can keep up with the pace in order to have a chance to play. If his skating was adequate, his chances of succeeding would be higher, since we like his smarts and attention to detail. He's not a super-skilled player, but makes enough smart plays in all three zones that he could find a way to make it as depth player in the NHL, with value shorthanded.

	PLAYER	TEAM	LEAGUE	HEIGHT	WEIGHT	POS	GRADE
NR	SPOTT, TYLER	GREEN BAY	USHL	5'9.75"	168 *	LD	ND
	HOCKEY SENSE		COMPETE		SKILL		SKATING
	5		6		5		6

Tyler Spott is an undersized puck moving defenseman and was trusted in all situations for a Gamblers team that was forced to rebuild this year. Despite not being the biggest or strongest player on the ice in many situations, Spott didn't give a lot away physically in a lot of situations. He uses his skating to his advantage and has a strong lower body and skating base which makes him difficult to separate from pucks or get leverage on in puck battles. Spott is crafty in regard to his stick work, he leaves very few sticks unchecked in front of his own net and has excellent stick position on the penalty kill in our viewings. Spott is reliable but not dynamic on the breakout, he doesn't commit a lot of glaring mistakes or turnovers. Spott uses his defensive partner as an outlet to relieve pressure if his first option up ice isn't available in a lot of instances and passes up opportunities to skate the puck up the ice in some instances. Spott is efficient with the puck in the offensive end and ran the power play with some effectiveness but doesn't possesses the high-end offensive skill or is a real shooting threat from the top of the zone which limits his pro upside at this point. He will have time to continue to develop his skill in the college ranks. Tyler will be off the Northeastern possibly as soon as this fall but more likely fall of 2020.

	PLAYER	TEAM	LEAGUE	HEIGHT	WEIGHT	POS	GRADE
NR	STANGE, SAM	EAU CLAIRE NORTH	HIGH-WI	6'0.0"	187 *	RW	ND
	HOCKEY SENSE		COMPETE		SKILL		SKATING
	5		5		5		6

Stange started the season with Team Wisconsin U18 in the Midwest Elite League where he was impressive against some of the top talent in the Minnesota High School ranks. Stange went on to dominate most of his Wisconsin High School opponents, leading Eau Claire North to their 1st ever State Tournament bid before losing to eventual State Champion, University School. Stange finished the season with Sioux City down the stretch and into the playoffs where he didn't look at all out of place, playing primarily a bottom six role for the Musketeers. Stange is a good skater, with above average explosiveness, especially with the puck. His work ethic and attention to detail in his game is very good but lacks NHL level offensive skill. Stange's work ethic and skating abilities give him a pro ceiling of being a potential worker bee on a skill line or a checking style winger in the bottom six. He is often first in on the fore-check and has crafty stick work in order to steal pucks off his opponent and win possession down low and protects the puck well along the walls. Stange has a slightly above average shot and release and displayed good range with the ability to score from the top of the circles but most of his goals are dirty, workmanlike goals around the paint. Stange ran the point on the Power Play for his high school team, as he was easily the most skilled player on the team but doesn't project as that type of offensive player at the next level. Stange's hockey sense and ability to read the play was an asset on the penalty kill and showed good anticipation and the ability to break up plays and potentially create shorthanded opportunities with his speed. Sounds like Stange will be heading to the USHL full time next season before heading to the University of Wisconsin down the road.

"I don't see a lot of skill there, he was invisible in the State Tournament, University School really shut him down." - NHL Scout, April 2019

"Someone might take him late, but the ceiling isn't high enough for him to be on my list." HP Scout, Dusten Braaksma

	PLAYER	TEAM	LEAGUE	HEIGHT	WEIGHT	POS	GRADE
NR	STAIOS, NATHAN	WINDSOR	OHL	5'9.0"	168	LD	ND
	HOCKEY SENSE		COMPETE		SKILL		SKATING
	5		5		6		5

Nathan Staios had an okay season for the Spitfires after being drafted 17th overall in his OHL-draft year. He finished the season with 29 points in 64 games, including 9 goals -- while being used in all situations. He also chipped in with 2 assists in 4 playoff games.

Staios is an offensive-defenseman who likes to activate at the offensive-line. He's got some skill and when given enough time and space, he was able to stand out and generate some points. There's an assertiveness to his offensive-game when controlling the puck and he looks to be a difference maker. His approach blended well with his compete on some nights. He's a diminutive defenseman with a compact frame which left him at a physical disadvantage along the boards; but, he did show some plus recovery skills, and can change his tempo to match the urgency of a play, though this wasn't always consistent. Under-pressure, he had mixed results; showing the ability to execute behind the goal-line on some plays, but getting overwhelmed on others. His anticipation grade is average. He doesn't identify passing lanes or skating lanes as quickly as we would like and this left him unable to penetrate with his passing, even with the man-advantage to the degree we wanted to see. At 5-on-5 this was more pronounced, where he was unable to match the pace of play at times, and had difficulty interpreting when he could pinch effectively.

Arguably the biggest issue for Nathan is his size and skating combo. He's an average skater but does have decent lateral mobility when walking the line and can side-step hits occasionally in his own-zone. For a player of Nathan's stature and mental attributes, it's imperative that his speed be much better and his isn't. In order for him to develop properly, he's going to have to refine his skating mechanics, develop a lot of strength, and learn how to interpret certain play-types quicker than he currently does.

"He really struggled in my viewings of him. He turned over a lot of pucks struggling with forecheck pressure." - HP Scout, Mark Edwards, May 2019

NR	PLAYER	TEAM	LEAGUE	HEIGHT	WEIGHT	POS	GRADE
	STARIKOV, LEV	DES MOINES	USHL	6'6.75"	200 *	LD	ND
	HOCKEY SENSE		COMPETE		SKILL		SKATING
	4		4		5		6

This can't have been the year that Lev Starikov wanted. After missing the 2018 NHL Draft window by just two days, the 6'6" Russian import was very much on the radar having played the entire 2017-18 season with Windsor (OHL). After just four points and a minus-11 start through 32 games, Starikov was released and left the league. Des Moines (USHL) picked him up, but it netted middling results. The big lefty was used sparingly and sometimes not until games were well in-hand. Seven assists and a minus-1 rating in 25 games is all that he cared to muster. This highlights the crux of the issue: compete. Lev just kind of loops around out there, rarely engaged, often taking the easy way out of plays that he could otherwise challenge himself with. He's a casual player who doesn't like to get too involved physically, though his strength is evident when he offers a shove. He doesn't rev it up with his skating or show off his at-least-moderate skill level. He is very content to power pucks around the boards and be done with the play. He was forced into turnovers quite a bit in Windsor. . Which is disappointing, because he has the ability to carry the puck in space and not make a mess with it. He can also make some snappy outlet passes, plus he has a heavy shot that never comes out of the garage. He is a very competent skater for his size and coordinated. He looks very comfortable with his frame and the wheels underneath it. Defensively, he relies on his pokecheck more than anything and it's unclear what he is willing to do on any particular shift to stymie an attack. There will be less talented players selected in the 2019 draft class, and not that Starikov is a world beater by any means, but the drowsy brand of hockey that he exhibits is his most off-putting quality.

"Frustrating player to watch because I think he could be a legit NHL prospect if he gave more effort, I hate to see kids squander their talent. Maybe with the right coach and mentor he can reinvent his game and attitude, I hope so." - HP Scout, Dusten Braaksma

NR	PLAYER	TEAM	LEAGUE	HEIGHT	WEIGHT	POS	GRADE
	STEEVES, ALEXANDER	NOTRE DAME	BIG 10	5'11.0"	185	LC	ND
	HOCKEY SENSE		COMPETE		SKILL		SKATING
	5		5		6		4

After spending what seemed like forever in the USHL (3 seasons) Steeves finished his freshman campaign with University of Notre Dame where he registered 7 goals and 2 Assists in 39 games, playing primarily a bottom six role for the Irish. Steeves didn't see much in the way of Power Play time which is an area of his game where he can be effective with the added time and space. Steeves has some offensive skill and can make plays but needs time and space to execute. Steeves skating was the big red flag for scouts last year in his 1st draft eligible year as a late 99 birthdate. While he has added some strength in the last year, his skating hasn't really taken the jump scouts were hoping. Steeves has a decent top gear when he gets going but needs the space to get there as his first couple strides is his major stopper at this point. Steeves showed an improved defensive game in his freshman year where his effort away from the puck was better than it was in the USHL and is willing to block shots and work on the Penalty Kill. His shot is an asset but didn't get in enough situations to showcase it this season.

"Steeves was on my watch list of NCAA draft eligible players to watch this year but it was clear early on he doesn't think or play the game fast enough right now." HP Scout, Dusten Braaksma

NR	PLAYER	TEAM	LEAGUE	HEIGHT	WEIGHT	POS	GRADE
	STEVENSON, KEEGAN	GUELPH	OHL	6'0.75"	183 *	LW	ND
	HOCKEY SENSE	COMPETE		SKILL		SKATING	
	6	6		4		4	

The six-foot-one, 175-pound forward spent the 2015-16 season with the Soo Thunderbirds Midget AAA team and, posted 17 goals and 12 assists for 29 points in 21 games. He was selected by Guelph in the sixth-round, 102nd overall, in the 2016 OHL Priority Selection.

Keegan is an example of a player who we think is a good Junior player but his skillset doesn't transfer to the NHL. He works hard and has fairly good hockey sense but we don't see him as an NHL prospect. His skating is big weakness and so is the fact that he does not possess much skill. He may get drafted but we would not be willing to select him at this point of his development. We see him as having a productive OHL career and then helping a CIS team down the road.

"I overheard another team's Scout who likes him. I don't see it." – NHL Scout, October 2018

"Not enough there, I don't see him as a draft." – NHL Scout, November 2018

"Not a draft for me. Skating doesn't look fixable." – NHL Scout, April 2019

"Our ratings say it all. He's a hard working player but the lack of skill and weakness in the skating department took him off my list of players with a draftable grade very early in the season. That said, he was a nice pick by Guelph where they got him. He's a productive OHL player. I do know of one Scout who has time for him as a draft worthy player." – HP scout, Mark Edwards, May 2019

NR	PLAYER	TEAM	LEAGUE	HEIGHT	WEIGHT	POS	GRADE
	STIENBURG, MATTHEW	ST. ANDREWS	HIGH-ON	6'0.75"	182 *	RC	ND
	HOCKEY SENSE	COMPETE		SKILL		SKATING	
	5	7		5		5	

Steinburg is a Halifax native who has played the past two seasons with St. Andrew's College in Ontario. This year, he was the captain of the team, and also played 3 games in the USHL with Sioux City. He's committed to play college hockey at Cornell University.

First and foremost, Steinburg is a very physical player. He likes to finish every hit possible, and he's a threat for opposing defensemen on the forecheck. He's very strong on his skates and really tough to contain along the boards and in front of the net. He was an offensive player with his team this year, leading them in scoring. Despite this, he projects more as a grinder at the pro level. His offensive skills are average at best. There is great velocity on his shot, but he doesn't have a quick release. At the level he played, his shots were often just too powerful for prep goaltenders to handle. His skating is a flaw; he's strong on his skates but doesn't generate good speed, lacking fluidity and agility. He's an up-and-down winger on his wing and goes hard to the net. He's not very good at changing directions quickly, as he lacks the proper footwork, agility, and quickness to do so. On the power play, he could be useful in front of the net; he's tough to move from there and can screen the goalie's view with his big frame. At the prep level, on the power play, he was used in a shooting role. We have a hard time seeing this happen at the pro level, though. We don't see him adding a lot of value to the PK unit due to his lack of footspeed and anticipation. This is not a good combination for shorthanded situations. Steinburg does compete hard each night, not taking many shifts off. If Steinburg can improve his quickness, his very physical brand of hockey could bring him to an NHL 4th-line grinder role at some point. That said, there's a lot of work ahead of him in terms of skating and overall skill level.

	PLAYER	TEAM	LEAGUE	HEIGHT	WEIGHT	POS	GRADE
NR	STRONDALA, VOJTECH	TREBIC	CZE-2	5'7.0"	154	LC	**ND**
	HOCKEY SENSE		COMPETE		SKILL		SKATING
	6		6		5		6

Strondala is a late 2000-born player who split this past season by playing in the 1st and 2nd men's league in his home country. He's a diminutive forward who skates well and has a good compete level in all three zones. He has active feet, keeps them moving and likes to annoy the opposing defensemen with a good forecheck. He gets outmuscled along the boards due to his lack of size and strength, and has to be smart to win those puck battles, notably with his quick stick. He's always gives a great effort on the backcheck and he's a smart player away from the puck. He's limited offensively as far as pro potential goes, as his skill level is average. He has good vision and he's more of a passer than he is a shooter. He doesn't have a good shot. In order for him to score, he needs to be near the net. As he continues to play at higher levels, it will get more difficult for him to get there due to his size limitations. He has value on the penalty-killing unit; he has good hustle and anticipation, which makes him efficient there. He might get a look late in the draft by a team, but he's not on our draft list.

"Small guys with the combo of average skill and lacking high end skating are going to be up against it to make my list." - HP Scout, Mark Edwards, May 2019

	PLAYER	TEAM	LEAGUE	HEIGHT	WEIGHT	POS	GRADE
56	STRUBLE, JAYDEN	ST. SEBASTIANS	HIGH-MA	6'0.0"	194 *	LD	**C**
	HOCKEY SENSE		COMPETE		SKILL		SKATING
	4		7		6		7

Jayden Struble checks a lot of boxes for us. Struble isn't overly big but is a very quick and agile defenseman that brings a good amount of strength and physicality. Jayden plays an agitating style that has shown to be highly effective in getting his opponents off of their games. Struble spent the 18/19 season with St. Sebastian's Prep School in Massachusetts where he registered 10 goals and 40 points in 28 games as well as finishing his season for the Boston Junior Eagles at the USA National Tournament in April. Struble plays a high-octane game at both ends of the ice and plays physical in all three zones. He doesn't hesitate to step up on players to attempt big hits in the open ice or on his pinches down the wall Jayden has no issue with protecting his goalie or teammates when the need arises and sometimes looks to be seeking out these opportunities. If there is a drawback to his physical style right now, it's that he can take himself out of position trying to deliver big hits and can get running a little hot and take bad penalties from time to time. His judgement in some situations is lacking but isn't a major concern at this stage. Struble's all-around skating ability allows him to challenge opponents and keep an aggressive gap without fear of getting beat wide or losing containment. He does an excellent job keeping plays out of the middle of the ice and then sealing off the play along the boards. Struble moves the puck quickly out of his own end, he is equally comfortable skating the puck or passing it out of his own end. In some viewings Struble showed some tunnel vision on the breakout in attempting to hit the homerun pass and stretch the ice, firing it up into the neutral zone hoping his forward can get a stick on it for a tip into the zone. Struble has the skating and skills to play with more poise and with time he should learn to slow things down and simplify in some instances. Offensively, Struble excels at the top of the zone running the Power Play, he has above average puck skills and his footwork allows him to walk the blue line and open up passing and shooting lanes.

Struble is creative, will come down from the point when he sees an opportunity and uses the boards well to get the puck to scoring areas or to teammates in the zone. He has good range on his shot and has shown the ability to score from high in the zone both with his heavy one-timer as well as his quick snap release. He is a bit raw in the hockey sense department but has shown in recent months of making strides. Often in prep school he was the alpha on the ice, and this led to some poor judgement at times. Struble projects as a two-way defenseman who's versatility puts his ceiling at the NHL level as a top two pairing defenseman. We are hearing Struble may be heading to the BCHL next season before heading to Northeastern in 2020.

"He's a good skater, has plenty of skill. Our area guy likes him. He might be gone before the 4th round.- NHL Scout, February 2019

"He's getting a lot of love. He's getting a lot of views. I can see him crashing the top 60." - NHL Scout, March 2019

"It's all about how you rate his hockey sense. I always find it more difficult to access the high school players. I've talked to guys who think he'll go in the 1st round though. I can't quite get there." - NHL Scout, April 2019

"So tough to evaluate him playing against terrible teams." - NHL Scout, May 2019

"He has a combination of skill and physicality that not many other defensive prospects have in this draft, I'm a fan of this kid, I have him high up in my rankings." HP Scout, Dusten Braaksma, May 2019!

26	PLAYER	TEAM	LEAGUE	HEIGHT	WEIGHT	POS	GRADE
	SUZUKI, RYAN	BARRIE	OHL	6'0.25"	178 *	LC	B
	HOCKEY SENSE	COMPETE		SKILL		SKATING	
	6	5		8		7	

Ryan Suzuki was the first overall selection in the OHL draft 2 years ago. , He produced 75 points in 65 games, including 50 assists on a mediocre Barrie squad. Internationally, he produced 8 points in 5 games while complimenting high-end players at the Hlinka, and at the U18's he

Suzuki is one of the most talented yet polarizing players in this year's draft. There's less than a handful of players who possess the dynamic offensive-skill set that he is capable of showing on any given night. The most impressive offensive-attribute he has is his playmaking ability. With the exception of Hughes and possibly the USNTDP's Trevor Zegras, there might not be a better passer in this year's class. When you blend his vision, accuracy, and touch with the puck, it allows him to make dynamic passes while going at top-speed. We've seen him carve through multiple players, while faking a shot before threading no-look passes that land directly on the tape, leaving the opposing defenses helpless. Furthermore, he's capable of saucer-passes, sharp stretch passes, no-look drop-passes, and fast one-touch passes which allowed him to dictate Barrie's powerplay, where he was comfortable both at the half-wall and along the point at times.

What really separates Ryan from other playmakers in this draft is his ability to mask his intentions with the puck on his stick. There are very few players who are as deceptive as Suzuki when he's weighing his options with the puck. One of the primary reasons for this is his ability to blend his shooting mechanics into his passing. Although he's an instinctive playmaker, Ryan also features a good shot. His release point is excellent but it's his body mechanics behind the shot that allow him to contort his frame so that he can manipulate shooting and passing lanes. This gives him the ability to exaggerate fake-shots before threading sharp high-percentage passes into open-lanes that were previously closed after getting the defense to bite on the initial play-type. Everyone on the ice knows that Suzuki is looking to pass, yet his play is rarely telegraphed which is a testament to his ability to fake opposing players, he's exceptional at it. Suzuki also possesses other high-end offensive-skills that compliment both his shooting and passing ability. His hands are some of the best in this draft as well, showing the ability to effortlessly pull the puck through his opponents and make highly technical-dekes from stationary positions, while in motion, and even when thrown off-balance. One of the better goals we watched from him this season was a double-clutch drag-move from his knees that he turned into a shot. His hands force his opponents to respect him, giving him additional time and space, which allows him to further take advantage of the rest of his skill-set.

Suzuki has shown an inability to shift his intensity when the game calls for it. There's been several games we've watched where Barrie really needed Suzuki to increase his effort and compete-level, yet he's shown an inability and an unwillingness to do so. Furthermore, Suzuki has been primarily a perimeter player in most of our viewings. He has excellent skating mechanics which are highlighted by impressive-edges, giving him the ability to remain elusive when going through traffic, but he doesn't use his skating or his edges to penetrate through traffic nearly enough. In almost every game we've seen him, he's had an opportunity to drive past a defender or skate into open-ice towards the slot-area, yet consistently has attempted to make perimeter passes. When Suzuki is carrying the puck, there's far too many plays where the puck is going back outside the middle of the ice, as opposed to inside the middle-area or towards the front of the net. Away from the puck, Ryan has a lot of work to do as well. He's able to generate pressure on the forecheck, battle along the boards, and help support his defense, but he's inconsistent in almost every game we've seen from him in these areas.

When we discussed where he wanted to rank him, an area we noted was how difficult it would be for him to match-up against the NHL's top centres if he didn't evolve his game substantially in terms of intensity, compete, and defensive presence. When we discussed what he would look like on the wing, it was difficult to see how he would take advantage of his offensive-gifts to the same extent he could as a center, let alone how he was going to win board-battles against bigger players at the next-level. Lastly, Ryan does display some aspects of hockey-sense at an excellent level, such as his vision and positioning away from the play, yet has a lot of difficulty assessing when he needs to shoot the puck. He has an excellent shot as mentioned above, yet that's not translating into goals, which is primarily due to how often he's willing to give up a high-percentage shot in order to make a pass.

Suzuki has the potential to become a top-6 center who can run a powerplay. However, our ranking of him, reflects how many hurdles he's going to have to overcome. He's going to need to greatly improve his effort-level in order to fulfill his offensive-potential, and learn how to be more selfish when the play calls for it. Lastly, Ryan isn't a player who you can put into a forechecking role, so if he doesn't develop properly, he's most likely going to bust, which makes him one of the riskier picks out of the top-end talents. There's a ton of potential but it comes with a lot of development needed in order to fulfill it.

"I was in Barrie last night and I saw him (Suzuki) two weeks ago. He was awful." - NHL Scout, November 2018

"He's the best pure passer in the draft, especially off the rush. Problem is he passes too often when he should shoot and he plays on the perimeter." - NHL Scout, December 2018

"Kaliyev, the London kid (McMichael) and Suzuki all have talent but none of them have any 'want to'. Wasted talent and players I don't want any part of where they will be taken (selected in draft)." NHL Scout, March 2019

" Zero desire to take pucks to the dirty areas and wants no part of any physical battle." - NHL Scout, March 2019

"He has skill, he can make plays but I don't see heart and desire. Sometimes he looks like a kid who isn't having fun." - NHL Scout, March 2019

" Suzuki was the most difficult player for me to rank. He's so talented, but sometimes when watching him I wondered if he had a pulse. If there is a player who can make our ranking look bad down the line, it's this kid, he'll need to find the ' on-switch' though and it seems as though that is easier said then done " - HP Scout, Brad Allen

	PLAYER	TEAM	LEAGUE	HEIGHT	WEIGHT	POS	GRADE
NR	SWANKLER, AUSTEN	SIOUX FALLS	USHL	6'0.0"	181 *	LC	C
	HOCKEY SENSE	COMPETE		SKILL		SKATING	
	5	5		6		4	

Confident, agitating winger. It was a real mixed bag all year from the rookie forward. Swankler started the year in Waterloo before being moved early in the season to Sioux Falls. The most consistent thing to his game is his ability to bother, provoke, and draw attention. He can wake up a drowsy game with an extra poke at a covered puck or with a facewash for the fun of it. Based on his actions in scrums, it seems like he's willing to back that up too. Swankler's skating stride is pretty loose and it gets out and away from him, so he's not generating maximum power with how wide it gets. This makes trouble for tight turns. On nights when he's leaving a little in the tank, he gets caught in the middle on a fair amount of plays. In the postseason, to his credit, he was working hard and won a surprising amount of races to pucks, so the top speed is clearly there. The hands occasionally flash, usually with a toe-drag maneuver, but they aren't consistent. He still kind of chops the puck up a little bit and fails to negotiate tighter spaces. The power play time in Sioux Falls really help bolster his production, as he's not a regular creator of even strength offense. He's a bit headstrong when he has the puck too; with his swooping style, he's always in a rush and is sometimes unwilling to make a simple play, some obvious opportunities pass him by.

We have noticed that in tighter game situations, his ice time dwindles a bit down the stretch because of his puck management and lacklustre defensive game. His passing accuracy and timing needs some work, he looks much more comfortable as a shooter anyhow – it fits his style and personality a little better that way. He is definitely on the raw side and as a late August 2001 birthday, he has a little bit more racetrack than some 2019 eligibles. He improved his ability to get around the rink over the course of the season and started to figure out the league a little bit more consistently later in the year.

" I have some time for him. Simply put, he's a pain in the ass to play against. Almost everything he does out there agitates the opposition and probably some Scouts. The way he celebrates goals, after the whistle stuff, and it's not like his penalty minutes are off the charts, so he manages to get away with it or not cross the line. Funny thing is he didn't show any signs of having this type of game in his AAA years." - HP Scout, Dusten Braaksma

NR	PLAYER	TEAM	LEAGUE	HEIGHT	WEIGHT	POS	GRADE
	SWETLIKOFF, ALEX	KELOWNA	WHL	6'2.5"	188 *	LC	ND
	HOCKEY SENSE	COMPETE		SKILL		SKATING	
	6	5		5		4	

Swetlikoff joined the Rockets halfway through the season after playing the first half of the season in the BCHL with the Vernon Vipers where he amassed 19 points in 27 games. In the WHL he eventually worked his way up to a top 6 role with the Rockets, ending up registering 14 points in 32 games. Not the most offensively inclined player, Swetlikoff was used as more of a shutdown centre. He's is a big power centre who is smart in his positioning and puck decisions. On top of this he also has a heavy shot when given time to get it off. Skating needs to improve as he lacks short area quickness and can sometimes be a bit plodding. We like the smarts and he does pay good attention to the little details in all three zones and has some value playing shorthanded. His skill level is average and won't ever be a big point producer at the next level.

NR	PLAYER	TEAM	LEAGUE	HEIGHT	WEIGHT	POS	GRADE
	TANUS, KRISTIAN	LEKI	FIN-2	5'8.0"	160	LW	ND
	HOCKEY SENSE	COMPETE		SKILL		SKATING	
	6	6		5		5	

Tanus is a second-year eligible player who was passed over in last year's NHL Draft. This season he played at different levels, mostly on a loan with LeKi in Finland's 2nd men's league where he had a lot of success (44 points in 33 games). He also played 17 games in Liiga, where he scored 4 goals and 6 points.

Tanus is a smart offensive forward who can play both down the middle and on the wing. He has some very good smarts, good poise with the puck, and excellent vision. He's an effective player in all three zones thanks to his superior hockey sense. He's always involved in his zone to support his defensemen and help them retrieve pucks down low and start the transition game from his own zone. He's more of a playmaker on the ice; he likes to feed the puck to his linemates in scoring areas. He doesn't possess a heavy shot, and it's tough for him to score when he is far from the net. He needs to be closer to the net to score. He does, however, have a quick release, but it lacks velocity. He's an agile skater, but for his size, his top speed and acceleration are not good enough to make it as a full-time NHLer. He's the kind of player coaches love to trust in any situations on the ice. He's a valuable player shorthanded due to his high hockey IQ and tenacity. It's more difficult for him to protect the puck when playing against stronger players; with his size, he's limited in what he can do along the boards. Overall, Tanus is a player we like because of his work ethic and hockey IQ, but there's not enough speed or skills in regards to his size to think of him as a legit NHL prospect.

NR	PLAYER	TEAM	LEAGUE	HEIGHT	WEIGHT	POS	GRADE
	TAPONEN, ROOPE	HIFK JR.	FIN-JR.	5'11.5	166 *	G	ND
	HOCKEY SENSE	COMPETE		SKILL		SKATING	
	5	6		5		5	

Taponen was Finland's top goaltender in U-18 play this season. He played in the junior league with the HFIK U20 team. He's an average-sized goaltender who can be victim to his size when he gets beaten above his shoulder going down too quickly. He's technically sound; he has quick reflexes and does a good job covering the lower part of the net with his quickness and good pads. He struggles tracking the puck when he has traffic in front of him. Because of this, teams take advantage, mostly in power play situations. On the international stage, he had some tough moments playing for

Finland's U-18 team. In August, at the Hlinka-Gretzky Cup, he didn't look very good. Nor did he make up for it at the most recent U-18 tournament in April. He has hasn't showed any elite athletic abilities for a smaller goaltender, which is another strike against him. He's a good competitor in his crease, not quitting on any pucks. With his size and some of his poor international performances, we think his chances of getting drafted are slim.

	PLAYER	TEAM	LEAGUE	HEIGHT	WEIGHT	POS	GRADE
85	TEPLY, MICHAL	LIBEREC	CZE	6'3.0"	187 *	LW	**C**
	HOCKEY SENSE		COMPETE		SKILL		SKATING
	5		5		5		5

Teply is a big forward from the Czech Republic split this past season between the men's league and 2nd division men's league in his home country. He had 2 assists in 15 games in the top men's league. On a loan with HC Benatky nad Jizerou, he had 10 points in 23 games. Teply was a regular with the Czech U-18 team this season, playing for them at the Hlinka-Gretzky tournament, The Five Nations' tournament in February and the U-18 World Championships in April. He also played with the U-20 program at the November Four Nations' tournament, and at the World Junior A Championships.

Teply is more physically advanced than most of his Czech teammates; he's big, strong and makes good use of his size when battling for the puck (and to protect it). He does his best work down low and along the boards, where it's tough to take the puck away from him. He struggles to take advantage of chances because his skating is not good enough right now; he lacks speed and agility. There's a lot of work that needs to be done for him to improve his quickness and acceleration. We also didn't see a big improvement in his skating compared to last year. He has good velocity on his shot, but does need to improve his release; his shots often get blocked before they can reach the net. He's not a natural goal-scorer and has always had trouble scoring in international tournaments against his age group. On the power play, he likes to play from the half-wall on the left side of the ice, getting pucks on net from there near the faceoff circle. With his size, we think he should be more of a net presence on the power play, rather than playing on the outside like he has done on the Czech power play in international tournaments. He has had success because of his size advantage, not necessarily his skill level. He's not a dumb player on the ice, though. He can make some good passes to his teammates, but with the puck on his stick, he tends to be more of a shooter than a passer. He has decent two-way presence and works hard on the PK. Teply is a player who has regressed in our rankings since the Hlinka-Gretzky tournament. The positives are still there, but we don't think there's enough puck skills and speed with him.

	PLAYER	TEAM	LEAGUE	HEIGHT	WEIGHT	POS	GRADE
100	TIEKSOLA, TUUKKA	KARPAT U20	FIN-JR.	5'9.0"	146	RW	**C**
	HOCKEY SENSE		COMPETE		SKILL		SKATING
	6		5		6		6

Tieksola was one of the top scorers in the Finnish junior league, with his 60 points in 51 games. With Finland's U-18 team during the past season, he had 19 points in 20 games.

Tieksola is an above-average skater with quick feet that has some real good offensive skills. He lacks ideal size right now, and it can be rough for him as a result when competing against bigger players in Liiga, even his own age group at times. He's going to need to hit the gym a lot in the next couple of years, as he needs to add a lot of mass to his frame. He's got excellent puck skills in tight spaces; we love the way he handles the puck in those situations. He's at his best when he has the puck on his stick, and has the ability to make plays offensively. He has showed nice acceleration when rushing the puck in the neutral zone, attacking opposing defensemen with a lot of speed. He's a threat offensively due to his speed, but also his good wrist shot and very quick release. He could still improve the velocity of his shot, however. He's got excellent vision as well; he sees the ice well and also has great puck poise in the offensive zone, as he can wait until the last second to make a slick pass to a teammate. With more space on the ice, such as on the power play, he's more effective and can display his great puck skills and vision more often than at even strength. In addition to his lack of strength, a problem with Tieksola has been consistency. He can be dangerous in one game and barely noticeable the next. This was frequently the case in international events: he would have one good game followed by two bad ones. Consistency is, without a doubt, something that he'll need to improve upon in order to make the NHL ranks one day. Tieksola is undersized, but possesses a good skill level. In addition to finding more consistency in his play, he needs to get bigger and stronger physically to have a chance. The team that will draft him will bet on his skill level and hope he can improve those other aspects in Liiga before he can make the jump to North America.

NR	PLAYER	TEAM	LEAGUE	HEIGHT	WEIGHT	POS	GRADE
	THOMPSON, TYCE	PROVIDENCE	H-EAST	6'0.25"	166	RW	C
	HOCKEY SENSE	COMPETE		SKILL		SKATING	
	6	6		5		5	

Thompson is a 99' DOB that is coming off an impressive freshman season for Providence College, scoring 8 goals and 17 assists in 42 games for the Friars. Tyce doesn't have the size of older brother Tage (Buffalo Sabres) but does have a lot of the same characteristics as far as style of play. Thompson plays a smart, detail-oriented game and while not having great size, he uses his body surprisingly well, especially in puck battles where he is able to seal off opponents and use leverage to come away with pucks. Tyce works hard in these areas as well and looks to have added some strength in his freshman year. While Thompson hasn't been an offensive powerhouse, at least on the score sheet, up to this point in his career he doesn't have some offensive skill to his game. He has a good arsenal of shots that he can get off in the offensive zone, and while he isn't a dynamic playmaker, he possesses good vision and understanding of the offensive zone. Tyce's work ethic and hockey smarts will give him a chance to get to the pro level someday so we wouldn't be shocked to see a team draft him in his final draft eligible year. Even if he doesn't get drafted, there will be scouts on him for the duration of his NCAA career and look to sign him as an NCAA Free Agent.

"Bit of surprise he didn't get taken last year but the offense just wasn't there, I guess. I like this player, I think he made progress this year, just not sure it was enough for me to draft as a 99'. More of a Free Agent prospect for me. HP Scout, Dusten Braaksma

"Really like his work ethic but thought the rest of his game was just average for me." - NHL Scout, March 2019

28	PLAYER	TEAM	LEAGUE	HEIGHT	WEIGHT	POS	GRADE
	THOMSON, LASSI	KELOWNA	WHL	6'0.0"	188 *	RD	B
	HOCKEY SENSE	COMPETE		SKILL		SKATING	
	6	7		7		7	

After being selected 53rd overall in the import draft, Lassi Thomson had a strong first year with the Kelowna Rockets. He became the top defenseman for Kelowna and stood out on the powerplay after finishing with 17 goals on his way to 41 points in 63 games. On top of this, Thomson was named WHL Western Conference Rookie of the Year, and a Western Conference Second Team All-Star.

Thomson is a versatile two-way defenseman whose best attribute is his ability to excel in transition, where he is a threat both as a skater and using the full width and length of the ice as a passer. His skating is characterized by a fluid stride and impressive edges which allowed him to routinely peel-off pressure in his own-end of the ice, as well as cut aggressively down the wings which led to him generating consistent scoring chances off the rush. His straight-line speed and agility allow him to knife through the neutral zone once he gets going, but he could use extra power so that he can further increase his straight-line speed. His passing ability features sharp-outlet passes that he's capable of generating under-pressure and when in motion, but there were games where he had some inconsistencies which led to unforced icing's and turnovers as well. As a result, we wouldn't label Lassi as a high-end playmaker but a good one. He does have tools that allow him to compensate when his passing isn't consistent, including a set of hands and skill level that are above-average, which gives him the ability to beat the first forechecker. Another important aspect to Lassi's game is his confidence when handling the puck under-pressure, he likes becoming the primary option when driving play through the neutral-zone and isn't afraid to challenge the defense. Lastly, Thomson processes the play at a good level, this extends to when he is carrying the puck while going at top-speeds, where he showed the ability to react to closed and open skating lanes quickly.

In the offensive-end and when quarterbacking the powerplay, Lassi showed several impressive tools that allowed him to finish second in rookie scoring for WHL defenseman. His confidence and skating extend to the offensive-line, where he showed poise, patience, and lateral mobility that allows him to re-open and readjust both his passing and shooting lanes while under pressure at a high-rate. When Lassi was given or created openings, he rarely showed high-end vision but still made calculated one-touch passes and was an efficient distributor. However, it's his slapshot that stood out the most in our viewings. His slapshot features a reduced wind-up, fluid mechanics, and a good amount of velocity given his build. Lastly, his shots were accurate, specifically for the amount of power he can generate behind them.

Defensively, Thomson showed a good combination of defensive awareness and physicality. He can be prone to shifts where things don't go his way, which leads to multiple clumsy and careless plays but he also displayed a good compete level and was willing to attempt to recover on defensive errors for the most part. He had further inconsistencies at tracking players without the puck as he sometimes lost his man on plays out of the corner and was occasionally late getting into shooting lanes. Furthermore, although aspects of his defense need work, he did show determination, grit, and the willingness to play larger than his size along the boards when the play called for it. Lastly, he was capable of making quick-decisions below the goal-line during forechecking sequences, both with and without the puck.

Overall, Thomson had a solid first year in North-America, projecting to be a potential top-four, puck-rushing defenseman who could slot in as a 2nd-powerplay option if his development goes well. For him to make it at the pro-levels, he will need to continue to develop his defensive-reads and become more consistent with his puck-management.

"He was really good on my most recent trip." – NHL Scout, February 2019

"He had a good finish and probably solidified himself as a first rounder." – NHL Scout, April 2019

"He's not coming back next year so it's another hit to their Memorial Cup hosting team." – NHL Scout, May 2019

"My issue is all in the hockey IQ department. I have seen some game where he really struggled making decisions and they were costly mistakes. I was a bigger Lassi fan last year in my limited viewings than I am now after more looks this year. I have him lowest rated amongst our guys who have a say on him." – HP Scout, Mark Edwards

82	PLAYER	TEAM	LEAGUE	HEIGHT	WEIGHT	POS	GRADE
	THRUN, HENRY	USA U-18	NTDP	6'2.0"	190 *	LD	C
	HOCKEY SENSE		COMPETE		SKILL		SKATING
	5		6		5		6

Sizeable, two-way defenseman. Thrun was productive in USHL outings – potting 23 points in 28 games despite not having a lot of access to power play time. The Massachusetts native had plenty of ups and downs as the year progressed and left some question marks in his wake. Chiefly among them is: What type of defenseman is Thrun going to be? He is blessed with a projectable frame and capable skating. The offensive tools are far from overwhelming and his defensive play wavers from terrific to highly suspect depending on the game. Outside of spending a lot of time supporting Cam York, the frontman of this NTDP defense, Thrun can't really lay claim to much more. He moves fairly well for a player of his size, despite not having the smoothest mechanics in the world. His posture is a little bit hunched over and his legs are a little straight and stiff, but it doesn't appear to hold him back significantly given how he carries himself on the ice. There is nothing remarkable about his technical tools in virtually any regard. He owns a pretty heavy shot, but the rest of his puck skills don't move the needle. He doesn't treat the puck like grenade and he can catch passes just fine though. His defensive game is pretty inconsistent and it has looked better with York, even if on his off-side, than it does with others. He doesn't look comfortable battling in front of his own net and when he does get there, his body positioning is on the poorer side. Against rush chances, he lets the game come to him a good bit of the time and the results are mixed. When facing sustained attacks without York, he seems to get crossed up too often. He'll switch sides indiscriminately or double-up on an already-marked man for no obvious reason. We don't see a lot of communication from Henry on the rink, perhaps he requires a vocal partner to help keep his wits about him. His puck poise leaves plenty to be desired. Beyond some pretty egregious turnovers on the breakout this year, there has been some rushed (and failed) clears because he just doesn't have a great feel for the timing of the game. On the flip side, he's generally a positive when pinching to keep plays alive at the attack line. He's a heavy pincher, not in terms of quantity, but in terms of how he attacks the play. If he doesn't get puck, he's getting man – maybe both – it's the most assertive sequence we're liable to see from him on any given night. However, the Harvard commit doesn't give us a lot of confidence that he'll be able to carry a puck or be a PP1 player at the next level.

"I really like Henry. I think he's really intelligent and has underrated skill. Bigger kid than I thought too." - NHL Scout, December 2018

18	PLAYER	TEAM	LEAGUE	HEIGHT	WEIGHT	POS	GRADE
	TOMASINO, PHILIP	NIAGARA	OHL	5'11.75"	178 *	RC	A
	HOCKEY SENSE		COMPETE		SKILL		SKATING
	7		6		7		7

Philip Tomasino had a great draft-eligible year by fitting well with a talented offensive-team in Niagara. He produced 72 points in 67 regular season games, including 34 goals. In the playoffs he produced 7 points in 11 games.

Tomasino is a swiss-army knife forward whose versatility made him effective. He's a unique-player in the sense that he's more than the sum of his parts in areas on the ice, that in theory he should struggle in. Specifically, with how dangerous he can be around the net-area and on the forecheck, despite his average-height and thin-build. The main attributes that allow him to counteract his physical limitations are his fearlessness, his agility, and his creativity that's produced through an impressive level of hockey-sense and puck-skills. He was assertive on the ice and showed a good compete-level in most of our viewings. This allowed him to forecheck aggressively, where he used impressive straight-line speed and anticipation to generate pressure on opposing defenses. For a player of his build, he was great at winning puck-battles by thinking quickly and reacting dynamically to active-sticks and physical-contact. Additionally, he was stronger on the puck in the corners than his size would suggest, showing an advanced stick-game and understanding how to use leverage effectively. He was equally as effective in-front of the net and around the goal-line as he was on the forecheck. Using his creativity to generate high-end plays. For example, we've seen Tomasino receive a pass in one-motion before making a no-look spinning between the legs-pass to his teammate in-front of the net. These types of plays were executed at a good-level due to Tomasino's high-end puck-skills. His hands allow him to experiment on the ice without turning the puck over too often; he also timed his move-set well, rarely attempting a pre-set move or forcing a low-percentage play. As a result, he showed plus decision-making which resulted in pucks rarely dying on his stick regardless of his creativity. His hands also allowed him to get underneath the puck in a hurry, which allowed him to elevate pucks in-tight to the net area. Another reason he could produce in-tight to the net were due to his edges, which are arguably the most impressive element of his skating. They allow him to make athletic plays that few other forwards in this draft can make, and this gave him the ability to escape pressure in-tight spaces and around the net area, as well as move laterally across the high-slot which allowed him to mix-up his options. The last attribute that defined his net-front presence is his willingness to play bigger than his size. He consistently attempted to weave and knife his way through high-traffic areas in order to make high-percentage plays in-front of the net.

Arguably the most improved area of Tomasino's game that made us more comfortable with his skill-set was his execution-rate when driving down a lane during rush-sequences. In some viewings, he was effective primarily around the goal-line, or during the powerplay where he was effective both in the slot area and around the net. However, as the season progressed, Philip showed the ability to beat defenders using his agility and hands, as well as score a bit more frequently from the hashmark area. Although his release is good, he doesn't generate a lot of power on most of his shot attempts. So, he's still less effective while shooting in-motion when coming down the wing than when he's in-tight to the net. Areas of improvement include his consistency on a game-to-game basis and filling out his frame so that his style of play can further translate at the NHL-level. Lastly, there's shifts where he's stagnant in the defensive-end and doesn't support his teammates at the level needed.

As the season progressed, he's forced our hand into showing us that he can make more NHL translatable plays and show enough in the way of high-end puck skills to believe he can become a top 3 line NHL'er.

"He's skilled and will compete. I've change my top OHL based prospect a few times this year but this kid has been my biggest riser." - NHL Scout, March 2019

"He works but doesn't compete. There is a difference." - NHL Scout, April 2019

"Tomasino solidified his spot on our list by remaining consistent and having better projectable skating than some other OHL forwards that were around the same tier" - HP Scout, Brad Allen

	PLAYER	TEAM	LEAGUE	HEIGHT	WEIGHT	POS	GRADE
NR	**TOPOROWSKI, LUKE**	**SPOKANE**	**WHL**	**5'10.75"**	**179 ***	**LC**	**C**
	HOCKEY SENSE		COMPETE		SKILL		SKATING
	5		7		5		7

Despite not having the offensive impact some might have expected Toporowski played a large role on a WHL contender. Luke generated 49 points on a deep Spokane roster despite very limited powerplay opportunities.

Toporowski is a player with some clear standout attributes, as well as areas that need work. His skating is explosive and he is extremely powerful in his stride, this stood out in every viewing. On top of this his effort level was great which maximized his skating ability. He constantly wants to be involved in the play, and played almost every shift to make an impact. Throughout the year he was a great PK'er and a presence on the forecheck. Offensively he was strong on pucks down low, and few at this level can knock him off the puck because of his excellent balance. Toporowski has a good release on his shot, though it was sometimes inaccurate. We found him lacking in creativity and slightly limited by a lack of refined puck skills. Because of this much of his offense came from speed plays off the rush and good passes from teammates. Did not generate many chances for others with his passing, but this was more due to not having advanced vision than any selfishness.

	PLAYER	TEAM	LEAGUE	HEIGHT	WEIGHT	POS	GRADE
55	TRACEY, BRAYDEN	MOOSE JAW	WHL	6'0.0"	177 *	LW	**C+**
	HOCKEY SENSE	COMPETE		SKILL		SKATING	
	7	5		7		5	

Brayden Tracey is a first-round pick of the Moose Jaw Warriors who had a phenomenal rookie season this year. Tracey gradually earned more opportunity as the year went on and played a large role on the WHL's most dangerous line with Justin Almeida and Tristan Langan. Tracey finished with 36 goals and 45 assists, good for 81 points, and won the WHL Eastern Conference Rookie of the Year award.

Tracey's defining attribute is his hockey-sense. In our viewings, he was good at recognizing where he needed to be away from the puck by consistently moving into the right spots on the ice. This extended to both stationary play and when joining the rush, showing the ability to adjust to what the defenseman were attempting to do and reacting accordingly. This allowed Brayden to get behind defensive-coverage, and force the opposition to react to his movement. His hockey-sense extended to when he was carrying the puck and when he was on the powerplay. Moose Jaw ran a 1-3-1 formation with Tracey in the high-slot, this is where he shined, showing the ability to make quick one-touch passes to his teammates while under-pressure, while also recognizing when he had an opening to release his high-end wrist-shot. Although Tracey has a slight-frame, his shot generates a surprising amount of velocity. This is due to his technical shooting mechanics, specifically with his foot-work. He doesn't set-his feet, consistently staying on one-foot before the shot comes off his stick which allows him the ability to move inside the shot motion; this results in a further increase in leverage, which results in further power. Furthermore, Brayden features one of the better release-points in this class, his body mechanics present few tells, his bottom hand doesn't drag down the stick during his release, yet he still has a surprisingly accurate shot. His soft-hands are another attribute that enhance his release, giving him the ability to quickly change the angle of his shot, this allowed him to score goals in our viewings where he was capable of dragging pucks around screens and when driving down the wing. Although he generates power in his release point, his power doesn't translate in his skating-stride, specifically within the first-few steps. It takes Brayden some time to get up to his top-gear, but once he reaches it, it's slightly above-average. However, the skating mechanics aren't below-average, so with added-strength he should be able to develop better skating.

Although offensively-gifted, Tracey does have concerns away from the puck, which is the primary reason why are ranking of him doesn't reflect his point production. His most glaring weakness is in his compete-level which we consider one of the most important attributes when ranking a player. There're shifts where he is willing to backcheck aggressively, and is willing to shift-gears to go after loose pucks, but in some viewings, he's not consistently engaged and can drift into the background when he doesn't have the puck. He has sequences where he looks to have given-up on a play after being dispossessed, and is unwilling to forecheck at the required pace at times. Additionally, he's not a player who's going to weigh-heavy against opposing defenses and although he can be feisty, it's a fleeting trait that's rarely seen from him. There can be a lack of urgency in Brayden's game depending on the play and shift.

Tracey has the skill-set to become a middle-6 forward who features duel-threat elements to his game and can develop into a primary shooter, however, in order for him to reach his potential, he's going to have to invest in the play away from the puck and compete at a significantly higher-level going forward.

	PLAYER	TEAM	LEAGUE	HEIGHT	WEIGHT	POS	GRADE
104	TUOMISTO, ANTTI	ASSAT JR.	FIN-JR.	6'4.0"	190	RD	**C**
	HOCKEY SENSE	COMPETE		SKILL		SKATING	
	5	6		5		4	

Tuomisto is an intriguing prospect out of Finland who has great size and an intriguing skillset. This past season, he played in the junior league and posted some great numbers offensively (35 points in 45 games). He also played for Finland's U-18 team at various tournaments this year. He didn't play in Liiga because he wanted to keep his NCAA eligibility.

Tuomisto has great size and is still growing into his body. Now at 6'04", once he's done gaining strength, he could be a massive player. In his prime, he could even be around 210-220 pounds. He has some offensive potential, but he's still very raw and inconsistent. When he's on his game, he makes a good first pass with good accuracy. He will, however, need to learn to make quicker decisions with the puck. Sometimes, there's too much hesitation from him when faced with pressure. He's calm with the puck on his stick, but we would still like to see him make quicker decisions. His puck-management is inconsistent as well; he can struggle to make passes into the transition on some occasions, whereas in other games he can be really good with his transitional play. He posted some good numbers this year in the junior league, but he's still pretty raw on the power play. The aforementioned decision-making issues can be a big problem for him in this regard as well. Although he has a big heavy shot from the point, we would like to see improve his release and get his shot off faster. His skating abilities are a work-in-progress; his footwork is average and he can rush the puck out of his zone. Once he reaches his top speed, he does generate some good speed for a player of his size. He does need to improve his acceleration and fluidity, as his footwork is currently working against him in regards to playing in the NHL. Tuomisto is a good competitor. He doesn't back down from any confrontations, and is starting to use his size more efficiently as time goes on. Tuomisto is intriguing because of his size and the fact that he's pretty raw, but has a lot of things he needs to improve in the years ahead. He could still be a future NHLer at some point.

"Liked him last week. (Five Nations) big kid who played hard in a shutdown role." – NHL Scout, November 2018

"He's not bad. Best I've seen him play though so I want to see more." – NHL Scout, November 2018

	PLAYER	TEAM	LEAGUE	HEIGHT	WEIGHT	POS	GRADE
NR	TURAN, OLIVER	ACADIE-BATHURST	QMJHL	6'5.0"	212 *	RD	**ND**
	HOCKEY SENSE	COMPETE		SKILL		SKATING	
	4	5		4		4	

Turan was drafted by Drummondville in the 2018 CHL Import draft. After starting the season with the Voltigeurs, he was later traded to the Titan for another Slovak defender (Michal Ivan). Turan had a tough time adjusting to the speed of the QMJHL; his footwork is below-average and he had a hard time keeping up with the speed of the QMJHL forwards. Not only was his footspeed was an issue, but the speed at which he makes his decisions became an issue for him this year. When he was under pressure, he would panic too much with the puck, resulting in too many turnovers. In the offensive zone, he has a decent shot, but he needs to get it off faster on net, as many of his shot attempts were blocked this past season. Turan has great size, at 6'05" and over 200 pounds, but he could still be stronger and have a better compete level along the boards. He's definitely a long-term project that will need to fill out his frame. He also has a ton of work to do to improve his puck skills and skating abilities. He's not someone we would draft based on his below-average skill level, but he could be back next season with the Titan in the QMJHL.

	PLAYER	TEAM	LEAGUE	HEIGHT	WEIGHT	POS	GRADE
4	TURCOTTE, ALEX	USA U-18	NTDP	5'11.0"	189 *	LC	A
	HOCKEY SENSE		COMPETE		SKILL		SKATING
	9		8		7		8

Although Alex Turcotte was injured a couple of times throughout the season, he found his game early and never looked back when he was on the ice, having an excellent year for the USNTDP by finishing with 87 combined points, including 34 points in 16 games in the USHL. He continued his success internationally, by having one of the programs best performances at the U18-Five-Nations and was good while dealing with illness at the U18's. He's scheduled to play for the University of Wisconsin in the 2019-2020 season.

Turcotte's defining attribute is his hockey-sense. He's one of the smartest players in this draft and as a result is one of the safest projectable players in this class. His hockey IQ allows him to execute plays at a higher rate than any other forward on the program. His puck management is one of the main reasons why we have ranked him above the other high-end forwards featured in the program, with the exception of Hughes. His awareness allows him to have a high-panic threshold which allows him to assess his options rapidly which has resulted in him turning the puck over less frequently then some of the other higher-end players featured in the program. Away from the play, he's adept at putting himself in good position to receive passes in traffic, and is very good in his own end of the ice, using his superior positioning to intercept passes and block shooting lanes. Additionally, his anticipation allows him to recognize transitional play quickly, and recognize openings. His playmaking ability and vision both compliment his ability to read the ice, where he's capable of making high-end passes at full speed and from stationary positions on the powerplay. Although he plays a more stream-lined game at times than some other high-ranked forwards, he still has a lot of skill but reserves it for the appropriate play, which speaks to his hockey-sense. Although Alex has a thicker-frame, it doesn't prevent him from getting around the ice due to impressive skating mechanics. He moves very efficiently and doesn't' have much in the way of wasted movement with his upper-frame, furthermore he's a powerful kid which allows him to get up to an impressive top-gear very quickly since he can accelerate rapidly. Due to his hockey-sense and skating, he's efficient when changing his pace of play. This compliments his motor well, as he's shown a very good level of consistency with his compete level in most of our viewings. His compete extends to the forecheck where he battles effectively, using his frame to weigh-heavy on defenses and his anticipation to take away passing lanes, resulting in increased pressure. He also uses his frame to penetrate defenses and get into heavy traffic areas around the goal-line, where he uses his hockey-sense to anticipate rebounds and loose pucks at a good-level.

Although he's a high-end playmaker, his shot isn't far behind his passing ability. He does lack some of the more refined mechanics when looking at his release point, in terms of his footwork and how much he bears down into his release, but he does display a plus release overall, and manages to generate a good amount of velocity on his shots. When looking over areas of improvement for Alex, there's not too many attributes that stand-out as negatives if any at all, but that's what makes Turcotte such a complete and well-rounded player and is one of the main reasons we have had Alex ranked in our top 5 from the beginning of the season.

Turcotte projects as a two-way, cerebral center who can match-up against other teams top-lines. He needs to continue to develop physically and refine his shooting mechanics to a degree, but otherwise is a 200-foot center with one of the higher-floor and ceiling combinations in this draft.

"He's a great player. Based on the awful rankings I see out there for him right now he's going to be a surprise on draft day. He's top 6 all day long."

"I've seen him a few times since he's been back from injury. I like him but I think Zegras it better. I think Zegras is more naturally gifted skill wise...better offensive player." NHL Scout, January 2019

"He's a fast, competitive guy. He'll drive it wide. I don't think he has as much skill or creativity as some of the other high-end guys though. He's in my top 15 though. - NHL Scout, January 2019

" Really like the kids game. Awesome interview too. I'm talking like in my top 5 interviews ever." - NHL Scout, January 2019

" I like the way he gets inside and he's not afraid to go to the net." - NHL Scout, January 2019

"I change my mind on Zegras, Boldy and Turcotte all the time. They are really close. I'll be trying to sort those three out in the second half." - NHL Scout, January 2019

" I think he's one of the most complete players in this draft and would've been in several other drafts as well.- NHL Scout, April 2019

" There was a stretch there after he got healthy where he was just lights out." - NHL Scout, April 2019

" He was sick at the U18 and still played pretty well." - NHL Scout, May 2019

" I've been watching him play since Bantam. He's a Swiss army knife kind of player, can play any way you want and be effective, personally I'd have no qualms with using a top 5 pick on him, I want character, leadership and maturity. He checks all those boxes and has excellent skill to go with it." HP Scout Dusten Braaksma, May 2019

" I feel like I've been the President of is fan club for two years. Saw him pretty early in his OHL Draft year and was sold. on him. He's got everything I want in a player. His hockey sense is off the charts, he plays fantastic in all three zones, he competes hard, he's skilled and he drives to the net. If he ends up being 4th on our list, he'll be one of our top 4th ranked players ever." HP Scout, Mark Edwards, April 2019

NR	PLAYER	TEAM	LEAGUE	HEIGHT	WEIGHT	POS	GRADE
	UBA, ERIC	FLINT	OHL	5'11.75"	193 *	RW	ND
	HOCKEY SENSE	COMPETE		SKILL		SKATING	
	5	5		6		4	

The winger played his Minor Midget AAA hockey with the Kitchener Junior Rangers. The Firebirds selected him in the 9th round in the 2016 OHL Draft. Uba played in all situations but slightly lacks in the skating and hockey sense areas. Skating looks ok in straight lines but drops off in the agility areas.

His shot is reasonably accurate with a decent release but not all that hard. He lacks at taking the puck to the net and tends to both play and shoot from the perimeter. He was solid on the penalty kill but that talent alone won't get you to the next level. He competed ok but did have his moments where he seemed to drop off in that area, maybe it's a bit of conditioning, not sure. We feel that Uba is a solid junior player but does not have transferable talent to project him a future NHL'er.

"Pretty good shot but just ok feet, lacks a bit in skating department when you put his whole resume together. Not a draft for me." - HP Scout, Mark Edwards, May 2019

NR	PLAYER	TEAM	LEAGUE	HEIGHT	WEIGHT	POS	GRADE
	VAN DE LEEST, JACKSON	CALGARY	WHL	6'6.25"	222 *	LD	ND
	HOCKEY SENSE	COMPETE		SKILL		SKATING	
	5	5		4		4	

A former first round WHL selection, Van de Leest played in a shutdown defensive role for the Calgary Hitmen this year. Finished with 1 goal and 21 points without substantial powerplay time.

Jackson is a bit of a throwback style big defenseman, standing a massive 6'6 and playing a very defensive game. In the defensive zone is Van de Leest's biggest area of strength as he utilizes his reach and size advantage to contain play to the outside and knock pucks loose. Not as overwhelming in puck battles as he could be, with smaller players sometimes out-quick-ing him in the corners. Skating is below average with very poor acceleration and agility. Takes a while to get his big frame rolling and this often puts him at a disadvantage, as he cannot afford to give up a step. Was sometimes susceptible to getting beat by speed off the rush, and lost a lot of races to pucks. With the puck plays a very safe style, throwing it off the window very often. Didn't display much ability to make a quality breakout unless he was given plenty of time. When given time he could make solid tape to tape passes, but needs to improve his distribution under pressure. Didn't display the ability to open up shooting lanes in the offensive zone, rarely moving laterally with the puck, and rarely moving off the blueline. Van de Leest needs to improve his skating and abilities with the puck to have a shot with the way the game is going.

37	PLAYER	TEAM	LEAGUE	HEIGHT	WEIGHT	POS	GRADE
	VLASIC, ALEX	USA U-18	NTDP	6'5.75"	193	LD	B
	HOCKEY SENSE	COMPETE		SKILL		SKATING	
	5	6		5		6	

Alex Vlasic was the largest defender featured on the program, and finished with 27 points in 61 games. In the USHL, he produced 15 points in 27 games, including 13 assists. At the international stage, he played a the U18-Five-Nations tournament and had a decent showing at the U18's, finishing with 1 assist in 7 games. He's slated to play for Boston University next season.

Vlasic is one of the rawest players in this class that requires the most projection out of any player featured on the program and in this draft in general for that matter. He has a remarkably long-frame which gives him the ability to take up a ton of space on the ice. It's rare to find a player with his level of coordination given his stature which creates an interesting package. His physical tools are highlighted by his reach. He's an aggressive kid which compliments his stick-play. He can make unorthodox stick-on-puck plays, reach around players, generating takeaways at unique-angles, and can use his stick to generate a tremendous amount of leverage in the corners. Furthermore, Alex can play a physical-brand of hockey when the play calls for it, specifically with his cross-checks which have resulted in several clean takeaways in our viewings. His length extends to the offensive-zone, where he can generate a lot of velocity on his slapshot as well. In the defensive-end, Alex's length gives him the ability to cover lost-ground, so when he does get beat wide, or is late to react in transition, he can recover in unorthodox ways. His tools also help compensate for his hockey-sense, which is the hockey equivalent of a smorgasbord. Rarely have we scouted a player who can anticipate a play-type using spatial awareness yet fail to generalize this to several other areas of the ice even though the play-type is similar. For instance, he can fail to interpret his gap or assess the time he has to cut off a skating lane behind the goal-line; yet at the offensive-blueline, can show impressive spatial-awareness when anticipating his time and space when activating in an effort to generate an offensive-play. His level of disengagement without the puck could be a factor when accounting for this, his focus seems to go up substantially in some of our viewings based on how involved he is around the puck. This extends to his vision as well. When he's focused, he can make accurate stretch-passes and react dynamically to the play in the offensive-end. We've seen him fake slapshots before recognizing quickly an open-passing lane, threading a sharp and accurate pass towards the circle resulting in an impressive primary assist. Yet, he can completely misfire a higher-percentage passing option off a routine play-type without pressure. His Jekyll and Hyde approach extends to his shot-selection as well. At times he can harmlessly float high-shots without accounting for lanes, yet at times bears down into a release that he purposely places behind screens, generating a dangerous scoring chance as a result. The most concerning aspect of Vlasic's game when projecting his skill-set is in regards to his hands. He can drag the puck in-tight to his body occasionally and can use his length to protect the puck at an average-rate but he also has a tendency to mishandle the puck which makes him susceptible when he over-handles the puck or when he tries to make a more dynamic play. That being said, when he is decisive, he has the ability to surprise with an impressive play that does require some skill. This suggests that there might be untapped offensive-potential depending on which version of Alex Vlasic you believe is the real one. What we are sure of is that he needs to more consistent in order to develop into the version we like on the ice.

The most important area that Alex needs to continue developing besides his puck-handling is in regards to his skating. For a kid his size, he does have above-average mechanics. He can't always maintain a deep-knee bend and when fatigued, it's very difficult for him to activate his core and maintain a proper posture which was noticeable when a lot of speed was required, but there is a decent amount of fluidity to his skating for how tall and thin he is. Though, as expected with any large kid who needs several years of development to physically mature, Alex has trouble generating power which hinders his acceleration and ability to stop and start as quickly as we would like. What makes his skating attributes unique, is that it's nowhere near as bad as you would expect given his current build. Overall, the biggest hurdle in attempting to project Vlasic is that it relies on his ability to put on a substantial amount of muscle which isn't done on a linear developmental curve. In other words, Vlasic needs a lot of developmental time and work compared to most other prospects in this class.

As you can imagine from this write-up, Alex is a polarizing prospect within our staff and that's to be expected when considering how many areas of further development are needed when projecting his game. If Vlasic does develop properly, then we see him becoming a mobile-shutdown-defenseman who can match up against prominent power-forwards due to his length and size. If everything goes right for Alex, he might be able to chip in offensively as well.

"Make him 6'0" or 5'11" and tell me where you would be willing to draft him?" He's not going (drafted) anywhere high. Not enough there." - NHL Scout, September 2018

"Five Nations was on big ice and that helped hide his biggest weakness (handing the puck under pressure) Throw out that event." - NHL Scout, December 2018

"I'm starting to drop him a bit, but he's been a tricky one to evaluate. I liked him at overseas but not since." - NHL Scout, January 2019

"Lack of urgency and he never impacts the game. He's not Logan Stanley but there is some Logan Stanley (in his game). He is smarter but he doesn't have Stanley's nastiness that showed up every once in a while and Vlasic skates better. Puck skills are similar." - NHL Scout, January 2019

"Very laid back kid in my interview. Reminded me of my Mattias Samuelsson interview last year. He might rub some guys the wrong way but I think he's probably fine though." - NHL Scout, January 2019

"(Laughs) Sure, ask me about the guy I have no idea what to do with. Last time I saw him he was so bad defensively...especially mentally. He was flat footed, caught on the wrong side of the play, puck watching, didn't pick up his man but then he made some puck plays that came out of nowhere. I can't figure him out." - NHL Scout, February 2019

"I'm not sold on him because he's inconsistent, but from doing some digging, he's going in the first round, that much I do know." - NHL Scout, March 2019

"He's been really struggling for me. I just dropped him out of my first round." - NHL Scout, March 2019

"I think there will be a significant difference from what Alex's game looks like now compared to where it could be in 5 years" - HP Scout, Brad Allen

"I saw him in midget, he was raw but had potential 1st Round pick written all over him. Fast forward to now, he has some intriguing tools but nothing stands out and makes me want to say 'you have to get this guy', I just haven't seen the progression." HP Scout, Dusten Braaksma January, 2019

"I worry that he's going to be a less tough Jared Tinordi." - NHL Scout, March 2019

"There's too much bad that comes with the good. He's outside my top 30 now." - NHL Scout, March 2019

	PLAYER	TEAM	LEAGUE	HEIGHT	WEIGHT	POS	GRADE
NR	VORLICKY, MIKE	EDINA	HIGH MN.	6'1.25"	183	RD	ND
	HOCKEY SENSE		COMPETE		SKILL		SKATING
	5		6		5		6

Vorlicky is a 2nd time eligible-NHL Draft prospect who elected to play his senior season for Edina High School rather than heading to the USHL. Michael captained his Edina Hornets to the Minnesota High School Class AA State Championship. After his High School season, Vorlicky joined the Madison Capitols to finish the season and was instantly their best defenseman in their final 6 games, registering 3 assists for the Capitols. Vorlicky is a smart two-way defenseman that has NHL caliber skating ability. On his puck retrievals, Vorlicky gets a step ahead of his forechecker by quickly identifying pressure and quickly turns pucks out of his own end either using his feet or accurate passing ability. When exiting his own end, Vorlicky is one of the better passing defenseman in this draft. He quickly surveys the ice and can stretch the ice both north-south and east-west and uses his defensive partner effectively. His passes find players tapes in stride which allowed his team to play a fast game that was difficult for opponents to defend. Vorlicky lacks some dynamic offensive skill that potential #1 defenseman at the next level have. Michael is able to skate up the ice into the offensive zone effectively but lacks some playmaking ability on his zone entries. Vorlicky can run the point on the power play effectively due to his mobility and passing accuracy but lacks the dynamic skill to really create high end scoring chances consistently and likely projects as a 2nd Power Play option at the next level. Vorlicky's excellent skating ability allows him to defend against the rush well, he has a good gap at the blueline and an active stick that can force players into mistakes. Vorlicky doesn't project as a top defenseman at the next level but has excellent skating, hockey sense and has a good understanding of his game and the things he does well therefor has a potential ceiling of being that stabilizing presence for a defensive partner that likes to take chances and jump into the play. Vorlicky will be heading to the University of Wisconsin in the fall.

"No secret among scouts in my area that I'm a fan. He's a really mature kid, it shows in his style of play and his attention to detail, he by no means is a high end NHL prospect right now but I believe if he doesn't get drafted, he will have a few NHL suitors when his college career is done." HP Scout, Dusten Braaksma, May, 2019

"I think there are a lot of defenseman in this draft that fit into this mold, would not shock me if he got drafted by someone." NHL Scout, March 2019

NR	PLAYER	TEAM	LEAGUE	HEIGHT	WEIGHT	POS	GRADE
	VUKOJEVIC, MICHAEL	KITCHENER	OHL	6'3.0"	205 *	LD	C
	HOCKEY SENSE	COMPETE		SKILL		SKATING	
	5	7		4		7	

Vukojevic didn't develop into the two-way defenseman that he flashed in the playoffs last season, but he still had a decent year, producing 29 points in 68 games, including 3 goals. In the playoffs he had 1 assist in 4 games. At the U18's, he had 2 assists in 7 games in a defensive-role.

Michael is a mobile shutdown defenseman who plays a physical brand of hockey. His greatest asset is his skating ability; which features good posture, a proper knee-bend that allows for a full-extension, and sharp-pivoting. He's a strong kid which gives him a powerful stride and this allows him to skate the puck out of high-danger areas when he can't find a passing option. His two-step area quickness also allows him to pressure opposing offenses quickly and his plus backwards mobility allows him to maintain an adequate gap most of the time in our viewings. Under-pressure, he was better as the season progressed at identifying his options below the goal-line, which led to a lower turnover rate than we had seen at the beginning of the year. One of the more impressive aspects of Vukojevic's game is his ability to play with bite but contain it when it's necessary. He rarely threw himself too far out of position when looking for a hit in our viewings. The main issue that Vukojevic has in regards to his skill-set, is that his puck-skills are below-average. He can recognize when to activate at the offensive-line and identifies seams at an okay rate, but when he's attempting to extend a play when in possession of the puck, it can backfire. He's not great at receiving passes while going at top-speeds and lacks the skill-set necessary to slow down pressure at the offensive-line. He generates points by delivering hard-one-timers through traffic and finding quick passing options that don't require a high-degree of difficulty. When he keeps his game simple, he's at his best. He won't get drafted for his offensive-skill-set, he'll get drafted for his mobility and his willingness to battle effectively in own-end. If he develops properly, then he has a chance of becoming a bottom-pairing shutdown defenseman who can move the puck out of his own-end, while receiving some penalty-killing time.

"Struggles with speed wide, and doesn't think the game well. It's early but he's a no draft for me right now." - NHL Scout, October 2018

"He really has a difficult time handling any sort of forecheck pressure. Maybe a late pick but that's about it." - NHL Scout, October 2018

"Not for me." - NHL Scout, October 2018

"Big guy who skates ok, but what is he going to be at the next level? He's not for me." - NHL Scout, November 2018

"He's low on skill and hockey sense. If he's 6'0" rather than 6'4" we are not even talking about him." - NHL Scout, December 2018

"I'd draft him at some point but it would be pretty late in the draft." - NHL Scout, May 2019

"I saw much better things from him after Christmas but he's still not a guy I'd take before the 6th round." - NHL Scout, May 2019

"He made my list just on the physical attributes along. They give him a chance." - NHL Scout, May 2019

"He was a big faller for me. I liked the physical tools I saw in limited viewings last year but he started his decline for me at the Hlinka and it continued into the fall. His puck game was very poor in my viewings." - HP scout, Mark Edward

NR	PLAYER	TEAM	LEAGUE	HEIGHT	WEIGHT	POS	GRADE
	WARNER, NATE	ST CLOUD C	HIGH MN.	6'0.0"	177	LC	ND
	HOCKEY SENSE	COMPETE		SKILL		SKATING	
	6	5		5		7	

Warner first impressed us in the Fall Elite League where he was over a PPG player for Team Great Plains, registering 5 goals and 13 assists in 17 games. Warner missed the second half of the MNHS season due to injury but returned to the St. Cloud Cathedrals lineup for the playoffs and led the Crusaders to the Class a Minnesota State Title. In 10 regular season games, Warner registered 11 goals and 22 points. In the sectional playoffs and State Tournament, Warner was close to unstoppable, racking up 8 goals and 10 assists in 6 games. Warner is an excellent skater with a top gear that was difficult for any team in the Minnesota high school ranks to contain. Warner's speed is NHL caliber but his ability to make plays and generate offense at a high speed is what made him so dominate in both the fall elite league as well as in the Minnesota High School League. Warner has an extra gear with the puck and uses it well as he enters the offensive zone to create space for himself and teammates and does a good job finding teammates coming into the zone late. Warner also likes to use his speed to gain the edge on his defenseman and take the puck to the net, which he seemed to be able to do at will in a lot of viewings. Warner plays a heady two-way game, he uses his instincts to snuff out plays on the back check and then can quickly turn plays the other way in transition. Warner is one of the youngest players available for this year's NHL draft. Warner will either be returning to SCC for his senior season next year or could head to Des Moines (USHL) who drafted him in the 5th Round in the 2017 USHL Phase 1 Draft. Warner was a St. Cloud St. commit but has switched his verbal commitment to University of Minnesota when Bob Motzko left St. Cloud for Minnesota.

	PLAYER	TEAM	LEAGUE	HEIGHT	WEIGHT	POS	GRADE
99	WARREN, MARSHALL	USA U-18	NTDP	5'10.5"	169 *	LD	**C**
	HOCKEY SENSE	COMPETE		SKILL		SKATING	
	4	6		5		7	

Mobile, offensive defenseman. Warren wasn't given much power play time at all this year, which suppressed his point totals a good bit. His modest four goals and nine assists in 26 USHL games are not eye-catching, but he was only second in plus/minus and shots among U18 d-men to Cam York. While still inconsistent and raw, the Boston College commit showed a good deal of improvement as the season wore on. His skating has improved and he seems to be generating more power out of his stride. His edgework is also on the rise, though really tight turns still elude him, as maybe he has a little wider stance than many blueliners that are his size. After blending in for a lot of games early in the year, Warren improved his ability to carry the puck across lines. He has yet to really combine his puck carrying ability and his knack for jumping into plays as the fourth man to create or finish a quality scoring chance. That's a tough ask at any level, but Warren could probably add a layer to his game still that would better support his own rushes. When he is able to follow-up on an offensive foray as a late man, Marshall likes to be a shooter. He doesn't have an over-powering shot, in fact, his snap shot might just be his best weapon as he's cruising in. For a player of his type, one-timers - both as the triggerman and the setup man – are just not currently in his wheelhouse. His hands have improved, but it's not clear that he's going to get to a level where he can beat reliable defensive players with his skill. The combination of skating and skill, however, should be plenty to beat high forecheckers with regularity at the next level.

Defensively, Warren needs a lot of refinement still. He keeps wonky, inconsistent gaps – even against rush chances that originate from outside the dot line. His pivots are oddly timed and executed. As a result, he ends up getting all turned around by better players coming down the wing who have a plus skillset. It looks like he wants to be a more aggressive style defender and shutdown plays earlier, but by the time the buzzer goes off in his head, the play has only progressed to a point where it's too late to be an aggressor. So he loses his shoulder squared-ness and the ability to use his stick to dictate the terms of the attack, and then he's left to rely on his skating to recover an advantage. His skating helps, but it looks like just average hockey sense will keep him as an unkempt defensive player for the foreseeable future. He looks athletic and coordinated, but not overly hockey strong yet. He doesn't play the game with a lot of physicality by default. There doesn't appear to be much drop off in his game if he has to switch from LD to RD. There's a lot of development arc left to eat up on Warren in terms of ceiling, but that said the floor is quite low too.

"He wasn't good in Europe, he really struggled there and it opened my eyes a bit. Hockey Sense was an issue." - NHL Scout, May 2019

"I probably like him more than some other guys. He has some skill and works hard. He can skate and was good on the PK too." - NHL Scout, May 2019

"Whichever team drafts him needs to have patience. I think he's a 3-4 year college player but I like this player more than some others on our staff. I think he fits into today's game well. He has some sandpaper to his game which you need as an undersized defenseman." HP Scout, Dusten Braaksma, March 2019

	PLAYER	TEAM	LEAGUE	HEIGHT	WEIGHT	POS	GRADE
NR	WASHKURAK, KEEAN	MISSISSAUGA	OHL	5'10.0"	184 *	LC	**C**
	HOCKEY SENSE	COMPETE		SKILL		SKATING	
	6	8		5		5	

Keean Washkurak had a solid-season for Mississauga, becoming one of the more consistent points producers on the team. He finished the season with 47 points in 66 games, and had 3 additional points in 2 playoff games. He was invited to the U18 squad where he was featured in a depth-role, finishing with 1 assist in 7 games.

Washkurak is a two-way energy winger who keeps a relentless-pace. He's not the biggest kid but he plays much larger than his size and is willing to battle against anyone in order to come away with the puck. This made him an effective agitator, and gives him the ability to make defenses uncomfortable with the amount of pressure he can put them under. When he's in control of the puck, he's flashed some decent skill and has learned how to use it more than he did in his previous season. He's capable of showing above-average hands at times and can extend his toe-drags into his release point. This gives him the ability to switch the angle of his shot but he's unlikely to threaten from above the hash-marks. Where he had the most success when we watched him, was around the front of the net, where he was quick to track rebound opportunities and bury quick shots in one motion off of passes. His vision is better then his release, he can thread some above-average passes through multiple players and is capable of making accurate passes while going at his top-speed. The biggest problem facing Keean is that he's an energy winger who has average-skating ability. He's a smaller kid so it's important that he can really fly around the ice to press the action but his stride is short and choppy and this diminishes his effectiveness; resulting in several performances where he wasn't able to be as effective away from the puck as he needed to be. Despite his inconsistencies, he still is a committed kid and plays a sound 200-foot game for the most part. Although there's some skill and he has a good on-ice mentality, he may need to fix his skating mechanics to have a chance of playing in the NHL.

"He works his *** off, he has a high end motor and he's F***ing tough. That puts him on my list if nothing else." - NHL Scout, January 2019

"He makes it difficult to pass on him. He's the player we all (Scouts) want to reward with a pick but sometimes it's just out of our control. - NHL Scout, March 2019

"He has a chance because of the compete and the intangibles." - NHL Scout, May 2019

"I like Washkurak. He can play on my Junior team any day and he's a guy you root for because of his work ethic. He's kind of like a Rees with less skill. He doesn't have the finishing talent." -HP Scout, Mark Edwards, March 2019

	PLAYER	TEAM	LEAGUE	HEIGHT	WEIGHT	POS	GRADE
NR	WEBBER, CADE	RIVERS ACADEMY	HIGH-MA	6'5.75"	194 *	LD	**ND**
	HOCKEY SENSE	COMPETE		SKILL		SKATING	
	4	6		4		7	

Cade Webber is a big, mobile defenseman out of The Rivers School in Massachusetts. Webber registered 12 goals and 26 points for Rivers School as well as seeing 7 games with the NTDP where he mainly saw bottom pairing or 7th d-man minutes. Webber has some physical attributes that got our attention, and had a decent season overall while playing for multiple teams this past season. He's scheduled to play for the Penticton Vee's in the BCHL next season.

Webber is a shutdown defenseman who uses an aggressive stick. The first thing that stands out about Cade is his size, he has a large frame which is also very-long, giving him an advantage when it comes to his stick-play. The tool that stands-out that gets him into position to use his active-stick is his four-way mobility. Despite his age and size, Webber is a fluid and coordinated skater who can make sharp-turns and pivots. This allows him to cover a lot of ground quickly and close his gap before his opponents can react. Along the boards, he battles using his stick more than his body; his physical game needs further development since he doesn't use his frame as instinctively as his stick. He's shown decent work under-pressure and can make the occasional outlet-pass but he's not a puck-moving defenseman at this time. In the offensive-zone he struggles, and doesn't have plus offensive-awareness or the puck-skills needed to be a consistent threat with the puck. There's a solid, yet raw defensive-package to work with in Webber's game, but he's going to need to continue to refine his decision making in his own-end and learn to use his frame more effectively, in order for it to be untapped.

NR	PLAYER	TEAM	LEAGUE	HEIGHT	WEIGHT	POS	GRADE
	WEIGHT, DANNY	USA U-18	NTDP	5'11.5"	177 *	LC	ND
	HOCKEY SENSE	COMPETE		SKILL		SKATING	
	5	6		4		4	

It was tough to find time for Danny Weight this season on a stacked U18 team. In USHL play, he only found 15 points and a plus-2 rating in 23 games. At the end of the season, Weight was the only 2019 eligible sent down to the U17 Team for the postseason instead of joining his teammates at the U18 World Junior Championships. The narrative goes a long way to telling the tale for Doug's son. While he has some decent hockey sense, particularly when the puck isn't on his stick, there just isn't a very palatable skill and skating package to be had. His skating is rather bland and doesn't possess enough pop to it. It seems to weaken when he has the puck on his blade too, as he easily succumbs to back pressure. The first step has improved, but that's about as far as the positives really go. He competes along the boards to get pucks and he isn't scared of contact. His hands are not fast enough to get any respect from defensemen. His shot is better than his playmaking skills, but that's not really enough to be considered noteworthy. Danny regularly gets to the net looking for loose change. Perhaps he'll have better luck and more ice time in Penticton (BCHL) next season, but he has a ways to go before being on the NHL prospect radar.

NR	PLAYER	TEAM	LEAGUE	HEIGHT	WEIGHT	POS	GRADE
	WILDER, HENRY	HOTCHKISS	HIGH-CT	6'1.0"	185	G	ND
	HOCKEY SENSE	COMPETE		SKILL		SKATING	
	7	6		6		7	

Wilder is a player that because of playing in the New England prep league and recently committing to Boston College after USA Hockey U18 Nationals has kind of flown low on the draft radar. He is not the prototypical NHL sized goalie as just over 6-feet tall although he succeeds because of this athletic abilities and ability to read plays. He played on a mediocre prep team which for Wilder was good as he saw lots of rubber and was the backbone to his team's success. His rebound control is solid and overall his goaltending techniques are strong in skating, positioning, and puck tracking. Will most likely return to school for senior year and play juniors at the front and back-end of the season. He has USHL, BCHL and other junior level options. Wilder is a strong character kid that looks to always improve his game off the ice as well.

NR	PLAYER	TEAM	LEAGUE	HEIGHT	WEIGHT	POS	GRADE
	WILLIAMS, JACK	SPRINGFIELD	NAHL	6'3.25"	175*	G	ND
	HOCKEY SENSE		COMPETE		SKILL		SKATING
	4		6		5		5

It seems like scouts have been waiting for Jack (Jonathan) Williams draft year for years now. Williams was a highly profiled goalie throughout his years in the St. Louis Junior Blues AAA program which lead to him being draft by Chicago (USHL) in the 3rd round of the 2017 Phase 1 Draft as well as the London Knights in the 2017 OHL Draft. Williams has had NHL size for a few years now, now the rest of his body is starting to catch up to his frame as he has added some strength. Williams relies on his athleticism, his game is not very technically sound at this stage. Williams loses his crease and his positioning. Due to his high compete factor in the crease, he doesn't give up on saves which leads to him scrambling and being out of position. Williams had a very up and down season for the Springfield Jr. Blues, there were stretches of the season where he was nearly impossible to beat and others where he really struggled in consecutive games. Williams is a Michigan State commit but will likely need a couple more years in junior hockey, refining his game before he is ready for NCAA minutes.

NR	PLAYER	TEAM	LEAGUE	HEIGHT	WEIGHT	POS	GRADE
	WILLIAMS, JOSH	EDMONTON	WHL	6'1.0"	194 *	RW	ND
	HOCKEY SENSE		COMPETE		SKILL		SKATING
	5		5		6		5

Josh Williams did not have the season we were expecting finishing with only 33 points in 66 games. Williams opened the season with a strong showing at the Hlinka/Gretzky cup but failed to build on this in his time with Medicine Hat and then Edmonton. He was the 5th overall pick in the 2016 WHL draft.

Williams greatest strength lies in his ability with the puck. Makes good decisions and has the balance and hands to play in traffic. He's got a good shot; he flashed some of his good shooting skills at the Hlinka/Gretzky cup with 5 goals in 5 games. Skating really holds him back as he has no extra gear, can make some tight turns with decent explosiveness but overall his footspeed is a weakness. Not consistently an assertive player and seems to be more or less a product of his linemates at times. There is room for improvement with Williams as he has had strong showings like at the Hlinka/Gretzky cup, but he has to improve on his assertiveness and aggressiveness to reach the next level in his game.

"Big faller with a lot of scouts is my guess." – NHL Scout, May 2019

"Saw him in Medicine Hat on back to back nights before the trade and he didn't impress." – HP Scout, Mark Edwards, May 2019

5	PLAYER	TEAM	LEAGUE	HEIGHT	WEIGHT	POS	GRADE
	WOLF, DUSTIN	EVERETT	WHL	5'11.5"	156 *	G	C
	HOCKEY SENSE		COMPETE		SKILL		SKATING
	8		6		6		6

Dustin Wolf was featured on a team that finished first in their division and was one of the top three teams in the WHL. However, Dustin wasn't a by-product of his team, his play elevated their level of success. He finished the season with excellent numbers, including a .936 save-percentage and a 1.69 GAA in 61 starts. He wasn't as successful in the playoffs but did manage to make it to the division finals, posting a .914 save-percentage and a 2.02 GAA in 10 games. He played on the Hlinka team for the U.S but had mixed performances and finished the event with a .909 save-percentage and a 2.65 GAA.

Wolf is one of the best puck-tracking goalies available in this class, and he has to be due to his size. When we look at the modern-NHL, there's been a substantial decrease in smaller goalies being able to develop into NHL-calibre netminders. However, there's been a bit of a resurgence recently, with the best of them being Saros; so, we are going to use him as a comparison model when breaking down Wolf's game at the same age. Wolf is almost as good as tracking the puck as Saros, with the exception of behind his goal-line and when evaluating where the puck is through screens. Juuse manipulated his frame to look around screens more than Wolf, and Wolf has a tendency to remain over-extended in his butterfly or stay crouched very low to the ice. He comes off his post as well as Saros did but does it in different fashion. You could make an argument that off high-danger shots in-tight to the net, Wolf is able to remain more-square on the first attempt, but the difference is marginal. Where Saros definitely has Wolf beaten out is in terms of his fast-twitch and overall dexterity at the same age. Juuse could transition into and out of his butterfly at a more rapid-rate, and was more explosive laterally, giving him an advantage on one-time options across the slot-area. Additionally, Juuse showed the ability to make rapid-adjustments at a more consistent-level then Wolf; though Wolf is also a good skater. Saros's gift is in his ability to readjust dynamically to certain play-types, where Wolf needs to be more structured and read the play at an even-higher level. That's going to be difficult for Wolf to do consistently at the NHL-stage. There's a tremendous amount of poise and patience featured in Dustin's game, rarely over-committing on a shot attempt and reacting very-well to skilled players in-tight to the net during breakaways and odd-man rushes. His glove is solid but not as good as Saros's was at the same age, but his blocker has looked very good in our viewings. One of the more concerning issues with Wolf's game, is that he's not as aggressive as we would like given his frame. Higher-end shooters at the pro-levels will have more room to work with then they did on Saros, since he was more aggressive than Wolf at cutting down angles on most shot attempts; though Wolf can develop this quality. The biggest drawback for Dustin is, that although he's athletic and can fully-extend, he's not as dynamic in his movement as we would like to see given his size.

Wolf was on our radar last season after having some very impressive performances for Portland, where he displayed hockey-sense that was bordering on elite. His reflexes, although good are not at the level we feel overly comfortable with though. That said, he still has one of the best mental-games in this year's draft which is why we have decided to still include him on our list. We wouldn't draft him high but towards the end of the draft, if he was available, then we would have a look.

"He's the litmus test to see how far excellent mental-attributes can really take a goalie who has been gifted good athleticism but not dynamic athleticism given his size" - HP Scout, Brad Allen

	PLAYER	TEAM	LEAGUE	HEIGHT	WEIGHT	POS	GRADE
NR	YAKOVENKO, ALEXANDER	MUSKEGON	USHL	5'11.0"	170*	LD	**ND**
	HOCKEY SENSE		COMPETE		SKILL		SKATING
	4		5		6		7

Yakovenko was recently deemed eligible for the 2019 NHL Draft as a 98' born playing in North America through a technicality. Yakovenko was 2nd in the USHL in scoring by defenseman with 19 goals and 33 assists in 56 games for the Muskegon Lumberjacks. For all the offensive production Alexander put up this season he played an effective and responsible game in his own end. Yakovenko is a strong skater with plus agility and explosiveness. He was highly effective in transitioning plays out of his own end. Alexander's strong skating ability is key to his defensive game, as his footwork keep him in good defensive position against the rush. There is still some development left for Yakovenko in the strength department as he can lose battles in front of his own net and along the walls but Yakovenko shows good compete in these areas. Offensively, Yakovenko is dynamic with the puck in the offensive zone; he can make some high risk decisions when on an Island, at the point that likely won't work out as often at the higher levels. Yakovenko sees the offensive zone well from the point and won't hesitate to bring himself and the puck down deep in the zone on the power play. Yakovenko has signed a professional contract for next season with Jukurit (Liiga) but it wouldn't shock us to hear his name called in Vancouver now that he has been deemed eligible.

	PLAYER	TEAM	LEAGUE	HEIGHT	WEIGHT	POS	GRADE
NR	YANTSIS, JONATHAN	KITCHENER	OHL	6'2.0"	210 *	RW	**ND**
	HOCKEY SENSE		COMPETE		SKILL		SKATING
	5		5		6		3

A big 6'2" forward who has grown since his OHL Draft season and who scored 50 goals and added 23 points in the OHL this year. Yantsis is a 1999 birth who is in his third season in Kitchener. He scored 5 goals in 59 games last season.

The thing that stands out about Yantsis for us is his skating. It's a big weakness and hurts his draft status for us. We would describe his game as being a good net front presence. His skill in the hands and shot departments have improved over the years. He is good at finishing from in tight. He lacks in the hockey sense department as he is a very one dimensional player. His play away from the puck needs work and he also lacks in the physicality department.

He's not really a puck possession player. He has a lot of success because of his size, he's stronger than a lot of the players he plays against and plays a good down low game. He gets inside position and out muscles guys in tight.

"Some stats Scout might draft him." - NHL Scout, March 2019

"He scored 50 goals so he might get drafted but I don't see the value." - NHL Scout, May 2019

"Really bad feet but he can shoot." - NHL Scout, May 2019

"His agent is a former Scout for us so I'd really like to like this kid more than I do. To me he's a 99 birth with really bad feet and too many holes in his game for me to spend a draft pick on him. Someone might take him but I'd bet more on an eventual free agent signing much like Brazeau in North Bay. If you draft him, he needs to play in the AHL next year because I don't want my draft picks ever playing overage OHL seasons. It was one of my reasons I didn't have interest in Durzi or Hollowell last season. I didn't think either were close to ready to play in the AHL this year and they would need to be drafted over-agers. Drafted players playing as over-agers tend to be missed picks much more often than they are huge success stories. - HP Scout, Mark Edwards

	PLAYER	TEAM	LEAGUE	HEIGHT	WEIGHT	POS	GRADE
12	YORK, CAMERON	USA U-18	NTDP	5'11.25"	171 *	LD	**A**
	HOCKEY SENSE		COMPETE		SKILL		SKATING
	8		6		7		7

Cam York solidified himself as the top defensive option on the program this season, finishing with 65 points in 63 games, and an additional 33 points in 28 games in the USHL. Furthermore, he saved his best international performance for the end of the season at the U18's, finishing with 11 points in 7 games, including 4 goals. He's scheduled to play for the University of Michigan for the upcoming season.

York is one of the most efficient defensemen in this draft class. His efficiency is a by-product of his hockey-sense and skating ability. To start, his anticipation both with and without the puck is excellent. He can dynamically adjust his pacing to match the intensity of a specific sequence which allows him to not only keep up with the play but at most times stay ahead of it. Due to processing plays rapidly and thinking two-steps ahead, York is excellent under heavy-pressure situations from the goal-line out. His vision compliments his reads off the forecheck, making him one of the better outlet passers in this class. It's rare to see Cam force a play or make questionable decisions with the puck. This extends to his puck-rushing ability. Though he prefers to find the stretch-pass, he's capable of using his impressive skating ability that features two-step area quickness, a fluid stride, and the ability to separate at top-speeds when transporting the puck. There's very little wasted energy within his skating mechanics and this allows him to play a lot of hockey without fatiguing at the same rate as most other defenseman. Furthermore, his skating ability and reads allow him to remain elusive which is important considering his average-frame, it's rare to see him get caught clean with a large hit. Defensively speaking, Cam maintains an excellent gap due to high-end spatial-awareness and excellent puck-tracking ability. When defending, he has a more modern and refined approach, making effective use of an active-stick and making well-timed defensive-plays that disrupt the opposing team's offensive-flow as a result. Although he's capable of delivering the occasional hit and doesn't mind bearing down when a game gets more physical in general, he still prefers a more structured and passive, yet calculated approach. That's not to say he doesn't compete; he simply adjusts his tempo depending on the play-type. His puck-skills are good, and he's capable of using them to protect the puck at the offensive-line and when he's attempting to drive-wide. In our viewings, Cam had a tendency to look to activate and use the back of the net to either set-up his teammates for high-danger scoring chances in-front of the net or quickly tuck the puck in on a wrap-around. He was adept at the latter-skill, and was very good at recognizing when he had a step on his opponents in order to take advantage of the goal-line in the offensive-end. Additionally, York has a plus release point that gets off his stick-quickly, this allows him to consistently get pucks through traffic since opponents have trouble taking away lanes in-time. That being said, his wrist-shot lacks velocity but the placements of his shots are usually directed towards deflection options. His vision also extends to the offensive-zone where he was responsible for quarter-backing the best 1st unit powerplay in junior hockey. He can thread sharp and accurate passes and needs little time to find an open-lane. Lastly, he does feature a good slapshot but prefers using his wrist-shot in most instances.

Despite all his offensive-gifts, Cam didn't produce at the rate his tools would suggest that he could or have many dominant performances in general for that matter. Which leads to the biggest area of concern in Cam's game at this time, which is that there were too many instances where he failed to assert himself on the ice. One of the primary reasons that could be responsible for this was due to the nature of the program in general. This was the best program team ever assembled; games were out of reach for their opponents as early as the first-frame at times. It's difficult for any player to maintain a high-compete when you know the game is basically over. This extends to the man-advantage, where Cam's abilities became secondary to that of Hughes, Boldy, Zegras and Caufield's. As a result, we were left wanting more, but having to take into consideration the unique developmental situation that York was under. Where Cam was more successful was on the international stage. During games where it was a win or go-home situation, we found that Cam stepped up and flashed more of his impressive skill-set, saving his best performance at the end of the season where he was dominant at the U18's. Although his international efforts alleviated our concern to a degree, it's still something we have had to take into consideration for our ranking.

Overall, York has the necessary ingredients as a player to project as a potential top-four mobile defenseman who can make plus plays in all three-zones. If he continues to assert himself going forward, he presents few risks which is why we have him ranked as an A-rated prospect.

" Interview was fine. Just not that interesting but he'll be fine. No red flags which is what we're looking for. To be honest you see his personality in his game. He's not an overly aggressive type of player on the ice" - NHL Scout, January 2019

" "Great defensively and has good vision. I think he's the type of player that NHL Coaches will appreciate." - NHL Scout, January 2019

" I think he'll go in that 18-20 range." - NHL Scout, January 2019

" He's their best defenseman and it's not close. I have really liked him some games versus college teams. The offence is not at the level that I thought it was last year." - NHL Scout, January 2019

" I'll be honest, I wasn't as high on him as others on our staff to start the year but I just saw him again last night and he's really grown on me. He's into my first round now." - NHL Scout, February 2019

" Had some ups and downs but really helped himself with a much better 2nd half." - NHL Scout, April 2019

" Based on what I'm seeing out there I think he's one of the most underrated players in the draft. I love his game and have him ranked top 10. He's ahead of Dach and Cozens." - NHL Scout, April 2019

" Early in the year I was wondering where was the player we saw as an underager? Then he showed up again. My #2 Dman and in my top 10." - NHL Scout, April 2019

" He's laid back Cali dude. I like him" - NHL Scout, April 2019

" He could become one of the best defenseman in this class if he learns how to develop that elusive 'it' factor to his game." - HP Scout, Brad Allen

" After Byram, he's the best defenseman I've seen in this draft." HP Scout, Dusten Braaksma, April 2019

" He was 10th on our pre-season ranking and our #2 ranked Dman. Moritz Seider pushed him down one notch on our final defensemen ranking After a mediocre first half of the season he returned to the form we saw last season. Outstanding in the second half and at the U18 in April." - HP scout, Mark Edwards, May 2019

" He's a California kid and it made me laugh when I had a few Scouts refer to him as Cali dude. They all mentioned how relaxed and laid back he was." - HP Scout, Mark Edwards, June 2019

NR	PLAYER	TEAM	LEAGUE	HEIGHT	WEIGHT	POS	GRADE
	YORK, JACK	BARRIE	OHL	5'11.75"	1790*	RD	ND
	HOCKEY SENSE		COMPETE		SKILL		SKATING
	5		6		5		6

Jack York was traded from Kitchener to the Barrie Colts, collectively finishing with 29 points in 61 games, including 7 goals. York is a two-way defender who plays at an aggressive-pace. His attack-oriented approach can be a double-edged sword for Jack though. On the one hand, it does allow him to make plus offensive-plays after activating at the line at the right-times, but he does have difficulty maintaining his offensive-reads. This puts him and his team in some bad-spots when he does pinch too aggressively. Though, he is a solid skater who can rush the puck and does compete when attempting to recover. There's a bit more offensive-upside in Jack's game when comparing him to Allensen, as he's shown decent lane-recognition and can fire some pretty hard-shots on net. His anticipation is above-average in all three-zones but it's his decision making that can lag behind. For example, he can anticipate a passing lane correctly and interpret the offensive-play type that's developing but he can then over-commit and throw himself out of position. Around the goal-line, he's shown a plus compete-level and can make the above-average outlet-pass on occasion too. The biggest concern with York is that he's not skilled enough to play with the mentality he has. He wants to be a difference maker but needs to know when to reign his game in, and hasn't learned how to do that yet.

	PLAYER	TEAM	LEAGUE	HEIGHT	WEIGHT	POS	GRADE
NR	YOUNG, TYLER	LAWRENCE ACAD.	HIGH- MA	6'0.0"	163 *	RW	**ND**
	HOCKEY SENSE	COMPETE		SKILL		SKATING	
	6	7		5		4	

Young is the son of former NHLer Scott Young, current Director of Player Development with the Pittsburgh Penguins. He is a player the has continuously grown physically through the recent years and his game also has trended in the right manner. As he has physically matured his shot has become stronger and has seen more success in the New England prep league as well as leading his team this past spring at U18 USA Hockey Nationals in points. Young is the late developing type that was not on radar of New England area players until recent. He plays a tough, hard-nosed style with physicality and versatile as will play penalty-kill, 5v5, and power play. Plays energy, up-temp way who competes in all three zones for pucks. Young is headed to Providence College in 2020-21 though could be a late round flyer in June.

	PLAYER	TEAM	LEAGUE	HEIGHT	WEIGHT	POS	GRADE
NR	ZAYTSEV, OLEG	RED DEER	WHL	6'0.75"	186 *	LC	**C**
	HOCKEY SENSE	COMPETE		SKILL		SKATING	
	5	6		5		6	

Zaitsev came to Red Deer after being taken 17th overall in the import draft thanks to a promising debut season in the MHL and impressive presence with the Russian u-17s. Zaitsev went on to produce 43 points in 66 games in a constant top 6 role with powerplay time. Zaitsev spent the majority of his season down the middle, but also showed the ability to play the wings.

Despite a slightly underwhelming first season Zaitsev has many positives to his game. Zaitsev is a powerful skater who is strong on his feet and difficult to knock off the puck. Zaitsev is also very competitive and physical, often throwing the body with big hits. On top of this he excels down low and along the wall in board battles, winning pucks consistently. Zaitsev is an effective decision maker with the puck but couldn't consistently find creative ways to break down a defense. There are some flashes of good vision and advanced instincts but these were not consistently on display with Zaitsev fading into the background too often. The potential to contribute more offensively is there with his skating and strong shot, but, he needs to develop more pure offensive instincts. As Zaitsev further adjusts to North America and a smaller ice surface there is major potential to show skill more on par with his early showings in international events.

NR	PLAYER	TEAM	LEAGUE	HEIGHT	WEIGHT	POS	GRADE
	ZAITSEV, DMITRI	RUSSKIE VITYAZI	RUS JR	6'0.0"	190 *	RW	ND
	HOCKEY SENSE	COMPETE		SKILL		SKATING	
	5	6		6		6	

Dmitri Zaitsev had a solid season for Russkie Vityazi Chekhov, finishing with 26 points in 56 games, including 13 goals. He went pointless in the playoffs but one note about his point-totals, is he accumulated 23 of his 26 points at even-strength and wasn't used on the top-powerplay in our viewings, getting 2nd-powerplay minutes instead. His play in the MHL gave him an opportunity to play for Russia at the U18-Five-Nations, where he didn't look out of place while getting some top-line minutes at times. Zaitsev is a high-energy winger who has some impressive-puck-skills. We've seen some creativity in his game by attempting difficult dekes and trying various between the leg passes near the goal-line. Though his execution has been mixed in his attempts, we have seen him bury the puck as well. He has a good release point that features above-average mechanics ranging from his footwork to identifying his shooting placement through screens. His top-speed is also above-average and he's a decent forechecker who uses his frame and stick in tandem to try and take-away the puck. He can beat goalies from above the hashmarks, but he's also willing to enter heavy-traffic and jam home a rebound if he gets a chance as well. He did enough in our viewings to consider him with a late pick since there's a good blend of compete, skill, with additional untapped potential given that he wasn't featured in a top-role for his team.

5	PLAYER	TEAM	LEAGUE	HEIGHT	WEIGHT	POS	GRADE
	ZEGRAS, TREVOR	USA U-18	NTDP	6'0.0"	166 *	LC	A
	HOCKEY SENSE	COMPETE		SKILL		SKATING	
	8	6		8		7	

Trevor Zegras increased his draft-stock after an injury to Jack Hughes gave him the opportunity to showcase himself as the first-line center for the program, an opportunity he took advantage of. He had an excellent year for the USNTDP by generating 66 points in 53 games in the development program, and an additional 40 points in 26 games in the USHL, including 15 goals. He's slated to play at Boston College in the 2019-2020 season.

Zegras is one of the best playmakers in this class who can make unique plays by using his dynamic passing ability. He has excellent vision and can make passes that are remarkably precise for how low-percentage some of his passing attempts can be. For instance, we've seen him make no-look spinning passes from one-knee that most players can't make from a standing position. His talent-level allowed him to make offensively-gifted plays, relying on his posture and wide-base when skating with the puck on his stick. His skating mechanics are very good, featuring an activated core, a deep-knee bend, and a straight-back which allows him to generate separating speed, making him dangerous off the rush. Furthermore, he's capable of making his impressive passes while going at full-speeds and as the year progressed showed improvement in his execution rate with the puck as a result of attempting higher-percentage passing plays more frequently. Although his straight-line speed is a plus, it's his ability to change his directions rapidly using a combination of his edges and advanced fakes that set him apart from most other skaters. There are times where Trevor will purposely telegraph his intentions when skating into a lane to manipulate the defense and draw them in before using his edges to completely change directions, resulting in additional space to make a play. He's a deceptive skater, a deceptive thinker, and has the ability to hide his stick-mechanics. This results in opposing goalies having trouble determining if he's attempting a pass or putting himself in position to shoot, which at times leaves both goalies and defenses vulnerable as a result. His ability to adjust play and slow it down with his gear shifts, while being able to manipulate opposing players, speaks volumes to his hockey-sense which is high-end. Although Zegras is an instinctive playmaker, his shot is advanced, featuring a fast release-point that works well with his ability to mask his shooting mechanics. Although his shot is dangerous, in some of our viewings, he wouldn't use it consistently despite having a high-percentage shooting option.

This was more pronounced on the powerplay, where he would routinely look to thread passes through heavy traffic regardless of having a good angle to shoot from. When he wouldn't opt to pass or shoot, he showed a very good set of hands that made him dangerous when attempting to cut towards the net area. Trevor anticipates the play at a high-level and this complimented his hands, allowing him to make consistent offensive-zone entries while under heavy-pressure as well.

Although Zegras is very talented, there are elements to his game that made us uneasy. As an example, he does have an excellent set-of-hands, and although he's capable of using them at the right times to beat his opponents and create additional space, he also showed that he can use them at the wrong-times. This led to several unforced turnovers and poor puck-management. Additionally, his moxie that he displays when carrying the puck can work against him. He's not afraid to challenge multiple-players or control the play for extended periods of time, but sometimes held the puck too long and reduces his options as a result. Though, as the season progressed and towards the U18's, Trevor showed development in the above attributes, reducing his turnover rates and not forcing the play to the same extent as he was early in the year. Although Trevor has some work to do with reigning in his talent, he has also developed in attributes he was weaker in as the season has progressed away from the play. An example of this is in his compete level. He's become better at skating down pucks during forechecking sequences and his attention to detail in his own-end has continued to develop, showing the ability to intercept passes, position himself well, and support his defense. Lastly, he increased his tenacity during physical altercations and board battling sequences and kept up his improved pace at the international stage.

Zegras has the potential to become a top-6 playmaking center who can play the half-wall on the powerplay. The talent was always there but the maturity wasn't at the beginning of the season, however he's impressed us down the stretch by becoming a more efficient and detail-oriented player.

"The Sonny Milano concerns have gone away for me. His hockey sense and skill level are really high end." - NHL Scout, January 2019

"He needs to get stronger and improve his defensive play but he's been consistently better for me than Boldy or Turcotte and those guys. He's been the second best guy after Hughes in all my recent viewings." - NHL Scout, January 2019

"He's after Hughes for me on that team. Just ahead of Turcotte." - NHL Scout, January 2019

"F***ing kid had a 2 on 1 and all he had to do was make the simple pass, but no, he had to pull some fluff bullsh** fancy dangle garbage and the Russian D (defenseman) took it away from him." - NHL Scout, February 2019

"He had a 3 on 2 last night and he went to his backhand and tried a spin-o-rama to send it. That stuff is what scares me when I'm ranking him." - NHL Scout, February 2019

"There's no debate about his skill but we could debate the level of his compete and hockey sense. It's not great at times." - NHL Scout, March 2019

"I don't think he's a dumb player, he just plays a selfish game too often." - NHL Scout, March 2019

"His best assets are his skill and his brain. Skating is good, he won't blow by people but he's shifty as hell." - NHL Scout, April 2019

"Skating is like Patrick Kane" - NHL Scout, April 2019

"I think Zegras developed into the player Ryan Suzuki could have developed into but hasn't, not yet anyway." - HP Scout, Brad Allen

"I got mixed reviews on feedback from interviews. Some Scouts really liked him, others not so much. I didn't love some of the details but as you can see by our ranking, it wasn't enough to drop him on our list." - HP Scout, Mark Edwards, June 2019

2020 NHL DRAFT TOP 31

RANK	PLAYER	TEAM	LEAGUE	HEIGHT	WEIGHT	POS
1	Alexis Lafrenière	Rimouski Océanic	QMJHL	6'1"	192	LW
2	Lucas Raymond	Frölunda HC J20	SuperElit	5'10"	165	RW
3	Quinton Byfield	Sudbury Wolves	OHL	6'4"	194	C
4	Anton Lundell	HIFK	Liiga	6'1"	183	C
5	Cole Perfetti	Saginaw Spirit	OHL	5'10"	185	C
6	Alexander Holtz	Djurgårdens IF J20	SuperElit	6'0"	183	LW
7	Noel Gunler	Luleå HF J20	SuperElit	6'0"	176	RW
8	Dylan Holloway	Okotoks Oilers	AJHL	6'0"	192	LW
9	Marco Rossi	Ottawa 67's	OHL	5'9"	179	C
10	Yaroslav Askarov	SKA-Varyagi im. Morozova	MHL	6'3"	163	G
11	Justin Sourdif	Vancouver Giants	WHL	5'11"	165	C
12	Seth Jarvis	Portland Winterhawks	WHL	5'9"	165	RW
13	Justin Barron	Halifax Mooseheads	QMJHL	6'2"	192	D
14	Connor Zary	Kamloops Blazers	WHL	6'0"	174	C
15	Tim Stützle	Jungadler Mannheim U20	DNL U20	5'11"	165	C
16	Jamie Drysdale	Erie Otters	OHL	5'11"	165	D
17	Kaiden Guhle	Prince Albert Raiders	WHL	6'3"	187	D
18	Jacob Perreault	Sarnia Sting	OHL	5'11"	198	C
19	Braden Schneider	Brandon Wheat Kings	WHL	6'2"	209	D
20	Jan Mysak	HC Litvinov	Czech	6'0"	176	C
21	Vasili Ponomaryov	MHK Krylia Sovetov Moskva	MHL	6'0"	176	C
22	Hendrix Lapierre	Chicoutimi Saguenéens	QMJHL	6'0"	165	C
23	Ty Smilanic	U.S. National U17 Team	USDP	6'1"	168	C
24	Will Cuylle	Windsor Spitfires	OHL	6'2"	201	LW
25	Jake Sanderson	U.S. National U17 Team	USDP	6'1"	170	D
26	Rodion Amirov	Tolpar Ufa	MHL	6'0"	168	LW
27	Tyler Kleven	U.S. National U17 Team	USDP	6'4"	190	D
28	Helge Grans	Malmö Redhawks J20	SuperElit	6'2"	183	D
29	Jake Neighbours	Edmonton Oil Kings	WHL	5'11"	201	LW
30	Marat Khusnutdinov	Vityaz Podolks U18	Russia U18	5'9"	152	C
31	Blake Biondi	Hermantown	HIGH MN	6'0"	185	C

2020 NHL DRAFT PROSPECTS

AMBROSIO, COLBY
RC - Tri-City Storm (USHL) - 5'09" 168

Smart, industrious center who earned a fair amount of ice time on the best team in the USHL. With a dozen goals and assists in 57 games, Ambrosio made a good impression with Tri-City as a rookie from the Buffalo Jr. Sabres. In midget, he played with (and out-scored) Luke Tuch, another prominent '02. He has an infectious work rate and plays the game with a ton of pace on every shift. He motors around the rink quickly but is also very intelligent about where to go and what to do when he gets there. Colby doesn't over handle the puck; he gets it and moves it efficiently. It's easy for smaller, inexperienced players to let plays die with them, but the Welland, Ontario native does a fine job mitigating that. He has shown his worth as a puck retriever, he's first to a lot of pucks. The skill level hasn't blossomed yet, as again, the puck isn't on his stick a ton during games but he did get power play time and cashed on it. In the same way that he quickly dishes pucks, his release and finishing moves show a lot of promise too. And though nine of his points came with the man advantage, he still maintained a plus-11 rating which was fifth best among the club's forward group. He'll likely have the opportunity to feature a little bit more prominently next season, which will hopefully give him the confidence and ability to be impactful against the top-end teams in the league – as he fell a little short in that regard this past year. The underlying skill level and the incredible pace at which he plays the game makes him a player to watch closely for 2020.

AMIROV, RODION
LW - Tolpar Ufa (MHL) - 6'00" 168

Rodion Amirov had a very productive year for the Russia U18 squad and Tolpar of the MHL. He produced 22 points and 9 goals for the Russian U18 team, and 26 points in 31 games, including 13 goals for Tolpar. In the playoffs, he continued producing with 6 points in 8 games, including 4 goals. At the Hlinka, he produced 2 assists in 5 games, then at the World-Junior-A-Challenge, he produced 3 points in 6 games, and at the U18's he was named one of the top players of the event with 9 points in 7 games, with 6 goals. Beating out Podkolzin and other prospects at the events in terms of generating points. Amirov is a quick-striking sniper who has an excellent, yet varied shot. Both his snap-shot and wrist-shot are excellent, featuring quick-releases. He presents to the goalie with a static posture while simultaneously identifying opening seams. He's one of the better shooters in the 2020-class and is one of the top-Russian prospects heading into next-season as a result. He's not just a shooter though; he's adept at finding back-door options and is good at recognizing the position that his teammates want him in, so that he can receive the puck. Furthermore, he's dangerous in-tight to the net due to his puck-tracking ability and doesn't just score high-skilled goals. His hands are very-quick, and he used them to freeze goalies before getting off his wrist-shot which led to some very important shoot-out goals on the international-stage. Rodion needs to further increase his separating speed and continue to gain some size, but the talent is already there.

ANDRAE, EMIL
LD - HV71 U20 (Jr SuperElite) - 5'09" 183

Emil Andrae split his season between two teams. On HV71's U18 team, he served as an alternate captain, and had a strong offensive season with 4 goals and 22 assists for a total of 26 points in 28 games. He was also given the opportunity to play 23 games for HV71's U20 team, where he managed to record 2 goals and 5 assists for a total of 7 points in 23 games.

Andrae is a very offensive-minded defenseman who almost serves as an extra forward at times and plays a high risk, high reward type of game. He needs to learn to play a more polished, simple game, as every pass cannot be a deciding one. He skates the puck up ice elegantly, as he is an excellent skater with slightly above-average top speed and fantastic mobility and elusiveness. He can twist and turn with ease, and has an impressive puck-control while doing so. He is well-built and has a low center of gravity, which allows him to be steady and keep his balance, even when pressured by physical opponents. As Andrae often gambles with his decisions, it's fair to say that his play is inconsistent and he will have to adapt his game if he wants to be able to play in the SHL or even HockeyAllsvenskan in the near future. He likes to find the long stretch pass from his own zone and does so successfully (more often than not) and it's obvious that he is confident that he will succeed. His short passing game is actually pretty good, he still tries to make the deciding play here as well, but he has the vision and creativity to make really good plays to set up his teammates for scoring chances. He keeps his feet moving and is not afraid to stickhandle to create time and space for a smart pass. While his shot is not very hard, he has a quick release and good accuracy to it and it will give the goaltender enough trouble. He has a knack of finding openings through opponents who are trying to block his shots. Defensively, he does a good job staying close to the puck-carrier with his fine skating abilities, and he is very aggressive when an opportunity to steal the puck appears. Even though his biggest strengths lie in his offensive game, his defensive game isn't too bad. Despite not being a big, tall defenseman, he doesn't shy away from getting physical in front of the net and in the corners; he will throw his body around to stop attackers. There are times where he gets overly aggressive and exposes himself out of position, and overall, his defensive awareness is inconsistent.

Andrae played 23 games for Sweden's U-17 squad and produced 4 goals and 9 assists for a total of 13 points. He was mainly playing on the first pairing with fellow top 2020 prospect Helge Grans. If he can polish his game and mix it up with more low-risk plays, he could potentially be a guy for the top rounds in the 2020 NHL Entry Draft.

ASKAROV, YAROSLAV
G - SKA-1946 St. Petersburg (MHL) - 6'03" 163

Yaroslav Askarov had an incredible year internationally and played very well for St. Petersburg. He finished the season with a .921 save percentage and a 2.37GAA in 31 games played. In the playoffs, he produced a .898 save percentage. Internationally he was featured at the Hlinka, the U19-World-Junior-A-Challenge, the U18 Five-Nations, the World U17's and the World U18's. His best performances were at the U18-Five Nations where he helped Russia win the tournament, the World-Junior-A challenge where he posted .954 save-percentage and a 1.26 GAA in 4 games, and the U17's where he helped Russia capture a silver-medal while posting a .948 save percentage and a 1.40 GAA in 5 games. Yaroslav Askarov is one of the best goalie prospects of the last decade and has the same level of potential as Andrei Vasilevsky. He's remarkably talented, yet shows the modern-day characteristics that we look for when evaluating goalies. His skating ability is excellent; he has a narrow-stance which gives him the ability to push off laterally at an explosive-rate. Additionally, his movement allows him to rarely over-extend and he's capable of rapid-adjustments needed for error-correcting after misinterpreting the initial play-type. His fluidity blends into his anticipation, allowing him to take-away angles consistently. His reflexes are excellent but a bit behind a goalie like Saros at the same-age, but he does have the advantage in height. His compete-level is matched by his poise; he plays with ice in his veins and doesn't seem to get affected by the moment, usually elevating in critical situations instead of buckling. We haven't been more excited about a goalie-prospect in years.

BARRON, JUSTIN
RD - Halifax Mooseheads (QMJHL) - 6'02" 187

Barron is a Halifax product and was drafted by the Mooseheads with the 13th overall pick in the 2017 QMJHL Draft. In his second season with the Mooseheads, he established himself as one of the top defensemen on the team, finishing with 41 points in 68 games and playing in all situations on the ice. He also played for Team QMJHL against team Russia in November, as the youngest player selected by Team QMJHL. Before the season, he was also a key player for team Canada at the Hlinka-Gretzky Cup in August.

He took a big step in his development this season by improving his offensive output, getting more power play time this year compared to his rookie season. He also was very efficient when manufacturing offense at even-strength, as 27 of his 41 points came at 5-on-5 this year. Barron has good size. As he continues to progress, he will continue to get stronger physically, which will help with his plays in his own end and enable him to win more one-on-one battles. He's a good puck-rusher; he has great top speed and an effortless stride, generating some real good speed if he has room to skate in front of him. His hands are okay, but he will often use his great speed to beat guys wide instead of using his stickhandling skills. In the offensive zone and on the power play, he has an accurate shot from the point that he keeps low and hits the net with regularity. His shot is above-average and he often will prefer to use his wrist shot over his slapshot. He has above-average smarts as well, but we've seen him make some questionable decisions in our viewings this year, so it's something he'll need to improve on for next season: keeping his game simple. He's not an overly physical or aggressive defenseman, but he's capable of throwing some good hits along the boards when needed and it's something he'll need to be more consistent with in the years ahead. Barron has very good potential with his size and skating abilities. He's one of the top prospects from the QMJHL for the 2020 NHL Entry Draft.

BEAUDOIN, CHARLES
RW - Shawinigan Cataractes (QMJHL) - 6'00" 174

Beaudoin was the 2nd first-round pick for Shawinigan in last year's QMJHL Draft (11th overall). The Bromont product had a tough first year adjusting to major junior, as he finished the year with 9 goals and 18 points. He also took part in the Under-17 Hockey Challenge in November (playing for Team Black) but went pointless in 5 games.

Beaudoin has good size and can be tough to handle along the boards when he's using it to his advantage. He works hard, but when things don't go his way, he doesn't work well. He needs to learn to let the game come to him and not overly commit himself. This tendency leaves him out of position often. Beaudoin's best asset is his ability to score goals; he has the potential to score a lot of goals in the QMJHL due to his good shot and quick release. He can be a poison in front of the net or in the slot on the power play. His on-ice vision and smarts are average, though, he's shoot-first type of winger and he doesn't always make the best decisions with the puck. Sometimes, he won't see an open teammate, can try to force plays and end up turning the puck over. He's got to work on his skating also, as his feet are heavy and his speed is only average. In order for him be drafted next season, he'll need to get quicker and improve his decision-making.

BEDNAR, JAN
G - HC Karlovy Vary (Czech) - 6'04" 185

Jan Bednar had an excellent season, splitting time between the Czech U19 league and the Czech league, while developing in Karlovy Vary's system. With the U19 squad, he produced a .917 save-percentage and a 2.39 GAA in 22 games, and at the men's level he produced a .917 save-percentage with a 2.73 GAA in 10 games. In relegation, he had a .915 save percentage and a 2.59 GAA in 5 games. Internationally, he was less successful, posting a .848 save percentage at the U17's and a .902 save-percentage in 2 starts at the U18's. Bednar is a fluid, butterfly-style goalie who takes up a lot of the net. He can seamlessly transition from his reverse-VH into his butterfly; and can extend into transitioning out of his butterfly effortlessly. He's a tall goalie that knows how to "stand-tall" in his crease when in his butterfly position by maintaining excellent-posture. His athleticism is high-end, showing the ability to fully-extend on certain shot-types. His glove-hand was well above-average when we got to see him on the ice and he can make difficult stops in combination with his long-legs when he looks to fully sprawl across the ice-surface. In order for Jan to take the next step for us this up-coming season; he's going to need to read the play quicker behind the goal-line, , continue to refine his stance so that it's more narrow from a standing-position, and learn how to recover without falling onto his chest during secondary save-attempts as often as he currently does.

BENNING, MICHAEL
RD- Sherwood Park Crusaders (AJHL) - 5'09" 170

Benning is a Denver University commit who opted for the college route over the WHL. This season he was a force in the AJHL, with 61 points in 60 games to tie for the leagues defenseman scoring lead. Numbers like these have not been registered by a 16 year old defenseman in the AJHL since the 1980's and watching Benning he is clearly a special player. Benning exudes extreme calm and confidence on the ice, never panicking under pressure and making creative plays when others would be throwing the puck away. When he is on the ice the game runs through him. Benning is dominant on the breakout at this level, easily shaking forecheckers and firing pinpoint passes to streaking teammates. Benning also has the ability to jump in to the rush and can knife his way through the neutral zone with great agility and awareness. He has the unique ability to make a play as soon as he sees it and every move he makes looks unforced and deliberate. In the offensive zone he also shines, demanding the puck on the blueline and has the quickness to embarrass forwards rushing out to challenge him. Benning shows the rare ability to attack the slot as a defenseman and is constantly surveying the ice for open teammates. Benning dominates on the powerplay with excellent distribution skills, but could work on his shot further as he is a likely powerplay quarterback at the next level. Defensively Benning has an excellent stick and plays with an extremely aggressive gap, constantly utilizing the cross pressure technique through the neutral zone. He tries to dictate the oppositions move with a very proactive approach. Sometimes this leaves him in trouble as he can gamble a bit too much and hang himself out to dry. While not dominant in puck battles he has a good understanding of how to use leverage and body positioning to box out bigger players. Benning is a new age defenseman who has the potential to be an offensive force at the NHL level someday.

BIAKABUTUKA, JEREMIE
RD - Val-d'Or Foreurs (QMJHL) - 6'03" 194

Biakabutuka was the 17th overall selection in the 2017 QMJHL Draft out of the Collège Charles-Lemoyne Midget AAA program on the South Shore of Montreal. In his first season, the big defenseman saw some good ice time as the year went on, and played a regular shift all year long. He saw his ice time on the PP and PK units increase over time. Physically, he was definitely ready to play major junior this year. He's strong along the wall and even if he's not super aggressive physically, he's more than adept to clear out the front of the net because he's got great strength. He's got good hockey sense and made some smart pinches during the year while supporting the rush and creating an extra option for his teammates in the offensive zone. On the power play, he can be a threat because of his great slapshot from the point; he'll need to improve his release and get his shot off more quickly, though. He only had 56 shots in 65 games this season; he'll need to use his shot more often next season with added ice time on the power play. Other areas he'll need to improve on are his footwork and overall skating abilities, and he needs to play at higher pace and be quicker on the ice. Biakabutuka is a great athlete who comes from a family of athletes (his uncle Tim was a star running-back for Michigan in the NCAA and the Carolina Panthers in the NFL). He was not selected in November for the World Under-17 Hockey Challenge, but will certainly want to prove people wrong next season in his NHL draft year.

BIONDI, BLAKE
RC - Hermantown High (MNHS) - 6'00" 185

Biondi had a highly productive sophomore season for the Hawks, registering 28 goals and 27 assists in 25 regular season games. Biondi also saw some time with the USNTDP U17 team where he was able to step into the lineup and produce from the start. Biondi then finished the season with Sioux City (USHL) where he fit in nicely in their top six down the stretch and into the playoffs. Biondi is a speedy goal scorer that can use his speed to drive the edge on defenders and has the hands to finish around the net area. Biondi is a strong and explosive skater; he is difficult to contain off the rush as well as separate from pucks down low. Blake's shot has pro upside; he displays an accurate, quick and deceptive release point. Biondi has been rumored to join the USNTDP for 19-20 but has not made any plans public. His USHL rights are owned by Sioux City (USHL) who will make a push to get the power forward in the lineup full time next season. Hermantown is an annual contender for the Minnesota Class A State title, which is a big draw for Minnesota kids, so Blake has a lot of options for next season. Biondi's skill set and hockey sense give him top six upside at the NHL level and will make him a highly scouted prospect next season wherever he decides to play. Biondi is committed to play for his hometown Minnesota Duluth Bulldogs in the future.

BLOMQVIST, JOEL
G - Karpat U20 (Jr. A SM-Liiga) - 6'01" 176

Blomqvist is the top goaltending prospect out of Finland for the 2020 NHL Entry Draft. He was the national team's top goalie at the U-17 level this season. He also played with the U-18 national team at the February U-18 Five Nations' Tournament, and was with the team at the April World Under-18 Hockey Championships but didn't see any action there. Back home in Finland, he split the season with Karpat's U18 and U20 teams, posting some real good numbers at both levels. He's a good-sized goaltender standing at over 6'01" and still growing. He covers a lot of space in his net and doesn't leave a lot of room for shooters. He makes himself look big in net by challenging opponents aggressively at the top of his crease. He's agile and has good athleticism, as he showed us strong post-to-post pushes. His puck-tracking is solid, and he has a good compete level, as he never quits on any puck and can make 2nd and 3rd saves regularly. He's got to work on his consistency, however, in addition to the fact that he can lack focus at certain moments in games. He should be back in the U20 league next season in Finland, but could also challenge for some ice time in Liiga. He should be Finland's top guy next season with the U-18 national team, starting with the Hlinka tournament in August.

BOLTMANN, JAKE
RD - Edina HS (MNHS) - 6'00" 180

Boltmann is a physical stay at home defenseman out of Edina High School. While Boltmann's offensive development has leveled off, his skating and defensive zone awareness continues to trend in the right direction. Boltmann plays a heavy game in all three zones; he is able to step up on players and deliver big hits and plays with a lot of physicality in his own end. Boltmann doesn't have high end playmaking offensive skill but he can consistently exit his own end reliability, both using passing and skating. In the offensive end, Boltmann has a heavy point shot but doesn't get into a lot of situations to utilize it yet. He defers a lot from the point and plays a more stay at home style that takes very few chances and will give up the offensive blueline easily. His gap control is good, but his foot speed and agility make him susceptible to getting beat wide if he loses positioning and containment. Boltmann is a prospect that has been considered high end for the last couple seasons but seems that High School hockey is no longer a challenge for him and could use a move to Junior hockey this year in order for his development to continue to progress. Boltmann is a University of Minnesota commit.

BORDELEAU, THOMAS
LC - USA NTDP-17 (USHL) - 5'09" 172

Highly skilled centerman with a very unique path to this point. The son of former NHLer, Sebastien Bordeleau, Thomas was born in Texas but when his father signed in Switzerland he spent a good portion of his youth overseas. When the Bordeleau's returned to Quebec, Thomas developed in the Belle Province. He last played AAA with College Esther-Blondin, where he was second in the midget circuit in scoring with 64 points in 38 games. Because he has U.S. citizenship, he was eligible to make the jump to the NTDP. In terms of overall scoring, he led the U17s with 39 points – 22 of which came in 34 USHL games. Bordeleau plays a cool, composed game with the puck. He has a lot of subtle skill and can do some very advanced things with the puck on his tape. His arrays of unique finishing moves, bolstered by a plus shot, are potentially lethal at this level. He skates just as well with the puck as he does without it. Despite only being 5'9", he does protect the puck well and can make just enough space for himself to get loose. He's a good skater, but maybe not explosive at the top-end which is probably more of leg strength issue than a mechanical flaw. Sometimes he looks a little too cool for school, and it makes us question his compete level a bit – especially on the backcheck. Against sustained attacks, if he's even close to being positionally correct, he is often late to react to his checks anyhow. His decision making will be something to watch as he becomes accustomed to – and gets a fair shot at - the league next season. The offensive tools, particularly with his finishing ability, will make him a very tempting piece for NHL clubs in 2020.

BOURQUE, MAVRIK
RC - Shawinigan Cataractes (QMJHL) - 5'10" 165

Bourque was the 3rd overall pick in the 2018 QMJHL Draft and had a great rookie year, finishing with 25 goals and 54 points, good for the top rank among players from the 2018 draft class. Bourque had a slow start with the Cataractes, but by the month of November, he was fully adjusted to the QMJHL. He had 7 points in his first 15 games of the year, but finished with 47 points in his last 49 regular season games and added 5 points in 6 playoff games against the top team in the league (Rouyn-Noranda).

Bourque is a decent skater who demonstrates good quickness in tight, but will need to improve his acceleration and top speed. He's very good on the power play, already scoring 10 of his 25 goals this year on the man-advantage. There, he would often play on the right wing around the faceoff circle, and he scored many goals with his one-timer. He likes to handle the puck from the half-wall; he's got an above-average shot and his vision is excellent. He can find teammates with some high-quality passes in the offensive zone. It is tough to defend against him; he is as good a scorer as he is a playmaker. His hockey sense is really good as well; he sees the ice very well and has great anticipation, knowing before anyone else where the puck will end up. He'll need to get stronger and faster, but he's got great hockey IQ and makes players around him better. Even at his size, he's not afraid to go to the net looking for rebounds (he scored quite a few goals from two feet from the net this year). Along the boards, he's not a physical player, but he's not soft either. His physical implication will get better as he continues to get stronger physically. Bourque has good potential, and his rookie season was a great example of what he can do on the ice. It was impressive to see him perform like he did with Shawinigan, one of the worst teams in the league this year. Bourque has the talent to be one of the top players from the QMJHL for the 2020 NHL Entry Draft.

BOWEN, ETHAN
C- Chilliwack Chiefs (BCHL) - 6'02" 161

A top prospect in western Canada throughout the WHL bantam draft process, Bowen fell in the draft when he chose the college route with a commitment to North Dakota before even playing a junior game. Bowen played this season for his hometown Chilliwack Chiefs, recording 39 points in 58 games. Bowen is a long and lanky centre who plays a very cerebral style. Bowen is not very powerful as a skater, but faster than he looks as he covers a lot of ground with a long fluid stride. Bowen will look like he's gliding while pulling away from a player. With the puck on his stick Bowen has the ability to attack defenses with good hands, and a very strong variety of passes he can execute. Bowen excels passing on his backhand which adds a major dimension for defenses to account for. Currently he is a better player without the puck with good anticipation, taking smart routes to support puck carriers on the breakout, and getting in to dangerous spaces after floating high in the zone offensively. Bowen has excellent tools defensively with good natural positioning and engagement. He also has a good stick and can use his reach to recover the puck. At times Bowen can appear to lack intensity and would benefit from more constant engagement. Bowen should have a strong showing next season in the BCHL as his skills expand and he becomes more of an offensive focal point for his team.

BRISSON, BRENDAN
L/LW - Shattuck St. Mary's (USHS) - 5'10" 168

Brisson is a late 01' birth date who is coming off a highly offensively productive season with the Shattuck St, Mary's prep team where he led them in points with 42 goals and 59 assists in 55 games. Brisson also saw 6 games this past season with Green Bay (USHL) who drafted him in the 10th Round of the Phase 1 draft in 2017. Brisson is an up-tempo player that likes to make things happen off the rush as he enters the offensive zone. Brisson shows good vision and timing off the rush where he can quickly feed pucks through lanes and likes to move East-West and force defenses to adjust with the puck on his tape. Brisson will have to add more North-South to his game to be as effective at the upper levels as teams are better at taking the middle of the ice away but Brisson has the skill to make this adjustment going forward. Brisson's skating isn't dynamic but possesses a decent top gear, especially with the puck. The red flag for Brisson right now is he is a late 01' birth date and how much better will his skating get, even with some added strength? Brisson shows good effort at both ends, he is able to win puck battles along the boards in his own end and has the skill to move pucks reliability to get the puck out of the zone. Brendan doesn't bring a lot in the way of physicality and relies on his hands and puck skills to win puck more than using his body to move opponents off pucks. Brisson will no doubt be moving to junior hockey next season before heading to the University of Michigan in the future.

BURNS, BRADY
LC - Saint John Sea Dogs (QMJHL) - 5'07" 145

Burns was a nice surprise this year with the Sea Dogs after being drafted 29th overall in June 2018. The Nova Scotia native had a good season, finishing with 29 points in 65 games, outscoring a lot of players who were selected before him (including his teammate Josh Lawrence – by one point).

Burns played mostly at center in the 2nd half of the season, but played some games on the wing in the first half. He's undersized, listed at 5'07" and 145 pounds (though he does look a bit bigger on the ice). Nevertheless, his size will be without a doubt a topic of discussion in his NHL draft year. Burns doesn't play like a smaller player, though; he has a great motor and a great compete level. His lack of size and strength does affect him during the year; his level of energy goes up and down due to fatigue and results in inconsistent performances. Burns has decent speed, but his main asset is his hockey IQ. He thinks the game really well, is a very smart playmaker, and makes players around him better. It was a tough year in Saint John this year, as they were the second-worst team in the league. There was either not a lot of talent or talented teammates with no experience. With more experience in the league, Burns could become a good player shorthanded. He has good anticipation and hustle, which could make him a good player on the PK unit. He'll need to improve his shot; it's average at the moment and in order to score his goals, he usually needs to be close to the net to be successful. Overall, Burns has a lot of qualities that we like, but next season will be a better indicator to determine whether or not there is potential for the NHL with him – or to say that he's just a very good junior player.

BUTLER, CAMERON
RW - Peterborough Petes (OHL) - 6'04" 198

We had him ranked 34th and Peterborough ended up taking him with the 27th pick in the OHL-draft. He had a solid-season with the Petes, where he managed to get powerplay time along the half-wall and play with some other talented players. He finished the season with 26 points in 64 games, including 18 goals. At the World U17's, he went pointless and had a disappointing performance overall despite flashing his talent. Butler is a towering winger, with an excellent tool-set. The most impressive aspect of his game are his puck-skills; his length allows him to make highly technical dekes and he can curl the puck in-tight to his body rapidly, giving him an excellent release-point. Additionally, he's good at anticipating the play, giving him the ability to use his impressive skating-ability to weave through players when attempting to drive down the right-wing. He was dangerous with the man-advantage, showing the ability to shoot in one-motion and he generates a lot of power off his shots; beating goalies clean by overpowering them. The biggest issue with Butler's game heading into next season is that he's prone to inconsistent stretches where he doesn't dictate play nearly to the degree his tools suggest that he can.

BYFIELD, QUINTON
LC - Sudbury Wolves (OHL) - 6'04" 214

Quinton Byfield had a tremendous season for the Wolves after going 1st overall in the OHL-draft, and finishing with the best point totals out of any OHL-rookie forward since Travis Konecny. He won the OHL-Rookie-Of-The-Year-Award after producing 61 points in 64 games, including 29 goals. He was one of the main reasons that the Wolves managed to make the playoffs, and finished with 8 points in 8 games, including 3 goals. At the U17's, he produced 3 points in 5 games for Canada Black. Byfield brings tremendous tools packed into a massive-frame. He's an excellent-skater given his age, size, and mechanics. His skating and take-over-mentality gives him a high-octane motor, which he used to overwhelm and physically impose himself down-low, and around the net-area. His puck-skills are very-good. He can beat opponents cleanly 1-on-1, and can make creative-dekes given his wing-span and ability to rapidly pull the puck. His hands extend into his release point, giving him the ability to suddenly shift-angles with his length, and he can wrap-pucks at extreme-angles in-tight to the net. Quinton isn't a selfish player, and is also a capable passer, demonstrating the ability to execute give-and-go sequences and cycle-plays while in full-motion. He's mature for his age away from the puck, and used his length and pace in our viewings to help his defenseman out on most nights. Byfield is the complete-package but it wouldn't hurt for his development if he continued becoming a true 200-foot-player and adding another level to his already impressive puck-skills. Another reason we are excited about Quinton's development is due to his age; he's one of the younger players in the class, yet is one of the most complete.

CHABRIER, BRANDON
RD - North Jersey Avalanche (T1EHL) - 6'00" 152

Brandon split the 18/19 season between Portledge Prep School and North Jersey Avalanche U16 (T1EHL). Chabrier is a 1st Round 11th overall draft pick of the Lincoln Stars (USHL) and a Northeastern University commit. Brandon was also drafted in the 12th Round of the OHL Draft by Flint. Brandon is a plus skater that uses his feet to be an effective puck rusher out of his own end. Chabrier has excellent four-way directional skating and the hands to match which make him difficult to corner and force into turnovers. Chabrier picks his spots well to join the rush and does a good job finding the soft spots off the rush to get into position for scoring opportunities. Chabrier displays dynamic puck moving ability at the top of the zone and possesses a good array of shots he can use to get pucks through to the net from the point position. For all the offensive upside Chabrier has, his best asset at this point is his defensive game. Brandon is able to use his skating to close off opponents on the rush and quickly eliminate scoring chances before they can develop. Chabrier brings a decent amount of physicality, he has shown the ability to time and finish guys along the boards off the rush as well as play physical against opponents in the crease area. Chabrier is a player we will be closely watching next season to see how he adjusts to Junior hockey which will ultimately determine his NHL draft value.

CHOUPANI, MATT
RC - Lac St-Louis Lions (LHMAAAQ) - 5'10" 172

Choupani was one of the most improved players in Midget AAA this season, finishing 2nd overall in scoring and amassing a total of 108 points (54 goals) in 58 games with the Lac St-Louis Lions this season. He made some big improvements in his skating and consistency compared to last year, and it really showed in terms of results. He was drafted in the 9th round by Blainville-Boisbriand last year and committed to Northeastern University; he's expected to go the NCAA route now. Choupani has an excellent wrist shot with a quick release. He has great puck skills; he's a threat one-on-one and controls the puck very well in tight spaces. He sees the ice well and he's a good playmaker as well. He is as good a finisher as he is a playmaker. As previously mentioned his skating has improved since last year; his speed is better, but mostly he's moving his feet way more and being more active on the ice. He's not an overly physical player and his compete level is fine; depending where he plays next year, he'll need to be stronger physically to play against bigger players. He's not a liability away from the puck, and gives an honest effort backchecking and in his zone to get the puck back.

CHROMIAK, MARTIN
LW - HK Dluka Trencin U20 (Slovakia U20) - 6'00" 179

Chromiak is a Slovak prospect who had a great year in the Slovak U20 league, with 46 points in 39 games. This was good for 6th overall in league scoring and top among U-17 players in the league. He also played internationally for his country in various tournaments during the year at both the U-17 and U-18 levels. Chromiak has excellent on-ice vision and the ability to make some high-end passes to his teammates. He's got good puck poise and doesn't rush any plays, as he likes to slow them down and open things up for his teammates on the ice. He's a right-handed shot, but usually plays on left wing. On the power play, he likes to run things on the left-side half-wall position. He has good hands, good one-on-one abilities and an accurate shot (either wrist or snapshot). He's solid both with and without the puck, has good smarts and strong positional game. In order for him to become a better prospect for the NHL Draft next season, he'll need to improve his skating abilities, acceleration and top speed. Also, he has decent size, but we would like to see him get more involved physically and engage more along the boards. Chromiak could be a good candidate to come over to the CHL next season for his NHL draft year, or possibly go elsewhere in Europe such as Sweden or Finland. He could also play in Slovakia's men's league, as he played 2 games with HK Dluka Trencin this season. Interesting player to keep tabs on and see where he ends up playing for his NHL draft season.

CIKHART, JAN
LW - Bili Tygri Liberec U19 (Czech U19) - 6'03" 187

Cikhart is a power-forward from the Czech Republic who played in the Czech U19 league, where he had 31 points (18 goals) in 40 games. He's a big kid who's has quick feet and above-average speed. He moves well for a kid of his age and size. He's still growing into his body and will need to add more weight to his frame. He's still a bit awkward on the ice in his movements; he can lose balance at times, but that should improve with time as he gets stronger. He's a shoot-first type of winger. He's got an above-average shot with a quick release. He can sometime shoot from anywhere in the offensive zone, but he has not showed much vision and creativity yet in the offensive zone. His hockey sense is average at this point; he needs to slow down the play a bit more and take a look at his options, not just shooting for the sake of shooting. He's got a good compete level, he's engaged physically, and once he gets stronger he'll be better to win those puck battles compared to right now. Intriguing prospect with his size and shooting abilities. He is one to keep an eye on next season if he can improve other aspects of his game.

CLANG, CALLE
G - Rögle BK U20 (Jr. SuperElite) - 6'02" 176

Calle Clang is a super-athletic goaltender playing for Rögle BK U20 in the SuperElite league. He started in 24 games this season, recording a 2.82 GAA and a .907 save percentage. He won 50% of his starts. He also played two games with his club's U-18 team, where he posted a 3.05 GAA and a .907 save percentage.

Clang has an interesting combination of size and athleticism. He covers big chunks of the net, but can still make those important desperation saves to save an otherwise sure goal. He plays a super-aggressive style where he forces shooters to make a move. He comes out from his crease to challenge shooters, and he anticipates their shots really well. He can be this aggressive since he is very vocal with his defenders and sets out to save the first shot and an occasional rebound, relying on his defender to collect loose pucks and rebounds. As most modern goaltenders are, he is great with his catching glove and his blocker side is slightly above-average. Openings can be found at the five-hole level and by moving him sideways. Even though he is super-quick in his lateral movements, he tends to make big moves, and he can be caught out of position before he fully recovers. His aggressiveness combined with his size makes him a big presence in net, and he makes himself look even bigger than he actually is. Clang competes super hard and battles for every loose puck and for a line of sight in every single situation. He is also very strong and can fight his way through screens and opponents blocking his sight. What's impressive with Clang is how he manages to stay calm and composed at all times, despite his rather vivid playing style. He rarely gets riled up and keeps his focus on his own game at all times. His skating is good, and so is his balance. He maneuvers around the crease and the net with ease. He can handle the puck and distribute hard, accurate passes as well, which is always appreciated by his forwards on the transition. Internationally, he played 10 games for Sweden at the U-17 level and played excellent for his team. He was also a part of the U-18 team that won the U-18 World Championships as their third goaltender.

COMMESSO, DREW
G - USA NTDP-17 (USHL) - 6'01" 170

Quick and agile goaltender with a really strong technical foundation. Commesso joins the Program from St. Sebastian's School in Massachusetts. The U17 starting goaltender position can be a taxing chore because of the nature of the team and the competition they face, so the 3.48 GAA and .889 save pct. behind a 5-12-4 record is far from relevant. Probably the most obvious trait of Commesso's is his movement in the crease and how easy he makes it look. He's a good skater and his shuffle ability is a big plus already. There's obviously going to be some core strength issues for a goalie this young in terms of keeping his shoulders upright when making those bigger pushes and it doesn't help that he's naturally a compact butterfly net minder, but it's something we expect to improve fairly quickly. Where the compact style comes in handy is in his rebound control, he does a really fine job getting soft on shots that hit him in the body and it prevents him from regurgitating a lot of pucks into the slot. On rushes that originate on or outside the dot line, he's an overlap setup with his short-side post that morphs into a RVH integration. This is a little bit unique in terms of utilization for an American goaltender, but it really jives well with his skill set actually. He's a low-setup goalie in his butterfly, so the overlap allows him to keep a shoulder on the short side instead of just relying on an extremity and his lateral quickness can compensate for the long side. He actively directs rebounds into unproblematic areas with his blocker and his pads on a consistent basis. He has the glove of a former baseball player, and looks very comfortable looking pucks into his mitt and catching them clean. High glove shots are looking like a work in progress for him because of how reliant he is on that compact butterfly style. His stick positioning is surprisingly good for a player of his age and he looks very comfortable playing the puck outside of the net. We've spotted a few instances where Drew's second- and third-save mechanics show a little bit of panic, but he generally holds up well and keeps himself in good shape to square up to the next shot. He does have a tendency to get backed up into his crease with traffic around. He's a smart player who tracks the puck well, so he can make it work for now – but he'll need to be able to fight through traffic that attempts to box him into the deeper blue. The Boston University commit was also the 11th overall pick in the QMJHL American Draft by Quebec. Given the technical makeup of this young goalie at 16, there's reason to believe he could be the first goalie chosen in the 2020 NHL Entry Draft.

CORMIER, LUKAS
LD - Charlottetown Islanders (QMJHL) - 5'08" 170

Cormier was one of the top rookies this year in the QMJHL, finishing the year with 15 goals and 36 points. With his 15 goals, he ranked 2nd all-time in QMJHL history for goals by a 16-year-old defenseman. Cormier's game got better as the year progressed; he amassed 25 points of his 36 points after the Christmas break.zxssQ

He was drafted 4th overall by Charlottetown in the 2018 QMJHL Draft. This year, he played in November at the World Under-17 Hockey Challenge, and in April, he was selected to take part in camp for Team Canada at the U-18 World Championships. Cormier is an excellent puck-moving defenseman; he's very quick to move pucks out of his zone either by skating them out or with a quick pass out of zone. He's got good footwork and he's quick to retrieve pucks in his own zone. He makes quick decisions and is quick to move pucks into transition. In the offensive zone, he's got great puck poise and he's active with his feet when he's trying to create offense. What makes him dangerous is he's got the ability to create plays on his own with above-average puck skills, but he also possesses excellent on-ice vision to create chances for his teammates on the ice. He's good at using his quick feet to move around on the blueline in order to find better shooting or passing lanes. He's tough to defend against one-on-one because of his skill level, footwork and elusiveness on the ice. Defensively, he's a smart defender, but his lack of size is a concern for the NHL. He's not tall, but he's quite strong physically for a 5'08" defenseman, so he's not overmatched as often. However, he's still limited against bigger forwards down low in his zone or in front of his net due to his lack of height. There's a lot to like with Cormier; he's your prototypical small puck-moving defenseman that we see more and more of in today's NHL. He's got things to improve on, but he was highly impressive in his rookie year in the QMJHL.

COULOMBE, ANTOINE
Goaltender- Shawinigan Cataractes (QMJHL) - 5'11" 186

Coulombe was the first goalie selected in the 2018 QMJHL Draft (35th overall) by Shawinigan. He made the Cataractes' lineup out of training camp and was put in a tough situation, playing a lot of minutes on a bad team. His numbers took a hit, as in 41 games he maintained a goals-against average of 5.19 and a save-percentage of .863%. Similar to Jonathan Lemieux last season in Val-d'Or, Coulombe was rushed to the league, or at least not protected enough. We are hoping that he can bounce back next season like Lemieux did this season with the Foreurs. The Montmagny native is an average-sized goaltender, standing around 6'00", and we are hoping he can grow an inch or two in the summer as this would help his cause for the NHL. He's an athletic goaltender with quick lateral movements who does a good job covering the lower part of the net. He's steady in his net; he's not usually overly-aggressive and covers a lot of space due to his strong technical base. He had some struggles with his rebound-control this season, but also he saw a lot of pucks. Shawinigan had all kinds of difficulties this year getting pucks out of their zone, so there was a lot of pressure on their goaltenders to make saves repeatedly. Even with that tough year, we are not too worried about his future as a good QMJHL goaltender, but as far as the NHL goes, he'll need to have some great performances in the future in order to overshadow the concerns in regards to his size.

CRNKOVIC, KYLE
LW- Saskatoon Blades (WHL) - 5'06.5" 153

Crnkovic was drafted 10th overall in the WHL bantam draft. After beginning the year injured Crnkovic came in and produced 31 points in 52 with his role beginning on the bottom lines before working his way in to the top 6. He also represented Canada Black at the world u17s registering 5 points in 5 games. Crnkovic is an undersized winger with excellent compete and instincts. He sees the play developing both offensively and defensively, as he made advanced timing passes and jumped in to passing lanes for interceptions. He is an adept puck handler with the ability to beat a defender in one on one situations. Crnkovic does a good job of using his quickness in the corners but is still sometimes physically overmatched due to his small stature. Despite his size limitations Crnkovic does not shy away from physicality and competes as hard as anyone, he is going in on every 50/50 puck. While Crnkovic doesn't have the elite skill and skating to be a top prospect at his size, he should make a big impact in Saskatoon next season.

CUYLLE, WILL
LW - Windsor Spitfires (OHL) - 6'02" 201

Will Cuylle came onto the Spitfires after getting drafted 3rd-overall in the OHL-draft. He scored a pair of goals in his first OHL game, in what was the start of a productive rookie-season. He finished with 41 points in 63 games, including 26 goals. In the playoffs, he had 3 points in 4 games, including 2 goals. Internationally, he played for Canada Black at the U17's, finishing with 3 points in 5 games. Cuylle is a power-winger who can snipe the puck. His greatest attribute is his wrist-shot. He has an elite release-point and needs no-time or space to get it off his blade. He's a powerful kid who knows how to rotate through his shot-motion, and processes the placement of his shot rapidly; this extends to his hand-eye coordination. The result is a shot that's both capable of over-powering net minders but can beat them by shifting his-angle so they misinterpret the initial point of contact off his blade. Although not a gifted playmaker, he can interpret open-lanes and put himself in positions to receive passes; he can also use his frame to barrel his way into traffic while waiting for his teammates to set him up. Away from the puck, he's capable of overwhelming smaller players with his frame on the backcheck and can body players along the boards. There's a tremendous tool-kit built into Will, he just needs to increase his pace at times and become more consistent.

DAVID, ALEXANDRE
RC/RW - Acadie-Bathurst Titan (QMJHL) - 5'08" 173

David was drafted by Acadie-Bathurst 26th overall in the 2018 QMJHL Draft. He had a tough rookie season with the Titan, battling injuries and playing on the worst team in the league. An offensive-minded player, he produced only 2 goals and 5 points in 49 games. He's a good skater with a good burst of speed; his skating abilities are the best part of his game. He has good hands and can be a threat one-on-one. However, he needs to get more involved in the tougher areas of the ice; he's currently a perimeter player. He's versatile, though, as he can play both down the middle and on the wing. This season with the Titan, he only had 38% success rate in the faceoff circle. Next season, look for his role on the team to expand; he should get top-6 minutes. He has above-average smarts and good awareness in his zone; he has the potential to become a good player shorthanded due to his speed and anticipation. His size will be an issue for the NHL Draft if he doesn't produce at a very high level next season.

DESNOYERS, ELLIOT
LW - Moncton Wildcats (QMJHL) - 5'11" 178

Desnoyers was the last pick in the 1st round of the 2018 QMJHL Draft when he was selected 18th overall by the Moncton Wildcats. He had a decent first year in the league with his 31 points in 61 games; he was physically ready for major junior after having played two seasons of Midget AAA hockey with the St-Hyacinthe Gaulois. He's a strong player on his skates who skates well and plays hard. He was highly-touted coming through the minor hockey system in Quebec, but he has really done a good job rounding out his game (he's not considered to be a high-end skills' guy). He plays with some good intensity along the boards. He can finish his hits and does a good job protecting the puck down low. He's not afraid to go to the net; a lot of his goals come from close to the net on rebounds or redirections in front of the net. He works hard on the PK unit too; he's got value there as well, making him a solid two-way player. Next year it will be interesting to see how Desnoyers' offensive upside can grow, and that should tell us a whole lot about his NHL potential for the 2020 NHL Entry Draft, because the rest of his game is solid.

DESROCHES, CHARLIE
RD - Saint John Sea Dogs (QMJHL) - 5'10" 165

Desroches is a P.E.I. native who had a good rookie season in a tough situation with the Saint John Sea Dogs; he finished the year with 10 goals and 27 points. The Sea Dogs selected him out of the Selects Hockey Academy program in Connecticut with the 32nd overall pick in the draft, even though he was touted as one of the best defensemen eligible in this draft class. At the time, he was committed to Northeastern in the NCAA, but changed his mind after he was selected by the Sea Dogs. He has good skating abilities, is a good puck-rusher and is quick to skate the puck out of his zone. He's got good footwork, and he's quick to retrieve pucks in his own zone. His good footwork helps him when defending against quick forwards. In the offensive zone, he does a good job moving around to find a better shooting lane. He possesses a hard shot from the point and does a good job keeping it low. He is a good puck-distributor from the point, not elite, but well above the norm. He's got to learn to make simple plays instead of the low-percentage play, but this is something that every young offensive defenseman needs to learn at some point. Defensively, it was not easy to evaluate Desroches this year, as Saint John was frequently overmatched and spent a ton of time in their own zone.

Obviously, he'll need to get stronger physically in order to become more difficult to play against in his own zone. By being stronger physically, he's going to be better at moving guys from the front of the net or at least just be stronger on their sticks to prevent them from getting rebounds. His positional game needs some work, which is also common in young offensive defensemen. We like Desroches' potential; we are looking forward to seeing how he does next year on a better Saint John team. He's got the skills to make some significant noise next year in the QMJHL, and in regards to his standing in the NHL draft.

DOUCET, ALEXANDRE
LW - Magog Cantonniers (LHMAAAQ) - 5'10" 190

Doucet was the 4th-leading scorer in the LHMAAAQ this season and led the league in playoff goals with 21 in 15 games. Doucet was drafted in the 6th round by Val-d'Or in 2018, after playing his QMJHL Draft year in Midget Espoir.

Doucet is a good goal scorer. He is not a flashy skater, but once he is in the offensive zone, he's very good down low and around the net. He's strong physically and is tough to contain along the boards at the midget level due to his excellent puck-protection game and the fact that he uses his size well. When he doesn't have the puck, he puts good puck-pressure on his opponents on the forecheck, and he's quick to force opponents into rushing their decisions with the puck. He also has good anticipation and is capable of intercepting passes in the neutral zone with a good stick. He's going to have to work on getting quicker in the summer in order to make a smoother transition to the QMJHL with Val-d'Or next season. There's a lot to like here with Doucet, and he's going to a team where he should get quality ice time next season.

DRYSDALE, JAMIE
RD - Erie Otters (OHL) - 5'11" 165

Jamie Drysdale was selected 4th overall in the OHL draft and lived up to his selection. He finished the season with the most points from the backend for the Otters, finishing with 40 points in 63 games, including 7 goals. He played for Canada Black at the U17's, finishing with 4 assists while captaining the squad and played for Canada at the U18's, where he finished with 2 assists in 7 games. Drysdale is a modern-day, puck-rushing defenseman who sees the ice-well and his options quickly. He had very-good four-way mobility and impressive edges which give him escape ability down below the goal-line, which is critical given his size. He's defensively responsible and uses his mobility to get in the way of shooting lanes; he also aggressively cuts down his gaps. He can make quality outlet passes but looks to become the transport option regularly; using advanced spatial-awareness to weave through traffic, generating transitional zone-entries at a very-high-rate. He breaks down opposing offenses when walking the line, using his lateral mobility and quick wrist-shot. His hockey-sense extends to the offensive-end, where he makes well-timed reads and activated correctly in most instances. Although he's efficient at the offensive-line, he isn't too dynamic, so we will be looking to see if he further develops his offensive-creativity.

DUFOUR, WILLIAM
RW - Chicoutimi Sagueneens (QMJHL) - 6'02" 180

Dufour was acquired by Chicoutimi from Rouyn-Noranda in the blockbuster Noah Dobson deal at the QMJHL trade deadline. He was originally drafted 6th overall in the 2018 QMJHL Draft. With the two teams this year, he amassed 9 goals and 21 points in 55 games. He saw his ice time increase significantly once he joined Chicoutimi, as they were in rebuilding mode and featured other good young players such as Hendrix Lapierre and Théo Rochette among their forwards' group. In Rouyn-Noranda, he mostly played on the 4th line due to playing on a stacked team.

Dufour is a big kid, standing over 6'02". With time, he'll add more mass to his frame and be tougher to handle physically for defensemen throughout the league. He won't ever be known as a physical player, but if he can play around 200 pounds, he'll be tough to handle by just playing a heavy game down low. His bread and butter will be his offensive game, mostly his shot and goal-scoring abilities. He's got a great shot, but he needs to use it more often (86 shots in 55 games this season). He has the ability to score from anywhere in the offensive zone with this shot. We've seen it at the midget level, where he was a threat to score from anywhere in the offensive zone with that booming shot. He can be used on the point on the power play in order to be featured in shooting situations, as was the case sometimes this year with Chicoutimi. However, he's much better playing on his off-wing in the "Ovechkin spot," where he can one-time pucks from the faceoff circle. His shot is powerful and heavy, and he can release it quickly. He needs to work on its accuracy, though. He's got work to do with his skating, even more so now with Chicoutimi. He's not a great skater, and his lack of speed and fluidity will be more visible on the big ice surface in Chicoutimi. Skating is an area of his game that will be heavily focused on next season in terms of progression level. He's a slightly one-dimensional forward; he's a scorer and doesn't have much value in his play away from the puck or shorthanded. Chicoutimi will be a heavily-scouted team next season, and should be among the league's top contenders. Dufour should have a top-6 role on the team and see plenty of ice time on the power play as a result.

EVANGELISTA, LUKE
RW - London Knights (OHL) - 5'11" 165

Luke Evangelista is a player we liked when watching him in Oakville in minor midget. Much like Foudy, he struggled with London at the start due to his strength. That said, we were slightly disappointed in his performance this season, as he only produced 2 assists in 27 games, but didn't have the same opportunities to play as some of the other rookies featured in this class. He did get a bit more playing time at the U17's, where he produced 1 assist in 5 games for Canada White. Evangelista is a small-winger who has some skill in his game. He's a capable playmaker who is comfortable assessing his options along-the-wall and can anticipate the play well, which allows him to find options quickly. His puck-handling is good, and we've seen him look to pull the puck rapidly from his backhand to his forehand while moving laterally in-tight to the net which has resulted in some high-end chances. There's a good extension when he's going at his top-gear but he didn't play with a consistent-pace and he had trouble using his skill-set while going at full-speed. He was at his best when slowing the play-down and making sharp-passes instead. In order for Evangelista to stand out next-season, he's going to have to get significant stronger and identify how he can assert himself into the game at a better-rate.

FABER, BROCK
RD - USA NTDP-17 (USHL) - 5'11" 176

Mobile and intelligent two-way defenseman. It's tough for a lot of the U17 defensemen to find points at the USHL level, but Faber's ten points in 35 games is a respectable figure and was second-best among club d-men. His minus-11 rating was tied for the best mark among U17 rearguards as well. Coming off of an impactful bantam season in Minnesota where he was named the bantam player of the year by Youth Hockey Hub, Brock joined the Development Program and quickly became one of its most reliable defensemen. Faber has very few holes in his game and his development will focus mostly on just increasing his ceiling as opposed to fixing glaring issues. He displays very smooth four-way mobility and strong edges. His first step quickness is really good. Brock handles the puck well and looks to have a plus shot, favoring a quick wrister rather than a big back scratcher. Because of his high-end hockey IQ, he already plays a composed, mature game for his age. His puck poise is strength and he really does a good job not to compound problems – when a simple play is the best play, he doesn't complicate things any further than that. He keeps proper gaps and positioning defensively against both rush chances and sustained attacks. The Notre Dame commit has a really terrific foundation to work off of which will allow him to really focus in on getting stronger and more skilled. The transition from Cam York to Brock Faber heading up the Program's blueline looks like it will be rather seamless given their respective skill sets and playing styles. There's plenty of ground to eat up on his development arc, but the late August 2002 birthday ought to be on the radar for the NHL Entry Draft's first round.

FARRELL, SEAN
LW - USA NTDP-18 (USHL) - 5'09" 174

Playmaking winger who spent the entire season with the U18 Team. Sean Farrell was the lone 2020 eligible that suited up at the U18 World Junior Championships for the United States; he registered two assists in seven contests. While only being used on the lower lines and the penalty kill for the majority of the season, Farrell had eight goals and 11 helpers in 28 USHL contests on the season. Impressively, he sported a plus-19 rating and took zero penalties. While he doesn't possess much in the way of game breaking skill, the Harvard commit is a good skater but he'll need to add a little more quickness to his rather hunched-over posture at his size. He has plus technical skills, but leaves the puck exposed a little too often. He does set up some easily catchable passes from his forehand or backhand. He needs to improve his puck protection abilities and/or make some more space for himself in order to really maximize his playmaking abilities. His hockey IQ is in the average range, maybe just a tick above. He did get some experimental time at center towards the later stages of the year, but his game lacked the completeness to really impress in that spot. He's not much of a finisher, so being in the middle might be a more traditional fit, but that feels like a lot of ice to manage for him. While Farrell plays an honest game, he's rather docile and it causes his game to blend into the ice some nights. He doesn't need to be an overly emotional player in order to get drafted, but he'll need a draw or a hook to shake the tag of being a generic, offensive winger. He may well get the opportunity for more ice time and offensively gifted linemates after being selected first overall in the 2019 USHL Entry Draft by Chicago.

FINLEY, JACK
C- Spokane Chiefs (WHL) - 6'05" 203

The big centre was taken 6th overall in the bantam draft. This season he had a modest 19 points in 63 games, but raised his productivity in the playoffs with 8 points in 15 games. Finley wasn't really in a position to produce strong numbers, playing in a lower lines checking role with no powerplay opportunities. Finley was utilized in a defensive role because he had the strength and smarts to excel in it against much older players. Finley is at his best battling for pucks along the boards and using his big frame. He also saw a lot of penalty kill time as he has strong positional discipline to take away lanes. Finley skates okay for a bigger guy but could stand to further improve in his explosiveness and agility. In the offensive zone Finley is strong off the cycle where he can use his size and reach to wall off defenders. Finley also has good hands for a big man and can handle the puck in traffic. On top of this he is a smart puck mover and decision maker who isn't going to hurt your team. There were instances where he showed above average vision but that was not consistent. Next season Finley will be a leader for a Spokane team that likely loses a lot from this season.

FOUDY, JEAN-LUC
RC - Windsor Spitfires (OHL) - 5'11" 168

Jean-Luc Foudy had a pretty decent year for the Spitfires due to getting ample-playing time while being used in all situations. He finished the year with 49 points in 63 games, including 8 goals. In the playoffs, he finished with 1 assist in 4 games, but was a difference maker at the U17's, where he produced 4 points in 5 games, including 4 assists. Foudy is an explosive, playmaking center who looks to drive-the-play. The main attribute that allows him to dictate play at times is his skating ability. Similar to his brother, he features an excellent set of skating mechanics and can gear-shift rapidly; opponents magnetize to him as a result of his skating. His skating ability allowed him to generate the most clean-transitional-zone-entries out of almost any other 2020-draft-eligible prospect. His offensive-instincts feature a pass-first mentality, and he would look to use his cross-over and pivots to open-up lanes to set-up his teammates. Although he features a slightly below-average-frame, he's willing to enter high-traffic areas, including taking direct routes towards the net. Although he displays impressive-tools and keeps a very high-pace which is an attribute we emphasize, there's aspects to Liam's game that keeps us from placing him as one of the higher-end prospects in this class, which is reflected in his rankings heading into the season. His decision making and anticipation lag behind his skating. He identifies options when they are stationary at a much higher-rate than when his teammates aren't set in position. Furthermore, he's not overly creative and looks to rely on his skating instead of his hockey-sense when breaking down opposing defenses. It's worked for him to a degree but in order for him to translate, it will be an area he will need to continue to develop into heading into next year.

FOWLER, HAYDEN
LC - Erie Otters (OHL) - 5'10" 185

Hayden was drafted 19th overall back in the 2017 OHL Draft by the Soo Greyhounds. He was traded to Erie during his rookie season. He only played in 25 games this season and had 8 goals and 10 assists prior to suffering a broken clavicle. His lack of games played cost us valuable viewings but he has shown us signs of being a sniper in the past. Fowler was just nine days from being eligible for the 2019 NHL Entry Draft rather than 2020.

His shot is a strength, it features a quick release and has proven to be quite accurate. He's smart player who makes good decisions with the puck. He anticipates the play well and finds quiet ice. He has shown good vision and soft hands, skill is not an area of weakness. His skating is just average lacking both a powerful stride and explosiveness. he returned in March and had 4 goals in 7 games so He'll hope to build off that in his NHL Draft season

FRANCIS, RYAN
RW - Cape Breton Screaming Eagles (QMJHL) - 5'08" 173

After a surprising first season in the QMJHL, Francis encountered more difficulties in his second season in the league. He was unable to beat his personal highs from the year before. Francis is a smart winger from Nova Scotia who sees the ice very well and makes players around him better. If he's put on a line with some snipers, he'll get the puck to them in scoring areas. His playmaking abilities are the best part of his game. His lack of strength and skating abilities are things he'll need to improve for next season. The strength facet will come with time, but for his size, skating will definitely need some big improvements. Right now, he's a bit of a one-dimensional player. His play away from the puck will need to get better. He has a good compete level, but his lack of strength hurts him when fighting for loose pucks along the wall. He's at his best on the power play with more time and space to make plays on the ice; once he starts seeing more ice time there, his production will go up as a result. Next season, we expect Francis to be a top-6 winger for the Screaming Eagles, and he needs to produce at a high level in order to get a look at the 2020 NHL Entry Draft.

GRANS, HELGE
D - Malmö Redhawks U20 (Jr. SuperElite) - 6'02" 183

Helge Grans has had a spectacular season where he split his season between three leagues. He played 11 games with his clubs U18 team in which he put up 4 goals and 10 points. His main team, on which he was a regular was his clubs U20 team where he was the highest scoring defenseman with 5 goals and 12 assists for a total of 17 points on a team that struggled to score goals and get wins all season and finished dead last in the southern SuperElite league. Grans fell under the spotlight as the only bright light on his team and eventually made his debut for his clubs men's team in the champions hockey league and followed up by getting dressed for 5 games in the SHL as well, without recording any points. Grans has very good size as he is listed as 6'2", but he skates and moves around like he is much smaller as he is very mobile and his stride is very smooth and fluid. For a kid his size, his lateral movement is super impressive and he showcases it very well, especially when quarterbacking the power play, dancing on the blueline. He is a solid two-way defenseman with very impressive puck skills and fantastic hockey sense, it's very rare to see him get stressed and throw away pucks at random as he plays with great composure and a calmness to his game that transfers over to his teammates. His ability to read the play makes him super confident in his decisions and he distributes the puck perfectly with crisp tape to tape passes. Grans's offensive zone game is strong and his short passing game and mobility on the blueline make him a threat even from a distance. His shot is both powerful and accurate and he can release shots quickly from the blueline to avoid getting his shots blocked at the same time as he won't hesitate to actually shoot when the shooting lane opens up. He is also strong on defense as his gap control is excellent and he reads the play superbly in his defensive zone to break up passes. While defense isn't his strongest attribute, he has the size and strength to muscle opponents off the puck as well as the high hockey IQ to break up the play with pure smartness. Grans played in 21 games for Swedens U17 team this season and put up 10 assists in those games, and even if his point total isn't too impressive, he was a star on that team and he could dominate games and control the pace of the games on his own at times. If this young, puck-moving, two-way defenseman can continue his strong development, he will be a hot prospect going into the 2020 draft.

GREIG, RIDLEY
C/LW - Brandon Wheat Kings (WHL) - 5'11" 155

An 8th overall Bantam draft pick, Greig had a promising rookie season in which he tallied 35 points, and slotted in to a middle six role for the Brandon Wheat Kings. Greig plays a cerebral game that is mainly offensively oriented at this point. The leagues physicality gave him some issues as he had a difficult time playing through contact and regaining the puck. Skating he was solid but unspectacular, not generating a ton of power out of his lower body yet. With the puck on his stick Greig was very adept as a passer showing above average vision and flashing the ability to make plays for others. He also possesses a quick release and accurate shot that will improve as he adds more strength. Greig has the potential to make a large offensive impact next year as he moves in to a larger role and further adapts to the size and strength of the league.

GROSHEV, MAXIM
RW - Reaktor Nizhnekamsk (MHL) - 6'00" 181

Maxim Groshev had a solid-season, firmly cementing himself as one of the better power-forwards heading into the 2020-season. He played for Reaktor Nizhnekamsk, where he produced 20 points, including 7 goals in 47 games. At the U19-World-Junior-A challenge, he produced 3 points in 6 games, and at the U18's, he produced 4 points in 7 games, including 3 goals; it was a very solid performance overall. Groshev is a space-creating, power-forward who can clear-out the front of the net and generate a ton of pressure on the forecheck. Although his physical stats appear average, he's a well-built kid who plays a tenacious and physical-brand of hockey. He has a very-high compete-level and keeps an excellent pace as result. He's also a decent-skater who looks to take direct-routes to the net; looking to penetrate through heavy-traffic. He's also got a good-blend of skill. He can find the open-man while in transition and gets a lot of leverage on his release-point. He can compliment other skilled-players on a line by going to the tough areas and coming away with the puck, while creating havoc down-low.

GUAY, PATRICK
LC - Sherbrooke Phoenix (QMJHL) - 5'09" 166

Guay comes from a hockey family. His father played in the QMJHL, playing one game in the NHL with Buffalo before moving on to Austria, Germany and Switzerland. Guay's older brother, Nicolas, plays for Drummondville, and his sister Alexie has committed to Boston College for next season and has played for Canada at the Women's Under-18 World Championships for the past two years.

Guay plays for his local team, the Sherbrooke Phoenix, who drafted him with the 5th overall pick in the 2018 QMJHL Draft. He had a slow start to the season, but once he made the adjustment and was healthy, he became a fixture on Sherbrooke's top-6 forward group. He finished the year with 18 goals and 36 points in 54 games. He's good on the power play when he has more room to maneuver; he's got quick hands and quick vision. His lack of size and speed hurts him at even-strength, and it's more difficult for him to make an impact in those situations compared to the power play. He's a calm kid on the ice; he doesn't get rattled by a lot and his poise with the puck is impressive. He's not afraid to shoot the puck on net, averaging over two shots per game this year. In the years to come, this will only improve with more ice time in offensive situations. He's a smart player who is not a liability in his own zone or away from the puck, but his size will provide some limitations when facing a big forward in a matchup. Guay has some good offensive tools, and there is no doubt he'll be a great QMJHL player. In order for him to have NHL potential, however, the key will be improving his speed. Without that, the NHL will be tough to reach for him.

GUHLE, KAIDAN
LD - Prince Albert Raiders (WHL) - 6'03" 186

Dominant at all previous levels, Guhle was taken with the 1st overall whl pick. Kaidan is the brother of Anaheim Ducks prospect Brendan Guhle. This season Guhle had 17 points in 65 games while playing a 3rd pairing role and only occasional 2nd PP. Prince Albert had a deep and old defence group that suppressed the amount of ice time he was able to earn. Guhle captained Canada Red at the u-17 where he had 3 points in 6 games. Guhle immediately stands out for his exceptional skating, which would be good for a player any size but is especially impressive with how big he is. Guhle had multiple plays where flashed a high skill level and was able to make some good offensive plays on the blueline. However he had limited opportunity and sometimes looked like he was lacking the confidence to play up to his talent early in the year. One thing Guhle brought all year was a massive physical presence. He showed a knack for landing big hits, and was sometimes downright dominant physically. Guhle also excelled defensively with his skating and reach a strong deterrent for attackers. Guhle consistently stopped rushes and broke up cycles while rarely making any big mistakes. With the puck Guhle at times lacks deceptiveness in what he's doing, and can telegraph his play. As the year went on he got more and more assertive, and started to play to his abilities. Next season Guhle will surely have a bigger role and will make an impact closer to what he is capable of.

GUNLER, NOEL
RW -Luleå HF (SHL SWE-1) - 6'01" 176

Noel Gunler was a dominating force for Luleå HF U20 at the start of the season, where he put up 27 goals and 19 assists for a total of 46 points in just 31 games. He was so dominant that it almost looked like he could score at will and he was the top goals scorer and point producer in the SuperElite North. After his fantastic performances in the U20 team, he got promoted to play for his clubs SHL team, where he dressed for 15 games and put up 2 goals and 3 assists for a total of 5 points on a team that finished with the highest point total in the regular season. Gunler is an offensive sniper with a deadly shot. He has a fantastic release and doesn't hesitate to shoot when given the opportunity and he reads the offensive play well enough that it seems like he is in a position to shoot every time he gets the puck. Even though he is mainly a shooter, his playmaking skills are well above average as he sees the ice well and can thread through passes with great precision. He has good size and is physically strong and can fence off defenders and protecting the puck with his body until he finds a teammate to distribute the puck to. He creates offense mostly by outsmarting the opposition and utilizes his fluid stickhandling to be a constant threat. His skating needs to improve, not that he is a bad skater by any means, as his first few strides are strong and he is well balanced, but he doesn't possess the same top speed as his fellow Swedish top prospects. Gunler does his work in the offensive zone and he is honestly not too viable in the two other zones as his defensive skills and mindset is his biggest weakness. He tends to be super passive in the defensive zone and his reads aren't all that great as he also tries to create offense by leaving the defensive zone early. He also lacks the ability to transition the puck from defense to offense and both his zone exits and zone entries need improvements, but if you're looking for a highly skilled goal scorer that doesn't have to drive the play, Gunler might be your guy. Internationally he played 8 games for team Sweden and put up 2 goals and 3 assists in those games for a total of 5 points. He was surprisingly cut from Swedens U18 world championship roster, the reason why remains a mystery as he should've been one of the biggest stars on that team.

GUSHCHIN, DANIIL
RW/LW - Muskegon Lumberjacks (USHL) - 5'08" 165

Speedy, dangerous offensive winger. After a very strong showing at the Hlinka-Gretzky Cup, Gushchin made a very successful USHL debut on a strong Muskegon Lumberjacks team in 2018-19. His 16 goals and 36 points in 51 games featured him prominently on the team's ledger. The speedy Russian winger is a dangerous weapon that has the ability to make something spectacular happens on any shift. The combination of puck skills and skating prowess make him a chore to contain. Gushchin has terrific hockey sense and supports the puck very well. He gets the puck and moves it, but he doesn't wait around admiring his play, he gets on his horse to help support the puck. He's a competitive player who doesn't wilt despite less than ideal size. The slick Russian import has an innate sense of danger that makes him really difficult to hit. Very much a talented passer, its Gushchin's release that makes him a threat even if he can't negotiate his way in close to the net. He's a sharpshooter through and through, and he also supplements his goal scoring ability with an array of quick, confident finishing moves when in tight. He motors around the ice with great speed, but Daniil is also a start and stop player with excellent agility, shiftiness, and edgework. The skill and skating package alone would be enough to justify him being on the 2020 radar, but the puck retrievals, the compete, and the hockey sense make him almost impossible to ignore. This is a player who plays like he loves the game.

HALLIDAY, STEPHEN
LW - Central Illinois (USHL) - 6'03" 220

Halliday was taken 1st overall in the 2018 Phase 1 USHL Draft out of the Toronto Marlboros Midget Program, and was able to step right into the Flying Aces lineup and be a contributor in their top six throughout the season. Putting up impressive numbers for an underage rookie, he had 10 goals and 24 assists in 55 games. Halliday was picked up by Dubuque in the USHL Dispersal Draft this spring after Central Illinois suspended operations. Halliday is a hulking power-winger who possesses a good combination of power and skill. Halliday is effective below the dots and off the boards, where he can use his big frame to protect the puck and dictate the play. Halliday has some good hands, particularly in tight areas to move the puck to teammates and slide pucks through traffic. Halliday played more of a playmaking style in his rookie year in the USHL, but possesses an NHL-caliber shot and release that he needs to learn to facilitate better, often passing up golden scoring opportunities for the extra pass. While Halliday has pretty good footwork and agility in regards to his skating, if there is a stopper in his game right now it's his straight-line skating and speed. Halliday is effective in having the puck on his tape and slowing the game down, but in games that are up-tempo and end-to-end, he struggles to keep up with the play and have an effect on the game. Despite having such a developed physical frame, Halliday isn't overly physical and defers to his stick skills to win pucks rather than brute force. Despite his lack of footspeed, Halliday has a high ceiling due to his puck-possession game and ability to make plays in tight areas and will be a player that will be closely tracked for the 2020 NHL Draft. Halliday will likely play one more season in the USHL before heading to the University of North Dakota in the fall of 2020. Stephen was also a 3rd round, 41st overall pick by Niagara in the 2018 OHL Draft. Hardie, James

HARDIE, JAMES
LW - Mississauga Steelheads (OHL) - 5'11" 161

James Hardie had a good rookie-season for the Steelheads by finishing the season with 22 points in 62 games, including 15 goals. In the playoffs he produced 1 goal, and at the U17's, he produced 2 points in 5 games. Hardie is a shoot-first winger who skates aggressively without the puck. He has plus skating mechanics and a good top-gear which afforded him the opportunity to generate pressure off the forecheck. Furthermore, he plays bigger than his size and is willing to throw his weight around in order to generate takeaways. His bread and butter is his shot, which features a good release and he was consistent at identifying seams through traffic when attempting to use it; he also looks to challenge players and use them as screens to mask his shooting angles. His playmaking lags behind his shooting ability at this time, but he does have a decent-feel for finding soft-ice away from the puck; which gives him the opportunity to receive passes from his teammates and bury the puck in the back of the net. We will be looking to see if James can continue to round-out his offensive-game and increase his consistency heading into next year.

HIRVONEN, RONI
LC - Blues U20 (Jr. A SM-Liiga) - 5'09" 154

Roni Hirvonen is one of the more talented Finnish forwards heading into the 2020-class and had a tremendous season for the Blues U20, finishing with 55 points in 50 games, including 21 goals in Jr. A SM-Liiga. In the playoffs, he produced 15 points in 11 games, including 3 goals. He also played internationally; producing 2 goals at the U17's and went pointless in 3 games at the U18's on a team that lacked chemistry for much of the event. Hirvonen is a dynamic center with excellent puck-skills. His hands are some of the best in this class. He can make lightning quick-dekes and has a lot of confidence when handling the puck, showing a high-level of creativity and deceptiveness. He's also good at recognizing when he should use his puck-skills and when he shouldn't, which makes him a cleaner-player who doesn't turn over the puck often. He has a very-good release point and can extend his dekes into his release; he also features an advanced understanding of how to hide his shot placement behind screens. Although he's very talented, Hirvonen hasn't had the impact internationally we would expect from him given some of his performances in league-play. So, there are inconsistencies within his game in terms of always using his skill out on the ice. Lastly, although his skating mechanics are okay, Roni isn't a strong or big kid and needs to fill-out his frame as much as he can this off-season. He's scheduled to play for Assat in Liiga next season.

HOLLOWAY, DYLAN
C/LW - Okotokos Oilers (AJHL) - 6'01" 192

This season Holloway had a massive season between international and league play. Holloway represented his country three times this season, first at the Hlinka, then for Canada west at the WJAC, and finally at the world u18s. At each stop Holloway was a top player. In the AJHL Holloway finished second in league scoring with 88 points in 53 games. Holloway excels in large part thanks to his great anticipation offensively and defensively as he is always moving in to good spots. He is fast and powerful on his skates, with the ability to rush the puck end to end. Holloways skating is high end with a blazing fast top speed and strong edges that allow him to make deceptive cuts with the puck. What makes Holloway stand apart is the plays he can execute while at high speeds. He thinks the game very fast and can recognize what his options are without having to slow down to think. He plays excellent give and go hockey utilizing his teammates very well. Holloway has strong vision that allows him to still generate offense and make plays when the pace slows down, excelling off the cycle and half wall. On top of his skills, he has a strong motor and is constantly looking to do whatever he can to make an impact. Holloway is a major positive defensively and clearly cares about this end. Next season Holloway will play at the University of Wisconsin and appears ready to handle the speed and physicality of college next season.

HOLTZ, ALEXANDER
LW - Djurgården IF U20 (Jr. SuperElite) - 6'00" 183

Alexander Holtz is one of the most highly touted prospects from Sweden in many years. Holtz was a regular for Djurgården IF U20 in the SuperElite league and was one of the biggest contributors on a young, talented team. He put up impressive 30 goals and 17 assists in 38 games in the SuperElite, which made him the best goal scorer in the entire league. He was also a big part of his team's success as they went on to win the bronze medal at the Swedish championships. He also got rewarded with 3 games in the SHL with very limited ice time. Holtz is the most intriguing pure goal scorer Sweden has produced in many, many years. His offensive gifts are close to limited and he is a pure sniper in the offensive zone and he can score from basically everywhere inside the blueline. Holtz will do whatever it takes to score a goal and given time and space, he will bury it. His shot is elite and he releases his wrist shot quickly and fires hard, accurate shots on goal. On the powerplay, he is stationed at the left faceoff circle to be able to fire away bombs with his one-timer. What makes Holtz extra dangerous is his ability to create scoring chances, without the need to be set up by his teammates as he has brilliant stickhandling skills and can deke his way around any defender to get a shot off. Another aspect of his offensive game is that he is ridiculously good on breakaways as he can beat the goaltender with his shot and dangle him out of his skates with his flawless technique and puck control. Even though his shot and flashy stickhandling may be his strongest attributes, his fine playmaking and vision cannot be neglected, he sees the ice well and has the ability to set up his teammates for scoring chances with accurate passes, even though he prefers to shoot the puck himself, given the choice. He anticipates the play well and has a nose for sniffing up areas close to the net where he can make an easy tap in or find a nice, juicy rebound. Holtz is not afraid of driving to the net, as he is strong and does just about everything to score a goal and even if this doesn't always result in him scoring, he can create havoc in the offensive zone where his teammates can capitalize. Holtz has a strong, powerful stride and even if it isn't very explosive and light, he gains some good speed with his long, strong stride. He is very well balanced when skating, his center of gravity is rather low and his core and legs are strong and keeps him from losing balance and getting bumped off the puck. He is very ambitious and has made great improvements to his skating from last season as well as during this season. He works hard all over the ice and his mentality is to win every single battle out on the ice, but he tends to get too eager to create offense and scoring goals that he leaves his defensive responsibilities early from time to time to get a head start on offense. However, he is viable in the defensive zone and he gives good support to his defenders by covering dangerous areas and killing angles, generally with his long stick which he keeps active to disrupt the play. He does a decent job on the backcheck, where he works hard to catch up, but he usually has the longest way back of all the players on the ice. If he wants to further develop and grow as a player, this is one aspect of his game he needs to improve in order to help his team with more than just goal scoring. Holtz played 13 games for Swedens U17 team this season where he put up 9 goals and 9 assists for a total of 18 points and helped his team clinch the bronze medal at the World under-17 hockey challenge. He was also one of the biggest contributors on Swedens U18 team during the season where he played 17 games and put up 10 goals and 12 assists for a total of 22 points and was a leading player for his team as they went on to wins the U18 world championships for the first time ever. He was also a part of the U18 team that came in second place at the Hlinka Gretzky tournament at the beginning of the season.

HUNT, DAEMON
LD- Moose Jaw Warriors (WHL) - 6'00" 196

Selected 15th overall in the bantam draft, Hunt was able to step right in to the line up and make an impact. This season Hunt recorded 20 points in 57 games, and made Canada's u18 team as an underage player. Hunt is a steady defenseman who played on a pairing with Josh Brook for much of the year. Physically strong, he never looked like a rookie in battles. Hunt is an above average skater who gets low and can get where he wants on the ice smoothly. Hunts defensive game is his strength as he has a good stick, takes smart angles, and can mirror an attacker. On the breakout he forced plays or got it out without possession far too often, Hunt was rarely willing to take a risk. The same issue limits his offensive game as Hunt is currently just a shooter from the point. With the departures of Brook and Woo next year hunt will have the opportunity to be a #1 defenseman, lead the powerplay and show improved offensive abilities and puck game.

IACOBO, FABIO
Goaltender- Victoriaville Tigres (QMJHL) - 6'02" 190

It was a big jump for Iacobo this season, coming from a prep school like Stanstead College to reaching the QMJHL, where he encountered a lot of ups and downs. He still showed some good potential, and was named to the rookie All-Star team at the end of the year. He backed up Tristan Côté-Cazenave all year long, but got a bit more playing time when an injury led to him being thrust into the number one role for a short period. Iacobo is still very raw technically; he can over commit at times and move himself out of position as a result (he swims a bit too much in his crease). He's got great size and he's a good athlete. He covers a lot of space in his crease. When he loses track of the puck, he still can make the save without seeing it due to his big frame. He's got an excellent glove; he made some very nice glove saves in our viewings of him this year. He's got to work on his consistency, much like any young goaltender. There's a lot of work to do with his technique, but when you watch Iacobo, he does look like a pro goaltender due to his size, athletic abilities and calm demeanor. Next season, his playing time should be interesting to see, as Côté-Cazenave should be back for his overage season. Another goaltending possibility is Nikolas Hurtubise, a 2002-born goaltender pushing to make the team as well.

JARVENTIE, ROBY
LW - Ilves U20 (Jr. A SM-Liiga) - 6'01 161

Roby Jarventie had a very good year for Ilves, producing 31 points in 40 games, including 14 goals. He was a ppg in the playoffs, scoring 3 goals and an assist in 4 games. At the U17's he had less success, scoring 1 goal in 6 games. Jarventie is a highly-mobile winger who is dangerous off the rush. He's got excellent skating ability with good mechanics. He can get up to his top-speed very quickly and has tremendous separating-speed. He's capable of carving through defenses and attacking the net directly, where he looks to use his impressive-wrist shot that features reduced tells with his static looking mechanics. He's willing to attack directly and looks to challenge defenseman when driving towards the net. He's a bit stream-lined at times, so he needs to continue to round-out his game but there's a good set of tools built into one of the younger draft-eligible forwards featured in this class.

JARVIS, SETH
C/RW- Portland Winterhawks (WHL) - 5'09" 164

The 11th overall bantam draft selection. Jarvis got a strong start to his WHL career with 39 points in 61 games while playing a middle six role. Jarvis also played for Canada red at the work u17 registering 5 points in 6 games. Jarvis is a dynamic offensive winger who plays the game at a high pace. Jarvis is a great skater who is always low and explosive with the burst and strength to drive the net off the wall. Jarvis is a threat in transition with good speed and instincts against an unsettled defense. Jarvis also showed some good passing instincts especially with passes from down low to the slot, taking advantage of overcommitted defenders. Jarvis has a smaller frame but plays with intensity and had a decent amount of success in board battles this season. Next season Jarvis should be an offensive leader for Portland and has potential to make a major offensive breakthrough

JOHANNESSON, ANTON
LD - HV71 U20 (Jr. SuperElite) - 5'09" 154

Johannesson hasn't played much this season due to an injury early on, but played 3 games for HV71's U18 squad, where he put up 2 points in the form of assists. He was mainly on his club's U20 team, where he played 8 games and managed to put up 1 goal and 1 assist for a total of 2 points.

While the viewings of him were few, he showcased his excellent skating abilities by moving around smoothly with quick feet and fantastic puck-transporting skills. His top speed is above-average for his age group, and he has impressive puck control. He is able to keep control of the puck and stickhandle at high speeds. Johannesson a small-ish offensive defenseman who can create plays with his vision and passing skills as he finds the simple, low-risk passes to his teammates. He is a great puck-carrier and possession player, and he is often the player making the zone entry into the offensive zone. In the offensive zone, he is active and wants to participate in his team's offense by providing good support to his forwards, and he is always open for a pass. He moves smoothly on the blueline and can be found trying to stickhandle there at times when trying to find an opening for his shot, which is not very hard, but sneakily accurate. His defensive game is what needs to improve the most. He makes good reads, but lacks the physical abilities to overthrow opponents and steal the puck. His opportunity to get away with the puck is by anticipating where rebounds and loose pucks will end up.

KAISER, WYATT
LD – Andover HS (MNHS) - 5'11" 165

Kaiser is a slightly undersized but smart, puck moving defenseman that has the ability to quickly identify pressure and move the puck out of his own end or use his partner as an outlet to relieve pressure in his own end. Kaiser has ok skating agility but still has room for improvement. His explosiveness with the puck is a plus as he shows a good gear in order to separate from pressure. Kaiser plays a smart, effective game when it comes to his puck decisions, Wyatt doesn't make a lot of high-end skill plays throughout the course of the game, but he can gain zones effectively, both with his feet and his passing ability that can stretch the ice sheet. In the offensive end, Kaiser makes reliable, low risk plays at the point position. He is calm under pressure and can cover a lot of ice in order to keep pucks in the zone. Kaiser has plus shooting ability from the point that includes good one-timing ability and can be used as the trigger man on the power play. Kaiser was drafted by Dubuque (USHL) in the 2018 Phase 1 Draft in the 7th Round and is a Minnesota Duluth commit.

KEHRER, ANTHONY
RD – Sioux City Musketeers (USHL) - 5'11" 196

Kehrer is out of the Rink Hockey Academy in Winnipeg and just finished his rookie season with Sioux City (USHL) where he played in all situations for the Musketeers. Anthony was a key piece to their backend all season long and was among the league leaders in ice time despite being one of the youngest players in the USHL this season. Kehrer is an excellent all-around skater, which is a cornerstone to his game, both offensively and defensively. He plays a smart and mature two-way game and makes a lot of plays that may not register on the score sheet but help his team win hockey games. His first initial strides are explosive and allow him to escape the fore-check effectively and gain zones with the puck on the breakout. Offensively Kehrer plays an effective but simple game, he can rush the puck effectively out of his own end and makes reliable plays at the point but isn't dynamic in his skill yet. His mobility is an asset at the point as he can open up lanes to pass and shoot as well as get around the point challenger and bring the puck down low when he needs to. Defensively Kehrer keeps a good gap and can handle things in front of his own net due to how physically developed he is already. Kehrer is a University of Wisconsin commit.

KHUSNUTDINOV, MARAT
LC - Vityaz Podolsk (Russia U18) - 5'09" 152

Marat Khusnutdinov didn't get to factor into many games in league play, just playing one game before factoring into 10 more games in the playoffs, where he produced 10 points in 7 games. At international events, he produced 5 points in 6 games at the U17's, and at the U18's he was featured in a depth-role, producing 3 points in 7 games. Khusnutdinov is a dynamic, two-way center who makes up for his smaller-stature with the ability to play larger than his size. Some other smaller forwards in the 2020-class lack skating ability but Marat isn't one of them; he features fluid cross-over mechanics and needs only a couple of steps before getting up to his top-gear. He's more quick, then he is purely fast but he can catch unsuspecting defenseman off-guard. His hands are bordering on elite, and as a result he has one of the most impressive arsenals of moves featured in this class. His shot is one of the best in this class and features advanced-mechanics. He's also a duel-threat player who can make very high-end passes and has shown plus vision. His hockey-sense is high-end and he plays a solid two-way game; there's awareness within his game that's noticeable on each shift. He didn't get a lot of playing time last season, but he's one of the more interesting Russian prospects heading into the draft.

KING, BEN
RW- Swift Current Broncos (WHL) - 6'00" 169

King was selected 13th overall in the bantam draft by Swift Current. This season he made a strong impact with 26 points in 48 games on a team whose leading scorer only had 31 points in 20 more games. With his position on this team King was given a ton of opportunity but also had linemates who weren't always on his level. King is a smooth and fast skater who can weave his way through the neutral zone and evade checks. King has good passing instincts and can make very creative reads. He is able to make plays attacking through the defence as a passer and was able to see cross ice lanes when they were open. He is at his best with the puck on his stick and had to take on the role of a line driver this season. It helps that King has above average hands that he uses to keep the puck away from defenders and maintain possession. King is very adept as a playmaker off the rush but also showed good instincts in settled 5 on 5 situations. Right now his shot is very weak and needs significant improvement for King to become less predictable and a more diverse offensive threat. King also has some work to do on his physicality and intensity as right now he is a bit weak and can be too much of a perimeter player at times. Next season King should be his team's top offensive threat as it once again looks to be a rebuilding year

KLEVEN, TYLER
LD - USA NTDP-17 (USHL) - 6'04" 190

Sturdy, physical defenseman who plays a big man's game despite his age. Fresh out of North Dakota high school (Fargo Davies High), the 6'4" blue liner proved to be just about the most overtly physical player on either of the USNTDP teams this past season. No doubt it was a tough year on the score sheet for Kleven, as he was limited to just three points and the worst rating among team blueliners at minus-23. Despite that, he showed the potential to do much greater things in due time. Those point totals do not accurately reflect his skill level. While he isn't going to be dangling anyone off of a rush chance, he handles the puck at around an average level right now – which isn't a red flag for his size and style of play. We would like to see him support his partner more on the breakout and get a little more involved in handling the disc so that comfort level increases. He has a hot shot when he's able to really take his time and hammer it. Kleven makes good reads defensively, even in situations where he ends up isolated; he mitigates risk at an advanced level for his age group. His reach is terrific and he plays with a real heavy stick. Despite being a powerful hitter, he doesn't run around chasing hits. He'll finish some players off, but most of his body contact is designed to separate his man from the puck. The University of North Dakota commit isn't shy about bullying players in front of his own net either. He gets around the ice just fine and he looks comfortable with his size already. His first step quickness could use some lubrication certainly, but his skating is not a negative by any means. How far Kleven moves up the draft board will really depend on his ability to transition the puck. The worry is that if he's just used as a support player and doesn't "lead" a pairing of his own, the ability to reliably move the puck may die on the vine and really hurt his stock.

KNAZKO, SAMUEL
LD - TPS U20 (SM-Liiga) - 5'11" 170

Knazko is a Slovak defenseman who played in Finland this year for TPS' U20 team. He amassed 17 points in 49 games, which made him the top-scoring U-17 defenseman in the league and 5th overall in the league in his age group. He played for Slovakia's U-18 team throughout the year as well. He had a good showing at the Hlinka-Gretzky Cup in August, but had more difficulties in April at the World U-18s, where Slovakia was demoted to the 2nd division for next year's U-18s. Knazko played in the 2018 U-18s as a 15-year-old, which made him the youngest player in Slovak history to play at the U-18 World Championships. He's a good puck-moving defenseman who makes a good first pass out of his zone. In the offensive zone, he has good puck-distribution skills. On the power play, he can be an asset; he's got a good point shot and finds good shooting lanes. He's a good puck-handler; he's got soft hands and can beat guys one-on-one when rushing the puck. With the puck on his stick, he needs to make quicker decisions. That was an issue with him at the April U-18s; his slow decision-making got him into trouble against a quick forecheck from other teams. We want to see him work on improving his footwork and overall speed as well. These are only average at this point, and he can get caught flat-footed in the neutral zone and doesn't have the speed to get back in position in time. There's some potential with Knazko and his good offensive flair, but other parts of his game need to improve in order for him to be a high pick in next year's draft.

KUBICEK, SIMON
RD- Seattle Thunderbirds (WHL) - 6'02" 179

Kubicek came to North America as the 89th selection in the import draft. A late birthday, Kubicek had a strong first season with 28 points in 61 games. To start the year Kubicek had limited powerplay time, but eventually worked his way up to the first unit. Kubicek also played for the Czech u18 team, first at the Ivan Hlinka, and then at the world u18 where was an assistant captain. Kubicek has a hockey brain and is a very solid decision maker who rarely hurts his team while effectively moving the puck out of his zone. Kubicek had good awareness for when to hold the puck and when he had no option but to chip it out, doing a very good job managing risk. He also has a good shot along the blue line that he could get through lanes pretty consistently. With the puck Kubicek does a good job drawing his man out to the point before smartly moving the puck to a teammate in open space. Defensively he is very sound, with good approach angles and gap control. Kubicek also has some bite to his game and plays with a physical edge. While for his size not a bad skater, Kubicek is not exceptional and was sometimes caught flat footed on the blue line. Improving his burst and fluidity would lead to a huge advancement to his game. Kubicek will have the opportunity to play a top pairing role again next season, and with a season to adjust to North America under his belt should thrive.

KUNZ, JACKSON
LW - Shattuck St. Mary's (USHS) - 6'02" 196

Kunz is a 1st Round, 9th overall pick of Green Bay in the 2018 USHL Phase 1 Draft out of Shattuck St. Mary's, where he played this year, registering 22 goals and 22 assists in 33 games. Kunz missed a chunk of the 18/19 season due to injury but was able to return at the end of the season and saw two games for Green Bay at the end of the year where he was impressive in both games. Kunz has excellent size and strength which translates to his skating, as he has a powerful stride that gets him to top gear quickly. Kunz likes to play with a physical edge but isn't reckless about it. He uses his size to his advantage when it's there but doesn't take himself out of the play. Kunz certainly likes to play a power forward type of game, but his strongest asset right now is getting into position to utilize his shot. Kunz has benefitted from playing with playmakers in his time at Shattuck St. Mary's, but he also has great hockey sense in being able to identify where he needs to get to on the ice for his teammates to get him the puck in scoring areas. Kunz is good at getting his shot off in traffic and has shown the ability to beat goalies straight up in one on one situations. His playmaking can best be considered vanilla at this point, while it isn't dynamic; it also gets the job done. Kunz can take advantage of defensive lapses and has the skill and vision to pass through lanes but doesn't create a lot of chances out of nothing. Kunz will likely be off to Green Bay (USHL) next season before heading back to his hometown of Grand Forks North Dakota where he will play for The University of North Dakota in 2020.

KUZNETSOV, YAN
LD - Sioux Falls Stampede (USHL) - 6'03" 201

Kuznetsov is a big Russian defender who was a rookie in the USHL this season with Sioux Falls. He didn't have a ton of success offensively this season with Sioux Falls, with just 4 points in 34 games. He did show more offensive potential at the U-17s in November. He's a two-way defenseman with great size and skating abilities. He's capable of logging a ton of ice time, as he did at the U-17s in November. He has decent acceleration and top speed for his size, and he's capable of skating the puck out of his zone. He has above-average smarts and keeps things simple with the puck. He has good puck-moving abilities on the power play and also possesses a hard shot from the point. His puck skills are decent at this point, and he was a capable player on the power play. However, he's still a bit raw, and didn't really do much in terms of offense at the USHL level this past season. Defensively, he's great along the wall and used his size very well to retrieve pucks. He's also good on the penalty-killing unit, making good use of his long stick to block passing and shooting lanes. He's also not afraid to block shots in front of his goaltender. He covers a lot of ice with his size, long stick and solid positioning game. He's expected to play college hockey next season at the University of Connecticut, a rare 17-year-old freshman in the NCAA.

LAFRENIÈRE, ALEXIS
LW - Rimouski Oceanic (QMJHL) - 6'01" 192

Lafrenière had a strong 2018-2019 season and played a ton of hockey. He started his season with a great performance at the Hlinka-Gretzky Cup, where he captained Team Canada and amassed 11 points in 5 games to lead the tournament in scoring (tied with Vasili Podkolzin). With Rimouski in the QMJHL, he was named MVP of the league during the regular season and finished 3rd in scoring with 105 points. He also played for Team Canada at the World Juniors in Vancouver, scoring 1 goal in 5 games and receiving limited ice time from the coaching staff. Lafrenière has made some good strides with his play away from the puck during this past season, even though his play away from the puck was heavily focused on at the World Juniors by the coaching staff. There's no doubt that he's a better two-way player now compared to last year. Nevertheless, his offensive game remains his bread and butter: his ability to create offense, his elite on-ice vision and how he always does a good job of making his linemates look better (case in point: Jimmy Huntington this season). In terms of high-end puck skills, Lafrenière is really good at handling the puck in tight spaces and his puck-protection game has improved. He has gotten stronger physically, and it's much tougher to take the puck away from him compared to his rookie season. His shooting abilities enable him to score from just about anywhere in the offensive zone; the excellent release on his wrist shot leads him to pick corners really well. This year, he was either used on the power play at the point or at the half-wall position. We think that the latter is a better spot for him long-term, but Rimouski was running short on puck-moving defensemen on their power play and there's no better puck-moving player on the team than Lafrenière. If there's an area of his game that needs work, one could point to his skating abilities. Currently, they are good enough and won't hinder him at the NHL level, but he could establish himself as more of a threat off the rush if he had better speed and the added ability to beat defenders one-on-one using that great speed. If he can work on his acceleration to the point where he could reach his top speed faster, this would be a big plus for him heading into his draft year next season. His top speed is fine; when he can reach it in the neutral zone, he can be very dangerous in one-on-one situations. He just needs to find a way to reach that top speed faster and more often.

Lafrenière is a premier prospect for the 2020 NHL Entry Draft. Rimouski should be among the league favorites next season in the QMJHL, and it should go without saying that he should land a bigger role with Team Canada at the 2020 World Juniors.

LAPIERRE, HENDRIX
LW/LC - Chicoutimi Sagueneens (QMJHL) - 5'11" 173

Lapierre is a Gatineau product and the top pick in the 2018 QMJHL Draft. In his first season in the QMJHL with Chicoutimi (when he played) he was fairly successful, averaging just under a point per game (45 points in 48 games). Unfortunately, he faced some injury problems, battling a separated shoulder that made him miss the U-17 Hockey Challenge, and also missed some games with a concussion in the 2nd half of the season. He was also part of Canada's U-18 training camp for the World Under-18 Hockey Championships in April, but was cut once more CHLers joined the team following their respective eliminations from playoff contention.

He played both on the wing and at center this past season. He mostly played on the wing in the first half of the season, moving to center in the 2nd half. His faceoff abilities will need some work, as he only had a 44.6% success rate in the regular season and 31% in the playoffs. Lapierre is an above-average skater, and his best quality is his vision. He sees the ice very well, and he's an asset on the power play, as he can make some high-quality passing plays for his teammates. He can be a difference-maker on the man-advantage with more space on the ice, and made a really good impact on Chicoutimi. He's got above-average smarts and makes his linemates better on the ice. He's a pass-first player, but will need to take more shots on net, as he averaged just over two shots per game. He has to be a little more selfish on the ice, and that will translate to more goal-scoring success. He's got an above-average shot with a quick release. He has a solid work ethic, but he's not a physical player and will need to get stronger physically, although his compete level is good. He had a great postseason in the opening round against Rimouski; despite losing 4 straight games, he amassed 5 points in the process and was his team's top player along with fellow 2020-eligible Théo Rochette. The young forward will be among the most talked-about players in the QMJHL next season on a good young team in Chicoutimi, not to mention one of the top prospects out of the QMJHL for the 2020 NHL Entry Draft.

LAVALLÉE, CHARLES-ANTOINE
Goaltender - Moncton Wildcats (QMJHL) - 6'02" 209

Lavallée was the 40th overall pick in the 2018 QMJHL Draft out of the St-Hyacinthe Midget AAA program. The big goaltender made Moncton out of training camp and was featured in 19 games this year as the backup behind veteran Francis Leclerc. He barely played in the second half of the season, as Leclerc was in net for all but 6 games. He has great size, covering a lot of space in front of his net, and he's a great athlete. He's quick in his movements, demonstrating good post-to-post quickness, and he's quick in his recovery. Technically, he's still a bit raw. He can get caught out of position and lose track of the puck as a result. He's got to work on his rebound-control, as he can give up some bad rebounds in the slot. Next season, he'll be the number one goaltender due to Leclerc moving on. He'll need to show more consistency, and his durability will be tested with a big workload next season.

LAWRENCE, JOSH
RC - Saint John Sea Dogs (QMJHL) - 5'07" 164

Lawrence was the 15th overall pick in the 2018 QMJHL Draft by Saint John, but would have been a higher pick had it not been for his NCAA commitment with Boston University. In the summer, he decided to join the Sea Dogs and forego his NCAA eligibility. It was a tough first season in the QMJHL for Lawrence on a bad team in Saint John. He saw a lot of ice time in his first season, but it was not a good situation, notably due to the team's record. Developing players in these situations is pretty tough. Lawrence is an undersized player with good skating abilities, including above-average speed. In order for him to play in the NHL at his size, he'll need to improve his speed a bit more. He's got good hockey IQ, he sees the ice well, and he's an above-average passer with a quick release on his shot. He's good off the rush and in counter-attacking situations due to his high skill level. It's more difficult for him to create offense from working the puck down low and battling along the boards due to his lack of size and strength. Due to his size, he's more of a perimeter player in the offensive zone. He can't win those one-on-one battles in front of the net or in corners when matched up against bigger players, but does a good job controlling the puck from the half-wall or the point on the power play. He's got good puck poise and a good hockey IQ to create scoring chances for his teammates or himself. He needs to learn to pay more attention to his defensive game, as his compete level away from the puck needs to get better. He does cheat a bit and tends to leave the defensive zone too early at times. Lawrence is slotted to be the Sea Dogs' number one center next season, and will need a good bounce-back year. He has his work cut out for him to establish himself as a high pick next season; his size will be an issue because he doesn't have any elite quality (such as a Cole Caufield in regards to his shot). Nevertheless, his point-production should see a big improvement with more experience next season, and the Sea Dogs should be a better team.

LEVI, DEVON
Goaltender - Lac St-Louis Lions (LHMAAAQ) - 6'00" 174

Levi is a late-born player (born on December 27th, 2001) who has played the last three seasons in Midget AAA with the Lac St-Louis Lions in the West Island of Montreal. It's unusual for a quality player like Levi to play three full seasons in Midget AAA, but after his second season, Levi established himself as the league's top goaltender. This year, he had a good season once again, despite the Lions struggling with injuries all year long. However, they had an amazing run in the playoffs, and Levi had some great performances in the semi-finals against the almost-impossible-to-beat Lévis Chevaliers, causing one of the biggest upsets in league playoff history. Levi was drafted by the Blainville-Boisbriand Armada in the 5th round of the 2017 QMJHL Draft (the closest team to his hometown) but decided to go the NCAA route, committing to the University of Vermont in April. He's expected to play for Carleton Place Canadians in the CCHL next season before reporting to Vermont the year after. Levi is an average-sized goaltender, but has good puck-tracking and really does a great job anticipating the plays in front of him. His hockey IQ is excellent. He's quick to move from post to post, and there's no quit with him. He can make some really nice saves on 2nd and 3rd rebounds. He's really good to handle the puck outside of his crease; not many midget goaltenders have the skills and confidence to handle the puck like he does. He's very calm in his crease and has sound rebound-control. He's got to work on his glove side a bit; with heavy traffic in front of him it becomes a bit tougher for him to track the puck. Levi will make a good NCAA goaltender and was a great midget goaltender, but the jury is still out on him as a NHL goaltender. Joining the CCHL next season will be a bigger challenge for him, but it's not a league that is known to issue many draft picks. He'll need to be dominant, because there's also a size-related question mark with him.

LUNDELL, ANTON
LC - HIFK (Liiga) - 6'01" 183

Anton Lundell is the top Finnish prospect heading into the 2020-class. He dominated Jr. A SM-liiga competition for HIFK, producing 15 points in 10 games with 6 goals, before moving to play with the men's team in Liiga, where he had superb numbers for his age. As a 17-year-old, he produced 19 points in 38 games, including 9 goals but was held pointless in the playoffs in 12 games. He was featured in a lot of events internationally, including suiting up for the WJC-20 team, where he produced 4 points in 7 games while displaying some chemistry with Kakko. Lundell is a cerebral – two-way – playmaking center who can make unique plays happen all over the ice. He has some of the best vision offered in this class and can find teammates through heavy-traffic and while going at top-speeds as a result. His hands are bordering on dynamic and can turn player's inside-out as a result. He's a quick-thinking and creative player, who can use the back of the net to bank pucks back to himself much like one of our top-rated prospects last year could, Vitali

Kravtsov. His hockey-sense makes him highly-adaptive and he showed the ability to drive-a-line for extended periods and also made his teammates better as a result of his unselfish, yet well-timed move-set. Lastly, he's a responsible 200-foot-center, who doesn't lean out to far in advance and is capable of defending with his frame and stick. The biggest area for Lundell to continue to improve heading into next season will be his two-step area quickness and his top-gear. He's a good skater but it would help if he can continue to develop it.

MALIK, NICK
G - HC Ocelari Trinec U19 (Czech U19) - 6'02" 174

Nick Malik had a decent-season, dominating the U19 league but having less success in the Czech2 league. In the Czech U19, he produced a .932 save percentage with a 2.41GAA in 6 games and a .960 save-percentage with a 1.74GAA in 8 playoff games. In the Czech2, he finished with a .903 save percentage and a .305 GAA in 26 games. Internationally, he was featured at a variety of events, including the Hlinka and U17's. Malik is a highly reflexive goaltender that has a lot of talent. His athleticism is the most prominent trait that's featured in his game; when breaking down his athletic ability, his reaction-time stands out the most. He processes play-types well in-tight to the net and has the ability to fully-extend; producing impressive saves as a result. His butterfly mechanics are a plus and he has good overall mobility. His glove-hand is also above-average but it's his blocker-side that lags behind the rest of his skill-set. High-skill players have taken-advantage of Nick on that side in our viewings, and he has trouble identifying how to square up to shooters properly that have the far-side option available when it's on his blocker-side. Additionally, he has the tendency to lose concentration and let in goals that his talent-level suggests he shouldn't let in. Malik is very skilled but he needs to prolong his concentration for a full 60-minutes.

MCCLENNON, CONNOR
RW - Kootenay Ice (WHL) - 5'08" 151

McClennon was the 2nd overall WHL bantam draft pick, and was a prolific scorer at every level he has played. This season McClennon had 29 points in 46 games with significant powerplay time, but even strength minutes mainly separate from Krebs on a weak team. He had a dominant showing at u-17s registering 11 points in 5 games and constantly generating high danger chances. McClennon is a high end shooter who has a deceptive and accurate shot that he gets off quick. He especially excels at changing his angle and release point to shoot around a screen, displaying this ability constantly off the half wall on the powerplay. McClennon is a tricky player who has a great mind for the game with his ability to draw extra attention with his shot threat before making smart passes, and has plays where he clearly outthinks the opposition. McClennon hustles and plays the game hard with intensity and passion, never giving up on pucks. He battles like a player much bigger than he is and was never afraid of physical contact which leads to some of his missed time due to injuries. Though he didn't play a ton with Krebs, in the times he did he displayed the ability to play off of an elite talent and occupy a more complimentary role. McClennon is quicker than he is fast with an explosive first few steps and the ability to turn on a dime. McClennon should find a lot of success next season as he further adjusts to the league and the young team around him improves.

MCDONALD, KYLE
RW - Windsor Spitfires (OHL) - 6'04" 187

Kyle was drafted by Windsor in the 2nd round #25 overall in the 2018 OHL Draft. He started with a limited role with Windsor mostly on 4th line, but was given some opportunity to move up in the lineup with injuries on the team and he played well and showed what kind of player he can be. Unfortunately Kyle got hurt midway through January and was shut down for the rest of the season.

He showed strong offensive awareness and a killer instinct to use his big frame to get the puck into high percentage scoring areas before releasing a hard, accurate wrist shot. He doesn't play a particularly physical game given his size, but was using his size to his advantage in puck battles. He demonstrated strong puck control, and uses his reach to his advantage to position himself effectively to avoid being checked off the puck. He shows an ability to make hard, accurate passes at high speed, and made quick plays in the offensive zone, often setting up his teammates for prime scoring chances.

MEIERS, JOHNNY
LF – Eagan Hs (MNHS) - 5'09" 170

Meiers is a speedy, puck hound that put up solid offensive numbers for an Eagan team that lacked a lot of offensive depth. Meiers was forced to provide a lot of the offense for Eagan, registering 18 goals and 31 assists in 24 regular season games. Meiers isn't the most gifted player when it comes to size and strength at this point but plays a much bigger game than his digits would suggest. Meier's has good hockey sense and knows where he needs to be on the ice and uses straight lines and quick feet to get there. Meier wins a lot of races to loose pucks and the races he doesn't win, he is able to out work or out smart his opponent into coming away with the puck. Meier's shows good awareness with the puck and knows when he needs to move it quickly, especially in the neutral zone where he limits mistakes and gets pucks deep in the offensive zone with consistency. While Meier's offensive skill cannot be considered high end at this point, he is a smart player, processes situations quickly and can get himself and the puck into scoring areas. Meier's likes to drive the paint with the puck but can also make plays from the perimeter, what limits Meier's offensive upside at this point is he isn't skilled enough to create time and space for himself, so he is forced to rely upon his hockey sense and work ethic in tight spaces. Meier's is a 3rd round pick of Sioux Falls (USHL) in 2018 and a Colorado College commit for 2021. This offseason will be important in determining Meier's NHL upside. Johnny will need to get a lot stronger to be effective with his style of play at the upper levels, but his hockey sense and work ethic will give him opportunities going forward.

MERCER, DAWSON
RC/RW - Drummondville Voltigeurs (QMJHL) - 6'00" 173

Mercer is a product of Newfoundland and was Drummondville's top pick in the 2017 QMJHL Draft (8th overall). He made some very nice progress this season and became an excellent two-way player for the Voltigeurs. Mercer had a great second season in the QMJHL, scoring 30 goals and 64 points in 68 games and also had 16 points in 16 playoff games. In the playoffs, he was one of their top players, outplaying some of their veterans. He's a smart player at both ends of the ice and a great playmaker. He sees the ice well and can find his linemates very quickly on the ice. He's unselfish and willing to take a hit to make a play. He has a good work ethic and compete level, but he's not very strong physically just yet. He still works hard along the boards and can finish his hits. He creates a lot of scoring chances either for himself or his teammates due to his play along the boards. He was used regularly on both special teams; he became one of his team's top players shorthanded thanks to his anticipation and hustle. On the power play, he can be used in different ways; either from the half-wall where he can control the puck more or in front of the net, where his quick stick helps him gets to loose pucks quickly. He'll need to improve his shot in order to become a bigger threat to score goals. He could see his velocity improve as well; right now he's not a high-end goal scorer. He has great hands, can dangle with the best of them and he's a threat one-on-one. We would also like to see him improve his speed; his skating is decent, but by adding some speed he could be even more dangerous off the rush. Next year, Mercer will have an even bigger role on Drummondville due to lot of key players leaving, and will also get more attention from opposing defense compared to this year.

MERCURI, LUCAS
RW/C - Salisbury Prep (USHS) - 6'03" 192

Mercuri was in his first season of prep hockey with Salisbury, after playing the previous two seasons with Châteauguay in the Quebec Midget AAA league. He was the 19th overall pick of the 2018 QMJHL Draft by Val-d'Or, but elected to go play south of the border this season. He has also committed to play college hockey at the University of Vermont.

Mercuri is a big body that can play on both wings and also at center, although he projects more as a winger at the pro level. He has very good puck-protection skills along the boards, and has really taken advantage of his size in the past two years to help him assert his level of play. His passing game and his poise with the puck are two parts of his game that are really underrated. He was over a point-per-game player this year with Salisbury, and was also a point-per-game player with Châteauguay in his QMJHL draft year. He has a heavy shot, but needs to improve the quickness of his release. He's a good stick handler for a player of his size, as he is good in tight spaces and very good on the power play near the opposing net. Mercuri has above-average smarts and vision; he can useful on the PK unit with his good, long, active stick that he uses to block passing lanes. The biggest flaw in Mercuri's game is his skating; there's work that needs to be done there. He has heavy feet, and his acceleration and top speed are only average. He'll be an interesting player to follow next season. He should be back with Salisbury, as no USHL team owns his rights. Alternatively, he could go the QMJHL route instead of towards the NCAA.

MIETTINEN, VEETI
RW - Blues U20 (Jr. A SM-Liiga) - 5'09" 159

Veeti Miettinen had a dominant year while playing for the Blues, generating 61 points in 48 games, including 27 goals. In the playoffs he produced 11 points in 11 games, including 5 goals. At the U18's he produced 4 points 5 games and had one of the better international performances we viewed this season at the U18-Five-Nations. Veeti is a diminutive, yet dynamic winger who anticipates the play at a very-high level. He's a fearless player regardless of his size and can score goals from well-out. He has some of the better shooting mechanics in the 2020-class, featuring impressive-footwork and excellent dexterity which allows him to take sharp-passes in one-motion and bury the puck. His passing ability is also extremely impressive; he looks to generate scoring chances for his teammates by slowing down while finding streaking players that are driving towards the net, and has the ability to use saucer-passes that require a high-degree of finesse to make them happen. Veeti is also a very capable deker, and can beat opponents with a creative-attack when using his hands. His skating is a work in progress, he's very weak and doesn't generate a lot of power, so that's the main area of improvement that we will be looking at when heading into the season.

MILLER, JOE
RC - Blake School (MNHS) - 5'09" 149

Joe Miller was drafted in the Phase 1 USHL Draft in the 2nd Round, 30th overall by the Chicago Steel. Miller at the top of a talented crop of players now coming up through the Blake School youth system. Miller registered 16 goals and 33 Assists in 25 regular season games for the Bears. Miller is an undersized but elusive forward that is difficult to get a body on and separate from the puck due to his quick skill. Miller is fearless and doesn't let his lack of size effect how he plays or how effective he can be. He consistently gets himself and the puck to scoring areas and does an excellent job creating space with the puck on his tape. His two-way game will need to continue to develop if he is going to be an effective center at the next level, especially if there isn't another growth spurt coming in the next year. Miller understands the game well offensively and moves the puck quickly in the neutral zone in the transition game. His skating has good fundamental and as he adds some strength, he should become even more difficult to remove from pucks. Miller gets the most out of his game at the High School level, and while he did see one game with the Steel in 18/19, scouts will need to see him against some bigger and stronger competition next season to see if his skill can translate to the upper levels. Miller is a University of Minnesota commit but is likely a couple years away from suiting up for the Gophers.

MILLER, MITCHELL
RD - Cedar Rapids Roughriders (USHL) - 5'10" 204

Raw, two-way blue liner who has yet to really establish his identity as a defenseman. Miller really thrust himself on to the radar with a strong Hlinka-Gretzky Cup tournament, but it may have set the bar a little high for what he was able to do at the USHL level. With just four goals and 16 points in 48 games, Miller had a hard time really distinguishing himself on a defense corps that really could have used a pacesetter. That said, he wasn't always put in the most favorable spots to produce considering his usage and the team's tactics. The Honeybaked product is interesting because there's some puck-rushing upside backed by some tight-gap, aggressive defending. The downside is just how unpredictable Miller can be because he still has a very much undefined and unrefined style of play. He looks a little unsure of himself sometimes even. Oddly, he looks the most comfortable when he's going full speed with the puck on his stick. He even looks like a better skater with the puck than without it, which is not a terribly common sight. The right-handed rearguard isn't shy about whipping pucks on net either, and he has the capability to get some good power on those tries. There's a good skill base to work with and the skating is a plus. His lateral skating and agility are strengths. The North Dakota commits likes to gap up and cut down plays before they start. That style seems to be borne out of necessity than preference though, as his play against sustained attacks is not very inspiring. Too often, he'll just end up going to the top of his own crease and just give away any leverage he once had on the situation. The closer to his own net the play gets, the more uncomfortable it looks for him. Beyond finding his way in terms of what type of player he wants to become, his hockey sense will be a top priority to track next season – as of right now, it might only be average at best.

MOORE, LLEYTON
LD - Oshawa Generals (OHL) - 5'09" 165

Lleyton Moore had a good season, even though he ended up getting dealt in a block-buster trade with Oshawa from Niagara and his introduction to that team was delayed due to an injury. He produced 10 points in 28 games, including 2 goals on the IceDogs, and an additional 3 assists in 6 games for Oshawa. For a rookie, he logged some heavy minutes in the playoffs and performed pretty well, contributing 5 assists in 15 games. At the U17's, he was relied on heavily by Canada White, producing zero points but that wasn't reflective of his impressive performance. Moore is a diminutive, puck-rushing defenseman who has excellent hockey-sense and can skate the puck. He's an assertive player who can drive-play at times due to the combination of his confidence and anticipation. His spatial-awareness allows him to identify soft-ice and lanes quickly, where he looks to use his fluid skating and take-advantage of what's offered. He's displayed really-good puck-retrieval and uses his edges in conjunction with his poise to remain elusive. At the offensive-line, he's good at re-opening his lanes and has a good-touch with the puck which allows him to breakdown defenses. The next step for Lleyton will be further improving his extension within his stride and putting on as much mass as possible given his small-stature.

MORRISON, LOGAN
RC - Hamilton Bulldogs (OHL) - 5'11" 170

Logan Morrison was drafted 18th overall in the OHL-draft and started out the season with a shoulder-injury which reduced the amount of games he was able to play. After returning from injury though, he was very productive, posting 34 points in 47 games, including 14 goals. In the playoffs, he had a lone assist in 4 games. Morrison is a fairly-smart, two-way center who has some well-rounded skill too. He's good at recognizing transitional play through the neutral-zone and has the vision necessary to fire sharp-passes at a high-rate. Although he's more of a playmaker in our viewings, he has a decent wrist-shot as well that features a plus release point, and he knows how to put himself in position to be dangerous with it. Although there's some talent in Logan's game, there's a significant flaw that he needs to improve in order to develop well. His skating leaves a lot to be desired given his average-frame. His stride is compact and jagged, and he's not a strong-kid yet; he needs additional power so that he can become more elusive in tight-spaces. Despite his skating set-backs, he had great numbers, so it will be interesting to see how he does next-season.

MUKHAMADULLIN, SHAKIR
LD - Tolpar Ufa (MHL) - 6'02" 170

Mukhamadullin is big defenseman out of Russia who played at both the U-17 and U-18 levels in international tournaments for his country this season. Back home, he split the past year between the MHL for Tolpar Ufa and with Salavat Yulaev Ufa in the U-17 and U-18 Russian junior leagues. He has great size; he's tall, strong and dominant along the boards. He plays a simple game with the puck on his stick. If no options are available, he won't try to force plays and will use the glass to get puck out of his zone. Not much offense out of him, but he has a booming shot from the point. He's limited in terms of his hockey sense, puck skills and offensive abilities. He's a good stay-at-home defenseman with a good physical game along the boards and a good active stick. He is a willing shot-blocker on the PK unit. He's got to work on improving his footwork and overall agility, as these are the major flaws in his game right now. Mukhamadullin was one of four players on the Russian team at the World Under-18 Hockey Championships in April.

MURRAY, JACOB
LD - Kingston Frontenacs (OHL) - 6'02" 192

Jacob Murray had an okay season for the Frontenacs after getting drafted 13th overall in the 2018 OHL-draft. We had him 47th overall in his minor-midget year, so we weren't as high on him as others but Kingston was a team that had room for Murray to make the team out of camp. When we watched him, he had difficulty keeping up with the pace of play, specifically when under heavy-forecheck pressure. Although he theoretically should be a good puck-retriever because of his speed, he turned it over more often than we would like see. Additionally, he struggled with his outlet passes and was inconsistent with his playmaking. Lastly, Murray needs to further refine his puck-skills so that he can become a more consistent transporting option. There's some potential in Murray's game but he needs a lot of development to bring it out.

MYSAK, JAN
LW - HC Litvinov (Czech) - 6'00 " 176

Jan Mysak had a tremendous season despite dealing with an injury for a couple of months. His .23 ppg in the Czech league for a U17 player ranks third, behind Pavel Zacha and Jiri Hudler. In the U19-Czech league he had 21 points in 9 games with 13 goals, and managed 7 points in 31 games in the Czech-league. In relegation play, he finished with 9 points in 6 games, including 5 goals. He played internationally at both the U17's and U18's, but wasn't as dominant as he was in league play. Mysak is a cerebral, two-way winger who uses his hockey-sense to think two-steps ahead of his opponents. He's a skilled-player that prefers to rely on his mind instead of his hands. He displays poise with the puck and has vision that extends through heavy-traffic; he's also very good at positioning himself effectively away from the play. His release point is very-good and he understands the time and space he has to bury the puck. His skating ability is also one of the better aspects of his game. His mechanics are sound and he is very fluid which allows him to skate without much wasted movement. He's already playing against men and succeeding, finding himself on Litvinov's top two-lines at times, so he's advanced for the class of 2020 in terms of his maturation.

NEIGHBOURS, JAKE
LW- Edmonton Oil Kings (WHL) - 5'11" 196

Neighbours was taken with the 4th overall pick in the WHL bantam draft. This season he got off to a hot start but slowed down as he struggled with injuries and fell from his early season role to finish with 24 points in 47 games. He spent some time on the first powerplay in a net front role and early in the year was on the top line before returning from injury in a depth scoring position. Beyond league play he captained Canada white at the world u17s and registered 6 points in 5 games. Neighbours one standout trait in his game is his smarts. Neighbours gets himself in to good positions and can quickly diagnose a play and make the right read. His brain allows him to maximize his physical tools. Neighbours is not an explosive skater, he has decent short area agility but lacks pull away speed in open ice which limits his ability to threaten off the rush. Neighbours has soft hands that allow him to make plays in front of the net where he can quickly corral a puck and make a move on the goaltender under pressure. His physical strength also stands out as he has a solid, compact frame that allows him to seek out contact and more than hold his own in board battles. Next season Neighbours should be a leader on a strong Edmonton team and gain more offensive opportunity.

NIEMELA, TOPI
RD - Karpat U20 (Jr. A SM-Liiga) - 5'10" 157

Niemela is an offensive defenseman from Finland. This past season, he played for Karpat's U20 team in the Finnish junior league. He had 8 points in 39 games in his league, which was the 2nd-best among all U-17 defensemen in that league behind Samuel Knazko. Internationally, it was a busy year for Niemela, as he played on the national U-17 and U-18 teams this season.

Niemela is really good at rushing pucks out of his zone. He is very efficient when it comes to moving pucks out of his zone, either by making a quick first pass or using his good skating abilities to skate the puck out. He's a decent skater with quick first few strides, but his top speed remains average. He has some work to do on improving his agility and backward skating. He's got to make quicker decisions with the puck as well, as he can encounter difficulties in his zone when under pressure and can turn pucks over too frequently, like he did at the April U-18s. He's got to learn to make more simple plays with the puck and not try low-percentage plays, as he does too often. Niemela makes good reads in the offensive zone and can be like a 4th forward, jumping in the play nicely. He's got a good, hard shot from the point and above-average vision that gives him value on the power play. He has average size and will need to get stronger in the years ahead. His defensive game will also need to get better in order for him to become a better pro prospect down the road for the NHL.

NOVAK, PAVEL
RW - Motor Ceske Budejovice U19 (Czech U19) - 5'09" 161

Novak was a top goal-scorer in the Czech U19 league this year, scoring 29 goals in 31 games. He also played 20 games in the 2nd men's league in the Czech Republic. He was a regular on the Czech U-17 and U-18 teams throughout the year; he started the year by playing at the Hlinka-Gretzky Cup in August. Overall, with the U-17 team this season, he had 15 points in 16 games and 6 in 12 games with the U-18 team. He's at this best on the power play with more time and space to make plays. He's got a very good shot, good velocity and a quick release. He's capable of playing the point on the power play, where he can be a threat to score from the point with his good wrister or snapshot. He can also play on the half-wall on the power play, where he can be more of a playmaker. He's good at slowing down the play and utilizing his patience with the puck to open passing lanes for his teammates. He's a bit undersized at the moment; he'll need to get stronger physically in order to compete better along the wall and be better competition in the years ahead. We also want to see him be more engaged at even-strength. He's not very active on the ice and we want to see that compete level improve. For a player of his size, we would also like to see his skating abilities improve. All these aspects are average at this point, and we want to see a quicker acceleration and more explosiveness overall. He was one of the lone Czech forwards to really make an impression on us this season and should be one of the top prospects from the Czech Republic for the 2020 NHL Entry Draft.

NYBECK, ZION
RW - HV71 U20 (Jr. SuperElite) - 5'08" 176

Zion Nybeck came to HV71's organization this season and has been a revelation for his team. He played 14 games with his new club's U-18 team, in which he put up 17 goals and 6 assists for a total of 24 points. He was a regular on the U20 team, where he put up 17 goals and 26 assists for a total of 43 points in just 35 games. His numbers are really impressive considering his height, however, he is extremely skilled and gifted with fantastic technique hockey sense. Nybeck always works very hard on both sides of the puck, and he is a loyal team player. His skating is average, as he lacks elite top speed, but he is mobile and can twist and turn on a penny if needed. He's got good footspeed, but since he lacks power in his stride, he's not able to gain very much speed on open ice. He struggles in a lot of areas due to his small frame, as he cannot make a claim for the high-danger areas without getting pushed away. The physical elements of his game are non-factors, and he will struggle in the corners and in front of the net. He does have an explosive offensive skillset, though, as he anticipates the play and can find teammates with nifty passes due to his vision and smarts. He's not really a pass-first type of player, it's just that he can't gain access to the areas of the ice where his shots threaten the goaltender enough as his shot is pretty weak, although he releases his wrist shot really quickly.

Nybeck played 16 games for Sweden's U-17 team and managed to put up 7 goals and 2 assists for a total of 9 points. He was also part of the team that placed third in the World Under-17 Hockey Challenge, in addition to the Swedish U-18 team that came in first place in the U-18 World Championships in Sweden. Nybeck was also awarded an individual prize as the best player in the domestic U-18 league.

O'ROURKE, RYAN
LD - Sault Ste. Marie Greyhounds (OHL) - 6'02" 181

Ryan O'Rourke had a solid rookie campaign for the Greyhounds, finishing with 22 points in 62 games. He had an additional 2 assists in 11 playoff games. He played for Canada Black at the U17's where he produced 6 points in 5 games, including 3 goals. O'Rourke is a two-way defenseman who some bite to his game. He's got a good-frame on him and was willing to use it to by imposing himself on his opponents both in open-ice and along the boards. Ryan keeps a good pace in own-end and was solid under-pressure due to his impressive anticipation which extends-out to all three-zones. He's not the fleetest skater, and has some choppiness in his stride at this time but made decisions quickly and had solid vision when we viewed him which helped compensate for his average-skating. At the offensive-line, he was very good at activating, which resulted in several impressive plays when we viewed him. His shot is a plus and he can drag the puck in-tight to the body to suddenly change the angle of his release point. O'Rourke needs to continue to fill out his frame and develop another gear in his stride by refining his mechanics when heading into next season.

OVCHINNIKOV, DMITRI
LC - Sibirskie Snaipetry Novosibirsk (MHL) - 5'10" 154

Ovchinnikov split his season between two leagues. He played 10 games for Sibir Novosibirsk U-17, where he put up 7 goals and 10 assists for a total of 17 points. He also played 40 games in the Russian MHL league and recorded 2 goals and 5 assists for a total of 7 points.

Ovchinnikov is not very big, listed as 5'10" and 154 pounds. He will always be one of the smaller players on the ice. He makes up for his lack of size with his fantastic hockey sense. He sees the ice well, with excellent vision, and has the ability to control the pace of the game to fit his strengths and needs. He has great offensive creativity, and his stickhandling and puck skills allow him to be able to pull a deke out of nowhere to beat opponents one-on-one everywhere on the ice. His short passing game is incredible, and he finds a way to set up his teammates for scoring chances almost every shift. His shot is weak and lacks velocity, but his shots are so smart that he can find openings anyway. However, don't expect him to be able to beat a goaltender with a free line of sight. Even though he is not very big or strong, he tries to hold onto the puck until his linemates are open or until he can find a safe pass, but he can easily be outmuscled and stripped of the puck as well. When that happens, he will battle hard to get it back. He competes super hard all over the ice to win loose pucks and to steal them from the opposition. He can get abused for a couple of shifts but will always keep coming back to the contested areas without a second thought. He doesn't just compete hard, he competes smartly. His reads are superb, both offensively and defensively. He will break up passes with clever reads in all three zones. His skating is fluid and smooth but lacks natural, raw power and top speed. He can easily avoid getting hit with his quick feet and lateral movements, but when he gets caught, he is totally stuck.

Ovchinnikov is a player that is just as viable at the first-line center position as he would be as a third-line center. He is super-smart, loyal to his team and a very good offensive two-way player. Hopefully, he can grow and get taller and stronger during the summer, but he is a very interesting prospect for the 2020 NHL Entry Draft.

PASHIN, ALEXANDER
LC - Salavat Yulaev Ufa (MHL) - 5'08" 154

Pashin was a good performer with the Russian U-17 team this season, and also played 17 games in the MHL where he had 10 points. He's an undersized center with great smarts and a great compete level. He's always moving his feet, and likes to annoy the opposing defense with a quick forecheck. He wins a lot of puck races with his good speed and hustle.

He plays bigger than his size, getting involved in traffic and not backing down from anyone. He's fearless on the ice. He sees the ice very well; he's mainly a playmaker and makes his linemates better. He has decent top speed and good acceleration. He has good puck skills and good one-on-one abilities. His good, lower center of gravity helps him to protect the puck against bigger players. He has value as a penalty-killer thanks to his good sense of anticipation that helps cut down passes and create turnovers. He'll need to get bigger and stronger in the years to come, but we like the compete level and skills of this player.

PERFETTI, COLE
LC - Saginaw Spirit (OHL) - 5'10" 185

Cole Perfetti had an excellent rookie season for the Spirit after getting drafted 5th overall in the OHL-draft. He was named the rookie of the month in both February and March, while also becoming the top leading rookie scorer in franchise history by finishing with 74 points in 63 games, including 37 goals. In the playoffs, he produced 14 points in 16 games, including 8 goals. He also played at the U17's for Canada White, where he finished with 9 points and had the most assists on the team with 7. What makes Perfetti a prolific scorer is his hockey-sense and release. He has one of the top wrist-shots featured in the 2020 class and is an elite-thinker. It's a lightning quick release that generates a tremendous amount of power due to how good Cole is at redistributing his weight to get underneath the shot. He needs very little time and space to put it in the back of the net and that's due to his anticipation. Perfetti is adept at reading what his opponents are attempting to do, and then dynamically reacting to their movement. He's an average skater, who has very little power in his lower-body, but his hockey-IQ allows him to slow the tempo-down and he has a remarkable level of poise when controlling the puck. He's one of the few underage players we viewed this year who amazed us with some of the plays he was capable of making. In order for Perfetti to continue to develop successfully, he needs to increase his strength so he can generate more power in his stride; while further refining his mechanics.

PERREAULT, JACOB
RC - Sarnia Sting (OHL) 5'11" 198

Jacob Perreault was one of the leading rookie scorers and named to the OHL all-rookie first team. He finished the season with 55 points in 63 games, including 30 goals. In the playoffs, he finished with 2 assists in 4 games and at the U17's where he played for Canada Red, he finished with 2 goals in 6 games. Perreault is a duel-threat center who has a versatile-attack at his disposal. He's one of the better shooters out of the 2020-OHL-class and can score in multiple ways, using a quick-strike style of play. He features an excellent wrist-shot and understands how to generate torque; his slapshot features a reduced wind-up that made him very successful with the man-advantage, where he showed that he can take difficult passes in one-motion; and he has a sharp backhander that he looks to use in-tight to the net. Additionally, Jacob can catch goalies by surprise by shooting off-angle and doesn't hesitate when given a high-percentage shot. His hockey-sense is good; he reacts dynamically to what's available in-front him and has the skill necessary to dictate play, though he doesn't drive play as much as his skill-set would suggest he can. The reason for this due to his balance and consistency. He's a decent skater who relies more on his sharp-edges than other aspects of his mobility but he's off-balance too often which results in him turning the puck-over and getting out-muscled despite his thicker-frame. Furthermore, he has games where he can be largely invisible before flashing his impressive skill-level, so we will be monitoring his shift-to-shift play next season to see if it improves.

PETERKA, JOHN-JASON
LW/RW - RB Hockey Akademie (Czech U19) - 5'10" 181

John-Jason Peterka had an excellent season, out-scoring the next highest point producer in the U19 league by 14 points and finishing with a 1.96 ppg-rate. He finished the year with 45 goals and 94 points in 48 games. He played internationally for the German squad at the U18s (Div1), where he produced 8 points in 5 games, with 2 goals. Peterka is a very-fast sniper with a lot of raw-upside. The first thing that stands out about the kid is his speed. He's capable of rapid-gear shifts and has impressive acceleration. Additionally, he can make plays while going at his top-speed and has soft-hands, though at international events when the competition was increased, he did have more trouble guarding the puck. He's not just a shooter though, showing the ability to thread the puck, this was pronounced on the half-wall and below the goal-line with the man-advantage. Although he's very quick and skilled, he lacks attention to detail away from the play at this time. He's unable to recognize how he should block lanes using his speed in his own-zone and needs a lot of coaching in order to develop a more well-rounded game. It will be interesting to see how he adapts to the DEL, where he's scheduled to play for EHC Munchen, since we think he might be too green for a top men's league.

PETERSON, DYLAN
RW/C - USA NTDP-17 (USHL) - 6'04" 185

Rangy, offensive forward with a huge frame. Peterson made the jump from the Canadian Midget/AAA circuit where he easily led his CIHA White club in scoring to come to the USNTDP. While the dual citizen (USA/Canada) didn't produce as much as he probably wanted with just three goals and 11 points in 31 USHL games, the adjustment period for him going against much tougher competition can't be overstated. This is where the rubber meets the road for the Boston University commit, as he can no longer just bowl his way through lesser competition. While the numbers might not have been there, he definitely had some games where he really looked the part and was poised to breakout. He owns a very high skill level and he looks comfortable with the puck on his stick for extended periods of time. The 6'4" forward uses his big frame to protect pucks and make space for himself at a very advanced level for his age. His hockey strength is a plus as well, as he shows good balance and edgework while shielding off defenders from stealing pucks from him. He's a plus skater with good puck poise and hockey sense. It will be interesting to see if he finds himself spending more time at center or at right wing next year, as he has shown the propensity to do both. Dylan could probably stand to move pucks a little quicker and work his way towards the net with more regularity. There are times when he takes a lap around the offensive zone, but it's a lot of perimeter play that amounts to little pay off. He's young for the 2020 draft class, as he's an August 2002 birthday, which adds a bit more to his allure. If all the potential energy that Peterson harnesses turns kinetic at some point next year, he could end up in the upper reaches of the NHL's first round.

PIERCEY, RILEY
RW - Barrie Colts (OHL) - 6'03" 185

Riley Piercey was taken 16th overall in the OHL-draft, and had some flashes when he was on Barrie. He finished the season with 14 points in 60 games, including 3 goals. Although Barrie missed the playoffs, he did play internationally, going scoreless in 5 games while playing for Canada White. Piercey is a mobile-power-forward who has a lot of tools. He's a kid who has a lot of length and a projectable-frame that he has yet fill out but that doesn't stop him from swarming players on the forecheck. He's willing to throw his weight-around and can play a tenacious-checking brand of hockey. His motor compliments his skating, he's a natural skater for a kid his size and can generate good straight-line speed. He didn't produce as much as his tools would have predicted, and this is a result of having questionable hockey-sense. He doesn't always know how to involve himself in the play, and doesn't read his teammates intentions at the consistency needed to extract the value of his tools. Although he's offensively raw in terms of evaluating where he needs to be on the ice at times, there's still some upside.

PILLAR, JOSH
C- Kamloops Blazers (WHL) - 5'11" 165

Pillar was selected 14th overall in his bantam draft. He made a strong impression this year in Kamloops playing down the middle on the third line with 22 points in 68 games. Piilar has speed that jumps out at you when you watch him play. He is explosive with a powerful stride and excellent acceleration; he was one of the best skaters amongst the WHL rookies. Pillar is a hard worker who did well in an energy role where he had to be engaged defensively and play physical. Pillar has some offence to his game with a lot of individual chances generated off the rush thanks to his speed and a good shot. The question with him is whether he has the ability to slow the game down a bit and generates chances in settled situations. Pillar has not yet shown strong playmaking and offensive instincts. Pillar has one high end skill and a lot of areas where improvement will have major benefits.

POIRIER, JEREMIE
LD - Saint-John Sea Dogs (QMJHL) - 6'00" 192

Poirier was the 8th overall selection in the 2018 QMJHL Draft. In his rookie season, he amassed 21 points in 62 games on a struggling team. Poirier is a highly-skilled offensive defenseman. He has good puck skills and skating abilities. He loves to rush the puck from his own zone and has excellent hands. He handles the puck like a forward sometimes, and he's a threat one-on-one due to those puck skills. His skating abilities are above-average and his good footwork helps him defend against speedy forwards. Poirier does flash some good skills, but does struggle with his decision-making. His hockey IQ is average at best. For a player with his skill level, he doesn't generate a ton of offensive chances once in the offensive zone. He creates plays with his feet, but as a playmaker from the point, it's more difficult. He's got a good point shot; he needs to work on his shot-selection and also his accuracy. Defensively, his compete level needs to improve. Currently, it's too easy to play against him in his own zone and in his position, it should be more difficult. He's not a physical player along the boards or in front of the net, and that will need to improve next season as well. Poirier does a lot of nice things on the ice with the puck, but the results from those nice plays are missing. He looks good with the puck on his stick, but we want to see more results out of him. That was a problem for us in his QMJHL draft year, and also this past season.

PONOMARYOV, VASILI
LC/LW - MHK Krylia Sovetov Moskva (MHL) - 6'00" 176

Vasili Ponomaryov had an excellent season in the Russian Junior league, producing 29 points in 37 games, including 20 assists. He was a dominant force at the U17's for Russia, producing 8 points in 6 games, with 4 goals. Ponomaryov is a dynamic player who plays a fast-paced game. His skill-level is very-high and it compliments his creative-attack. He looks to challenge defenders and use his hands to break them down before identifying the most dangerous-play he can make. Although he produced more assists than goals, he's a duel-threat forward who has good footwork behind a quick-snap-like release. His playmaking is also very good and he can make difficult passes while going at top speeds. He's not the fastest player in a straight-line, relying more on his quick pivots and edges to remain elusive. His motor helps compensate for some of his skating though, as he's constantly in motion and attempting to make a play. He's a highly adaptive player with a variety of ways to put points up on the board. He's coming into the 2020 season as one of our top Russian prospects.

PROKOP, LUKE
RD- Calgary Hitmen (WHL) - 6'03.75" 202

A highly touted bantam, Prokop was selected by Calgary with the 7th overall pick in his draft. This season he played top 4 minutes in a shutdown role with 10 points in 62 games. Prokop is big and rangy with good skating ability that allows him to take away time and space. He can be a physical presence, throwing hits that separate the man from the puck consistently. With his great reach defensively he was able to break up multiple rushes before they crossed the blueline. Prokop can sometimes lack in his decision making and was occasionally caught in no man's land defensively because of indecisiveness. Offensively Prokop's game is mainly limited to his big point shot as he rarely pushed the limits or risked making mistakes. With his shot and skating ability there is potential for him to do more offensively when put in that role. With the puck he can be effective with his breakout passes, but looked like a different player when he was under pressure. Prokop's game has a ton of room for growth but there is a good foundation with his size and skating.

PUUTIO, KASPER
RD - Karpat U20 (Jr. A SM-Liiga) - 5'11" 172

Puutio was a strong performer internationally for Finland this season, playing at both the U-17 and U-18 levels. Back home, he played in the junior league for Karpat's U20 team, where he had 4 points in 31 games. He was also on the U-18 team, where he had 12 points in 10 games. Puutio is not very flashy, but plays a very efficient game at both ends of the ice. He does just about everything well on the ice; he can move pucks quickly out of his zone and be physical when he needs to be along the boards. Puutio is a solid two-way defenseman; offensively, he has good vision and a quick release on his shots from the point, but he also does a good job getting his shot through. He has good mobility, a good active stick in the defensive zone and a good compete level. These are attributes that make him an effective player in his zone. He has a good hockey IQ and above-average smarts that bode well for his future. Puutio is one of the top defensive prospects from Finland for 2020, and should be one to keep an eye on next season, whether he plays in the junior league or Liiga.

QUINN, JACK
RW - Ottawa 67's (OHL) - 5'11"-170

Jack was Ottawa's 2nd round pick #39 overall in the 2017 OHL Draft. He was awarded rookie of the year in 2017, he was up and down with the 67'S and the Kanata Lasers last year as a 16 year old. When he started the season he was on the 4th line playing a limited role, but as the season went on he quickly establish himself as a good 200 ft player. He ended the year with 32 points in 61 games. Jack is a late '01 birthday.

Jack's hockey IQ is outstanding and he knows where everyone else is on the ice, his vision on the ice is outstanding he is very good at slowing the game down in front of him and finding the open man or finding open spot in zone for scoring chances. Jack is also a very good stickhandle with the puck as he has turned a number of defensemen inside out 1 on 1. Jack has the ability to control the game when he has the puck on his stick, the puck seems to always find him or follow him on the ice, and he has a good release on his shot, very deceptive. Jack needs to focus more on taking puck hard to the net and going to the dirty areas and creating more chances for himself as on some nights he likes to stay on the perimeter too much. With his high hockey IQ his defensive awareness was really good for Ottawa, he understands where to be in the zone, and seemed to know where the puck is going to be as well. He was really good on the PK for Ottawa knowing when to pressure the puck carrier and when to stay back and use his stick to break up passes. He is very good at not putting himself in bad situations to get hit hard based on his size. Jack needs to focus on getting stronger and faster next year, and he can be a key contributor for Ottawa success next year, and contribute a lot on the offense as well.

RAFKIN, RUBEN
RD - Tri-City Storm (USHL) - 5'11" 188

Rafkin is a prospect from Finland who has been playing in America since 2016-2017, having played with the Selects Hockey Academy for 2 years before making the jump to the USHL this season. In his rookie season in the USHL, he had 10 points in 38 games and also amassed 90 penalty minutes. He was a key player with Finland's U-17 team, playing in exhibition games in August versus Sweden and Russia, the November U-17 Hockey Challenge and in February at the European Youth Olympic Festival.

Rafkin is of average height, but he's extremely strong and very advanced physically compared to his peers. He loves to play a very physical game; he hits hard and keeps opposing forwards honest when they rush the puck on his side of the ice. He needs to be a bit more poised in his zone and not run around as much for the big hit, though. He's a powerful skater with good acceleration and decent top speed. He loves to rush the puck out of his zone and has good hands to handle it in traffic, allowing him to make plays in the offensive zone. He's strong on the puck; when he's rushing the puck, it's tough to take it away from him. In the offensive zone, he has a big shot from the point and can create offense with his feet by being very active and jumping into the play. He's tough to play against; he plays an in-your-face physical game and has a mean streak. One thing we want to see him improve on is his puck-management. He can be victim to some bad turnovers at times with his strange decision-making Rafkin will play for Lincoln in the USHL next season, as he was acquired in a trade from Tri-City. He's committed to play college hockey at Denver University.

RATZLAFF, JAKE
RD - Rosemount HS (MNHS) - 6'03" 205

Ratzlaff is a 6th Round Draft pick of Green Bay (USHL) in 2018. Ratzlaff is a towering, rangy defenseman that has developed physically the last couple of years and as a result, his skating and footwork has made good progress. Ratzlaff's footwork and stick work allows him to quickly eat up ice and take away time and space effectively around the blue lines and in the neutral zone. Ratzlaff has good pucks skills and has shown the ability to stretch the ice coming out of his own end. His long, powerful strides allow him to rush the puck up ice when the play calls for it. Ratzlaff showed decent offensive upside this year, with 10 goals and 15 assists in 24 games for Rosemount. Jake has a booming, right-handed slap shot from the point. Defensively, Ratzlaff still has some things to sort out at times. He can rely on his size advantage a bit too much in some instances which comes across as lackadaisical play in some situations and needs to show more urgency in getting to pucks and on the opposition in the corners. Ratzlaff does do a good job cleaning things up in front of his own net, he is active in checking sticks in the slot and shows good awareness and clears pucks out of danger well. Ratzlaff is the prototypical defenseman when it comes to size and skating ability, how he adjusts to having less time and less of a size advantage at the upper levels of amateur and professional hockey will likely determine his NHL upside, but a lot of the tools are there and Jake will be a highly scouted prospect in 19/20 wherever he plays. Ratzlaff is a University of Minnesota commit and given his size advantage at the High School level, we're not sure what another season of High School hockey will do for his development so it's likely Ratzlaff will at least spend some of next season in Green Bay

RAYMOND, LUCAS
RW - Frölunda HC U20 (Jr. SuperElite) 5'10" 165

Lucas Raymond had an extremely strong year good year with the Frölunda HC U20 where he produced 48 points including 35 assists and tied his league for second place in the scoring race. In the playoffs, he scored 9 points in 6 games including 5 assists. He also made his debut in the SHL as a 16-year old and appeared in 10 games recording 2 assists and did not look out of place at all. He also played 4 games in the Champions hockey league where his team won the Internationally he appeared for his nations U17 team and U18 team. With the U17 squad, he scored 17 points in 13 games and he was a dominating force offensively in a duo with Alexander Holtz. With the one year older U18 team he managed to put up 21 points in 17 games, including a hatrick in the U18 world championship final against Russia where his nation won the gold on home soil. He was also a part of the team that won the silver medal at the Hlinka Gretzky tournament earlier on the season. Raymond may be the player that is the funniest to watch in the SuperElite, as he has a super explosive offensive skillset as well as a super high level of competing. His offense is super creative and irrational and he can do unexpected things with the puck, anytime, anywhere as he's got fantastic hands and puck control, superb stickhandling and amazing vision. His 35 assists in the SuperElite is a testament to his vision and passing skills, but what makes his offensive skills so fantastic is that he can stickhandle his way around anyone as his hands are extraordinary and his excellent quickness and foot speed allows him to be a threat on open ice as well. He skates with a low center of gravity and is hard to catch as he is evasive and always keeps his feet moving. He has the ability to gain a lot of speed and he really can handle the puck at high speed and make a play by passing and shooting the puck at a high speed too. Raymond's shot is lethal, especially his wrist shot, with a little time and space he will almost certainly score and he also get his shot off in tight areas with great velocity. Even though Raymond is a superstar, he has the ability to make his teammates better and he has great work ethic with a superb two-way game he is a factor in all three zones. His compete is super high as he hates to lose the puck, he always fights hard to get it back and won't stop the pursuit until his team has possession of the puck. Raymond really drives his team's offense and he won't wait for a play to happen, but instead, he creates the play he wants, always with exuberant creativity and playfulness. Although Raymond's got few weaknesses to his game, he lacks a bit of size, but he does have the speed and mobility to make up for it. He has proven that he is a game winner and a big performer in big games as he scored 2 goals in the U18 Swedish championship final and led his team to the gold medal and then a couple of weeks later scored three goals in the U18 World Championship final game against Russia. Other than this he also, as mentioned above, won the Champions hockey league. Other mentionable achievements this past season: Hlinka memorial silver medal, U18 Swedish championship playoffs MVP, U20 SuperElite most points by a U17 junior, U20 SuperElite best forward, U17 WHC all-star team, U17 WHC bronze medal. It will be exciting to see if he can improve even more in his draft year as he will be one of the top prospects for the entire 2020 draft going into it. We will most likely see him play for Frölunda HC in the SHL next season.

REID, LUKE
RD - Chicago Steel (USHL) - 6'00" 185

Two-way defenseman who just missed the cut for the 2019 NHL Entry Draft. Reid holds dual American-Canadian citizenship, but represented the United States very well at the Hlinka-Gretzky Cup. After a strong season with the Penticton Vees (BCHL), Reid made the jump to the Chicago Steel of the USHL. He wasn't used as on the power play, but managed 19 points in 60 games while leading the team in plus/minus by a decent margin at plus-15. Despite being used in mostly defensive situations, Luke can snap the puck ahead on the breakout. He puts a lot of pace on his passes and he has a plus shot that he probably doesn't pursue enough. Reid checks off a lot of boxes and has a high floor, even if he doesn't have a particularly elite skill that stands out. The biggest drawback for Reid is that he seems to play the game without a lot of confidence and he exhibits a low panic threshold. One begets the other, but the way he often conducts himself on the rink doesn't jive with the tools that he owns. Despite being a very competent skater, he plays with a loose gap and it puts him in a tougher position more often than not. He has technical skills and breakout ability, but when he feels pressure, his puck poise drops considerably. Reid has better hockey sense than he shows; we would love to see him play with more composure and a killer instinct next season to really boost his draft stock. He's a University of North Dakota commit but is likely to return to the USHL in 2019-20.

RENWICK, MICHAEL
RD - Hamilton Bulldogs (OHL) 5'11" 170

Michael Renwick had a decent-year for Hamilton, although he only managed to play in 18 games. He finished with 3 points, including 1 goal and at the U17's; he was featured on Canada White but didn't produce a point in 5 games. Renwick is a raw-two-way defenseman who can activate at the line. He's at his best when he keeps things simple in his own-end, and can read off his partner at an okay level; this extends to reading transitional play when he looks to make an outlet-pass. He's not a puck-moving defenseman who relies on his skating, but he does use his skating to generate offensive-chances at the blueline. The offensive chances he generates are dependent on his ability to interpret when he has enough time and space to make a play, and we've seen him produce chances by getting his wrist-shot and slapshot through traffic, or by making a clean-pass. Michael needs to work on his ability to remain calm and collected when an opponent is bearing down on him in his own-zone; he has trouble anticipating play when the pace is high and makes poor decisions as a result when there's too much pressure. If Renwick can clean that part of his game up, then he can continue to develop into a useful defender for Hamilton next-season.

ROBINSON, DYLAN
RC - Oshawa Generals (OHL) - 6'01" 170

Dylan Robinson was drafted 28th overall in the OHL-draft and came in with some promise after finishing as the MVP of the OHL-cup, but had a forgettable year and suffered an injury; we expect him to get traded this off-season. He produced 7 points in 34 games, including 2 goals after receiving limited ice-time. At the U17's, he produced 1 goal in 5 games for Canada White. Robinson is a two-way center who can play a detail-oriented game off the puck. He's not a high-end offensive-player but can make accurate passes while in motion, and doesn't mind engaging in traffic. Additionally, he's a bigger kid who can hit-hard and can weigh-heavy on opponents. In order for Dylan to develop, he needs to further develop his skating and puck-skills; he's a raw-offensive-player with the puck on his stick at this time.

ROCHETTE, THÉO
LC - Chicoutimi Sagueneens (QMJHL) - 5'09" 153

Rochette grew up mostly in Switzerland, but due to his Canadian passport, he was eligible for the QMJHL Draft. Drafted 7th overall by the Chicoutimi Saguenéens, he had a solid rookie season in the league with 43 points in 59 games and also scored 4 goals in 4 playoff games in the opening round against Rimouski. A bit unusual for a rookie in this league, Rochette's game got better as the season progressed and played his best hockey in the last two months of the season and in the playoffs. Rochette is a smart center. At this stage of his career, he is already dependable at both ends of the ice. He's not the biggest player and is also not an elite skater. Those two things should hurt his draft stock a bit next season if he doesn't grow a couple of inches in the summer (and if he doesn't improve his skating). He's got decent speed and a good burst of speed, but for a center of his size, he definitely needs to add an extra gear to his skating. He's got a decent shot with a quick release. He's got above-average hands, good puck skills and good one-on-one abilities. He's got a good compete level, he keeps his feet moving and works hard in all three zones. With what we saw last year, there's not much doubt that Rochette will be a very good player in the QMJHL. The question with him will be whether or not he will become a good NHL prospect. He's not big and not fast, but he has some good offensive skills and a good hockey IQ. He'll be followed closely next year in Chicoutimi, playing alongside some other draft-eligible such as Hendrix Lapierre and William Dufour.

ROEPKE, CASEY
LD - University School (WIHS) - 5'11" 170

Roepke is coming off a Wisconsin High School state title with University School of Milwaukee. Roepke saw some games with Green Bay (USHL) toward the end of the season and eventually settled in and played some good games with the Gamblers. Roepke is a smooth skating defenseman who still needs to add some strength in order for his straight-line skating to smoothen out a bit. His stride has some good technical aspects but lacks explosiveness and the ability to separate from fore checkers. Defensively, Casey plays a smart and effective game, he sorts out situations quickly in his own end and can make up and covered for some mistakes by his defensive partner in a lot of viewings. Roepke's puck skills are good, he is able to stretch the ice and is an accurate passer coming out of his own end. In the offensive end, Roepke uses a quick release to get shots through to the net and has decent vision of the zone but lacks some game breaking offensive ability and projects as more of a two-way defenseman than a high point producing, power play defenseman. Casey can move the puck effectively from the point position and makes few major mistakes.

ROLSTON, RYDER
RW - USA NTDP-18 (USHL) - 6'00" 165

Energetic, goal-scoring winger. Son of Brian Rolston, Ryder spent most of the year with the U18 Team before being demoted late in the season. The demotion did allow Rolston to be a featured piece on a team, as opposed to the depth role that he was used in for much of his U18 time. All together, he found 14 goals and 24 points in 34 USHL games. Committed to Notre Dame, Ryder offers a lot in the skating department. He has terrific multi-directional mobility with a very smooth stride. His skating speed jives well with the high level of pace that he plays with. Sometimes, he's even a little too fast for his own good, as he can over-skate plays at times. Controlling the puck at top speed has sometimes been problematic for him as well, despite having really slick hands; he still lets some pucks roll away from him at very inopportune times. Like his dad, Rolston's calling card is his shot. He has a lightning quick release and is capable of whizzing pucks past goalies even from mid-range. He does a good job finding a way to get a stick on pucks near the net or to negate icings. His playmaking and vision are not impressive and his overall hockey sense is questionable. Defensively, he really struggles with coming back through the middle and maintaining proper body positioning. He's also not nearly as hockey strong as we'd expect. There are times where he supports the play well, but he still needs to improve on his ability to get open. Too many of his scoring chances are from streak-and-shoot attempts off the rush. The bullet shot and the wheels that come with it is the entrée here, if he can add some greater dimension to his game, his draft stock would improve immensely. Rolston was selected 2nd overall in the 2019 USHL Entry Draft by Waterloo.

ROODE, BENJAMIN
RD - Acadie-Bathurst Titan (QMJHL) - 6'05" 207

Roode was the Titan's 1st pick in the 2018 QMJHL Draft (14th overall) and played 66 games with them this past season. Roode has obvious great size and decent agility and mobility for a player of his size at this age. He's more of a defensive defenseman at this point in his development, as he only had two assists this past season. He's got to improve his decision-making with the puck and move it faster in the transition. Defensively, he relies on his size to win one-on-one battles, as well as a good active stick to knock pucks down. He's still raw with his offensive skillset and was not featured in a positive situation, with Acadie-Bathurst finishing the year as the worst team in the league. It was tough to shine and improve his offensive game playing on such a bad team who didn't have possession of the puck for much of each game. Next year, it will be important to see him make some progression in terms of his play with the puck, in addition to his offensive game, in order to become a better NHL prospect. Defensive defensemen are not really what teams are looking for in today's NHL.

ROSSI, MARCO
C - Ottawa 67's (OHL) - 5'09" 170

Marco came into the league as a highly touted player from Europe, Ottawa selected him #18 overall in 2018 Import Draft. Marco is a late birth coming from Austria, you would think that his first year in North America there would be an adjustment to his game, Marco came in and was dominant for Ottawa all year round and you couldn't tell he was only 16 years old.

He ended the year with 65 points in 53 games with a very impressive +51 on the year. Marco is a very good two-way centre with good skill and smarts to his game that plays an excellent 200 foot game. Rossi displays strong skating abilities, utilizing a fluid stride to generate quality speed. He is arguably at his best in possession were he shows quick and skilled hands along with a creativity with the puck. Rossi makes quick and strong decisions and possesses the ability to generate offensive opportunities for both himself and his line mates. He thinks the game very fast and can recognize what his options are without having to slow down to think. He played excellent give and go hockey with his linemate Felhaber. Marco has strong vision that allows him to still generate offense and make plays when the pace slows down, excelling off the cycle and half wall. Rossi uses his speed well as he aggressively forechecks and utilize a quick stick to strip opponents of possession. Marco does possess a good release, so when he can effectively get to the scoring areas he becomes dangerous. His quick feet and edges in combination with his puck control can make him elusive with the ability to create space in otherwise tight areas. He is a player who shows great awareness in the defensive zone and positional awareness. He played every situation for Ottawa this year. Powerplay, penalty kill, 5 on 5 etc. Rossi can easily end up in the top 30 players for the 2020 NHL Draft, he needs to build off his excellent 1st season with Ottawa, and continue to work on his skating ability and strength with and without the puck.

ROY, PIERRE-OLIVIER
LW - Gatineau Olympiques (QMJHL) - 5'10" 167

Roy was the 9th-overall selection in the 2018 QMJHL Draft by Gatineau. In his first season in the QMJHL, the former Lévis Chevalier finished the season with 7 goals, 26 points in 56 games. Roy is an intelligent winger who plays a mature game at both ends of the ice. Next season, look for him to improve on those offensive statistics by playing a regular shift on the top-6 in Gatineau, in addition to being a regular on the power play. He sees the ice well; he makes players around him better thanks to his high hockey IQ and excellent vision. Roy can play on any line on a team and find way to contribute. He's not a big player, but he's strong on his skates and has a good compete level. He will play big roles on both the PP and PK units next season with the Olympiques. His skating abilities are decent; he has quick feet but doesn't generate great top speed. He's got some work to do on improving his speed for next season. Look for him to continue to progress offensively next season, slowly but surely becoming an important piece of the Olympiques' rebuild. He's in a similar spot as many QMJHLers next season: next season will determine if he's going to project more as a real good junior player or have NHL potential.

SANDERSON, JAKE
LD - USA NTDP-17 (USHL) - 6'01" 170

Very raw, offensive-minded defenseman. Coming from the Edge School and the Calgary Flames Bantam teams, Jake Sanderson has rapidly put himself on the 2020 NHL Draft radar. With just seven points and a minus-22 rating in 22 USHL games, Sanderson offers no apologies about how raw he is as a defenseman. A fairly upright skater who isn't too tough to knock to the ice, the son of former NHLer Geoff Sanderson still gets around the rink pretty well. It's not very pretty from a mechanical perspective, but he covers the ground that he needs to. What's more is that he really trusts his edgework and his ability to change directions to bail him out of tight situations. He has a plus shot and is threatening with the one-timer, particularly on the power play. While it's not always obvious on puck retrievals, Sanderson can get a head of steam about him and carry the puck across multiple lines. We would like to see these flashes of skill occur with more regularity, but there is an undercurrent of very useful talent for this U17 captain. There's still a lot of work for Sanderson to do defensively. His anticipation of the timing of plays is lacking and it causes him to make pivots and reaches that range from unproductive to awkward. The reality of the situation is that Sanderson is just not very refined at the moment; however, he has shown the propensity to really be an impactful blue liner at this level. If he's able to really smooth out his game as a whole, the North Dakota commit could end up as the premier U.S. d-man taken in the draft. In the meantime, he was also a fourth round selection of Winnipeg (nee Kootenay) of the Western League which, if nothing else, introduces another potential avenue for the Montana native to pursue.

SAVOIE, CARTER
LW- Sherwood Park Crusaders (AJHL) 5'09" 170

The brother of Matthew Savoie, Carter is a standout in his own right. Already committed to Denver University, Savoie had a huge first year in the AJHL with 73 points in 58 games good for 5th in league scoring. Savoie is a highly intelligent offensive winger who drives whatever line he is on. Savoie is a great skater who utilizes crossovers and a downhill skating style well to generate speed through the neutral zone. He also has good edges that allow him to cut away from traffic while maintaining his speed. Savoie is a problem for the opposition off the rush with the vision to see layers coming in with him on the attack. He also has a quick release on his wrist shot that can catch goaltenders off guard. Savoie has the hands necessary to play in traffic and is slippery and hard to contain in close quarters. With his exceptional hands Savoie can often draw defenders in before using his high end vision to fire a cross ice pass to a now open teammate. Savoie competes hard and has the want and will to recover pucks. Savoie has multiple options for where to play next season with the Winnipeg ICE recently acquiring his rights along with his brother. Wherever he ends up, look for a dominant offensive season.

SAVOIE, NICOLAS
LD - Quebec Remparts (QMJHL) - 6'00" 174

Savoie was touted as a first or second-round pick in last year's QMJHL Draft, but was eventually drafted in the 4th round by the Remparts due to his NCAA commitment with Providence College. Savoie had a decent first season with the Remparts, playing in 56 games and amassing 12 points overall. He missed some time due to a broken jaw suffered as a result of a bad hit. Savoie has good skating abilities and footwork. He's an average-sized defender, but with his quickness, he can quickly retrieve pucks in his own zone and can skate it out of his zone with ease. He's good to skate the puck away from pressure, but needs to pick his spots better and not too try too much on his own. His decision-making with the puck also needs to improve next season, as he's got an average hockey IQ and needs to improve his shot-selection from the point. He's got to be more poised and patient with the puck rather than rush his plays. He needs to get stronger physically and be more assertive in his battles along the boards and in front of the net. Savoie should be a regular on the Remparts' top-4 on defense next season, and will contribute at both ends of the ice for them.

SCHNEIDER, BRADEN
RD- Brandon Wheat Kings (WHL) - 6'02" 210

Schneider is a late birthday who was the 12th overall selection in his bantam draft. This season Schneider stepped in to a major role on a young Wheat Kings defence and did an admirable job with 24 points in 58 games. He also played for Canada at both the Hlinka and u-18. Schneider is not the type to wow with his offensive game, rarely executing high-end plays. Schneider does move well enough and make good enough reads with the puck that his is not a liability on this end. His main strength however is in the defensive zone where Schneider uses his size and above average skating ability to smother opponents. Schneider does a great job at breaking up the cycle and corralling forwards in front of the net. For a big player Schneider moves well with a powerful stride once he gets going and an average first few steps, on a couple occasions he was beat wide but he is competent defending all but the fastest attackers. In transition Schneider fairly consistently moves the puck out but could stand to be a bit more patient as there are games where he can seem to be throwing it away a bit too early when there is a better play available. Part of this is due to somewhat limited puck skills as Schneider doesn't really have the ability to hang on to it and beat a fore checker. Schneider should continue to be a defensive force and minute eater for Brandon next season.

SCHINGOETHE, WYATT
LC - Waterloo Black Hawks (USHL) - 5'10" 205

Thoughtful, two-way center that really looked comfortable in all situations as a USHL rookie. Schingoethe was on the USNTDP radar, but elected to sign a tender with Waterloo instead. For a 16 year old, Wyatt really featured prominently on the Black Hawks and he handled it all with aplomb. At 33 points in 62 games, he was outpaced by a very select few 2020 draft eligibles. He looks and carries himself bigger than the 5'10" he's listed at. In fact, he looks quite rangy out there and highly intelligent to boot. He can play center and wing, power play and penalty kill, offense and defense – the adaptability that he has shown at such a young age really hints at a ton of promise. He thinks the game really well and demonstrates some defensive nuances that are typically not figured out by players until they're older and more experienced. Right now he only shows flashes of hands and finishing skills, the Notre Dame commit doesn't give the aura of game breaking skill or even an overly powerful shot yet. The skating package is a plus and his closing speed is particularly noteworthy. Working from a very strong and well-rounded foundation, if Schingoethe really augments his technical skills to the point that he can reliably beat players at this level, he'll quickly become one of the most sought after American players for 2020.

SEBRANGO, DONOVAN
LD - Kitchener Rangers (OHL) - 6'00" 179

Donovan Sebrango had a very successful rookie season with the Rangers, finishing with 26 points in 62 games, including 7 goals. In the payoffs, he was pointless, but at the World U17's, he had 2 assists in 5 games for Canada Black. Donovan Sebrango is a two-way defenseman who can rush the puck, while also delivering some bite. He doesn't mind standing up for himself or his teammates, and although he has an average-frame, he's not afraid to use it. His skating mechanics are not the best, he features a sloped posture but it hasn't prevented him from having impressive overall mobility. He has impressive two-step area quickness which made him difficult to catch on the forecheck, and used his mobility to penetrate through the neutral-zone consistently. His ability to find soft-ice away from the puck made him dangerous in the offensive-zone; showing good chemistry with his defensive-partners and reading off their reactions well, so that he could get into position to get his shots towards the net. His vision is ahead of his release point – he can thread sharp passes through traffic and had a good-rate of execution when trying to develop plays.

SEDOFF, CHRISTOFFER
LD - HIFK U20 (Jr. A SM-Liiga) - 5'11" 159

Sedoff is a mobile two-way defender from Finland. This past season, he played for HIFK's U20 team, amassing 3 points in 32 games. He also took part in various U-17 tournaments for Finland throughout the year. He's not a big point-producer just yet. In U-17 tournaments versus his own age group, he didn't stand out in any way in the offensive zone. He plays a simple game with the puck, and his offensive game is still raw at this point. He's pretty good in his own zone; he has good mobility and a good stick that helps him cover as much ice as possible. He's quick to apply pressure to the puck-carrier and cut down on his opponent's time and space quickly with a strong gap. He's not the biggest defenseman, but he has a decent physical game along the boards and competes hard in his zone. Sedoff should be back next season in the U20 league and could also challenge for a spot in Liiga if he can improve his offensive game.

SEED, NOLAN
LD - Owen Sound Attack (OHL) - 5'11" 168

Nolan was Owen Sound's 1st round pick #15 overall in the 2018 OHL Draft. He came into his first season in the OHL and he played an impressive 60 games for the Attack as a 16 year old.

Nolan is an effortless skating two-way defenseman, his first couple strides are very strong, and there's times on the rush where he's able to break away from defenders with his speed. Nolan has shown good puck skills; he has an above average shot from the point and would like to see him use it more often. He seemed to have played in more of a defensive role for Owen Sound on the back end, he only had 10 points. He is a smart Defensemen and has great anticipation on the ice. He's good at reading and reacting to plays in front of him, and at getting himself into position before the play develops. Seed is very good at making quick and accurate decisions in transition and knowing when to jump into the play or sit back. He also has excellent puck retrieval skill, as he gets back quick to get the puck and goes on the offense effectively. With a full year under his belt, next year is where we would likely see Nolan have more of an offensive role for Owen Sound on the back end. If he can feed of his OHL Draft year he should be able to post some points.

SEELEY, RONAN
LD- Everett Silvertips (WHL) - 5'11" 175

One of the most talented defenders in his age group, Seeley was taken 20th in his bantam draft class. This season he was largely relegated to a 6th/7th defenseman role on a veteran Everett blueline, recording only 9 points in 52 games. Despite what the numbers suggest Seeley possesses a lot of talent, constantly making plays that stood out in our viewings. Seeley is a great skater who has the lateral agility to make moves in the offensive zone and quickness to beat a fore checker. When combined with above average puck handling she was able to attack the defence of the rush and attempt risky plays. He does a great job with his passing on the breakout, consistently getting his teammates clean exits and giving them pucks at the right time. Defensively Seeley is still a bit weak due to his lack of size and a bit raw in his instincts as he could sometimes lose his man in front of the net. Seeley showed a ton of progression over the year and had some games where he was a standout. He is a player we like to have a very strong draft year as more opportunity opens up in Everett.

SIMONTAIVEL, KASPER
RW/LW - Tappara U20 (Jr. A SM-Liiga) - 5'9" 179

Kasper Simontaival had a very good under-age season while playing for three-different teams. He has developed through Tappara's system, playing for both their pro team in Liiga, producing 2 assists in 5 games and at the Jr. A level where he produced 27 points in 27 games, including 9 goals. He was loaned to LeKi in the Mestis league, producing 14 points in 21 games, including 5 goals. At the international stage he played in several tournaments including the Hlinka, Champions HL, U18 Five-Nations and World U18's. Simontaival is a stocky sniper who can also distribute the puck. He's a highly coordinated kid who understands how to generate power through his whip-like release. Although he produced more assists than goals, several of his secondary and primary assists were the result of overwhelming net minders with his shot, making it difficult to absorb rebounds which gave his teammates opportunities to bury the puck. His hockey-sense is good, and this gives him the ability to mix-up his options making him difficult to read, specifically off the rush. His vision extends to back-door and trailing options. The biggest area of improvement needed for Kasper is in regards to his skating. For a short and stocky player, it's important he has excellent speed but Simontaivel doesn't at this time, he needs to further increase his acceleration and edges so that he can become more elusive given his build.

SMILANIC, TY
LW/C - USA NTDP-17 (USHL) - 6'01" 167

Hustling, offensive forward with an infectious work ethic. Smilanic and Thomas Bordeleau were neck and neck on a tier unto themselves in terms of U17 scoring this past season. The Colorado native did find nine goals and eight assists in 33 USHL games. With three assists in two games, he also tied for the team lead in scoring during their very abbreviated playoffs. The first thing to notice about Smilanic is that he plays the game like he absolutely loves it. He's highly competitive and his work ethic is off the charts. He backs that up with a really interesting skill set. His shot improved over the course of the year, but still isn't quite good enough to beat goalies from mid-range. He has nice set of mitts on him, and he can control the puck outside the plane of his shoulders. That said, there are times where he's moving just a little too quick for his own good and pucks can just bounce away from him without provocation. He's fast and nimble as he motors around the ice, but he plays with a high center of gravity. He's not very hockey strong and is pretty easy to knock off the puck and knock off of his skates. The biggest question mark for Smilanic is his hockey sense. Too often we see him just in another player's lane or right on top of a teammate in a way that makes little sense. The U17 Team naturally has a slew of undeveloped players by trade, so next season will be a big test for how Ty's mental game grades out. If all systems are go on that, this has the makings of a first round caliber player – if it's determined that he works harder instead of smarter, that will certainly muddy the waters considerably. Another angle on this is that Smilanic was a third round pick in the WHL Draft by Regina, and the door hasn't closed on that avenue either – as the worker bee forward remains without a college commitment.

SMITH, JACK
L/LW – St. Cloud Cathedral (MNHS) - 5'11" 181

Jack Smith is a 1st Round 13th Overall pick of Sioux Falls in the 2018 Phase 1 USHL Draft and is committed to The University of Minnesota Duluth. Smith is coming off a Minnesota Class A State Championship for St. Cloud Cathedral where he put up 24 goals and 29 assists in 25 games. Smith was dominating in the State Playoffs, putting up 7 goals and

8 Assists in 6 games. Smith is a physical, power forward that brings good two-way effort night in and night out. His skill is not dynamic at this stage, but his work ethic and hockey sense put him in a lot of situations to excel and contribute. Smith played a lot of 2019 with NHL Draft prospect Nate Warne, when Warner was in the lineup and Smith was the worker on that line, getting the puck on the fore-check and forcing turnovers from the opposition. Smith plays a heavy game, finishing-his checks and battling in the tight areas of the ice. Smith's plan for 2019-2020 is undermined at this stage but he is physically ready for junior hockey if he chooses to go that route. Smith is a July 02; DOB so is one of the youngest players in this 2020 draft class.

SOUCH, CARTER
C/LW- Edmonton Oil Kings (WHL) - 5'09.5" 150

Taken 75th overall in his bantam draft Souch has had a major rise over the past couple seasons, Souch is a late birthday who played half a season last year before cracking the lineup fulltime this year and recording an impressive 45 points in 68 games without significant powerplay time or top linemates. Watching Souch it is immediately evident how much energy he brings to the game. Souch is a strong skater who is constantly attacking at full speed and is a major factor on the backcheck. He also brings a strong playmaking element with the ability to make difficult reads at top speed. Souch has vision that allows him to exploit holes in the defence and create dangerous chances for teammates. Souch can also take on a defender one on one with the puck skills to beat a defender inside and speed to go wide. Souch is small which can make him a bit of a nonfactor in boards battles but he works hard enough to make up for it. With his limited strength he has a fairly underdeveloped shot that can make him a bit one dimensional as a passer. Souch is a player who we would not be surprised if he had an even bigger breakout next year as one of Edmontons most dangerous players.

SOURDIF, JUSTIN
C/RW- Vancouver Giants (WHL) - 5'11" 163

Sourdif was the 3rd overall pick in his bantam draft class, and had a promising debut season registering 46 points in 64 games for a strong Vancouver team. Sourdif consistently played in the top 6 on the right wing, but saw no powerplay time making his totals even more impressive. Sourdif also played at the u-17s for Canada Red where he wore an "A" on his jersey. A deceptive playmaker, Sourdif made some extremely advanced passes showing excellent timing and awareness. Sourdif has the look of a high end playmaker and possesses the full arsenal of passes to go over around and through defenders. Also presents a shot threat with a quick release that he used to catch goalies off guard. IQ was exceptional, playing beyond his years without the puck constantly finding soft spaces in the defence. Showed good abilities skating through the neutral zone, finding gaps in coverage and showing great change of pace ability. Sourdif's skating features excellent ages, and great shiftiness in tight areas, allowing him to shake defenders on his back. Sourdif could stand to improve his top speed to become an even more dynamic threat. Consistently gives effort and plays lot bigger than his size, Sourdif was unafraid to take and initiate contact going to the dirty areas. Sourdif is a top prospect coming out of the WHL for next year.

SPEARING, SHAWN
LD - Peterborough Petes (OHL) - 6'01" 183

Despite Shawn being a 4th-round selection in the 2018 OHL-draft, he managed to make the Petes out of camp and ended up as Merkley's partner at times as well. He had a decent season despite modest numbers; finishing with 3 points in 37 games, including 2 goals. In the playoffs he was pointless. Spearing is a modern-day shutdown defenseman who has a versatile defensive-game. He's not the biggest kid for his role, but he makes up for it with an impressive compete-level and can use his frame to physically overwhelm players. He maintains a steady-gap and is good at assessing offensive-plays; getting himself in position to block-shots or take away a passing lane. His skating is mixed; he has two-step area quickness but his straight-line speed is a work in progress. As a result, he looks to move the puck up with outlet passes more than transporting out himself. He's calm and poised under-pressure along the goal-line which helps him identify his passing options too. In the offensive-end, Shawn keeps things simple, looking to get his shot through traffic, but also attempts shot-passes. His offensive-game is far more raw than his defensive-game at this stage though. Spearing needs to continue to refine his skating mechanics and develop more creativity and confidence at the offensive-line so that he can further-develop his two-way game.

STÜTZLE, TIM
LC - Jungadler Mannheim U20 (DNL U20) - 5'11 165

A shoulder injury forced Stützle to miss a total of 12 weeks, playing just 21 league games, but he sure made the most of the games he got. He scored 23 goals and 55 points, and added four goals and 11 points in five playoff contests, winning the DNL championship with Jungadler Mannheim. In addition, Stützle appeared in international action for Team Germany at the U17, U18, and U20 levels. He led Germany to promotion from the U18 Div. 1 A World Championships with a tournament-best nine points in five games.

After playing most of his DNL rookie season on the wing, Stützle transitioned to centre for large parts of the 2018-19 campaign. He's a dynamic, all-around offensive player who tries to make something happen every time he touches the puck, both as a playmaker and a scorer. Stützle is an excellent skater with great speed and agility. That, along with his excellent puck skills, allows him to easily beat defenders one-on-one and drive to the net for scoring chances. He possesses a strong shot arsenal with a very quick release on his slap shots and wrist shots, creating power through rapid upper-body movement rather than body strength, and great accuracy. But, he also displays very good vision and excellent passing ability to set up teammates. At times, Stützle can still be too selfish, which is a regular occurrence for players of his quality in a weak junior league. He prefers to play centre, but if we wants to play that position at the next level, he'll have to continue improving his defensive game in his own zone.

STRANGES, ANTONIO
LC/LW - London Knights (OHL) - 5'10'' 179

Antonio Stranges was drafted 21st overall in the 2018 OHL-draft and had a productive rookie-season. He finished with 34 points in 66 games, including 13 goals. In the playoffs, he wasn't as effective, producing 2 assists in 11 games. Stranges is an elusive, playmaking center with a lot of skill. What makes the kid stand out is his ability to swivel on his edges; it makes him remarkably elusive when he's cutting aggressively and it also allows him to mask his intentions with the puck. He's good at saucing passes over extended-sticks when recognizing his openings and has some savviness to his game. He can switch up the tempo of a shift with his quick-striking style of offensive-attack but has some poise that gives him the ability to slow-down the play when he needs to as well. His shooting mechanics are a bit strange in the sense that he's equally as dangerous on his backhand as he is on his forehand, but this does give him a significant advantage when attacking in-tight to the net. Lastly, Stranges has an excellent set of hands, giving him the ability to turn players' inside-out with his move-set. Although Antonio is skilled, he's not overly consistent; he was dominant on some shifts and invisible in others, so it's important for him to come prepared next-season since he's expected to be one of London's leading offensive catalysts.

SVEJKOVSKY, LUKAS
RW- Vancouver Giants (WHL) - 5'09" 158

Svejkovsky spent last season playing in the BCHL before joining Vancouver for this season. Svejkovsky's numbers were held back by limited playing time and opportunities with 26 points in 67 games. These numbers obscure Svejkovsky's offensive game. Svejkovsky was one of his team's best playmakers, constantly making wow passes where he was the only guy in the rink that saw it. When Vancouver gave him a half walk powerplay opportunity he excelled and could pick defenses apart utilizing the cross ice and high slot pass, manipulating sticks of the opposition before making a great pass. Svejkovsky is a flawed player at this point. While a good skater he is not elite and with his size his lack of pull away speed clearly disadvantaged him at times. Svejkovsky is extremely underdeveloped physically and in some instances was a defensive liability due to his inability to compete in board battles. With added strength and opportunity Svejkovsky has the potential for a major breakout next season.

SZMAGAJ, ETHAN
RD - Waterloo Black Hawks (USHL) - 5'10" 178

Slick, offensive defenseman. Szmagaj just missed the cut for the 2019 NHL Draft by three days, which may end up being really beneficial to the University of Michigan commit. He didn't see a ton of ice time all season, and it was especially limited in the playoffs - where he was essentially just a power play specialist. While he did play a full 62-game docket, it's a little misleading given his utilization. Szmagaj netted 17 points, nine of which came with the man advantage, and a plus-15 rating. Ethan plays a fairly unique style. He's a heady, pace-pushing defenseman who shows a lot of upside. He has a projectable foundation of technical skills. His edges and agility are also a plus, but he probably needs more out of his first two steps to shake forecheckers in the manner that he aspires to. He really likes to pivot and try to go against the grain but just can't quite sell it well enough yet. He's also an aggressive style defender who wants to break up plays in the neutral zone before they become a problem. One of the big advantages that Szmagaj features over some other blueliners of his ilk is that he's a feisty competitor and looks very athletic. It's a very raw player, but one who could really shoot up the development arc with some added ice time in 2019-20.

TERRY, ZACH
LD - Guelph Storm (OHL) - 6'01" 187

Zach Terry had a solid first year for the Storm despite getting limited ice-time. Once Sean Durzi was brought on board, it reduced his ice-time, which resulted in less points then he could have produced. His finishing stat-line was 5 points in 51 games, including 2 goals. At the U17's, he didn't produce any points in 5 games but had some good moments there as well. In Oakville minor-midget, he quarter-backed the powerplay, showing some offensive-ability but didn't get that opportunity with Guelph in his rookie season. Terry is a two-way defenseman who has some versatility in his game. He's above-average at anticipating the play when the flow of the game is coming back towards him, which made him decent under pressure, and he showed a quality-first-pass that hit the mark at a good-rate. He didn't like to rush the puck as much as he looked to make quick and clean passes that had a high-percentage of hitting. His decision making is good and he doesn't force his play types, playing a more structured game on the backend. He's a bigger kid and is good at using his frame to pin players and force them to play extended minutes along the boards. At the offensive-line, he can use his anticipation and reads to activate, and displayed a heavy shot as well when he could find a lane. He's not a dynamic puck-carrier and needs to continue to work on his skating but he has some upside.

THOMPSON, JACK
RD - Sudbury Wolves (OHL) - 6'01" 172

Jack Thompson was selected 30th overall in the 2018 OHL-draft, and had an excellent rookie season for the Wolves while getting third-pairing responsibilities and 2nd-unit powerplay-time. He finished the season with 16 points in 52 games, including 6 goals, and in the playoffs, he produced 5 points in 8 games. He also played internationally for Canada Red at the U17's, where he went pointless. Thompson is a smart, two-way defenseman with looks to activate in the offensive-end. He has impressive anticipation which he uses to react dynamically around the goal-line in his own-end, as well as pinch aggressively while looking to get his shot off. His release point is above-average and he's good at assessing when his lanes are open and closed. His decision making was solid, and he doesn't over-extend at the offensive-line. In the defensive-zone, he keeps a good pace which made him good at recovering when he was caught out of position, and he's willing to sacrifice his body in order to block a shot. His skating mechanics allow him to keep up with some of the quicker forwards who attempt to beat him-wide and he can join the rush as a result of them as well. Heading into next-season, Thompson is expected to play a bigger role, including manning the top-powerplay unit.

TOLNAI, CAMERON
C - Ottawa 67's (OHL) - 6'01" 180

Cameron was Ottawa's 6th overall pick in the 2018 OHL Draft, Cameron played for the Oakville Rangers who dominated the SCTA that year and won SCTA player of the year honours. He played a limited role most of the year for Ottawa with the depth that they had up front. When he got the opportunity to play you would see some flashes of his upside. He has a good frame and uses his body and puck skill to protect the puck well. He uses his stick effectively on loose pucks and in puck battles to strip opponents of the puck with ease. He is a good skater with a powerful stride; he has shown a good top speed and acceleration to separate himself from opponents. Tolnai is incredibly difficult to knock off the puck and when in possesession he rarely makes a mistake. His vision allows him to find teammates effortlessly and distribute the puck effectively to his teammates. Away from the puck he provides his teammates a solid outlet and supports teammates in board battles as a high man. He did play on Ottawa PK this year and was really affected, his awareness defensively is outstanding. Tolnai is very complete player but adding some mass to his frame could make him that much more effective in the offensive zone. Next year with more of a role for Ottawa Tolnai should thrive and would greatly benefit him. With some added strength and balance, he should continue to be a force at the next level.

TUCH, LUKE
LW/RW - USA NTDP-17 (USHL) - 6'01" 197

Grinding, power forward type of winger. A product of the Buffalo Jr. Sabres and brother of Vegas winger Alex Tuch, Luke found 16 points in 30 USHL games with the U17 Team. At the World U17 Hockey Challenge, he was limited to just a single goal in five games. There aren't a lot of secrets about what Tuch is all about right now; he's that third piece on a scoring line that does the bulk of the grunt work. He plays a heavy game and does a lot of good work along the boards and on the forecheck. He is one of the most physical players on this version of the NTDP. Tuch readily goes to the front of the net to try to cause a stir. While he isn't a stellar defensive player, he does play the penalty kill regularly as well. The Boston University commit has a plus shot and is a surprisingly good passer when he has time to make a play. When in doubt, he'll just whip a puck at the net and try to follow it there. All told, the skating and skill package is just average right now. He does think the game well and he competes pretty hard to compensate for his tools still being unpolished though. He's a left wing by trade and it makes sense given his player type, but he was used at right wing at times this year and it felt like a slightly uncomfortable disadvantage for him. To really slide up the draft boards next winter, Tuch will need to improve his skill level.

TULLIO, TYLER
RC - Oshawa Generals (OHL) - 5'09" 161

Tyler is the son of the Generals owner, but unlike what we have seen in junior hockey leagues several times in the past, Tyler was worthy of a roster spot on an OHL roster without any assistance. Tyler had a successful rookie season in Oshawa where he posted 15 goals 27 assists for 42 points in 60 games. Tyler showed some production in the playoffs with 6 points in 14 games, with his team upsetting the Ice-Dogs as part of their run. At the U17's, he wasn't as productive, producing 1 assist in 7 games for Canada Black but didn't get a lot of minutes on the ice and was used on the penalty-kill as opposed to the powerplay.

Tullio is a smallish yet competitive playmaking center. He looks to find his teammates with crisp passes and has extended vision. He plays bigger than his size in terms of finishing his checks and can take a direct approach to the net as well. When the pass isn't there, he's shown that he can shoot the puck at an above-average level. His release-point is above-average and he can generate a decent amount of leverage when looking to go top-shelf. One of the more impressive aspects of Tyler's game was that he competed hard and showed grit to overcome his size disadvantage. So there would seem to be heart to go with some skill out there. The biggest area we are looking for Tyler to continue with his development is in regards to his over-all strength and also in his ability to generate more when he is carrying the puck.

TUSSEY, NOAH
LC - Stillwater HS (MNHS) - 5'11" 174

Noah Tussey is a 6th Round pick of Sioux City (USHL) in the 2018 Phase 1 Draft and is coming off a strong sophomore season for Stillwater HS, registering 13 goals and 22 Assists in 25 Regular Season games. Tussey saw a 3 game call up to Sioux City as well, registering 2 goals. Tussey is an up-tempo skater with above average explosiveness off the hop. For all his skating ability, Tussey doesn't excel in the transition game as one might think and does a lot of his offensive work below the dots and in front of the opposing net. Tussey shows good strength both in the ability to set up in front of the net and win ice against defenseman but also in protecting the puck down low in the cycle game. Tussey doesn't display high end, one on one offensive skill but can make plays in tight areas and see's the ice well. Tussey brings a good amount of physicality in puck battles and on the fore-check which adds to his power forward profile. Tussey will likely be returning to Stillwater HS next season but will likely see some time in the USHL as some point as well. Noah is a University of Minnesota commit.

VALADE, REID
RW - Kitchener Rangers (OHL) - 5'10" 161

Reid Valade was drafted 17th overall in the OHL-draft, and had a decent year for the Rangers. He finished his season with 20 points in 62 games, including 5 goals. In the playoffs, he was held pointless in 4 matchups but did generate 2 assists in 5 games with Canada Black at the U17's. Valade is a north-south skating winger who looks to use his puck-skills to make a difference on the ice. His skating mechanics are good and he already generates a decent amount of power despite his lighter-frame. He uses his skating in combination with his hands to pull-the-puck to the outside and cut towards the goal-line frequently. He likes to assert himself into games and looks to challenge defense both with and without the puck. He can make sharp-passes while going at full-speeds but he's not as good at finding soft-ice or putting himself in position to receive a pass back. There's a good pace to his game and he's good at hustling back to his own-end of the ice as well.

VEILLETTE, WILLIAM
LC - Chevaliers de Lévis (LHMAAAQ) - 5'11" 165

Veillette spent the majority of the season with Lévis in the LHMAAAQ due to Shawinigan already having four 16-year-olds on their team. Veillette also needed an extra season in Midget AAA. He played 6 games with the Cataractes and took part in the U-17 Hockey Challenge as an injury replacement. With Lévis, he amassed 53 points in 34 games. He's the kind of player who could rise next season and be higher on different draft boards than originally thought, as he's an underrated player since his QMJHL draft year. With his limited experience in the QMJHL, he could surprise more than a few folks next season when he makes it for good. Shawinigan drafted Veillette in the 2nd round of the 2018 QMJHL Draft with the 28th overall pick. He's a good skater with decent top speed and a good burst of speed that he can used to surprise defenders by going around them. He's got above-average smarts and a good arsenal of shots. He likes to have the puck on his stick, and on the power play, he's dangerous from the half-wall, where he likes to control the puck. He's good a good compete level and good awareness away from the puck. Next season, with a good group of young players such as Mavrik Bourque, the Cataractes could start making some noise in the QMJHL. Veillette is a key player in this rebuild and could become a key player for them next season rather quickly.

VIERLING, EVAN
LC - Flint Firebirds (OHL) - 6'00" 154

Evan Vierling had a solid season after getting drafted 2nd overall in the OHL-draft. He had an opportunity to play a sizable role with the Firebirds, resulting in 27 points in 60 games, including 6 goals. He was featured at the U17's on Canada Red, producing 3 points in 6 games. Vierling is a two-way, playmaking-center who can make high-skilled passes. He plays with confidence and poise, giving him the ability to transition the puck over all three-lines; he's also a fluid skater with plus skating mechanics. He's a quick-thinking player who sees the ice-well and this allowed him to set-up his teammates with efficient plays. He's dangerous from the hash-marks area and out due to his ability to find his teammates with back-door passes but can also threaten around the goal-line. His shot lags behind his playmaking ability but he looks to release the puck at the right times, in high-percentage areas. The biggest area of improvement for Evan will be in developing his power so that he can become a more explosive-player, as he has a tendency to play at one-gear a bit too frequently. He also isn't the most creative or dynamic player, he plays a more stream-lined game which is fine but it wouldn't hurt to see him make unique play-types.

VILLENEUVE, WILLIAM
RD - Saint John Sea Dogs (QMJHL) - 6'01" 163

Villeneuve was the 2nd overall pick in the 2018 QMJHL Draft but had a hard time in his first season in the QMJHL. It was a tough transition to major junior hockey for Villeneuve, notably due to Saint John's position in the standings and the fact that he was spending too much time in his own zone. His confidence suffered during the year due to his poor play and poor team success. Villeneuve has good size and smarts at both ends of the ice. He can rush the puck, but his skating didn't improve a lot from midget to the QMJHL and his lack of speed hurt him this year. He encountered more difficulties separating himself from the pack when in possession of the puck, and couldn't get away with it. It was tougher for him to create space on the ice. From the point, he has an average shot. He only scored once this year, but he's not a big threat from the point on the power play. He sees the ice well and he's capable of making a good first pass, but his decision-making needs to be quicker in order for him to be more successful at the QMJHL level. In midget, he was rock-solid defensively and very good one-on-one, using good body positioning and a good active stick. This past season, however, it was really hard for any player to shine on the Sea Dogs, especially in a defensive role. This was the case for Villeneuve. Look for him to rebound next season after a big summer of training. The potential is still there, as he has good size and two-way smarts. The key for him is to continue to work on his skating, footwork, improve the velocity of his shot and make quicker decisions with the puck.

WIESBLATT, OZZY
RW- Prince Albert Raiders (WHL) - 5'10" 187

Selected 25th in the bantam draft, Wiesblatt broke into the league in a big way this season. Wiesblatt earned his way on to a line with Cole Fonstad almost immediately and was with him all year putting up 39 points in 64 games. Towards the end of the year and playoffs Wiesblatt even began to play a role on the powerplay. Wiesblatt also was an assistant captain for Canada black at the u17s, with 3 points in 5 games. On the ice Wiesblatt plays a very high tempo game and is always buzzing around. He is an explosive skater who can push the pace of play with his feet. Wiesblatt also thinks fast and can execute plays at high speeds. His game also revolves around his hustle, there are very few on the ice that will out compete Wiesblatt. He is tenacious and chippy constantly getting under the oppositions skin and using his sturdy frame to throw crushing hits. Skill wise Wiesblatt has pretty good hands and can make plays one on one. He has not shown high end passing abilities and mainly excelled off the puck offensively this season, with a good sense for when to dart into a scoring area. Wiesblatt already does a ton of little things right and doesn't have any clear areas of weakness. It will be interesting to see how he develops next year with more offensive responsibility.

WILLIAMS, JACK
RW - Selects Hockey Academy (Midget) - 5'11" 170

Smooth, offensive winger with a creative flair. Williams was limited to 38 games with the Selects Academy midget program in South Kent, Connecticut, but his 29 goals and 57 points in that abbreviated season put him on pace to be among the leaders on his club had he have been able to play the entire season. The Maine native also spent time in the USHL with the U17 NTDP and the Muskegon Lumberjacks. With Muskegon he had three each of goals and assists in nine appearances and also potted some goals in the playoffs. In a lot of instances, affiliate players don't often find a lot of ice time when they're thrust on to competitive teams late in the season, but Jack made it difficult to keep him on the bench – he earned a regular shift more often than not. Seems like more of a playmaking winger at this point, but one that is willing to go to the net and battle more than many creative passers like him. He has really noteworthy vision and is not afraid to make some adventurous, but often well thought out, passes. He has a plus shot that is really bolstered by a snappy release. One of his most outstanding traits is how effective he is with misdirection. He's very good at manipulating defenders with head, shoulder, and/or stick movements. He has a bit above average speed, but nothing more. His stride is good mechanically, so he should be able to add on to his speed and quickness without much of an issue. Jack is better on the forecheck than the backcheck. As an added bonus, he can really dig in and get underneath guys to really affect defensemen on breakouts. He has that defensive "viscosity" at a young age, which gives the impression that there's a lot of room for defensive upside if that development arc is pursued. The Northeastern commit goes to the net with regularity and he battles, but only right up to the whistle (or even a little short of it, if he feels the play should be stopped). We have not seen him so much as have a chat with any opponents much less partake in a shoving match after the whistle. He seems to have zero interest in that and given his penalty minute totals historically, it seems as if Lady Byng was a mentor of his. In the game proper, he does fight to get pucks back – so there are definitely competitive juices that flow through him. His vision and hockey IQ meeting up with his underlying skill level really makes for an intriguing prospect with potentially first round caliber upside. He was selected first overall in the QMJHL American Draft by Saint John.

WONG, NICHOLAS
RC - Kingston Frontenacs (OHL) - 5'09" 170

Nicholas Wong was drafted 38th overall in the 2017 OHL-draft and was traded in the Murray deal with Kingston, splitting time between Oshawa and the Frontenacs as a result. He produced 10 points in 37 games, including 5 goals with the Generals and had 15 points in 29 games, including 8 goals with Kingston. Wong is an undersized-center with a lot of skill. He's a weaker player who lacks physical-tools and as a result has difficulty getting any separating speed. To compensate, he's developed good puck-skills and can beat opponents one-on-one with a creative-attack. He's also a capable playmaker who can thread sharp-passes through difficult seams and has an above-average release point as well. Wong also featured a decent compete-level but is still kept to the outside too often. The biggest area of improvement Nicholas needs to make heading into next season is filling out his frame so that he doesn't lose as many battles along the boards, and continuing to refine his skating mechanics.

ZARY, CONNOR
C/LW- Kamloops Blazers (WHL) - 6'00" 175

Zary was unheralded coming in to the WHL as a 37th overall bantam draft pick, who has only blown past expectations since. A late birthday, Zary would have pushed for a first round position if he was in this year's draft. Zary was his team's top player and had 67 points in 63 games, with a particularly strong end of season push to drag his team in to the playoffs. He was also extended an invite to Canada's u18 team where he had 7 points in 7 games. Zary is a very crafty player who excels in the small details to make a big impact. Zary excels with the puck on his stick where he can control the pace of the game. Zary is excellent at utilizing changes in his speed to suck defenders in to the position he wants them in, and has vision a step ahead of the play with great anticipation. From below the goal line Zary could pick teams apart as a passer and showed excellent ability to play coming up the half wall, displaying cross seam passing, and the ability to interchange with the defenseman, where he would often burn his check on a fake drop pass. Zary is creative as a passer, finding unique ways to make plays through the defence and is also a shot threat with a very accurate wrister. He also excels as a driver of play through the neutral zone where he can spot holes in coverage as they open up and knife his way in to the zone despite lacking high end speed. Zary is able to think fast and can make great decisions seemingly as soon as the puck is on his stick. Next season expect Zary to challenge for a first round position and continue to put up impressive scoring totals.

2021 NHL DRAFT PROSPECTS

ALLEN, NOLAN
LD - Saskatoon Blazers, (SMHL) - 6'01" 180

Allen was the 3rd overall draft pick to the WHL with the powerhouse Prince Albert Raiders. He starred for team Saskatchewan at the Canada winter games, recording 6 points in 6 games. Allen dominated the SMHL with 35 points in 39 games as well as a playoff leading 21 points in 13 games, winning the leagues defenseman of the year. The slippery two way defender got in to 7 WHL games and registered an assist, but looked beyond his years in his call up chances. Allen was excellent with the puck, beating forecheckers and showing extreme confidence under pressure. Allen's mobility and skating are excellent allowing him to make high end plays and attempt plays others could not. On top of this he has a high end offensive mind, constantly finding ways to get involved in the play. Allen made a stronger impression than any other draft eligible and has a good chance to earn a major role for the defending WHL champions next season.

ARCURI, FRANCESCO
C - Don Mills Flyers (GTHL) - 6'00", 187

Francesco is an offensively gifted player who displays great creativity in puck possession. He is most noticeable when he's creating time and space in possession and passing or shooting the puck. Francesco possesses a good, quick release and accurate shot. Throughout the season consistency has been an issue but possesses a quick-strike ability to change the game in an instant. He displays good anticipation, decision-making and playmaking skills on the offensive side of the puck. In the offensive zone he is very comfortable behind the opposition net and sees the ice well from that area. Francesco displays good skating mechanics and mobility in order to make plays in a tight areas, however, he could improve his top-end speed. Francesco could improve his play on the defensive side of the puck especially if he's going to play centre at the next level.

AVON, JON-RANDALL
C - Peterborough Petes (OMHA-ETA) - 5'11", 165

Jon-Randall is a smooth skating forward who possesses high-end speed and is among the fastest players at the Minor Midget level. Leading the Petes in scoring through the regular season, he has been a consistent riser in the draft rankings the more we see from him. At first glance Jon-Randall's speed, pace and work ethic are his most prominent tools. With his quick first step and top-end straightaway speed he has the ability to create space in one-on-one scenarios and effectively turn defenders on a regular basis. He generates most of his offense off the rush with his speed and can beat defenders wide or through the middle. Throughout the season he has really improved his hands when at full speed and can get a shot off or make an effective pass to a teammate but should continue to refine his consistency in this area. Occasionally in transition he just runs out of room to make a skilled play. He would benefit from cutting harder laterally across the ice on his rushes to get more pucks to the front of the net. Once inside the offensive zone, Jon-Randall possesses good deception forcing goalies to respect both the shot and the pass. He possesses a good shot with a strong release and good velocity helping to be a Top-5 goal scorer in the ETA. Jon-Randall has been on an upwards trajectory all season long and with his excellent work ethic and mix of speed and skill he projects to be a top-6 forward at the OHL level and should play as early as next season.

BÉDARD, ANTHONY
RW/LW - Trois-Rivières Estacades (QMAAA) - 5'08" 126

Bédard is not the biggest player, but his size does not seem to affect him in any way. He is a hard-working forward who brings a lot of energy to a team. Whether it is during a power play or a 5-on-5 situation, he is always around the net, screening the goalie, or trying to get rebounds. One of his greatest qualities on the ice is his skating; he's a fast skater who applies a good forecheck and finishes his checks every time he has a chance to. Used on both special units during the season, he's a smart player who rarely makes a bad decision. He's a winger who is capable of winning an important faceoff, mostly on the penalty kill when needed. Bédard is pretty light on his feet and will need to add a lot of mass to his frame, even more so due to the style of play he has. He has an above-average shot with decent velocity, but will need to improve its release. He's not a high-end skills' guy, but his work ethic and compete level makes him a dangerous and tough player to play against. He's a complete hockey player and there's not many like him in Québec. In the QMJHL, he'll be able to contribute at both ends of the ice and also be a bit of a pest. He might need extra time in Midget AAA next season, but Bédard could become an excellent 2nd liner in the QMJHL in a few years.

BEHRENS, SEAN
LD - Chicago Mission U16 (HPHL U16) - 5'06", 148

Sean is committed to the University of Denver (NCAA) for the 2022-23 season and is signed to the United States Development Program U17 team for the 2019 season. He was drafted by the Sarnia Sting in the 7th round (129th overall) in the 2019 OHL Priority Selection. Sean is an undersized yet mobile defenseman with high-end offensive skill. He is a fluid puck mover that can generate offense in various ways with his feet or his stick. He is an excellent skater who is agile and quick on his edges allowing himself to build speed and change direction on a dime. With the puck on his stick he possesses an excellent an ability to stare down opposing players when carrying the puck through the neutral zone leaving them guessing what he was going to do with the puck. Sean possesses strong offensive instincts to see skating lanes open up and attack them with speed and agility. In the offensive end, he is a dual threat as a passer and a shooter displaying strong anticipation and ability to put himself in scoring positions. When he finds a shooting lane, Sean possesses pretty good shooting accuracy picking his corner. Defensively, he showed good ability despite his size to step up in the neutral zone and strip the puck transitioning it into offensive so quickly. Sean is hard to knock off the puck using his excellent skating and agility to evade checks. With his excellent skating, hockey IQ and offensive skill Sean possesses a high ceiling as top pairing defender and powerplay specialist at the next level.

BELLIVEAU, ISAAC
LD - Cantonniers de Magog (LHMAAAQ) - 6'00" 174

Belliveau was the 25th overall pick in the 2018 QMJHL draft selected by the Rimouski Oceanic; he played 1 game this year with Rimouski. With Magog in midget AAA he made some big progress in his game and finished 2nd in the league for points for defensemen. He finished the year with 8 goals; 40 points in 41 games and with his team won the Quebec Midget AAA playoff championship for a second straight year and also lost for a second straight year in the Telus Cup final. Belliveau made the biggest progress with his decision making; he's making quicker decision now and has cut down on turnovers. On the power play he does a good job putting pucks on net, keep his shots low helping the cause of his teammates in front of the net. He's more of a two-way defenseman than rather a pure offensive point getter from the backend. In his zone he's active along the board and uses his size well to win puck battles and gets involved in the physical part of the game. He's got to improve to be even more efficient at the major junior level is skating ability and footwork. There are some holes on Rimouski defense with key players leaving and Belliveau will have all the opportunities to earn ice time and playing time next season on a squad who should be amongst the top teams in the league and a team that will be heavily scouted with Alexis Lafrenière in his draft year.

BENIERS, MATTHEW
LC/LW - USNTDP U17 (USHL) - 6'00" 163

Beniers began the 2018-2019 season with the USNTDP U17 team but it didn't take long for it to be obvious he could hold his own with the U18 club and eventually settled into the top 9 with the U18 squad, playing 20 games and earning a spot on the roster for the U18 World Championships despite being the youngest player at the National Development Program. Matthew displays high end hockey sense and instincts that allows him to be in the right place on the ice consistently. He is not a possession player as much as he is a quick strike player. He makes quick decisions with the puck due to his hockey sense and ability to think the game at another level. His skating ability and explosiveness allows Beniers to be quick to loose pucks and pressure the puck carrier all over the ice. He is crafty in regards to his stick work and can catch opponents from behind and force turnovers or strip pucks. A much underrated part of his game is in the faceoff circle where he is highly effective in using his body and buying time for support in the event he doesn't win the draws cleanly. Matthew has excellent individual skill that can beat defenders in one on one situation. Beniers has the skill and power in his game to beat defenders when they are on his back, he uses his creativity to get himself out of situations where it looks like he is out of options and can create scoring chances out of nowhere. Beniers played on mostly on the wing with the U18 team but projects as a high end two-way center down the road. He should move back to the middle next year where he will surely benefit from the additional time and space as well as give him opportunities to develop his two-way game. As it stands right now, Matthew is on track to be a very high end prospect for the 2021 NHL Draft. Beniers remains uncommitted to an NCAA program at this point but is a highly sought after prospect due to the fact he looks to be on track to be ready for college hockey in his draft year of 2020-2021. Beniers was a 13th-round draft choice by Quebec in the 2018 QMJHL Draft.

BIGGAR, ZACH
LD - Kensington Wild (NBPEIMMHL) - 5'11" 172

Biggar is a P.E.I. native who played for Kensington in the NBPEIMMHL this past season. He also played for his province at the Canada Games, as well as the Gatorade Challenge (where he unfortunately got hurt on the first day and missed the remainder of his team's games). Biggar had a good year with his Midget team; he's got good size and can move around the ice very well. Currently, he's more of a stay-at-home defenseman, but we still feel that there's some offensive potential with him that could be developed in the years to come. He keeps things simple at even-strength and makes sure to defend well before thinking about offense. He'll make some pinches here and there, but we see more raw offensive potential when he's on the power play. His mobility makes him a good option for the man-advantage; he's got good hands and can distribute the puck, but will also skate into gaps to take a shot if he's given room. He's got decent footwork and overall skating abilities. Before making the jump to major junior, however, we would like to see work to improve it. Defensively; spacing and timing allows him to take opposing players out of the play if they get in too close. He's got a good active stick and he's a good defender one-on-one due to his smarts and positional game. He plays with confidence; he's self-assured with the puck and also knows how to play within his limits. Biggar has a lot of raw talent, his game needs some polish, but he's a player with a high ceiling. Depending who will draft him, he could either make a QMJHL team as soon as next year or possibly go play Junior A (similar to fellow P.E.I. native Jordan Spence did last year) and gain experience and improve his game before moving on to the next level.

BOLDUC, ZACHARY
LC- Trois-Rivières Estacades (QMAAA) - 5'11" 154

Bolduc is a player with really good offensive skills; he demonstrated it by finishing the season among the top-10 scoring leaders in the LHMAAAQ with 54 points in 42 games. When Bolduc has control of the puck, he is really difficult to stop on the ice due to his excellent puck-protection and good speed. He is the kind of player who is capable of taking both offensive and defensive responsibilities. Bolduc has been very successful on the power play during this season by demonstrating an excellent vision of the game and making spectacular passes. Due to his good hockey IQ, he always knows what to do on the ice and where to be on the ice. He was also very important to his team in terms of face offs, on both sides of the ice, by winning 53% of them. Physically, he is not scared to take and distribute hits along the boards. He is the kind of player that every team in the league would have liked to have. However, one of the things he needs to improve on is his consistency. He didn't have a good Canada Games' tournament in February by his standards, but that was the only blemish in his season for 2018-2019. Bolduc is a complete and versatile player with great hockey sense, and will make a team really happy on draft day. There's some interest in him south of the border as well, and playing in the NCAA is an option for him. He's expected to play for Mount St. Charles prep school next season in Rhode Island. He was also drafted in the 2nd round 21st overall by Sioux City in the phase 1 of the USHL draft.

BOUCHER, TYLER
RW - Avon Old Farms School (USHS-Prep) - 6'00", 190

Tyler is committed to Boston University (NCAA) for the 2021-22 season and is signed to the United States Development Program U17 team for the 2019 season. He was drafted by the Ottawa 67s in the 7th round (143th overall) in the 2019 OHL Priority Selection. Tyler is a nice sized power forward with an all-around skill set. He plays a very heavy and physical game mixed in with good offensive skill. He shows a strong work ethic in all three zones leading to him winning most battles and 50/50 pucks. He is a very smart player who understands the importance of puck possession. Tyler is patient with the puck and always seems to make a smart play with it. He is reliable in his own zone as he is a very strong player who's hard on the puck. In the offensive zone he displays great puck protection ability and playmaking ability. He is a pass first player but has a strong nose for the net as well. He is a strong skater who's very hard to knock of his feet. He doesn't have blazing speed, but he moves up and down the ice fairly well. Overall Tyler is a skilled power forward who plays a solid two-way game and already has a pro frame.

BOURGAULT, XAVIER
C/RW - Shawinigan Cataractes (QMJHL) - 5'11" 155

Bourgault made Shawinigan out of training camp was a bit of a surprise as he was committed to go play one year at Stanstead College to get himself ready physically for the QMJHL. There was some question mark if physically he would be ready to play full time in the QMJHL but he did end up playing the full season with the Cataractes. He played in 62 games during the season and also played at the World under 17 hockey challenge. Bourgault can play on the wing and at the center position; he struggles with his faceoff this season averaging 37% which is often the case with 16 years old center in the league. He's an above average skater, he's got good quickness and some quick burst that can be useful when trying to beat a defenders going wide on them. He has quick hands in tight and an above average release on his shot. He's too inconsistent as his play is really up and down. We would like to see him become more consistent in his performance and effort level. He lacks strength physically and needs to get stronger to have more of an impact along the boards and win more puck battles. He has above average smarts, good awareness away from the puck and he's not a liability in his own zone. We expect to see Bourgault to take a big step next season with Shawinigan and become a top 6 forward for them and one of their top offensive contributor.

BOUTIN, CHARLES
LW/LC - Blizzard du Séminaire St-François (QMAAA) - 5'09" 149

Charles Boutin is a rookie forward who had the biggest impact on the Blizzard's score sheet this season, as he scored nine goals and added 17 assists, good for 26 points in 41 games. With his frame (5'9" and nearly 150 pounds), he currently fits a below-average template. However, his excellent hockey sense and strong individual skills place him among the players with the best potential in 2019 QMJHL Draft. His skating is one of his main strengths; he has a very good skating technique with fluid strides and a fast force of acceleration. His soft hands allow him to be able to get rid of his opponent in one-on-one situations, in addition to opening up more space for him to stickhandle. He likes to have the puck on his stick and initiate zone entries by himself. His vision of the play is such that he is able to execute accurate passes to his teammates, which is why he was used on the point on the power play. Boutin knows how to position himself in the offensive territory to offer himself as an option, and does not hesitate to fight hard for the puck in the corners of the rink. He can play as a centerman or as a winger. We believe that at least an additional half-season at the Midget AAA level could be beneficial for his development, although he possesses several strengths that lead us to believe that he could make the jump next year to the QMJHL. When he reaches physical maturity, he will be a top-6 player at the next level.

BOUTIN, OLIVIER
LD - Chevaliers de Lévis (LHMAAAQ) - 5'09" 161

Boutin is a defenseman with great hockey IQ on both sides of the ice, with and without the puck. He was stellar offensively in the first half of the season, but his numbers slowed down a little in the second half and during the playoffs. He showed good abilities to escape pressure and exit his zone effectively, moving the puck up quickly with a strong first pass or by skating it out of the zone himself. Boutin possesses great feet to skate effectively forwards and backwards, and uses this to his advantage to maintain good gap control to defend the rush or close in on his opponents quickly in the defensive zone, also using his edgework and stick-positioning to force opponents into turnovers. Offensively, he uses his IQ to make effective plays on the rush when his team has possession in the offensive zone, looking to make a play to forwards in high-scoring areas. At the same time, he does not force plays or get into turnover trouble. At 5'09", Boutin doesn't possess a big frame, but his quickness to retrieve loose pucks makes him hard to pressure on the forecheck. He is not the most physical defenseman, but will get the job done defensively with this smarts instead of his physical game. At the next level, Olivier has the potential to become a 2-way defenseman with offensive upside.

BROWN, CADEN
C - St. Louis AAA Blues U16 (T1EHL) - 5'10.25", 158

Caden is committed to the University of Wisconsin (NCAA) for the 2021-22 season and is signed to the United States Development Program U17 team for the 2019 season. He was drafted by the Kitchener Rangers in the 8th round (151th overall) in the 2019 OHL Priority Selection. Caden is a strong playmaking centre with high-end hockey intelligence and skill that translates effectively to the OHL level. He moves well on the ice displaying a wide skating base and a powerful stride using his long legs to cover the ice efficiently with only a few strides required. He currently lacks a quick first step, which is an area for improvement as it takes more ice for him to reach his top speed. Caden uses his long stride to create separation in transition where he is most effective and likes to have the puck on his stick to make controlled zone entries. With his strong hockey intelligence he puts himself in position to make a play by anticipating the play very well and making calculated decisions. In the offensive zone, Caden is a strong facilitator with the puck electing to be a pass-first centre and showing excellent vision to see plays develop and find open teammates with a pass. On the powerplay, Caden showed an ability to distribute the puck efficiently from the blueline or the halfwall. He is not afraid to drive to the slot for shooting opportunities but thrives making plays from the perimeter. His shot is good and he would benefit from shooting the puck more and being more assertive with his shot when the opportunity exists. Defensively, Caden provides an effective stick in the neutral zone and tracks back well helping his defensemen to defend effectively and win puck battles. He is very strong in the faceoff circle winning draws cleanly showing good reliability especially when the game is on the line. He is solid on his skates but does not tend to initiate contact with opposing players. Caden has the potential to be a top line centre at the OHL level and his responsible defensive game, effective faceoff ability and high-end hockey intelligence and playmaking skill should allow him to make an impact on any team he plays for next season.

CHAYKA, DANIIL
LD - Guelph Storm (OHL) - 6'02" 187

Daniil Chayka was selected 7th-overall in the OHL-draft and had a productive rookie-season on the backend while also winning an OHL-title. He finished the season with 14 points in 56 games, including 5 goals. In the playoffs, he registered zero points in 20 games. He played for Russia at the U17's and produced 2 points in 6 games. His team was also featured at the memorial-cup, where he went pointless in 4 contests. Daniil is a raw, two-way defender who has a lot of upside given his tools. He's a gifted skater who can pivot and move laterally at a very-good level when readjusting his lanes at the offensive-blueline. He has a good-set of hands, and can challenge opponents one-on-one, which led to a couple of impressive goals this season. Furthermore, he's a quality-outlet passer whose has extended vision. He's not just an offensive-oriented defender though. He's got a good frame on him, and uses it effectively at an above-average rate. He also can close his gaps quickly due to his acceleration and plays at a decent-pace in his own-end. Although there's a lot of upside in Chayka, he still lacks detail in his defensive-assignments at times, and can lose his man in coverage as a result but competes and attempts to recover at a good-level. Furthermore, although he can flash impressive offensive-plays, there's' times where he has been stagnant at the line. Chayka is a young and promising defenseman who we think has the potential to be one of the better OHL-defenseman featured in the 2021 class.

CLARKE, BRANDT
RD - Don Mills Flyers (GTHL) - 6'01", 177

Brandt has a high hockey IQ combined with talent that makes him the most dynamic offensive defensemen in this draft. Brandt displays innate composure when playing the puck that is rare amongst players his age. Whether it is towing the offensive zone blueline to open shooting and passing lanes, puck retrieval scenarios with oncoming forecheckers in his defensive corner, or making sure of the right pass in breakouts, Brandt has the smarts and skills to execute. His skating mobility, short area quickness, and edge work is what sets him apart from his peers as he is able to set himself up for multiple moves. His anticipation in understanding what opponents and teammates are going to do and reacting accordingly showcases his hockey IQ. He usually maintains good gap control but this would be one area of improvement for him. At times he can back up too far into his zone instead of cutting down the angle upon entry. While he is not afraid of contact he does not go out searching for it. With his height plus weight and tremendous skating ability it would be great to see him add a more physical presence to his game. He has a good shot release and can get it off quickly through opening up shooting lanes, but he does not possess great power. Brandt should transition into a top four role in the OHL next season and projects to be a top pairing defender who can also be a powerplay specialist.

DAIGLE, NICOLAS
LC - Chevaliers de Lévis (LHMAAAQ) - 5'08" 150

Daigle was drafted by Rimouski in the 4th round 61st overall in the 2018 QMJHL draft and was later traded to Victoriaville during the QMJHL trade deadline for D'Artagnan Joly. He was the captain of Levis midget AAA team who broke all kind of records this season in the LHMAAAQ and went 41-1 in the regular season. The undersize center had a lot of success winning the MVP honor of the CCM challenge in December and finishing 3rd in league scoring with 72 points in 39 games. Daigle is ultra and competitive center who plays well in all three zones and makes his linemates better on the ice. He's not a high end offensive upside type of prospect but he does a bit about everything well on the ice and he's a leader on and off the ice. He needs to improve his shot to be more of a threat with the puck on his stick in the offensive zone at the next level. He has an excellent hockey IQ, vision and competes level. He sees the ice well and he's a good playmaker. Good defensive awareness, with his work ethic and anticipation he will make a good player shorthanded. He'll be a regular next season with Victoriaville and should start on a bottom 6 role and slowly but surely during the season climb the team depth chart.

DEAN, ZACHARY
LC - Toronto Nationals (GTHL) - 6'00" 161

Dean is originally from Newfoundland, and made the move this season to the top midget league in Ontario (GTHL) to join the Toronto Nationals. This season, he amassed 89 points in 66 games and also had a great showing at the Canada Games, representing his province with 15 points (13 assists) in 7 games. Dean has great offensive upside and is as good of a scorer as he is a playmaker; he has high-end skills to go along with a great work ethic. He's got an above-average shot with a quick release. He brings many facets to the game; if he can't produce offensively, he can play a physical game and make himself valuable in other ways. Very agile on his skates, his great top speed and acceleration make him tough to contain for opposing defensemen. He's dangerous one-on-one, as his great hands combined with his speed makes defenders back up, giving him more room to make plays offensively. He has a good compete level, is not shy to use his body to make plays in the offensive zone and down low. He's got good hockey sense and anticipation that makes him a complete hockey player, and also has value playing shorthanded. Dean was standout performer at the Canada game for his province and put on a show at the Gatorade Challenge as well showing his high end skills over the course of this event. There's a lot to like with Dean, and he is one the top players available in this year's draft class. Dean was drafted by Madison in the phase 2 of the USHL draft.

DEL MASTRO, ETHAN
LD - Toronto Marlboros (GTHL) - 6'02" 184

Ethan is a fluid skating defensemen who has the ability to move the puck around the ice efficiently through passes or skating the puck up himself. Playing with a competitive edge, Ethan embraces the physical side of the game and can lay big open ice body checks in transition. Ethan utilizes good balance and strength in his base to be able to play through contact and uses his intelligence as a defensemen to play with average gap control. He would benefit from improving his decision-making on both sides of the puck. Ethan can be guilty of cheating and taking unnecessary risks in transition. Ethan provides a sturdy defensive presence with limited offensive upside. Offensively, he would benefit from improving his puck facilitation skills and shot velocity. Because of the physical nature of his game and his competitive spirit Ethan can sometimes tow the line of being undisciplined. Ethan possesses some intriguing tools for the next level but will need to improve his overall decision-making in order to make an impact at the OHL level.

DUKE, DYLAN
C - Detroit Compuware U16 (HPHL U16) - 5'10" 165

Dylan is a dynamic center who possesses high-end hockey intelligence, skill and leadership qualities. He is an excellent skater with a smooth stride, balance and agility who is fuelled by his lower-body strength for a quick first step and acceleration. His game begins in the defensive zone where he displays smart positioning and an active stick to assist his defensemen in creating turnovers. Once he wins the puck battle he showed high-end anticipation to make smart breakout plays, often stretching the ice and leading to odd-man scoring opportunities. His innate ability to anticipate and sense where his teammate are on the ice at all times separates him from many of his peers. Offensively, Dylan is a complete prospect with high-end shooting and passing skill. With the puck on his stick he possesses excellent vision to see passing lanes that do not even appear to be there making high-end plays with his stick. Dylan is a dangerous threat anywhere in the offensive zone creating for shooting rom the side of the net, half wall or the blueline. He has the ability to shoot the puck from anywhere displaying excellent shooting range but carefully picking his shots and showing strong accuracy. Dylan plays in all situations while displaying excellent compete and drive to score. Should he decide to pursue the OHL route he will be able to step into an OHL lineup next season and make an impact in this league and is the type of player a general manager can build a team around.

EKLUND, WILLIAM
C - Djurgården IF U20 (Jr. SuperElite) - 5'08" 154

Eklund divided his season between two teams. In his clubs U18 team he played 26 games in which he recorded 10 goals and 12 assists for a total of 22 points and served as an alternate captain. He also played 13 games for his clubs U20 team where he put up 1 goal and 2 assists for a total of 3 points. Eklund is a small technically gifted centerman that also is viable on a wing. He possesses great hands and can stickhandle through a crowd while skating at a somewhat high speed. He is a little magician with the puck and he sees the ice well, but lacks a bit of timing in his passing game to be an effective offensive player and he tends to always end up in the corners or behind the opposing net, instead of taking the puck to the net. His work ethic is high and he is a team player and he takes his defensive duties seriously. Defensively he does a good job at killing angles and is giving great support to his defenders. While he doesn't play a physical game, he does play a smart game on both ends of the ice and his hockey IQ is rather high. His shot is seriously weak and needs improvements and he doesn't shoot very hard or accurate. Eklund played 11 games for team Sweden's U17 team and recorded 2 goals and 8 assists for a total of 10 points.

ENRIGHT, ISAAC
RD - Pembroke Lumber Kings (HEO) - 6'01" 165

Isaac was a key contributor on the backend for one of the top teams in the league and quickly established himself at the beginning of the season as a high-end prospect. Isaac is an intelligent two-way defenseman that you really need to watch closely to appreciate just how talented he is. He possesses a large frame however he doesn't play an overly physical game but can play with an edge when he wants to. He is an effortless skater that possesses a beautiful stride and impressive foot-speed which he often showcases rushing the puck up the ice or to push the pace in transition. Isaac consistently makes plays at top speed and is capable of doing things with the puck that other defenseman is unable to. In the offensive zone he handles the puck with confidence and is excellent at managing and distributing the puck. His mobility on the blueline allows him to generate offense by eluding defenders and creating shooting and passing lanes. Defensively, his high-end skating allows him to quickly close the gap and limit his opponents time and space. Once he retrieves the puck in the defensive zone, he usually makes a smart decision with the puck whether it's making an accurate breakout pass or a chip off the glass to alleviate the pressure. At times he can be guilty of trying to do too much with the puck and can skate himself out of options forcing him to make difficult plays that aren't available.

GALLAGHER, TY
RD - Detroit Compuware U16 (HPHL U16) - 6'01" 175

Ty is a smooth skating two-way right shot defenseman who possesses high-end offensive potential and the ability to be a top-pairing defender at the OHL level. He skates very well and his feet provide the foundation to his mobile game. In transition, he makes smooth pivots allowing him to be in position to defend showing good edgework and speed both forwards and backwards. Defensively, he possesses such a smart stick to strip pucks and transition into offense so quickly and efficiently. When playing in one-on-one coverage he plays strong defense using his size and frame to keep opponents to the outside. Ty possesses the confidence and intelligence to move the puck effectively with either his feet or his hands, correctly selecting the most appropriate zone exit strategy to safely and efficiently move the puck up ice. He possesses good deceptive qualities to his game to keep opponents guessing where he will go with the puck. Ty has the skill and maturity to run a team's powerplay showing good puck movement selecting his shooting lanes well and distributing the puck at the right times. His low quick release allows him to get shots off fast without letting the defense time to set. His shot arsenal includes a slap shot and snap shot – both of which are highly effective with good accuracy. Ty displays high offensive upside but can also provide quality defensive minutes and is reliable in all three zones.

GAUCHER, NATHAN
RC - Gaulois de St-Hyacinthe (QMAAA) - 6'02" 176

The younger brother of Val-d'Or rookie Jacob Gaucher, Nathan is also a center with above-average physical maturity, as he swings the scales at nearly 180 pounds from the top of his 6'2''. In his freshman year with St-Hyacinthe, he quickly established himself as the top center of the team, completing his rookie season with 18 goals and 15 assists for 33 points in 42 games. He also got an invitation to the Canada Games to represent Team Quebec. He is a forward who has a lot of tools to his arsenal, making him a dominant player throughout his age group. His skating is one of his main strengths; his stride is powerful, large and well-balanced. He likes to accelerate in the neutral zone while in possession of the puck, attacking opposing defenders at full speed once in the offensive territory. He is effective in puck-protection situations because he uses his size as well as his long reach to have the advantage over his opponents. He brings a physical dimension to the game; he likes to complete his checks and constantly get involved with good body checks. His wrist shot is powerful, sometimes inaccurate, but still one of his favorite weapons. His handling of the puck is good and he uses his presence in control of the puck well to open gaps and additional space to stickhandle. Gaucher has been used in all kinds of situations this season, scoring important goals on the man-advantage while doing a good job a man short or in more defensive situations. Much like his older brother, he can be very useful when taking important face-offs at critical moments. He is effective on the forecheck with his stick and he is strong along the boards in his battles for the puck. Although he is one of the youngest of his age group (considered a late-born player), Gaucher has the necessary skills to jump directly into the QMJHL next year.

GAUDREAU, BEN
G - North Bay Trappers Major Midget (GNML) - 6'02" 165

Ben played Minor Midget last season as an underage goaltender and chose to play his OHL Draft year with the '02 Major Midgets helping lead his team to an undefeated 36-0 regular season. Ben is a big-bodied goaltender who is one of the most physically mature among goalies in the age group. As a butterfly style goalie, he tempts shooters to go high on him but shows strong reaction and explosive power to make saves. He uses his frame to his advantage making himself look big in goal and sometimes even extending his upper body a few extra inches to make a save up high. Tracking pucks with attention and focus, Ben challenges shooters at the top of his crease and takes away shooting angles while displaying excellent confidence and a good level of calmness to his game. His movements in the crease are often calculated and not hurried, which compliments his positioning and pro style of goaltending. On dump-ins, he regularly leaves his net to play the puck showing good passing skill at appropriate times but also shows good awareness when to set the puck up for his defensemen. He plays well between the whistle and never gives up on pucks showing strong compete and composure. Ben has shown some inclination at times to overplay his angles by sliding too far on his pads in his butterfly position but has also shown an ability to use his edges and athletic ability to recover and make saves. Ben was the top goalie available in the OHL Priority Selection and projects to be a starter in the OHL.

GILL, JUSTIN
LW/C - Vikings St-Eustache (LHMAAAQ) - 6'00" 175

Over the course of the season, Gill has consistently improved and was rewarded with more and more responsibilities by the coaching staff. Like other prospects, he started the year on the team's bottom-6 and made his way up in the lineup. Despite starting the campaign as the fourth-line center, Gill finished the season second in the Vikings' scoring leaders. When the season ended, he was playing on the top-6 and on power play while still killing penalties. Gill isn't the most creative player, but he does have some tricks up his sleeve to make his way offensively. He has good straight-line speed and keeps his plays effective both with and without the puck. Once in the offensive zone, Gill tries to find the soft spots to receive the puck and release good one-timers. He is not afraid to go into the dirty areas of the ice to create scoring chances. In his own zone, he will quickly put pressure on the puck-carrier with an effective active stick and will keep tight coverage of his opponent. His skillset should land him a spot on a middle-6 anywhere in the league.

GOURE, DENI
C- Chatham Cyclones (MHAO) - 5'10" 160

Captain of his team and a centre that can play and excel in any situation, Deni is a workhorse and the offensive catalyst for the Cyclones. He has one of the best releases in Minor Midget when given the time and space in the offensive zone and has a game-break ability. All of his shot types are powerful and accurate, and he does possess the skill to drag and shoot, changing the angle from which his shot is released. While his shot is outstanding he is also a playmaker and if necessary can deliver a tape-to-tape saucer passes to set up his teammates. Possessing good size, he can out muscle and punish opponents, and his work ethic and defensive ability are also noteworthy. Deni's skating technique is okay but he will need to improve his footspeed in order to create separation at the next level. Deni has already played Jr. B games with the Chatham Maroons scoring 2 goals and earning 2 assists. He scored 53 points in 32 games during the Alliance regular season accounting for much of the offense on a weak Chatham team. Deni has the ability to step into an OHL lineup next year and produce offensively with his electric release.

GRATTON, DYLAN
LD - North Jersey Avalanche U16 (AYHL U16) - 6'00" 157

Dylan is a smooth skating left-shot defenseman who possesses intriguing size with plenty of room left to fill out. As a rangy defender, his skating stands out as a strength displaying pretty good overall technique, mobility and smooth edgework. In transition, he pivots well to the inside or outside remaining in position to make a play. His long and powerful stride provides him with good straightaway speed and allows him to get up and down the ice with ease. He is often most noticeable in the offensive transition and is quick to join the rush adding numbers and earning quality scoring chances. He possesses excellent vision inside the offensive zone and pretty good anticipation to jump up and make offensive plays both with and without the puck. Dylan's defensive game continues to be a work in progress and his decision-making is an area for improvement to be more effective in one-on-one coverage. Dylan provides a unique mix of size, skating and offensive skill and has the potential to be a top pairing defenseman at the OHL level with a high-end offensive skillset.

GRUSHNIKOV, ARTYOM
LD - CSKA Moskva U18 (Russia U18) - 6'02" 176

Grushnikov made his mark playing as an underager on Russia's U-17 team this past season at different tournaments throughout the year. He led all Russian defensemen in scoring at the U-17 Hockey Challenge in November with 4 points in 6 games. Even as a 15-year-old, he already has great size. More importantly, he has great poise with the puck and doesn't look his age on the ice. He was often the quarterback of the Russian team, showing his good poise from the blueline. He's not overly flashy offensively, but makes the smart and effective plays from the point. He sees the ice well and makes quick decisions with the puck. He has decent mobility and used his stick well to defend one-on-one and knock pucks down from opponents. He's already quite strong for a player of his age, and that helps him compete well along the boards and in front of the net. We would like to see him improve his quickness a bit in the years ahead so that he can be more of a factor when rushing the puck, because at this point, he doesn't rush the puck a lot. He prefers using his passing abilities to activate the transition game for his team. Still very young, Grushnikov should be a key player next season on Russia's U-17 team and possibly U-18 team as well, if he continues his good progression.

GUENTHER, DYLAN
LW - Northern Alberta X-Treme Prep (CSSHL) - 6'01" 188

The first overall draft pick in the WHL bantam draft. Guenther got in to 8 regular season games with the Edmonton Oil Kings, recording 4 points. He dominated the CSSHL on a line with Matthew Savoie, registering 58 points in 28 games, and 16 points in 5 playoff games on the way to a league championship. At the Canada winter games he had 13 points in 6 games to lead his team. Guenther is a dynamic offensive threat with a creative mind for generating plays. He is constantly finding soft space offensively and doesn't need the puck on his stick a ton to make an impact. Guenther is a dangerous shooter with a lightning quick release who will immediately give WHL goaltenders problems. He is a good skater but does not have blow you away speed and clearly wasn't yet strong enough for the WHL. Look for him to step in to the lineup on a strong Oil Kings team next year and excel offensively.

GUÉVIN, JACOB
RD- Trois-Rivières Estacades (QMAAA) 5'09" 164

Guévin is an offensive defenseman who really likes to carry the puck to the offensive zone. He may not be the biggest defenseman, but he is very fast and has good skills, which allows him to get rid of his opponents pretty easily and quickly. Defensively, he is very good in terms of his gap control, always placed at the right place in front of his net. He also skates very quickly backwards and uses his stick well, which makes him really good in one-on-one and one-on-two situations. He's an undersized defenseman and has to use his smarts rather than his strength in order to defend his own zone. He's in tough down low when facing bigger players who can take advantage of his lack of strength. During breakouts, he always has his head up and makes a good first pass to his players. Guévin also played on the first power play unit for his team, where he was always calm with the puck while making good and quick passes to his teammates.

He finished the season with 25 points in 42 games and was one of the top defensemen for Team Québec at the Canada Games in February. Guévin committed to the University of Nebraska-Omaha in the month of March, making the likelihood of reporting to a QMJHL team doubtful for next season. He was also drafted by Muskegon in the phase 1 of the USHL draft.

HARRISON, BRETT
C - London Jr. Knights (MHAO) - 6'00" 154

Brett continues to prove himself as the top prospect out of the Alliance who thrives in puck possession. He has a very desirable frame with the reach and puck protection skills to shoulder off checks while maintaining possession. That being said, he doesn't just rely on his size as his high hockey intelligence allows him to think the game on another level compared to his teammates and most opponents. His first step isn't outstanding, but he accelerates well utilizing his long stride to help him get him moving quickly. At top speed he sees the ice quite well and regularly stickhandles the puck around and through defenders with ease. Once he gets the puck on his stick his game speeds up. In transition, Brett possesses the tremendous ability to not force passing or shooting lanes when they do not exist, and instead makes simple, but smart plays. Brett is also a patient attacker; he is skilled and smart enough to out wait and suck in defenders before feathering accurate passes to teammates. At times throughout the year Brett played like a top-5 prospect in the draft but struggled with consistency from game-to-game, especially in the playoffs. Having already had some Jr. B game experience with the London Nationals, Brett should be able to make the jump to the next level next season as a centre without being a liability five-on-five and projects to be a first line centre in the OHL.

HAYES, AVERY
RC/RW - Hamilton Bulldogs (OHL) - 5'08" 161

Avery Hayes was drafted in the 6th round of the OHL priority selection and had a decent rookie-season for the Bulldogs. He produced 18 points in 64 games, including 7 goals. In the playoffs, he contributed 1 assist in 4 games. We have limited viewings of Hayes but he did perform well when we viewed him. He's a small kid who lacks size and doesn't generate a ton of speed which has held him back from producing as much as his skill would suggest he could. However, he's displayed poise and a maturity when handling the puck, and had several impressive plays that resulted in high-quality scoring chances. His shot features a decent amount of velocity and he can shoot the puck in-tight to his wheelhouse which made him effective from a stationary position. Though he's skilled, he has a lot of work to do away from the play, and needs to continue to develop how quickly he reads off his teammates. Additionally, he needs to assert himself in the game more often and needs to physically mature.

HÉBERT, JULIEN
LW - Chevaliers de Lévis (LHMAAAQ) - 5'11" 170

Hébert is a feisty winger whose game has consistently evolved and improved over the course of the season. Playing up and down in the lineup throughout the year, Hébert was given more responsibilities. He started the season on the fourth line, while his coach used him on penalty kill unit. At the end of the season, Hébert was playing on the top two lines and got some time on power play while still killing penalties. Despite not being the most creative player, he has the abilities to complete talented players like Roy and Nadeau by positioning himself well in all three zones. Once in the offensive zone, Hébert is at his best below the faceoff dots, as he worked efficiently to make his way to the net and tried to create some traffic. He is not afraid of initiating or receiving contact, going into the dirty areas of the ice to create scoring chances. In his own zone, he will quickly put pressure on the puck-carrier with an effective active stick and will keep tight coverage. He's a jack-of-all-trades and his game projects well at the next level. His skillset should land him a spot on a middle-6, but if he can find chemistry with other talented players, he can be a top-6 forward in the long run.

HOLMES, JACOB
LD - York Simcoe Express (OMHA-ETA) - 6'00.5" 170

Jacob is a smooth skating defender who plays an intriguing two-way game. He possesses good size that projects well at the next level. He thrives in possession making key plays with the puck and driving play to the net showing good puck movement and offensive potential. Starting in his defensive end, Jacob keeps his head up exiting the defensive zone and can move the puck either with his feet or by stretching the ice with a crisp tape-to-tape pass. When carrying the puck, he has very good awareness for where his teammates are on the ice and starring down defenders while making no look passes providing an element of deception to his game. In his own end, he is consistently engaged in the play and battles hard in the corners and out front of the net to win pucks. In transition, he displays good gap control to stay tight to attacking forwards and limit their time and space. Jacob is an intriguing defenseman for his strong two-way game and offensive upside who projects as a top pairing defender at the OHL level.

HUCKINS, COLE
LW/LC - Stanstead College (CAHS) - 6'03" 180

Huckins is a New Brunswick native who has been playing with Stanstead College for the last two seasons in the prep ranks, and this year had 27 points in 18 games plus 8 points in 7 games playing for New Brunswick at the Canada Games in February. Huckins is a power-forward who is still growing into his frame and learning to use his size more and more. He's an above-average skater, and he's tough to contain when using his speed and size to get around defenders. He's tough to handle down low and around the net. He's got good hands, and can score from many different ways, either with his hard shot (he's capable of scoring from anywhere in the offensive zone) or from in-close, using his size to get to rebounds or tip pucks in front of the net. He works hard, demonstrating a good effort at both ends of the ice, in addition to good support down low to help his defensemen retrieve pucks when playing center. He needs to improve his level of awareness on the ice; we've seen him get hit hard too often on the ice and that could lead to injuries in the future. He also needs to use his teammates more; they will help him create more offense by building that trust. Huckins is one the top power-forwards available from this draft class, but it's still unknown at this time what his intentions are for the future in regards to the QMJHL (compared to the NCAA). However he was drafted by Waterloo 28th overall in the USHL draft.

HUGHES, LUKE
LD - Little Caesars U15 (Midget) - 5'10.75" 155

Luke is the youngest of the three Hughes brothers and is a dynamic puck moving defenseman with high-end offensive instincts indicative of the new age defenseman. His skating is excellent including strong agility and footspeed allowing him to change directions on a dime. On the offensive side of the puck, he is a fourth forward and is not shy to jump up into the offensive zone to outnumber the opposing team and create scoring chances. He is consistently at his best in possession using his puck handling and skating to carry transition attacks up ice and aggressively looking to generate offense once gaining the offensive blueline. Luke consistently displayed good overall awareness, showing quickness on puck retrievals along with an ability to recognize and escape pressure with his footwork. Luke's defensive game, however, still requires some improvement to be a reliable option at the next level but has shown improvement over the course of the season. Luke has the ability to take over any game with his skillset and projects to be a top pairing defenseman at the OHL level with an ability to quarterback a powerplay but will need to continue honing his game on the defensive side of the puck to be an everyday reliable defender.

JANICKE, JUSTIN
L/LW - Maple Grove HS (MNHS) - 5'08" 160

Justin is following the path that his older brother Trevor did, Justin has committed to the USNTDP for 19/20 and is also a Notre Dame commit for 2022. Janicke isn't a big kid at this stage but possesses powerful skating and shows the ability to takes himself and puck to the net frequently. Janicke possesses some decent skill but his big assets at this stage is his skating and goal scoring ability, he can try to play too much of a skill game at times but is highly effective when he simplifies his game and focuses on his strengths. Justin registered 19 goals and 30 assists in 24 Regular season games as a sophomore for Maple Grove High School. Janicke can play with some edge, especially in regard to his stick work where he can be aggressive and chippy with his hooks and slashes. Despite not being very big or strong yet, Janicke plays a good power forward game in which he can possess the puck down low and make plays off the cycle. Much like his older brother, Justin plays with good effort and compete at both ends of the ice.

JOHNSTON, WYATT
C - Toronto Marlboros (GTHL) - 5'11.75" 151

Wyatt is an intelligent hockey player who utilizes his smarts to be a fantastic playmaker and defensively responsible forward. Utilizing good stick handling skill, poise and puck control he is able to spread the puck around the ice creatively. As a centre for his line, Wyatt also displays great ability and understanding of when to help out down low and is effective in facilitating breakout passes. His passing ability in general is a strength in his game and can deliver pin point, cross-ice passes exemplifying his playmaking skills and great vision. Throughout the course of the year, Wyatt has shown a very competitive drive to his game as he is not just an offensive playmaker but a two-way forward with good defensive skills and instincts. Wyatt will need to continue to hone and refine his skating to be an effective player at the next level. While Wyatt displays great playmaking skills, his goal scoring abilities have been inconsistent and would benefit from a year at the junior level. Overall Wyatt's intelligence and composure with the puck combined with his vision and ability to execute passes makes him a strong playmaker and an intriguing prospect who could develop into a top-6 talent with two way upside, high IQ and playmaking ability.

KIDNEY, RILEY
LW/C - Cole Harbour Wolfpack (NSMMHL) - 5'10" 154

Kidney has been a big riser all year long; he's consistently gotten better as the season went on. In the most important games, he was usually one of the best players on the ice. Kidney is a highly-skilled center; he's quick and agile with good edges and balance. He'll need to improve his top speed and acceleration, but he's so smart and has such great anticipation that gets to where he needs to be. Kidney is a playmaker; he sees the ice well, protects the puck and can open up passing lanes with quick fakes and stutter steps. He's creative and can find ways to buy himself the extra second that he needs to make a play. Kidney is made even more dangerous by his quick and accurate shot release. He can finish when he moves into the dangerous areas of the ice. There will almost certainly be an adjustment period at the junior level, as his style of play relies on protecting the puck with his body. He needs to get physically stronger over the summer in order to compete better with bigger players at the next level. Kidney started the year on the wing, but moved to center to take on more defensive responsibilities. He's good at using his agility to take away time and space and clear the puck down the ice. Kidney is one of the most intelligent players from this draft class and will make a QMJHL team happy on draft day.

KUKKONEN, KYLE
RC - Maple Grove HS (MNHS) - 5'10" 165

Kukkonen is a late 02' birthdate who was drafted in the 5th Round by Madison (USHL) in the 2018 Phase 1 Draft. The Michigan Tech Commit registered 18 goals and 29 assists in 24 games for Maple Grove High School. Kukkonen saw a 3 game call up to the Madison Capitols this season where he scored in back to back games and seemed to be able to be able to handle the older, faster league well in a small sample size. Kyle plays a sound two-way game and uses his impressive quick bursts of speed to pressure puck carriers and turn pucks over as well as draws penalties on his opponents. His work ethic\, speed and crafty stick work allows him the strip pucks on the back check in the neutral zone and quickly turn plays north. In the offensive end, Kukkonen is a quick puck mover that doesn't need a lot of time and space to make plays. He hasn't quite figured out how to best use his speed offensively yet but still has some time to sort that out. Kukkonen played much of the season on a like with Justin Janicke, these two have played together up through youth and bantam hockey and work well off each other, with Janicke heading to the NTDP for 19/20 it will be interesting to see if Kukkonen can keep his offensive development trending upwards. Kukkonen has quick hands in traffic and has shown the knack for feeding pucks through tight lanes and through traffic.

LAMBOS, CARSON
LD - Rink Hockey Academy Prep (CSSHL) - 6'00" 200

Lambos was the 2nd overall bantam draft pick to the Winnipeg Ice. This season he put up 30 points in 23 games for Rink Hockey Academy, and played 5 games with Kootenay, scoring a goal. Lambos was a standout at the Canada winter games where he captained Manitoba and had 7 points in 6 games. He is a physical specimen with great instincts. Lambos is strong beyond his years and a powerful skater which allows him to confidently patrol the ice. He is a great puck rusher who can take it end to end or hurt you with a smart breakout pass if you over commit. Lambos has a very hard shot, with a lethal one timer, and is always activated offensively looking to generate a chance. His physicality stands out with punishing hits on much older players in the WHL. Lambos should have little trouble translating his game to the Winnipeg Ice next season.

LANGLOIS, JÉRÉMY
LD - Cyclone de Québec (Espoir) - 5'11" 180

Langlois is without a doubt one of the best 15-year-old players to have played at the Midget Espoir level this season. With the Cyclone, he compiled an impressive total of 29 points, 12 goals and 17 assists in 32 games, remarkable statistics for a rookie defender. The left-hander is characterized by his excellent mobility and the level of ease with which he carries the puck alone on the breakout, allowing the play to progress forward while having an impact offensively. He has a good first pass and uses his well-developed vision to find gaps and identify partners with smart passes. He controls the play very well from the point, acting like a quarterback when his team plays on the man-advantage, showing sound puck-management by circulating it effectively while forcing the opposite team to move. Langlois also has some excellent shots, whether it's his one-timer or his wrist shot that he is able to put on net. He is also able to find his teammates' stick-blades to create redirections. In addition, he knows how to buy extra time from the offensive blueline, using dekes and head moves, which allow him to create additional space for himself. Langlois has a sense of anticipation that helps him pinch at the right time without getting caught out of position. His backward skating skills allow him to be effective defensively in one-on-one situations. He has the necessary tools to make a very good defender in the QMJHL. He will be an important part of the Blizzard in 2019-2020.

LAVOIE, ELLIOT
LW - Chevaliers de Lévis (LHMAAAQ) - 6'00" 177

Elliot is another player who saw limited ice time due to the skilled players ahead of him in Lévis. His size and quick hands allow him to be an effective player along the boards and in tight spaces. When receiving a pass from his defensemen, he uses his body-positioning to shield himself away from opponents, and can quickly pivot to look up ice and pull the puck across his body to complete passes to his center or to the weak-side winger with speed. He didn't show a lot offensively, but at the Gatorade Challenge, he showed an ability to combine his speed with a quick release and accurate shot to score goals off the rush and by positioning himself in scoring position around the net. With his size and style of play, he needs to improve on his edgework. If his performance at the Gatorade Challenge is any indication, expect to see him to be an offensive leader in Lévis next season. He has the potential to be a top-6 forward at the QMJHL level.

LEGAULT, CHARLES-ALEXIS
RD - Lac St-Louis Lions (QMAAA) - 6'02" 190

Legault came into this season as arguably the top defenseman available from Quebec, and a player who could challenge for the top pick in the draft. Unfortunately, Legault saw his season cut short in early September and his future is still unknown. He's big, strong and very mobile on the ice for a player of his stature. He can do a bit of everything on the ice; he can rush the puck quite easily with his skating abilities and puck skills. He can defend well and play a physical game along the boards. On the power play, he's a threat because of his big shot from the point. He's definitely a risky pick with his injury and due to missing so much time this year. A lesser-known aspect of his game that we couldn't really figure out this year: how smart is he? How high is his hockey sense? From what we saw in August and September and last year in Bantam AAA, Legault had all the tools to be a premiere defenseman in this draft class. It will be interesting to see what happens to him next season if he's back playing hockey. All indications pointed to him leaning towards going the NCAA route, and with his injury, it makes even more sense now. We ranked him based on potential, but also took into account the risk that comes with him. Legault was drafted by Muskegon in phase 2 of the USHL draft.

L'HEUREUX, ZACHARY
LW/LC - Châteauguay Grenadiers (LHMAAAQ) - 5'11" 187

L'Heureux finished the year with 21 goals and 31 assists for a total of 52 points in 41 games, along with an impressive 10 goals and 13 points, which he amassed while playing for Team Quebec at the 2019 Canada Games in Red Deer, Alberta. L'Heureux had a very good year despite not having had much help by playing on a weak Châteauguay team. He was not only one of the best rookies in the league, but was also one of the best players in the entire Midget AAA circuit. The 5'11", 187-pound forward is dynamic with excellent skating skills and great offensive abilities. He possesses a strong stride to the outside, which allows him to create time and space off the rush and to eventually find a way to the prime shooting areas. L'Heureux has the ability to beat defensemen in many ways, whether it is with speed to the outside or with the use of nifty stick work, and he always gets his shots through. The young forward protects the puck well on open ice and his strong edges make it hard for opponents to knock him off the puck. L'Heureux also showed throughout the year that he's capable of being a QB on the power play, as he showed a great ability to make smart entry decisions in an effort to set up in the o-zone, even when under immense pressure. The knack on L'Heureux is his shift-to-shift consistency and the fact that he sometimes tends to stay on the perimeter. All in all, L'Heureux has the skills and skating abilities to thrive at the next level and any team would be lucky to get him at the draft. L'Heureux was drafted by Cedar Rapids in phase 1 of the USHL draft.

LOCKHART, CONNOR
C/RW - Kanata Lasers (HEO) - 5'09" 170

Connor is a dynamic forward with a high-end skillset and should be considered a top prospect for the OHL draft. He was dominant at the AAA level, demonstrating quick speed, great stickhandling abilities and a high hockey IQ. He has the ability to separate himself with his acceleration and has a very quick first few steps, allowing him to effectively drive the play through the neutral zone on the rush. He can hit his teammates at high speed on the breakout with perfectly placed, hard passes and controls the game at times when he is on the ice. He played top minutes in all situations for Kanata in the HEO last season and can play a physical game defensively. He can cause turnovers with his anticipation and defensive awareness. Throughout the season, he showed an ability to score in multiple ways. He has a hard wrist shot, but could improve on his shooting accuracy when he lets off a quick release. Connor possesses high-end playmaking abilities and vision, and is a consistent threat when he has the puck in the offensive zone.

LUCIUS, CHAZ
RC/RW - Gentry Academy U15 (NAPHL) - 6'01" 160

Lucius dominated the inaugural season of the Gentry Academy for the U15 team. His stats aren't important because the level of a lot of the competition on the schedule wasn't high end, but the opponents Gentry did play that were on par with their talent level, Chaz dominated the play in those games as well. Lucius is a pure goal scorer who uses his hockey sense to be in scoring situations. Chaz played much of the year with his younger brother Cruz who is considered one of the top 04' born players in North America at the stage. Chaz has much more size than Cruz and showed excellent power and technique to protect the puck and drive the crease and middle of the ice. Chaz has quick hands and excellent shooting ability, he can get his shot off in stride, off the rush and find the corners with little time and space. His skating is fairly raw at this stage. Chaz has a good top gear but still has a lanky frame, as he gains some strength and fills out his frame, he should add some explosiveness to his skating but has good agility. Chaz has high end two-way instincts and for all he brings in the offensive end of the rink, he can be equally impactful in his own end, using his high-end hockey sense and compete to snuff out and breakup plays in his own end. Chaz will be heading to the USNTDP this fall before heading to the University of Minnesota in 2022.

LYSELL, FABIAN
RW - Frölunda HC U18 (Jr. J18 Elite) - 5'09" 157

Lysell split his season between two teams, Frölunda HC U16 that was a dominant force in the U16 league and demolished all competition, where he put up a mighty record of 34 goals and 33 assists for a total of 67 points in only 21 games as his team went on to win the Swedish U16 gold in a dominating fashion and he was awarded the prize as the U16 MVP. He also played 20 games for his clubs U18 team where he put up 10 goals and 9 assists for a total of 19 points and was a part of that team winning the Swedish U18 championships too. As his numbers show, Lysell is an offensive, point producing machine and a very dynamic player. He's got fantastic hands and puck skills and great determination with the puck and is considered a game changer as he doesn't wait for a play to happen, but makes the play happen. Lysell can dangle defenders out of their equipment and he can be very spectacular to watch and even though he plays a flashy game, he still manages to be effective with his chances and capitalizes really well. His go to move is the toe-drag where he sets the puck up for a wicked wrist shot with good accuracy. He is is the smaller side of the spectra and the physical game isnt a strenght to his game, but he skates extremely well, with a low center of gravity he can explode with his first few strides and really take off and gain good speed and its impressive to see him stickhandle and managing the puck at his top speed. His vision and reads are superb as he anticipates when to go to certain areas and where the puck eventually will end up. His defensive abilities are hard to judge since his teams haven't really played in the defensive zone all season, but he has done a good job at covering his d-man in the defensive zone and makes good defensive reads too. He won't throw his body around to bump players off the puck, but he might lift some stick to pickpocket the puck from the puck holder.

Lysell played 9 games for Team Sweden U16 this season and recorded 10 goals and 9 assists for a total of 19 points which ultimately is a production of 2.11 points per game, against international competition.

MACDONALD, CAMERON
LC/LW - Selects Hockey Academy (USHS) - 6'02" 180

MacDonald was a big-time scorer this season in the prep ranks with Selects Hockey Academy, scoring 72 goals and 126 points in 52 games. He also was featured during the Winter Canada Games playing for Nova Scotia, where he only had 2 goals (2 points total) in 6 games on a disappointing Nova Scotia team. Before making the move to the USA prep ranks, MacDonald broke the Nova Scotia Bantam goal record, with 54 goals in 33 games last season. He's a big, strong two-way forward. He gives an honest effort in his own zone, can block shots in his zone and show good support to help his defensemen retrieve pucks deep in their zone. As a power-forward, he is learning more and more to use his body to increase his efficiency all over the ice. For a big kid, he skates well; his top speed and acceleration are good. He's very dangerous if he goes untouched in the neutral zone; his combination of size and speed is really tough to handle for prep school defensemen, as proven by his statistics this year. He's got a very good and heavy shot, and can get it off in no time with his quick release. He likes to play from the half-wall area on the power play, but also can do a good job in front of the net, where he's tough to handle. His compete level is a bit inconsistent, he needs to bring his A-game more often. MacDonald is not committed to any NCAA school at this point but did sign a tender agreement with Sioux Falls before the USHL draft.

MAILLOUX, LOGAN
RD - Toronto Marlboros (GTHL) - 6'02" 209

Logan has great size for his age and projects really well at the next level. Logan displays good speed and a powerful stride to be involved in rushes up the ice showcasing his skating ability. He has an OHL caliber shot already with his powerful point shot through traffic with either a slap shot or snap shot. However, when he is not able to get his shot off he can be quiet offensively as he does not really facilitate creative passes. While Logan displays good gap control because of his long stick and range with his reach he can struggle at times with pivots and can get beat to the outside by oncoming offenders. Logan will also need to become better in puck possession as he can fumble the puck at the blue line and needs to become more aware to quickly get pucks out of the corner. Showcasing a great physical presence and willingness to use his size to lay big open ice hits which will be beneficial to any OHL club that drafts him. His intriguing size, good skating ability and great shot should allow him to transition into the OHL next season.

MALATESTA, JAMES
LW - Lac St-Louis Lions (QMAAA) - 5'09" 155

Malatesta's regular season was riddled with injuries, but that didn't stop the rookie forward from having a fantastic end-of-season. During the regular season, he had a hard time finding offense, only scoring 12 points in 22 games. Even if Malatesta didn't find the back of net too often in those 22 games, he was still playing very good hockey and creating lots of scoring chances. His strong play earned him a spot on Team Québec at the Canada Games, where he had 5 points in 6 games against some very strong competition. Malatesta plays a North-South game and has a very good release on his shot. He is a powerful skater who is hard to stop in the open ice. He is not overly big, but he never shies away from contact and likes to deliver the body from time to time. His strong shot makes him a threat when he gets close to the slot and is why he is often used on the power play. Malatesta has improved throughout the year when using his powerful stride to take the puck hard to the net and not settle for shots from outside range. Malatesta was the second-leading scorer on the Lions in the playoffs, where he netted 11 goals and 23 points in only 16 games and was an integral part of his team's success. Overall, Malatesta has the skills to be a producer at the next level if he can stay healthy. He was drafted 53rd overall in phase 1 of the USHL draft by Lincoln.

MCCALLUM, LANDON
C - Brantford 99ers (MHAO) - 5'09.5" 153

Landon is a centerman that seems to impact the game every shift as he is always looking for an advantage over his opposition. Wither that means beating them with his skating and speed, maneuvering skillfully with his stick, or mentally frustrating them with his mind games, he's always looking for the leg up. He is willing to engage physically and can deliver solid hits, but he can also be distracted by playing the mental game and sometimes this does not benefit him or his team. When focused, his compete level is quite desirable and he displays both great offensive and defensive awareness. Moving with the puck Landon finds and winds through open ice with speed and skill. He can drive wide, or use his hands to confuse and deke defenders. On the powerplay he is exceptionally capable of managing the attack as he understands where he needs to be in order to receive the puck. Once he has possession he has the vision to see where teammates are going and the ability to accurately distribute to them. With his skill set, feisty-ness, and junior hockey experience as a call up for the Stratford Warriors, he should be able to move onto the next level with ease and develop into a highly skilled pest in a few years' time.

MCTAVISH, MASON
C - Pembroke Lumber Kings (HEO) - 5'11.75" 174

Mason is a dynamic offensive forward who has the skill set and potential to make an impact at the next level. He was awarded the Most Valuable Player of the Year in the HEO league this year. He showed the ability to dominate his opponents and take control of games. He possesses great speed and explosive acceleration. He adjusts his speed when he has the puck to draw defenders in before speeding up to beat them wide. He has the ability and skill set to battle, retrieve loose pucks and carry the play end-to-end. His exceptional puck control and confidence in the offensive zone is what sets Mason apart than any player in the league. Mason ability to control the puck along the boards in the offensive zone is his major assets; he will use his size to protect the puck down low, use his reach and takes the puck to the net when given the opportunity, a major factor which led to him finishing the season with 47 goals in 41 games. Mason has an uncanny scoring ability as he can beat you many different ways from up high to down low, on the power play and penalty kill; he is a threat every time he's on the ice. Mason demonstrates incredible offensive awareness, finding ways to get himself into high percentage scoring areas before shooting and finding open teammates with hard, accurate passes.

He has a quick release, and an accurate, hard wrist shot. His quick hands and skill set in tight make him a consistent threat in the offensive zone when he has space. Consistency in work ethic will give Mason the opportunity to be offensive impact as a 16 year old in the OHL next year.

MELANSON, JACOB
RW - Weeks Major Midget (NSMMHL) - 5'11" 182

Melanson is a highly-skilled winger. He has good size and skating abilities, as well as smarts, patience and soft hands. This season with the Weeks, he had 20 goals and 41 points in 32 games and also played a big role with Nova Scotia at the Canada Games and Gatorade Challenge. One of the most highly-touted prospects coming into the season after dominating at the Bantam level, Melanson had to adjust to playing on a younger team near the bottom of the standings. He was always the focus of the opposing team when he was on the ice, and while it may have frustrated him at times, it forced him to learn to play at a faster pace. He has all the tools to be a very good forward at the junior level. He's good at both ends of the ice and has good skill. He can stickhandle in tight corners, and he has the patience and vision to find the perfect moment to make a play and catch the defense off-guard. Melanson is strong on his skates, has good edges, and a hard, accurate shot that can power through goaltenders. Melanson has good work ethic; he's the type of player who wants to have the puck on his stick when the game is on the line. He can play with a bit of an edge, as seen during the Canada Games, but need to display a bit more consistency from game to game in that regard. Melanson got a few games in at the Junior A level near the end of the year, even managing to put up a 3-point game against 20 year olds. There will be another adjustment period for him to cross at the major junior level, but there's no question that Melanson is ready to play there as early as next year.

MIANSCUM, ISRAEL
LW - Forestiers d'Amos (LHMAAAQ) - 6'01" 194

Mianscum came into this season with a lot of hype after leading Midget Espoir last year in points as a bantam-aged player. This season, he was in a tough situation with Amos, who was not good once again this season. Mianscum didn't get a lot of help offensively on his team. He still found a way to score 21 goals and 35 points in 36 games this season. However, he was cut by Team Quebec for the Canada Games. One of our biggest problems with him this season was his compete level. We like the size-and-skills package that he offers, but his compete level was a big disappointment in our viewings with him this season. The fact that he played on a bad team does play a factor when analyzing this when we saw him, but it doesn't explain all of it. However, when we saw him at the Gatorade Challenge in late April, there's was no issue with his compete level there. He was a dominant player at this event, leading the event with 13 points in 5 games. He's got a power-forward frame and plays a heavy game down low in the offensive zone. With good players around him, he showed that he can be one of the best players from this draft class. He's got a heavy shot and sees the ice well, too. His skating abilities made some nice progress this season; he's not a speedster, but gets to where he needs to be. He does use his size well down low. When he is at his best, he's tough to contain for opposing defensemen. He's physically mature, and that should help him when making the transition to the QMJHL next season. Mianscum was drafted by Sioux City in the USHL Draft.

MITTELSTADT, LUKE
LD - Eden Prairie HS (MNHS) - 5'11" 181

Luke was recently drafted by the Madison Capitols, 2nd overall in the USHL Phase 1 Draft. Luke is the younger brother of Casey and has been recognized for a couple years as the best of his age group in the Minnesota youth hockey ranks and Luke showcased that skill this season as a Sophomore for Eden Prairie HS and was a key contributor to their run to the State title game. Mittelstadt registered 3 goals and 25 assists in 25 regular season games as well as 2 goals and 5 assists in 6 playoffs games. While Mittelstadt brings excellent offensive upside, he plays a mature, smart defensive game. Mittelstadt uses his skating effectively in his defensive game. Mittelstadt has a strong and agile base that keeps him from getting beat wide and makes some difficult plays against the rush seem routine. Mittelstadt was a regular on the Power Play for the Eagles and was effective in creating scoring chances from the point. Mittelstadt has a good shot that he gets off his tape quickly and shows good poise under pressure at the point. Mittelstadt will likely be heading back to Eden Prairie HS this coming season and while he is still two years away from NHL Draft eligibility, he will be a closely monitored prospect as potential top prospect for the 2021 NHL Draft. Like both his brothers, Luke is a University of Minnesota commit.

MOTORYGIN, MAKSIM
G - Dynamo Moscow U18 (Russia U18) - 6'00" 163

Motorygin is a good-sized goaltender for a late 2002 birthday (born December 24th, 2002). This past season, he played for the Dynamo Moscow U-18 team, and also saw ice time for Russia at the U-17 Five Nations' Tournament in Sweden this past February. He's active in his crease, he plays with authority and has great poise. He competes hard to track pucks with traffic in front of him and to collect loose pucks and to save rebounds. He's got a super-quick catching glove and can make some really good glove saves. He has good athleticism and balance.

MYKLUKHA, OLEKSII
RC - RB Hockey Akademie (Czech U19) - 5'10" 154

Myklukha was born in Poland, but has represented Slovakia and Ukraine internationally in the past. Most recently, he played for Slovakia at the U-17 Four Nations' Tournament in Plymouth this past December. This season, playing for the Red Bull Akademie in the Czech U-19 league, he was one of the top U-17 players in the league along with teammate John-Jason Peterka and Pavel Novak. He finished 2nd after Peterka in terms of point-per-game ratio for U-17 players in the league. He's a late 02' birthday, which makes him eligible for the 2021 NHL Entry Draft. Myklukha is undersized and his skating abilities are only average. He lacks good acceleration and a good top speed to be more effective at his size. He has some good smarts, he sees the ice well and he's a good player shorthanded. Thanks to his anticipation, he's able to read plays pretty quickly. He'll need to improve his shot, as it lacks velocity at the moment and it is tough for him to score from long distances. With his size, scoring and winning position battles in front of the net from 5 feet in are also difficult. He's more of a playmaker, as he has good puck poise and good vision as well. It will be interesting to see where he ends up next season. He's eligible for the CHL Import Draft, or he could also go play somewhere in Europe if he leaves the Red Bull Akademie.

NADEAU, OLIVIER
RW - Chevaliers de Lévis (LHMAAAQ) - 6'01" 200

Nadeau is a skilled two-way power forward who has contributed in numerous areas of the game with his skillset. Playing alongside Joshua Roy, he was one of the leaders on the team, playing on both special teams for Lévis. This demonstrates his ability to be effective and valuable at both ends. He possesses a good shot that he can release quickly and a good scoring touch around the net. It is tough to move him out of the front of the net with his imposing frame, resulting in a lot of traffic in front of the goaltender. He's willing to take some punishment in front of the net as well. Nadeau uses his high hockey IQ in order to position himself properly in all three zones and makes high-percentage plays all over the ice. The biggest weakness in Nadeau's game is that he has slow starts in his first three steps. He has heavy feet and lacks quickness in his strides, but he compensates with intelligent positioning. He displayed a good physical presence, showing a willingness to compete in the corners and in front of the net to win the position. As a prospect for the next level, Nadeau projects as a high-IQ power-forward who will do the dirty work in front of the net and along the boards, with a nice scoring touch around the net. In order to be even more successful, he'll need to work on his skating.

NAUSE, EVAN
LD - Newbridge Academy U-18 (PSHF) - 6'01" 175

Nause is a New Brunswick native and he's coming off his second year playing with the U-18 team at Newbridge Academy. Nause is an excellent skater; a quick, skilled puck moving defenseman who has shown a lot of improvement as the year went on. When Nause is engaged, he's quick and shifty. He's great at starting the rush from his own end with a good breakout pass, his good hands and ability to protect the puck. His defensive game has improved as well; he's gotten bigger and stronger and can quickly close gaps, catching the offense off-guard. He sees the ice well and does a good job identifying open men and shutting them down. There's a lot of power in his stride, allowing him to quickly get to top speed and making him very difficult to knock off the puck. Nause has quick hands and can make quick, short passes in tight. Nause really got to shine during the Gatorade Challenge and Canada Games, where he played against higher-level competition. He's shown that he has the tools required to be a top defenseman at the junior level. He's still a bit raw, and you can see that when attempting to project him. There's another level he might be able to reach in the next couple of years if his development goes the right way. He was drafted by Sioux Falls in the USHL Draft, but he's not committed to any NCAA schools yet.

OLAUSSON, OSKAR
LW - HV71 U20 (Jr. SuperElite) - 6'00" 165

Late born 2002, Olausson split his season between HV71 U18 and U20. With his clubs U18 team he put up 17 goals and 8 assists in 19 games for a total of 25 points. He also played 11 games for his clubs U20 in the SuperElite league and recorded 1 goal and 3 assists for a total of 4 points.

Olausson plays a smart game where he utilizes his strengths to the maximum to gain advantages on the opposition. He skates really well as he's got great top speed, good acceleration and has the ability to sustain his speed for longer durations of time, if needed. He is a technically sound skater and what really makes him stand out is how clever he utilizes his skating as he knows exactly when to slow down and just glide and when to explode with his quick first couple strides to gain access to certain areas of the ice where he will be able to receive a pass. He distributes the puck well as he often makes the low percentage play and plays a give-and-go type of game where he can disorient opponents by moving the puck quickly and taking a new position on the ice. His hands are okay, but could benefit from getting improved, although he can control the puck at high speed and beat defenders 1 on 1, he is still most effective when keeping things simple. His shot velocity is average but he has the ability to pick his spots and his shooting accuracy is crazy as he finds a way to thread be puck past shot blockers, to pick his spot over the goaltender's shoulders and the goaltender won't even be able to see the puck at all. Even though he is a great offensive player, he is a two-way player and his defensive game is strong as he makes fantastic reads and player hard. He can capitalize on his size and bump opponents off the puck as well as blocking shots and killing penalties. He is highly viable in all three zones and even if its still too early to tell, he looks like a really great prospect for the 2021 draft. Olausson also played 8 games for Sweden's U17 team where he managed to put up 7 goals and 4 assists for a total of 11 points and he had a spectacular showing in the 5-nations tournament in Tranås, Sweden in February.

ORR, ROBERT
LC/LW - Lac St-Louis Lions (QMAAA) - 5'11" 166

Orr is a natural point-producer with great stick skills and fine overall offensive instincts. He has a great touch in the slot and can elevate the puck in tight spaces, which makes him a great finisher. He is a good skater with strong mechanics, speed, and great lateral ability. The problem with his skating is that he does not use it enough. He is often flat-footed, which causes him to turn pucks over a lot, especially against stronger opponents, and on the forecheck he doesn't use his speed to put any pressure on the opposing team's defense. Rarely this year did we see Orr apply his skating abilities and it truly separated him from the pack, and allowed him to dominate with the puck, and create plays completely by himself. He has a quick release and accurate shot, and he usually gets his shots off while in stride, which makes it hard on goalies. Orr could definitely simplify his game more at times as he sometimes gets caught trying to make 1 or 2 extra moves rather than using his quick shot. Defensively, like most players with Orr's skillset at his age, he needs to be more responsible. When playing on the wing he is too soft along the wall and shows no interest in getting into the shooting lanes. Orr racked up a total of 43 points in 50 games between the regular season and the playoffs, and if he isn't in the QMJHL or playing south of the border next year, he will likely be one of the top scorers in all of Midget AAA next season.

OTHMANN, BRENNAN
RW - Don Mills Flyers (GTHL) - 5'11" 153

Brennan is a fluid skater with good mobility and possesses one of the best shots in the Minor Midget age group making him an offensive threat on every shift. He has a knack for putting the puck in the net with tremendous accuracy and power combined with intelligent offensive zone positioning. In addition to scoring goals, Brennan also displays really good vision and playmaking skills using his linemates and making them better. His hard shot and excellent release to get it off at his top speed is what separates him from others. Brennan also showcases a willingness to be physical in tough contests, which compliments his game well and demonstrates his compete level. Brennan's skating mechanics are fluid displaying strong edges, power and mobility. While he is a skilled player his stickhandling skills do not stand out as a strength in his game. Brennan is a high-end winger who is capable of scoring goals at will or setting up teammates and projects to be a top line winger at the OHL level.

PALODICHUK, JOE
LD - Hill Murray School (MNHS) - 6'00" 165

Palodichuk logged a lot of minutes for Hill Murray in the run to the Minnesota State tournament, playing in a it of key situations including the Penalty Kill. For Palodichuk to be trusted in those situations as just a 03' DOB speaks to the mature all-around game he possesses. Palodichuk's offensive numbers don't jump off the page, with just 3 goals and 9 assists in 24 regular season games, however Joe was used primarily in defensive situations and was not a regular on the Power Play. Palodichuk is a smart defenseman that keeps a good gap, he showed the ability to break up plays before they get started in the neutral zone. Joe can make accurate seem passes coming out of his own end but can seem lackadaisical at times in his puck retrievals, he identifies pressure well but doesn't look to be in a hurry to retrieve the puck and puts himself under pressure when he doesn't have to. He can handle things at the High School level but will need to play with more urgency in these situations to control the game with the same effectiveness. Palodichuk was recently drafted in the 5th Round, 68th overall in the 2019 NHL Phase 1 Draft by Fargo but will likely be returning to Hill Murray for 19/20 where he should get more offensive opportunities.

PAQUET, FÉLIX
LD - Cantonniers de Magog (QMAAA) - 6'01" 187

Félix Paquet is a defender who made excellent progress as the season advanced with the Cantonniers. Demonstrating some signs of reluctance and keeping his style of play relatively simple early in the year, he began to show more confidence in his decision-making in the mid-season in addition to winning in physical maturity; he is now swinging the scales at almost 190 pounds from the top of his 6'1". He completed the regular season with a personal record of one goal and 12 assists for 13 points in 42 games, while posting an excellent plus-34 rating. Using his great calm while in possession of the puck, Paquet is effective on the rush, managing to make good first precise passes that allow for an effective transition. His decision-making is good and he excels at getting rid of the pressure when an opposing forward pursues him deep in his own zone in puck-retrieval situations. Although he has been further recognized for his defensive qualities this season, the left-hander still has good offensive strengths, leading us to believe that he could very well become a reliable top-4 defender at the next level by having an impact at both sides of the rink. Paquet is particularly effective at maintaining his opponents in one-on-one situations, since he is able to manage his positioning and distance with the puck-carrier, regularly blocking pucks with his stick and body. A regular on the penalty kill, he also saw playing time this season on the second power play unit. Since he rarely makes mistakes, he could stand to use his imposing frame a little bit more to his advantage by being more physical in his own territory. Paquet will be the number one defender on the Cantonniers' blueline next year.

PASTUJOV, SASHA
RW - Detroit Compuware U16 (HPHL U16) - 5'11" 175

Sasha is a high-end playmaker who also possesses an ability to score in tight to the goal. Lined up on his off wing, he displayed a low and wide skating stride that provides him with strong stability and protection as a puck carrier. He is an agile skater and shows good ability to cut laterally into the slot while maintaining control of the puck and driving it hard to the net. Sasha's overall skating and mobility are good but his footwork could be improved to elevate his game to an even higher level. Throughout the season he showed a good ability to beat defenders on the outside or inside with his hands and speed. On multiple occasions, he used his speed and puck handling skill to carry the puck with confidence through the neutral and offensive zones while keeping his head up. Sasha's best attribute is his playmaking skill using his high-end hockey intelligence and anticipation to make elite level plays with his hands. He has the ability to anticipate and see an open teammate throughout the offensive zone and deliver a crisp tape-to-tape pass. While his playmaking skill is special he can also shoot the puck. His shot range in our viewings was primarily limited inside the faceoff circles using his hands and physical drive to the slot to score while relying on his playmaking skill at further distances. Sasha is a high-end playmaker whose skating, hockey IQ and work ethic combine to make him one of the top wingers available in the OHL Draft.

PEART, JACK
LD - Grand Rapids HS (MNHS) - 5'09" 171

Recently drafted 7th overall in the 2019 Phase 1 USHL Draft by Fargo, Jack Peart is a highly skilled but undersized defenseman out of Grand Rapids High School. Peart is a strong and explosive skater who despite his size is difficult to separate from the puck. He skates with a wide base that shields the puck well and has good separation speed coming out of his own end. Peart can lead the rush out of his own end but isn't reckless about it. If the puck can get to where it needs to be with an outlet pass, he is just as willing to use that than his feet to get the puck there. His ability to quickly identify pressure and go through his reads is as good as anyone currently in the Minnesota High School ranks. In the offensive end, Peart is able to set the table effectively from the point, his ability to walk the blue line and open up lanes and be confidence under pressure is impressive for a player his age. The game many nights ran through Peart having the puck on his stick. How Peart is able to develop his defensive game in the next couple of seasons' will ultimately determine is draft stock and NHL upside. The vision and offensive skill are there to be a power play specialist, but if he can sort out some of the things in his own end, he could develop into a top NHL Draft prospect for 2021.

PELLERIN, MAXIME
RW/RC- Trois-Rivières Estacades (QMAAA) - 5'11" 160

The greatest quality Pellerin has is his ability to keep control of the puck even if he is battling against multiple players. He's very good at handling the puck in tight spaces. He protects the puck well. Even when he loses control of it, he is extremely quick to take it back. Offensively, he has a very good vision of the game, and is capable of making great passes. He's effective on the power play, where he can use his good vision and good puck poise. Pellerin can play both on the wing and at center; he usually plays on the first or second line and won 57% of his face-offs' when used at center. Pellerin has a good shot as well as a good shot release. However, he's got to work on the accuracy of his shot. He's a good enough skater for this level, but will need to keep working on his skating to improve his speed in order to play at another level next season. He finished the season with 42 points in 42 games and also played for Team Quebec at the Canada Games, playing on a line with Bolduc (his Trois-Rivières teammate) and Zachary L'Heureux of Châteauguay. Pellerin has top-6 upside for the QMJHL, either as a center or on the wing.

PINELLI, FRANCESCO
C - Toronto Red Wings (GTHL) - 5'11.5" 172

Francesco is a skilled two-way power forward who can contribute in numerous areas of the ice with his versatility and overall skillset. Francesco possesses a good, long stride and can produce good speed that will translate well to the next level. Francesco is a communicative leader who plays on both the powerplay and penalty kill for the Red Wings showcasing his value to the coaching staff in multiple ways. He possesses a hard shot that is evident on his one-timers from the right circle when set up on the power play and good scoring ability on breakaways. He uses his high hockey IQ in order to make passes in the offensive zone, setting up his teammates and shows an ability to play at a high speed but can also slow down the game when in possession, creating time and allowing for things to develop. Francesco is sound in his decision making in order to facilitate quick breakouts or knowing when to support defensively. Displaying a good physical presence showing a willingness to compete in the corners or lay a devastating hit. As a prospect for the next level, Francesco projects as a first line centre who can play a complete game and lead a team with all the intangibles.

PLANDOWSKI, OSCAR
RD - Selects Hockey Academy 15U (USHS) - 6'01" 170

Plandowski is a Halifax native, but played this past season with Selects Hockey Academy and the previous year with OHA Edmonton prep. He comes from a hockey family, with his father being an NHL scout and his mother a power-skating coach back home in Nova Scotia. This past season, the offensive defenseman had 53 points in 48 games, including 8 goals and an added 4 points in 6 games at the Canada Games playing for Nova Scotia. He made some nice progress over the course of the season; mostly in terms of decision-making. He kept his game more simple and cut down on the turnovers that we saw at the beginning of the season. He's a good defenseman to rush the puck out of his zone; he has above-average skating abilities and is quick to retrieve pucks in his own zone. He's got above-average puck skills, good poise with the puck in the offensive zone and some good creativity with the puck to create scoring chances. He's got a good point shot with above-average velocity and does a good job keeping it low for tips and rebounds. He's got a good compete level, is good one-on-one and, if needed, will play a physical game along the boards. He had a great showing at the Canada Games even if his province (Nova Scotia) was a disappointment in Red Deer. He was a more consistent performer compared to Cam Whynot, the other highly-touted defenseman. Plandowski is committed to play college hockey at Quinnipiac University and in May he was drafted in the USHL by Green Bay.

POWER, OWEN
LD - Chicago Steel (USHL) - 6'04" 214

Sturdy, two-way defenseman with great size. A product of the Mississauga Reps midget program, Power jumped right into being a top-four defenseman in the USHL as a November 2002 birthday. Already imposing at 6'4" and over 200 pounds, Power plays a composed, reliable game. He was a 2nd round selection in the OHL Draft in 2018, but elected to go the USHL route to preserve his commitment to the University of Michigan. As the season wore on, Owen displayed even greater confidence in his game. He's a tight gap player who is on top of attackers and the puck in all three zones. His reach disrupts a lot of plays at this level. He also wasn't shy about jumping into the rush. His shot and ability to one-time pucks is a major weapon. He led all USHL rookie blueliners in goals with 11, his 25 points was second in that same subset behind 2019 eligible Zac Jones. Already a good, coordinated skater for his size, Power plays the game very coolly and with terrific puck poise. With Chicago's #1 defenseman aging out of the league for next season, Power will likely take on the full complement of responsibilities. Provided he passes that litmus test, the Ontario native will remain on track to be a top-15 pick in 2021.

PUNNETT, CONNOR
LD - North Central Predators (OMHA-ETA) - 6'0.5" 179

Connor possesses intriguing size that projects well with room to still fill out and add strength to his frame. He is a physical defender who has two-way potential if he can improve his decision-making and hockey IQ. Connor is an average skater who possesses good speed but a slow first stride that causes him to be behind the play at times and vulnerable on rushes to the outside that expose his lateral foot speed. Defensively, he plays incredibly physical angling forwards to the outside and finishing his checks. His strength his most noticeable along the boards where he initiates contact to separate opponents from the puck. At times, Connor can make good plays with his feet or stick to move the puck up ice; however, consistency remains an issue. Connor can make irresponsible decisions with the puck making risky reads showing average anticipation and leaving his team exposed to odd-man opportunities against. Connor will need to improve his quickness and hockey IQ in order to be successful top-4 defender at the next level.

RATY, AATU
LC - Karpat U20 (Jr. A SM-Liiga) - 6'00" 170

Aatu Raty is the younger brother of Aku Raty who is a 2019 eligible-player, playing on the same-line both for their team and at international-events. He's the more skilled of the two brothers and has already dominated the junior-circuit with Karpat's U18 and U20 squads. He played the majority of his games in Jr. A SM-Liiga, where he produced 31 points in 41 games, including 17 goals. In the playoffs, he continued his productive-ways with 12 points in 10 games, including 4 goals. At the international-level, he played in several different-events, including both the U17 and U18 tournaments and had his most productive tournament at the U18-Five-Nations where he produced 5 points in 4 games. Raty is a line-driving winger, who plays with a lot of confidence. He looks to take the puck from the outside and move towards the circles, using his body and length to protect the puck while identifying his options. His length works well with his hands, as he's shown the ability to rapidly adjust his shooting-angle; he can also make extended toe-drag dekes and beat opponents cleanly by pulling the puck around them before cutting to the net. He's a multi-faceted and versatile player who shows good hesitation when carrying the puck and can make high-end no-look passes look relatively easy as well. His skating ability is a plus and he's coordinated, which gives him deceptive skating mechanics when he looks to suddenly shift-lanes. He's going to be one of the top players featured in the 2021-draft and is the best Finnish prospect heading into it.

REYNOLDS, PETER
LW - Shattuck St.Mary's U16 (USHS) - 5'10" 165

Reynolds is a New Brunswick native who has been away from his home province for 3 years already, having played the last two seasons at Shattuck St. Mary's and the one before in Boston. This season with the U-16 team, he was playing a year up finished the year with 71 points in 51 games. He added 9 points in 7 games at the Canada Games, where he was his province's top player. He's one of the more skilled players from this draft class, has a great shooting arsenal and above-average speed. He likes to have the puck on his stick and make plays offensively. He's got an excellent release and can score from anywhere in the offensive zone. Reynolds is as good as a scorer as he is a playmaker. He at his best on the man-advantage, where he has more room to make plays be a threat on the ice. Defensively, he's not a liability; he has above-average smarts and anticipation to intercept some passes. At the Canada Games he was dominant; his mix of his skills and compete level was really tough to counter for opposing teams. In the game against Ontario where New Brunswick was badly outplayed, Reynolds found ways to make things happen every time he was on the ice, which was super impressive. He's committed to Boston College and he was also drafted by Chicago in the USHL draft in May.

RICHARD, GUILLAUME
LD - Blizzard du Séminaire St-François (QMAAA) - 6'00" 148

Guillaume Richard had an excellent offensive rookie season with 27 points (seven goals and 20 assists) in 38 games. Richard also participated in the Canada Games, where he helped Team Quebec win the gold medal in an important role by being used in all kinds of situations; five-on-five, power play and penalty kill. He is a defender who is very comfortable when carrying the puck on his stick and bringing it from one zone to another, thanks to his excellent skating abilities and his puck handling skills. He constantly offers offensive support when the opportunity arises. He is also very effective when quarterbacking the power play, where he circulates the puck effectively from the point and manages to create additional space under pressure by making some dekes with his fast hands and head moves that compromise the opposition. His abilities allow him to bring pucks to the net with his good slapshot or his accurate wrister. With his excellent mobility, Richard is able to accelerate quickly with his first strides and is patient in puck-recovery situations deep in his own zone. His defensive game remains the element on which he must continue to improve over the coming months. Having reached an agreement with the University of Maine for the 2021-2022 season, it would be surprising to see him back in the QMAAA next year, as he should move into the USHS with the Mount St. Charles Academy team.

ROBIDAS, JUSTIN
RC - Cantonniers de Magog (QMAAA) - 5'07" 162

Justin Robidas is an exceptional player with an extraordinary hockey sense among all the eligible skaters at the 2019 QMJHL Entry Draft. He is a very intelligent forward who knows how to make his teammates better and who has a remarkable work ethic. Playing at center, he is able to make plays as well as score goals. The 15-year-old rookie distinguished himself in the faceoff circle as well, with an efficiency ratio of around 70%, particularly exceptional given the high number of draws he took as the top center for Magog. A heart-and-soul leader, Robidas quickly paid his dues within the team's lineup in order to establish himself as his team's offensive mainstay while contributing in all facets of the game. Used on the first power play unit, the right-hander can also fulfill tasks shorthanded or take charge of important faceoff's in critical situations. In his first QAAAA season, Robidas had an impressive 53 points (28 goals and 25 assists) in 35 games. He has also had an excellent postseason, scoring on seven occasions and adding 15 assists, good for 22 points in 14 games, a crucial contribution to the Cantonniers' second consecutive conquest of the Jimmy-Ferrari Cup. He also took part in the Canada Games, where he lined up as the captain of Team Quebec. In a leadership role, he helped his team win gold against the Ontarians, with 10 points (five goals and five assists) in six games. Possessing elite on-ice vision, Robidas manages to identify his teammates with the help of judicious passes that have the effect of opening the play. His skating is one of his main strengths; he has a very smooth and stable stride in addition to having a lot of power in his legs to accelerate quickly. He loves exploiting this facet of his game by signaling himself in transition, making use of his speed and force of acceleration in the neutral zone to gain space and attack the enemy territory at full speed. His undeniable puck handling skills such as his stickhandling and agile hands allow him to stand out when he is in possession of the puck, making him a constant threat. He always manages to create something. Thanks to his strong hockey sense, Robidas is effective at anticipating and knowing where to position himself in order to be first on a loose puck or to intercept a passing attempt. He has an excellent, powerful and accurate wrist shot that is rarely off-target, and he also has very good hand-eye coordination that allows him to deflect shots from the point. It also explains his success in the faceoff circle. Responsible defensively, he does not hesitate to backcheck deeply to help his defenders. Although he is not a very tall skater, there is no doubt that Robidas will be a dominant player in the QMJHL and has all the tools required to eventually become a captain of one of the 18 clubs. He is ready to make the jump for the next level next year, and was our top-ranked prospect for this year's QMJHL draft.

ROLOFS, STUART
LW - Kanata Lasers (HEO) - 6'02", 188

Stuart is a large forward at the AAA level with quick hands and high offensive skill. He exhibits very strong puck handling abilities, and skates well with the puck on the rush, using his size and skill to protect the puck. He has the skill to deke through multiple defenders at a time and control the puck along the sideboards with ease. He has a hard, accurate wrist shot and a quick release, and has a tendency to skate to high percentage scoring areas before shooting. Stuart is also an effective playmaker and has great vision in the offensive zone. He can make long, accurate passes on the tape at high speed. Stuart will want to continue to improve on his foot speed to make a similar impact at the OHL level.

ROUSSEAU, WILLIAM
G - Vert et Or du Séminaire St-Joseph M18 (LHPS) - 6'00" 158

Playing with Séminaire St-Joseph in the LHPS in the M18 category, Rousseau has compiled impressive statistics at the end of the regular season, as his personal record shows: 14 wins, one defeat in regulation and another in overtime in 16 games. He also posted an excellent 1.75 goals-against average and a .930 save percentage. His great numbers convinced Hockey Quebec to invite him to the Winter Canada Games in February, where he had to content himself with the role of backup to William Blackburn of the Élites. He was only featured in one game during the preliminary round. Rousseau is a goaltender who covers the lower part of his net well with his pads. His lateral movements are good, and he shows agility on his skates in addition to good balance. He has good technique that allows him to control rebounds appropriately, and he seems comfortable playing the puck outside of his crease. It will be interesting to see where the goaltender from Trois-Rivières will play next year, as he is without a doubt one of the best players at his position for this year's draft. He's committed to play college hockey at Nebraska-Omaha in the NCAA.

ROY, JOSHUA
LW/C - Chevalier de Lévis (LHMAAAQ) - 5'11" 180

All year long, Roy displayed high-end skills, leading the Lévis Chevaliers to a 41-1 record. He was also a heavy topic of discussion for the 1st overall selection all year long. Sound in all facets of the game, he has good straight-line speed and balance, but still needs to work on his acceleration and first steps. Roy is great with his ability to read the play and anticipate what comes next, which allows him to excel at both ends of the rink. On the offensive side of the puck, Roy possesses an elite scoring touch, but also likes to hold onto the puck and control the pace of the game in the offensive zone. As a shooter, he possesses excellent shot velocity and accuracy with his wrist shot and snapshot, fooling goalies while subtly changing his shooting angles. Even if he is more recognizable by his scoring abilities, Roy can make high-end plays in all three zones. He will make you pay for lazy coverage in the offensive zone with cross-ice offensive zone saucer passes from anywhere. Roy is more of a cerebral player, but his lack of compete level at even-strength leaves us with question marks. This season, he could finish a game with 2 or 3 points in a game despite not being as dominant as that stats' line would tell us. He's lethal on the power play; he amassed 40 of his 88 points on the power play this season. With more space and time on the ice, he's a very dangerous player. Roy's 88 points this season was the 7th-highest point total for a 15-year-old in the history of the LHMAAAQ. Roy will most likely make an impact right away in the QMJHL next year, and it might not take long before he becomes a top-6 forward for the team that selects him in June. He was part of the Team Quebec squad that won gold at the Canada Games, amassing 13 points in 6 games. His midget team was upset in the playoffs by Lac St-Louis in the league semi-final, and Roy was not as good in the playoffs as he was during the regular season (11 points in 11 playoff games). In late April at the Gatorade Challenge, he didn't stand out as much as we would have liked, but you've got to keep in mind that other top picks from previous drafts didn't have amazing performances at this tournament either. He can play both on the wing and at center, but will most likely start his junior career on the wing. Areas slated for improvement in order for him to reach his full potential: his compete level, in addition to quickness on the ice.

ROY, TRISTAN
LW - Cantonniers de Magog (QMAAA) - 6'02" 184

Tristan Roy is a very mature physical left-winger for a 15-year-old rookie with the Magog Cantonniers in the QMAAA. He completed the regular season with 11 goals and 10 assists in 42 games, seeing regular ice-time on the first power play unit. He had a great postseason, averaging more than one point per game with 10 goals and six assists in 15 games, helping Magog claim its second consecutive championship by scoring the winning goal in overtime in the fourth game against the Lac St-Louis Lions. Roy is a power-forward who could be very dangerous in front of the blue paint. He uses his impressive size and individual attributes to his advantage to recover pucks and make his presence felt in the slot. He has a very good wrist shot with good velocity and knows how to use opposing defenders as a screen before releasing it. When he reaches his top speed, he becomes difficult to maintain and steal the puck from, as his strides are powerful and well-balanced. The overall mechanics of his skating remains the main element Roy must work on if he wants to have a bigger impact at the next level. He is an effective player in puck-pursuit; he is tenacious with his stick and regularly manages to steal pucks from opponents in addition to completing his checks. He is dominant along the boards and manages to win his battles. Evolving both on the power play and the penalty kill, the left-handed forward is not afraid to use his body to block shots. Given his mature frame and the attributes that characterize his game, there is no doubt that Roy will be a good top-6 player in the QMJHL. He could even make the jump to the Q as early as next year.

SAGANIUK, COLBY
C - Pittsburgh Penguins U16 (T1EHL U16) - 5'05" 134

Colby was arguably one of the best U15 American prospects for the 2019 OHL Priority Selection but his NHL upside is questionable at this time due to his 5'5" frame. While his skating and talent are high-end, he will need to add size to become a top-end NHL prospect by the 2021 Draft. He was selected by the Erie Otters in the 2nd round (37th overall) in the 2019 OHL Priority Selection and has signed with the United States National Development Program U17 team for the 2019-20 season. Colby is an undersized centre who is one of the most dynamic and offensively gifted players available in the OHL Draft. The foundation to his game is his excellent skating, which allows him to make an impact in all three zones. He is extremely light and agile on his skates showing excellent speed and acceleration and often forcing opponents to take penalties on him to negate clean quality scoring chances. His skating allows him to move laterally with ease and change direction on a dime making him a slippery player who avoids contact. Colby's excellent work ethic mean his feet are always moving to make a play or pressure the puck and win races to the puck. Throughout our viewings, Colby thrived with possession and liked to have the puck on his stick to control the play making him most dangerous in transition with his speed and skill. His soft hands and feet allow him to create space with the puck to make a play. He displayed strong passing skill with an ability to stretch the ice north-south or east-west making strong tape-to-tape passes. Despite his size, Colby displayed a willingness to drive the puck through the slot and to the front of the net showing good drive and determination in the tough scoring areas. He played in all situations and is an offensive threat even on the penalty kill where he scored multiple shorthanded goals in our viewings using his speed and hands to create clean breakaways. Colby displays pretty good anticipation, intelligence and hockey sense in all facets of his game. His high-end skillset projects he will be a top-6 forward at the OHL level.

SAMOSKEVICH, MATTHEW
RW/C - Shattuck St. Mary's (US-Prep) 5'10" 170

Matthew is a late 02' birthdate but despite his age and being eligible to play on the U16 team, Samoskevich played up with the prep team this past season and it was evident early on he was the most dynamic offensive player on the roster. Matthew put up 36 goals and 38 assists in 51 games for the Sabres. One area of Samoskevich's game that improved in the last year is his skating. While he has had the agility and strength on his skates, he has added another gear when it comes to explosiveness off the hop which allowed him to win more puck races and have the puck on his tape more this season than in previous season's. Matthew can play a multifaceted game offensively, he is able to play a power game below the dots, as he is strong on the puck and uses his body well or he can play and up-tempo game and generate off the rush. His vision and ability to read the play at this stage is among the best in his draft class. While Samoskevich is not a defensive dynamo at this stage, he does show effort and compete to come back into the play but will just need some time to understand his roll in his own end, as he is very eager at times to get on the offense before things are sorted out in his own end. Samoskevich was drafted in the 4th round by Chicago in 2018 and saw some action for Chicago down the stretch and into the playoffs where he impressed but was not a regular in the lineup throughout the playoffs despite not at all looking out of place in the USHL. As of now Samoskevich is committed to the University of Michigan and due to his late birthdate and developmental track, its not improbably that Samoskevich will be playing his NHL Draft year in the NCAA ranks.

SAVAGE, REDMOND
C/RW - Detroit Compuware U16 (HPHL U16) - 5'10" 160

Redmond is a skilled two-way forward with average size who can play centre or wing. He can play in all situations from operating on the top powerplay unit to the 5 on 3 penalty kill. He has a relentless work ethic and does not lose many battles. Throughout the year he has either played wing on the top line with Duke and Pastujov or centered his own line. He has the ability to be the go-to guy on any given game for this Compuware team that is full of talent. He possesses game breaking offensive skill. He displays above average skating and stickhandling ability, he also has goal scoring and playmaking ability, but his most impressive characteristics are his work ethic and versatility. He can struggle with consistency at times as he is not very noticeable in some games. As he continues to grow and fine-tune his skills, he has the potential to be an impactful top-6 forward at the next level.

SAVOIE, CHARLES
LC - Vikings St-Eustache (LHMAAAQ) - 6'01" 161

Charles is a skilled center who led his team in scoring during the regular season. He possesses good puck skills, vision, and a quick wrist shot, which makes him a multi-faceted offensive threat. He was at his best on the power play unit, where he could handle the puck for a little bit longer and drag attention to himself before making nice cross-ice saucer passes to an open player. While he's not the fastest skater, Savoie has a smooth stride that allows him to skate with agility. This makes him dangerous in one-on-one situations against opposing defensemen. Despite not being the most physical, Savoie displayed good anticipation and good reads on the ice, which gave him opportunities to create turnovers in the offensive zone. On the defensive side of the puck, he could be more engaged in the play and compete better for loose pucks. All-in all, Savoie is a skilled center who has the potential to play on a top-6, but will have ensure that his compete level becomes more consistent in order to ensure his potential.

STANKOVEN, LOGAN
RW- Thompson Blazers, (BCMMHL) - 5'08" 170

Stankoven was take 5th overall in the WHL bantam draft by the Kamloops Blazers. This season he tore up the BCMML with 101 points in 38 games to lead the league by almost 40 points and earn MVP honors. When his midget season concluded he got in to 13 WHL games including playoffs and registered 3 points in a third line role where he didn't look out of place. Stankoven is a high end offensive driver who thrives on controlling play with the puck on his stick. He has great instincts as a passer, seeing the play as at opens up and creatively utilizing his teammates. He is very undersized but is extremely tenacious to make up for it. Stankoven was willing to put his body on the line and batted against much older players, never showing any quit or backing down. Stankoven has the ability to make a play out of nothing and should be one of the top rookies in the WHL next season.

STILLMAN, CHASE
C - Sudbury Wolves (GNML) - 5'10.25" 155

Chase is a highly intelligent two-way centre who can anticipate the play and make an impact in all three zones. Both with and without the puck he shows high compete level making creative and smart decisions playing the role of both facilitator and finisher. He is a good skater who displays good speed but only average acceleration lacking the extra gear to turn defenseman on the outside on a consistent basis. Offensively, he is a threat both as a passer and shooter and keeps defensemen guessing on his next move. The key to Chase's game is puck possession where he makes smart reads and more often than not makes the right play with the puck. Without possession, he anticipates where the puck is going to be and puts himself in position to make a play offensively. Chase's shot is not the hardest but it is accurate allowing him to pick his corner. Without the puck, he displays good relentlessness to never give up while tracking back and playing an honest game that will be favourable to coaches at the next level. Chase is smart enough to step into an OHL lineup next season as a 16-year old and projects to be a top-6 forward by his 18-year old season.

STRINGER, ZACK
LW - Lethbridge Hurricanes (WHL) - 6'00" 150

Stringer was the 8th overall bantam draft pick by his hometown team. This season Stringer had 41 points in 30 AMHL games, in his second season of midget hockey after playing as an underage last season. He joined Lethbridge for the end of the season getting 4 points in 8 regular season games and earning his way into the playoff lineup where he registered 3 points in 6 games. Stringer plays an extremely smart complimentary style of game. He excels as a passer and recovering dump ins where he seemingly comes out with the puck every time. With the puck on his stick he quickly analyzes all of his available options and makes great quick reads. He excels as a playmaker from beneath the goal line where he found open teammates on the point and the home base area with consistency. Plays with a ton of effort, forechecking hard and diving in front of shots for blocks. Skating will be his big hurdle to overcome as he has a very awkward hunched over style and clearly lacks strength and explosiveness. For having such a strange looking stride he still got around okay with speed to keep up with the pace and excellent balance. Next season Stringer should immediately enter the Lethbridge top 6 in what might be a rebuilding year.

TINLING, DOVAR
LC - Lac St-Louis Lions (QMAAA) - 5'11" 165

Tinling finished the regular season with 42 points in 29 games, along with 16 points in 15 playoff games. His numbers put him among the top 10 for points-per-game average and he was an instrumental part in his team's quest for the Jimmy Ferrari Cup, in which they fell short to a very strong team from Magog. Tinling is a pass-first player with an uncanny ability to find his linemates in the right spots for quality scoring chances. Tinling was a wiz on the powerplay this year, usually teamed up with Matt Choupani and Chris Duchesne. He always found a way to create space and feather pucks through the seams to the open man. He makes smart decisions with the puck and shows great poise in the offensive zone. His puck skills are among the best in the league, and his accurate wrist shot allowed him to score 24 goals throughout the regular season and playoffs. The worst parts of Tinling's game are his overall work ethic and commitment to defensive play. Tinling fails to win battles along the wall due to a lack of effort and not being strong enough on his stick. He can also be found trying to leave the o-zone too quick. Another problem with Tinling is his unwillingness to get into the shooting lane. He is often late to assignments and shots from the point consistently get to his team net. Lastly, he will need to improve his skating and compete level if he wishes to be a dominant player at the next level. Tinling was drafted 23rd overall in the USHL draft by Des Moines but still not committed to any NCAA schools.

WALLSTEDT, JESPER
G - Luleå U20 (Jr. SuperElite) - 6'03" 205

Jesper Wallstedt is the most highly touted Swedish goaltender since. He decided to join Luleå HF's organization this season and figured in 4 games for his new clubs U18 but he was mainly with the U20 team where he started 21 games recording a 2.65 GAA and a .901 save percentage. Wallstedt is way ahead of the curve in his age group and has been starting games in the SuperElite since he was 14-15 years old and still have a couple of years until his even draft eligible. Wallstedt has got great size and covers a lot of the net even as he sits down in his butterfly. He is a modern goaltender who combines size with athleticism. Wallstedt tends to rely a bit too much on his size and he could really benefit from being a little more aggressive and anticipating than he is right now. As most modern goaltenders he has a quick catching glove in which he looks really confident. His angling needs improvement, he covers the near post well, but he leaves big chunks of open net high on the far post which skilled shooters can easily exploit. That is not good, especially since he goes down to his butterfly position way too early in an effort to cover the ice and hope that the shooter will hit him, instead of trying to read the play and anticipate the shot. He does however, anticipate passing plays really well and keeps his stick active to break up passes through the crease. Wallstedt has improved his skating and feet movement during the season and he is now more active, with small, controlled movements which allow him to have full control of where he is positioned. He is constantly calm and composed, which is impressive since he is very young. His authority is also impressive and he is very vocal with his defenders, letting them know exactly what he wants them to do. He needs to work on his mental toughness as he struggles with recovering from conceding a bad goal, when this happens he crawls deeper into his net which results in him covering less net than before and he starts to look anxious. Super interesting prospect for the 2021 draft and with more time to develop and get experience, we expect him to continue to grow as a goaltender and hopefully he will be a player for the earlier rounds at the draft.

WHYNOT, CAMERON
LD - Valley Wildcats (NSMMHL) - 6'01" 177

A lot was expected of Cam Whynot coming into his second season of Midget, and he responded with a very good season with 13 goals, 40 points in 35 games with the Valley Wildcats. Whynot has a deep toolkit; he's a great skater who is smooth and efficient, with a 6'01" frame. He can rush the puck easily out of his zone; he's the best pure puck-rusher in this draft class. He really opens up ice for himself with his agility, evading checks and creating space. Whynot is a workhorse defenseman, he's been leaned on heavily throughout his minor hockey, but especially this year where he was commonly playing every second shift, and he rarely ever came off the ice in special teams' situations. Whynot needs to simplify his game a bit in the offensive zone and be more patient with the puck. We would like to see him create more offense on the power play with his playmaking and vision. He does a good job creating offense thanks to his skating abilities and puck-rushing abilities, but his hockey IQ is only average at this point in his development. There were times during the season it felt like Whynot could take over a game, but was a little too passive. He's a guy who could take off up the ice and create offense by himself, but often times he saw plays and made passes that his teammates were not able to execute on or quick enough to take advantage of. His resilience is the other concern; there have been times where he's struggled to push back after a bad start. However, there have been nights throughout the season where Whynot has singlehandedly kept his team in the game, and most of his 13 goals coming at key moments. Whynot is one of the best defensemen available in this draft class. During the USHL Draft, he was drafted by Des Moines with the 129th overall pick

WILMER, JEREMY
C - North Jersey Avalanche U16 (AYHL U16) 5'06" 120

Jeremy is an undersized pure offensive center who plays at a faster speed with the puck on his stick and has dominated the American AYHL U16 (62 points in 22 games) and T1EHL U16 (61 points in 25 games) leagues this season. He displays pretty good speed, acceleration and agility with the puck using his skating to weave through defenders or create space for himself in the offensive end. At his size, Jeremy does need to add size and strength to become stronger on his skates to compete consistently in puck battles and be stronger on the puck. With the puck on his stick, Jeremy has quick hands and an innate ability to deke through defensemen to create his own scoring chances. He creates scoring chances both with and without the puck using his strong anticipation skills and has high-end playmaking and finishing skill. Despite his high-end offensive skill, Jeremy's play away from the puck in his own defensive zone is an area for improvement. He tends to float without the puck and looks disengaged on the backcheck failing to cover his man and being soft in coverage situations. Improving his defensive zone awareness and displaying a consistent work ethic would improve his ability to make a high-end impact at the next level. Jeremy is a highly skilled offensive player who projects better as a winger at the next level due to his lack of defensive play, but has the skill to be a top line forward at the OHL level.

WINTERTON, RYAN
C - Whitby Wildcats (OMHA-ETA) - 6'0.25" 156

Ryan is a smart power forward who displays pretty good vision to see passing lanes before they develop and getting teammates the puck. Throughout the season he was consistent and reliable for the Wildcats playing a key role on a Top-10 Minor Midget team. Ryan displayed strong two-way qualities to his game while playing all three forward positions. Showing smart defensive characteristics, he back checked consistently and came back into the corners to help out his defensemen ensuring that his team had regained control of the puck before turning up ice. In transition, Ryan skates well using his speed to pressure opponents and create turnovers or make a move in the offensive end. Offensively, he displayed good playmaking ability but was also willing to go to the tough areas for quality scoring opportunities. He does not rush his decisions with the puck showing good patience and composure while often making efficient and smart decisions. Ryan's release is not the most lethal in the draft but with time and space he can still fire an accurate shot past a goalie. To improve his release, he could work on developing its' quickness, velocity and changing his shooting angles. Throughout the season, Ryan used his frame to effectively battle for pucks along the perimeter showing good puck protection and cycling ability. With room still to fill out and add strength, Ryan could add a more consistent physical edge to his game by finishing his checks. Ryan projects as a top-6 centre at the OHL level because of his skating, vision and power forward style of game while being responsible in all three zones and could make the jump as early as next year, depending on the depth of his drafting team.

GAME REPORTS

Team Canada vs Team Finland, World Junior Summer Showcase, Aug 2 2018

Canada –

Raphael Lavoie (2019) – Lavoie had a very impressive game for Canada, showing high-end tools combined with his excellent physical gifts. He's rangy but has very soft hands which were on full display as he weaved through heavy traffic on an end-to-end rush, resulting in his best scoring chance of the game. His length allows him to catch goalies off guard on more severe angles, almost catching Lehtinen several times due to this. His skating mechanics for his size have improved from last season and he was consistently driving past the Finnish defense. He found soft-ice several times and had plus decision making, showing little hesitation with the puck on his stick. Although he was brought in as the 13th forward as an injury replacement, he was arguably Canada's most impactful forward.

Joel Teasdale (2019) – Teasdale didn't get too many opportunities offensively; however, he did make a couple of efficient passes, one of which was a cross ice pass through the slot area that almost resulted in a high-end scoring chance. He didn't make any poor decisions that resulted in bad play but he didn't do enough to really stand out either.

Matthew Welsh (2019) – A small goalie that used his impressive lateral movement to compensate against Finland. His push offs were powerful, unfortunately he was unable to hold his edges and inadvertently threw himself out of position on the first goal he let in, despite reading the play correctly. His best save came off a cross ice pass in the high-slot which he squared up to very quickly, absorbing a hard wrist-shot into his equipment resulting in no rebound.

Finland

Teemu Engberg (2019) – Flashed some offensive ability throughout the game but didn't maintain puck possession for extended periods of time. He looked to rush down the wings on several sequences and fired off a couple of shots. His release point was a plus, there was velocity on his shot and he could shoot the puck while going at top speeds. When he ran out of room during one drive attempt, he remained poised and didn't cause a turnover under pressure, instead making a subtle no look chip pass to his defenseman off the boards.

Linus Nyman (2019) – Nyman was one of the more effective Finnish forwards out there today, finding soft-ice in the high-slot area consistently both at even strength and on the powerplay, where he was effective at both setting up his teammates and creating scoring chances for himself. Unfortunately, during a back checking sequence which required him to break into his top gear, his skating mechanics didn't allow him to generate much in the way of straight-line speed and when combined with his size, it shows why he has been passed over in previous draft classes despite flashing offensive tools.

Kaapo Kakko (2019) – The most talented forward on Finland unfortunately didn't get an opportunity to establish himself after getting injured relatively early in the first period, he did not return.

Santeri Salmela (2019) – Salmela had a very effective shut-down game for Finland today. He's not going to flash a dynamic skill-set and didn't get any opportunities offensively; however, he played a very clean and calculated game in his own-end. He processed the play quickly both with and without the puck and made several fast and efficient passes that led to transitional zone exits for Finland. He wasn't just relying on his stick play, as he showed a willingness to play the body and was effective during a couple of board battling sequences. Fans won't notice him often but he continuously made plus plays.

Aleksi Anttalainen (2019) – Played on the top pairing for Finland and had a solid all-around game. He's grown a bit since his draft year which has helped him establish his physical presence. Despite been undersized, he's built like a tank and is extremely strong, which was evident after having success pushing larger Canadian players off the puck. His shot was hard from the point but never threatened. He didn't get caught out of position very much and complimented Laaksonen well.

Otto Latvala (2019) – A massive defender with excellent reach. Latvala played the body effectively and used his stick to try and take away lanes at a plus rate. Didn't show any transitional puck rushing ability and look uncomfortable holding onto the puck for extended periods of time in the offensive-end but did get off a couple of quick wrist-shots that found their way through traffic. His best sequence came off a Canadian forecheck where he remained calm under pressure and used his stick to regain control of the puck after temporarily losing it. Looked like a big stay at home defender with plus tools.

Anttoni Honka (2019) – Honka had a mixed game for Finland today. He displayed excellent tools, highlighted by impressive edges, lateral mobility, straight line speed, soft hands and a sharp first pass. He took advantage of these traits to create several clean transitional zone exits and entries. In the offensive-end, he had a plus read from the point where he recognized that he couldn't get his shot through traffic, opting instead to purposely shoot wide and create a bank pass into the crease area that resulted in a scoring chance. Despite showing above average reads when walking the line at times, his decision making in his own left something to be desired. He did have a couple of good defensive sequences showing the ability to process play quickly while under pressure but when given extended time to think, he put himself out of position. This led to Canada's first goal of the game, where he was aggressive instead of passive against Rasmussen. He quickly closed his gap on Rasmussen as he skated over the blueline and attempted a poke check but missed the poke check and over-skated the puck, leading to Rasmussen getting time to walk in alone on net. On the overtime winning goal, he lost his man in coverage and was unable to recover in time; he showed frustration knowing he was caught out of position on the sequence. He was also indirectly responsible for the 3rd goal against, after making a poorly timed pinch at the offensive blueline, giving Canada an odd-man rush. He was directly and indirectly responsible for 3 of Canada's goals today despite showing a high-ceiling.

Team USA vs Sweden, World Junior Summer showcase, Aug 2 2018

USA

Jack Hughes (2019) – Hughes was the best forward for the U.S Squad today, which should be highlighted considering he's one of the youngest players here. His ability to shift gears deceptively allowed him to drive wide on a Swedish defenseman before making a crisp pass in the slot area, resulting in a high-end scoring chance. He scored after flashing his agility near the right circle, side-stepping a defender before firing a quick and low shot that surprised Ahman. Had a nice defensive play against Hugg, where he stripped him off the puck after tracking him effectively below the goal-line. He played a complete game today and carried play for a relatively flat U.S squad in stretches.

Matt Anderson (2019) – Anderson had a steady presence on the back-end. He was physical when necessary and showed good gap control when challenged by a Swedish forward on one play. He looked aware out there, wasn't caught out of position in the neutral zone or offensive-end, and made a couple of quick transitional passes. Though, there was little in the way of offense displayed in his game.

Sweden

Erik Aterius (2019) – Aterius had a couple of moments where he made something happen on the ice. He's thick for his build and I felt that hindered his forechecking ability in terms of getting to loose pucks as quickly as he naturally could if he was in better shape. That said, he was tenacious in a board battling sequence and showed some separating speed against Drury, where he gained a step which drew a penalty after skating hard into the slot. Wasn't afraid to take a direct route to the net.

Rickard Hugg (2019) – Hugg had one of the best performances I've seen from him. He was Sweden's most impressive forward, and had multiple high-end scoring chances which led to 2 goals. He opened the scoring on the first shift of the game after receiving a stretch pass that set him in on a breakaway, where he fired a quick snap shot. His second goal came off a fortunate bounce in-front of the net where it landed directly on his stick; he was in the right place at the right time. He flashed impressive edges throughout the game, using them to create space for himself when under pressure.

Marcus Sylvegard (2019) – Sylvegard was noticeable on the ice for Sweden and generated several quality chances. His skating looks awkward, there's a lack of knee bend when he's attempting to generate power in his first couple of steps that hindered his acceleration, despite showing adequate straight-line speed. He looks to drag the puck and find shots through defenders, but there's a lack of high-end skill that led to him having mixed results. His best chance came near the slot area but he fired an inaccurate shot over the bar. He did have a plus back checking sequence that helped negate a scoring chance, and showed a 200-foot game.

Tom Hedberg (2019) – Hedberg was cast in a shutdown role and received penalty-kill time. Despite not been overly big for his role, he did show impressive strength along the boards and was capable of keeping up with players like Tkachuk in-front of the net. On one play, he used a quick stick to backhand the puck out of danger in-front of the crease which took away what could have been a high-end chance. His positioning was good overall and on one sequence where he fell behind the play, he recovered by using a stick-lift before pressing himself into his opponent around the crease area. He didn't show any offense today.

Adam Ahman (2019) – Ahman is an undersized goalie who showed some poise under pressure but wasn't overly impressive. He had some high-end glove saves, and it was consistent all game. Specifically, in the first period he had his best save where he moved across and took a high-shot away with a quick glove hand. There were a couple of notable weaknesses technically however. His lateral push-offs weren't on point, and it left him scrambling to square up in time on some cross-crease attempts. He also showed an average transitional butterfly, he didn't get down to the ice as quickly as he should have on several different sequences. This could be considered a glaring flaw considering he only stands 6 feet. He also had some difficulties in his post integration which led to Norris's goal in the 3rd period after failing to drop into his reverse V-H in time to take away the bottom part of the net. It was a soft goal and helped the U.S gain momentum. He let in 5 goals overall but had some decent moments as well.

Czech Republic vs USA, Hlinka Gretzky Cup, Aug 6 2018

Czech Republic

Martin Lang (2019) – Martin Lang had a poor game for the Czech's today. One of the better shooters on the team, he didn't put himself in prime positions to score and seemed to be a step behind the play when put under pressure. His inability to play at the pace that the States set caused him to force several passes leading to turnovers. Another area of his game that looked concerning was his motor when he didn't have the puck on his stick, he looked like a passenger who wasn't interested in getting involved; it was a tough day for the talented forward.

Michal Teply (2019) – Teply had some flashes of playmaking and one on one skill against the U.S but wasn't consistent which could be said for the majority of his teammates. He showed impressive vision during a passing play where he drove down the left wing before making a spinning pass into the slot area which landed on the tape of his teammate. On another sequence in his own-end he showed soft-hands which he used to pull the puck around multiple opponents. His best scoring chance came in the slot area but he didn't get much on the shot.

Matej Toman (2019) – Toman was effective on the penalty-kill but much less effective at even-strength in today's match up. During one sequence, he recognized a sloppy drop-pass attempt by Foster in his own-end, then used a poke check to put himself on a breakaway where he attempted to cut before shooting glove side, the release was quick but Wolf was in position and read the play well. On another short-handed attempt, he sprung his teammate in on a partial breakaway after delivering a crisp pass from the neutral zone to the offensive blueline. Despite his efforts on the penalty-kill, he didn't form much in the way of chemistry with his linemates.

Jaromir Pytlik (2020) – Jaromir has good size, especially for his age but lacked lower body strength based on today's viewing. This led to an awkward stride, yet despite his stride he still had plus two-step area quickness and displayed energy on the forecheck. He looked to drive down the wings and cut to the outside. His best chance came from a drive around the back of the net where he then spun and delivered a quick wrist-shot that was absorbed by Wolf. He played an up-tempo style and looked to attack but wasn't overly effective today.

Martin Huga (2019) – Hugo Has showed two-way characteristics but also had some lapses at the offensive-blueline that caused two goals against. He was used in all situations and looked to use his frame and reach to aggressively close gaps when on the penalty-kill. He showed poise while under pressure during one sequence during a forecheck, where he distributed the puck quickly along the boards to alleviate danger; additionally he didn't get caught while holding the puck in his own end, showing clean transitional zone exits for the majority of the game. In the offensive-end he did a decent job at quarterbacking the powerplay, showing above average puck-skills but was caught twice when attempting to move the puck which led to two shorthanded breakaways.

Nick Malik (2020) - Malik flashed his high-end tools but didn't get much help from his defense. He displayed a strong glove hand and was good at absorbing shots in his butterfly. His reflexes are impressive and this allowed him to make several high-end saves, including a couple of breakaway saves and saves in tight to his net. One area of concern was his inability to get squared-up on backhand shots that were delivered while in motion. He had difficulty assessing the release point. He allowed 4 goals but two of them were on breakaways, a third was a perfect wrist-shot that went bar-down over him and the other was a hard slap shot that was delivered right in-front of his net after a defensive error. It was difficult to fault him on any of the goals he gave up, but there were some technical issues that he displayed today as well, despite having considerable upside.

USA

Arthur Kaliyev (2019) – Kaliyev had an okay game today. He flashed his excellent release on a couple of occasions. His best chance came in-front of the net area where he fired a quick wrist-shot on Malik after finding soft-ice despite heavy traffic around him. He had another dangerous chance from the left circle but the shot went wide, though the shot generated a lot of velocity and was dangerous. The most glaring concern based off today's game was that his skating didn't look overly improved from last season and there was a lack of pace in his play.

Grant Silianoff (2019) – Silianoff had a great game for the U.S and formed the best line out there with Mastrosimone. He displayed good passing ability throughout the contest. None was more impressive than his long stretch pass that sprung Jutting in on a breakaway. On one of his other primary assists, he drove down the left wing before making a subtle drop pass that set up Mastrosome for the opening goal of the game. Later in the game, he drove down the right wing and recognized that the Czech net minder wasn't completely square to him so he shot a low and hard wrist-shot that went in the back of the net. Silianoff displayed a varied attack and showed that he could think the game quickly while in motion.

Aaron Huglen (2019) – Huglen didn't get too many opportunities, however he was sprung on a breakaway and showed adaptive deking, slowing down the play which stalled Malik before he pulled to his backhand and tucked the puck five hole. The move displayed a good set of hands.

Robert Mastrosimone (2019) – Mastrosimone was arguably the most impressive forward on the ice in today's game. Although Salianoff had more points, Mastrosimone showed a 200-foot game and had several excellent defensive plays to go along with his 2 goals. He showed chemistry with Salianoff and together they broke down the Czech defense consistently throughout the game. He scored the opening goal on an impressive wrist-shot that had pinpoint accuracy and was released quickly. On his second goal, he showed little hesitation before slapping a puck far-side on Malik, so he showed the ability to score with different shot types. Furthermore, his ability to anticipate the play was also on display which allowed him to put himself into position to get off his shots. His most impressive sequence didn't lead to a point. He dashed in after a loose puck in the corner, after anticipating where the Czech defender was going to try and bank the puck off the boards, he used his own stick to recollect it and then made a spinning no-look pass into the slot area that resulted in a terrific scoring chance. Defensively, he was used in a 5-on-3 situation and had a well-timed block at the top of the slot which resulted in a cleared puck at a critical time. Shortly after, he recognized a Czech forward who was attempting to rush the puck up the side-wall, where he then squeezed him out and separated him from the puck, showing the ability to hit despite his smaller stature. Mastrosimone displayed a multi-faceted yet creative attack while breaking down the Czech team today.

Mike Koster (2019) – Koster played with bravado and a high degree of confidence when handling the puck, especially during powerplay situations when he was given more room to work with. He had several clean transitional zone exits and entries, showing poise and the ability to navigate through soft-ice and open up space for his teammates as a result. He had mixed decision making though. On one play while on the powerplay, he made a telegraphed drop pass that resulted in a breakaway chance. Defensively, he threw himself out of the play and left his man unattended directly in-front of the net which required one of Wolf's best saves of the game. Furthermore, once in the offensive-end, he displayed some tunnel vision, not looking to assess his options as much as he was looking to drive down a lane and create for himself. The showed the ability to carry the puck but his defensive game and decision making were not at the same level in today's game.

Dustin Wolf (2019) – An undersized goalie who's taking over the reigns from Carter Hart this upcoming season. Wolf looked dominant despite his stature, showing excellent puck tracking ability and anticipation of the play. He had an impressive glove-save on a breakaway early and on another short-handed attempt he displayed fast and efficient lateral movement which turned what could have been a difficult save into a routine stop. His best save came from a point blank wrist-shot from the slot area where he showed high-end push-off mechanics allowing him to square up, cutting the angle down very quickly before absorbing the wrist-shot into his blocker side. Arguably the most impressive aspect of Wolf's game was that he made almost every difficult and high-end scoring chance look easy to handle. He has several traits that are necessary to compensate for his size and earned a shutout against the Czechs.

Russia vs Finland, Hlinka Gretzky Cup, Aug 6 2018

Russia

Yaroslav Likhachyov (2019) – Likhachyov had several impressive playmaking sequences against Finland. He had the primary assist on Guschin's goal, after feeding him from the boards while under heavy pressure and setting him up for a breakaway. On another sequence, he got behind defensive coverage before making a crisp saucer pass that went over a Finnish defender's stick, which set up his teammate for a scoring chance. He was making decisions quickly with the puck on his stick, but largely played around the perimeter and wasn't consistent out on the ice.

Arsenii Gritsyuk (2019) – Gritsyuk scored twice for Russia but was largely invisible, rarely controlling play with the puck on his stick or setting up his teammates. His first goal came after he fired a low shot that generated a rebound which he managed to collect before firing an additional low shot that beat the Finnish netminder. His second goal was a result of putting himself in good position for a rebound that was kicked directly to him after Chinakhov shot a low shot from the left circle. Arsenii was decisive on both goals.

Daniil Gushchin (2020) – Gushchin was one of the most impressive players on the ice, consistently generating scoring chances using his improved straight-line speed. At last years U17's, his high-end puck skills and release were evident but he was still developing a base. In today's viewing, he showed that he's improved his speed by generating additional power. His shot has also benefited from his increased strength. He fired several pucks that had a lot of velocity behind them and were threatening. He scored on a breakaway after using his separating speed to rush in before he fired a quick wrist-shot. He assessed his options on the goal quickly and recognized that the Finnish goalie wasn't squared up. On several other sequences, he created for himself, cutting aggressively towards the net before using his shot. Despite his smaller frame, he was effective on the forecheck and wasn't afraid to throw his weight around when needed. It felt like every time he touched the puck he made something happen out there and is capable of making dynamic plays at top speeds.

Vasili Podkolzin (2019) – Podkolzin was the best player on the ice today, showing a complete 200-foot game while displaying his dynamic offensive skillset. He had a tremendous block after aggressively moving laterally during a penalty-kill sequence and diving in-front of a point blank slapshot. He was hurt on the play but recovered. On another sequence, he competed hard in the corner and managed to come away with the puck leading to possession for his team. He scored after separating himself on a breakaway and using his frame to protect the puck while being aggressively backchecked. He made a highly technical deke, faking a backhand before pulling the puck quickly to his forehand, the Finnish netminder was thrown out of position and bit hard on the move due to Podkolzin's body positioning. He's highly coordinated and shifty, which allows him to make exaggerated dekes while in motion. He showed today that he can be multi-faceted by having the ability to set up his teammates or generate scoring chances for himself, furthermore he competed hard in all three zones and looks like a natural leader out on the ice, which is probably why he Captains this team.

Daniil Gutik (2019) – Gutik had an excellent game for Russia and showed chemistry with Podkolzin out on the ice. His puck skills are bordering on elite, he's capable of very impressive dekes that he can make while in motion which benefits him when paired with other talented teammates when attempting to create off the rush, during give and go sequences, and during cycling plays. He dictated the tempo of the game when on the powerplay and at even-strength, showing poise, patience and awareness. Plays rarely died on his stick and he generated scoring chances for his team consistently. He had an impressive give and go sequence, using his hands to breakdown a Finnish defender before passing the puck off below the goal-line to his teammate who then set him up in-front of the net for a tap in goal. His skill level allows him to make difficult plays look effortless at times and he was dangerous on a shift-to-shift basis.

Finland

Leevi Aaltonen (2019) – Aaltonen flashed his speed and played a tenacious two-way brand of hockey. He had one excellent shift where he flew down the left wing, fired a hard wrist-shot that was mishandled by the Russian netminder, recollected the puck before spinning and attempting an additional shot. On the same sequence, he delivered a hard hit in the neutral zone and wasn't afraid to get physical against larger opponents in general. On the penalty-kill, he used his skating ability to create pressure effectively, forcing the Russians to make low percentage plays at times.

Henri Nikkanen (2019) – Nikkanen was one of the more prominent Finnish forwards against Russia, flashing impressive puck-skills and a hard shot. He skates with a wide base and this hinders his initial steps, which doesn't allow his legs to keep up with his head at times. This was seen during a neutral zone play, where he correctly read the play away from the puck and generated a takeaway, however he was unable to capitalize after gaining possession because his acceleration didn't allow him to separate himself during transition, as a by-product he was backchecked and lost possession. On another sequence in his own-end, he attempted to transition the puck out of the slot area but was stripped again due to his initial steps hindering him. That been said, during a backchecking sequence, he did show that once he gets past his first few steps he can generate above average straight-line speed. His best scoring chance came after he made a deke that gave him room to get off a quick wrist-shot that was labelled far side, requiring a difficult stop.

Anton Lundell (2020) – Lundell was the best player for Finland, carrying his international play from last season to today's game. He displayed excellent puck-skills in the neutral zone. The puck was caught in his skates, but he quickly kicked the puck to his stick, then made several impressive dekes before making a no-look bank pass off the boards to his teammate which resulted in a clean transitional zone entry. He was one of the only Finnish forwards who generated sustained puck possession for his team in the offensive-end. On another play, he found soft-ice in the left circle and masked his intentions with the puck before releasing a hard-wrist-shot that missed short-side. His body mechanics made it difficult for the Russian defense to figure out if he was passing the puck off or looking to shoot. Lundell showed intelligence, composure, puck-skills and was varied in his approach. His play was impressive given how disjointed Finland was in stretches.

Slovakia vs Sweden, Hlinka Gretzky Cup, Aug 6 2018

Slovakia

Dominik Sojka (2019) – A big center who faired well at the U18's last year. His play carried over on the defensive side against Sweden. He was detail oriented in his own end and understood when to support his defense. On one play, he positioned himself properly to help move the puck up for his defense along the boards leading to a transitional zone exit and on another defensive play he used his frame below the goal-line to come away with the puck. Against Soderblom who has similar height, he displayed the ability to contain players his own size and was physical when necessary. Unfortunately, despite showing a strong defensive presence in the middle of the ice, his offensive game was limited. He parked himself in front of the net on the powerplay and had one decent chance but otherwise didn't show the ability to control play, overwhelm on the forecheck, or create scoring chances for himself. He didn't show any dynamic quality based off todays viewing.

Maxim Cajkovic (2019) – Despite been the most talented forward on this team and one of the most talented Slovakian prospects in recent memory, Cajkovic was given 2nd line and 2nd powerplay time. With less talent to work with, Maxim didn't get many prime scoring opportunities. Despite this, his first shot of the game was mishandled by Wallstedt, giving him a primary assist on a play that should have never developed. He did have a couple of sharp and accurate passes that were difficult to make, yet he made them with a high-degree of precision and his release point made him threatening from the outside, where the majority of his chances were generated from. Cajkovic plays an explosive game at a high tempo but wasn't able to get into a rhythm and was largely shutdown but he didn't have a lot to work with and was going up against a good group of defenders.

Michal Mrazik (2019) – Mrazik didn't carry over his successful U18 performance last season to today's game against Sweden. He's a large winger with an above average shot but unfortunately had very few looks and was unable to generate much in the way of offense despite getting first line minutes. He had a poor performance overall.

Samuel Knazko (2020) – Knazko had a solid game for Slovakia despite being one of the younger defenders on the ice. He had an excellent defensive play early against Holtz where he used a stick-lift to mitigate a quality scoring chance. His play down-low around his own goal-line was good, showing efficient passing skills and containing his play, rarely putting himself in bad position. He had a couple of crisp outlet passes from his own-end. He was used on the top powerplay but had little success since Slovakia failed to control play throughout the contest, that said, he did show plus agility and poise at the line as he side stepped an aggressive Swedish player before attempting to get a shot through traffic that was blocked. He also attempted to transition the puck over the neutral zone but didn't have as much success. Overall, his skating ability, vision, and poise were noticeable.

Patrick Kozel (2019) – Kozel was bombarded in goal by Sweden but was the only reason the game was close. He showed a plus butterfly, lateral mobility, post integration and composure as he made several quality saves. His most notable save was midway through the third period, where he moved laterally and used a quick glove hand to take away a prime scoring chance. He never looked overwhelmed and read the play well despite playing against several quality forwards who generated off the rush. His rebound control helped take away secondary shots and the shots that were mishandled, he squared back up to consistently. Three of the four goals he let in were impressive plays that he had little chance on. He was Slovakia's best player.

Sweden

Elmer Soderblom (2019) – Soderblom looks like he has begun developing his raw tools. Frolunda has a fantastic development program and Soderblom looks to have benefited from it based on today's viewing. He's the tallest kid on the ice and last year he was unable to generate power in his first few steps because of his size but that wasn't the case here. He was tenacious on the forecheck and was able to help create off the rush with one of the fastest players on the ice in Raymond. Raymond fed him a nice pass in the slot area, which was fired low by Soderblom from the high slot. The release point was quick and he handed the shot while in motion. He had another prime scoring chance off a pass from Raymond down near the goal-line but inadvertently over-skated the play and put himself out of position. He has plus hands and skill for his size and seems to have put his raw tools together based off today's viewing, there was a lot to like about his game.

Arvid Costmar (2019) – Costmar generated several high-end scoring chances for himself despite playing in a bottom 6 role. He was dangerous off the rush and showed the ability to shoot while going at top speeds. His first plus scoring chance resulted in a rebound due to the speed at which he can release his shot. His shots generated a lot of velocity which made him dangerous from the high-slot. He had a powerful slapshot on the powerplay from the left circle that resulted in a big rebound and later he generated another scoring chance at the time of the net. His combination of speed and shooting ability made him stand out.

Albin Grewe (2019) – Grewe had an excellent game for Sweden despite been overzealous on one hit which resulted in him sitting in the box for half of the third period. He scored the opening goal for Sweden after showing patience and poise before walking into the bottom of the right circle and firing a shot over Kozel who had no chance. His release point is masked by a lack of body movement, it's difficult to pick up and he needs very little time to generate power behind it, it's an impressive release. Furthermore, he displayed the ability to generate off the rush, using his impressive two-step area quickness and straight-line speed to weave into high-traffic scoring areas. He's not afraid to take the puck to the net directly, and looked to catch the Slovakian defense off guard. There was an element of craftiness to his game. He was one of the better forwards for Sweden.

Lucas Raymond (2020) - Raymond was the best player on the ice for either team in today's game. He was the offensive catalyst for the best line which included Holtz. His speed was apparent, generating several high-end chances by driving past his opponents and setting up his teammates or creating for himself. In previous viewing's, he has shown more of a shooting mentality, but here he looked more balanced in his approach, utilizing his teammates at the right times and generating for himself when he found soft-ice. His release point lacks tells and he generates significant power while moving at top speeds, making him very dangerous off the rush. Furthermore, he was processing the play quickly, which allowed him to be a multi-faceted threat, showing high-end passing ability to compliment his shot. His vision was exceptional in today's game as well, threading several quality passes over out-reached sticks and finding backdoor options consistently. He took over the game, generating chance after chance while showing elite tools.

Alexander Holtz (2020) – Holtz wasn't far behind Raymond in today's effort. He was thinking the game at a high level and seemed to be two steps ahead of the opposition on most plays. He had a beautiful primary assist off a saucer pass that landed on the tape of his teammate on one sequence but looked to pass too much, showing an unselfishness which led to decreased scoring chances. Unlike Raymond who looked to generate with his speed, Holtz looked to use his hockey smarts to control the pace and tempo of the game. There was an efficiency to his game both at even strength and on the powerplay, not always staying in one or two gears but shifting between several gears depending on what was given to him. Holtz showed a high level of skill and adaptability on the ice today and was dominant in stretches.

Karl Henriksson (2019) – Henriksson was the beneficiary of playing with Holtz and Raymond on the top-line. He showed impressive speed when driving over the neutral zone on one sequence and on several others showed that he could keep up with Ramond and Holtz. He scoring a goal after putting himself in a prime position where Holtz fed him an excellent pass which was discussed above. On another sequence he used his speed to drive down the left wing and made a backhand pass to his teammate which resulted in a prime scoring chance. Karl displayed skill and speed which complimented his teammates well, he didn't look out of place on the top-line.

Jacob Gronhagen (2019) – Gronhagen is similar in size to Soderblom but seemed to lack a step, which isn't unexpected given his hulking build. However, he did show plus passing ability early, making a nice no-look backhand pass into the high-slot which generated a scoring chance. He also took a direct route to the net on another play, and showed some grit when attempting to battle down-low against the Slovaks. His best scoring chance came off a rush where he fired a wrist-shot with a whip-like release that went over the net. He looked to have interesting tools out there but wasn't as effective as Soderblom.

Victor Soderstrom (2019) – Soderstrom was paired with Bjornfot in today's match up and looked impressive. He's an agile and efficient skater, highlighted by two-step area quickness which allowed him to alleviate the forecheck consistently. One of the main reasons the Slovaks couldn't generate much in the way of offense when Soderstrom was on the ice was due to his puck retrieval ability. When a puck was dumped, Soderstrom acted quickly and showed accurate passes to his teammates while under pressure. He looked comfortable when walking the line and had plus hands which allowed him to breakdown the defense on a couple of sequences. His wrist-shot had a plus release point and he found the post late in the third period on one of them. He quarterbacked the top powerplay, and was efficient as distributing the puck but didn't get too many opportunities to generate with his shot due to Holtz dictating play along the half-wall.

Tobias Bjornfot (2019) – Bjornfot had a complete game for Sweden and displayed several impressive qualities. He has a very efficient stride which allowed him to carry the puck up the ice effortlessly on several sequences and looked comfortable weaving in and out of traffic. His defensive reads were on point. During an attempted offensive zone entry by Slovakia, Bjornfot read the play in advance and stripped a Slovak off the puck before passing it off quickly which resulted in a counter attack. Similar to Soderstrom, he had little trouble finding open teammates while under pressure along the boards and had several stretch passes that were accurate. When walking the line, he looked to release a couple of quick wrist-shots, one of which found its way through traffic, resulting in a difficult save for Kozel. He played a simplified offensive game but was excellent all around and showed a combination of poise and intelligence with significant skating ability.

Philip Broberg (2019) – Broberg is the largest defender out of the top-end guys on the backend for Sweden and used his size to deliver a crushing hit to Cajkovic as he attempted to enter the zone with speed. He's advanced physically but he also showed decent agility for his size. This was seen when he drove wide before cutting aggressively around a Slovakian defender during a pinch which resulted in a highlight reel goal, his speed caught his opponents by surprise and Kozel couldn't set himself in time to move laterally, it was an impressive sequence. Furthermore, he played a more physical brand of hockey than most of his defensive teammates but was still capable of showing finesse when transitioning the puck up the ice. He had a great game for Sweden.

Jesper Wallstedt (2021) – Wallstedt is the youngest goalie featured at the tournament and it showed in stretches. His nerves got the better of him on the first shot of the game, as he bobbled a routine butterfly save, leading to a rebound goal. After the initial goal, he had to remain focused despite Sweden out-shooting Slovakia 2-1 going forward. This was where the young netminder showed impressive composure, as he made a breakaway save and a shorthanded save during a 2-on-1 sequence during critical points in the game. He had an element of calmness in the crease and looked composed considering his age. Technically speaking, he stayed down in his butterfly in stretches for too long, and had difficulty squaring up to lateral passes on some plays. This led to the 2nd Slovakia goal as he didn't square up in time, though was given time to do so. It's rare to see a goalie of his age featured at this tournament and despite letting in two questionable goals, he stayed composed and flashed a lot of upside.

Canada vs Slovakia, Hlinka Gretzky Cup, Aug 7 2018

Slovakia

Dominik Sojka (2019) – Unlike yesterdays game where Sojka largely showed off his defensive ability, against Canada Sojka had a couple of plus offensive sequences. He rushed down the left wing and distributed the puck to Mrazik who chipped a shot in on net. Later in the opening frame he used his large frame to counteract the Canadian defense and put himself in a prime scoring position, he fired a low and hard wrist-shot which required Gauthier's most difficult save of the period. Although Slovakia was overwhelmed for the majority of the game it was good to see the big center create some offense, though he didn't flash plus puck skills or controlled play. Lastly, his skating mechanics are a plus but he's still growing into his frame which causes him to lose a step at times against the quicker players out on the ice, this was evident against Cozens who peeled off of him and created a high-end scoring chance because of it.

Maxim Cajkovic (2019) – Cajkovic had a slow start against Sweden but was slightly better against Canada. He's still not getting opportunities on the top line with Sojka and Mrazik which is putting him at a disadvantage but unlike yesterday where he was largely making plays around the perimeter, he was instead using his plus skating ability to cut through high traffic areas while attempting to create off the rush. His split the defense in the second period which led to one of Slovakia's only scoring opportunities. He had a primary assist on a powerplay goal after delivering a powerful one timer that was difficult to control and required a kick save leading to a rebound which resulted in a goal for Slovakia. Although he has tremendous speed, he's not attacking his defensive blueline at the rate he theoretically could based off today's game.

Michal Mrazik (2019) – Mrazik had a better game today against Canada than he did against Sweden. One area of concern is that he was having trouble keeping up with the pace of play yesterday and again today there was a lack of generating off the rush due to his below-average skating ability. He stands upright and his arms are not tight to his body when he's attempting to take off, his mechanics appear loose, but he is a massive winger and it will take time for him to develop that aspect of his game. Where he improved today was in his ability to find soft-ice and read the play in the offensive-end so he could put himself in good positions to shoot. He had multiple high-end scoring chances, where he generated velocity in his wrist-shot, however some of his shots were inaccurate.

Martin Chromiak (2020) – Chromiak was more noticeable against Canada than he was against Sweden. He generated a scoring chance after feeding Sojka down near the right circle early in the game. On another play, he drove down the left wing and created an additional scoring chance while going at top speeds. He had a nice defensive read at the line and created a turnover before rushing back over the neutral zone as well. He's one of the younger Slovakian forwards but showed flashes of an above average offensive game today.

Samuel Knazko (2020) – Knazko was good yesterday and here again today, he displayed a 200-foot game with a high-level of maturity for his age. He had an excellent defensive stick early, stopping a Mutala cross-crease pass attempt that would have resulted in a high-end scoring chance. Shortly after, he made an excellent defensive recovery play by keeping up with Cozens before using an active stick to strip him off the puck just as he was about to shoot. During forechecking sequences, he remained composed and made subtle passes that were effective which minimized Canada's scoring opportunities for the most part. When in transition, he showed the ability to move the puck up the ice which led to an offensive opportunity, and during Slovakia's second goal, he pinched correctly and put himself in a position to get the rebound which went to his teammate instead. Knazko has been impressive in the first two contests.

Oliver Turan (2019) – In last years viewings, he rarely generated offensive opportunities, mostly playing a shutdown game. However, here he managed to make several nice plays from the line, one of which directly resulted in a Slovakian goal. On one play, he was pressured by two different players simultaneously but managed to use his improved hands to deke past his opponents before making a nice pass that led to extended zone time. On another sequence that was similar, he showed good hesitation and poise at the line while faking a shot before making a no-look pass to his teammate who scored, giving him the primary assist. Defensively, he had some trouble containing the faster Canadian players which should be expected given his 6'5 fame, however he did level a Canadian forward in the slot on one play.

David Borak (2019) – Although the final score was 4-2 for Canada, without Borak's 54 save performance, it would have been far worse, he was easily the best player for Slovakia and stood on his head throughout the game. He's undersized standing 6 feet, however he demonstrated plus lateral mobility, reflexes, agility and a fast glove hand which he used to make several high-end saves. On a couple of sequences, he had to push from left to right aggressively while sprawling out with his pads and took away several high-end one timers. Although he had impressive lateral mobility, he was good at holding his edges when he needed to, his crease containment was a plus. This was seen on one save specifically on Clarke, after almost over-extending his movement, he stopped on a dime and threw himself in the opposite direction which allowed him to take away what looked like a sure goal with his blocker. His glove was consistently positioned well, against Parent he made a point blank save that required little movement to demonstrate this. On saves that required extension, he demonstrated good flexibility which is important given his size and his reflexes were largely up to the task. He was tremendous and had arguably the best goaltending performance of the tournament so far.

Canada

Graeme Clarke (2019) – Clarke had a good game against Slovakia, consistently finding soft ice to set up his impressive wrist-shot. He wasn't afraid to go into high traffic areas with the puck on his stick where he showed soft-hands and an affinity for dragging the puck around opponents sticks before letting his wrist-shot off. His shot is difficult to pick up, he has few tells in his body mechanics, can shoot while simultaneously dragging the puck and the release is fast. He scored a goal using the above mechanics and had several high-end scoring chances that required excellent saves by Borak. He showed instinctive goal scoring ability in today's viewing and was willing to enter high-traffic areas to get his shot off.

Jamieson Rees (2019) – Rees played with energy and generated several scoring chances for both himself and his teammates. Similar to Clarke in that he found soft-ice and released a shot that had good velocity, however the mechanics weren't as refined. That been said, he came out from below the goal-line and had an impressive pass that was threaded through multiple players in the crease, resulting in a primary assist. He didn't look like a primary scoring option or display high-end talent but he did generate chances in spurts and showed a plus motor.

Alexis Lafreniere (2020) – Lafreniere wasn't very impressive against Switzerland but faired better against Slovakia, displaying deceptive and creative elements to his game. When Lafreniere attacks from the left wing, he's excellent at masking his intentions with the puck and freezing his opponents which opens up additional options. Furthermore, he's a multi-faceted offensive threat, meaning his shot is equal to his passing ability. He took advantage of this trait against

Slovakia, consistently feinting the shot before using his vision to try and set up his teammates from the right side. He displayed a quick processor which allowed him to evaluate quickly if his shooting or passing lanes were taken from him, where he then adapted, giving him multiple looks through-out the game. He scored Canada's opening goal after rushing down the left wing and firing a quick wrist-shot over Borak on the blocker side. Overall, he didn't control play as often as we have seen in previous viewings, but his play picked up considerably from yesterday.

Ryan Suzuki (2019) – Suzuki had an excellent game against the Swiss but here he was quiet. Ryan did put himself into a couple of prime scoring positions and had one excellent scoring chance after firing a wrist-shot in the high-slot that required a difficult stop. Although Suzuki has more of a playmaking mentality on the ice, he does have an impressive release point. Unfortunately for all his skill, he played at a lower tempo and not at the pace that his skill level is currently at. In today's viewing, we were hoping to see more energy out of him, his motor based off today's game was concerning.

Kirby Dach (2019) – Dach showed improved skating ability and improved shooting mechanics from last season against Slovakia. He generated off the rush after coming down the right wing and shooting a quick wrist-shot which hit the post. Last season, he didn't generate as much velocity on his shots and was unselfish in prime scoring chances, which didn't happen in today's game. Additionally, he demonstrated impressive hand-eye coordination after shooting a puck out of midair from the crease area which hit another post. Known more for his playmaking, Dach didn't disappoint, threading a beautiful pass on the powerplay that resulted in a primary assist from below the goal-line. He demonstrated that he can threaten in the offensive-end in multiple ways and generated several high-end plays.

Peyton Krebs (2019) – Krebs picked up where he left off yesterday, by using his skating ability and excellent puck skills to create several scoring chances. He displayed his speed during a short-handed chance, splitting the defense before getting stopped short-side. Krebs is at his best when he's attacking the net and not playing on the perimeter and here today he was consistently going into high-traffic areas to make plays. He generated both from a stationary position and off the rush, using his vision and playmaking ability to consistently set up his teammates when his lanes were closed. If it wasn't for Borak, Krebs would have had a multi-point night and was one of Canada's most noticeable players.

Dylan Holloway (2020) – Holloway had an excellent game for Canada, combining a plus motor with impressive mobility and an instinct to attack the net directly. He caused a shorthanded turnover by using his speed at the defensive blueline which led to a shorthanded breakaway chance. Later in the game he scored after moving laterally across the slot and shooting a low wrist-shot five-hole. He was doing most of his work off the rush and played at a high pace. One area that wasn't as impressive based off today's viewing was that he didn't generate much in the way of power on his shots, but he's on of the younger players featured here so there's plenty of time for him to continue to develop that aspect of his game.

Dylan Cozens (2019) – Cozens was Canada's best player today, driving play and controlling the game from start to finish by using a varied and impressive tool-kit. Due to his size, puck-skills and skating ability, he was able to control the tempo. If he didn't see any additional room to skate, he would slow play down and use his hands to maintain puck possession before making passes behind him to trailing teammates. Though, he also had to slow down play as a result of running out of room at times. On one sequence, he recognized a speed advantage against Sojka, and peeled right past him into the high-slot while on his backhand. The play showcased a powerful lower frame and explosive acceleration from Cozens. During a transitional zone entry, he had two Slovakian players draped over him, forcing him to fall to a knee on the ice, however he showed impressive core strength and puck tracking ability, as he continued to make a clean transitional zone entry despite the pressure, it was arguably his most impressive play yet didn't result in a point. Lastly, he was capable of generating both from a stationary position and off the rush, rarely making the wrong decision. Today's game was a standout one for Cozens who looks to have multiple ways to breakdown opponents while playing a rare power center game.

Justin Barron (2020) – Barron demonstrated excellent four-way mobility and impressive feinting mechanics while walking the line. Although one of the younger kids on the team, he's one of the better skaters, his lateral mobility is the best aspect of his impressive skating, showing advanced cross-over mechanics. His lateral movement when combined with his fakes at the line made it very difficult for Slovakia to track what he was going to do with the puck which allowed him to consistently re-open shooting lanes to his liking, this was emphasized on the powerplay, where he stood out the most.

Matthew Robertson (2019) – Robertson showed a 200-foot game and had a couple of impressive offensive sequences. He had a plus pinch at the line, reading the play correctly before carrying the puck hard into heavy traffic and releasing a heavy wrist-shot that required a stop. Additionally, he featured the hardest slapshot from the backend today, which led to several rebounds. He also was capable of getting his shot through traffic at a consistent level.

Bowen Byram (2019) – Byram played a controlled and efficient 200-foot game for Canada on the backend. His mobility is impressive, showing effortless skating ability that helped him seamlessly transition up and down the ice throughout the game. His hockey smarts were on full display, rarely getting caught out of position in both the defensive and offensive-end and showed several controlled transitional zone-exits and entries. One of his more offensive plays came early after he drove down the right-wing and aggressively cut across the crease area, though he was knocked off the puck it showed that he can switch from a finesse-oriented approach to a tenacious one depending on the situation. There was a high level of versatility and adaptability present in his game today.

Michael Vukojevic (2019) – Vukojevic showed good positioning in his own-end, making it difficult for opposing teams to get inside on him, while also showing a willingness to release his shot from the point. Michael has impressive physical tools which gives him the ability to play a heavy game when necessary, and against some of the larger Slovakians, he managed to use these tools to mitigate scoring chances while keeping them largely on the perimeter. At the offensive-line, he wasn't overly creative or showed much in the way of puck skills, however from the point he got several opportunities to get his shot through traffic where he demonstrated velocity and kept his shots between the ankles and knees to increase potential tipping options. He played a streamlined game today and his offense appeared somewhat limited despite having some good defensive sequences.

Braden Schneider (2020) – Schneider had a clean and effective game in his own-end for Canada while playing largely mistake free in the offensive-end. He had an excellent recovery sequence for his partner Guenette who was caught at the blueline and lacked the straight-line speed to recover, however Schneider recognized this and managed to re-position himself in time to pivot and poke the puck away from a Slovakian forward who was looking to gain control and go on the offense. On another defensive play, he demonstrated impressive skating ability and board play, skating hard to a stray puck in the corner before pinning his opponent along the boards which led to a zone clear. Lastly, during a Slovakian rush, he assessed his gap spacing correctly and delivered a perfectly timed hit which took away a potential scoring chance. He didn't do anything flashy and wasn't overly involved offensively, but made several heads-up defensive plays while playing at an impressive pace when necessary.

Kaedan Korczak (2019) – Similar to Schneider in the sense that he didn't do anything flashy, however he made clean plays that led to several transitional zone exits for his team. The best play that summarizes Korczak's game against Slovakia was when he helped support his defensive partner by closing his gap aggressively, then using his reach to poke the puck loose on a Slovakian puck carrier leading to a turnover which was the catalyst for Canada transitioning out of their own end. Smart, simple and effective hockey was demonstrated by Kaedan out there.

Czech Republic vs Russia, Hlinka Gretzky Cup, Aug 7 2018

Russia

Yaraslav Likhachyov (2019) – Likhachyov didn't control play but he did show flashes of high offensive skill during the opportunities presented to him. He scored a wrist-shot goal after driving down the left wing and cutting across the left circle, the shot surprised Malik who didn't get an opportunity to set which gives an idea of how quick the release was, it was a deceptive release as well. Later in the game, he showed good edge work as he cut across the goal-line aggressively before recollecting the puck in the corner and threading a sharp pass through traffic. likhachyov didn't need a lot of room with the puck on his stick to make some high-level plays out there, though he was inconsistent with his play.

Egor Chinakhov (2019) – Similar to Abramov in the sense that when he did get the puck he displayed a good amount of skill but didn't get too many touches with the puck. He had a well executed give and go sequence with a teammate which resulted in a quick backhand goal directly in-front of the net, he took a direct path into the slot despite heavy traffic on the play. In the neutral zone, he showed good anticipation and a plus read without the puck while using an active stick to turn the puck over before passing it up to the ice. He had an additional stand out offensive moment when he took another direct route to the net that resulted in a scoring chance.

Daniil Gushchin (2020) – Gushchin wasn't firing on all cylinders but showed his dynamic skill-set at times. He looks to have improved his lower body strength from last season which has helped increase his acceleration based on today's game, this is important considering his small stature. He used his speed to win races to stray pucks down-low and didn't need a lot of time or space to get off his powerful wrist-shot. His best chance came from the right circle but he fired the puck over the bar. On one play, he skated down the slot area and attempted to go through the Czech defense, attempting a one-handed pull move in tight to his body, so he was willing to get creative out there and try difficult moves. The kid was playing with confidence but we've seen more offensive output from him in previous viewings.

Vasili Podkolzin (2019) – Podkolzin had an average game today despite scoring a goal. He wasn't developing chemistry out there with Gutik and Nikolaev but still made some plus plays. He had a decent wrist-shot from the right circle early but it wasn't until later that he used his speed and agility to cut around Suhrada that he flashed his dynamic qualities. He drove wide on the Czech defenseman while skating down the right wing and then faked a backhand shot before pulling the puck to his forehand and firing it past Malik who had already bit on the initial fake, it was an impressive goal. He also flashed his two-way play by aggressively backchecking Raska before getting into an altercation that landed him in the box. He's had better games in our viewings but still showed moments of why we consider him a first rounder.

Sergei Alkhimov (2019) – Alkhimov had a solid effort without the puck for Russia. He established a forechecking presence early and often, showing good quickness for his frame and a high-octane motor. He was constantly moving his feet and was rarely stationary, consistently putting pressure on the Czech defense. He had a nice board pin below the goal-line which resulted in a turnover and an opportunity for his team. On the penalty-kill, he wasn't afraid to get into shooting lanes and blocked a hard slapshot with his thigh which left him in pain but he returned and played a tenacious game the rest of the way. He didn't get going offensively but he established a presence on the ice without the puck and was a plus factor for his team in the win.

Yaroslav Askarov (2020) – Askarov had an impressive game for Russia and earned a shutout. Unlike last years international Russian goalie crop, Askarov isn't undersized, standing 6'2 and showed advanced technical mechanics for his age. His transitional butterfly and post integration were impressive and his mechanics didn't leave a lot of room for the Czech's to shoot at. He was slightly late at squaring up on shots coming down on his right-wing occasionally, but showed a fast glove hand that was consistent at controlling rebounds throughout the game. One of his better saves came off an awkward bounce from the boards that resulted in a quality scoring chance directly in-front of the net where he had to react quickly. Another interesting aspect to his game was that he looked to play the puck at a high-rate and had well timed passes that helped transition his team out of the zone. There was a lot to like about his game based on today's viewing, though he never dealt with sustained pressure or too many high-quality scoring chances either.

Czech Republic

Martin Lang (2019) – Lang had a much better game today than he did yesterday against the States by having a couple of quality plays for an otherwise flat Czech forward group. He was involved early by firing a severe angle spinning shot that required a save, he then showed high-end skating mechanics as he tracked down the puck and hustled back into his own-end. On the same sequence, he took a pass and transitioned the puck back up ice resulting in an offensive zone draw, it was a smart play. He showed the ability to deke adaptively as opposed to using pre-set moves on another sequence, after attempting a drag that failed, he pulled the puck away from a Russian stick and made a quick move to give him more space before attempting a backhander. On the powerplay, he was used along the half-wall and had a nice passing sequence out of a shot fake before rushing down near the crease area and firing a puck that hit a body in-front of the net. There's still a lack of energy from him away from the puck but the skill and release is there.

Simon Kubicek (2020) – Kubicek had an above average game and demonstrated that he can play a 200-foot game. He's got a thick frame but that didn't seem to prevent him from walking the line comfortably while showing plus lateral mobility which allowed him to re-open up shooting lanes while on the man advantage and at even strength. He looks to fire the puck and displayed a heavy slapshot from the point, he also put himself in good position to receive passes for his one-timer, however his slapshot's were largely off target, showing a lack of accuracy in today's contest. Furthermore, he wasn't waiting for lanes to clog or for heavy traffic to potentially screen Askarov, he wasn't overly patient but he's eligible in 2020 so there's a lot of time for that aspect of his game to grow. On one powerplay sequence, he took a terrible interference penalty which was poorly timed and took away the momentum the Czech's were starting to generate. On the defensive side, he had a couple of quality transitional passes out of his own-end and showed some chemistry with Has when they were paired together. There was some potential in Kubicek based off today's viewing.

Martin Huga Has (2019) – Has had a solid game for the Czechs and made less mistakes while holding the puck along the offensive blueline than he did yesterday. He had an excellent hit in the defensive-end, levelling his opponent which led to a turnover. On another defensive play on the penalty-kill, he took away the bottom part of the net on a block that might have prevented a goal and was reading the play well. When walking the line with the main advantage, Has distributed the puck efficiently, but wasn't overly dynamic, there seems be a lack of creativity with how he breaks down defenses based off today's game but there's upside here.

Sweden vs Switzerland, Hlinka Gretzky Cup, Aug 7 2018

Sweden

Elmer Soderblom (2019) – Soderblom was less effective against the Swiss than he was against Slovakia however he had the best shift and sequence of the game. During a forecheck, he used his reach to turn the puck over on Villa behind the net which resulted in four different scoring chances generated through Soderbloms vision and shooting ability. His best chance of the sequence came after finding soft ice directly in-front of the slot and firing a quick wrist-shot that went over the net. Despite his range, he can shoot in-tight to his body, his shooting mechanics are pretty good for such a tall player. He hit the post late after using his reach to redirect a puck past the Swiss netminder after parking himself in-front of the net but it stayed out. He had some impressive moments where his high-end tools were on display again.

Albin Grewe (2019) – Grewe wasn't as dangerous as he was against Slovakia due to not finding as many open shooting lanes as his previous effort. His best sequence came off a rush where he passed the puck off resulting in a high-end scoring chance but he didn't generate too many looks. One area to note with Grewe is that he continues to play a high-energy game. His motor compliments his plus puck skills well, and when combined with his fearlessness for driving into high traffic areas, it left a good impression despite not generating too many quality chances.

Lucas Raymond (2020) - Raymond was tremendous yesterday and continued to dominate again today. He was creating off the rush and generated several high-end plays throughout the contest. He loved to generate on either wing. If he's on his wing, he looks to pull the puck around his opponents and either set up his shot for the far-side but if he feels the angle isn't there or the lane is blocked he looks to set up on his teammates on his backhand. There were several high-end passing plays he threaded through heavy traffic on his backhand off the rush. He scored two goals. The first was shothanded after skating down his off wing and letting go a quick snap-shot. It's difficult for goalies to pick up his shot not just due to how fast it comes off his stick but also due to how fast he can change the angle with the amount of speed he generates when on the rush. His second goal came in tight to the goal-line, displaying a strong stick while out competing the Swiss defense before tucking it in on his backhand. Raymond has out-played Holtz through the first two games and is carrying over what we saw from him last season to this tournament. He's a special player.

Alexander Holtz (2020) – Holtz wasn't as good today as he was against Slovakia but did show that he can be versatile without the puck. He played the body during a couple of forechecking sequences, it was evident that he is still developing that aspect of his game since he didn't look too comfortable throwing his weight around, but he did deliver a puck separating hit on one attempt down below the goal-line. Similar to yesterday, he used his intelligence to slow the play down to his liking before delivering a crisp pass onto the tape of his teammate for a scoring chance. Similarly, on another play, he slowed down and evaluated the ice before delivering a quick snap shot on net. He didn't control play to the same extent as he did yesterday.

Jacob Gronhagen (2019) – Gronhagen had an effective game for Sweden, generating several high-end scoring chances. Similar to Soderblom in regards to his height plus shot combination, but he releases the puck differently than Elmer, it comes off his stick slower but picking up the release point is difficult due to his length. He used his shot from the high-slot throughout the game and showed better accuracy here than he did against the Slovaks. He also distributed the puck effectively. In the neutral zone he made a quick passing play to help transition the puck up the ice and made a nice backhand pass around the goal-line which set up Raymond for a high-quality scoring chance.

Victor Soderstrom (2019) – Soderstrom was quiet from the offensive blueline until the third period where he started showing his high-end skill with the puck. In the first two frames, he wasn't attempting to breakdown the opposition with his hands or skating ability, opting instead to shoot low wrist-shots quickly from the point. However, in the third period, he used his soft-hands to beat a Swiss player one-on-one which opened up a shooting lane for him where he shot a low wrist-shot that went five-hole. Defensively he wasn't overly engaged because the Swiss were unable to generate many opportunities after the first period.

Tobias Bjornfot (2019) – Bjornfot used his impressive four-way mobility to minimize the Swiss forecheck while looking composed and in control out on the ice. There was one specific sequence against the half-wall in his own-end where he showed zero panic in his game despite dealing with an opponent who was hovering around him. Soderstrom tapped his stick on the ice to let him know he can pass it back but Bjornfot anticipated the Swiss players movement and stick well, showing excellent composure on the sequence. When he was caught out of position slightly, his skating allowed him to recover and he was good at gaining position after losing it. His transitional breakouts were effective and on one sequence after the Swiss netminder let in a sharp angle goal, Bjornfot rushed down the left wing and attempted the same shot-type, so there's an element of adaptability to his game. He read the play well and thinks quickly in all three zones based off today's viewing.

Philip Broberg (2019) – Broberg had a very impressive game yesterday against the Slovaks, and here again he had an excellent game, flashing tremendous puck rushing ability while showing a high-level of decisiveness in his play. He's a big kid but found find soft-ice when attempting to rush the puck. This can be attributed to his straight-line speed which is high-end. Furthermore, he used his speed to regain defensive position when caught and played the body on one sequence after losing position in-front of the net. His outlet passes were accurate and he didn't over-extend himself despite looking to carry the puck, making quick decisions that led to several scoring chances. He scored a goal from the line after walking in and firing a low wrist-shot short-side through a screen. He's shown through these first two games at this tournament that he can score in multiple ways and is anticipating the defense at a plus rate. He showed a combination of size, skating ability, and scoring instincts all while playing a 200-foot game.

Joel Wahlgren (2019) – Wahlgren outplayed his twin-brother today by generating several chances. He had a nice offensive-sequence early where he recognized an open skating lane and took off before cutting directly in-front of the net, but failed to get his stick on the puck to get a shot off. Later in the game, he set up a prime scoring chance for Gronhagen in the slot area after he delivered a sharp pass from the left circle while in motion. He had a couple of additional plays that made him noticeable on the ice and contributed to his team. He was better today than he was yesterday against Slovakia.

Oscar Bjerselius (2019) – Bjerselius had several quality scoring chances in today's game, demonstrated a nose for the net, yet had mixed results when attempting to transition the puck. He had his first major scoring chance of the game in the slot area but fired a hard wrist-shot over the bar from a stationary position. Towards the end of the third period, he had two back to back excellent scoring chances after finding soft-ice in the slot area, his accuracy was better on these shot attempts which were both labelled glove-side. Furthermore, he looked to carry the puck in transition often, but didn't seem to recognize active sticks or pressure as much as he could have which led to a couple of turnovers. He didn't showcase high-end offensive skill but put himself in good scoring positions and played with an above average motor today.

Karl Henriksson (2019) – After playing relatively good against Slovakia while complimenting Raymond and Holtz, Henriksson had a game to forget today. He looked rushed when he was carrying the puck and over-extended himself on several sequences while showing poor decision making. In the neutral zone, he over-skated a Swiss player who had the puck which led to a clean transitional zone entry against. On the powerplay he rushed down the left wing and skated himself into a situation where there was no passing or shooting lane, so he quickly made a hard-backhand pass up the middle of the ice, inadvertently clearing the puck out of the zone for the Swiss. In the defensive end, he made a no look backhand pass when attempting to transition which was immediately picked off, while attempting to recover he was a step behind the play and took a hooking penalty. He played at a good pace but forced play and made poor decisions overall.

Ludvig Hedstrom (2019) – Hedstrom had a good game and had several successful sequences. Early in the first period, he pinched successfully and made a sharp pass into the slot area that should have resulted in a goal but the puck was missed by his teammate. The pass on the play was threaded through multiple players, it was impressive. Early in the third period, he carried the puck through all three zones and fired a severe angle wrist-shot that caught the Swiss netminder off guard, it was an important goal but should have been stopped. Later in the period he had a nice defensive read while showing an active stick, he also transitioned the puck effectively in spurts.

Hugo Alnefelt (2019) – Despite having to stop under 20 shots, Alnefelt had to come up with some critical saves early in the game when the game was scoreless and the Swiss were pressing. His best save early was off a lateral pass across the slot area which forced Alnefelt to fully extend before getting his blocker on the puck. Later in the game he showed the ability to make a high-end recovery save while coming out of his butterfly, the rebound fell directly in-front of him and was shot low, yet he showed impressive flexibility while creating a full extension pad save. His rebound control was consistent, both when absorbing shots in his butterfly and when redirecting the puck into the corners. There was a high level of calmness and composure in his game. He earned a shutout over the Swiss but made several quality stops despite facing a limited volume of shots.

Switzerland

Theo Rochette (2020) – Rochette had the best sequence against Canada after making a beautiful no-look backhand pass below the goal-line which should have resulted in a goal, and here again today, he was one of the best forwards for the Swiss. He played the half-wall on the powerplay and had several impressive passes that were accurate. He made one pass that was threaded through multiple Swedish defenders and landed on the tape of his teammate for a high-quality scoring chance directly in-front of the net, the play showed poise and plus vision. On another passing attempt, he made a no look backhand pass that required a high-degree of difficulty while in motion that led to an additional scoring chance. He was a catalyst for offense and was the Swiss forward who demonstrated the highest level of hockey sense, puck control and skill in today's viewing.

Simon Knak (2020) – Knak was the other forward with Rochette who had several high-end plays. Despite having poor skating posture in today's viewing, where he stood too upright and didn't generate much in the way of power giving him average acceleration, he still managed to create off the rush and attempted several cuts to the net. He had the most shots generated out of any Swiss forward and his best chance came off a tipped shot during the powerplay which showed a good level of hand-eye coordination. He was one of the most noticeable forwards for the Swiss and appeared to have some talent.

Yves Stoffel (2019) – Stoffel had a couple of impressive sequences against Sweden. He had an impressive neutral zone play where he used plus two-step area quickness and his edges to cut around a Swedish defender before attempting to drive down the wing with the puck, he competed hard on the play. On another play he demonstrated above average hands, threatening one-on-one before firing a shot far side that was absorbed. He was one of the few forwards who was capable of challenging the Swedish defense in spurts.

USA vs Finland, Hlinka Gretzky Cup, Aug 7 2018

USA

Arthur Kaliyev (2019) – Kaliyev displayed several high-end offensive tools against Finland, and was more consistent than he was against the Czechs. He started off early, aggressively cutting to the net while trying to pull to his backhand before getting his stick pressed. Throughout the contest he looked to peel from below the goal-line and use his excellent wrist-shot that features both a high-end release point while generating a lot of power. He scored a goal during an impressive give and go sequence, using his quick shot to bury the puck before the Finnish goalie could move laterally across in time. His shooting instincts were noticeable and he was dangerous but he hasn't taken over many shifts and has made plays primarily in spurts.

Robert Mastrosimone (2019) – After dominating the Czech's, Mastrosimone had another impressive game, displaying the ability to make plays both with and without the puck. Against Finland, Robert displayed a multi-faceted shot, using a reduced wind up in his slapshot, dragging the puck to change the angle of his release point during multiple sequences and on one attempt using his blade in-front of the net to redirect the puck. Without the puck, Mastrosimone looked to create pressure against the Finnish defense, stripping an unsuspecting Loponen who was turning just as Mastrosimone used a stick lift and generated a takeaway. He then skated down near the bottom of the left circle and made an accurate pass to his teammate who buried the puck. It was a momentum swinging goal. He's shown the ability to be dangerous in multiple ways through his first two games of the tournament and has played with a good pace while showing intelligence on the ice.

Nicholas Robertson (2019) – Robertson demonstrated a take over mentality with the puck on his stick, carrying play for much of the game. He was used on the powerplay and had the most noticeable high-skill sequence out of any player on the ice today. He had the puck in the neutral zone and with a Finnish forechecker aggressively attempting to knock him off the puck, he used plus agility to side step the check before showing impressive hands to drag the puck in-tight to his body to bypass a second Finnish player, then transitioned the puck over the offensive blueline and used his edges to create a spinning no-look backhand pass to his teammate across the slot area. The pass missed but the sequence showed several tools at Robertson's disposal. Through out the game he consistently controlled the puck to generate several impressive and clean transitional zone entries. He looked to shoot more than pass and release point was a plus, however there were tells in his body mechanics, so there was a lack of deception to his approach at times. He did mix up his options though, giving him a primary assist after quickly assessing a give and go sequence with Kaliyev down below the goal line. He was impressive in today's contest and played at a high pace.

Luke Toporowski (2019) – Toporowski played efficient and effective hockey for the U.S while showing elements of a 200-foot game. He scored the first goal of the game after drifting across the slot area and redirecting a Feenstra point shot. On another sequence, he aggressively cut to the net and showed a good amount of skill before releasing a hard and low wrist-shot. In the neutral zone, he made a heads-up play and intercepted a pass before transitioning the puck up the ice. On another sequence, he made a sharp pass to his teammate from the goal-line to out in-front of the net which resulted in a redirect goal, giving him the primary assist.

Sam Colangelo (2019) – Colangelo was effective in spurts against Finland. He has a big body and used it to guard the puck before aggressively cutting down the right side of the ice and using a backhand to forehand deke, tucking the puck past the sprawled out Finnish goalie. On another sequence, he used his big frame to position himself properly in the slot area and generated a wrist-shot that was blocked but was quick to act and attempted a second additional shot. On another sequence, he was hit but absorbed it and created a high-end scoring chance on the powerplay. He didn't look deterred in heavy traffic areas and was took a direct approach to the net that led to his goal. One area that held him back today was his first few steps didn't look overly impressive, it took him a bit of time to generate power in his stride, but he's young.

Luke Reid (2020) – Reid had an impressive defensive game for the U.S while showing a high-level of composure in a coupe of pressure situations. His most impressive defensive sequence came off a two one one situation after his defensive partner Webber, tripped at the line. As opposed to aggressively cutting down the puck carrier which would have resulted in a potential scoring chance for the other Finnish forward, he quickly skated in the middle of the slot and used his stick to block the passing lane, he then recognized that Rati was looking to shoot and made an excellent and well-timed block. Additionally, on the Finnish forecheck, Reid used his frame effectively to counteract takeaway attempts and helped generate several transitional zone-exits. He's talented offensive defenseman but he wasn't using his skill as much as we would have liked to have seen from him. Regardless, he had some good plays that contributed to his team.

Mike Koster (2019) – Foster used his puck carrying ability to breakdown the Czech defense, and that occurred again today. During one sequence on the penalty-kill, he aggressively carried the puck over the offensive-line and cut to the net, drawing a penalty and taking away the Finnish powerplay. Unlike yesterday, where he was demonstrating some tunnel vision in his approach when transitioning over the offensive-line, against Finland he wasn't forcing his options and letting the play develop more naturally, allowing to make more efficient and effective plays. His better moments came when he would freeze the defense and make accurate passes that set up his teammates. One area to note, is that despite Koster's willingness to become a puck transporter, the top-end gear was lacking.

Michael Feenstra (2019) – Feenstra hit the post early against the Czechs and here he looked to shoot the puck from the line when he was given the opportunity, which led to a primary assist after his low wrist-shot was tipped in-front of the net. His release point is above-average but he hasn't shown any dynamic qualities while walking the line yet. Unlike some of his defensive teammates, Feenstra has size, showed the ability to transition the puck cleanly out of his own-end with an accurate first pass and looked to shoot the puck.

Cade Webber (2019) – Webber is a gigantic kid, standing 6'6, yet unlike most players with his build, he demonstrated a surprising amount of coordination and fluidity in his movement. This allowed him to counteract an aggressive Finnish forechecker on one sequence, quickly pivoting and staying in-front of his man before angling himself and using his frame to pin his opponent into the corner. On another forechecking sequence, Webber showed the ability to move the puck quickly when the play called for it. Using a short and fast chip pass to his teammate, though after recollecting the puck he did run into a closed skating lane, but tried to use his size to bulldoze himself through his opponent. On several other sequences, Webber used his reach effectively to disrupt the attack. Although he didn't generate from the offensive-blueline, Webber displayed defensive acumen and plus mobility for his size leading to several important defensive plays.

Dustin Wolf (2019) – Wolf had a good game for the U.S while making several well-timed stops to keep momentum for his team. As discussed against the Czech's, Wolf is undersized but demonstrated again elite puck tracking ability. In one-on-one situations with either a shooter whose received a pass during a defensive breakdown or on breakaways, it's apparent than Dustin can track his opponents body mechanics and breakdown the play they are attempting to generate in advance which allows him to get positioned before the play develops. During two separate breakaways, he was already in position before his opponents attempted their shot, and his ability to assess the angle of a high-percentage shot was impressive. That been said, unlike yesterdays game where he posted a shutout, Wolf did allow an unscreened wrist-shot go by him from the top of the right circle and later allowed another wrist-shot from the right circle get over his glove, though there was traffic on the second goal. Additionally, despite his puck tracking skills, his size can limit him when he's attempting to look around and track play through screens, he had trouble with some points shots, resulting in multiple shots going off the post on him.

Finland

Leevi Aaltonen (2019) – Aaltonen had flashes out on the ice but wasn't as consistent as some previous viewings. He's a tremendous skater who can accelerate quickly and create pressure off the forecheck but didn't generate turnovers or force the defense as much as he has in other viewings. His best sequences primarily came on the powerplay where he set his teammates along the point and the half-wall. He had the primary assist on Lundell's goal after drawing the attention of the defense to him before making a sharp pass across the high-slot. His best scoring chance came in the slot area where he fired a hard wrist-shot wide but did find soft-ice.

Henri Nikkanen (2019) – Nikkanen was relatively quiet at even strength but had a couple of plus plays with the man-advantage. There was a lack of pace to his play but he does have a good amount of skill that allows him to control the tempo of a play at times. This was seen during set-up where he distributed the puck before putting himself in good position for a one-timer. In today's game, he would have been more effective if he was willing to hit another gear, but didn't change his pace to match the American's.

Anton Lundell (2020) – Lundell has had success at previous international events like the U17's and U18's last season, here again he contributed to his team, despite his team looking flat for much of the contest. In previous viewings, he shown more of a playmaking element to his game, but today he scored off a wrist-shot that went through heavy traffic and over Wolf's glove while on the powerplay. He recognized the screen option and the shot was very accurate. Like a lot of his teammates, he wasn't consistent but he flashed his plus puck skills when attempting to transition over the line offensive-line.

Kasper Simontaival (2020) – Simontaival had a difficult game for Finland, making some poor decisions with the puck on his stick at times and having trouble keeping up with the pace of play. On one sequence when he was on the powerplay, instead of playing a simple game when distributing the puck, he forced a difficult pass that was easily read by the States, resulting in an unforced turnover. On another sequence when carrying the puck over the blueline, he was stripped off the puck and seemed unaware of the American opponent's backcheck. On other sequences, he was unable to penetrate or create space for himself with the puck on his stick.

Aku Raty (2019) – Raty showed off a plus wrist-shot and was one of the few Finnish forwards who had multiple looks at the net today. He scored after transitioning over the offensive blueline and firing a hard-wrist shot that fooled Wolf. The placement was good and his release point was a plus. He attempted several other shots and tried to utilize screens to mask his shot placement. Today, he had a shooters mentality but didn't demonstrate much in the way of playmaking ability or control play for extended periods of time.

Mikko Kokkonen (2019) – Kokkonen had a solid, yet unspectacular game for Finland, displaying good hockey sense. He's shown the ability to shoot the puck and walk the line effectively during the powerplay in previous viewings, but here he didn't generate much offense at both even-strength or on the powerplay. However, in the defensive end he did have some good moments. Kokkonen has improved his skating mechanics and showed plus edges, which allowed him to alleviate pressure while carrying the puck from behind his own-goal line, where he made several accurate and safe passes to help move the puck up the ice. He had one sequence where he made multiple quick passes to help keep puck possession while in transition, he was making decisions quickly out there. I wish he would have attempted to be more assertive in the offensive-end but he didn't get too many touches with the puck and Finland had difficulty generating offense in general.

Kalle Loponen (2019) – Loponen distributed the puck efficiently on the powerplay while demonstrating plus feinting mechanics that helped open up passing lanes. He was consistently skating into open-ice through the circles during several powerplay opportunities and faking wrist-shots before making sharp cross-ice passes to his teammates. His passing accuracy was solid and he ran the powerplay more efficiently than any other Finnish defender today. His best sequence came after making a difficult keep-in play at the line before firing a wrist-shot which found its way through traffic. He was assessing his time and space well, while also demonstrating some grit despite being undersized in the defensive zone.

Livari Rasanen (2019) – Rasanen was arguably the best player on the ice for Finland today. He made a well-timed stick lift which took away what would have been a high-danger shot from Kaliyev very early in the contest. Shortly after, he supported his defensive partner and skated aggressively after a stray puck before making a long, yet accurate stretch pass to his teammate. On another sequence, he carried the puck through all three-zones while killing a penalty. He was comfortable and assertive in his decision making with and without the puck. He was stripped by Mastrosimone which led to a back-breaking goal, but he made several plus plays to compensate for that sequence. After getting stripped, he was the first to try and recover and showed determination out there against the U.S forecheck, not getting deterred when getting hit or when dealing with pressure.

Canada vs Sweden, Hlinka Gretzky Cup, Aug 8 2018

Sweden

Elmer Soderblom (2019) – Soderblom continues to look dangerous in-front of the net. His size and length are impressive but it's the hand-eye coordination and offensive-awareness away from the puck that helps him redirect shots into the back of the net like he did today against Canada. He had an excellent hit on Krebs so there was sandpaper in his game and on the forecheck he looks to finish his checks as well. He didn't have too many consistent shifts but the raw tools stood out.

Albin Grewe (2019) – Grewe was hurt late in the third period but before his injury he had a couple of offensive sequences where he used his edges and impressive straight-line speed to attack around the net area. He was primarily kept to the outside today but he did have a prime scoring chance in the slot area where he shot the puck over the net, he elevated the puck quickly on the play. There was a lack of chemistry displayed on his line which didn't help him generate as many offensive chances as some previous viewings. That been said, he still showed that he can make plays while in motion today.

Lucas Raymond (2020) - Raymond has been excellent all tournament and that continued today against Canada. It was an interesting match-up in terms of Canada's mobile defense going up against Lucas's impressive skating ability. He didn't create as many offensive opportunities as some previous efforts but that didn't stop him from drawing a hooking penalty by using his separating speed on one play and on several others, he was driving down the wings while looking for a passing option or a shooting lane. His most impressive sequence came after collecting a puck that was tipped off Holtz stick, he pulled the puck to his backhand while moving through the slot area and made an accurate backhand pass to Holtz creating a give and go sequence that led to Sweden's opening goal. His speed, skill and multi-faceted offensive skill-set makes him dangerous every time he touches the puck.

Alexander Holtz (2020) – Holtz was Sweden's most dangerous player against Canada. In some previous viewings he tended to be too unselfish at times but that wasn't the case today where he looked to shoot consistently. He found soft-ice throughout the game and released several impressive wrist-shots that were difficult for Maier to pick up. His body mechanics masked his release due to shooting without a lot of movement, this combined with the ability to change angles on his shot rapidly made it dangerous every time he touched the puck. He rang two posts and scored on a beautiful shot that had excellent placement from the right circle. Furthermore, he looks to use screens and was aware of when he needed to re-open his lanes, he wasn't forcing play and that's; been a consistent theme throughout this tournament.

Tobias Bjornfot (2019) – Bjornfot had an effective two-way performance against Canada but continues to show a stream-lined approach at the offensive blueline. He has the ability to shift gears when pressured in his own-end and once again showed a high-panic threshold when dealing with the forecheck. On one sequence he protected the puck properly before transitioning cleanly out of his own-end, on a similar sequence Suzuki cut him off but instead of forcing the play, Bjornfot peeled off the pressure and found his defense partner for an additional zone exit. Plays like the two above are characteristic of his overall performance so far at this event, he was moving the puck efficiently while showing poise and awareness. In the offensive-end he was opting for accurate yet simple passing plays and managed to get his slapshot through traffic which was redirected for a goal. He wasn't displaying any dynamic qualities out there though, which has been a continuous theme dating back to his U17's.

Philip Broberg (2019) – Broberg used his impressive four-way mobility to both transition the puck while also making several excellent recovery sequences. He's a powerful skater and this allows him to cover ground rapidly, which was showcased throughout the game against Canada. On one sequence the puck was turned over at the line and he needed to recover quickly with Rees pressuring him but he's willing to expend his gas tank when needed on the defensive side of the ice and did so during the sequence. On several other plays he transitioned the puck cleanly through all three zones and looked to cut from the outside, though unlike previous games, he was matched by Canada's mobility and gap control which forced him to the outside. His best scoring chance came after moving laterally across the slot and delivering a high-wrist shot that was gloved down after coming off the half-wall. In the defensive-end, he showed physicality and over-extended himself which led to Canada's game winning powerplay goal with less than 2 minutes left, however he was good at containing his physical presence for the most part. His stick was active and he used it to counter several cross-crease pass attempts and demonstrated an impressive defensive presence when going up against Canada's top players. This was an important test for Broberg and he faired well overall. The one area that was average on some sequences was his decision making during the powerplay, where he rushed certain plays leading to unforced turnovers but that's to be expected at times with his approach.

Albert Lyckasen (2019) – Lyckasen didn't create much in the way of offense but had a couple of notable defensive plays against Canada. His most impressive play was the result of a clean transitional zone exit while under pressure, he showed plus edges and looked aware in his own-end at times. In the neutral zone, he was good at recognizing when the play was transitioning which allowed him to remain in decent position.

Ludvig Hedstrom (2019) – Hedstrom was paired with Broberg and faired well in his own-end at even strength and on the penalty-kill. He showed good edges to spin out of a check that still clipped him but his recovery was a plus. On other forechecking shifts, when he was physically pressured he still managed to generate plus plays for the most part and his best defensive play came during a 2-on-1 sequence against where he made a well-timed sprawling play that stopped the pass attempt. He didn't get going offensively or carry the puck very often but showed that he can play against top competition today.

Jesper Wallstedt (2021) – He's the youngest player at this event and against Canada it showed on some plays. In previous viewings and this one, he continues to go down too early depending on the shot location and type. Another area that needs work based on today's game and others is that he tends to remain in his reverse V-H too long when his opponents come out from behind the net. Despite staying on the ice too long in stretches or going down too early, Wallstedt played with an impressive level of composure and when factoring in his age this point should be highlighted. Despite going up against some of the most skilled players in this tournament, he never looked rattled or out of place. His best save was a result of moving laterally and kicking out his left pad which stopped Lafreniere who had received a great pass from Dach. He was playing a minimalist and blocking style, instead of relying on reflexes or making saves that required full extension.

Canada

Alexis Lafreniere (2020) – Lafreniere had a good game for Canada but wasn't overly dominant on any shift. He showed impressive offensive-awareness on his goal by tracking the puck properly off the boards and turning into position to take the puck in one-motion before firing a quick wrist-shot into the back of the net. On another sequence he set himself up in a high-traffic area in-front of the net to receive a pass that led a high-quality scoring chance and on an additional play he broke down the defense using a quick deke to re-open his shooting lane before firing a shot wide. In today's contest he displayed an advanced understanding of how to re-open shooting and passing lanes while in motion. This combined with his deceptive release point and impressive passing skills made him a threat.

Ryan Suzuki (2019) – Suzuki had a good game for Canada and played at a better pace then some other viewings, while also showing some intensity. You can't deny the kids skill, he's a multi-faceted offensive threat but during some games last year and at this event, he's looked unengaged at times but that wasn't the case today. He competed hard for loose pucks, took a big hit, pressured the defense and at one point was upset with his teammate and let him know about it. He played with energy and when you combine that with his impressive skill-set it becomes very noticeable. Ryan consistently set up his teammates and was adept at masking his intentions with the puck on his stick, this led to his primary assist on Canadas opening goal after he threaded a pass to Williams in the right circle from below the goal-line.

Peyton Krebs (2019) – Krebs wasn't as dangerous against Sweden as he has been in some previous games but continues to show a varied attack characterized by deceptive gear shifts and the ability to process the play quickly while going at top speeds. His best scoring chance came after driving down the right wing and cutting directly towards the net before attempting to fire a quick wrist-shot far side, he changed the angle of his release while in tight to his body on the play. Below the goal-line he had a couple of impressive passing as well.

Kirby Dach (2019) – Dach had a great game for Canada by skating hard while simultaneously using his vision to set up his teammates for impressive scoring chances. He's a difficult player to contain due to his length, size and edges, which he used in combination when below the goal-line and around the net area to create havoc on several shifts. I would still like to see him shoot a bit more but today he did peel off a check and take a direct approach to the net and get his shot off. He also used his size effectively to set up screens and played a factor on Byrams game winning goal due to his presence in-front of the crease. Dach has excellent tools and has been consistent in using them during this event so far.

Dylan Cozens (2019) – Cozens wasn't as dominant against Sweden as he has been in some previous games but he still played a complete game. On the forecheck, he had a physical presence and this allowed him to generate a takeaway that led to a high-end scoring chance for his team. He continues to play with a lot of confidence when carrying the puck. This allowed him to make some high-risk plays near the offensive blueline where he protected the puck while on his backhand before peeling off pressure and re-opening his skating lanes. When his lanes were taken, he made quick decisions and wasn't forcing play, making accurate passes to his teammates consistently throughout the game. He didn't have any real high-end scoring chances today though.

Sasha Mutala (2019) – Mutala has had a quiet tournament up to this game and although he only generated a couple of offensive chances, he was excellent away from the puck. His best offensive chance came after driving down the right-wing before releasing a quick wrist-shot that was labelled short-side, his release point is high-end. On the defensive-side, he was used on the penalty-kill and had several impressive plays. He showed good defensive awareness and used his stick to intercept a pass attempt before clearing the puck. On other sequences he backchecked effectively and applied pressure. With less than a minute to go, he stripped Holtz off the puck before making a clean transitional zone exit and fired a pass to Cozens which should have resulted in a primary assist but Cozens missed the open net after the goalie was pulled.

Josh Williams (2019) – Williams was dangerous for Canada today, needing very little time to get his shot off and was consistent at putting himself in good position to be set up for scoring chances around the slot area. He scored Canada's opening goal after receiving a pass from Suzuki and wiring a hard wrist-shot far-side, the placement was excellent. Later in the game he received a pass from Dach and almost buried his second goal of the game, the amount of power he was generating on his shots from a stationary position was impressive. Furthermore, he was effective in spurts on the forecheck and competed hard away from the puck. The skill and shot stood out against Sweden.

Bowen Byram (2019) – Byram played a complete game for Canada both with and without the puck. Byram isn't the biggest defenseman but he wasn't afraid to step-up and deliver puck separating hits which he did on a couple of sequences. His ability to assess the movement of opponents gives him the opportunity to time his checks appropriately and that was noticeable here. His transitional puck moving was on point, using his skating ability and poise while carrying the puck to make several clean transitional zone-exits and entries throughout the game. When walking the offensive-blueline, he had a coupe of exaggerated body feints that helped him re-open his shooting and passing lanes. He scored the game winning goal for Canada after firing a quick seeing-eye shot through traffic thajt found the back of the net on Wallstedt's glove-side. He was patient and controlled on the ice, rarely skating himself into corners or putting himself in a position where he had to make low-percentage plays.

Kaeden Korczak (2019) – Korczak had an excellent defensive game for Canada. He matched Broberg's skating ability with his gap control and defensive reads. On one sequence when Broberg was driving down the left wing after entering the zone, he cut off the skating lane in advance and used his stick to generate a takeaway before clearing the puck on the penalty-kill, shortly after, he anticipated Holtz's slap-pass and intercepted the puck resulting in an additional clear. Late in the game on the penalty-kill, Broberg attempted to cut below the goal-line and create a scoring chance but Korczak read the play in advance again and took away the angle for Broberg which led to a low percentage shot at a critical time. It was fitting that the final seconds of the game was him defending against Raymond with excellent positioning and anticipation, keeping the Swede to the outside and using a check to push him into the corner, taking away any chance Sweden had to generate a high-percentage shot. His play won't end up on the highlight reel but his defensive reads were impressive.

Matthew Robertson (2019) – Robertson had a good two-way game for Canada. Despite getting caught while attempting to carry the puck out of his own-end which resulted in Holtz's goal, Robertson played with poise in his own end and used his reach to counter his opponents. He showed some offense after skating from the left-circle towards the slot area before releasing a quick wrist-shot that went bar-down over Wallstedt who had gone down too early.

Finland vs Czech Republic, Hlinka Gretzky Cup, Aug 8 2018

Finland

Leevi Aaltonen (2019) – Aaltonen continued to play with speed against the Czech's but wasn't effective in driving play or creating plays today. He had mixed puck retrieval results and was unable to find soft-ice in prime scoring areas. The one aspect of his game that has remained consistent throughout this tournament despite having an off game was his motor, he's constantly moving out there and managed to grab a couple of stray pucks.

Antti Saarela (2019) – Had one solid sequence where he rushed the puck up the ice and got a shot off before finishing his check along the boards, he took a direct route and wasn't afraid to physically engage, otherwise he didn't create offensively.

Anton Lundell (2020) – Despite having a nice defensive read on the penalty-kill where he used his stick to knock a cross-ice pass attempt out of the zone and a decent rush attempt where he transitioned through all three zones, this was Lundell's least effective game of the tournament. He also ended up getting called for a trip that led to the game winning powerplay goal and was visibly frustrated on the play.

Kasper Simontaival (2020) – Simontaival played well for Finland today, looking to attack consistently. He managed several scoring chances for his team, finding soft-ice to get his wrist-shot off while driving down both wings. His best sequence was a result of patience, poise, and plus puck skills as he out-waited his opponent before dragging the puck around him near the net-area resulting in a scoring chance. This was his best game of the tournament and it showed that he has a good amount of offensive-upside when he's on.

Aarne Intonen (2019) – Intonen was inconsistent but flashed some skill against the Czechs. He had a dangerous give and go sequence that came close to resulting in a goal, he was decisive on the attempt. His best sequence came on an individual effort while driving down the left wing. He dragged the puck around his opponent before quickly pulling the puck from his forehand to his backhand while attempting to shoot it far-side, it slipped off his stick but the play demonstrated good hands and a willingness to attack directly.

Patrik Puistola (2019) – Puistola was around the puck in the offensive-end more than most of the other Finnish forwards. There was an element of elusiveness to his game, peeling off aggressive defenders and using his edges to create opening for himself. He split the defense on one attempt and on another, peeled off a Czech before getting a low wrist-shot through traffic. His release was quick but there was a lack of power generated on his attempts. Patrik also demonstrated a shoot-first mentality.

Juuso Parssinen (2019) -Parssinen didn't have a great game by any stretch but had arguably the nicest play of the game. He went end-to-end with the puck while showing a decent set of hands before firing a backhander off the post that fooled Malik.

Mikko Kokkonen (2019) – Kokkonen had a solid two-way effort for Finland. He was making decisions quickly under pressure, and found open passing lanes consistently. During the powerplay, he was distributing the puck efficiently and was using a combination of feints and lateral mobility to freeze the Czech defense to re-open lanes. His defensive awareness was notable on one sequence, where he had his back-turned to the pass but stayed with his man in-front of the net and made a well-timed stick-check, assessing the Czech's body language in order to make the play despite not having vision on the puck. He scored a beautiful goal that further displays his plus release. He found soft-ice in the left circle after calling for the puck and wired a heavy wrist-shot short-side. An attribute to note about his shot is that he continues to release heavy shots despite displaying limited movement, he was good at masking the release, there's not much in the way of tells for goalies to pick up on. I found his offense to be lacking before this game, but here he demonstrated more confidence when carrying the puck and was more assertive on the ice.

Samu Koskenkorva (2019) – Koskenkorva wasn't effective in the offensive-end but he had several plus defensive plays. He's not going to show up on the highlight-reel in today's game but he played bigger than his size, wasn't afraid to play physical when needed, and demonstrated a good level of compete out there. His best sequence came off the faceoff where he corralled a loose puck before skating the puck out of a high-danger area resulting in a clean transitional zone exit, on the same shift he recognized when he needed to transition from offense to defense quickly and made an additional defensive play that stopped a Czech player from cutting below the goal-line.

Czech Republic

Martin Lang (2019) – Lang was inconsistent for the Czech's but had flashes, which has been a common theme this tournament. His best sequence came after aggressively tracking down a puck in the slot area and stripping a Finnish player who had just obtained it, he used his stick to generate a take-away and then passed it back to the point before finding soft-ice and getting his shot off far-side which was stopped. He had an additional shot near the same area, at the left circle which is where he's shown to be at his most dangerous but both shots were fired without traffic and were handled relatively easily. Despite having a quick release, he didn't look to change angles or shoot around screens today.

Adam Raska (2020) – Raska had a couple of quality sequences for the Czech's today. He had the primary assist after making a nice no-look backhand pass from the slot area that set up Has's opening goal of the game. In the defensive-end, he had a fantastic shot block on Kokkonen which resulted in a clear. At times, he was attempting to do a little too much with the puck and over-extend himself but he still had some good moments.

Michal Teply (2019) – Teply was active against Finland, generating several quality-scoring opportunities in the slot area, he also scored the game winning goal in over-time on the powerplay by rifling a wrist-shot from the right-circle. He wasn't looking to pass the puck as much as he was attempting to find soft-ice in the slot area to get his shot off, which he found consistently. He generated the most high-danger chances for the Czech's but his release point was slightly delayed, it allowed the Finnish netminder to get set on every attempt and even on his goal there appeared to be a screen. Furthermore, his puck-skills looked average in today's game.

Marcel Barinka (2019) – Barinka set up the game winning goal for the Czechs. He wasn't very consistent but on the poweplay, he threaded a pass through the crease that resulted in a goal that was called off quickly, the pass was crisp and accurate though. He demonstrated good backchecking ability which helped create pressure on Intonen's best scoring chance. On the game winning goal, he made a sharp pass to Teply from the left circle to the right circle. He was able to find open seams with the man advantage.

Jaromir Pytlik (2020) – Pytlik wasn't consistent but had several drives where he managed to hold onto the puck and use his frame effectively. He's one of the younger players but he's big and played with a good pace for his size. His best sequence came after driving wide while skating behind the net before threading a pass into the slot area that landed on the tape of Beranek for a goal.

David Homola (2019) – Homola didn't do anything flashy but was effective in his own-end. He had several plus transitional zone-exits showing a good first pass and making decisions quickly under pressure. There was poise to his game and he didn't over-extend himself, he played simple yet effective hockey for the Czech's today.

Simon Kubicek (2020) – Kubicek wasn't as effective as some of his previous games but he still had a couple of impressive moments. His best sequence came after making an accurate pass out of his own-end. After the Finns came back over the zone shortly after the pass, he made a fast defensive-read near the his own-net and boxed out a Finnish forward which took away scoring chance. He was in good position to block a hard point-shot shortly after the above sequence as well. Offensively he didn't really get going but he upside was still notable.

Martin Huga Has (2019) – Hugo Has was the best player on the ice for the Czech's today, showing an effective two-way game with a high-level of consistency. He opened the scoring for the Czech's after finding space to get a wrist-shot off from the left circle. He's rangy and it allows him to change the angle of his shot quickly, the release was above-average. He quarterbacked the powerplay and was successful at creating options for his teammates. There was a plus level of poise, patience, lateral mobility, and puck-skills displayed when he was walking the line in the offensive-end. In the defensive-end, he used his length to counteract The Finns, and managed to prevent Puistola's attempt at cutting wide on him during one play by using his length and frame. One area to note with Has during this game was that he was aggressive at closing his gap on certain sequences, he was forcing the Finns to react to his movement and wasn't passive. Has has had an impressive tournament so far and is continuing to carry his play from the U18's to the Hlinka.

Russia vs USA, Hlinka Gretzky Cup, Aug 8 2018

Russia

Yegor Spiridonov (2019) – Spiridonov has been inconsistent all tournament and that continued today against the U.S. He had a nice rush where he looked to use a screen before firing a low wrist-shot that required a decent save but with that exception he generated only one other decent look. He did display an element of creativity late in the third by attempting a between the legs tuck-in play near the goal-line but it didn't result in a goal. After a decent showing at the U18's last year, Spiridonov has yet to show much in the way of sustained offense.

Mikhail Abramov (2019) – Abramov didn't take over any shifts but he generated in spurts and complimented his line with Likhachyov and Gushchin well. He had the primary assist on Likhachyov's goal after passing across the slot area after finding an opening. His best assist came off the draw, where he won the faceoff and made a move around his opponent before finding an open seam to thread a pass through the crease that gave Likhachyov a tap in. He showed that he can be a duel-threat in this game, generating chances both from his shot and passing ability. He was making decisions quickly in the offensive-end as well.

Yaroslav Likhachyov (2019) – Likhachyov scored two goals as a result of finding soft-ice in high-percentage scoring areas and needed little time to bury the puck. His most impressive play wasn't a result of his goals but instead of a rush down the left wing where he showed impressive hands and the ability to draw his opponents to him before making a backhand saucer pass that landed directly on the tape of Abramov's stick for a goal. Today he showed that he can make plays while in motion and broke down the U.S dynamically, there wasn't any pre-set moves or an attempt at forcing the play, he adjusted quickly to what was presented to him and shifted the play when needed. He demonstrated skill and a willingness to go to heavy traffic areas when needed.

Oleg Zaitsev (2019) – Zaitsev wasn't a factor offensively. He did show impressive balance and won a board battle along the half-wall in the offensive-end by angling his body properly to separate the U.S opponent from the puck which led to a Russian scoring chance but with that exception, he had difficulty getting going.

Egor Chinakhov (2019) – Chinakhov was tenacious on the puck in spurts. He had a great scoring chance early where he fired a hard wrist-shot that difficult for the U.S netminder to absorb, this game and previous games have demonstrated that he doesn't need much time for the puck to settle down in-front of him before he can release his shot. His best sequences though came away from the puck. He displayed a plus motor and was aggressive when attempting to track-down loose pucks. He applied pressure to the U.S defense and was noticeable despite not having blazing speed.

Daniil Gushchin (2020) – Gushchin had another stand-out performance against the U.S. He was generating chance after chance by using his speed and a direct approach to the net before getting his powerful wrist-shot off. He didn't give up on secondary opportunities, this was displayed on his first goal where he banged home his own rebound, he tracked the puck well on the play and got the puck up in a hurry. His second goal was more of a result of Likhachyov's fantastic pass but Gushchin's positioning allowed him to bury the chance. During several different sequences, he made quick decisions with the puck and continues to make the right decisions in the offensive-end consistently, there wasn't any tunnel vision in his play. He's been a dynamic player for Russia so far during this tournament and has carried over his successful play from the U17s.

Vasili Podkolzin (2019) – Podkolzin displayed dynamic offensive-ability against the U.S. His skating stride was a bit unorthodox dating back to the U17's followed by the U18's last season but that doesn't seem to hinder him due to his agility and puck-skills. He had the most impressive one-on-one move of the game, turning a U.S player inside-out at the right circle using his length and coordination to drag the puck past him. His shot was dangerous all game and he managed a one-time slapshot goal from the right-circle after receiving a good pass from Gutik. He scored an additional goal after cutting down the right-wing and using his hands in-tight to the net before firing a quick-shot that went far-side. The most impressive element of his game today was his ability to transition seamlessly from attempting an individual play to a team-oriented play, if he doesn't like his options he can quickly become his own option and it made him very difficult to defend against.

Daniil Gutik (2019) – Gutik had a great game for Russia and flashed a high-compete level against the States. He has length, a ton of skill, and has shown impressive vision throughout this event but today he was winning the majority of his board battles and was using his length and intelligence to effectively track and takeaway the puck from the U.S. One sequence that highlighted this was when he made a quick stick-lift along the half-wall before making a sharp pass that resulted in a scoring chance near the high-slot. He didn't use his hands as often as has in previous viewings but he was decisive and aggressive in his approach. His primary assist was a result of peeling off his opponent before baiting the U.S netminder with a fake-shot, after Mullahy squared up he delivered a hard-pass to Podkolzin. Lastly, he's going to need to continue to use his length and frame to be effective away from the puck since he's knock kneed to a degree, it hinders his ability to push off effectively and generate power.

Ilya Nikolayev (2019) – Nikolayev had his best performance of the tournament so far, flashing a multi-faceted skill-set. He had the most impressive primary assist in the game which can't be understated since there was several impressive passing plays. After receiving a pass near the right-side of the crease, he made a beautiful no-look pass that landed directly on Mironov's stick resulting in an easy goal. He had multiple high-end scoring chances as well. One of them was a result of Gutik's work where he received the pass and made a quick deke which readjusted his shooting lane before firing a quick wrist-shot. On another, he skated the puck into the slot area and showed impressive hands that completely fooled the U.S defender who bit on the initial move, this allowed Ilya to get a hard-wrist-shot on net that resulted in a difficult stop. He was also impressive away from the puck and flashed a 200-foot game. On one play, he skated down towards his own-net area to support his defense and quickly chipped the puck up ice resulting in a clean transitional zone exit. On a backchecking sequence he managed to aggressively skate-down a U.S player and generate a takeaway. He's not as talented as Gutik or Podkolzin but he has complimented them well in spurts.

Roman Bychkov (2019) - Bychkov had a good two-way effort for Russia. He's not the biggest defender but he displayed a heavy point-shot which resulted in the last goal of the game. He received a pass from Abramov, moved laterally to re-open his shooting lane before firing a powerful slapshot that went right through Mullahy. Mullahy was tracking pucks better than his save percentage indicated today so it was pretty impressive to see him get beaten clean from that far out and speaks volumes to Bychkov's slapshot based on today's viewing. He didn't display any dynamic qualities but he was effective.

Artemi Knyazev (2019) – Knyazev transitioned the puck effectively with his skating and passing ability but continues to show a lack of offensive-touch in this tournament. He had a well-timed pinch early in the game and on the same shift he read the play correctly away from the puck in the neutral zone resulting in a clean take-away after he used his stick. He had plus anticipation in all three-zones but when at the offensive-blueline he didn't display much in the way of skill and his shot appeared to be weak again, opting to try and get it through open-shooting lanes as quickly as possible. He has yet to demonstrate a high-end offensive attribute during this tournament.

Dmitri Tyuvilin (2019) – Tyuvilin was impressive on both sides of the puck against the States. He had an active-stick and this resulted in mitigating a couple of rush attempts by the U.S. Furthermore, on the powerplay he used above-average edges and showed poise countering the U.S forecheck before transitioning the puck up ice. In the offensive-end, he was good at assessing when he could pinch and this allowed him to get several impressive scoring chances throughout the game.

Ilya Mironov (2019) – Mironov is the biggest defender on the backend for Russia and made his presence felt by delivering heavy shots on net. He scored after pinching and finding soft-ice behind U.S coverage where he made no mistake burying a hard and low wrist-shot past Mullahy. Despite having power in his shot, his skating mechanics and stride appeared average to below average. He had some difficulty in his own-end at times as a result but his length does counteract speed coming down on him too.

USA

Arthur Kaliyev (2019) – Kaliyev had a mediocre game despite scoring a goal. Around the goal-mouth and slot area he's dangerous which was demonstrated during his goal where he tracked the puck and fired home a puck in tight to the net during a powerplay. He has pro size and a high-end release but in each game at this tournament so far, we have questioned his motor and he did nothing to ease those concerns against Russia. There wasn't much in the way of compete or secondary attempts to recover during transitional play from Arthur and he looked one-dimensional out there.

Josh Groll (2019) – Groll displayed impressive straight-line speed and balance today. He was skating well out there and this allowed him to make an old-school dump and chase play where he chipped the puck over a defender before using his skating to track it down resulting in offensive-zone time. During a rush through the neutral zone he was met with a heavy hit but demonstrated good balance by staying on his feet. His best chance was a wrist-shot in the high-slot but it was blocked. He also had a nice backchecking sequence where he was aggressive and managed to break up a play that was forming. His most notable attributes were his compete and his motor.

Robert Mastrosimone (2019) – Mastrosimone wasn't very effective against Russia despite scoring a goal. Although his goal was impressive. He demonstrated poise, patience, and plus hands as he dragged the puck past a defender then fired a low-wrist shot through the Russian netminder. He changed the angle of his release while in motion and this completely fooled Askarov. His other notable moments came during the powerplay where he took advantage of more space and made some quick and decisive plays. On one play, he received a hard but inaccurate pass from Reid near his left skate but managed to control the puck and was aware that due to the nature of the pass that a Russian forward near him was going to close in on him quickly, so he fired a sharp pass to his teammate that reset the powerplay before a turnover occurred. It was subtle but kept the play alive and demonstrated his awareness in the offensive-end. The biggest drawback to his game today was his inability to move the puck through the neutral zone due to his average first few steps.

Nicholas Robertson (2019) – Much like Mastrosimone in the sense that Robertson didn't generate a lot of offense and when he did it was primarily with the man-advantage. His best chance came after he out-waited his opponent which allowed a shooting lane to re-open, he then wired a hard-wrist-shot off the bar, the release was good on the attempt. On another shooting attempt he demonstrated that he can change the angle of his shot rapidly and it generated a good amount of power. He's had a good tournament so far but this was a weak game for him and much of the U.S team who were out-played from start to finish. This game further enhanced that he has had difficulty creating chemistry away from the man-advantage at times, he hasn't played with his teammates as well as he could have.

Luke Reid (2020) – Reid was the best player on the ice for the U.S against Russia. He had a tremendous hit in the defensive-end against Gushchin who was attempting to side-step him during a one-on-one sequence, but Reid tracked his body movement well before slamming him down to the ice with a puck separating hit. He was skating hard today and had several clean transitional zone entries at the offensive-blueline as a result. When walking the line, he flashed a good set of hands and was able to move laterally while also using feints which made it difficult for the Russian defense to contain him at times. He had the primary assist on Colangelo's powerplay goal after delivering a heavy slap-shot from the blueline that was redirected. This was his most impressive game of the tournament.

Switzerland vs Slovakia, Hlinka Gretzky Cup, Aug 8 2018

Slovakia

Dominik Sojka (2019) – Sojka played a complete 200-foot game and was the catalyst for several offensive plays. He's still not displaying much in the way of puck skills which doesn't allow him to challenge in one-on-one situations effectively, however he did use his vision to set up his teammates such as Chromiak and Mrazik. He had the primary assist on Mrazik's first goal after successfully using his length and size to overwhelm the much smaller Delemont along the boards before making an accurate pass to Chromiak in the right circle. He had an excellent scoring chance after finding soft-ice in the slot, but placed a snap-shot over the bar, the release was quick. He had an excellent defensive play late with his team leading by one goal, skating aggressively from below the goal-line and using his frame to block a shot, it was well-timed and helped secure the win.

Maxim Cajkovic (2019) – Cajkovic was the most skilled play on either team, so this was his opportunity to get back on track after having a lack luster start to the tournament, however despite scoring a goal that showed off his elite shooting mechanics, he flashed his talent as opposed to consistently utilizing it. He started out poorly, displaying tunnel vision and missing his teammate in the high-slot who was open for a quality scoring chance while he was driving down the right wing. On another sequence, he put himself in a prime scoring position but didn't get the puck off his stick fast enough. However, as the game progressed he started playing better. He out-competed two Swiss players below the goal-line to gain back possession on one sequence, and on another used his frame to angle himself away from pressure which allowed him to gain possession during a forecheck. He has very little options to pass the puck to at even strength since he's been continuously used on the second line, however he scored a tremendous goal from the high-slot, showing his lightning quick release, the shot went bar-down and had power, there was no chance for the Swiss netminder on the play. He showed impressive vision below the goal-line after making a no-look spinning pass out to the high-slot and on another sequence, he showed patience before attempting to distribute the puck to his teammate who arrived late to his pass attempt. Another notable moment for Maxim was when he used his explosive skating ability to aggressively backcheck during a giveaway by his teammate, resulting in a takeaway, so it was good to see him flash a defensive side to his game. The last aspect to note, is that there was an intensity to his game, which translates in his motor, he's got an excellent combination of skill and pace, he just didn't display it for the full 60 minutes out there. That been said, he should have dominated today and didn't.

Michal Mrazik (2019) – Mrazik had two goals against the Swiss, though both goals weren't overly impressive. His first goal was after he cut down the right-wing and shot a severe angle wrist-shot near the goal-line that should have been stopped. He also scored an empty net goal after receiving a pass in the right circle. Mrazik's biggest issue based off this game and others, is that he is continuing to have difficulty generating offense without the support of his teammates. He needs to be put on a line with players who can pass him the puck and use their skills to create additional ice for him to use. The main reasons for this are due to his food speed, his first few steps and skating mechanics need work, plus he demonstrated average to below-average hands, which doesn't allow him to make space for himself or breakdown the defense off the rush. He's got a good combination of size, shooting instincts and an above average release but the puck skills and skating are holding him back here.

Martin Chromiak (2020) – Chromiak flashed potential against Switzerland and scored the game winning goal for his team. His skating ability stood out, and he used it in multiple sequences when attempting to create off the rush. On one sequence, he pulled to his backhand while driving down the left-wing before stutter stepping to try and throw off his opponent before continue to cut behind the net. Although he didn't generate a scoring chance off the play, he was aware of his options and was assessing what he could do against the Swiss defenseman dynamically, not looking to make a pre-set deke or force a play. His skating was also noticeable on the empty net goal where he separated from the Swiss and hit the post before recollecting the puck and getting a primary assist. His goal was impressive, he contorted his frame, dropping his posture as he snapped a shot in one motion from the right circle that went far-side.

Patrik Kozel (2019) – Kozel fought through some shaky moments and ended up making several impressive saves at critical times throughout the game. He had some difficulty tracking the puck on several plays. On one of them, Delemont drove down the wing and lobbed a puck on him, however he lost it between his pads and required helped from his defense. On another sequence, he lost track of the puck below the goal-line and moved laterally in the opposite direction of the puck before having to quickly attempt to recover by pressing into his post, it almost resulted in a bad goal. The first goal he gave up was a turn around shot that was lobbed in on him without any traffic, simply going over his glove, he was visibly upset with himself after it went in. However, in circumstances where a goalie isn't completely on his game, you look for him to compete and battle back, which is exactly what Kozel did out there. In the last half of the game, he has several high-end saves, flashing above-average lateral mobility, plus reflexes and used his glove hand well. His best series of saves came off of Knak's attempt at a hattrick, as he tracked the puck through multiple players and quickly transitioned into his butterfly to take away the first shot, before kicking out his left pad to take away the second attempt. He was better against Sweden but he showed impressive mental attributes today.

Switzerland

Simon Knak (2020) – Knak was the most dangerous Swiss player on the ice against Slovakia, scoring 2 goals while coming close to scoring a third. He's still having trouble digging his skates into the ice, which makes him look like he's skidding on water at times, but despite his skating mechanics he generated several impressive offensive-plays. He scored his first goal of the game after delivering a fantastic slapshot from the right circle. The puck came off his stick in one motion and the mechanics were impressive, Kozel had little chance on the shot. His second goal was the result of finding soft-ice in-front of the slot area and taking advantage of a misdirected poke by a Slovakian defenseman which put the puck directly on his tape, he needed little time to get the puck off his stick and into the back of the net. His most impressive sequence didn't result in a point but he displayed soft-hands and good puck control while below the goal-line before making a great no-look backhand pass out into the slot area. Today, he displayed a varied attack, setting up his teammates while showing impressive vision, and shooting quick shots that were difficult for Kozel to get squared up to. Furthermore, he was consistently around the puck and can make plays in tight-spaces. He's rarely trying to create from the perimeter opting to attack around the net instead. Despite being younger than the majority of his teammates, he's been arguably the most dangerous forward for the Swiss at this event and has displayed a high-level of assertiveness and decisiveness in the offensive-zone.

Theo Rochette (2020) – Rochette continued to display a combination of vision, intelligence and the ability to control the tempo of a play with the puck on his stick against Slovakia. He centered the top line with Stoffel and Knak and was the catalyst again for several impressive offensive plays. Based off this game and others from this event, he's shown a playmaking mentality, however he did get one high-scoring chance that required a difficult stop by Kozel as well. He's good at recognizing open and closed lanes and took advantage of them, threading several high-end passes to knak and Stoffel throughout the game. One of his better plays was when he used a shot fake at the right circle which froze the Slovakian defender before making a sharp pass that resulted in a scoring chance. The Swiss are a one-line team at this tournament, and a large part of their success is run through Rochette.

Yves Stoffel (2019) – Stoffel was constantly in motion out there and generated multiple breakaway chances while short-handed, he also had one of the most impressive offensive sequences of the game. He didn't score on his breakaways but he created pressure and showed good positioning away from the puck which helped generate them in the first place. On his best play, he skated aggressively down the right wing, used plus puck-skills to carry the puck into heavy traffic, despite getting hit, he managed to swing a pass through a Slovaks legs which resulted in one of Knak's best scoring chances. The play demonstrated his plus edges, puck-skills, and vision.

Noah Delemont (2020) – Delemont had several plus transitional plays but also was a liability in his own end at times. He's undersized and slight, relying on his edges to mitigate pressure in his own-zone. On one sequence, he made an impressive spin move, resulting in a clean transitional zone exit before entering the offensive zone and cutting aggressively towards the net which resulted in a scoring chance. On several other sequences, he demonstrated fluid skating mechanics that allowed him to separate before transitioning back up the ice. He looked comfortable trying to create offense from the offensive-blueline and threatened with a low and hard point shot that made its way through heavy traffic. However, in his own-end he wasn't as assertive without the puck and had difficulty with the Slovakian forecheck due to his size and lack of decisiveness. He was directly responsible for the Slovaks game winning goal. The puck drifted in on him when he was in the slot area, where he then routinely chipped the puck up the middle of the ice resulting in a takeaway. On the same sequence, he skated down below the goal-line and collected the puck but tried to carry it under heavy pressure instead of making the smarter, safer and quicker play which would have been to chip the puck off the side boards to his teammate. As a result of attempting to carry the puck, he was stripped by Sojka, leading to Sojka's primary assist. Despite making poor decisions at times in his own-end, the puck-moving skill-set was present against Slovakia today.

Canada vs Sweden, Hlinka Gretzky Cup, Aug 9 2018

Sweden

Elmer Soderblom (2019) – Soderblom continues to look dangerous in-front of the net. His size and length are impressive but it's the hand-eye coordination and offensive-awareness away from the puck that helps him redirect shots into the back of the net like he did today against Canada. He had an excellent hit on Krebs so there was sandpaper in his game and on the forecheck he looks to finish his checks as well. He didn't have too many consistent shifts but the raw-tools stood out.

Albin Grewe (2019) – Grewe was hurt late in the third period but before his injury he had a couple of offensive sequences where he used his edges and impressive straight-line speed to attack around the net area. He was primarily kept to the outside today but he did have a prime scoring chance in the slot area where he shot the puck over the net, he elevated the puck quickly on the play. There was a lack of chemistry displayed on his line which didn't help him generate as many offensive chances as some previous viewings. That been said, he still showed that he can make plays while in motion today.

Lucas Raymond (2020) - Raymond has been excellent all tournament and that continued today against Canada. It was an interesting match-up in terms of Canada's mobile defense going up against Lucas's impressive skating ability. He didn't create as many offensive opportunities as some previous efforts but that didn't stop him from drawing a hooking penalty by using his separating speed on one play and on several others, he was driving down the wings while looking for a passing option or a shooting lane. His most impressive sequence came after collecting a puck that was tipped off Holtz stick, he pulled the puck to his backhand while moving through the slot area and made an accurate backhand pass to Holtz creating an impressive give and go sequence that led to Sweden's opening goal. His speed, skill and multi-faceted offensive skill-set makes him dangerous every time he touches the puck.

Alexander Holtz (2020) – Holtz was Sweden's most dangerous player against Canada. In some previous viewings he tended to be too unselfish at times but that wasn't the case today where he looked to shoot consistently. He found soft-ice throughout the game and released several impressive wrist-shots that were difficult for Maier to pick up. His body mechanics masked his release due to shooting without a lot of movement, this combined with the ability to change angles on his shot rapidly made it dangerous every time he touched the puck. He rang two posts and scored on a beautiful shot that had excellent placement from the right circle. Furthermore, he looks to use screens and was aware of when he needed to re-open his lanes, he wasn't forcing play and that's; been a consistent theme throughout this tournament.

Tobias Bjornfot (2019) – Bjornfot had an effective two-way performance against Canada but continues to show a stream-lined approach at the offensive blueline. He's got the ability to shift gears when pressured in his own-end and once again showed a high-panic threshold when dealing with the forecheck. On one sequence he protected the puck properly before transitioning cleanly out of his own-end, on a similar sequence Suzuki cut him off but instead of forcing the play, Bjornfot peeled off the pressure and found his defense partner for an additional zone exit. Plays like the two above are characteristic of his overall performance so far at this event, he was moving the puck efficiently while showing poise and awareness. In the offensive-end he was opting for accurate yet simple passing plays and managed to get his slapshot through traffic which was redirected for a goal. He wasn't displaying any dynamic qualities out there though, which has been a continuous theme dating back to his U17's.

Philip Broberg (2019) – Broberg used his impressive four-way mobility to both transition the puck while also making several excellent recovery sequences. He's a powerful skater and this allows him to cover ground rapidly, which was showcased throughout the game against Canada. On one sequence the puck was turned over at the line and he needed to recover quickly with Rees pressuring him but he's willing to expend his gas tank when needed on the defensive side of the ice and did so during the sequence. On several other plays he transitioned the puck cleanly through all three zones and looked to cut from the outside, though unlike previous games, he was matched by Canada's mobility and gap control which forced him to the outside. His best scoring chance came after moving laterally across the slot and delivering a high-wrist shot that was gloved down after coming off the half-wall. In the defensive-end, he showed physicality and over-extended himself which led to Canada's game winning powerplay goal with less than 2 minutes left, however he was good at containing his physical presence for the most part. His stick was active and he used it to counter several cross-crease pass attempts and demonstrated an impressive defensive presence when going up against Canada's top players. This was an important test for Broberg and he faired well overall. The one area that was average on some sequences was his decision making during the powerplay, where he rushed certain plays leading to unforced turnovers but that's to be expected at times with his approach.

Albert Lyckasen (2019) – Lyckasen didn't create much in the way of offense but had a couple of notable defensive plays against Canada. His most impressive play was the result of a clean transitional zone exit while under pressure, he showed plus edges and looked aware in his own-end at times. In the neutral zone, he was good at recognizing when the play was transitioning which allowed him to remain in decent position.

Ludvig Hedstrom (2019) – Hedstrom was paired with Broberg and faired well in his own-end at even strength and on the powerplay. He showed good edges to spin out of a check that still clipped him but his recovery was a plus. On other forechecking shifts, when he was physically pressured he still managed to generate plus plays for the most part and his best defensive play came during a 2-on-1 sequence against where he made a well-timed sprawling play that stopped the pass attempt. He didn't get going offensively but showed that he can play against top competition today.

Jesper Wallstedt (2021) – He's the youngest player at this event and against Canada it showed on some plays. In previous viewings and this one, he continues to go down too early depending on the shot location and type. Another area that needs work based on today's game and others is that he tends to remain in his reverse V-H too long when his opponents come out from behind the net. Despite staying on the ice too long in stretches or going down too early, Wallstedt played with an impressive level of composure and when factoring in his age this point should be highlighted. Despite going up against some of the most skilled players in this tournament, he never looked rattled or out of place. His best save was a result of moving laterally and kicking out his left pad which stopped Lafreniere who had received a great pass from Dach. He was playing a minimalist and blocking style, instead of relying on reflexes or making saves that required full extension.

Canada

Alexis Lafreniere (2020) – Lafreniere had a good game for Canada but wasn't overly dominant on any shift. He showed impressive offensive-awareness on his goal by tracking the puck properly off the boards and turning into position to take the puck in one-motion before firing a quick wrist-shot into the back of the net. On another sequence he set himself up in a high-traffic area in-front of the net to receive a pass that led a high-quality scoring chance and on an additional play he broke down the defense using a quick deke to re-open his shooting lane before firing a shot wide. In today's contest he displayed an advanced understanding of how to re-open shooting and passing lanes while in motion. This combined with his deceptive release point and impressive passing skills made him a threat.

Ryan Suzuki (2019) – Suzuki had a good game for Canada and played at a better pace then some other viewings, while also showing some intensity. You can't deny the kids skill, he's a multi-faceted offensive threat but during some games last year and at this event, he's looked unengaged at times but that wasn't the case today. He competed hard for loose pucks, absorbed a big hit well, pressured the defense and at one point was upset with his teammate and let him know about it. He played with energy and when you combine that with his impressive skill-set it becomes very noticeable. Ryan consistently set up his teammates and was adept at masking his intentions with the puck on his stick, this led to his primary assist on Canadas opening goal after he threaded a pass to Williams in the right circle from below the goal-line as well.

Peyton Krebs (2019) – Krebs wasn't as dangerous against Sweden as he has been in some previous games but continues to show a varied attack characterized by deceptive gear shifts and the ability to process the play quickly while going at top speeds. His best scoring chance came after driving down the right wing and cutting directly towards the net before attempting to fire a quick wrist-shot far side, he changed the angle of his release while in tight to his body on the play as well. Below the goal-line he had a couple of impressive passing as well.

Kirby Dach (2019) – Dach had a great game for Canada by skating hard while simultaneously using his vision to set up his teammates for impressive scoring chances. He's a difficult player to contain due to his length, size and edges, which he used in combination when below the goal-line and around the net area to create havoc on several shifts. I would still like to see him shoot a bit more but today he did peel off a check and take a direct approach to the net and get his shot off. He also used his size effectively to set up screens and played a factor on Byram's game winning goal due to his presence in-front of the crease. Dach has excellent tools and has been consistent in using them during this event so far.

Dylan Cozens (2019) – Cozens wasn't as dominant against Sweden as he has been in some previous games but he still played a complete game. On the forecheck, he had a physical presence and this allowed him to generate a takeaway that led to a high-end scoring chance for his team. He continues to play with a lot of confidence when carrying the puck. This allowed him to make some high-risk plays near the offensive blueline where he protected the puck while on his backhand before peeling off pressure and re-opening his skating lanes. When his lanes were taken, he made quick decisions and wasn't forcing play, making accurate passes to his teammates consistently throughout the game. He didn't have any real high-end scoring chances today.

Sasha Mutala (2019) – Mutala has had a quiet tournament up to this game and although he only generated a couple of offensive chances, he was excellent away from the puck. His best offensive chance came after driving down the right-wing before releasing a quick wrist-shot that was labelled short-side, his release point is high-end. On the defensive-side, he was used on the penalty-kill and had several impressive plays. He showed good defensive awareness and used his stick to intercept a pass attempt before clearing the puck. On other sequences he backchecked effectively and applied pressure. With less than a minute to go, he stripped Holtz off the puck before making a clean transitional zone exit and fired a pass to Cozens which should have resulted in a primary assist but Cozens missed the open net after the goalie was pulled.

Josh Williams (2019) – Williams was dangerous for Canada today, needing very little time to get his shot off and was consistent at putting himself in good position to be set up for scoring chances around the slot area. He scored Canada's opening goal after receiving a pass from Suzuki and wiring a hard wrist-shot far-side, the placement was excellent. Later in the game he received a pass from Dach and almost buried his second goal of the game, the amount of power he was generating on his shots from a stationary position was impressive. Furthermore, he was effective in spurts on the forecheck and competed hard away from the puck. The skill and shot stood out against Sweden.

Bowen Byram (2019) – Byram played a complete game for Canada both with and without the puck. Byram isn't the biggest defenseman but he wasn't afraid to step-up and deliver puck separating hits which he did on a couple of sequences. His ability to assess the movement of opponents gives him the opportunity to time his checks appropriately and that was noticeable here. His transitional puck moving was on point, using his skating ability and poise while carrying the puck to make several clean transitional zone-exits and entries throughout the game. When walking the offensive-blueline, he had a coupe of exaggerated body feints that helped him re-open his shooting and passing lanes. He scored the game winning goal for Canada after firing a quick seeing-eye shot through traffic that found the back of the net on Wallstedt's glove-side. He was patient and controlled on the ice, rarely skating himself into corners or putting himself in a position where he had to make low-percentage plays.

Kaeden Korczak (2019) – Korczak had an excellent defensive game for Canada. He matched Broberg's skating ability with his gap control and defensive reads. On one sequence when Broberg was driving down the left wing after entering the zone, he cut off the skating lane in advance and used his stick to generate a takeaway before clearing the puck on the penalty-kill, shortly after, he anticipated Holtz's slap-pass and intercepted the puck resulting in an additional clear. Late in the game on the penalty-kill, Broberg attempted to cut below the goal-line and create a scoring chance but Korczak read the play in advance again and took away the angle for Broberg which led to a low percentage shot at a critical time. It was fitting that the final seconds of the game was him defending against Raymond with excellent positioning and anticipation, keeping the Swede to the outside and using a check to push him into the corner, taking away any chance Sweden had to generate a high-percentage shot. His play won't end up on the highlight reel but his defensive reads were impressive.

Matthew Robertson (2019) – Robertson had a good two-way game for Canada. Despite getting caught while attempting to carry the puck out of his own-end which resulted in Holtz's goal, Robertson played with poise in his own end and used his reach to counter his opponents. He showed some offense after skating from the left-circle towards the slot area before releasing a quick wrist-shot that went bar-down over Wallstedt who had gone down too early.

Canada vs USA, Hlinka Gretzky Cup, Aug 10 2018

Canada

Alexis Lafreniere (2020) – Lafreniere had a commanding game for Canada against the U.S. He displayed good chemistry with Parent today which led to two of Canada's goals. He opened the scoring for Canada after finishing a give and go sequence with Parent before using his soft hands to drug the puck past a defender's stick and then fired a hard wrist-shot under the arm of Wolf, the release point was high-end and it's a difficult shot to puck up due to Lafreniere's limited movement before he shoots. On the powerplay, he found Parent in the left circle for a primary assist. Another aspect of his game that stood out was his ability to enter the offensive zone cleanly while carrying the puck due to his ability to interpret pressure and where it's coming from rapidly. There are few players that are at this tournament if any that can assess how much time and space they have to make a play as well as Lafreniere.

Ryan Suzuki (2019) – Suzuki was notable in spurts but never really dominated any shifts or had consistent play. He continues to showcase his multi-faceted offensive skill-set, looking dangerous when releasing his impressive wrist-shot while also making high-end and difficult passes look relatively easy at times. When the speed of the game picked up and it became more physical it felt like Suzuki became less of a factor at times. He also was largely kept to the outside and had difficulty penetrating the defense when carrying the puck in the offensive end.

Jamieson Rees (2019) – Rees played with energy in a depth role and was effective in spurts. He used his speed in an attempt to generate from the left-wing, this led to him hitting the post after getting everything on a slap-shot from the left circle. He scored a goal by putting himself in good position in-front of the slot area and finding the puck in heavy traffic and shooting it past Wolf.

Peyton Krebs (2019) – Krebs had a solid game for Canada at both ends of the rink. He had several impressive scoring chances as a result of using his hands in motion while attacking the net slot area. His shots were hard but they were also largely inaccurate today. Despite his shot not finding its home, his passing ability was also present, showing an impressive combination of vision and passing ability to find his teammates consistently throughout the game. He set up the game winning goal after transitioning the puck from his own-end before showing impressive agility while skating into the slot area before stopping up and finding Williams with a pass. On the defensive-end, he displayed a high-compete level in order to knock the puck off his opponent resulting in a zone clear as well.

Kirby Dach (2019) – Dach was snake bitten against the States but one of the direct results of his inability to get a goal was due to his mixed decision making when assessing if he should pass or shoot, which is uncharacteristic of him. He's a primary playmaker and is a pass first-player with the mentality to look for his teammates, so it's expected that in certain high-scoring areas, he will still opt to pass off the puck. However, on one sequence as an example, he was sprung on a breakaway and instead of looking to generate a shot, he turned away from Wolf and kept the puck on his backhand, clearly showing the tell that he was going to pass back to Lafreniere who was coming in behind him, he then passed the puck off on a clean breakaway. He had a great scoring chance during a 2-on-1 with Krebs but he was slightly out of position which forced his shot wide when he attempted to shoot in one motion. He was still very good in certain sequences and can pass the puck at a high-level but his assessment of when to look for his shot was lagging behind his ability to assess when he should pass at times during today's game.

Dylan Cozens (2019) – Cozens scored arguably one of the most bazaar goals of his young hockey career but with that aside he used all his tools to dictate play on several shifts throughout the game. His shot has been mixed in certain contests throughout the tournament but today it was on point which made him dangerous when he had the puck. He snapped a hard wrist-shot that rang off the pipe from the right circle from a stationary position on the powerplay on one sequence and on several others, he threatened with it. On the last play of the game, he received a pass from Byram after finding soft-ice in the slot and rifled home a hard wrist-shot over Wolf's glove, however the game had ended before the puck crossed the line but due to a rule that no video review could be used, the goal counted. Regardless, the shot and the placement were excellent. Another aspect of his game today that stood out was his ability to transition the puck using his powerful stride to create separational speed. The last area of his game to note is that he was adept at switching his motor on the fly, adapting to soft-ice, open passing lanes, and clogged lanes at a high rate. This caused him to rarely force the play.

Xavier Parent (2019) – Parent had his best game of the tournament and contributed for Canada. He was playing with energy and threatened consistently with his shot. He set up lafreniere's opening goal and scored on the powerplay after firing a hard-wrist shot that had excellent placement. He's at his best when he plays at a fast-paced brand of hockey and today that was the case. In some previous viewings, his decision making was mixed and he had a couple of unforced turnovers, and although he had one in his own-end when attempting to exit the zone, for the most part he was reading the play and reacting well, leading to good decisions.

Sasha Mutala (2019) – Mutala had a couple of offensive flashes. He had a prime scoring chance all alone in the slot area, holding the puck for a second before pulling to his backhand but Wolf read the play well. He had a tremendous pass across the slot area to set up his teammate but it didn't result in an assist. On another sequence he used his frame to guard a puck that was knocked to him in the defensive-zone, under pressure he used a spin before transitioning back up ice and made a nice drop-pass to Cozens which set him up for a prime scoring chance. He wasn't a consistent offensive threat but he flashed his high talent level.

Samuel Poulin (2019) – Poulin, like Mutala is featured primarily in a depth-role, so it's difficult for them to find their game due to their decreased ice-time but he still had some impressive plays. He was dangerous while driving down the wing on one sequence and fired a hard and low wrist-shot that required Wolf to be alert. On another play, he showed plus creativity as he attempted to pull the puck between his legs in the slot area to quickly change angles of his shot. He also managed to create off a wrap-around late in the game and showed good skating ability.

Josh Williams (2019) – Williams displayed his shot and the ability to open himself up and find soft-ice to make it a threat. He was largely invisible for the majority of the game, but like most good shooters, he doesn't need a lot of time or space to generate scoring chances and that's what happened when he received a pass from Suzuki and fired home a high-end wrist-shot that Wolf was unable to track. Wolf has impressive tracking skills and good angles so for him to mistime when he needed to cut the angle down is a testament to how fast Williams can get his shot off. He scored the game winning goal after taking a pass from Krebs and firing a hard wrist-shot past Wolf's glove while in full motion. He didn't need anytime to settle the puck down. He only displayed one dimension to his game today but it was a very impressive dimension.

Justin Barron (2020) – Barron flashed his impressive offensive tool-kit while walking the line against the U.S. He has excellent four-way mobility characterized by impressive crossover mechanics which gives him the lateral mobility necessary to open-up his shooting lanes at a consistent rate. On one sequence, he faked his slapshot before simultaneously using his hands and feet to change the angle of his attack, then with his head up, he made a no-look pass to his teammate in the high-slot resulting in a good scoring chance. He's good at exaggerating his posture and movement which made it difficult for his opponents to read where he was attempting to transition the puck. This applied to both the defensive zone and offensive-end. He did make a defensive mistake that directly led to a goal against as a result of relying on his skating ability a little longer than he should have but overall, he was impressive.

Nolan Maier (2019) – Maier had a difficult start to the game for Canada but showed a competitive edge and battled back while making several difficult saves. He's not the biggest kid but he's technically above-average and read the play relatively well. His best save was during a 3-on-1 sequence where he correctly read the pass across the crease and sprawled across while kicking out his right pad to take away what looked like a sure goal, it was an athletic save and it came at a critical time during the game. Several of the goals that went past him were the result of impressive shots, however he was caught during a draw after failing to transition into his butterfly in time during Robertson's second goal of the game of a draw.

USA

Arthur Kaliyev (2019) – Kaliyev has had a disappointing tournament so far despite producing, unfortunately that continued against Canada. His best chance came in the slot area where he fired a wrist-shot that went wide. His release point is excellent and he needs no time to assess where he wants to place the puck however his play away from the puck left a lot to be desired. During sequences that required Kaliyev to enter another gear in order to try and retrieve the puck and during backchecking plays, his effort level was average to below average. Furthermore, in a game where the play was transitioning back and forth constantly with a lot of speed been used on both sides, Kaliyev was notably a step behind on some shifts. This was a result of his below average two-step area quickness and skating mechanics. He has an excellent shot but he had relied on too much while not showing other attributes consistently.

Aaron Huglen (2019) – Despite Huglen playing in a depth role, he managed to generate several offensive chances early in the contest. He scored the second goal of the game after collecting the puck below the goal-line and making a lacrosse-style volley that surprised Maier. The goal displayed an impressive level of skill. Shortly after his goal, he found himself on a partial breakaway after getting behind the Canadian defense, he opted to shoot a low wrist-shot far side but Maier cut down the angle. He had an impressive forechecking sequence as well, out-competing a Canadian defenseman for a loose puck before delivering a sharp pass around the net resulting in a high-end scoring chance for his team. His play tapered off after the opening frame but it was still one of his more noticeable performances.

Robert Mastrosimone (2019) – Mastrosimone started slowly but picked up his play in the second half of the game, generating several offensive chances for his teammates. Despite having average mobility and a busy stride he used his head to keep pace with the opposition. On one sequence, he jumped directly over the boards at a perfect time to intercept a pass in the neutral zone and on another play, he generated a three-on-one scoring chance after reading Barron's movement as he transitioned over the offensive-blueline and stripped him of the puck before moving it back up ice, then set Salianoff up for a prime scoring chance with a sharp and accurate pass. In the third period he fired a heavy wrist-shot that handcuffed Maier that almost resulted in a goal. He showed today that he can play with faster players and against faster players than himself by anticipating the play while also making decisions quickly. The last area to note with Mastrosimone is that he was once again a multi-faceted offensive-threat by being dangerous near the goal-line and from the high-slot both with his pass and his shot.

Nicholas Robertson (2019) – Robertson had a game to remember by recording a hattrick while flashing a high-octane motor. On the defensive side he made an excellent diving stick-on-puck play that took away a cross crease pass attempt and wasn't afraid to play deep in his own-end. Although his diving play was impressive and at times he played deep in his own-end to support his defense, it was his offensive game that really stood out. He scored three goals showing a diverse array of shots and skills. His opening goal was from a stationary position while on the powerplay in the left circle, where he picked the top corner, the release was impressive and the shot had velocity on it. His second goal of the game was the result of him getting a jump on Suzuki off the draw directly after Suzuki had taken a faceoff, he quickly got behind the defense and shot a low backhand shot before Maier could enter his butterfly. The third goal of the game was a result of Robertson burying an accurate wrist-shot that popped the bottle while in motion. He showed he can score in multiple ways out there. One interesting aspect of his game is how reliant he is on slipping checks with his elusive play due to not having a great top gear.

Josh Nodler (2019) – Nodler had a good performance for the U.S. by making several impressive passes while also threatening with his shot. He played the half-wall on the powerplay and was an efficient puck distributor. He had the primary assist on the opening goal of the game by delivering a sharp and accurate pass across the ice to Robertson who was parked in the left circle. He displayed the ability to shoot in motion while moving laterally across the high-slot before releasing a dangerous wrist-shot that missed far-side. On another sequence, he made a sharp pass to his teammate for another quality scoring chance near the goal-line. This was one of his better performances at this event.

Luke Toporowski (2019) – Toporowski had a complete game for the U.S. He had an aggressive backchecking sequence on Cozens who wasn't aware of Luke who then used a stick-lift to generate a takeaway before moving the puck back up ice. On another defensive-play, he helped support his defense by keeping Krebs to the outside who was attempting to cut towards the net. His most impressive play was a rush through all three zones where he received a pass that was behind him in his own-end, he pulled the puck between his legs with one hand while in motion then took off up the ice before side-stepping Schneider and entering the offensive-zone where he got a quick wrist-shot on net before falling to the ice, It was an impressive display of skill. He also scored a goal by being well positioned in-front of the slot area and fired a quick shot that went past Maier who wasn't set on the play.

Luke Reid (2020) – Reid had a good defensive effort game against Canada, displaying the ability to play bigger than his size when needed while showing some poise under pressure. He has plus edges and used them to spin off pressure behind his own goal-line, he also displayed grit by taking an elbow by Lafreniere directly in the face but never attempted to draw the penalty by embellishing during the sequence, opting to play hard and show that it didn't affect him. He did a good job of boxing out the much bigger Dach around the net area on one sequence and got into an altercation with him briefly, he wasn't backing down out there. He transitioned the puck smoothly into the offensive zone on a couple of different plays and skated hard when caught out of position which was seen during a rush attempt by Rees.

Mike Koster (2019) – Koster had a good two-way performance against Canada and once again showed a high-level transitional skillset. His mobility is decent and he can generate a separating gear which was noticeable against a fast Canada squad. When he was carrying the puck, he displayed confidence and poise which led to several clean transitional zone entries and exits. He threatened with his shot from the blueline, showing a reduced wind-up which allowed him to get his shot off quickly. Even though he didn't lean too heavily into his shots, they generated a decent amount of power and he managed to get a couple through traffic. One play that was good to see was when he stuck up for Wolf when a Canadian player refused to move after the whistle in-front of his goalie, so he grabbed the bigger opponent and attempted to throw him to the side despite being on the smaller side. One play that he would want back was in the last 30 seconds of the game. He decided to try and end the game with a shot from his own-end but it missed the net, resulting in an icing. His decision was the catalyst for Canada's game tying goal in the last second of the game.

Dustin Wolf (2019) – Wolf played better than his state line would suggest. He wasn't as confident today as he was in previous viewings at cutting down angles and didn't read the play in heavy traffic as effectively either. However, he did still show impressive reflexes and had the best save of the tournament so far. After giving up a rebound, Krebs had an open net to shoot at but Wolf lunged across and got his glove on the point-blank shot, it was a remarkable effort. Furthermore, although technically sound, the play demonstrated that he can break his technique in order to make an unorthodox save when called upon to do so. One other area to note was that he didn't look shaken after giving up any of the goals that went by him, he remained calm and poised throughout the fast-paced game.

Russia vs Sweden, Hlinka Gretzky Cup, Aug 10 2018

Russia

Yegor Spiridonov (2019) – Spiridonov has had a disappointing tournament but he was more active in the offensive-end this game and competed consistently. He had a deflection in traffic after tipping a shot from the point, and he looked to generate low wrist-shots through traffic. He had a terrific backcheck where he used a well-timed stick-lift to take the puck away before transitioning back into the offensive-end. On the powerplay he was used along the half-wall and managed a couple of impressive transitional zone entries before stopping up to set up the man-advantage. Although it was a better performance, he still didn't dominate a shift or flash any dynamic qualities.

Yaroslav Likhachyov (2019) – Likhachyov skated well today and attacked the Swedish defense while displaying impressive hands. He wasn't always successful and coughed the puck up a couple of times however he also drew two penalties as a direct result of using his quick hands to gain an advantage on the Swedish defense who were forced to hook him. He made a tremendous pass on his backhand that was threaded through a tight-seem but his teammate mishandled the puck. He was better last game but he certainly flashed skill out there today and looked to penetrate the defense. He doesn't need linemates to create plays and he showed that he can be a primary driver of play at times.

Daniil Gutik (2019) – Gutik was average against Sweden and didn't really get any high-end scoring chances. He was most dangerous on the powerplay where he used extra space to set up his teammates. He executed a crisp pass across the slot to Podkolzin for what could have been a high-end chance but Vasili fanned on the attempt. Behind the goal-line he flashed his superb hands while also demonstrating poise under pressure to maintain puck possession before setting up Amirov for a good scoring chance in the slot area. With the exception of those plays he was relatively quiet considering his talent level.

Vasili Podkolzin (2019) – Podkolzin was the best Russian on the ice, showing a variety of high-level attributes to penetrate the opposition. He took a bit of time to get going and missed on a good chance early but as the game progressed he became increasingly dangerous. He's unorthodox in the sense that he gets around the ice fine despite having an awkward stride and his shot is very dangerous despite having a lot of movement before the release point. This could be seen when he cut across the slot area before pulling the puck and firing a shot far-side and on several other plays. He scored the only Russian goal after a brilliant end to end rush where he split through the defense and from his knees, backhanded a shot past Alnefelt.

Rodian Amirov (2020) – Amirov had a good offensive effort, getting multiple shots on net and consistently finding open skating and shooting lanes. His best chance came from the slot area after receiving a pass from Gutik and firing a low shot short-side. Another area to note is that after firing his initial shots he skated hard and competed when attempting to get the puck back.

Ilya Nikolayev (2019) – Nikolayev had a couple of impressive sequences against Sweden. He looked to attack the defense one-on-one and was successful using his quick hands to evade sticks and bypass players. He had an excellent block from his knees in his own-end that stopped a scoring chance as well. Although against Sweden he wasn't as effective at getting his shot off as he was against the U.S.

Roman Bychkov (2019) – Bychkov was used on the powerplay and looked to fire the puck as often as he could. He's got a big wind-up but he was capable of using it as a fake to get the Swedish defense to bite before moving to re-open his lanes. He also displayed a capable first pass and didn't do anything in the defensive end to hurt his team. His shot appeared to be his most impressive attribute based off today's performance.

Artemi Knyazev (2019) – Knyazev had a couple of plus transitional plays and dealt with pressure relatively well in his own-end yet still has shown little in the way of offensive-upside. He fired a couple of point shots that were low and well-timed with screens however he still hasn't looked confident holding onto the puck for extended periods of time or attempted to penetrate the defense with skill. That been said, he was calm and assertive in his own-end when dealing with pressure, rarely getting caught off guard. During sequences where he required to enter another gear, he was able to, and this allowed him to skate the puck out of dangerous areas of the ice on a couple of shifts.

Dmitri Tyuvilin (2019) – Tyuvulin had a solid two-way performance against Sweden. He had a terrific shot blocking sequence where he got in the way of two separate scoring attempts before skating hard after the puck, he inadvertently took a penalty on the play but he showed a good level of compete on the sequence overall. Under pressure, he looked calm and collected when holding onto the puck, though he did have mixed results with his first pass, some of them were inaccurate. On the powerplay he carried the puck and showed above average mobility before making a couple of clean transitional zone entries. When walking the line, he used a couple of fakes to re-configure his lanes and was active.

Yaroslav Askarov (2020) – Despite getting limited action in the first frame, Askarov showcased several impressive attributes. It's difficult for a goalie to zone in on the play when only facing a few shots, yet his best save came when he had limited shot volume and directly after coming out from the locker room during the intermission. He read Raymonds pass attempt and pushed off laterally across the crease where he kicked out his pad and absorbed Holtz's shot. During a penalty-kill, Holtz broke down his defense which required Askarov to come out and make two impressive back to back saves. His rebound control was a plus, as were his reads and glove hand. He would have liked to have the game winning goal back, he was caught by Henriksson cheating off the post when he expected a pass to be delivered in the slot to Holtz, but with the exception of the game winning goal, he was solid.

Sweden

Elmer Soderblom (2019) – Soderblom didn't get too many opportunities offensively and wasn't overly involved in the play. His best plays were away from the puck where he used his size and showed plus anticipation to take away shooting lanes resulting in multiple blocked shots. His best scoring chance came off a backhander attempt where he used his length to try and tuck the puck far-side. His hands looked above-average out there today. His wrists are flexible, he has length, and he's coordinated which allows him to create scoring chances one-on-one.

Lucas Raymond (2020) - Raymond had an average game based off his previous work at this tournament but was still impressive relative to most other kids on the ice. He was dangerous on the rush as the game progressed and continues to display a versatile attack. He recognized when his shooting and skating lanes were blocked and showed good pivoting mechanics to stop up and turn on a dime to create passing plays. He set up Holtz for a prime scoring chance early in the second that required the best save of the game by Askarov. He plays with a lot of speed and as a result when he slows his play down, it threw off the Russian defense and allowed him additional room to make plays. The game winning goal was a result of this, as he burst down the left wing before stopping up and passed the puck across the high-slot to Henriksson for the game winning goal. His vision and skating ability were his most notable attributes today.

Karl Henriksson (2019) – Henriksson played well with Raymond and Holtz, showing some chemistry off the rush. He had a prime scoring chance after finding himself in the slot area and getting a pass from Raymond that he fired far-side, the shot missed but it was hard and came off his stick at an above average rate. He scored the game winning goal after recognizing that Askarov hadn't squared up and was cheating off his post. It was good to see him adapt to what the Russian netminder was giving him on the fly instead of opting to attempt the pass to his teammate. He's had a mixed tournament for us but he flashed some offense today and continues to play with speed.

Alexander Holtz (2020) – After looking to shoot the puck more against Canada, Holtz once again had several impressive scoring chances. He was robbed point blank by Askarov at the start of the second but the main takeaway from the attempt was how quickly he could get leverage under the puck in one motion from the pass. During the powerplay he rushed down into the slot area and fired two consecutive shots that generated a lot of power and were difficult to gauge. He was slowing the play down at the start of this tournament but has adjusted his game and is playing with more speed while also being more assertive on the ice when looking to shoot in his last couple of performances.

Tobias Bjornfot (2019) – Bjornfot had a very impressive defensive game while also transitioning the puck consistently. Against an impressive Russian forward group, Bjornfot seemed to have all the tools necessary to shut them down, with the exception of Podkolzin's tremendous rush, Tobias was sound defensively. He had well timed shot blocks, good poke checks, and used his frame to keep his opponents to the outside when they attempted to drive wide. His most impressive play that highlighted this was against Gushchin, where he anticipated the small Russians cut towards the net and used his frame to angle him to the side resulting in a lost scoring chance. With Podkolzin pressure him, he demonstrated his impressive four-way mobility, skating backwards with the puck before pivoting and angling his frame away from Vasili's stick, he then carried the puck cleanly through all three zones. He showed today and in other viewings that he can stop players from driving wide on him, deflect shots with his stick, block shots, get into shooting lanes in advance of the play, and make sharp and accurate outlet passes to get the puck out of his own-end. Unfortunately, like in previous viewings, he's still showing a rudimentary offensive game.

Philip Broberg (2019) – Broberg was excellent against Russia, showing a 200-foot game in another stand-out performance. He's been difficult for teams to contain and that was no different today, he showed his speed and transitioned the puck effortlessly at times. He had an end-to-end rush that was only matched by Podkolzin's attempt, where he drove wide on the defense and cut across the crease before shooting a low backhander that went off the post and bounced towards Askarov. He scored the opening goal of the game after recognizing that the Russian netminder was screened, shooting a hard wrist-shot from the blueline that went in blocker side. He didn't flash much skill in the offensive-end but his shot was powerful and he used his skating ability to create chances. On the defensive side he was impressive. He used his frame to effectively battle in the corners and delivered a couple of well time checks to disrupt the Russian attack, he also positioned himself well and used an active stick to break up a couple of plays. The drawback here and in some other contests is he still has had inconsistencies when trying to pass the puck to his teammates, has shown mixed decision making at times and hasn't displayed high-end skill or advanced fakes at the line.

Hugo Alnefelt (2019) – Alnefelt had a solid performance for Sweden, showing plus reads and athleticism. He's capable of fully extending during primary and secondary scoring chances and this allows him to take away a large portion of the net away, specifically with low shots. During attempts that were labelled high, he was good at assessing his angles and cutting them down aggressively before squaring up. Additionally, his rebound control was impressive and he absorbed several shots throughout the game. Another area to note was that he was good at finding pucks through heavy traffic on point shots and displayed plus reflexes when he needed to extend himself.

Windsor Spitfires vs Guelph Storm, Sept 20, 2018

Windsor -

Piiroinen, Kari (2019) – Piiroinen played well in his first start of the season for the Spitfires, showcasing a technical butterfly and good rebound control while picking up the win. He was tested early and often yet offered very little in the way of rebounds due to absorbing the majority of shots he faced. Furthermore, he transitioned into his butterfly quickly, sealed his arms within his butterfly which offered little room for shooters, and didn't go down too early on most shot attempts. Another aspect of his game that stood out was his crease containment, he rarely threw himself out of position while using plus edges. Lastly, he's not the biggest goalie, standing 6 feet but was willing to challenge shooters to cut down the angle on most shot attempts.

Ladd, Grayson (2019) – Ladd was featured on the second pairing with Starikov and had a solid outing by playing a physical and up-tempo brand of hockey in his own-end while also anticipating the play in the offensive-end at times. In the defensive side, he showed that he could out-compete his opponents during loose puck situations along the boards. On one specific play he out muscled two separate players while demonstrating that he understood how to use leverage to win the physical battle, his motor and willingness to engage bigger guys despite his smaller size stood out. In the offensive-end, he had a well-timed pinch that led to a quality scoring opportunity, but rarely held the puck for extended periods of time.

Staois, Nathan (2019) – Staois was featured on the top pairing and had a decent two-way effort. Despite being an undersized defenseman, he was willing to commit physically and competed, recovered quickly during a couple of defensive lapses and showed good lateral mobility while walking the line. He made a defensive error early, not settling down and recognizing his options before throwing a pass that landed on the stick of a Guelph player, this led to a scoring opportunity but Staois was quick to react and attempt to cut down his gap which disrupted the play. During a couple of dump-in sequences, he was quick to collect the puck before looking to find his options and his lateral movement gave him escape ability. In the offensive zone he didn't threaten too often but did show plus lateral movement as he skated around a player before delivering a hard shot from his knee that went over the top of the net.

Starikov, Lev (2019) – Starikov's a massive defender standing 6'7 but has a decent amount of coordination for his size and flashed a unique set of tools. He maintained a solid gap on a couple of different sequences, but had inconsistent positioning at times caused by over-playing his man. On sequences where he lost a step, he showed that he can recover. On one play, he was cut aggressively on but made a diving poke check that caused a turnover. Around the goal-line and around the net area he didn't take advantage of his physical gifts at the rate he could have, showing little in the way of a mean streak or physically overwhelming smaller players, instead relying on his length too often. At the blueline he was featured on the powerplay and scored a goal directly after a Spitfire powerplay expired by pinching at the appropriate time and getting two separate opportunities on the same sequence. His wrist-shot generated power and looked more threatening than his slapshot today.

Cuylle, Will (2020) – Cuylle had a successful OHL debut, scoring his first goal and consistently threatening with the puck on his stick. He displayed good anticipation away from the puck in the offensive zone and this allowed him to find soft-ice consistently. He's a big kid and wasn't afraid to position himself in high-traffic areas around the slot area which is where the majority of his scoring chances came from him. His goal was the result of finding soft-ice and getting a quick and low wrist-shot off from a stationary position. On other shooting attempts, he showed that he can shoot while in motion and generated power.

Foudy, Jean-Luc (2020) – Despite playing on the 4th line, Foudy stood out with his impressive skating mechanics and playmaking skills. Similar to his brother, he's an excellent skater who displayed an efficient and powerful stride that also featured a deep knee bend. His speed forced the Guelph defense to respect him and this gave him time to find his teammates with accurate and sharp passes throughout the game. Although he showed a passing instinct more than a shooting instinct, he did mix up his options by showing an awareness of when his passing lane was closed or open and generated primarily off the rush. He had the primary assist on the game winning goal in overtime, where he threaded a crisp pass across the slot to his teammate after coming down the wing with speed.

Guelph -

Chayka, Daniil (2021) – Despite being the youngest player featured in the game, Chayka was given responsibility on the top-pairing and looked mature for his age in all three zones. He played with a good level of composure and was aware in his own-end of the ice, but wasn't overly tenacious in his own-zone either. He's already a pretty big kid and is also highly mobile, showing good skating mechanics which allowed him to transition the puck up the ice. In the offensive-zone, he didn't look overly flashy or try anything dynamic but moved the puck efficiently on the powerplay at times.

Woolley, Mark (2020) – Woolley had a solid two-way performance for Guelph. In his own-end, he delivered a couple of clean shoulder hits, one of them knocked his opponent to the ice and separated the puck. Under pressure, he assessed his options well and made several transitional plays that led to clean zone exits by passing the puck up the ice. He delivered the best hit of the game in the neutral zone, where he caught his man in open-ice and delivered a momentum swinging hit. In the offensive-zone, he had a well-timed pinch which led to a scoring opportunity after he fired a low wrist-shot that resulted in a big rebound.

Bertuzzi, Tag (2019) – Bertuzzi didn't control play often in the offensive zone but did generate several scoring chances throughout the game and displayed plus puck skills. He looked to cut wide and was aggressive at entering high-traffic areas, this gave him two prime scoring opportunities that he didn't manage to execute on but the positioning during the attempts were good. He had several nice passing plays while in motion and on the powerplay he showed a plus set of hands in the slot area, pulling the puck quickly around his opponent while assessing how much time and space he had.

Primeau, Mason (2019) – Despite getting first line minutes, Primeau rarely was engaged offensively and didn't do enough to really stand out. He was active on the forecheck during a sequence early and generated a takeaway from below the goal-line, on another shift he managed to fire a wrist-shot short-side from the right-circle but it never threatened and with the exceptions of those plays he didn't generate too often.

Guelph Storm vs Sudbury Wolves, Sept 21, 2018

Guelph Storm

Chayka, Daniil (2021) - Chayka was more involved offensively today than he was in his previous outing and had a couple of nice defensive reads away from the puck. When walking the line during the powerplay, he showed poise, out-waiting his opponent who had pressured him at the line and attempted to cut off his passing lane, Daniil assessed the time and space he had before moving laterally to re-open his passing lane which led to a redirection scoring chance. His best scoring chance came late in the high-slot where he fires a hard wrist-shot that missed the net far-side, his shot was hard to pick up and he generated a lot of momentum without a lot of movement. In his own-end he still didn't display a high-end motor but used his frame and positioning to position Sudbury players who were attempting to cut in on him, to the outside. He had an excellent diving sequence late during a 2-on-1 where he read the pass attempt correctly and took away what would have been a high-quality scoring chance.

Woolley, Mark (2020) – Woolley had a good game for the Storm on both sides of the puck. His skating mechanics hinder his ability to quickly evade pressure on the forecheck but Mark demonstrated an excellent first pass against Sudbury to compensate for his mobility, consistently finding his teammates despite having limited time on most attempts with hard and accurate stretch passes. His best pass was an end-to-end stretch pass which he threaded through multiple playesr and landed on the tape of Bertuzzi which set up a high-percentage scoring chance for the winger. His defensive positioning away from the puck was above-average and he used his big frame effectively during down-low sequences around his net area. In the offensive zone, he fired hard and low slapshots with a reduced wind-up and had success getting them through traffic; his opening slapshot hit the post.

Bertuzzi, Tag (2019) – Bertuzzi didn't have any stand-out shifts or drive play for his line but he did have a couple of high-end scoring chances. He had a nice one-touch give and go sequence with his teammate in the high-slot resulting in a quality scoring chance during a powerplay, yet similar to yesterday he shot the puck wide. On another attempt, he moved laterally aggressively across the slot to re-open his shooting lane while under pressure before getting a low shot. His best scoring chance came after receiving a pass from Woolley which gave him a lot of time and space to set up his shot but he telegraphed the location with his mechanics. Although he did display better accuracy today, his rate of execution wasn't high.

Sudbury Wolves

Ross, Liam (2019) - Ross had a solid effort for Sudbury resulting in a goal while also shutting down Guelph on the penalty-kill. He's a big kid and drove a Guelph opponent into the side of his own-net early which resulted in a penalty but the power generated was impressive on the hit. His defensive positioning was passable on the penalty-kill and he wasn't afraid to clog-lanes when needed. Offensively, he kept his game simple at the blueline, but he did have a terrific pinch which resulted in his first goal of the season by finding soft-ice near the slot area before firing a hard wrist-shot while in motion, the shot fooled Popovich. Away from the puck, he had a good play in the neutral zone resulting in a takeaway after anticipating a pass attempt.

Wawrow, Drew (2019) – Wawrow won't show up on the highlight reel for his performance but he had an impressive defensive game, showing a combination of poise and elusiveness under pressure which allowed him to transition the puck out of his own-end consistently. He displayed plus edges by spinning off and pivoting suddenly while simultaneously assessing the play quickly during sequences where he was tasked with moving the puck to his teammates and did so at a high-rate throughout the game. He wasn't as effective in the offensive-zone as he was in the defensive-zone, but did have a nice play where he was pressured but side-stepped his opponent before delivering an accurate pass. He rarely made mistakes and was a big reason why Sudbury managed to transitional cleanly out of their own-end.

Byfield, Quinton (2020) – Byfield came into today's game with a lot of hype and lived up to that hype by having a solid offensive performance which included a primary assist and his first goal of the season. The first thing that stands out about Quinton are the tools, he has a big frame yet is elusive and very coordinated for his build and age. Furthermore, he demonstrated high-end puck-skills, and when combined with his agility and power, it made him difficult to contain during rush sequences and during one-on-one situations. His primary assist came off a quick and hard wrist-shot from the right circle which was difficult to absorb and his goal was the result of a breakaway where he showed a deep knee bend that allowed him to stay ahead of the defense that was chasing him before burying a backhand goal. On that goal and other plays, he showed that he can use an impressive set of hands while in motion, specifically on a play in the neutral zone, he had the puck get behind him but kicked it from his skate before pulling the puck with one-arm, the skill was apparent. Byfield also displayed a willingness to use his size effectively when entering high-traffic areas and wasn't playing on the perimeter, showing a tenacious approach at times when carrying the puck. Lastly, his wrist-shot didn't have tells and was difficult to read, yet he was good at assessing his passing options as well.

Murray, Blake (2019) – Murray had a relatively quiet game where he didn't get himself in a position to score. He did have a strong sequence below the goal-line where he controlled the tempo of play and found his teammates with a couple of sharp passes that reached the offensive blueline and on a couple of other sequences delivered some accurate passes but was largely kept to the outside and looked comfortable playing from the perimeter. He did manage to get his shot off at the bottom of the right circle, the release point was very good, but he never managed to find soft-ice consistently and rarely threatened despite showing impressive offensive tools.

Hamilton Bulldogs vs Barrie Colts, Sept 22 2018

Hamilton -

Jenkins, Frank (2020) – Jenkins was Renwick's defensive partner and faired slightly better in his own zone but still had difficulty with the forecheck at times. He was given a lot of time and space to make a bank pass up to his teammate on one play, but mis assessed the forecheck and turned the puck over. Behind his own-goal line, he was physically out muscled and lost control of the puck on a couple of different sequences. That being said, he did have success at times at finding an open-teammate with a first pass that allowed a breakout to happen but it wasn't at a consistent level.

Renwick, Michael (2020) – Renwick had a difficult game in his own end of the ice for the Bulldogs. He had difficulty assessing how much time he had under pressure and was responsible for turning the puck over multiple times in his own-end. When holding the puck, there was a lack of assessment and forced passes. During a pinch attempt, he did generate a good passing play that resulted in a high-end scoring chance, but was caught behind the net which resulted in an offensive chance against as well. It was a difficult game for Michael.

Fleischer, Tim (2019) – Fleischer made some opportunistic plays around the net area and was effective in spurts. He showed good composure in the neutral zone while protecting the puck and made several accurate passes throughout the game. His best scoring chances came off of rebound opportunities where he positioned himself well. Tim didn't display any dynamic qualities out there though.

Kaliyev, Arthur (2019) – Kaliyev was dangerous on the powerplay and processed offensive plays quickly. He wasn't consistent at even strength and wasn't a factor in loose puck battles or races to pucks but he was extremely dangerous from stationary positions in the right circle on the powerplay. His puck-skills stand out and they allow him to be deceptive with his release point. He scored a goal from the right circle by faking a slapshot before changing the angle and burying a sharp off-angle wrist-shot. Furthermore, both his slapshot and wrist-shot were dangerous today yet he was still capable of assessing his passing options while setting up his release which allowed him to distribute the puck efficiently as well. Arthur's skills stood out but so did his lack of motor at times.

Barrie -

Allensen, Nathan (2019) – Allensen competed and was physical in his own zone while also getting some powerplay time. He played with a mean streak today despite being a smaller defender by delivering a crushing hit in the high-slot on one play, and working hard along the boards consistently while not being afraid to play with an edge. He made life difficult for players who were looking to gain a position in the slot area and was aggressive when attempting to box out his opponents. His gap control was above average and he used an active stick to intercept a pass attempt on one play. He had some powerplay time but with the exception of a low slapshot from the point, he didn't generate much in the way of offense but did display a motor.

Piercey, Riley (2020) – Piercey had a decent game for the Colts by having an effective forecheck and creating pressure against the Bulldogs defense that looked overwhelmed on some shifts. He competed hard without the puck and on a couple of sequences along the boards in the offensive-zone showed that he was willing to physically engage. He had two prime scoring chances, one from the left circle where he looked to put the puck short-side and another where he aggressively cut into a heavy traffic area and delivered a backhand shot that resulted in an assist. He played at a good pace, was tenacious at times and stood out in spurts despite receiving limited minutes.

Suzuki, Ryan (2019) – Suzuki had an effective two-way performance for the Colts but let his playmaking instincts cloud his ability to gauge when he had an open-shooting lane at times which reduced the amount of scoring chances he should have had. He showed a good amount of deception in his game both at even-strength and on the powerplay, where he would use head fakes and angle himself to misguide his opponents into thinking he was going to shoot before delivering some impressive passes. However, he tended to look for the pass despite having found himself in a prime scoring chance directly in the slot area, this was a consist issue today and occurred multiple times. Away from the puck,

Seattle Thunderbirds vs Portland Winterhawks, September 22, 2018

Seattle

Mount, Payton- Confidence grew throughout the game. Played a strong possession game in the 3rd and made a couple nice low to high passes.

Hamaliuk, Dillon- Finished the game with a goal and two assists. Looked strong on the puck and was really pushing guys around out there. Has above average puckhandling ability and made some creative moves in the offensive zone. Both his assists were plays where he forced a turnover, went around the defenseman and made a nice pass to a teammate for a tap in. Dillon was throwing checks whenever he had a chance with a couple of really big hits.

Huo, Samuel- Lanky center played a very defensive game. Used his reach to disrupt plays and poke pucks away. Lacked touch with the puck on his stick.

Bryks, Graeme- Was involved in the play a lot but looked really raw and unpolished. His hands and skating really look like a work in progress but he had a couple plays where he flashed above average vision.

Kubicek, Simon- Was out there on the first powerplay unit and made a lot of safe, low risk passes. He was very effective on the breakout as well and also played solid defensive game forcing forwards away from dangerous areas.

Lee, Jake- Looked in control of every situation he was involved in tonight. Barely put a foot wrong, with the puck getting out of his zone on a tape to tape pass every time he touched it. Lee did not force anything and did a great job using his body to hold players off until the right play opened up. Very hard and accurate shot that he got on net a lot. Defensively his positioning was excellent both on the rush and in the zone, keeping play to the outside. He showed that he is physically clearly stronger than almost anyone out there.

Williams, Owen- Scored a goal after jumping in to the rush as a trailer. Williams looks like an above average skater with some offensive instinct.

Portland

Newkirk, Reece- Reece was very calm and confident whenever he was on the ice. Had a couple nice passes to his teammates with one leading to a solid chance in the high slot. He did look somewhat reluctant to shoot the puck.

Jarvis, Seth- Very good first WHL game as the 16 year old picked up 2 goals. Jarvis is very quick and used his speed to split the D on a couple occasions, drawing penalties two shifts in a row. He also showcased a high end release on both of his goals with two finishes up high that gave the goalie no chance.

Hanas, Cross- Showed a lot of speed on the rush and was very confident carrying the puck through the neutral zone. He had a nice assist by outwaiting a sliding defenseman and giving his teammate a perfect backdoor feed. Overall his vision as a passer looked good as he showed a lot of creativity. Lack of strength really showed as he was easily outmuscled when he engaged in battles.

Hanas, Clay- Solid skating defenseman had a tough night. Hockey sense looked suspect with a couple passes straight to the other team's tape. He was also badly outmuscled by a forward driving the net for a goal against.

Niagara Icedogs vs Mississauga Steelheads, Sept 23 2018

Niagara -

Constantinou, Billy (2019) – Constantinou flashed a two-way game against the Steelheads while also getting some powerplay opportunities. He was pressured in his own-end at times but responded well, displaying plus agility while protecting the puck, though he also had a couple of turnovers as a result of failing to escape along the goal-line at times. Another thing to note in the defensive zone was that he kept a good pace and tracked his man well when they were carrying the puck. One of his better sequences came on the powerplay after the puck was turned over, he maintained a good gap and used an active stick to generate a takeaway before transitioning back up ice. At the offensive-line he looked comfortable under pressure and used several shot fakes to freeze opponents before distributing the puck.

Sopa, Kyen (2019) – Kyen Sopa wasn't consistent on a shift-to-shift basis but did generate a couple of scoring chances throughout the game while showing that he wasn't afraid to drive to the hard areas of the ice. He flashed some skill while driving down the right-wing and releasing a quick wrist-shot that caught Ingham flat-footed but was stopped. On other sequences he attacked the net and had a couple of dangerous give and go sequences, showing an accurate shot and made a couple of passes.

Tomasino, Phillip (2019) – Tomasino had a solid performance while playing with Thomas and Lodnia, he didn't drive play to the same degree they did but he also showed that he can be more than a passenger with other skilled players. He displayed an above-average amount of offensive-awareness by finding soft-ice in high-percentage shooting areas several times throughout the game. Furthermore, he was good at assessing when he needed to mix up his passing and shooting options and had a plus rate of execution.

Mississauga -

Harley, Thomas (2019) – Thomas Harley had a solid offensive game while quarter-backing the powerplay yet was mixed in his own-end of the ice and had difficulty reacting to transitional play away from the puck at times. Harley looked to pinch, his most successful attempt came from the boards where he flashed some skill while carrying the puck while cutting through the slot area before delivering a backhand on net. He was consistent at getting low shots from the point through traffic during the powerplay due to being able to gauge when his lanes were open and closed for the most part. Although he was an offensive catalyst at times, his defense wasn't consistent. He did have an active stick on one play and defended a one-on-one situation well, but on several others, he misinterpreted his gap and his positioning, which directly led to goal against. In the neutral zone, he was late to react to certain transitional plays, and this led to him taking a critical penalty that cost his team a goal. Lastly, his motor and pacing was below-average, he didn't make life difficult for the opposing team.

Hardie, James (2020) – Hardie displayed tenacity and a shoot-first mentality against the Ice-Dogs. He wasn't afraid to enter high-traffic areas and looked to challenge the defense during one-on-one situations. He preferred to shoot the puck and showed an above-average release while also using screens to deceive Dhillon. On the forecheck, he played much bigger than his size, throwing his weight around consistently and forcing the defense to play heavy minutes below the goal-line.

Reisnecker, Filip (2020) – Reisnecker is looking to duplicate some of Leon Draisaitl's success after coming over from Germany and was successful in doing just that by scoring a goal today. He took a big hit down below the goal-line where he was caught with his head down and was taken out of the game but made a return and didn't play with any hesitation or fear as a result. He wasn't overly consistent but did show both plus passing skills and the ability to shoot the puck from distance. He fired a hard and low wrist-shot while in motion that was placed well that went into the back of the net and had a couple of impressive give-and-go sequences with his teammates. There was versatility within his skill-set.

Schwindt, Cole (2019) – Schwindt wasn't a driver of play but did generate scoring chances by scoring a sharp goal after finding soft-ice in the slot area with the man-advantage, he didn't hesitate on the shot and shot is in one motion which didn't give Dhillon time to get set. Later in the game he had another prime scoring chance and showed that he can elevate the puck quickly. He managed to find soft-ice and was consistent at anticipating where his teammates were attempting to find him.

Washkurak, Keean (2019) – Washkurak had an excellent offensive performance, finishing with 4 points while playing at a high-pace which made him a factor both with and without the puck. He was relentless on the forecheck and created pressure which led to a turnover where he collected the puck and made a quick backhand pass to his teammate in the slot for a prime scoring chance. That play set the tone for his game the rest of the way, consistently moving his feet and remaining active which allowed him to out-pace Niagara on some shifts. He buried a quick wrist-shot off a pass across the top of the crease but his most impressive effort came on an individual rush where he drove down the right wing before moving the puck through heavy traffic, where he delivered a quick wrist-shot that went off a skate and into the net. Keean had difficulty finishing in some of our viewings last season but didn't have that issue today.

Edmonton Oil Kings vs. Medicine Hat Tigers, September 26, 2018

Edmonton Oil Kings

Alexander, Jacson- Played a very solid game tonight with almost no mistakes. Was calm under pressure, constantly making the right play on the breakout. Offensively was engaged but didn't show much creativity with the puck on his stick.

Alistrov, Vladimir- Had a very slow start but picked it up as the game wore on. After the first period he seemingly had a shot on goal every shift. Alistrov generated odd man rushes with his surprising speed and showed the ability to both pass and shoot in these situations. He looked unengaged when the puck wasn't on his stick.

Robertson, Matthew- Played the game with a ton of confidence. Whenever Robertson had the puck on his stick he was calm and looking to make a play. This payed off with some nice moves to beat forwards at both the offensive blueline and on the forecheck. Occasionally this backfired as Robertson got a bit too relaxed with the puck resulting in turnovers. For such a big guy he is an excellent skater and showed his agility and speed often. Didn't get beat in a one on one all game and had a couple plays where he stood the opposing forward up before they even gained the blueline. Showed off his tools, but needs to clean up on some of his decision making.

Neighbours, Jake- The 16 year old Neighbours did not look out of place at all. He was making his presence felt physically every time he was on the ice, finishing checks whenever he could. He also showed confidence carrying the puck to gain the offensive zone with possession. Was not particularly assertive offensively mostly making safe plays to maintain possession and going to the net.

Medicine Hat Tigers

Williams, Josh- Had a very understated game but did a lot of little things right. Williams was seemingly coming out of every battle he was involved in with the puck on his stick. When he got the puck however he wasn't creating much, really only generating one high quality chance (with a nice pass on a 2 on 1) all game. Smarts showed with Williams jumping passing lanes to pick off pucks 3 separate times, and making some subtle little pick plays to open up room for his teammates. Solid game but would have liked to see more.

Rybinski, Henrik - Was on a line with Williams and had a very difficult game. Puck was on his stick a ton but didn't lead to many positive results as he was turning it over almost everytime. He seemed like he was trying too hard to force the play today.

Sioux Falls Stampede vs Central Illinois Flying Aces, Fall Classic, Sept 27 2018

Stampede

Johnson, Ryan (2019) – Johnson didn't get too many opportunities at even strength but he did play on the powerplay and was efficient at distributing the puck, while also using his speed in his own-end to escape the forecheck. On one defensive play early, he was decisive in closing his gap but the decision making could have been better. He didn't gauge or assess the angle of his opponents' potential shot and rushed him down which opened up a passing lane in-front of the net. That being said, when under pressure, he used his excellent mobility to alleviate pressure before delivering accurate passes to his teammates. When quarterbacking the powerplay, he showed deceptive fakes and good pivoting skills to re-open his lane on occasion and was good at assessing when his lanes were clogged. He was the catalyst for a Stampede powerplay goal by spinning off pressure before making a pass down near the goal-line. It wasn't Ryan's best offensive or defensive effort but he flashed his high-end tools.

Kuznetsov, Yan (2020) – Despite being one of the younger players on the ice, Kuznetsov demonstrated plus defensive awareness and made smart and quick decisions with the puck while under pressure. He's a big kid, coming in at 6'3 and 200 pounds and used his frame effectively to drive the Aces players to the outside on several sequences. Furthermore, he displayed an above average gap and made it difficult for opponents to feel comfortable in high-traffic areas. When under pressure both at the offensive-blueline and around his own goal-line, he looked calm and comfortable, reading the play well an rarely coughing up the puck. His best sequence wasn't flashy but it was effective. In his own-end while under pressure from two different Aces players, he used his frame to guard the puck and kept his head up before making a nice bank pass to his teammate which led to a transitional zone exit. He wasn't as engaged in the offensive-end but his read away from the puck and his poise were what stood out.

Piironen, Valtteri (2019) – Piironen didn't threaten in the offensive-zone but he battled hard in the corners and used his frame effectively against larger opponents such as Halliday. On one shift, Halliday attempted to cut but Piironen drove him to the outside and did a good job of pinning him along the boards. He drew a penalty after peeling off pressure behind his own-net and didn't look overwhelmed for the most part. The offensive-side looked limited out there today though.

Lee, Andre (2019) – Lee wasn't effective with the exception of one high-end scoring chance at even-strength, yet he had several dangerous chances on the powerplay, and managed to score as well. His goal was a result of finding a loose puck in the slot area before quickly spinning and wiring a wrist-shot far-side, he didn't hesitate on the play. He had a couple of point-blank scoring chances down-low and was a problem on the powerplay for the Aces by showing plus anticipation and showing good setting himself up in prime scoring chances. Despite the goal and the powerplay moments, there was very little consistency throughout the game at 5-on-5.

Flying Aces –

Driscoll, John (2019) – Driscoll had a quiet game for the Aces but was effective on the defensive-side on some critical plays. His best sequence came under heavy pressure, where he had to identify and respond quickly to a dump in chase sequence where he had an opponent draped over him, yet maintained his composure and balance before getting the puck out of a dangerous part of the ice. His anticipation spread to the neutral zone, where he jumped into the play to stop transitional zone-entries and for the most part did a decent job of containing the Aces players around his own-net area.

Siedem, Ryan (2019) – Siedem had a difficult game for the Aces by failing to react and respond to pressure in his own-end of the ice or generate from the blueline despite getting top powerplay time. During several different forechecking sequences, he was unable to assess or evaluate where he should put the puck on time, and even when given space to make outlet passes his accuracy and timing were mixed. He had several forced and unforced turnovers and didn't show much in the way of recovery on the plays he needed to. That being said, occasionally he did make a play that moved the puck up under pressure and did manage to deliver a couple of hard shots from the point, but overall, it wasn't a reliable defensive performance.

Breen, Lynden (2019) – Breen had success on the powerplay while demonstrating above average vision but was much less successful at 5-on-5, where he was kept to the outside for most of the night. He had a primary assist on the powerplay, after threading a pass from the goal-line to the slot area where Janicke managed to get behind coverage. At even strength, he had difficulty generating much in the way of offense with Halliday who was on his line.

Halliday, Stephen (2020) – Halliday was the first overall pick in the USHL Futures Draft but didn't live up to his pick position against the Stampede. He's an enormous kid, standing 6'3"220 but had difficulty using his size to get in-front of the net area and generate much in the way of offense. He did show composure under pressure at the offensive-blueline on one play and made a quick move to give himself a bit more space with the puck which led to extended zone time, and he also showed that he can use his frame to absorb impact and be a problem along the boards but at even-strength, he wasn't able to get going. On the powerplay, he was slightly more successful and did recognize when he needed to look for redirections on a couple of different sequences.

Janicke, Trevor (2019) – Janicke looks to have developed his one-on-one skill and showed a plus motor in today's game. He scored two goals, the first was a result of him finding soft-ice behind coverage during a powerplay and burying a quick wrist-shot that he got off his stick before the goalie could slide over. His second goal was from a stationary position where he used his frame to generate additional power on his one-timer, it was a heavy shot that went bar-down from far-out. Last year, he had difficulty assessing when he should attempt to use his skill-set and when he shouldn't and that was the case against the Stampede as well. He looked to drive possession and make plays but he was demonstrating a one-track mind out there, constantly looking to engage one-on-one even if there was a less flashy but more efficient play to make. Away from the puck, he was featured on the top penalty-kill and did a decent job of taking away lanes and helped generate a short-handed scoring chance on one sequence. Despite some inconsistencies, Trevor had a quality game.

Muskegon Lumberjacks vs Fargo Force, Fall Classic, Sept 28

Lumberjacks –

Afanasyev, Yegor (2019) – Afanasyev was the most dominant player on the ice for either team highlighted by impressive puck skills and a dangerous release. He flashed high-end hands early, making a well executed between the legs deke from the right circle to re-open his shooting lane before firing a backhander wide. He didn't miss most of his shot attempts after that initial one, landing himself a hattrick while showing a versatile range of shot types. He scored his first goal from above the right circle with a powerful yet well placed slapshot that went bar-down, the shot had a reduced wind-up making it more difficulty for the goalie to set. His second goal was a quick wrist-shot from the left circle, his release point stood out on the attempt. His third goal was the result of a re-direct in-front of the net where he used his length to tip home a point shot. Yegor showed that he's more than just a shot though, making several high-end moves while also showing precise and creative passing. It was a standout performance where he forced you to take notice of him. His line of Kile and Bjork was the best of the game and he had a consistent presence on the powerplay as well.

Gaffney, Alex (2020) – Gaffney showed an above average level of tenacity and grit for his size and was willing to compete both with and without the puck despite being at a physical disadvantage given his 5'7 frame. His best scoring attempt came in the slot where he attempted to re-direct the puck on net but the main takeaway was that he was willing to enter high-traffic areas and take punishment both when trying to get into scoring areas and along the boards. Without the puck he had his best play, using an active stick to disrupt a play at the defensive-blueline before moving back up ice. On another shift, he aggressively backchecked and attempted to engage with his larger opponent. Gaffney did get thrown around at times and was knocked off balance on a couple of shifts but it didn't deter him, though he also never got going offensively either.

Gushchin, Daniil (2020) – Gushchin didn't have a standout performance like we have seen him have at the U17's and Hlinka but he still was noticeable on the ice by generating several clean transitional zone entries both at even strength and on the powerplay. Daniil is capable of making high-end plays while in motion and this allowed him to use his speed and skill to weave through heavy traffic at the line before setting up his teammates. Additionally, he used bursts of speed to drive down the wings before firing quick wrist shots on net. His best chance came off a shot in the slot area with traffic but he wasn't able to get into the slot area as much as some previous viewings, opting for off-angle shots at times. Additionally, his passing was mixed today, although he was successful at carrying the puck over the offensive line, he made a couple of poorly placed drop passes which made it difficult for his teammates to maintain control.

Force –

Fiedler, Cedric (2019) – Fiedler was moved up to the second pairing today and stood out more than in his previous performance at the Fall Classic by combining his aggressive approach that he displayed with some physicality. His mobility was noticeable yesterday and here again, he used it to close his gaps quickly before relying on his size and stick to overwhelm his opponents. This led to his secondary assist, after using his frame to knock a lumberjack's player down to the ice from behind his goal-line, he collected the puck and made a short pass that led to a breakout and eventual goal. On the penalty-kill he used his stick to disrupt a scoring chance in the slot area and was alert around his net area. The biggest drawback to his performance was that he had trouble pacing himself at times, he tracks players aggressively who are carrying the puck which inadvertently throws himself out of position, causing him to expend additional energy to recover. He also wasn't bad under pressure when dealing with the forecheck behind his net but he tended to absorb hits instead of trying to evade them. Similar to yesterday, he didn't generate much in the way of offense at the line but did have a well-timed pinch to keep a puck in.

Huglen, Aaron (2019) – Huglen didn't threaten offensively as consistently as he did in yesterday's viewing. His best shift was early in the game, where he showed a willingness to take a hit to make a play which extended his teams offensive-zone time, followed by making a diving pass back to the blueline and then generated an additional scoring opportunity. Unfortunately, that shift was a fleeting moment in an otherwise quiet game for Aaron. His best scoring chance came off a quick wrist-shot in the slot area but with the exception of that play, he didn't use his tools effectively to put himself in a position to score.

Nodler, Nosh (2019) – Nodler had a good performance for Fargo, showing the ability to anticipate the play both with and without the puck. In previous viewings, Josh for the most part has shown a pass-first mentality and against the Lumberjacks that was the case again. He was good at recognizing where his teammates were attempting to position themselves in advance, but his execution was semi-mixed depending on the pass attempt. That being said, in the offensive-end, he entered high traffic areas both at even strength and on the powerplay and was rewarded for his efforts by scoring a late goal in-front of the net area off a quick wrist-shot. Away from the puck, he had a great interception in the neutral zone and read the play in advance before transitioning back into the offensive-end. In both Nodler's games at the Fall Classic there's been a lack of puck-skills shown and the only attempt in today's game resulted in losing the puck, so that element hasn't been on display.

Sioux City Musketeers vs Green Bay Gamblers, Sept 28 2018

Musketeers –

Kehrer, Anthony (2020) – Kehrer had a standout performance on the backend for the Musketeers. He mishandled the puck early in his own-end yet showed a good amount of poise under pressure before finding his teammate in the neutral zone with a crisp pass. He displayed a variety of body and head fakes, quick hands, and was willing to take a hit under pressure to make a play. Down-low in the corners, he was willing to battle and compete yet had the hockey sense necessary to anticipate pressure in advance so that he rarely had to. Despite being very young, Kehrer demonstrated today that he could force the opposition to react to him before he needed to react to them, and this allowed him to make several impressive plays in both his end and at the offensive blueline, using advanced head and body fakes, a quick set of hands, and the confidence needed to use them together to re-open lanes where he managed to thread a couple of passes and set himself up for a good scoring chance in the high-slot. Furthermore, he showed impressive cross-overs and had a powerful base, giving him plus four-way mobility. His biggest mistake resulted in a goal after Zabaneh managed to get behind his coverage in the neutral zone but with the exception of that play, Kehrer flashed a lot of talent.

Krenzen, Nolan (2019) – Krenzen played a relatively quiet game but had a couple of moments where he stood out. His best plus sequence was the result of supporting his defenseman before pivoting behind his goal-line and carrying the puck out of the zone under heavy pressure. On the sequence, he was knocked off balance but managed to stay on his feet. He was used on the penalty-kill and had a key block at a critical moment in the game in the third by anticipating a shooting lane in advance. The shot stung him but he played through it.

Pasanen, Tommy (2019) – Pasanen is a large defenseman who took advantage of his tools in spurts against the Gamblers. He's not slow for his size and maintained a relatively good gap for most of the game, however it was his reach and strength that stood out the most. There was one play where Green Bay was trying to transition over the offensive blueline, but Pasanen used an aggressive stick to knock the puck resulting in a turnover. Down near his goal-line, he was competing hard for a puck and ended up knocking his opponent to the ice effortlessly before lunging for the puck behind the net, the play resulted in an additional take away and possession for his team. At the offensive-line, he had difficulty getting his shot through traffic, rarely recognizing when his lane was open or closed and didn't flash much in the way of skills that would indicate he could re-open them if he wanted to. That being said, he was solid defensively and attempted to be active offensively despite not having a lot of success in that area of his game.

Kallionkieli, Marcus (2019) – Kallionkiele flashed an impressive offensive tool-kit which led to a 2-goal performance against the Gamblers while playing on the top-line and getting powerplay time. His second goal was the goal that stood out. He was having success at finding soft-ice today and managed to get open in the right circle where he took a pass in one motion, needing little time to put it in the back of the net. The release point was a plus and he generated a lot of velocity on the shot which didn't allow the Gamblers netminder to move over in time, the placement was exactly where it needed to be as well. One aspect of his offensive game to note based off today's viewing was that he rarely looked for his teammates even if they were open, opting on occasion for lower percentage shots instead of making the pass. Furthermore, although his skating mechanics were fine, showing a long stride with a relatively deep-knee bend, he had a bit of trouble generating power in his first few steps. The kid can shoot the puck but his hockey sense and vision don't seem as developed based off this viewing.

Brink, Bobby (2019) – Brink is a relatively small forward standing 5'10 "160 but didn't play like one out there. He displayed a fearless brand of hockey, willing to not only compete against larger opponents than himself during board battling sequences but deliver big hits as well. Although his skating mechanics were awkward, he got around the ice at an okay rate and this complimented his high-octane motor. He was constantly pressuring without the puck, which resulted in a successful backcheck in the neutral zone. When he did have the puck he was dangerous too, this was primarily a result of having the ability to change his tempo on the fly by adapting to what the Gamblers were giving him in the offensive-zone. This allowed him to have success both at even strength and when playing the half-wall on the powerplay. He almost scored the opening goal after being left-open at the bottom of the right circle where he delivered a hard one-timer from his knee. Later in the game he scored the 5th goal for the Musketeers during a 2-on-1 sequence where he quickly buried a cross crease feed past the sprawled out netminder. He showed that he can pass the puck as well, making well-timed and accurate passes consistently while recognizing when he needed to re-open his lanes. The biggest takeaway from Bobby was that not only did he have a great motor today, but he showed that he had the ability to contain it while using it to shift the tempo and momentum of the play. This speaks to potential high-end hockey sense. It was an impressive performance where he displayed a good amount of hockey sense.

Gamblers –

Mylymok, Luke (2019) – Mylymok had an average game for the Gamblers. He did have a successful recovery sequence where he recognized that his defenseman was in trouble and quickly skated to collect the puck and get it out of danger. With the puck however, he largely played a perimeter game and didn't play at a high pace. His best offensive sequence was when he moved laterally over the high-slot before making a soft pass to his teammate which set him up for a scoring chance, he also fired a couple of shots on net but nothing that was threatening. Luke wasn't very hard to play against and wasn't able to pressure the opposing defense or create any sustained offense.

Zabaneh, Nicholas (2019) – Despite being the extra forward, Zabaneh came in and made a statement for his team by having arguably the best offensive game out of any Gambler. He showed plus mobility early when transitioning through all three-zones and getting the puck deep. On the same shift, he found soft-ice directly in-front of the net with the net largely open but fanned on the shot attempt. He showed plus anticipation away from the puck that led to one of the better defensive sequences of the game. He anticipated a bank-pass attempt up the side-wall but quickly intercepted the pass attempt, he then recognized another zone clear attempt and knocked it down and finished off his shift by using an active stick near the left point to intercept yet another clear attempt, it was an impressive sequence. With the puck he was dangerous as well, as he found soft-ice behind coverage and was sprung on a breakaway scoring five-hole on a quick wrist-shot that didn't allow the netminder to set. He also demonstrated that he can pass the puck and set up his teammates with some sharp passes in the offensive-zone. His skating, anticipation both with and without the puck and scoring instincts were present today.

Ottawa 67s at Kitchener Rangers, September 28, 2018

Kitchener Rangers –

Vukojevic, Michael –2019 Vukojevic is a big and sturdy defenseman who possesses a heavy stride playing top pairing minutes on the Rangers blueline. He displayed good physical defensive traits to his game playing hard man-on-man and angling opponents to the boards. His mobility is slightly above average but he was exposed at times making sluggish pivots on the defensive rush giving opponents a step on him. He moved the puck well in this game delivering good passes to advance the rush; however, he did not appear to be entirely comfortable handling the puck for any length of time. Vukojevic scored a goal in this game on a hard one-timer off a faceoff win. He would benefit from improving his puck skill and playmaking abilities to improve the offensive aspects of his game.

York, Jack – 2019 York displayed good two-way defensive traits to his game playing in all situations and being involved in the play in all three zones. He demonstrated an ability to jump up into the offensive rush and displayed good hands and decision making with the puck. He played as the Rangers powerplay quarterback and distributed the puck well taking shots on net when the shooting lanes were there. One area where he struggled and is an area where he could improve his game is defending the middle of the ice.

Xhekaj, Arber –2019 Xhekaj possesses attractive size but played very sheltered minutes on the Rangers blueline in this game. He displayed an active stick and angled opponents towards the perimeter in the defensive zone. His foot speed and anticipation seem to still be a step behind as he adjusts to playing on an OHL blueline.

Sebrango, Donovan –2020 Sebrango showed some offensive skill and potential from the back end in this game playing primarily at even strength and powerplay. He played a depth role but contributed to moving the puck up ice on his shifts. He showed good instincts pinching in off the point on the powerplay looking for the backdoor feed. He also earned his first OHL point assisting on Michael Vukojevic's 2nd period goal.

Valade, Reid –2020 Valade had a slow start to the game and was primarily stuck in the neutral zone unable to make clean zone entries or create sustained offensive zonetime. In the 2nd period he got his feet moving and earned some good offensive zonetime on a different line cycling the puck along the perimeter but unable to drive the net. He would benefit from adding strength to his frame to improve his board play and offensive zone presence.

Ottawa 67s –

Clarke, Graeme –(2019) Clarke displayed some good creative playmaking aspects to his game but for the most part was defended tightly and didn't get much open ice. He made several clean offensive zone entries and showed awareness to stop up inside the blueline, assess his options and find the open teammate. He showed an ability to sustain the forecheck retrieving pucks, earning body positioning and cycling pucks down low when no play exists. On many shifts including the powerplay he was looking for the soft ice in the slot but did not receive any clean opportunities. On one shift he was tempted to try the lacrosse-style shot from behind the net. He made some careless decisions with the puck throughout the game and could improve his overall decision-making and risk assessment.

Peric, Lucas –(2019) Peric is a mobile defenseman who took a regular shift but was prone to making mistakes and causing turnovers. He played in all situations including the powerplay and penalty kill. As the powerplay quarterback he struggled to distribute the puck smoothly and his passes seemed off the mark.

Quinn, Jack –(2020) Quinn is a versatile forward who played in all situations including powerplay, penalty kill and 4-on-4. He was engaged throughout the game displaying good puck pursuit winning battles and taking pucks to the net. He contributed to some good offensive zonetime displaying hands and confidence at the blueline and then initiating the cycle down low.

Tolnai, Cameron –(2020) Tolnai is a smart player who thinks the game well and displayed average speed and acceleration. He displayed good situational awareness making smart, low-risk plays. He would benefit from adding strength to his frame and getting stronger on his skates.

Maggio, Matthew –2021 Maggio was slotted on the 67s second line and earned a regular shift. He displayed average straightaway speed but would benefit from improving his foot speed and first few strides. He struggled on zone entries and got held up a lot in the neutral zone. His biggest asset is his shot and the Rangers defended him tight which resulted in 0 shots on goal.

Spokane Chiefs vs Kootenay Ice, September 29, 2018

Spokane

Arbuzov, Egor- The Russian import played a very low risk game in big minutes partnered with Ty Smith. Made the safest play he could every time resulting in few mistakes and few notable plays. Passing was off a bit as he was missing a lot of easy passes and giving teammates difficult pucks to handle. He showed a little bit of patience with the puck in the third period leading to two nice point shots through traffic.

Beckman, Adam- Did not stand out for any particular trait in his game but was frequently making good plays and involved in chances. The biggest tool for Beckman seemingly is his brain as he constantly found himself in the right place at the right time. Had a nice assist where instead of taking an open shot on the 3 on 2 he hesitated, drew the defender and passed to a teammate for a redirect into the back of the net.

Toporowski, Luke- Toporowski had a huge game today and was borderline dominant every time he touched the ice. Skating really sets Toporowski apart as he is excellent in all areas from straight line speed, to edge work. Most impressive was his balance, as he was able to easily explode through checks and drive past defencemen. Almost every shift it seemed like Toporowki would steal a puck and then explode up ice to create a dangerous chance. On the forecheck Toporowski did an excellent job of forcing turnovers as he gave defencemen no time or space to make a play. In the offensive zone he was consistently getting pucks in to dangerous spots and unleashing his heavy shot.

Kootenay

Orzeck, Nolan- One of the few Kootenay players who had a good game. Orzeck is a puck moving defenseman who skates well and did a great job as one of the few guys actually getting the puck out of his zone with possession today. Passing was always on point so teammates could take it in stride. Nolan also made a couple nice pinches in the third to keep the play alive.

Krebs, Peyton- Things were not really coming off for Krebs today as he tried to do too much. Throughout the game Krebs showed a very good stick to create turnovers and also intercepted a couple of passes. On the offensive end almost everything he did was resulting in a turnover throughout the first two periods. He looked flat and lacking in a breakaway gear. Finally came out to play in the third and scored a nice goal where he outraced two defencemen to a loose puck and ripped a shot low blocker that the goalie had no chance on. Also had a few shifts where he picked Spokane apart from outside with his passing. Looked like his normal self in the third, but the game was already lost by that point.

McClennon, Connor- McClennon had a pretty good night especially when compared to the rest of the team. McClennon showed that he processes the game very fast. He made an awesome one touch pass to spring a teammate for a breakaway. Also picked up an assist showing great deception, as he looked like he was about to shoot, pulling 4 players from the opposing team to him before feeding a teammate coming around the net.

Muskegon Lumberjacks vs Sioux City Musketeers, Fall Classic, Sept 29 2018

Lumberjacks –

McDonald, Cameron (2019) – McDonald had a good game for the Lumberjacks at both ends of the ice, using his speed and escape-ability to come away with the puck in the corners. He's quick and he needs to be given his 5'9 frame, using it to carry the puck over all three-zones on a shift or two, but he primarily looked for stretch passes to move the puck up and was successful at doing so. He showed a high-degree of finesse with his pass attempts that resulted in an impressive accuracy despite some of them being difficult passes to make. Furthermore, he was efficient in his puck distribution when walking the line and moved the puck quickly from the point during powerplay opportunities. Under pressure, he didn't panic and some of his better sequences resulted from cleanly getting the puck up the ice despite having bigger opponents aggressively trying to cut off his skating and passing lanes. On a couple of different shifts, he demonstrated a solid gap as well. Despite being a small defenseman, he showed that he was capable of angling larger forwards away from the net area during drive attempts.

Belpedio, Nic (2019) – Belpedio had a solid defensive effort for the Lumberjacks and played bigger than his size, he also managed to shut-down Kallionkieli in one-on-one situations and keep him to the outside despite his size and speed. Nic isn't a big player but he had no problems getting physical along the boards when necessary and had the most impressive block of the game, diving aggressively while sacrificing his body to block a point-blank shot from the bottom of the left circle late in the game while trying to protect the lead. He also showed vision and had one of the best stretch passes of the game from his own-end that landed on the tape of his teammate and led to a transition up the ice.

Skinner, Hunter (2019) – Skinner had a good game for the Lumberjacks by playing physical while being decisive at both ends of the ice when the puck was on his stick. Around the net area, he used his big frame to push players and redirect them into the corners. He had a couple of hard yet accurate passes both from his own-end and at the offensive blueline which resulted in a high-quality scoring chance. His best play came from behind his own-goal line where he used his strength to out-muscle a player while competing for a loose puck, then fired a hard pass that landed on the tape of his teammate resulting in a clean transitional zone exit. His power transferred over from his physical play into his slapshot as well, as he demonstrated the ability to generate a lot of velocity from the offensive blueline.

Afanasyev, Yegor (2019) – Afanasyev had another impressive performance but didn't control play to the same extent that he did against Fargo. Late in the first period, he had a prime scoring opportunity after getting behind coverage but missed on his shot attempt, however shortly after he buried another chance directly in-front of the net. He scored yesterday off a deflection and a stationary wrist and slapshot, but today he showed that he can score while in motion and with little time to find his shot placement. It was a goal scorers' goal, and the release point looked high-end. He flashed his puck-skills by dragging the puck quickly around an overzealous Musketeer player early in the game but wasn't using his hands as often as he was in our previous viewing. One area of concern today was that he was a bit too opportunistic when looking for the stretch pass and as a result wasn't playing deep enough in his own away from the puck at times. That being said, he still looked dangerous and demonstrated that he doesn't need much in the way of time or space to the puck in the back of the net.

Gushchin, Daniil (2020) – Gushchin had a good game for the Lumberjacks, showing the ability to set up his teammates while also generating high-end scoring chances for himself by using his speed. He had an assist off the Lumberjacks first goal after transitioning over the offensive blueline before moving laterally and finding his open teammate. He played the half-wall on the powerplay where he's shown the ability to be dangerous and that was the case today as well. He looked to peel off pressure along the boards and create space for his teammates so that he could feed them the puck for scoring chances but was good at interpreting when his shooting lanes were open as well. He scored a goal by being in the right place at the right time when a rebound came right to him in-front of the net area. His speed and skills were on display out there.

Musketeers –

Kehrer, Anthony (2020) – Kehrer had some impressive sequences against the Lumberjacks, showing poise, confidence and the ability to make plays in tight spaces at both ends of the ice. In his own-end, he played a mature game, looking composed in heavy pressure situations and demonstrating plus hockey sense with a blend of skill to help minimize defensive turnovers. On one sequence near his own blueline, he was under pressure but managed to guard the puck and get through traffic resulting in a transitional zone exit. Behind his own goal-line, he had briefly retrieved the puck with a forechecker bearing down on him, he used a head fake and switched his positioning to misdirect his opponent before calmly making a backhand pass around the boards to his defensive partner resulting in a clean exit. At the offensive blueline, he didn't get too many opportunities, but he did have a successful pinch where he recognized open-ice before attempting a give and go sequence with his teammate below the goal-line that almost resulted in a quality scoring chance. Despite limited ice-time, he stood out.

Pasanen, Tommy (2019) – Pasanen is a large and rangy defenseman who showed an above-average level of four-way mobility given his frame. He maintained a proper gap on most sequences and was aggressive with his stick which helped break up a rush attempt. Behind his own-goal line, he was collected when dealing with physical opponents and made a couple of crisp outlet passes. His best offensive chance came after joining the rush and receiving a drop pass from Pospisil but his shot was deflected before he could get it off. He looked aware and showed plus physical traits out there.

Brink, Bobby (2019) – Brink demonstrated a high-octane motor and was part of the best line of the night on either team, featuring Kallionkieli and Pospisil. He was aggressive and tenacious on the forecheck, constantly competing against multiple players, and displaying a big gas tank, rarely slowing down despite impressive output. His pressure kept the Lumberjacks playing heavy minutes below their goal-line at times. With the puck on his stick, Bobby looked to get his shot off which he managed to do on a couple of chances. During one attempt, he displayed the ability to drag the puck tightly to his body to counteract a shot block attempt, he demonstrated on the paly that he was capable of shooting around a screen. Lastly, Brink played with speed and was constantly in motion, he had a noticeable performance.

Kallionkieli, Marcus (2019) – Kallionkieli generated the most scoring chances out of any forward on the ice against the Lumberjacks. One area that was noticeable early and often was that he had a shoot first mentality to back up his impressive release point and this led to several quality scoring chances. He hit the post off a reduced wind-up slapshot from the left circle during the powerplay, he came very close to hitting another crossbar during a wrist-shot that he fired while moving laterally over the slot and arguably his best chance came earlier in the game during a 3-on-1 sequence. A shooting mentality can be a double-edged sword at times, and in Marcus's case, that's what happened during his best opportunity. He collected the puck after an errant pass attempt from his opponent at the offensive blueline who was caught badly out of position but instead of looking to use head fakes or slow the play down to create additional options for himself, he rushed directly into the slot area and telegraphed his intentions with the puck on his stick. Another area to note with Kallionkiele's game was that he showed that he has the tools to play as a multi-faceted threat. Despite his tunnel-vision at times, he did have some impressive passes, his best being a no-look spinning backhand pass to his teammate during the powerplay that resulted in good scoring chance. Although he displayed talent, the biggest area of concern based on today's viewing was his hockey sense. He played a fast game with a good pace and a shoot-first mindset but he didn't display the ability to slow the game down, utilize his teammates effectively or mask his intentions enough with the puck on his stick.

USNTDP vs Sioux Falls Stampede, Fall Classic, Sept 29 2018

USA –

Thrun, Henry (2019) – Thrun had a quality two-way performance for the States, anticipating the play well at both ends of the ice while keeping his game simple and largely mistake free. I say largely since he did get stripped during a forechecking sequence behind his own-goal line while attempting to carry the puck which almost led to a goal but with the exception of that play, Thrun had success at moving the puck out of his own end by making crisp outlet passes. In the offensive-end and neutral zone, his skill-set was noticeable. He was good at assessing when the play was transitioning, and at the offensive-blueline he had several well-timed pinches resulting in extended zone-time. There was one attribute that was below-average today, which was his ability to gauge if his lane was open or closed from the point. Several of his shots were blocked and during his best shooting opportunity after finding soft-ice, he attempted a pass that resulted in a turnover instead. His best shift started from the offensive-blueline where he made a well-timed pinch followed by a successful pass before having to transition back to defense, where he made a good read away from the puck in-front of the net and intercepted a cross-crease pass before moving the puck out of a high-danger area. Regardless of some mistakes, he largely played a clean and efficient game in each zone.

Vlasic, Alex (2019) – Vlasic had a strong defensive effort against the Stampede. He's a large, rangy and coordinated kid who can recover better than most defenseman his age due to his length. There were a couple of plays where a quick Stampede forward looked to cut around him and although it appeared Vlasic was a step behind, he would use his active-stick and frame to give himself the opportunity to recover. The end result was Alex consistently taking away scoring opportunities for the Stampede. He was physically engaged along the boards but kept his game contained, allowing him to maintain good positioning. Another reason he wasn't overly active at times was due to his defensive partners; Fensore looked to use his speed to rush the puck at times so Vlasic played passive during those types of sequences. Lastly, on the defensive side he handled a three-on-one situation well despite it resulting in a goal and had a couple of accurate and well-timed passes. In the offensive-zone, his wrist-shot came with a lot of torque due to his height and length resulting in a powerful shot but it missed the net far-side. His best offensive moment was the result of a successful pinch where he received a pass from the left-circle and found Boldy across the slot for an open-net goal. He fooled the Stampede defense on the play and didn't give his opponents many tells as to what he was going to do with the puck. It was a good offensive flash from the big defender.

York, Cam (2019) – York had a strong game for the U.S while getting paired with Warren for much of the match. Warren is a very mobile player but tends to over-skate the play at times and throw himself out of position, this is where Cam came in and did an excellent job maintaining good gaps and positioning to help compensate for his partner. Furthermore, he was fast to recognize his options while under pressure and had several sharp passes that landed on the tape of his teammates when moving the puck up the ice. From the blueline, Cam had success getting his quick wrist-shot through traffic and picked up the primary assist on the 4th U.S goal. He received a drop pass at the line then quickly drove down behind the goal-line where he made a no-look pass directly in-front of the net resulting in the goal. His puck protection, speed, vision, and offensive awareness were all displayed on the play. Like Vlasic's pass, Cam gave no tells with his body movement and head positioning which made it difficult for the stampede defense to recognize when they needed to take away the lane with their sticks. Lastly, York's efficiency can't be under-stated, his intelligence allows him to anticipate plays and as a result he can reserve or expend at the right times giving him the ability to log heavy minutes.

Warren, Marshall (2019) – Warren played with speed and had a physical edge in his game which made him difficult to play against at times. His speed can be a double-edged sword for him depending on the play. There're times when he uses his speed to transition effortlessly up the ice and he had several pinches resulting in scoring opportunities but he tends to over-skate the play which results in him needing to recover. For instance, when transitioning from offense to defense, he read the play accurately but wasn't starting and stopping by using his edges at times when he should have, and as a result didn't have the gap needed to contain his opponents. That being said, he played with effort and grit, and despite not being the largest kid, he showed a fearlessness on the ice when engaging bigger players. Unfortunately, he was injured after closing his gap aggressively in the last minute of the third and appeared to take a hit to the head that resulted in the game tying goal but he did get up after and get back to the bench. Warren didn't have the best gap or positioning at times but he played at a high-pace, flashed an excellent set of tools and demonstrated that he can play a physical game when needed.

Fensore, Dominick (2019) – Fensore had a great game for the U.S and stood out despite being the smallest defenseman out on the ice. He displayed chemistry with Vlasic who gave him the opportunity for him to use his speed to transition the puck while also activating into the play in the offensive-end. He had arguably the best defensive sequence out of any defender today. The sequence started at the offensive-blueline where he managed to fire a shot that was blocked before collecting his own rebound and fired another quick shot from the high-slot. He then transitioned to defense where he read a pass attempt directly in-front of his net area and extended his stick to deflect the puck behind the net. He then moved the puck around the boards before having to deal with a developing odd-man re-entry play which he read correctly while positioning himself properly, and last but not least, he then used his quickness to recover for his teammate in the corner by skating down a loose puck during a board battling sequence and passed it successfully out of the zone. He also had an impressive shoot-out goal, showing an above-average release that went bar-down. For a defender of his size to have a chance, he needs to be smart and quick, and in today's game he demonstrated both, it doesn't hurt either that he's one of the youngest kids in the draft so there's a bit more time for him to grow.

Farrell, Sean (2020) – Farrell is one the younger kids featured on this squad but that didn't stop him from having an impressive offensive game where he threatened off the rush consistently. He seemed to always be in motion and used plus agility to create additional room for himself. His best offensive sequence came after out-waiting his opponent while moving laterally over the high-slot before feeding his teammate a nice pass that resulted in a quality scoring chance. Furthermore, his wrist-shot was quick to come off his stick and he had no trouble firing it off the tape while in motion. That being said, his one-timer from a stationary position wasn't the hardest shot you'll see. Farrell flashed the ability to both shoot the puck and pass it, and more importantly demonstrated plus hockey sense today to take advantage of his skills.

Caulfield, Judd (2019) – Caulfield displayed chemistry with both Beecher and Boldy and was excellent in his own-end of the ice without the puck. He had a short-handed breakaway which he generated for himself by using his length to create a turnover before showing above-average straight-line speed to gain some separation. He came in with speed to back the goalie up giving him additional room to tuck the puck upstairs, but he misfired on his quick snap-shot that went over the net. Throughout the game, Judd showed a high-degree of creativity, consistently using his length to drag the puck past active sticks before attempting to set up his teammates. He showed a wide-range of moves and a good level of agility for his size, which made it difficult for his opponents to read what he was attempting to do at times with the puck on his stick. His shot came off his stick quickly but he didn't look to drag the puck or suddenly changed angles given his length. Furthermore, he was capable of making several impressive plays while off-balance but he looked to plant both feet which allowed Howe to read his shot attempts. Physically, he was engaged and had a couple of successful defensive plays where he used his size to his advantage to knock a Stampede player off the puck, this applied to the forecheck where he forced the Stampede to play heavy minutes. It was a good two-way effort for Caulfield who flashed a plus set of hands, vision, and creativity and competed at both ends of the ice.

Lindmark, Owen (2019) – Lindmark wasn't consistent out there but he created a couple of scoring chances for himself by outskating his opponents. He demonstrated power in his lower-frame which allowed him to out-race a Stampede player for a puck resulting in a breakaway. He fired a quick wrist-shot far-side that was stopped on the play. On a couple of other shifts, Lindmark managed to generate off the rush where he again would look to shoot the puck and played with a shoot first mentality. One other aspect of his game to note was that he was successful at recognizing when his shooting lanes were open and would use his mobility to shift the lane when he was coming through the high-slot area.

Boldy, Matthew (2019) – Boldy wasn't always a consistent threat on the ice, but that didn't stop him from having the best primary assist of the game, scoring a goal, hitting the crossbar, and getting two separate breakaways in overtime. One thing that was consistently displayed in each play described above was they were generated with high-end skill. His hands are some of the best in this class, and he used impressive hand-eye coordination early to knock a high saucer-pass down, then seamlessly transitioned the puck to his stick before threading a seeing-eye pass through heavy traffic for the opening goal. Another play that showcased his hands was during an entry attempt over the blueline, where he pulled the puck between his legs and made an additional move to create room, he almost put himself off-side but had the balance and the awareness to keep the play alive which resulted in an additional goal. He rung a puck off the crossbar midway through the game after finding soft-ice in the high-slot, the shot was powerful and there weren't many tells in his mechanics. In overtime, he had two breakaway opportunities and had an additional opportunity in the shootout, he didn't score on any of them but he displayed a versatile move-set and has the ability to make highly technical dekes look relatively easy. Lastly, he processed the play quickly and displayed a high-level of creativity when controlling the puck

Stampede –

Johnson, Ryan (2019) – Johnson showcased the ability to escape under pressure in his own-end by using his mobility and hockey sense. He was decisive with the puck on his stick in the D-zone, recognizing that he had limited time and space to move the puck out of tightly controlled areas of the ice before transitioning over the blueline by either using his own impressive straight-line speed or by making accurate stretch passes. He wasn't afraid to take a hit and is willing to use the frame he has to lean on his opponents during board battling sequences. His positioning was above-average but there was a couple of plays where we would have liked him to play with a bit more pace when attempting to cover a shooting and passing lane. In the offensive-end, he was used on the powerplay but wasn't able to generate too many scoring opportunities due to being heavily pressured at the line which forced him to distribute the puck quickly.

Red Deer Rebels vs Saskatoon Blades, Oct 2, 2018

Red Deer

Zaitsev, Oleg (2019) - Played a very safe and reliable game, centering Red Deers first line. He did a great job supporting the puck and being a breakout option low through the middle. Zaitsev also did an excellent job battling along the boards in both zones, coming out with the puck the majority of the time. On top of this Zaitsev threw a couple big hits, playing a hard physical game. Offensively did not show a ton of creativity but made a lot of solid passing plays and crashed the net hard. Scored one goal but could have had 3 if he hadn't missed a couple open nets.

Bains, Arshdeep (2019) - Not consistently noticeable but did show some solid speed and confidence through the neutral zone on a couple occasions. Got an assist by slowing up of the rush and making a cross ice pass to the trailer who walked in to score.

Anders, Ethan (2019) - Battled really hard to make saves in traffic but let in a couple of weak goals where he looked a bit slow. Cleanly beat five hole on one goal and didn't have the greatest rebound control with two goals coming off outside shots he left on the doorstep.

Saskatoon

De La Gorgendiere, Aidan (2020) - Looked extremely confident playing on Saskatoons top pairing. Above average skating and very good decision making, this allowed the rookie to consistently complete clean breakouts. Defensively did a great job controlling where the forwards went with his stick. Only real rookie moments came on cycle and battles where he clearly did not have the strength to outmuscle opponents.

Malysjev, Emil (2019) - Very poor first couple of periods for the lanky defenseman. He really struggled handling the puck on passes and puck retrievals, with pucks consistently bouncing off his stick. With the puck under control his decision making was solid making some very good reads on regroups. His skating is a bit awkward looking.

Dach, Kirby (2019) - Not an excellent game by his standards but consistently showed some of his elite tools. Dach has an effortless look to his skating, where he barely looks like he's moving but is gliding past the player beside him. By far the strongest part of Dach's game is his passing ability, the way he sees the ice is unique and he plays with a different rhythym that opens up a lot of lanes. He has a very good understanding of how to draw the attention of players and open space before moving the puck. His passing was mainly on display on the powerplay where everything ran through him as he picked up a pair of assists. Had a couple concerning plays where he but himself in dumb spots and took a couple of huge hits as a result. Would also like to see a bit more compete in his game as he can look very low energy and reluctant to physically engage.

Robbins, Tristan (2020) - Speedy forward who earned more ice time as the game went on. Generated a couple solid chances with his skating and played a very strong energy game. Also was very strong on the PK filling lanes very well. Looked a little bit lacking in his puck handling ability and didn't generate much in settled offense situations.

Maier, Nolan (2019)- Maiers athleticism in net looks great as he got across quickly for a couple excellent saves off cross ice passes. There were three goals against on deflections, and another on a 3 on 1 where he didn't have much of a chance. He really stepped up in the third period with some really big saves to keep his team in it. Aggressively cuts off angles playing very far off the goal line.

Team Northeast vs Shattuck St. Mary's Prep, October 3rd, 2018

Team Northeast

Koster, Mike (2019) - Despite the loss Koster played one of the more complete games this scout has seen him play in the last couple years. Koster's skating and offensive play has always been on display in previous viewings but in the past his decision making has been questionable. In this game he showed the ability to pick his spots and his decision making on when to join or lead the rush up ice was very good. Koster was good on his puck retrievals and supported his defensive partner well on breakouts which has been a concern in the past. Koster scored on the Power Play in the 2nd period by using a nice shot fake to get around the opponent challenging him at the point, showed good poise moving across the zone waiting for a shooting lane to open up and fired a wrist shot near the faceoff circle that beat the goalie on the glove side.

Pinoniemi, Garrett - 2019 It was fairly quiet night offensively for Pinoniemi who seemed to fight the puck when under pressure and he struggled in the faceoff circle, losing some draws cleanly. Pinoniemi skates well and can cover a lot of ice which allowed him to be an asset on the back check and provide back pressure to help his defense close gaps.

Shattuck St. Mary's

Lacombe, Jackson – 2019 Displayed good skating and edgework both in defending and with the puck on his stick. Lacombe was on the point on the Power Play and while his footwork allowed him to move around on the top of the power play effectively, he didn't use his skills to get the puck down to the dangerous areas of the zone enough and there for didn't create a lot of chances on the PP.

Gonchar, Mikhail - 2019 Gonchar has good size and his skating and footwork are above average. Mikhail played a sound game defensively, using his long reach to challenge the puck carrier and forced them to rush plays as they entered the zone.

Kunz, Jackson – 2020 Kunz displayed good size and speed and played a power forward style with the puck in his limited ice time. Jackson left the game late in the 1st period after taking a big hit along the boards at his own blueline and didn't return to the game.

Samoskevich, Mackie – 2021 Samoskevich was the most offensively skilled player on the ice for either team in this game. It reflected by his 1 goal and 2 assist performances. Mackie displayed high end skill at an up tempo pace and showed the ability to beat his man one on one on a number of occasions. On his goal Mackie showed good explosiveness in his skating to track down a loose puck in the neutral zone and gain the edge on the defender and score with a backhand to forehand move. Samsoskevich also beat his defender one on one on one of his assists using a quick stick handling move and then made a nice backhanded feed to #14 who scored on the play. Samoskevich is a late 2002 birthdate so his draft year is a couple years away but he looks to have all the makings of a highly sought after prospect for that draft.

Sault Ste. Marie Greyhounds vs Peterborough Petes, Oct 4 2018

Sault Ste. Marie -

Calisti, Robert (2019) – Calisti played larger than his size and had a couple of solid defensive plays throughout the game. One of his more notable sequences was during an attempted zone entry over his own blueline by an opponent, he gauged time and space well before delivering a clean puck-separating hit then collected the puck and transitioned over all three zones, resulting in a clean offensive zone entry. In his own-end, he assessed the play in advance behind his own-goal line on a couple of shifts, and was consistent at tracking his opponent, showing good support for his defensive partner on one play in particular that allowed him to move the puck back up the ice. There was little in the way of offense or puck skills shown by Calisti but he was adequate in his own-end and flashed the ability to transport the puck.

O'Rourke, Ryan (2020) – O'Rourke displayed two-way qualities against Peterborough but didn't play with a lot of pace in his own-end and lacked the mobility necessary to keep up with some of the quicker players. His pivoting and balance were average, and this led to him been susceptible when mis-interpreting his gap. That been said, he did manage to stay in-front of his opponents on some shifts and used his body and stick to take away lanes at times but wasn't physically engaged enough. He was used on the top powerplay unit and showed decent quarterbacking skills, particularly with his poise when holding onto the puck before looking for an open teammate. He showed the ability to use body and shot fakes to re-position his passing and shooting lanes but didn't have any plays that showed too much in the way of high-end skill or creativity.

Carroll, Joe (2019) – Carroll had a below-average game while playing on the third-line for the Greyhounds by not being engaged in the offensive-zone consistently. His play was largely kept to the perimeter, which was a result of him rarely looking to drive into heavy traffic areas despite showing a good amount of fluidity on his skates. He did position himself properly to receive a pass in a good scoring area near the slot on one sequence and his best offensive-sequence came off a give-and-go where he passed it to his teammate in the high-slot before skating near the goal-line where he received a pass and attempted to backhand it past Jones. With the exception of that scoring chance he looked to pass the puck and made a couple of soft-passes showing decent skill. Other areas to note were that his motor and pace were average, he failed to drive play, and despite having a fluid stride his posture is upright and he lacks a deep knee-bend.

Kerins, Rory (2020) – Kerins had a couple of good scoring chances while playing on the top-line and getting powerplay time. Rory wasn't afraid to get into high traffic areas. One play that demonstrated this was during a puck carrying rush where he attempted to weave through heavy traffic. On the powerplay he looked to be at his most dangerous by finding soft-ice in the slot area and had a couple of high-end scoring chances as a result. Although he didn't execute at a high-rate at times, he displayed an above-average motor and seemed to be constantly in motion, rarely sitting back and watching play, instead trying to involve himself in it.

Peterborough -

Jones, Hunter (2019) – Jones was largely the reason that Peterborough came away with the victory. He's a big kid but moves like a goaltender half his size, displaying excellent crease containment due to his edges, impressive lateral mobility, good reflexes and fluid post integration. The above package allowed him to make several high-end saves ranging from point-blank extended pad saves in-front of the crease, to saves that required him to move across his net rapidly to take away one-timer options. He allowed two-goals on breakaways, but he assessed the shot locations correctly. Despite facing several high-percentage shots while playing in-front of a defense that looked overwhelmed at times, Jones made difficult saves look relatively easy by reading most plays well in advance and squaring up to shooters correctly, it was an impressive performance.

Spearing, Shawn (2020) – Spearing had an above-average game in his own-end but was rarely a factor on the other side of the ice. He positioned himself well to receive passes from his defensive partner, and as a result was above-average at moving the puck up the ice with transitional outlet passes under pressure. He wasn't overly physical but did engage along the boards when necessary and when he was caught behind the play on a couple of different sequences, he competed hard to try and gain back his positioning. At the offensive line he had trouble getting the puck through traffic and wasn't a factor in generating much in the way of scoring chances.

Butler, Cameron (2020) – Butler had an average performance against the Greyhounds, getting a couple of quality opportunities but having mixed execution and failing to anticipate the play both with and without the puck on some plays. He's a big kid and used his size to drive-wide while attempting a direct approach to the net on one shift which resulted in a shot short-side. On another sequence he showed below average anticipation, reacting late a defensive play by his opponent who closed his gap on him quickly and took away his passing lane as he was carrying the puck during a 2-on-1 sequence, but he did have a high-end scoring chance directly in-front of the net however the puck skipped over his stick, again he was slightly late to react to the play. After a whistle, he was involved in a physical altercation and didn't mind mixing it up as well.

Cermak, Erik (2019) – Cermak didn't get too many opportunities while playing on the 4th line but did receive some powerplay time where he had his best scoring opportunity. With the man-advantage, he found soft-ice in-front of the net and shot a quick wrist-shot that required a difficult stop, it was his best scoring chance of the game. On another sequence he was involved along the boards and tried to pry the puck free but his forecheck for the most part was average, he didn't manage to generate much in the way of sustained pressure.

Sioux City Musketeers at Green Bay Gamblers, October 5th 2018

Sioux City Musketeers

Kallionkieli, Marcus – 2019 The first thing that stood out about Marcus's game tonight was his skating. While it's not real explosive yet, he possesses a long, powerful stride that makes him deceptively quick to pucks and closing on players on the fore-check. Marcus didn't do much to drive the offense or create chances in this game but showed willingness to compete for pucks and drive the net when the opportunity presented itself.

Brink, Bobby – 2019 The Denver University commit was held off the score sheet in this game but provided solid effort in all three zones. Brink showed fast skill with the puck. An example of this was in the 3rd period when he makes a slick stick handling move with speed to gain the edge on the defenseman coming into the offensive zone and proceeded to drive hard to the net for a good scoring chance. Brink also showed good awareness in the offensive zone where he won a battle along the half wall and took the puck to the slot, showed good poise with the puck to get the defenseman to challenge him and then zipped a pass over to the far side defenseman for a one-time shot that the goalie had to make a good glove save on. Brink didn't shy away from any areas of the ice and played a much bigger game than his size would lead you to believe.

Kehrer, Anthony – 2020 Kehrer was one of the better players for either team tonight. Anthony displayed great skating ability and edgework, both in defending one on one and with the pick on his stick. Kehrer displayed his footwork and elusiveness coming out of puck battle in his own end, where he used a slick pivot to escape pressure and zip a pass on his teammates tape to exit the zone. Kehrer was good along the wall in his own end by competing and winning battles. On a 5 on 3 Penalty Kill he won a 2 on 1 battle behind his own net and proceeded to draw a penalty in the sequence and the proceeded to have a key shot block on the ensuing 5 on 4 penalty kill to finish the PK. Kehrer showed the ability to walk the line effectively in the offensive end. Kehrer played his off side and had no trouble making plays on his backhand to hold and move the puck in the offensive zone.

Kraws, Ben – 2019+ The Miami (OH) commit was on his game tonight and only got better as the game went on. Kraws was under siege for much of the game and was able to keep his team in the game and preserve the 1 goal lead late in the game. Kraws played a sound game structurally, very few times was he caught out of position or scrambling and controlled his rebounds well the entire game. Kraws displayed a good combination of size and athleticism, making some excellent east-west saves.

Frisch, Ethan – 2019 Frisch is a bit undersized but played bigger than his 5'11" stature in this game. Frisch used his above average skating ability to keep a good gap and positioning when defending against the rush. On one sequence, Frisch was able to force the puck carrier to the outside on the rush and finish his check on the half wall, separating his man from the puck. Frisch was sound in executing his breakouts, both using his feet and accurate passing ability. Frisch went through his reads quickly and was able to find the open man effectively for much of the game. When an outlet pass wasn't available Frisch showed the ability to skate the puck out of his own zone and find a teammate in the neutral zone or gain the red line and dump into the offensive zone. Very few turnovers or errant passes were committed when the puck was on Frisch's stick tonight and he was dynamic with the puck at the point of the power play.

Green Bay Gamblers

Mylymok, Luke – 2020 Mylymok displayed his high end skill in assisting on Green Bay's goal when he used his quick hands and stick handling ability on a 2 on 2 line rush to beat his defenseman as he entered the offensive zone, creating a 2 on 1 where he fired a quick shot to the goalies far pad where the rebound kicked right out to his teammate for an easy tap in goal. Mylymok's offensive skill was on display and his skating is explosive with the puck on his stick. Luke showed good 2-way effort and broke up a couple plays on the back check as well. Mylymok showed the skating and skill to be a Draft prospect for 2020.

Giroday, Chris – 2019 Giroday played a reliable two-way defensive game for much of the night. His defensive positioning and stick where an asset tonight, as he did a good job challenging plays at his own blue line and taking away time and space from his opponent. Played a physical game in front of his goalie and cleared the front of the net well on outside shots. Chris got himself into some difficult situations a couple of times by not moving the puck quick enough is his own end.

Rimouski Oceanic at Drummondville Voltigeurs, Oct 5th, 2018

Rimouski Oceanic

#11 Lafrenière, Alexis (2020) – With no Salda in the lineup, Lafrenière played on the point on the power play and was also featured on his usual spot at LW on the top line. His line had some scoring chances and some good pressure on some shifts, but overall, Lafrenière didn't stand out in this game as we have seen in the past. His skating and pace were only average. He showed a good compete level in all three zones, but for his standards, this was not a great game for him.

#56 Innis, Christopher (2019) – Solid all-around game from Innis, who saw some good ice time in all situations tonight. Innis is not very tall, but is very strong on his skates and it showed in his battles along the boards. It was also tough to beat him one-on-one. The only problem he had defending in this game was against the speed of the opposition, as he was beaten wide a couple of times. Good stick in the defensive zone blocking passes and knocking pucks down. Good anticipation as well, as he knew where the puck would go and was effective when moving them out of his zone quickly, with a good first pass.

#42 Bernard, Jacob (2019) – Thought he did a good job putting pucks on net tonight, and made simple plays that made him efficient at both ends of the ice. Not a flashy defenseman but he showed good smarts and took advantage of his opportunity tonight.

#92 Ellis, Colton (2019) – He was weak on the first goal he allowed, but was solid the rest of the game for the Océanic. He made several key saves in the first two periods to keep Rimouski in this game, and in the 3rd, the Océanic were able to put the game away with some timely goals. His puck-tracking was solid, and he did well on the 2nd and 3rd rebound-saves. He demonstrated a good work ethic fighting off those pucks and making those saves.

#94 Massicotte, Zachary (2019) – His footwork and agility are below average, and for this reason, he had trouble against speedsters during this game. He didn't look good defending against Dawson Mercer in the first period, which made him look bad on one sequence. He had a good physical presence in his own zone and used his big body well along the boards.

#24 Bizier, Mathieu (2019) - Strong effort in all three zones, especially in the defensive zone, where he really did a good job coming back deep in his own end to support his defensemen. No quit from him when playing away from the puck; saw some good effort on the backcheck. He played a mature game away from the puck. Offensively, he had some shifts with Lafrenière in this game but couldn't materialize enough offense consistently. With the puck, he had some ups and downs in the first two periods, but had his best effort in the 3rd period.

#88 Janvier, Frederyck (2020) – A 16-year-old player who made the jump from the LHPS to center Rimouski's 4th line this year. He's tiny, but plays much bigger than his listed size, and was physically involved every time he was on the ice. Combined with his work ethic, this factor made him noticeable. He played the pesky-player role on his line, and has good enough speed to annoy the opposing defensemen on the forecheck.

Drummondville Voltigeurs

#6 Baker, Jarrett (2019) – Baker was solid tonight, playing more than usual with Nicolas Beaudin out of the lineup. He played hard in his own zone and threw some good hits when needed. He was solid on the PK unit, clearing the front of the net, and making good use of his stick to take the puck away from the Rimouski forwards.

#4 Pelletier, Thomas (2019) – Pelletier showed good skating abilities in some sequences tonight, which helped in getting himself out of trouble in his own zone. He didn't try much offensively, though, as he mostly preferred to dump the puck in the Rimouski zone once past the red line. He was solid when it came to defending one-on-one; he used his body well and threw some good hits along the boards. He showed improved footwork from last year, which did help him a lot in those one-on-one confrontations. However, I wish I would have seen more plays with the puck out of him today.

#16 Dion, Jacob (2020) – Called up for this game to replace Beaudin, Dion, who was drafted last June by the Voltigeurs, showed some interesting things on the power play with his quick puck movements and ability to rush the puck. He had quality ice time on the power play, but his even-strength opportunities were limited.

#29 Turan, Oliver (2019) – A big presence on the blueline, Turan was not overly physical. He made good use of his long stick on some sequences, including one where he broke up a passing play on a two-on-one chance from the opposition. Skating, mobility and footwork will need to get better, and his reaction time was slow as well.

#19 Mercer, Dawson (2020) – He was one of the best forwards, if not the best Drummondville forward today. Mercer showed excellent skill level throughout this game, with excellent speed off the rush. Really dangerous one-on-one, and Rimouski attempted to play physical against him in the first period but he didn't seem to be bothered by it, as he had other good moments in periods 2 and 3.

Shawinigan Cataractes at Sherbrooke Phoenix, October 6th, 2018

Shawinigan Cataractes

#65 Nussbaumer, Valentin (2019) - On the power play he played on the point, and didn't have his best moments in the first period. He was better in periods 2 and 3, however. There was some questionable decision-making early-on in the game, but this also improved after the first period. He showed good flashes offensively with his skill and speed. He has the speed to beat defensemen wide and showed it on some occasions during this game. He had some good scoring chances in the game but couldn't finish, and his shot could stand to improve. He was also a good playmaker in today's game; he created some good scoring chances for his linemates. If they had had more finish, he could have had 2 or 3 assists in this game. With the puck, he did some good things, but without the puck he was a bit lost in his own end and will need to get better playing away from the puck.

#11 Martin, Jeremy (2019) - Solid effort in today's game from Martin, who showed a good compete level battling for pucks and was quick to put pressure on the puck-carrier in the neutral zone trying to create turnovers. He kept his feet moving, which made him effective today. He scored the 2nd Shawinigan goal mid-way in the 3rd period while going to the net and taking a pass in the slot from Gabriel Denis – he then made a nice deke in front of the Sherbrooke goaltender.

#15 Denis, Gabriel (2019) – Liked his puck-protection game down low and how he used his body to keep possession of the puck. He worked hard in all three zones and made a nice feed to an open Jeremy Martin for the Cataractes' 2nd goal of the game.

#22 Bourque, Mavrik (2020) – It was a quiet game from him. I counted one good scoring chance where he took a quick wrist shot on his off-wing that came close to beating the Sherbrooke goaltender. He saw ice time regularly at even-strength and on the power play, but was not a factor.

#79 Beaudoin, Charles (2020) – Beaudoin is still adjusting his game to the major junior level. He was hit hard three times in this game. He was a bit slow reacting to plays out there. He showed his quick release on one scoring chance on one play, but that was his only highlight in the offensive zone.

#98 Bourgault, Xavier (2021) – He saw ice time on the power play and at even-strength, but struggled when battling for pucks along the boards. Bourgault is still immature physically and lost most of his one-on-one battles against bigger and more physical opponents.

Sherbrooke Phoenix

#32 Joncas, Alexandre (2019) - He was the most efficient defenseman from Sherbrooke today. He kept his game simple, and moved the puck smartly without being flashy. He was good defending one-on-one by playing his man well. Not a big upside as far as the NHL Draft goes, but he was solid today.

#72 Bellamy, Jaxon (2019) – Bellamy had a bad first period where he struggled in possession of the puck and made too many mistakes. He calmed down his game in periods 2 and 3. His decision-making while in possession of the puck was still too slow, however, and was prone to turnovers. He played on the power play; he took some good point shots. His puck-distribution on the man-advantage could stand to be better.

#29 Poulin, Samuel (2019) – Poulin was really good in the first half of the game, playing like a true power-forward: using his size and vision to make plays offensively. He was strong along the boards and was protecting the puck really well down low. He made a great play down low protecting the puck, then feeding a teammate in front of the net for the 2-0 goal. He made another similar play where he showed excellent vision from below the faceoff dots. His game dropped a bit in the 2nd half after he made a bad pass that was intercepted, which led to the first Shawinigan goal of the game.

#81 Okuliar, Oliver (2019) – Feet are heavy, but gets around the ice well enough for this level and heads to the tough areas of the ice. Still, his lack of speed hurt him when trying to create separation between himself and his coverage. Good down low and he's strong on the puck. I also liked his playmaking abilities from down low.

#10 Guay, Patrick (2020) - He showed quick decision-making and an ability to make some good passes for his linemates in the offensive zone. A bit undersized, it can be tough for him along the boards early-on in his QMJHL career. He made smart plays with and without the puck, he showed good awareness in his zone, and provided good support coming back deep in his zone.

Hamilton Bulldogs vs Peterborough Petes, Oct 6 2018

Bulldogs –

Mutter, Navrin (2019) – Mutter had an ineffective game for Hamilton while playing on the 4th-line. He showed a lack of puck-skills that caused his passes to be too sharp and miss their intended targets for the most part, while also failing to protect the puck properly as a result. He's a big kid with decent skating and forechecked aggressively in spurts, but never really generated consistent pressure or delivered a takeaway. He did attempt a couple of passes near the goal-line to his teammates but they were largely inaccurate, his spacing away from the play was also mixed.

Avery, Hayes (2021) – Hayes had a standout performance for Hamilton despite being the youngest player in the game. He's a slight player and lacks power in his first-few strides, but he compensated well with plus anticipation and having a high-panic threshold when getting pressured. Although his straight-line speed didn't impress today, his agility did, side-stepping several players that allowed him additional time and space with the puck, this allowed him to have good puck-management and keep plays alive. He scored his first goal of the season after skating down towards the left-side of the slot after receiving a pass from Kaliyev during a 2-on-1; he shot the puck quickly and in one-motion while also opening himself up properly. His most impressive play showed poise, patience, and confidence while moving laterally through the slot before out-waiting Jones who went into a butterfly, he then fired a hard wrist-shot that pinged off the crossbar. The shot came off his stick with a surprisingly amount of velocity. Away from the puck, he had a nice stick-deflection play that redirected a point-shot in the corner.

Kaliyev, Arthur (2019) – Kaliyev was dangerous today but also showed some concerns away from the puck on both the forecheck and in his own-end of the ice. His offensive-game stood-out, showing a lethal release point that led to a wrist-shot that hit the crossbar, but it was largely his passing that looked crisp out there. On the powerplay, he was slotted in the right-circle and forced his opponents to respect his shooting option which allowed him to create space for his teammates, he then threaded several passes around the goal-line, this led to a secondary-assist on one play. He had a primary assist after feeding a nice pass across the slot to Avery as well, it was timed properly and he made it difficult for

Jones to make the read. Away from the play, Kaliyev displayed a lack of engagement along the boards, next to zero-compete on some forechecking sequences, and a lack of effort on the backcheck as well. Though, after Peterborough fought back in the game to make it 3-2, Arthur did show a gear change and hustled a little more, so to his credit, he showed he can shift his tempo, but that tempo was still lagging behind relative to most other players on the ice.

Morrison, Logan (2020) – Morrison had a difficult game for the Bulldogs. He had a clean-transitional zone-entry on one play, but on another he slowed down while carrying the puck despite having open-ice which forced his teammates offside. He was caught with his head down while moving over the offensive-line and was met with a big hit that shook him up a bit. On the forecheck, he was unable to compete well due to poor skating mechanics and a lack of power in his frame.

Petes –

Spearing, Shawn (2020) – Spearing was used on the third-pairing but did a decent job around his goal-line by physically engaging, keeping his opponents mostly to the outside and along the boards, as well as supporting his defenseman at times. He's not the biggest kid but had no problem using his frame to counteract the Bulldogs forecheck, and he moved the puck under-pressure at a decent rate, though offensively, he didn't get too many touches with the puck or generate scoring chances.

Butler, Cameron (2020) – Butler had an inconsistent game for the Petes, but did show good anticipation and positioning away from the play, which allowed him to have a couple of good-looks throughout the game. The first thing that stands out about the kid is his release point, although he fanned on his opening attempt, and missed the net on another, it was quick. He showed the ability to change the angle of his release-point on his goal, by curling the puck around the Bulldogs netminder who had gone down to early. The play that led to his goal also showed good poise when handling the puck and the ability to find loose pucks in traffic around the slot-area. He's a big kid, but didn't engage physically as much as I would have liked to have seen and never drove-play or dictated the tempo of play on any shift.

Jones, Hunter (2019) – Jones had an above-average performance for the Bulldogs, showing good rebound control from shots labelled for his crest-area, a good glove-hand, and the ability to read plays well. His lateral movement let him down a couple of times, and this resulted in two of the goals scored against him. On the first, he didn't generate enough power in his initial push-off while moving side-to-side, and the 2nd goal was on the powerplay, where he failed to push off properly from his butterfly which left a lot of net open. That being said, he showed the ability to mentally-rebound, keeping his team in the game with some excellent point-blank saves when the Petes were down by a single goal. Furthermore, his rebound control was solid, and he was calm in the crease. There was very little in the way of panic or extra-movement in his game.

Chicago Steel at Madison Capitols, October 12, 2018

Chicago Steel

Treloar, Travis – 2019 Treloar displayed a plus motor all game, especially in regards to pressuring the puck carrier. His work ethic on the back check allowed his defenseman to be aggressive at their own blue line and have a good gap against the opponent. Treloar scored in the 3rd period by retrieving the puck after an offensive zone faceoff, circled out of the corner and drove the net along the goal line and out muscle the defender to jam the puck past the Madison goalie at the side of the net. Travis didn't display much in the way of high end puck skills or playmaking ability in this game but was able to create possession and offensive zone time due to his hard work in all three zones.

Groll, Josh – 2019 Groll wasn't a contributor on the score sheet in this game; however his play around the puck in all situations was key to his team's success tonight. Groll used plus skating and hockey sense to disrupt the puck carrier on the fore-check as well as applying back pressure. Groll had some key shot blocks in his own zone, especially on the Penalty Kill. An example of Groll executing the little things was on the penalty kill where he blocked a shot/pass at the top of his own zone, which allowed a clear down the ice, toward the opponents goal, Groll exploded out of the zone, chasing down the puck in the offensive zone and forcing the Madison goalie to cover the puck and Madison to take a defensive zone faceoff which killed the rest of the penalty. Groll was around the puck all night and won a lot of 50/50 battles, sometime against bigger opponents. Groll also displayed a plus shot release and power on a quick release from above the faceoff circles that the Madison goalie was barely able to fight off.

Power, Owen – 2019 Power is one of the youngest if not the youngest player in the USHL this year, being a late 2002 birthdate but he doesn't look it physically. Power has a big frame and long reach, which he used well when in a defensive posture against the rush. Power showed the willingness to jump in the play, both in the offensive end as well as joining the rush coming out of his own end however not much came of this as he wasn't able to get into the correct lane to receive a pass and on a couple occasions Power didn't show enough urgency to get back after the play went the other way. Power displayed a big shot from the point on a one-timer, despite only take a half wind up on the attempt, the puck came off low and hard, however there was no screen in front and the Madison goalie was able to make the save with no rebound. Owen displayed decent straight line skating for his size but needs to continue to work on his awareness and footwork as he was late and slow on a couple of his pivots and had his opponent had more skill, he could have been burned on a couple line rushes with players getting beyond him.

Reid, Luke – 2019 Reid played the point in the #1 PP unit and was effective in quickly moving the puck to the open side and using his east-west movement to get the opposing penalty killers to move and open up ice for his teammates. Reid showed good 2-way capability when he showed good escape ability with the puck in the neutral zone and skate the puck into the offensive zone for a shot on goal and then proceeded to hustle back to disrupt a line rush heading the other way. While Reid puck movements out of his own end didn't do much to stretch the ice, he moved the puck quickly and used his defensive partner well to alleviate pressure from the fore-check which allowed for clean zone exits.

Mastrosimone, Robert – 2019 Mastrosimone was easily the best player on the ice for either squad in this game. Mastrosimone registered 2 goals on the evening and easily could have had a couple more throughout the night. Robert didn't display many weaknesses in his game tonight. While his skating stride is not the most technically sound, Robert gets around the ice well and is able to find holes in the defense. Mastrosimone showed a good two-way game on his first goal where worked hard behind his own goal to eliminate a scoring chance and allow his team to gain possession and exit the zone. Mastrosimone proceeded to use his speed to catch up to the play coming into the offensive zone, where a blocked shot found Mastrosimone's tape as he came down the middle of the slot and used his quick release to beat the Madison goalie under the bar. Mastrosimone showed good skill and creativity on an offensive zone faceoff where he went to his forehand and executed a shot on goal right on the drop of the puck that the Madison goalie was ready for. Shortly after this play Mastrosimone scored his 2nd goal where he showed good compete and work ethic to out-work two Madison defenseman behind the net, circled the cage on his forehand and quick shot that beat the goalie on the short side. Mastrosimone also passed up a tap in goal at the back door later in the game to try to setup a teammate at the other side of the net. This may have been due to the situation of the game more than his hockey sense or scoring drive.

Lindmark, Owen – 2019 Lindmark played a solid 3rd line center for USA in this game. He competed at both ends of the ice, showed the willingness to get over top of pucks at both ends and had a big shot block in the 2nd period while the game was still close. Lindmark showed good explosiveness in his skating and was often first on the fore-check in a lot of instances. Lindmark executed his roll well in this game, and did well in the faceoff circle. The struggle for Owen this season in regards to his draft stock is will he be put in enough offensive situations to display his skill.

York, Cam – 2019 York was ok in this game. He didn't do much to stand out or drive play at either end; however was effective in exiting his own zone, both using his feet and skating as well as his vision and passing ability. York displayed the ability to stretch the ice east-west by finding players in stride on the other side of the ice on the breakout as well. York had one good scoring chance coming down from the point where showed his quick, powerful release but shot the puck high and wide of the net.

Beecher, John – 2019 Beecher was USA's best and most consistent forward in this game. While Beecher's skating doesn't look overly impressive at first glance, he is deceptively quick and has an efficient and powerful stride. An example of this was in the 2nd where he was able to drive through the slot with the puck, splitting the defenseman and drawing a penalty. Beecher showed excellent compete in all area's often using 2nd and 3rd efforts and physicality to win puck battles for his team and was in and around the puck all evening. Another area of his game that was impressive was in the faceoff circle where he won a lot of draws, many cleanly against some veteran faceoff guys on Minnesota. Beecher displayed a true Power Forward style in this game, something not many other players on this USA squad can do.

Thrun, Henry (2019) – Thrun was the most offensively active defenseman for USA in this game. Thrun made good reads with the puck in his own end was able to find teammates with passes up the seam and stretch the ice in both directions. Thrun moved down the slot from the point and nearly scored on a tip from the slot on a feed from Hughes. Looked like the puck might have actually crossed the line but there was no review on the play. Thrun showed good creativity by using the boards not only to move the puck to his defensive partner to relieve pressure but to open up additional lanes up ice. While Thrun's footspeed is not at the level of some of his teammates, he used his hockey sense and active stick to defend one on one effectively in this game.

Hughes, Jack – 2019 Hughes did a good job showcasing his skill in this game, however in doing so he hung onto the puck too long in a lot of instances and committed some turnovers. Hughes wasn't able to create space for himself that he is used to having when he plays against his peer group. The older, more experienced Minnesota team did a good job keeping Hughes on the perimeter for a lot of the game. Having said that Hughes was still able to execute some scoring chances by feeding teammates who were able to occupy some of the space he created for others. There is room for improvement with his shot, as it didn't appear to be overly powerful nor did the release look to be overly quick.

Helleson, Drew – 2019 Played an effective stay at home game for a defensive squad that only dressed five defenseman. Helleson used his footwork and body position well both in defending 1 on 1 as well as with the puck in shielding his opponents and buying time for himself. He showed good defensive positioning in one sequence versus a very fast player in Sammy Walker, keeping him to the outside and stripping him of the puck.

Rowe, Cameron – 2019 Rowe showed excellent athleticism on a couple high-end saves on grade "A" scoring chances. Rowe did a good job take away the lower half of the net as well as battling to find pucks in traffic. Has efficient east-west movement and tracked the pucks east to west, not over committing with his movements. Late in the game Minnesota was able to beat Rowe over the glove on a couple of scoring chances.

Boldy, Matthew – 2019 Boldy played a bit too much of a 1 on 1 game where he held onto the puck too long, either committing turnovers at the blue lines or in the offensive zone, missing opportunities to find teammates in the offensive end. Boldy has good skill with the puck, however against this experienced Minnesota team, his game was too one dimensional for it to be as effective as it could have been. Showed good hockey sense to find open lanes and get puck possession in the offensive zone.

Moose Jaw Warriors vs Spokane Chiefs, October 13, 2018

Moose Jaw

Hunt, Daemon- Don't think he really had a misstep all game, seemingly always being in the right spot defensively and offensively. Skating is very fluid and powerful, winning every puck race he was put in. His skating also allowed him to play with a great gap, giving attackers little time and space off the rush. Has a booming shot from the point that he did an excellent job finding lanes with, and keeping it low with 3 points coming off point shots. Looked a bit lacking in confidence with the puck, playing with almost no risk to his game. As only a 16 year old, this should come and Hunt looks like he will have a very bright future.

Tracey, Brayden- Tracey was excellent, with his high end skill level noticeable every time he was on the ice. Great stickhandler with the puck on a string and the ability to make players miss in the open ice. Also could seemingly take any pass and control bouncing pucks effortlessly. Has a very unique rhythm to his game, passing at the right time to open a play up consistently. Absolutely no panic in his game as he did not look like he made a single forced play all game, really dictating the tempo when he had the puck. Did an excellent job forcing turnovers all over the ice with excellent stick checks, often picking players pockets. Compete was consistently high throughout the game, looking like he wanted to make a difference every shift.

Spokane

Beckman, Adam- Role has grown as he was lined up on the first line and PP units today. Will not blow you away on any one play but over the course of a game he makes a lot of smart high percentage plays. Has an excellent sense for when to move the puck and rarely turns it over because of this. Attacking he is always a threat to either pass or shoot and doesn't give the defender much of a sense on what he will do. Also extremely willing to pay the price and crash the net, seemingly right in the action on all of Spokane's good chances.

Toporowski, Luke- His hustle and skating ability are both elite. He generated multiple breakaways every game through his intense puck pressure and explosiveneds. He excels protecting the puck down low using his body as there are very few players at this level able to knock him off a puck. Skill level is just average without ridiculous creativity or stickhandling ability so mainly generates chances through speed and strength. Toporowski was very effective on the penalty kill, doing a great job at destroying breakouts and taking away shooting lanes in the zone.

Fargo Force at Sioux Falls Stampede, October 13, 2018

Fargo Force -

Mancinelli, Michael - 2019 Played a tidy, two-way game. Showed good smarts, got to the right side of the puck often. Just an average skater, a little choppy. Didn't really show off much in the way of puck skills on the night, as he didn't have it a lot. Plays a little further down the lineup and seems to have a less offensive role than you'd expect from a prospect at this level. This was one of his first games with a new club as well.

Sioux Falls Stampede -

Cameron, Matt - 2019 2000 birthday. Impressed with some really nice hands plays. Can beat different caliber/types of players at this level with regularity it seems. Scored a pretty goal to boot. Very capable skater. Has enough skill, confidence and flash to his game that he's worth keeping on the radar after being passed over 2018.

Johnson, Ryan - 2019 Showed wonderful multi-directional mobility, set in a good, low stance with a deep knee bend. Very calm under pressure. Plays the game almost too calm sometimes and it causes some of his passes against the grain to get tipped by the hardest working forecheckers. Made two multi-line rushes, but his teammates seem to have some trouble recognizing what their respective roles are on a defense-carry zone exit -> entry. Smart and effective defensively. He was willing to stand in there to make a play against bigger opponents. He had an effective breakout passer all night.

Decisive and intelligent. Really shows a great grasp of the flow and momentum of players, even if he can't see them – terrific understanding of the geometry of the game. Had a really strong and poised start. Tailed off a little bit later in the game. Oddly, didn't play the last minute of a tied game, nor did he take either of the first two shifts of overtime (played the third shift only). Still showed he was very much in control at this level already.

Brynas IF u20 at AIK u20, October 13, 2018

Brynas u20

Soderstrom, Victor (2019) - Played a quick, simple passing game for the first 40 minutes of the game. When his team struggled he had to seize the game and skate the puck himself, which he did successfully. Always a offensive threat from the blueline and creates offense with superb outlet passes. Super smooth skating and with excellent stickhandling, it looks like absolutely no one can take the puck off of him.

Aik u20

Karlstrom, David (2019) - Karlstrom keeps his feet going in all three zones and drives hard to the net, creating time and space for his linemates. Takes great responsibility two-ways and is not afraid to get physical. Distributes the puck well and gives good support all over the ice. He scored the 1-0 goal on a rebound.

Sjolund, Samuel(2019) - Sjolund is a left-handed defenseman with good mobility and decent speed. His physical attributes are pretty well-rounded. However, his play with the puck is way too inconsistent.He can make a great outlet pass one shift and then miss an easy pass for an icing call on the next shift. His shot is hard and hits the net most of the times, but there is not much creativity from the blueline.

Hedlund, August Hedlund had a quiet game today, against a team who played its third game in three days. He was calm and confident all game long, makes small quick movements and has superb reflexes. His communication with his defenders is strong and sharp.

Team Southwest vs NDTP-U17, October 14, 2018

Team Southwest

Docter, Grant – 2019 Used his hockey IQ and footwork to escape fore-checker with his outlet passes up ice. Despite not being big in stature, Docter was able to play physical against his opponents and uses leverage well to win battles and outmuscle for pucks. Docter registered one power play assist in this game and displayed efficiency and playmaking at the top of the Power Play.

Pitlick, Rhett – 2019 Pitlick scored one goal in this game with a nice give and go down low from the half-wall on the power play and beat the USA goalie with a well-placed shot over the blocker inside the far post. Pitlick showed fast skill with the puck and was able to drive the offense for stretches with the puck on his tape.

Luedtke, Josh – 2019 Luedtke was the best player on the ice for either team. Josh made his presence felt at both ends of the ice. Despite being an undersized defenseman, Luedtke was physical against his opponent, one instance, stepping up at the blue line and delivering a big hit on the puck carrier entering the zone. Luedtke scored a beautiful even strength goal in the 2nd where he came down the slow from the point where he found soft ice and received a pass and made a quick toe drag around the defender and fired a quick shot for the hash marks that beat the USA goalie over the glove. Luedtke excelled on the breakout, using his vision and skill to find teammates tape at the far blue line from deep in his own end to spring a breakaway chance.

Lavelle, Shane – 2019 Lavelle used his speed well to consistently take the puck to the net as well as be effective in the fore-check and back-check in forcing turnovers. Lavelle played an effective power forward style and he was the worker for his line in winning puck battles and gaining possessions but did very little to drive offense or create chances in the offensive end.

Boltmann, Jake – 2019 Boltmann plays a sound defensive game, consistently keeping a sound gap against the rush and keeping plays away from the middle of the ice. Boltmann was solid on his puck retrievals and did well to be aware where the pressure was coming from and moved the puck quickly out of his own end or to his defensive partner. Boltmann made good reads in the defensive zone and physically handled his opponents in front of his own net on a number of occasions. Boltmann was paired with Luedtke in this game and was a stay at home presence for Luedtke who likes to play an aggressive rover style from the back end.

USNTDP-U17

Tuch, Luke – 2020 Tuch played a prototypical power forward game today and was difficult to defend in 1 on 1 situations where he protected the puck well and used his strong skating base to shield defenders and drive plays toward the net. Tuch showed good hockey sense when he was able to identify his defender being flat footed as he entered the zone with the puck and aggressively took the puck to the net for a grade "A" scoring chance.

Gallatin, Owen – 2020 Gallatin is an undersized defenseman that was able to use his quick feet and hands to be an effective puck mover throughout this game. Away from the puck, Owen struggled identifying coverages in his own end quick enough and needs to ass strength to defend 1 on 1 more effectively.

Brynäs IF at Djurgården IF Oct 14 2018

Djurgården

DIF# 33 LD Björnfot, Tobias (2019): Great LD with good size and good skating. Mostly a very mature game from the 16 year old player that played in SHL the day before. Skated good, released the shot a couple of times but not that super accurate shot. Quick hard direct shot. Super talent but didn't had one of his best games. Made some dangerous moves at own blue and lost the puck. Was driving through 3 players but it looked very risky and he had team mates that would have been player to dropped the puck to. One good hit on the board.

DIF # 44 RW Grewe, Albin (2019): Excellent super talent that already made some games in SHL thanks to his skills. Played with high energy, good speed and with great poise. Was delivering some great accurate passes, good long passes. Always completed his hits and tried to play aggressive game. Was expecting him to shoot lot more. Great speed and close gap on a very high level. A couple of times where he could have used his teammates and where he gave me the impression that he wasn't even aware of having them with him. Was starting to move the puck more to his teammates later on and the 3-2 goal was nicely prepared by Grewe moving the puck. An eye for the net and the speed was shining both with puck and without. Was stopping to skate when chasing the opponent and it led to 2PIM for tripping. 1+1, 1 SOG, PIM 2.

DIF # 10 RW Holtz, Alexander (2020) - Difficult to believe that this guy is just 16 years old and plays with 4-year-old players and still shines as he does. He has great poise and shows very little understanding that he is the youngest. Use the speed and drives in to net. Good positioned. Good passes both backhand and forehand. Creates a lot. Some occasions it looks like he has very much luck being on the right spot but I am convinced it's his hockey sense that place him there. Very mobile and moves his over body very quick to get a extra quicker new direction. Was moving with his teammates a lot especially behind the 4-2 goal. Was looking to have some miscommunication with # 15 but otherwise excellent. Wonderful direct shot and good in PP with Grewe. Placed himself in front of the goal but had difficulties to stay there but I liked the attitude. 1 A, 2 SOG

DIF #19 CE Bjerselius, Oscar (2019) - Looked like he had good possibility to create gap from opponent, liked the pressure in the legs when skating. Nice quick chipping passes. Was having a ok game but wasn't visulised to much either positive or negative. Decent faceoffs.

Brynas

BIF # 29 RD Söderström, Victor (2019) - Söderström is a great skater and use his speed and very smooth skating in the game. He was reading the game very good and sees his teammates for opening hard accurate passes that starts scoring chances. He has good communication with his team mates. Far from big but knows how to use the body. Made a good offensive hit on Grewe. A bit over confident in second giving some pucks away. Creative playmaker and a good accurate shot, unfortunately with no traffic in front of the net. Great positioning, great angling on opponents and very good reliability. He showed very good agility and created a lot by finding his team mates or a couple of time bringing the puck on a puck rush himself. In third he brought the puck through he ices, went between the 2 Ds and delivered a shot that clinger hard in the frame. Even with that skills I liked his balance and considered that he played for his team at first. His vision and quick reaction of the game impressed me with awareness of team mates behind him that could take a quick pass between the legs backwards and heading to the net for a scoring chance. Potentially some small inches to far against wrong pillar when DIF had a 3 against 2 rush which lead to DIF doing 4-2. Great attitude during the game and even though the numbers I find Söderström one of my favorites and already ready for senior games. 2 SOG.

Saskatoon Blades vs Calgary Hitmen, October 17, 2018

Saskatoon

De La Gorgendiere, Aiden- It was a tough game for him with a couple major lapses in defensive coverage, resulting in wide open players in front. He was doing a good job with his passes when he had time but against a heavy forecheck was mostly throwing it away.

Malysjev, Emil- Looked really slow today, and really struggled to change directions keeping up with his check in the defensive zone. With the puck was making solid decisions but his passing was very unrefined, giving teammates a lot of passes in the feet.

Dach, Kirby- Doesn't look as dominant as you would expect but he finds a way to get his points. Passing is always on, right to where his teammate needs the puck and never in feet. He uses a very long stick which is a key to how he plays. Is amazing at stealing pucks and deflecting passes using his massive reach to get his stick to places most players cannot. He also uses his stick length to pass from a ton of different spots often reaching with his stick to pass around players. Offensively has added more to his game as he's a lot more of a shot threat now. This is especially noticeable on the powerplay where he is now a lot less predictable.

Robbins, Tristen- Best skater on the ice, can absolutely fly. Used his speed to be a real nuisance on the forecheck, giving defencemen no time to get the puck under control. Also had a really nice inside out move on a Calgary defenseman to go in for a breakaway that he put off the post. Had a couple passes where he showed decent vision.

Calgary

Fiddler-Schultz, Riley- Relentless and skilled player. Physically you can tell he's a bit overmatched but he works hard enough and is smart enough to make up for it. Did a great job anticipating the play defensively to get in passing lanes. Offensively he was at his best with the puck on his stick, getting a lot of shots on net and making some good moves on defencemen.

Halifax Mooseheads at Sherbrooke Phoenix, October 20th 2018

Halifax Mooseheads

#50 Lavoie, Raphaël (2019) - It was the Lavoie show in the first period; he made things happen in different ways with his excellent puck skills, vision and great wrist shot. He scored a highlight-reel goal going around Crête-Belzile and beating Sigouin from his backhand. He was quieter in the 2nd period, and in the 3rd period, he had some flashes in the offensive zone. Lavoie did good work with his long reach protecting the puck, and once he was able to hit his top speed, he was intimidating for the Sherbrooke defensemen dealing with him one-on-one. Lots of talent here, but I would like to see him work harder and be more consistent from shift to shift.

#67 Parent, Xavier (2019) – Parent had maybe one or two scoring chances in this game. One of these was from the slot, where he took a good one-timer, but overall, he was not a big threat on the ice. His skating didn't look as good as I remembered from the past 2-3 years of scouting him. He lacks some explosiveness, and as a smaller player, this is a key asset for him to have. He made a couple of questionable decisions with the puck, including one on a 2-on-1 rush.

#20 Barron, Justin (2020) – Barron was solid today, playing his usual strong two-way game. He was good on the transition with some good passing plays and moved pucks effectively out of his zone. He was tough to beat one-on-one, quickly putting pressure on the puck-carrier. He has the mobility and positional game to be effective in a shutdown role. He played in all situations today.

Sherbrooke Phoenix

#32 Jonas, Alexandre (2019) – Made simple passing plays while in transition. His decision-making is okay, but if he was quicker at making his passes, he could create more offense. On one sequence where he had Poulin open to receive a pass (which would have led to a scoring chance off the rush), he didn't see him quickly enough, which cancelled the opportunity. He played a smart game at both ends of the ice. He is not the biggest defenseman, but competed well and worked hard. He's good at playing within his limits. At his size, he had some problems when he was matched up versus Lavoie.

#72 Bellamy, Jaxon (2019): Struggled with the pace of the game, was slow retrieving pucks in his zone and had some tough shifts in his own zone. He didn't get many shifts on the power play and was not a factor in this game, as he had very few puck touches.

#14 Jentzsch, Taro (2019) – The 18-year-old German didn't get much done offensively today, but was good on the PK with good hustle, anticipation and an excellent stick. Loved his work ethic, but didn't see much in terms of offensive skills. He did some good work down low cycling pucks with his linemates.

#29 Poulin, Samuel (2019) - Poulin had some good scoring chances in this game; he had a good first period, showing good flashes of his skills and an ability to use his size to his advantage. He was quieter the rest of the game and finally scored on a rebound in front of the net late in the game to make the score 4-2 Halifax. Liked his work along the boards and his technique to protect the puck, and how he used his body to shield opponents away from the puck. He had trouble finishing plays today, missing on some good scoring chances.

#81 Okuliar, Oliver (2019) - Skating is rough, feet are heavy. He worked hard down low and on the forecheck. He created a scoring chance with an aggressive forecheck that caused a turnover. He was involved in the tough areas and was often near the puck. He's a smart player.

Vancouver Giants vs. Kelowna Rockets, October 21, 2018

Vancouver

Valenti, Yannik- Nothing overly flashy in his game but played an extremely smart positional game. Was excellent with controlled pressure on neutral zone regroups and the forecheck. Also did a great job making himself available to teammates for a pass, playing a very mature game off the puck. Skating and skills appeared to be just average as outside of a couple nice carries through the neutral zone he didn't have a ton of noticeable moments.

Sourdif, Justin- Showed an extremely high level of talent throughout the game, with a couple of high end skill plays. Instantly stands out on the ice as a guy that's always playing with a ton of energy. With the puck on his stick Sourdif showed a very unique ability to beat players one on one both with his skating and stickhandling. In one particularly impressive sequence off the rush he opened up, faked a drop pass which the defender bit on, then turned the corner and threw a dangerous pass to a teammate in front. Also showed a really good understanding of where the soft spaces in the offensive zone are as he constantly found himself wide open in a dangerous area, scoring a goal off of a play like this.

Byram, Bowen- Stands out for his effortless skating, and some of the best lateral mobility of any defenseman in the draft. With the exception of one really bad turnover as the last man Byram consistently showed excellent decision making. He is the type of player who makes plays with the puck that will maintain possession for his team, never forcing a risky play or throwing the puck away. Extremely confident in the offensive zone getting involved without the puck and especially with the puck on his stick. Two goals were started off of him making an opposing team player miss at the blue line before exploding into open ice and making a dangerous play. Defensively had a great stick, managing to disposes any player that came close to him.

Kelowna

Thomson, Lassi- There are a couple areas of Thomson's game where he is a very clear standout. Whenever he has the puck on his stick Thomson shows high level hands, and is very confident making moves at high speeds. Deked his way into the offensive zone on a couple of occasions. Basically any time he touched the puck in his own zone it was getting out as he did a great job settling down the puck and finding a good tape to tape pass. In the offensive zone Thomson excels at finding a shooting lane and also has a very heavy point shot.

Korczak, Kaeden- Not the best game for Korczak as his passing and decision making looked a little bit off. Defensively was still rock solid, with very good positional play and a willingness to engage physically. Did an excellent job of breaking up the other teams cycle and winning the puck back for his team on multiple occasions. For a big guy is a very fluid and explosive skater, going all the way from behind his net into the other teams zone as he blew by everyone on one shift. Was up top on Kelowna's powerplay and did an okay job of moving the puck around but telegraphed the play a couple times allowing the other team to jump the lane.

USA U18 vs Dartmouth, October 22nd, 2018

USA U18

#30 Knight, Spencer (2019) – Only played the first half of the game and gave up one goal before leaving to give the rest of the game to Rowe. He had, on a couple of sequences, some issues playing the puck behind his net that resulted in turnovers. No chance on the only goal he gave up, as it was a great scoring chance in front of the net after a Dartmouth forward was left uncovered there.

#27 Rowe, Cameron (2019) – Rowe had some issues tracking pucks in the half of the game he played, but seemed to be playing with more confidence in the 3rd period. He was soft on the first goal he gave up, as he was too slow covering the puck with his glove. Overall, he gave up three goals but was able to hold onto the lead in the 3rd period to get Team USA the win.

#7 Vlasic, Alex (2019) – In the first period, he was too passive in his own zone and also took bad angles when attacking the puck-carrier. This left him in a bad position to defend. He doesn't have the best footwork, but does generate a decent amount of speed. He made a nice play on Team USA's 3rd goal with a nice pass/shot that was deflected by Boldy in the slot.

#4 Helleson, Drew (2019) – He made some good decisions even when under pressure with the puck on his stick. He made some surprising moves when rushing the puck, and showed some good stickhandling work beating guys one-on-one. Good defending as well, good gap control, and he was always quick to put pressure on the puck-carrier in the defensive or neutral zone.

#5 Webber, Cade (2019) – Huge kid who was called up this week to replace Marshall Warren on the team. Love the size and how he moves well for a 6'5" defenseman. He didn't get any power play or PK ice time. His footwork could be more fluid, there's some minor tweaking that could be done to improve his fluidity. The game can be a bit fast to him as far as decision-making goes; there's a big adjustment coming from prep hockey to play versus an NCAA team.

#24 McCarthy, Case (2019) – Struggled a bit with his passing game when he was under pressure today. When not under pressure, he made some good passes, but rushed them a bit otherwise and turned the puck over as a result. On the power play, he took some hard shots on net, and showed off his good one-timer as well. Good defending one-on-one, showed good gap control, and threw some good hits.

#2 York, Cam (2019) – Demonstrated a fluid skating stride. He started getting more active in the offensive zone in the 2nd half of the game, where he used his feet more to make a difference in the game offensively. Good at rushing the puck out of his zone; with his fluid footwork, it can be easy for him to escape pressure and get the puck out of his zone. He was the lone defenseman on the power play (1st unit).

#3 Thrun, Henry (2019) – Solid game from Thrun tonight. There was nothing flashy, but he was effective playing alongside York on the back end at even-strength. He did a good job in the offensive zone to get open and receive passes from his teammates. He did a good job on Team USA's 2nd goal, where he jumped into the rush and made a nice pass to Zegras to put his team up 2-1. He didn't get power play time, though.

#6 Hughes, Jack (2019) – With his acceleration, it was too easy at times for him to create separation and make zone entries tonight. His speed was really on display on the man-advantage, given that he had more space on the ice. He made a great passing play to Zegras for the opening goal of the game. Another great playmaking play was on the game-winning goal, where he did a good job waiting an extra second before passing the puck to Caufield just to freeze the opposing goaltender.

#11 Zegras, Trevor (2019) – Zegras scored two goals tonight from two great setups from teammates, where he had an open cage to shoot at. Love the puck skills, but not that he was still outmuscled too often along the boards against Dartmouth tonight. His physical immaturity has shown in these mini-series versus NCAA teams. He did, however, make a couple of weird decisions with the puck, turning it over.

#9 Boldy, Matthew (2019) – Boldy was a two-way force tonight; he scored Team USA's 3rd goal with a nice tip in front of the net. Strong effort on the backcheck; he made two great plays there that I noticed where he was able to pick the puck away from an opponent with his good active stick. Boldy didn't show any high-end skill level or skating abilities, but showed high-end smarts.

#29 Weight, Danny (2019) – His footwork and overall quickness are average at best. With the puck on his stick, he has a hard time creating separation from his opponents. He showed some good smarts in all three zones, and was good along the boards as well.

#13 Caufield, Cole (2019) – Scored the game-winning goal in the 3rd period on a 2-on-1 rush with Jack Hughes feeding him a perfect pass. He didn't have a big impact in this game outside of that goal, however. In fact, he encountered some struggles playing against a more advanced physical team like Harvard. He didn't get many opportunities to use it, but he does have an excellent release on his wrist shot, as demonstrated on his goal.

#21 Farrell, Sean (2020) – Liked his speed and hustle throughout this game; he was playing on the 3rd line with Lindmark and Rolston. His speed and acceleration are good, and he used his low center of gravity well to protect the puck along the boards. He scored Team USA's 6th goal of the game with a good shot on a 2-on-1 rush. However, I would like to see him make smarter plays and use his linemates better.

#12 Rolston, Ryder (2020) – He showed some glimpses of a good skating stride down the wing on a couple of sequences where he went around opposing Dartmouth defensemen. He missed his defensive coverage on Darmouth's first goal, leaving his man open in the slot. He scored Team USA's 4th goal of the game.

#17 Beecher, John (2019) – He showed good support in his own zone, helping his defensemen retrieve pucks down low. He didn't create much offensively, centering the 4th line between Moynihan and Caulfield. He didn't show much in terms of creativity and playmaking abilities today.

Saint John Sea Dogs at Moncton Wildcats, October 25th, 2018

Saint John

#13 Villeneuve, William (2020) – Good one-on-one defending, good positional game, and a very good active stick to pokecheck pucks away or extend his stick to block passing lanes. Offensively, he would always keep his play-selection simple, taking simple wrist shots from the point with good accuracy. One of these led to Saint John's 1-0 goal.

#44 Poirier, Jeremie (2020) – He showed some good skating abilities on some sequences and an ability to dangle the puck one-on-one in the offensive zone. He played on the power play, but was not a big factor in this game.

#58 Desroches, Charlie (2020) – He was really good tonight, outside of a couple of mistakes in his own zone. For one of these sequences, he played the puck instead of the man, only to be deked by Jeremy McKenna. Overall, he was good, showing quick puck-moving skills and using his feet well to rush the puck out of his zone and into the offensive zone. He was involved in the offensive zone, often playing like a 4th forward on the ice.

#18 Lawrence, Josh (2020) – Good use of his speed tonight, good puck rushes into the offensive zone and made some good zone entries all night. Really good in the faceoff circle tonight; one of his faceoff wins led to the opening goal of the game. He was involved in the play, despite not being the biggest player on the ice, and had some good scoring chances close to the net.

#88 Cajkovic, Maxim (2019) – Not very involved on the ice. We would like to see him work harder to get the puck back. Not many puck touches on the ice - when he had the puck in the offensive zone, he had a tough time getting his shot through to the net. He played on the top line with Lawrence and also saw a good amount of ice time on the power play.

#25 Prikryl, Filip (2019) – Filip showed some good work down low and along the boards in this game from him. He demonstrated good puck-protection behind the net, and created a couple of scoring chances for teammates there. He showed good vision on these plays, setting up his teammates from behind the net. He showed some flashes in the first period and was quieter during the rest of the game.

Moncton

#21 Spence, Jordan (2019) – Throughout this game he showed some very good poise with the puck, was never in panic, and always seemed to make the smart plays with the puck. Good first pass out of his zone. Quick, accurate passes that helped out his team's transition game. He finished the game with an assist; he did a great job coming back to stop an odd-man rush by Saint John, stealing the puck on a great backchecking effort and started the quick transition that led to the Jakob Pelletier goal that put Moncton up 3-1. Not overly big and not an outstanding skater, but Spence shone with his smarts and puck-moving abilities tonight.

#11 Pelletier, Jakob (2019) – He showed good smarts and vision in this game. He racked up 3 points and also came close to adding a 2nd goal, but was robbed by D'Orio. Pelletier is a quick skater, and he's quick to put pressure on the puck-carrier. Good top speed and quick acceleration. Not a big guy, but plays bigger than his listed size and goes to the net with no hesitation. He plays in all kind of situations for the Wildcats and is a pretty complete player.

#9 Desnoyers, Elliot (2020) – Not a whole lot to say about his offensive game today, but he was strong along the wall, showing good physical maturity in one-on-one battles (especially for a 16-year-old). He's tough on his skates and it's tough to take the puck away from him. Good compete level from him; he kept his feet moving all the time.

London Knights vs. Ottawa 67's, October 26, 2018

London

McMichael, Connor (2019) - McMichael displayed good skill to his game, generating several of London's offensive opportunities in the 1st period while in transition. Connor shows average skating abilities but can reach a fairly good top speed. Improving his stride and first step would only enhance his game. In possession McMichael shows good awareness of his surroundings and can be a threat to pass or shoot. Connor recognized time and space and would utilize defenders as screens releasing a shot. He was effective on the forecheck using a combination of a quick stick and willingness to finish his check to create turnovers. Connor was effective on the cycle tonight, and generated a few chances late in the 2nd for London.

Stranges, Antonio (2020) - Stranges had a strong game as he consistently made strong decisions both in possession and away from the puck. Antonio showed intelligence to his game and always seemed to be in strong position in all three zones. Stranges possesses good skating abilities, reaching a quality top speed, he also shown excellent edge work with his skating, along with an ability to make simple skilled plays with pace. Anthony also showed deceptive puck handling and puck protection skills. While Stranges kept his game fairly simple, he complemented his line mates very well.

Guskov, Matvey (2019) - Matvey displayed competitiveness to his game that was consistent throughout. He routinely was first to pucks and engaged in board and position battles, often emerging with possession or position. Guskov was arguably at his best along the wall and off the cycle as he showed good puck protection skills and was able to create a few scoring chances coming of the cycle and taking the puck to the net. I would like to see Guskov be more aggressive with the puck when coming off the rush and taking the puck hard to the net, there were a number of times he had a good rush but just kept to the outside and wasn't able to create and offence of that.

Tolnai, Cameron (2020) - Tolnai displayed skill to his game, however it was inconsistent. He showed impressive puck skills and was able to create space or simply beat a check with his 1-on-1 skills. Cameron made up for a lack of offensive opportunities by competing hard throughout and winning battles in the dirty areas. Tolnai was also strong on the forecheck where he used a quick stick and anticipation skills to create turnovers or force low percentage plays.

Quinn, Jack (2020) - Quinn is an undersized forward who used his skill and creativity to generate offensive opportunities. His strong edges and puck handling abilities allowed him to become elusive despite only average skating abilities. Quinn however is a deceptive skater and despite a stride that has room to improve he can reach a fairly good top speed. His creativity was his most intriguing attribute and while it did lead to turnovers occasionally it also allowed him to generate numerous chances offensively. He scored a beautiful goal toe dragging the defence turning him inside out and then had patient to outweigh the goalie and slide puck past London's goalie.

Clarke, Graeme (2019) - Clarke showed effectiveness on the power play and good recognition of time and space as he walked of the half-boards and release a quality shot through traffic. Clarke instinctively followed up his shot and was able deposit his own rebound, showing quick hands in tight on goalie. Clarke displays a hard and accurate shot, he needs to be quicker when receiving the puck, and he will stop the puck first then shoot allowing the defender to get in front of the shot. Graeme struggled 5 on 5 tonight, he needs to focus on being more consistent and more involved with the limited amount of ice time that he got tonight.

Calgary Hitmen vs Lethbridge Hurricanes, October 26, 2018

Calgary

Zimmerman, Cael- Displayed really good edge work and agility when in possession of the puck today. Had a couple impressive offensive zone shifts where he used quick changes of direction to beat his defender and generate a scoring chance. Had a couple nice passing plays as well, doing a good job using his teammates.

Van De Leest, Jackson- Towering defenseman didn't have much of an impact in this game. Decision making was not too bad but he is not a good enough skater to be a difference maker. Did do a good job using his reach and strength to keep players outside off the rush and in the offensive zone.

Lethbridge

Barlage, Logan- Big rangy centerman had a very strong night with the occasional shift where he looked dominant. Physical tools are excellent as he is bigger and stronger than most opponents. Mostly generated chances by using this physical advantage on weaker players to drove the net, or buy extra time. Showed average ability handling the puck and the ability to make good passes when given time and space. Seemed a bit slow to read and react to the play at certain times.

Cozens, Dylan- Motor is non-stop, competes as hard as he can every time he is on the ice. Also plays a very responsible defensive game, never selling out positionally for more offensive and staying on the defensive side of his check. In open ice he has excellent speed and can fly through the neutral zone with the puck. Handling the puck he lacks a bit of creativity and today was a bit too predictable. Shot is excellent with a great release but didn't get a ton of opportunities to use it tonight as his teammates were not always finding him.

Modo u20 at Västerås IK u20 October 28, 2018

Västerås ik u20

Olofsson, Albin (2019) - Olofsson is small and quick. Pretty good decision making, but did not manage to create many hot scoring chances. His shot is weak.

Modo u20

Popovic, Alexander (2019) Popovic is not big, at all. He skates really smooth and is very mobile, but needs to use that to his advantage more often. When he keeps his feet going, he has no problems getting away from forecheckers or rushing the puck up ice. Got passive in his defensive zone and were a spectator at times.
Can his puckskills handle his speed?

Wahlgren, Joel (2019) - Was totally invisible big parts of the game. Got a few quick released shots on goal, but did not seem to want to participate at all. His skating looked forced and he did not work hard for team success.

Wahlgren, Max (2019) - Was the standout this game. Used his frame to win battles to create scoring chances. Showed good hands when he scores 1-0 on a breakaway. His shot was however not very accurate and lacked power. Played the whole game on the outside and tried to go wide on defenders, but had some problems with defenders being better skaters than him. Needs to work harder both ways. Finished the game with 2 goals.

Sudbury Wolves vs. Ottawa 67's, October 28th, 2018

Sudbury

Ross, Liam (2019) – Liam displayed two-way capabilities to his game and was effective using his fluid skating abilities on both sides of the puck. Liam showed poise in possession and was able to escape pressure using his quick feet and strong edges to create space before moving up ice in possession. Ross saw the ice well and was able to simplify his game at times by making the quick read and outlet pass to a teammate. Liam was really good at reading the play and knowing when to jump into the play, or to step up in the neutral zone creating turnovers.

Murray, Blake (2019) - Blake had a strong game tonight, utilizing his hockey sense and vision to create scoring chances for him and his teammates. Murray was good in possession where he was able to dictate the pace of play despite average skating abilities. He recognized when to push the pace and attack with speed and when to slow it down and draw in a defender before slipping a pass to a streaking teammate. Blake vision and playmaking skills were good tonight on the power play making some backdoor passes for chances. Murray handles the puck well and showed creativity tonight, however he rarely looked to beat his check 1-on-1, opting to simplify his decision to avoid a potential turnover.

Ottawa

Clark, Kody - Kody was effective tonight. He showed his smarts and awareness, and his ability to find space and simplify his game when needed. However, he could stand to improve his decision making and play away from the puck in the neutral and defensive zones. Kody displays a heavy and accurate shot, however there were occasions were speeding up his release would have allowed for scoring opportunities opposed to blocked shots. He was also effective on the forecheck tonight separating puck from the defense and creating some turnovers.

Clarke, Graeme (2019) - Clarke played a smart, structured game, but failed to gain traction in the opposing end. Graeme has been productive offensively this season, but struggled tonight. Graeme forced the play off the rush, exposing the puck, and too easily giving up possession. Clarke scored a nice goal in the slot finding the open area, receiving the pass and getting the puck off quick not allowing the goalie much time to react. Graeme shows good anticipation in the offensive zone; he was just too inconsistent tonight with his play.

Södertälje SK at Linköping HC Oct 31, 2018

Linköping HC

LHC # 45 RD Lundmark, Simon (2019) - Stable Big right shooting RD using a long stick to angle the opponent and in forechecks. Good reading and quick passes. Already had 3 GP in SHL last season and probably a more defensive D. Good long first passes. Had one good rush from own net over the ice with decent speed. Thought he could be more mobile and show himself for teammates, shoot more from blue and could have moved more sideways on the blue to fool the goalie a bit more. 2 SOG but not very dangerous.

LHC # 27 LD Lyckåsen, Albert (2019) - Angle opponents good. One decent good shot that hit the frame. Legs move a lot but doesn't looks yet powerful, ok speed and not afraid of bringing the puck in to traffic in front of the net, continued to skate and led to a hocking penalty and PP. Was creating and started the game with long pass. 2 SOG, +-1

LHC # 41 CE Costmar, Arvid (2019) - Had an overall good game even I thought it looked like he was a bit cautious from time to time the first 2 periods. When he steps up playing the regular game with speed, he shines in J20. Not the quickest first steps but reads the game very good and play smart. He reacts quick and controls the body and feet to get the puck with him even when receiving bad passes when in speed. Was creating a lot of scoring chances. Quick using toe ins before delivering passes. Able to have 4 players on him but still seeing his team mates in front of net and able to deliver passes. Shots a lot but not always accurate. Had a hard shot in the pillar. He had 3 assists and was having nice mobility, reading and passes on 3-2 and 5-2 goals. 6-2 was a pass to 40 that could score in empty net. Costmar had good focus when being provoked, pushed back a little bit but left without getting them under the skin. 3 A, 17/23 FOW, 5 SOG

LHC # 22 RW Pedersen, Marcus (2019) - Angles the opponent good and active in defensive game away from the puck. Active forechecking and stole the puck quick directly from the bench bringing it to a scoring chance. Was seen jumping in front and screening the goalie. Plenty of good quick and accurate passes and good puck receiving's. Could shoot more and more accurate. Scored and behind 5-2 goal together with #41 & # 50. 1G+1A, 2 SOG

Södertälje SK

SSK # 6 LW Feuk, Lucas (2019) - Looked bigger then 6'0" and was visulised a lot with good speed. Created a lot of SSKs chances, brought puck over the ice with speed and head up. With speed and stick skills Feuk attracted up to 3 LHC players opening the ice for team mates. Very good quick reading. Creative pass backwards between the legs and backhand passes to team mates for scoring chance. Delivered an open ice when he arrived from penalty, not sure if it was planned or coincidence but it was effective. Provocations against LHC # 41 after whistle blows. Delivered some hard accurate shots. Lot of ice time and a leading position. Had a much better game then the number shows.

SSK # 52 RW Bingmark, Sam (2019) - First game in J20, not much visualized but delivered few decent shots. Good energy in the last period.

SSK # 87 Gustavsson, Hugo (2018) - He Was visualised a lot from time to time, made a very nice toe in and delivered the puck on the net. Moved a lot sideways with puck on blue. Got 2 SOG. OK speed over the ice and delivered a couple of nice passes.

Saskatoon Blades vs Kootenay Ice, November 1, 2018

Saskatoon

Dach, Kirby- Whenever he was on the ice Dach had a huge impact in every phase of the game. Played a completely mistake free game without being low risk, has a really good understanding of what plays need to be made out there. Dach has a great feel for when he needs to move the puck and make a play, never holding it for too long and often making an excellent play in one touch. His ability to handle a pass and send a perfect pass to another teammate in one sequence is excellent. Dach also has a great one timer that he got off a couple of times this game. Defensively Dach is always engaged and is a force at creating turnovers, he even had a PK shift this game where he looked dominant off his ability to take away lanes and steal pucks. Also showed excellent puck protection ability, with one play where he completely outmuscled a player while handling the puck under pressure with one hand on his stick to create a scoring chance. Shifts where him and Krebs lined up against each other were very high intensity.

Maier, Nolan- Only let in one soft goal where he had much of a chance this game. Maier is excellent getting across the crease on cross ice passes and making difficult saves. Plays a very aggressive style and is very explosive athletically. Had a couple of miscommunications with his teammates when handling the puck.

Kootenay

Krebs, Payton- Statement game from Krebs where he basically put the team on his back in leading them to a win. Showed more high end skill than I'd seen from him before and was executing some ridiculously difficult passes with ease. Krebs was primarily involved in 3 of Kootenays goals today showcase elite abilities on each. On his teams first goal Krebs threw an effortless spinorama on his defender in the open ice which he transitioned into a backhand shot that forced Maier into a difficult save and rebound that Krebs teammate put in. Another Kootenay goal involved a ridiculous saucer pass from Krebs, and another involved him stealing the puck from a defender before beating two players and slipping a shot five hole as he cut cross ice. For all the skill Krebs showed, his hustle stood out just as much. Krebs was racing in to beat out icings, throwing hits, and battling for the puck. Could see how much he was trying to raise his game with most of his dominant shifts coming against Dach, raising his game more as the game went on. Played almost every second shift for his team down the stretch with the teams gameplan basically being to get Krebs the puck.

Mississauga Steelheads vs. Niagara Ice Dogs – November 1st, 2018

Mississauga Steelheads –

MISS #9 LC Washkurak, Keean (2019) – Washkurak is not the biggest body out on the ice yet it did not hinder him from playing a strong support game in all areas of the ice and showed some physicality. He leveled #44 Thomas late in the game by Niagara bench that threw the opposing forward over the boards and into the bench. He also made a clean open-ice hit earlier in the game. He was given 2nd line center duties along with #74 Tippett and seemed to play in his shadows a bit offensively as line mate often opted to shoot rather than pass and Washkurak seemed to think pass first rather than shoot. He showed some speed with the puck on a few rushes and backchecking to break up plays. There were a few shifts whereby he went unnoticed and yet overall played a smart, two-way game. He looked the part of more of a playmaker than goal scorer.

MISS #11 RC Schwindt, Cole (2019) – Third-line center for the game although showed some skills and smarts during the game. Schwindt was simplistic in possession but made high percentage decisions. He utilized his size to shield the puck while generating speed to effectively elude a check. He used his body and reach to protect puck below the dots in possession to generate offense. One mark off would be his skating stride. For a bigger body he has decent speed, although his technique could improve as bit labored with head and arm action excessive, especially with initial steps. He took advantage in the 3rd period on the penalty-kill when #24 Ham fell and turned over puck, leaving Schwindt with breakaway in which he drew a penalty shot. On the PS he did not convert as made simple move staying on forehand as he cut across near crease making easy stop for goalie #30 Dhillon with left pad. He uses his body, competes on puck, and showed some glimpses of good stick skills with puck. He is a player to keep an eye upon as the season progresses. Schwindt could be a player starting to scratch surface.

MISS #15 RW Reisnecker, Filip (2020) – The German native was average in this game as was given limited ice time as 4th right winger. He showed his skill sets in spurts although somewhat inconsistent, especially not given full opportunity. He is a late 2001-birthdate, so he will have another season to adjust to North American game and earn more ice. He did show a solid stride.

MISS #21 LW Portokalis, William (2020) – The rookie '02 birthdate forward was given limited ice, 4th line LW line-up. He is a player that has very good puck skills and displayed them a couple of times in breaking the puck out off the wall around the Dman and then later in the game with nifty move around #82 Bukac through the neutral zone that drew a slashing penalty in the 1st period. You can tell he has some deceptive offensive skills and thinking. At some point you hope he gets more opportunity in the season.

MISS #37 LD Callaghan, Charlie (2020) – For most of the game Callaghan keep his game simple as 3rd pair Dman positioning himself well defensively to stay out of trouble and made good first pass on the outlets. He made a mishap in the 3rd period that led to the third goal against as he mishandled puck and did not move puck quick on easy, first option in the corner that eventually was turned over and #3 Jones goal. Overall, he looked average and still trying to find comfort zone in the OHL.

MISS #48 LD Harley, Thomas (2019) – Harley has the size and mobility as showed his defensive skills early in 1st period as he defended 1v1 on #13 Maksimov easily with position, stick, and transitioned puck well the other way. In his next shift in 1st period, an aggressive pinch on the offensive zone lead to 2v1 scoring opportunity the other way in which his goalie bailed him out. Harley hugged the boards and #9 Lodnia simply toe-dragged around him to start the break. This also happened in 2nd period whereby pinching again gave up 2v1 yet this time #71 Sopa scored upon. He will need to learn to pick his spots as likes to pinch and hold pucks in the offensive zone, yet sometimes will need better decision and peel out of zone and limit odd-man rushes. He made good puck decisions on breakouts and distribution on the power play. He joined rush as well after initiating breakout to try and generate offense. He sometimes got caught in neutral zone in odd positioning yet had good recovery in stride to catch opponent also using long reach to break play up. Took one long shift 2nd period on the power play resulted in bad turnover in neutral zone and got lucky on non-penalty call on #9 Lodnia to stop play. His mobility is good especially for size, although think his lateral movement and crossovers could improve as couple times got crossed over on more skilled, quicker forwards on 1v1 situations. Midway in 3rd period Harley displayed more offensive tools and skating as rushed puck into offensive zone creating scoring chance. His shot strength was average as did fire a few shots on net from the point. Harley showed tools and mindset that can be developed for the next level as you see the potential.

MISS #67 RW Varga, Adam (2019) – Third line RW that plays with some pace. Showed good speed and hustle, especially in a shift late in the 2nd period as made a good rush with puck done the wing for scoring chance, yet also hustled back on the backcheck to negate a Niagara rush.

Niagara Ice Dogs –

NIA #10 LD Howard, Mason (2019) – Big left-handed, rookie Dman on 3rd pairing that was average on impression. He kept his game simple in moving the puck on outlets, short shifts, and solid defensive positioning.

NIA #11 RW DeSimone, Jonah (2020) – Rookie winger with speed and quick steps. Given 4th line right wing line-up he received limited ice time.

NIA #19 LW Martin, Ian (2019) – You can see glimpses of Martin's offensive skills with his offensive thoughts, hands, and shot. Although being 4th left wing he did not receive a consistent shift to display.

NIA #26 RC Tomasino, Philip (2019) – Tomasino seems to be caught in a situation whereby in his draft year he is behind two veterans, NHL drafted centers in #3 Jones and #44 Thomas. In being the 3rd line center his opportunity is somewhat limited although that does not stop him from showing his hockey IQ at both ends of the ice. He does a good job in supporting his teammates in all three zones, as plays a 200-foot game. He did not receive any power play time and probably a factor in why his numbers are lower, yet still respectable. He made a great play in the 3rd period off the rush as he skated puck into the offensive zone and feathered a nice backhand pass to setup #72 Johnson in the slot and then on the same shift, he made great effort on a takeaway in the corner and fed #71 Sopa in the slot for scoring chance. The skills and smarts are certainly in Tomasino's game, you just wish he received more opportunity to display. He was strong at the face-off dot on the not as well.

NIA #68 RD Constantinou, Billy (2019) – Constantinou was a bit silent in thus game. He was given 3rd Dman pairing along with #10 Howard yet did see some PP time on the second unit. The skating skills with ability mobility were on display at times although he seemed to simply move puck more than rush himself like in the past. He had one hiccup in the 2nd second period while on the PP with odd puck decision that lead to a turnover in the neutral zone and he ultimately took a hooking penalty in recovery. He did pick up assist as simply moved puck in the OZ, and #28 Bruder goal was lucky as hit off Mississauga Dman skate on the crease. It did not appear the RHD had any shots on goal.

NIA #71 LW Sopa, Kyen (2019) – Smaller sized right-handed 2nd line left wing that showed effort each shift. For his size, he was willing to be physical and go into the dirty of the ice to gain puck possession. He scored nice goal with 1-timer finish off the inside of the post on 2v1 conversion off #44 Thomas pass. He read the play as it developed to get out into the open space and quickly fired puck for goal. He had a few other opportunities as he shows smart in the offensive zone and knows where to go without the puck to receive passes. There are aspects to his game, potential for high levels, and player to monitor this season.

NIA #72 RC Uberti, Jake (2020) – A bigger right-handed center in rookie season in OHL that centered the 4th line with limited time on ice. He did win one of the two face-offs taken. Tough game to really evaluate with TOI.

Charlottetown Islanders at Drummondville Voltigeurs, November 2nd, 2018

Charlottetown

#10 Budgell, Brett (2019) – Budgell was solid in a defensive role during this game, and was a key player for Charlottetown's penalty-killing unit. He demonstrated good stick work and anticipation. He was good and effective at how quickly he would put pressure on the puck-carrier and force players to make quicker decisions with the puck. He was good along the wall; I saw good puck-retrieval from him during this game. He did some good work along the boards to feed Pierre-Olivier Joseph on the on the Islanders' first goal of the game. However, his skating could be better, as he lacks some explosiveness in his stride.

#14 Alexandrov, Nikita (2019) – This was not a great game from Alexandrov, who showed some glimpses of his talent on some shifts, but was not a real offensive factor for the Islanders overall. His skating is good and fluid, and he is agile on his skates. He played on the top line and top power play unit, often paired with Budgell, but I didn't see him get any shifts on the PK unit.

#18 Dersch, Alexander (2019) – Another German import on the team, Dersch was solid in his own zone, played a physical game along the boards and even got into a fight in the 2nd period. He was playing on the top pairing at even-strength with Pierre-Olivier Joseph. Not a whole lot from him as far as offensive plays or puck touches, though.

Drummondville

#4 Pelletier, Thomas (2019) – It was a quiet game for Pelletier as far as puck touches and offensive plays. He struggled a bit when coming back to retrieve pucks in his own zone. He made some good defensive plays defending the rush, including one nice diving play to block a pass defending against a 2-on-1 rush in the 3rd period. He played on the PK, but did not get any ice time on the PP.

#16 Dion, Jacob (2020) – Dion was called up for this game, with Nicolas Beaudin still hurt. Not a whole of ice time at even-strength, but he did see some ice time on the 2nd power play unit. He didn't shy away from trying to create some offense by acting like a 4th forward on the ice and going deep in the offensive zone. He used his feet well by rushing the puck out of his zone; his good feet are his best asset.

#6 Baker, Jarrett (2019) – Baker played a solid physical game tonight in his own zone and also had a fight in the 2nd period. He used his feet well by skating the puck out of his zone and getting away from the forecheck. He defended well, making it tough on opposing forwards by playing an in-your-face physical game and challenging them physically along the boards.

#81 Simoneau, Xavier (2019) – Simoneau was great tonight. As usual, he showed a great compete level in all three zones. He didn't back down from anyone, and was involved in the physical game despite being the smallest player on the ice. He showed great patience with the puck; on some shifts, he would wait an extra second to find a teammate with a great pass. His decision-making was good, but he also makes quick decisions with the puck. In addition, without the puck, he showed good anticipation in the neutral zone, creating some turnovers as well in the neutral zone.

#19 Mercer, Dawson (2020) – It was a quiet game offensively for Mercer today, who was not really a factor despite playing in an offensive role and even getting power play ice time. He showed some improved work in terms of his play away from the puck, including some good involvement in his zone and good support by helping his defensemen retrieve pucks. He had a regular shift on the PK unit, which is a new role he has acquired this season.

Minnesota Magicians at Fairbanks Ice Dogs, November 2, 2018

Minnesota Magicians -

Jutting, Jackson - 2019 Workman-like game from Jutting. He came back into his defensive zone pretty regularly and with some vigor. He wasn't typically in the best position for success, but he was back there with effort. Made a few good passes, particularly crossing the attack line – snappy passes that were crisp and right on the tape. He did jump into a rush that started in his own zone that resulted in a 2-on-1 that he made no mistake about putting in from the right side. His hands are not particularly noteworthy, even in open space. His cause is halved by his lackluster skating. He has no explosion, particularly at top gear…there isn't much there. He has a quality shot release, he shows some playmaking upside…but the skill, skating, smarts package seem prohibitively unenticing. He was not productive in the faceoff circle either.

Dubuque Fighting Saints at Waterloo Black Hawks, November 2, 2018

Dubuque Fighting Saints

Maccelli, Matias – 2019 It was a fairly quiet game for Matias in regards to driving the play and creating offense for his team but used his hockey sense to be in position for a couple good scoring chances in the 3rd period that he wasn't able to convert on. On a few instances Matias didn't work hard to get back in the play on the back check and was late coming back to his own end.

Jackson, Dylan – 2019 Waterloo did an excellent job shutting down Dylan and his line in this game. Dylan did show a deceptive and quick release with his shot with good velocity on a shot attempt from the slot. Dylan displayed quick feet and hands with the puck on his tape but lacked the hockey sense to create time and space for himself in this game.

Waterloo Black Hawks

Drkulec, Ryan – 2019 Drkulec showed a good net front presents in this game, did well to get his body in front and screen the goaltender and get his stick in lanes for tip attempts. Showed good physicality in front and in puck battles. While Ryan's straight line skating is decent and has above average straight line speed, he lacks explosiveness off the hop and struggled being effective in the transition game where he was caught from behind on a couple of occasions.

Swankler, Austen – 2019 Swankler displayed powerful skating and a strong base, drawing a penalty as he drove down the slot. Austen showed god hand eye coordination with a nice deflection in front for a near goal that was eventually called no goal due to the puck not completely crossing the goal line. Swankler played a pass first game with the puck in the offensive zone and in doing so passes up some good scoring chances for himself. Austen made some nice plays in offensive zone entries to create controlled possessions for his team that creates some scoring chances as a result.

Firstov, Vladislav – 2019 Firstov displayed explosive skating by winning a lot of races to loose pucks. Firstov played with a physical edge in this game as well, initiating contact in a few puck races and in the corners. Firstov scored twice in this game, showing the ability to score in different ways, both on the Power Play. His first goal came from a down low position where he got the puck below the goal line and took advantage of a clear lane to the front of the net where he drove to the front and jammed the puck past the goalies pads. Firstov's second goal came from the half-wall position where he one-timed a pass from the faceoff dot area under the bar on the short side.

Charlettetown Islanders at Victoriaville Tigres, November 3rd, 2018

Charlottetown

Dersch, Alexander (2019) – He kept his game simple with the puck. There is nothing flashy about his game, but he also did a good job putting pucks on net. He's not very creative with the puck, but will opt for the simple play without getting into trouble. He was solid along the boards and to defend in his own zone.

Budgell, Brett (2019) – His footspeed hurt him when it came time to create separation between himself and his coverage. He was solid along the boards and often around the net while looking for rebounds or to tip some pucks in. That was his role on the power play.

Alexandrov, Nikita (2019) – He was moving his feet well today, which was the opposite of last night's game in Drummondville. He was more noticeable in the offensive zone; he was shifty and was making quick turns to avoid hits.

He flashed some good puck skills on some rushes, including one occasion where he came in with speed on his off-wing, which resulted in his best scoring chance of the night.

Victoriaville

#64 Iacobo, Fabio (2020) – Iacobo was solid, even if he allowed 4 goals in this game. He faced 43 shots overall and eventually he and the Tigres lost the game in overtime. He made himself look big in net, and was square to the shooters. With traffic in front of him, he was still able to track the puck well. He made couple of nice glove saves in this game, also showing a quick glove. He demonstrated good agility for a goaltender of his size, and doesn't waste any energy in his crease, as he's very calm there.

#12 Larochelle, Sean (2019) – Larochelle showed some good anticipation during this game. He made some good reads in the neutral zone to intercept some passes and create some turnovers. He's not an explosive skater, but has good lateral mobility and was capable of starting the transition game with a quick pass or by skating the puck away from pressure. He showed a quick release on his wrist shot, but his shots were lacking some velocity.

#18 Serdyuk, Egor (2019) – Scored the opening goal of the game after a neutral-zone turnover on the first shift of the game. On that goal, he put the puck five-hole on his backhand, beating the Charlottetown goaltender on a breakaway. He was not very noticeable on the ice, but one thing he did well was getting himself open to receive passes in the offensive zone and escape his coverage, much like he did on his 2nd goal. Not a big forward, and not a great skater either. He doesn't have much of a physical game.

#9 Abramov, Mikhail (2019) – Abramov is a good skater, has quick feet and is fluid on his skates. He encountered some difficulty along the boards when facing Charlottetown defensemen, who gave him a hard time and overmatched him physically. He made a good play along the boards, keeping possession of the puck and immediately feeding Morozov behind the net which led to the 3-2 goal (Serdyuk's 2nd goal of the game). He showed flashes of good vision and playmaking abilities in this game, but lacked consistency. He will need to get bigger and stronger in order to compete better along the boards.

Victoriaville Tigres at Drummondville Voltigeurs, November 4th 2018

Victoriaville

#12 Larochelle, Sean (2019) – He was active on the point on the power play, not staying still on the blueline. Doing so provided his teammates another passing option in the offensive zone. He joined the rush on some occasions, trying to create some offense. He made a couple of nice and quick first passes throughout this game, and scored Victoriaville's first goal of the game with a quick slapper on the power play.

#46 Sevigny, Vincent (2019) – He was solid in his own zone for the majority of the game. He was really good at blocking passing lanes on some odd-man rushes he faced. He had a sound positional game, and an excellent active stick. He played in all situations for the Tigres, including on the 2nd power play unit and as a regular on the PK unit. One big mistake he committed was when he couldn't handle Veleno's speed on one rush. He was caught flat-footed and had no chance of defending against Veleno's top speed.

#9 Abramov, Mikhail (2019) – He showed some good awareness in the defensive zone and supported his defense well down low. He also showed good anticipation to read plays, as well as good use of his stick in defensive situations. On the power play, he likes to play around the faceoff circle, creating some plays with his vision and playmaking from there. Victoriaville had trouble getting any consistent offense going in this game, and Abramov was not a factor offensively in this game (outside of a couple of nice passes he attempted).

#18 Serdyuk, Egor (2019) – Not very involved in the play. His skating, rather his lack of explosiveness, was showing today. He made some bad decisions while in possession of the puck, and overall didn't play a smart game. Much like the rest of his team, he didn't do much offensively in this game and was barely noticeable on the ice.

#70 Hurtubise, Nikolas (2020) – Hurtubise got his first career QMJHL start today, as Victoriaville was playing its 3rd game in 3 days. He was a bit nervous in the first period, but made some good saves to bolster his confidence. I liked how he fought hard for every puck. He stopped 14 of 16 shots in the first period, including his best versus Dawson Mercer on a breakaway with his right pad. He's not a tall goaltender; he had to work really hard to track pucks with heavy traffic in front of him. Overall, he did well in this game, even if he allowed 5 goals. His team didn't have a lot of energy or cohesion in front of him.

Drummondville

#4 Pelletier, Thomas (2019) – He was hit hard in the first period and looked a bit shaken up afterwards. He played at even-strength with Xavier Bernard, but received no power play ice time. He didn't get many puck touches in this game and was not a factor in this game offensively or in the transition game.

#6 Baker, Jarrett (2019) – Baker is not flashy with the puck, but made simple plays with it and made sure to move it quickly out of his zone during this game. He also used his feet to skate it out of danger. As usual, he was tough to play against physically and kept talking after whistles as well.

#29 Turan, Oliver (2019) – Turan made a couple of nice passes in the first period, moving pucks better than what we've seen so far this year. He made a nice play on the 2nd goal, taking a shot on net that was tipped in by Nicolas Guay at the front of the net. However, he didn't have any impact during the rest of the game, and was not very noticeable with the puck on his stick (but didn't make any big mistakes, either).

#81 Simoneau, Xavier (2019) – He worked hard in all three zones, and his compete level was excellent as always. He was involved in many scrums after whistles and didn't hesitate to get engaged physically. There were not a lot of noticeable offensive plays from him today, though. He was playing on the LW today, playing on an offensive line, and saw ice time on both the PP and PK units.

#19 Mercer, Dawson (2020) – Mercer had some ups and downs in this game, playing RW on the 3rd line. He also played on both special teams' units. He had his best scoring chance on the PK but was stopped by Hurtubise on a breakaway. In the first period, he was generating some good speed in the neutral zone to attack the offensive zone, but got away from this in periods 2 and 3.

U. of Minnesota at U. of Wisconsin, November 9thth 2018

University of Minnesota

Brinkman, Ben – 2019   Brinkman didn't see much ice time in any special teams situations tonight but saw his ice time increase as the game moved along and played regular shifts in the 3rd period with his team with a 1 goal lead. Brinkman scored his first NCAA goal in this game, and while it was a bit of a fluky goal, with one of his teammates in the goal and the Wisconsin goalie out of the play, the goal counted and changed the tide of the game. While his goal wasn't that impressive, as he had an open net to shoot at, Brinkman was good on the shift and nearly setup a goal right before his goal by shooting wide of the net that nearly connected on the back door. Brinkman showed good gap control against a speedy Wisconsin team and the willingness to step up on players coming into the zone in which he picked his spots well. Brinkman executed his puck retrievals well and moved the puck efficiently out of his own end.

U. of Minnesota at U. of Wisconsin, November 10th 2018

University of Minnesota

Brinkman, Ben – 2019 Brinkman built off his solid performance last night. His confidence with the puck continues to progress and showed the ability to rush the puck out of his own zone and up the ice but wasn't careless in doing so and picked his spots. Brinkman was quick to identify the fore-checker and move the puck quickly to his defensive partner or find a teammate up ice to exit the zone. In what was an emotional Rivalry game, Brinkman brought good physicality down low and in front of his own net. In the offensive zone, Brinkman showed a quick release with good velocity. Displayed quick hands in one sequence to come down form the point with the puck and cut through the slot and fire a backhand against the grain that just missed the far post. All in all Brinkman defended well and exited his own zone well in this game.

Czech Republic vs Finland, U18 Five Nations' Tournament, November 10th, 2018

Czech Republic

#29 Muzik, Radek (2019): His speed is okay, but if he's not moving his feet like he was today, he looks slow out there. He did score in this game, but it was a weak goal allowed by the Finland goaltender. Muzik has good size, but didn't show enough skills or speed today.

#18 Pytlik, Jaromir (2020): He had a quiet first 40 minutes, but better moments in the 3rd period. Overall, it was Pytlik's weakest effort in this tournament. He was not as involved, and had trouble creating offense for his team.

#12 Raska, Adam (2020): Not very noticeable offensively today, but he did show good speed and hustled hard. Good energy on the ice, but didn't do much in the offensive zone.

#19 Bernovsky, Jan (2019): Inconsistent performance from him today. He had his best moment at the end of the 2nd period. He made a great pass on the 4-2 goal. He has good size and his skating is decent. Also loved his quick release and above-average puck skills.

Finland

#6 Hatakka, Santerri (2019): Hattaka made numerous plays with his feet in this game; he showed a good ability to rush the puck out of his zone and into the offensive zone. Unfortunately, a lot of his offensive rushes ended up dying in the corner and no scoring chances were created from them. He didn't mind playing physical in his own zone, throwing some good hits, and his compete level in his zone was good. However, he left some question marks about his smarts and creativity in this game.

#7 Tuomisto, Antti (2019): He did a good job defending in his own zone and one-on-one today. Good body and stick positioning, and he played his man well. Not a flashy player offensively, but he played a simple game with the puck and was moving pucks quickly and accurately out there. He saw some ice time on the 2nd unit of Finland's power play.

#3 Loponen, Kalle (2019): The lone defenseman on Finland's 1st power play unit was once again not shy to get pucks on net. He has a quick release and an accurate shot from the point. However, he had trouble with his passes today, as he lacked some accuracy with them and his transition plays were not that effective as a result.

#4 Rasanen, Llvari (2019: His good footwork and overall agility on his skates helped him cover lots of ice in the defensive zone. He was quick to distribute pucks out there (mostly D to D rather to his forwards in his case). He was not really a factor in the offensive zone, playing more like a stay-at-home defenseman.

#36 Puistola, Patrik (2019): He showed good one-on-one abilities with his soft hands and an ability to finish plays by scoring the 3-1 goal. Not his best game, but he knows how to score and doesn't need many scoring chances to get a goal. Good nose for the net. Not the best skater, either, but he's shifty, which makes it tough to defend against him one-on-one in the offensive zone.

#15 Saarela, Antti (2019): Easy to notice out there with his great speed and great work ethic. Loves to have the puck on his stick and be involved in rushes, trying to beat defenders with his outside speed. He plays a bit too much on the perimeter, however. He has a thin frame and lacks the necessary physical strength to win those battles in front of the net or along the boards with enough regularity.

#10 Aaltonen, Leevi (2019): Loved his intensity tonight; he worked hard and brought some good energy to the game. Didn't always make the smart decision out there, however; he had some good scoring chances due to the opportunities that he created for himself, but there was not much in terms of playmaking/passing plays from him today.

#37 Parssinen, Juuso (2019): Strong game from Parssinen today, who had 2 goals playing on the 3rd line for Finland. He showed good speed on his first goal, scoring on a breakaway. On his second goal, he scored on a good backhand shot. His goals were bonuses today, as he played a strong game in his own zone. Liked his compete level in the defensive zone and on the PK.

#35 Tieksola, Tukka (2019): He showed a good release when he took shots on net playing on the team's 4th line. His speed was noticeable as well, quick acceleration out there.

Czech Republic U20 vs Russia U20, November 10, 2018

Czech Republic

Teply, Michal- Came out a bit flat and wasn't really noticeable until the third period. Is a bit slow but was good when he had possession in the offensive zone, protecting the puck and cycling very well. Scored a goal from the high slot with an excellent one touch release that was in a spot that gave the goalie no chance.

Hugo Has, Martin- Passing was a bit off today as he missed a couple easy ones and iced some pucks. Showed a lot of confidence carrying the puck and good instincts for when to use his feet to get up ice. Defensively he was very engaged and used his reach to keep players outside.

Russia

Dorofeyev, Pavel- Was a lot better today as he was more consistently involved in the play. Dorofeyev can be very slippery with the puck managing to slide past players in the offensive zone. He also makes some really crafty passes where he finds a lane that most players wouldn't see. Off the puck he does an excellent job sneaking around in defenders blindspots getting himself a nice back door tap in today. What is worrying about his game is how low intensity he can appear when his team doesn't have the puck.

Podkolzin, Vasili- Podkolzin plays the game all out, with absolutely no fear. Has an excellent first few steps which really suits his style of game. Podkolzin can also be very shifty and showed some good change of direction with the puck today, on top of his usual power game. With the puck Podkolzin made a lot of nice short support passes and is a guy who never gives up possession easily. On the forecheck Podkolzin always challenges the defence and makes things difficult for them. In battles he also frequently comes out on top simply by out working the opponent.

Sweden vs Czech Republic, U18 Five Nations' Tournament, November 11th, 2018

Sweden

#7 Bjornfot, Tobias (2019): Bjornfot showed excellent skating abilities in this contest. His mobility in his own zone was good to cover opposing forwards and eliminate space for them on the ice. He carried the puck out of his zone easily in order to escape the Czech forecheck. He didn't create much offense, though. He played physical in his own zone when needed; he was quick to put pressure on the puck-carrier with either his stick or by throwing hits.

#6 Popovic, Alexander (2019): Undersized but showed good mobility as well as an ability to rush the puck out of his zone and avoid the pressure of the forecheck. He played on the power play more, with Broberg out of the lineup. However, he was overmatched physically in his own zone and in front of his net due to his lack of strength.

#5 Lundqvist, Alexander (2019): He kept his game simple with the puck, making safe passes to get puck out of his zone but not taking risks. He was not a factor offensively. Good involvement physically, and good timing with his hits in the neutral zone.

#12 Costmar, Arvid (2019): Elusive on the ice. An okay skater, but possesses good agility that helps him avoid hits. However, he lacks explosiveness and acceleration. Good all-around player, liked his smarts at both ends of the ice. He played in all situations for his team today.

#21 Feuk, Lucas (2019): Inconsistent from shift to shift. Overall, his speed was okay, but he had a couple of shifts where he showed some good acceleration down his wing. Liked the skill level, but he was still too inconsistent and raw out there.

#22 Wahlgren, Max (2019): Liked his game along the boards, thought he used his size well there. Wahlgren was very involved in the play, playing a physical game along the boards and also using his size to go to the net.

#15 Andersson, Isac (2019): Got a goal by going to the net and finishing a nice pass by Henriksson on the 3-2 goal. He showed good commitment in the defensive zone. Also, good awareness and effort with his play away from the puck.

#20 Henriksson, Karl (2019): He got hurt early in the game with a high hit, but came back to have a good game. He made a real nice play on the 3-2 goal, using his good speed to go wide on a Czech defenseman and feeding the puck to Andersson, who finished the play near the net.

#24 Grewe, Albin (2019): He played with more grit today than during the rest of the tournament, and was eventually skating with a better pace out there. At times, he was too selfish with the puck, trying too many individualist plays on the ice instead of using his teammates. He did, however, make a nice play on the 2-1 goal, skating down the right wing, making a quick cut inside and then taking a quick wrist shot to beat the Czech goaltender glove side.

Czech Republic

#2 Parik, Lukas (2019): Made himself look big in net. Played a sound positional game and was calm in his crease. He has great size. He is not the most athletic goaltender, but never seemed out of position in his crease. He covered his angles well and challenged the shooters well, too. Rebound-control was solid today.

#4 Turecek, David (2019): A good-sized defenseman who saw a good amount of ice time today playing in all situations for the Czechs. His puck skills looked below-average today, and he didn't move around too well either; he looked average at best out there.

#18 Pytlik, Jaromir (2020): He showed good support down low helping his defensemen out often in this game. He used his size well, battling for pucks down low in his own zone and also in the offensive zone. He was able, in the neutral zone, to hit his top speed without being checked. This made it tough for Sweden's defenders to face him, as he was making his way to the offensive zone with a ton of speed. He scored a goal on the PP from the half-wall with traffic in front of the net.

Team Russia vs Team QMJHL, CIBC Canada-Russia Series, November 13th, 2018

Team QMJHL

#11 Harvey-Pinard, Rafaël (2019): Harvey-Pinard was named player of the game for Team QMJHL in a losing effort. He was one of the team's hardest workers, even with the game out of reach in the 3rd period. He was strong on pucks and showed no quit while checking guys and in defensive assignments. He showed good anticipation away from the puck in the neutral and defensive zones, knowing where the puck would go, and creating some turnovers.

#10 Lafrenière, Alexis (2020): It was an average game for Lafrenière's standards. He had some scoring chances in the 2nd period, working the puck from down low, but overall he didn't seem to gel with his linemates and didn't have a huge impact in the game. He was good along the wall, using his size well to protect the puck and absorb hits by Russians.

#12 Pelletier, Jakob (2019) : He played on different lines today. He worked hard and was quick on the forecheck and in puck-pressure situations. He had a couple of scoring chances, but like the rest of Team QMJHL, it was not a very good night offensively. He got his nose dirty in front of the net and in the tougher areas as well.

#29 Poulin, Samuel (2019): Poulin was playing in front of his local fans tonight, and had a solid night compared to his fellow draft-eligibles. He took some good shots on net in the first half of the game; he was not shy to do so. He was solid along the boards as well, taking advantage of his big frame. He was skating well and generating some decent speed down the wing. Usually he plays RW with Sherbrooke, but he was on the left side today.

#39 Legaré, Nathan (2019): Didn't think he skated well today. He didn't generate a lot of speed and also fell on his own one time, creating a Russian scoring chance. He was struggling to keep up with the pace of the Russians. His best moment came in the 2nd period, where he threw possibly the best hit of the game on a Russian defenseman, but overall, this was not his best game.

#50 Lavoie, Raphaël (2019): Another player on Team QMJHL who didn't have a good showing today. He had some good shifts in the 2nd period, but overall, he didn't generate much out there tonight. He looked like he was a step behind speed-wise. His best moments in the 2nd period happened when he started using his size and reach down low, but there were not enough of those shifts tonight. He was paired with Lafrenière, and they didn't seem to have much chemistry playing together. He has good hand-eye coordination; he knocked many pucks out of the air with his stick.

#4 Bergeron, Justin (2019): Bergeron was paired with Justin Barron today, and that was the team's best defensive pair. He played a smart and effective puck-moving game. He played with confidence, both in transition and while defending. His good footwork helped him keep up with the speedy Russians, and he was poised with the puck on his stick.

#25 Barron, Justin (2020): Outside of his mistake in front of the net on the Muranov goal, Barron was solid tonight. He was moving really well on the ice. He has excellent footwork and agility. He was moving pucks smartly and quickly in transition, and was also defending well one-on-one by playing his man well and being physical.

Prince Albert Raiders vs Medicine Hat Tigers, November 14, 2018

Prince Albert

Protas, Alexei (2019) - Very high IQ is evident whenever you watch him as Protas is always making plays for others as a passer. His skating looked better today as he was a little bit shiftier but he still needs major improvement in this area. Has a very good understanding of what way he needs to play to succeed.

Leason, Brett (2019) - Wasn't as noticeable today as he usually is, but was still amongst the best players on the ice. Showed off a lot of wiggle and elusiveness today, beating guys with change of direction rather than outracing them today. Release is awesome as he does a great job at quickly settling the puck down on difficult passes and getting shot off. Without the puck he was doing a great job driving the net on the rush, pushing defencemen back and opening a lot of space for his teammates.

Guhle, Kaiden (2020) - A lot more confident than usual today with the puck. Used his skating ablity a ton today beating forecheckers with both quick turns and pure speed. Below average passer, giving guys pucks that are just enough off that they can't make a quick play once they get it.

Medicine Hat

Sogaard, Mads (2019) - The 6'7 Dane is a massive presence in net who has exciting athleticism for a goalie his size. Sogaard did an excellent job tracking the puck through traffic, seeing over everyone to follow shots from the point. Also gets across the crease very quickly on east-west plays. Can sometimes look a little too enthusiastic and over slide on cross ice plays. Plays fairly aggressively which combined with his frame gives the opposition very little to shoot at.

Team Russia vs Team QMJHL, CIBC Canada Russia Series, November 15th, 2018

QMJHL

#10 Lafrenière, Alexis (2020) – Much better game for Lafrenière tonight compared to Game 1. He was a constant threat offensively and made things happen on the ice, whether it was in a setup role or a scoring one – he came close to scoring 2 or 3 times in this game. He can be like a shark when he sees a scoring opportunity; never looking super-fast, but when he sees an opportunity, he can reach an extra gear to take advantage of this opportunity.

#50 Lavoie, Raphaël (2019) – Lavoie also had a better game tonight after an average first game. He had a great scoring chance early in the first period after receiving a great pass from Lafrenière that sent him on a breakaway after he went wide on a Russian defenseman. He had another chance on the power play, but fanned on a nice pass in the slot. He used his size a bit more along the boards, and his long reach to protect the puck. On some shifts, we noted that with a better skating ability, he could have taken more advantage.

#29 Poulin, Samuel (2019) – Poulin was not as good as he was in the previous game, but still showed good acceleration and an ability to go wide on Russian defensemen on some shifts. Good along the boards, won his one-on-one battle. He had one or two scoring chances close to the net, but those were the only real scoring chances he had in this game.

#39 Legaré, Nathan (2019) – He skated better than in Game 1, but there's some work to do with his skating to improve acceleration and top speed. He used his body and was engaged physically against Russian defensemen on the forecheck. He flashed a good wrist shot while coming down his off-wing on one sequence in the first period, but that was his only real good scoring chance in this game. He struggled to contribute offensively in the two games he played.

#25 Barron, Justin (2020) – A quieter game today from Barron, and he had more iffy moments in this game. His passing game was not as good as it was on Tuesday. He didn't create any turnovers, but they were lacking some accuracy. Not very flashy today - he was less noticeable in the transition game and in the offensive zone tonight. In the first period, he made the pass to Morand that led to Team QMJHL's 1st goal.

Drummondville Voltigeurs vs. Gatineau Olympiques, November 16th, 2018

Drummondville

Simoneau, Xavier (2019) - Simoneau brought an impressive amount of speed and energy to the game on a consistent basis. Xavier possesses a good skill level to his game, but often utilized his speed and aggressive puck pursuit to quickly close on opposing puck carriers and create turnovers. Despite his undersized frame, Simoneau plays with some aggression and willingly engaged physically throughout the game. In possession Simoneau has a shifty and elusiveness to his game as his quick feet allow him to change direction well, while his puck handling ability makes him a threat to beat his check in a 1-on-1 scenario. Xavier consistently made quick and high percentage decisions in possession, leading to offensive opportunities.

Turan, Oliver (2019) – Turan possesses good size and strength to his game and excelled playing a simplistic defensive game. While Oliver was strong on the defensive side of the puck, he flashed the willingness to exploit open ice when it presented itself and was able to carry the puck up ice and into the offensive zone. Turan made consistently strong decisions despite being fairly simplistic in his approach on both sides of the puck. Oliver's feet have room to improve which will only help his ability to contain transition attacks. He also needs to work on his transition game as he was beat 2-3 wide with speed, and was too slow pivoting backwards; he needs to work on his angles better as well.

Gatineau

Aebischer, David (2019) - Aebischer played a non-flashy, but highly effective and consistent game. David doesn't possess high end offensive traits to his game but flashed some two-way ability to his game. Aebischer ability to show patience in possession, see the ice well and effectively make a first pass, allowed his team to fluidly transition from defense to offense. David possesses fairly good mobility and was able to effectively contain the opposition in transition. David would benefit from tightening his gaps, however his ability to angle opponents away from the centre of the ice, allowed him to be effective.

Likhachev, Iaroslav (2019) - Likhachev made a small impact in the game, not showing a willingness to be first to pucks, competing in puck battles and utilizing his generated speed to successfully forecheck and back-check. Most notably Likhachev was able to out skate an opponent to a loose puck resulting in a breakaway opportunity. Likhachev needs to be more consistent with his game; he took many shifts off tonight where you didn't even notice him at times in a high scoring game for Gatineau.

LePage, Connor (2019) – LePage showed an impressive work ethic throughout the game, consistently displaying an energetic style of play. LePage energetic style allowed him to generate turnovers, while his willingness to consistently finish his checks made him tough to play against and agitating. Connor's foot speed will need to improve as he lacks first step quickness which limits his ability to separate from a check. When Connor was able to find some separation from his check, he displayed a deceptively strong shot, showing a quick release, strong velocity and accuracy.

Sioux City Musketeers at Des Moines Buccaneers, November 16, 2018

Sioux City Musketeers -

Kallionkieli, Marcus - 2019 Surprisingly complete package of a player. Kallionkieli featured prominently on a top line with Bobby Brink and Martin Pospisil. The Finnish import also played on the power play and in 4 on 4 situations, he was used often throughout. On the power play he was used low near the post and in the slot. He scored by receiving a puck low, just outside the post out of a tripod and then was able to turn inside and bring it across the net mouth for a goal. Rangy winger with a good skating stride – very smooth. Generates decent speed, but isn't a blazer. Good change of direction skater, very good on starts and stops. Can withstand contact well despite a little bit of a lanky frame still. Effective forechecker and backchecker all night long. Very impressed by his smarts in all three zones. His ability to time switches and when to change lanes is very strong. Made a few good defensive plays on the night. Offers a plus shot and can score from mid-range at this level. Displays strong puck poise as well, adding to the smoothness of his overall game.

Brink, Bobby - 2019 Fast and industrious all night long. Part of a dynamite top line with Marcus Kallionkieli and Martin Pospisil. Offers a plus skill level from a technical perspective. Can easily make a first forechecker miss and with a head of steam can beat two. Uses defenders momentum against them with smooth skill and good anticipation. Can make skill plays at a high rate of speed. Strong puck carrying skills. Works himself open in the offensive zone. His first step quickness is impressive. Even more impressive is his closing speed. On the forecheck, he is in a defenseman's hip pocket at a jarring rate for this level. Has savvy beyond his years in terms of dictating where pucks and players are going next. He already knows he can move players with his guile or, defensively, give them something and take it away just that quickly. Played on the power play in the low spot and also the right point. Also worked on the PK. All situation player who noses his way into any area on the ice…shades of Brian Gionta in that regard.

Des Moines Buccaneers -

Paquette, Tyler - 2019 Used sparingly throughout the night. Maybe third line minutes. Fairly awkward skater who doesn't get a lot out of his stride. His feet stop moving when his hands activate, further reducing the effectiveness of lacking skating mechanics. Certainly has a shot, but he seems to struggle to find room to get it away. Doesn't seem to fully grasp how to migrate into the softer areas of the offensive zone to open himself up yet. Did play some penalty kill, though he didn't seem to have a strong penchant for defensive play at even strength.

Chicago Steel at Madison Capitols (4-3) Chicago, November 16th 2018

Chicago Steel

Mastrosimone, Robert – 2019 Robert wasn't a big factor in the game tonight and Madison did a good job against his line for much of the night. Mastrosimone displayed some of his offensive skill in moving the puck in the transition game and finding teammates in the neutral zone with speed but this was the only impact he had for the most part. Robert didn't have enough north-south in his game tonight to be effective and Madison did a good job taking away the middle of the ice which limited the effect Mastrosimone could have in this game.

Treloar, Travis -2019 Treloar didn't register any points in this game but was effective in the offensive end in regards to winning key puck battles along the wall, especially on the Power Play in order to sustain offensive zone possession for his team. Treloar lacked explosiveness in his skating but showed the ability to make plays with speed once he gets a head of steam with the puck.

Reid, Luke – 2020 Luke displayed flashes of sound puck moving ability both in using his feet as well as quick reads up ice however in certain situations Reid's hockey IQ would have lapses in judgement, in one sequence Reid retrieved a loose puck from around the faceoff circle, instead of taking the clear lane to gain his net and turn the play up ice, Reid turned and skating up the near half wall into traffic and turned the puck over in the process. Reid displayed good technical mechanics in most areas of the game tonight except in regards to his decision making.

Power, Owen - 2021 Being listed at 6'5" and 195 lbs. Obviously Power has a ways to go before he is grown into his big frame, however he displayed decent footwork and footspeed for his lanky frame. Power uses his reach well in defending one on one and is able to take away a lot of time and space in doing so. Owen displayed a good shot release from the point that he was able to get through traffic and on goal successfully.

Edmonton Oil Kings vs Kelowna Rockets, November 17, 2018

Edmonton

Robertson, Matthew (2019) - For a player his size Robertson is such an impressive skater, with the ability to stop and turn on a dime. Robertson looks very fluid with the puck on his stick, able to slip by opponents effortlessly sometimes and calmly beat his man at the offensive blueline. Lacks creativity as a passer and doesn't always involve himself offensively often too content to just sit around. Defensively he is engaged and with his size and skating is very difficult to beat.

Alistrov, Vladimir (2019) - One of Edmontons most dangerous forwards today as he was very engaged and competing hard. With the effort he brought today he was able to use his skills to make a lot of plays with the puck, creating dangerous chances on most shifts. Not an explosive skater but he is very fluid and has good top speed. Seems to be getting more comfortable with the pace of play, and was encouraging to see him compete hard today.

Kelowna

Korczak, Kaeden (2019) - As always was strong defensively and very willing to engage physically. Natural instincts are not consistently the best but had a great play today stepping up to intercept a pass in the neutral zone leading to his team scoring the game winner. Puck skills are not at a high enough level to make many plays in transition or the offensive zone.

Foote, Nolan (2019) - Offensively really only looked dangerous from the ringette line down as Foote is great at protecting the puck and has a very heavy shot, but lacks in the skating department. 2 goals coming off of very quick releases today where he had space and made the other team pay.

Thomson, Lassi (2019) - Probably the most creative offensive mind of all the WHLs draft eligible defencemen. Makes plays a lot of others wouldn't even attempt (had a perfect Elias Pettersson end board bank pass today). He is a real quarterback type with the puck as he is always in control with the puck and reading where pressure is moving. He does a great job at committing forecheckers and finding seams while moving up ice. Defensively he has a very strong stick and is proactive in breaking plays up. Skating is above average at this level but he could still stand to gain some quickness as he occasionally makes plays where he overestimates how fast he is.

USNTDP U18 at Dubuque Fighting Saints, November 17, 2018

USNTDP U18 -

Vlasic, Alex - 2019 Plays LD. Worked the PK and PP2 (right point). Generated a goal from the PP with a half-slapped one-timer from inside the top of the circle. For a big player at this age, he is really in control of his body, very coordinated, very calm at all times. Makes very intelligent reads, really good at anticipating…he knows what he wants to do with the puck before gets it. This is especially valuable to a player of his type, as he is not brimming with technical skills just yet. Nothing jumps off the page from that perspective, but he gets it and moves it quickly and smartly. Plenty capable skater, pretty fluid for his size at this age, good reach, really good risk mitigation. Opens up for his partner well, very reliable in all three zones. Not flashy. Isn't going to offer a lot of end to end rushes. But he has wit and size and mobility and he showed it off tonight.

Hughes, Jack - 2019 I'm not sure if anyone in this draft class will have had the puck on his stick as much as Hughes does any given night. He is the strongest puck carrier on a talented club and it's not particularly close. His stickhandling mixed with acceleration and speed are too much to handle in the USHL. His stutter step/stop n' go moves jive so nicely with his edge work and first step quickness that just getting a stick on him is an achievement for some would-be defenders. The quick misdirection sequences that he offers is that of the "hyper-speed superstars" that have germinated post-2005 lockout. Operates the power play from the right half boards. Spent most of the night at even strength with Trevor Zegras and Matthew Boldy. He whipped a number of shots towards the net and setup linemates for just as many. Hughes flummoxed the defense for most of the night, they were able to pin him against the boards in the corner one time, other than that, he was tough to nail while the game was close. Defensively, he really doesn't fit into a team concept. He just skates around briskly going from man to man, to lane to lane, to layer to layer freely and with no real, deliberate purpose…but his speed and presence are enough to force pucks to be coughed up by players who lack poise, so it's not a total loss. Hacked at some attack zone and DZ draws at a positive rate it felt like. Dropped to a knee to win an important defensive zone draw on his strong side when the game's outcome was still in doubt in its middle stages. Has all the improvisational skill of the best jazz pianist. Sometimes though you see linemates falling over themselves just to get out of his way though. How easy is it going to be to play with Jack Hughes at the next level? Or better, what type of player is going to work best with him – may be a challenge for his next organization.

Dubuque Fighting Saints -

Maccelli, Matias - 2019 Maccelli shows off some really nice hands, it looks like he has a nice array of finishing moves. Otherwise, his game is pretty hollow. He is quick, good stops. He actually relies on his ability to stop and go against the grain as his go-to get-away move when accepting passes along the boards, but he goes to it enough times that smarter defenders can anticipate it. Despite his first-step quickness, he doesn't offer anything more than average long speed. Doesn't seem very strong yet. Plays the right half boards on the PP. Forced a no-chance pass through the box that was picked off and led directly to a shorthanded goal. Doesn't seem terribly interested in backchecking. He was asked by his coach to serve a too many men minor on a team that dressed 22, one could read that one of two ways. He did make a couple of interceptions in the NZ, but wasn't able to make a lot with them in close quarters. This is a player that still needs some open space or weaker players to really thrive. The upside is in the stickhandling that he possesses, there's a good skill base from that perspective…but that may be all he offers at the moment.

Vancouver Giants vs Victoria Royals, November 18, 2018

Vancouver

Byram, Bowen (2019) - Played a very aggressive offensive game today, creating more chances than anyone else on his team. Byram is a dangerous player in transition who can knife through the neutral zone effortlessly. In the offensive zone he shows some great smarts with his ability to move without the puck and his decision making while he is in possession. Had an excellent play today where he slipped in to the slot faked a shot and had the patience to round 2 defenders he committed before firing high. Defensively he was generally very alert and aggressive with his angling. Is prone to the occasional shift where his intensity completely drops off and he makes weak plays.

Sourdif, Justin 92(2020) - Great decision maker with and without the puck who has an advanced understanding of timing and spacing. Very creative passer who does a great job at creating passing lanes with stick work. Overall very slippery and hard to contain with the puck on his stick.

Miner, Trent (2019) - Very confident between the pipes always looking calm and in control. Does a great job squaring himself to shooters and is tight technically, leaving very few holes. Had a couple plays where he couldn't generate enough power on his slide to make saves on cross ice passes. Excellent puck handler who loves to step out and try make a play.

New England Prep, November 18, 2018

Dexter School –

DEX #9 RC Farinacci, John (2019) – Farinacci should be one of the top prep players this season and showed his game early in the game scoring early in the first period off his own rebound down low on his off side as he followed his shot with his second shot getting some luck going off Dman shin pad out front for the 1st goal of the game. His second goal of the game was more influential as he made smart reload through the neutral zone with good stick position to help cause the turnover. He quickly peeled around in transition with linemate #24 McInnis starting the give-n-go from the offensive blue line in and snapped home a shot into the open net after the quick puck movement. He had a few other plays in the 1st period whereby he displayed his skill sets and offensive instincts as he stickhandled through defenders for high end scoring opportunities. He already has had early season success in USHL with Muskegon over weekend of action. Farinacci is one of the higher-end non-NTDP players for the draft looking forecasting for early round pick.

DEX #35 G Mullahy, Derek (2019) – It was a pretty easy game for the senior goalie as the depth of Dexter out matched Delbarton, thus limiting the pucks Mullahy faced. He only had to make two challenging saves the entire game whereby he had to show his athleticism and reads on the play to make the save. He played a confident game allowing no second chances, solid positioning, and hockey IQ. Would like to see Mullahy in a more challenging game later in the season.

Malmö Redhawks IF at Linköping HC Nov 18, 2018

Linköping

LHC # 27 RD Lyckåsen, Albert (2019): - Had speed in the game, rings in the puck on net, creates dangerous chances. Made some unnecessary risky roughing's which referee didn't saw. Angles opponents good and difficult to pass through. Good eyes. Quick release, quick turnovers, several good opening passes. A good toe in and towards the net. Was talking to referee a bit too much after a whistle resulted in that the referee took the faceoff out from offensive zone.

LHC # 12 CE Ekmark, Elliot (2020) - Used as RD in PP, angles his opponent good. Had good rushes and thought he could have turned in to the net more often. Quick and good side moving and shots from faceoff circle. Good reading and positioning. Good Faceoffs. 8 SOG, 8/10 FOW,

LHC #28 RD Zivlak, Ivan (2020) - Good opening passes to Pedersen several times. Didn't look to have his regular game however I have to remind myself that he is just 16 and some months and plays in J20 SuperElit. Was not much visulised for long times, looked a bit unfocused in some shifts and angry on the bench. Had 2 decent shots from blueline but without traffic. 2 SOG, usually not much happens backwards when Zivlak is on ice. While he was on the ice both goals where scored. +2, 2 SOG.

LHC #22 LW Pedersen, Marcus (2019) - Tall righthanded LW often found on the offensive blueline ready for long pass and a rush. Had good impact on the game although not any points in protocol. Pedersen was also giving quick long passes difficult to predict. Good creative and started several quick turnovers bringing the puck with speed. Looked to have some respect to steer in to the net and ended up behind the goal cage. Delivered a good shot but from very difficult angle, was going under the skin of the opponent after whistle blows. Did some unnecessary hits with the stick on the opponent, behind offensive net, that looked to be risky to get unnecessary penalties. 2 SOG.

LHC #32 LW Szurowski, Mateusz (2020) - Was used as LD in powerplay. Good passes in PP. Did some misreading and had risky passes in own zone. Skating very low almost sitting and difficult to take the puck from. Was competitive, wins the pucks.

LHC # 35 LW Persson, Albert (2020) - Very tall 16-year-old guy. Was making mostly notes about that he was not so much visulised and could have used his team mates better. Was delivering 4 SOG and 1 went in. Second goal was an empty net goal.

LHC # 24 RW Åhlin, David (2019) - Was gliding and bringing the puck to offensive zone with speed. Looked unscarred but still didn't go in to the net. Using a long stick with successful poking on opponents. Did some misreading and attacking opponent high leading to chances for MIF. Was not convincing me or made that much impact, (delivering good passes) that I sometimes can do.

Malmo

MIF # 28 CE Plato, Hampus (2020) - Was one of the top players in MIF shining with speed and passes, small right handed player. Lifting sticks to steal the pucks. Was looking to read the game very good, was often found on the spot where the puck ended up. Was balancing the provocations good resulting on opponent # 16 getting a penalty for roughing. Released a quick direct accurate wrist shot. Was getting under the skin on opponents. Competitive. Finnish hit. Strong at the board, keeping the puck with one arm and keeping opponent outside with the other. Was finding his team mates in very difficult angles with passes after pulling out the opponent's team before. Was talking a lot and questioning the referee and since not much people in the arena it was possible to hear lot of it from seating platform.

Prince Albert Raiders vs Lethbridge Hurricanes, November 20, 2018

Prince Albert

Protas, Alexei (2019) - The combination of vision and puck protection that Protas has allows him to be a very good playmaker at this level, sees the ice at a very high level when he can slow it down. Also has a deceptively good shot that he gets off in a hurry. First few steps are terrible but once he gets going he can skate pucks into the ozone and has deceptive speed.

Leason, Brett (2019) - At this level there's not much teams can do to stop Leason. He is such a powerful skater that the D has to play flawlessly on the rush to avoid getting beat, because once he gets a step he's too big and too fast to contain. Every shift you can tell that he wants to make an impact however he can, and he works hard in all areas of the ice. Calm and composed as a finisher with no panic even when he is under pressure, scoring 3 goals today. Has above average hands and can beat defencemen with his skill sometimes. Has great timing for getting himself into goalscoring areas.

Lethbridge

Cozens, Dylan (2019) - Out of all the players in the WHL Cozens might be the best skater. The combination of top end speed, agility, and explosiveness that Cozens has is freakish. Taking the puck into the offensive zone looks like a walk in the park for him most of the time. His transition play is easily his strongest area as he does a great job taking routes where he can give his teammates passing options, and receives pucks with speed. Defensively Cozens is also very attentive and is very good at disrupting plays with his speed and stick. On the downside Cozens often looks content to fade into the background and doesn't assert his abilities on a consistent basis. This is especially noticeable in the offensive zone where he can be a bit of a passenger sometimes even though he has the tools to be elite.

Barlage, Logan (2019) - Game really relies on his size and strength. Very heavy on the puck and difficult to knock around which lets him take the puck into traffic to generate chances. Also is heavy on the forecheck where he is unafraid to throw a check in order to separate a player from the puck. Strong shot but his release takes too much time.

Saskatoon Blades vs Lethbridge Hurricanes, November 21, 2018

Saskatoon

Dach, Kirby (2019) - Came out strong in this game generating a ton in the first period. Handling the puck very well today and using his stickhandling and agility to make things difficult for defenders one-on-one. Generally looked in the zone today dominating with and without the puck. Defensively Dach has a huge impact as he reads plays so well as they develop that he can get in positions to make plays.

Lethbridge

Cozens, Dylan (2019) - A fairly assertive game for him as he looked like he wanted to make an impact more frequently today. Shot release is excellent, can beat goalies clean at this level. At times Cozens can lack creativity and doesn't make the most of his dynamic abilities, also has a tendency to skate himself in to turnovers through the neutral zone by forcing something that's not there. Has the type of skating where if he gets a step on a defenseman he is gone.

Barlage, Logan (2019) - Quiet game offensively but played a strong physical game on the forecheck. Shot is very heavy when he has time and space to get it off.

AIK u20 at Djurgarden IF u20, November 21 2018

AIK u20

Karlstrom, David 2019 Smart, two-way centerman with good size. Skating needs to improve, but is not bad. Were very defensive in his defensive zone, got passive and were a spectator on the 4-1 goal. Made good decisions with the puck all night, feeding his wingers the puck and skated the puck zone to zone under control several times, showing some good stickhandling and awareness. Uses his body successfully to protect the puck along the boards. He did not create any scoring chances at all, had a weak offensive game.

Djurgarden IF u20

Bjornfot, Tobias 2019 Bjornfot played a solid two-way game through the whole game. He has good work ethic and is a leader for his team. He has good size, strength and battles hard in front of his own net and in the corners. Had some trouble getting the puck out of his own zone, trying to stickhandle and skate through forecheckers. Misread the situation and gave the opposition a breakaway which they scored their third goal late in the game. He often jumps the attack and got a quick release wrist shot. Quarterbacks the power play with good movement on the blue line and a shot that gets through traffic.

Holtz, Alexander 2020 - Holtz showed his explosive offensive skillset this game. Easily beat his defenders with exceptional stickhandling and powerful skating. He reads the game very well and creates scoring chances every time he is on the ice. Although he is a shoot-first type of player, he shows good vision and playmaking abilities too. Has a quick, hard shot and finds the areas of the ice where he can shoot, often. Leaves his defensive zone a bit early at times, creating chances offensively, but leaves a hole defensively. Skating needs to improve further. Finished the game with an assist. Top prospect for the 2020 draft.

Bjerselius, Oscar 2019 Bjerselius gives good support to his teammates all over the ice. He battles hard and reads the play really well, making interceptions and retrieves loose pucks. He does his work away from the spotlight, giving his forwards more time and space to attack. Bjerselius gets some time on the power play, but there is no upside to his offense. His shot is average and his hands does not seem to keep up with his good hockey sense. Has a short stride average top-speed. Bjerselius finished the game with a secondary assist.

Waterloo Black Hawks at Sioux City Musketeers, November 21, 2018

Waterloo Black Hawks -

Firstov, Vladislav - 2019 Firstov has a compact stride, but is pretty stiff-legged. His feet are pretty quick, but there isn't a good knee bend to his stride, so there isn't a lot of power there. That's augmented by the fact that he isn't a very hard worker. He disappeared for long stretches of this game. There was a little pep in his step when he got some extra shifts when Waterloo fell behind late. But his compete and engagement was touch and go all night. When he did locate pucks, the skill level wasn't overwhelming. He made one nice carry across two lines, other than that, his work from down low on the PP was the only thing that warranted attention. He needs some room to be effective and I'm not sure there's enough dynamic skill there or dynamic skating there to reliably make that room.

Drkulec, Ryan - 2019 Noticeably massive player at 6'5". First impression was that there wasn't going to much there considering how slow he is off the blocks. His first two or three steps don't go anywhere. But his top speed is actually very appealing. Most surprisingly, he made a couple of skill players – notably, working himself off the wall for looks. He had good spatial awareness too, his turns and stickhandles were very calculated. He showed he can get to the wall, engage in a battle and walk it off the wall. Naturally, he also makes a mess of things in the front of the net, but he isn't fully coordinated to be a deflection or put-back artist yet. He's a late 2000, so he's not too far off the curve...this is a player to put the magnifying glass on at the end of the year to see the level of progression – it could surprise.

Cameron, Matt - 2019 First game with his new team after a trade. Played limited minutes, but that seemed to increase a bit as the game went on. Showed that he's a plus skater and could work himself out of corners and off the wall with good small-area footwork and some nifty hands. Threw a couple of strong hit attempts. Good hockey sense.

Sioux City Musketeers -

Ford, Parker - 2019 Ford played a ton of minutes tonight. He's a real hard worker, a lot of hustle to his game. He's PK1 and PP1 as well. Not only does he work hard, but there's some skill underneath that work rate that's worth noting. Very strong skater, he's quick and fast. Very well balanced. In the rare event that he actually gets solid contact, he absorbs very well. Often times, he has the awareness to skirt hits, despite going to the dirty areas to make his living. Very agile, very good sense of where other players are that he can't see. Showed off some quick hands tonight, got himself off the wall and out of tight spots regularly. He didn't play ES with the big guys (Kallionkieli, Pospisil, Brink) but he does play down low and in front on the PP with them. He's not just a decoy, or a throwaway guy in front...he gets the puck often, and works it across the net line. His defensive play is advanced for his age. It's smart and he really gets underneath his check to dislodge them from a puck or to disrupt a would-be chance. Very hockey strong for his size. Has the coach's trust too. With less two minutes to go, protecting a one-goal lead, Sioux City called a timeout after an icing with their top line out there. Because of the timeout, they were able to make a line change and they took off perhaps the best line in the USHL to put on Ford and his unit. Ford rewarded the decision with the empty net goal to seal it.

Brink, Bobby - 2019 High-end motor, high-end skill player who plays all the time in all situations and is effective more often than not. Not only does he work hard, but he works smart. He identifies the biggest risk to his team defensively and jumps to sniff it out. In two particular cases, he was actually unsuccessful…both were a combo of a reach/body position shortcoming. That's the drawback on him: size. Though he plays bigger than his vitals, there's a reality to it that sometimes presents itself. Really great game awareness, he is quick to jump into the right spots on the rink on both sides of the puck. He can give and take passes of all types with ease. He wins a lot of puck battles. Made a terrific SH rush 1v1 against a defender, pulled in an angle change shot from the dot that beat a 6'3", NHL-drafted goalie under the bar to give Sioux City their first lead midway through the 3rd.

Complete player, competes hard, has the skills, the smarts, the skating, and the shot to be an impact player at the next level.

London Knights vs Mississauga Steelheads, Nov 22 2018

Knights –

McMichael, Connor (2019) – Wasn't consistent and didn't drive his line that featured Guskov at the start of the game, but was opportunistic, using his speed and his shot to threaten. He was good at finding soft-ice and getting in-between the young Mississauga defense, showing soft-hands and the ability to quickly change the angle of his release point. He had a primary assist, after firing a quick and low shot that bounced of Ingram's pad resulting in a rebound goal. Behind the goal-line he made an impressive one-touch pass out into the slot on another shift as well. Overall, he flashed his hockey sense, skill, and skating ability but not for a full 60 minutes.

Guskov, Matvei (2019) – Guskov was featured on a line with McMichael but rarely touched the puck out there today. He did have a really nice cut in the right-circle, where he showed deceptive passing ability by dropping a no-look drop-pass that set up a goal. His impressive passing ability was further displayed after he set McMichael in on a partial breakaway after making an accurate stretch pass from the neutral zone as well. Away from the play, Matvei was willing to commit to defense and played deep in his own-end of the ice at times.

Stranges, Antonio (2020) – Stranges played on the 4th line but also received powerplay time, showing flashes of his talent level. He had a couple of impressive transitional zone entries where he was willing to enter high-traffic areas while attempting to control the puck. The most impressive element of his skating on display today was his edges which allowed him to make sudden directional changes, this resulted in his best individual effort where he cut across the slot before dragging the puck in-tight to his body and releasing a wrist-shot that caught off Ingham slightly off guard. He missed a wide-open net on the powerplay, shooting the puck over the net, but he still got the puck off quickly. Overall, Antonio showed confidence when handling the puck and was notable in spurts.

Steelheads –

Harley, Thomas (2019) – Harley showed a good command for the game with the puck on his stick, away from the play he played at an average pace which resulted in several routine defensive plays that resulted in goals and high-end chances for London. He had a difficult opening period, where a puck ricocheted off of him into the net, and also poked the puck onto an opponent's stick which resulted in a goal after he failed to maintain an adequate gap against Foudy. His offensive skill helped counter some of his defensive lapses as he was efficient on the powerplay, showing poise and the ability to make sharp passes to his teammates, he also recognized when his lanes were open and closed. His transitional play was also a plus, finding teammates with his vision. His tempo and physical presence wasn't adequate, but his offensive-skill stood out.

Washkurak, Keean (2019) – Washkurak had several offensive zone entries and generated offense in spurts for the Steelheads. He's not the biggest kid, but he's willing to engage physically and enter heavy traffic to make plays. His best sequence came in the neutral zone where he showed a decent amount of agility while stepping multiple players before moving over the line and making a saucer pass to his teammate which resulted in one of the better scoring chances for the Steelheads. His motor and willingness to compete was there today.

Schwindt, Cole (2019) – Schwindt played in all situations for the Steelheads and played at a good pace while battling effectively by using his frame. He had a nice dump and chase sequence where he chased after the puck, recollected it along the boards before distributing it, he was also willing to cut aggressively towards the net area when carrying the puck. On the powerplay, he had a nice no-look backhand pass from below the goal-line, and on the penalty-kill he was willing to sacrifice his body to make a shot-block.

St. Thomas Academy vs Minnetonka Skippers, November 23, 2018

St. Thomas Academy

Christy, Rob – 2019 While Christy showed flashes of his speed and ability to be strong on the puck in this game, he was not consistent enough to have an effect and Minnetonka did a good job against his line all night and Christy's body language showed he was frustrated at times. Christy seemed uninterested at times in the game, especially away from the puck and in his own end. Christy is a draft prospect that has shown the ability of much more than he did in this game.

Minnetonka Skippers

Luedtke, Josh – 2019 Luedtke has always been an offensive defenseman that plays a rover style who likes to skate the puck up and down the ice, in this game Luedke showed he has made great strides in his reads coming out of his own end, rather than rushing up the ice when his first option isn't available, Luedtke was identifying his options earlier in his puck retrievals and showing more poise in his decision making and delivering the puck accurately to his forwards. Luedtke has recently switched his NCAA commitment from Northern Michigan to Denver and the growth in his play is likely a big reason for that. The only aspect lacking in Luedtke's game right now is size and strength to defend in one on one situations, however that was not needed a lot in this game as Minnetonka controlled most of the play.

Docter, Grant – 2019 Docter and Luedtke showed once again why they will again be one of the best defensive pairings in Minnesota High School hockey this year. Docter plays a smart two-way game that is a stabilizing presence for the more offensively minded Luedtke and executed his role well in this game. Docter is not without offensive skill; Grant made a quick sauce pass from the left point to the right face-off dot to set up a one-timer Power Play goal. Docter showed the ability to process situations quickly and always leaves himself outs with the puck. Docter runs under the radar due to his underwhelming point totals but is an excellent skater and puck distributer that consistently gets pucks out of his own end.

Björklöven at AIK, HockeyAllsvenskan, Nov 23 2018

AIK

#70 Broberg, Philip - Broberg has great size and is an excellent skater, considering his size. His game is really different in HockeyAllsvenskan, than it is with the juniorteam or even internationally. He makes good decisions, quick passes tape to tape and values when to take risks and jump the attack. Defensively he's got the strength and ability to skate, to defend really well even against men. Active stick defensively and is not afraid to play physical and use his body. Did a superb job in box play, getting the puck out of the zone and winning puck-battles. Has a good long, powerful stride that allowed him to beat the defenders on his left side and create scoring chances. Was a offensive threat from the first shift - to the end of the game, showcasing really good offensive instincts and movement on the blue line. Continued to challenge the defending team with good low shots through traffic and terrific passing. Beat his man 1-on-1 almost every try and there was a sense of great self- confidence. Has an under rated shot, its relatively hard, hits the net through traffic and has a quick release. Need to work on his puck-skills, this is obvious in high pace games. Overall he was one of the best players on the ice this game and has really grown in to the higher level of play in the HockeyAllsvenskan.

Holy Family Catholic Fire vs Wayzata Trojans, November 24, 2018

Holy Family Catholic

Pinoniemi, Garrett – 2019 Garrett was effective but far from dominates in this game. Pinoniemi used his speed to gain the offensive zone and did a good job getting himself and the puck to the middle of the ice. Pinoniemi saw a number of good scoring chances by finding the soft area's in the slot and making himself available for centering feeds but missed the net on a couple grade "A" scoring chances. Pinoniemi showed good creativity and vision to slide a feed down low from the slot for a scoring chance in one instance in the 1st period. Pinoniemi showed good hockey sense to get himself into scoring opportunities but lacked the finishing ability in the game.

Fechko, Trey – 2021 Despite likely being the youngest player on the ice in this game, Fechko's game was impressive in a couple of areas. First is his skating, Fechko displayed excellent agility and the ability to get to top speed quickly off the hop. Fechko played a fearless, physical style on the fore check and displayed impressive craftiness on the back check in pick pocketing puck carriers and forcing turnovers. Fechko showed good playmaking ability in setting up his team's goal in the 1st by threading a pass from the half wall to teammate at the far slot for a goal. Fechko is a 2003 birth year and just a freshman but played in all situations on the top line for Holy Family and looks to be one of the top 03's in the State of Minnesota, after playing games for Holy Family last year as an 8th grader.

Maple Grove Crimson vs Edina Hornets, November 24th, 2018

Edina Hornets

Vorlicky, Mike – 2019+ Vorlicky is a re-entry NHL Draft prospect. While Vorlicky popped up on the draft radar for some scouts last season, he didn't see the significant minutes on a deep Edina blueline last year for any teams to use a draft choice on him. This year will be a different story as Vorlicky logged a ton of minutes in this game for the Hornets, playing in all situations and registering a goal on the Power Play by taking advantage of the ice given to him and coming down the slot from the point for a shot on goal. Vorlicky is an excellent skating with NHL explosiveness as well as footwork and agility. He was able to use his skating to control the game with the puck on his stick and made a number of impressive rushes out of his own end as well as free up lanes from the point for quick shots on net. Vorlicky displayed a good physical edge when the situation called for it but didn't take himself out of the play in doing do. With the added ice time and situational opportunities Vorlicky will have this year he will be a player to watch as the season progresses.

Boltmann, Jake – 2020 Played a stay at home defensive game by using his footwork to be in good position against the rush and having an active stick in his own end. Skating lacks some straight line explosiveness but has good agility. Was able to stretch the ice east/west and north/south on outlets passes.

Maple Grove Crimson

Janicke, Justin – 2021 Despite being a 2003 born player and just a freshman, Janicke was an important piece to Maple Grove pulling the upset in this game and was one of the better players on the ice for either squad. Janicke's explosive skating allowed him to win races to lose pucks and have a lot of puck possession in this game. Justin displayed quick hockey sense in moving the puck quickly to open teammates in the offensive zone and in the transition game. Janicke finished the game with 1 Goal and 1 Assists, however was in on all 3 goals as he set a great screen on the goalie for the game's opening goal. In his goal that tied the game in the 3rd, Janicke showcased his explosive skating in winning a race to a puck that was cleared out of his own end off the glass and beat the goalie with a quick shot inside the far post as he drove the net. Janicke will likely be a NDTP invite for next season as he looks to be one of the top players of his age group.

Kukkonen, Kyle – 2020 Kukkonen showed good finishing ability on his goal on a 2 on 2 where he looked off Janicke who was driving through the slot and fired a quick shot through the goalies five-hole. While Kukkonen doesn't have a technically sound skating stride he possesses good top speed and it doesn't hold him back in his game at the stage. Kukkonen's hockey sense showed flashes of being good away from the puck as he played a smart defensive game in his own end but with the puck he tried to do too much and tried to stick handle and make a fancy plays when he had clear lanes for shots or passes.

Chicoutimi Saguenéens at Blainville-Boisbriand Armada, November 24th, 2018

Chicoutimi

#8 Kniazev, Artemi (2019): Kniazev really excelled today at carrying the puck out of his zone. His strong skating abilities make it look easy for him. He seemed to skate the puck out of his zone on every shift he had today. On the power play, he saw a lot of ice time and was even the lone defenseman on Chicoutimi's first power play unit. He also used his good wheels to retrieve pucks quickly in his own zone. In the offensive zone, he kept his feet moving, moving a lot in the offensive zone, which can provide additional options for his teammates. Another area in which he excelled tonight was his decision-making. He demonstrated real quick decision-making with the puck, and his passes were usually crisp and accurate.

#92 Lapierre, Hendrix (2020): Lapierre played on the LW of Chicoutimi's 2nd line, also receiving regular ice time on the power play (where he had his best moments tonight). He showed impressive vision and playmaking abilities on the power play; usually on the half-wall he made some high-quality passes to his teammates (who unfortunately couldn't finish). Lapierre showed good patience with the puck in the offensive zone and was also good along the boards to protect the puck by using his size. He has above-average speed, using it on a couple of sequences to beat an Armada defenseman wide.

#19 Rochette, Théo (2020): While he may be less flashy than Lapierre, the young Swiss/Canadian showed some good smarts and maturity in his play by playing a solid two-way game today. He backchecked hard and showed good support down low, helping his defensemen out. Not the biggest guy, but he didn't mind getting his nose dirty in front of the net and in the slot in the offensive zone. He did a lot of dirty work for his line along the boards and in front of the net. He's not a speedster, at least not that I saw today. His speed didn't look great; it was only average.

Blainville-Boisbriand

#7 Rannisto, Jasper (2019): Saw some physical play for him in his own zone. He also cleared the front of the net. Not a lot of plays where he was noticeable with the puck, and not many puck touches. He took some simple shots on net, but overall, didn't show much vision or creativity in the offensive zone. His footspeed looked only average.

#58 Bolduc, Samuel (2019): It was a quiet night for him compared to the night before, where he was more noticeable for his puck rushing abilities. Today there were not a lot of puck touches from him and he was not very noticeable on the ice. He showed a good, heavy slapshot from the point, but as far as offensive plays go, that's all we got from him today. When he was not under pressure, he made some good first passes. However, when he *was* under pressure, his decision-making was too slow and got him into trouble.

Vancouver Giants vs Saskatoon Blades, November 27, 2018

Vancouver

Byram, Bowen (2019) - Great agility and confidence stickhandling, you can tell he knows what kind of plays he is good enough to pull off at this level. Also has really good instincts for finding soft space as a trailer on the rush. In the offensive zone Byram is very good at shooting off of motion when he has the puck, is not a guy who needs time and space to get the puck off. When he goes D to D he is always tape to tape and commits his opponent to him.

Sourdif, Justin (2020) - Natural skill level is very high and is evident when you see him touch the puck. Very good hockey brain as he puts himself in good spots and makes some very clever passes. Defensively is a very strong stickchecker who is really good at finding the puck. Adding strength is going to be huge for Sourdif as he is very weak right now. Also has speed that is just average.

Saskatoon

Dach, Kirby (2019) - Some of his most impressive moments I have seen in this game. Stole a puck from Byram on the forecheck and proceeded to pick the short side top corner about as tight as you can on one of his first shifts of the game. Also showed a good combination of puckhandling and strength on some impressive net drives. It is impressive seeing such a big guy who has such good hands in tight areas. A few wow passes today with one seam pass for a breakaway that he threaded through 4 players on the other team. Gets creative in using the boards and goalie to make passes when he has no lane.

Muskegon Lumberjacks at Green Bay Gamblers, November 30th 2018

Muskegon Lumberjacks

Afanasyev, Yegor – 2019 It was a fairly quiet game for Afanasyev. Yegor displayed a good shot on one sequence off the rush shooting in stride, coming down the wing and did a decent job identifying and getting to the soft areas in the offensive zone to be available for scoring chances and was able to get some decent scoring looks in doing do, however he was unable to create much offensively with the puck on his stick and didn't get involved in the hard areas enough to be an impact player in this game.

Frisch, Ethan – 2019 While Frisch didn't register any points in this game, he was by far Green Bay's best defenseman, logging a lot of minutes in all situations. Frisch's skating allows him to cover a lot of ground in all areas of the ice. Frisch was able to track down and beat opponents to loose pucks in the neutral zone and as well as get to pucks in order to keep them in the offensive zone. Frisch was solid on the breakout and used his skating and vision to buy time and find

2nd and 3rd options coming out of his own end. It was an effective two-way game for Frisch and used his skating and footwork to close the gap quickly at his own blue line.

Giroday, Chris - 2019 Giroday saw a good amount of time on the Power Play in the game and did a good job moving the puck around the zone and made some very clean plays at the offensive blue line while under pressure to keep the puck moving in the offensive zone. Giroday connected on a good amount of his outlets and showed the ability to rush the puck if need be. Defensively, Giroday did well to keep plays to the outside on the rush but did get beat wide on a couple occasions, but showed good physicality and made players pay a price in front of the net.

Linkoping HC u20 at Sodertalje SK u20, December 1 2018

Linkoping HC u20

Pasic, Nikola 2019 Pasic is a fast, skilled, shot-first winger. He shoots all the time, seems to never even consider a pass. He skates really well with an intense, quick footed stride and low center of gravity, he would benefit from going harder to the net since he often plays the outside. He did stand out offensively scoring 2 goals and an assist, one of the goals being a beautiful spin-o-rama backhand shot. His overall game is flawed. He does not contribute at his own end, the only thing on his mind is goalscoring. His defenders looked frustrated at times and his line mates had to carry a large load in the d-zone.

Costmar, Arvid 2019 Scored a beautiful goal on an 2on1 on the box-play. Reads the play very well and is often at the right place at the right time. Has good vision offensively, but did miss some easy passes. His shot is very accurate and has a quick release, but is not very hard. Would like to see more offense from him, but overall he plays a smart, responsible two-way game.

Lyckasen, Albert 2019 Drives the play with effective passing and simple zone exits, seems to find always find an easy pass under pressure. Smooth skating and he can really skate the puck out of his d-zone and in to the o-zone under pressure. His hand-eye coordination is good and he knocked down pucks out of the air a couple times. Had success quarterbacking the power play and setting his team mates up for shots. Effective two-way defenseman with a modern playstyle. On 5 on 5 he struggled to create offense. He did not jump the play and rarely left the blue line Was one of the best players on the ice this game.

Ahlin, David 2019 Plays hard, intense and goes through traffic. Despite only being listed as 5'9", he's not afraid of physical play and he's going in to all situations with high speed. Offensively he plays a fast give-and-go type of game, with lots of intensity and energy. He could use to put on some muscle, he got pushed around at times and looked small beside other players.

Sodertalje SK u20

Feuk, Lucas 2019 Feuk slacked and looked uninterested, especially defensively. Tried to beat the defenders by leaving his defensive zone before his opposing defenders.

He is an outside player and avoided physical play until he got frustrated by the result at the end of the game. Got some good offensive instincts and scored his teams only goal.

Wang, Carl 2019 Did not impress this game. A give away along the boards led to the opposition getting the go ahead goal 24 seconds in to the game. He had a hard time getting out of his own zone, due to trying to do too much, with below average puck skills.

Strong defensively 1on1, he plays the body and utilizes his size along the boards. His defensive awareness around his own net needs improvement, gets passive and spectates. At the end of the shifts he looked gassed and were skating on straight legs.

Edmonton Oil Kings vs Regina Pats, December 5, 2018

Edmonton

Guenther, Dylan (2019) - The midget aged first overall Bantam Draft pick was an AP for the game tonight. Positionally he was all over the place and his age showed quite a bit. However with the puck his skill was evident and he looked very speedy. He uses this combination to play the game with a lot of pace. Scored his first career WHL goal.

Neighbours, Jake (2020) - Plays a very mature game making the right plays frequently. His hockey sense is clearly strong but I'm yet to see much of a creative element to his game. Also is lacking a bit of long speed as he doesn't gain a ton of speed in space.

Robertson, Matthew (2019) - Had his typical game with great defensive work, encouraging flashes of offense, and a couple dumb turnovers. Excellent defending 1 on 1s with reach skating and strength that make him tough to beat. Had one super impressive move at the blueline to attack the slot that he followed up with a forced pass. Hands and skill sometimes look like they could be above average. Jumps into the rush without the puck well often beating his backchecker up ice, and scored a goal from this today.

Regina

Sedov, Nikita (2019) - Really impressed today, looking more confident and comfortable than earlier in the year. Skating was fluid in all four directions though not explosive. Was making smart decisions with the puck all game and never seemed to be panicked. Was good breaking out under pressure frequently using a shoulder fake before grabbing the puck on dump ins to beat the first forechecker.

Saginaw Spirit vs Niagara Ice Dogs, Dec 6 2018

Ice Dogs –

Tomasino, Philip (2019) – Tomasino had a above-average two-way performance for Niagara, factoring in on the forecheck, as well as anticipating the play away from the puck in advance which led to a couple of takeaways. He's a smaller kid but is adept at angling himself when he's along the boards, which allows him to protect the puck at a consistent level when matching up against physically imposing players. His combination of balance, edges, poise, and awareness allow him to navigate around the goal-line and set-up his teammates which occurred several times throughout this game. His best sequence came after stripping the puck by using a fast stick-lift, then quickly distributing it to Thomas who missed an open-net by ringing it off the crossbar. He showed a nice set of hands as well; in the right circle he pulled the puck quickly around an opponent's stick before releasing a quick wrist-shot. He's still not showing a lot of confidence when attempting to generate scoring chances from the hash-marks out and is instead continuing to produce offense in-tight to the net. Lastly, he didn't generate much off the rush, but he didn't need to in order to be effective out there either.

Spirit –

Prueter, Aidan (2020) – Prueter had a decent game for the Spirit by playing larger than his size on a couple of different plays involving the forecheck, as well as cleanly transitioning the puck over the offensive-line as well. He didn't show any sort of high-end offensive-skill-set, but he did have a nice cut through the high-slot while carrying the puck before making a drop-pass to his teammate that resulted in a scoring chance. His most impressive pass was the result of a spin-attempt in the bottom of the right-circle where he threaded the puck through the slot, but it didn't result in a goal. Lastly, he didn't mind playing physically and was willing to engage along the boards, though he wasn't overly effective in any one area let alone the forecheck, overall.

Perfetti, Cole (2020) – Perfetti was the most dominant forward for Saginaw showing a broad-range of high-end offensive-skills and a dynamic element to his game generated through a combination of his hands and his release point. He was engaged early and made several impressive one-touch passes that resulted in a primary assist, as well as other high-end scoring chances. Furthermore, his passing showed the ability to think well ahead of the play, he has a natural hockey sense where he can adapt to make the necessary play in tight-spaces while needing little time. He had several scoring chances, generated primarily through his quick release and fast-hands. He found himself all alone in-front of the net after a defensive breakdown and showed the ability to quickly pull the puck from his forehand to backhand in one-motion but hit the post after running out of room on the short-side. Like the rest of his game, its difficult for the opposition to gauge his next play, and the move surprised Dillon. Lastly, he had arguably the best goal I've seen this year. He received a pass from the right-circle and shot the puck as he was falling to his knees, the release was very fast and the shot was a bar-down goal, the shot was dynamic. His other shot attempts, weren't far off his impressive goal, showing a lightning quick release and the ability to rapidly shift the angle.

Porco, Nicholas (2019) – Porco wasn't very involved in the play and rarely made a difference or contributed both in the defensive-zone or offensive-zone. He did use his speed to engage on the forecheck and delivered a couple of notable hits, using his frame effectively, but never managed to create much in the way of pressure or turnovers at a consistent level. He did attempt to get his shot-off but was largely unsuccessful, though he did make a couple of decent passes and did recognize when he had open-teammates at times. One of the more concerning aspects of this game was Porco's inability to handle the puck properly while going at full speed, he had one great opportunity while rushing down the right-wing but mishandled the puck. His best scoring chance came around the goal-line off a sharp-angle slapshot that missed the mark.

Millman, Mason (2019) – Millman had a solid defensive effort for Saginaw, which was needed considering how many injuries they had on the backend heading into this game. He wasn't perfect, overstepping the position he needed to maintain on a couple of different plays, this was a result of looking for a big hit at an inopportune time which we have seen him from in previous efforts as well. That said, he was very good at keeping Niagara largely to the outside and still used his tenacity and physical presence in the corners to effectively disrupt the play. His puck management below his goal-line was a plus, showing some awareness and the ability to deal with the forecheck while under pressure by making quick decisions and nice outlet passes that mostly hit the tape of his teammates. He was more consistent in this aspect of his game than some other previous efforts as well. His best sequence came from a backchecking effort where he skated aggressively after a Niagara player and broke up a breakaway scoring opportunity that resulted in no shot on net. Lastly, he skated well today, showing a fluid stride, plus edge-work and a decent top-gear, though his stride is a little short.

AIK at Vita Hästen, December 7th 2018

AIK

AIK #70 RD Broberg, Philipp (2019) - A player who showed excellent skating, powerful legs and great mobility. His backward skating is excellent and he use his speed for rushes. Broberg was leading his man with great passes, some very long first passes. Vita Hästen is a bottom team but Brobergs vision and play making skills are great. Broberg showed very good anticipation and usually was found in position before the plays. He has great vision for team mates and good control on the watch during PP. Broberg showed very mature game and was witnessed constructive communication with teammates and supportive communication on ice. I think Broberg developed during the season and not running on rushes in every single opportunity. He is less predictable. In first period he was running on a rush on the left side and showed great stick handling and vision, but without team mates he ends up with 3 players on him and is taken down. Would be fun to see him getting some shifts in higher lines but he is accepting his role great and I guess it will come eventually. Great Positioned for a pass and free shoot a couple of times both in regular setup and in PP but didn't got the puck. Had some good passes to Blackhawks prospect Mathias From and with speed he was gliding in to the slot and released a wrist shot. He has very good vision for the team mates, opponent and change directions quick at the board. He helped his team mates and was visualized for passes. He turns his head excellent. In second period he had some miscommunication or lack of communication with the goalie behind the net. I saw again what I have seen in previous games; after a mistake Broberg seems to place himself alone with head down a bit too long time, I would like to see that he shakes it off quicker and prepare for next shift. I assume this is a balance with his competitiveness that will develop further. Being 6'3" & 198 lbs I still find him a bit easy to move and falls a bit too much considering his size. Broberg released 3 SOG, all of them was saved by the goalie and would have required more traffic to be dangerous. He had TOI 12,58. Broberg once again proved that he is a very skilled offensive Defense-man.

WJAC, USA vs Canada West, December 9, 2018

USA

Brink, Bobby (2019) - Fairly quite game as Brink is not the most dynamic puck carrier. Brink does however have a very good sense of postioning and was excellent at receiving passes. This allows him to be a dangerous player offensively without dominating the puck. On the powerplay with more time and space he got to show off his vision and shot with some dangerous plays.

Mastrosimone, Robert (2019) - Showed good speed and a lot of creativity with a couple full flight dekes. Did a very good job defensively retrieving pucks as well and really drove his line. Had a couple passes that really highlighted his vision.

Jones, Zachary (2019) - Probably the most impactful player on the ice this game. His skill level is excellent with the hands and IQ to pull off a move almost anywhere on the ice, was very hard for fore checkers to contain. Was very efficient on the breakout both making excellent passes and using his skating as a one man breakout a couple times. Despite being a smaller defenseman he played a strong game defensively as he did a good job recognizing when his opponent was in a vulnerable position(puck rolling, on backhand, etc.) and attacking. Broke up two 2 on 1s in the third with this aggressive, decisive style. Top end speed is just okay but Jones is very agile and slippery.

Johnson, Ryan- His skating is on an elite level, as he has high end speed as well as the ability to stop and turn on a dime. Johnson can get himself out of almost any situation with his wheels. In the offensive zone had great instincts for getting himself in to the play as he had a couple dangerous chances in the high slot. Defensively had a great stick, which combined with the excellent gap his skating allows him to play with lead to a couple forced turnovers in the neutral zone.

Canada West

Blaisdell, Harrison (2019) - Speed and skill are just average but has a very good mind for the game. Was consistently putting himself in good spots to receive passes and did a good job of getting to spots where he could be a threat. Didn't have many standout plays either good or bad but was consistently making smart decisions.

Holloway, Dylan (2020) - The most consistently impactful forward for Canada West. Does all the little things and clearly pays attention to the details with excellent positioning. Was excellent at winning back pucks in battles. Skill level is very good and he stands out when he's carrying the puck as he skates well and can make plays at a high pace. Created a couple great chances for his teammates with his vision.

Newhook, Alex (2019) - Disappeared into the background for too many stretches this game. When he was on he had the vision and skill to make high end plays at this level. Wasn't carrying the puck through the neutral zone often but when he did he looked excellent. Would like to see more assertiveness from him.

Rizzo, Massimo (2019) - Hands are awesome but decision making was lacking. Often would seem like all he wanted to do was dangle guys and he would hold on to pucks too long, or force a very difficult play. Speed was also just average as he wasn't blowing by anyone. Could do a much better job balancing risk/reward.

Ahac, Layton (2019) - Very strong showing playing a smooth, confident game. Did a good job of putting himself in positions with the puck where he had a lot of options, never skated himself out of plays. Defensively had a great stick and was dispossessing players often.

Snell, Mason (2019) - Solid outing making very good decisions when he had the puck. Snell has very good feet that allow him to play with a tight gap through the neutral zone and contain quicker forwards in his zone.

Canada West vs Russia, World Junior A Challenge, Dec 12 2018

West -

Campbell, Alexander (2019) – Campbell was featured on a line with Newhook yet was the primary driver for his line throughout the game. He wasn't always able to penetrate through traffic but his pace and effort stood out despite being a smaller framed kid. He had a couple of quality scoring chances in the slot area and was able to set-up his teammates for quality scoring chances as well. His best sequence came early, where he generated a high-end scoring chance before making an aggressive stick-lift that caused a turnover and extended zone time for his team.

Holloway, Dylan (2020) – Holloway attempted to generate pressure away from the puck but was largely unsuccessful against a Russian defense that did a good job of moving the puck up quickly. He's a quick player and was tenacious in puck pursuit situations but had a lot of difficulty generating off the forecheck as well as making clean transitional zone entries. It wasn't one of Dylan's better performances, where he was ineffective.

Blaisdell, Harrison (2019) – Like most of Canada West, Blaisdell had difficulty generating offense due to Russia's impressive defensive game, but he did manage to generate a couple of quality scoring chances near the net area. He was more effective on the powerplay, where he was given additional time and space to try and set up his shot. Harrison didn't get too many opportunities into today's game at even strength and was largely ineffective overall.

Rizzo, Massimo (2019) – Rizzo was inconsistent in today's game but did show a decent amount of vision which featured quick one touch passes and the ability to find his teammates through tight-seems. He was also one of the only Canadian players who managed to make a clean zone entry, where he showed poise while carrying the puck. That being said, he had difficulty generating any sort of sustained offense.

Newhook, Alex (2019) – Newhook was featured on the top-line and the powerplay but was unable to take advantage of the minutes given to him. He did flash his offensive-skill by driving hard down the left-wing on one play, where he dashed past a Russian defender which re-opened a lane before threading a crisp pass to his teammate, but with that exception and one wrist-shot that missed short-side on the powerplay, Newhook failed to generate much in the way of offense. He was momentarily injured midway through the contest, so that might have had an effect on today's performance but he did stay in the game, but was kept to the outside and didn't show off any dynamic qualities.

Russia –

Bychkov, Roman (2019) – Bychkov had a solid two-way performance for Russia, showing good anticipation on dump and chase sequences at his own blueline, while quickly getting the puck moved towards the net area in the offensive-end. Under pressure on the forecheck, he was quick to assess his options and showed some tenacity by using his body along the boards when needed on some plays. He didn't flash a lot of skill at the line today, but he was effective at moving the puck out of his own-end and skated hard.

Nikolaev, Ilya (2019) – Nikolaev centered the top line for Russia and showed a tenacious two-way game. He's flashed a lot of skill in previous viewings but his most impressive attribute today was his willingness to battle hard along the boards and come away with the puck. He also had several hard backchecking sequences and although his skating is average, he was willing to empty the gas tank to compete in loose puck races and create pressure. Offensively, he wasn't the primary driver of play but he did set-up his teammates with quality passes and showed a level of deception with his movement.

Serdyuk, Egor (2019) – Serdyuk put himself in good scoring positions and was noticeable in spurts due to his aggressive attacking style of play. On one sequence which showcased this, he cut hard from the outside while driving down the wing and fired a shot that missed the net. On another sequence, he received a pass from Guskov in the slot area after finding soft-ice and fired a wrist-shot that required a difficult stop. He didn't flash any sort of high-end skill but was opportunistic in the offensive-end.

Podkolzin, Vasili (2019) – Podkolzin was the best player on the ice by a large margin, dominating both with and without the puck consistently throughout the game. He had a tremendous stick-checking sequence on the penalty-kill, an excellent backchecking effort which caused a turnover, and was playing at a pace that most of Canada West simply couldn't keep up with. One of his weaker attributes is his straight-line speed, but he managed to find open-ice regularly and use impressive edges to give himself space, which resulted in several clean offensive-zone entries. He was a threat on the powerplay from the half-wall, both by loading up on his slapshot that he timed correctly giving him a primary assist after the shot was too hard for the Canadian netminder to absorb, as well as delivering hard yet accurate passes that resulted in accurate puck distribution. Lastly, he challenged defenders one-on-one and was successful at using body fakes and patience to create openings to get his release off. It was another stand-out international performance from Vasili who at one point was triple teamed along the boards, which gives you an idea of the game he had.

Guskov, Matvei (2019) – Guskov had a decent two-way performance for Russia today. He had an excellent shift where he battled hard along the boards for a puck and then managed to find Serdyuk for one of the better scoring chances of the game. Away from the play, he had a good defensive effort where he kept his opponent to the outside before generating a turnover. One area to note with Guskov today was that he was primarily looking to set-up his teammates and was a little too unselfish at times.

Gutik, Daniil (2019) – Gutik didn't get too many opportunities in the offensive-end to showcase his very high-talent level, but he did compete better away from the puck then in some previous viewings. On one sequence in the offensive-end, he did flash his very impressive hands, using his reach and anticipation of active sticks which resulted in extended zone-time without a turnover, but for the most part it was his effort-level during forechecking sequences that looked improved from previous viewings. He still had some trouble using his frame effectively to generate leverage given his height and length, but he did compete better and looked involved away from the play which again, hasn't happened in some previous viewings.

Askarov, Yaroslav (2020) – Every international event we see, this kid has impressed and today he generated another quality shutout while showing a very-high skill level. He didn't have to make too many high-end saves, but he showcased a tremendous tool-set. A lot of the pucks around him were getting blocked due to quality defensive work in-front of him, but it also helped emphasize his ability to make rapid adjustments when needing to change his angle on the shots that were deflected to an additional opposing player resulting in secondary saves. His crease containment was impressive considering that he has explosive lateral movement yet stops very quickly and rarely over-played his positioning, he also was fluid with his post integration, and made a couple of impressive reactionary saves where he squared up in advance, cut down the angle, and anticipated the shots coming in on him. He has yet to show an attribute that wouldn't be considered above-average to excellent.

Windsor Spitfires vs Saginaw Spirit, Dec 16 2018

Spitfires –

Piiroinen, Kari (2019) – Pirroinen had a decent performance for the Spitfires by making some timely and difficult stops. He's not very big, but he's tall when in his butterfly, which allows him to take up more of the net against high-shot types than you would expect. His stance is semi-narrow at times allowing him to readjust using his edges effectively after misinterpreting the initial play. His edges allowed him to push-off laterally quickly, which gave him his most impressive save of the game, where he read a cross- crease pass before extending his pad to rob Prueter for a point blank save. He allowed 3 goals, one was through a screen after Wilde took a seeing eye shot from the point but the other two were similar in the sense that Kari was unable to determine the angle necessary on the far-side of the net to come away with the save. Furthermore, for an average-sized goalie, he displayed average reflexes and overplayed his position at times, but did show good edges and a solid butterfly technique as well.

Prueter, Aidan (2020) – Prueter wasn't consistent but did make some positive plays, while also staying in the game after taking a large hit when he was caught with his head-down during an attempted zone-exit. It was good to see him bounce back and compete despite appearing injured to some extent on the sequence. He had a point-blank scoring chance where he put himself in good position which was mentioned above, and had a solid forechecking sequence, showing he's not afraid to physically engage against larger opponents. Below the goal-line, he also moved the puck quickly on one play while under pressure.

Angle, Tyler (2019) – Angle had a solid two-way performance for the Spirit and became more dangerous in the offensive-zone as the game progressed. He was excellent on the penalty-kill, generating scoring chances by pressuring on the forecheck. This gave him a breakaway scoring chance where he bobbled the puck but still managed to get a backhand off. On another penalty-kill, he positioned himself well in the high-slot and delivered a low wrist-shot, though he failed to change the angle or threaten with any sort of power on the attempt. He also showed the willingness to engage in heavy traffic, cutting to the net aggressively on one sequence. Tyler scored the game tying goal after positioning himself near the goal-line and anticipating a pass that allowed him to jam in the puck on the short-side. In overtime, he broke out on a 2-on-1 where he slowed the play down enough to allow D'Amico to get into position which gave him a primary assist on a nice pass that landed on the tape of his teammate. In the defensive-end, he supported his defense and was willing to play the body along the boards, showing a plus compete level as well. He was arguably the best forward on the ice for either team.

Cuylle, Will (2020) – Cuylle made the fans happy by scoring the opening Windsor goal on teddy bear toss night, while consistently threatening with his impressive release for most of the game. He was one dimensional in today's game, but that dimension was him finding soft-ice and then releasing his wrist-shot that created several high-end scoring chances and a goal. His goal was the result of finding soft-ice in the left-circle, needing little time or space to generate a lot of velocity. His shot is unique in the sense that he can release it very quickly, he can change angles on his release from a stand-still position rapidly, yet the accuracy of his shot rarely decreases given how much power he can generate. Despite getting consistent scoring chances and being a threat, Will didn't drive play for his line or show much in the way of pace.

D'Amico, Daniel (2019) – D'Amico was one of the most consistent forwards for the Spitfire who came out flat, which required Daniel to drive play for his line at times, which he was successful at doing. He displayed a short and choppy stride but was effective around the goal-line due to his pivoting and edges which allowed him to remain elusive while assessing his options. He displayed good vision, making several impressive backhand passes that generated scoring chances as well. In his own-end, he was effective along the boards at times and competed. He scored the overtime game-winning-goal after adjusting his hips and opening them up for one-timer from the slot which elevated in a hurry over the sprawled-out Spirit netminder. He was one of the better forwards out there today.

Foudy, Jean-Luc (2020) – Foudy had an effective two-way performance for Windsor by using his impressive skating ability to cut aggressively towards the net area, which resulted in high-end scoring chances throughout the game. One of the first things that stands-out about Foudy is his willingness to challenge defenders one-on-one and use his explosive skating to drive into heavy traffic, this resulted in several plays in-tight to the net, as well as collecting an assist for his efforts. His shot never threatened, but he's shown in this game and others that he's a primary playmaker whose instincts are to look for the open-man, this allowed him to thread several nice-passes in traffic. In his own-end, he was responsible and showed good anticipation and awareness away from the play.

Spirit –

Perfetti, Cole (2020) – Perfetti had a solid two-way performance for Saginaw, showing a combination of anticipation, poise, and awareness out on the ice. The kid doesn't generate a lot of power in his first few steps or have much in the way of straight-line speed, yet he was consistent at managing the puck when he had it on his stick by showing advanced puck-protection skills and a calmness under-pressure that's rare for his age. He showed today, that he's the type of thinker that forces reactions to his play, and this freezes his opponents, so regardless if they can out skate him or physically over-power him, he still found a way to make plays before turning the puck over most of the time. His best scoring chance came after a give-and-go sequence where he attempted to fire the puck upstairs in-tight to the net, but his best play came away from the puck where he showed a willingness to expend his tank in order to take away a prime scoring opportunity after he caught up to his opponent and used a well-timed stick check. Perfetti is intelligent but at times looks like he lacks pace out there, so it was good to see that he was looking to be efficient as opposed to just not competing at the level necessary away from the play. On the forecheck, he couldn't impose himself physically, but did use his anticipation and a good stick to generate a takeaway at the goal-line on one sequence as well.

Porco, Nicholas (2019) – Porco had an above-average two-way performance for Saginaw by using a combination of skating and compete to generate opportunities. He continues to show an up-right awkward looking stride, yet he gets around the ice-well since he generates a lot of power in his lower-half. He used his powerful-stride to cut aggressively around an opponent early before firing a wrist-shot that required a glove-save by Kari. On a forechecking play, he used his frame effectively to overpower his opponent before finding his teammate with a sharp pass that landed on the tape for one of the better scoring chances of the game. On the powerplay, he showed a good compete level after falling to the ice but extending himself to maintain puck possession. Away from the puck, he had a solid backchecking sequence along the half-wall. Although he wasn't always consistent offensively, he played aggressively in spurts and used his skating to backup the Spitfires defense.

Millman, Mason (2019) – Millman had a solid two-way performance for Saginaw, using his frame and physical attributes to keep his opponents wide around his net area. He's an average-sized defenseman, but what he lacks in weight and height, he makes up for in compete. He's a battler who's willing to get physically engaged at anytime necessary, though, in today's game that was a double-edges sword for the kid. On one play, he was too aggressive and played too-high which through himself out of position. On another sequence, he over-extended his tank and then when it came time to take away a shooting-lane, he was too slow to get into position which allowed the opening Spitfire goal that Cuylle scored. However, he did make up for a few of his mistakes with solid play in the offensive-end by getting low shots through traffic and displayed decent playmaking skills by passing the puck into the slot area after activating which gave him a primary assist. He's not the most talented player on the ice but he competes, plays at a good pace, and shows that he cares with his style of play.

Sioux Falls Stampede at Des Moines Buccaneers, December 18, 2018

Sioux Falls Stampede -

Johnson, Ryan - 2019 The improvement of Johnson's puck rushing game is impressive and important, he's working himself into the middle of the rink more and showing the ability to more reliably beat forecheckers. Once again against Des Moines he showed great skating ability in all facets. He is a prototypical modern defenseman, in that he skates very well, he's not overly big, but he's very smart and he plays aggressively with his stick to disrupt plays at lines so that he doesn't have to defend so much. He did get out-muscled in a foot race situation in the later stages of the game…his pace wasn't the issue, but at the top of the route, so to speak, while Johnson was stopping, the attacker was able to get leverage on him and still keep the puck. Other than that, it was a strong game and it felt like he played over 23 minutes. The question is the finishing skills still. The ability to finish off plays whether it be shooting it or the setup pass deep in the attack zone…how much of that does he bring to the table right now? Maybe not quite enough.

Phillips, Ethan - 2019 Phillips was the most skilled player on the ice for the duration of the game. He made a number of strong rushes and skill plays for Sioux Falls. He skates extremely well with the puck on his stick and he plays with a ton of energy…he's practically gliding above the ice out there at times. Not only is he skilled, but he's also very smart. He makes good decisions all over the ice. Most notably, he made a perfect body play on a shorthanded rush going against him (he plays left point of PP1) by anticipating exactly what the attacker was going to do in the NZ and just through his rather small frame into the attacker's chest to disrupt the play. If there's one drawback, it's definitely size – he's listed at 5'9", 146 lbs. that may be underselling his weight, but he's certainly not even an average-sized player. He has a terrific skill foundation. There's a couple of times he bites off a little more than he can chew, but he pull off what he's trying to accomplish 4 out of 5 times and because he can make moves at full speed, he's a threat to beat many players in this league. Very fast player, can make himself even smaller to squeeze through attempts to pin him to the wall, hard worker, quick shot release. This is a player that could be a late riser depending on concerns about his frame.

Tabakin, Brandon - 2019 Wasn't on my watchlist coming into the game, but caught my eye with some very strong skating ability and some heady plays on both sides of the puck. Offers more puck skills, better passing, and at least one-line puck carrying than his stats would suggest he's capable of. Smaller player, but plays that modern, active-stick defense, and he has good hockey sense to boot. Has great awareness of his partner and how to switch off of players and when to take calculated risks. He's a 2000 birthday, so he was passed over in 2018, but is still worth keeping an eye on his progression.

Swankler, Austen - 2019 Plucky game for Swankler, but overall quiet. He seems more determined when there's a chance to start a riot than when the game is going on…which isn't to say he's a lazy player, but sometimes it seems like he leaves a lot more in the tank than other guys. Part of it too, could be the optics. He has a pretty loose and weak stride and his edge work isn't that great…as a result there's tough turns out there for him, so he doesn't commit too deep into either zone to compensate. Some shifts turn into monkey-in-the-middle for him. He played on PP2, but was asked to serve a minor penalty for a player who was given a misconduct. Showed a couple of lower-end skill plays, but nothing that jumped off the page. He did jam loose a covered puck in the 2nd which initiated a fracas…becomes the only player to eventually drop both gloves, then while tied up in the scrum, reaches over a linesman to throw a punch at a 6'3" Des Moines defenseman. He lucked out in that the officials concocted a way for everything to wash evenly.

Krannila, Jami - 2019 Industrious two-way forward. Really works from end line to end line on any shift that calls for it and he does so without hesitation. Plus-plus mobility and his top speed is very high-end. Plays the game very intelligently, with a high attention to detail for not only his age but also for it being his first year of hockey outside of Finland. He is a low setup player and looks almost as big as his very slight vitals, which may scare some clubs off at the end of the day. Worked on the power play. Showed good playmaking skills throughout. Stickhandling is a plus, but he probably can't reliably beat players one on one with hands alone yet. He needles into the little areas necessary to keep plays alive and he beats players to the spot on smarts and speed. Don't recall anyone able to get a lick on him during the game despite his size. Very noticeable in a positive way throughout, has an offensive skill set that's worth a look when combined with penchant for defensive play. Just missed the cut-off for 2018 as an October '00 birthday.

Muskegon Lumberjacks at USNTDP U18, December 19, 2018

USNTDP U18 -

Caulfield, Judd - 2019 Big, heavy player that works in down low without hesitation. Got underneath a defender and used his leverage to pry him away from the puck and keep a dying play alive. Had a few hits that were useful to the game. Played on the PK, but also made a bad PK change in the 2nd. Just an average skater but with above average strength and balance. His lackluster small-area footwork prevents him from being a better net-front presence. Along the same lines, I wasn't wowed by his offensive instincts either…even from a line of clearly manufacturer types, as opposed to organic creation types (John Beecher and Michael Gildon).

Helleson, Drew - 2019 Terrific game from Helleson. Flashed some nice hands over the course of the game and did challenge some Lumberjacks in the process. Led a strong rush down the middle and then widened out the attack and added depth…and was well-timed in doing so. Probably more of a good rush support d-man down the line than a rush leader, but good on him to have the confidence to go for it. Made a very good elusive play from a near stationary spot that shed the forechecker with ease. Still seems like a more defensive player at heart…frequented the PK. Had a shift with one good hit and then one so-so hit in back to back sequences. Looked considerably stronger from the last time I saw him and put his strength on display in no uncertain terms today…a stark contrast from earlier viewings. This was most complete and sterling effort from him in every way for my money.

Lindmark, Owen - 2019 Played in all situations and had a really strong game overall – scoring twice, getting five shots down on paper. Competed at both ends for most of the night. Played PK and was a net-front man on PP2…that's where he found his deflection goal. His game was good wall-to-wall, but there was a point where I wished he could get more engaged…not because he was lazy, but because he seemed to lack confidence. Immediately thereafter he exploded to take a shorthanded foray, then proceeded to undress the d-man and waste the goalie with a nice forehand-backhand finish. That seemed to put the necessary wind his sails for the rest of the day. Heady player with what looks like some untapped potential even just at the level he currently resides at. I'd be interested to see him in a larger role…played with the only 2020 eligible players on the club today (Sean Farrell and Ryder Rolston).

Warren, Marshall - 2019 Blended in for much of the game, even with various partners. Made one strong rush to create a chance late. Looked a little heavy handed at times. Likes to launch them, with intent to score, from the backline. Has a little bit of an elongated stride, and with more strength, he should be able to generate some good power out of it, but he's not all the way there yet.

Zegras, Trevor - 2019 Zegras is the forward who stepped up the most in the absence of Jack Hughes and he did a phenomenal job carrying the mail for the US. Displayed some superb hands and wonderful playmaking and vision. Big plus in the skating department too. He took on some of the PP QB duties as well. While he was maybe a little too fanciful at times with some adventurous passing, that also might be a product of him feeling the spotlight was on him with the team's best player out of the lineup. He showed all the potential tools of a very high end draft pick in his class.

Vlasic, Alex - 2019 Quiet game from Vlasic, as they tend to be. Features prominently on the PK. But he needs to be more imposing in front of his net and protect it with more urgency. Early in the game, he let a PP man slip underneath him and beat him back to his goalie and it ended up needing partner support to extinguish it. Beyond that situation, he doesn't use leverage very well to his favor, nor is he particularly hockey strong yet compared to his vitals. He supports the rush just fine from a tactical perspective, but doesn't have the technical skills to execute on it beyond that. Looks like he might offer a plus shot, but the passing and stickhandling are not interesting from a top prospect. Capable skater for his size and it should improve with leg strength. Took a blatant penalty by getting his hands into the head of an oncoming attacker…easily avoidable.

Fensore, Domenick - 2019 Super high-end mobility. Great edges, great starts and stops. His four-way mobility is outstanding. Made a change of direction play at the attack line that rattled the man marking him – very Gostisbehere like in that particular move. Made two long stretch passes, one in a compromised, pressure spot and they were both right on the money. Carries the puck well across multiple lines, even made a strong hands to beat a defender 1 on 1 in the NZ. Obviously the smallest player on the ice for most shifts, but he had one shift where he withstood a strong hit attempt that – while it knocked him off his feet technically – he landed on his feet and remained in the play, it merely lifted him off the ice for a second. Then made a good physical play in a 1 on 1 rush against him where he put both his hands right in the chest of the attacker trying to dangle him. Extremely intelligent in all three zones. Has a skill package that ought not to be passed up.

Turcotte, Alex - 2019 This was Turcotte's first USHL game since late October and it showed. He had a rough game all told. Fell twice in open ice, took a big hit in the NZ, couldn't connect on many of his passes because of poor timing or geometry. He seemed mentally fatigued by the end of the game more so than even physically. He is a plus skater. He made a strong NZ backcheck after a play was botched high in the offensive zone. The puck jumps off his blade. But as expected in a player's first game in a while, he just didn't have his game together. The talent base is evident and hopefully he'll return to form in short order.

Caufield, Cole - 2019 Very quick mitts and very mobile. Put out the first chance they could in a 4v4 situation where his strengths are more at a premium. Clearly has an offensive tool set and a skating base to work with, but he needs to make more of a push towards the net with proper arcs. Too often he was working in straight lines and not arcs, so he gained no leverage on defensemen…leverage he can't afford to lose at his size. He needed more open space to work with than a player of his skill level ought to it feels like. There were more than a few shifts where he was tough to notice today. Skill is one thing, deception and creation of space are another…needs to do a better job manipulating defenders with a skating and skill combination, instead of just one or the other.

Beecher, John - 2019 Big and very mobile to go along with smart and tenacious. Beecher's game is in the details and work effort. Just average puck skills on display, but he knows where to be and he plays the game the right way in all facets. Not overly hip to the organic rush offense, if he gets mixed up in that, he's better off being the guy that drives the net and makes a mess. He's better suited to create "manufactured" offense. Works on the PK. Strong in the dot.

York, Cam - 2019 Top-notch game from Cam York. Made so many good reads early on to disrupt plays in the NZ and he kept a good stick at the attack line to revive dying US chances. Plays the modern, mobile, aggressive (stick) style of defending but does it smartly and without a lot of risk.

Took on more PP quarterbacking duties with Hughes away…put out a very deflectable point shot that resulted in an early goal. Makes the game look very simple because his anticipation level is so high and his skating base is great. His technical skills are not elite, but if they come around, he could be a real gem.

Boldy, Matthew - 2019 Without Jack Hughes, Boldy seemed a little less engaged offensively with Alex Turcotte as his center…later got to play with Trevor Zegras. He was the triggerman on his line. Has some nice hands plays in controlled, slower situations. Nothing very noteworthy about his skating. In fact, he didn't offer a lot of pop in any regard for most of the game. Did make some nice cross seam passes that he has a knack for looking off. Not sure if this going to truly be an impact player/gamebreaker type player, but certainly has the tools to be a very strong complementary piece on a good line.

Thrun, Henry - 2019 Was really fighting it on RD with Cam York today. Made a few plays where he swapped to the other side when his partner was already engaged on the left that were not smart and it left the front of the net wide open. Made a graphic NZ turnover on a diagonal, telegraphed pass that led to a rush chance against. Then whiffed on an uncontested one-timer late in the game. He is a plus skater and he generates a good amount of power despite not having a very deep knee bend. Did make a strong catch and release play on his wrong side. Didn't show off a lot of other positives and unearthed a lot of questions about his decision making in the process.

Finland vs Sweden, U20 World Junior Championships, Dec 26 2018

Swe –

Fagemo, Samuel (2019) – Fagemo had a decent scoring opportunity midway through the first where he caught Luukonen flat-footed with a quick wrist-shot but it missed the net, later in the frame he drew a penalty by skating hard along the boards before getting tripped. Fagemo was relatively quiet in the second frame with the exception of one odd-man rush where he fired a spinning shot that missed the net at the bottom of the left circle. In the third period on the powerplay, Fagemo found soft-ice in the high-slot before receiving a pass which he rung the puck off the cross-bar, the release was quick. Overall, he was noticeable in spurts and was capable of generating both off the rush and from a stationary position on the powerplay where he displayed a shoot-first mentality.

Broberg, Philip (2019) – Broberg played limited minutes and wasn't much of a factor when he was on the ice. He had one shot in the first opening frame that wasn't overly threatening and never established his offensive-game at the line. In his own-end, he played the body effectively at times but also was caught under pressure, failing to assess his options at the rate he needed to. Overall, he had difficulty adjusting to the pacing of the game in all three zones.

Fin –

Kakko, Kaapo (2019) – Kakko had a relatively quiet opening frame but did manage one impressive shift where he showed poise while controlling the puck under pressure below the goal-line, at one point he lost the puck but used his reach to regain control before feeding his linemate for one of Finland's better scoring chances. Kakko was dominant on the powerplay in the 2nd frame, using his strength, puck protection and vision to control the play while setting up his teammates consistently from the half-wall. He had a dangerous forechecking sequence late where he stripped the puck off a Swedish defender below the net, then attempted a tuck-in around the goal-line before finding Heinola pinching from the point resulting in a great scoring chance. Despite being relatively quiet for the majority of the third, he came alive within the last couple of minutes, showing impressive vision while processing the play quickly which led to a great primary assist and also gave Nyman a prime scoring chance. Overall, Kakko showed excellent puck protection skills and used his frame to play a heavy puck possession game in the offensive-end.

Heinola, Ville (2019) – Heinola played a hard-two-way game and was one of the better Finnish defenders on the ice despite being the youngest on the backend. On one sequence he played his man one-on-one well, showing good balance while playing the body and taking the Swedish forward down to the ice. At the end of the first he made an accurate pass that was threaded through multiple sticks across the slot area in the offensive-end. Ville was tenacious away from the puck, showing a fearless brand of hockey and played at a high-pace, this resulted in an important recovery sequence as well, where he skated aggressively to catch up to Fagemo which reduced the forwards scoring chance. Most of his passes were accurate and sharp, needing little time to measure his options before distributing the puck both in the offensive zone and defensive zone under pressure. He was paired with Jokiharju and complimented his defensive partner while standing out on his own as well.

Lundell, Anton (2020) – Lundell had a good two-way performance for Finland, showing his intelligence both with and without the puck. Lundell had a good sequence in the opening period where he displayed plus playmakjng ability while transitioning through the neutral zone and in the second frame he was quick to support his defense when needed and was aware in his own-end, consistently assessing when Sweden was trying to penetrate the slot area and positioning himself accordingly. He consistently found a way to be involved in the play in the offensive-end and displayed the ability to gauge when he should shoot or pass the puck at a consistent rate. Despite his young age, he played a mature and poised game while also standing out.

Latvala, Otto (2019) - Latvala has been tasked with a shut-down role at this event and was consistent at doing so in the opening frame by using his impressive length to disrupt Elvenes after he attempted to transition over the offensive blueline. He supporting his defensive partner well on one sequence where his partner was beaten wide and he cut across to take away a skating lane resulting in a decreased scoring chance. On one sequence under pressure in his own-end, he peeled off pressure before finding his man, the play showed poise. Overall, his passes were consistently accurate, though at times they were too sharp making them more difficult to handle. Overall, he displayed average skill and was never threatening offensively but had a couple of decent defensive reads and used his tools effectively on some shifts.

Russian vs Denmark, U20 World Junior Championships, Dec 27 2018

Den –

Brinkman, Jonathan (2019) – Brinkman started slow and left the game for a period of time, but after returning, he stood out and was one of the more effective Danish forwards despite being the youngest. He was efficient on the powerplay the previous day and here again he showed plus vision with the man-advantage and was decisive. He was confident holding the puck and drew a penalty late against a larger Russian defender. His best scoring opportunity was the result of keeping the puck in at the blueline before driving down the left wing and shooting a short-side shot that he attempted to tuck under the bar. Brinkman played with some bravado and flashed some skill.

Grundtvig, Andreas (2019) – Grundtvig was noticeable for Denmark, demonstrating a good motor by playing at a high-pace when carrying the puck. He had above-average mobility and used his quickness to drive wide and try and overwhelm the Russian defense. Although he wasn't successful at scoring, he wasn't afraid of attempting to drive through high-traffic areas and was one of the few Danish forwards who generated scoring chances for himself off the rush.

Schultz, Phillip (2019) – Schultz was arguably the most effective Danish player on the ice today and showed leadership qualities by trying to help carry Denmark after they lost Rondbjerg due to injury. He started off strong by having a point-blank scoring chance in the opening minute by cutting through the Russian defense after surprising them. He was used on the penalty-kill and had a well-timed shot block as well as using his aggressiveness at the line which resulted in a couple of turnovers. His motor and tenacity compensated for his average skill-level and he generated offense consistently by driving play for his line.

Rus –

Podkolzin, Vasili (2019) – Unlike Svechnikov last year who wasn't given much of an opportunity out of the gate, Podkolzin was featured on the 2nd line with Morozov and Marchenko, while also getting quality minutes on the penalty-kill. He made the most of his opportunity, playing a tenacious two-way game that resulted in an impressive forecheck while also making life difficult in his own-end for Denmark. His playmaking was impressive and he had several solid sequences in the offensive-end which generated heavy minutes for the opposing defense. Although he wasn't able to flash much of his skill, he did show it in spurts, specifically on one play in the neutral zone where he used his soft-hands to guard the puck. It was a good start to the tournament for Vasili.

Morozov, Ilya (2019) – Morozov had a decent offensive performance for Russia by generating several powerful slapshots from the point. He's not the most mobile kid but didn't need to be out there today since the majority of play was controlled within the Danish zone, and this allowed him to get set and fire several powerful shots on net. Ilya also displayed some creativity at the line by faking several shots before passing it off to his teammates, while also making a clean no-look spinning pass to his teammate that landed on the tape. In some previous viewings he was relying too heavily on his slapshot, so it was good to see him mixing up his options out there.

Benilde St. Margaret's vs Holy Family Catholic, December 27th 2018

Holy Family Catholic

Pinoniemi, Garrett – 2019 Despite registering two goals in this game, Garrett was in large a perimeter player, struggling to get himself and the puck into high scoring areas and played too much of an individual game in this one, not utilizing his line mates as well as he could have. Pinoniemi showed flashes of compete for pucks along the walls but was not consistent in this regard. Garrett displayed good skill on the perimeter and was able to find guys when given the time and space but didn't do a lot to create space for himself or others in this game.

Fechko, Trey – 2022 Fechko is just a freshman and late 03' DOB but you couldn't tell that by his play in this one. Trey showed a tireless work ethic. Playing with Pinoniemi, Fechko was often the first one in on the fore check, where he competed hard for pucks and was physical on defenseman. Fechko showed willingness to pay the price in front and was rewarded on his goal in the 2nd period. Trey was a 9th Round Draft pick of Moose Jaw (WHL) last year and looks to be a very high pick in this year's USHL Phase 1 Draft.

Benilde St. Margarets

Mesenberg, Blake – 2020 Mesenberg displayed excellent offensive skill in this game. His quick hands allowed him to cut through the Holy Family defenders, defeating multiple players for a backhanded scoring chance. Mesenberg scored 2 goals in this game, one with a great release from the faceoff circle, beating the goalie over the glove on the short side, the other when he did a good job cutting to the slot with the puck off the faceoff and firing a quick shot that he followed up on and put in the rebound. Mesenberg had an excellent opportunity on a 2 on 1 where he got the puck in the slot but was too slow to get his shot off and was caught from behind by the Holy Family player.

Ferris State University at University of Minnesota, December 28th 2018

University of Minnesota

Brinkman, Ben – 2019 Brinkman got off to a difficult start in this game, giving up a goal when his gap on his opponent was too big and the Ferris State player was able to use Brinkman as screen and fire a shot that beat the Minnesota goaltender short side. Brinkman got lost in some defensive zone coverage's early in this game as well and lost his one on one positioning in a couple of instances. There certainly were some "freshman" moments for Brinkman in this game and seemed to really battle the puck in his own end; however Ben had some good plays at the offensive blue line that nearly resulted in goals for the Gophers. Would have liked to see Brinkman take off with the puck coming out of his own end more in this game, he had the space on a few outlets to skate the puck up ice and elected for the simple play. Brinkman lost his confidence early in this game and it just seemed to snowball for him from there.

Ottawa 67's vs Niagara Ice Dogs, Dec 28th 2018

67's –

Clarke, Graeme (2019) – Clarke had a decent first half but trailed off considerably in the second half of the game, rarely generating offense or standing out. He did show a couple of plays that flashed plus anticipation as he quickly distributed the puck both on the powerplay along the half-wall and at even-strength in the neutral zone without a lot of time or space. He found a couple of opportunities to get off his threatening shot that featured the ability to drag the puck in-tight to his body, which changed the angle. He also recognized when to use a screen to his advantage and attempted to mask his shot placement as well. Overall however, except for a few notable plays, he was inconsistent and showed a lack of acceleration and top-end speed needed to carry the puck for extended periods of time. As a result, he was unable to drive play.

Quinn, Jack (2020) – Quinn had a solid game for the 67's, consistently generating offense by playing at a high-pace while playing a fearless brand of hockey. He's not the biggest kid but was willing to enter heavy-traffic areas and take direct routes to the net area. This resulted in his best scoring chance of the game where he quickly pulled the puck to his backhand while cutting from the bottom of the right-circle before firing a quick backhander that fooled Dillon but hit the crossbar. There was an element of creativity to his passing, showing a combination of spinning and deceptive passes as well. The compete was there but his skill-set doesn't always match his energy, his passes were sometimes too sharp, and he sometimes overstepped his skill-set, making him less effective than if he was to play a more controlled game at times.

Okhotyuk, Nikita (2019) – Okhotyuk had a solid two-way performance for the 67's, showing a plus motor in his own-end while playing an imposing brand of hockey. He's a smart player but had a couple of turnovers in his own-end, ranging from falling to the ice while attempting to peel around the net, so simply passing the puck up to an opponent, but on each play, he displayed an impressive drive to recover. The best sequence that demonstrated this was after he passed the puck up carelessly along the half-wall while he was under-pressure, he was the first to skate aggressively back into position and block a shot. In the offensive-zone, he was threatening with both his wrist-shot and slapshot. With his wrist-shot, he showed the ability to quickly drag the puck to change the angle and his shot has velocity on it, but the accuracy wasn't there. Same for his slapshot, he can really hammer the puck, but his shot attempts all went over the net today. That said, his puck management at the offensive line was a plus and he distributed the puck fine, though his passes were too hard to handle at times as well.

Ice Dogs –

Tomasino, Philip (2019) – Tomasino had an above-average offensive performance for Niagara and was the only player to score for his team. He was impressive on the forecheck at times, being the first to race in after the puck and won a couple of board battles despite going up against larger opponents. He never consistently drove play or was involved in heavy cycling, but he did show flashes of high-end talent. On one play he made a quick slapshot from his knee that fooled the Ottawa netminder and rung off the post, and after cutting through the slot and receiving a well-timed pass he showed good patience and poise before making pulling the back to his backhand for his goal. He has a soft-touch and was willing to drive towards the net area despite his slimmer frame and was involved in the forecheck but didn't drive play or was overly consistent either.

Nichols/Belmont-Hill School Tourney December 28, 2018

Nichols School vs Rivers School –

NIC #7 LD Suda, Michael (2020) – The junior Dman was good for the most parts of the game as he will rush the puck to generate offense, run the power play, and distribute puck. He made nice stretch pass in the first period on Nichols first goal as recognized the line change and quickly transitioned puck to #12 Ricotta at the far blue line. There were a couple of defensive lapses whereby entire team got puck watching and gap control was not great that lead to Nichols falling behind. On the 5th goal against in played back and allowed the forechecker #7 Tresca to retrieve puck and set-up goal. He likes to usually play aggressively in defensive zone using his stick and body to separate opponent from puck. His strong skating ability allows him to cover ice. He showed his shot from the point a couple of times as well as good strength and accuracy. He will be one to monitor over next 18 months for 2020 NHL Draft.

RIV #7 RW Tresca, Philip (2020) – He is a bit undersized although plays with good pace and shows good offensive instructs around the net and in the offensive zone. He reads plays well and showed it on the first goal for Rivers as got into position to grab #6 Cormier point shot and fire the rebound home quickly 5-hole in the 1st period. He is good at finding the soft softs around the ice to get the puck and has good speed and offensive abilities off the rush. He made the play of the eventual GWG in the 3rd period as he quickly beat the defenseman to the puck below the goal line and fed #5 McEachern going to the net. The Yale commit probably isn't on draft radar much for next season yet based on size.

RIV #8 LD Webber, Cade (2019) – Webber has been talked about on the draft scene for a few seasons although he is always quite average in every viewing for this scout. Sure, he has good size and mobility is decent for his stature although he does not play an offensive defenseman, nor does he play the aggressive, intimidating Dman. There are times where you see a glimpse yet not enough consistency in game for a high round pick. Yet there are also times whereby he throws the puck away losing possession or misses teammate on the breakout. He is more of a project. In the 3rd period with his team in the lead he got caught altercation away from the puck that lead to minor and misconduct penalty taking himself out of the finish of the game. Nichols then mounted 2-goal comeback, even though Webber's opponent fell short, the discipline was a question in this game as well.

Kimbell Union Academy vs Brunswick School –

KUA #11 LC Mazura, Thomas (2019) – His was probably the best player on the ice this day during the tournament. He has good size and moves well with good puck skills and vision. He reads plays well and not only is a threat offensively but also good defensively with reloads through the neutral zone and reliable in own end. He uses his reach well to get possession of pucks. He set-up the first goal as he quickly jumped on puck below goal line on a goalie mis-play and passed to #8 Mack for the tap-in on the crease. He was then more impressive on the 2nd goal in the period as created 2v1 rush with #5 Griffin as he received pass back in slot two-feet off ice he quickly showed good hand-eye and tapped puck down. Instead of quickly shooting it he fed it back to teammate for open-net goal. He was a player on the ice that made plays each shift and made teammates around him better. Mazura is a player the will highly likely be committed soon and will be stirring draft scene as the season continues.

KUA #18 RW Carrabes, Brian (2019) – He is a smaller, crafty winger with good offensive instincts. He showed his stick skills and offensive abilities in spurts. He will probably develop into good NCAA player as committed to BU, although would need more strength and commitment to the defensive game for the pro levels. To his credit he did throw a couple of good body checks early in the game. He had a handful of good scoring chances although did not covert to get on the scoresheet.

KUA #20 LC Merritt, Arlo (2019) – Merritt is Canadian native that moved to the New England prep ranks a couple of seasons ago. He has been in draft discussion leading up to this season. He plays a solid 2-way game and has the size which draws attention to scouts and coaches although his upside for the pro game is perhaps limited. His skating is solid and showed some offense here as scored 3rd goal going to the net and re-directed #22 Bennett pass after teammate drove puck wide and threw it across crease on Merritt stick. He has improved in confidence with the puck and trying to make an impact since last viewing.

KUA #26 LW Dore, Paul (2020) – Dore was good in this game although he did not find the scoresheet. He is strong and has a real sense of how to get to the soft, scoring spots. He is a shooter that likes play below the dots and gets his position to get shots on net. He has good size and skating ability is there. He will be one to watch moving forward.

BRWK #4 LD Moore, Cooper (2019) – Moore is a very solid defender who has been getting NCAA attention for years. He has good size who shows very good mobility, puck handle, and poise with the puck. He makes very good puck decisions as he knows when to peel off pressure or move the puck quickly in transition. He shows good hockey IQ. His team was a bit outmanned and talent level not to the grade of KUA making things difficult at times for the senior defenseman. He plays both ends of the ice very well and has all the developing skills sets and mind to become even better on college and possibly reach the pro level. He could certainly be a mid-round pick in June.

New Hampton School vs St. Francis School –

NH #22 LW Dunlap, Jake (2020) – He is on the smaller as late '01 birthdate and even though he did not get on the scoresheet in 6-2 win vs St. Francis. Although he made impact with his shifty play with the puck to open up lanes and scoring opportunities for himself and teammates. He competes all over the ice and shows good offensive thoughts. Will most likely be a solid NCAA player as not dynamic, high-end with speed, quickness, and strength.

Millbrook School vs Belmont Hill –

MIL #18 RC Neudorf, Kyle (2020) – He showed some glimpses of game. He showed his good stick skills as he was able to create some scoring chances in the offensive zone by puck skills and shot release. He can fire the puck with good velocity and made goalie make some good saves. He seemed to make more of impact in the first half of the game. His skating stride is a bit labored as will need to improve speed and quickness for the next levels although his game has potential with offensive instincts and hockey IQ.

BH #8 RC McGuire, Ryan (2020) – Belmont Hill was sort of a very vanilla team. They scored one goal vs Millbrook yet forward Ryan McGuire was a bright spot. He is average size although he skates well as showed some speed and agility with the ability to create offense. He made good reads on plays, handle the puck well, plays with some pace, and saw the ice offensively to set-up opportunities.

Finland vs Slovakia, U20 World Junior Championship, Dec 29, 2018

Fin –

Kakko, Kaapo (2019) – Kakko controlled play and was the primary driver at even strength. He's adept at angling himself and using his length to guard the puck while weighing heavy on the opposition, which he did consistently out there. On the powerplay, he was used down near the net area as opposed to the half-wall today and used his size and frame to screen Hlavaj effectively. Both at even strength and on the powerplay, Kakko made smart decisions with the puck and made several impressive one-touch passes by processing the play quickly. This was one of Kakko's more dominant performances so far at this event.

Heinola, Ville (2019) – Heinola had a good offensive-performance by demonstrating the ability to activate in the offensive-end at the appropriate times based on today's viewing. He was calm and collected in his own-end and has developed a decent amount of chemistry with Jokiharju but it was his offensive performance that stood out the most today. He had a well-executed neutral zone rush where he made a clean transitional zone entry that flashed some skill. When over the blueline, he was good at assessing defensive breakdowns and taking advantage of soft-ice. This led to a goal where he received a crisp pass from Kakko who found him alone in the high-slot, the shot placement was good and he didn't rush his opportunity. Today's game was his best offensive performance of the event so far.

Honka, Anttoni (2019) – Honka didn't stand out consistently but did have a couple of impressive flashes. He had a threatening rush showing off his plus edges by weaving in and out of heavy traffic while taking a direct approach to the net. In his own-end, he used his agility to counteract the Slovakian forecheck and fired a couple of accurate and sharp passes that landed on the tape of his teammates. Despite not logging heavy minutes, he flashed his impressive tools.

Lundell, Anton (2020) – Lundell was relatively quiet compared to previous viewings but that didn't stop him from making a beautiful toe-drag move while in full motion that led to a quality scoring chance as well as scoring a goal. On his goal, he found soft-ice at the bottom of the right circle and fired home a high wrist-shot after receiving a pass from Heinola who was cutting around the goal-line, the shot was well placed. He wasn't afraid to enter heavy traffic areas around the goal line as well.

Svk –

Hlavaj, Samuel (2019) – Hlavaj didn't play as well here as he did against Sweden, but he still showcased impressive reflexes and cut off his angles aggressively. His most notable attribute this game was his reactionary kick saves, making several of them against some of the better shooters on Finland. On a couple of sequences, he showed the ability to recover quickly, which helped alleviate shot types that he couldn't absorb. He dealt with the Fins constantly pressing below his goal-line, yet he was good at integrating into his post when in a reverse V-H and took up a lot of the net when doing so. The majority of goals he allowed were high-percentage shots that he didn't have much of an opportunity to stop.

Dlugos, Marcel (2019) – Dlugos had a decent game for Slovakia while being used in all situations. He was effective for the most part on the penalty-kill, where he used his imposing frame and length to counteract opposition in-front of the net. He was aggressive in spurts as well which allowed him to generate pressure against the Finnish forwards. Similar to Fehervary at last years event, Dlugos was used on the powerplay in-front of the net area to take advantage of his frame, this led to one of the better scoring chances for Slovakia but Marcel swung and missed the puck while he was alone in-front. There wasn't much in the way of skill displayed but he's big and he played an aggressive brand of hockey today.

Edina Hornets vs Chaska Hawks, December 29th 2018

Chaska Hawks

Pitlick, Rhett – 2019 Pitlick was in on all 4 goals for Chaska, registering 2 goal and 2 assists in this game, including the tying goal in the 3rd period as well as setting up the game winning goal late in the game. On the tying goal Rhett displayed good shot placement coming down his strong side, beating the goalie over the pad on the short side, just inside the post. Pitlick displayed a good motor in all three zones and continues to do an excellent job in pressuring the puck carrier and forcing the opponent to make quick decisions with the puck Pitlick displayed crafty stick work on the back check, stripping pucks from opponents on a number of sequences. While Pitlick works hard on the back check, On a few instances Pitlick exited his own zone a tad early looking for the "homerun" pass from Koster for a breakaway.

Koster, Mike – 2019 Along with Pitlick, Koster was also in on all 4 Chaska goals in this game, registering 1 Goal and 3 Assists which included the game winning goal late in the 3rd period. Koster continued to display excellent puck moving ability, both using his skating and passing ability. Koster played a much more controlled game from the back end, not leading the rush up ice with the puck as much and picked his spots to be aggressive better. Koster did commit one bad turnover when he attempted a stretch pass up the middle that was intercepted by an Edina player who went in on goal for a good scoring chance. Koster's excellent edge work and puck skills allowed him to open up plays in the offensive end and create space for his teammates on a regular basis. Koster displayed good one-timer ability on the game winning goal when he and Pitlick made a switch at the top of the power play and Koster ripped a one-time form the faceoff circle that beat the goalie inside the post. In his own end, Koster showed the willingness to take a hit to move the puck out of his own zone, something he hasn't always been willing to do in the past, relying on his skating and puck skills to avoid contact.

Edina Hornets

Williams, Nick – 2021 Williams is a late 2002 birth year, but despite his age Williams showed a mature game from the back end. Williams was paired with Mike Vorlicky in this game, which provides a stabilizing presence that allows Williams to showcase his ability to skate the puck out of his own zone. Williams has good combination of agility and puck skills that allowed him to get shots through from the point, one of which was deflected in front for a goal. Williams is a University of Minnesota commit and looked like he will be a prospect that will be tracked closely over the next two seasons for the 2021 NHL Draft.

Vorlicky, Mike - 2019+ Vorlicky was kept off the scoresheet in this game, but that's not to say he didn't create offensive chances, both with his accurate passing ability as well as his quick release from the point. Vorlicky continues to be Edina's best defenseman night in and night out, playing in all situations for the Hornets. Vorlicky made excellent reads coming out of his own end, consistently leaving him outs and finding ways to stretch the ice when available. His strong skating base allowed him to fight through checks and continue moving the play north. On a number of sequences Vorlicky was able to easily elude the speedy Pitlick on Chaska who is excellent at creating turnovers on the fore check and forcing defenseman into mistakes. Defensively, Vorlicky displayed good stick work in one on one situations and kept good position on his man defensively in front of his own net.

Nevers, Mason – 2019+ It was a rare quiet game from Nevers which probably proved to be the difference in the game for Edina. Chaska did an excellent job against Nevers line in this game and forced Edina's other players to beat them. Mason wasn't able to penetrate the middle of the ice with the puck like he usually does and was forced to play on the perimeter for much of his offensive zone opportunities.

Wayzata Trojans vs Holy Family Fire, December 29th 2018

Holy Family Fire

Pinoniemi, Garrett – 2019 Pinoniemi was able to register 2 assists in this game by using his vision and quick hands to open up passing lanes and find the open player in the zone. Pinoniemi used a nice shot fake from the slot and quick feed to a teammate on the backdoor for a Power Play goal. Pinoniemi did a good job protecting the pucks with a wide base and getting pucks into scoring areas but could have created more by showing some poise; in some cases his passes were blindly put toward the slot area with his teammate out numbered. While Pinoniemi displayed his skill and quick stick particularly in puck battles where he was able to strip pucks and gain possession, his game didn't come across very intense, especially away from pucks. There was a lot of wide turns away from the play in some situations and could of benefited from playing more of a North-South game and adding more straight lines to his game.

Fechko, Trey – 2022 Fechko showed a good combination of speed and skill in this game. Fechko didn't look like a freshman, as he was often first in on the fore-check on his line and consistently was able to pressure defenseman into turnovers or rushing their puck movements. Fechko showed excellent vision and playmaking ability down low at the goal line on the power play, in one instance making a quick feed to the back door, through some stick for the tying goal. Fechko showed good two-way play, often working hard to apply back pressure and taking away east west lanes with good stick position coming back to the play. Fechko has good explosiveness in his skating, tracking down a loose puck that got behind the opposing defenseman in the neutral zone for a breakaway scoring chance. Fechko continues to track well for the future as he is able to control stretches of the game as just a late 03 DOB.

Wayzata Trojans

Bergsland, Tommy – 2019 Bergsland is an 8th Round pick of Fargo (USHL) in 2017 and while he still remains uncommitted to an NCAA program and isn't considered a NHL Draft Prospect at this point, his play to start this season and in this game was worthy of a game report. Bergsland registered 1 goal and 2 assists in this game and was able to consistently create scoring chances in the offensive end using his ability to get shots off his stick quickly and through traffic. Bergsland scored on a one-timer from the slot on the power play. Bergsland did a good job taking advantage of the time and space Holy Family was giving him at the point and consistently put passes on his teammates tape from the point. Bergsland is a strong kid with decent size but his skating ability is underwhelming and lacks explusiveness he needs to separate from speedy fore-checkers, however has above average agility and used his stick and body position well in one on one situations.

Switzerland vs Russia, U20 World Junior Championship, Dec 31 2018

Russia –

Morozov, Ilya (2019) – Morozov had an okay performance for Russia. He failed to pin his man along the boards early which resulted in a Swiss goal in the opening minutes which shouldn't have happened given the difference in size between him and his opponent. In this game and some others, he's failed to impose himself physically at times and wasn't playing at a high pace in his own-end of the ice. That said, he did use his frame to block shots and take away lanes during the penalty-kill. Although he wasn't overly involved offensively today, he did saucer a beautiful pass in the neutral zone that led to a breakaway scoring chance, and grabbed his own shot attempt off the play as well. One other area to note is that he hasn't shown much in the way of creativity and we wish he would look for his teammates a bit more since he's shown that he can make a quality pass.

Podkolzin, Vasili (2019) – Podkolzin was dynamic in spurts for Russia today and helped get his team back on track after a horrible start. It was going to be interesting to see if he could maintain the level of compete at this event as previous ones given the difference in size and competition, yet Vasili has been tenacious and has shown the same fearlessness that's been consistent in several previous tournaments. Although this doesn't apply as much against the Swiss given their not the biggest team, he did have several key board battling wins today as well. He's yet to really bare down and shoot the puck as much as we have seen previously but he was displaying top-end playmaking skills out there. On an end-to-end rush, he managed to just barely stay on side while showing excellent puck control before passing the puck back to Marchenko who scored Russia's opening goal. The play showed his ability to assess his options while going at full speeds quickly. He was also effective below the goal-line today, and found his teammates regularly for quality scoring chances both in stationary positions and when in motion. Overall, this was arguably his best game of the tournament and showed off his rare blend of tenacity, intelligence and high-end skill.

Shashkov, Nikita (2019) – Shashkov had a solid yet under-the-radar game for Russia, showing plus playmaking ability while also competing hard yet wasn't flashy. He had several nice set-ups for his teammates below the goal-line despite being under heavy pressure from the Swiss D, this resulted in a primary assist where he threaded a pass-through multiple player before finding his open teammate who buried the chance from the slot. During a penalty-kill sequence he managed to out-compete 3 different Swiss players simultaneously by using his lower body strength to guard the puck.

Slepets, Kirill (2019) – Slepets had an excellent game while short-handed for Russia. Although his stride was short, Kirill generated power and used impressive edges to gain separating speed during breakaways and odd-man rushes. Ironically, he failed to score on his highest-percent chances but buried a wrist-shot in the high-slot from a stationary position, the shot was accurate and the release was above-average. Furthermore, he had a good passing sequence with Romanov during a 2-on-1 where he slowed down the play forcing the Swiss defender to over-commit before threading a cross-slot pass that landed on the tape of his defensive teammate. Slepets had a quality game and was a force on the penalty-kill.

Switzerland –

Nussbaumer, Valentin (2019) – Nussbaumer generated a couple of notable plays while showing a good amount of hockey sense away from the play. He was engaged early, after making a clean transitional zone entry on one sequence and then following that up by scoring the 2nd Swiss goal after parking himself in-front of the crease and putting home a wrist-shot which he elevated quickly. He generated a primary assist after making an impressive one-touch pass in the neutral zone and was used on the powerplay where he demonstrated decent puck movement as well. Away from the puck, he made a nice interception in the high-slot and had consistently good positioning. Although his hockey sense was on display, he failed to be the primary driver of play at any point.

Moser, Janis (2019) – Moser had some difficulties in his own-end at times but still moved the puck up the ice out of his own-end under pressure on a couple of plays, while managing to generate some offense from the backend as well. When controlling the puck below his own goal-line, he was calm and collected, making several crisp passes while using the boards to transition the puck. Against some of the higher-skill players such as Kravtsov, Moser did run into trouble by having an aggressive gap used against him which allowed his opponent to side-step him, though he was quick to try and recover. He had a seeing eye shot get though heavy traffic which led to Nussbaumers rebound goal and activated from the line which led to his best scoring chance of the game where he found soft-ice in-front of the slot area. On the play, he showed average puck-skills during his forehand to backhand move followed by his shot attempt, but the recognition that he should jump into the play was there. Overall, Moser was overwhelmed by the top-end talent of Russia but also had a couple of solid sequences and didn't look lost out there.

Holy Cross Crusaders at USNTDP U18, January 1, 2019

USNTDP U18 -

Zegras, Trevor - 2019 Zegras continued his strong play without Jack Hughes in the lineup. Showed off some very early creativity by earning an assist on a whirling pass to the front of the net from behind the end line. He's a very creative passer in general, though sometimes a little too adventurous for his own good and it creates unforced errors. He's quick on his feet and seems more confident about body contact now – more so receiving than giving, as he's not a physical player by design. He has a better sense now on when contact should occur, how to brace, and how to avoid it. Perhaps learning off of guys like Hughes and Caulfield for that. He did make a poor decision with the puck in the 2nd period while his team was changing. He attempted to buy time for the change, and instead of using his wheels to circle back once more, he elected to make a puck protect move and and was overcome, leading to a turnover. Later in the game, he had a pass to the front of the net that was banged out with some authority…it sent a speedy Crusader through the NZ and Zegras had a beat on him, caught the player and just put his body right in front of the puck carrier just above the hashmarks to brilliantly destroy the play. The Crusader player grabbed him by the head/neck area and pulled him down in the process, and Zegras was wrongfully charged with the hold – but he made a terrific play, not even allowing a shot against. He was about +6 in the dot while the game was still close too.

Turcotte, Alex - 2019 Has quickly rounded back into form after missing about two months. Played a standout game at both ends of the ice. Seemed poised and ready for virtually everything on the rink. A sensationally creative playmaker from any angle, in any part of the rink. Has a great sense for where players on both sides have moved to, even if he's not actively watching them. Can make subtle passes through seams and against the grain at a near-elite level. While he is creative, he isn't a player that you need to plead with to shoot either…early in the game he flew the zone on a good read to catch a two-line stretch pass leaving him on a clean 2-on-1 with Matt Boldy and then he looked off Boldy and snapped it home. There aren't too many passes that he can't catch either. Backchecked effectively, though against the colleges, it's not always a frantic pace…aided further by this being a New Year's Day afternoon start…but he played the hand he was dealt, and he made good on it and did so with a good degree of urgency. Very strong technical skater, exhibits really good footwork and his change of pace skating is advanced for his age…he knows when to rev it up and gear it down like an NHLer. Finished the game with two goals and an assist.

Boldy, Matthew - 2019 Little bit of a quieter game from Boldy, but when he had the puck he was quite noticeable. Made a few really high-end hands plays through out. Played in the slot on the power play on a top unit. A creative passer, but one who isn't quite good enough with the timing to get all of them through. Sometimes it feels like his game is just a touch too complicated for his skill level. It's difficult to keep up with Hughes, Turcotte and Zegras…even a player like Caulfield shows off some things that maybe Boldy can't quite do as consistently, and this hinges on – or is heightened by – the skating disadvantage that Boldy has on the aforementioned. Quiet game overall, but the skill level was still noticeable, as was his shot.

Dubuque Fighting Saints at Des Moines Buccaneers, January 4, 2019

Dubuque Fighting Saints -

Maccelli, Matias - 2019 Never seemed to really get engaged outside of one power play shift. Plays a perimeter game and doesn't move his feet a lot. Had zero interest in defense, which is not unusual. He will loosely cover a point man after a while, but he mostly hangs at the blueline, outside the dot line looking for a puck to be sprung to him. Made some creative passes, but most were low percentage. Plus, he wasn't moving his feet while making them, so he offered no real penetrating threat – which halved his own cause. His go-to move is still turning against the grain, above the half boards and then trying to figure out where to go from there. Shows off some decent hands and he means to be a good playmaker from the boards. In, what I imagine to be, an effort to prevent his stick from being slashed and then losing the puck…he takes his stick really far off the ice when stickhandling through a crowd…maybe further than necessary. Even though he's a low-setup player, that extra distance seems noteworthy. Seems to really struggle to make space for himself. Not a burner from a speed perspective either.

Des Moines Buccaneers -

Paquette, Tyler - 2019 Improved from the last time I saw him. Skating mechanics are still a little unkempt, but his speed and balance have improved…even his glide speed has improved. Made about five hit attempts in the game, including one in open ice…a couple very a bit half-hearted or awkward, but there's more effort in his game. Owns a fairly powerful shot and he works his way to the net well. He needs to do a better job getting himself available to take shots. Saw a little more jump in his game tonight and it felt like he was rewarded with some extra shifts as the game went on…may have helped that his team was ahead by 2 or more in that time as well…

Meyer, Brady - 2019 Big body that got pushed from center to wing as the game went on. Doesn't see a lot of ice, but when he does, he's not very involved. Watches the play, doesn't move his feet very well…when the puck comes to him, he's swarmed under and his passes are tipped regularly. Isn't particularly well-versed in the defensive zone to make up for it, nor does he throw his big frame around. Had another viewing or two of him in the past, but he didn't find enough ice or do enough to even warrant a report…seems like this is just his game.

Proctor, Kirby - 2019 Average skating defenseman with decent awareness. Can make short outlet passes reliably and has a good sense of when to move it against the grain. Willing to be physical at the point of attack, though he too often gets sucked outside the dot line in his setups and it causes him some trouble against skill guys who can make it back into the interior and protect the puck or are faster than him. One instance in particular saw him get walked at the defensive line on a play that he should have shaded 18 inches more into the interior of the rink and given the forward nothing…instead, he breathed life into a dying play

Bohlsen, Kaden - 2019 First game back after a month absence. Didn't look at all rusty. Jumped right back into the swing of things. Works hard at both ends of the ice. Used his big frame to protect pucks and he can protect and move at the same time with plus skating ability. Handles and moves the puck with ease. Made a couple of power moves towards the net that just wasted defenders. His first goal came from driving the net on the far post and tucking in a one-touch backhand off of a rebound. Second goal was an EN. Doesn't shy away from physical play…in fact, he demolished a Fighting Saint in the NZ that sparked a good crowd into a frenzy. Strong frame, strong skater, good skill base, very complete player and one who looks to be on the rise.

Russia vs USA, U20 World Junior Championship, Jan 4 2019

USA –

Hughes, Jack (2019) – Jack wasn't overly noticeable at even strength while playing on the third line, but on the powerplay along the half-wall, he was very effective. Russia controlled the play for much of the second half of the game and this didn't allow Jack too many touches with the puck at 5 on 5, but Russia took a couple of costly penalties and this allowed Hughes to showcase his talent. He was both elusive and shifty while dictating play by drawing defenders to him, setting up his teammates with efficient and accurate passes, while also showing excellent puck control. He had a primary assist after his shot-pass was put home in-front of the net. That play and others showed his ability to analyze lanes quickly and use his skills to re-open his lanes so that he could both fire the puck and pass at a high-rate. Away from the puck he was willing to play deep in his own-end but was out-muscled along the boards on several different sequences.

Logan Cockerill (NYI 2017) – Cockerill had an excellent game for the U.S both with and without the puck. It's unlikely he ever develops into a primary scorer or driver of play, but he was very effective at generating off the rush by using his acceleration. This led to the States opening goal, where he drove past Morozov down the left wing before finding Wahlstrom in the slot who buried the puck, Logan did a good job of drawing the Russian netminder into a potential shot before making an accurate pass. Away from the puck, Cockerill had arguably the best stick-on-puck play of the game, recognizing Kravtsov had found soft-ice with Primeau caught out of position, before darting in the Russians lane with his stick and ramping the shot attempt over the glass as a result. Logan is one of the more unheralded players on this team but played well.

Russia –

Slepets, Kirill (2019) – Slepets used his speed and motor to drive what turned out to be an excellent line for Russia that also featured Galimov. He wasn't as effective on the penalty-kill due to the U.S defense being able to match his speed for the most part but that didn't stop him from generating several impressive scoring chances down the wings at even strength. His most impressive sequence came while challenging Samberg 1-on-1, where he showed soft-hands by making an inside-outside move while simultaneously side-stepping his opponent, this gave him enough room to get a shot off. Away from the puck, he maintained the same pace that he did with the puck, and this allowed him to create pressure and despite his smaller stature he had no issues challenging the bigger U.S defense during board battling sequences. He played with heart and in a game where it took some of the better Russian players time to get involved, Slepets was ready from the opening drop of the puck.

Galimov, Artyom (2019) – Galimov was coming off a bad performance against the Swiss, but stepped up in a big way today against the U.S, showing an excellent set of hands which resulted in several scoring opportunities for Russia. He still wasn't effective without the puck, but when he had it on his stick, he showed creativity that allowed him to create space and drive play in spurts. His most impressive sequence was during a drive down the wing where he used a toe-drag while in motion before sliding behind the net and coming back out around before firing a spinning shot that was difficult for Primeau to pick up. Galimov showed skill and creativity against the States.

Shashkov, Nikita (2019) – Shashkov has primarily showed off his playmaking abilities up to this point in the tournament, yet today he generated several shots and was willing to enter high-traffic areas around the net which almost resulted in several goals. Despite not being the biggest kid, he played fearless in-front of the crease and was good at finding soft-ice. He scored a goal that redirected off his skate bit it was waved off, and later in the game he had an excellent chance off a kick save but couldn't capitalize on the rebound. While short-handed he generated good straight-line speed along the boards while side-stepping a hit, he then drove hard into his U.S opponent, challenging him while simultaneously attempting to drive towards the net as well. Shashkov had an above-average performance overall for Russia.

Podkolzin, Vasili (2019) – Podkolzin had a very good 200-foot game for Russia. He's young, but he's just as strong as a lot of the other kids here and demonstrated that against a big and mobile U.S defense who were unsuccessful at containing him consistently due to how tenacious Vasili can be on the puck. He's a competitive player and at points today seemed to will plays that a lot of other players simply couldn't make. On one sequence from a stand-still position, Podkolzin showed off his impressive puck skills which re-opened his shooting lane before firing a hard and low wrist-shot that required a difficult kick stop and generated a rebound. On another sequence, he put his head down and challenged a U.S defender while taking a direct approach to the net before passing it off in the goal crease which led to a quality scoring opportunity for his team late. Away from the puck, he was assertive and detail oriented, allowing him to position himself and intercept a couple of outlet passes that kept the U.S hemmed in their own end. Overall, Podkolzin was one of Russia's better forwards out there despite being one of the youngest, which is a testament to his talent level and determination.

Frölunda HC at Linköping, Jan 4, 2019

Linköping HC

LHC # 12 CE Ekmark, Elliot (2020) - 16 year old very unafraid player that was willing to battle and go in to the net. Ekmark had nice attitude. He came in from the bench and went directly to offensive faceoff circle, receiving the puck from # 8 from corner and more or less had 4 Frölunda players around him, went through 2 of them and released a shot from slot that went to a rebound from goalie pad that # 8 finished. Important goal at 19.45 in second that was only created due to Ekmarks willingness to go to the net. Delivered some nice quick accurate passes to # 41.

LHC # 41 CE Costmar, Arvid (2019) - Costmar had an ok drive, good mobility and good footwork, made some risky moves but also some nice toe ins. Good passes over centerline. Delivered a couple of shots on goal but without any traffic. Good part of the work behind 2-3 pp goal.

LHC #27 LD Lyckåsen, Albert (2019) - Good communication on ice. Reading the opponents very good and good stick checks. I thought he pushed out the opponents a bit too hard and got very difficult to change direction, making the opponent passing him. Was going good on the body and looked strong by the board.

LHC #22 LW Pedersen, Marcus (2019) - Did not see much of Pedersen. Made an open ice hit.

LHC # 3 RD Worge Kreu, William - In previous games he hasn't convinced me and my expectations on him considering Sabres drafted him, even though a 7th rounder. Today was some nice clever passes but to no one. Good reading at the board and quick long passes. Delivered a hard shot but wasn't accurate on the net. Looks thin and lot of frame to fill.

FRÖLUNDA

FHC # 22 CE Henriksson, Karl (2019) - Henriksson had good energy, good attitude and confidence. Great speed and search the way to the net with speed. Had some ok faceoffs. 2 A, 3 SOG

FHC # 45 RW Andersson, Isac (2019) - Good chemistry with # 38 and # 22. Had good drive. Was showing good work ethic and shot a lot.

FHC # 37 RW Söderblom, Elmer (2019) - 6'7" 216 lbs 17 year old RW that was good handling the puck and found his way to pass opponents. Scored the GWG with # 22 and # 45.

FHC # 3 RD Kumlin, Axel (2020) -Getting through the oppponents good and technically strong and confident at the board. Good attitude.

FHC # 23 C Åström, Filiph (2019) - Played in fourth line but when on ice he had good energy, went towards the net and looked strong.

FHC # 29 RW Engstrand, Eric - 6'4" 207 lbs 2000 born player that still is good on the skates and mobile. Was playing in first line and found his team mates good with passes. Shot 2 decent shots from blue line.

Modo u20 at Djurgarden IF u20 Januari 4 2019

Modo u20

Wahlgren Max 2019 Wahlgren did not really show up today. His offensive patterns this game was: outside, outside, outside. He got a couple shots on goal, but not from any high scoring areas. He did not get a lot of ice time during the later stages of the game.

Wahlgren, Joel 2019 Wahlgren had a good game, showing some good grit and work ethic.

He was one of the most active forwards for his team. He could have produced a couple more points this game if he had executed better when creating scoring chances. He went offside several times, failing to read the play properly. He could really benefit from start going through traffic and not staying on the outside all game long. Finished the game with a goal.

Popovic, Alexander 2019 Popovic skates superbly, which he proved in the first period when he cruised through the opposing team, going coast-to-coast. After that he really stopped skating, which is strange, considering it is his strongest asset.
When stopped skating, he looked average at best.

He did stand still in his own zone, spectating the play, without reading the play or even attempting to break up the play.

Nordin, Oscar 2019 Nordin is listed as a 6'2" big centreman, although he played like he thought he was 5'9". Instead of using his big frame to his advantage, he tried to stickhandle and finesse his way around the opposition. His skating mechanics are poor, skating with his knees together, but he does have good top speed. Did a good job in the faceoff circle.

Djurgarden IF u20

Holtz, Alexander 2020 Holtz is absolutely lethal when attacking. His shot is elite and so are his offensive instincts, where he always believe he can beat the defenders, no matter how many of them he faces. He sniffed his way to 4(!) breakaways this game, whereof 2 of them he stickhandled his way around 2 defenders and skated in for a breakaway.

His teamwork and two-way play have definitely improved during this season and he can be found deep in his own zone, helping his defenders more frequently now than he was before. He does still cheat defense at times to try to get a head start on opposing defenders.
Holtz finished the game with 2 goals and several great scoring chances created for himself and his linemates.

Bjornfot, Tobias 2019 Bjornfot is a really good team player. Even though he is the leader on his teams' blueline, he still works hard every shift and sacrificed his body to block shot, both on 5on5 and on the box play. He got a lot of ice time and plays in all situations and does a good job, without really excelling in any. Bjornfot is extremely strong physically and uses it to his advantage when locking forwards to the boards in the corners and in front of his own net. He is active with his stick defensively and his reach is really good. A question mark defensively is his defensive awareness, since opponents seem to get good scoring chances when sneaking up on him from behind. Once again he makes mistakes at the end of the games. This time he collided with his defensive partner to allow a Modo forward to get a breakaway and scoring.

Brannstam, Alex 2019 Brannstam had an interesting game. He skates well and skated actively, which led to some created scoring chances.

He had a hard time handling the puck, it seemed to bounce off his stick more times than not. But when he controlled the puck he did provide the puck to his forwards with good crisp passes.

His shot was accurate and had good power today. Finished the game with an assist.

Bjerselius, Oscar 2019 Bjerselius was the first line centerman on a young Djurgarden team. He looked comfortable in the first period, almost lazy. It looked like he waited for his right winger #24 Walli-Walterholm to get the game going. He provided good defensive support, as he always does. However, this game he lost most man-to-man duels during the first half of the game. Bjerselius got the opportunity to perform offensively as the first line centerman and was put on the first power-play unit. He registered one shot, from a good area, but the shot was weak and easily saved by the goaltender. His passing game was terrible today, he missed easy passes and was overall careless with the puck.

Chicoutimi Sagueneens vs. Gatineau Olympiques, January 4th, 2019

Chicoutimi

Kotkov, Vladislav - Kotkov displayed a good combination of size and strength along with skill and speed to his game. Vladislav was able to display quick hands in tight as he found rebounds quickly and was able to make plays in tight spaces. While Kotkov has room to improve his first step, he was able to reach a good top speed which did make him imposing on the forecheck and tough to contain when attacking the offensive zone and scored a nice goal of the rush tonight with a quick wrist shot.

Bouthillier, Zachary (TOR) - Bouthillier was excellent in nets tonight for Chicoutimi, he was squared to the puck not giving Olympiques players at room to shoot, there wasn't any movement in the crease either, he was aggressive with his set up and challenging the players to shoot. Bouthillier is a very technically goalie, he had good rebound control, he sucked in a lot of high shots not giving any 2nd or 3rd chances, and he was good at kicking pucks to the corners with his rebounds. He showed good lateral movement going post to post, and was good at covering the lower part of the net. Bouthillier was also strong at fighting through screens or tracking pucks from out wide or from the point.

Houde, Samuel (MTL) - Houde displayed strong two-way attributes and skill to his game. A player who continually showed strong awareness of his surroundings, Samuel was an effective three zone presence, providing strong positional play. In possession Houde showed good vision and playmaking skills as he created for his line mates. Houde is still an effective trait as he flashed the ability to beat opponents in 1-on-1 scenarios. Houde's ability to anticipate put him in strong position throughout the game, as he was always on the right side of the puck. Houde was good tonight off the rush drawing defensemen to him and make a pass to a trailing forward coming in on the rush, he must have done this 4-5 times tonight.

Gatineau

Jones, Creed - Jones was strong in goal for Gatineau, showing impressive athletic abilities and strong reflexes. Creed's ability to anticipate the play along with his quick post-to-post movements allowed him to make multiple high-end cross-crease saves. Jones has good size; however his willingness to challenge shooters and play his angles effectively allows him to take away net and make saves. Jones also showed an ability to play the puck with effectiveness tonight allowing it easier to break out of the zone.

Finoro, Giordano - Finoro played with competitiveness to his game that allowed him to make small impacts on both sides of the puck. Finoro showed the ability to make simple skilled plays but generated the majority of his offensive opportunities but outworking his opponents. Finoro was often first to pucks and won his puck/position battles. Finoro flashed a deceptively good release and had effectiveness on the penalty kill. Finoro showed good skating ability tonight. Finoro had another strong night in the faceoff circle going 65% on draws.

Craig. Keiran (2019) - Craig played a simple but aggressive game tonight, showing good energy and competes. Kieran was good in a complimentary role, being first to pucks, winning his battles and getting pucks to teammates to make plays. While Craig was unable to create much on his own, he did flash a quick release which he was able to get off mid-stride and made an impact with his physical play and competitiveness.

USA vs Finland, U20 World Junior Championships, Jan 5 2019

USA –

Hughes, Jack (2019) – Hughes had his best game of the tournament, consistently making clean transitional zone entries and breaking down the Finnish defense with his skating ability. He showed his dynamic skill-set early, as he banked a pass off the boards to himself to evade an active stick and used his hands to safely protect the puck before moving up the ice. His passing was accurate, with his best pass coming from the right circle, where he made a precise backhand pass that went through traffic and resulted in one of the better scoring chances for the States in the 2nd frame. He almost scored the go-ahead goal after breaking through the defense and finding himself alone in-front of the net, but was denied by Luukonen. He saved his best for last and drove play at a higher rate at even strength than at any other point at this event.

Finland –

Kakko, Kappo (2019) – Kakko scored the golden goal for his Finnish team which capped off an impressive performance overall. He had a great chance during a 2-on-1 sequence where he flew down the right wing but seemed to hesitate slightly too long which resulted in a shot block. He made up for his missed chance by scoring the go-ahead goal with just minutes remaining by finding the puck in traffic and backhanding it over Primeau. Kappo was solid away from the puck as well, showing determination on the backcheck which gave him a takeaway in the neutral zone on once sequence, and he was aggressive during puck pursuit situations on the forecheck, at one point he took on two American defenders and came away with the puck still on his stick, showing his compete in the corner. Overall, it was another impressive performance.

Lundell, Anton (2020) – Lundell displayed good chemistry with Kakko and had one of his best performances of the tournament. In the opening minutes, he had a sequence which characterizes his play well, where he helped support his defenseman away from the puck in his own-end, then chipped the puck up the ice, then transitioned over the offensive-blueline before making a nice drop-pass that set up a scoring chance. He drew a penalty by cutting into heavy traffic while driving down the right-wing before side-stepping into the slot area while looking to release his wrist-shot. On other offensive sequences, he distributed the puck efficiently and wasn't afraid to enter high-traffic areas to try and make a play, this resulted in Anton getting the primary assist on the golden goal, where he had the initial rebound shot stopped before Kakko found the puck. Lundell didn't look out of place at this event and showed a cerebral two-way game out there today.

Honka, Anttoni (2019) – Honka had a difficult game for Finland which resulted in him losing ice-time as the game progressed. Although he had a moment of two where he used his agility to throw off the U.S during the forecheck, which gave him time to make a couple of passes that moved the puck up; Honka again, didn't play efficiently in his own-end and showed average processing ability. He took a bad penalty after coughing up the puck that led to a disallowed goal and never seemed to really find his confidence after that play. In the offensive-zone, he didn't get too many touches with the puck but when he did, they were largely ineffective. Although Honka's puck management was poor, he didn't give up competing, and was trying to make a difference, he just wasn't able to keep up with the faster pace of the game today.

Latvala, Otto (2019) – Latvala had a solid two-way performance for Finland by playing big in-front of his own crease and scoring an important goal from the point. As mentioned previously, Latvala is a towering defender and he used his leverage against smaller players well in-front of the net resulting in a couple of important tie-up plays which resulted in reduced rebound opportunities for the U.S. Under pressure on the forecheck, he was calm and collected, but was average with his breakout passes overall. In the offensive-zone, he didn't flash any sort of dynamic quality and didn't show any creativity but what he did manage to do, was get his shot through traffic and recognize when Primeau was screened which gave him his 2nd goal of the event. Although he did get burned by Cockerill on once sequence where his agility was taken advantage of it, his mobility held up enough to stay in-front of the U.S attack out there.

Muskegon Lumberjacks at Cedar Rapids RoughRiders, January 5, 2019

Muskegon Lumberjacks -

Afanasyev, Yegor - 2019 Not a ton of ice for Afanasyev in a herky jerky game. He didn't play on the top line, but was instead shuffled down in the lineup a little bit and only played PP2. He certainly didn't wilt from the physical contest. He threw his body around quite readily, but smartly. He also uses his body to protect pucks very well. He has a lanky but projectable frame…sort of uses it like a young Evgeni Malkin, and in that same vein, might be stronger than he looks out there. He's very coordinated and he plays the game with a lot of exuberance. He made a few good rushes during the game, showing off good stickhandling and feel for the time/space of the game. He got a couple shots away in the process. He has a plus shot, but is probably just an average skater overall. It looks like he has the athletic makeup to be a better skater in time…it doesn't hold him back much now because it's not a negative, but it's going to be something to work on.

Bukes, Colby - 2019 Bukes had a spectacular game and spent a ton of time on the rink. One of Bukes' best assets is his change of direction and escapability against the flow of a forecheck. Very mobile, very agile, and able to skate the puck up the rink. He moved pucks ahead with a lot of accuracy and success…though he did have one pretty graphic turnover.

Plays the game with an easy confidence and calm. Defends aggressively, but is pretty stout and smart about it. He is a '99 birthday, so it should be obvious that he's ahead of the game – and it is – but the skill package is getting good enough to consider now. The only thing lacking is his shot, which doesn't have a lot of zip on it.

Cedar Rapids RoughRiders -

Silianoff, Grant - 2019 Smart and pretty industrious. Silianoff plays the game with his head up and ready to contribute. He doesn't offer a lot in terms of technical skill, but he hustles and he's a slightly above average skater. Worked down deep into the defensive end as a sagging winger, going all the way to the net at times, but smartly – as Cedar Rapids commits the center to the wall often. He manned the mid-slot on PP1 all night. Has a quick release and a plus shot. Didn't really get a lot of clean looks, nor was he much of a setup man at ES. He's a player who will need to work hard to continue to really advance, but he appears to have a motor that's conducive to that improvement.

Minnetonka HS at Duluth East HS, January 5, 2019

Duluth East HS -

Donovan, Ryder - 2019 Tall, very thin player who has the skating stride of someone who has recently shot up a few inches. A little bit of an awkward stride and the first two steps leave something to be desired in terms of the energy they generate. His top speed is a plus though once he gets moving at about stride three or four. The thing that jumps out most about Donovan is what a circular style of game he plays…he doesn't stop on hardly any pucks, and he takes very circuitous routes back when backchecking. In one instance in the 2nd period, he had an opportunity to backcheck from the bottom of the attack zone circle and come back through the middle – he was likely going to be last man back anyhow – but instead he goes out of his way to loop behind the net while play is going the other way.

His understanding of the geometry of the game is poor and he takes poor angles to pucks and bodies. He doesn't give off the feel of having a lot of hockey sense with how he does his business out there. He carries pucks into teammates' feet, poor angles of attack, he calls for passes when he's not the best option, etc. His defense, when applicable, is almost roller hockey-like…sort of stalking, waiting for a player to pass through his "bubble" and then it's typically slash on the stick to see if you can force the puck to pop out the other direction.

He lined up at LW and C, but he plays the game all over the place and other players have to adjust to what lane he has drifted into. He hacks at faceoffs with no real purpose. He is tall and has a strong skill base. He can carry the puck with a head of steam and walk through many players at this level, he did so several times this afternoon, in fact. But this is a very rough product and it's unclear if enough pieces can come together quick enough to make this player any more than a late flier.

Växjö Lakers HC at Linköping, Jan 06, 2019

Linköping

LHC # 3 RD Worge Kreu, William - I have sometimes thought Worge Kreu looked a bit nonchalant and not so engaged. Today I felt that he had more energy. Was having a good confidence as last player but still within the limits to not be very risky. Worge Kreu did some puck rushes south north in center line that I haven't seen him doing. At one of them he delivered backwards a pass in front of net but no one was there to finish it. Worge Kreu was in good positioning for shots but team mates didn't notice him. Hoping to get a penalty he was staying lying on ice when the LHC took the puck on a 5-4 play.

LHC # 27 RD Lyckåsen, Albert (2019) - Good communication with # 48. Stone hard accurate passes, very quick on the skates, wonderful energy, Was reading the game very good, was stick poking successfully and was delivery good tackles. His backward skating looked to be very much with crossover when might would be quicker and more efficient straight backwards.

LHC # 20 LW Lycksell, Olle - Showed good speed and good hands, was turning the game quick and always searched himself towards the net both with puck or without it for rebounds and re-directions. Made one faceoff and lifted the opponents stick very quick and clever. Was very mobile and made himself available all over the ice. A nice toe in and a accurate shot.

LHC # 41 CE Costmar, Arvid (2019) - Many games in J20 Costmar looked to use higher speed in the last period, today he felt very motivated and with high energy from the start. It felt like the chemistry with Lycksell was good. Good speed, quick accurate passes. Nice quick released direct shot scoring 1-0 after prework from also # 20 & # 29. Good backchecking home & overall good faceoffs.

LHC # 22 RW Pedersen, Marcus (2019) - Good speed, good passes in to the slot. Good attitude and was fighting hard in the battles. Had issues receiving the passes. Made some risky slashes close resulting in penatlies. Delivered an open ice.

LHC # 53 RW Malinowski, Alexander (2019) - Undersized 4th line player with good skills and attitude that use speed when he gets icetime. Good passes, clever pass behind back towards slot. Battles to win pucks. Going on rebounds at the pillar.

Luleå HF u20 at AIK u20 Januari 6 2019

Luleå HF u20

Ramberg, Lucas 2020 Ramberg is a smooth skater and got no problems skating the puck forwards. He also showed some good hands when he stickhandled his way out of danger.

He lost a battle in front of his own net, which led to his team conceding the equalizing goal to force OT.
No points today, but an overall good performance by the young defenseman.

Jellus, Simon 2019 Jellus did well in a sheltered role as the fourth line centerman, where he did not play much on 5on5, but got the opportunity to lead the powerplay from the right side. He managed to show good playmaking skills on the powerplay against an aggressive opponent and he also did a good job in retrieving the loose pucks from rebounds with his big frame. He needs to work on his skating skills, where he skates with straight legs and crouched over back. Could also benefit from getting better educated on the tactical aspects of the game. He is a raw, unrefined talent. Finished the game with an assist on the powerplay.

Wallstedt, Jesper 2021 Wallstedt stepped up a notch from yesterdays game against Djurgarden. He was vocal all game long and guided his defensemen well. He made some great reflex saves and proved himself to be able to make quick lateral moves. Like most goaltenders, he is strong on his glove side. He had tendencies of going down in his butterfly too early, leaving big chunks of open net, high on his far side.

Muzik, Radek 2019 Muzik keeps on working very hard for his team. He could be a really useful player if he only could work smarter. His lack of hockey sense shows in him skating offside at a couple occasions. Today he kept his feet going, but his straight-legged skating prevents him from actually gaining any speed. He scored a fantastic goal where he showed great patience and skill. From the goal line, he waited for the goaltender to get down in the butterfly, to shoot the puck off the crossbar and in. He finished the game with a goal.

Nordanstahl, Isak 2019 Nordanstahl played a fine game as the third line centerman. He covered big areas of the ice with his hard two-way game. He has average size, but is very useful in all areas of the ice, without excelling in any. His skating is good enough to compete at this level. Had a weak game in the faceoff circle.

Oshawa Generals vs. Ottawa 67's, January 6th, 2019

Oshawa

Vallati, Giovanni - Vallati played a simple, low-risk style of defense that allowed him to be effective throughout. Possesses average skating abilities and overall mobility however his ability to simplify the game both in possession and away from the puck is what he struggled with tonight. Vallati showed good awareness in the defensive zone and utilized both his strength and stick to separate player from puck. In possession Giovanni struggled to make the simple outlet pass. Giovanni is a stay-at-home defender type that can fly under the radar.

Neumann, Brett (2019) - Neuman had a strong game for the Generals tonight. Despite his undersized frame Brett played hard throughout, showing a willingness to be first to pucks and go to high traffic areas. He was effective on the forecheck using a combination of speed, quick stick and willingness to finish his check to create a turnover. In possession Neuman wasn't overly creative but always made the right decision. He moved pucks quickly and showed intelligence to his game in his ability to find space in the offensive zone and remain positional sound on both sides of the puck.

Tullio, Tyler (2020) - Tullio didn't have his strongest offensive performance, however was still highly effective which showed intriguing versatility to his game. Tyler played hard throughout the game, finishing his checks and utilizing his speed to forecheck successfully. Tullio can become an agitating presence with his willingness to play physically with speed. Ty was very strong on the penalty showing good awareness and anticipation, while his ability to read the play throughout the game put him in ideal positioning to create turnovers or generate offense

Ottawa

Quinn, Jack (2020) – Quinn displayed skill to his game throughout, but made an early impact scoring his team's first goal. Quinn was able to utilize his speed to drive wide past the opposing defender before releasing a shot on goal that handcuffed the goaltender. Quinn however adding strength to his game would only enhance his skating abilities. Quinn displayed quick feet and was consistently moving in the offensive zone, finding space effectively. His quick stick allowed him to create turnovers on the forecheck. Quinn was passive on the forecheck but utilized his ability to anticipate the play to create turnovers.

Rossi, Marco (2020) - Marco was arguably the top performer in the game. He scored the opening goal of the game walking off the half-boards, beating his defender with a slick one-on-one puck handling move, before releasing a shot that was both heavy and accurate over the goalies glove hand and just under the cross-bar. Marco dictated the pace of play in possession and showed an uncanny ability to raise the play of his line mates with his vision and playmaking skills. Marco was always on the right side of the puck show excellent positional awareness and overall hockey sense to his game. Marco was a fun player to watch overall tonight, should be a fun player to watch next year.

University School at Edgewood Crusaders, January 8th, 2019

University School

Roepke, Casey - 2020 Roepke displayed excellent skating ability and explosiveness with the puck. Casey took a couple risky paths with the puck coming out of his own end and committed some turnovers in the process but for the most part, controlled the game with the puck on his stick for much of the night. Defensively there is some room for growth in his game as he can be aggressive in one on one situations coming into his own end which took himself out of the play and got lost in some coverages in his own end as well. Casey excelled in the offensive end where he moved pucks quickly and accurately around the zone and did a good job under pressure at the point. Roepke displayed a quick and powerful release on one shot from far out that rang off the post but finished the game with 2 goals and 2 assists and make plays with the puck in all 3 zones.

Mann, Ethan – 2021 Mann is a University of Wisconsin commit as of this past fall. Ethan is still a tad undersized at this stage but that didn't prevent him from being effective against larger players. Mann displayed quick hands and made quick plays with the puck that helped him register 3 assists in this game. Mann showed a quick stick both in open ice and in pick battles which allowed him to win battles against larger opponents. Mann displayed good hockey sense and was in the right positions on the ice in order to be around the puck a lot in this game. Mann's hockey sense and quick skill at this stage will likely make him a higher round pick in this year's USHL Draft and a possible invite to the NDTP Evaluation Camp as well as a late round OHL Draft Prospect despite his intentions to play College Hockey.

Sioux City Musketeers at Fargo Force, January 10, 2019

Sioux City Musketeers -

Kallionkieli, Marcus - 2019 Disappointing follow-up on Kallionkieli. Particularly regarding his hockey smarts…on closer inspection, they're no better than average. He failed to make the right reads defensively without other defenders filling in where they belonged first…then he figured it out. When he had to make the choice and the attack against was still forming and ambiguous, he hesitated and/or chose incorrectly. He had a few looks in open ice but didn't generate as much as I thought maybe he could have. He left a little meat on the bone in the attack zone for most of the night, despite getting his goal. His goal could have been scored with a shovel, on the heels of Pospisil getting leveled in front.

Kallionkieli also took a big hit trying to sneak in to the attack zone along the boards. It was a tough night overall, and he did some damage to the perception of potential technical skills and his smarts.

Fargo Force -

Bohlsen, Kaden - 2019 First game with his new team after being traded two days prior from Des Moines. Didn't find a lot of ice time as he works to get acclimated. Quiet start, first guy off most of the time. He warmed up to the game as it went on and started becoming more physical. He even tried to mix it up with skilled pest Martin Pospisil (SC) after a whistle, and it seemed as though Pospisil wanted nothing to do with it. Bohlsen is a solidly-built player, thick frame, strong skating base. He didn't get a lot of puck touches tonight, and was about a -2 in faceoffs on the night, but not for lack of effort. Worked both ends of the rink diligently. But, all told, there wasn't a lot of ice for him in his first game.

Nodler, Josh - 2019 Overall it was a good night for Nodler and he saw plenty of ice time, including PP and PK time. I think immediately this is a player with upside, but one who needs to really zero in on a niche. He's just an average skater overall, he has a little bit of a wide base and there's a bit of hitch step in there that holds him up…but he can skate backwards pretty well for my expectations, he did that a few times tonight and the transitions in and out were clean. He's not high on technical skills, but he doesn't chop the puck in half either. He has enough to make a little room for himself or buy a little time in open ice, but probably doesn't have enough to beat a competent player 1vs1. Looks to have some brains and a desire to work. He even took a few faceoffs tonight despite being a winger. This is one of those players that you could see working his way into being a defensive specialist down the line if he a) improves his starts/stops game and b) fully embraces that role. The latter can be tough for a lot of players. Nodler ought to be on the radar, as there's enough there to keep an eye on.

Niagara Ice Dogs vs Kingston Frontenacs, Jan 11 2019

Ice dogs –

Tomasino, Philip (2019) – Tomasino had a solid offensive-performance for Niagara, showing the ability to be dangerous off the rush. In some previous viewing, Philip was primarily threatening and creating chances around the goal-line and although he managed a secondary assist after making a quick pass below the net area in this game, it was his ability to generate while cutting laterally across the slot-area that stood out today. He had a high-end chance after making a quick-move that showed good-timing and awareness with his spacing by tipping a puck over an extended stick which gave him a point-blank chance alone in-front of the net. After that chance, he drove down the left-wing before displaying impressive lateral agility, cutting aggressively through the slot before firing a snap-shot short-side that fooled the Kingston netminder. He generated in spurts and rarely drove play, but he did flash offensive-talent, edge-work that allowed him to remain elusive, and the ability to process the play quickly enough to make fast plays in tight-spaces.

Frontenacs –

Wong, Nicholas (2020) – Wong had a difficult evening for the Frontenac's due to his puck-skills not being able to compensate for his lack of physical tools against Niagara's backend. Nicholas was willing to compete but was primarily kept to the outside, getting out-muscled and overwhelmed when attempting to cut to the net area. He adapted to a degree, threading a couple of impressive and sharp passes that resulted in high-end shots for his team from the outside since he couldn't drive through the middle of the ice. He rarely managed to find soft-ice to get off his plus release and didn't show the ability to make the opposing team respect his skill-set. In some games with a lot of pace, both Wong's lack of speed and size allow him to get shutdown and become ineffective.

Constantinou, Billy (2019) – Constantinou had a poor performance against his old team. Billy competed hard in-front of the net and his man-to-man coverage was okay; however, his puck management was off. There were several different plays where he attempted to make outlet passes to alleviate pressure, but his passing was inaccurate and there was a lack of attention to detail with how he was managing his breakouts. As an example, as opposed to using his pivoting ability while remaining patient to try and re-open passing lanes, he instead rushed his options and as a result turned over the puck consistently. Despite the drawbacks he had in his own-end of the ice, he did show impressive puck rushing ability which did lead to clean transitional zone-entries while going through heavy traffic. From the backend, he rarely generated scoring chances and his best scoring chance came during a 5-on-3 where he had his shot blocked in the slot after failing to recognize his lane was closed.

Brand, Evan (2019) – Brand had difficulty keeping up with the pace of Niagara's attack in his own-end, but competed hard, and used his frame effectively in-front of the net at times. He was willing to engage physically along the boards, but had trouble separating the puck from players using his leverage and length. From the point, he managed to generate a couple of shots that made their way trough seams, this led to getting a primary assist after one of his shots was redirected in-front of the net. Lastly, although his edges and coordination aren't bad for his size, his lack of acceleration and top-end speed hurt him out there today when attempting to deal with a quicker Niagara team.

Rowe, Lucas (2019) – Rowe had a poor offensive-game for Kingston, as he was unable to use his speed effectively to penetrate Niagara's defense. He had a couple of decent rushing plays where he side-stepped two Niagara players in the neutral-zone before gaining the line, and on another sequence, he aggressively cut-wide while driving down the right-wing which led to an okay pass attempt in-front of the slot. However, he never managed to cut through heavy traffic and as a result looked to generate from the outside which he was unsuccessful at doing. On one shot attempt, he made himself an option and received a pass across the left-circle but didn't shoot the puck in one-motion which allowed the Niagara goalie an opportunity to get set. On a couple of passing attempts, he failed at assessing when his lanes were closed which resulted in a couple of turnovers.

Beraldo, Adrien (2019) – Beraldo was one of the better Kingston players on the ice today, making plus plays at both ends of the ice. He had a nice sequence early where he recognized pressure in the neutral-zone before peeling off and generating an offensive-zone entry. In his own-end, he made clean outlet passes under-pressure and hesitated correctly to re-open a lane which showed some poise. He also showed decent anticipation at the offensive-line today, pinching correctly at times. As a result, he scored a goal after finding soft-ice at the bottom of the left-circle before releasing a wrist-shot that was accurate and threatened after rushing through the slot before firing a wrist-shot on another. His puck management has been poor in some previous viewings, as well as his puck-control at the offensive-line, but against Niagara he had one of his better showings.

Rögle BK u20 at Sodertalje SK u20 January 12 2019

Rögle BK u20

Mrazik, Michal 2019 Mrazik had problems to keep up with the pace of the game. He had to cheat his defensive responsibilities to create space between him and the defenders to even create a scoring chance. He did not really play a team-based game since he did not get involved in any type of defense or battles for the puck. He did score two goals, the first one was a pass that got defected by the defenders stick and the second one was a well-placed one-timer from in close.

Bergvall, Love 2019 Bergvall was one of the tallest players on the ice. He struggled defensively and parked his big frame in front of his net when he did not know how to keep up with Sodertaljes forwards. He has a long reach and a decent defensive stick. He would benefit from being more flexible with his stickhand, now it was cemented high up on the shaft, which prevented him from making hard passes. His shot was hard and low but took some time to release.

Clang, Calle 2020 Clang had a big part in this win. He saved 90,62% of the shots, where many of the shots were high scoring chances. He played very aggressive and forced the shooters to make a move. He moves quickly, both when skating and making saves. However, he does move a lot and makes big movements which means he is out of position at times. He is very athletic and made a couple big desperation saves to save his team from conceding goals. Clang showed great skills with the puck on his stick and could pass the puck to the offensive blueline without any problems.

Sodertalje SK u20

Wang, Carl 2019 Wang started the game very well, he initiated offense, played the body and made simple plays. Further into the game, he disappeared more and more. He got passive defensively and got stressed with the puck. He even got benched in the third period.

Feuk, Lucas 2019 Feuk was totally invisible for big parts of the game. He skated offside, gave up on loose puck and seemed to be uninterested in hustling to score goals. He was easily caught by defenders, even though he jumpstarted the attacks by leaving his defensive zone early, since his skating needs improvement. He did finish the game with two assists from two shots that got defected.

Waterloo Black Hawks at Tri-City Storm, January 12, 2019

Tri-City Storm -

Saville, Isaiah - 2019 Very compact butterfly goalie who plays pretty deep in his net. Never wavers from playing the entire game on his knees, even on hard rims, he's down to the ice. At 6'1, a very low setup RVH style, this may pose a challenge for him at the next level if he doesn't find a way to keep a shoulder up near the post…further, keeping his shoulders up as he slides across post to post would be helpful too, as he has a tendency to slide back towards his goal line on the pushes, even if the shooter isn't at a deep enough far-side angle to necessitate that depth change. Saville doesn't do a great job filling the net. His glove often overlaps with his hip…with his fingers pointed towards the play, instead of out or up and away from his body. It's not uncommon for him to have overlap outside the posts in a style that already makes him smaller in net. His glove placement suggests he has lazy hands, and given how few times he telescopes out for pucks with his glove and how even fewer hit it in a blocking style because of the aforementioned overlap, there's probably some merit to that. It's easy to push Saville back into his paint, he really has a hard time establishing himself at his spot both by choice, but also by force. Traffic will force him back to the goal line and he's not anchored enough to fight through it from his typical stance. He does do a fair job making his rebounds predictable because of his style and the limited amount of save selections he has. Not very aggressive in playing the puck and looks to be only an average skater. He has a decent foundation to build off of, as he won't let a lot of pucks through him. But he needs to really build on this base and get more comfortable in finding ways to be aggressive and reduce the amount of visible net to shooters to have a chance at the professional level.

USNTDP-U18 at University of Wisconsin, January 12th 2019

USNTDP-U18

Warren, Marshall – 2019 Warren was solid in this game. He defended in one on one situations well by using his skating and sound positioning. Showed good strength along the wall against larger opponents and won puck battles in his own end. Marshall showed good hand eye coordination in batting down pucks and in receiving and controlling errant passes. Warren made a number of subtle plays that don't show up on the scoresheet but contributed to his teams win in this game, whether I be getting pucks out of the zone or using 2nd and 3rd effort to win puck battles.

Turcotte, Alex – 2019 Turcotte continues his impressive play since returning from injury. Turcotte's playmaking ability was on display, as he was able to thread passes through traffic. Turcotte made a quick pass to find Boldy in the slot for a goal on the Power Play. Turcotte scored by driving the net hard and getting position and leverage on his checker. Turcotte competed hard in the corners and was able to win a good amount of his one on one battles.

Beecher, John – 2019 Beecher was listed as the 4th line center on the line chart but was still able to log a good amount of ice time with his play on the Penalty Kill where he was effective. Beecher opened the scoring when he can down the wing with speed and shot in stride with a quick release that beat the Wisconsin goalie far side just inside the post. Beecher played a good two-way game, breaking up some plays with back pressure on the back check as well as showing his ability to read the play and breakup plays in his own zone.

Vlasic, Alex – 2019 Vlasic displayed some decent offensive thoughts and ability in the offensive zone, coming down from the point and finding Turcotte in front on the Power Play. While Vlasic showed pretty good mobility in his skating, however his stride lacks explosiveness due to its mechanics which resulted in him losing races to loose pucks. Vlasic struggled on some of his breakouts, blindly throwing passes where no teammates were and seemed to struggle when his first read wasn't available.

Thrun, Henry – 2019 Thrun played his offside as a left shot defenseman, but didn't seem to have an issue making plays off the wall in the offensive zone. Thrun moved the puck quickly D to D and was able to get shots through to the net. Thrun lacks some footspeed in some areas of his skating but used his stick and body positioning to defend one on one. Thrun showed good hockey sense in his ability to read the play and has a good stick in the defensive zone.

Zegras, Trevor – 2019 With Alex Turcotte back in the lineup, Zegras moved to left wing on the top line with jack Hughes and Alex Caufield where their line dictated the play in the offensive zone. Zegres showcased high end skill with a quick one-touch pass to setup a goal by Cole Caufield at the backdoor as well as a slick backhand feed off the boards at the offensive blueline to find Jack Hughes coming down the middle of the ice. Zegres showed good physicality on the fore-check by finishing his checks as well.

Saskatoon Blades vs Portland Winterhawks, January 12, 2019

Saskatoon

Kirby, Dach (2019) - Played with a real desire to make a difference and was using his shot more often today. Passing ability and IQ are elite as he makes plays where he clearly outthinks the opposition. When he plays with patience and outwaits players he is dominant. Great job using his reach to get the puck around the goalie on his goal. Was mishandling a lot of pucks today, and cheated leaving the defensive zone a couple times. His package of skills are unique and he stands out on the ice.

Crnkovic, Kyle (2020) - Played a super smart game, making very smart decisions with and without the puck. Scored with a great shot as the puck carrier on a 2 on 1 where he did an excellent job showing pass before sniping it with a quick release. Receives passes with a soft touch which allows him to make plays the second he gets the puck. Showed a good understanding of spacing and changed paces to open up gaps and allow teammates to get involved in plays.

Maier, Nolan (2019) - Not his night. Had a ton of plays today where he didn't track the puck well and looked like he was constantly scrambling. Let in multiple soft goals, with many coming at deflating times for his team.

Portland

Hanus, Clay (2019) - One of the best pure skaters amongst WHL draft eligibles with excellent agility and speed. Despite this doesn't always maximize this tool as he can skate himself into bad spots and attacks too north-south. Did a good job activating offensively in the rush and off the blue line where he was dangerous without the puck. With the puck he doesn't have a ton of creativity in his decision making. Jarvis, Seth- Consistently dangerous player who shows a ton of skill with the puck. Keeps defenders off balance playing a very shifty, unpredictable style. Was really strong protecting the puck for a smaller player, walling off significantly bigger players. Feet are always moving offensively and took really smart routes in to scoring areas and puck battles. Newkirk, Reece- Fairly quiet game as 3rd wheel on a line with Glass and Blichfeld. Very smart passer who understands how to get pucks around and through defenders. Consistently solid decision maker with and without the puck. Has a bit of a pest element to his game and was frequently in the mix after the whistle.

Vancouver Giants vs Victoria Royals, January 13, 2019

Vancouver

Byram, Bowen (2019) - Aggressive finding seams in the offensive zone and looked very natural making decisions on when to go. Generates a ton of offense off the rush where he is dangerous as a puck carrier and trailer. Was strong making plays in transition and is really good at drawing pressure and creating space. Has occasional turnovers where he doesn't take a look and just throws the puck away.

Sourdif, Justin (2020) - Looks like he's continued improving from the beginning of the year and was asserting himself much more. Sourdif is very shifty and crafty with the puck. Does a great job using his eyes and body positioning to deceive defenders and consistently makes skilled passes. Competes hard and is excellent at causing turnovers on the forecheck. His overall hockey IQ is very impressive.

Victoria

Fizer, Tarun (2019) - One of the few Victoria players with any real standout moments. Fizer is a very strong skater who did a good job getting in spots where he could receive passes and attack with speed. In the O-zone wasn't as dangerous as Victoria was generally limited to outside shots.

Youngstown Phantoms at USNTDP U18, January 15, 2019

Youngstown Phantoms -

Kuntar, Trevor - 2019 Seems like he wants to play a power forward style of game…there's some battle to him, a little bit of sandpaper. He made one carry where he shrugged off a checker and carried it deep along the boards, but based on the rest of the night, that was an anomaly…as he was knocked off the puck rather easily and often for the duration. The skating is a minus here. It's a real rough stride, especially the first step. He doesn't generate a lot of power or speed from it, he doesn't have a strong base to stay on the play/puck. His feet stop moving when he goes to make plays with his hands in any regard. Though he worked himself into decent position in the NZ because of the blue line lock style that Youngstown featured early, his coverage in the defensive zone was spotty. The game just sort of whizzed by him and he was waving his stick indiscriminately at passers by. I don't think he anticipates the play well enough to be a weapon in that regard. Played net-front on PP2 and was on what seemed to be the second line all night, but there isn't enough technical skill underneath the warts to see NHL potential.

Malone, Jack - 2019 Quick and hard working forward. His feet churn quickly and he can zip around the rink at a pretty good clip. His stride might not be that powerful, but the RPMs in his feet propel him plenty. Probably just a "B" skill level, good hands, good passing, but not a gamebreaker. Did generate goal off of his hard work though…received a pass curling high in the NZ, turned it into a semi-break, got a weak shot on and then gathered his own rebound to light the lamp. Threw one good hit, attempted and missed/narrowly hit on another. Played slot and down low on PP1. Took some faceoffs, but mostly lined up at RW. Presents an interesting blend of traits that are worth tracking.

USNTDP U18 -

Gildon, Michael - 2019 Gildon had a very passive game and didn't get involved too much. This isn't atypical for his season to date, as he is used pretty sparingly at the bottom of the lineup card. Offers much less in the way of skating and skill compared to the players ahead of him on the depth chart. Just a beat behind the play in virtually all facets.

Moynihan, Patrick - 2019 Excellent skater on a really strong skating base. Multi-directional mobility in spades. Smart and competitive player. Really works to keep plays alive and has the skill to do so consistently. He showed off a couple of quick hands plays early on that impressed. Not only that but his vision was surprisingly good, playing up in the lineup, he didn't miss a beat. He made three terrific passes across the net line in the first 25 minutes of the game. He doesn't waste a lot of time with getting shots away, he can whip them pretty good…even if they're in close to his feet or a little bit behind him. He actually looks much taller on the rink than his vitals indicate. May be a real hidden gem surrounded by a lot of high-end talents at the rate he has progressed this season.

Hughes, Jack - 2019 Pretty much the Jack Hughes came you come to expect. Speed, skill, transition hockey, playmaking, he had in firing on all cylinders in his first USHL game in five weeks. As usual, he made several creative, if not adventurous, passes that led to scoring chances. He had a couple of in-close looks as well, that were held out of the net early in the game before the dam was burst. He ended up with a three point night as part of a big win. One thing that's interesting about Hughes is that he never really stops moving, and that sounds like a positive, but sometimes you see him leaving areas – particularly in the attack zone – that he might be better served to settle into for a beat or two… for a couple reasons: that's a soft area where he's open to shoot or make a play and because I think a high-end player will expect him to be there. There were two instances in the NZ where he was trying to run a weave with another player and Hughes took what should be considered the wrong lane given the circumstances. He was -5 in the dot while the game was still in the balance. Reasonably, these remarks have an "over scouting" feel to them…

Regina Pats vs Kootenay Ice, January 16, 2019

Regina

Sedov, Nikita (2020) - His strongest game I have seen, calm and in control with the puck today. Great job QBing the PP distributing well to both sides and holding PKers in his shooting lane to open things up for teammates. Passes were consistently on the tape and moved at the right time. Very fluid player who can distribute pucks and showed good sense offensively. Needs to add some strength as he can get outmuscled down low.

Kootenay

McClennon, Connor (2020) - Tenacious and unafraid of contact despite his smaller frame. Battled hard but didn't really show a ton skill wise today. Took 2 massive hits today which were both on plays where he put himself in very bad spots, and as a result left injured.

Krebs, Peyton (2019) - One of the league's top playmakers and most dynamic players. Was skating really well today, generating a ton of clean zone entries. Excels on odd man rushers both as a shooter and passer, consistently making unique plays. Makes some unreal anticipation passes where he sees where the guy is going to be open before he's there. Very hard to contain from down low as he protects the puck so well and loves using 10-2 turns to spin away from defenders while surveying the ice for passes. Compete level is through the roof, as he never lets himself get outworked for pucks.

Fargo Force at Sioux Falls Stampede, January 16, 2019

Fargo Force -

Fiedler, Cedric - 2019 Sizable defender who sort of gallops around the rink. Not a very fluid skater, has a little hitch step that makes the whole operation look questionable. Very reactive defender who on more than one occasion was left just flailing. Early on, he made a horrendous turnover against a very easy forecheck…it led directly to an "A" scoring chance. Didn't show much in terms of puck skills or reliable outlet passing. He doesn't defend nearly enough to make up for these deficiencies.

Bohlsen, Kaden - 2019 Bohlsen wasn't seeing top-six minutes in this game and played a heavier game as opposed to a skill game as a result. He had more than a couple very good, very deliberate forechecks that jarred pucks loose. He made three strong hit attempts and was a plus in the dot. Showed good hockey sense and took the right angles to almost every puck and board battle. Plus skater under a big, scalable frame.

Nodler, Josh - 2019 Good work from Nodler tonight. Got a tip-in down-low on PP1 to open the scoring. Showed some of his limitation later when he received a pass in the low NZ with a chance to break through, but he just didn't have a good enough burst with the puck on his stick and was lassoed by the d-man quickly enough to negate a chance. Just an average or slightly above average skater overall, augmented though, by a good work ethic. He just has "C" level hands in space. Not sure he offers enough from a pure tools perspective to be a player, but he's worth tracking.

Sioux Falls Stampede -

Phillips, Ethan - 2019 Little quieter game than usual for Phillips, but it was also a game that didn't feature a lot of attack time for long periods on either side. He continues to show he's a high-end skater with a good shot, very strong hockey sense, and "B" level skill. He works hard at both ends of the rink too. His size can sometimes make it tough for him, but he works his way into the areas he needs to and has a good sense for the timing of the game.

Tabakin, Brandon - 2019 Mobile defenseman with crafty hands. His game is maybe a little too complicated for its own good sometimes…this was evidenced early on when Tabakin threw two picks away trying to do too much with it. Further, he's sometimes a little impatient defensively…he's aggressive, he wants to turn pucks over go the other way, and sometimes he picks his spot wrong or he gets his shoulders off their line and gifts an area that the puck carrier didn't earn. At the line he has the change of direction skating that buys him a lot of real estate. Even behind the net, his skating and head fakes and misdirection allow him to shake forecheckers reliably. He has the puck skills to match too. It's odd to see such low point totals for the season, because it doesn't jive with his talent level.

Johnson, Ryan - 2019 Fluid skater. Very modern style, stick-first defender. Was very casual and not very aggressive in pushing the offensive pace. Had one strong rush that originated in the NZ, but he failed to negotiate the puck to the interior, or even back to his forehand once he got in to the scoring area. He shows flashes of 1st round potential from a skill perspective, but so much of the time he handles the puck in such a non-chalant fashion. I don't know that he's not too calm for his own good sometimes. I'd like to see him take over the play a little more often than he does. He lets a lot of the game come to him…which isn't to say he doesn't manage it well, because he does…he's in the right spots often. But you get the sense that there's more there if he ever wanted to rev it up. He did sneak down to the top of the circle to get a quick one-timer off to break a mid-3rd period tie. Well-placed shot, but not powerful.

Swankler, Austen - 2019 Really showed some good reads tonight, more so than any previous viewing. Very dialed into the game. He took some really terrific angles on the forecheck. He sniffed out a few breakouts in the NZ too. His closing speed is the most impressive part of his skating package. Swankler's stride is a little bit loose, but the top speed is strong. His forechecking is aided by a good reach too. Plus, his willingness to be physical. He made one good NZ hit and took a big run at another one late, but didn't get all of it. Just "C" hands, kind of chops the puck up a little bit. Looks like a player that isn't quite used to his own size yet too from a coordination standpoint.

Lincoln Stars at Madison Capitols, January 17th 2018

Lincoln Stars

Pinto, Shane – 2019 It was a bit of an off game for Pinto in this game. Pinto missed on two excellent scoring chances, one where he shot over the top of the net on a Grade A scoring chance in the slot as well as didn't convert on a back door play with the goalie out of position, scoring chances he hasn't missed on much of this season. Pinto did make some good defensive reads and plays, especially on the Penalty Kill where his active stick took away lanes and intercepted passes, one of which created a shorthanded chance but Pinto, being late in his shift on the PK got caught from behind by the Madison defender who made a good play to negate the breakaway. Pinto showed some poor judgment late in the game where he attempted a drop pass at his own blue line with the game tied that almost resulted in a goal. While Pinto struggled for stretches of this game, this was a bit of an outlier for him so far this year.

Skinner, Hunter – 2019 In his first game with Lincoln since being traded from Muskegon, Skinner was Lincoln's best defenseman in this game, making plays at both ends. Skinner showed excellent skating mobility and explosiveness to escape pressure but also in joining the rush and getting back in the play quickly when the play goes the other way. Skinner has good vision of the ice and moved the puck effectively at both ends and was able to shield the puck to buy himself time and always left himself outs with the puck. In the offensive end, Skinner showed a good one-time with velocity and the ability to get it off even if the passes were not on a tee for him. Skinner saw the offensive zone well and moved the puck accurately in the zone which resulted in 2 primary assists in this game.

Lee, Justin – 2019+ Lee is a slightly undersized defenseman but played bigger than his size in this game. While he didn't register any points, Lee was key to Lincoln exiting their own end quickly and used his plus skating ability to defend against the rush and using position and leverage to keep opposing players to the outside. His footwork allowed him to change and open up lanes from the point and move the puck in the offensive end.

Power, Jordan – 2019 Power showed the skating ability to join and lead the rush out of his own end but made some poor decisions and took some aggressive lanes with the puck that resulted in turnovers in key situations and could of benefited from simplifying his game coming out of his own end. Power did a good job identifying pressure and communicating with his defensive partner. Power didn't show a lot of playmaking ability in the offensive end.

Hlavaj, Samuel – 2019 Samuel joined Lincoln after the World Junior and getting his 3rd start for the Stars in this game. Hlavaj displayed aggressive positioning; challenging shooters in 1 on 1 situation however saw a few shots get through his body and seemed to battle with some pucks on the glove side. Hlavej showed good athleticism, making some good saves in moving laterally and takes away the lower portion of the net well.

Lopina, Josh – 2019 Lopina was slotted as the 3rd line center. Lopina has good size and has good skating speed and agility but didn't create much offensively in this game. Lopina didn't show the ability to use his speed or size to his advantage and struggled getting the puck to scoring areas but was effective and physical on the fore-check and made a couple good defensive plays in the neutral zone to breakup some line rushes by Madison.

Sioux City Musketeers at Madison Capitols, January 18th 2019

Sioux City

Stange, Sam – 2019 Stange, playing the 1st of a 2 game call up from his Eau Claire North High School Team certainly had an adjustment period early in the game, playing on the top line with Martin Pospisil and Jordan Steinmetz. Stange tried going against the grain and reverse the play in his own end a couple of times that resulted in additional defensive zone time for his team but eventually did a better job of getting pucks out of the zone along the wall. Stange showed an explosive first couple strides and good top end speed and once he adjusted to the speed of the game, eventually settled in and made some good plays with the puck. Showed his explosiveness late in the game when he challenged the play at the point and chipped the puck out of the zone and won the race to the loose puck and scored the ENG, sealing the win for Sioux City.

Kallionkieli, Marcus – 2019 Marcus showed good stick handling in tight areas and a good compete level along the boards, where he initiated contact and was able to use his size to his advantage in protecting the puck and winning puck battles but struggled to create chances on his own. Marcus failed to get the puck out of his own end or get pucks deep in the offensive end on a couple situations and made some errant passes in the neutral zone that stalled some line rushes. In the offensive zone Kallionkieli saw a couple good scoring chances that he didn't convert on, one of which was missing the net with teammates in front on the power play, as he came down from the half wall one on one with the goaltender, resulting in the puck to wrap around the boards and out of the zone.

Kehrer, Anthony – 2020 Kehrer stood out as Sioux City's best defenseman in this game. His puck retrievals and plays with the puck under pressure were very good and showed the ability to stretch the ice both north and south and east and west coming out of his own end. Anthony showed great skating agility and explosiveness in order to separate from the fore-check. In the offensive end, Kehrer had a lot of clean zone entries with the puck and would look for opportunities to come down from the point. Kehrer's skating ability allowed him to keep a good gap in the neutral zone and challenge players to make plays at the blue line, forcing offside plays on a couple of instances.

Kraws, Ben – 2019+ Kraws is a tall lanky goaltender that takes away the lower part of the net well. While Kraws wasn't challenged a ton in this game, but he made some hard saves look routine late in the game and was calm when traffic was near the crease. Kraws is in his 2nd year of draft eligibility and in this game looked much more comfortable and confident than a year ago.

Everett Silvertips vs Kelowna Rockets, January 18, 2019

Everett

Seeley, Ronan (2020) - Smooth skating defenseman showed very well. Made a couple nice plays on the breakout where he used his skating and change of direction to create passing options. Generated many shots with a couple coming from dangerous spots. Looked confident and mobile walking the blue line. Showed traits offensively that could allow him to emerge next season.

Kelowna

Korczak, Kaeden (2019) - Solid skater and plays a strong defensive game. Good at keeping attackers to the outside and frequently wins his battles. With the puck is a very rigid stickhandler and was consistently spraying his passes behind/in the feet/in front of his teammates. Also makes too many plays where he just throws the puck off the window without even thinking.

Thomson, Lassi (2019) - Tools are very impressive. Thomson is one of the better players in the league leading a breakout. Used the whole ice as a passer spreading the defense with accurate cross seam breakout passes, stretch passes, and utilizing the middle of the ice. When he decides to the lead the rush Thomson is great as he has the hands and edgework to beat players in open ice. He really standouts with his ability to cut past players and maintain speed. Has a strong physical aspect to his game as he throws checks when he can. Makes lots of very creative plays that show how well he processes the game. In the O-zone he is a threat with his big one timer.

Foote, Nolan (2019) - Solid but unspectacular game. Foote plays heavy and showed a good ability to skate through checks. He competes hard and is strong in battles, winning with good body work and a heavy stick. Good instincts offensively with his passing and play without the puck. Plays a ton, rarely off the ice for more than a couple minutes as he's used on both PK and PP on top of heavy even strength usage.

Sioux City Musketeers at Chicago Steel, January 19, 2019

Sioux City Musketeers -

Pasanen, Tommy - 2019 Huge, strong, physical defender. Good skating base for his size, pretty quick…really no flaws in his skating game for his size. He really loves the battle…to the point where he will ignore the puck and stick to the front of the net just to give someone the business. Really makes it a point to put players down in front or along the boards and isn't afraid to use his stick to do it. Pretty loose gap player…maybe not even gaps against the rush, but just his ability to manage space is not a fit for the modern game. He is so intent on playing a passive, defensive style that it's to his detriment defensively…he makes trouble for himself by not keeping 70/30 pucks in the zone or allowing a talented player to build up too much speed in the NZ against him. It looks like he would have a plus shot, but his puck poise is so low that he just whips things into traffic from 60 feet without the care to make a better play if one were available.

Stange, Sam - 2019 First shift of his second USHL game of the season started with a good NZ pickpocket and then a good attempt at a second. Didn't end up finding a lot of open space, but he seemed to have B/C skill level when he did have the disc. Plus skater, good quickness…but particularly his closing speed is remarkable. He can get up on puck carriers quick. Good balance too. A couple of times he stopped his feet on plays that it seemed obvious how he could support the puck…they were always in situations when the puck was or was likely to be in his team's possession. Not sure if it was tentativeness not to make a mistake defensively given his inexperience at this level, or if it's a hole in his game…but hopefully he improves on his ability to get open and support the puck, because otherwise he shows good anticipation. Above average shot release.

Chicago Steel -

Treloar, Travis - 2019 Easy player to lose in the grand scheme of the game. Did feature on the PK with first unit time. He has a really good shot…he one-timed home a mid-range bomb on a major power play that broke the game open. Other than that, he doesn't move the needle much in the game…below average skater that doesn't appear to bring much else than a shot. Even if he had some skill (which he may very well have), he isn't quick or savvy or strong enough to use it any pertinent way.

Abruzzese, Nick - 2019 Smart, playmaking center. Plus skater. Good head for the game, communicates with teammates well on the rink. Skill level is maybe C+/B-, but it's nothing next level. How well can he work in a tighter, faster game is the question…and I think that will be a real challenge for him. If he's as adaptable as he is smart, he's got a fighting chance.

Scored on a cross-ice tap in at the top of the crease. It was a good read to cut in far post and the defenseman Pasanen took the player down the middle instead of managing the lane, leaving Abruzzese wide open for first goal of the game. He does come back defensively, but only because he's a veteran it looks like…not because he's a particularly sticky defensive player. Two-way play might not be his default setting, but he puts in some effort – it's appreciated. Just a bit below sea level on faceoffs tonight. Despite being a '99 at this level, there are still times when he just boots the puck or whiffs on it…you'd really like that to be worked out of your system by now in his situation ideally.

HV71 u20 at Djurgarden IF u20 January 19 2019

HV71 u20

Holmstrom, Simon 2019 Holmstrom was very active and involved from the first puck drop. He has only played a couple games since the return from his latest injury and it was at times obvious he was a bit rusty, but he gave it his all and competed hard at all times.

He worked as hard defensively as he did offensively, in spite of the fact that his strengths lie in his offensive abilities. He was dominant on the power play, where no one could steal the puck from him. He did look like he really wanted to impress but sometimes held the puck for too long instead. No points today, but an overall good two-way performance.

Alnefelt, Hugo 2019 Alnefelt did come up big a couple times, saving his team from conceding sure goals. Those saves looked panicky and he showed tendencies to fall forwards. This led to him lying down, swimming in his own crease rather often. He goes down to his butterfly early, leaving big chunks of open net high above his shoulders.

Gronhagen, Jacob 2019 Gronhagen is BIG and strong! And not surprisingly is he lacking speed and explosivity. However, he does think the game very well, making smart, well-thought decisions. He did show that he wanted to compete and he did not want to lose this game

Sarnia Sting vs. Peterborough Petes, January 19th, 2019

Sarnia

Sproviero, Franco (FA) - Sproviero had a strong game demonstrating several skills to his game. He displayed strong vision to feather passes through seams which led to Sarnia 2nd goal. He possesses good acceleration and puck skill to create scoring chances. He is a strong skater with good edgework. As the game progressed he began to shoot the puck demonstrating an accurate shot including one shot that he placed right under the crossbar, blocker side on Jones. Franco showed a strong work ethic tonight, was hard on pucks and very seldom took a shift off.

Rees, Jamieson (2019) - Rees is a smart center who displayed good potential as a playmaker and a scoring threat. As the game progressed he began shooting the puck more. He drove the slot and scored top corner off a loose puck for his 1st goal of the game, showed good awareness to jump into the rush to create a 2 on 1 which led to his 1st goal. He is a good skater who possesses good speed and can attack defenders inside or outside. He was responsible for taking late game offensive and defensive zone draws. Jamieson played a really good 200 foot game tonight for Sarnia. He showed well on the half wall of the power play retrieving pucks and moving pucks efficiently.

Peterborough

Čermák, Erik (2019) - Erik displayed some good offensive skill and puck possession using his speed to carry the puck into scoring areas. He made a great toe drag move to cut into the middle of the ice and showed a good release on his slap shot for a quality scoring chance. He is a good skater who used his speed to back check and help out in the defensive zone. He showed creativity making good passes through defenders and possesses good instinct for loose pucks. He also set up another power play goal with a great cross-crease pass to backdoor for an easy tap in goal.

Robertson, Nick (2019) - Robertson displayed strong hands as the go-to shooter and triggerman in Peterborough line-up. He displayed an intelligence to know where to be on the ice and how to create separation and become open in the offensive zone for a one-time shooting opportunity. His release and scoring ability are amongst the best in the OHL, and it showed on his first goal of the night, found open spot in slot, took onetimer and beat goalie high glove side. He was engaged in all zones and provided a strong presence along the boards in the defensive zones battling and recovering pucks.

Jones, Hunter (2019) - Jones played a strong game for the Petes tonight, making 31 saves on 34 shots. He wasn't tested much early in the game, but made a few big saves when necessary, once on a breakaway and again in the second period in close on the rush. He showed quick reflexes and did a great job covering the net up high. He had little chance on the first goal against, which was a perfectly placed one timer that was put top shelf from the edge of the crease. He had good vision through traffic and was controlling his rebounds better as the game wore on.

Portland Winterhawks vs Tri City Americans, January 20, 2019

Portland

Hanus, Clay (2019) - Had a very good game today, getting more out of his tools than he usually does. Mobility is excellent, can move in any direction so fast. Is very good at shooting the puck while in motion, either of a drag or as he receives a pass. Competes really hard and despite the occasional misread have some confidence in him developing in this area. Sometimes with the puck doesn't really seem to know what to do with the puck when his first options are taken away.

Jarvis, Seth (2020) - Always around the puck, and works to win it. Jarvis compete level is excellent and he is always one of the hardest workers on the ice. Generated a ton of chances today with his passing as he was moving the puck to the right areas with good timing. Continues to impress more and more with each viewing.

Newkirk, Reece (2019) - Centered a line with Jarvis and Dureau today where he got to showcase more than he does with Glass and Blichfeld. Always puts himself in good positions and because of this could handle defensive responsibility at the centre ice role. Also showed more skill in his puckhandling ability as he was making plays to beat players in the ozone when forced.

Tri City

Sasha Mutala (2019) - When he has the puck in the zone you can see his skill but doesn't really bring it in the neutral zone or dzone. Had some plays where he beat defenders with really good edgework, but generally a pretty quiet night.

Boyko, Talyn (2021) - Massive goalie is not eligible until 2021 but had a phenomenal game, leading Tri City to an upset tonight. Looked raw and was a bit over active in net but recovered for some very nice desperation saves. Athletic tools are definitely there.

Frölunda HC u18 at AIK u18 January 20 2019

Frölunda HC u18

Svensson, Liam 2019 Svensson has great size and skates pretty decent. He showed good puck skills, but not often enough. Looked lazy and uninterested for most of the game. He did not want to engage in any physical play, whatsoever.

AIK u18

Vikman, Jesper 2020 Vikman was a big presence in net all game. He has good size, but stands a bit crouched at times, making him smaller than he actually is. He competed hard and were vocal with his defenders. Did not get put to any big, physical tests since the opposition did not really want to battle in front of the net.

Madison Capitols at Central Illinois Flying Aces, January 21, 2019

Central Illinois Flying Aces -

Breen, Lynden - 2019 Diminutive, nimble centerman with a good work ethic. Breen does a lot of things fast and well. His legs churn quickly, his mind moves quickly, he gets set and puts his stick down for faceoffs quickly…he's a Rudy, essentially. Quick feet and is very quick off the blocks. His top speed is good, but I'm not sure I see a real pull away gear. That could be a product of stride length and leg speed, he has the upside to have that next gear based on technique. He'll need to be fast if he wants to make it, because he's not very hockey strong and he has trouble withstanding contact and remaining on his blades. Just a little better than average hands and a weak shot. He is defensively responsible though and a heady passer, which he showed all night. He worked both PP1 and a later-wave PK shift. Was tasked with defending a one-goal late after the previous shift of players gave one up, but he, too, was unsuccessful in preserving the lead. Was a plus player in the dot today. Offers a lot of detail work, and the upside for more. Which is nice because the skill isn't overwhelming…but it's tough to watch him and not see a little bit of a young Paul Byron.

Janicke, Trevor - 2019 Good pace, especially early from Janicke. Sort of a hulking style of player at times, looks a little bigger than his vitals. Only one real hit attempt in the game though, he's not much of a bruiser. Certainly more of a shooter. He tried to put a couple on today, but missed. Including a one-time chance from the left side of the power play that missed well wide. Has strong top speed. He's a good worker. Very competent skater…legs are churning a good bit while he's out there. He took longer than average shifts today at least, his first shift may have been 100 seconds. He works and communicates well on the ice. Maybe just average hockey sense though…there are things in the game he can eyeball and figure out the geometry of, but there's certain things he can't sense…so it's a little hit or miss in this regard. He ends up with the puck behind his own end line to start the rush an odd amount of times – may be coaching related. He has the hands to navigate the less clustered parts of the rink, but when he gets in tight, he's just a little short in this regard…but his hands aren't slow, probably "B" hands. Janicke constantly cheats on faceoffs by never coming to a full stop and he really crowds the dot. He may be more clever by half in these scenarios, because it seems like he often goes "over" the puck and misses it. Was put out on PP1 and PK2 duties. Was put over the boards to defend a late lead, but was unsuccessful. Then was put on to battle back from a late deficit and was unsuccessful. He didn't take the faceoff on either of his last two in shifts in those crucial spots.

Saginaw Spirit vs Peterborough Petes, Jan 24 2019

Spirit -

Porco, Nicholas (2019) – Porco had a solid performance for Saginaw by using his speed to generate scoring chances consistently throughout the game. He has a powerful first-step and although he skates upright, he still has a good knee bend that allows him to generate power which each stride. This allowed him to pressure at the blueline when in the defensive-end which gave him a takeaway, as well as separate himself on a breakaway where he elevated the puck on his backhand in-tight to the net. He also found soft-ice consistently in the slot area and displayed okay vision, though the creativity wasn't on display. Although he played a north-south, streamlined type of game, he rushed the puck while displaying the ability to generate offense while going at his top-gear.

Perfetti, Cole (2020) – Perfetti wasn't consistent and didn't drive play but he did flash a dynamic offensive-skill set. One attribute that stood out was his ability to mask his intentions with the puck, it was difficult for the Petes defense to tell when he was going to shoot or pass. This was largely due to his posturing when carrying the puck. He also showed plus anticipation and used it to find soft-ice in the slot area before he fired a bar-down wrist-shot goal that the Petes netminder had no chance on, it was a high-end release point. In the corners, he was largely ineffective, getting easily out-muscled and thrown off the puck but that didn't prevent him from attempting to drive through heavy traffic, which resulted in an impressive individual effort where he side-stepped a Petes player and skated in alone before firing a quick wrist-shot short-side that required a high-end save.

Millman, Mason (2019) – Millman had a solid game for the Spirits, playing a physical brand of hockey that resulted in several impressive hits while maintaining a heavy presence in the corners. He made a nice recovery play where he backcheck aggressively after a turnover occurred and used his frame properly to throw a Petes player off a puck which negated a point-blank scoring chance. Although his edge-work and pivoting never stood out, he increased his pace in his own-end when needed which allowed him to keep his opponents largely to the outside. Under-pressure, he moved the puck but not too efficiently, just enough to get the job done. In the offensive-end, he showed the ability to fake a shot in order to readjust his lane but never flashed any sort of high-end offensive-skill. Millman largely played a shutdown game and did it well.

Petes -

Spearing, Shawn (2020) – Spearing had a solid two-way performance for the Petes while playing on a line with Merkley. He had one of the more impressive defensive sequences in the game where he maintained a good gap, kept his opponent to the outside, then delivered a clean hit, followed by a good box-out effort in-front of the net that showed a plus compete level while using his frame and stick to angle himself under his opponent. Lastly, he anticipated a shot and got into the lane to block it properly where he it was angled into the corner; those above plays characterized his complete defensive game that he showcased out there, showing good man-to-man coverage, rarely getting beaten wide, and showing an attention to detail away from the puck. In the offensive-end, he managed to get his shot through traffic and showed some deception by trying a shot-pass that was close to getting redirected in-front of the net. He also moved laterally well at the line and displayed enough two-step area quickness to cover ground when needed, though his straight-line speed was lacking due to a short-stride and a lack of a proper knee-bend.

Butler, Cameron (2020) – Butler was decent for the Petes, flashing his impressive tools while also scoring on a goal on the man-advantage. With Robertson at the top-prospects game, it was an opportunity for Cameron to step-up, but he wasn't overly effective at even-strength, showing only flashes as opposed to a complete offensive game. He didn't manage to use his impressive skating and size to pressure effectively enough on the forecheck which has occurred in some previous viewings but did anticipate some plays away from the puck in the neutral zone. He scored a snap-shot goal from the left-circle which Prosvetov had little chance of getting too, the shot generated a ton of power and was shot in one-motion. On a rush down the right-wing, he showed plus agility for his size, moved laterally quickly to dodge a Spirit defenseman before trying to find his teammate but the pass was disrupted.

Frölunda at Linköping, Jan 24. 2019

FRÖLUNDA

FHC # 11 LW Fagemo, Samuel (2019) - 2000 born LW that constant during the game used his good speed and was shooting quit much and accurate. He works home and use the speed for good forechecks. Fagemo placed himself good and was moving to be visualized and available for shots. He was good in defending by locking the stick for opponents. Fagemo did a nice pass backwards in front of the net that was difficult to read. Fagemo got a hit but took it good; he noticed the hit in advanced.

FHC # 22 LW Nässen, Linus (2019) - Nässen only got 2.48 TOI. I Only noticed a nice delivered pass in to the slot and one decent SOG.

Youngstown Phantoms at Tri-City Storm, January 25, 2019

Youngstown Phantoms -

Kuntar, Trevor - 2019 Not very effective tonight. His skating and hockey strength are not up to par, and they limit his impact on the game. The overall skill package is also pretty limited, which is augmented by the fact that he can't use his hands while his feet are in motion.

Malone, Jack - 2019 The boxscore was not charitable to Malone, who was one of the few players who showed up tonight for Youngstown. As usual, he played in all situations. Showed off his very quick feet and smart forechecking throughout. He has a strong frame that has a lot of potential in and of itself. He works well in open ice, and can make skill plays while he's moving. His skating/skill/smarts/work ethic package give off the impression that he'll be a versatile player as he moves up the ladder. Even for Youngstown, he can play C and RW depending on the situation. The development path for Malone may end up being based on his ability to make skill plays in tight spots, I'm not convinced he can do that yet…but if he can, it changes his trajectory significantly. There's a lot to like in this package…even if the ceiling isn't remarkably high, he looks like a player that's going to be able to carve out a role for himself as a pro.

Tri-City Storm -

Pinto, Shane - 2019 First game with first place Tri-City after being traded from last place Lincoln. Pinto didn't play more than third line minutes as he assimilates to his new team. He only saw power play time later in the game. He was pretty quiet early on. As the game went on, and he got some more shifts, he warmed up and looked more comfortable. Played exclusively on the wing tonight, mostly drawing defenders wide to set up players coming down the center lane with speed. He finished a couple hits tonight. He doesn't rev up his skating a lot, but he can move surprisingly well with his long stride. Namely, with his closing speed on loose pucks or players in compromised position with the puck. His stride isn't pretty, but he can move when he needs to. Notched the goal that doused a mini-rally in the 3rd. It was a 2-on-2 rush where he pushed the d-man back, used some nice moves to work his way into the middle, the d-man surrendered his leverage and Pinto shot a BB into the top part of the net with a wicked release. It will be interesting to track how Pinto reacts to having some talent around him, he had a lot of freedom…and had to take a lot more…in Lincoln. Pinto left Lincoln representing over one-third of their total offense output.

Jones, Zac - 2019 Very competent skater, but nothing electric for a player of his size. Jones does show some flashes of skill, but it looks like mostly junior skill and not a lot that's transferable. He has a plus shot, preferring the wrist shot from distance over a big wind-up. His release isn't terribly enticing though. Defended around his net fairly well all net. He wasn't tested a ton by the opponent or by the game script, so he wasn't defending all that much. He did make a challenging clear on the PK in the middle part of the game. In fairness to Jones, who plays a ton, this was the start of a three-game weekend for him and he may have been conserving energy in a game where Tri-City jumped out to an early lead. He played LD all night, PP1, and some second-shift PK time.

Attard, Ronnie - 2019 Leggy defensemen with a high center of gravity. Pretty quiet game overall, didn't make a lot of rush attempts – which had been noted in previous glimpses. Just an average skater with a fairly inefficient stride. The skill level didn't impress too much, but he was paired with Zac Jones most of the night, who did a little more of the heavy-lifting in this regard. Attard has a plus shot and played in all situations all night. Including RD at ES. This was the first game of a three-game weekend for Attard, which may have influenced his play tonight.

Duluth East Greyhounds at Prior Lake Lakers, January 25th 2019

Duluth East Greyhounds

Donovan, Ryder – 2019 Donovan logged a ton of minutes in this game, MNHS doesn't track ice time but he likely played half of the game. Donovan showed good anticipation at the top of the penalty kill, aggressively attacking the points and showed the willingness to block shots and created shorthanded scoring chances for his team. Donovan has an extra gear with the puck and showed the willingness to drive the net but also was able to pull up and slow the game down in the offensive zone and get the puck to scoring areas. Duluth East was shutout in this game but Ryder created a lot of scoring chances in this game that his line mates were not able to convert on. Donovan also showcased a good one-time from the half wall on the power play. At times Donovan looked to lack effort and willingness to compete for pucks but some had to do with the number of minutes he's asked to play and him picking his spots. Donovan showed is stretches the willingness to be physical and use his size in battles.

Prior Lake Lakers

Jutting, Jackson – 2019 Jutting isn't an explosive skater but it didn't affect his game as he was quick to jump on loose pucks and showed the ability to read the play, take good angles to pucks and know where to be on the ice to have the puck on his stick a lot. Jutting showed a good compete level in all zones and was a key part of his team pulling the upset in this game. Jutting was impressive in the faceoff circle, winning many drawls cleanly, especially when he was head to head with Ryder Donovan. Jutting was on the point on the power play where he was efficient with his puck movement and showed a quick release from the point on his teams 2nd goal that was deflected in front.

University of Wisconsin at University of Minnesota, January 26th, 2019

University of Minnesota

Brinkman, Ben – 2019 Despite hardly getting any time on Special Teams this season, Brinkman continues to be an effective shut down defenseman for the Gophers and was their best defenseman in this game. Brinkman's gaps were extremely good in this game, which isn't always easy on the large Olympic sized Ice sheet that the Gophers play on, but Brinkman's skating agility and footwork is high end. Brinkman was physical along the walls, delivering some big hits throughout the game as well as making things hard on the Wisconsin forwards in front of his own net. Would have liked to see Brinkman get more involved in the offensive end, however did show good puck skills to stickhandle around a

Wisconsin player and come down the slot where he was hooked and drew a penalty on the play. Brinkman picked his spots to skate the puck out of his own end but did a good job not holding onto the puck for long stretches and progressed through his reads and moved the puck accurately, especially in the neutral zone where time and space is at a minimum. Despite playing top 4 minutes, out of Minnesota's 6 defenseman that took regular shifts, Brinkman was the only defenseman to not finish the game in the minus.

Val-d'Or Foreurs at Drummondville Voltigeurs, January 26th, 2019

Val-d'Or

#21 Guenette, Maxence (2019): Not very active in the offensive game; he preferred to play a non-flashy, safe game. Guenette was playing on the 2nd power play unit and didn't take good shots on net. His shot selection was poor, and he was slow to get his shot off (one of them was blocked and led to a scoring chance by Drummondville). He has good footwork and smarts and that helps him with his play in his own end, but he failed to make an offensive impact.

#77 Biakabutuka, Jeremie (2020): His decision-making was a bit slow, and this hurt him against a speedy team like Drummondville. He did show some good puck skills; he made some good passes throughout the game and showed good vision in the offensive zone. However, his footwork was average; in his own zone, he didn't move his feet well and that hurt him when attempting to contain opposing forwards or to retrieve pucks.

#92 Michel, Jeremy (2019): He flashed some of his skills today. He was shooting the puck well and made things happen in the first two periods of the game. Unfortunately, he played on the perimeter too often in the offensive zone. He could have had more success by playing more in the tougher areas of the ice. He has decent speed and played regularly on the power play (mostly in the half wall position).

#24 Gaucher, Jacob (2019): The big center didn't get very many opportunities to touch the puck today and was not very noticeable on the ice in offensive situations. However, Val-d'Or was overmatched in general in terms of puck-possession time. He worked hard away from the puck; he was often seen coming back in his zone supporting his defensemen to retrieve pucks behind his net.

Drummondville

#81 Simoneau, Xavier (2019): This was a much better performance from him compared to last night against Rouyn-Noranda. He showed how good of a passer and playmaker he can be by making some very nice passes to his linemates all game long. Good puck poise in the offensive zone, which helped him make those nice passes to his teammates. His compete level and work ethic was on par with his usual level; he played a physical, in-your-face type of game. He's quick and agile on his skates, but his straight-away and top speeds are only average.

#19 Mercer, Dawson (2020): He was a regular on the 1st power play unit, but he didn't get many puck touches, as the puck was usually on the sticks of Veleno, Beaudin or Comtois. Throughout the game, he showed a good release on his wrist shot, but he needs some work in regards to his accuracy. He had some good scoring chances, but didn't take good shots on net. His shots were often found in the goalie's crease. Liked his agility on the ice. His speed is fine, but he does a good job beating guys one-on-one due to his agility and footwork.

USNTDP U18 at Muskegon Lumberjacks, January 26, 2019

USNTDP U18 -

Helleson, Drew - 2019 Not a great game from Helleson. His hands seemed pretty heavy night in the rare instances where he was hanging on to it. Most of the time he was just sliding pucks to his partner. Transition skating looks a little rough. He takes a lot of unnecessary contact because of the lack of overall fluidity to his game…just not very smooth in any area, still a raw player in all facets. Needs to do a better job managing his triangle for starters. Pucks get in close on him – offensively or defensively – and he gets antsy quick.

Thrun, Henry - 2019 Had a fine night, in a game that his team dominated much of. He's a plus skater and really generates some good straight line speed. His stride isn't beautiful when moving laterally, but it's very serviceable. He's a little straight-legged, but he gets around the rink fine. He doesn't do anything fancy with the puck. He doesn't handle it like a grenade either. His puck carrying skills aren't meaningfully enticing. Thrun doesn't show the plus skill level necessary to get pucks into the interior of the rink or to beat defenders. In fact, Thrun pushes himself into the gutter almost immediately when he has the puck in space, which really halves his cause. Made two unforced errors to start the 2nd period…one of which was a whirling no-look pass that went right to the tape of a Lumberjack without a clear recipient in sight. Later, he snuck into the slot for a one-time attempt but whiffed. He doesn't have a very strong shot that he can reliably get away anyhow.

Knight, Spencer - 2019 Didn't face a shot on net for more than 15 minutes of game action to start. Kept himself occupied with some stick plays though. He made a good two-line pass to spring a PP breakout. Later in the game, he tossed some backhand sauce while looking off a forechecker. On the PK in the 1st, he made a really good read to scoop the puck along the end boards to the far side to help get a clear…Muskegon had had possession for a good stretch before then, this wasn't a dump-in, this was a very aggressive in-zone play. Very good skater. Anticipates the play very well. Wasn't challenged early, only facing two weak shots in the 1st, he didn't yield a rebound on either of them. He erased a Henry Thrun mistake early in the 2nd with no rebound either. Made a great save to mop up a rebound with a strong push all the way to the other post and then zipped up the puck for good. He is so well anchored for a young goalie, even on big pushes he never loses his net. Very composed, very poised. Has a good grasp of who the threats are, who can/might shoot the puck and doesn't waste a lot of energy or movement to challenge players that he doesn't believe to be a shooting threat. Which means he isn't getting up and down all game…very economical. He's a reverse VH goalie in terms of post integration, but it's used much more responsibly than some young goalies coming through these days. He doesn't go right into that setup on plays that develop in the circles…he uses it on plays that develop below the end line, which is better use. Particularly because even average players are able to make that low angle shot over the shoulder these days. The goal that he surrendered was not very stoppable given the circumstances. There's no reasonable way that a goalie can shut that down after having to make the initial push that he did…he would have needed to really have his stick strongly positioned right on the money. It was an otherwise flawless victory for Knight.

Muskgeon Lumberjacks -

Bukes, Colby - 2019 Pretty typical game for Bukes. Really good skater, made a few good puck plays and did a lot to drive what little offense Muskegon could muster tonight. Did get beat to the inside defending Danny Weight because of a mistimed crossover. Did get a good enough piece of John Beecher in the NZ to eventually spill him to the ice. Seems to model his game after Kristopher Letang in a lot of ways.

Afanasyev, Yegor - 2019 Leggy winger. Good multi-directional fluidity to his skating stride, but is a little goofy with the straight line speed with his hunched over posture and loose stride. Becoming a frustrating player to track in some ways, tonight was a good microcosm of that. Made a good support play in the NZ, but then fumbled the puck away with a weak hands play at the attack line. He flies the zone often, it appears to be by design, as he's not the only player that does it on the team – but he seems designated for the task on his line. He did beat out an icing on one such hail mary play. Finished a good hit in the NZ in the later stages while the game was still close. He just seems very raw in terms of technique and details…what's troubling is that he might be getting more raw by the week. He has not tracked upwards from where he was at the beginning of the year…the skill level has not improved and I think his decision making should be questioned.

Chaska Hawks at Bloomington Kennedy Eagles, January 26, 2019

Chaska Hawks -

Koster, Mike - 2019 Offensive defenseman who was not shy about jumping into the play. Even took a faceoff and played center for a shift. Sound puck carrier for this level, but not electric. He has a plus with a strong release. Plus mobility to boot. Didn't spend a lot of time defending because his group at the puck more often than not in a game that became non-competitive fairly quickly. Seems pretty raw at defense and full well knows he can step up and make some plays that wouldn't ordinary work at higher levels. Otherwise, he seemed calm and poised throughout. It was a big night for Koster statistically…registering six points in an 8-0 win.

Pitlick, Rhett - 2019 Pitlick showed that he was plenty capable of doing whatever he wanted in the game tonight. His skating and puck skills are very advanced for this level of play. He's a remarkably good skater, who has all the fluidity necessary for a player his size to get out of tight spots. He has superb hands and can carry the puck around the offensive zone without much trouble until something he likes opens up. Because of the non-competitive nature of the game, Pitlick wasn't challenged to defend for most of the night. He's not much of a start and stop player, he typically circles around trying to force some action…which won't work against a higher caliber opponent certainly. It's interesting how similar his style of play is to Jack Hughes…and maybe with the same potential fault: is anyone else on the same page as Pitlick? Or is it just his pure skill that opens up things enough at this level of play? I award points for creativity…but some passes that Pitlick comes up with are – charitably – adventurous. How he fits in when he's not the best player on the ice by a tier or two will be interesting to track.

Hamilton Bulldogs vs Mississauga Steelheads, Jan 26 2019

Bulldogs –

Kaliyev, Arthur (2019) – Kaliyev showed off his impressive offensive gifts but also showed his flaws out on the ice today. He played at one gear and that gear wasn't as a good pace away from the puck, there was several opportunities for him to compete for loose pucks yet he showed no urgency. When he had the puck on his stick, he had a different approach by aggressively cutting from the goal-line on his forehand before releasing a hard-wrist shot that went over the top of the net as an example. On another sequence, he again showed a better compete level when challenging the defense and goalie with the puck by making a high-skilled drag deke before pulling the puck to his backhand. On the powerplay, he wasn't as effective with his one-timer as previous viewings, but still put himself in good position. Overall, Arthur showed little in the way of compete, pace, or intensity but did flash his dangerous shot and excellent set of offensive skills.

Mutter, Navrin (2019) – Mutter had a decent game for Hamilton, showing the ability to take a hit as well as deliver one while also showing decent vision. He was stepped up on by Harley but didn't move an inch, and later in the game delivered a hard hit along the boards that upended his opponent. His best sequence came after he made a clean offensive-zone entry before making a nice backhand pass to his teammate at the top of the right circle which set up a scoring chance. Although his shot appeared average in terms of the mechanics and velocity, he did manage an assist after Ranger was unable to cover the puck properly. Although Mutter didn't flash much skill or offensive ability, he played a physical brand of hockey and found his teammates on occasion.

Steelheads –

Harley, Thomas (2019) – Harley had an above-average offensive performance and made accurate transitional passes up the ice consistently, however his defense was mixed in several attributes. Thomas had a solid defensive sequence early where he used his frame effectively to counteract a Bulldog player along the boards behind his goal-line, then used his length to push the puck up the side-wall which generated a defensive clear. Later in that period he had an aggressive stick that disrupted an offensive-rush while maintaining a solid-gap. Unfortunately, as the game continued his defense suffered due to improper gaps and a failure to recover on sequences that required him to change his pace. In the offensive-zone he was efficient but not as effective in some previous viewings, but he did score a powerplay goal after firing a quick wrist-shot from the point that found its way in the back of the net. Harley continues to show defensive lapses and an inability to elevate his pace when the play calls for it away from the puck.

Schwindt, Cole (2019) – Schwindt had a decent two-way performance for Mississauga. He was notable on the forecheck and was willing to engage physically along the boards which resulted in several effective sequences where he created pressure against the Bulldogs. He was used on the powerplay and showed some deception, faking his pass before attempting a wrist-shot short-side, he also was decent at finding his passing options today. He found himself all alone in-front of the net after a mix-up but was unable to bury the puck, so there were some execution issues too.

Washkurak, Keean (2019) – Washkurak played at a high-pace and had a couple of quality rushing sequences where he set-up his teammates as well as having a high-end scoring chance himself. He makes up for average skating mechanics with his compete level and had no problem physically engaging when needed. Furthermore, he looked confident when carrying the puck through the neutral zone and found his options quicker today then in some previous viewings, he never flashed any high-end plays and wasn't overly consistent though.

Prueter, Aidan (2020) – Prueter had a solid game for the Steelheads and was the most engaged player for his team early. He was effective at creating pressure while showing a plus motor and set up his line-mate Hardie for a quality scoring chance while also showing a level of creativity by making a no-look backhand pass around a defender. He was equally as engaged away from the play and showed that he was willing to expend his gas-tank during backchecking sequences as well. His shot never appeared threatening but his passing skill was present against the Bulldogs, and he played a sound two-way game while executing at a high-rate by making plus decisions with the puck.

Ranger, Joe (2020) – Ranger had an impressive game for the Steelheads and was largely the reason they came away with a point. He had some difficulty setting down early and let in a leaky goal after failing to absorb a harmless wrist-shot, but after that goal he settled down and made several highlight-reel saves. His best save was the result of him moving laterally and fully extending his pad during a 3-on-1 sequence where he read the play well in-tight to the net. All game, he battled and made several breakaway saves showing plus athleticism and reaction time. The two main areas he was exploited were his rebound control and inconsistently squaring up properly when facing a potential passing option depending on the play. Overall, it was a great performance from the young netminder.

Leksands IF at Linköping HC , Jan 26 2019

Linköping HC

LHC # 27 RD Lyckåsen, Albert (2019)

Lyckåsen was considerable invisible and didn't looked explosive today. He was angling the opponents mostly good, tried to pass by the opponent on the board but unsuccessfully. Went out a bit to hard and far out, made the other D had to cover up ending in penalty and BP. Thought that Lyckåsen could have moved a bit more on the blue line sideways to open opportunities. Last minutes in third period Lyckåsen looked more as he usually does. Mid 3rd period he was able to quickly receive and control the pass at blue line and passing the D and creating a chance. A bit later he was aggressive and quick with a stick-check and able to keep the puck in offensive zone.

LHC # 41 CE Costmar, Arvid (2019)

Costmar made some tricky passes, used the board for creative passes to himself. He had Some nice passes between the leg and heading toward the net waiting for scoring chance. A good level of provoking infront of the net. Stick check efficient and high with good intensity. Stressing the opponent high and quick. Takes his guy good. Costmar was visualized everywhere on the game and with decent speed. Receives / delivers a collision/ open ice good. Standing low on the skates and with good balance. Delivered a good direct shot. Quit often and also today Costmar seems to be more intense and with more speed the closer the end comes.

LEKSAND

LIF # 77 LD Lundqvist, Alexander (2019)

6'2" LD that looked confident and calm. Delivered a dangerous pass in to own slot. Looked as average skater but anyway decent speed. Stands up and shows his presence. Found position quick towards the slot to be available for shot. Delivered good accurate passes and especially a long opening pass to # 71 in pp. Goes in to the heat at the net. Decent hockey sense on J20 level and with lot of hockey in the family including drafted father and Nick Lidström as uncle.

Djurgarden IF u20 at AIK u20 January 26 2019

Djurgarden IF u20

Bjerselius, Oscar 2019 Bjerselius really took big responsibilities defensively. He was well positioned and competed hard in his defensive zone. He had problems with his puck game and only passed the puck sideways and backward… This led to him showing zero offense.

Grewe, Albin 2019 Grewe did everything but play hockey this game.His first shift consisted of two big hits and getting called for a 2-minute penalty för interference. The only thing he did defensively was trying to find opponents to hit. He was strong on the puck and showed some powerful skating up the wing

Bjornfot, Tobias 2019 Bjornfot played a brave game today, he was first to the puck in the corners at all time, most times coming out of the corners with the puck on his stick. He also did a good job when transporting the puck up ice. Bjornfot missed his marking a couple times in his defensive zone but was saved by his goalie.He also got beat 1on1 on the outside on AIKs first goal. He seems to play with more self-confidence now than he has earlier during the season.

AIK u20

Broberg, Philip 2019 Broberg was surprisingly playing with the juniors today. He had a couple of good shots in the first period but wasn't as driving offensively as he could and should have been. His skating is extraordinary and he has a powerful stride which he really showed defensively when he caught forwards trying to beat him on the outside with ease. Finished the game with an assist in Overtime.

Karlstrom, David 2019 Karlstrom filled the role as the third line centerman very well in this defensive tilt. He was strong when battling along the boards and protected the puck exemplary by using his body. He was positioned well, to be able to pick up loose pucks and shutting down the oppositions counterattacks. No points today and no sign of any offensive upside besides his hockey-iq.

Seattle Thunderbirds vs Kamloops Blazers, January 27, 2019

Seattle Thunderbirds

Lee, Jake (2019) - Not Lee's best game as his skating looked a couple steps slower than earlier in the season with the exception of a few plays. Really struggled with his passing as well as he had a lot of passes where he put teammates in bad spots where they had to control the puck on their backhand or in their feet. Very good at using simple body and head fakes to beat forecheckers.

Rybinski, Henrik (2019) - Change of scenery has really been good to him. Before a trade from Medicine Hat he looked like a completely different player. Rybinski was an extremely creative passer today making multiple plays across the grain to set teammates up for good chances. Also made a lot of good lever passes to hit players joining the play from behind him. Was also tenacious in his forechecking, applying constant pressure on defenders when he had the chance. Rybinski could use more explosiveness and speed as I felt his skating was simply average. Also would have liked to have seen him be a bit more of a shot threat as him passing got a little predictable as the game wore on. Overall very good game as I felt Rybinski went out to make an impact each shift.

Kamloops Blazers

Pillar, Josh (2020) - Excellent speed and skating was immediately noticeable. Combined with a great work ethic this made Pillar a very noticeable player on each shift he had. Showed some skill but clearly not at a level yet to be an offensive difference maker consistently.

Zary, Connor (2020) - Did a very good job at dictating the game while he was on the ice. The game was played at his pace as he constantly slowed the play down off the rush and found open teammates. In the offensive zone he showed very good vision, making some very difficult passes. Thought he used his strong edgework and balance very well to create space for himself off the cycle. IQ, and especially the speed at which he processed the game stood out. Not an especially fast skater, but had solid shake in open ice.

Shattuck St. Mary's Prep at St. Andrews College, January 27, 2019

Shattuck St. Mary's Prep

Lacombe, Jackson – 2019 Jackson drove possession for SSM in this game. He displayed very good offensive skill in being able to skate the puck out of his own end as well as showing good awareness in reading the play and executing stretch passes, on one instance, realizing St. Andrews was attempting a change, Lacombe quickly fired a pass to one of this forwards at the far blue line that was called off sides but likely would have been a breakaway opportunity for his team. Lacombe tied the game at three in the 3rd period with and end to end rush, protecting the puck as he gained the edge on the St. Andrews defender and beating the goalie, short side over the shoulder with an excellent backhand pass. Lacombe wasn't overly competitive in his own end and didn't defend well in front of his own net and got lost in some coverage but there was no denying his offensive impact on this game from the back end. He controlled the game with the puck on his stick and was active in the offensive end. His skating and quick footwork allowed him to defend against the rush well and made some good timed poke checks and closed opponents off well.

St. Andrews College

Steinburg, Matthew – 2019 Steinburg is a Cornell Commit and a Sioux City (USHL) affiliate who has already saw 2 games in the USHL this season. In this game, Steinburg blocked a shot on the PK, resulting in a 2 on 1 and made a nice pass over for the Short Handed goal as well as scored the game sealing Empty Net goal in the final minutes. Steinburg is a big body and his physical presence was known in all three zones in this game, delivering big but legal hits, both along the wall as well as in the open ice. His skating is raw but his mechanics are not bad and with a little time and strengthening will add some explosiveness. Matthew showed good hands and board play in keeping pucks alive and working to create separation on his opponents and played a prototypical Power Forward game.

Saginaw Spirit vs. Ottawa 67's, January 27th, 2019

Saginaw

Porco, Nicholas (2019) - Porco displayed an offensive spark to his game and good overall potential. He was involved in the play moving pucks up ice and joining in on the rush. He demonstrated an ability to play in all situations including the power play and penalty kill. There were times where offensive chances were lost as he held the puck for too long, attempting to make one last move before finding a teammate.

Perfetti, Cole (2020) - Perfetti is a smart centerman who displayed good awareness on the ice and managed to generate some scoring chances while entering the offensive zone with speed carrying the puck. He played in all situations including some shifts as the power play quarterback where he displayed good puck movement. His intelligence makes him difficult to play against because he is always in position in the defensive end to make a play. He provides great support to his defenseman and takes care of his own end first before transitioning into the offensive rush.

Ottawa

Okhotyuk, Nikita (2019) - He was the best defenseman in this game and looked like he had taken his game to another level compared to previous viewings. He was very physical in this game delivering clean hard hits to separate the opponent from the puck. He made several high-end breakout passes to stretch the ice and efficiently move the puck. He is sturdy on his skates demonstrating good strength and balance. He possesses a limited amount of offensive instincts. Nikita was hard to play against for any Saginaw forward coming into the defensive zone.

Clarke, Graeme (2019) - Clarke displayed some intriguing skills at the showcase. He skates well and showed some skill entering the offensive zone with speed to carry the puck to the net for a quality scoring chance. He displayed good determination to keep his feet moving and skate through checks. He showed an ability to create scoring chances in multiple ways including by crashing the net and using his shot off the rush. He had a limited amount of ice tonight, but when he was out there he made somewhat of an impact.

Bahl, Kevin (ARZ) - – Showed great puck control in this game. Has the size to absorb contact and protect the puck, and the skill to make plays under pressure and while taking contact. He was guilty of trying some overly complicated plays at times throughout this game, which led to giveaways. He was strong tonight at reading the play in front of him and knowing when to jump up in the neutral zone creating some turnovers.

Drummondville Voltiguers vs. Gatineau Olympiques, January 29th, 2019

Drummondville

Ivan, Michal (FA) – He was good tonight at sneaking in from the blueline in the offensive zone very effectively, and has the skill to keep his shooting and passing options open in the offensive zone when he has the puck. Scored a goal in this game by sneaking down from the point, receiving and pass and beating a defender one on one to get closer to the net and improve his shooting lane. Is a strong skater and uses his edgework to his advantage in the defensive zone, creating space for himself with effective stops and tight turns. He had a strong first pass out of the zone tonight, he very seldom spent time in his own end when he had the puck on his stick.

MacLeod, Gregor (FA) - Macleod is most noticeable because of his skating and speed which he uses to beat defenders to the net and win puck races. With the puck he shows good agility and shifty skating to turn off defenders while maintaining control of the puck. He was primarily kept to the perimeter in this viewing. He displayed a good release but needs to find shooting lanes more consistently to take his game to the next level. Gregor needs to be more patient in his own end, he was leaving zone too early trying to go on the offense.

Simoneau, Xavier (2019) - Simoneau is an undersized yet skilled center who shows impressive creativity and offensive skill. He is a strong skater using his smaller frame and lower center of gravity to exude power through his legs making him difficult to knock off the puck. Exiting the defensive end, he carried the puck well showing good stick handling and instinct. In the offensive end, he showed he was not afraid of contact or skating into the dirty areas and engaging physically to battle for pucks. He showed high hockey IQ on the power play tonight for Drummondville.

Gatineau

Bizier, Mathieu (2019) – Bizier had an overall quiet game showing some flashes of skill and intrigue but struggling to make a consistent impact offensively. He showed flashes of work ethic on the back check skating hard to disrupt the puck carrier. As the puck carrier, he showed some patients in traffic to hold onto the puck and make a play. One area of particular concern is his overall hockey intelligence, which could be improved to elevate his game as a consistent offensive scoring threat.

Aebischer, David (2019) – David was skating well in this game, using this to his advantage when closing gaps on opponents and transitioning to offense. When skating into the offensive zone, he did well to not force plays and would make the most of what was available to him. He had a strong first pass, didn't show panic in his game when pressure was on him. He made a number of good passes to teammates trailing him on the rush, putting his teammates in good positions to shoot. He showed good puck movement on the power play tonight as well.

Cedar Rapids RoughRiders at Lincoln Stars, January 30, 2019

Cedar Rapids RoughRiders -

Silianoff, Grant - 2019 Hard working game as usual for Silianoff. That doesn't represent him being effective in the game however. It was a tight game, and Silianoff has neither the skating prowess or technical skill to get separation in this situation. He laid a decent pass in the low NZ for a player attempting to cut through both d-men as he crossed the attack line, but even that was just a little off-timed for the situation and the rush failed. He did backcheck and do work without the puck. Hardly took a shift off. Little bit of a wide skating base and not a very strong stride…he chops around the ice ok, but his top speed is low…no next gear.

Francis, William - 2019 This game puts Francis on the map for me. He was a complete afterthought in previous glimpses earlier in the year, but has evolved a great deal in that time. His skating has improved remarkably. His first step is now rather explosive for his size. Overall, his skating is a plus for his size/age. It has gotten much more refined. His balance is still poor, and he's easily knocked off his feet. His back skating isn't all the way there yet, particularly his stops…he's gaining too much backward momentum and putting too much of it on his heels. Still the overall improvement is noteworthy. He is using his body to his advantage much more as well. Won a few board battles with strength and leverage. If he's initiating contact, he's ok…when he's trying to absorb contact, that's when he ends up on his wallet. Has looked confident jumping into the rush more. Early in the game he jumped into the rush and got a weak wrist shot on. Later, he whiffed on a wide open wrister coming back to him from low as he went jumping into the slot. While those were unsuccessful attempts, they represent potential. In the 3rd, he made a great, explosive jump into the zone off of a won NZ faceoff, gained the line, beat a man with hands, and drew a penalty going to the net.

Lincoln Stars -

Hlavaj, Samuel - 2019 Athletic, butterfly+ style goaltender. Has quick legs. Goes to the reverse-VH post setup very often, but sometimes has a little trouble exploding out of it to shooters. Needs to do a better job adding that depth. Part of the issue could be some issues in tracking pucks and shooters…his head and body movement suggest that he might loose track of shooters that roam around the slot while pucks are in the corner…his save selection and depth double down on this. He's not particularly well-anchored, perhaps a product of having some quick, reflexive feet. His technique is wonky through big pushes…stick and glove placement need to be more consistent and proper. He does like to come out and play pucks…he hit on a fairly high percentage of these plays. The goal against came the shift after the 2-0 goal in the 3rd, but it was a product of a bad turnover…still Hlavaj's body language gave the impression that he read it off the stick poorly. The report sounds more negative than his game tonight dictated…he certainly has potential and a good foundation of skills to build off of.

Skinner, Hunter - 2019 He clearly wants to be an active, agile offensive defenseman but he just doesn't quite have all the physical or technical traits to make it work as often as he wants…particularly in tight space. The potential for him to jump out of the Jeremy Roy tier he's in now towards what he likely sees himself as – Kristopher Letang, is deep in there. Skating is good, the edge work makes it for him. He could stand to get a little more out of his stride with a little deeper knee bend and leg strength. He has decent hands, which might undersell it a bit given what he was able to do in a spell of 4-on-4 play during the middle portion of the game. He showed off some mitts, some good fakes, misdirection, etc. but just couldn't quite explode through it to shed a checker. He did score the opening goal of the game. Didn't look like he handled it clean, but the puck didn't explode off his blade when he was able to corral it. He made a couple good hits to shutdown rushes. He's physically engaging and stands his ground very well in this regard. He actually looks a little uncomfortable defending the front of his net when he can't get engaged in a battle…got caught reaching once or twice in a situation like this. He sometimes cheats a little bit with positioning against rush chances, he doesn't get his shoulders square and play from a good position and out…instead, he will rush it and see if he can swipe it and get transition. He did get walked hard right at the line in the 3rd period. It was head-shakingly disappointing. Missed more outlet passes than maybe you'd expect, even if some of them were challenging or geometric. That said, he's just a handful of games into playing for a last place team who just dealt its top two scorers…perhaps an adjustment period to the talent around him is in order.

Power, Jordan - 2019 Quiet defensive game for Power. Just an average or slightly above average skater. He defended near his net smartly and coolly all night. He isn't quite quick enough to get to the walls and jam pucks loose and away from danger. Despite hanging out in the defensive zone a lot, he didn't seem willing to engage physically in hardly any case. Didn't display much in the way of offensive prowess or puck skills when he did have the opportunity.

Central Illinois Flying Aces at Sioux Falls Stampede, January 31, 2019

Central Illinois Flying Aces -

Siedem, Ryan - 2019 Not a particularly enticing game from Siedem. Started out trying to bait a forechecker by moving laterally across the defensive zone, but Siedem was fooled by him, lost the puck, and then fell trying to recover. Made a horrific turnover late in the 3rd standing still on the blueline. Just an average skater with a laissez-faire attitude towards the game. He doesn't display a lot of urgency in any situation…on the plus side, he doesn't panic a lot either. Seems to be about a half-beat behind in the defensive zone. Quarterbacks the power play from the top. Setup a one-time goal off of a won faceoff. Had a lot of trouble catching passes all night…probably missed about three or four passes that hit his blade.

Janicke, Trevor - 2019 A game that you come to expect from Janicke at this point. Hard working, good pace, good speed. He plays in all situations and was a monster in the faceoff dot. It's a little surprising he isn't a little more physical, he only made one hit attempt in the game…on the smaller Jami Krannila. Janicke was effective at both ends all night. He covered the front of his net a couple of times when both of his d-men vacated to the boards. Finished on a rebound near the net by cutting through the high-rent area with a purpose. Despite his work rate and penchant to play 200 feet, he still looks like he'd be better served at right wing at the next level as I don't think I see him being able to manage the puck in the middle of the ice as well.

Breen, Lynden - 2019 Breen blended in with the ice tonight for the most part. He exhibited his normal speed and hustle game. Has a good eye for the details of the game, good hockey smarts and he was used in all situations. Didn't do anything that stuck out in the game overall and seemed the fight the puck a couple of times. Breen doesn't offer a lot of upside, but he's a player that could wedge himself into a niche and improve on it to the point that he gets a look.

Sioux Falls Stampede -

Swankler, Austen - 2019 Highlight of the night for Swankler was when he broke the tie in the 3rd with a nifty toe-drag that opened up room for him to walk into the slot and put one far side. Other than that, it was a rather forgettable game for him. A couple of noteworthy errors later in the game: Made a poor pass on a rush attempt to Ethan Phillips that Phillips had to corral and it cost them a better chance. In another instance, very late in a shift, he had a clean look to get a dump-in and change…but before he hits the line, he elects to throw it into a largely-vacant wing in the NZ.

So, there was some good and bad for Swankler tonight, who didn't play a ton, but did see some power play time. He gets around the ice ok, but it's not pretty. His stride pushes out to the side instead of back and through the blade, so he doesn't get nearly the maximum power out of it.

Krannila, Jami - 2019 Detail-oriented, two-way center who plays bigger than his vitals. Very good speed, augmented by his high-end work rate. He stood in and took some hits to make plays, including one that would have led to a late-shift zone exit had his linemate not let him down. Not only that, but he threw some strong hits with a purpose throughout. One of which started the 2nd period that cleared a d-man right off his feet. And even when he wasn't making punishing hits, he has the spatial awareness to stand-up/slow down players to allow time for others…he stood up a forechecker who tried to slip past him after Krannila dealt a pass across the net line.He takes great angles on fantastic reads. His feel for the game is near elite. Plays the left point of the PP. A long wrist shot on the PP led to a rebound goal. On a later PP, he sprinted back from his left point position to cover for Ryan Johnson who had lost a puck at the right point to a checker who was on a clear-cut breakaway from center ice in. Krannila comes all the way across the ice diagonally, reaches around and tips the shot attempt wide of the net without committing a penalty or wiping himself or his goalie out. Same sequence: He receives the puck behind his net, from a standing start, shakes a forechcker, carried it across three lines, and dealt a great pass to an open player cruising down the slot for a scoring chance. Later in the 3rd, he makes a strong multi-line rush and then passed to setup a scoring chance. Later in the sequence, he zips from the end wall in his attack zone all the way back to the top of his own circle to perfectly pick off a Trevor Janicke cross-ice pass on a 3-on-2 to thwart the opportunity and get a clean zone exit. The smaller Finn only struggled in the faceoff circle tonight, everything else was exquisite. He has skill, playmaking ability, skating, work ethic, defensive acumen, and he has a master's degree understanding of the game already…

Phillips, Ethan - 2019 Over-skated quite a few plays tonight…a little jumpy for whatever reason. One of those over-skates was in the DZ and it led to a chance against. He did it again in the attack zone and it cost him a chance on his own strong rush to the net early in the 3rd on the PP. He did scoop in an errant pass from Austen Swankler on a rush chance and salvaged the whole try. He also finished a hit in this game, which isn't typically in his portfolio. Nothing spectacular skill-wise from Phillips tonight, but he continued to work hard, he is responsible defensively and he makes good reads.

Tabakin, Brandon - 2019 Not quite as aggressive with the puck as I've seen him in the past, but still a major factor in the breakout. Very fluid skater, great edges, great at starts/stops, escapability, and agility. Quick and accurate puck mover who swings the net with gusto to start the rush. He still needs to be more aggressive near his net defensively, and maybe even across the board, his intensity could improve. He's an older player that could probably offer a little more, if he's permitted to on a strong roster. The skating and skill package is very much worth keeping an eye on.

Johnson, Ryan - 2019 Looks like the leash may have been loosened on Johnson slightly, or he's taking better advantage of his opportunities. Early in the game, he made a number of surprisingly confident rushes that we hadn't seen a ton of in the first half of the season. At the line, he made a real shifty hands play that fooled a winger badly, but the puck rolled just under his blade as he was preparing to fire. Later, he took almost a full round-the-world tour of the offensive zone then set up a chance for a teammate. His hands are improving in a tangible, game-effecting way. As usual, he was on point defensively, looked very confident tonight…took on players, offensively and defensively, more than usual and was willing to take on hit attempts – most of which he ducked out of and/or absorbed coolly. If Johnson puts together more games like this down the stretch, his stock will be back on the rise.

Chicago Steel at USNTDP U18, February 1, 2019

USA-

Matthew Boldy (2019) - Boldy had about an average game for him. He ended up getting a helper on the game winning goal where he made a play to get the puck to Turcotte on a zone entry. He was rather quiet in the first period but got better as the game went on. He's such a talented player and is hard to contain him for an entire game. He's very creative and deceptive with his stickhandling and did well to create scoring opportunities for himself and his teammates throughout the game. His skating isn't a major asset, but I wouldn't say it's a problem either. Overall it was a decent not great game for Boldy.

Alex Turcotte (2019) - Turcotte, much like Boldy took a while to get going tonight but played decent overall. He picked up the primary assist on the game winning goal by Vlasic. He out muscled the Steel player to get the puck over to Vlasic who tapped it in. Turcotte wasn't a dominant force like usual tonight but still played solidly and had an impact on the game. He's very skilled, very strong and very fast. He also has a relentless work ethic. When he's at the top of his game he is right up with there with Hughes as one of the best players in this draft class. The fact he was still able to make an impact on this game when things weren't going his way early say a lot about him. He should continue to play well and keep moving up the draft board.

Judd Caulfield (2019) - Judd played one of his better games of the season. He doesn't always use his large frame to his advantage but tonight he did. He was strong on the forecheck and played a heavy game. His line combined for three goals and he had a goal and assist. His goal came on a tip where he provided a strong net front presence and his assist came on a nice play where he faked a shot, froze the goalie, and found Weight in front for a tap in. Judd has the making of an NHL power forward, but he needs to play with more of a mean streak and more urgency.

Trevor Zegras(2019) - Zegras was quiet on the score sheet tonight but he created plenty of opportunities and was very noticeable. He's got an elite skill set and a hockey IQ to match. He plays with a confident swagger and isn't afraid to make any play. His shot isn't heavy, but it is accurate, and he has demonstrated that this year. He makes his line mates better and he can play either the center or wing. He's a special talent and should be selected in the top ten of the draft.

Cole Caufield (2019) - Caufield had an off game tonight as he couldn't get much going. He did have a few decent opportunities and had four shots on net. The obvious thing with Cole is the size but it doesn't seem to affect him too much. He is usually able to make plays on the walls and forechecks relatively well. The best thing about Caufield is his ability to disappear in the play and then find open space to get an excellent scoring chance. His shot speaks for itself and he also has a nice set of hands. In this game tonight, I would've liked to see him move his feet to beat guys wide instead of pulling up and looking for a pass. He had a few opportunities to take the puck to the net but opted to pull up. He's a deadly offensive weapon and should rebound.

John Beecher (2019) - Beecher has been inconsistent throughout the year. This was one of his off games. He was unnoticeable for most of the game and wasn't hard on the puck. He has very enticing size and speed and needs to use it more often. In the third period he blew by a defenseman to basically give himself a breakaway but didn't finish. The speed he showed on this play was very impressive, and this is a glimpse of why he can be an NHL player. He is a borderline first round pick right now and needs to be more consistent if that is going to happen.

Alex Vlasic (2019) - Vlasic had a very solid game scoring the game winning goal and tallying an assist. He crashed the net hard and tapped the puck into an empty for the goal. He's very solid and steady defenseman who moves the puck well. His size and reach are huge assets for him. He skates well for his size and rarely gets beat. Despite his two points tonight his offensive upside may be limited as he gets to the next level.

Marshall Warren (2019) - Warren had a very good game. He's a very good skater and puck mover. He took the puck end to end which resulted in Gildon's goal in the first period. He plays a physical game and doesn't shy away from contact. He has a bit of a slender build but should be able to fill out as he ages. He does not play the power play but does have offensive upside to his game. He likes to join the rush and act as a fourth forward because of his skating ability. He's a great player who should make a solid NHL defenseman.

Dom Fensore (2019) - Fensore was all over the ice tonight. He's an extremely mobile defenseman who moves up and down the ice with ease. He recorded the primary assist on a shot from the point on Caufield's tip in goal. He is very undersized, but it does not affect him. He has a very active stick and is too quick to get beat in the defensive zone. His skating is another level as far as most draft eligible defenseman. He is able to rush the puck with tremendous speed and carves his way through the opposition. Overall, he is a very exciting player with offensive flare and tremendous upside.

Cam York (2019) - York is the best defenseman on this team and one of the best in the class. He is an extremely smooth skater and dices his way through opposing players. He makes tremendous outlet passes that are almost always tape to tape. He is an excellent powerplay quarterback and has a quick accurate wrist shot he loves to use from the point. He did not have his most outstanding game tonight, but he is always very solid. He should be off the board in the mid first round, and whatever team takes him should be very excited.

Chicago Steel

Robert Mastrosimone (2019) - Mastrosimone is a dynamic winger with great speed and skill. He was noticeable in this game and played well. He recorded two assists where he displayed his speed and skill. His first assist was a helper on the powerplay where he made a nice cross ice pass. The second assist came where he got caught on a breakaway but was able to recover and make a pass out front for the goal. He is a little bit undersized but plays tough and with a chip on his shoulder. He is a very smooth skater in open ice. He could get stronger and work on his play on the walls.

Nick Abruzzese (1999)- Nick is a small playmaking center. He displayed incredible hockey IQ in this game. He is a very smart player who always makes the right pass. He is strong despite his size and is a strong and fast skater. He was held off the point sheet tonight but was very dangerous. He leads his team in points and it's easy to see why. He displayed some very smooth hands and creative playmaking. He is in the last year of his draft eligibility. He would be a great late round flyer with upside for a team looking for skilled forwards.

Travis Treloar (2019) - Travis has very smooth hands and used them a lot in this game. He is a bit undersized and a little bit weak on the puck. When he was given time and space in this game, he was able to make some nice plays. He is not an overly quick skater and was not able to tally any points. His overall skill set is legit, and he may be worth a draft pick in the late rounds. He needs to continue to contribute more for this team and get faster and stronger.

St. Paul's School vs St. Sebastians, February 1st 2019

St. Sebastians

Struble, Jayden – 2019 Struble was Sebastians most active defenseman he used his excellent skating ability to drive play at either end of the ice. Struble was always looking for opportunities to join the rush but wasn't careless in the regard and picks his spots well. Showed good effort to get back and break up plays that go the other way. Struble played with good physicality, one instance stepping up on player at offensive blueline and delivering a big hit to separate him from the puck as well as setting up a shorthanded goal in his own end by finishing his player along the wall and taking the puck away and flipping a pass to the neutral zone that created a 2 on 1 shorthanded opportunity that his team converted on

Saint John Sea Dogs at Blainville-Boisbriand Armada, February 2nd, 2019

Saint John

#88 Cajkovic, Maxim (2019): He flashed some of his talent tonight in a losing effort and with not much help around him. He took some good shots on net, mostly using his quick wrist shot to get pucks on net, but often those were shots from far. He played on the point on the power play; I thought his passes were hit-and-miss, as he missed some easy passes, but showed some dynamic qualities in the offensive zone. On certain sequences, he showed real quick hands, handling the puck in one-on-one situations. He possesses a good wrist shot. His skating looked average, and he will need to work on getting quicker in order to create more separation.

#44 Poirier, Jérémie (2020): His footwork was good today. He showed good lateral agility and used his skating to help him retrieve pucks and also to escape pressure from the forecheck. He flashed some of his abilities to rush the puck out, but nothing came out of it as far as creating scoring chances. He had a couple of turnovers and didn't see much ice time in the second period. Overall, he didn't do much today, but moved well and moved pucks quickly in the neutral zone. Unfortunately, not a whole lot of offense was created by him as a result.

#18 Lawrence, Josh (2020): Lawrence had a couple of good flashes in the offensive zone, showing some good vision and playmaking abilities. For a smaller guy, his speed was not excellent and lacked explosiveness. He took some good shots on net; he has a good release on his wrist shot. He lost his man behind his own net, and that led to the 2-1 goal (which proved to be the eventual game-winner).

#13 Villeneuve, William (2020): Real tough game for the #2 overall pick of the 2018 QMJHL Draft. He started the game with a nice play, breaking up a 2-on-1 rush with a nice dive to block the cross-ice pass. It was downhill from that point on, as he was slow to retrieve pucks in his own zone. His footspeed and skating were both average at best. There were a lot of turnovers from him in the 2nd period, with one costing his team a goal after he failed to clear the puck out of his zone at the start of the 2nd period. A key to his game last year was his ability to rush the puck out of his zone. He didn't do much of that today, and didn't look very confident with the puck on his stick. He struggled with his puck-management for most of the game, and his shot from the point didn't have much behind it.

#12 Burns, Brady (2020): Burns was one of the best Sea Dogs today. He was always around the puck and was working really hard all over the ice. Undersized, but played in the tough areas of the ice and was involved out there. He made smart plays all game long, demonstrating his excellent hockey IQ and playmaking abilities, even if his teammates couldn't always finish his plays. He played a feisty game and didn't back down, despite his size. It's tough for him to win his battles versus the older and stronger players, but that didn't stop him. He scored the lone goal for the Sea Dogs off a rebound, and also had another one called back by the referee in the 3rd period.

#14 Drover, Alex (2020): Loved his ability to rush the puck into the offensive zone. He showed good skating and shooting abilities throughout this game. This is the part of the game that he excels at, and that will make him a successful junior player. He'll need to work on his compete level by winning more puck battles out there, and improve his play in his own zone. At this point, he's a bit of a one-dimensional player who happens to skate and shoot the puck well.

#25 Prikryl, Filip (2019): Net presence on the power play; big frame that can be useful in front of the goalie to obstruct his view. His skating is poor; he is not very agile and lacks the necessary speed to create separation between himself and his opponents when rushing the puck. Today he struggled with the pace of the game. He didn't show much creativity and vision in the offensive zone, and his best work was done down low and in front of the net.

Blainville-Boisbriand

#58 Bolduc, Samuel (2019): He made it look easy to rush the puck out of his zone today, with his reach and excellent skating ability. He often made guys miss in the open ice; he didn't mind taking some risks when rushing the puck. On some occasions, we saw him deke an opponent just in front of his net. It may have been a dangerous play, but with his reach, he was able to beat that player. His passes were very crisp with very good velocity, to the point where sometimes his teammates had trouble receiving the pass because of how hard the puck got to them. On the point on the power play he likes to shoot the puck, as he possesses a very hard slapshot. However, he'll need to find better shooting lanes, or elect to move the puck quickly to a teammate instead, if there's no real shooting option.

#89 Tourigny, Miguel (2020): Tourigny was called up from Midget AAA after the team had traded Pascal Corbeil to Baie-Comeau. A similar player, Tourigny has quick feet and a quick stick, which helps him defend in his own zone. Despite being undersized, he's not afraid to get involved physically, as he threw a couple of nice hits. Good skater to rush the puck as well.

#47 Pinard, Simon (2019): Really loved his compete and involvement level along the boards tonight. He won a lot of puck battles and was intense on the forecheck. He looked to be playing with the best confidence we've seen from him this season. He showed off his good hands in the offensive zone on a very impressive sequence in the first period, but couldn't finish and score a goal. On the power play, he was often used on the half-wall, and showed some good vision and playmaking abilities from there.

#91 Lacombe, Thomas (2019): He had a couple of chances to score in the game, but couldn't materialize on any of them. He could have scored in the first period following a 2-on-1 rush, but William Villeneuve made a nice dive to intercept a pass going back his way that could have been a very good scoring chance. He showed some good speed and hustle out there. However, he is still learning a new league and making adjustments to his game after joining the Armada at the trade deadline. He played in the NAHL in the first half of the season.

Sarnia Sting vs North Bay Battalion, Feb 3 2019

Sting –

Jamieson, Rees (2019) – Rees had an average performance for Sarnia, rarely managing to penetrate high traffic areas or generating high-end offensive chances. He did show the ability to anticipate when his lane was closed, making a nice no-look backhand pass that set up his teammate early in the game on 5-on-5, but for the most part he was ineffective at even strength. On the powerplay, he was used in-front of the net area, and on one play made a nice cut to the net while attempting to tuck the puck in. His motor and pace and willingness to drive his line wasn't on display at the normal rate as some other viewings but he flashed his skill at points during the game.

Perreault, Jacob (2020) – Perreault was also largely ineffective at even-strength like Rees, however when given more time and space to use his shot on the powerplay, he was more effective and efficient. One area where he had some success today was with his transitional offensive-zone entries, showing plus agility as he side-stepped his man on one sequence and on another, he showed fluid crossovers to cut aggressively while skating over the blueline. He scored a powerplay goal during a scramble which left him with an open-net but was most dangerous around the goal-line where he showed a good-touch with the puck and made a couple of plus passes, the best being a sharp turning pass that resulted in a high-end chance.

Leufvenius, Hugo (2019*) – Leufvenius displayed the ability to generate high-end chances around the net area and didn't need much time or space to get off his threatening shot. He's a big and strong kid with broad shoulders and used them to barrel his way through heavy-traffic around the goal-line at times where he displayed plus hands that helped him keep control of the puck. His power translated to his shot, needing little time to gain leverage and fire pucks upstairs. This resulted in two-goals and the game winning goal. Although his agility and straight-line speed were average, he was good at getting behind defensive coverage to compensate for his skating ability as well.

Guy, Brayden (2019) – Brayden Guy was largely ineffective for Sarnia but did display plus hands on one sequence where he showed the ability to beat his opponent one-on-one under pressure. On another sequence he had a nice backchecking play despite his poor skating, so the effort was there on some shifts, but it didn't translate into much in the way of scoring chances in today's game.

Kamerrer, Colton (2020) – Kamerrer had a below-average game for the Sting. He was largely ineffective in the offensive zone and was responsible for a goal-against after failing to help support his defensive partner on one sequence. Arguably his best play was in the defensive-end after he managed to keep Coe to the outside when he was aggressively attempting to cut towards the net area, Colton stayed with him and maintained a solid gap on the defensive read, unfortunately on another defensive sequence, he didn't anticipate where he needed to be positioned after his defensive partner lost the puck in the corner, this allowed a Battalion player to come out in-front of the net and bury the puck. In the offensive-zone, he rarely touched the puck and never threatened, showing no dynamic or high-end offensive skill.

Reesor, Ashton (2019) – Reesor had a decent game for Sarnia, using his frame effectively to keep Battalion players at Bay in-front of the net and showed the ability to move the puck under-pressure at an above average rate today. His passing wasn't perfect, he did misfire a couple of stretch passes that failed to transition the puck up the ice, but around his goal-line, he made simple and effective passes up the boards at times. His best play came by anticipating an open-passing lane across the high-slot before diving forward with his stick and disrupting the pass-attempt, the play showed effort and some ability to read the play away from the puck in advance. Like Kamerrer, Reesor failed to offensively get engaged at the blueline, opting for simple plays and trying to move the puck down-low the odd-time he touched it.

North Bay –

Coe, Brandon (2020) – Coe was the most impressive forward on the ice for either team today, generating chances off the rush by using his speed, while also displaying an effective forecheck. He's a big kid and wasn't afraid to use his frame on the forecheck and during board battling sequences, this led to two of the bigger hits in the game, where he stapled Rees along the boards on one play and was the catalyst for a North Bay goal despite not getting an assist after delivering a devastating hit that resulted in a takeaway. His physical efforts complimented his pace and skating ability, which allowed him to drive play at times, where he showed the willingness to enter heavy traffic areas, this resulted in the opening goal of the game. Brandon drove hard towards the net and scored on his backhand, showing patience and poise as he waited for the Sarnia netminder to react before he made his move. Another important element that was on display today was his ability to gauge when he should shoot and pass, he took advantage of high-danger shot locations but also knew when he should distribute the puck too. Lastly, he made a nice move that beat his opponent one-on-one by tucking the puck between the defender's legs. It was an impressive performance by the young forward.

Primeau, Mason (2019) – Primeau had an effective offensive-game for the Battalion, generating several shots while also setting up his teammates in spurts. In some previous efforts, Mason had trouble getting involved offensively, but that wasn't the case today, he stood out and made some nice plays. He had the primary assist on the opening goal after recognizing that Coe was open in the slot and had several other sharp passes that hit the tape of his teammates while he was in motion. Although he had shot the puck several times, Primeau did have difficulty getting the puck in the net since he continues to lack the power to get much leverage on his shot, the accuracy was also mixed. Furthermore, he didn't display soft-hands or drive into heavy traffic as much as you would like given his size.

Rose, Simon (2019) – Rose had a decent two-way performance for the Battalion, scoring a goal with a low, seeing eye-shot from the point, while also moving the puck out of his own-end under pressure at a decent rate. One of the bigger areas of concern with Rose is regarding his combination of size, skating and pace, he's a smaller defenseman but his pace in all three-zones was lacking. He did physically engage at times, including against much larger players. There was no one attribute that stood out, but he was an overall plus player for his team out on the ice.

Czech Republic vs Finland, U18 Five-Nations, Feb 5 2019

Czech Republic –

Parik, Lukas (2019) – Parik had a decent performance for the Czech's while holding Finland to 3 goals. He's not the most athletic netminder, but he covers a ton of net and uses a blocking style approach. He had several impressive saves in-tight to the net where he remained tall in his butterfly and showed good coordination on his blocker side when attempting to absorb rebounds and deflect pucks. He had a calm presence in net and rarely threw himself out of position. His size allowed him to see the point well, which allowed him to position himself for point shots in advance on most attempts.

Poizl, Daniel (2019) – Poizl had a solid defensive effort for the Czech's, using above-average acceleration to chase down loose pucks quickly, making him effective during recovery and dump and chase sequences. Early in the game he lost his footing, but maintained composure and completed a nice bank pass off the boards, which set the tone for the rest of his performance, where he quickly distributed the puck behind his goal-line consistently. In the offensive-end, he was used on the powerplay, but didn't show any dynamic qualities from the offensive-blueline, opting for quick passes but not much else.

Raska, Adam (2020) – Raska was featured on the Czech's top line which proved to be the most effective. He scored the 2nd goal of the game after finding soft-ice at the bottom of the right circle before quickly shooting a wrist-shot far-side which was accurate. His best sequence came late in the third period where he cut aggressively towards the net resulting in a quality scoring chance, before collecting the puck again and cutting in-tight to the crease. He had no trouble attacking heavy traffic areas but overall his performance was average.

Teply, Michal (2019) – Teply was the most consistently dangerous option for the Czech's which resulted in a hattrick, he also played on the top-powerplay-unit along the half-wall. He didn't drive play like his state-line would suggest, but he also didn't need a lot of time or space to get off his deceptive shot. His first goal occurred on the powerplay, where he recognized that he had enough room to skate in and shoot a hard-wrist shot that had a quick and accurate release. His other two goals were the result of him changing the angle rapidly by spinning into his release point with his back initially turned to the play, again the release point was impressive. Although his shooting was on display, his playmaking didn't stand out and he rarely controlled the puck in the offensive-zone.

Psenicka, Ondrej (2019) – A towering kid who's the largest player on this Czech squad, Ondrej had some notable shifts and generated offense in spurts. One of his better sequences came while driving through the neutral zone, he evaded a big hit showing a good amount of dexterity for his size before driving behind the goal-line and looking for options. One area to note, was that for such a bid kid, he played at a good pace and some plus offensive chances as well.

Muzik, Radek (2019) – Muzik had an impressive game for the Czech's by contributing with two goals and competed hard. Although a big player, Muzik was able to consistently find soft-ice and took advantage of it which resulted in his opening goal, where he fired a quick wrist-shot that went five-hole. His second goal was the result of a deflection, showing that he can use his length to his advantage. On another play, he stopped up and quickly assessed his options before finding a clear passing lane. Although he played well, his skating stride was awkward.

Finland –

Loponen, Kalle (2019) – Loponen had a solid two-way performance for Finland, demonstrating that he can play bigger than his size and contribute at both ends of the ice. He generated a big, yet clean hit early that knocked a larger player down to the ice, the hit was well-timed and stopped a transitional play. In the offensive-zone he played on the top-powerplay, and showed that he could distribute the puck with accurate and sharp passes. His shots managed to get through traffic but they weren't threatening, however, he did have a well-timed pinch where he skated aggressively down the left-wing and fired a hard-wrist shot that went over the net. Away from the play, he was quick to recognize when he needed to transition back to defense and didn't over-commit on the offensive side of the puck, showing a responsible defensive game.

Rasanen, Livari (2019) – Rasanen had a solid defensive performance for Finland. He didn't do anything notable in the offensive-end but defensively Rasanen had a couple of great defensive plays. One of his more notable defensive sequences was during a 2-on-1 rush against, where he assessed the passing lane quickly, and took away the pass resulting in no shot. Along the boards, he was tenacious and worked hard and he also fired a couple of accurate out-let passes under-pressure that landed on the tape. Rasanen has shown us a more reserved style of play but he's been effective at shutting down players and making smart decisions with the puck, which he did in today's game.

Hatakka, Santeri (2019) – Hatakka showed confidence when carrying the puck, utilizing his plus skating ability to transport the puck under pressure. He was calm and poised in his own-end and had no issues holding the puck and rushing it up ice which resulted in clean transitional zone entries. He used his skating ability to have an effective pinch at the line as well, where he streaked down the right-wing while assessing his options. That being said, despite moving the puck well, he didn't generate much in the way of offense.

Aaltonen, Leevi (2019) – Aaltonen used his excellent speed to drive play at times but was also largely kept to the outside when he gained the offensive-line. Leevi showed high-end acceleration and used it to drive the Czech defense back which resulted in giving him some room to work with, but his execution and decision making was mixed. Although he was unable to show off any high-end passing ability today, he did have an excellent rush down the right wing where he fired a hard-wrist shot that went over the Czech netminder, the release was hard and he managed to shoot in one-motion. Aaltonen's tools stood out, but with the exception of his goal, he had trouble creating sustained offense.

Puistola, Patrik (2019) – Puistola was arguably the most consistent and impressive Finnish forward on the ice today despite not scoring. He has a high-talent level which stood out today in different situations on the ice. For instance, he made a beautiful pass from his own-end which found Simontaival for a primary assist. During a powerplay sequence while under pressure, he displayed one-on-one skill by quickly pulling the puck around an aggressive forechecker and gained the offensive-line before making a quick pass that resulted in extended zone time. His best sequence came along the boards, where he was strong on the puck against two larger opponents, managing to use his plus edges to evade getting pinned and ended up skating hard down the left-side before setting up his teammate. In some previous viewings, Patrik has demonstrated a plus release point but today he showed duel-elements in the offensive-zone and flashed both tenacity and skill.

Simontaival, Kasper (2020) – Simontaival had a good game for Finland, flashing a plus release and soft-hands which resulted in two-goals, he also played on the top powerplay unit. Although he's not quickest kid, especially given his small stature, Kasper made up for it with his natural talent. His first goal was as highlight-reel goal where he turned a larger Czech defender inside out before going bar-down, it was arguably the most impressive goal of the game. His second goal came on the powerplay at the left circle, where he walked into a shot that was accurate and quick to come off his stick. He scored a third goal was called back but the play demonstrated good hand-eye coordination as he tipped it out of mid-air while in heavy traffic. Simontaival didn't drive play but he needed little time or space to become a threat in the offensive zone.

Raty, Aku (2019) – Raty wasn't consistent but he did flash an impressive tool-set, displaying speed, and making difficult plays while in motion. His best scoring opportunity came in the slot area where he dragged the puck in-tight to his body which allowed his shot to get through traffic. On that play and others, he looked to use the defense in-front of him as a screen to make his shot more difficult to read, and he played at an above-average pace away from the play as well.

Parssinen, Juuso (2019) – Parssinen showed a mature game both with and without the puck, flashing hockey sense and a good release point. On two separate plays, he positioned himself properly and supported his teammates in the offensive-zone which allowed him to regain control of the puck after his teammates temporarily turned it over. Although not very quick, he showed poise and confidence when holding the puck, this resulted in a nice forehand to backhand move while driving down the right-wing before shooting a backhander that required a difficult save. On another play, he recognized that he could use the defender as a screen and shot a hard-wrist shot around his opponent. He was able to shift the tempo of the game at times and flashed a good hockey IQ.

Sweden vs Russia, U18 Five-Nations, Feb 5 2019

Sweden –

Alnefelt, Hugo (2019) – Alnefelt was largely the reason that Sweden remained competitive against Russia. He's a big and athletic goalie which was highlighted by several well-timed saves requiring full extension is his lower body. He was good at anticipating shot fakes and moved fluidly when attempting to stop cross crease shot attempts. Hugo's rebound control was only average today, he had trouble absorbing shots at times but was quick to react and attempt to recover as well. Both goals he allowed were difficult to stop and overall, he had an impressive performance.

Grewe, Albin (2019) – Despite getting rocked with a clean hit while attempting to gain entry in the offensive-end early, Grewe remained in the game and ended up driving play at times for Sweden. He played a tenacious and fast-paced game which made him relatively effective on the forecheck in spurts, and he used his plus edges to cut aggressively towards the goal-line on a couple of different sequences. When under pressure, he showed a soft-touch with the puck and made a couple of skilled plays but had difficulty generating shots on net. It was a decent performance overall.

Raymond, Lucas (2020) – Raymond didn't have one of his better performances today due to being largely kept to the outside when attempting to attack. He did use his impressive edges to spin off pressure while handling the puck at the offensive-blueline which resulted in extended zone-time while showcasing his puck-skills, but with the exception of that play, and one other where he cut directly out in-front of the goal-line on the powerplay, he had difficulty generating any sustained offense and was shutdown.

Holtz, Alexander (2020) – Holtz had one of the more difficult games we've seen from him this season. His acceleration is behind his linemates, Henriksson and Raymond, which didn't allow him as much time or space to create offense as usual. The end result, was him largely getting shut-down. His best opportunity came late in the third period where he managed to find open-ice and fire a hard wrist-shot while driving down the right-wing. Arguably Alexander's biggest weakness is his skating, although above-average, it prevented him from evading an aggressive Russian team, making him looked overwhelmed on some shifts. Lastly, he did look to physically engage at times, so he's willing to make a hit if the opportunity is there.

Johansson, Albert (2019) – Albert had a decent two-way performance for Sweden. He had a clean transitional zone-entry showing poise while carrying the puck on one sequence, and managed to generate a couple of hard point shots both at even-strength and on the powerplay. Away from the puck, he maintained decent positioning, and was able to move the puck under pressure behind his own goal-line at an above-average level on most shifts.

Henriksson, Karl (2019) – Although Karl didn't get too many opportunities to generate offense when established in the offensive-end, he was very consistent at using his speed to cleanly transition the puck over the offensive-blueline. He centered the dynamic line of Holtz and Raymond, yet drove the play on the line the most today, which is rare compared to most other viewings of this line at other international events. On the powerplay, he played the half-wall and had moderate success moving the puck, but never was overly dangerous. His speed, ability to assess open-ice, and confidence when carrying the puck stood out. However, so did his inaccurate passes that were too sharp at times.

Russia –

Chistyakov, Semyon (2019) – Chistyakov was arguably the best Russian defender today. He played with poise in all three-zones and was making quick decisions that led to several transitional plays. Behind his own-net, he made quality tape-to-tape stretch passes, in the neutral zone, he showed displayed poise under-pressure while assessing his options, and in the offensive-end, he quickly distributed the puck both at even strength and on the powerplay. Although he's small, he displayed a physical aspect to his game by levelling Grewe as he attempted to gain the offensive-line, and showed good pivoting which made him elusive. Overall, it was a very impressive performance, showing smart decisions both with and without the puck.

Bychkov, Roman (2019) – Bychkov had an above-average two-way performance for Russia. He used his skating ability to make impressive recovery plays when caught out of position at times, and was good at assessing his options in his-own end under pressure. He also showed confidence by aggressively carrying the puck over the offensive-line and cut near the goal-line before looking to thread a backhand pass, on one attempt. He didn't get too many opportunities in the offensive-end, but was good at moving the puck up the ice and displayed an aggressive and physical game when attempting to disrupt the Swedish offense. Although he's not a large defender, he played at a high-pace and shutdown some of the more skilled players on the ice.

Gritsyuk, Arseniy (2019) – Gritsyuk wasn't a primary driver of play on most shifts but he did display a good amount of skill when the puck was on his stick. He scored the 2nd goal of the game for Russia after finding an opening in the slot-area and firing an accurate wrist-shot. On a two-on-one sequence, he did a good job of masking his passing option and on additional plays, he showed plus vision when looking for his teammates.

Podkolzin, Vasily (2019) – Podkolzin wasn't as effective today as most other previous international viewings, but he still played a solid two-way game and generated high-end scoring chances for both himself and his teammates. His line of Nikolayev and Zaitsev was very effective which was in large part due to the intensity Vasily displayed on the forecheck. His best scoring opportunity came late after he went end-to-end before generating a hard wrist-shot where he used a screen before releasing the shot.

Sheshin, Dmitri (2019) – Sheshin had a good performance for Russia, showing the ability to play larger than his size and compete at a high-level which complimented an impressive motor. He found soft-ice on several different plays, and as a result, had a couple of threatening shots on net, though his best chance went wide it did show a decent release point as well. He had a tremendous backchecking effort on a potential 2-0 play for Sweden, where he jumped over the boards and quickly covered ground which allowed him to catch up and knock the Swedish forward off the puck, he then skated hard back up ice to try and get involved. There was a ton of hustle in the kids' game.

Zaitsev, Dmitriy (2019) – Zaitsev had an impressive performance for Russia, displaying skill while playing at a high-pace. He flashed a good set of hands by dragging the puck while remaining onside as he transitioned over the offensive-line on one play, and on a couple of other plays, he used his hands to negate active sticks while looking for his teammates. One notable quality was his ability to drive down a lane before setting up effective drop-passes which resulted in a couple of plus scoring chances. He had a good forechecking sequence where he assessed Hedstrom's outlet pass attempt, knocked the puck down and then delivered a clean hit which knocked the Swedish defender off balance. Dmitri also showed the ability to move the puck efficiently in tight-spaces which led to his best sequence of the game where he worked his way through traffic and found his open teammate before pressuring again on the forecheck. He played the half-wall on the powerplay and had impressive puck distribution as well. Overall, Zaitsev showed skill, vision, and played at a high-pace.

Amirov, Rodion (2019) – Amirov had a solid performance for Russia which resulted in him opening the scoring after finding himself alone at the bottom of the right circle and shooting into an open-net. He also had the first breakaway attempt of the game, opting to shoot the puck but it missed the net. His forechecking ability stood out, as he anticipated the opposing players movement well, which allowed him to intercept pucks. Rodion's hockey sense looked above-average in today's viewing, finding openings to generate offense and made good decisions both with and without the puck at a consistent level.

U.S.A vs Finland, U18 Five-Nations, Feb 7 2019

U.S -

Boldy, Matthew (2019) - Boldy had a game that showcased some of his better attributes such as his creativity with the puck, and some of the attributes that we have grown wary of overtime, such as unforced turnovers and the need to try and make a high-skill play when a simple and more effective play would have worked better. There was several examples of this throughout the game around the goal-line, where he had creative no-look spin-passes that created scoring chances in the slot, but also would have low-percentage between the leg shot attempts that missed the net and would lead to lost possession. The creativity, skill, and ability to make plays while in motion were evident, but so were the unforced plays that led to a lack of execution against Finland.

Zegras, Trevor (2019) - Zegras showcased his impressive passing ability, this attribute was emphasized with the man-advantage where he made several sharp-passes through tight-seems that landed on the tapes of his teammates. His turnover rate wasn't as high as Boldy's today and it was good to see him show more selfishness and look to get off his quick release on a couple of scoring chances as well. Along the boards, he was engaged physically and showed some bite in his game as well. Zegras was also willing to enter high-traffic areas which gave him several point-blank scoring chances, one of which he buried on the side of the net. Despite showing off his playmaking skills, he still forced a couple of passes that resulted in turnovers as well.

Turcotte, Alex (2019) - Turcotte was the best U.S player out of the big draft eligibles out there against Finland, playing a calculated yet controlled game that showed off his two-way attributes. One of the plays that really stood out was off a failed shot attempt that was blocked, where he raced down the puck, out-competed two Finnish players to retrieve it and made a nice backhand pass that resulted in a keep in. It's plays like that and others that showed his high-execution rate with the puck and the ability to gauge when he needs to enter another gear to make a play happen. He scored the U.S's first goal by being in the right place at the right time in the slot area, sliding a quick shot under the Finnish netminders pad.

Rolston, Ryder (2020) - Rolston showed the ability to play with speed in a complimentary role, making several plays that required a quick processor out on the ice but also showed that he needs to continue to refine his hockey sense and learn to play slower with the puck at times. He played at a very-high tempo and played at times too quickly as a result. He rushed through the slot area under heavy traffic then lost control of the puck but was willing to finish his check. On a couple of others plays, he rushed his shot and passing option which led to poor execution. On one play he mis-fired in the high-slot and on a spinning pass under-pressure he didn't get enough woof on the puck. He did show the ability to backcheck using his speed, competed aggressively, and still made a couple of impressive plays while going at top speeds.

Beecher, John (2019) - Beecher had difficulty assessing how much time and space he had to make plays at times, and was largely kept to the outside, however he did use his speed away from the play well, which allowed him to have several impressive backchecking sequences. Beecher has difficulty handling the puck or making the right play under pressure while going at top speeds at times, and that occurred several times in this game. One of the more notable plays that demonstrated this was when he fell at the offensive-line when attempting to transition the puck and another involved mis-timing a pass while driving around the goal-line. He was not effective in the offensive-zone but was solid in picking up his man in his own-end and skated hard.

Finland –

Puistola, Patrik (2019) - Puistola was engaged offensively in spurts against the States and capitalized on a couple of plays. On Finland's opening goal, he rushed down the left-wing during an odd-man rush and used a head fake that made him look like he was going to pass before firing a quick and low shot that forced Knight to cough up a large rebound that led to a primary assist. In some other viewings, Puistola has shown the ability to play bigger than his size, and on one play against Helleson, he out-muscled the bigger defenseman along the boards. He played on the half-wall during the powerplay and was good at distributing the puck while also looking composed when assessing his options under pressure.

Rasanen, Livari (2019) - Rasanen didn't flash a lot of high-end skill or show off any dynamic elements to his game, but his execution rate was high, and he was in good position away from the play which allowed him to intercept the puck as well as come up with well-timed shot-blocks. Rasanen compensates for his average offensive game by making detail-oriented plays. As an example, away from the play, he slowed down Zegras just enough using his frame while Zegras was trying to pass him to make sure he couldn't help compete along the boards but he didn't draw an interference penalty, subtle yet effective plays like that one is the reason Rasanen was effective out on the ice.

Aaltonen, Leevi (2019) - Aaltonen had a decent game for Finland, generating chances by using his speed. He's had some difficulty in this event and others in terms of assessing when he should shoot or pass. On one play, he found open-ice in the left circle but instead of skating in and looking to get a high-quality shot off, he passed it into a closed lane while attempting to find his teammate. On another rush, he generated a low shot that could have resulted in a rebound opportunity, so he showed improvements as the game developed in terms of picking his spots to shoot. Despite his small stature, he engaged physically on the forecheck, and his skating complimented his pace well, he plays at a very high-rate.

Peterborough Petes vs Ottawa 67's, Feb 7 2019

Petes –

Robertson, Nicholas (2019) – Robertson played one of the best games I've seen him play this season, dominating play on both sides of the ice. He was involved early with the puck, making skilled one-on-one moves that forced the 67's to respect him. This allowed him to create space for himself where he generated nearly a dozen high-end plays that involved threading passes while at full speed to his teammates through multiple opponents, as well as cutting aggressively through traffic using his impressive move-set which broke-down the 67's defense. His shot was very dangerous in this match up, showing an advanced drag which, he extended into his release to suddenly change angles. For his size and strength, he generates a surprising amount of velocity on his wrist-shot which he managed to get through traffic several times. Although he didn't score during the game, in the shootout he did have a quick wrist-shot that went five-hole for a goal. His compete level and anticipation allowed him to take advantage of his reads away from the puck, generating several interceptions on pass attempts by the 67's. Furthermore, he made several well-timed stick lifts and was strong on the puck. Although his weakest element is his skating, he out-hustled his opponents which allowed him to cut wide and beat defenders. His skill was matched by his compete level, and it allowed Nicholas to drive play consistently throughout the game and stand out on a shift-to-shift basis.

Butler, Cameron (2020) - Butler generated offense in spurts but wasn't very consistent or dangerous with the man-advantage where he played from the half-wall. He was able to drive down both wings and threaded a couple of sharp passes that led to quality scoring chances, and his best scoring chance came in the high-slot where he released a hard wrist-shot around a screen that required a difficult stop. Lastly, Butler didn't use his size too well on the forecheck and didn't disrupt the Ottawa defense as much as he has in some previous efforts.

Jones, Hunter (2019) – Jones started this game poorly, letting in two goals that he misread. The first goal was during a scramble and was a high-percentage shot from the left-circle, but he didn't use his edges properly and pushed too aggressively when attempting to move laterally, throwing himself out of position. On the second goal, he mistimed a wrap-around that he was late to the post on. However, after letting in the 2nd goal which was soft, Jones fought back and showed mental toughness by recomposing himself and gaining back his structure. The result was several well-timed and impressive point-blank saves in the two periods that followed. He showed a combination of hockey sense, mobility and reflexes which allowed the Petes to stay in the game. It was an important showing for Jones who has started letting in softer goals as the year has progressed but showed that he can fight back after starting slowly.

67's -

Rossi, Marco (2020) – Rossi had a solid showing for the 67's, flashing his impressive playmaking skill-set both at even-strength and on the powerplay. He continues to show creativity and composure when holding the puck, and this allowed him to out-wait and breakdown the Petes defense consistently. Unlike a lot of other smaller players, Rossi had shown that he can use his size to his advantage, anticipating lanes in advance and using his impressive edges to remain elusive under-pressure. Lastly, he had a nice drive directly in-front of the net in this game, which he has consistently shown in some other viewings as well, he doesn't play scared and doesn't back down from larger players, showing a competitive element to his game.

Okhotyuk, Nikita (2019) – Okhotyuk had an okay game for the 67's. He wasn't as effective as some previous viewings due to not using his skating ability enough to become the puck transporting option out of his own-end as consistently as other viewings, though in the third period, he did have a good zone-exit where he did use his skating and frame properly to angle himself away from an opponent while under pressure. At the offensive-line, he was again more passive and didn't activate into the play as often as some other games, opting instead for quick yet simple plays. Lastly, in his own-end, he wasn't as physically engaged and didn't play at the pace we've become accustomed to over the course of the season.

Clarke, Graeme (2019) – Clarke was used in a depth-role and wasn't very noticeable in today's game. He did find soft-ice on a couple of occasions and used openings to fire his impressive wrist-shot off but his shots were inaccurate. Away from the play, he did skate aggressively and did show some compete but never moved the needle in a positive away consistently both in the offensive or defensive zone.

Nichols School Showcase –February 8th, 2019

St. Andrews College –

SAC #4 RD Agnew, Jack (2019) – A late '00 birthdate RHD with decent size and solid mobility and puck skills. He made smart plays around the ice to move the puck in outlets and showed some offensive abilities as well. He is a good puck moving Dman and distributes on the power play too.

SAC #21 LC Carogioello, Frankie (2020) – He is a smaller forward that is elusive to defenders and creative with the puck. He scored the first goal of the game in the first period as he peeled out of the offensive corner off the goal line and recognized the time and space and fired low shot to far side beating goalie. He is committed to Miami and will be a solid college player, although if gains more speed and strength could gain more attention.

SAC #27 RW Stienburg, Matthew (2019) – The late '00 right winger who is making draft attention seemed to be fairly quite offensively early. He did show his captain, leadership on the PK as he blocked a couple of shots and sacrificed for team. The skating stride is average as his speed and agility could use improvement. He is the power forward who works well below the dots and will come up with pucks in corners and along the wall. He certainly has good shot, although appeared to be player that needs set-up linemate to receive pucks for scoring opportunities. He did score team's forth goal in the 3rd period as he received some open ice down the right wing and snapped puck high, short-side over glove. He has good size frame and showed physical style at times. He could be a late round flyer at this point for the draft.

SAC #29 RW Bowie, Brendan (2019) – Bowie is on the smaller side and might be playing in the shadows of Stienburg. He certainly has good hockey intelligence as made good reads on plays with and without the puck. He has good stick skills as well to elude defenders and created scoring chances. He again showed smarts with the puck in puck protection in making sure made good decision on passes and limit any turnovers. He seemed on most shifts to make plays and impact positively for team using his agility and skating, smarts, stick skills. Delta Hockey Academy Midget Prep –

DHA #4 LD Smythe, Kurtis (2020) – Smythe showed a solid skating stride and good puck handle to avoid pressure and outlet puck.

DHA #6 RD Sexsmith, Joel (2020) – He showed that he can skate and handle the puck although a few times he played risky knowing that he was last defender back yet still tried to maneuver around the forecheck himself instead of moving the puck. Sexsmith has some skill sets although will need to improve puck decisions.

DHA #7 RW Latimer, Carson (2021) – Latimer played down the right wing using his powerful stride to gain speed in trying to beat defenders. He had some good puck skills as well with the speed along with offensive instincts, so there is potential in the young prospect.

DHA #9 LC Plummer, Krz (2020) – He picked up tripping, slew foot penalty early in 1st period in the game then started to play hockey a bit as game progressed. Although he did like entering the offensive zone and would often cut across the slot, east-west instead of changing his entry and being deceiving. One time it led to turnover at offensive blue line. It was an up-n-down performance.

DHA #11 LD Ardanaz, Nicholas (2020) – Ardanaz was only NCAA commit on team with most drafted or headed to the WHL. He was average size LHD with good mobility and range in skating. He handled the puck well and showed offensive style as would join or even lead rush with the puck. In the 2nd period he got a bit lax on his passing, instead of snapping passes tape-to-tape. You can see he possesses some good skill sets and skating abilities.

DHA #31 G Sim, Drew (2021) – He is young although good size goalie certainly above 6-foot. He was making smart reads and controlling rebounds well, showing good composure as well in net. He handled the puck well outside his crease too. His team as the game progressed got tired, giving up more chances against, and Sim made saves and was solid outing although could have had some more defensive help.

DHA #33 LC Horstomann, Tyler (2020) – He was physically good size and showed glimpses of his skills. He created nice give-n-go with #9 Plummer in 2nd period for good scoring opportunity.

Culver Military Academy –

CUL #13 LD Cox, Spencer (2019) – He is average size LHD although moves well as agile on his skates to elude pressure and skate puck up the ice offensively. He handled the puck well. All around he showed a good game with poise, smarts as good puck decisions and was effective player on the blue line at both ends of the ice. Made good passes all game and distributed on the PP from the top. Cox was one of the better players on the ice for team.

CUL #20 LD Lohrei, Mason (2019) – He is a big LHD with good mobility for his lanky size. He has a long reach that he utilizes in the defensive zone well to break up plays closes gaps as well. He will keep it simple and make a good first pass although he did not show much offensively after making initial breakout pass. There is potential with his body and overall athletic tools although he will have to learned to put it altogether. Not sure he is worthy enough of a draft pick, more so a player to monitor in the years.

Nichols School –

NIC #7 LD Suda, Michael (2020) – He got involved early with nice rush up ice through defenders showing his stride, strength, and stick skills to release solid backhand shot on net for a scoring chance. He picked up PP assist in 1st period as he quickly feed a back-door pass from below the dot to #21 Gonter. He plays in all situations from the 5v5 to PP and PK and it is almost too much as often leads to long shifts. He is talented player although could be more effective if he would slow the pace down at times instead of forcing puck up the ice with his skating. It appears Suda has the green light at any time from the back end. Yet he will play physical and brings offensive talent from the blue line. He would benefit from playing in a more challenging league with a better supporting cast around him.

Shattuck Prep –

SSM #2 LD LaCombe, Jackson (2019) – On first shift he and his defensive partner kind of parted ways in the defensive slot area allowing #21 Gonter to straight right through for scoring opportunity early. LaCombe then played a solid game showcasing his strong mobility and puck handle for player his size. He made solid puck decisions in outlets and rushing the puck up the ice himself. He did a good job turning the puck up quickly in transition to start the offensive rushes. Defensively he was solid in positioning and utilized his reach and strength effectively. He possesses strong shot and will get on the scoresheet with his passing rather than scoring Dman. He owns physical tools and skills sets to develop into a solid prospect.

SSM #8 LC Shlaine, Artem (2020) – Shlaine was a bit quite in this game. He did not factor on the score sheet although he usually displays good offensive skill sets and knowledge with puck possession and playmaking. He did not do a whole lot in this opening game of the showcase.

SSM #12 LC Brisson, Brendan (2020) – Brisson scored the 3rd goal for team on a tap-in play at the crease that was really made off the awareness of linemates #19 Rollwagen and #14 Lee. Otherwise Brisson was kind of on the perimeter in this game as did not notice any skill or effectiveness to the game's outcome. He is a smart player as made some plays in tight areas with the puck as recognized the pressure.

SSM #19 RW Rollwagen, Tyler (2019) – Rollwagen is solid power forward style winger that made some plays in the offensive zone. He made nice play on the 3rd goal showing his vision as made crafty seam pass to #14 Lee for the goal yet showed his awareness with initial puck entry into the zone. Later in the game he also recognized his opponent on him on the crease and simply rolled away from the pressure and created a good scoring chance. He will probably need some junior experience and NCAA time to develop his game.

SSM #22 RW Samoskevich, Matthew (2021) – He was the most dangerous player on the ice all night for Shattuck. He has the late '02 birthdate so he should gain lots of draft attention over the next two seasons as well. He made great feed from the wall after entering the offensive zone in the 1st period to #11 Norman going to the far post for the tap-in goal. He displayed good skill sets with good puck possession, skating to break away from pressure, and showcasing his hands and shot. He could have easily had a few more goals as he ripped it off the post a couple of times and the goalie robbed him as well on a few shots. He did score a nice goal in the 3rd period as he displayed his speed into the zone and stuck a shot from top of circle short-side over blocker. Samoskevich is certainly a player to monitor for the higher levels and draft in coming years.

SSM #23 RD Morrow, Scott (2021) – Morrow has certainly gained size the last year or so and his skating ability has improved as well with his mobility and edge work. His stride and lateral movements were more fluid and with that and his stick handling ability he showed good composure with the puck from the back end. He made good puck decisions all game, recognizing pressure, and effectively transitioning puck quickly to offense. He plays positionally well and makes smart reads on plays. He is a player with good potential for the future.

Russia vs Finland, U18 Five-Nations, Feb 8 2019

Russia –

Vaschenko, Nikita (2019) – Vaschenko had an effective two-way performance for Russia. He has a thicker build and he took full advantage of it at both ends of the ice. At the offensive-line, he delivered a clean, yet powerful puck separating hit that resulted in a takeaway and in his own-end, he was aggressive along the boards and used his frame effectively to drain the Finnish forecheck. He scored a goal at the point off a seeing-eye shot that floated over the Finnish netminder but with the exception of his goal, showed little in the way of offensive-skill. He was tenacious, competed hard, and contributed.

Bychkov, Roman (2019) – Bychkov was arguably the best player on the ice for either team through the first half of the game before trailing off slightly in the second-half. His offensive-skill set stood out, as he drove down the right-wing before making a nice between-the-legs drag move that gave him additional space to attempt a backhand pass near the goal-line. He scored a goal after receiving a difficult pass to handle in the neutral-zone, where he spun with the puck before gaining the offensive-zone, skated aggressively down the right-wing and buried a quick wrist-shot that went five-hole. In his own-end, he used an active stick, had a decent gap, and on one sequence where he needed to recover after failing to assess how much time he had to make a pass under pressure, he was the first to physically engage in an attempt to recover. Bychkov skated well, was effective at both ends of the ice, and had offensive-flashes that stood out.

Chistyakov, Semyon (2019) – Chistyakov had an efficient defensive-effort for Russia, showing a quality outlet-pass and plus hockey-sense. He never stood out for any flashy or creative plays, but he was very effective at determining his passing options quickly and firing accurate passes that allowed his teammates to transition up the ice cleanly. Furthermore, when his options were limited, he showed confidence when carrying the puck through the neutral zone which led to a good transitional-zone-entry at the blueline. Behind his net area, he was quick to identify pressure and assessed how to make himself an option for his defensive-partner away from the puck consistently.

Nikolayev, Ilya (2019) – Nikolayev had some difficulties at the start of this tournament and that translated over to today's viewing as well. He wasn't as involved in the play as we're used to seeing, wasn't as effective on the forecheck as he's been in some previous viewings, and looked lethargic at times. He did suffer a knee injury at the mid-way point but came back and started playing better towards the end of the game. His best sequence was on a forecheck, where he out-muscled his opponent before threading a solid-pass to his teammate, but never displayed dynamic qualities which we have seen from him at other international events. One area to note regarding Ilya was that he was taken off the line with Podkolzin and struggled.

Podkolzin, Vasili (2019) – Podkolzin had an okay performance for Russia, showing flashes of his impressive offensive-game but rarely drove play and wasn't as much of a factor as the game progressed, though he was noticeable in the first-frame. He started out of the gate playing at an impressive-pace. Along the boards, he delivered one of the better hits in the game, leveling a Finnish opponent before taking the puck back. He had one impressive deke before spinning off pressure and finding his teammate, but overall, he didn't penetrate heavy traffic or drive-play to the same degree as most other performances that we've seen.

Chinakhov, Egor (2019) - Chinakhov had an opportunistic performance, where he didn't drive play, but did find soft-ice away from the play which led to several high-end scoring chances. He had multiple breakaway attempts by getting behind the defensive-line undetected but on both attempts his shot never really threatened and he didn't show off anything dynamic. However, in the shootout, he did have a nice wrist-shot goal that showed a quick release and was accurate. Furthermore, he had a crisp pass from the top of the right-circle which set up one of the better Russian scoring chances of the game. Although Egor was offensively involved at times, his pace, tools, and skill-set didn't overly impress.

Groshev, Maksim (2020) – Groshev had a good performance for Russia by getting involved on the forecheck and causing the Finnish defense to play heavy-minutes. Maksim displayed a high-octane motor out there and when combined with his thicker frame, it allowed him to generate consistent pressure which made his opponents make mistakes. When he had the puck, he showed decent vision, setting up his teammates in the slot-area on a couple of different attempts. Furthermore, he played a fearless brand of hockey, taking direct-cuts near the goal-line towards the net area, that resulted in a couple of scoring chances. He was one of the better forwards on either team.

Finland –

Tuomisto, Antti (2019) – Tuomisto had a solid two-way performance for Finland. He was good under-pressure in his own-end, specifically when he was willing to transport the puck himself, this led to a couple of transitional rushes. On one rush attempt, the puck was turned over but he showed an excellent compete level on sequences where he was forced to recover, and showed power as well by stick-lifting his opponents multiple times. His ability to assess his time and space in the offensive-end was a plus today, moving the puck well both at even-strength and on the powerplay, but he's still primarily looking to get his shot-off through traffic as quickly as he can, as opposed to re-opening lanes by faking pass and shot attempts. Although he can be efficient at the line, there continues to be a lack of high-end offensive-skill shown too. Lastly, his outlet passes were inconsistent, showing mixed accuracy and a lack of ability to gauge how sharp they need to be.

Aaltonen, Leevi (2019) – Aaltonen had a plus offensive-performance for Finland, using his speed to threaten and generate chances. He's a smaller kid but showed that he's willing to go to the front of the net where he buried a rebound-goal and he also scored in the shootout after firing a quick-wrist shot past the Russian netminder. When given an opportunity to settle-down on scoring chances like he had in the shootout, he evaluates where he should shoot better. When he was under-pressure, he mis-assessed his placement for some of his shots as well as how much soft-ice he had at times. This has been a continuous theme for us with Aaltonen; he has excellent speed but it comes with a price for him, where he needs to be able to process the play that much quicker so that he can make the right plays while going at his top-gear, but the results have been mixed.

Tieksola, Tuuka (2019) – Tieksola had a better showing against Russia than his previous efforts at this event, showing the ability to control the puck in tight-spaces, while also showing plus vision. He was more consistent today and as a result, stood out more on the ice. On one sequence, he drove the puck through all three-zones before delivering a soft-backhand pass to his teammate for a quality scoring opportunity. He played the half-wall with the man-advantage and showed some poise under-pressure while simultaneously assessing his options, this led prolonged possession during some powerplays. Although he's slight and was easily knocked off the puck, he didn't mind taking a hit but he also primarily stayed to the outside and was distributing around the perimeter, rarely attempting to threaten by penetrating into heavy traffic.

Flint Firebirds vs Sudbury Wolves, Feb 8 2019

Firebirds –

Cavallin, Luke (2019) – Cavallin had a difficult night that resulted in him getting pulled and replaced at the beginning of the 3rd period. He wasn't getting much in the way of help from his defense, as they were largely unable to keep Sudbury to the outside or clear the puck on secondary shots. However, Luke showed average to below-average hockey sense behind his goal-line, which resulted in him consistently mis-reading plays, he also had difficulty putting himself in position to square up on secondary scoring chances due to not been able to readjust if he misinterpreted the initial shot or pass. This was largely due to not staying up on his edges properly and using a vertical-horizontal too frequently when an opponent was cutting on an angle. Furthermore, his reflexes appeared average and his lateral mobility didn't allow him to move fluidly on certain shot types. Areas where he showed some plus mechanics including his ability to track pucks through screens, and his glove-hand was decent out there.

Kolyachonok, Vladislav (2019) – Kolyachonok had an okay two-way performance for Flint, showing plus puck skills while making a couple of defensive reads, though his pace was concerning. Arguably his best defensive effort came from interpreting shot locations in advance which allowed him to make several blocks, including two subsequent blocks on one sequence. It's important to note he was still willing to sacrifice the body to some degree even with the game completely out of reach. Another good aspect of his defensive effort was that he was willing to play with an edge;

during a board battle he aggressively tossed an opponent off balance which caused a turnover. The last area that he was consistent in was his ability to find a first-pass option along the boards while below the goal-line. Areas of concern defensively included mis-assessing when he could transition out of the zone away from the play which threw himself out of position at times, and he was caught flat-footed due to not moving his feet-enough, this caused him to take a penalty on one shift. In the offensive-end, he manned the point on the powerplay and showed the ability to fake a shot before distributing the puck and showed plus cross-over mechanics and edges which allowed him to carry the puck while re-opening lanes.

Uba, Eric (2019) – Uba was a none factor in this game, showing little in the way of urgency from the opening shift, especially away from the play. You could count on one hand the amount of touches he had with the puck in the offensive-end, but he did have one impressive sequence where he showed a soft-touch with the puck by threading the puck between an opponent's legs before quickly firing a hard snap-shot that required a glove-save. In his own-end, he didn't backcheck or support his defense effectively along the boards.

Keppen, Ethan (2019) – Keppen was one of the few Flint players to get on the scoresheet and had a nice defensive sequence as well but was largely inconsistent and was unable to create pressure on the forecheck. At the defensive line, he managed to generate a takeaway which gave him an opportunity to break in on a partial breakaway, but he showed a choppy and short-stride that didn't allow him to completely separate which resulted in a routine save since he had to fire the puck before the defense caught up to him. He's got a decent frame and showed a willingness to enter high-traffic areas around the net, this resulted in his goal off a rebound after having his initial shot stopped. Although he scored and did some good things in his own-end, Ethan lacked any sort of high-end or dynamic element to his game and showed average skating mechanics when extending into his top-gear.

Vierling, Evan (2020) – Vierling had a difficult game for Flint due to having poor puck management that resulted in him turning the puck over several times. He did manage to generate a couple of clean transitional zone-entries but regardless if he attempted to cut through the high-slot or wide, he seemed to lack the puck-protection skills necessary to hold onto the puck that's needed to drive play for extended periods of time. To his credit, he was also one of the only Flint players who was capable of generating any sort of offensive chances for his team, making several well-timed passes while in motion that helped set-up his teammates. His passing continues to look more impressive than his shot, he was able to find soft-ice and showed decent hockey sense at times, but his release point, velocity, and mechanics didn't allow it to threaten at any-point. Away from the play, he was willing to play deep in his own-zone and did at times attempt to support his defenseman, though the pace wasn't always consistent or very good.

Wolves –

Ross, Liam (2019) – Ross had an above-average two-way performance for Sudbury, using his frame effectively to weigh-heavy along the boards and keep opponents to the outside, as well as chip in on the stat sheet. He's a big body and used it to effectively press players up against the glass, as well as deliver some good hits. His passing was decent today, he had a couple of quick passes out of the zone that resulted in Sudbury getting to transition the puck. In the offensive-end, he activated at the correct time which resulted in him scoring a wrist-shot goal from in-tight to the net after a blocked shot dropped near him. It was better than some previous efforts overall.

Byfield, Quinton (2020) – Byfield had a solid two-way performance for Sudbury, using his combination of high-end tools while keeping an impressive pace that overwhelmed Flint's defense for most of the game. He was more dominant in the first-half of the game than the second but that was due to his team being up by 5 goals before the half-way point in the 2nd period. Before that mark, he created pressure on the forecheck and stripped the puck off a Flint defenseman who had difficult with a pass, he then cut aggressively towards the net and flashed a set of soft-hands by pulling the puck from his forehand to his backhand which resulted in a goal. On another play, he showed some creativity while rushing in on a breakaway by making a one-handed backhand deke attempt but mis-timed the move. Byfield played an unselfish game and consistently found his teammates which led to several plus give-and-go sequences as well. Away from the play, he was impressive defensively, showing a good two-way game as he stopped a potential high-danger shot in the slot area by using his length to disrupt a shot-attempt and created pressure at the defensive-line which never allowed Flint's defense to get as engaged as they would have liked.

Murray, Blake (2019) – Murray had a hattrick against Flint, showing an impressive release point while consistently finding soft-ice due to Flints poor defensive effort. He scored in multiple ways, including a sharp wrist-shot from the slot area that was very accurate, going top-corner for his most impressive goal of the night. He showed some creativity as well, trying a no-look between the legs backhand shot near the crease area, though a more effective and simple play would have probably had a better result. Away from the puck he was solid, making a couple of good defensive reads, his best being at his own-line where he generated a high-end scoring chance after using his frame and stick to generate a takeaway. Although Murray produced, he did have some drawbacks, such as lacking pace, he never drove play, and he was unable to find his teammates consistently, showing average vision. Most of his work was also done in stationary positions where he relied on his teammates to set him-up for scoring chances. Furthermore, his skating continues to look average, standing too up-right and not looking fluid when taking off.

Thompson, Jack (2020) - Thompson had a solid two-way performance for Sudbury, displaying plus anticipation and the ability to recover. He had a great defensive-sequence where he was caught out of position but aggressively backchecked and used his stick to take away a high-quality scoring chance, he then raced after his opponent and delivered a big hit in the corner. When Flint was attempting to cut wide-on him, he showed plus edges and maintained a solid-gap which kept them mostly to the outside as well. In the offensive-zone, he activated properly which resulted in a great scoring chance where he had an open-net but missed wide. On another play he showed a good release point while in motion in the high-slot. He also displayed the ability to recognize when he should shoot through-screens, which resulted in a difficult glove save by Cavallin on one attempt.

Rouyn-Noranda Huskies at Blainville-Boisbriand Armada, February 8th, 2019

Rouyn-Noranda

#16 Beaucage, Alex (2019): Beaucage took some good shots on net tonight, mostly on the power play, where he would play on the left wing and take shots from the faceoff circle (this is where he scored in period 3 on the power play). His shot has great velocity, and he gets it off quickly. He made some good passes as well during the game. He is a talented passer, and made quick decisions with the puck in the neutral zone to find his teammates going full speed towards the offensive zone. His pace was average at best, though, as he lacks explosiveness and it is hard for him to gain his top speed quickly from his starts. Even his top speed is not great. He worked hard, showing a good compete level at both ends of the ice, and was involved along the boards and in some scrums as well.

#4 Bergeron, Justin (2019): Liked his offensive flair during the game. He didn't shy away from joining or leading the rush. He's a smart player offensively, and always tries to create offense when he has the puck on his stick in the offensive zone. He possesses a good, quick wrist shot and didn't hesitate to put pucks on net. He's very active from the back end, acting very much like a 4th forward on the ice. His footspeed is average, and he can be slow to react to speedy forwards going on his side of the ice, and also when retrieve pucks in his own zone. He had very limited power play time, as he's been put on PP2 (with Noah Dobson taking a PP1 role and playing most of the two minutes). He was okay defensively, he was quick to put pressure on the puck-carrier, but I'd like to see him use his stick to block passes and passing lanes more.

#6 Régis, Samuel (2019): Not a spectacular game from Régis, but he was, as usual, very efficient on the ice and played a mistake-free game. Not big and doesn't have the best footwork, but he played very smartly out there. He played well within his limits; he made some good rushes into the offensive zone, moved the puck safely into transition and didn't take many risks out there. He was solid in his own zone, read the play well and (despite his size) protected the puck well down low and absorbed hits well along the boards, keeping possession of the puck.

Blainville-Boisbriand

#58 Bolduc, Samuel (2019): Some good puck-carries out of him earlier in the game from him; he generated very good speed with his powerful strides, often beating the first forechecker easily. On the power play, he didn't hesitate to throw pucks on net, but his one-timer was blocked often before reaching the Huskies' net. He was a bit slow moving pucks in transition on some sequences, such as on one occasion when he had an open man in the neutral zone and waited too long before making his pass, resulting in a turnover. He didn't played physical enough in his game, with his strength and size he could have done more to make a difference versus the Rouyn-Noranda forwards in his zone.

#47 Pinard, Simon (2019): Another good game from Pinard today, who scored a very nice goal on the power play in the first period. He went through the Huskies' defensemen, showing quick hands, before beating Émond with a backhand shot. He showed decent speed, but he also showed a nice burst of speed that he used to beat defensemen wide. He was solid away from the puck, doing a good job getting into the shooting lanes and blocking shots late in the game with the game on the line. He worked hard in all three zones and competed well along the boards.

Sioux Falls Stampede at Waterloo Black Hawks, February 9, 2019

Sioux Falls Stampede

Johnson, Ryan – 2019 Johnson's skating ability has been well documented this year and he used it well in eluding pressure in all three zones when he had the puck. In one sequence, Johnson showed good hands to match his footwork as he came out from behind the net and made a quick move around fore-checker to exit his zone. The next sequence of the play is where Johnson still struggles at times, instead of taking advantage of the open ice he had and using his skating to lead the rush up ice, Johnson attempted a long stretch pass when it wasn't necessary or available that resulted in a nothing play for his team. While Johnson has made slow but steady strides in his overall game this season, he struggled in this game in striking the right balance of when to have poise with the puck and knowing when he needs to move it quickly. Defensively, Johnson uses his feet and good stick to defend against the rush and was difficult to go wide and gain leverage on due to his clean pivots. In the offensive end, Johnson played a simple game, he is able to walk the blue line effectively and showed he can cover a lot of ground in order to keep pucks in the offensive end but didn't do a lot to create offensive chances either 5 on 5 or on the Power Play.

Krannila, Jami – 2019 Krannila displayed high end skill and speed in this game. For a smaller player he showed the ability to protect the puck well, in one sequence he was able to shield the larger defender with his free hand as he gained the edge and drove the net for a scoring chance. Krannila showed good vision in the offensive zone, was able to create space and open up lanes with his skill and agility. Despite his size, Krannila showed the willingness and ability to get the middle of the ice in the offensive end and was willing to pay a price to get to areas of the ice he needed to. Krannila setup the tying goal in the 3rd with an excellent cross slot pass. Krannila only registered one assist in this game but was a key part of Sioux Falls come back in this game.

Romano, Anthony – 2019 Aside from his Empty net goal to seal his teams comeback, it was a quiet game for Romano. He displayed good speed and explosive skating and had a good motor in all three zones but didn't do much to create offense but showed good speed with the puck. Romano was robbed by Waterloo goalie on a one-timer on a 2 on 1 late in the 2nd period. Romano showed some sand paper and physicality along the boards and in front of the offensive net and did win some battles down low to sustain offensive zone time.

Swankler, Austen – 2019 Swankler struggled to be effective in this game; he attempted to beat too many defenders 1 v 1 which resulted in turnovers. Swankler failed to get the puck deep in the offensive zone by trying drop passes at the offensive blue line on a couple of sequences that resulted in wasted zone entries. Swankler has good hands in traffic and was able to create time and space for his teammates but failed to get them the puck. Swankler isn't an explosive skater but displayed decent top speed, it just took him too long to get there on a couple of instances and he was caught by back pressure or lost races to loose pucks.

Phillips, Ethan – 2019 Phillips was the one consistent piece on his line of Swankler and Romano. Phillips was noticeable in using his motor on the fore-check and competing for pucks using 2nd and 3rd efforts. Phillips did good work on the Power Play on the half wall and showed good versatility in his playmaking ability from that position. Showing a good mix of puck decisions and moving up and down the wall to open up plays.

Waterloo Black Hawks

Firstov, Vladislav – 2019 Firstov showed glimpses of his offensive skill, especially late in this game where he protected the puck well down low and made a great feed to the slot that just missed connecting for the tying goal but wasn't a consistent factor throughout the game. Firstov was "one and done" in too many puck battles and didn't show much willingness to get his nose dirty until late in the game when his team had surrendered its lead. His skating stride isn't technically sound but showed decent top end speed with the puck. There are times when his skating looks sluggish but it looks like it comes from lack of effort more than anything else.

Blumel, Matej – 2019+ Blumel opened the scoring early as he turned on the jets and beat his defender to the net to put in a rebound as he came out of the penalty box. Blumel displayed a good top gear with the puck as and used it to get back on the back check as well. Blumel ran the point on the power play but also showed the ability to get in a shooting position on the half wall where he displayed excellent one-timing ability on the power play where he was able to get a heavy shot off. Blumel's speed was difficult to contain when he had the puck and drove the offense in the transition game for his line in transition.

Schingoethe, Wyatt – 2020 Wyatt played a solid 2-way game and was physical, on one play, challenging Ryan Johnson at the point and delivering a big hit on him to get the puck out of his own zone. Schingoethe showed a strong base in front of the net, gaining and holding position on his defender on a number of occasions as well as along the wall where he had leverage on his opponent and worked hard to be over pucks and won battles for his team. Wyatt showed good vision of the ice and was able to find teammates in transition. Schingoethe continues to look like a solid prospect for the 2020 NHL Draft.

Sweden vs Finland, U18 Five-Nations, Feb 9 2019

Sweden –

Nybeck, Zion (2020) – Although Nybeck didn't consistently stand out, he flashed offensive-talent on a couple of different plays, specifically in the third period. He's a smaller kid but was willing to enter heavy traffic in order to make plays, this mentality led to his goal where he collected a rebound and showed off a fast-set-of-hands by evading sticks before pulling the puck to his backhand for the goal. Shortly after that play, he made a nice pass near the blueline which was saucered from his backhand, giving him a primary assist on a wrap-around goal. Both offensive plays displayed high-end puck skills.

Bjornfot, Tobias (2019) – Bjornfot had a poor performance for Sweden, showing below-average puck management while not reacting quickly enough at either end of the ice. We have seen Tobias perform well in some previous games but that wasn't the case today, his outlet passes were inconsistent, his puck carrying below the goal-line was mixed, and he ran out of room while assessing his options during forechecking sequences. At the offensive-line, he showed a lack of creativity or any high-end offensive-skill.

Gunler, Noel (2020) – Gunler displayed a high-end release point but also showed mixed decision making both with and without the puck at times. Like the rest of his team, Sweden didn't get going until the third-period but Noel stood out. He displayed confidence rushing the puck through the neutral-zone and evaded a check while side-stepping with the puck. He was used on the powerplay but didn't put himself in good positions to release his shot, opting instead to remain at an off-angle while distributing the puck near the goal-line for the majority of his powerplay time. However, at even strength, he did find soft-ice near the bottom of the left-circle which led to his goal, where he elevated the puck quickly over the Finnish goalie. On another shot-attempt, he showed the ability to be dangerous at an off-angle at the right-circle, wiring a puck off the crossbar, the velocity and release point were impressive. Lastly, he drove through traffic in-front of the slot, giving him his best shooting-angle of the game but opted to look for a pass that resulted in what should have been a high-end scoring chance becoming a dead-play.

Raymond, Lucas (2020) – Raymond had a plus performance for Sweden by being the only consistent driver of play for his hockey team, which has been a common theme for him all season. He showed a good compete level, two-step area quickness, and excellent anticipation to generate pressure. When he was carrying the puck, he worked well in tight-spaces, using his soft-hands while simultaneously surveying the ice to help set up his teammates. Furthermore, he was good at masking his intentions, shifting his body-mechanics quickly to fake shots before attempting to thread pucks through traffic.

Holtz, Alexander (2020) – Holtz has had a difficult game for Sweden due to failing to execute with the puck on his stick. He had an opportunity early while driving down the right-wing but his shot never came off his stick properly, resulting in a routine save. After the whistle he looked down at his blade, trying to figure out what happened on the attempt and that moment encompassed the rest of his performance. On the powerplay, he put himself in good scoring positions but when he had prime-chances, he missed the net. When he wasn't shooting, he was passing but at times forced his passes resulting in turnovers as well. He did have a couple of good touches with the puck and a clean offensive-zone entry showing above-average straight-line speed but otherwise had a forgettable game.

Finland –

Loponen, Kalle (2019) – Loponen had a good offensive-performance for Finland, showing the willingness to get involved in the play while also displaying above-average hockey sense. His first goal was a low seeing-eye shot at the line, he had a reduced wind-up on his slapshot and managed a lot of velocity. His other goal was the result of recognizing when he should join the attack which allowed him to join an odd-man rush where he put himself in good position to bury a wrist-shot upstairs over Alnefelt for the goal, he managed to shoot the puck in one-motion. In his own-end, he looked to move the puck off the boards quickly and at times stepped-up to deliver a hit in order disrupt transitional play.

Rasanen, Livari (2019) – Rasanen was a steady presence on the backend for Finland, showing plus man-to-man coverage, while managing to effectively box-out players in-front of the net. He wasn't flashy and kept his game simple, but that's what allowed Livari to be effective, by staying within his game and not overextending himself. At the blueline, he looked to quickly get the puck deeper in the zone and in his own-end, he made several well executed outlet passes that landed on the tape of his teammates.

Tuomisto, Antti (2019) – Tuomisto had a decent two-way performance for Finland, showing better outlet passes that led to more efficient breakouts in his own-end. In some other viewings, he tended to fire passes that were inaccurate and too sharp, but in today's game he showed better accuracy. He showed some grit after the play as well, getting in the face of a Swedish opponent, so there's an edge to him depending on the situation. That edge didn't translate to an overly physical game and at times he was a little late to assess what Sweden was attempting to do but he also was decent under-pressure and didn't panic when below the goal-line. In the offensive-end, he faked a shot before attempting to re-open his lane which was important considering in most other viewings, he played a steam-lined game that didn't involve much in the way of lane adjustment when walking the offensive-line.

Aaltonen, Leevi (2019) – Aaltonen had a solid performance for Finland, slowing his game down and assessing his time and space better than some other games at this event. Instead of attempting to skate circles around his opponents or use his motor inefficiently, Leevi looked to stop-up and create chances and switch-gears to make him less predictable. He was also effective along the half-wall on the powerplay, setting up his teammates while also identifying when he had enough space to walk into the left-circle before firing a wrist-shot that went in blocker side. The shot was released through a screen and was accurate. Furthermore, he assessed when he should shoot and when he should pass it off at a more consistent rate today.

Raty, Aku (2019) – Raty had a decent game for Finland, generating in spurts while showing a plus release point. Aku has shown that he likes to carry the puck through the neutral zone but has had mixed results assessing how much time and space he has, that was the case today as well, where he's a little late when trying to move over the line on an angle and as a result forced his teammates offside occasionally. That being said, he also managed a couple of clean entries which resulted in extended zone-time. On the forecheck, he was effective, this led to his opening goal of the game where he pressured correctly, collected the puck near the net area and fired a hard wrist-shot that went over Wallstedt's glove, the shot was bar-down. He scored another goal in motion in the slot-area after receiving a pass after cutting directly towards the net area, the shot was off his stick in one motion and showed good placement. Like Aaltonen, there's times where he plays with a plus motor, but he's still having trouble with turning it down in his own-end of the ice, this resulted in a poor penalty. Overall though, Raty was a plus player for his team and was dangerous.

Tieksola, Tuuka (2019) – Tieksola was one of the best forwards on the ice for either team, showing very good agility, as well as good straight-line speed which complimented his plus motor. In some other viewings of him at this tournament, he's disappointed but today he was much more involved in the play and looked to game a difference early and often. He was deceptive when carrying the puck by using his edges and pivots to rapidly change direction which allowed him to create additional time and space in order find his teammates. He's shown at this event and others that he's a pass-first player, threading some impressive and technical passes while going at full-speeds. The biggest areas of improvement in today's viewing was Tieksola's willingness to drive-play and attack through heavy traffic. On one sequence, he weaves through multiple players while going at a high-speed, which led to a primary assist after he generated a rebound by crashing the net. In the defensive-end, he showed a willingness to sacrifice himself to make a shot-block and was hurt on one attempt but competed through the shift. He was excellent overall today.

Miettinen, Veeti (2020) – Miettinen was excellent for Finland, generating over a dozen scoring chances for his team, while also showing the willingness to drive-play. He started the game off well, displaying a good skill-level that allowed him to beat a defender one-on-one before firing a wrist-shot that he elevated quickly. His decision making was a plus, as was his vision, finding his teammates consistently while setting them up for scoring chances throughout the game. Furthermore, he was poised when holding the puck and assessed his options at a plus rate. Although under-sized, he was willing to take a direct-route to the net but he also looked light and weak, showing little in the way of power when attempting to accelerate. That being said, he compensated well by showing a good motor and was very consistent today, dominating possession at times as a result.

Russia vs USA, U18 Five-Nations, Feb 9 2019

USA -

Beecher, John (2019) – Beecher flashed his excellent skating ability and high-end tools, but also showed why his play doesn't translate into a high-rate of execution as well. He had several impressive rushes that showed off his skating mechanics. For a kid his size, his fluidity is exceptional, as is his straight-line speed which he used to barrel down the wing before releasing a wrist-shot on one-attempt and a pass across the slot area on another. His passing was below-average this game though, in large part to his inability to soften his pass-attempts, this extends to his precision when attempting to thread his passes through traffic. He was decent on the forecheck and showed some tenacity after the whistle after getting into an altercation with Spiridonov. Overall, it was another showing from John that flashed his tools but also flashed why they don't always translate into points.

York, Cam (2019) – York was decent for the U.S on the backend against Russia. He started the game off strong, showing the ability to carry the puck over the neutral zone before making a quick move that showed some agility as well. The Russians forechecked aggressively but York's anticipation allowed him to keep up with the pace of play for the most part, making quick decisions that helped alleviate pressure. Although he won't weigh-heavy on opponents often due to his smaller stature, he still physically engaged to a degree and used an active stick to make life more difficult for his opponents. At the offensive-line, he was a bit quiet, not generating too many scoring chances overall.

Rolston, Ryder (2020) – Rolston had some difficulty to start against Russia but played better in the last-half of the game. He looked to use his speed to skate past the Russian defense, but had some difficulty establishing himself on the forecheck during some chase sequences. However, he did get his offense going in spurts, shooting in a rebound goal after putting himself in good position, while also contributing on the powerplay with a pass that was redirected in-front of the net very late in the game.

Thrun, Henry (2019) – Thrun had some solid moments for the U.S, showing an active-stick, a good compete-level, and above-average hockey-sense in his own-end. He had a good read during a 2-on-1 against sequence where he anticipated the pass attempt and got himself in-front of the lane which took away the chance. Along the boards in his own-end, he was strong on the puck while competing against two-different Russian players, he won the board battle and managed to take off and gain a clean entry in the offensive-end. That entry sequence was extended to prolonged time for the U.S attack, where Thrun pinched correctly and made several crisp passes to his teammates when cycling the puck down-low. It wasn't all good moments for Henry though, after activating at the offensive-line at the wrong-time, he was thrown out of position which resulted in an odd-man rush that led to a goal against. Overall though, Thrun had some good moments.

Caufield, Cole (2019) – Caufield generated scoring chances consistently throughout the game and at times showed his high-end release point. Although he some difficulty penetrating through traffic at times, he still was dangerous at off-angles due to how quickly he can elevate the puck and how much velocity his wrist-shot can generate, this led to several quality scoring chances and a late goal where he found soft-ice in the slot before firing an accurate wrist-shot that went past Askarov's blocker. Cole was decent with his puck distribution on the powerplay as well, but at times didn't show a high-panic threshold, making inadvertent turnovers. An example of this was when he needed to react quickly after running out of room so he made a spinning no-look pass that was intercepted easily. That being said, Caufield demonstrated again that he needs very little time to get off his tremendous shot and find the back of the net.

Zegras, Trevor (2019) – Zegras had an okay two-way performance for the States. He had an excellent defensive play on a backchecking effort which resulted in a takeaway and later in the game made a good read that resulted in an interception off a pass by Zaitsev, he also showed a willingness to get engaged down below the goal-line and support his defenseman. Although the defensive-side of his game was good in spurts, his offensive-game was sloppy. He showed his creativity off, attempting to make several high-end one-touch passes but the results were mixed. Furthermore, although he's usually deceptive with the puck, he telegraphed some of his intentions out there, specifically on an odd-man rush where he didn't look to use his head to fake Askarov before attempting a cross-crease pass, this made it an easy tell to pick up for the Russian keeper.

Boldy, Matthew (2019) – Boldy had a poor offensive-performance for the U.S, but did have a good backchecking effort on one sequence where he stick-lifted a Russian player from behind in the neutral-zone before making an accurate pass that transitioned the play back around. Boldy did have some good moments where he made efficient give-and-go sequences with his other skilled teammates and did show off some creativity, but a common theme that has developed at this event and in the USHL as well is inconsistent puck-management and that occurred here again far too often.

Turcotte, Alex (2019) – Turcotte started this game strong, but tapered off towards the final frame. He had some impressive flashes, cutting down the wings while feeding technical passes to his teammates but didn't play consistently at the same pace we've normally seen from him. On one play in the neutral-zone, he tried to do too much with the puck by attempting to weave through multiple players and ran out of room, resulting in a turnover, so it felt like Alex was attempting to do too much by himself at times. That being said, he still flashed impressive offensive-gifts and processed the play quickly while under pressure.

Russia -

Burenov, Nikolay (2019) – Burenov had a stand-out offensive performance from the backend for Russia. He maintained a decent gap and made some accurate outlet passes in his own-end but it was his shot that stood-out today. He activated at the offensive-line and found soft-ice in the high-slot where he received a pass and scored a bar-down wrist-shot goal that went over Knights glove. On his second-goal, he had a seeing-eye wrist-shot go through heavy traffic and find its way over Rowe. It was a game where Burenov looked offensively engaged and was dangerous as a result.

Gritsyuk, Arseniy (2019) – Gritsyuk was arguably the best player on the ice today for Russia, driving play in spurts while competing at a high-level. With a game that mattered, Arseniy stepped up in a big way, dictating the tempo of play by showing poise under-pressure and making smart-decisions with the puck on his stick. He had several high-end passes to his teammates which resulted several chances as well as goals being generated. Furthermore, he did most of his work off the cycle and around the goal-line, recognizing open and closed lanes well while under-pressure. He also scored a goal for his team after finding soft-ice, the release point was impressive on the shot. Away from the play, he battled aggressively and at one point through himself down to the ice to intercept an outlet pass attempt. It was an impressive performance from the kid.

Nikolayev, Ilya (2019) – After having a slow start to the tournament and getting injured at one point, Nikolayev had a good performance against the U.S, playing a physical-brand of hockey while also showing his impressive puck-skills. He was engaged from the opening whistle, delivering several clean hits along the boards and pressuring away from the puck. In a one-on-one situation, he flashed his quick set of hands, making a nice outside-to-inside deke by rapidly pulling the puck before delivering a sharp wrist-shot that required a point blank save. He had a primary assist after moving the puck up quickly to his open teammate and overall was much more effective than some previous viewings at this event.

Spiridonov, Egor (2019) – Spiridonov had his best game of the event, showing an impressive forecheck and cycling effectively. He has a good frame for physical play on him, and today he used it effectively while showing a good motor as well. In some previous viewings he had trouble generating scoring chances, but against the U.S. he managed to find soft-ice consistently which resulted in several high-end scoring chances. His release-point isn't overly dangerous and he failed to show the ability to change the angle of his shot but he did score a goal during an odd-man rush where he put himself in good position to receive a pass while in motion. There wasn't any sort of creative element to Spiridonov who played a more streamlined game but he was effective out there and showed a good compete-level.

Zaitsev, Dmitri (2019) – Zaitsev had another solid showing for Russia by using his motor to make the U.S uncomfortable and by getting involved offensively. He attempted a couple of dekes and moves that failed but the creativity was there. As an example, after receiving a pass from Nikolayev near the crease area, he tried a quick between the legs move pass that was intercepted, on another attempt, he tried a pull-deke around a defender but couldn't get by him. That being said, his rate of execution was a plus overall, he also scored a goal after getting sprung on a partial breakaway where he fired a sharp wrist-shot over the glove of Knight from just above the hashmarks.

Sheshin, Dmitri (2019) – Sheshin had another good offensive-effort for Russia. He played on the half-wall on the powerplay showing good poise and puck-control, he also made quick decisions under-pressure which resulted in him keeping pucks alive along the boards. He scored a goal after finding soft-ice and shooting a hard wrist-shot that went top-corner. His motor and pace were consistent again, and he had no problem engaging physically.

Flint Firebirds vs Barrie Colts, Feb 9 2019

Firebirds –

Kolyachonok, Vladislav (2019) – Kolyachonok played a solid defensive game which involved some physicality and the ability to shift his gear when the play was picking up pace. He had a great hit in own-end which caused a turnover after a streaking Colts player attempted to cut into the middle of the slot, and he was willing to engage after the whistle. He was quick to move the puck from behind his goal-line and had above-average positioning overall. Although he was used on the powerplay, he wasn't really a factor in terms of generating offense on most shifts but didn't turn the puck over or stand out for the wrong reasons either.

Keppen, Ethan (2019) – Keppen had a solid two-way performance for Flint, showing a versatile game that featured the willingness to enter heavy traffic, as well as compete aggressively for loose pucks along the boards. He won a board battle early in the neutral zone and then showed above-average crossover mechanics giving him enough lateral mobility to bypass his opponent and create a clean offensive-zone entry. That play sparked his game, he was active and was skating hard for the majority of the game, which drew a penalty behind the net at one point. He scored a tap-in goal after finding soft-ice in the slot area after receiving a pass from the right circle and was consistent at setting up his teammates as well.

Vierling, Evan (2020) – Vierling had a quality two-way performance for Flint, showing plus playmaking ability which gave him several assists. He made quality stretch passes that landed on the tape of his teammates and was also capable of making sharp passes while going at top-speeds. He several high-end scoring chances where he found soft-ice in the slot-area, but his shot was relatively average today compared to his playmaking. He was used on the penalty-kill and had a heads up read at the defensive-line which resulted in a quality short-handed chance as well. Evan was consistent and stood out, showing a decent amount of talent but failed to show any dynamic element as well, never challenging one-on-one or showing high-end creativity.

Colts –

Allensen, Nathan (2019) – Allensen had a quality two-way performance for Barrie, showing plus skating mechanics and a willingness to compete hard to obtain the puck in his own-end. He raced after a loose puck near his goal-line and beat his opponent to it which allowed for a transitional breakout early and was engaged throughout the game after making that play. He was used on the powerplay and was decent at distributing the puck but lost his poise when under heavy pressure which resulted in a forced spinning pass that missed its mark. However, he did activate at the offensive-line at even-strength on one sequence which resulted in one of Barrie's best scoring chances after he gloved down a loose puck and set up his teammate in the slot area for a great scoring chance. He never threatened with his shot from the point, didn't display high-end talent, but was serviceable and skated hard.

York, Jack (2019) – York had a mixed game for Barrie, pinching too aggressively at times which put him behind the play and resulted in prime scoring chances for Flint. He was used on the powerplay with Allensen, and moved the puck well, but never managed to breakdown the Flint defense or show off much in the way of vision since he was unable to thread passes in heavy traffic. His skating was a plus and he used it to generate clean offensive-zone entries and extend offensive-zone time for his team. In his own-end, he assessed his options well enough to move the puck up and on one sequence he had a nice give-and-go sequence while under pressure.

Suzuki, Ryan (2019) – Suzuki had a mixed game for Barrie. He was inactive in the first half of the game, rarely showing the willingness to engage physically away from the play or cut aggressively through traffic when carrying the puck except for one play where he attempted to split the defense and ended up crashing into the goaltender. However, it was a different story in the third. After receiving quality powerplay time, Suzuki started flashing his talent, distributing the puck with excellent one-touch and no-look passes, showing a high-level of deception that made it difficult for Flint to read. In the middle of the third, he showed his hands, dragging the puck in-tight to his body which allowed him to shoot around a screen and fool the Flint goalie. Suzuki was inconsistent but came alive and took over the third period by using his talent.

Baie-Comeau Drakkar at Blainville-Boisbriand Armada, February 9th, 2019

Baie-Comeau

#29 Légaré, Nathan (2019): His decision-making was poor; he took some good shots on net when sometimes a pass would have been a better decision to make. He looked like he had tunnel vision, as he didn't use his teammates out there enough, opting to shoot the puck sometimes from low-percentage angles. His skating was below average; he's strong on his skates but didn't generate much speed, and looked heavy on the ice while struggling with the pace. Not much in terms of physical play from him today, as his best hit came from when he had a collision with a referee in the neutral zone. On the power play, he was used in the slot and was trying to get passes that he could one-time on the net. The Armada, however, did a good job covering him in the slot. His best scoring chance came on a breakaway, but he was stopped by the Armada goaltender and hit the post on the rebound.

#8 Merisier-Ortiz, Christopher (2019): Not very noticeable out there tonight, though he showed some of his good footwork and skating abilities on the power play in the 3rd period. That was, unfortunately, pretty much it for him in this game in terms of being noticeable. He played with veteran Pascal Corbeil, and Corbeil made most of the transition plays (puck rushing and puck moving) on that defensive pair.

Blainville-Boisbriand

#58 Bolduc, Samuel (2019): Didn't play with a heartbeat in the first period, was not very active in his own zone and was too soft on one play deep in his own zone which led to the 2-0 Baie-Comeau goal. There was a lack of aggressiveness in his game tonight. He needs to use his big frame more in his own zone. He had more of a pulse in the 2nd period, making more plays including a nice stretch pass at one point, but he was still too soft in his own zone. Not many puck rushes from him today, and he didn't have many chances to shoot the puck on the power play, either.

#7 Rannisto, Jasper (2019): Didn't like his decision-making tonight. He made a bad cross-ice pass in the neutral zone that ended up being a turnover that led to a Baie-Comeau goal. He also had a couple of his shots blocked, as his shot release was not quick enough, and he was also unable to find a shooting lane. His footspeed is average at best, and he struggled defending versus speedy forwards.

#21 Rochon, Antoine (2019): He worked hard today, and I liked his compete level throughout this tough game for the Armada. Did a good job getting into the shooting lanes and blocking some shots in his own zone. He made a nice feed to Corbeil on a 2-on-1 rush that led to the Armada's first goal of the game. Skating was decent and he kept his feet moving out there. He was one of the few Armada forwards who was at least noticeable tonight.

Spokane Chiefs vs. Kootenay Ice, February 9. 2019

Spokane

Beckman, Adam (2019) - Excellent game with his puck distribution, making almost no bad plays. Generated a ton of zone entries on cross ice passing and does a good job moving the puck away from pressure. Made some more difficult passes on the powerplay with a couple nice feeds to the high slot and cross seam. Would like to see him attack with a bit more pace as he seemed to slow it down a bit too much today.

Toporpwski, Luke (2019) - As usual Toporowskis work rate and speed really stood out. Thought he was a bit wasteful with the puck today with a lot of plays forced. Lacks in creativity with the puck and does not have high end skill level. Can get tunnel vision with the puck sometimes instead of taking advantage of all his options.

Kootenay

Krebs, Peyton (2019) - Cannot think of one game where Krebs has not gone out and competed hard. Almost every positive Kootenay play today primarily involved him. Great at gaining the zone as he constantly found the hole and showed the explosiveness in his skating to push defenders back. Was also great on pucks down low both with his board work to recover it in battles, and protecting it from the opposition with change of direction and strength. Dangerous playmaker with an excellent understanding of how much room the opposition selling out to stop him opens up.

McClennon, Connor (2020) - Was impressed by his constant hustle today. Despite being a smaller player is very unafraid on the ice. Was a very willing shooter today as he threw it on net whenever he had a chance, would have liked to see him attempt some more passes instead of shooting a low percentage shot.

USA U18 vs Sioux Falls Stampede, February 15th, 2019

Sioux Falls

Phillips, Ethan (2019) - Phillips created plenty of scoring chances for his team in this game. He is an undersized winger with plenty of skill who is also not afraid to go to the dirty areas. He took some big hits, but he wasn't fazed by them. He skates very well and gets up and down the ice very quickly. He has a smooth set of hands and very intriguing playmaking ability. He plays the point on the first powerplay unit and displayed great vision and a hard one timer. He recorded an assist on their only goal. He made a nice give and go play on a 3 on 1 rush for a goal by Berglund. He had plenty of nice rushes and he does well to get in on the forecheck and pester opposing defenseman. Phillips was one of the few bright spots for Sioux Falls in this game.

Johnson, Ryan (2019) - Johnson displayed fantastic skating ability, lateral movement, and change of direction. He has great escape ability where he displays shiftiness and great edge work. He stayed calm and did a solid job moving the puck up the ice. He almost seems a little too nonchalant at times as he trusts in his abilities a little too much. Everything about his game was very smooth. He did not seem to want to get involved offensively as much as he probably could. He didn't see as much powerplay time as he should have, which was strange because he has intriguing offensive tools. When he did see the powerplay it was for thirty seconds or less, but he showed nice vision and a want to put the puck on net. Due to his slim frame he is a stick first defender and makes sure to keep himself between his man and the net.

Jami Krannila (2019) - Krannila was just average in this game. He was pretty quiet for most of the game but did show some good signs. He has a low center of gravity which contributes to his strong stride and puck protection ability. He did a good job of drawing defenders to him and finding an open guy for a scoring opportunity. He was a fairly quick skater but did not show game breaking speed. He had five shots on a goal but not many real threats of scoring. He seemed to lose interest in his shifts quickly and turn on cruise control. He did a good job in his own zone playing a sound positional game and having good awareness.

Anthony Romano (2019) - Romano displayed a strong skating stride and above average speed. He was very good on the penalty kill and very responsible in all three zones. He did not display high end skill but more of a power forward style of play. He has a lot of energy and got in hard on the forecheck. He showed his speed where he outraced Matt Boldy for a lose puck and gave himself a half breakaway. He took the puck hard to the net and drew a penalty on the same play. He did not appear to be a guy who can drive the offense on his own, but he has decent offensive ability and played a solid 200-foot game.

USA

Helleson, Drew (2019) - Helleson had a very solid game tonight. He did a good job knowing his options before getting the puck, then executing the play he wanted to make. He skated with the puck a little more than usual tonight to create offense opposed to his normal stay at home style of play. His skating and his hands were both impressive tonight and seem to have improved from the start of the season. He played physical in his own zone and made it hard on opposing forwards to get the puck to the net. He played within himself tonight and did a nice job for his team.

Rolston, Ryder (2020) - Rolston showed a lot of confidence in his abilities tonight carrying the puck and creating offensive opportunities. He has great acceleration when carrying the puck and does a great job pushing the defensemen back. He has a quick and accurate wrist shot that he loves to get off on the rush. He scored the first goal of the game when he drove the net and tipped in a pass from Owen Lindmark. He picked up and assist on the second goal of the game where showed great quickness. He walked up the wall, cut to the middle of the nice and fired a wrist shot that was tipped in by Matt Boldy. It was a very good game for Rolston and his confidence has been growing over the past few weeks.

Boldy, Matthew (2019) - Boldy was on his game tonight. He had six shots on net and was dangerous all night. He displayed fantastic hand eye coordination when he tipped in Rolstons shot to put his team up 2-0. He had one rush where he showed great speed and deceptiveness where he made the defenseman bite on a shoulder fake. He walked in alone but was gloved by the goalie. Boldy could've had a huge night but was unable to figure out the goaltender. This game was a very positive step for Boldy going forward as his skill and creativity was on full display. He did a great job keeping possession of the puck and limiting turnovers as well.

Thrun, Henry (2019) - Thrun had a very good game tonight. He's a rock back there for this team as he doesn't make many mistakes and plays a very solid game in all three zones. He moved the puck up the ice quickly and made tape to tape passes. He didn't get beat in his own zone and plays very well in 1 on 1 situations. He demonstrates very good foot speed and has a very good-sized frame. He never plays too flashy, but tonight he showed fantastic vision and offensive ability when he followed up the play, took a drop pass from Lindmark and found Moynihan in an opportune scoring position. Moynihan was able to score giving Thrun an assist on the play. He had a very solid game all around.

Sioux Falls Stampede at USNTDP U18, February 15, 2019

Sioux Falls Stampede -

Phillips, Ethan - 2019 Very strong game from Phillips. He was an offensive catalyst and looked more confident with the puck than he had in the past couple viewings. Setup a 19 year old with his first career goal – it was the only goal of the night for the Stampede. Really impressed with how Phillips elevated his game against a tough US defense. He plays a smart game and the skill and drive to standout.

Krannila, Jami - 2019 Krannila really upped his game in a big spot. He's always very engaged in games, but tonight he was really tracking the puck and the play well. He was Sioux Falls' best player. He sniffed out and disrupted a lot of creative NTDP plays that most others at this level can't figure out. He turned some pucks over and generating odd man rush chances against with good NZ play. Traditionally, he's more of a setup man, but tonight he called his own number a bunch. He had five shots on the night, no one on the team had more than three. I'm not sure there was a single shift where Krannila didn't get a touch on the puck in a positive way. Played all 200 feet as usual…smarts, speed, and a dedication to his craft.

Johnson, Ryan - 2019 In a quick-tempo game, I think we learned a lot about Johnson's skill level right now. He has some trouble stringing consecutive elite plays together. He can turn on a dime against the momentum of the play and lose forecheckers easily, but it's that next play that isn't quite on the money. On individual plays, he has the skills…his hands are improving, his skating with the puck is improving, his passing is fine. It's that next play that isn't there yet. Johnson's feet and hockey sense didn't allow him to be fooled too much defensively tonight…but he didn't look quite as confident about stepping to make plays as he had been in previous viewings…tough to blame him, not only was this the first of a three-game weekend, but it was against a stacked team. He also lost a foot race to Matthew Boldy that negated an icing, which is a little odd in and of itself. In a game where a lot of players on both sides seemed to dial it up, I'm not sure if Johnson did…or was able. Which isn't to say he played poorly, but everyone else was pushing the pace just a little bit more.

USNTDP U18 -

Zegras, Trevor - 2019 Played LW with Jack Hughes and Cole Caulfield. Made two early turnovers…one was a creative stop and go move against Ryan Johnson who sniffed it out. The other was a poor decision trying to carry the puck through the NZ and right in the middle of the ice, he tried to switch on his puck protection mode and that led to a 3 on 1 the other way. Zegras didn't really have his skating legs tonight overall, he seemed to have a bit of an off night. He didn't have as much ice to work with either, with Hughes occupying the middle…so that may have something to do with it.

Hughes, Jack - 2019 First USHL game for Hughes in a month. He didn't seem to miss a beat. He made two unreal passes in his first few shifts. He had Zegras on left and Cole Caulfield on his right tonight. It was a pretty typical Hughes game, minus him missing a puck touch when he got a loose for a semi-breakaway in tight which washed a scoring chance. I have a growing concern about his hockey sense, particularly when the puck isn't on his stick…but that doesn't necessarily mean defensively. There's more than a couple times in games where he simply runs into his teammates, or crosses into lanes that do not belong to him and it surprises some of his linemates. Defensively, he's a looping mess that seems to have free reign to just apply pressure where he sees fit and everyone else has to adapt. But even in transition, when it's just starting, if Hughes doesn't have the puck – sometimes you see the cracks showing. No real question that he's the most technically skilled player in the draft class, but does his head for the game really match his hands and feet? That's a high bar that his extremities set, but I wonder how well he plays with others in a faster, more structured environment.

Boldy, Matthew - 2019 Boldy never ceases to impress with the hands plays he can make. He is exceedingly creative with the puck. He has a good feel for the game, but sometimes he's too complicated for his own good. He relies on a lot of tricky stuff and a lot of cross-ice passes to make his mark in games...that probably isn't a very sustainable way to make offense at the NHL level. The question is: Is trying this stuff now to see what he can pull off and far he can push himself from a talent development standpoint? Or is he going to tie himself in a knot at the next level trying to stop on a dime, touch a puck behind himself, spin off a defenseman, and then try to drop a cross-ice sauce pass over two sticks? Alleviating some of these concerns is the meat that exists to Boldy's game...he's not just sizzle. He plays a good two-way game too. He can settle in and be the third wheel, trigger man if the situation arises. He isn't a dynamite skater...but he did win a foot race against a terrific skater in Ryan Johnson to negate an icing in the middle portion of the game. It's not likely enough to hold him back significantly.

Hamilton Bulldogs vs. Ottawa 67's, February 15th, 2019

Hamilton

Mutter, Navrin (2019) - Mutter showed good power forward potential combined with a strong work ethic down below the hash marks. He is an average skater who displayed a good burst of speed and acceleration in open ice. On several shifts he drove hard to the net disrupting the goaltender and looking for rebounds or loose pucks. He was strong tonight at getting pucks deep in corners and attacking Ottawa defense. He was physical in all 3 zones tonight, he had a couple good strong open ice hits.

Kaliyev, Arthur (2019) – Kaliyev moves very well given his size showing good speed and acceleration. He is at his best when he's moving his feet showing fluid movements. He showed some intriguing skills including a good release and flashes of hands. He has a more difficult time creating by himself and needs a linemate to play with and help create with him. Despite his imposing frame, he was not as physically dominant as he could be in this viewing. I was disappointed in Kaliyev game tonight; he seemed to not be engaged at all at the start of the game. He kept to the outside a lot throughout the game, even on the rush or power play. Arthur didn't like to go to the areas in the offensive zone to be effective. It was my first viewing this year of him and i was disappointed in his compete level.

Morrison, Logan (2020) - Logan had a solid showing in this viewing. He displayed impressive puck control and protection skills which alongside his vision allowed him to feed his line mates and makes the most of opportunities on a regular bases. He showed a good and accurate release on his goal in the 1st period. He was able to accept the pass and get the puck off quick, not allowing goalie time to react to the shot.

Ottawa

Okhotyuk, Nikita (2019) – Okhotyuk has good vision on breakout passes in transition. His ability to close down angles on attacking players limiting the time and space was very evident tonight. He showed great hustle on offensive zone rush, then back check where he finished a big hit on the attacking player. Not afraid to battle in the corners and mix it up physically. While he is able to get up and down the ice well, his overall skating ability could use work. He seems to always make the simple play in his own end and not panicking with the puck with pressure on him.

USNTDP U18 at Chicago Steel, February 16, 2019

USNTDP U18 -

Turcotte, Alex - 2019 Turcotte with speed and space can cause any defender in his peer group some trepidation. He just eats up ice with the puck so fast and he's moving you exactly where he wants you to go with his quick stickhandling.

Made a perfect little saucer pass from behind the left post out to Jack Hughes in the right dot on the power play to setup the tying goal…one of his four assists on the night. Added shorthanded goal when he was left alone in front and Boldy found him. He was actually stopped on the initial try while standing at the top of the crease, but stuck with it and cashed on his own rebound. Finished a couple of hits on one particularly energetic shift…the second of those hits helped contribute to a turnover that led to a goal. On the plus side for Turcotte, this was one of the few viewings I've seen where he didn't take a real big hit either. Very complete center, with wheels and hands that are tough not to notice. May be just about the best overall playmaker in the draft class from a puck distribution perspective.

Thrun, Henry - 2019 Still tough to get a read on what kind of defender Thrun wants to be. He is very inconsistent in how he plays the game. Started out with an offensive push…made a good cross ice that led to a chance from the right point. Then did a good job keeping playing alive at the left point. Made a couple of smart, and above all – heavy – pinches….meaning, he attacked the puck ruggedly and finished a hit in a way that allowed for even money for the forward covering for him the puck did get past him. From the 2nd period and forward, he seemed to dial it back. In fact, he really started to over-skate plays…sliding too far back in the defensive zone with the puck on the wide side, over-skated a PK scrum that cost them a clear, over-skated a support opportunity that caused him to end up with a wonky gap, which he tried to recover from with an aggressive play outside the dots and Mastrosimone walked right around him…Thrun came up with feathers. He's a better lateral and back skater than he is moving up the ice. Doesn't seem to offer much puck carrying upside or exciting offensive tools. He's probably going to need a more firm career track/player type.

McCarthy, Case - 2019 Traditional, defensive defenseman with good ability to physically close off plays intelligently and effectively. Not much on puck skills, no puck poise, is prone to forced and unforced errors alike, and just a below average to average skater. Lacks confidence in space and with the puck. Not a good enough outlet passer against no or limited pressure for this level. He committed three unforced errors in this regard in the 1st period alone. Looks like he might have a heavy shot tucked away in there, but he has a tough time keeping it down and useful. Made a pretty graphic error against a quick rush chance, where he stopped moving his feet, reached, lost positioning and couldn't recover. He clearly stuck a body part out and tripped the attacker, but it went unpunished. The game just moves a little fast for him overall, and above all, he just doesn't have the puck skills to match…it feels like he knows that and it causes him added strife. In a little bit more structure, with less of an all-star team around him, he might be able to feel more comfortable just playing the game that he can play…but whether an NHL team wants that game going forward is a fair question, as his base line technical skills are substandard.

York, Cam - 2019 Standard game that we have come to expect from York. Calm, cool, collected…occasionally revving it up in a way that reminds you he is still the most skilled defenseman on the team. After a sleepy start, he made a nice multi-line carry in response to the 2-1 goal by Chicago. His stick positioning is always right on the money…points his blade right at the puck and has the skating and smarts to hang around in every play. Made a big open ice hit in the 3rd, which was the only uncharacteristic thing about York's night. The only question for York is: how big is the skill upside really? Tonight would make you guess that he's not quite a #1 d-man down the road…probably more of a #2.

Fensore, Domenick - 2019 Active, aggressive defender who makes great reads in all three zones. Made a nice offensive play in the zone to walk low, fake a shot and then Gretzky turn against the grain before finding Vlasic on a cross-ice feed. Plays the game with a lot of confidence, really plays on his toes. He isn't afraid of giving or receiving physical contact despite his size. The skill package is tantalizing on top of some of the best skating in his draft class. He did seem to lose his net twice…just seemed like he lost track of exactly where he was and felt like he was closer to his net than he was. He doesn't like to get pushed back into the paint as it doesn't match his style nor is it beneficial for him to do battle in the trenches. Fensore attacks the top of the route to borrow a football term…he does everything he can to not let the game play him. And he looks very capable of that at LD or RD.

Chaska Hawks at Chanhassen Storm, February 16, 2019

Chaska Hawks

Warnert, Blaine – 2019+ Warnert was dominate in this game, registering 3 goals and dominating his opponents using his size and speed. Warnert doesn't have great explosiveness off the hop but displayed a good top gear. His size and long reach allowed him to dominate in 1 on 1 situations. Warnert showed good awareness in knowing when to go to the net and getting his stick available for passes as he drove the paint. Warnert may not be a draft prospect due to his lack of explosiveness but he checks a lot of other boxes and will be an intriguing pro prospect given his size and scoring ability.

Pitlick, Rhett – 2019 Registering 4 assists in this game, Pitlick's playmaking ability was well on display throughout the game. One sequence Pitlick was able to quickly control the puck on the half wall and zip a pass through a small lane to Warnert on the backdoor. He see's lanes and is able to get passes through traffic consistently. Pitlick's awareness and hockey sense came into question with a couple of his decisions with the puck, one where he didn't take advantage of the time and space he had to drive the net, instead choosing to circle back along the half wall and essentially skate the puck out of a scoring area. Pitlick has a lot of skill and made things happen more often than not with the puck on his tape but as his competition gets tougher at the high levels, he will need to add some simplicity to his game.

Koster, Mike – 2019 Koster showcased his playmaking ability in this game, often leading and joining the rush coming out of his own end. On one instance he held onto the puck too long while circling the offensive zone, resulting in a turnover and a 2 on 1 going the other way. Despite the one glaring turnover, Koster was able to execute a good amount of offensive zone entries with control and consistently setup things in the offensive end. Koster moved the puck quickly and confidently in all 3 zones and controlled the game from the back end. Koster's skating isn't explosive but has above average agility and when combined with his puck skills, made him difficult to pin down on the fore-check and he was able to escape pressure easily for most of the game. Koster's defensive awareness and gaps could have been better in this game, however with his opponents not having a lot of offensive skill, Koster was able to easily recover in a lot of instances and it didn't cost him in this game.

Leksand IF u20 at AIK u20 february 16 2019

Leksand IF u20

Lundqvist, Alexander 2019 Lundqvist was a big presence since he is a big defender, he did however not play big. Sure, his reach with his defensive stick is really good. But he did not use his body in any way. His breakout passes were terrible and were more likely to hit someone on the knee than on the tape of the stick. He was somewhat successful at quarterbacking the power-play, with good passing. However, his lateral movement was not smooth at all and every single one of his shots was blocked by the first forward.

Ronnqvist, Viktor 2019 Ronnqvist had a solid game, without getting tested properly. He competed hard for rebounds and loose pucks and showed great lateral speed. He is very small for a modern goaltender, but today he came up big with his speed and athleticism.

AIK u20

Broberg, Philip 2019 Was this really Broberg? He was a humongous disappointment and did not show any of the advertised skills he is supposed to have. Sure, he proved his smooth skating at times, but rarely took advantage of it. He totally fanned on shots, missed the puck and fell. He missed passes and got icing calls against him. He did score his teams only goal with a lucky bounce from a shot from the blueline.

Hedlund, Hedlund had a night he will want to forget, fast. He stood deep in the net and did not challenge the shooters as he usually does. Some of his actions resulted directly to goals against. He looked like he lacked self-confidence. Both he and his defenders had a terrible game.

Sjolund, Samuel 2019 Sjolund moved the puck well. He also got the opportunity to quarterback the first power-play unit ahead of Philip Broberg. He struggled on the power-play, he was strangely positioned on the blue line and did not move at all at times. He was a complete mess defensively but managed to avoid being on the ice for most goals against.

Karlstrom, David 2019 Karlstrom had a weak game, just like the rest of his team. He played with a lot of tenacity and played with more grit than he usually does. He really needs to improve in the faceoff circle.

Tri-City Storm at Waterloo Black Hawks, February 17, 2019

Tri-City Storm -

Jones, Zac - 2019 As usual, Jones logged a ton of time…most of which with '99 Ronnie Attard. Wasn't a particularly noteworthy game from Jones. He was good defensively, but struggled with the offensive parts of his game. He missed a number of outlet passes tonight…his first PP shift of the game was a disaster: off of a won faceoff, he carried the puck a clear five feet outside the blueline, made a no-chance stretch pass into traffic, and then fumbled a point pass out to center and got the puck tangled in his feet on the attempt at a quick regroup. Doesn't appear to offer enough pluses in the skating and skill categories to warrant a lot of fanfare.

Pinto, Shane - 2019 Really engaged in the battle right off the hop today. Very active stick, engaged in some body contact. Skated hard both ways all game. He was dictating terms off of faceoffs, communicating with players about what he wanted, telling them where to setup, etc. He made a great stick lift and pass to lead to the first goal. Setup the winning goal with a nice sauce pass on a 2 on 1, the initial shot was rejected, but the rebound kicked right to him behind the net and he made a quick pass to a cutting Attard who cashed from in-close. Pinto had five shots, his line (with Brendan Furry and Ian Murphy) had 12 of TC's 23 shots in the contest. Pinto has a good head for the game and really good hand-eye coordination…he can pick passes out of the air with regularity and he gets a stick on a lot of pucks when he's cruising through the slot. He was also about +8 in the OZ/DZ dots tonight. The only drawback to Pinto is that he's only about an average skater, maybe even a touch below that…otherwise, he's a player…and he may have the best hands in the USHL (not including NTDP players).

Attard, Ronnie - 2019 Fits into the mold of a bigger, shoot-first offensive defenseman with limited hockey sense. Almost a dead ringer for former NHLer Cody Franson in terms of style. He can around the ice all right, his skating isn't terribly nimble…looks like he has one really dominant leg and another that he can't generate as much from. His lateral skating seems only seems to go one direction and his change of direction step is almost non-existent. So he can't shake defenders at the line as readily as you would like. At this level, he does a fine job negotiating shooting lanes, but unless the skating and skill package improve, that seems like it will evaporate as he moves up the ladder. He is very aggressive at playing defense, but not so much in a physical way…he just follows guys all over the place and then doesn't recede back towards his net…he'll just park himself up near his own blue line at times, and while the back side of the play rotates back towards the net, he'll routinely leave a forward to work his spot. Attempted to make what would have been a poorly-timed defensive change…stayed on, got the puck and then just threw it lightly away into the NZ…it was cleanly picked up by Waterloo, skated in with speed and it led to Waterloo making it a one-goal game in the 3rd. Attard took three penalties in the first two periods as well, one of which on the PP, as a puck got by him in the mid-layer of the offensive zone. He scored by cutting way down into the zone to follow-up on a 2 on 1 missed opportunity, Pinto fed him at the top of the crease for a lay-up.

As usual, he spent almost the entire night on the ice and paired with Zac Jones…but it's the younger Jones who cleans up Attard's messes more often than not. I'm not convinced there's enough pro skills in Attard's repertoire to make him an NHL player.

Waterloo Black Hawks -

Blumel, Matej - 2019 Blumel has a unique playing style that doesn't really match a particular mold. He plays a lot for Waterloo – tonight he was mostly on his off-wing – and he goes at ES, PP and PK. He doesn't have good footwork… goofy, wobbly stride, but he gets around the ice ok…particularly his long speed without the puck, he gets really low like a speed skater almost and can gain some ground. He's not physical, but there's a lot of "friction" with other players, even his own teammates, he always seems to be in someone's kitchen. High volume shooter…he's a ready, fire, aim player. He did get left alone in front at one opportunity, but didn't have a useful move at the ready to score. Good worker, not a very high-end skill set. Eight shots, and no points today.

Firstov, Vladislav - 2019 Nothing much from Firstov today…seemed to not play for about 13 minutes of game time from the mid-1st period til early in the 2nd for no obvious reason. He made one neat stutter-step play that allowed him to carry a puck to the middle of the attack zone on his forehand…but outside of that, he didn't have a lot of room out there. He booted two standard passes…one of which was a wide-open, easy pass on the power play…Firstov continues to struggle to accept passes. Previous concerns about his skating and skill level were not at all ameliorated today.

Drkulec, Ryan - 2019 No room for Drkulec tonight. Very few puck touches, but did end up with an assist thanks to a late-shift Ronnie Attard NZ turnover. He tried to make some puck protection moves off the wall and use the leverage of his frame and the boards a few times, but he just couldn't get the coordination and the timing down. He took a remarkably selfish and pointless penalty after a minor to moderate collision that he took exception to…came back right at that perp and cross-checked him to the ice 10 feet in front of the referee who was eyeing it the entire way. Drkulec and NHL clubs are in a potentially tough spot, as he probably isn't as far along as you'd like him to be at this point in the year, and he's a late 2000 birthday by just a fraction…probably isn't ultimately worth a draft pick in 2019.

Prince Albert Raiders vs Moose Jaw Warriors, February 18, 2019

Prince Albert

Guhle, Kaiden (2020) - Guhle has grown a ton as the season has gone on and his confidence has clearly increased. Decision making was much better today as Guhle played with some more risk which lead to him making better plays. Skating ability always stands out, but today coupled that with better puckhandling to make some skilled plays. Generated some offense from the blueline today as well.

Protas, Alexei (2019) - Stood out with his puck protection down low. Huge frame that no one could push around or get around to reach the puck. Uses this ability to set up his teammates once a second defender commits to stopping him or he sees an open lane. Speed in open ice is deceptive and surprisingly does a very good job generating zone entries as a puck carrier. First step and agility however do hold Protas back.

Moose Jaw

Tracey, Brayden (2019)- Extremely smooth hands, with a lot of high skill plays today especially in receiving the puck. Had good intensity on the forecheck today and also had a couple nice interceptions on good anticipation plays. With the puck Tracey was very creative in finding passing lanes and had an excellent release on his shot. Great offensively without the puck which really shows on the powerplay where he plays the high slot role better than anyone else I've seen this year. Raised his game in the third period, with two goals and a primary assist to bring his team within range of a comeback. Fairbanks Ice Dogs vs Janesville Jets, February 22nd 2019

Alaska Fairbanks Ice Dogs

Reid, Nate – 2019 Despite giving up 4 goals in regulation, Reid displayed excellent technical attributes throughout this game. While he is listed at 6'2" he plays smaller in the net, particularly in the butterfly so this is an area of his game that he needs to improve on. Reid was aggressive in challenging shooters in one on one situations But as a result lost his crease on a few too many instances and was caught out of position. Nate communicated with his defenseman well on break outs and helped identify where the pressure was coming from. Nate made an excellent save in overtime on a 2 on 1, not biting on the head fake and staying square to the shooter.

Janesville Jets

Brady, Cole – 2019 Brady showed good East West movement, particularly on the penalty kill Where his team struggled to take away passing lanes and forced him to move laterally a lot. Brady made an excellent blocker save 1 on 1 when the puck was turned over in the slot. Brady tracked loose pucks well and was quick to cover them in traffic. It wasn't the best performance from Brady in this game but he made enough key saves to give his team a chance to win In a shootout where he made 3 very impressive saves and looked calm and composed against all three shooters.

February 23, 2019 Brynäs IF at Örebro HC

BRYNÄS

BIF # 90 LW Boqvist, Jesper - The regular quick feet and good hands was used by Boqvist and he was bringing in the puck breaking in towards the net with speed. Boqvist stressed the puck holder good with the stick. Won several pucks and after one aggressive stick check ended with an Assist for 2-1 goal.

BIF # 8 RD Söderström, Victor (2019) - Wow, its amazing that a 17-year-old and quit small guy can do in Swedish Top league. He has super smooth floating skating and very good mobility especially sideways and backwards. Söderström was changing speed, stopped and started with the puck made him difficult to beet. He loves to build speed and showed a very good rush bringing the puck bringing over central ice and towards net. He is very good in receiving and giving quick accurate pass and manage to get the puck under control picking it down with the knee. Söderström positions himself very good and makes his team mates knowing where he is using his stick in the ice ready for pass. He communicates good with his team mates on the bench and on ice. Söderström looked very calm and mature and moved his head and showed good vision.

Rögle BK u20 at Brynas IF u20 february 23 2019

Rogle BK u20

Mrazik, Michal 2019 Mrazik looked like he was enjoying his game, he played with playfulness and lots of energy. His stride is very short and makes him lose speed. Even though he cheats his defensive responsibilities and leaves his defensive zone early to get a headstart on offense, defenders have no problems catching up on him. He showcased great hands and stickhandling a couple times, dangling his way around the offensive zone, but most of the times he did not get a shot away at the end. When he's not having the puck on his stick, he just parks his big frame in front of the net. Without moving or even trying to move, he just stands there waiting for shots to deflect, but it leads to him not being a part of his team's offense.

Brynas IF u20

Persson, Viktor 2020 Persson is another small, right-handed, offensive defenseman coming out of Brynas. His movement pattern looked great offensively and he could read where the puck would end up and where his teammates would go. He gave himself time with the puck by anticipating the play and did succeed in being constructive with the puck. His skating was smooth, with a low center of gravity and his top end speed was also pretty good. As a smaller defender, playing against older guys, he almost always went for the poke check instead of a bodycheck. However, he had no problems getting in battles in front of his own net. Suffers a bit from playing on an extremely weak team.

Kvist, Oskar 2019 Kvist played on the fourth line, where he has been stuck all season long.

He did not really contribute more than some grit and it seems like his skating has taken a step backward. He wasn't active offensively more than a few hits and his defensive game had flaws. Kvist had great character and worked hard all game.

Luleå HC at HV71 Feb 24 2019

HV71

HV71 # 18 RW Nybeck, Zion (2020) - Future potential topdraft Nybeck is far from a big player but he is mobile and skates well, checks with the stick high and his offensive mindset makes him having big impact on the ice even if he is 3,5 years younger than some or the players. Nybeck reads the ice very good and has good speed and positions himself on the right spot. Although he is so young, he attracts Luleå players on him but he stays focused on the hockey.

HV71 # 65 LD Andrae, Emil (2020) - I like the attitude of Andrae and he skates full speed to the bench and gets under the skin of Luleå players. Andrae had nice eyes for the game and delivered plenty of good first passes. He puts good pressure and forecheck good. Andrea showed great hands and delivered dangerous quick wrist pass for scoring chance. With speed in center line he came through and had tick tack pass with # 20.

HV71 # 20 RW Holmström, Simon (2019) - Due to injuries and unclear of where he plays Holmström has been a player I have not seen Holmström live this season. Seeing him with the expectations of being a 1st rounder I would question that at least if seeing this game. He is excellent skater, tall, mobile and when he uses his legs his stride is more efficient then most. He both pulls away and catch other players good. Holmström checks high and quick. He is calm with the puck and is not stressing away the puck before he has a good alternative. He pulls penalties by his skills and reputation. He is excellent in giving passes and receiving passes and together with his mobile skating in all directions he positions himself quick on good places and delivers crispy passes. He goes on net. No question that Holmström is an excellent player but for most of the game he didn't shine of confident and I would at some few times liked to see him moving a bit in position on the line and communicated higher and with the stick to show his availability. If this would be the only game, I would have seen Holmström I belive I would have considered him as a very good player, potentially a late 2nd rounder – early 3rd rounder except of for 2 things. During 3rd period in 2 shifts period Holmström seems to release the break and went like crazy around the offensive zone, winning pucks by corner and poke checks. If that is a level of speed Holmström is using frequently during the games I think he stays in the first rounds discussions. He also tried to score a Zorro goal from behind the net. Not sure how much his previous injuries are keeping him back but I hope to see him the 13th March next time to confirm the correct level.

HV71 # 10 CE Grönhagen, Jacob (2019) - 6'6" and 209 LBS Grönhagen is clearly visualized and used his body, delivering some slashing, one nice big hit, screens the goalie, delivered hard accurate passes and was strong by the board. He also makes it painfully for Luleå players in front of HV71 net.

Luleå HC

LHC # 10 LW Gunler, Noel (2020) - Future top prospect 2020 I have seen quit many games with during the last years but can't say he was shining today. Gunler reads the game very good and breaks HV71 and wins pucks several times. Gunler looks smaller then registered 6'1". Gunler was strong and quick by the board with puck. During some turbulence after referee's whistle Gunler was a bit over energized and the lines men that pulled him away told him that he was lucky that the referee just wanted to send him for 2 minutes penalty. Gunler has great puck receiving skills and controls the puck quick but a couple of times in own zone he kept the puck to long and gave HV71 the chance to win the puck back.

LHC # 19 CE Jellus, Simon (2019) - Was good on receiving hard passes, was positioned good a couple of times but took too long time and didn't managed to release any shots on goal. Plenty of good faceoffs and was showing good anticipation. In BP he was angling the opponent good keeping them on the outside of the box.

LHC # 52 RW Muzik, Radek (2019)- The tall Czech was showing ok anticipation at time but wasn't visualized much. Registered for 1 SOG but I didn't saw any shots.

LHC # 3 RD Korencik, Marek (2019) - The big Slovak that is Captain for Luleå was looking strong and aggressive making it difficult in front of Luleå net , received a big hit and took it good. Wasn't visualized very much but lifted his energy in 3rd period.

HV71 at Brynas IF February 25, 2019

Brynas IF

Soderstrom, Victor 2019 Soderstrom had a slow firsts period. He played it very safe with the puck and did not contribute much to the offensive game and finished the period with a -2 plusminus rating. He did gear up for the second period, where he took more initiative with his effortless, smooth skating. He moved the puck really good out of his own zone, both by skating it and passing it. He had two great moments when he skated the puck end-to-end showing fantastic awareness, hands and skating. His move where he freezes his skating for a moment, just to increase the speed is looking out to work just fantastic even on this level. Soderstrom battles hard defensively, lifting sticks, going to the corners and so on. But he does lose some battles when he gets outmuscled since he is rather small. Overall he reads the play very well and is not afraid of facing bigger and stronger guys, but he needs to add mass and weight. He finished the game with a goal, which was his 7th point of the season. That tied him for 5th in most points by an u18-defender in a single season in the SHL.

Barrie Colts vs Ottawa 67's, Feb 28th 2019

Colts –

Suzuki, Ryan (2019) – Suzuki played at a higher pace today than in some previous viewings which resulted in a better effort away from the puck. Ryan has very good skating mechanics and a fluid stride, both of which were on display early and often, resulting in an impressive back-checking sequence that resulted in a takeaway and a defensive zone clear for his team. He used his fluid stride to carry the puck and transition over the offensive blueline on several different plays. Although he failed at executing his one-on-one move-set and at times over-extended himself by attempting to drive through multiple players by himself, it was good to see him attempt to penetrate through traffic as opposed to keep the play largely to the outside which has been an on-going concern from the start of the season. On the powerplay, he made several impressive one-touch passes that resulted in a couple of secondary assists, however at even strength, he forced a couple of unnecessary passes, most of them being backhand passes while he was driving down the wings. Despite his offensive turnovers, he showed more effort and had decent positioning in his own-end and still made several high-end offensive plays. The biggest area of concern was that he continues to play without wanting to be involved along the boards, at times he avoided any physical contact and looked afraid to engage.

Allensen, Nathan (2019) – Allensen had a solid game for Barrie, using his skating ability to race after loose pucks in the defensive-zone, and showing an attention to detail while keeping up with the pace of the play. On one play that showcased this, he recognized an open-passing lane despite being partially turned away from the play and used his stick to disrupt a pass in the circle. He's not very big but he continues to demonstrate the ability to play with some grit and player larger than his size, this allowed him to box-out opponents at times and finish his checks when needed. Under pressure, he was above-average, showing decent anticipation of how much time and space he had to work with. Where Nathan struggled in this viewing and some previous ones, is his inability to assess how much power he needs on his outlet passes, he passes mostly at one speed and that's hard, which results in icing's and turnovers depending on if the pass requires a softer touch. Furthermore, he was ineffective in the offensive-zone and rarely touched the puck on the offensive-blueline.

York, Jack (2019) – York had a solid two-way performance for Barrie, showing a combination of mobility and anticipation in both the offensive and defensive zones. He did have a major mistake where he overplayed an opponent in the corner which inadvertently put himself out of position and led to a goal against but for the most part was above-average in his own-end of the ice. Arguably his most impressive play came away from the puck where he anticipated a pass in the left circle, intercepted the puck and rushed up the ice which resulted in a quality scoring chance. He played on the 2nd powerplay and buried a hard-wrist shot far-side after recognizing that he had soft-ice that he could skate into to improve his shooting angle.

Ottawa 67's –

Rossi, Marco (2020) - Rossi wasn't as dominant as some previous viewings, but still showed impressive offensive-skills and the ability to process the play quickly in tight-spaces despite being under heavy pressure. He's capable of shifting his skating gear, and this allowed him to deceive the defense in-front of him, finding opening before quickly distributing the puck to his linemates. Unlike Allensen mentioned above, Marco has an excellent touch which allows him to fire fine-tuned passes of different types, including backhand saucer passes, short one-touch passes and sharp passes while in motion and while off-balance. Despite his small stature, he's shown the tendency to drive towards the net if there's an opening and this led to his best scoring chance today where he cut across the crease aggressively while attempting to tuck the puck. Furthermore, when he did turn the puck over, he was the first to compete and attempt to recollect it.

Clarke, Graeme (2019) - Clarke was used on the 4th line at even strength and due to the 67's playing without the lead the entire game, he was rarely. That said, he was used on the powerplay at times, where he had a couple of decent plays, but nothing that resulted in a high-end scoring chance against. He was unable to find as much soft-ice with the man-advantage as some previous viewings as well.

Okhotyuk, Nikita (2019) – Okhotyuk had one of his most impressive games of the season for me, playing with confidence, poise, and tenacity. In some previous viewings, he wasn't as willing to carry the puck himself and become the option so that he could transition the puck through the neutral zone, but against Barrie that wasn't the case. He consistently used his impressive and powerful skating ability to rush the puck out of high-danger areas, as well as pinch aggressively which resulted in a couple of great scoring chances. His best scoring chance came by rushing down the left-wing after pinching correctly before firing a hard off-angle wrist-shot that just went over the bar. His wrist-shot lacked accuracy, but the velocity was there. On one sequence, he used his frame to direct an opponent into the boards, then carried the puck through all three-zones before delivering a sharp-pass, that play, and others really stood out in a dominant performance. One area to note with Okhotyuk is that he still had some trouble executing his outlet passes at a high-rate, but when he chose to carry the puck instead, it compensated for how hard some of his pass attempts were to handle. Nikita played at a high-pace, was physically engaged, and stood out at both ends of the ice, activating more aggressively than in some other games.

Ottawa 67's vs Hamilton Bulldogs, March 1 2019

67's –

Rossi, Marco (2020) – Rossi came out of the gate a bit flat, but after taking a high-hit and inadvertently losing control of the puck, he found his game. He made a skilled-pass that he threaded into the slot from the half-wall resulting in a high-end scoring chance early, and in the third period his talent took over. He had several dynamic sequences which generated scoring chances, and he scored the game-winning goal after a beautiful tic-tac-to play that had him jam in the puck through the five-hole in-front of the net. Away from the puck he was willing to compete against larger players but was efficient with his energy in own-end, extending his gas-tank when needed. It was a complete game that started flat but ended with him having the strongest third period out of any player on the ice.

Clarke, Graeme (2019) – Although Clarke continues to play on the 4th-line, he was put on the top powerplay unit and made the most of his opportunities early by burying a rebound in-front of the net. He had an excellent shift in the second period where he battled hard along the boards and used his stick to strip the puck before controlling it for over a minute, finding Okhotyuk who had pinched for a scoring chance, and later carrying the puck around the side board and up through the high-slot before firing through traffic. Despite playing on the 4th line, Graeme had several offensive-chances and showed plus offensive awareness away from the puck, setting himself up well to release his high-end shot.

Quinn, Jack (2020) – Quinn played an effective two-way game, showing a good motor and the willingness to engage in heavy traffic. He had a great scoring chance early in-front of the crease area where he quickly pulled the puck from his forehand to backhand before trying to slide the puck through the Hamilton netminder, but it went wide. On another sequence, he went end-to-end, showing a set of soft-hands as he attempted to carve through the Hamilton defense, but he was unsuccessful, the play did show some fearlessness though. On another player, he showed above average cross-over mechanics as he cut wide in order to re-open his shooting lane before firing a low shot. His last notable play involved a nice no-look backhand pass. Overall, he complimented his line well and was consistent.

Okhotyuk, Nikita (2019) – Okhoytuk had a solid two-way performance for the 67's, yet did have some difficulty with his passing, especially when attempting to move the puck out of his own-end under pressure, the execution wasn't as good as in some previous viewings. Nikita had a great defensive sequence where he recovered by skating hard to regain position during an odd-man rush against and sacrificed his body, taking a heavy shot around the shoulder area, the play might have stopped a potential goal. On another sequence, he cut off his opponents skating lane quickly and delivered an emphatic hit. During several board battling plays, he used his frame and stick effectively, and when combined with his high-compete level, managed to out-battle Hamilton when they were on the forecheck. In the offensive-end, he pinched correctly at times, and this resulted in a couple of scoring chances. Overall, Okhotyuk's physical presence was notable and he was a plus factor in his own-end despite having difficulty with his passing at times.

Bulldogs –

Kaliyev, Arthur (2019) – Kaliyev was dangerous in the offensive-end of the ice for Hamilton, yet still showed red flags with his play in terms of pace and skating. Kaliyev opened the scoring for the Bulldogs, firing a hard wrist-shot from the right-circle in one-motion after receiving a cross-slot pass on the powerplay. His pace wasn't too bad in the opening frame and he did attempt to compete away from the play against Bahl who out-weighs him by quite a bit. He scored a second-goal after receiving a great pass into the slot where he fired a hard seeing-eye wrist-shot that probably should have resulted in goaltender interference but didn't. When he was shooting from a stationary position, he flashed his puck-skills, utilizing screens to pull the puck around his opponents to re-open his shooting lanes and had a slot of success by being deceptive with his release point. Dipietro had a lot of difficulty tracking where Kaliyev was attempting to place the puck both when he was in motion firing the puck and from a stand-still position. Furthermore, he mixed up his shot types, showing a dangerous slap-shot, as well as his wrist-shot. Away from the play there was a couple of decent reads and he did attempt to engage physically, but the skating keeps him from being able to effectively forecheck and backcheck. Lastly, his pivoting left him flat-footed which made him rely on his hands a bit too often at times.

Mutter, Navrin (2019) – Mutter didn't have too many notable plays except for one high-end scoring chance where he drove hard to the front of the net and almost put home a quick wrist-shot that went wide, on the same sequence, he showed his physical play along the boards and delivered a big hit. Later in the game, he delivered another big-hit that moved the 67's defender off balance, but overall, he was quiet and didn't generate much in the way of offense.

Morrison, Logan (2020) – Morrison moved the puck efficiently in the neutral zone on a couple of different plays and on one attempt, skated through the high-slot before firing a wrist-shot that trailed wide. He was better in the first-half of the game than the second-half, where he was largely kept to the perimeter and had trouble keeping up with the intensity of the play due to his size and skating combination.

Waterloo Black Hawks at Fargo Force, March 1, 2019

Waterloo Black Hawks -

Firstov, Vladislav - 2019 Had one chance in the middle of the attack zone with the puck on his stick, but wasn't able to explode through his check nor protect the puck against him. That was of only two times Firstov was intricately involved all night it seemed like…the other one did net him an assist on a turned over puck that he fed across the net line for Ohrvall to slam home. Otherwise, Firstov was tough to find.

Fargo Force -

Nodler, Josh - 2019 Not a lot of ice time for Nodler early on. But he saw some time with the puck on his stick in the 2nd. He has some okay hands, but it's not smooth yet. He still has a tendency to chop the puck into pieces. He's a little too antsy in all facets actually, he can really over-play the game sometimes and it's to his distinct detriment…spends just a little too much time chasing the game around.

Zabransky, Libor - 2019 Zabransky is a plus skater…particularly lateral and back skating. Competent in all three zones. Plays with a good gap, pretty good stick positioning. He isn't super high on puck skills, but he doesn't treat the puck poorly either. He's better than he looks, as silly as it sounds…he plays the game on his heels (he even shoots a lot of fadeaway wrist shots from his back foot, when he could stand in and make a better play). On even routine plays, he puts his heels right on the offensive blue line…just lets the game play him too much. If he was more active and aggressive and poised, he would be a much more interesting prospect. He has the skating, shot and hockey IQ to at least be worth a look…but his feel for the game or his confidence in his game is lacking…even as he drops a level from the WHL to the USHL as a 19 year old. Played most of the night at RD with newcomer Ethan Frisch on his left. At one point, he rushed a D-to-D pass that caused Frisch to have to catch the puck in his own crease…in the crease on an unsolicited pass from the right half boards.

Frisch, Ethan - 2019 First game in Fargo for Frisch who was acquired from Green Bay. He was used to playing a lot in GB, and while there is more going on with this Fargo team, he still found himself out there quite a bit...particularly as the game wore on...including some PP2 time. Early on, he made a really nice NZ defensive play where he stuck to his man across two lanes and didn't allow the center line while no other threats existed on his back side because Waterloo was trying to change. Next shift, he made a big hit, followed by a perfect pokecheck to end two plays successively. He was very physical tonight...the most physical I've seen him, but it looked very natural. He seems solidly built even if he doesn't have a big frame. Shows some flashes off skill, but not quite as consistently as you'd like...his drawback may be just being an average skater at his size. He is calm and smart, but very competitive. Has a better slapshot than wrist shot, despite him bricking out on a one-timer later in the game. A very strong game that he spent playing on the left side (with Libor Zabrasnky) despite being RHS. This player checks off a lot of boxes at the end of the day.

Huglen, Aaron - 2019 First game back in the USHL for Huglen since leaving Roseau High School. His ice time picked up as the game went on...ended up with some PP2 time. Skating isn't a plus overall, but his edges are sharp and his turns are very tight. Closing speed is a plus as well. But his first step and his long speed aren't noteworthy. Very smart player. He diagnoses things so quickly and he's always aware of what could happen next. He's a start and stop player and is constantly making little angle adjustments for best results. Made a nice NZ pickpocket early in the game that seemed to give him his confidence pretty quickly. In what was a very tight game, Huglen setup four high quality scoring chances in the 3rd period alone for Fargo...four of probably their five highest quality scoring chances of the entire night. Subtle, but strong technical skills...doesn't make big swooping moves unless he needs to...he sets up defenders to fail and then executes on it.

Bohlsen, Kaden - 2019 Bohlsen played the middle and found a decent amount of time tonight...including the second unit of both special teams units. Was a slight plus in the dot tonight. Plus skater on a really sturdy frame. The technical skills don't jive too well with his size and skating yet. Needs to be a little more creative coming off the wall, there isn't a lot of unpredictability there. Needs to be better at separating his top-half body mechanics and his bottom-half body mechanics...right now everything is a little too square. He doesn't look terribly confident in his ability. This is a longer-term player who has a lot of room left on his development arc. If the skills don't eventually come around, it's a player that a team might have some luck re-programming as a fourth line worker.

Mora IK u20 at Sodertalje SK u20 March 2 2019

Mora IK u20

Edstrom, Adam 2019 Edstrom with his 14 games SHL experience from this season was expected to shine in this game. He had his shining moments and a lot of flawed moments. Edstrom is big, and I mean BIG. Listed at 6'6" he was the biggest player on the ice with a wide margin and he could move and skate impressively well considering his size. This is why it was so disappointing to see him standing still offensively and not using his body at all in any point of the game, except for blocking shots. He has all the tools to be a fantastic power forward, good skating, good hands and stickhandling, his hockey IQ was okay and his shot was powerful. Too bad he played softer than a kitten. He was fantastic at killing penalties and played a fulfilling two-way game. Edstrom did finish the game with an assist

Eklund, Charles 2019 - Eklund showcased excellent skating abilities with great foot speed and an intense technical stride. He is rather small and weight less than a feather, this combined with his speed made the defenders take penalties to stop him. On the powerplay, he was positioned behind the net, which makes absolutely no sense at all. He worked hard all over the ice, but didn't really provide any offense while having the puck on his stick. His hockey sense was below average and so was his hands and shot.

Norgren, Oliver 2019 Norgren probably one of the best games in his life today, with 39 saves and a save percentage of 92,86 he kept his team in the game and basically stole 1 point from Sodertalje. He is not big, but he makes up for the lack of size with impressive speed to make some acrobatic, desperation saves. Unfortunately, he is forced to make these saved since he doesn't read the play very well and his defenders did a terrible job in front of him. His biggest weakness besides his lack of size was his catching glove. He catches right, but he struggles to actually catch the puck, dropping it and having to go down and block it on the ice.

Sodertalje SK u20

Feuk, Lucas 2019 Feuk keeps on playing on the outside of the defenders, never wanting to get in closer to the high danger scoring zones. He did create some offense this game, but he was too far away from the goal to actually be a threat. He fired his heavy shot a lot, as he often does, but yet again had problems hitting the net. Feuk is a player who excels on the power play when given more time to process his actions. He failed once again to prove he can contribute on 5on5, this may be because of his below average skating abilities. He did score a goal on a long defection in the third period.

Fairbanks Ice Dogs at Springfield Jr. Blues, March 2, 2019

Springfield Jr. Blues -

Williams, Jack - 2019 Not a very smooth goaltender. He fights through a lot of aspects of his game…parts of which that do not complement each other well. He sets up with very low hands and his glove even drifts down to fingers-out, this brings his shoulders lower and forward…the advantage is that it's easier to get down into the butterfly and not let pucks get through your body as easy, which Williams does do well…but it also should help with puck tracking, but Williams struggles and sort of thrusts and jabs his body around, losing positioning to find pucks that are not in threatening areas. Doesn't appear to be a very skilled skater, but his shuffle ability is a positive. It does look like he thinks the game pretty well, but doesn't have the physical characteristics to convert it. His rebound control is faulty, to the point that he can easily punch things away from him that are going to hit him in the chest pad from a ways out. He's always jolting around and stiff, so rebound control suffers immensely. His stick positioning is not refined. And his shoulder rotation is jagged and not consistent with the play, it also leads him into some overlap with the side of the net that appears unintentional considering how much he enjoys dipping into the RVH setup. His over-reliance on that post setup cost him his only goal of the match with two seconds left in the 2nd frame. This is a goalie that is a long way from home and for him to be fighting the game as much as he does, it would take a lot of work to get where he needs to be. Michigan State doesn't have the reputation of being goaltending factory either.

USNTDP U18 at Madison Capitols, March 2, 2019

USNTDP U18 -

Gildon, Michael - 2019 Played with Jack Hughes and Cole Caufield all night, but it didn't do anything to snap Gildon into action really. He plays a clunky game…sort of a hulking, sluggish skater. He doesn't show any creativity or notable puck skills. It was tough for him to keep up with Hughes' freewheeling style and Gildon doesn't have the hockey sense to be a third wheel that makes room for guys. He's a beat and a half behind most plays.

Caufield, Cole - 2019 Disappointing outing from Caufield, but perhaps he was tapped out from a 4-goal effort the night before, and a four point night the game prior. He was with Gildon and Hughes, which puts a lot of weight on Caufield's shoulders because of Gildon's limitations and the amount of attention that's always paid to Hughes. Caufield was content to play in the perimeter tonight and seemed a quarter beat behind on getting open. The Caufield calling card is him getting lost in the woods and then quickly emerging and snapping home a quick shot in the interior. That just wasn't timed right for him tonight. He seemed much less engaged in the game overall and didn't participate even a little bit defensively. Didn't show off much explosive skating either, which he had shown in the past…wasn't very willing to challenge defenders, instead he opted to go wide and then defer the puck the others. Low residue game for Caufield… almost no impact tonight.

Moynihan, Patrick - 2019 Quick player, good speed, but better off the blocks. Feet are always going and poised to make a break towards the puck or a man. He's always working, but he works smart. He readily covers for pinching d-men, he regularly provides overlap support to avoid linear/flat rushes, he fetches puck from anywhere you need him to and he moves them quick. That's the biggest takeaway for me with Moynihan…plays never die with him. He has good hands, he plays the game at such a high pace…a pro pace. Played with Turcotte and young Beniers (late '02). Setup Turcotte with a real nice side angle chance with a quick pass where he looked off the defender to give himself the lane. Moynihan has shown all year that he can play with talent and not look at all out of place…moreover, he's a positive, active contributor…tonight was no exception.

Vlasic, Alex - 2019 Not much change or evolution to Vlasic. Big man, big reach, but doesn't cover a lot of ground in foot races. He moves laterally pretty well, his back skating is improving. Skating is overall just average. He made a good, well-timed hit in the corner early, but that was extent of his physicality for the night. Had one skate into the zone with the puck, picking up a dead NZ puck, but it resulted in a very weak backhander from a low angle. He doesn't have a lot of puck poise, nor does he earn any space or respect with his limited puck skills. My concern is that he doesn't look uncoordinated, or freshly tall and still growing into his body. He looks comfortable – and while not a finished product of course – but just not a very toolsy player at the end of the day.

Madison Capitols -

Papp, Kristof - 2019 Skinny player, who plays the game with some vigor and urgency, but ultimately doesn't quite understand how to channel it yet. Looks a little uncoordinated, for lack of a better word…maybe out of control would be more appropriate. Not very hockey strong, but he did throw a hit into Jack Hughes that got him squarely in the corner. Played on the PK, but wasn't very attentive…too many loops, not a lot of lane integrity. He needs to be better with his starts and stops, but I'm not sure how comfortable he is making a good, hard stop. Was about -6 or -7 in the DZ and AZ dots. Did surprise with a couple of skill plays: Made a good pass to setup a 2 on 1 tap in. And then broke away from Case McCarthy from center in and made a nice cross-crease move to beat Rowe and give Madison a 3rd period lead. He's a long way off, but he's worth keeping an eye on.

Lavelle, Shane - 2019 Plus skater. Looks to be cut from the new-school power forward mold, but he's not ripe yet. Played limited minutes in his second ever USHL game. Made one nice pass to the slot. Next shift he made a strong backcheck late in a shift. There is a hint of some skill to go along with the size and good skating…but it's not prevalent yet. Details are lacking…in one situation, he had trouble corralling a poor pass that was behind him. He bats it along and then engages in a board battle. But rather than getting the puck to center – which he had the opportunity to do – he elected to take on that battle about three feet inside his line, which is an unnecessary risk.

Charlottetown Islanders vs Blainville-Boisbriand Armada, March 2nd, 2019

Charlottetown

#51 Cormier, Lukas (2020): Great performance from Cormier tonight, who showed good creativity with the puck in the offensive zone and made some nice passing plays to his teammates. He read the play well, knew when to pinch in the offense zone and did a good job as a 4th forward on the ice, by either leading or jumping into the rush. He got a ton of ice time tonight, playing on the 1st pairing of every power play and seeing top 4 ice time at even-strength. He made good and quick decisions with the puck on his stick all game long, playing like a veteran out there with great maturity on the ice.

#6 Laaouan, Noah (2019): He played a safe game in his own zone; not a whole lot of flashes from him today. He was paired with Cormier, who did most of the puck-moving and transition work for that D-pair. Good active stick when defending. He didn't stand out in any positive or negative way today, which considering his style is probably not a bad thing.

#10 Budgell, Brett (2019): He worked really hard out there and was involved in the physical part of the game. He played center, which has been the case for him since late January after playing mostly on the wing since he joined the QMJHL. He was under 50% in the faceoff circle with 11 faceoffs taken. He had one great scoring chance alone with the goaltender, but couldn't finish on the backhand. He did some good work along the boards, showing a good compete level. He won his fair share of battles and was good on the forecheck, applying good puck pressure.

#14 Alexandrov, Nikita (2019): Did a lot of his work down low, and this is how he created some of his scoring chances. He didn't create much off the rush; his skating game was not good today as he didn't beat anyone with his speed. He lacked explosiveness out there as well. Most of his good moments were created from behind the net and working the puck down low. At the same time, he was easily knocked down during the game. Not sure if this was a skate-related issue, but he fell down quite a lot today. He played in every situation but was not a big factor in this game. I didn't like his passing game, either, as he tried a lot of no-look passes (often on the backhand) that either went nowhere or to an Armada player's stick. He did, however, show good work ethic on the backcheck and played sound hockey away from the puck.

#24 Fortin, Xavier (2020): He showed some good hustle and speed during this game. There was a good explosiveness to his stride and he worked hard in all three zones. He did a good job keeping his feet active and playing with some good energy. Not the biggest guy, but played a feisty game out there tonight. He did a good job attacking the offensive zone with speed, and on one sequence, he made a very nice feed to Budgell (who unfortunately couldn't get the puck past the Armada goaltender).

Blainville-Boisbriand

#58 Bolduc, Samuel (2019): Not a strong game from Bolduc, but he had some decent moments in the game where he flashed his tools. He had couple of nice rushes with the puck from his own end where he showed his great top speed. When not under pressure, he showed his ability to make a good crisp pass to a teammate, and took some good shots on net from the point on the power play. However, he was inconsistent throughout the game and also was too passive in his own zone.

#47 Pinard, Simon (2019): He used his speed to create some scoring chances for himself in this game, keeping his feet moving and demonstrating good agility. He had some decent scoring chances during the game, but had trouble getting quality shots on net or finishing plays.

Ottawa 67's vs Mississauga Steelheads, March 3 2019

67's –

Rossi, Marco (2020) – It was the Rossi and Falhaber show today for the 67's on a line that consistently dominated possession in the offensive zone, especially in the 1st and 3rd frames. Rossi's a smaller player but understands how to utilize his size so that it's an advantage out there. His pivoting and edge work make him elusive, and he used both skating attributes combined with his impressive balance to negate bigger players who were attempting to knock him off the puck. He set up his teammates consistently with impressive passes and executed difficult passes at a very-high clip today. His most impressive pass was a no-look saucer pass under pressure down below the goal-line that resulted in a primary assist. His hockey sense away from the puck was very good and this allowed him to play a heavy cycle-game and drain the Steelheads defense, breaking them down, this also resulted in him having several high-end scoring chances, but he couldn't find the back of the net. The only attribute that looked flat out there was the power he generates on his wrist-shot, and his straight-lines speed wasn't at the same level as his agility, but it was another dominant performance for the talented forward.

Clarke, Graeme (2019) – Clarke was used on the 3rd line today so he was given a bit more playing time than other viewings, but was inconsistent, rarely generating much in the way of offensive chances despite getting some powerplay time as well. One of the primary reasons for this was due to his average skating which didn't allow him to keep up with the pace of play at times, he stays somewhat up-right, and his knee-bend isn't as deep so his power in his first few steps is still lacking. That said, he did have a terrific backchecking effort late in the game which helped preserve Dipietro's shutout and showed his compete as well. He scored an empty net-goal, but his best scoring chance despite his goal was off the rush when he found soft-ice and wired a puck that missed far-side. Clarke continues to show the ability to handle the puck with quick hands which allows him to release the puck off impressive toe-drags, but he was unable to get it through traffic consistently today.

Nikita Okhotyuk (2019) – Okhotyuk had a quiet yet effective game in his own-end for the 67's, playing up to the pace of the game and using his physical brand of shutdown hockey to mitigate the Steelheads forecheck. He was going up against competitive players who won't quit or slow down on the forecheck such as Schwindt and Washkurak but used his frame to angle the puck away from them, pinned them, and generally out-muscled them along the wall. Under pressure, he made several quick passes around the boards to help move the puck before he turned it over and was stable overall. In the offensive-zone, he showed another well-timed pinch which helped set-up Maksimovich for a quality scoring chance but was largely effective in own-end and not the offensive-end. His most impressive sequence occurred under-pressure where he showed some creativity in escaping physical contact when carrying the puck through the slot area, as he pivoted and angled himself to fake his direction before moving it up the ice.

Quinn, Jack (2020) – Quinn had a mixed game offensively for the 67's, executing relatively poorly compared to some other viewings early, but was sharper in the 3rd frame. He played with speed, and this allowed him to have an efficient end-to-end rush where he beat an opponent one-on-one, but his hands looked average today. Late in the game he had a beautiful saucer pass that sprung his teammate in for one of the better scoring chances in the game as well. His offensive-skill set wasn't matching his pace but he still had some flashes and plus plays for his team.

Steelheads –

Harley, Thomas (2019) - Harley had an effective two-way performance for the Steelheads by playing relatively well under pressure in his own-end and moving the puck efficiently both at even-strength and on the man-advantage. He had a good defensive-play early, stripping the puck off Rossi with by using his stick and length, and on a couple of different sequences used his impressive skating ability to carry the puck out of the zone. His passing was sharp, he executed at a high-rate and made several tape-to-tape passes while skating at top speeds. This game was an important one to monitor Harley's pace and willingness to engage physically, but there weren't many times during the contest where he needed to try and use his frame, his elusiveness and passing ability were effective enough in this match-up. He did attempt to leave the zone too early on occasion, and on one play specifically, this caused an odd-man rush, his pace was also lacking when attempting to recover on the play. In the offensive-zone, his puck distribution was solid, making quick passes that led to several scoring chances, but his ability to recognize when his shooting lane was open, was mixed, this was magnified when his telegraphed slap-shot resulted in a very important zone clear during a 4-minute powerplay where the Steelheads had the 67's gassed out. Overall, it was still a solid performance for Harley.

Prueter, Aidan (2020) – Prueter was overwhelmed physically and had difficulty keeping up with the pace of play at times but competed hard and was willing to engage with much larger players than himself. He didn't manage to generate too many scoring opportunities and was largely kept to the outside but did have the odd-pass that kept the play alive in the offensive-zone, but it still wasn't one of his better games.

Schwindt, Cole (2019) – Schwindt tried to generate off the forecheck as he's done in most of our other viewings but was largely ineffective out there today due to the 67's swarming him behind the goal-line and around the net area. That said, he still showed his high-level of compete and did use his frame to aggressively attempt to gain back the puck during dump-and-chase plays. He also attempted to drive into heavy traffic and came close to having a high-end scoring chance at the top of the crease, but the puck skipped on him.

Washkurak, Keean (2019) – Washkurak had an okay two-way game for the Steelheads, where he generated offense in spurts and had one of the best scoring chances of the game during a powerplay sequence but was robbed by Dipietro who made a sprawling save. Like Schwindt, Washkurak plays at a high-pace most of the time, but his average skating really stood out in a bad way this game where he was a step-behind when chasing down loose pucks and couldn't consistently generate offense as a result. On one 2-on-1 sequence, he failed to recognize how much of an open shooting-lane was given to him as he rushed down the left-wing and opted to pass at the wrong time, resulting in a failed opportunity at a critical time in the game. One other area to note was that he telegraphed his play at times, there was a lack of deception when he was holding the puck.

Hardie, James (2020) – Hardie was largely ineffective but did have a good supporting sequence on the forecheck where he recollected the puck after Schwindt was tied up and unable to retrieve it himself. In his own-end, he showed poise under-pressure before passing the puck behind his own-goal line to his defense and on one offensive play around the goal-line, he showed a bit of creativity where he faked his skating direction before attempting a quick wrap-around.

Central Illinois Flying Aces at Green Bay Gamblers, March 3rd 2019

Central Illinois Flying Aces

Janicke, Trevor – 2019 Janicke showed good 200 ft effort and a good motor throughout the game. His compete level stayed consistent, even as the game never really seemed within reach for his team. Trevor didn't display a lot of offensive skill in this game but managed to get some shots through defenseman off the rush and displayed a quick release point as he shot in stride. Handled himself well in the faceoff circle, winning a few draws cleanly for his team.

Breen, Lynden – 2019 Not a noticeable player as far as driving offense and creating chances in this game. Made a few careless plays with the puck in crucial areas of the ice that resulted in turnovers and plays going the other way. Showed a good top gear with the puck and had he showed better judgement on some offensive zone entries, his speed was creating separation from defenseman on a few instances.

Halliday, Stephen – 2020 Halliday is a big kid and is easily identifiable out on the ice but didn't always play to his size in this one, often avoiding competing in hard areas and being soft along the walls for a player with his size. His skating needs work, he has a decent top gear but his feet are sluggish off the hop and limit his ability to contribute in the transition game. Halliday has some intriguing skill but his ceiling will be limited going forward if his skating doesn't improve.

Siedem, Ryan – 2019 It was a pretty average game from Siedem. He didn't do much to create in the offensive zone or create off the rush. Siedem managed the puck ok on breakouts but lacks explosiveness in his skating which forced him into making quick but vanilla plays with the puck, either going off the glass and out of the zone or rimming around the boards to relieve pressure.

Baie-Comeau Drakkar vs Drummondville Voltigeurs, March 6th 2019

Baie-Comeau

#29 Legaré, Nathan (2019): Not a great game for Legaré, who had only one good scoring chance that I could count in the game. He didn't even get the best shot off on that chance from the slot. He didn't play with a ton of pace out there, and was not really a factor in the game. Not super physical either; I only saw him throw one good hit all night and wanted to see more intensity out of him, especially in such a big game against a top team like Drummondville.

#8 Merisier-Ortiz, Christopher (2019): He was good at keeping pucks in the offensive zone from the point. With his good footwork and agility, he was also able to block quite a few attempts by Drummondville to get the puck out of their zone shorthanded. He showed good agility and footwork all game long. He was good at retrieving pucks deep in his own zone and kept things simple, making good decisions. He moved the puck well on the power play as well, and got an assist on Baie-Comeau's first goal of the game.

Drummondville

#19 Mercer, Dawson (2019): Not a great game from Mercer. He had some chances offensively, but struggled in terms of shooting the puck. At some point, he missed a wide open net. He has a good shot, but needs to work on his accuracy.

#81 Simoneau, Xavier (2019): Excellent compete level as usual from Simoneau, who didn't back down from anyone and was tough to play against. There's no fear in his game. At some point he was even battling hard against 6'05" Sacha Roy of Baie-Comeau. He played in the tough areas in the offensive zone, including the front of the net on the power play, and didn't stay on the outside. He made some nice passes in the offensive zone, showing good vision. Even at his size, he showed good abilities when protecting the puck, often spinning and keeping the puck away from his opponent by using his strong lower body.

Duluth East Greyhounds vs St. Thomas Academy Cadets, March 7th, 2019

Duluth East Greyhounds

Donovan, Ryder – 2019 Donovan registered a power play assist on Duluth East's lone goal. While Donovan wasn't dominate in this game he showcased his skating and hands throughout the game. Donovan displayed an excellent top gear with the puck, especially through the neutral zone. A couple examples of Donovan showcasing his hands and playmaking was in the 2nd period as he entered the offensive zone was able to pull the puck back away from the poke check and then feed a slick pass through the defenders stick and feet to teammate driving down the slot for a scoring chance as well as earlier in the game shorthanded where he gained the edge on the defender and used his reach and body to protect the puck from the puck check and slide a centering feed to his open teammate who was driving the net who proceeded to miss with a shot over top the open net. Donovan showed good effort on the back check, using his speed to get back and breakup a 2 on 1 with a stick check at the last second to keep the game at 1-0. Ryder needs to add more stops and starts to his game, on one instance he likely could have banged home a rebound in front but he skated past the net as the goalie struggled with the rebound and made some questionable or lackadaisical decisions with the puck in his own zone. Used his body well along the wall with the puck and played with a little bit of an attitude with some stick jabs behind the play and after whistles; you could tell he was into the game. All in all Donovan did what he could in this game but lacked the playmakers around him to get his team over the top. Heard he will likely be heading to Dubuque (USHL) sometime next week to finish up the season.

Rouyn-Noranda Huskies vs Drummondville Voltigeurs, March 8th, 2019

Rouyn-Noranda

#4 Bergeron, Justin (2019): He really struggled with his decision-making and puck-management all night long. He usually does a good job moving pucks, but tonight had trouble making a pass and would turn the puck over. He had trouble with the speed of the Drummondville forecheck, who gave him less time to make plays. His lack of footspeed hurt him when defending against the speedy forwards from Drummondville, and he was also slow to retrieve pucks in his own zone.

#6 Régis, Samuel (2019): A rare bad game from Régis, who is usually very consistent from game to game. He had trouble handling the Drummondville forecheck, and most notably all the difficulty in the world when he was matched against Xavier Simoneau, who made him commit errors repeatedly with his aggressive in-your-face play. Régis was not a factor in moving pucks or offensively tonight.

#16 Beaucage, Alex (2019): Not a good game from Beaucage, who had difficulties with the pace of the game. He was really slow to get going when not moving his feet. He had some chances in the game but mishandled the puck on some attempts. He flashed his shot on some sequences, but overall, I didn't like his decision-making and how the pace of the game was too fast for him.

Drummondville

#6 Baker, Jarret (2019): He played a safe and hard game in his own zone. He was always there to defend his teammates, and did a good job clearing the front of his net. He made it tough for opposing forwards by hitting them, slashing them and throwing a lot of trash talk their way. His footwork is decent; he skated pucks out of his zone when he had to and has enough speed to retrieve pucks in his own zone while avoiding the forecheck.

#81 Simoneau, Xavier (2019): He was very good tonight, playing not only the skills game, but also as a great agitator. He drew two penalties within the first five minutes of the game, and had Rouyn-Noranda players chasing him all game long. He was very tenacious on the forecheck and gave a ton of headaches to Samuel Régis of Rouyn-Noranda. He created many turnovers in this game due to his relentless forecheck. He also showed some good vision on the power play, making some very nice cross-ice passes, but his teammates couldn't finish those plays.

#19 Mercer, Dawson (2020): Got an assist on the 1-0 goal, but it was not a great game from Mercer tonight. He didn't make much of an impact in the game, but tried to play a physical game and his level of intensity was good. I didn't like his pace, as he didn't skate well and was lacking some explosiveness out there that would have helped him create some separation. He didn't beat anyone one-on-one with his speed or stickhandling.

USNTDP U18 at Lincoln Stars, March 8, 2019

<u>USNTDP U18</u> –

Lindmark, Owen – 2019 Played mostly RW tonight, only took one shift at center. He just kind of rotated in as needed, and didn't really have regular linemates. He was a regular on the second PK unit and was about +3 on important face offs. Good worker who drives the net hard. Pretty smart player, good frame. Speed is a plus, even if it takes him a little bit to rev it up. Didn't have a chance to showcase skills tonight, as he saw little ice time.

Zegras, Trevor – 2019 Good skating, playmaking center. Zegras supports offensive plays well. Not only he is well balanced and tough to knock off the puck, but he also has a very heavy stick. It's tough to take pucks from him, and he can hack away 50/50 pucks to his advantage. As he has done all season, Zegras was a playmaker tonight and a very creative one at that. Certainly one of the most creative, if not adventurous, playmakers in the draft class. He makes a number of no-look and behind-the-back passes. He can do this at any place on the ice – and both off of organic opportunities and manufactured ones. He did get blown up in open ice trying to buy time on one particular rush, it seemed to catch him by surprise, as he made almost no effort to spin off of it, despite ample room to do so. Not an effective defensive player. Just kind of loops around, as he's not a start-and-stop player. He didn't use his body a single time tonight for any purpose, he lets his stick do the talking…that's not uncommon for the season either. Good shot release, not a terribly accurate shot. Made a brutal turnover to start the 3rd period where the US was up 4-1, where he was stripped clean carrying it through his own slot and it was converted immediately into a goal that started a four-goal 3rd period rally from Lincoln.

Zegras is a talented playmaker and he has good wheels, however the details of his game are still a bit lacking. I wonder if he wouldn't be better served starting out as a winger at the next level, just until he matures a bit.

Turcotte, Alex – 2019 Intelligent, complete center. He just supports plays so well, on both sides of the puck. His conceptual recognition of proper spacing and gap is beyond his years. He has terrific closing speed and his timing for the game is tough to match in his age group, always playing at the right pace it seems like. Outside of a few crisp passes, he didn't have a lot of flashy plays tonight or big swooping rushes. He did some grunt work in front on the power play. 50/50 on important draws. Strikingly, for some reason that's beyond my recognition, a smart player like Turcotte should not get blown up in every game…but once again tonight, he eats a hip in the offensive zone and it knocks him flying. Rarely do players that have his skating ability and his smarts get tagged as much as he does…it may be the worst thing that can be said about his game in general. In overtime, he had a green light chance to return the favor by drilling a Lincoln playing coming through the slot with the puck…he stopped short and allowed the scoring chance. That was a disappointing finish to his night.

Hughes, Jack – 2019 Offensive catalyst via nimble puck carrying most of the night. Really terrific playmaker across multiple lanes once he enters the offensive zone. His elite level skating and stickhandling was on display as usual. He took a number of shots tonight. Many from in close, as he doesn't have a laser certainly. The one long shot he attempted was a 1T from the right point on the power play, but his stick exploded instead. Drove the net with the puck on a 2 on 1 and went backhand roof from the top of the crease. Prior to that, he cut towards the slot to bang one home from the top of the crease. On the flip side, he made a horrific turnover looping around and doing too much at the top of his offensive zone…he really isolated himself on the play, got double-teamed and really chased the loss by trying to stickhandle out of it instead of getting it deep or even just tossing it to the side boards. It led to a breakaway, but Vlasic caught the guy and negated it. Doesn't offer anything from a defensive perspective tactically, but does offer a lot of pressure due to his speed when he wants to participate in that area. Without the puck, Hughes doesn't seem to read the play at any more than an average-ish level. He fails to cut off fairly obvious lanes in the NZ and even on offense, sometimes he runs himself into a disadvantage in terms of his lane/layer selection. He's super effective at zone entries with the puck on his stick, that rate appear to drop rather markedly when he has to support the rush. Was 50/50 on important face offs on the night.

Beecher, John – 2019 A mobile tank of a center. He's smart and downright crafty at seeking out pucks on the forecheck. He's a very effective penalty killer. Very detail oriented away from the puck. Physical…can really develop some punishing hits, he can separate from the puck, he can protect the disc in traffic…he really gets body usage at a young age. Despite this imposing style, he's actually a little less aggressive in offensive situations than you'd want. He defers a lot and is so ready to cover for point men or be the third man high that it seems to curtail his offensive potential enough to make me question what kind of ceiling he really offers. Just average puck skills, above average shot…but he really doesn't look all that comfortable with the organic rush offense that the NTDP plays…he looks like he's just ready to be an NCAA player where goals are scored because eight guys cram into the slot and pucks pinball in. I'd really like to see what he looks like as "the man" or at least one of the men on a higher level team, but going to Michigan probably delays that thought a bit. He's a hockey player, no question…he really looks the part. But what kind of upside does he really possess?

Rowe, Cameron – 2019 Rowe can be tricky to make a diagnosis on because he makes a lot of the right moves when shots aren't coming and a lot of bad ones when shots do come. He looks good in his stance, even though he's not a very good skater, he does make good adjustments in the crease. I like his glove depth, even though it does leave him a little susceptible to goals going under his elbow. He mostly just leans on the post for his post integrations, where most goalies use the reverse-VH these days, he opts for this rather infrequently actually. He does have an odd hitch step when figuring out the depth in his crease…tough to read what that is, but it may be a safety step for him in terms of figuring out where he is in the net…it does look like he checks for markings pretty often during the game to figure out where he's at. The issue for Rowe is when shots are taken…it's just not smooth, it's not calculated. The movements in the crease when a shot isn't going to be taken almost look rehearsed when compared to the save selection and reaction when shots are taken. Rowe guesses a lot, he loses anchoring, he goes into scramble mode – which is total chaos for him – pretty quickly…typically these days, when you see a goalie leaning or using the overlap post setup, that means that a goalie is probably comfortable standing up and making a save (Nabokov often, Hellebucyk and Rinne to lesser extents), but Rowe doesn't make stand-up stops. He drops right into the butterfly, but without a good enough challenge to the shooter to make up for the angle (and net) that he gives up with this approach.

Lincoln Stars –

Skinner, Hunter – 2019 Skinner was a little under siege in this one from a defensive point of view. The US Team had him turned inside out a couple of times as Skinner continues to battle with defensive consistency – based somewhat on him being unsure of what style of d-man he really wants to be I think. Offensively, he was game and made a few good rushes. He ended up warming up to the game quite nicely, and was a big part of the Lincoln comeback – assisting on both goals with the extra attacker in the last two minutes. He also walked Rowe with a terrific shootout move, but he just missed the net with it. At the rate of improvement he has shown in the USHL, this is a player that could really explode in the next 12-18 months, but he needs to keep the pace. He has some nice hands on him, he can hit a moving puck, he can make some strong body contact, but he's not yet as impactful as you'd like him to be at this level.

Rouyn-Noranda Huskies vs Sherbrooke Phoenix, March 9th, 2019

Rouyn-Noranda

#4 Bergeron, Justin (2019): Way more effective tonight than he was last night in Drummondville; his puck-management way better. He was moving pucks well in transition and took some good shots on net from the point, usually using his wrist shot. He's got good offensive flair, and it showed tonight, as he knew when to put pressure and play like a 4th forward. He saw more PP time tonight, as the 2nd unit of the PP was getting more ice time. A bit slow in terms of retrieving pucks deep in his own zone, due to his slow footwork and the fact that he is an average skater.

#6 Régis, Samuel (2019): He was paired with Dobson today and performed better than yesterday by moving pucks faster. If he was in trouble, he just gave the puck to Dobson, who was there to help him out. He didn't stand out, but was back to his regular self, playing a smart and safe game in his own zone.

#16 Beaucage, Alex (2019): He fell down too often on the ice today. He was not strong on his skates, and even if his compete level was good, he didn't win enough one-on-one battles. He flashed his shot on some sequences, but it was not a good viewing overall for Beaucage today, for the second game in a row. His skating is a big concern for me. He played a smarter game today than he did yesterday in Drummondville, but still not enough to be an impact player.

Sherbrooke

#5 Jacques, Jérémy (2019): It was just an okay game from Jacques, who has a long reach and a long stride, but doesn't generate great top speed when rushing the puck or when trying to get away from the forecheck. Not very strong on his skates; fell down too often when battling one-on-one. He didn't show great vision or great passing abilities in the offensive zone. Those qualities could lead to more offense out of him. Still very raw as a prospect, though.

#10 Guay, Patrick (2020): Not very noticeable offensively at even-strength. His skating looked average and not very explosive. He worked hard at both ends of the ice, showing good commitment to his play without the puck and making some good backchecks. Offensively, he was more noticeable on the power play with more space on the ice, and he also touched the puck more frequently on the man-advantage.

#14 Jentzsch, Taro (2019): He worked hard at both ends of the ice. Good along the boards, winning puck battles there. Speed was okay, but not top-tier.

#29 Poulin, Samuel (2019): Not a great game from Poulin, but he still made some interesting plays throughout the game, this being a positive viewing for him. He worked hard on the backcheck and showed good commitment in the defensive zone to help his team. He was strong on the puck; it was tough to take it away from him. He did some good work protecting the puck with his body, using his back to shield defensemen away from him. He took some good shots on net, showing some good velocity on his shot.

#37 Peach, Bailey (2019): Quick feet and good acceleration. He had an excellent rush where he used his outside speed to beat a defenseman wide and cut to the net for a scoring chance. If he could generate more of those rushes, he would be a more consistent offensive threat. Overall, he didn't create much today, and needs to find ways to create more offense instead of relying on his speed. Need to see more smart plays out of him.

Sioux Falls Stampede at Waterloo Black Hawks, March 9th, 2019

Sioux Falls Stampede

Krannila, Jami – 2019 Krannila showed high compete and high skill in this game. He didn't shy away from battles and won a good amount of them using his quick hands and body position to separate his opponent from the puck. Krannila showed his high-end skill when he tied the game in the 3rd period, collecting a pass that was behind his body as he was coming into the zone, passed to himself between the legs to get the puck in front of him, gained control and beat the goalie with a quick backhand to forehand move. Krannila was involved in the play and was noticeable from start to finish in this game.

Johnson, Ryan – 2019 One of the worst games we have seen from Johnson this season. Johnson hung onto the puck too long in a lot of instances and didn't leave himself with a lot of outs, resulting in turnovers. In one sequence early in the game, Johnson tried to turn away from a fore checker along the half wall and fell, resulting in a turnover and the game's opening goal. A miscommunication with his goalie on a puck retrieval behind his own net resulted in a scoring chance against and also showed poor awareness on a defensive zone faceoff where he left the front of the net to attempt a slap shot clearing attempt up the boards, only to fail to get the puck out of the zone and leaving his man wide open in front of the net for a goal against. Johnson made some lackadaisical plays with the puck coming out of his own end, which is an area where he usually is very assertive and confident. Johnson is a talented skater and puck mover but struggled early in this game and just couldn't get it back on the rails after that.

Phillips, Ethan – 2019 Phillips scored on the power play when he was left wide open on the back door for a tap in goal, aside from that wasn't overly noticeable in this game. Phillips had flashes of his plus edgework and quick hands in traffic but didn't create a lot offensively in this game.

Romano, Anthony – 2019 Hardworking two-way player. Showed good awareness to pick off a Waterloo outlet pass as he came onto the ice, entered the offensive zone and used a quick release and the defender as a screen to beat the waterloo goalie on the short side with a well-placed wrist shot. Efficient in the faceoff circle.

Swanker, Austen – 2019 Aside from missing the net on two, point blank scoring chances to start overtime, this was one of Swanklers better games this scout has seen this season. Simply put, Swankler was a pain in the ass all night. He was involved and physical from start to finish. Always seemed to be in the middle of everything after the whistle and looked to visibly get under the skin of his former team on a number of occasions. Swankler showcased his quick hands in traffic and made some excellent plays with the puck to setup scoring chances for his team. Swankler made a nice toe drag around defender but lacked the explosiveness in his footwork to separate from defender and get the puck to the net.

Waterloo Black Hawks

Blumel, Matej-2019+ Showed explosive skating in transition, taking the puck end to end, eluding the pressure and turning quickly up ice and made a quick cut through the slot for a shot on goal that the Sioux Falls goalie made an excellent glove save on. Matej showed the ability to jump into lanes and take the puck to the slot area on the number of offensive zone possessions but was held off the score sheet in this one.

Firstov, Vladislav-2019 Firstov tallied two assists in this game and showcased good offensive awareness and instincts, is able to find the soft areas of the offensive zone and gain position on defenders in the slot. Firstov didn't affect the game much in his own end and still seems unengaged some shifts but is getting better in the compete area and is using his teammates better in order to generate space for himself in the offensive zone. Skating stride isn't technically sound but it isn't a hindrance on his game at this stage.

Sudbury Wolves vs Niagara Ice Dogs, March 9 2019

Wolves -

Ross, liam (2019) – Ross had a difficult game for the Wolves by failing to distribute the puck behind the goal-line clearly under-pressure and failing to recognize transitional play from the blueline in time which led directly to a critical goal-against. Behind his own-net, he couldn't recognize his time and space, this caused him to force passes around the boards that were intercepted by Niagara. His outlet passes were also off the mark, landing in his teammates skates or missing the intended target entirely which caused an icing at one point. In-front of the net on the penalty-kill, he was more successful, showing a willingness to use his frame to pin elusive opponents such as Tomasino along the boards and showed decent hockey sense when anticipating passing lanes that where been used by Niagara. In the offensive-zone, he failed to recognize how quickly the puck was going to transition and this led to a 2-on-1 against that resulted in a goal that put Sudbury in a tough spot. He never threatened or showed plus puck skills at the line either.

Thompson, Jack (2020) – Thompson had a poor night for Sudbury, failing to distribute the puck cleanly and quickly up to his forwards while getting out-muscled in-front of the net area resulting in Niagara being able to impose themselves in-front of the net at times. On one sequence, he did show a willingness to expend his tank completely while trying to recover for his defensive partner who made a bad pass in the neutral zone, and he did battle in-front of the net, so it wasn't due to getting out-worked as much as it was that he didn't have the strength to impose himself on some of his older opponents. His best scoring chance came late in the dying seconds of the game after he made a clean transitional zone entry while carrying the puck and fired a hard-wrist shot that went over the net but never stood out at the offensive-blueline.

Murray, Blake (2019) – This was an important game for Murray in terms of assessing how he would perform in a high-paced game against a quality team, and the end-result was him being a negative for his team after turning the puck over more than a handful of times with zero scoring chances generated in the offensive-end. He had two positive plays which occurred away from the puck, the first was an interception in the neutral zone which stopped Niagara from transitioning, and the other was when he skated aggressively to a puck in his own-end before an opponent could get to it. The rest of the game was Murray being kept to the perimeter, not being able to find soft-ice, and not being able to make quick decisions when given limited time and space. It was a poor effort and a bad performance.

Byfield, Quinton (2020) – Byfield had a decent two-way performance for Sudbury, showing a good motor away from the play that allowed him to take advantage of his impressive tools, and was one of the only major catalysts offensively for his team, though he was also inconsistent and was kept to the perimeter too often. He was able to create pressure on the forecheck by skating at a high-pace but this rarely resulted in disrupted plays. Furthermore, he was unable to use his frame or skating ability to carve through Niagara's defense. His best scoring chance came as a result of recognizing that an Ice Dogs defender was flat-footed, he extended his reach to poke the puck to his teammate which resulted in 2-on-1 opportunity, but his teammate misfired the pass forcing Quinton to take an off-angle shot in-tight to the net which was handled. His other scoring chance was the result of him pivoting and finding an open-seam through traffic where he fired a seeing-eye wrist-shot quickly that required a save by Dillon. Away from the play, Byfield had a couple of notable defensive plays by using his motor and frame to help support his defense, but he also was too opportunistic when attempting to leave the zone at times, this caused him to play higher than he should on some plays.

Niagara –

Tomasino, Philip (2019) – Tomasino had a solid performance for Niagara by generating scoring chances around the goal-line and out-competing his opponents for loose pucks while on the forecheck. He's not very big, but he was strong on the puck in the corners and is adept at angling himself to give himself leverage which allows him to come away with pucks that you wouldn't think he would be able to get against larger opponents. This led to several prime scoring opportunities for both himself and his team, the best of which, was when he cut aggressively through the slot and out-waited Ukko-Pekka before firing a wrist-shot that just missed the net. Furthermore, he was good at making quick passes while skating down the wings, but never really threatened from the hashmarks out. Lastly, his pivoting and edge work was on display, he made one failed deke attempt that showed off his excellent agility, where he attempted to pull the puck around a defender who attempted to hit him but missed after he side-stepped him while at top-speeds. He didn't regain control of the puck on the play, but it was an impressive level of agility and showed how elusive he can be.

London Knights vs Saginaw Spirit, March 9 2019

Knights –

McMichael, Connor (2019) – McMichael was not much of a factor in the offensive-end when it came to threatening with his release or generating off the cycle or off the rush against the Spirit. He had a couple of well timed one-touch passes that helped set-up his teammates in-tight to the net but was largely kept to the perimeter and didn't manage to find an angle within the hashmarks to get off his shot. In some previous efforts, Connor has shown an average motor by keeping an inconsistent pace, yet today he was better at shifting his gear away from the puck when the play called for it. This was displayed during a good defensive sequence where he skated aggressively after a loose-puck in the corner, transitioned up the defensive-wall, then kept tight man-to-man coverage before intercepting a pass that was labelled for the slot and used his stick to deflect the puck out of danger. This also applied to the forecheck and backcheck where he switched his pace to match the play needed to generate a takeaway, this resulted in extended zone-time for London at a couple of points. He didn't drive play or factor in offensively, but it was good to see him extend his motor and show a better overall effort and compete level out there away from the puck.

Stranges, Antonio (2020) – Stranges was inconsistent like McMichael in the offensive-end but did flash his agility and skill. He took advantage of a deflected puck off a skate which allowed him to generate a sharp-backhander in the slot area. On one sequence, he showed plus agility, opening his hips to quickly change directions while carrying the puck through the neutral zone before firing a low-wrist shot from the left-circle. His release point was quick, and there was some velocity on the shot-attempt as well. His best sequence came after making a sharp pass in the slot under-pressure showing a good amount of decisiveness, he then maintained a good pace and generated a takeaway in heavy traffic while skating aggressively through the slot area, which allowed for continued possession.

Guskov, Matvei (2019) – Guskov flashed plus vision and anticipation both with and without the puck on his stick but was largely invisible for long stretches of the game. He had an excellent sequence in the neutral zone where he helped support Stranges along the boards before anticipating a passing lane getting taken away, so he out-waited his opponent before finding a target which created a transitional breakout for his team. He had an excellent high-skill pass from the bottom of the right-circle, which led to a primary assist on the only London goal of the game by making a no-look spinning backhand pass while in motion. The pass landed directly on the tape of his teammate. Guskov continues to frustrate in my viewings, flashing high-end talent before not getting involved enough at a consistent rate.

Spirit –

Millman, Mason (2019) – Millman had a difficult game for Saginaw, showing poor puck management and generally looking more fatigued than some previous viewings. He plays with some bite and despite looking lethargic; he did manage to get under the skin of Formenton after battling with him in-front of the net. He still competed and played with some bite while attempting to box-out his opponents, but his checks lacked the same jam in this game as some other ones. Furthermore, his gaps were not tight today and he was caught out of position on a couple of different occasions, once while flat-footed which led to a high-percentage chance against, and on another while he attempted to leave the neutral-zone which required a recovery effort by him. While under-pressure he didn't make accurate passes consistently, which caused several turnovers as well. It was a forgettable performance by Mason.

Perfetti, Cole (2020) – Perfetti had one of his best offensive-efforts of the season which resulted in a 4-goal game, including an empty-netter. He needed little time or space to bury the puck in the slot and crease areas. His best goal was off a broken play which caused the puck to redirect directly to his stick, where he capitalized by firing a low yet fast wrist-shot. He was in the right-place at the right time which is a common theme for the kid. His other goals were also impressive, one was an in-tight backhander that trickled in and the other was him finding soft-ice on the powerplay behind coverage where he fired the puck in one-motion after receiving a sharp-pass from McLeod. Away from the play, although not fast or strong, he still managed to be a factor by intercepting pucks after anticipating the play in advance below the goal-line, and on a backchecking sequence he used a stick-lift to generate a takeaway. Perfetti continues to display hockey sense and the ability to put the puck in the back of the net.

Porco, Nicholas (2019) – Porco had a below-average performance for Saginaw, rarely factoring in on the forecheck despite playing with speed and having size, while also largely being kept to the perimeter. He did have a couple of impressive flashes though. On one play specifically, he made a quick no-look pass that was threaded between two London players in the slot-area, but his teammate wasn't expecting it. On another sequence, he used an active-stick on the penalty-kill to generate a takeaway despite being gassed out near the end of his shift. Lastly, he did use his speed in spurts to generate scoring chances and a couple of clean transitional zone entries over the offensive-line but again, nothing consistent or overly threatening.

CREDITS

Once again this year I'm very pleased with our team of people at HockeyProspect.com. I want to thank all our scouts for all their hours spent in the rinks, and also for the time spent on their computers writing reports. We also thank Kathy Kocur for her assistance with photography and translation efforts. This was also year two for my 12 year old daughter helping out as well. She also has to put up with my *slight* grumpiness during the busy month of May as we put this book together.

I hope you enjoy our 2019 NHL Draft Black Book and want to say thank you for your support. We couldn't continue to produce it each year without it.

Thanks to all these fine people who contributed to this book.

Jerome Berube	Andreas Eklund
Brad Allen –	Russ Bitely
Dusten Braaksma	Janik Beichler
Liam Loeb	Ron Berman
Justin Sproule	Sean Del Giallo
Michael Farkas	David Cozzi
Johan Karlsson	Tyler Brown
Mitchell Avis	Ben Whittle
Conor Mulligan	Chad Landry
Scott McDougall	Pier-Olivier Plouffe
Blake Damerow	Charles Lassonde
Dan Markewich	

Kathy Kocur – Photographer, editing translations.

Leah Dyck - Website Interviews.

Alyssa Edwards -Data entry and font styling.

enjoy the draft and your summer,

Mark Edwards

© 2019 HockeyProspect.com